W9-BBK-210

C.W. Manwaring.

A DIGEST

OF THE

EARLY CONNECTICUT

PROBATE RECORDS.

COMPILED BY

CHARLES WILLIAM MANWARING,

Member Connecticut Historical Society.

Vol. III.

HARTFORD DISTRICT,

1729—1750.

Volumes I and II were originally published
in 1904, Volume III in 1906.
Reprinted 1995 by Genealogical Publishing Co., Inc.
Baltimore, Maryland 21202
Library of Congress Catalogue Card Number 94-74584
International Standard Book Number, Volume III: 0-8063-1471-0
Set Number: 0-8063-1472-9
Made in the United States of America

PREFACE.

Herewith is presented to the public the third and last volume of " Manwaring's Digest of Early Connecticut Probate Records," which completes a digested transcript of the first fifteen books of original record, and brings the work down to the year 1750. Beginning with the year 1800, there exists a complete modern card index of the records, the original books of which are as yet in a much better condition than those which are included in this work. There remains, therefore, a period of fifty years (1751 to 1800), the original books of which, it is hoped, will yet be compiled as a continuation of Mr. Manwaring's labors; for it is a period of great interest and importance, including as it does the events leading up to the War of the Revolution and the years of the war itself, during which there were many matters of both individual and collective interest which would be disclosed by such a compilation, and would tend to fill many a gap in the line of ancestry, a subject which is now engaging the attention of many of the descendants of our oldest families, and which will become more and more important and valuable as time goes on. Could Mr. Manwaring have been spared to us for a few more years, this continuance of his labors would have been his greatest pride and pleasure, for it was his constant thought and hope. But he has been gathered to his fathers, and, if it is ever done, others must complete that which he has so faithfully, conscientiously and perseveringly begun.

Of the volume before us, it may be said that to take it up and carry it to a conclusion without the guiding hand of its originator and leading spirit, had been a task that would have been far more difficult had it not been for an intimate knowledge of the personal ideas and wishes of the author, whose acquaintance and friendship has transformed the task to a pleasurable duty.

Nothing has occurred during its preparation to call for any more explanations than have already appeared in the prefaces to the first and second volumes, yet it has been considered advisable to remind the reader (as was done in the second volume) that the *first* volume contains in its first thirty-two pages a list showing the changes made in the different Probate Districts of Connecticut from the beginning, and also what towns were comprised by them at every change, as this list is of inestimable value as a time and money saver to those engaged in the work of tracing their ancestry, as well as to professional genealogists.

To make each volume as complete and convenient as possible in itself, we also repeat here a list of abbreviations used throughout the work, as follows:—Invt., Inventory; Adms., Administration and derivatives; Dist., Distribution and derivatives; Recog., Recognizance, Recognized, etc.; W. R., Windsor Records; P. C., Private Controversies; Cert., "Certified by;" and Test., "Attested by."

To compile a work of this kind and extent without making mistakes is simply beyond human ability, one reason alone being that no two persons could read, sense and translate the old records exactly alike. Another good reason is that none of us are infallible. The effort, then, should be to make as close an approximation to correctness as possible, and this has certainly been done by the author. Beyond this, time, aided by the circulation and practical use of the work, must be depended upon to reveal the errors that really have been made; and when enough of these discoveries have been collected to warrant it, they should and will be published as a supplement to the main work. In the meantime errors that are discovered in season to be embodied in the work itself, but after the sheets have been printed, are gathered in a separate chapter of "Errata" and published in each volume. Thus, following this preface, will be found a list of all errors discovered to date; and an invitation is hereby extended to all using this work to make known any real error which they may discover, for in this way only can a great work like this be sifted, perfected and made an authority.

Some confusion is found in the original records as to the date of *death* of the testator and the date of the *inventory*. Unless proof is found from other sources, such as town or church records, it is difficult to determine from the probate records, as written, what is intended.

As an illustration of the difficulties encountered in a work of this kind, and as a sample of the quaint old records from which this work has been compiled, we give here photographic plates of the will of a man who was one of Hartford's leading citizens in his day and generation — Gregory Wolterton, the first Townsman (Selectman) Hartford ever had. On the page opposite each plate is given a translation in type, line for line, of the original, including orthography, capitalization and punctuation, or lack of the same. It will also be noticed that while the testator himself gives the name of Wolterton or Woolterton, it is given as *Winterton* in the certification before the Clerk of Court; and also appears as *Winterton* and *Wilterton* in other parts of the old records.

Plates are also given of the monument erected to the founders and settlers of Hartford, on the east and north faces of which are inscribed their names. This memorial stands in the church-yard of the old First Church of Hartford, which is now in the very heart of the city.

A portrait of Mr. Manwaring forms the frontispiece of this volume, and is a good likeness of him as he appeared in the later years of his life.

Thus is finished, with this volume, a work of which, with all its faults, any man might well be proud, and which will preserve its author's name till the end of time.

Obituary.

It is with regret that we announce the death of Mr. C. W. Manwaring, genealogist and member of the Connecticut Historical Society, and author and compiler of this work, who passed away on Saturday evening, August 19, 1905, in Hartford, Conn., where he had resided many years.

Charles William Manwaring was born in Waterford, New London County, Conn., May 9, 1829, and was a descendant of one of the oldest families in Connecticut, the Manwarings being among the earliest settlers of that State, and their genealogy being easily traceable for many generations before the settlement of the New World. In his young manhood he became a builder and contractor, but his love for books and research led him to take up a line of work which has resulted in his leaving behind him a monument more enduring than stone, and a work which will be more and more appreciated as future generations come and go.

Mr. Manwaring was about seventy years old when he conceived the idea of putting into a concise and durable form the contents of the original books of probate records of Connecticut, part of which were in the State Capitol and part in the Halls of Record at Hartford, and all of which, from excessive use and lapse of time, are fast approaching a condition when access to them will be obtained with difficulty. Having conceived the idea, he immediately began the work of putting it into a practical form, and for the remaining years of his life labored incessantly under great physical disability, and succeeded in producing the work of which this is the closing volume. While it is a work of great value to reference libraries, genealogists, and all who are interested in tracing their ancestry, it is also a pioneer work in its line, pointing the way to what may be done in other parts of the State and in sister States in the way of putting their ancient and valuable records into a form that will forever insure against their loss or destruction. Only great patience, determination, courage, and an abiding faith in the merits of the work could have brought about its production, especially at such an advanced age, and Connecticut was fortunate in possessing among her citizens one who was equipped with such necessary qualifications, and the State has recognized his labors by purchasing copies of the work for official use.

It is a sad fact that on the day following the completion of his great compilation, he succumbed to the fatal disease which at last took him away (a cancerous affection of the throat), thus showing with what great courage and suffering he must have pursued his labors on the latter part of his work. For nine months he patiently bore his affliction until death released him, leaving a work that will preserve his name forever.

ERRATA.

VOLUME I.

Page.

3—The following items should be added to the inventory of Samuel Allyn :—

	£ s d
It. in hogsheads, payles, tubbs and earthen ware,	) 00-19-00
It. 2 spinning wheeles.	) 00-07-00
It. in crookes, Grid iron, fire pan and tongs,	) 00-13-00
It. his workeing tooles,	) 02-02-00
It. a muskitt and sworde,	) 00-13-00
It. a table, and forme, and other lumber,	) 00-10-00
It. in cattle : one cowe, one heifer, 1 yearling,	) 12-00-00
It. two swynes,	) 04-00-00

5—Will of Joseph Clarke is duplicated on page 108.

16—line 7 from bottom, for 1644, read *1649.*

33—l. 31, for Elizabeth Standly, read Elizabeth *Loomis.*

49—l. 28, after Cole, erase *son of James Cole, late of Hartford.*

97—l. 4, for 1665, read *1655.*

l. 9, for Commisin, read *Tommisin.*

102—l. 16 from bottom, for Marcy Bushnell, read *Mary* Bushnell.

l. 6 from bottom, for William Adgate read *Thomas* Adgate. The entry in the Court Record is William Adgate, but from other authority it is evidently an error of the Recorder.

118—l. 12, for 1659, read *1661.*

119—l. 6 from bottom, erase *John, age 33 years 29 May, 1683.*

120—Erase l. 1-4, and insert *Will of Samuel Greenhill that two-thirds of the land of said Samuel Greenhill, deceased, did belong to Thomas Greenhill, deceased. They also find that the one-half of that two-thirds of Land did belong unto the Children of Jeremiah Addams, viz., John Addams, Hannah Addams, Sarah Addams, and that one-third part of that half doth belong to Nathaniel Willett's Children. And that one-quarter of that third part doth belong to Zachary Sanford in Right of his wife, and for that proportion the.*

125—l. 16, for Cophall, read *Coxhall.*

l. 2 from bottom, for Foyse, read *Joyse.*

134—l. 33, for Abyah, read *Abigail.*

Page.

141—The following should have appeared on this page:

OLDAGE, RICHARD, Windsor. Died 27 January, 1660. Invt. taken by Deacon Gaylord and Humphrey Pinney.

And shortly after an Inventori was taken of the estat that he left conserning which before his death he had before witnes said that his will was that his sonn in law John Osbon should have all that he had and he was to alow him maintenanc whilst he lived and so was to take all and paye all.

Witnes: *Mat:Grant, Tho:Dibble.*

	£—s-d.
Imprimis his howse and home lott 8 ac 3 quartus valued at	40- 0-0.
wood land and swamp nere pine meadow 13 ac	10- 0-0.
ten ac of swamp neare adjoyning valued	01- 0-0.
one the east side of the great river aboue namerok 12 rodd wide valued at	02- 0-0.
below namerok 12 rodd wide vald at	04-01-0.
goods with in howse valued in all	11-11-0.
	68-11-0.
the state indebted to Mr Henery Clarke	0-11-0.
for rates to the towne	0-03-3.

the men that valued the state ware Deacon Gaylard, Houmpery Pinne.

149—l. 19 from bottom, for 1665, read *1655* (twice).

152—l. 2 from bottom, for her, read *hee* (twice).

153—l. 10 from bottom, for Howard, read *Steward.*

166—l. 12-14, Court Record, 7 September, 1693, refers to Estate of Christopher Wolcott, son of Simon and Martha (Pitkin) Wolcott, who died 3 April, 1693, and should have a separate title.

l. 24, Erase *Allyn.* The sentence ends with Mary.

194—l. 16, for Samll, read *small.*

199—l. 5, for Joseph Gaylord, read *Josiah* Gaylord. (The name is written Jos. in record.)

202—l. 18 from bottom, for 1667, read *1676.* For Will dated, read *Proven.*

Will of John Goodrich, Jr. is duplicated on page 308-9.

207—l. 19, for sister, read *sisters.*

209—l. 26, for 1664, read *1674.*

210—l. 1, for John Howkins, read John *Judd.* After Mary, add *Judd.*

218—l. 5 and 6, for 18 February, 1655, read *3 February, 1657.* Erase Thomas b. 23 April, 1659 (he had died), and Mary, b. 8 May, 1667 (she had died).

Erase l. 7 and 6 from bottom, and insert *To his five sons and daughter Elizabeth, to each 62-13-04.*

219—l. 14 from bottom, for John Cornish, read *James* Cornish.

220—l. 20, for 19 March, 1661, read *2 Jan., 1665.*

223—l. 8, for 1699-1700, read *1669-70.*

l. 10, for 1699, read *1669.*

l. 16, for 1699, read *1669.*

Page.

237—l. 26, for daughter, read *sister.*

241—l. 2 from bottom, for Josiah, read *Joshua.*

242—l. 2, for Josiah, read *Joshua.*

244—l. 15, for 1665, read *1655.*

246—l. 13 from bottom, for Ferris, read *Terry.*

250—l. 23, for (Vol. VI), read *(Vol. IV).*

253—l. 7 from bottom, erase *and* at end of line.

254—l. 11 from bottom, for Joseph Stow, read Joseph *Hand.*

259—l. 12 from bottom, for Sister's abovesed, read *Sister Abegel's.*

l. 8 from bottom, for foote, read *for.*

260—l. 2, after poorter, insert *the wife of Samuel Porter, twenty shillings. Also, I give unto.*

l. 6, for said John bacon, read *land belonging to the school.*

l. 7, for forever, read *sener.*

l. 12, for John Haynes, read *Joseph* Haynes.

l. 5 from bottom, insert *Will dated 21 April, 1670.*

261—l. 19, for 1688, read *1668.*

269—l. 8 from bottom, for my son Joseph, read my son *John.*

273—l. 17 from bottom, for Jacob Wells, read *Ichabod* Wells.

276—l. 8 from bottom, erase *and Thomas Robbins.*

l. 3 from bottom, for Martha Robbins, read Martha *Boreman.* For Thomas Robbins, read *Mr.* Robbins.

295—l. 18, for James, read *John.* Erase *(Part gone......) Gates,* and insert *Penfield, one of the legatees.*

296—l. 22, for son, read *sons.*

297—l. 19, for Henry, read *Mary.*

298—l. 18, read *Joseph, James and Isaac Curtice, and Mr. Kimberly. Lt. James Treat,* etc.

l. 4 from bottom, for John Kelly's, read *John Kelsey's.*

302—l. 24, for Father's, read *husband's.*

316—l. 4, erase *Hanna Hall.*

323—In distribution to heirs of John Hosford are the names: To heirs of John Hosford, Jr.; to Timothy Hosford; to Esther Phelps, widow; to Sarah, wife of Joseph Phelps; to Samuel Hosford; to Nathaniel Hosford; to Mary, wife of Josiah Owen, Jr.; to Obadiah Hosford.

350—l. 9, for 1681, read *1684.*

351—Will of John Pratt is duplicated on page 500.

355—l. 2, for Mary, read *Naomi.* An error of the Recorder corrected from original document.

362—l. 7 from bottom, for Daniel Smith, read *Samuel* Smith.

363—l. 20 from bottom, for Arnot, read *Arnold.*

364—l. 13, for Arnot, read *Arnold.*

381—l. 12, for Mr. Welles', read *Mrs.* Welles'.

l. 21, after Ichabod Welles, erase remainder of sentence.

Page.

386—l. 18, for William Boardman, read William *Burnham.*

391—Insert NOTE. "Now in October, 1687, Sr. Edmund Andross took upon him the Government of this Colony. And the Records of the Acts of the next County Courts of the County of Hartford (Except the records of the Inferiour Courts of Common pleas holden in the time of Sr. Edmund Andross his Government) are recorded in the fifth book of the records of the Sd. County Court No. 5, which beginns May 20th, 1689."

393—l. 15 from bottom, for Mary X Beppin, read Mary X *Crippin.*

394—l. 11 from bottom, after *Thomas,* erase remainder of paragraph.

396—l. 9, for John Allyn, read *Capt. Thomas* Allyn.

l. 14, for 23 March, read 23 *May.*

397—l. 9, after John, erase *(Dec.).*

404—l. 15 from bottom, for 1st son, read *third* son.

407—In distribution of Estates of John Bissell, Sen. and Jr., 15 March, 1693-4, *Hezekiah Bissell* should be included.

420—l. 15 from bottom, after Olmsted, erase *Abigail Butler.*

l. 6 from bottom, erase *onely whereas,* and insert *orally. Whereas, etc.*

433—l. 5, for Elisol, read *Elijah.*

445—l. 6, for 27 March, read 27 *November.*

l. 7, for 16 December, read *26* December.

l. 12, for James Forbes, read *John* Forbes.

447—l. 18, for Widow, read *Wife.* For Samuel *Griswold,* read Samuel *Gaylord.*

448—The ante-nuptial agreement of Josiah Gilbert has no connection with preceding estate, and should have a separate title.

452—l. 10, after *by,* insert, *my father in.*

458—l. 22, for Sarah Hall, read *Mary* Hall.

459—l. 17 from bottom, for 1690-1, read *1690.*

l. 16 from bottom, for 1691, read *1690.*

l. 15 from bottom, for 1690-1, read *1690.*

475—l. 17 and 18, Court Record, 5 April 1703-4: is misplaced, and should appear under estate of Benjamin Judd, on page 474.

l. 10 from bottom, for Mary Jones, read Mary *Janes.*

l. 17 from bottom, for Mary Jones, read Mary *Janes.*

482—The following will should have appeared on this page:

(Will on File.)

LOOMIS, JOHN, Windsor. Will dated 27 August, 1688. Exhibited 4 Dec., 1688. No Court Record found.

John Loomiss senior doe beinge of a competent understandinge and memory ordayne and appoynt this my Last will and Testament

In primis my will is that my eldest son John shall have a double portion of my estate in Land yt to bee acounted for part that he have already beene posessed of and by this I give liberty to bee assured of

Page.

my will is that all my land on both sides ye River shall be
equally devided betweene all my children now livinge I leave
itt in charge in my will yt there bee indeavered of all
a ready complyance to agree in ye devission itt beinge
so small devissions I know not how to pleas myself nor them
my will is yt my daughter Elizabeth shall have equall
portion with my sons excepting John of ye moveable estate
my will is yt my wife shall have ye product of ye thirds of
all my land as longe as she lives and that ye house
homested & barne Remayne to my wife as longe as
she lives and ye free dispose of itt amongst my children
when she dies & thatt ye 3d prt of my moveable
estate of what she shall chuse to bee to her free
dispose amongst my children
my will is yt my son Thomas's two sons shall have ten pownd
a pees of my moveable estate
I apoynt my wife and son John Executors of this my
will always provided yt my Just debts shall bee payd
out of my moveable estate and if itt will not reach
every one proportionable shall abate
my will is that   (illegible)
by my wife at her death

I subscib my hand
John Loomys Sr

Wittness:
Abigaill Aling,
Nathanale Porter.

485—l. 20, For Nathaniel Gladden's, read Nathaniel *Stoddard's.*
486—The will of John Merrells was not probated. See agreement for
settlement of his estate, pp. 258-9, Vol. II.
489—l. 15, for George Drake, Jr., read *Job* Drake, Jr.
490—l. 13, for Henry Wolcott, read *John* Wolcott.
491—l. 20, erase *Richard Newell.*
     l. 9 from bottom, for Hannah Smith, read Hannah *North.*
     l. 4 from bottom, after Children: read *Thomas North, Joseph
North, Mary Searles and Sarah Woodruff.*
     l. 3 from bottom, erase *&* at beginning of line.
501—l. 5 from bottom, for Page *10,* read Page *110.*
509—l. 4 from bottom, for Mary, read *Marah.*
515—l. 8, at beginning insert *William Ward, John Ward, Phebe Hall,
Sarah Hand.*
517—l. 12-14, Court Record, John Webster, is duplicated on pp. 132-3,
Vol. II.
518—l. 3, after Ichabod Welles, erase *Jacob.*
533—l. 27 from bottom, for Eleazer, read *Elizabeth.*
537—l. 26, for Thomas Hoskins, read Thomas *Hopkins.*
541—l. 7 from bottom, for Samuel, read *Mary.*
543—l. 17 from bottom, for 4 May, read *7 July.*
544—l. 18, add, *To Susannah Butler, to Cornelius Holybut, to Ann Butler.*

Page.

547—l. 8, after Hannah, insert *to David*.

549—l. 17, for John Deming, read *Jonathan* Deming.

557-8—Court Record (Vol. IX) 6 October, 1719, is misplaced, and should appear under Estate of Jonathan Gillett, Sen., on page 201.

564—l. 5 from bottom, for 1695, read *1698*.

566—l. 6 from bottom, after Mary, add *to Nathaniel*.

570—l. 5 from bottom, for (Vol. VIII), read *(Vol. VII)*.

575—Court Records, Estate of Thomas Newberry, should not be separated from same Estate on pp. 489-90.

578—l. 11 from bottom, for son, read *friend*.

581—Court Records, Estate of John Sadd, should not be separated from same Estate on pp. 502-3.

583—l. 12, for 1698-9, read *1698*.

592—Distribution of Estate of Jonathan Welles should not be separated from same Estate on pp. 517-8.

593—Erase *Note:* lines 3 and 4.

597—l. 17, erase *John Whiting*.

l. 18, erase *Widow Hannah*.

598—l. 16, after Abigail 13, insert *John 11*.

605—INDEX TO ESTATES. l. 5 from bottom, after Atherton, Major Humphrey, erase *Hartford*.

606—l. 27, for Beckley, Samuel, read, Beckley, *Nathaniel*.

l. 37, for Benton, Samuel, read, Benton, *Edward*.

620—Add Stiles, Henry, Windsor, ... 152

621—l. 24, after Wadsworth, Elizabeth, erase (Farmington) and insert *Hartford*.

VOLUME II.

Page.

16—Court Records Timothy Baker are duplicated on page 152.

25—l. 2 from bottom, after Father, insert *Nathaniel*.

26—l. 2, for John Boarn, read *Thomas* Boarn.

l. 17, after Joseph, insert *to Nathaniel*.

30—l. 7 from bottom, after Susannah, erase *Porter*.

l. 6 from bottom, erase *to Samuel*.

38—l. 5 from bottom, for Richard Case, read *Rachel* Case.

39—A former will of William Cheeny, dated 1699, not probated, mentions wife Hope, and Anne, daughter of his cousin Benjamin Hand.

42—l. 14 from bottom, for 2nd daughter, read *sd.* daughter.

45—l. 3 from bottom, for Daniel Hoyt, read *David* Hoyt.

Page.

49—l. 11 from bottom, for Sarah Benton, read Sarah *Burton.*

    2 from bottom, after David Cornwall insert *deceased.*
for Sarah Benton, read Sarah *Burton.*

    1 from bottom, for Stephen Cornwall, read *Stephen Cornwall's Children.*

52—l. 24 and 30, for Poole, read *Toole.*

57—l. 16, for Palidence, read *Patience.*

60—l. 25-35, Agreement, 5 August, 1718, Estate of Josiah Elsworth is duplicated on page 384.

62—l. 21, for Joseph Kimberly, read *Abraham* Kimberly.

80—l. 2 from bottom, after Jonathan, insert *to Joseph.*

90—The Estate of Joseph Lewis, Simsbury, should not be separated from record of same estate on Page 330, Vol. I.

95—l. 15-26, Court Record, 22 March, 1723, Estate of William Miller is duplicated on page 548.

98—l. 23, Insert *NORTH, JOHN, son of Samuel North. Court Record, Page 106—1st. March, 1707-8; This Court appoint John North to be guardian to his son Josiah North, a minor, age 2 years.*

    l. 26-27, after age erase remainder of sentence.

112—l. 29, for Henry Belding, read *Gideon* Belding.

114—l. 14, for 2 August, 1707-8, read 2 August, *1708.*

119—l. 24, for Thomas Stodder, read *John* Stodder.

120—l. 17, for Samuel Stow, read *Nathaniel Stow, Jr.*

127—l. 3, for 1708, read *1705-6.*

133—l. 1, for Page 8, read Page *82.*

144—l. 6 from bottom, for Thomas Gipson, read Thomas *Crippin.*

147—l. 2 from bottom, for Benjaimn, read *Benjamin.*

152—l. 6 from bottom, for He died, read *Taken.*

158—l. 16 from bottom, for Mary Wright, read *Mercy* Wright.

164—l. 16, for 12 April, read *26* April.

167—l. 16 from bottom, after Jonathan, erase *Jr.*

    l. 10 from bottom, erase *To the heirs of John Bull, decd.,* and insert *To Thomas, Nehemiah and John Bull, children to John Bull, decd.*

    l. 9 from bottom, after Susannah, insert *Porter.* For Sarah Bull, read Sarah *Hart.*

171—l. 12, for Marcey Butler, read *Mary* Butler.

172—l. 6, for Lydia, read *Mary.*

173—l. 18 from bottom, for David Chapman, read *Jabez* Chapman.

176—Court Records, 25 July, 1721, and 26 July, 1721, Estate of John Chester, have no connection with preceding Estate, and should have a separate title.

177—l. 12, for Jemima, read *Mary.*

178—l. 8, for Jonas, read *Josias.*

Page.

184—l. 5 from bottom, Court Record, 4 October, 1725, Estate of Isaac Crane, has no connection with preceding Estate, and should have a separate title.

192—l. 10, for Samuel Wolcott, read *Sarah* Wolcott.

196—l. 8, after daughters, insert *Mary and Susannah.*

202—l. 1, for Hartford, read *Haddam.*

l. 2, for Sarah, read *Susannah.*

217—l. 19, for February, read *January.*

218—l. 23, for Samuel Harris, read *Daniel* Harris.

l. 24, for Samuel Cadwell, Jr., his daughter Thankful Cadwell, read *Samuel Bidwell for his daughter Thankful Bidwell.*

l. 25, for Hannah Savage, read Hannah *Sprague.*

220—l. 4, after (Vol. X):, insert *2 March, 1724-5.*

229—l. 31-35, Court Records, 3 November, 1724:, and 1st. March, 1725-6: are misplaced, and should appear under Estate of Jonathan Hollister on pp. 230-1.

230—l. 20-29, Inventory of Jonathan Hollister is duplicated on page 530.

233—l. 15, after estate:, insert *to Mary Hooker.*

bottom line, for Root, read *Foot.*

bottom line, erase *Corning.* The last sentence should read *Joseph Foot and her father,* etc.

238—l. 1, after (Vol X): insert *7 July, 1724:*

239—l. 14 from bottom, for Middletown, read *Farmington.* (The inventory calls him of Wethersfield.)

247—l. 12, after 7 November: insert *1727:*

252—l. 31-33, Court Record, 17 May, 1733: Estate of John Lewis, is misplaced, and should have a separate title.

256—l. 15, for 19 years, read *9* years.

261—l. 3, after Deborah, insert *Drake.*

265—Erase l. 15 and 16, and insert *NORTH, JOHN, Farmington, son of Thomas North. Invt. £39-12-07. Taken 2 February, 1709-10, by Samuel Newell, Sen., and Joseph North.*

l. 23, for son, read *brother.*

l. 28-29, Court Record, 8 April, 1701: is misplaced, and appears under Estate of John Warner, Middletown, on page 131.

l. 30-35, Court Records, 6 April, 1713: and 4 October, 1714: are misplaced, and should appear under Estate of Thomas North, Farmington, on same page.

266—l. 1, for 17 November, read *7 December.*

268—l. 19, for Elizabeth Wadsworth, read *Mary* Wadsworth. The record reads Elizabeth, but is clearly an error of the Recorder.

l. 9 from bottom, after Thomas, erase *Jr.*

269—l. 3, after Olcott, erase *Jr.*

273—l. 8, insert *comma* between Jonathan and Humphrey.

280—l. 13 and 12 from bottom should be transposed. John was the eldest son, but had died.

Page.
292—l. 4, for Richard Seamore, read *Ebenezer* Seamore.
　　l. 23, for Ebenezer Gilbert, read Ebenezer *Seamore.*
　　l. 3 from bottom, for Jonathan Pomeroy, read *Joseph* Pomeroy.
298—l. 10, for Thankfull Smith, read *Nathaniel* Smith.
300—l. 13, for Noah Spark's eldest son, read *Noah Sparks, eldest son.*
307—l. 20, for Mary Steele, read *Marcy* Steele.
312—l. 32-41, Record of Distribution on file 27 January, 1742-3, Estate
　　　of John Thompson, is misplaced, and should appear under
　　　Estate of John Thompson on page 352, Vol. III. John
　　　Thompson, a son, is named as a legatee.
313—last word, for durgget, read *drugget.*
322—l. 14, for Hannah Bird, read Hannah *Birge.*
336—l. 13 from bottom, for John, read *Stebbin.*
340—l. 18 from bottom, after Daniel insert *Bidwell, Sen.*
356—l. 6, after William, erase *and to John.*
361—l. 7, for marirage, read *marriage.*
370—l. 10, for Marcy Churchill, read *Mary* Churchill.
379—l. 4, for Mary Dunham, read *Marcy* Dunham.
380—l. 14 from bottom, for 1718, read *1716.*
387—bottom line, after her, insert *decease.*
397—l. 13, for (Vol. X), read (Vol. IX).
　　l. 22, for Francis Wetmore, read Francis *Whetmore* (Whitmore).
　　l. 30, for Francis Wetmore, read Francis *Whetmore* (Whitmore).
　　l. 35, for Francis Wetmore, read Francis *Whetmore* (Whitmore).
404—l. 10, for Newell Strong, read *Hewett* Strong.
　　l. 15, insert *comma* between Samuel and Giles.
416—l. 11 from bottom, erase *Mary 10;* after Abigail, erase *8.*
　　　　　　　　(The page in record is broken.)
443—l. 26-7. This Court Record is misplaced and should have a separate
　　　title.
450—l. 7, for Mary White, read *Sarah* White.
452—l. 23, for 1721-3, read *1721-2.*
453—The last nine lines on this page, Court Records, Estate Mrs. Abiah
　　　Wolcott, are duplicated on page 626.
455—l. 10, for Joseph Bodwitha, read Joseph *Bodurtha.*
456—l. 16 from bottom, for about, read *above.*
460—l. 11, for Benjamin, read *Henry.*
　　l. 18, for 3 August, 1724, read 3 August, *1725.*
464—l. 32, for Hooker, read *Holcomb.*
465—l. 2 from bottom, for Marah Belding, read *Mary* Belding.
469—l. 2 from bottom, for Martha Boardman, read *Hannah* Boardman.
473—l. 6, for Daniel, read *David.*
476—l. 13 from bottom, for Daniel Strong, read *Samuel* Strong.
478—l. 3 from bottom, for 9 November, read *19 March.*
　　l. 13 from bottom, for Daniel, read *David.*
483—l. 11 from bottom, after *Timothy,* insert *comma.*

Page.

489—l. 8-13. These Court records are misplaced and should appear under Estate of Nathaniel Cooke on same page.

491—l. 32, after Hill, erase *comma* and insert *period I give to my daughter Mary.*

511—l. 5 from bottom, for Thomas Gates, read *Joseph* Gates.

l. 3 from bottom, for Shaylor, read *Fuller.*

NOTE.   John Gates, a son, had already received his part.

512—l. 15 from bottom, erase *(was she not a daughter?)*

514—l. 21, for 2 September, read *3 October.*

l. 22, for William Goslin, read *Abraham Fox.*

515—l. 13 from bottom, after John, erase *Jr.*

525—The estate of Jonathan Higley should not be separated from the record of the same estate on page 398.

526—l. 24, for sons, read *sums.*

541—l. 18, for LOVEMAN CHILDREN, read *LOVEMAN, THOMAS, JR.*

544—l. 6, for John Pratt, read *Joseph* Pratt.

549—l. 25, for Daniel Strong, read *Samuel* Strong.

551—l. 20, for 7 February, read *7 March.*

554—l. 26, for Sarah Hewitt, read Sarah *Newell.*

557—l. 9, for Grant, read *Junior.*

573—l. 21, for Mary Hammond, read Mary *Hanchet.*

576—l. 6 from bottom, after Aaron, erase *(David).*

579—l. 3, for Mary Watson, read Mary *Ashley;* for Sara Ashley, read Sarah *Watson.* The record reads as stated, but an error was made by the Recorder. See Court Record—3 February, 1718-9, page 306.

581—l. 10, insert *Will dated 25 July, 1728.*

588—l. 18, for Hananh, read *Hannah.*

l. 22, for son, read *sons.*

l. 26, for Jonathan Hall, read Jonathan *Hale.*

600—l. 3-5, Court Records, 6 June and 5 September, 1727, are misplaced, and should appear under Estate of Capt. William Warner, Wethersfield, on pp. 600-2.

l. 9, insert *Will dated 15 October, 1726.*

601—l. 6 from bottom, for 1725, read *1726.*

605—l. 27, after age erase *12.* (The page in record is broken.)

624—l. 14 from bottom, insert *Will dated 16 December, 1725.*

625—l. 9, insert *Will dated 9 February, 1726.*

627—l. 14 from bottom, for Daniel, read *David.*

628—l. 15, for *Died,* read *Invt. taken.*

629—l. 12, for Eleazer, read *Ebenezer.*

643—INDEX TO ESTATES, add *Hopkins, Joseph, Hartford, 1712..235*

675—Erase from Index, *Giles, Samuel, 404.*

681—Add to Index, *Hooker, Giles, 404.*

683—Erase from Index, *Humphrey, Jonathan, 273.*

692—Add to Index, *Pinney, Humphrey, 273.*

VOLUME III.

Page.

5—Court Record, 4 April, 1732, Nathaniel Bacon, is duplicated on page 462, Vol. II.

10—The last two lines do not seem to belong to this Estate; probably should follow Estate of James Bate on page 353, Vol. II.

15—l. 4 from bottom, the Court Record reads Jonathan Bulkeley, as stated, but from other sources it is evident that the name is *Buckland*.

16—l. 1, for *BULL, ISAAC,* read *BULL, DANIEL.*

l. 8, Erase *BULL, SUSANNAH,* and add Court Record, 7 October, 1729:, to preceding estate.

18—l. 4 from bottom, for 5 April, read *25* April.

19—l. 32, for 20 May, 1739, read 20 May, *1731:*

21—l. 2 from bottom, for additional record Estate of Peter Butler, see page 390.

27—l. 19, for Nathaniel Goodrich, read Nathaniel *Goodwin.*

28—l. 22-24, This Court Record is misplaced and should appear under Estate of Nathaniel Cooke, on page 489, Vol. II.

54—l. 10 from bottom, for Daniel, read *David.*

4 from bottom, for Daniel, read *David.*

55—l. 9, for Daniel, read *David.*

65—l. 29, for Elizabeth Gross, read Elizabeth *Gooff.*

67—l. 3 from bottom, after September:, insert *1730.*

72—l. 26, for 31 January, 1731, read *4 April, 1732.*

80—l. 6-9, The Court Record of Joseph Loomis is as given, but is thought to be an error of the Recorder, and should really belong to the Estate of Nathaniel Loomis, immediately preceding.

81—l. 4, for Daniel Loomis, read *David* Loomis.

83—l. 6-22, This Court Record is misplaced, and should appear under Estate of Daniel Markham, on Page 256-7, Vol. 11.

88—l. 15, for Giles Hooper, read Giles *Hooker.*

91—l. 2, for *75* shillings, read *5* shillings.

92—l. 20, for *John Phelps, the 2nd son,* read *John Phelps 2nd., son,* etc.

97—l. 26, for *28 April,* read *1 May.*

l. 28, for *her,* read *him.*

100—l. 10 from bottom, for Hannah Richards, read *Esther* Richards.

103—l. 25-27, Court Record, 3 July, 1733, is misplaced, and appears under Estate of Joshua Robbins on page 449.

112—l. 5 from bottom, for Samuel Smith, read *Simon* Smith.

Bottom line, for Samuel Smith, read *Simon* Smith.

Page.
113—l.   9, Insert: Page 41 (Vol. XVI) 5 November, 1751 : Mary Smith, alias Flower, Adms., exhibited an account of her Adms., which is accepted by the Court, and moves for distribution. Whereupon this Court appoint and impower Capt. Daniel Webster, Abraham Merrell and Samuel Moodey, of Hartford, to distribute the estate, viz.: To the relict, her right of dowry and 1-3 part of the personal estate; to Justus, the eldest son, a double share; and to Nathaniel, Elizabeth and Hannah Smith their single share.

      l. 12, after December, insert *1732-3.*

115-116—The Court Records, Joseph Spencer, Haddam, are misplaced, and should appear under same estate on page 301, Vol. II.

117—l.   3 from bottom, erase STOCKING, ELISHA, and add Court Record, 1st February, 1732-3: to preceding Estate.

      l. 2 from bottom, for *of the,* read *of Daniel Stocking.*

131—l.   7, add: Page 82 (Vol. XVI) 3 December, 1752: Return of setting out dowry to Elizabeth Cole, alias Whaples, relict of Thomas Whaples, of Farmington.

147—l. 22, for Marcy, read *Mary.*

158—l.   8 from bottom, for David Gates, read *Daniel* Gates. Add *George Gates* to agreement, 7 September, 1734.

161—l. 21, for Noadiah Taylor, read *John* Taylor.

163—l. 11, for Timothy Grant, read Timothy *Loomis.*

167—l. 26, for David Pinney, read *Daniel* Pinney.

168—l. 20, for $5, read £5.

175—Court Record, 28 March, 1734: John Lane, is duplicated on page 410, Vol. II.

      l. 15 from bottom, for Corp., read *Capt.*

178—l. 18 from bottom, after Hannah Lord L. S., add *widow of William Lord.*

195—l.   9 from bottom, for 1722, read *1728.*

196—l.   9 from bottom. It was probably *Daniel* Sedgwick, not *Samuel,* who chose a guardian 1st April, 1735: An error of the Recorder.

201—l.   5 from bottom, add: Page 87 (Vol. XVI) 13 February, 1753: Sarah Smith, widow of Samuel Smith, of Middletown (Kensington parish), moves for dowry.

215—l. 14, for Daniel, read *David.*

      l. 18, for Daniel, read *David.*

      l. 23, for Daniel, read *David.*

      At end, add: Page 21 (Vol. XVI) 30 April, 1751: Jonathan Yeomans, aged 17, son of Elisha Yeomans, Tolland, deceased, chose Joshua Wills to be his guardian.

218—l. 11-14, Court Record, 2 August, 1737: is misplaced, and should appear under Estate of John Andrews, Middletown, on pp. 139-40.

Page.

240—l. 17-36, Court Record, 6 May, 1755: should follow Estate of Thomas Cadwell, on page 422, Vol. I.

253—l. 21, for March, *1734*, read March, *1741*.

274—l. 7, for Daniel, read *David*.

281—l. 14, for William Barnard, read William *Burnham*.

312—l. 6 from bottom, add: This Court appoint Mrs. Elizabeth Newberry to be a guardian to Benjamin Newberry, 13 years of age, and Thomas Newberry, about 11 years.

342—l. 9, after December, insert *1741*.

357—l. 7 from bottom, for Daniel, read *David*.

362—l. 25, for eldest, read *youngest*.

366—l. 2-6, Court Records, 24 December, 1742; and 5 April, 1743: are misplaced, and should appear under Estate of Sergt. Joseph Wetmore, on page 129.

369—l. 3, for 1738-40, read *1739-40*.

376—l. 4, for Page 112-113, read Page *111-112*.

    l. 6, for 30 November, 1742, read 30 November, *1743*.

384—l. 7 from bottom, add *To Joseph Baker, Jr.*

388—l. 13 from bottom, the Court Record reads Bolman, as stated, but from other sources it is evident that the name is *Boardman*.

403—l. 13 from bottom, for 1744, read *1745*.

434—l. 22-25, This Court Record is misplaced, and should appear under estate of Jacob Merrells, p. 546, Vol. II. There was an agreement signed 13 December, 1742, between Abigail Merrells, the widow, and Jacob, Zebulon, Elisha, Asa, Joshua and Abigail Merrells.

437—l. 8, for Mary Wilson, read Mary *Wilcox*.

456—l. 3, add: Page 63 (Vol. XVI) 19 May, 1752: Richard Shaw, a minor, 15 years of age, son of John Shaw, late of Hartford decd., chose Samuel Wright of Hartford to be his guardian. Recog., £500.

465—l. 7 and 6 from bottom, for Daniel, read *David*.

480—l. 22, add: Page 37 (Vol. XVI) 5 October, 1751: This Court appoint Daniel Williams of Wethersfield to be a guardian to David Williams, about 7 years old, son of David Williams of Wethersfield, deceased. Recog., £600.

488—l. 2 from bottom, for *Died 3 October, 1748. Invt.*, read *Invt. 3 October, 1748.*

536—l. 7 from bottom, for Ebenezer Goodwin, read Ebenezer *Griswold:*

566—l. 11, add: Page 51 (Vol. XVI) 4 February, 1752: Jabez Hall, a minor about 14 years and six months old, son of Giles Hall, Middletown, deceased, made choice of Jabez Hamlin, Esq., of Middletown, to be his guardian. Cert: by *Joseph Southmayd, J. P.*

Page.
567—1. 6, for Samuel, read *Lemuel.*
    1. 29, for Samuel, read *Lemuel.*
569—1. 6 from bottom, for Simon Kinsbury, read Simon *Kingsbury.*
571—1. 28, for Hope Fox, read *Hosea* Fox.
583—1. 23, add: Court Record, Page 67 — 17 May, 1748: An account of administration exhibited by Lydia Lee, Admx.
634—1. 6 from bottom, for 1750, read *1752.*
649—1. 11 from bottom, insert: Page 28 (Vol. XVI) 17 June, 1751: Mary Smith, daughter of Nehemiah Smith, late of Glastonbury, deceased, made choice of her uncle Gideon Hollister to be her guardian. Cert: *Thomas Pitkin, J. P.*
660—1. 7, for Osgood, read *Osborn.*
665—1. 13, add: This Court appoint John Arnold, Jr., to be a guardian to William Stow, a minor son of Ebenezer Stow, 11 years old; to Martha Stow, aged 9; and Elizabeth Stow, aged 7. Recog., £500 for each minor.
668—1. 9-13, Court Record, 29 May, 1749: is misplaced, and should appear under Estate of Samuel Thompson, on pp. 354-5.
687—1. 15 from bottom, add: Page 87 (Vol. XVI) 13 February, 1753: William Rockwell, guardian to Isaac Williams, late of Middletown, decd., moves for distribution of land lying in common with heirs of Sarah Williams.
696—1. 12 from bottom, add: Page 96 (Vol. XVI) 13 April, 1753: Elijah Yeomans, aged 15, son of Elijah Yeomans, late of Tolland, decd., made choice of Joshua Wills of Tolland to be his guardian. This Court appoint Joshua Wills to be a guardian to Oliver Yeomans, aged 13, Eunice aged 8, and Elisha aged 6 years.

Will of Gregory Wolterton,

HARTFORD, 1674.

Photographed from the Original, on file in the Office of the Probate Court at Hartford, Conn.

I Gregory Wolterton of Stratford upon the River of
Chrastroke doe make this my last will and testament
wherin I give unto my wife Jane Wolterton the sum of twenty
pound to be payd her within ... ... as if myself prouid ... ...
if he in sig as the defect I doe also give unto John my wife
for dwelling and liberty and use of the thre rome while she ... last
... ... is meet to be gardon but not for so let it away to any
but for to use it for her owne use during the time of her life and
for to use some part together and be meet for her conveniency
and liberty for to let her firewood in the yard I doe also give unto her
the sum pound to be payd her by ... ... by my Stratford during
the time of her life I doe also give unto Hamett Wolterton the sum
of mahors wolterton that had his passage in ... ... in ... England
of mahors wolterton ... ...
...

I Gregory wolterton of hartford upon the River of
Conictacoote doe make this my last will and testimement
wherein I give unto my wife Jane wolterton the some of twenty
pound to be payd in movebel goods as it prised & provided that
it be in such as she desire I doe also give unto Jane my wife
her dweling and liberty and use of the nue roome which was last
bilt which is next to the garden but not for to let it away to any
but for to use it for her owne use during the time of her life and
for to use some part of the seller and the ouene for her Convenienty
and liberty for to set her firewood in the yard I doe also give unto
her six pound to be payd to her every yeare by my excecktor during
the time of her life I doe also give unto James wolterton the son
of mathew wolterton that live in Ipsage in sufolke in owld Ingland
ten pond if he be living if not to his Childeren eaquelly divided I also give
unto Mathew waller of nue londen five pound I give also unto
Rebecka waller ten pound I give unto sara waller five pound
I give unto John shepeard sener the son of Edward shepard one peese
of land by estemation fower ackers be it more or les lying and
buting upon benieme harbor east paul peck south John bidall north
and upon paul peck and John bidall west and he is for to pay twenty
shilings to his father Edward shepard twenty shilings to his sister
Debbera fairbankes and twenty to his sister sara Tomson and twenty
shilings to his sister Abegeles Childeren I doe heereby give
unto hanna lord and to mary lord the daughters of Thomas lord
that is deseased five pound a peese and the things that are left
in the trounke that wer the mothers for to be devided butwin them
and Mary for to have trounke and also to the sones of wiliam
waller deseased at lime that is to say to wiliam waler ten pound
to John waler ten pound to samull waler ten pound and to mathew
waler ten pound mor over I give to wolstone brockwood seaner ten
pound and to wiliam brockwod his son ten pound also I give to bethia
stoken the daughter of samiuell stoken five pound.
I give unto samuell stoken seaner forty shilings and also unto
steven hopcines seaner forty shilings I doe also give unto na
thanill standly twenty shilings also to mary poorter the wife of
John porter seaner twenty shilings also unto hanna poorterr the
wife of samuell poorter twenty shilings also I give unto the
wife of Isacke Moore of farminton twwenty shilings also I
give unto Mr John whiting paster of the Congregation five pound
also I give one parsell of land lying in hoccannum sixe ackers
be it more or les abuting on the great River west on Nathanile
bakon south and on the land belongingen to the scoole North and upon
the upland east unt Mr James Richards and John whit sener and
to whome they shall apoint as foffees in trust for the only use &
behoufe for the maintinence of the ministry of the mennistrey
of the south side of the Riveret the Church wherof Mr whiting is now
pastor, more over I give unto Elisebeth Antrewes the wife of
John Andrews juner forty shilings also I give unto Mr Joseph Haynes teacher
at the owld meeting house forty shilings also I order unto dority lord
lord the daughter of thomas lord deseased twenty shilings
and more over I give unto John mirels and his Ayers for ever booth my
howsing & tanyard & all that I have and all my land that Is undisposd

...nome Iordayne and appoint... of ... to his my last will & Testament ... & to ... to all & singler my loueing friends Mr James
... and John w[hi]t... ... to the ouer sett for his my last
will & Testament as witnes my hand and sealle this present ... of July
1674

Gregory Wolterton

signed & sealed in
presence of vs

James Richards

John w[hi]te

Aug[ust] 26 1674
These may Certifie that Gregory Woollterton did in the presence of
John while and my selfe (witnesses aboue subscribed) sygne seale
deliuer and declare the within and aboue so writeing to be his
last will and Testam[en]t.   as Attests James Richards. Asst

me John whise made oath in court Sept[embe]r 3 1674. that Gregory winterton
signed sealed & deliuered this as his last will & Testament in presence of m[aste]r James
Richards & himselfe as attests   John Allyn Secret[ar]y

whome I ordayne and apoint sole excetor to this my last will
will & testement I doe also desire my loving frinds Mr James
Richards and John whit sener for to be overseers to this my last
will & testiment as witnes my hand and seale this seventene of July
1674   Gregory wolterton
Signed & sealed in
presence of us
James Richards
John White

Augt 26, 1674

These may Certifie that Gregory woollterton did in the Presence of
John white and my selfe (wittnesses above subscribed) signe seale
deliver and declare the within and above sd writenig to bee his
last will and testamt

as Attests James Richards Assist.

Mr John White made oath in court Sept 3 1674 that Gregory winterton
signed sealed & delivered this as his last will & Testament in
presence of Mr James Richards & himself as Attests

John Allyn Secrety

EAST FACE

Monument in memory of the Founders and Settlers of Hartford, Conn. — Erected in the old churchyard of the First Congregational Church.—Now called the Center Cemetery.

PROBATE RECORDS.

VOLUME XI.

1729 to 1732.

Page 158-9.

Ackley, Samuel, Haddam. Died 18 January, 1729-30. Invt. in land, £337. Taken by James Spencer, John Bate and James Cone.

Court Record, Page 27—1 September, 1730: Adms. to Hannah Ackley, the widow, who exhibits an inventory. Accepted and ordered to be recorded and kept on file.

Page 44 (Vol. XVI) 28 November, 1751: An account of Adms. on the estate of Samuel Ackley was now exhibited in Court by David Gates, Adms. Accepted. Also, the sd. Adms. moves for a distribution, whereupon this Court appoint and impower Moses Rowley, John Persivel and John Fuller, of East Haddam, to dist. the estate, viz., 1-3 of the moveable estate to the relict of the deceased, also 1-3 part of the real estate; and to David Ackley, only child, all the residue of sd. estate, both real and personal, to be to him and his heirs forever.

Dist. File: 20 May, 1752: To the widow, Hannah Gates; to David Ackley, only son. By Moses Rowley, John Fuller and John Parsivel.

Page 265.

Adams, Esther, Hartford. Died 30 October, 1732. Invt. £15-00-01. Taken 6 December, 1732, by Timothy Cowles and Nehemiah Smith.

Court Record, Page 78—5 December, 1732: Adms. to Joseph Cowles, and, with Daniel Bidwell, recog. in £200.

Page 84—6 March, 1732-3: Exhibited an inventory. Accepted, ordered to be recorded and kept on file.

Page 325-6-7.

Allyn, Dea. Thomas, Middletown. Invt. £1204-18-04. Added, £949-10-00. Taken by Jabez Hamlin, Solomon Adkins and Nathaniel Bacon. Will dated 1 December, 1733.

I, Thomas Allyn, of Middletown, do make this my last will and testament: Imprs. I give to my wife Hannah Allyn fourty pounds out of my moveable estate, also the use of one-half of my dwelling house and cellar, and the use of one-third of my barn and yard and orchard and of all my improved lands; all this so long as she continues my widow. Item. I give to my daughter Elizabeth, and to her heirs forever, my lot on which my dwelling house now stands, from the highway eastward so far as my lot extends, with all the buildings, yards and orcharding upon the said land, and also westward from said highway the whole breadth of my lot unto the highway on Stony Hills, about 75 acres. Also, I give her the sixty acres of land lying in the long lots on the east side the Great River, which I bought of brother Jonathan Smith. Also, all my right in uncle Thomas Allyn's new division on the east side the Great River: i. e., my own right as heir to him, and what I bought of my brethren; and also the one-half of all my rights to undivided lands and commonage. Also, two-thirds of my sheep, and the one-half of all my other stock and moveable estate whatsoever (after her mother has taken the fourty pounds I have given her in what she pleaseth), hereby obliging my said daughter Elizabeth or her heirs seasonably to pay the one-half of my just debts and funeral charges and half the legasie hereafter mentioned. Item. I give to the children of my daughter Hannah Gilbert, deceased, and to her heirs forever: Imprs. I give to her eldest son, Allyn Gilbert, the west end of my new field lot which my house standeth on, about 70 acres. Item. I give to her second son, Nathaniel Gilbert, all my right in the long lot on the east side the Great River, which was originally uncle Thomas Allyn's, about eight schore acres. Item. I give to her two daughters, Hannah and Dorothy Gilbert, one-third of my sheep and one-half of all my other stock. Also, I give them the half of my right in undivided lands and commonage so far as to make each of their portions half as much as one of their brothers. Item. I give to my four grandchildren, Allyn, Nathaniel, Hannah and Dorothy Gilbert, 10 acres of land at the west end of my lot in the new division on the east side ye Great River. Item. I give five pounds in money to be improved for the religious instruction of the children in the New Feild Quarter, and my will is that the minister who shall have the pastoral charge of the people in said Quarter shall be desired to spend a convenient time in the month of June annually in giving pious and Godly instructions to the children. And I do appoint the committee for the school in said Quarter to receive and improve said money for the above-said, ordering them to pay said minister annually six shillings. I appoint my two sons-in-law, Nathaniel Gilbert and Jonathan Allyn, executors.

Witness: *Zacheus Candee,*   THOMAS ALLYN, LS.
          Joseph Blacke,
          William Rockwell.

    Court Record, Page 103—1 January, 1733-4: The will and inventory now exhibited in Court, proven, and both accepted and ordered to be recorded and kept on file.

Will and Invt. on File.

    Arnold, Josiah, Haddam. Died 22 June, 1733. Inventory taken 2 July, 1733, by Benjamin Smith, John Fisk and Thomas Brooks, Sen. Will dated 15th June, 1733.

Know all men by these presents: That I, Josiah Arnold of Haddam, in the County of Hartford and Colony of Connecticutt, in New England, being of a languishing state of body and hastening to my dissolution, yet of sound mind and memory, do make and ordaine this my last will and testament, viz.: First of all, I comend my spirit into the hands of Him that gave it, and my body unto the earth, to be buried in decent Christian burial as my executors shall think fit. And as to these worldly goods wherewith God hath blessed me, I give and bequeath them in manner following, viz.: Imprimis: I give and bequeath to my well-beloved wife Abigail the use and improvement of 1-3 part of all my real estate, both buildings and lands, during her natural life; and 1-3 part of all my personal estate, goods and chattells I give her to be at her own disposal forever. Item. I will and bequeath to Francis and Josiah Arnold, sons of my brother David Arnold, a piece of land containing 39 acres and a 1-2, lying at the south end of Turkey Hill, bounded south on Saybrook line, east on land of Abraham Tyler, north on land of Hannah Tyler, and west on William Scovill's land. Item. To my well-beloved daughter and only child, Rhoda, I give and bequeath all the remaining part of my estate, both real and personal, moveable and imoveable, to be her own forever. Item. I ordain and appoint my brother David Arnold and my well-beloved wife Abigail the sole executors of this my last will and testament. In witness whereof I have hereunto set my hand and seal.

Witness: *Phineas Fiske,*   JOSIAH ARNOLD, LS.
Joseph Munger, Mary X *Smith.*

Court Record, Page 96—29 June, 1733: Will proven.

Page 146-7.

Bacon, Andrew, Middletown. Invt. £570-13-03. Taken 5 August, 1731, by Israhiah Wetmore, William Ward and Joseph Rockwell.

Court Record, Page 53—22 September, 1731: Adms. to Anne Bacon, widow. Recog., with James Tappin, £300.

Page 55.

Bacon, Beriah, Middletown. Invt. £517-07-02. Taken 27 ———, 1730, by John Collins, Joseph Rockwell and Nathaniel Bacon. Will dated 9 May, 1729.

I, Beriah Bacon of Middletown, do make this my last will and testament: I give to Anne, my wife, the 1-3 part of my moveable estate and the use of 1-3 of each parcel of land during life, and which room she shall choose in my dwelling house, with convenient sellering, during her life. I give to my eldest son, Beriah Bacon, my dwelling house and the lott it stands upon, which I bought of John Ranney, and 8 acres of my other half-mile lott which lyeth southward of the highway my house stands by, to be taken out of the north end, upon the east side, half the width of sd. lott; but and if that width cuts off all the brook towards the south part of the 8 acres, then it shall run so wide as to leave convenient watering in the remaining parts of sd. lott southward of the sd. 8 acres. This I give to my son Beriah and to his heirs forever. I give to my son Pierpont Bacon the remaining part of my aforesd. half-mile lott lying southerdly of the highway by my dwelling house. After his brother Beriah has had his 8 acres, the remaining part I give to my son Pierpont and to his heirs forever. I give the remainder of all my lands and moveable estate to be divided equally amongst all my children, sons and daughters, each one an equal share. I make my wife, Anne Bacon, sole executrix.

Witness: *Nathaniel White,*   BERIAH BACON, LS.
John Bacon, 3rd, Joseph White.

A codicil, dated 19 April, 1730: The executrix may advance some part of the moveable estate to the daughters in case of need (as of marriage before they come of full age), such advances to be a part of their portions.

Witness: *Joseph White,*   BERIAH BACON, LS.
John Churchill.

Court Record, Page 21—2 June, 1730: Will proven.

Page 63—4 April, 1732: Tabitha Bacon, a daughter of Beriah Bacon of Middletown, chose her uncle Nathaniel Bacon to be her guardian. Recog., £100.

Page 73—4 August, 1732: This Court appoint Ann Bacon, alias Gill, the relict of Beriah Bacon, late of Middletown, and her present husband Joshua Gill to be guardians to Beriah Bacon, age 12 years, Pierpont Bacon, age 8 years, Ann 10, and Bethia Bacon, age 4 years. Recog., £200.

Dist. File: 13 June, 1733: Dist. of the estate as followeth: To the widow, Anne Bacon; to Elizabeth Passewell, to Anna Bacon, to Tabitha Bacon, to Beriah, eldest son; to Pierpont Bacon.

Page 1 (Vol. XII) 28 March, 1731: Dist. of the estate of Beriah Bacon exhibited in Court by Ann Gill, executrix, Nathaniel Bacon and William Rockwell.

Page 233.

Bacon, John, Middletown. Will dated 30 October, 1732.

I, John Bacon, Sen., of Middletown, do make this my last will and testament: I give unto Mary, my well-beloved wife, all my right and interest in any lands or moveable estate whatsoever that she brought with her or stood possessed of when I married with her, that are now in being, and also two cowes which I now have: all this I do give to her and her heirs forever. Also I give unto her the improvement and use of my dwelling house which I now dwell in, and the yard before the doore to the highway, and the garden southward of the house, and liberty to fetch water from the well, and the rent of all my lands in Hartford; these I give to her for her comfort during her natural life. And I do hereby prohibit her receiving any tenant into my dwelling house without the consent or liberty of my son John Bacon. I give unto my daughter Sarah 1-2 of my brass kettle and all the pewter ware which I now have which did belong to her mother, my former wife Sarah. Also I give unto her all my Wongunk swamp which lies against the end of the meadow of her husband Nathaniel Brown. I do hereby order my son John Bacon to pay to my sd. daughter £10 out of my moveable estate. All this I give to my sd. daughter and to her heirs forever. I do further give unto my wife Mary 1-3 part of my swine, Indian corne and flax, and the whole of a parcel of yarn which she hath prepared for cloth. And my will is she shall have 3 bushels of wheat and 2 bushels of Indian meal from my grist mill yearly so long as my sd. mill shall continue in order, or during her natural life. I give unto my son John Bacon, whom I likewise make my only and sole executor, all and singular my houseing and lands and all other estate, whatsoever and wheresoever the same shall and may be found or belonging unto me by any lawfull means (he paying my funerall charges, just debts and legacies), all by him freely to be possessed and injoyed forever.

Witness: *John Collins,*   JOHN BACON, LS.
Nathaniel Collins, William Rockwell.

Court Record, Page 77—17 November, 1732: Will proven.

Bacon, Nathaniel. Court Record, Page 63—4 April, 1732: Nathaniel Bacon, as guardian, exhibits in Court a receipt bearing date 31 January, 1731-2, from John Bacon, that he had received from his guardian, Nathaniel Bacon, all the estate due from said guardian to him.

Bailey, Christopher. Court Record, Page 91—17 May, 1733: Christopher Bailey, a minor, 15 years of age, chose Seth Wetmore, of Middletown, to be his guardian. Recog., £100. Cert: *Giles Hall, J. P.*

Page 122-123.

Bancroft, Ephraim, Windsor. Died 1st May, 1731. Invt. £87-13-00. Taken by John Cady, Samuel Osborn and David Bissell. Will dated 17 October, 1727.

I, Ephraim Bancroft, Sen., of Windsor, do make this my last will and testament: I give to my son Nathaniel my house and homestead, both upland and meadow, and orchard adjoining, lying in Windsor, to him and his heirs forever. Also, that part of my lott that I bought of Joseph Owen running from the common road or highway eastward to the end of Three-Mile ————, I give to my sons Nathaniel and Thomas, to be equally divided between them. Also, after my decease, I give my moveable estate to my son Nathaniel and his heirs forever. I give to my son Ephraim, besides what I have already given him, 10 shillings in money or that which is equivalent. I give to my daughter Sarah 1 cowe besides what I have already given her. I give to my son John £7 in money or other pay equivalent, to be paid out of my estate by my son Nathaniel. I give to my son Daniel £5 in money or other pay equivalent, to be paid by my son Nathaniel. I give to my son Thomas all my lands lying on the west side of the road or highway running down to the Great River, on which Thomas's house now standeth. This I give him besides what I have given to him in this my last will and testament. Also my will and pleasure is that my teeme tackling shall be equally divided between my son Nathaniel and my son Thomas. I do hereby appoint my son Nathaniel Bancroft and Jeremiah Bissell, of Windsor, my executors.

Witness: *Edward Hunting,*   EPHRAIM BANCROFT, LS.
Ebenezer Stiles, Sarah Pinney, Jr.

Court Record, Page 48—6 July, 1731: Will proven.

Page 84-5.

Banks, John, Middletown. Invt. £373-10-11. Taken 23 December, 1730, by John Sage, Samuel Gipson and John Warner.

Court Record, Page 34—5 January, 1730-1: Adms. to Elizabeth Banks, widow.

Page 25 (Vol. XIII) 22 March, 1737-8: William Banks, age 14 years, son of John Banks, chose William Rockwell to be his guardian. Recog., £50. Cert: *Giles Hall, J. P.*

Page 1 (Vol. XIV) 6 April, 1742: Sarah Banks, a minor, 17 years of age, and Mary Banks, a minor, 12 years of age, daughters of John Banks, chose William Rockwell of Middletown to be their guardian. Recog., £200.

Page 30-31.

Barbour, David, Hebron. Invt. £1300-03-00, plus. Taken 3 December, 1729, by Samuel Waters, Joseph Phelps and Samuel Curtis. Will dated 2 October, 1729.

I, David Barbour of Hebron, in the County of Hartford, do make this my last will and testament: I give to Hannah, my wife, £30 in current money of the Colony; also 1 black mare and 1-3 part of my buildings and household goods, debts and moveable estate during her naturall life; and also the improvements of all my real and personal estate for the careful bringing up of my children until they arrive to lawful age, and then the sd. improvements to return to the sd. children as they shall come to lawfull age. And after her death the sd. 1-3 part to return to each child to whome it belongs, as hereafter mentioned. I do likewise make Hannah, my sd. wife, sole executrix.   I give to my son David land adjoining Morris Tilletson's land and Jacob Root's land, together with 1-2 of my common and undivided right of land, and also part of the orchard on the east side of sd. highway, for 6 years forward after my son David come to lawfull age, and no longer.   I give to my son Stephen the remainder of my land on the east side of the highway; also my homestead with the buildings thereon, together with 1-2 of my common or undivided right of land, for which the sd. Stephen shall pay £5 money to each of the sisters within two years after he comes of age.   I give to my daughter Hannah £10 current money of the Colony; also the other two of my daughters, viz., Temperance and Mary, an equal legacy with Hannah save the £10 as above given, which gift or legacies to my sd. daughter shall be in my other lands already laid out in three certain parcells as far as these three parcells will do, and the moveables to make the remainder.   I make Capt. Hezekiah Gaylord and Sergt. John Phelps, of Hebron, my overseers.

Witness: *Nathaniel Stiles,*   DAVID BARBOUR, LS.
Asaell Phelps, Samuel Curtice.

Court Record, Page 9—6 January, 1729-30: Will proven.

Page 80—6 February, 1732-3: David Barbour of Hebron, age 16 years, chose Joseph Phelps of Hebron to be his guardian. Recog., £100.

Page 90—17 May, 1733: Temperance Barbour chose Joseph Phelps to be her guardian. Recog., £100.

Page 53 (Vol. XIII) 27 December, 1739: Mary Barbour, age 14 years, chose Israel Post of Hebron to be her guardian. Recog., £200. Cert: *Joseph Phelps, J. P.* And Stephen Barbour, a minor, 15 years of age, chose Moses Case of Hebron to be his guardian.   Recog., £200.

Page 18-19.

Barbour, Lieut. Josiah, Windsor. Invt. £817-01-00. Taken 7 January, 1729-30, by Jacob Drake, Job Loomis and Timothy Loomis. (See File for date and names.)   Will dated 1st April, 1726.

I, Josiah Barbour of Windsor, "wheel wright," do make this my last will and testament: I give unto Sarah, my wife, for her to have and injoy, 1-3 part of my lands, some portions that I purchased of Ebenezer Gilbert and Ebenezer Spencer, and also of Ebenezer Williams's land that belonged to Mark Kelsey, and 1-3 part of the land I purchased of Josiah Cooke and Joanna his wife.   I also give unto my wife, for her to have and injoy only for and during ye time she shall happen to live and remain my widow, my parlour or lower room of my dwelling house, also 1-2 part of the west end of my barn.   Also, I give to her a feather bed, a mare and a cowe, to be her own forever, and one year's provision.   The reason why I have not given unto my wife any more of my moveable estate is because that I had none of her estate left her by her former husband, for she disposed of the same unbeknowne to me, and she may dispose of my estate (if given) as she did her former husband's and so leave herself destitute. I give to Nathaniel Barbour, my eldest son, besides what I have already given him by deed of gift, all my land in the lower field on the west side of the road to Windsor, 1-3 part of the land I purchased of Ebenezer Williams that belonged to Mark Kelsey, 1-3 part of the land I purchased of Josiah Cook and Joanna his wife, and also 1-3 part of the land I purchased of Ebenezer Gilbert and Ebenezer Spencer; also, 1-3 part of all my undivided land that shall be laid out by virtue of any right belonging unto me. Also, I give to son Nathaniel Barbour £20 in money, to be paid him by his brother Aaron Barbour. I give to my son Jonathan Barbour, besides what I have already given him by deed of gift, 2-3 part of the land purchased of Ebenezer Williams that belonged to Mark Kelsey, 2-3 part of the land I purchased of Josiah Cook, also 1-3 part of the meadow land I purchased of Ebenezer Gilbert and Ebenezer Spencer, also 1-3 part of all undivided lands. I give him £20 as money, to be paid him by his brother Aaron Barbour. I give my son Aaron Barbour my home lott, dwelling house, barn, and all edifices erected on the same, with other lands. Also, I give him all my "wheel wright's" tools. I give to my two daughters, Abigail Brown and Rebeckah Drake, to each of them £80 in current pay or 2-3 money. I give unto my daughter Abigaill £5 more. I give to my grandchildren: to Elizabeth Drake, if she continues to live at my house till she comes of age, the sum of £20 in current pay or 2-3 money; and to Hannah Drake £15 as money. I make my sons, Nathaniel Barbour, Jonathan Barbour and Aaron Barbour, executors.

Witness: *Charles Whiting,* JOSIAH BARBOUR, LS.
Samuel Howard, John Dod.

A codicil, dated 9 December, 1729: I, the sd. Josiah Barbour, by this present codicil, do ratify and confirm my last will and testament, and do give to my wife Sarah 10 bushels of Indian corne, 6 bushels of rie, and 20 pounds of flax and a barrel of sider, and all the pork, butter and suit in the house, to be paid to her, my sd. wife Sarah, immediately after my decease. And whereas I have ordered a legacy to be paid by my executor to my two grandchildren, Elizabeth Drake and Hannah Drake, my will is that Elizabeth Drake shall have one of the feather beds and one of the blankets my wife made since we married, and Hannah Drake the other feather bed and two blankets which she made since she came here, and the middle brass kettle, as part of their legacies, to be valued at inventory price; but my wife Sarah shall have the use of them during her natural life.

Witness: *Elisha Pratt, Sarah Pratt,* JOSIAH BARBOUR, LS.
Hannah Loomis, Timothy Loomis.

Court Record, Page 8—6 January, 1729-30: Will proven.

Page 49—3 August, 1731: The executors exhibit receipts under the hands of the heirs.

Page 155-6.

Barbour, Ruth, Windsor. Invt. £84-10-06. Taken 30 November, 1731, by Nathaniel Drake, John Cook, Jr., and Henry Allyn. Will dated 13 November, 1716.

I, Ruth Barbour of Windsor, thought it best to make this my last will and testament: After my just debts and funerall expenses are paid, my will is that what is wanting of my son Benjamin and John Barbour's portion, and also of Sarah Barbour's portion, according to their father Samuel Barbour's last will, shall be made up to each of them out of my estate. Further, I freely release my son Joseph Barbour from that 20 shillings per annum that he was to pay unto me by his Father Barbour's will. I fully discharge my son Benjamin Barbour from paying for his dyet while he has been with me, provided he demand nothing of my executors for what work he has done for me, nor for the corn or meat I have had of him. I give to my son John Barbour my mare and a steer, and all my right in the oxen that sd. Joseph Barbour bought of Josiah Barbour, and also hay to keep them this winter. I give to my daughter Sarah my best bed and furniture, also a pig and four bushels of corne and two of rye. I give to my son-in-law, Samuel Barbour, 20 shillings in money besides what he owes me. I give to my grandson, William Barbour, 5 shillings in money. Lastly, my will is that the remainder of my whole estate be divided to and among my children hereafter named, in equal shares, viz., to David Barbour, Joseph Barbour, Benjamin Barbour, John Barbour, Mary Brown, Ruth Phelps, Elizabeth Loomis and Sarah Barbour. I make my son Joseph Barbour sole executor.

Witness: *Matthew Allyn,*   RUTH X BARBOUR, LS.
        Thomas Marshall.

Court Record, Page 86—December, 1731 : Will proven.

Page 83, 93.

Barbour, Sarah, widow of Lieut. Josiah Barbour, Windsor. Died 1730-31. Invt. £50-02-08. Taken 4 January, 1730-31, by Thomas Marshall, Thomas Filer and Timothy Loomis. Presented by Deacon Nathaniel Drake, Remembrance Sheldon, Adms., and Hannah his wife.

See File: We, the subscribers, being the only heirs of the estate of our honoured mother, Sarah Barbour deceased, relict and widow of Lt. Josiah Barbour of Windsor, do hereby mutually agree to divide the estate as followeth: To Enoch Drake, eldest son, his double portion; to Benoni Trumble and Sarah his wife, to Remembrance Sheldon and Hannah his wife, and to Nathaniel Drake, to each of them their single portions. To which agreement we, the subscribers, do hereby bind ourselves, all to each and each to other, and each of our heirs, in the full and just sum of £50 of current money of this Colony, to be paid by him or them that shall refuse to stand to the above agreement to him or them that shall stand to and abide by the same. 30 February, 1730-1.

ENOCH DRAKE, LS.	REMEMBRANCE SHELDING, LS.
NATHANIEL DRAKE, LS.	SARAH TRUMBLE, LS.
BENONI TRUMBLE, LS.	HANNAH SHELDING, LS.

Witness: *Giles Elsworth,*
        Timothy Loomis.

Court Record, Page 33—5 January, 1730-1: Invt. exhibited by Nathaniel Drake and Remembrance Sheldon, Adms. Accepted.

Page 37—7 February, 1730-1: Agreement exhibited and confirmed by the Court.

Page 194.

Bate, James, Sen., East Haddam. Invt. £1032-19-01. Taken 13 April, 1732, by Daniel Brainard, Timothy Fuller and John Holmes. Will dated 24 December, 1729.

I, James Bate, Sen., of the Township of Haddam, on the east side of the river, in the County of Hartford and Colony of Connecticut, have thought it my duty to make my last will and testament: My will is my wife Mary Bate shall, at my decease, have 1-3 part of my moveable estate wholly at her own dispose, according to her own choice; also, that during her widowhood she shall injoy and have the full profit and benefit of my house, barn, orchard and homelott, as also the benefit of my land lying by the Cove, so far as she may have occasion for it on account of firewood. My will is that my grandchild, Elizabeth Fuller, have £20 out of my estate, and no more, since her mother in her lifetime had sundry things out of my estate which I have taken no particular account of. My will is that all my estate (besides what I have here absolutely disposed of), both real and personal, wheresoever it is to be found, whether in buildings, lands, cattle, or in other things, shall be equally divided among my 7 children, viz., Rebeckah, Ruth, Alis, Mary, Anne, Abigail and Unis. And for as much as there will be found in my Book of Accounts sundry things which some or all of my children have already received, some more and some less, my will is that when each child's part is set out to them that what is found on account shall be considered as so much of their portion already paid. I appoint my wife, Mary Bate, sole executrix.

Witness: *Stephen Hosmer,*   JEAMES BATE, SEN., LS.
Thomas Knowlton, Joseph Spencer.

Court Record, Page 69—6 June, 1732: Will exhibited. Annah Bate, a minor, 16 years of age, Abigail 13 years, and Eunice Bate, age 10 years, chose their mother, Mrs. Mary Bate, as their guardian. Recog., £150.

Page 73—4 July, 1732: The will of James Bate, exhibited last June, being fully proven, John Comstock the 2nd, of Lyme, in right of his wife Rebeckah, daughter of James Bate, moves this Court for a distribution. This Court appoints Deacon Daniel Brainard, Lt. John Holmes and Daniel Cone, distributors.

Dist. File: 15 November, 1732: To Mary Bate, widow; to Rebeckah Comstock, eldest daughter; to Ruth Gibbs, to (Elec) Alice Hall, to Mary Comstock, to Annah Bate, to Abigail Bate, to Eunice Bate and to Elizabeth Fuller (granddaughter), to each of them the sum of £158. By Deacon Daniel Brainard, Lt. John Holmes and Daniel Cone, distributors.

Page 51 (Vol. XII) 5 October, 1736: John Bate, a minor son of James Bate, chose his brother Samuel Bate to be his guardian.

Page 328.

Belding, Gideon, Wethersfield. Invt. £79-18-00. Taken 28 December, 1733, by Jacob Williams, Benjamin Wright and David Goodrich.

Court Record, Page 103—1st January, 1733-4: Adms. granted to Elizabeth Belding.

Page 8 (Vol. XII) 6 August, 1734: Elizabeth Belding, widow, moves this Court to set out moveables for her support, the estate being reported insolvent. Thomas Deming and Benjamin Wright appointed commissioners. Elisha Belding, a son, 19 years of age, chose Josiah Churchill to be his guardian. Ruth Belding, age 16 years, chose her uncle Daniel Belding to be her guardian, also appointed guardian to Ebenezer Belding, age 3 years. Elizabeth, age 14 years, chose her mother, Elizabeth Belding, to be her guardian. And this Court appoint the widow guardian to Hannah, age 11 years, Hezekiah 8 years, Sarah 7 years, and Gideon 5 months old, all children of Gideon Belding deceased.

Page 35 (Vol. XV) 30 March, 1747: Ebenezer Belding, a minor, 16 years of age, son of Gideon Belding, chose Daniel Belding of Wethersfield to be his guardian. Recog., £300.

Page 119.

Bidwell, Zebulon, Hartford. Invt. £201-19-09. Taken 7 April, 1731, by John Meekins and Nehemiah Olmsted.

Court Record, Page 42—6 April, 1731: Adms. to John Bidwell, Jr.

Page 68—22 May, 1732: Mary Bidwell to be guardian to her child, Stephen Bidwell, age 1 1-2 years. Recog., £50.

Page 75: At a Court of Probate held at Hartford, 4 September, 1750, this Court allows to Jonathan Rose, who married the widow of Zebulon Bidwell, of Hartford, decd., guardian to Stephen Bidwell, son of the decd., for keeping sd. minor till he was 4 years old (3 years and 6 months), the sum of £17-10-00. Allowed for Court fees allowing this account £0-12-00.

Page 2 (Vol. XVI) 26 August, 1750: Stephen Bidwell, a minor, aged 20 years, son of Zebulon Bidwell, made choice of his uncle John Bidwell to be his guardian. Recog., £400.

Page 331.

Biggelow, Daniel, Hartford. Died 14 May, 1733. Invt. £119-05-08. Taken 5 June, 1733, by Timothy Cowles and Nehemiah Olmsted.

See File: At a Court of Probate held att Hartford in and for the County of Hartford, on the 3rd day of June, Anno. Dom. 1733, set out to the widow, Elizabeth Biggelow, the relict of Daniel Biggelow, late of Hartford decd., for her necessary support, £16-16-09 of moveables.

Court Record, Page 92—5 June, 1733: Hannah Biggelow, a daughter of Daniel Biggelow, chose William Bidwell of Hartford to be her guardian, also appointed guardian to Martha Biggelow, age 11 years, and Daniel Biggelow, age 8 years. Recog., £150.

Page 94—3 July, 1733: Adms. granted to William Bidwell.

Page 100—6 November, 1733: William Bidwell, Adms., exhibited an account of his Adms. and supposes the estate to be insolvent. Five months allowed for the presentation of claims.

Page 106—5 February, 1733-4: William Bidwell, Adms., presented a further addition of debts. And this Court appoint Joseph Cowles and John Pitkin, of Hartford, commissioners to receive and examine claims against the estate.

Page 55 (Vol. XII) 1st June, 1737: This Court appoint Elizabeth Biggelow to be guardian to her children, viz., Elizabeth, age 8 years, and Thankful, 6 years of age.

Page 167-8.

Biggelow, Joseph, Hartford. Invt. £1494-15-04. Taken 23 September, 1731, by Joseph Cook, Joseph Webster and Samuel Webster. Will dated 4 September, 1731.

I, Joseph Biggelow of Hartford, do make this my last will and testament: I give unto Sarah, my wife, 1-3 part of all and singular my moveables or personal estate at her own disposal. I give to my wife the use of the half of my dwelling house, the half of my orchard, and the half of all the other buildings now standing upon the land whereon I now dwell, and 1-3 part of all my land, for and during her natural life. I give unto my three sons, Joseph, Elisha and Josiah, all my houseing and land, to be equally divided between them (yet so as that my wife shall have the use above mentioned). My will is that my three sons above mentioned shall pay to my three daughters, Sarah, Mary and Abigail, £80 in money to each of them. I give unto my kinsman, Jonathan Williams, £10. I appoint Capt. John Whiting, of Hartford, and my wife Sarah Biggelow, and my son Joseph Biggelow, to be the only executors.

Witness: *Nathaniel Stanly,* JOSEPH BIGGELOW, LS.
John White, Jacob White.

Court Record, Page 61—19 February, 1731-2: Will proven.

Page 99—9 October, 1733: The executors exhibit an account of their Adms., and report the estate indebted £178-13-09 more than the moveable estate.

Page 5 (Vol. XII) 31 May, 1734: The executors, per act of the General Assembly of 9 May, 1734, now give notice of sale of land, Wednesday, 19 June, at 2 of the clock, at beat of drum, to the highest bidder, land with house, barn, shop and orchard on it, to say 10 acres and 1-2, the lott bought of John Williams, shoemaker, on the road to Wethersfield.

Page 187.

Bissell, Jonathan, Windsor. Invt. £263-15-04. Taken 25 November, 1731, by Thomas Elsworth, Ebenezer Bissell and Thomas Judd. Court Record, Page 63—4 April, 1732: Adms. granted to Bridget Bissell, widow, and Jonathan Bissell, son of the decd.

Page 321.

Blake, Jonathan, Middletown. Invt. £341-03-03. Taken 12 November, 1733, by John Harris, Joseph Johnson and Stephen Blake. Will dated 9 October, 1733.

I, Jonathan Blake of Middletown, do make this my last will and testament: I give to my wife Mary room in ½ of my house and barne and homelott, and also, half of my pasture that I bought of William Ward; also, half the land that I bought of John Andrus; also half of a piece of land I bought of Samuel Eglestone; the use of all my husbandry utensils and 1-3 part of my personal estate during the time of her widowhood. I give to my son Daniel all that piece of land that my father Johnson gave my wife in the northwest quarter of lands in Middletown, he paying to his sisters £160 money as they arrive at lawful age. I give to my son Jonathan Blake the equal halfe of my house and barne and homelott, with the buildings upon it, also the equal half of my pasture that I bought of William Ward, also the equal halfe of the land I bought of John Andrus, also half of the land I bought of Samuel Eglestone, he paying £40 money to his sisters when he arrives to lawful age. I give to my son Stephen Blake the equal halfe of lands as given to my son Jonathan Blake, he paying £40 to his sisters when he arrives to lawful age. Also, I give to my two sons, Jonathan and Stephen, all my interest in commonage or undivided lands in Middletown on the west side of the Great River, in equal proportion. I give to my five daughters, Mary, Elizabeth, Prudence, Mercy and Sarah, all my interest in land, divided or undivided, on the east side of the Great River in Middletown. Also, I give them £240 money, to be paid by their brothers as above specified, in equal proportions. I appoint my wife sole executrix.

Witness: *Benjamin Wetmore,*   JONATHAN BLAKE, LS.
Jabez Hamlin, John Cornwall.

Court Record, Page 101—15 November, 1733: Will exhibited by Mary Blake, widow, and well proven by the witnesses thereto. And it appears in sd. will that the testator gave to his eldest son Daniel a piece of land which in right sd. testator had not power to dispose of, and ordered his eldest son to pay legacies to his daughters as they come of age. And Daniel appeared in Court and objected against sd. will. And it appears that the sd. Daniel had nothing to pay sd. legacies with. Therefore sd. will is not approved. The Court grant Adms. to Mary Blake, widow, who gave bond with Joseph Johnson of £400.

Page 30 (Vol. XII) 1st July, 1735: Mary Blake, widow, Adms., exhibits an account of her Adms. Accepted.

Page 24 (Vol. XIII) 7 March, 1737-8: Jonathan Blake, age 16 years, son of Jonathan Blake, chose his uncle Stephen Blake to be his guardian. Recog., £100. Cert: *Giles Hall, J. P.*

Blancher, Elizabeth. Court Record, Page 17—7 April, 1730: Elizabeth Blancher desires to take the guardianship of her child, Richard Norton, age 13 years, which this Court approves. Recog., £50.

Page 88.

Boardman, Elizabeth, Middletown. Invt. £115-05-06. Taken 23 December, 1730, by John Sage, Samuel Gipson and John Warner.

Court Record, Page 34—5 January, 1730-31: Adms. to Mrs. Elizabeth Banks, of Middletown.

Page 268.

Boardman, Samuel, Middletown. Invt. £112-04-00. Taken 29 November, 1732, by Nathaniel White and Ebenezer Hurlbut.

Court Record, Page 87—3 April, 1733: Adms. to Stephen Boardman, the widow desiring the same, and he recognized with Lieut. Tho: Cadwell. Exhibit of an inventory, which was accepted and ordered on file.

Page 334.

Boardman, Sarah, Wethersfield. Died 23 January, 1732-3. Invt. £103-00-06. Taken 2 March, 1732-3, by Samuel Steele, Isaac Riley and Ebenezer Dickinson. Will dated 25 March, 1727-8.

I, Sarah Boardman, of Wethersfield, widow and relict of Mr. Samuel Boardman, being very aged, do now make this to be my last will and testament: Whereas, it pleased my husband (of happy memory) to endow me with six pounds a year, to be paid to me annually by my two sons, David and Joseph, in equal proportion, I do give unto my sd.. sons such part as remain unpaid to me by them. And whereas, my said husband was pleased (by his last will) to give me £70, to be at my dispose, and some part of the £70 hath never yet been distributed to me, I do hereby give that part unto my two sons, David and Joseph Boardman, in equal portion, forever. Item. I give to my daughter, Abigail Boardman, wife to my son David, one pair of cobirons. Item. I give to my daughter, Mary Boardman, wife to my son Joseph Boardman, one heifer now two years old. Item. The remaining part of ye sd. seventy pounds, with what I have gotten by my industry, I give to William Warner, Sarah Warner and Hannah Warner, my grandchildren, in equal proportion. And I do hereby appoint my sons, David and Joseph Boardman, and my daughter, Mary Warner, executors.   SARAH X BOARDMAN, LS.

Witness: *Edward Bulkley,*
Joseph Treat, Josiah Riley.

Court Record, Page 90—1 May, 1733: The will now proven. David Boardman refused the trust and Mary Warner accepted. Will and inventory ordered to be recorded and kept on file.

Page 163-4.

Buckland, Charles, Hartford. Died 23 December, 1731. Invt. £51-10-04. Taken 27 January, 1731-2, by Timothy Cowles, John Meakins and Joseph Pitkin.

Court Record, Page 59—1st February, 1731-2: Adms. granted to Esther Buckland, widow. Also, this Court appoint her guardian to Charles Buckland, 11 years of age. Recog., £50.

Page 64—4 April, 1732: The Adms. reports the estate insolvent. This Court appoint Lt. John Meakins and Ensign Joseph Pitkin commissioners, and direct them to set out to the widow the sum of £17-12-02.

Page 11 (Vol. XII) 1st September, 1734: Charles Buckland, age 14 years, chose Joseph Shepherd of Hartford to be his guardian. Esther Buckland, Adms., exhibits now an account of her Adms., which this Court accepts.

Page 140-1.

Bulkeley, Rev. John, Colchester. Invt. £689-14-10. Taken by Samuel Loomis and Nathaniel Foster.

Court Record, Page 53—22 September, 1731: Adms. granted to Patience Bulkeley, with John Bulkeley, son of the deceased.

Page 20 (Vol. XVII) 10 May, 1754: Mr. Oliver Bulkeley, one of the heirs to the estate of the Rev. Mr. John Bulkeley, late of Colchester deceased, now moves to this Court that dist. be made of the real estate. The Court so order, viz.: To the heirs of John Bulkeley, Esq., deceased, a double share, and to Gershom, Charles, Peter and Oliver Bulkeley, and to Sarah Bulkeley alias Welles, Dorothy Bulkeley, Patience Bulkeley alias Lord, and Lucy Bulkeley alias Lord, to each of them their single shares of sd. estate. And appoint Israel Foot, Samuel Filer and Alexander Phelps, distributors. Also, this Court order the distributors to set out to Mrs. Patience Bulkeley, relict, her thirds of the estate.

Bulkeley, Jonathan. Court Record, Page 2—2 August, 1729: Jonathan Bulkeley, a minor, 14 years of age, with the consent of his mother and father-in-law, Elizabeth and James Forbes, chose Joseph Pitkin to be his guardian.

Bull, Isaac. Court Record, Page 86—22 March, 1732-3: Isaac Bull, a minor, 18 years of age, son of Daniel Bull, late of Jamaica, Long Island, decd., chose Daniel Bull of Hartford to be his guardian. Recog., £100.

Page 10 (Vol. XII) 19 September, 1734: Caleb Bull, 15 years of age, son of Daniel Bull, late of Jamaica, L. I., chose Aaron Bull of Hartford, his brother, to be his guardian. Allowed.

Bull, Susannah. Court Record, Page 4—7 October, 1729: Susannah Bull, a minor, 13 years of age, chose Mary Bull, her mother, to be her guardian.

Page 320-1.

Bunce, John, Hartford. Invt. £538-06-08. Taken by Jonathan Olcott and Jonathan Steele. Will dated 16 July, 1730.

I, John Bunce of Hartford, do make this my last will and testament: I give unto my wife Mary Bunce the use and improvement of all my houseing and lands during life, and all my moveable and personal estate to be at her own dispose as she pleases, to and amongst my children. After my wife's decease I give all my houseing and lands, the moiety or half-part thereof, unto my son James Bunce, and the other moiety or ½ part thereof unto my grandsons, Jacob, John and Isaac Bunce, to be equally divided to them, my sd. son James Bunce 1 part, and my sd. grandsons, Jacob Bunce, John Bunce and Isaac Bunce, the other part, to be to them and their heirs forever. Binding and obliging my sd. grandsons, when they are of lawful age and come into possession of what I have given them, to pay 20 shillings apiece unto their father (my eldest son) John Bunce, Jr., per annum during his natural life. I give unto my sd. son John Bunce 20 shillings besides what I have formerly given him, to be paid him out of my estate. I give unto my three daughters 5 shillings apiece besides what I have formerly given them, to be paid out of my estate.

Witness: *George Wyllys,*   JOHN BUNCE, LS.
John Dod, Elizabeth Wyllys.

And further, I, the above-named John Bunce, do make this codicil to my aforewritten will: that my son John Bunce shall have liberty to dwell in my house, which is now the dwelling house of my son James, in case he shall live to survive me and my wife, during my sd. son John's natural life if he my son John shall desire and require the same. And further, it is my will that my son James and my grandchildren, Jacob, John and Isaac, to whom I have given the 1-2 of my houseing and lands, shall have an equal right in my well to use the water thereof as they have occasion. And further, to explain what is above written wherein it is my will, that he shall have my house which I now dwell in for his property after me and my wife's decease.

Witness: *Thomas Ensign, Jr.,*   JOHN BUNCE, LS.
Hezekiah Lane, John Dod.   7 October, 1733.

Court Record, Page 100—6 November, 1733: Will exhibited by Mary Bunce, widow, and James Bunce, son of sd. deceased. There being no executor named in the will, Adms. with the will annexed was granted to the widow and son, and the sd. James Bunce recog. in £300 with Moses Cook.

Page 101—4 December, 1733: Invt. exhibited. Estate insolvent.

Page 108—5 March, 1733-4: James Bunce and Mary Bunce, Adms., exhibited a list of debts due from the estate, £70-13-11; also the account of debts due to sd. estate, amounting to £2-13-00; which account this Court accepts.

Page 14 (Vol. XII) 26 November, 1734: Per act of the General Assembly, 9 May, 1734, directing James and Mary Bunce, Adms., to sell land to the value of £37-03-03 at vandue. Report of sale.

Page 17—2 December, 1734: Land sold to John Skinner, Jr.

Page 1 (Vol. XIII) 1st March, 1736-7: Jacob Bunce, a grandson to John Bunce, showing that by the last will of his grandfather there was given a homested, 1-2 to James Bunce and the other half to Jacob, John and Isaac Bunce, to be divided equally between them; and whereas, there is no person to divide the estate, the sd. Jacob, being now 21 years of age, together with James Bunce, one of the heirs, moves this Court to appoint freeholders to dist. sd. estate. Whereupon this Court do appoint Ensign James Church, Deacon John Edwards and John Skinner, Jr., with the assistance of John Bunce, the father and natural guardian to the sd. John and Isaac Bunce, distributors. If ye sd. John Bunce neglect or refuse to joyn in makeing a division, then the sd. James Church, John Edwards and John Skinner shall make the division.

Page 8—2 June, 1737: Report of the distributors appointed to make division of a certain lott of land, formerly belonging to Mr. John Bunce of Hartford, to Jacob, John and Isaac Bunce, sd. lott of land being the homelott of the testator, bounded north partly upon a highway and partly upon land belonging to the heirs of John Richards, late of Hartford; west on land belonging to Jonathan Steele partly, and partly upon land belonging to Jonathan Mason; east partly upon land belonging to the heirs of John Colwell, and partly upon land belonging to Benjamin Catlin, and partly on land belonging to Jonathan Mason; and south on land belonging to sd. Mason. We have viewed sd. lott of land, and have divided or sett out to Jacob Bunce 1 1-2 acres of sd. land, at the south end of sd. lott, extending northward from Jonathan Mason's land, the wedth of sd. lott, 12 rods.

Dated 3 June, 1737.   JOHN EDWARDS,
           JAMES CHURCH, JOHN SKINNER, JR.

Page 20 (Vol. XIV) 5 April, 1743: Isaac Bunce, a minor, 16 years of age, son of John Bunce, chose Samuel Flagg of Hartford to be his guardian. Recog., £50. Jared Bunce, age 12 years, and Abigail, age 10 years, this Court appoint their mother Abigail Bunce to be their guardian. Recog., £50. Lucretia Bunce, a minor, 13 years, chose her mother, Abigail Bunce, to be her guardian.

Page 23—24 May, 1743: Application being made to this Court that a dist. of the estate of John Bunce, according to the will of the deceased, be made, this Court do appoint James Church, Joseph Cook and Jonathan Seymour, of Hartford, to divide the estate accordingly.

Page 26—7 June, 1743: Report of the distributors.

Page 20 (Vol. XVI) 4 April, 1751: Whereas, there is a motion made to this Court that dist. be made to the heirs of John Bunce, late of Hartford decd., of 2 lotts of land lying in a tier of lotts west of Cooper Lane in Hartford, whereupon this Court appoint John Skinner, Daniel Steel and Thomas Hopkins to make division of sd. land.

Page 24—29 May, 1751: Report of the distributors.

Page 299.

Burnham, Martha, Wethersfield. Will dated 7 August, 1733.

I, Martha Burnham of Wethersfield, do make this my last will and testament: I give and bequeath 5-6 of all my estate unto my children now living, viz., my son Eleazer Gaylord, Martha Wilcocks, Elizabeth Gaylord, Sarah Bissell and Hannah Orvis, unto them equally alike; and the other 6th part I give unto my grandchildren, the children of my son Samuel Gaylord deceased, viz., to Samuel Gaylord, 1-3 part of sd. 6th part; to Eleazer, his brother, 1-3 part, and to Millicent, 1-3 part of sd. 6th part. And whereas, my sd. son Eleazer Gaylord is indebted to me by a note of £14, payable to me, and £5 he has lately received of Mr. John Russell, and 20 shillings he oweth to me an another account, my will is that my estate be all apprised, allowing he oweth me £20, and after it is apprised if the sd. £20 be more than his 6th part, then he to pay what that is more than his 6th part to the rest of the legatees, being allowed 12 months to pay it in. And if he don't pay it within 12 months after my decease, my executor to recover the same by the £14 note. I ordain my son-in-law, Nathaniel Gaylord, sole executor.

Witness: *Daniel Williams,*   MARTHA BURNHAM, LS.
Daniel Harris, Benjamin Woodbridge.

Court Record, Page 97—4 September, 1733: Will proven.

Page 342-3.

Burr, Thomas, Sen., Hartford. Will dated 5 April, 1722.

I, Thomas Burr, inhabitant in Hartford, do make this my last will and testament: To my son Thomas I give the house that he now liveth in, and barn, and homelott belonging to them. I also give to him 1-2 my lott called the Blue Hill lott. To my son Samuel I give him the house that I live in, and the barn, and the homelott belonging thereunto. I also give to him the other half of my Blue Hill lott. I also give to my son Samuel my lott lying in Pine Field, otherwise called the Brick Hill swamp lott. Those houseing and lands thus exprest I give to my sons Thomas and Samuel forever. I give to my son Joseph £20, which I order to be paid equally between my three sons, Samuel, Jonathan and Daniel. To my son Benjamin I give £20, which he hath already received. To my son Jonathan I give my lower lott in the meadow on the east side the Great River, to him and his heirs forever. To my son Isaac I give £10, which I order to be paid equally between my sons Samuel and Jonathan. To my son Daniel I give my upper lott in the meadow lying on the east side of the Great River, and all my undivided land on the east side of the Great River, to him and his heirs forever. To my daughters, Sarah and Hannah, I give three cowes. To my daughter Ann I give one cowe, which she hath already received. To my daughter Abigail I give one cowe. And all the rest of my stock I give to my two sons, Jonathan and Daniel, equally to be divided between them, as my cattle and my horse, my swine and my sheep. I give also to Daniel that lome and tackling that he now works with. It is to be understood that my will is that all my household implements, as bedding, all cloth, and puter, brass, iron, wood, tin, books, tables, chairs and chests, these goods thus exprest I give to my three daughters, that is to say, my daughter Sarah and my daughter Hannah and my daughter Abigaill, equally to be divided between them. It is to be understood that my will is that my daughters, Sarah and Hannah, shall have the use of the north end of my house (that was given to Samuel) as long as they shall live unmarried, and 1-3 of the cellar, and a piece of land big enough for a garden for them, all which shall be for their use as long as they shall live single.

Witness: *Nathaniel Goodwin,*   THOMAS BURR, LS.
Richard Goodman, Samuel Welles.

Postscript, dated 20 May, 1739: My mind and will is that all my undivided lands lying in that tract of land called New Bantom shall be equally divided betwixt my three sons, Thomas, Samuel and Jonathan. And I do now appoint my two sons, Jonathan and Daniel, to be the executors.

Witness: *Nathaniel Goodwin,*   THOMAS BURR, LS.
Thomas Sandford, Daniel Butler.

Court Record, Page 104—5 February, 1733-4: Will proven.

Page 289.

Burton, Samuel, Middletown. Died 23 April, 1733. Invt. £81-12-08. Taken 13 June, 1733, by John Penfield and Nathaniel White.

Court Record, Page 93—3 July, 1733: Adms. granted to Sarah Burton, widow.

Page 24 (Vol. XII) 1st April, 1735: Sarah Burton, Adms., exhibits an account of her Adms., which is accepted.

Page 25 (Vol. XIII) 7 March, 1737-8: Samuel Burton, age 17 years, son of Samuel Burton, and Sarah Burton, age 14 years, chose Benjamin Cornwall of Middletown to be their guardian. Recog., £200.

Page 33—3 October, 1738: Sarah Burton, the widow of Samuel Burton, with Francis Smith, her husband, assent that Mr. John Clark of Middletown may be guardian to Daniel Burton, age 11 years, and Benjamin Burton, age 9 years, children of Samuel Burton. Recog., £300.

Page 54—4 September, 1739: Sarah Smith, the wife of Francis Smith, alias Sarah Burton, Adms. on the estate of Samuel Burton, moves to this Court for a dist. of the moveable estate of sd. deceased to the heirs surviving, she having exhibited an invt., which is on record:

	£ s d	
To Sarah Smith, alias Sarah Burton,	16-07-10	1-3
To James, the eldest son,	8-03-07	
To Simon, Samuel, Daniel, Benjamin, Mary and Sarah Burton, to each of them their single shares,	4-01-09	1-2

And appoint Capt. Nathaniel White and Ensign John Gains, of Middletown, distributors.

Page 139-40.

Butler, Joseph, Hartford. Invt. £611-12-06. Taken 30 August, 1731, by William Gaylord and Henry Brace.

Court Record, Page 51—7 September, 1731: Adms. granted to Esther Butler, widow, and Gideon Butler, son of the decd.

Page 349 (Probate Side, Vol. XII): Know all men by these presents: That we, Samuel Shepherd and Eunice his wife, Thomas Bull in right of his wife decd., Bethia Butler, Rebeckah Butler and Esther Butler, all of Hartford, in the County of Hartford, being the only female heirs to the estate of our honoured father Joseph Butler of sd. Hartford decd., have received of our brother Gideon Butler, Adms. on sd. estate, our full and whole portion of all and every part of our right in sd. estate, and do hereby covenant for ourselves and heirs that neither we nor they shall at any time challenge or have right to any part or parcel of sd. estate, and do hereby discharge our sd. brother and his heirs to sd. estate of any further challenges or demands of any part of sd. estate, real or personal, acknowledgeing we have received in full our whole portion, and do agree that this shall be a full settlement and final determination of the premises. In confirmation hereof we have hereunto each of us set to our hands and seals and acknowledged the same before the Court of Probate, this 2 day of March, 1735-6.

SAMUEL X SHEPHERD, LS.	REBECKAH X BUTLER, LS.
EUNICE X SHEPHERD, LS.	BETHIA X BUTLER, LS.
THOMAS BULL, LS.	ESTHER X BUTLER, LS.

Court Record, Page 41—2 March, 1735: Agreement exhibited and accepted by the Court.

Page 264-5-6.

Butler, Joseph, Wethersfield. Invt. £1000-00-00. Taken 28 February, 1732-3, by Edward Bulkeley, Samuel Collins and John Kirby. Will dated 8 July, 1725.

I, Joseph Butler of Wethersfield, do therefore make this my last will and testament: Imprs. What I have already by deed of gift conveyed to and settled upon my sons Richard Butler and Gershom Butler, both now living, and my son Charles Butler decd., is what my small estate will allow to each of them respectively as so conveyed, and my will and mind is that neither they nor either of them or neither of the rest of their children shall have or injoy any further part, share or portion of my estate, lands, goods or chattells, but be utterly debarred and excluded from any further share or part thereof or demand thereon, the sd. lands so conveyed to them and sd. heirs respectively as aforesd. only excepted and saved. I give, grant, devise and bequeath all the rest and residue of my houses and sd. lands lying in Wethersfield or in Middletown, within sd. County, or elsewhere, not disposed of by deeds as aforesd., to my three sons now living with me, viz., Benjamin Butler, Joseph Butler and Charles Butler, to be holden to them and to their heirs and assigns forever in the proportions and shares following: that is to say, to my sd. son Benjamin 3-7 parts of the whole of my sd. houseing and lands not so disposed of, and my other two sons last mentioned, viz., Joseph and Charles, to have the remaining 4-7 parts equally between them, they paying the legacies hereinafter mentioned. I give to my daughter Mary Butler 2-3 part of all my personal and moveable estate, and order my sd. son Benjamin to pay to her the sum of £25 in current money, and my sd. sons Joseph and Charles shall pay her the sum of £20 like money, each of them. I give to my wife Mary Butler all the rest of my moveable or personal estate of what kind soever, the same being 1-3 part, and also the use and improvement of 1-3 part of all my houseing and lands, for and during the term of her natural life. And I do make my wife sole executrix.

Witness: *Timothy Stevens,*   Jo. BUTLER, LS.
Dorothy Stevens, Tho: Kimberly.

Court Record, Page 81—6 February, 1732-3: Case continued, two of the witnesses being deceased.
Page 84—6 March, 1732-3: Will proven.

Page 229-30.

Butler, Peter, Middletown. Invt. £271-05-06. Taken 2 November, 1732, by Joseph Rockwell, Thomas Stow and William Rockwell.

Court Record, Page 76—13 November, 1732: Adms. to Phebe Butler, widow, with Nathaniel Brown. Recog., £400.

Page 46 (Vol. XIV) 7 August, 1744: An account of Adms. was now exhibited in Court by Phebe Butler, alias Hamlin, and Edward Hamlin, her present husband, Adms. Account accepted. The sd. Adms. move this Court for a dist. of the moveable estate. Ordered as followeth:

	£ s d
To the widow Phebe Butler, alias Hamlin, her thirds,	20-13-08
To Mary, Lucia and Rebeckah Butler, to each,	13-15-09

And appoint Benjamin Adkins, Jonathan Allin and Joseph Clark, distributors.

Page 56—5 March, 1744-5: Report of the distributors.

Page 234.

Camp, Elizabeth, Kensington. Invt. £110-14-09. Taken 30 November, 1732, by Thomas Hart and John Root. Will dated 24 July, 1728.

I, Elizabeth Camp of Kensington, in the Township of Middletown, within the County of Hartford, do make this my last will and testament: I give to my three daughters, Elizabeth, Abigail and Mary, all my wearing apparell, both linen and woolen, to be equally divided among them. And all my other estate, both real and personal, I give to my two sons, Samuel and Caleb Galpen, to be equally divided among them. I do appoint my two sons above mentioned, Samuel and Caleb Galpen, executors.

Witness: *Josiah Boardman,*   ELIZABETH X CAMP, LS.
Isaac Peck, Rebeckah X Hart.

Court Record, Page 78—28 November, 1732: Will exhibited.

Page 288.

Case, Daniel, Simsbury. Died 28 May, 1733. Inventory taken 29 June, 1733, by Nathaniel Higley, Daniel Addams and Reuben Slater. Will dated 25 May, 1733.

I, Daniel Case of Simsbury, do make this my last will and testament: First of all, I give and bequeath unto Penelopy, my wife, 1-3 part of my houseing and lands during her life, the use of 1-3 part of my moveable estate during her life, also my best horse and my best cowe to be her own forever. Nextly, I give all my houseing and lands to my four sons, namely, Daniel, Dudley, Zacheus and Ezekiel, to be equally divided between them, and also all my wearing apparell, and also 1-2 of my tools and team tackling, equally between them. Nextly, I give all the remaining part of my moveable estate to my two daughters, Mindwell and Susannah, to be equally divided between them. I do appoint James Case and my wife Penelopy to be executors.

Witness: *James Hilyer,*   DANIEL CASE, LS.
Jonathan Case, Nathaniel Westover.

Court Record, Page 93—3 July, 1733: Will exhibited.

Page 97—29 June, 1733: This Court appoint Penelope Case to be guardian to Daniel, age 13 years, Mindwell 11, Dudley 9, Susannah 7, Zacheus 4, and Ezekiel 2 years of age, children of Daniel Case decd. Recog., £400.

Page 53 (Vol. XIV) 5 February, 1744-5: An account of Adms. was now exhibited in Court by the executors: Paid in debts and charges, £10-09-02; and received, £9-08-06. Daniel Case, eldest son, now moves this Court to make dist. of the real estate and also of the personal estate according to the will of the sd. deceased. This Court appoint Capt. Nathaniel Holcomb, Joshua Holcomb and Andrew Robe, of Simsbury, to divide the estate and make return of their doings to this Court.

Page 286.

Case, John, Simsbury. Died 22 May, 1733. Invt. £1340-00-00. Taken 8 June, 1733, by Joseph Case, John Humphrey and Daniel Addams. Will dated 14 September, 1730.

I, John Case, Sen., of Simsbury, do make this my last will and testament: I give to my well-beloved wife Sarah 1-3 part of my now dwelling house and barn, with 1-3 part of my improveable land during her natural life, and also 1-3 part of my moveable estate forever. I give to my son John a certain piece of land lying on the east side of the river in Simsbury, being 12 acres that his barn now stands upon, sd. land lying westward of Buttolph's house, north of the highway, bounded northerly side on Josh. Holcomb's land. I give to my son Daniel the pasture lott that his house stands upon, with 4 rods south of his dwelling house and so running west 1 1-2 rods, south of the south corner of sd. Daniel's land, straight through the lott to the west end, and also the 2 1-2-acre lott that bounds south upon sd. pasture and north upon Samuel Adams's land. I give to my son Jonathan my homelott that I now dwell upon, with all the buildings thereon. The remaining part of all my lands I give unto my sons John, Daniel and Jonathan, to be equally divided between them, except that I give to my son John £10 more than an equal part. I give to the heirs of my daughter Mary, 10 shillings to her son and 5 shillings to each of her daughters, besides what I have already given her in her lifetime. I give to my daughter Sarah so much in moveable estate as to make up £60 as money with what I have already given her, with this promise, that my wife Sarah quits all her claim in the law that she has or may have unto lands that descended to her from her Father Holcomb equally to my sons, John, Daniel and Jonathan; but, if not, I give unto my sd. daughter 10 shillings. Also I give unto my daughter Hannah

£60 in moveable estate with what she has already received, in the whole £60 as money. I appoint my three sons, John, Daniel and Jonathan, executors.

Witness: *Andrew Robe,*   JOHN CASE, LS.
Esther Higley, Timothy Woodbridge.

Court Record, Page 93—3 July, 1733: Will proven.

Page 14 (Vol. XII) 13 November, 1734: Jonathan Case, executor, moves this Court that a division be made of some part of sd. estate not particularly given or divided in his will. This Court appoint John Humphrey, Joseph Humphrey and Joseph Hoskins, of Simsbury, to make a division of such part of the estate so given by the will.

Dist. per File: 16 March, 1742: To John Case, to the heirs of Daniel Case, to Jonathan Case, and to Sarah Case, widow relict of the decd. By Joseph Humphrey, John Humphrey and Joseph Hoskins.

P. S.—We think it reasonable and necessary, and do therefore order, that John Case, his heirs and successors, shall have the liberty and use of a passway through the north side of the Bissell lot distributed to the heirs of Daniel Case, for him to go from the highway to his land by the river with carts, cattle, etc., as they shall have occasion.

This distribution was allowed   JOSEPH HUMPHREY,
by the Court, 5 February, 1744-5.   JNO: HUMPHREY,
Test: Joseph Talcott, Clerk.   JOSEPH HOSKINS.

Inventory on File.

Chamberlin, John. Transient person, who died 26 November, 1730, at the house of Jonathan Ashley in Hartford. Invt. £6-17-08. Taken 14 December, 1730, by Zebulon Mygatt and Garrad Spencer.

Court Record, Page 37—2 February, 1730-1: Adms. granted unto Jonathan Ashley of Hartford, who accepted that trust in Court and gave bonds accordingly.

Page 306.

Chipman, Joseph, Haddam. Died 17 January, 1733. Invt. £351-15-06. Taken by Nathaniel Spencer, John Bailey, Jr., and Ebenezer Arnold.

Court Record, Page 97—4 September, 1733: Adms. to Annah Chipman, widow. Recog. with Samuel Bailey of Haddam. This Court appoint Mrs. Anna Chipman, relict of Joseph Chipman decd., to be guardian to Elizabeth Chipman, age 11 years, Abigail 9 years, Joseph 5 years, and Annah 1 year old. Recog., £300.

Page 67.

Church, Richard, Colchester. Invt. £224-13-09. Taken 17 June, 1730, by Nathaniel Foote, John Bulkeley, Jr., and Ephraim Foote.

Court Record, Page 19—5 May, 1730: Adms. to James Church, son of the deceased.

Page 26—4 August, 1730: Invt. exhibited by Ensign James Church.

Page 210-11.

Clarke, Daniel, Haddam. Died 28 April, 1732. Inventory taken by Jared Spencer, Elijah Brainard and Hez: Brainard. Will dated 24 April, 1732.

I, Daniel Clarke of Haddam, in the County of Hartford and Colony of Connecticut, do make this my last will and testament: I give to my wife Mary the use of 1-2 of my dwelling house and half my barn, and the use of half my lands now under improvement, during the time that she shall remain my widow, and also 1-3 part of all my personal estate. I give to my eldest son Daniel my dwelling house, barn and homestead, viz., all the land which I have there adjoining and 15 acres of land which I bought of the Town, abutting on the 7th division lott on Haddam West Side, laid out on the right of William Ventrus, and a piece of land on the east side of the Great River given me by the Town, adjoining land of Lt. William Brainard, and 1-4 part of all my right and title in and to the undivided lands on both sides the Great River, and my fulling mill, and taintor hooks and bars, and all the tools belonging to sd. mill, and also my press. I give to my son Hezekiah a certain piece of land which I had of Capt. Caleb Cone, lying near the house of Richard Wakeley, and — acres of land more or less on the southeast side of Cedar Pole Hills, and the 1-2 of all my lands in the upper meadow, both meadow and swamp, except what I have herein given to Daniel, and 1-4 part of all my right and title on both sides the Great River. I give to my son James 100 acres of land lying at a place called the Otter Pond, all in one piece, where it shall best suit him, and 1-4 part of all my right in the undivided land on both sides the river. I give to my son Joseph the 5th division lott on Haddam West Side, laid out on the right of Samuel Spencer, containing 20 acres, and 21 1-2 acres of the 5th division lott, laid out on the right of Mr. Nicholas Noyes. Sd. whole lot contains 75 acres. And 13 acres of the 8th division lott, laid out on sd. Noyes's right. Sd. whole lott contains 45 acres. And also my own 8th division lott, laid out on my inhabitant right, and also the 8th division lott laid out on the right of Samuel Spencer, and also 1-4 part of all my right and title in and to the undivided lands on both sides the Great River. I give to my four daughters, viz., Abigail, Sarah, Deborah and Mary, all my lands which I have not given to my four sons. Also, I give to my four daughters all my personal estate of all sorts, except what I have already disposed of in this will. I make my wife Mary sole executrix.

Witness: *Caleb Cone, Jr.,*   DANIEL CLARKE, LS.
Richard Wakeley, Jr., Hezekiah Brainard.

Court Record, Page 74—3 October, 1732: The last will and testament of Daniel Clarke, late of Haddam decd., was now exhibited in

Court by Mary Clarke, executrix. Sd. will being proved, is with the invt. approved and ordered to be recorded.

Page 16 (Vol. XII) 13 December, 1734: Daniel Spencer of Haddam, in right of his wife, moves this Court for a division of some part of the real estate given by will of the decd. to the four daughters, viz., Abigail, Sarah, Deborah and Mary, and their heirs forever. This Court appoint Elijah Brainard, Thomas Brooks and Hezekiah Brainard, of Haddam, to divide sd. estate in equal proportions according to the will.

Page 41—19 March, 1735-6: Report of the distributors.

Page 37 (Vol. XIII) 5 December, 1738: James Clark, age 18 years, and Deborah Clark, age 16 years, children of Daniel Clark, chose their brother Hezekiah Clark to be their guardian. Recog., £500. Cert: *Hezekiah Brainard, J. P.*

Page 87—20 April, 1741: Mary Clark, 12 years of age, daughter of Daniel Clark, chose Daniel Spencer of Haddam to be her guardian. Recog., £200. Cert: *Hezekiah Brainard, J. P.*

Page 152-3.

Clark, Joseph, Farmington. Invt. £468-19-02. Taken 2 December, 1731, by Deacon William Gaylord, Isaac Goodwin and Samuel Welles.

Court Record, Page 57—December, 1731: Adms. to Elizabeth Clark, widow, who, with Ebenezer Smith of Hartford and John Welles of Farmington, recog. in £200.

Page 16 (Vol. XIII) 1st November, 1737: Elizabeth Clark, alias Shepherd, and Daniel Shepherd, her present husband, Adms. on the estate of Joseph Clark, exhibited an account of their Adms: Paid in debts and charges, £70-18-09. Which account is accepted in Court and ordered to be filed. This Court appoint Daniel Shepherd to be guardian to three of the children of Joseph Clark, viz., Jemima, age 13 years, Joseph 11 years, and Abijah 8 years. Recog., £200.

Page 48—12 April, 1739: Daniel Shepherd, guardian to the heirs of Joseph Clark, viz., to Joseph, Abijah and Jemima Clark, informs this Court that sd. minors having right in the 11th allottment of land in Farmington, bounding east on Hartford bounds, west on a highway, north on a highway or 12th allottment, and south on the 10th allottment, in sd. Farmington, as may more fully appear on record, which land above described lyes in common or joynt tenancy with Mr. John Whiting and Thomas Cadwell, of Hartford, and Abigail Woodruff, of Farmington, and the sd. Shepherd, in behalf of sd. minors, moved that freeholders be appointed to assist him as guardian in making a division of sd. land: Whereupon this Court appoint Deacon William Gaylord and Timothy Skinner of Hartford to assist sd. guardian in makeing a division, that the sd. minors may have the benefit of the improvement in severalty.

Page 2 (Vol. XIV) 23 September, 1742: Daniel Shepherd of New Hartford having resigned his guardianship to Joseph Clarke, age 16 years, and Abijah Clark, minor children of Joseph Clarke, these minors now make choice of Aaron Clarke of Windsor to be their guardian. Recog., £500.

Page 23—4 May, 1743: Daniel Shepherd of New Hartford, in right of his wife, who was the relict of Joseph Clark, and Adms. on sd. estate, moved to this Court for a dist. of the moveable estate of the deceased, and also that his sd. wife's dowry in the real estate may be set out to her as the law directs. Whereupon this Court appoint Ozias Goodwin and Jared Spencer of Hartford and Samuel Welles of Farmington to set out 1-3 part of the buildings and lands of the deceased by bounds for Elizabeth Clarke alias Shepherd, for her right of dowry, and also to make dist. of the moveable part of the estate to the widow and heirs, viz.:

	£ s d
To Elizabeth Shepherd, relict of the decd.,	25-08-01
To Joseph Clarke, eldest son,	25-08-00
To Abijah Clarke and Jemima Clarke, to each of them,	12-14-00

Page 89-90.

Colyer, John, Hartford (Weaver). Invt. £622-13-02. Taken 13 November, 1730, by John Sheldon, Nathaniel Goodrich and Aaron Cooke. Will dated 7 July, 1730.

I, John Colyer of Hartford, do make this my last will and testament: I give to my son John Colyer all my houseing and lands, whatsoever and wheresoever, to him and his heirs forever. I give unto my beloved wife Elizabeth 1-3 part of all my personal estate, to her and her heirs or to her own proper use and dispose, and 1-3 part of my real estate in houseing and lands during life. I give unto my four daughters, viz., Elizabeth, Eunice, Thankfull and Mary, each of them £40 as money. I appoint my wife Elizabeth to be my sole executrix.

Witness: *Nathaniel Goodwin,*   JOHN COLYER, LS.
Jonathan Bull, Joseph Hoskins.

In addition to the inventory: The testator's right in the Five Miles and his right in the western lands purchased by Hartford and Windsor.

Court Record, Page 36—12 January, 1730-31: Will proven and invt. exhibited.

Page 39 (Vol. XII) 3 February, 1735-6: Mary Colyer, age 16 years, a daughter of John Colyer decd., chose Wilterton Merrell to be her guardian.

Distribution on file, 27 March, 1739: An agreement, signed by

WILLIAM GOODWIN AND ELIZABETH HIS WIFE,	THANKFULL COLIER,
JOSEPH OLCUTT AND EUNICE HIS WIFE,	MARY COLIER.

Page 35-102.

Cole, Mabell, widow of John Cole, Kensington. Invt. £99-02-05. Taken 24 December, 1729, by Thomas Hart and Samuel Thompson. An addition of £4-19-06 was made to the inventory.

Court Record, Page 4—4 November, 1729: Adms. granted to John Cole, eldest son.

Page 100.

Cohoon, Nathaniel, Colchester. Invt. £731-01-11. Taken 2 April, 1731, by Israel Newton, John Johnson and Thomas Adams.

Court Record, Page 22—March, 1731-2: Adms. to Jane Cohoon, widow, and Joseph Taylor, of Hebron. Inventory exhibited, ordered to be recorded and kept on file.

Page 50—7 September, 1731: Martha Cohoon, 16 years of age, a daughter of Nathaniel Cohoon, chose Joseph Taylor, of Colchester, to be her guardian. Recog., £100.

Page 75: A Probate Court held at Hartford, 27 May, 1748. Present, Joseph Buckingham, Esq., Judge; Jos: Talcott, Clerk. This Court order that the original inventory and administration bond, and the administration account on the estate of Nathaniel Cohoon, late of Colchester, deceased, be transferred to the Court of Probate in Colchester, in the district of Hartford, there to be kept in that office.

Cook, Joseph. Court Record, Page 11—3 February, 1729-30: Joseph Cook, a minor, 17 years of age, chose Joseph Barbour of Windsor to be his guardian. Recog., £50.

Page 251-2.

Cooke, Martha, Hartford. Will dated 1st March, 1731-2.

I, Martha Cook, widow, do make this my last will and testament: Imprimis. I give to my three daughters, Martha Cook, Mary Merrells and Annah Cooke, all my moveable estate, to be equally divided amongst my sd. three daughters, including the £5 that my daughter Mary hath already received. And further, my mind is that my daughter Annah shall have my bedd and all the furniture belonging to it, to be reckoned in her part of the moveables. I give to my six children, Aaron Cooke, John Cooke, Moses Cook, Martha Cook, Mary Merrells and Annah Cook, all real estate, to be equally divided amongst them. I do hereby constitute my son Aaron Cooke and my son John Cooke to be executors.

Witness: *Nathaniel Stanly,*   MARTHA COOKE, LS.
Anna Stanly, Sarah Stanly.

Court Record, Page 75—10 October, 1732: Will proven.

Page 95—7 August, 1733: John Cook exhibited an agreement for the settlement of the estate of Mrs. Martha Cook decd. in the following manner: This writing witnesseth, that we, the subscribers, have mutually agreed that this entry shall be the rule of dividing the estate which our mother left us, and the whole of it, that is to say, her interest in the land sold to Mr. Joseph Pitkin, and all the lands in this town or elsewhere that belongs to our said mother, or may hereafter, that is, equally to each of us.

As witness our hands:	MARTHA HOOKER,	AARON COOK,
In presence of us:	ANNA COOK,	JOHN COOK,
Jno: Whiting,	MOSES MERRELL,	GILES HOOKER,
Tho: Hooker.	MARY MERRELL.	MOSES COOK.
28 March, 1733.		

We, the subscribers, do acknowledge that we have recd: the sum of one hundred and twenty pounds apiece each of us, which was given by our hond: father, Aaron Cook, by will.

| Witness: *Jno: Whiting,* | GILES HOOKER, | MARTHA HOOKER, |
| *Tho: Hooker.* | MOSES MERRELL, | MARY MERRELL. |

Joseph Talcott, Jun., Clerk.

Page 16 (Vol. XIV, Probate Side): We, the subscribers, being appointed by the Court of Probate held 13 September, 1742, to make partition of the estate of Mrs. Martha Cook according to her will, have made the following division: To Lieut. Aaron Cook, in the meadow lott, 2 1-2 acres and 20 rods, being 1-2 mile and 20 rods in length, and 2 rods 5 foot and 1-2 foot wide, which lyeth on the north side of the sd. lott; also, to Anne Cook, land of the same length and breadth; also, to the heirs of Mary Merrells, alias Mary Cook, land of the same length and breadth, butting north on the land of sd. Anne; to John Cook, land of the same length and breadth, butting north on the sd. Mary; to the heirs of Moses Cook, that piece of land called the little orchard, and also, in the aforesd. meadow lott, 6 foot 9 inches in breadth and the same length as above mentioned, lying on the north side of sd. meadow lott; and also to Martha Hooker, the whole of the right that belonged to the above-named Martha Cook decd. in the lott called the Neck lott, and also in the abovesd. meadow lott about one acre, it being 14 ft. and 6 inches wide, same length as above, butting north upon the land divided to John Cook, September, 1742. The above distribution was allowed on the first Tuesday in December, 1742.

JOHN MARSH,
OZIAS GOODWIN.

Page 270-1.

Cooper, Thomas, Middletown. Invt. £705-00-00. Taken 27 March, 1733, by William Ward, William Whitmore and Joseph Rockwell.

Court Record, Page 87—10 April, 1733: Adms. to Abigail, the widow, who recog. with William Whitmore in £500. Mrs. Abigail Cooper, widow, appointed guardian to her two children, viz., John, age 13 years, and George, age 9 years.

Page 104—5 February, 1733-4: Lamberton Cooper, age 16 years, chose his uncle Francis Wetmore to be his guardian. Recog., £100.

Page 62 (Vol. XIII) 1st April, 1740: John Cooper, age 20 years, and George, age 16 years, chose their uncle Francis Whitmore to be their guardian. Recog., £500. Cert: *Joseph White, J. P.* Abigail Cooper, Adms., exhibited in Court an account of her Adms., which account it appears in debts and charges the sum of £61-10-05 was paid, and received £3, which account is accepted and ordered to be kept on file.

Page 189.

Cornish, Benjamin, Simsbury. Died 1st April, 1732. Invt. £31-01-06. Taken 27 April, 1732, by Samuel Pettibone, James Hillyer and Samuel Pettibone 2nd.

Court Record, Page 67—9 May, 1732: Adms. to James Cornish of Simsbury.

Page 74—3 October, 1732: The estate insolvent. John Humphrey, Jr., and Samuel Pettibone, the 2nd, appointed commissioners.

Page 4 (Vol. XII) 7 May, 1734: Joseph Cornish, Adms., exhibits an account of his Adms. Accepted.

Page 12—8 October, 1734: Pursuant to an act of the General Assembly, 9 May, 1734, this Court do order Josepĥ Cornish, Adms., to make sale of so much land as will procure the sum of £25-08-10, and make return thereof to this Court.

Page 311.

Cornwall, Isaac, Middletown. Died 25 August, 1733. Invt. £83-10-00. Taken 28 September, 1733. Will dated 25 August, 1733.
The last (nuncupative) will of Isaac Cornwall, late of
Middletown, decd.:
I give to Fletcher Ranny and Joseph Ranny a yoke of steers comeing 4 years old, and my brindle cow. And I give to Elisha Wilcoks a yoke of steers comeing three years old, and my red pide cow. I would not have you take it to pay any debts that I owe to their father, for I don't mean so, nor I would not have you take it so, but I give it them freely and voluntarily.

Middletown, November ye 5th, 1733.

Mary Ranny, Esther Ranny and Abigail Wilcoks personally appeared before me, Jabez Hamlin, Justice of the Peace for Hartford County, and upon oath declared that they were with Isaac Cornwall the day before his death, and that the sd. Cornwall the day before his death pronounced what is within written and desired them to be witnesses thereof. And further, that the sd. Esther wrote what is on the other side presently after, and that at that time he was, to the best of their judgement, *mente sana,* and died the night after.   MARY X RANNY,
        ABIGAIL X WILCOCKS, ESTHER RANNY.

Jurant Coram. Jabez Hamlin, Just. Peace.
The adverse party being
cited, but not present.

Court Record, Page 96—29 June, 1733: Jacob Cornwall, Adms., a brother of the deceased, gave bond with Richard Seymour of Hartford for £200.

Page 98—2 October, 1733: The nuncupative will exhibited by Joseph Ranney. Deferred.

Page 100—6 November, 1733: Jacob Cornwall appeals to the Superior Court from the judgement of this Court in approveing sd. will.

Page 60-61.

Cornwall, Samuel, Middletown. Died 6 April, 1730. Invt. £631-19-04. Taken 1st May, 1730, by George Phillips, Daniel Hall and Joseph Rockwell. Will dated 16 March, 1729-30.

I, Samuel Cornwall of Middletown, do make this my last will and testament: I give unto Phebe, my wife, the one equal third part of all my household goods, moveable estate and stock, of what name soever, forever. I give to my wife the improvement of 1-3 part of my dwelling house and buildings, all my homestead, and all other my improveable lands, during her natural life. I give to my eldest son Samuel Cornwall a double portion in the whole of my estate after my just debts are paid. And it is my will that the whole remainder of my estate be divided equally amongst all the rest of my children, and that my sons shall have their portions in lands and my daughters shall have theirs in moveable estate so far as it will go. And if my daughters shall have any part of my land set out to them, they being designed to sell the same, they shall first make tender of the same to some of their brothers, my sons. I constitute my wife Phebe my sole executrix.

Witness: *George Phillips,*   SAMUEL CORNWALL, LS.
John Kilbourn, Joseph Rockwell.

Court Record, Page 23—5 June, 1730: Will and invt. exhibited. Approved.

Page 32 (Vol. XIV) 16 November, 1743: Phebe Cornwell, the widow and executrix of the last will of Samuel Cornwell, now moves to this Court that distributors may be appointed to distribute the estate according to his last will: Whereupon this Court appoint Capt. George Phillips, Deacon Solomon Adkins and Mr. James Ward, of Middletown, distributors. Ebenezer Cornwell, a minor, 14 years of age, son of Samuel Cornwall, late of Middletown, chose Mr. William Rockwell to be his guardian. Recog., £200. Cert: *Jabez Hamlin, J. P.*

Page 282.

(Add. Invt. in Vol. XII, Page 391.)

Cornwall, Capt. Timothy, Middletown. Invt. £1429-13-10. Taken 24 January, 1732-3, by Joseph Rockwell, John Collins and Samuel Dwight. Additional inventory of his clothes, which just came from Ireland, and some other things, valued at £72-12-06: apprised 1st November, 1734, by Joseph Rockwell and John Collins.

Court Record, Page 92—5 June, 1733: Adms. granted unto Peter Wolcott and Susannah Wolcott his wife, late widow of the sd. deceased. Recog. with John Anderson.

Page 328.

Cowle, Joseph, Wethersfield. Invt. £518-03-10. Taken 18 December, 1733, by Benjamin Wright, Jacob Williams and David Goodrich. (One and 3-4 acres of land in Fairfield Swamp.)

Court Record, Page 103—1st January, 1733-4: Adms. granted to White Cowle, widow, who recog. in £200 with Jacob Williams of Wethersfield.

Page 19 (Vol. XII) 4 February, 1734-5: White Cowle, Adms., exhibited an account of her Adms., which is accepted.

Page 42—31 March, 1736: White Cowle, age 13 years, daughter of sd. deceased, chose David Goodrich of Wethersfield to be her guardian. Recog., £100.

Page 11-12-13-14.

Cowles, Nathaniel, Sen., Farmington. Invt. £406-07-00. Taken 22 November, 1729, by Isaac Cowles, Sen., and Daniel Andrews. Will dated 16 January, 1727-8.

I, Nathaniel Cowles, Sen., of Farmingtown, do make my last will and testament: I give to my wife, Mary Cowles, 1-3 part of my personal estate to be at her own dispose to her own children, and the use of 1-3 part of my houseing and lands during life. Unto my daughter, Thankfull, I give £5 besides what I have given her before she married. Unto my grandchildren, Esther Cowles and Nathaniel Cowles: to Esther 5 shillings, and to Nathaniel 20 shillings, when they come of age. I give unto my daughter Phebe £25, to be paid to her when she comes of age or at marriage. Unto my sons Timothy, Benjamin, Joseph, Samuel and Daniel, I give each of them all the rest of my estate or right of all the divisions of land in Farmingtown that I have or shall have. I make my wife Mary Cowles and my son Timothy Cowles executors.

Witness: *Isaac Cowles, Sen.,*   NATHANIEL COWLES, SEN., LS.
John Treat, Isaac Cowles, Jr.

Court Record, Page 6—2 December, 1729: Invt. now exhibited. Will proven.

Page 330-1.

Cowles, Timothy, Farmington. Invt. £144-10-08. Taken 4 June, 1733, by Isaac Cowles and Daniel Judd.

Court Record, Page 91—17 May, 1733: Adms. to Content Cowles, the widow, who recog. with Capt. Isaac Cowles of Farmington.

Page 8 (Vol. XII) 22 July, 1734: Content Cowles, Adms., exhibited now an account of her Adms., which this Court accepts.

Cramer, John. Court Record, Page 13—3 March, 1729-30: John Cramer, a minor, 14 years of age, chose John Curtice to be his guardian. Recog., £50.

Page 65-66.

Craw, John, Bolton. Invt. £272-19-00. Taken 1 July, 1730, by Samuel Brown and Jonathan Strong. Will dated 21 March, 1730.

In the name of God, amen. I, John Craw, of the Town of Bolton, in the County of Hartford and Colony of Connecticut, in New England, do make this my last will and testament: I give to my wife Rebeckah one cowe and one mare, together with 1-3 part of the rest of my personal estate, forever: and 1-3 part of my house and improved land during her life. And unto my well-beloved son Jacob Craw I give my house and the 50 acres of land on which the house stands, together with all my moveable estate, excepting my wife's legacies, he paying out the legacies contained in this my will and testament, by him freely to be possessed and injoyed. And to my son Jonathan Craw I will and bequeath £40 current money of this Colony. And to my son Joseph Craw I give £40 in like money. And to my son Ebenezer Craw £40 of money. And to my son John Craw I give £5 of lawful money. And to my son Richard Craw I give the sum of £5 of lawful money. And to my daughter Catharine Hills, and to her heirs, the sum of £15 lawful money. And to my daughter Elizabeth Sherman I give the sum of £15. And to my daughter Mary Craw I bequeath the sum of £30 lawful money. And to my daughter Rebeckah Craw I give £5 of lawful money. And to my daughter Deliverance Hills I give £15 of lawful money. And the abovesd. legacies to be paid out by my son Jacob Craw in 13 years from the date hereof. I appoint my wife Rebeckah and my daughter Mary Craw to be executors.

Witness: *Samuel Brown,* JOHN CRAW, LS.
Jonathan Strong, Hepzibah Spencer.

Court Record, Page 25—4 August, 1730: Will and invt. exhibited.

Page 72—27 June, 1732: Joseph Craw of Bolton, a minor, 15 1-2 years of age, son of John Craw, chose his brother John Craw of Coventry to be his guardian. Recog., £50.

Page 24 (Vol. XII) 1st April, 1735: Ebenezer Craw, 15 years of age, son of John Craw, chose his sister Mary Craw to be his guardian. Recog., £50.

Page 269.

Crowfoot, Margaret, Wethersfield. Invt. £35-15-09. Taken 27 March, 1733, by Samuel Deming, David Boardman and Timothy Baxter. Will dated 14 March, 1733.

I, Margaret Crowfoot, widow, of Wethersfield, do make this my last will and testament: I give unto my son Joseph the sum of 2 shillings current money. I give all my moveable estate whatsoever to my son Ephraim and daughters Elizabeth, Mehetabell and Sarah, and to Margaret and Mary, my granddaughters, to be equally divided amongst them. I appoint Elizabeth and Mehetabell, my daughters, to be executrixes.

Witness: *Samuel Deming,* MARGARET CROWFOOT, LS.
Timothy Baxter.

Court Record, Page 86—3 April, 1733: Will now exhibited by Elizabeth Hollister, an executor named in the will.

Page 293.

Curtice, Jonathan, Wethersfield. Inventory taken 1 August, 1733, by Samuel Collins, Benjamin Wright and Jacob Williams.

I, Jonathan Curtice, of Stepney Parish, husbandman, do make this my last will and testament: I give to Hepzibah, my wife, whom I also make my sole executrix, the 1-3 part of all my lands, buildings and edifices for her improvement during her natural life; also, 1-3 part of my moveable estate to be her own forever. Nextly, I give to my son Thomas Curtice my dwelling house and barn, and 25 acres of land with the orchard upon it, butting south and east on highways, west on Samuel Collins, and so to run north until it make ye 25 acres. Nextly, I give to my son Eleazer

Curtice 18 acres of land butting north and east on a highway, west on Samuel Collins, and so running north till it makes 18 acres, for his own. Nextly, I give to my son Jonathan Curtice 12 acres of land next my son Eleazer Curtice, butting north upon the sd. Eleazer's land, east upon a highway, west on Samuel Collins, and to run south till it make the sd. 12 acres; also the half of my lott in Wethersfield Meadow, which lott contains by estimation 3 acres, which is 1 1-2 acres butting east on a highway, the south side of it butting on the heirs of Mr. Nathaniel Hooker, to be his own forever. Next, I give to my son John Curtice 12 acres of land next my son Jonathan, butting north on Jonathan's land, east on a highway, west on Samuel Collins, and to run south till it makes the sd. 12 acres; also the 1-2 of my lott in Wethersfield Meadow, the north side thereof, butting east on a highway, south on my son Jonathan, and north on Josiah Churchill, to be his forever. Next, I give to my daughter Anne Curtice £100. Next, I give to my daughter Abigail Curtice £100. Both of which is to be made out of my moveable estate if there be sufficient; if not, out of that and my remaining lands. All the rest of my estate I will to be divided to my sons, Thomas, Eleazer, Jonathan and John, in equal proportions.

Witness: *Joseph Butler, Sen.,*   JONATHAN CURTICE, LS.
Richard Butler, Jonathan Collins.

Court Record, Page 95—7 August, 1733: Will and invt. exhibited by Hepzibah Curtice, the widow.

Page 53.

Day, John, Hartford. Invt. £820-18-10. Taken 29 April, 1730, by Joseph Barnard, Ozias Goodwin and Samuel Edwards. Will dated 16 November, 1725.

I, John Day of Hartford, do make this my last will and testament: I give to my wife two cowes, with a full 1-3 part of the remainder of my moveable estate, as also all my right in the mill; and after her decease I give it to my son William and his heirs. I give to my son John Day 40 shillings, to be paid out of my weaving tackling. I do confirm to my several sons the deeds of gift I have formerly made to them of my lands, to them and their heirs. I give to my son William and to his heirs my 3-acre lott in the Long Meadow. I give to my son Joseph my loom with all the appurtenances thereto belonging. All the rest of my moveable estate not before given I give to my daughters, equally to be divided among them, only my daughter Sarah shall have the value of £4 more in them than either of her sisters. And I appoint my wife Sarah to be sole executrix.

It being before omitted, I add: I give to my wife the use of 1-2 of my house during her widowhood, and 1-2 the cellar, the houseing to be on the south part.

Signed and sealed and declared in presence of   JOHN DAY, LS.
Timothy Woodbridge,
Joseph Wadsworth, Jonathan Olcott.

Court Record, Page 19—5 May, 1730: Will proven and inventory exhibited.

Page 47-8.

Deming, John, Wethersfield. Died 25 November, 1729. Invt. £32-07-05. Taken 23 January, 1729-30, by Samuel Benton, Jonathan Robbins and Noadiah Dickinson.

Court Record, Page 9—6 January, 1729-30: Adms. granted to Mary Deming, the widow, and Nathaniel Deming.

Dennison, Anne. Court Record, Page 47—4 June, 1731: This Court appoint Mercy West of Tolland to be guardian to Anne Dennison, one of the daughters of Joseph Dennison of Stonington decd. Recog., with Amasa West of Tolland, in £300.

Page 258.

(Add. Invt. in Vol. XII, Page 352.)

Denslow, John, Windsor. Invt. £115-19-09. Taken 25 December, 1732, by Israel Stoughton, Peletiah Allyn and John Allyn. Additional invt. of £277-04-10. Taken 14 February, 1733-4, by Israel Stoughton, Peletiah Allyn and John Allyn.

Court Record, Page 83—22 February, 1732-3: Adms. granted unto Samuel Osborn, who gave bonds with Jacob Osborn of sd. Windsor.

Page 41 (Vol. XII) 19 March, 1735-6: Additional inventory exhibited and accepted.

Page 60 (Vol. XIII) 5 February, 1739-40: Samuel Osborn, Adms., exhibited an account of his Adms: Paid in debts and charges and lost estate, the sum of £73-03-04. Which account is accepted and ordered on file.

Page 81-157.

Dewey, Joseph, Hebron. Invt. £148-03-02. (Personal estate.) Taken January, 1730-31, by Samuel Loomis and Samuel Curtice. Will dated 4 December, 1730.

I, Joseph Dewey of Hebron, in the County of Hartford, do make this my last will and testament: I give unto my nephew Charles, son of my brother David Dewey of Westfield, in the Province of Massachusetts Bay, this farm on which my house and mill stands, lying partly in Hebron and partly in Colchester, together with the house in which I now live, the mills and barn and all the implements belonging thereto, only reserveing for Benjamin Taylor the use of the sd. farm and all the mills and buildings thereon in common or partnership with the sd. Charles Dewey for 10 years, to commence at the time of my decease. I give unto Israel and Jabez, sons of my brother Israel Dewey of Stonington decd., 147 acres of land I have lying near to John Trot in Hebron, to be equally divided between them, according to its survey on record under Samuel Curtice's hand. I give to my nephew Charles Dewey 1 meadow lott in the North Meadow in Hebron, near Mr. Bliss. My will is and I hereby order my executors hereafter named to dispose of my farm lying in Hebron near where Baxter lives, containing 142 acres, in the payment of my just debts; also 3 lotts in the Little Meadow near to Samuel Caulkin's, in Hebron, I order my executors to sell toward the payment of my debts; 32 acres of land lying in Hebron on the Plaine by Mr. Bliss, together with all the land I ought to have of Nathaniel Dewey of Lebanon, in Lebanon, and also the land or right of land in the place called Union (excepting 50 acres in sd. Union, which I will to be set out to Isaac Burroughs, my cousin), I order my executors to sell, and the money received to be improved towards the payment of my just debts, saving only £100 thereof, which I give unto my friend and executor hereafter named, John Bulkeley, Jr., of Colchester. I order my executors to sell the land which I have lying by the land of Lemuel Fitch, of sd. Colchester, for the payment of my debts, reserveing £100 which I give unto my friend John Bulkeley, Jr. I give unto the sd. John Bulkeley a piece of land which I have lying on the road from Colchester to Glastonbury, by the brook called Salmon Brook, and in Hebron. I give unto the sd. John Bulkeley and my nephew Charles Dewey 16 acres of land lying on the hill called Chesnut Hill, in Colchester, equally to be divided between them. I give unto Benjamin Taylor and the sd. John Bulkeley, Jr., all the interest and property which I have in the iron works in Colchester, also all common rights of land in Hebron and in Colchester. I give unto my honoured uncle Dewey, father to Nathaniel Dewey of Lebanon, £10; to Gershom, Charles, Peter and Oliver Bulkeley, sons to the Reverend Mr. John Bulkeley, £5 each, as also to Dorothy, Patience and Lewce Bulkeley, £5 each. As a condition of the aforesd. divises to my sd. nephew Charles Dewey and Benjamin Taylor, I do order that they shall saw in my sawmill, to sd. Charles Dewey bequeathed, timber, plank, and boards sufficient for the building of a house for the sd. John Bulkeley, Jr., if he shall build in Colchester and require the same of them. I hereby appoint Mr. John Bulkeley, Jr., of Colchester, together with Benjamin Taylor of Hebron, in the County of Hartford, to be the only executors of this my last will and testament.

Witness: *Joseph Wright,*   JOSEPH DEWEY, LS.
Nathaniel Otis, Josiah Gilbert, Jr.

Court Record, Page 33—5 January, 1730-31: Will exhibited and proven.

Page 160.

Dewolph, Charles, Middletown. Invt. £407-04-02. Taken 31 December, 1731, by Nathaniel White and John Arnold. Will dated 4 December, 1731.

I, Charles Dewolph of Middletown, in the County of Hartford, do make this my last will and testament: I give to my wife Prudence 1-4 part of all my moveable estate and the use of my dwelling house and all my improveable land within the bounds of the Town of Middletown so long as she shall live a widow bearing my name, and the use of all my moveable estate during the term of her widowhood. I give to my two sons, John Dewolph and Stephen Dewolph, that 32 acres of land in Glastonbury which I had of Thomas and Sarah White, to be divided equally between them. I give to my two sons, Symon Dewolph and Joseph Dewolph, my dwelling house in Middletown and all the lands in Middletown, both upland and meadow, and swamp, which I had of Thomas White, after their mother's decease or marriage. I give to my daughters, Prudence, Elizabeth, Sarah, Mary and Rebeckah, 2-4 of my moveable estate after their mother's decease or marriage. I give to all my sons and daughters all that land which was given by my father to me and my heirs within the bounds of Lyme, to be divided equally among them, that is, if it should ever be recovered, but my advice to my children is not to try for it. I make my son Symon Dewolph sole executor.

Witness: *Nathaniel Savage,*   CHARLES DEWOLPH, LS.
     John Savage,
     Joseph White.

Court Record, Page 58—4 January, 1731-2: Symon Dewolph, executor, declined the trust, and this Court grant Adms. unto Prudence Dewolph, widow.

Page 95—7 August, 1733: Prudence Dewolph, Adms., exhibits an account of her Adms., which is accepted by the Court.

Page 103—1st January, 1733-4: Joseph Dewolph, a minor, age 14 years, chose Thaddeus Welles of Glastonbury to be his guardian. Recog., £100.

Page 312-343.

Dickinson, Eliphalet, Wethersfield. Invt. £633-01-01. Taken 30 October, 1733, by Jacob Williams, Benjamin Wright and Gideon Goodrich. Will dated 6 February, 1728-9.

I, Eliphalet Dickinson, of the Town of Wethersfield, do make this my last will and testament: I give to my wife Rebeckah her thirds, and also a dowry of £20 money. I give to my three sons, Obadiah, Eliphalet and Eleazer, an equal part of my land, to them and their heirs forever, all my lands which I shall die seized of, they and each of them paying equally out of my moveable estate to my three daughters, Sarah, Rebeckah and Eunice, £50 apiece. I appoint my wife Rebeckah Dickinson executrix.

Witness: *Amos Williams,*   ELIPHALET DICKINSON, LS.
Jonathan Lattimore, Philip Goff.

Court Record, Page 97—4 September, 1733: Will exhibited and proven.

Page 92.

Dix, Leonard, Wethersfield. Invt. £887-17-10. Taken 24 December, 1730, by Samuel Wright, Ebenezer Belding and Jonathan Belding, Jr. Court Record, Page 36—15 January, 1730-1: Adms. granted to Abigail Dyx, the widow.

Page 7 (Vol. XII) 2 July, 1734: Leonard Dix, age 17 years, and Abigail Dix, age 14 years, children of Leonard Dix, chose their father-in-law, William Nott, to be their guardian with their mother, his wife. And this Court appoint sd. William Nott to be guardian to several other of the children of sd. decd., viz., Rebeckah Dix, age 12 years, Jerusha Dix, age 10 years, Jacob Dix, age 7 years, and Charles Dix, about 7 years of age. Recog., £500.

Page 101 (Vol. XIII) 30 November, 1741: This Court appoint Elisha Griswold to be guardian to Charles Dix, about 11 years of age, son of Leonard Dix, late of Wethersfield. Recog., £300. Certified to this Court by *David Goodrich* that Jacob Dix, son of Leonard Dix, chose Elisha Boardman of Wethersfield to be his guardian. Recog., £300.

Page 326 (Vol. XIII, Probate Side): We, the subscribers, being sole heirs to the estate of Leonard Dix, late of Wethersfield, do hereby fully and mutually agree that the disposition hereafter particularly set and affixed to either of us of real or personal estate shall be our part or portion or demand of, in or to the estate of the sd. decd.:

	£ s d		£ s d
To Leonard Dix,	235-19-06	To Rebeckah Dix,	69-09-11
To Jerusha Dix,	67-13-06	To Charles and Jacob	
To Hannah Dix,	66-19-08	Dix,	131-17-06
		To the widow,	46-01-03

For a full confirmation of all the foregoing, we acknowledge we have received, this 2nd February, 1741, and do hereby discharge each other of any further demands upon the sd. estate. And have hereunto set to our hands and seals:

ABIGAIL X BLYNN, LS.	REBECKAH DIX, LS.
ELISHA GRISWOLD, LS.	ELISHA GRISWOLD, GUARDIAN
ABIGAIL GRISWOLD, LS.	TO CHARLES DIX, LS.
ELISHA BOARDMAN, LS.	ELISHA BOARDMAN, GUARDIAN
HANNAH BOARDMAN, LS.	TO JACOB DIX, LS.

Court Record, Page 108—2 February, 1741-2: Jonathan Blynn of Wethersfield, in right of his wife, formerly the relict of Leonard Dix decd., moves this Court that her right of dower on sd. Dix his estate may be set out to her by freeholders as the law directs: Whereupon this Court appoint Jonathan Belding, John Stilman and Ephraim Williams to set out 1-3 part of the real estate of the sd. Leonard Dix decd. to the sd. Jonathan Blynn and Abigail his wife, as her dowry.

Page 109—2 February, 1741-2: Agreement exhibited and confirmed by the Court.

Page 76.

Dixwell, Bathshua, Middletown. Invt. £54-12-09. Taken 4 March, 1730, by Joseph Rockwell and Robert Warner.

I, Bathshua Dixwell, formerly of New Haven, now resident of Middletown, being fallen into old age, do make this my last will and testament: I give to my daughter Mary Collins, under whose care I now am, and to her children, all that part of worldly goods that I shall die possessed of. I give to my son-in-law, John Collins, my husband Dixwell's Bible forever. My son-in-law, with Mary his wife, to be sole executors. Dated 8 June, 1727.

Witness: *John Hamlin,*   BATHSHUA DIXWELL, LS.
       Seth Wetmore.

Page 300.

Doolittle, Abraham, Middletown. Invt. £288-07-09. Taken 27 August, 1733, by John Collins, Joseph Clark and Joseph Doolittle.

Court Record, Page 96—29 June, 1733: Adms. to Martha Doolittle, widow. Recog., £200, with William Marks.

Page 18 (Vol. XIV) 1st March, 1743: An account of Adms. was now exhibited in Court by Martha Doolittle, alias Martha Marks, Adms. on sd. estate, which account is accepted.

Page 90 (Vol. XV) 14 February, 1748-9: Martha Doolittle, alias Marks, Adms., having exhibited an invt. of the estate of sd. deceased, and also an account of Adms., informing this Court that there is nothing to divide but real estate, this Court do appoint Capt. Jonathan Allyn, Lt. Nathaniel Gilbert and Joseph Clark, of Middletown, to divide the real estate, viz., 1-3 part of the buildings and land to Martha Doolittle, alias Marks, for her improvement during life, and to Abraham Doolittle, eldest son, his double share or 2-3 thereof, and to Ebenezer Doolittle, the youngest son, his single share.

Page 36-7.

Dracke, Elizabeth, Windsor. Invt. £100-plus. Taken 12 January, 1729-30, by John Palmer, Job Drake and John Cooke, Jr. Will dated 22 June, 1728.

I, Elizabeth Dracke, widow, of Windsor, do make this my last will and testament: I give to my son Jacob Dracke, of Windsor, my partison, my silver spoon, my silver dram cup and drinking glass. I give my wearing apparrel, except my silk hood and silk scarf, to my daughter Elizabeth Griswold, my son Jacob Dracke, my daughter Sarah Wolcott, and the four children of my daughter Mary Porter decd., to be equally divided into four parts, and Elizabeth shall have one, Jacob one, Sarah one, and the children of Mary one. And that part of my apparrell which shall be distributed unto the four children of my daughter Mary decd., my will is that that part shall be equally divided into five parts, of which Mary Pettebone shall have one part, Catharine Dracke two parts, Lydia Porter one part and Anne one part, they being the four children of my sd. daughter Mary Porter. I give to my granddaughter Elizabeth Gillett 20 shillings money. I give unto my grandson Moses Griswold 20 shillings money. I give to my granddaughter Elizabeth Newbery 20 shillings money. I give to my granddaughter Catharine Dracke my silk hood and scarf, my best iron pot and iron kettle, and a brass kettle of mine that was once the honoured Capt. Clarke's. I give to my granddaughter Hannah Dracke 20 shillings money. And the residue of my estate I give to my son Jacob Dracke, daughter Sarah Wolcott, and Catharine, Lydia and Anne, three of the children of my daughter Mary Porter decd., to be divided into four parts, of which my son Jacob shall have two, my daughter Sarah one, and the three last-mentioned children of my daughter Mary one. And my will is that in the division of this last part among sd. three children that the whole shall be divided into four parts, and that Catharine shall have two parts, Lydia one part, and Anne one part. I make my son Jacob Dracke to be my sole executor.

Witness: *Ebenezer Phelps,*   ELIZABETH DRACKE, LS.
Samuel Philley, Henry Allyn.

Court Record, Page 13—3 March, 1729-30: Will and invt. exhibited and proven.

Page 290.

Drake, Job, Windsor. Will dated 14 March, 1732.

I, Job Drake of Windsor, do make this my last will and testament: I give to my wife Elizabeth the use of all my estate during her natural life. I give to my son Jeremiah Drake that lott where I now dwell which I had of my father, and that which I have which was Joshua Wills's—to him forever, he allowing to his mother what is above given to her, and to my daughter Rebeckah the use of the new house during the time she shall remain a single woman. I give to my daughters Elizabeth and Rebeckah, and to my granddaughter Eunice Drake, my lott that bounds north on the land of Thomas Stoughton and south on the land of Samuel Moore, to be divided amongst them share and share alike, saving only to my wife her legacy aforesd. I give to my daughter Rebeckah £25 out of my moveable estate, she to take it in household goods or in cattle. I give to my grandson Jonathan Drake my right, interest, share and part of a land called the Equivalent Land. I give to my son Jeremiah all my lands in Windsor not above disposed of, whether already divided or undivided, to him and his heirs forever. I give all my right, interest, share and part of the lands called the Western Lands to my daughter Elizabeth, my daughter Rebeckah, and son Jeremiah, and my granddaughter Eunice Drake forever, share and share alike. My will is that after the death of my wife Elizabeth, if any of my moveable estate shall be left not disposed of to pay my debts, that it shall be equally divided between my three children and my granddaughter Eunice Drake, each one to share alike. I appoint my son Jeremiah Drake and my son Joseph Rockwell to be executors.

Witness: *Timothy Edwards,*   JOB DRAKE, LS.
Joseph Drake, Eliakim Cook.

Court Record, Page 94—3 July, 1733: Will exhibited.

Page 62.

Drake, Joseph, and Sarah, his wife. Invt. £91-10-06. Taken 24 June, 1730, by Timothy Cowles and John Bidwell.

Court Record, Page 17—7 April, 1730: This Court discharges Timothy Easton of Hartford from being guardian to Lemuel Drake, and appoint Capt. Ciprian Nichols of Hartford to be guardian to sd. Lemuel Drake, a minor, about 6 years of age. Recog., £50.

Page 20—11 May, 1730: Whereas, Sarah Drake, widow of sd. decd., who was appointed Adms. 25 April, 1728, and took Adms. on her deceased husband's estate, had died without finishing her Adms., this Court grant letters of Adms. unto David Bissell of Windsor, and he reports the estate insolvent. And Joseph Drake and Matthew Grant, with David Bissell, are appointed commissioners.

Page 22—2 June, 1730: This Court appoint Timothy Easton to be guardian unto Joseph Drake, son of Joseph Drake. Recog., £50. Joseph Cooke of Hartford appointed guardian to Ebenezer Drake, age 5 years. Recog., £50.

Page 65—11 April, 1732: Lt. Samuel Marsh of Hartford to be guardian to Samuel Drake, age 4 years, son of Joseph Drake. Recog., £50.

Page 111 (Vol. XIII) 2 March, 1741-2: This Court now grant Adms. on the estates of Joseph Drake and his wife, both decd., unto Joel Rockwell of Windsor, the former Adms. being departed this life and Adms. not finished. Recog., £200, with Joseph Rockwell of Windsor.

Page 149.

Deuplessey, Francis. Invt. taken 1 July, 1731, by Joseph Backus and John Edwards, consisting:

	£	s	d
In personal estate,	68-08-10		
In six casks of molasses, 703 gallons, @ £0-03-00 per gallon,	105-09-00		
In six barrells of sugar, @ £5 per hundred,	61-11-06		
In money, etc.,	14-10-06		

Estate in New England.

Will dated 21 April, 1731: In the name of God, amen. Whereas I, Francis Deuplessey, late of the Island of Barbadoes, in the West Indies, but now of the Town and County of Hartford, in the Colony of Connecticut, in New England, have by the blessings of God Almighty obtained and acquired a small estate in divers parts of this world, and knowing that it is appointed unto men once to die, that I might set mine house in order, have heretofore made and ordained my certain will and testament, in due form, wherein I have disposed of all that estate which God has given me in the West Indies, West America and elsewhere (excepting what I have here in New England), after my decease, to my brother Lewis Deuplessey of London, Gent.; my sisters, Elizabeth Deuplessey and Mary Anne Deuplessey, of London aforesd.; and my brother, Peter Deuplessey, of Barbadoes, aforesd., and in the sd. will have appointed my good friends, Capt. Thomas Mapp and Mr. Joseph Bailey, of the Parish of St. Phillips, in Barbadoes aforesd., to be the executors of that will, and have left the sd. will in the hands of Mr. John Dallison, of Barbadoes aforesd., merchant at Barbadoes aforesd., which will and testament, so far as it relates to all my estate (excepting what I have in New England as aforesd.), I do hereby establish and confirm and will not have anything herein contained to be so inventoried as to make void the same. And as to that small estate which I have here in New England, I make, ordain and appoint this to be my last will and testament, as follows: viz.: Imprs. My will is that my just debts should be punctually paid by my executors hereafter named, in these presents appointed, after which: Item. I give and bequeath unto Mr. Francis Beteille of Boston, in New England, merchant, and to my good friend Mrs. Susannah Beauchomp, of Hartford aforesd., daughter of Mr. John Beauchomp of sd. Hartford, all such debts and demands as are due and comeing to me or that hereafter shall be recovered by my exeutors or in my name of and from Mr. Stephen Boutiwan and James Boyard, of Boston aforesd., to be equally divided between the sd. Francis and Susannah, and in such proportion to be to them and their heirs forever. Item. All the rest of my estate, of what kind or nature soever, which I have here in New England, I hereby devise and bequeath unto the sd. Susannah Beauchomp, to be to herself and to her heirs forever. I appoint Mr. Samuel Mather, of Windsor, and Mr. William Pitkin, of Hartford, executors to all my estate in New England aforesd., and restraining it to that only. In testimony whereof I, the sd. Francis Deuplessey (being now *sana memoria*), have hereunto set my hand and seal.

Witness: *John Edwards,*   DEUPLESSEY, LS.
Ebenezer Williamson, J. Gilbert, Jr.

Court Record, Page 53—11 May, 1731: The executors declined the trust, and Adms. was granted to John Beauchomp of Hartford, one of the principal creditors.

Page 245-6.

Dutton, Joseph, East Haddam. Invt. £157-11-00. Taken 4 February, 1733-4, by John Spencer, John Church and Jabez Chapman. Will dated 1st September, 1733.

I, Joseph Dutton of Haddam East Society, do make this my last will and testament: I give to my wife Mary Dutton 1-3 part of all my household goods, and 1 good, gentle and easy beast, horse or mare, to be provided out of my moveable estate, with convenient furniture for her to ride upon, and 1 good cow and six sheep, all which she shall have power to dispose of as she shall judge most for her comfort. And my will is that my son Samuel Dutton shall provide sufficient fodder and pasturing for sd. creatures during her widowhood. Also, I give to her 1-4 part of all the grain that my sd. son shall raise from the farm on which I now dwell, yearly, excepting he and she shall otherwise agree. Also, it is my will that my sd. son shall provide for her a sufficiency of convenient firewood during her widowhood, and 1 barrel of syder, and what apples she shall have occasion for, yearly, if the orchard will afford it; also, the choice of any 1 room in my now dwelling house during her natural life. I give to my 3 sons, Benjamin, David and Thomas Dutton, all my creatures that shall not be otherwise disposed of before my decease or by this my last will, that is to say, 1-2 to Benjamin, and ye other half to be divided between David and Thomas equally, which they shall have besides what they have already received. I give to my son Samuel Dutton, besides what he hath already received in deed of gift bearing date with these presents, some cattle that I formerly set out to him. All my carpenter and husbandry tools I give to my son-in-law, Matthew Smith, to be delivered to him out of moveable estate. I give to my daughter, Rebeckah Gates, besides what she hath already received, a table and a brass pan, and the best of the coverlids, and a featherbed, after my own and my wife's decease. I give to my daughter Ruth Millard and to my grandson William Selby, besides what my sd. daughter Ruth and sd. grandson's mother hath formerly received, all the remainder of my household goods not before disposed of, and that which they have received shall be reckoned with what remains, and shall be equally divided between them. I appoint my wife and son, Samuel Dutton, executors.

Witness: *Mary Smith,*   JOSEPH X DUTTON, LS.
Jabez Chapman, Daniel Booge.

Court Record, Page 105—5 March, 1733-4: Will exhibited by Samuel Dutton, executor named in sd. will. Proven.

Page 56 (Vol. XII) 15 June, 1741: Know all men by these presents: That we whose names are underwritten do acknowledge that we have received in full of Samuel Dutton, executor of our honoured father's (Joseph Dutton's) will, all that is given in sd. will to us the subscribers.
10th April, 1734.   MATTHEW SMITH, | DAVID DUTTON,
Witness: *Thomas Millard,*   BENJAMIN DUTTON, | THOMAS DUTTON.
     William Selby.

Know all men, that we who are the under-subscribers acknowledge that we have received in full of Samuel Dutton all that is given in the will of our honoured father to us the under subscribers.

7th day of May, 1734.   THOMAS MILLARD,
Witness: *David Dutton,*   RUTH X MILLARD.
         William Selby.

October the 30th, 1738: Know all men, that I, William Selby of East Haddam, acknowledge that I have received of Samuel Dutton all that was given me by the will of Mr. Joseph Dutton.

Witness: *David Dutton,*   WILLIAM SELBY.
         Thomas Millard.

May 28th, 1744: Then we, Daniel Gates and Rebeckah Gates, have received of Samuel Dutton all that was given us by our honoured father in his will.   DANIEL GATES,
Witness: *Nathan Fisher,*   REBECKAH X GATES.
         Judah Gates.

The above is a true copy of the original, and recorded by me.

Jos: Talcott, Clerk.

Page 247-274.

Edwards, Samuel, Hartford. Invt. £2547-13-03. Taken 2 December, 1732, by John Skinner, James Church and Jos. Talcott, Jun. Will dated 3 November, 1732.

The last (nuncupative) will of Samuel Edwards, late of Hartford decd.: The evidence of the honourable Joseph Talcott is: "And as soon as I came to him he said: 'I have altered my mind as to what I intended to give my wife, and I give her £800.' The addition to the minutes of his giving his wife £800 I put in writing the morning after he died, that his relations might know what part and how."

Sworn in Court.   JOSEPH TALCOTT.
Test: Jos: Talcott, Jun., Clerk.

I, Eunice Talcott, Junr., well remember that being att Mr. Samuel Edwards's the night before he died, my father comeing into the house where Mr. Edwards lay sick, I told Mr. Edwards my father was come. He said, "Well, it is well, but I might have one thing altered. I will give my wife more than I have." And when my father came up to the bed, Samuel Edwards said: "I have altered my mind as to what I intended to give to my wife, and I might have that legacy altered. It must be £800." Signed this 3rd day of November, Anno Dom. 1732.

Sworn in Court.   EUNICE TALCOTT.
Test: Jos: Talcott, Jun., Clerk.

Att a Court of Probate held att Hartford, in and for the County of Hartford, on the 23rd day of April, Anno Dom. 1733: Then the Honble.

Joseph Talcott and Eunice Talcott, the above subscribers, in Court this day were sworn to the evidence above written, and under oath declared that the testator, Samuel Edwards, was of sound disposeing mind and memory at the time when he altered the legacie given to his wife Jerusha and made it £800.

Sworn to in Court. Test: Jos: Talcott, Junr., Clerk.

Page 235-6.

Eglestone, Benjamin, Windsor. Invt. £23-08-10. Taken 24 November, 1732, by Thomas Stoughton and David Bissell. Will dated 16 December, 1729.

I, Benjamin Eglestone of Windsor, do make and ordain this my last will and testament: Although I have given my children portions according to my ability formerly, yet I think it wisdom to make this following small addition to prevent future trouble: Imprimis. I give unto my son-in-law, Samuel Osbond of Windsor, to complete his deceased wife's portion, 5 shillings. I give unto my daughter Marcy Miller 5 shillings. I give unto my daughter Sarah Bliss 5 shillings. I give unto my daughter Dorothy West £5. I give unto my daughter Esther Osbond, of Enfield, 5 shillings. I give unto my son Benjamin Eglestone the remainder of my goods and chattells whatsoever, who is obliged to take care and honourably to maintain the testator as long as he liveth. And my son Benjamin Eglestone I constitute my sole executor.

Witness: *Thomas Stoughton,*   BENJAMIN EGLESTONE, LS.
Joseph Harper, Robert Thompson.

Court Record, Page 78—5 December, 1732: Will exhibited and proven.

Page 125.

Eglestone, Corp. John, Windsor. Invt. £609-12-10. Taken by Nathaniel Drake, Timothy Loomis and Henry Allyn. Will dated 17 June, 1730.

I, John Eglestone of Windsor, do make this my last will and testament: I give to Esther, my wife, the 1-3 part of my real estate during life, and 1-3 part of my personal estate forever. I give to my three sons, James Eglestone, John Eglestone and Edward Eglestone, all and singular my houseing and lands wheresoever, to be equally divided between them and to be injoyed by them and each of them forever, only reserving my wife's thirds therein during her natural life. I give to my daughter Esther Filley, besides what I have already given her, 2 shillings and 6 pence. I give to my daughter Stiles, besides what I have already given her, 18 pence. I give to my other five daughters, Abigail Eglestone, Dorcas

Drake, Anne Clark, Dameras Eglestone and Martha Eglestone, £6 apiece. Finally, I make my wife Esther to be sole executrix.

Witness: *Matthew Allyn,*   JOHN EGLESTONE, LS.
Thomas Moore, Henry Allyn.

Court Record, Page 49—3 August, 1731 : Will exhibited and proven.

Page 196.

Eglestone, Thomas, Windsor. Invt. £363-07-08. Taken 9 May, 1732, by Nathaniel Drake, Job Loomis and Henry Allyn. Will dated 4 February, 1731-2.

I, Thomas Eglestone of Windsor, do make this my last will and testament: I give to my wife Grace so much of my moveable estate as she shall see cause to improve or make use of, so long as she remains my widow, and also 1-3 part of my houseing and land during her natural life. I give to my son Thomas Eglestone 2 acres of land I bought of Samuel Bissell, and 10 acres of land lying at Pequanock Path, and also all my right and interest in the Equivalent Land, so-called, and 1-4 part of the undivided lands in Windsor Common, to him and his heirs forever, but not to be by him sold to any person whatsoever except to one of his brothers, provided they or either of them shall offer to him so much for the same, or any part thereof, as any person shall offer him for the same. I give to my son Jedediah Eglestone the whole of that lott on which he dwells, viz., the lott I bought of Cook and Marshall, except what I have already given him by deed of gift; also 1-2 of my lott in the western lands, and 1-4 part of my right in the undivided land in Windsor; also 1-2 of my lott in the Great Meadow, he paying to my daughters hereafter named the sum of £8 money. I give to my son Joseph Eglestone my dwelling house and barn and homelott, and 1 acre of land adjoining thereto; also my lott in the Little Meadow; also 1-2 of my land laid out to me in the 1 1-2 Mile Division in the undivided lands in Windsor; also 1-2 of my lott in the Great Meadow, he paying to my daughters the sum of £50 money. I give to my son Ephraim Eglestone 10 acres of land lying at the place called Mile's Hole; also my meadow lott lying on the east side of the Great River; also 1-2 of my land laid out to me in the 1 1-2-Mile Division of Town Commons; also 1-4 part of my lands in the undivided lands in Windsor, he paying to my daughters the sum of £12 money. And further, my will is that my six daughters, viz., Hannah, Isabell, Deborah, Mary, Mindwell and Esther, have paid to them by my sons Jedediah Eglestone, Joseph Egleston and Ephraim Eglestone, the sum of £70 money. And my will is that my sd. sons Jedediah, Joseph and Ephraim pay to my daughter Grace Whaples the sum of 10 shillings money, and to her children, viz., Thomas and Abigail Whaples of Hartford, the sum of £5 money each. And as to the remaining part of my moveable estate (if any there be), my will is that my sons Thomas, Jedediah, Joseph and Ephraim, shall divide it equally between them. And I appoint Grace, my wife, to be sole executrix. And I do desire Capt. Henry Allyn, my son Jedediah Eglestone, my son Ephraim Eglestone, and Isaac Loomis, to be overseers.

Witness: *Josiah More, Hezekiah Parsons,* THOMAS X EGLESTONE, LS.
Henry Allyn, Timothy Loomis.

Court Record, Page 70—6 June, 1732: The executrix refused the trust, and Adms. was granted to the widow and Joseph Eglestone, a son of the sd. deceased.

Page 65.

Ensign, James, Hartford. Invt. £222-06-08. Taken 15 January, 1730, by Thomas Richards and Joseph Webster.

Court Record, Page 15—3 March, 1729-30: Adms. to James Ensign.

Page 43-4.

Forbes, David, Hartford. Invt. £622-04-10. Taken 11 February, 1729-30, by Daniel Dickinson, John Benjamin and Timothy Williams. Will dated 25 December, 1727.

I, David Forbes of Hartford, do make this my last will and testament: My will is that, after my just debts are paid, my wife Sarah shall have and injoy 1-3 part of my personal estate, with this proviso, that at her decease she shall give it (ware and tare excepted) among my daughters according to her discretion, and that during her natural life she shall have the improvement of 1-2 part of my dwelling house, half the barn, 1-2 the orchard, and half the land lying between sd. orchard, and half of the pasture joining thereto, about 3 acres, together with the improvement of 1-3 part of the rest of my improved land. I give to my son David, besides what I have already given by deed of gift, 1-3 part of my right to the common or undivided land in Hartford east side, to be and remain to him and his heirs forever. Unto my son William I give 1-2 of my dwelling house, 1-2 of my barn, 1-2 of my homelott, 1-2 of my orchard and pasture adjoining, together with the 1-2 of the above-mentioned house, barn, orchard and pasture after the decease of my wife, together with a piece of meadow, about 6 acres, called Crow's lott, which is bounded north on my son David's land, west on the heirs of Clark, south on Mr. Pantry's land, and east on the Great Bridge Crick, 1-2 part of my outland at Hougonum called Moody's and Hopkins's lott, the remaining part of Dicke's lott, together with a right to a 1-3 part of my undivided land above mentioned, to be and remain to him and his heirs forever. I give to my son Solomon an upland lott at Hougoanum containing 12 acres, on the west side of the country road, bounded east on sd. road, south on land belonging partly to Timothy Williams and partly to John Benjamin, west and north on Timothy Williams; a piece of meadow land containing 4 acres, called Sandford's lott, bounded west on the Little Bridge Creek and east on the Great Bridge Creek, south on land belonging to the heirs of John Crow deceased, and north on land of Mr. Pantry; the remaining half part of the lott called Moody's and Hopkins's lott, together with a right to the third part of my undivided land; to him and his heirs forever. And my will is that my son Solomon be put out to some good trade according to the discretion of my executors. I give to my daughter Sarah, to my daughter Catharine, to my daughter Mary, for their portion, £30 to each of them, to be paid out of my personal estate after my wife has had her thirds thereof; and if that don't make up the sum mentioned, my will is that my son William pay 2-3 and my son Solomon 1-3 of what is wanting. My will is that Mr. William Pitkin and wife Sarah be my executors.

Witness: *Samuel Woodbridge,*   David Forbes, ls.
Elizabeth Woodbridge, Margaret X Colt.

Court Record, Page 13—3 March, 1729-30: Will and invt. exhibited.

Page 20—28 May, 1730: Solomon Forbes, age 16 years and 4 months, chose his brother David Forbes to be his guardian. Recog., £50.

Page 42—6 April, 1731: Catherine Forbes chose her brother David Forbes to be her guardian. Recog., £50.

Page 115-16-17.

Foster, Thomas, Middletown. Invt. £924-11-00. Taken 28 May, 1731, by Daniel Hall, Edward Foster and Joseph Rockwell. Will dated 25 February, 1730-1.

I, Thomas Foster of Middletown, in the County of Hartford, do make this my last will and testament: I give to Margaret, my wife, 1-3 part of my personal estate, also the use of 1-2 of my dwelling house (which end she shall choose), also one of my cellars, 1-3 part of my barn, 1-3 part of all my improved land, the odd room and well. I give unto my only son John Foster my dwelling house and barn and homestead, and all the buildings thereon, also that lottment of land over the Crick near the red house so called, also my lower Pond lott on the east side of the Great River, reserving his mother's thirds. I give to my son John Foster my best chest, also 2-3 of my propriety right in commons and undivided lands, and all other of my lands in Middletown not disposed of by will; also I give to my son John Foster all my stock of leather and hides, also all my husbandry tools and my shop tools. It is my will that after my just debts are paid and my wife's thirds allowed to her, that what remains of my stock of creatures shall be equally divided between my son John Foster and my daughter Elizabeth, now the wife of John Kent. I give unto my son John Foster all my wearing apparrell. I give unto my daughter Elizabeth Kent, besides what I have given her already, that lottment of land which I now have lying near unto Capt. Daniel Hall, also 1-3 part of my right in the mines and in my lands there, and also 1-3 part of my propriety right in commons and undivided lands in Middletown. I make my son John Foster my only executor.

Witness: *William Ward,*   THOMAS FOSTER, LS.
Edward Foster, Joseph Rockwell.

Court Record, Page 46—18 May, 1731 : Will and invt. exhibited and accepted.

Page 127 (Vol. XV) 1st May, 1750: Margaret Foster, widow and relict of Thomas Foster, now moves to this Court that dist. be made of the estate of the deceased according to the last will, whereupon this Court appoint James Ward, Ephraim Adkins and John Bacon to set out to the sd. widow what is given to her in the sd. will, and make return thereof to this Court.

Page 302-3.

Fox, Joseph, Glastonbury. Invt. £530-15-07. Taken 6 July, 1733, by N. Talcott and Abraham Fox.

Court Record, Page 97—4 September, 1733: Adms. to Esther Fox, widow.

Page 87 (Vol. XIII) 20 April, 1741: John Fox, a minor, age 15 years, son of Joseph Fox, chose Thomas Sparks of Glastonbury to be his guardian.

Page 51 (Vol. XIV) 11 December, 1744: Noah Fox, a minor, age 15 years, son of Joseph Fox, chose Hosea Fox of Glastonbury to be his guardian. Recog., £200.

Page 21 (Vol. XV) 5 August, 1746: Samuel Fox, a minor, 15 years of age, chose Thomas Sparks of sd. Glastonbury to be his guardian. Recog., £500.

Page 39—2 June, 1747: Joseph Fox, age 14 years, chose Thaddeus Welles of Glastonbury to be his guardian. Recog., £500.

Page 95—1st Tuesday in April, 1749: An account of Adms. was now exhibited in Court by Esther Fox, Adms., which account is accepted. The Court order the estate distributed: To Esther Fox, widow, her thirds of moveable estate; to Hosea Fox, the eldest son, his double part in the real estate; to John, Noah, Samuel and Joseph Fox, the rest of the sons, to Esther Fox and Beriah Fox alias Risley, daughters, to each of them their single portions of sd. estate. And appoint Col. Thomas Welles, Capt. Jonathan Hale and Elizur Talcott of Glastonbury, distributors. And also order the distributors to set out to the sd. widow her right of dowry of the real estate, viz., 1-3 of the buildings and lands.

Page 112—5 December, 1749: Report of the distributors.

Page 98-175.

Fuller, Edward, Colchester. Invt. £124-18-00. Taken 25 January, 1731, by Ensign Samuel Waters of Hebron and Nathaniel Foot of Colchester.

Court Record, Page 39—2 March, 1730-31: Invt. exhibited by Elizabeth Fuller, the widow; the estate insolvent. And the Court order £22-10-00 to be set out as necessaries to the widow.

Page 64—17 January, 1731-2: Adms. account accepted.

Page 161.

Garret, Francis, Simsbury. Invt. £179-17-07. Taken 26 August, 1731, by Joseph Case, Samuel Pettebone and Michael Humphrey. He died 24 June, 1731. Will dated 23 June, 1731.

I, Francis Garret of Simsbury, do make this my last will and testament: I give to my wife, Sarah, 1-3 of my lands during life and 1-3 part of my moveable estate forever. I give to my two sons, John and Francis (and if the child to be born is a son, to him also), to all of them, all my lands in Simsbury, in equal shares. I give to my daughters, Sarah and Susannah (and to the child that is to be born, if a daughter), to each of them, in money £5. If my wife Sarah should be put to difficulties either to pay my debts (my moveables not being sufficient) or to support the children, she may sell my house and lands in Simsbury to defray the charges thereof at the discretion and advice of the Judge of Probate for the County of Hartford, who is humbly desired to see that what is left might be reserved for my heirs after the reasonable allowances as above said. I constitute my wife sole executrix.

Witness: *Abraham Sydervelt,*　　　　　FRANCIS X GARRET, LS.
Samuel Pettibone, 2nd., Michael Humphrey.

Court Record, Page 60—1st February, 1731-2: Will and invt. exhibited and proven by Sarah Garrett, widow.

Page 1 (Vol. XV) 3 December, 1745: Francis Garrett, a minor, 16 years of age, son of Francis Garrett of Simsbury, made choice of his father-in-law Joseph Woodford of sd. Farmington to be his guardian. Recog., £400. Cert: *Asahell Strong, J. P.*

Page 8—4 February, 1745-6: John Garrett, 19 years of age, did on this day, with the consent of his mother, Sarah Woodford, formerly Sarah Garrett, who was guardian to sd. minor, make choice of William Woodford to be his guardian. Recog., £500.

Page 273.

Gilham, Jeams, Hebron. Invt. (personal estate), £22-16-10. Taken 2 June, 1732, by Jonathan White and Samuel Curtice.

Court Record, Page 69—5 June, 1732: Adms. to Rev. John Bliss of Hebron, who gave bond with Samuel Rowley. Exhibit of inventory.

Page 88—10 April, 1733: The estate represented insolvent. Samuel Curtice and Stephen Post appointed commissioners to examine claims.

Page 278.

Gill, Joshua, Middletown. Invt. £376-10-08. Taken 25 May, 1733, by Nathaniel White and John Gains.

The 26th day of April, 1733, I, Joshua Gill of Middletown, in ye County of Hartford, do make this my last will and testament: Imprimis. I give to my wife Ann all that part of the moveable estate which she brought with her, or the value of it, and likewise 3-4 of the remainder of all my moveable estate. This I give to my wife and her heirs forever. And further, I give to my wife the use of my dwelling house and land or the land adjoining thereto down to the Pond, and all my other improved lands except 1-3 part of my mowing land which lyeth within Pecowsit Field. This I give to my wife so long as she lives a widow bearing my name. My will is that my executors shall sell that piece of land which I have now lying in the Half-Mile Lott on the east side of the Great River, adjoining to Lt. Savage and John Hale's land, as soon as may be, and the effects of it to be laid out in building a little house, or repairing the house I now live in, for the comfort of my wife if she think needful, and she to have the use of it so long as she remains a widow. Further, I give to my wife £5 money yearly, to be paid to her, so long as she lives a widow, by my executor, and lands to be sold as is needful to provide the sd. £5 yearly. I give to my brother Richard Gill, after my wife has had her part of my moveable estate, the remaining part. This I give to my brother Richard and his heirs forever. And further, I give to my brother Richard the use of 1-3 part of all my mowing land lying within Pecowsit Field, so long as my wife lives. I give to my two brothers, Richard Gill and Ebenezer Gill, after my wife's decease or marriage, what then remains of my buildings or lands, howsoever it may be butted and bound, I give the whole of it to be divided, my brother Richard 2-3 of it, and to my brother Ebenezer the remaining third. This I give to my 2 brothers, Richard and Ebenezer, and their heirs forever. And I make Deacon Joseph White and my brother Ebenezer Gill to be executors.

Witness: *Jonathan Smith,*   JOSHUA GILL, LS.
Joseph White, Francis Smith.

Court Record, Page 83—3 July, 1733: Will exhibited and proven.

Page 164-185.

Gillett, Aaron, Colchester. Invt. £1171-16-01. Taken 2 January, 1731-2, by John Skinner, William Worthington and John Bulkeley, Jr.

Court Record, Page 33—5 January, 1730-31: Adms. to Hannah Gillett, widow.

Page 62—7 March, 1731-2: The Adms. shows this Court that there is not sufficient moveables to pay the debts. Then was set out to her £13-13-10 (for) necessaries to keep house.

Page 66—2 May, 1732: Adms. account accepted.

Page 92—5 June, 1733: Upon motion of Hannah Gillett and Jonathan Gillett, liberty is given to sell lands to the value of £723-04-00, with directions for advertising the sale.

Page 1 (Probate Side): Know all men by these presents: That we, Lemuel Stores and Hannah Stores, both of Colchester, in the County of Hartford and Colony of Connecticut, (which sd. Hannah was the daughter and only heir of Aaron Gillett, late of Colchester deceased), have received of our honoured mother, Mrs. Hannah Chamberlin of sd. Colchester, administratrix on the estate of the sd. Aaron Gillett, all the estate of the sd. deceased that did belong to the sd. Hannah Stores or that ought to be set out to her, with all the rents and profits of sd. estate, whether arising out of the real or personal estate, to our full content and satisfaction. And we do therefore hereby, for ourselves, our heirs, executors and administrators, forever acquit, exonerate and discharge our father, Mr. Joseph Chamberlin, and his wife, the sd. Adms., and all other persons concerned with or for the sd. Adms. in the management of that affair, from any claim, challenge or demand to be made by us or our heirs for any part of the estate abovesd. more than what we have recd. as above said, and do hereby ratify, confirm and establish any disposition or conveyance or conveyances that have been made by the sd. Adms. of the sd. Aaron Gillett's lands pursuant to ye trust reposed in her. And for confirmation of what is above written they have hereunto set their hands and seals, the 18th day of October, 1749.

Signed and sealed Dc. in presence of   LEMUEL STORES, LS.
Jno. Bulkeley,   HANNAH STORES, LS.
Alexr. Clark.

Colchester, October 18th, 1749: Personally appeared Lemuel Stores and Hannah his wife, and acknowledged this instrument to be their free act and deed.

Coram: John Bulkeley, Assistant.

Received Febry.
7th, A. D. 1749-50, and recorded
at length by me. *Jos: Talcott, Probate Clerk.*

Inventory on File.

Gillett, Elias, Windsor. Invt. £18-05-00. Taken 13 March, 1731-2, by Jacob Drake and Daniel Loomis.

Court Record, Page 61—29 February, 1731-2: Adms. granted to William Kelsey of Hartford, and the sd. Adms. informed this Court that the estate is insolvent, as he supposeth. This Court order him to make further inquiry and report to this Court 1st April next.

Page 222.

Gilman, Solomon, Hartford. Died 8 August, 1732. Inventory taken 3 September, 1732, by Roger Pitkin, Gabriel Williams and John Goodwin.

The last will and testament of me, Solomon Gilman, of Hartford: I give to my wife Hannah the use of 1-2 part of my upland lott on the west side of the highway, viz., 1-2 the orchard, 1-2 the plowing land to the meadow, the use of 1 1-2 acres of grass land in the meadow lott next to the abovesd. upland (in what part she shall see cause to take it), and the use of 1-3 part of my clear land on the east side of the highway, together with one lower room and one chamber in my dwelling house (which she shall choose), with what part of the cellar she shall need, to be for her use during life, and the use of 1-4 part of my barn. I also give her 1-3 part of my household stuff, except the bedding, and then I give her one bed (which she shall choose), with the furniture belonging thereto, and one cowe, to be for her use and intirely at her dispose forever. I give to my son John the remaining part of my upland lott lying west of the highway, and my meadow lott lying next to that; and, after my wife's decease, that part of sd. land on the west side of the highway which she improves, with the buildings and fruit trees thereon, and the improvement of 3 acres of land in my upper meadow lott, bought of William Mann and Joseph Barnard, during the term of 10 years. And after 10 acres are measured off my lott on the east side of the highway next to the street, I give him 1-2 of the remaining part of the sd. lott so far eastward as a brook or run of water which comes out of Morton's meadow. Also, I give him a gunn and a colt which he has used. I give to my son Solomon that piece of land voted to me by the Proprietors of the Five Miles in Hartford, the improvement of 1-3 part of what remains after my son John's three acres are set out of my upper meadow lott, for the term of 10 years. And if it should so happen that my son Solomon should not hold the sd. piece of land granted me by the Proprietors above mentioned, then I give him 1-2 part of my land eastward of the Long Plaine Brook to the east end of my lott. Likewise, I give him a colt, a gunn and two steel traps which he has improved, to him and his heirs forever. I give to my son Josiah 1-2 part of my land lying east of the brook that comes out of Morton's meadow. And if my son Solomon holds the above-mentioned piece of land granted me by sd. Proprietors, then my will is that my sd. son Josiah injoy the whole of my land from sd. brook that comes out of Morton's meadow to the east end of my lott, to be and remain to him and his heirs forever. Likewise, I give him the improvement of 1-3 part of my upper meadow lott, John's three acres excepted, for the term of 10 years. I give to my son Daniel 10 acres of land on the east side of the highway and butting west thereon, and the remaining half-part of my land as far eastward as the brook that comes out of Morton's meadow, and the improvement of the remaining 1-3 part of the upper meadow lott during the term of 10 years; and after the expiration of the term of 10 years, my will is that the whole of the upper meadow lott be equally divided between my son John and my son Daniel, and so to remain to them and their heirs forever. I give to my daughter Hannah, besides what she has already received, 20 shillings. To my daughter Mary, 20 shillings. To my daughter Mabell and my daughter Sarah, £30 to each of them. I

ordain that my wife Hannah and son John and my brother Richard Gilman be the executors.   SOLOMON GILMAN, LS.
Witness: *William Pitkin,*
Daniel Williams, John Coult.

Court Record, Page 74—3 October, 1732: Will and invt. exhibited.
Page 39 (Vol. XII) 3 February, 1735-6: Josiah Gilman, a minor, 16 years of age, son of Solomon Gilman, chose his brother John Gilman to be his guardian. Recog., £100.
Page 54—1st February, 1736-7: Daniel Gilman, age 14 years, son of Solomon Gilman, also made choice of his brother John Gilman to be his guardian. Recog., £100.

Page 69.

Goodman, Richard, Hartford. Invt. £137-07-08. Taken 11 June, 1730, by Aaron Cooke, Obadiah Spencer and John Sheldon.
Court Record, Page 25—7 July, 1730: Adms. to Richard Goodman, son of the deceased. Exhibit of inventory.
Dist. File: 4 April, 1757: To Richard Goodman, eldest son; to Timothy Goodman, to Benjamin Burr in right of his wife Mary Goodman, to Daniel Ensign in right of his wife Abigail Goodman. By Timothy Phelps and Hezekiah Marsh.

Invt. in Vol. XII, Page 388-9.

Goodrich, Hezekiah, Wethersfield. Invt. £1643-11-01. Taken 4 September, 1732, by Nathaniel Burnham, Martin Kellogg and Joseph Woodhouse.
Court Record, Page 68—20 May, 1732: Adms. granted to Honour Goodrich, widow, and Eleazer Goodrich and David Deming of Wethersfield. Recog., £400, with Ozias Goodwin of Hartford.
Page 43 (Vol. XII) 6 April, 1736: Inventory exhibited by Honour Goodrich, widow, and David Deming, Adms.
An agreement, made this 23 day of August, 1753, by and between Honor Perrin, of Wethersfield, who was sometime the wife of Mr. Hezekiah Goodrich, deceased, on the one part; Elizur Goodrich, Jun., of said Wethersfield, who is the only son of the said Hezekiah Goodrich, deceased, on the second part; and Charles Whiting, of Norwich, in the County of New London, and Honor his wife (which sd. last named Honor is the only daughter of the sd. deceased), on the third and last part, is as followeth, vizt.: That the sd. Honor Perrin shall have and hold during her natural life, as her right of dower in and of the real estate of said Hezekiah Goodrich deceased, one full third part thereof, to be set out to her on her request in severalty, and one-third part of personal estate of sd. deceased after the debts are paid and satisfied, to be

her own forever. That the said Elizur Goodrich, Jun., shall have and
hold two-third parts of all the said estate, both real and personal (excepting only the right of dower of the sd. Honor Perrin, as before mentioned), to be to him and to his heirs and assigns forever. That the said
Charles Whiting and Honor his wife, in right of the said wife, shall
have and hold one-third part of the estate (excepting the right of dower
as aforesaid), to be to the said Honor, the wife of the said Charles Whiting, and to her heirs and assigns forever. In witness and confirmation of
the foregoing agreement, the parties have hereunto set their hands and
seals.

HONOR PERRIN, LS.   CHARLES WHITING, LS.
ELIZUR GOODRICH, LS.   HONOR WHITING, LS.

Page 130.

Goodrich, Josiah, Tolland. Invt. £2696-12-03. Taken 9 to 30th
August, 1731, by Jonathan Delano, John Abbott and Zebulon West. Will
dated 14 March, 1728-9.

I, Josiah Goodrich of Tolland, do make this my last will and testament: I give unto Sarah, my wife, £60 worth of my household goods,
such of them as she shall choose, such excepted as was mine before my
marriage to her. I give to my sd. wife £180 money or bills of public credit,
and further the use, benefit and interest of the remaining part of my estate
for one year after my decease, and the use of my building until my eldest
child comes to be of age, and then two rooms of my house (which she
shall choose) during the time she shall be my widow, with this exception,
viz., that my funeral expenses and such charges for some mark or sign
whereby it may be known where my body lies, as my sd. wife shall order.
Nextly, my will is to give the remainder of my estate as follows, viz.: I
give to my eldest son, Josiah, £225; to my son Aaron, £200; to my son
Samuel, £200; to my son John, £200. I appoint the Reverend Mr. Stephen
Steele of Tolland, Mr. Elisha Micks and my brother Elizur Goodrich, of
Wethersfield, executors.

Witness: *Joseph Baker,*   JOSIAH GOODRICH, LS.
John Huntington, Daniel Elsworth.

Court Record, Page 50—3 August, 1731: Will exhibited and was
proven 5th October, 1731.

Page 51—7 September, 1731: Rev. Stephen Steele is appointed guardian unto Aaron Goodrich, 12 years of age, son of Josiah Goodrich.
Recog., £100.

Page 55—5 October, 1731: Elizer Goodrich of Wethersfield to be
guardian unto Samuel Goodrich, 10 years of age. Recog., £100. And this
Court appoint Col. John Stoddard of Northampton to be guardian unto
John Goodrich, age 3 years, and David, age 2 years. Col. Stoddard,
Martin Kellogg and Elisha Micks of Wethersfield acknowledged them-
selves joyntly and severally bound in a recog. of £600.

Page 53 (Vol. XIII) 7 August, 1739: One of the sons of Josiah Goodrich, late of Tolland, by his attorney, Joseph Gilbert, Jr., of Hartford, appeals from the judgement of the Probate Court, in approveing the will of Josiah Goodrich, to the Superior Court.

Page 5 (Vol. XIV) 22 May, 1742: Capt. Elizur Goodrich, by and with the consent of the other executors and heirs to the estate of Josiah Goodrich, moves to this Court that distributors may be appointed to make division of the estate according to his last will. This Court appoint Capt. Samuel Chapman, Zebulon West and Ebenezer Nye, of Tolland, distributors.

Distribution:

We, the subscribers, being appointed by ye Court of Probates in ye County of Hartford to make division and partition of ye estate of Josiah Goodrich, Esq., late of Tolland, to ye heirs according to his last will, have made partition of ye houseing and lands, or real estate, that being all that was shown to us to be distributed by ye executors to ye heirs of ye said deceased, vist.:

To Josiah Goodrich, eldest son, ten acres of land that was of his father's homestead. Also, one farm of 204 acres, lying southward of the meeting house, abutting partly on ye Rev. Mr. Steele's land, on Ephraim Grant's land, and on ye heirs of Barnabas Hinsdale. Also, ten acres purchased of Samuel Benton; value, £450.

To Aaron Goodrich, second son, 133 acres of land lying on Willimantic River, a part bought of John Yeomans decd., abuts south on a line drawn parallel to ye northward line of Isaac Benton's land; value, £400.

To Samuel Goodrich, third son, sundry pieces of land containing in ye whole 262 acres: One piece, 90 acres, lying on the hill east of Shubal Sturns, Jun., it being a lot purchased of Samuel Benton; also, 41 acres commonly called Stone House Meadow, abuts on Samuel West's land; also, 40 acres that abuts on Daniel Cook's land; also, 27 acres lying on Skungamug River, both sides, abuts on Daniel Cook, Doct. Bernard, Mr. Steele and Hez: Loomis. Also, four acres that was purchased of Joseph Rice, at a place called Rice's Neck; also, 17 acres (it being a part of the farm purchased of John Yeomans), abuts south on Isaac Benton's land, east on Willimantick River; also, 43 acres, abuts on land of Tho: Eaton and Joseph Baker; the whole in value £400.

To John Goodrich, fourth son, the remaining part of ye homestead or farm of land, excepting half an acre (further described in David's part), with the buildings, together with the tradeing shop that stands joyning to ye northwest corner of sd. dwelling house, wee say the said remaining part of ye homestead excepting ye said dwelling house and half acre aforesaid, to ye said John; in value, £400.

To David Goodrich, youngest son, half an acre of land at ye northwest corner of ye homestead, 14 rods in length north and south, and six rods in width east and west, abutting north on Mr. Steele's land, together

with the dwelling house and appurtenances (except the shop) ; in value,
£400.

<table>
<tr><td>The foregoing division was made by
4 June, 1742.
Accepted in Court, 4 January, 1742-3,
and ordered to be kept on file.</td><td>SAMUEL CHAPMAN,
EBENEZER NYE,
ZEBULON WEST.
Test: Jos: Talcott, Clerk.</td></tr>
</table>

Page 318.

Goodwin, William, Hartford. Invt. (personal estate), £94-06-08.
Taken 3rd November, 1733, by John Marsh and John Pratt. Will dated
1st March, 1727-8.

I, William Goodwin of Hartford, do make this my last will and
testament: I give to my wife her thirds. I give to my son William
Goodwin all my estate, both personal and real, to be to him and his heirs
forever, excepting only what I shall hereafter order him to pay to his
sisters. I give to my daughters, Sarah, Mary, Rebeckah, Violet and Susannah, £20 apiece, to be paid them by my son William, my executor, out
of my estate at an inventory price. And my will is that if my two daughters, Violet and Susannah, shall live a single life unmarried, that they shall
have a liberty to dwell in my dwelling house, either by themselves or with
their brother, as they can agree. And my will is that Violet shall have
10 shillings a year paid her by my son William, or the use of one acre of
land in the south meadow, during her being unmarried. And my will is
that what my daughters have had already of me, or what they shall have
of me before my decease, shall be part of their £20. And I make my son
William Goodwin my executor.

Witness: *John Pitkin,*   WILLIAM GOODWIN, LS.
Joseph Pitkin, Mary Pitkin.

Hartford, July the 23rd, Anno Dom. 1733: I, William Goodwin, do
now make a schedule, addition or codicil to this my last will, in which
I did make my son William Goodwin my executor, and did in sd. will
order him to pay some legacies, as in sd. will reference thereto being had
will appear. And now do further add and will that my two daughters that
now live with me, viz., Violet Goodwin and Susannah Goodwin, shall
have liberty to live in and have what use and improvement of the east
end of my dwelling house, as also my cellar, as they shall have occasion
for, so as not at all to hinder my wife, son William or any of his family
of their necessary use of the ovens or cellar as they shall have occasion.
Further, my will is that my sd. daughters shall have the use of my well
and liberty to improve part of my land in my garden as may be needful
and convenient for their use for a garden. And the foregoing I give the
use of during the time they or either of them continue single or not married. And in respect to any difference that may or shall happen to arise
between my children as to the use or improvement abovesd., I desire my

loveing friends, Ensign James Church and Mr. John Edwards, to advise and determine between my children. I do also further will that my executor do pay out of my estate the following legacies: To my daughter Violet Goodwin, £50; and to my daughter Susannah Goodwin, £40, besides what I have given them in my aforesd. will. And this I give them and their heirs forever.

Witness: *Joseph Talcott,*   WILLIAM GOODWIN, LS.
Jeames Church.

Court Record, Page 99—6 November, 1733: Will, with codicil, exhibited.

Goslin, Mary. Court Record, Page 27—2 September, 1732: Adms. granted to Mary Goslin, daughter of the decd.

Page 28—6 October, 1732: Mary Goslin, Adms., exhibits an account of her Adms., which this Court accepts.

Green, Sophia. Court Record, Page 57—17 December, 1731: Sophia Green, a minor, 14 years of age, whose father is deceased, chose Thomas Marks of Middletown to be her guardian. Recog., £50.

Page 102-3.

Griswold, Michael, 2nd, Wethersfield. Died 20 April, 1731. Invt. £919-06-04. Taken 11 May, 1731, by Michael Griswold, Nathaniel Burnham and Jacob Griswold. Will dated 2nd April, 1731.

I, Michael Griswold, 2nd, of Wethersfield, do make this my last will and testament: I give unto my son Benjamin Griswold my homestead, about 11 acres of land, with the house and barn and orchard thereon standing, except the improvement of 1-2 of sd. lands, buildings and orchard, which I reserve to my wife Mary during her widowhood; also except the blacksmith shop and tooles thereof, and the ground which sd. shop covers, which I reserve for my son Michael during the time he shall see cause to uphold and work in sd. shop, and no longer; and also one acre of land across the highway near sd. homestead, which I purchased of my brother Samuel Griswold, and lying next to the homelott of George Northway, excepting the use of sd. acre which I reserve for my wife during her widowhood; and also 2 acres of land lying in the Great Meadow in Wethersfield, which I purchased of Eliphalet Dickinson; he, said Benjamin, paying upon my decease to my daughter Prudence the sum of £20 money or equivalent thereto. I give to my son William Griswold 1-2 of my lott at Newington and lying on the north side of sd. lott there, and my desire is that my sd. wife, upon my decease, do by deed of gift convey to sd. William the 1-2 of my lott that I hold in her right at Besitt Plaine, viz., the north side of sd. lott; but in case my sd. wife shall neglect or refuse to convey sd. half of sd. Besitt Plaine, then my will is that she pay to the sd. William out of my moveable estate what the sd. land shall be valued at upon my decease. I give to my son Michael Griswold the other half of my lott at Newington, lying on the south side of sd. lott, and my smith shop and tooles, and also the use of the ground it covers, while he the sd. Michael shall uphold and use the same, and also my paceing mare. I give to my son Phineas Griswold 1 1-2 acres of land lying across the way, purchased of my brother Samuel Griswold, being part of the homelott of my honoured father Thomas Griswold, excepting 1-3 part of the yearly produce, which I reserved to the use of my sd. father during his natural life; and also 1-2 of the house and land now standing on sd. lott and to be divided between sd. Phineas and Ensign Michael Griswold upon the decease of my sd. father; and also my windmill lot. I give to my daughter Prudence £20 money and also a heifer and calf, which, with what she hath had, is all her portion. I give to my daughter Kezia the 1-2 of my Besitt Plaine lott, on the east side of sd. lott, and 5 roods of land in the Great Plaine, concerning which lands my will or desire is that my sd. wife (upon my decease) do convey sd. half of sd. Besitt Plaine lott and sd. 5 roods in the sd. Plaine to Kezia by deed of gift. I give to my wife Mary the improvement of the 1-2 of my house and orchard and homelott whereon they stand, and also the improvement of 1 acre lying across the way next the homelott of George Northway, during the time she shall continue my relict or widow; and also all my part of the team and all the tackling thereon, and husbandry implements, and all other my moveable estate; also 2 cowes and all my sheep and family provisions and winter corne on ye ground, I give to my wife and my son Benjamin for the payment of my just debts and support of my family as need shall require. I appoint my wife and my son Benjamin Griswold to be my executors.

Witness: *Nathaniel Burnham,*   MICHAEL GRISWOLD, 2ND, LS.
Michael Griswold, Nathaniel Griswold.

Court Record, Page 44-6—4 May, 1731: Will and invt. exhibited and proven.

Page 272.

Griswold, Shubael, Windsor. Inventory taken by Nathaniel Pinney, Joseph Barnard and Nathaniel Pinney, Jr.

Court Record, Page 88—13 April, 1733: Adms. to Phebe Griswold, widow, who, with her brother Joseph Cornish, of Simsbury, gave bond and exhibited inventory.

Page 30 (Vol. XV) 6 January, 1746-7: Shubael Griswold, a minor, age 17 years, son of Shubael Griswold, late of Windsor deceased, chose John Phelps the 2nd of sd. Windsor to be his guardian. Recog., £600.

Page 332.

Griswold, William, Wethersfield. Invt. £154-09-00. Taken 1st March, 1733-4, by Michael Griswold and John Robbins.

Court Record, Page 83—22 February, 1732-3: Adms. to Benjamin Griswold of Wethersfield, who gave bond with Daniel Robbins and Elisha Griswold.

Page 91—5 June, 1733: Exhibit of inventory.

Page 255-279.

Hamlin, John, Esq., Middletown. Invt. £571-03-00. Taken 14 June, 1733, by John Collins, Solomon Adkins and Jeames Ward; also Nathaniel White, Ebenezer Hurlbut and Joseph White. Will dated 21 October, 1732.

I, John Hamlin, Esq., of Middletown, do make this my last will and testament: I give to my wife, Sarah Hamlin, if she survive me and see cause to dwell in my house, she shall be comfortably maintained. If she see cause to remove to her own children, she shall be paid £5 money annually for seven years or so long as she bears my name. I give to my wife a guinea which lieth in my secretore, which is in consideration of the great trouble she hath in my present sickness, and also a suitable mourning suit. And the reason why I have given her no more interest in my estate is because before our marriage I proposed to her that I would renounce all property in or use of any estate belonging to her, but that it should be wholly to her and her heirs; and that she should wholly renounce all property in or right to my estate after my decease, but that it should be disposed of to my heirs, unto which proposalls I suppose she consented, and accordingly have performed them on my part. I give to John Hamlin's children in this form following: my grandson Giles Hamlin shall have the house and homestead, and my three granddaughters, Mehetabell, Elizabeth and Mary, to each of them £60. My will is that my granddaughter Mehetabell shall have 14 acres which her husband hath fenced in on my farm, in lieu of her £60. My will is that my granddaughter Mary shall have an equal half share with my four children, Esther, Mary, Sibbell and Jabez, in the division of my moveable estate, and that what wants to make up her £60 to be paid by her brother Giles, when he comes of age, to my granddaughter Mary King.

N. B.: My sister Mehetabell Hooker to have the desk in the shop that was my father's. I renounce to my daughter Johnson any former debt that stands upon the book against her. I give to our pastor, Rev. William Russell, £5; and to the Church £5. I give to my grandsons, Hamlin John Hall, Hamlin Blake and Hamlin Johnson, to each of them an ewe sheep. I give to my grandson John Hamlin my seal ring when he comes of age. I give to my daughter Sibbell Dwight my silver salt cellar, and to my granddaughter Esther Hall my two-handled silver cup; to my granddaughter Sibell Dwight my silver porringer and silver dram cup. I ordain my son Jabez Hamlin sole executor.

Witness: *John Rockwell,*   JOHN HAMLIN, LS.
———— *Wetmore, William Rockwell.*

Court Record, Page 81—6 February, 1732-3: Will proven.

Hamlin, Nathaniel, Middletown.   Invt. £1224-09-09.   Taken 18 November, 1731, by John Collins, Joseph Rockwell and William Whitmore. Finished 3 April, 1732. Exhibited in Court 6 June, 1732.

Court Record, Page 71—6 June, 1732: Adms. granted to Sarah Hamlin, widow.

Page 10 (Vol. XIII) 7 June, 1737: This Court appoint Richard Hamlin of Middletown to be guardian to William Hamlin, a minor, 12 years of age, and Harris Hamlin, aged about 5 years, sons of Nathaniel Hamlin, the mother of sd. minor consenting thereunto. Recog., £200. An account of Adms. on Nathaniel Hamlin's estate was exhibited in Court by Sarah Hamlin, the relict of sd. decd., alias Sarah Bacor, and Nathaniel Bacor, now husband to the sd. relict, by which account it appears they have paid in debts and charges, with what is allowed the widow for bringing up her children, the sum of £94-18-04, which account is accepted by the Court. This Court do appoint Nathaniel Bacor to be guardian to Sarah Hamlin, a minor, aged 9 years, daughter of Nathaniel Hamlin. Recog., £150.

Page 25 (Vol. XIV) 7 June, 1743: Nathaniel Bacon, in right of his wife, who was the relict of Nathaniel Hamlin, late of Middletown, moved to this Court that her right of dower may be set out to her in the estate of the sd. deceased: Whereupon this Court appoint Nathaniel Gilbert, William Rockwell and Joseph Wright, of Middletown, to set out her rights of dower, viz., 1-3 part of the buildings and lands, by bounds.

Page 27—5 July, 1743: Return of the setting out of the widow's dowry. Accepted.

Page 281.

Hamlin, William, Middletown.   Inventory (probably none taken). Will dated 16 May, 1733.

I, William Hamlin of Middletown, do make this my last will and testament: Imprimis. I give to my son Richard Hamlin what I have given him by deed of gift already. I give to my son Nathaniel Hamlin's heirs what I gave their father by deed of gift in his lifetime. I give to my son Edward Hamlin what I have given him by deed of gift already, and also to run eastward up to ye top of Stony Hill, so called, the breadth of his own land, and ye land I give to Daniel and Esther Hurlbut. I give to my son Charles Hamlin my homelott with the buildings and fences upon it, and also my pasture lying between Capt. Hall's and Jabez Hamlin's land. Also I give to my sd. son Charles all my long meadow and long meadow swamp. Also I give him my little meadow by the bridge on this side the Ferry River. Also my boggy meadow called Sansor's Point. Also I give him all the rest of my estate not disposed of in this my will, obliging him to pay all my just debts, funeral charges and legacies. I give to my daughter Susannah what household stuff and land I have given her, and also the equal half of my pasture in the northwest part of the Town Plat. Also I give her my dun mare. I give to my daughter Esther what household stuff and lands I have given her, and also the equal half of my pasture in the northwest part of the Town Plat. I give to my grandson Timothy Cornwall all my interest in the pond on the east side the Great River; but if he should dye before he comes to inherit it, my will is that his sister Rebeckah Cornwall shall have it. I give to each of my grandsons a £10 right of my right of the interest in the common and undivided lands in Middletown. I give to my respective friends, the Rev. Mr. William Russell and Jabez Hamlin, to each of them £5 money, and desire them to be overseers and to assist my executor. I appoint my son Charles Hamlin sole executor.

Witness: *John Collins,*   WILLIAM HAMLIN, LS.
James Ward, Jr., Thomas Hurlbut.

Court Record, Page 92—5 June, 1733: Will proven.

Page 304.

Hart, Stephen, Sen., Farmington. Invt. £939-04-00. Taken 27 September, 1733, by Isaac Cowles, John Hart and John Newell. Will dated 3 September, 1728.

I, Stephen Hart, Sen., of Farmington, do make this my last will and testament: I give unto Sarah Hart, my wife, the use and improvement of 1-2 of my now dwelling house and barn, and the use and improvement of 1-3 part of all my improved lands during the time of her life, and 1-2 part of my household goods to dispose of among my own children at her own discretion, and one cow. I give unto my sons, Timothy and Daniel Hart, all my houseing and lands, divided and undivided, to be equally divided between them, and husbandry tooles, with their arms and ammunition, and tools for the making of wheels. And further, I give unto my daughters, Sarah, Anne and Abigail, as followeth: Abigail to have £50 at her marriage if it happens so to be, or at my decease, to be paid by my executors. And the other half of my household goods not given to be equally divided betwixt all my three daughters above named. Further, I do constitute my wife Sarah Hart and my son Timothy Hart my sole executors.

Witness: *Isaac Cowles, Sen.,*   STEPHEN X HART, LS.
Robert Porter, Solomon Whitman.

Court Record, Page 97—29 June, 1733: Will and invt. exhibited and approved.

Hawley (Harley), Robert. Court Record, Page 98—2 October, 1733: Robert Hawley, formerly of Boston, now of Bolton, a minor, 16 years of age, chose Gideon Post of Bolton to be his guardian. Recog., £100.

Page 284.

Hills, Benjamin, Hartford. Invt. £243-10-08. Taken 30 March, 1733, by Nathaniel Fitch, Daniel Dickinson and John Benjamin.

Court Record, Page 93—3 July, 1733: Adms. to Elizabeth Hills, widow, and Samuel Hills, a brother, who gave bond with John Hills, a brother.

Page 44 (Vol. XII) 13 April, 1736: This Court appoint Samuel Hills to be guardian to two of the children of Benjamin Hills decd., viz., Oliver, age 7 years, and John, 5 years, their mother desiring the same.

Page 6 (Vol. XV) 4 March, 1746: An account of Adms. was now exhibited in Court by Elizabeth Hills and Samuel Hills, Adms. Accepted.

Page 8—4 February, 1745-6: John Hills, a minor, 16 years of age, son of Benjamin Hills, chose Joseph Cowles of Hartford to be his guardian. Recog., £200. Oliver Hills, now 18 years of age, also made choice of the sd. Joseph Cowles to be his guardian. Recog., £200. Cert: *Ozias Pitkin, J. P.*

Page 177.

Holcomb, Rebeckah, Simsbury. Will dated 14th Aprill, 1731.

I, Rebeckah Holcomb of Symsbury, in Hartford County, do give unto my daughter Rebeckah Holcomb all my moveable estate, after my decease, that was given to me by my husband Thomas Holcomb by his last will, to her and to her heirs forever. My daughter Rebeckah to be my executrix.

Witness: *Joshua Holcomb,*   REBECKAH X HOLCOMB, LS.
Ruth Griffin, Consider Holcomb.

Court Record, Page 66—2 May, 1732: Will exhibited and proven.

Page 104-5-6.

Holcomb, Capt. Thomas, Simsbury. Died 5 March, 1731. Invt. £869-03-07. Taken 7 April, 1731, by Benjamin Addams, Joshua Holcomb and Nathaniel Higley. Will dated 13 May, 1729.

I, Thomas Holcomb of Simsbury, in the County of Hartford, do make this my last will and testament: I give to my wife, Rebeckah, 1-3 part of my moveable estate, to her and her dispose forever, my two guns only excepted. Also, I give her the improvement of the 1-3 part of all my improveable land during all the time she remains my widow, and also the improvement of 1-2 of my dwelling house, both lower and upper rooms, and cellar. I give to my eldest son, Thomas Holcomb, 6 acres of land lying on the north end of that land I bought of Bissell, west of that I have already given him, being the north corner of my land. I give unto my son Daniel Holcomb 3 acres of land where his house and orchard now standeth, and that free from any incumbrance of improvement by my widow. I give unto my five younger sons, viz., Daniel Holcomb, Consider Holcomb, Return Holcomb, James Holcomb and Enoch Holcomb, all my lands within fence, both meadow and upland, with all the remainder of the land I bought of Bissell, with all the land given and measured out to me in the last division, and also my lott of land under Popatunock, to them in equal shares. I give to my four younger sons, Consider, Return, James and Enoch, with my two daughters, Elizabeth and Rebeckah, all the lands that shall or may be set out to me, or properly appertaining to my estate, my Town division agreed on, to them in equal shares; but in case the Town division shall be nullified and a division be made to the proprietors, that then my will is that my two eldest sons, Thomas and Daniel, shall have equal shares with my six other children last named, if such a division be made to the proprietors. I give to my sons, Consider and James, my dwelling house and barn, with my fourth part of the grist mills at the Falls to be to them in equal shares. I give to my two sons, Return and Enoch, my two guns. I give to my two daughters, Elizabeth and Rebeckah, £20 to each. I appoint my wife Rebeckah and son Daniel executors.

Witness : *Nathaniel Higley,*   THOMAS HOLCOMB, LS.
John Griffen, Samuel Higley.

Court Record, Page 44—4 May, 1731 : Will and invt. exhibited.

Page 87—22 March, 1732-3 : James Case of Simsbury, guardian to James and Enoch Holcomb, moves this Court for a distribution of the estate. Capt. Benjamin Addams, Jonathan Holcomb and Daniel Case appointed distributors. James Holcomb, 17 years of age, and Enoch Holcomb, 15 years 6 months, sons of Capt. Thomas Holcomb, chose James Case of Simsbury to be their guardian. Recog., £200.

Dist. File: 15 June, 1733 : To Thomas, to Daniel, to Consider, to Return, to James, to Enoch, to Elizabeth Gross, to Rebeckah Holcomb. By Benjamin Addams and Jonathan Holcomb.

Page 225.

Holmes, Jonas, Wethersfield. Invt. £583-07-05. Taken 30 May, 1732, by Jonathan Curtice, Jacob Williams and Daniel Goodrich.

Court Record, Page 76—5 September, 1732 : Adms. granted to Sarah Holmes, widow, and Benjamin Wright of Wethersfield. William Holmes, a minor, age 17 years, son of Jonas Holmes, chose his mother, Sarah Holmes, to be his guardian. Recog., £200.

Page 5 (Vol. XII) 4 June, 1734 : Sarah Holmes now being deceased and not having finished her account of Adms., this Court grant letters of Adms. unto Richard Holmes of Gilford, son of the decd.

Page 11—1st September, 1734 : Richard Holmes, Adms., exhibits an account of his Adms., which is accepted.

Page 13—29 October, 1734 : Pursuant to an act of the General Assembly, holden at New Haven, directing Benjamin Wright, Adms., to sell so much of the land of the sd. deceased as will procure the sum of £141-18-01: Whereupon this Court directs the Adms. to make sale of the land at Rocky Hill, in Wethersfield bounds, which land bounds north on the heirs of Jonathan Ryley decd. and Nathan Robbins, south on Daniel Edwards and on the heirs of Jonathan Smith, easterly on a highway, west on a highway leading to Middletown and on Thomas Morton, Nathaniel Robbins, Daniel Edwards and Stephen Riley.

Page 48—31 March, 1736: This Court directs Benjamin Wright, Adms., to make sale of the dwelling house of the sd. decd. at Wethersfield, Rocky Hill, and 2 acres of land adjoining, which land is bounded east on the deceased's own land, west on the road leading to Middletown, and south on John Church his land, which land is to be sold for defraying the sum of £141-18-00 and charges oweing; if he can sell it in two months to good advantage; if not, to report to this Court for further order.

Page 7 (Vol XIII) 10 May, 1737: Return of sale of land by Benjamin Wright to Thomas Butler, consisting of 2 acres with house and barn, sold for £145-00-00.

Page 285.

Hollister, Ephraim, Glastonbury. Invt. £115-10-06. Taken 29 June, 1733, by Jonathan Hale and Josiah Miller.

Court Record, Page 93—3 July, 1733: Adms. granted to Elizabeth Hollister, widow. Recog. with Josiah Hollister.

Page 105—5 February, 1733-4: Elizabeth Hollister, Adms., exhibited an account, and there not being moveables sufficient to pay the debts, this Court do set out to the widow the value of £19-02-11 in moveables.

Page 23 (Vol. XII) 14 March, 1734-5: This Court impower and direct Elizabeth Hollister, with Josiah Hollister, to sell so much of the lands of the sd. decd. as will procure the sum of £35-08-08 to answer the debts due from the estate.

Page 25—14 April, 1735: Josiah Hollister is appointed guardian to Ephraim Hollister, a minor, 10 years and 3 months old, son of Ephraim Hollister.

Page 122 (Vol. XV) 22 March, 1749-50: Hill Hollister, a minor, 19 years of age, son of Ephraim Hollister, late of Glastonbury, made choice of Timothy Porter, Jr., to be his guardian. Recog., £500.

Page 72.

Hooker, Samuel, Sen., Farmington. Invt. £1595-19-10. Taken 28 September, 1730, by John Porter, Isaac Cowles and Daniel Wadsworth. Will dated 21 July, 1730.

I, Samuel Hooker, Sen., of Farmingtown, do make this my last will and testament: I give to Mehetabell, my wife, 1-2 of my now dwelling house and barn, and homelott that my house stands upon, and 1-3 part of all my improveable land in the meadow, during the term of her natural life, and to be used and improved by my two sons, Giles and William, for her use and comfort. And further, I give all my right in the mill or mills in Hartford, on the east side of the Great River, and half my household goods, and two cows, to be at her own dispose to give to my own children, and all the silver and plate. I give to my son Samuel all the right I have or ought to have in the lott of land that fell to my honoured father, called the Blue Hills, lying east from Southington, and 1-4 part of the reserved lands within the bounds of Farmingtown that of right belongs to me that is not yet laid out, and one large gun that was formerly John Cole's, to him and his heirs forever. I give to my son Giles Hooker my dwelling house and lott that my house stands upon, and all that lott lying upon the east side of the highway, and the barn that stands upon the aforesd. lott of land, except one acre of the land that lyeth next to Ensign Samuel Lee his lott, and all the land they lyeth within the place called Indian Neck that I have any right unto (except three roods that I purchased of Clark Carrington), and 38 acres of land at a place called Long Swamp. And further, I give one lott of land that was my honoured father's, lying within the first division of land west from the Town, or the 150 acres that by right will fall to me from Mr. Hezekiah Wyllys, which the sd. Giles shall choose, and all the moveable part of my estate that is not otherwise disposed of by this will. I give unto my son Thomas Hooker 33 acres of land that lyeth in a place called the Dead Swamp, and 96 acres of land that lyeth west from the Town in a place called the first division, and 1-4 part of the sequestered land that of right belongs to me in Farmingtown. I give to my son William Hooker one acre of land that was formerly Joseph Barns's, lying east from the Town street, from the southerly part of the sd. lott next unto Ensign Samuel Lee's house and homelott, and 32 acres of land lying at Long Swamp which I had of John Porter, and 3 roods of land at a place called Indian Neck that was Clark Carrington's. Further, I give unto my two sons, Giles and William Hooker, all the remainder of my lands, divided and undivided, that lyeth within the Common Field or elsewhere, that is not disposed of, both outlands and ye sequestered, and all that is not before mentioned, to be equally divided betwixt them, always provided that the aforenamed William Hooker pays his equal proportion of debts justly due from me. This to the above-named Giles and William Hooker and their heirs forever. I give unto my daughter Esther Stiles one horse, or horse kind, besides that which is given her already. I give unto my daughter Mehetabell Hooker so much out of my estate as to make her equal in estate with her sister Esther Stiles. I make my wife Mehetabell and my son Giles Hooker executors.

Witness: *Isaac Cowles, Sen.,*   SAMUEL HOOKER, LS.
Daniel Wadsworth, Timothy Porter, Jr.

Court Record, Page 27—1st September: Will proven.

Probate Side, Ante Page One: A receipt, dated 21 May, 1742: Received of my brother Giles Hooker, executor to the estate of my honoured father Samuel Hooker deceased, the full of all debts, dues, legacies or demands whatsoever, ariseing or accrueing to me by virtue of the last will and testament of my sd. father, or any other ways due, payable or belonging to me from sd. estate, and do hereby fully and absolutely acquit and discharge him the sd. executor and the sd. estate from all and every part thereof.

The above is a true copy of the original receipt.

Pr. DANIEL COITT,
MABELL COITT.

Test: Jos: Talcott, Probate Clerk.

Page 24-5.

Hoskins, Robert, Sen., Simsbury. Died 8 November, 1729. Invt. £510-00-00. Taken 20 November, 1729, by Nathaniel Holcomb, Joseph Case and James Hilyer. Will dated 16 April, 1728.

The last will and testament of Robert Hoskins of Simsbury, in the County of Hartford: I give to my wife, Mary, 1-3 part of my moveable estate. I give her 3 acres of meadow land in the south end of my meadow, called Owen's meadow, to her forever. I give her the 1-2 of my house and house lott and orchard and barn, and the priviledge of 1-2 of the cellar during her natural life. Also, I give her 1-3 part of all my real estate or lands which I have not disposed of by deed, to be and remain to her during her natural life. I give to my eldest son Robert Hoskins, besides what I have already given him by deed of gift or otherwise, a tract of marsh land on the east side of the mountain which I bought of Mr. John Moore of Windsor. I give to my son John Hoskins, besides what I have heretofore given him by deed of gift or otherwise, the 1-2 of my lott in the lower meadow which I had of my father, being in the whole 20 acres. I give to my son Joseph Hoskins, besides what I have already given him by deed of gift or otherwise, all my meadow called Owen's meadow, excepting three acres which I have given to my wife. I also give him the home lott adjoining on the sd. meadow, on which he hath built a barn, and to extend northward as far as the cross fence now standing between the old orchard and the young orchard. Also, I give him 1-2 of a field of improveable lands between Owen's Brook and Bissell's Brook on the Plaine. Also, I give him the 1-2 of my 300-acre grant or division that lyeth between my house and John Case's. I give to my son Daniel Hoskins, besides what I have given him by deed of gift or otherwise, the 1-2 of my lott in the lower meadow. Also, I give my son Daniel a piece of land of about an acre lying within the meadow fence, to the brow of the hill as the fence now standeth, being a young orchard. Also, I give him 1-2 of a field of improved land of 12 acres lying between Bissell's Brook and Owen's Brook. Also, I give him the 1-2 of my 300-acre land or division. I also give him 12 acres on Owen's Brook, lying between his land which I gave him by deed of gift and land which I gave Joseph by deed of gift. I give to my daughter Mary, the wife of Joshua

Holcomb decd., £40 in money besides what I have already given her. I give to my daughter Thankfull, now the wife of Benajah Humphris, £40 as money besides what I have already given her. All other rights, titles, reversions and remainders not heretofore mentioned I give and bequeath to my six children, Robert, John, Joseph, Daniel, Mary and Thankfull, in equal shares. I appoint my wife Mary Hoskins and Joseph Hoskins, my third son, to be executors.

Witness: *William Buell,*   ROBERT HOSKINS, LS.
Joell Gillett, Samuel Higley.

Court Record, Page 9—6 January, 1729-30: Will proven.

Page 178.

Hosmer, Capt. Thomas, Hartford. Invt. £2954-14-11. Taken 25 April, 1732, by Joseph Skinner, Isaac Sheldon and John Whiting. Will dated 10 January, 1731-2.

I, Thomas Hosmer of Hartford, do make this my last will and testament: I give unto my wife, Anne Hosmer, 1-3 part of all my lands in Hartford for her improvement during life, also 3 rooms (one lower room and two chambers) in my dwelling house, which she shall choose, the third part of my cellar, and the 1-3 part of my barn, for her use during her widowhood; also give her 1-3 part of my household stuff, 1-3 part of my stock of cattle and other creatures, and my negro woman, to be at her own dispose forever. Likewise I give her one of my negro boys, viz., Ceaser, for her service so long as she remains my widow. If she marry, the boy I give to my son Stephen. I give to my eldest son Thomas Hosmer, besides what I have conveyed to him by deed of gift, all my land (excepting 15 acres that I shall otherwise dispose of) lying and being on the east side of the highway at the west division, always provided that my son Stephen shall have the use of 1-2 the mowing land for two years, and then to return to his brother Thomas, and half the apples in the orchard for the space of six years. I also give to my son Thomas my negro boy named Hanniball, he paying £20 to his brother Stephen towards building his house, for him, my sd. son Thomas, his heirs and assigns forever. I give to my son Stephen Hosmer, besides what I have conveyed by deed of gift, 15 acres of land lying and being on the east side of the highway at the west division, bounding north on the heirs of Mr. Hain's land and south on land I have given to my son Thomas. I also give him £20 towards his house, which his brother Thomas is to pay, for him, my sd. son Stephen, his heirs and assigns forever. I give to my son Joseph Hosmer 1-2 of my land, excepting six acres that I shall otherwise dispose of, at home, both meadow and upland, with my dwelling house, barn and other edifices thereon erected, the sd. land to be measured out and bounded on the north side. Also I give to my son Joseph the northern half part of my lott of land lying below Rocky Hill. I give to my son John Hosmer the remainder of my land (excepting 4 acres that I shall otherwise dispose of) at home, both meadow and upland, lying southward of the land which I have given to my son Joseph. And likewise I give to my son John the southern half part of my lott of land below Rocky Hill. I give to my four sons, Thomas, Stephen, Joseph and John, all my right, share, part and interest of, in and to the large tract of land called the Western Lands, belonging to the Proprietors of Hartford and Windsor, to be equally divided between them. I give to my sons, Joseph and John, between them, my team, one yoke of oxen and two old horses, and all the utensils belonging to the team. I give to my daughter, Sarah Hosmer, 2 acres of meadow land at the east end of my meadow land, and 1-2 the breadth on the north side; also that lottment of land lately laid out on the right of my grandfather Thomas Hosmer decd., in the Five Miles of land, commonly so called, on the east side of the Connecticut River in Hartford, for her my sd. daughter Sarah forever. I give to my daughter, Anne Hosmer, 2 acres at the east end of my meadow land, half the breadth thereof, and bounded north on the land given to my daughter Sarah; and also I give to my daughter Ann that alottment of land laid out on the right of my father Stephen Hosmer decd., in the Five Miles of land, so called, on the east side of the Connecticut River in Hartford, forever. I give to my sd. two daughters, Sarah and Ann, after my just debts and legacies herein given are paid, all my moveable estate whatsoever that shall remain, with my interest, share and part in the boalting mill adjoining to the lower gristmill in Hartford, to be equally divided between them. I appoint my wife and son Thomas executors.

Witness: *John Knowles,*   THOMAS HOSMER, LS.
John Cole, Rachel Knowles.

Court Record, Page 66—2 May, 1732: Will and invt. exhibited and accepted.

Page 220-2.

Hubbard, Richard, Sen., Middletown. Invt. £59-19-01. Taken 23 August, 1732, by Ephraim Adkins, Joseph Rockwell and Nathaniel Brown. Will dated 14 July, 1731.

I, Richard Hubbard, Sen., of Middletown, do make this my last will and testament: I give to my wife Martha the 1-2 of my household goods and stock and other moveable estate, and the improvement of the other half of my household goods and stock and other moveable estate, and of my homelott and long meadow lott, so long as she continues my widow. I give to my daughter Martha what I have given her by deed of gift, viz., £45 in land and the products of about 30 acres more, which was £25, and £7-17-06 which she has already received, the whole being £77-07-06. I give to my daughter Elizabeth what I have given her by deed of gift, which amounts to £44, and 1-2 of an acre of land on the Neck at 20 shillings, and £24-10-04 in moveables and money which I advanced by the sale of lands to pay her debts after she was a widow, the whole being £69-10-04. I give to my daughter Hannah ye lands and goods, £69-13-00. I give to my daughter Mary lands and goods, £69-16-00. I appoint my wife Martha sole executrix.

Witness: *Solomon Adkins,*   RICHARD X HUBBARD, LS.
Edward Foster, Stephen Winstone.

Court Record, Page 75—5 September, 1732: Will and invt. exhibited and approved.

Page 235-6.

Hubbard, Samuel, Hartford. Invt. £336-07-06. Taken by Thomas Ensign, Jr., and Jonathan Steele.

Court Record, Page 79—19 December, 1731: Will exhibited with invt. by George Hubbard, executor named in the will, who refused the trust and was appointed Adms. (the will not found). Also the heirs exhibit an agreement:

We, the subscribers, Samuel Hubbard, George Hubbard, John Hubbard, Esther Butler, Thomas Lee in behalf of Elizabeth his wife as well as in his own behalf, Isaac Lee and Mary Lee his wife, and John Gurney and Sarah his wife, being the children and children-in-law of Samuel Hubbard, late of Hartford deceased, and interested in his estate, do hereby agree upon a division for ourselves severally and respectively, and our heirs, as followeth: That is, that the sd. John Hubbard's share or part of sd. estate shall be £50 in lands or else in current bills of public credit. And the part or share of the sd. Esther Butler, Elizabeth wife of Thomas Lee, and Mary wife of Isaac Lee, shall be each of them so much as to amount to £50 each with what they have had heretofore given them out of sd. estate. And the part or share of the sd. Sarah wife of John Gurney, besides what hath already been given her, shall be all the moveables belonging to the sd. estate, provided all the debts be paid out of them. And all the remainder of sd. estate shall be equally divided between the 2 elder brothers before mentioned, to-wit: Samuel Hubbard and George Hubbard. In witness whereof we have hereunto set our hand and seal this 19th day of December, 1731.

Then personally came before the Court of Probate, holden at Hartford, Samuel Hubbard, George Hubbard, John Hubbard, Esther Butler, Thomas Lee, Isaac Lee, and John Gurney, and acknowledged their voluntary act and deed.

Approved by the Court,

SAMUEL HUBBARD, LS.
GEORGE HUBBARD, LS.
JOHN HUBBARD, LS.
ESTHER X BUTLER, LS.
THOMAS LEE, LS.
ISAAC LEE, LS.
JOHN GURNEY, LS.
J: Talcott, Clerk.

Page 175-6.

Huchisson, Joseph, Hebron. Invt. £458-14-04. Taken 17 March, 1732, by Samuel Gillet, Obadiah Dunham and Samuel Rowley. Will dated 1st February, 1731.

I, Joseph Huchisson of Hebron, in the County of Hartford, do make this my last will and testament: I give to my wife Mary Huchisson the bed we now lye on, and a great brass kettle, and four pewter platters, these things forever; also, the use of my dwelling house and the improvement of the third part of my improved land in Hebron, and of my barn so much as is necessary, for her during the term of her natural life unless she marry, then she should have the use of neither house, barn or land forever. I give to my son Jonathan Huchisson my gunn and broad axe, to be his own free and clear forever; and also that farm which lyes on Glastonbury line, the whole of it as it is bounded in a certain deed on record. I give to my son Aaron Huchisson my dwelling house and barn, as also half this lott which I now live on, the north half, with all the fences and fruit trees thereon, and half that land which lies over the brook. I give to my son Joseph Huchisson the south half of this lott which I now live on, and half of yt land over the brook. Furthermore, my will is that all my lands and buildings should be apprised, and that my sons Jonathan, Aaron and Joseph Huchisson shall be equally alike in estate as to number of pounds when my estate is all apprised. I give to my youngest son Israel Huchisson so much of my estate as to make him equal with the rest of my aforesd. sons. I give and bequeath unto my daughters, Mary, Ann and Rachel Huchisson, to each of them 2-3 so much of my estate as I do give to my sons. And my will is that my wife and my brother Hezekiah Huchisson be my executors.

Witness: *Obadiah Dunham,*   JOSEPH X HUCHISSON, LS.
Esther Dunham, Samuel Rowlee.

Court Record, Page 65—31 January, 1731: Will and invt. exhibited and approved.

Page 250.

Huffman, John Casper, Simsbury. Invt. £161-03-00. Taken by Thomas Holcomb and Joshua Holcomb. He died 21 March, 1732. Will dated 13 March, 1732.

I, John Casper Huffman, do make this my last will and testament: Imprimis. I give unto my maid and nurse, Else Griffin, the half of my estate, both personal and real—the real estate to be hers during life and then to descend to her daughter Martha if she arrives to the age of 21 years, if not, then to Else Griffin, her heirs and her assigns forever. I give to my countryman, John Hendrik Nearing, all my right and title to a piece of land that he and I hold in equal share, lying in Simsbury at a place called Pond Hill, about 7 acres in the whole between us both, more or less, and also I give him my right to two acres of land at the Pond Marsh adjacent, held also in common, more or less. I give to sd. Mr. Nearing all my books after my decease. After my just debts are paid I give unto my nurse, Else, the remaining part of my estate, real and personal, to her and her heirs forever, in consideration of her long and difficult service, reserving to Mr. Nearing the liberty to his own use to improve or lease a certain copper mine supposed to be found in sd. land,

he or his leases paying what they may damnify that land by such improvement. I appoint my friend Else Griffin to be sole executrix.
Witness: *Timothy Woodbridge,*   JOHN CASPER X HUFFMAN, LS.
Ann Nearing, Thomas Holcomb.

Court Record, Page 68—22 May, 1732: The last will of John Casper Huffman, deceased, was now exhibited in Court by Else Griffin, executrix, who accepted the trust. The will was proven, and, with an inventory, was ordered recorded and kept on file.

Page 292.

Humphrey, Deacon John, Simsbury.   Died 31 December, 1732. Inventory taken 2 March, 1732-3, by John Pettibone, Jr., Joseph Cornish and Samuel Pettebone the 2nd.

Court Record, Page 93—3 July, 1733: Adms. granted to Michael Humphrey, son of the deceased.

Page 214 (Probate Side, Vol. XIII): A distribution of the estate of Deacon John Humphrey, late of Simsbury, made by agreement of us, Sarah Humphrey, widow, John Humphrey, Benajah Humphrey, Michael Humphrey and Daniel Humphrey, all sons to the sd. decd., and Joseph Case and Hannah Case (formerly Hannah Humphrey, daughter of the sd. decd.). A list of all the goods, chattells and lands of the sd. decd. to be distributed among the surviving heirs of the sd. decd. In witness to the above-written agreement we have hereunto set our hands and seals this 3rd day of March, 1732-3.

Signed and sealed:

Witness: *John Pettibone, Jr.,*   SARAH X HUMPHREY, LS.
Benjamin Mills.   JOHN HUMPHREY, LS.
HANNAH CASE signed and sealed   BENAJAH HUMPHREY, LS.
in presence of *Joseph Mills,*   MICHAEL HUMPHREY, LS.
Josiah Case.   DANIEL HUMPHREY, LS.
JOSEPH CASE, LS.
HANNAH CASE, LS.

Page 51.

Hurlbut, Jonathan, Kensington.   Invt. £716-00-10.   Taken 17 April, 1730, by Thomas Hart and Samuel Smith.   Will dated 25 March, 1730.
I, Jonathan Hurlbut of Kensington, do make this my last will and testament: I give to my wife Abiah Hurlbut her thirds during life. To my eldest son Stephen Hurlbut I give 100 acres of the east end of my lott in Middletown whereupon he now dwells. To my second son Jonathan Hurlbut so much of the remainder of sd. lott as amounts to £5 in current bills of public credit. To my third son Josiah Hurlbut 20 acres of the west end lott whereupon my dwelling house now stands. The re-

mainder of my land and buildings within the bounds of the sd. Kensington I give to my two younger sons, Isaac Hurlbut and James Hurlbut. The remainder of my sd. lott in Middletown and all the remainder of my personal and moveable estate I give to my four daughters, Abiah, Sarah, Mary and Martha. I do hereby appoint Capt. Isaac Hart, of Kensington, executor. My will is that my children give full confirmation of that land and houseing I sold to my wife's brother Abraham Gillett whereupon he now dwells.

Witness: *William Burnham,*   JONATHAN HURLBUT, LS.
Isaac Lee, Joseph Porter.

Court Record, Page 18—5 May, 1730: Will exhibited. Capt. Isaac Hart refused the trust. This Court appoint Abiah Hurlbut, the widow, and Josiah Hurlbut, the son, Adms. The will was proven, and, with inventory, to be recorded and kept on file.

Page 14-15-16-17.

Joanes, Thomas, Colchester. Invt. £1232-03-06. Taken 6 November, 1729, by Nathaniel Foote, Samuel Loomis and Israel Newton. Will dated 27 October, 1729.

I, Thomas Jones of Colchester, in the County of Hartford and Colony of Connecticut, yeoman, do make this my last will and testament. I give to my wife Mary Jones her thirds of my estate; also give to my sd. wife my negro gall Nanna during the life of my sd. wife. If she survive her sd. mistress, then my will is she, being apprised, shall return to any one of my children that will take her and pay out to the rest of my children equal shares of what she shall be apprised at, only reserving to himself or herself their own part. And if it so happen that the sd. negro gall have any issue during the life of my sd. wife, that then they shall belong to my children, and that they be so disposed of as that all of them may equally share in the profit of them. And as for my real estate, with the remainder of the personal, I give and bequeath the same in manner following: That is to say, to my three eldest sons, viz., James, Jabez and Jonathan, I give my farm lying on each side of the road near to Mr. James Newton's. My will further is that my sons, James, Jabez and Jonathan, shall pay to their four sisters, viz., Mary, Lewcey, Rachell and Sarah, £60 money to each of them, that is to say, after so much of sd. estate as shall be valued or apprised at £100 be reserved and set aside for each of themselves, viz., James, Jabez and Jonathan, and so observing this rule until the whole of that part of my estate be divided among these my aforenamed sons and daughters. And for as much as it is probable that my sd. son Jonathan may be ever under an incapacity to act and do for himself, if he die without issue, my mind and will is that his brothers, having had a tender regard to take care and provide for him, that that part of my estate willed to him shall be equally divided between them. And also I give unto my youngest son Joshua my farm on which I now dwell, it lying adjoining to Lt. Harris's farm on which he now dwells; and my will is that, this farm being apprised, my sd. son shall, after an £100 worth thereof be set aside for himself, pay to my youngest daughter Lurenia the sum of £60. I do now name, ordain and appoint my wife Mary Joanes, and my brother Nathaniel Cohoon and Mr. James Newton, both of Colchester, executors.

Witness: *John Bulkeley, Jr.,*   THOMAS JOANES, LS.
William Treadway, Josiah Treadway.

Court Record, Page 7—2nd December, 1729: The last will and testament of Thomas Jones, of Colchester, exhibited in Court by Mary Joanes, widow, and Nathaniel Cohoon and James Newton. Will proven.

Page 37—2 February, 1730-1: Adms. accompt exhibited in Court and accepted.

Page 40—13 March, 1730-1: Whereas, James Joanes, Benjamin Graves and Mary his wife, and Lucy Joanes, have quitted and made over their whole right and title and claim unto Joshua Joanes and Lurenia Joanes of that part or parcell of land given them the sd. Joshua and Lurenia by the will of their father Thomas Joanes; and also the sd. James Joanes, Benjamin Graves and Mary his wife, and Lucy Jones have bound themselves by bond in the sum of £200 that all the younger children shall, as they come of lawfull age to act, also quitt their claim of sd. parcells of land unto Joshua and Lurenia. All which appears on the files of the Court of Probates in the County of Hartford: This Court do therefore order and appoint Messrs. John Bulkeley, Jr., Nathaniel Foote and James Newton, of Colchester, to distribute the estate of the sd. deceased to and amongst the widow and children of the sd. deceased Thomas Jones, and that they set out to every one what lands shall be theirs according to will, by meets and bounds.

Page 315.

Kelsey, Hannah, Hartford. Invt. £55-12-03. Taken 19 March, 1732-3, by Joseph Talcott, Jr., and Jonathan Olcott.

Court Record, Page 91—24 May, 1733: Adms. to Obadiah Spencer of Hartford. Exhibit of inventory.

Page 98—2 October, 1733: Recog. with Jonathan Marsh, of Hartford.

Keney, Ebenezer. Court Record, Page 68—22 May, 1732: Ebenezer Keney, a minor, 14 years of age, chose David Hills of Hartford to be his guardian. Recog., £50.

Page 102—12 December, 1733: David Hills, guardian to Ebenezer Keney, son of Ebenezer Keney decd., desires release and sd. Keney also desires it. Granted, and Ebenezer Keney chose his father-in-law William Haile of Glastonbury (alias Hall) to be his guardian. Recog., £200.

Kilbourn, Thomas. Court Record, Page 108—5 March, 1733-4: Thomas Kilbourn, son of Ebenezer Kilbourn, formerly of Glastonbury, 15 years of age, chose his mother Elizabeth Kilbourn to be his guardian. Recog., £50.

Page 39-40.

Kimberly, Thomas, Esq., Glastonbury. Invt. £2109-09-00. Taken 17 February, 1729-30, by Jonathan Hale and Abraham Kilbourn. Will dated 2 January, 1729-30.

I, Thomas Kimberly of Glastonbury, do make this my last will and testament: I give to Ruth, my wife, her thirds. I give to my three sons, Thomas, Samuel and John, the lott of land where I now dwell, that is to say, my sd. son Thomas to have 8 rods wide on the north side, Samuel to have 7 rods wide next to him, and my sd. son John to have 7 rods wide on the south side, provided my sons pay to their five sisters £80 apiece at the day of their marriage or when they arrive to the age of 21 years, which shall happen first. I give to my sons, each of them, a yoke of steers and a breeding mare. And I give to my sons my lands at Dimond Pond and that land called the "Pig-in-the-Pocke." And all the rest of my lands in the Township of Glastonbury to be equally divided between them, all which lands and estate above given to my sons to be to them forever. I give to my five daughters my lott of land lying at the Long Pond in the bounds of Colchester, to be equally divided among them. I give to my sons, Thomas and Samuel, all the rest of my moveable estate after my debts are paid. My sons Thomas and Samuel to be executors.

Witness: *Joseph Andrews,*   THOMAS KIMBERLY, LS.
Thomas Welles, John Hale.

Court Record, Page 13—3 March, 1729-30: Will proven.

Page 337.

King, Benjamin, Stafford. Will dated 20 November, 1732.

I, Benjamin King of Stafford, in the County of Hartford, do make this my last will and testament: I give unto Remember, my wife, whom I likewise constitute my only and sole executor, all my lands and moveable estate, all my household stuff, cattle and tools, and all my whole estate, both real and personal, ordering this my executor to pay all my debts out of sd. estate, and also to pay to my respective children as followeth, as they shall come of age: To my eldest son Benjamin, 5 shillings; to my son Samuel, 5 shillings; to my son Joseph, 5 shillings; to my daughter Elizabeth, 5 shillings; to my son Moses, 5 shillings; to my daughter Mary, 5 shillings. And all the remainder of my estate I leave with my executor to be disposed of for the comfortable maintenance and support of my eldest daughter Agnes, which never hath had the use of her reason, for which cause I order this my estate to be disposed of at the discretion of my executor for the comfortable maintenance of my child Agnes. And I do hereby order my executor to have the advise of my well-esteemed friend, Lt. John Huntington, of Tolland, in the disposal of sd. estate.

Witness: *John Pasco,*   BENJAMIN KING, LS.
Isaac Osborn, Rebeckah X Pasco.

Court Record, Page 101—4 December, 1733: Will exhibited by Remember King, the executrix named in the will.

Page 1 (Vol. XII) 1st April, 1734: Benjamin King, age 16 years, and Samuel King, age 14 years, chose their mother Remember King to be their guardian. Cert: *John Huntington, J. P.*

Page 111-112.

Knowlton, Thomas, Haddam, East. Died 25 December, 1730. Invt. £394-15-07. Taken by Daniel Brainard, Shubael Fuller and Thomas Cone. Will dated 15 September, 1730.

I, Thomas Knowlton, Sen., of Haddam, on the east side of the Great River, in the County of Hartford, do make my last will and testament: I give to my wife Susannah the sole benefit and profit of the remaining part of my homestead, together with the house and barn and orchard, and all the conveniences belonging thereto, as also my woodlott division on the common, during her life; and 1-3 part of my moveable estate forever. I give unto my son Thomas, besides what I have already done for him or given him by deed of gift, the piece of swamp and lowland lying at the mouth of Moodus River, as also my homestead, house, barn and orchard, and the lott on the commons, that is to say, the abovesd. swamp and lowland to be to his use and profit presently, but the other he shall not have the use and profit of until after his mother's decease and until his sisters hereafter mentioned have done with them according to the true intent of what is after mentioned, together with all my right and interest in the commons or undivided lands. I give to my daughter Mercy Bates one cow, and add nothing further to her, she having had her mother's estate. I give to my daughter Susannah Olcott nothing further than this (she having already had the main intended for her), viz., that at her mother's decease she shall injoy the house, barn, orchard, and homelott so far as my furthermost bars where there is a cross fence, to remain to her so long as she continue in her deserted condition or a single state. I give to my two daughters, viz., Lucy and Hannah, my division of land lying on Eight-Mile River, as also the remaining two-thirds of my moveables, to be equally divided between them. And if these my two daughters, or either of them, shall continue in a single state after my wife's decease, my will is that they shall have a good priviledge in the house so long as they continue in a single state, and no longer.

Witness: *Stephen Hosmer,*   THOMAS KNOWLTON, LS.
Nathaniel X Lord, Joseph Grover.

Court Record, Page 46—4 June, 1731: Will and invt. exhibited by the widow Susannah, who, with the son, were joyntly and severally bound. Adms. to the widow.

Page 339.

Labbe, Stephen, Wethersfield. Invt. £39-12-03. Taken by William Manley and Nathaniel Hale.

Court Record, Page 92—5 June, 1733: Adms. granted to Esther Labbe, widow, with Nathaniel Hale.

Page 12 (Vol. XII) 8 October, 1734: The Adms. exhibited now an account of their Adms., which this Court accepts.

Page 7.

Lewcas, John, Middletown. Invt. £26-11-06. Taken 2nd June, 1729, by Samuel Cotton and Zacheus Candee.

Court Record, Page 2—2 August, 1729: Invt. exhibited by Sarah Lewcas, widow. And this Court appoint Sarah Lewcas to be guardian to her son Joseph Lewcas, 7 years of age. Recog., £50.

Page 22—2 June, 1730: Sarah Lewcas, Adms., reports the estate insolvent.

Page 35—5 January, 1730-31: Sarah Lewcas, Adms., showing that part of his estate was a small frame house standing on Town land, and will not therefore go into the inventory, this Court advise to sell at vandue and return the avails to this Court.

Page 40 (Vol. XIII) 2 February, 1738-9: Joseph Lewcas, son of John Lewcas, chose his uncle Jacob Whitmore to be his guardian. Recog., £100. Cert: *Giles Hall, J. P.*

Page 58.

Lewcas, Samuel. Invt. £7-19-08. Taken by Abraham Fox and Gideon Hollister.

Court Record, Page 22—2 June, 1730: Invt. exhibited by Elizabeth Lewcas, who reports estate insolvent and prays the Court that necessaries be set out for her support, which is as follows, viz.:

	£ s d		£ s d
1 bed and furniture,	1-10-00	2 pewter spoons,	0-01-00
1 porridge pott,	0-18-00	1 water pail and hand pail,	0-02-00
3 milk bowls,	0-04-06	3 earthern potts,	0-02-08
1 Bible,	0-13-06	3 wooden dishes,	0-01-00
1 pewter plate,	0-02-00	2 chaires and 1 old barrell,	

The widow refused administration.

Page 241-2.

Loomis, John, Windsor.   Invt. £342-06-06.   Taken 1st December, 1732, by Joseph Newbery and Joshua Loomis.   Will dated 18 June, 1729.

I, John Loomis, of the Town of Windsor, do make this my last will and testament: I give to Esther, my wife, the improvement of 1-2 of my land within fence, and also my woodland, as she think fitt, during the term she shall continue my widow.   If she shall marry, then she shall have the 1-3 of sd. lands with the use of 1-2 of my dwelling house during life.   I give to my sd. wife Esther the 1-4 part of my household stuff and goods.   I give to my son John a double portion of my estate with my three daughters, and to be disposed of as in manner followeth, viz., that he the sd. John shall have all my lands after my decease, he paying the legacies to each of my daughters, to Esther, to Sarah and to Damaras, if any there be to pay, so much as to make each of them to have half so much as his double portion.   And he shall have three years time to pay out to them the sd. Esther, Sarah and Damarus their portion.   And also that they shall have each of them their equal part in moveables belonging to my estate.   I make and ordain my son John sole executor to this my last will.

Witness: *Simon Wolcott,*   JOHN LOOMIS, LS.
Isaac Loomis, Nathaniel Loomis.

Codicil, dated 20 June, 1729: That he only gave to his three daughters to each of them a single share in his estate, in his moveable estate and his lands on which his house standeth, that is, the meadow and upland to the Three Miles.   And I do give unto my son John all my lands in Windsor, laid out or in time to come may be laid out as a property to me or to my estate, and also all the right or property in any other town or place whatsoever.

Witness:*Thomas Skiner,*   JOHN LOOMIS, LS.
Nathaniel Loomis, Isaac Loomis.

Court Record, Page 78—28 November, 1732: Will and invt. exhibited, accepted and ordered to be kept on file.

Page 34.

Loomis, Nathaniel. Inventory taken 5 January, 1729-30, by Thomas More, Henry Allyn and Timothy Loomis, apprisers.   An inventory of the estate of Nathaniel Loomis, son of Joseph Loomis, both of Windsor, deceased.   The only estate presented was the only moiety or half-part of 40 acres of land lying in Windsor, lying in common with Stephen Loomis for the heirs of Stephen Loomis decd., which other half did formerly belong to Isaac Loomis deceased.   The whole 40 acres bounds northeastwardly on common and undivided land, northwestwardly on land ———————————, and southeasterly on land of Sergt. James Enno or land formerly surveyed to Capt. Daniel Clark and Mr. Thomas Hanford, and southwesterly on land of Ichabod Loomis in part and partly on land of Abraham Loomis. Which we apprise at 40 shillings per acre, £40 for the 20 acres. The above-written is a true inventory of the estate of the above-sd. Nathaniel Loomis as one presented by the Adms., namely, Joseph Stroud of Boston, and taken by us the subscribers under oath.

Loomis, Joseph. Court Record, Page 7—2 December, 1729: This Court grant Adms. on the estate of Joseph Loomis of Windsor, decd., unto Joseph Stroud of Boston, who accepted that trust, gave bond, and took letters of Adms. this day.

Page 261-2-3.

Loomis, Ensign Nathaniel, Bolton. Invt. £86-08-01. Taken 2 October, 1732, by Timothy Olcott and Daniel Griswold of Bolton. Will dated 6 January, 1729-30.

I, Nathaniel Loomis of Bolton, in the County of Hartford, do ordain this my last will and testament: I give unto my wife Ruth the use of 1-2 of my dwelling house and half of my improved land during her natural life; also so much of my moveable estate as shall be necessary for her comfortable subsistence. I give to my son Nathaniel Loomis 1-2 of my right in the common and undivided land in Windsor besides what I have already given him by deed. I give to my son Charles Loomis 1-2 of a parcell of land in Bolton I took as part of a 2nd division (the whole parcell is 16 acres, bounded east on Coventry). I give to my son Roger Loomis my 2nd division arising from my land. I give to my son Jerijah Loomis my homelott I now live on, with the buildings and appurtenances thereof, as it is bounded west on the highway, south on land I have given to Roger Loomis, east on common land, and north on Charles Loomis and Col. Allyn, 1-2 of which after my wife's decease. Also I give him 1-2 of about 20 acres in Hebron I had in exchange with John Bishop; also 1-2 of 15 acres of swamp north of John Bishop's land. I give to my daughter Ruth £80 to be paid her by my son Jerijah Loomis when she is 18 years of age. The other half of my lands in Windsor Town Commons to be equally divided amongst my sons. I appoint my son Nathaniel sole executor.

Witness: *John Bissell,*   NATHANIEL LOOMIS, LS.
Samuel Brown, John Bishop.

Court Record, Page 84—6 March, 1732-3: Will exhibited by Nathaniel Loomis, executor.

Page 313-14.

Loomis, Lt. Nathaniel, Windsor. Invt. £517-05-03. Taken 21 October, 1733, by William Wolcott, Hezekiah Porter and Samuel Bancroft. Will dated 26 May, 1729.

I, Nathaniel Loomis of Windsor, being now stricken in age, do make this my last will and testament: I give to my wife Elizabeth the use of the whole of my estate during widowhood, and 1-2 the moveables to be at her own dispose. I give to my brother Daniel Loomis my meadow at Podunk, he paying my sister Mindwell Loomis £20. I give to my brother Hezekiah Loomis land I bought of Nathaniel Bissell, he paying to my brother's children, Jonathan and Ebenezer, £5 apiece. I give to my brother Moses the homestead with the buildings, he paying to my brother Josiah Loomis £25 within two years after possession. I give to Daniel Gillett, 2nd, that part of the lott which I bought of Nathaniel Bissell west of the country road, he paying Hepzibah Loomis £30. The rest of my moveable estate not disposed of I give to be equally divided amongst my sisters and my wife's brothers and sisters living, and the children of those decd. I make my wife Elizabeth, with Daniel Gillet, my executors.

Witness: *Richard Skinner,*   NATHANIEL LOOMIS, LS.
Isaac Loomis, Noah Skinner.

Court Record, Page 99—6 November, 1733: Will exhibited.

Page 185-6.

Macklarren, Patrick, Middletown. Invt. £250-00-00. Taken 16 March, 1732, by John Warner, Samuel Gipson and James Brown.

Court Record, Page 64—4 April, 1732: Dorothy Macklarren, widow, declines Adms. on the estate of her husband Patrick Macklarren, late of Middletown decd. Adms. granted to Nathaniel Otis of Colchester, with Hezekiah Hucheson of Hebron.

Page 81—6 February, 1732-3: Nathaniel Otis, Adms., reports the estate insolvent, and moves to this Court that commissioners be appointed. This Court appoint John Bulkeley and Ephraim Welles of Colchester.

Page 11 (Vol. XII) 1st September, 1734: The commissioners on the estate of Patrick Maclarren, viz., Messrs. John Bulkeley and Ephraim Welles of Colchester, having had an order of this Court to adjust the claims of creditors on sd. estate, and by reason of Mr. Otis, the Adms., informing them that some effects belonging to the estate of the sd. decd. were in Scotland and some in Barbados, the sd. commissioners thereupon did not proceed according to sd. order, but the effects being come to hand this Court do order and appoint the commissioners to receive and examine all claims of the several creditors on the estate of the sd. decd., and how they are made out, and to act and doe in all things whereto their office as commissioners hath relation according to law, and the creditors on sd. estate are allowed 6 months to bring in their claims and prove their debts.

Page 8 (Vol. XIII) 18 May, 1737: The commissioners report interest on a bond to James Goodwin, merchant, of £100 sterling, with interest until paid, which was allowed until the decease of the sd. McLarren, sd. bond to be paid when an average is made.

Mallory, Judah, Middletown. Court Record, Page 6—November, 1729: Judah Mallory, a minor, 14 years of age, chose Capt. Joseph Southmayd to be his guardian. Recog., £50.

Page 119.

Markham, James, Middletown. Invt. £484-00-03. Taken 1st July, 1731, by Solomon Adkins, William Wetmore and Jonathan Blake. Will dated 7 April, 1731.

I, James Markham of Middletown, in the County of Hartford, do make this my last will and testament: I give to my wife Elizabeth (her thirds) during life; also I give to my wife my pasing mare. I give to my son James Markham a double portion of all my estate, both real and personal, accounting what I have given him by deed as part of his portion. I give to my son William Markham a single portion of all my estate, both real and personal, accounting what I have given him by deed. I give to my sons John Markham and Nathaniel Markham each of them a single portion. I give to my daughters, Elizabeth Foster and Abigail Markham, a single portion, except £5 to be deducted out of each of their portions. All above named having been helpful to git and keep my estate and living with me. I give to my daughters Mary Markham, Martha and Hannah Markham, each of them, half so much as one of their above-named brothers. Further, my will is that the gunn I gave my sd. William shall not be reckoned as part of his portion, neither the heifer I gave my daughter Elizabeth Foster shall be reckoned as part of her portion. And what my daughter Elizabeth Foster had of household stuff shall be reckoned as part of her portion. And I give to my son James Markham so much as to bye a good gunn and not to be reckoned as part of his portion. And the gunn I gave my son John Markham shall not be reckoned as part of his portion. And I order that my son Nathaniel Markham be put out to learn some good trade, and that he shall have a good gunn bought for him and not to be reckoned as part of his portion. I give to my daughter Abigail 1 cow-calf, not to be reckoned as part of her portion. Also, to my daughter Mary that great charge in money I have expended with doctors, &c., not to be reckoned as part of her portion. Also, to my daughter Martha that that is due by her indenture not to be counted as part of her portion. Also to my daughter Hannah her trade or time to learn it, a loom and tackling, not to be accounted as part of her portion. 'And further, my will is that the lands belonging to me shall be my sons', they paying to their sisters their portions in money or such spetia as they can produce at money prise. I appoint my wife Elizabeth Markham to be my executrix, and James Markham my executor, and desire Rev. William Russell and Mr. Jabez Hamlin overseers.

Witness: *Jabez Hamlin,*   JAMES MARKHAM, LS.
John Foster, Ebenezer Prout.

Court Record, Page 48—6 July, 1731: Will and invt. exhibited and approved. Hannah Markham, 14 years of age, daughter of James Markham, chose her uncle Benoni Houghton to be her guardian. Recog., £100.

Page 98—2 October, 1733: Nathaniel Markham, a minor, 14 years of age, son of James Markham, chose his brother William Markham to be his guardian. Recog., £100.

Page 21 (Vol. XII) 20 February, 1733-4: Daniel Markham, of Enfield, in the County of Hampshire, and the children of James Markham, late of Middletown, deceased (which children are James Markham, William Markham and John Markham of Middletown, and Nathaniel Markham of Haddam, the only sons of the deceased James Markham), supposeing they had right to some of the real estate in lands of the deceased by virtue of his last will, moved for a distribution thereof according to one law of the Colony directing the Court of Probates to appoint freeholders to divide such estate, and summoned Jonathan Center and Martha his wife, Elizabeth Arnold, Martha Arnold, Mehetabell Arnold, Joshua Arnold, Rebeckah Arnold, John Arnold, Jun., and Ebenezer Arnold, to object if they see cause. The parties accordingly appeared, and this Court having heard the pleas, do not see cause to grant the plaintiffs' motion or to order said real estate to be divided by freeholders. Israel Markham, of Windham, one of the grandsons of Daniel Markham, appealed from the judgement of this Court unto the Superior Court, and recognized in £50.

Distribution from File:

	£ s d		£ s d
To the widow,	68-16-08	To Elizabeth Foster,	34-09-00
To James Markham,	173-14-06	To Mary Markham,	20-09-1Q
To William Markham,	122-10-04	To Abigail Markham,	34-09-00
To John Markham,	95-00-00	To Martha Markham,	20-09-10
To Nathaniel Markham,	43-00-00	To Hannah Markham,	20-09-10

We do order that the widow, during her natural life, shall have the use of one-third part of the dwelling house and barn, with convenient yard room, and one acre of land at ye rear of the homelot, with one-third of the fruit that shall grow in the orchard, and two acres and two-thirds of an acre at ye south end of ye eight acres lying at the rear of the homelot, with free liberty to pass from said land to the house and barn. And also two acres of land on the east side of the land by the river, and also one-third of the four acres of boggy meadow.

Middletown,   *Pr. Jabez Hamlin,* } *Distributors.*
27 November, 1733.   *William Rockwell,* }

We, the subscribers, do hereby allow, ratify and confirm the foregoing distribution. As witness our hands this 28 February, 1733-4.

ELIZABETH X MARKHAM, } *Executors.*
JAMES MARKHAM,   }

Exhibited in Court, 5 June, 1738. Accepted and ordered to be kept on file.

Test: Jos: Talcott, Jun., Clerk.

Page 346.

Marshall, John, Bolton. Invt. £556-03-03. Taken 23 November, 1730, by Hezekiah King, Benjamin Talcott and Ephraim Tucker.

Court Record, Page 38—12 February, 1730-1: Adms. to Damaras Marshall, the widow. Exhibit of inventory.

Page 316-345.

Meakins, Lt. Samuel, Hartford. Died 18 April, 1733. Invt. £1522-19-05. Taken 9 June, 1733, by Ozias Pitkin, Timothy Cowles and Nehemiah Olmsted.

Court Record, Page 95—5 June, 1733: Adms. to John Meakins, a brother. Recog., £500, with Thomas Burr of Hartford.

Page 2 (Vol. XII) 1st April, 1734: An account of Adms. was now exhibited in Court by John Meakins, Adms.: Paid in debts and charges, £101-16-03. Which account is allowed and ordered to be kept on file.

Page 7—2 July, 1734: An agreement for the settlement of the estate of Samuel Meakins was exhibited in Court under the hands and seals of the heirs of sd. estate, and acknowledged to be their free act and deed.

Agreement as per File: 18 March, 1734-5: Samuel Meakins, a brother to some and an uncle to others of the legatees. An agreement for the division and settlement of the estate of Samuel Meakins to the surviving heirs was agreed between us as follows: To John Meakins, 2-7 of the estate; to Mary Belding, 1-7; to Thomas and Sarah Spencer, 1-7; to Thomas Hurlbut and Rebeckah Hurlbut, 1-7; to John Arnold and Hannah Arnold, 1-7; to Mary Meakins and Sarah Meakins, with Joseph, Hannah, Abigail and Rebeckah Meakins (the children of Joseph Meakins decd.), 1-7 part. By Joseph Pitkin, Jonathan Hills and Joseph Cowles.

Merrells, Wilterton. Court Record, Page 34—5 January, 1730-1: Wilterton Merrells is appointed guardian to his children, Samuel, Hannah and Gideon Merrells. Recog., £50.

Messenger, Nehemiah. Court Record, Page 40—13 March, 1730-1: Nehemiah Messenger, 17 years of age, chose his father Daniel Messenger to be his guardian. Recog., £50.

Page 271.

Moodey, John, Hartford. Invt. £310-18-11. Taken 13 March, 1732-3, by Isaac Kellogg and Nathaniel Smith.

Court Record, Page 85—9 March, 1732-3: Adms. granted to Samuel Moodey, son of the decd., who gave bond with David Ensign.

Page 251 (Probate Side, Vol. XII): I, Sarah Moodey of Hartford, widow, with my children, heirs to the estate of John Moodey, agree on a dist. of sd. estate to the surviving heirs, viz., to the widow Sarah Moodey, to John Moodey, to Samuel Moodey, to Ebenezer Moodey, to Nathaniel Moodey, to Adonijah Moodey, to Sarah the wife of David Ensign, to Hannah Moodey, to Silence Moodey, to Patience Moodey, and to Samuel Moodey as guardian to Adonijah Moodey, to each of them their respective portions. In confirmation of the before-written, we, the abovesd. widow and heirs, have set to our hands and seals this 5th day of March, 1733-4.

DAVID ENSIGN, LS.	PATIENCE MOODEY, LS.
SARAH X ENSIGN, LS.	SARAH X MOODEY, LS.
SILENCE MOODEY, LS.	JOHN MOODEY, LS.
NATHANIEL MOODEY, LS.	SAMUEL MOODEY, LS.
SAMUEL MOODEY, GUARDIAN LS. to ADONIJAH MOODEY, LS.	EBENEZER MOODEY, LS.

Court Record, Page 108 (Vol. XI) 5 March, 1733-4: An agreement to settle the estate was exhibited in Court and accepted. Adonijah Moodey, a minor, 16 years of age, chose his brother Samuel Moodey to be his guardian. Recog., £50.

Moore, Peletiah, Estate, Windsor. Court Record, Page 5—4 November, 1729: Adms. to John and Ebenezer Moore.

Moore, Samuel, Estate, Windsor. Court Record, Page 99—6 November, 1733: Adms. to Damaris Moore, widow. Recog., £500, with John Moore.

Page 206.

Add. Invt. in Vol. XII, Page 232.

Moses, Aaron, Windsor. Invt. £66-16-09. Taken 22 May, 1732, by Giles Elsworth, Samuel Stoughton and John Allyn. Additional invt. of lands in Simsbury valued at £40-02-08, taken 2 December, 1735, by Joseph Case and Benjamin Addams.

Court Record, Page 67—9 May, 1732: Adms. granted to John Thrall of Windsor, who, with Joseph Cornish of Simsbury, recog. in £200. And the Adms. suspects the estate insolvent.

Page 76—7 November, 1732: John Thrall, Adms., exhibits an account of his Adms. and reports the estate insolvent. This Court appoint Roger Newbery and John Warham Strong commissioners.

Page 1 (Vol. XII) 28 March, 1734: Report of the commissioners.

Page 44—13 April, 1736: Additional invt. exhibited and accepted.

Page 7 (Vol. XIII) 18 May, 1737: John Thrall, Adms., exhibits a further account of his Adms. Accepted.

Page 10—7 June, 1737: Per act of the General Assembly, John Thrall, Adms., may sell land with Mr. Roger Newbery of Windsor to the value of £47-12-05, to answer debts due, at public sale.

Page 26—4 April, 1738: The sale of land brought only £33-16-00, the estate being insolvent.

Page 39—11 January, 1738-9: The creditors were paid on an average and gave receipts thereof, and the Adms. was granted a *Quietus Est.* by the Court.

Page 322.

Nearing, John Henry, Simsbury. Died 4 September, 1733. Invt. £322-14-10. Taken 2 November, 1733. Will dated 27 August, 1733.

In the name of God, amen. I, John Henry Nearing of Simsbury, see cause to ordain and appoint this my last will and testament: I give to my wife Ann Nearing the use of all my improveable lands during the time of her widowhood, and all my moveable estate, after my lawfull debts and funerall charges are paid, to her forever, except my carpenter and joyner tools and one iron bound trunk and one sea chest, these I give unto my two sons, John Henry Nearing and Emanuel Nearing. I give to my son John my trunk and my son Emanuel my chests, and the tools to be equally divided between them. I give unto my son John Henry Nearing the east end of my lott, from Mody Brook to the east end, and my lott called the Pond Hill lott, and that lott called the Pond Marsh lott, and 1-2 of that which I have in that lott called Thomas Griffin's great lott (the south side of sd. lott), which tracts of land I give to him and his heirs forever. I give unto my son Emanuel Nearing my house and barn and homelott, and meadow lott, and the west end of my lott called the great lott, from Mody Brook to the west end, and 1-2 of that lott I have in the lott called Thomas Griffin's great lott (the north side of sd. lott), which percells of land I give to him and his heirs forever. And I appoint my wife to be executrix.

Witness: *Joshua Holcomb,*   JOHN HENRY NEARING, LS.
Elizabeth X Gooff, Return Holcomb.

Court Record, Page 101—4 December, 1733: Will now exhibited by Anne Nearing, alias Nichols, who was the widow of sd. decd. Her present husband, James Nichols, appeared in Court and gave his consent that sd. Anne his wife should execute sd. will. This Court appoint James Nichols and Anne his wife to be guardian to the children of sd. deceased, viz., John Henry Nearing, age 12 years, and Emanuel Nearing, age 9 years. Recog., £200.

Page 9 (Vol. XIII) 7 June, 1737: This Court appoint Samuel Pettebone to be guardian to Emanuel Nearing, a minor, 12 years of age. Recog., £200.

Page 10—7 June, 1737: John Henry Nearing, now 16 years of age, chose John Humphrey to be his guardian. Recog., £200.

Page 153.

Newell, Rev. Daniel, Middletown. Invt. £517-10-10. Taken 30 December, 1731, by Joseph Smith and William Russell.

Court Record, Page 58—4 January, 1731-2: Adms. granted to John Newell of Farmington, who, with Daniel North, recog. in £300.

Page 105—5 February, 1733-4: John Newell, Adms., exhibited an account of his Adms.: Paid in debts, £10-03-06; and received, £37-05-08. Which account is accepted. This Court appoint Samuel Thompson of Farmington to be guardian to Abigail Newell, age 4 years, and Mary 2 years of age, children of Daniel Newell. Recog., £200. John Newell appointed guardian to Daniel Newell, 7 years of age. Recog., £100. Joseph Porter appointed guardian to Hannah Newell, daughter of sd. decd. Recog., £100. Nathaniel Newell appointed guardian to Ruth Newell, age 7 years. Recog., £100.

Page 29 (Vol. XII) 3 February, 1735-6: Mrs. Ruth Newell, the widow, moves this Court for an allowance for the bringing up of a child at the age of 4 years, which was born after the decease of sd. Mr. Newell. This Court allows her £4 per year, and £20 to be added to the Adms. account.

Page 296-7.

North, John, Jr., Kensington. Invt. £216-06-11. Taken by Thomas Curtice and Joseph Smith. Will dated 13 January, 1732.

I, John North, Jr., of the Parish of Kensington, in the Township of Middletown, do make this my last will and testament: I give the 1-2 of my land which my father gave me in Farmington, called the south lott (the north side of sd. lot), adjoining to his own land, I say I give the sd. half of the lott to my honoured father John North. And also I give to my sd. father all my moveable estate of what name, kind or nature soever. I give to my mother Elizabeth North all the rest of my lands which were given to me by my father as aforesd. And I appoint my honoured father John North and my mother Elizabeth North executors, requireing them to pay all my just debts.

Witness: *Samuel Hubbard,* JOHN NORTH, JR., LS.
Hezekiah Hooker, Isaac Lee.

Court Record, Page 95—7 August, 1733: The last will and testament of John North, Jr., late of Middletown, was now exhibited in Court, and being fully proved, is by this Court approved and ordered to be recorded. And John North, father of the sd. deceased, being appointed an executor of the sd. will, appeared in Court and refused the trust and desired that Benjamin Judd, Jr., of Farmingtown, might take Adms. on the estate, whereupon this Court grants Adms. on sd. estate unto the sd. Benjamin Judd, Jr., with the will annexed, and he gave bond with his father Benjamin Judd.

Page 90—1st May, 1733: Invt. exhibited by Benjamin Judd, Jr., and John Woodruff, Jr.

Page 6 (Vol. XII) 2 July, 1734: Benjamin Judd, Adms., exhibited an account of his Adms. Accepted.

Page 18—7 January, 1734-5: Benjamin Judd, Adms., may sell land to procure the sum of £21-04-10.

Page 96-7.

North, Joseph, Sen., Farmington. Invt. £243-10-01. Taken 30 January, 1730-1, by Timothy Porter, Isaac Cowles, Sen., and Giles Hooper. Will dated 24 April, 1724.

I, Joseph North, Sen., of the Town of Farmington, do make this my last will and testament: It having pleased God, in His holy, wise providence, to deny me heirs of my own body, I have already by deed settled the greatest part of my freehold estate upon my neare kinsman, Joseph Woodruff. It is therefore my special care now in this my will that my wife, who, through her great pains, prudence, and industry hath been a great builder of my house, may be comfortably carried through this world. Therefore, I do give unto Martha, my wife, and to her heirs and assigns forever, all my estate, both real and personal. More particularly I do give to my wife 2 parcells of land, both of them lying and being within the bounds of the Township of Farmingtown, viz., one percell of land lying neare a place called Purgatory, containing about 7 acres, be the same more or less, adjoining northerly on land of Samuel Cowles; also one parcel of land lying on the contrary side of the highway against Smith Gridley's house, containing 6 acres, be the same more or less, bounded as followeth: east with land formerly Joseph Smith's, west with the land of Thomas North, north with a highway, and south with land belonging to the heirs of William Judd. Also, I give unto my wife, to be at her own dispose forever, all my personal estate of all sorts without exception, which I now have or shall be mine at my decease. Also, I do give unto my wife, during the term of her natural life, the use and profit of my land in the Common Field neare the Round Hill; also that part of my house, barn and homelott whereof I made a reserve in the deed of conveyance I made to my aforesd. kinsman Joseph Woodruff. And further, if I, the sd. Joseph North, through necessity should in my lifetime make dispose of any particular thing or things willed to my wife as above entered (which my purpose is to avoid as much and as well as I can), that then my will is

that her right to the remainder should be no ways altered or weakened thereby. And I hereby make Martha my wife my only and sole executrix.
Witness: *John Hooker, Sen.,*   JOSEPH NORTH, LS.
Abigail Hooker, Sen., Sarah Hooker.

Court Record, Page 39—2 March, 1730-1: Will exhibited by the executrix, who declined the trust and was appointed Adms. with the will annexed.

Invt. on Page 290. Will in Vol. XIII, Page 331.

Northam, John, Colchester. Invt. £138-04-00. Taken 1st December, 1732, by Samuel Loomis and Joseph Wright.

Will dated 11 October, 1732: I, John Northam of Colchester, do make this my last will and testament: I give to my wife Hannah 1-3 part of my real estate during life, and 1-3 part of my personal estate to be her own forever. I give unto my son John, when he comes of age, 65 acres of land lying upon Diceson Stream, with all my divisions to be laid out in the undivided lands in Colchester excepting the sequestered commons, ye which I give, with all my moveable estate, to be equally divided amongst my 9 daughters by my executors hereafter named, as they shall come of age of 18 years or be married. I appoint my wife Hannah and my brother Noah Pomeroy to be sole executors.
Witness: *Ephraim Little,*   JOHN NORTHAM, LS.
Ebenezer Northam, Ebenezer Day.

Court Record, Page 94—3 July, 1733: Will returned to Colchester that the proofs may be amended, and Adms. granted to Hannah Northam, widow, with the will annexed. Recog., £200, with James Church.

Page 109—7 March, 1733-4: Will now returned, fully proven.

Page 332 (Probate Side, Vol. XIII) 11 April, 1749: We, the subscribers, Adms. *Cum Testimento* to the last will and testament of John Northam, late of Colchester decd., have set out and delivered to each daughter that part of the real estate that was willed to them, there being 8 remaining (one dead): Two divisions of land, one of 70 acres and one of 45 acres, the 70 acres valued as one-third better by the acre than the 45 acres. We set out to ye 5 eldest daughters, viz., Lurana, Hannah, Sarah, Ruhamah and Ann, that 70 acres on the east side of Dickinson's Stream, they paying to the other three daughters, viz., Abigail, Katharine and Experience, £10-10-00 to each. We also set out to Abigail, Katharine and Experience the 45 acres division joyning upon Middletown line, as it is upon record, to their satisfaction. *Noah Pomery,*
                         Hannah Foot.
21 April, 1749.   *Test: Joseph Talcott, Clerk.*

Page 96 (Vol. XV) 21 April, 1749: An account of Adms. was now exhibited in Court by Hannah Northam, one of the Adms. with the will annexed, by which account she has paid in debts and charges £135-19-00, which account is accepted. Also, the Adms. exhibits a report of the distribution of the real estate according to the last will of the sd. deceased, which is accepted by the Court.

Page 295.

Nott, Elizabeth, of Stepney, Wethersfield. Will dated 1st May, 1733: I, Elizabeth Nott of Stepney, Wethersfield, having certain lands and right to lands which descends to me by inheritance from my father, John Hall decd., which I have a mind to dispose of among my children, and which, by the free consent of my husband, William Nott, that I should dispose of sd. land and rights according to my mind, I do make and ordain this my last will and testament: I give to my son Thomas Nott my Beaver Meadow lott, containing four acres more or less, bounded west upon Beaver Brook, north on heirs of John Belding, south on land of Theophilis Sherman. To my sons Abraham and William Nott my lott in Dry Swamp, containing 8 acres more or less, bounded west on a highway, north on lands of Ebenezer Belding, south on lands of Daniel Boardman, east on land of Capt. Joshua Robbins, to be divided equally between them. I give to my son William Nott my lott lying in the middle tier of lotts at the head of Hog Brook, 10 acres more or less, bounded north on a highway, south on a highway, east on land belonging to Noah Waddams, west on land of my husband's. I give to my daughters Jemima and Elizabeth Nott my lott where my father lived, 6 acres more or less, bounded north on a highway, east on a highway, south on land of Samuel Smith, west on land of Sergt. Dickinson. My will and desire is that my husband William Nott should be the executor of this my will.

Witness: *Daniel Russell,*   Elizabeth Nott, ls.
Benjamin Wright, Gideon Goodrich.

This will was read in the hearing of William Nott, the husband of sd. Elizabeth Nott, and he manifested his free consent and concurrence to the whole of the above-written will. And as an evidence of his free consent and approving of the same, has hereunto set his hand and seal this 1st day of May, in the year above mentioned.

Witness: *Daniel Russell,*   William Nott, ls.
Benjamin Wright, Gideon Goodrich.

Court Record, Page 95—7 August, 1733: Will exhibited by William Nott.

Page 184, 259.

Olcott, Cullick, Hartford. Invt. £17-08-06. Taken 8 May, 1732, by Nathaniel Olcott and David Smith. Will dated 22 January, 1731-2.

I, Cullick Olcott of Hartford, doe make this my last will and testament: I give and bequeath to Susannah, my wife, 75 shillings in money. I give to my son Thomas Olcott all my goods, debts and moveable estates and lands, except £5, which I give to my daughter Hannah Olcott, and the above-written 5 shillings given to my wife. I make my brother Josiah Olcott sole executor of this my last will and testament.

Witness: *John Bonnell,*　　　　　　　CULLICK OLCOTT, LS.
Nathaniel Olcot, Thomas Olcot.

Court Record, Page 67—9 May, 1732: Will now exhibited by Josiah Olcot. Proven.

Page 239-345.

Osgood, Jeremiah, Middletown. Invt. £170-08-03. Taken 25 November, 1732, by John Collins, Ephraim Adkins and Jonah Strickland.

Court Record, Page 79—19 December, 1732: Adms. granted to Ephraim Adkins, and he reports the estate insolvent. This Court therefore appoint Seth Wetmore and Nathaniel Browne commissioners.

Page 103—1st January, 1733-4: This Court grant the Adms. further time to make up his account.

Page 9 (Vol. XII) 3 September, 1734: Report of the commissioners, viz., Nathaniel Browne, Seth Wetmore and Ephraim Adkins. This Court order an average to be made.

Page 102 (Vol. XV) 6 June, 1749: Jeremiah Hubbard Osgood, a minor, 15 years of age, son of Jeremiah Osgood, chose Samuel Galpin of Middletown to be his guardian. Recog., £600.

Page 148, 193.

Pasco, Jonathan, Stafford. Invt. £567-17-00. Taken 20 February, 1728-9, by Benjamin Howard and Samuel Warner. Will dated 23 January, 1728-9.

I, Jonathan Pasco, planter, of Stafford, in the County of Hartford, do make this my last will and testament: I give to my honoured and tender mother my house lott whereon my house stands, to her and her heirs forever. I give to John Burroughs, Jr., son to my sister Elizabeth deceased, 50 acres of land; also to Timothy Simmons, son of my sister Margaret, I give 50 acres of land, which these 50 acres lyes in the North Village of Stafford in one tract. I give to my brother John Pasco 100 acres of land in Stafford, lying northwest of John Clemmons's house lot. Also, I give to my brother James Pasco my home lott of 50 acres on ye west side of Town Street in Stafford. As to my moveable estate I dispose of it as followeth: To my intended spouse, Experience Church, I give my heifer and least brown steare, the rest of my stock to pay my debts and to be sold to pay any necessary charges, at the discretion of my execu-

tors, namely, my honoured mother, my brother John Pasco, and my
brother John Warner, whom I order to pay to my two sisters, Sarah Had-
locks and Margery Bement, £4 apiece. I give to Jonathan Pasco, son of
my brother John Pasco, my Cedar Swamp lott, to him and his heirs forever.

Witness: *John Graham,*   JOHN PASCO, LS.
Samuel Warner, Benjamin Rockwell.

Court Record, Page 16—3 March, 1729-30: Will proven.

Page 312.

Will on Page 340. Invt. on Page 219, Vol. XII, and Page 67, Vol. XXI.

Phelps, Abraham, Windsor. Invt. £1896-19-02. Taken by Israel
Stoughton, Jonathan Styles and Peletiah Allyn; David Elsworth, Samuel
Stoughton and Noah Bissell; 4 February, 1733-4, and 2 January, 1771.
Will dated 24 August, 1733.

I, Abraham Phelps of Windsor, do make this my last will and testament: I give unto my kinsman Samuel Stiles and Mary his wife all my
moveable estate. I give unto Jonathan Pinney, son of Humphrey Pinney
of Windsor, part of the lott which was my grandfather Pinney's, on the
east side of the Great River, viz., that part which lyeth on the east side of
the country road. I give unto John Phelps, the 2nd son of John Phelps,
my lott which was purchased of Joseph Phelps, lying on the east side of
the Great River in Windsor, being 12 rods in breadth, running from the
Great River 3 miles, conditioned that he pay unto my executor hereafter
mentioned the sum of £60 within six months. And if the sd. John Phelps
the 2nd doth not pay the aforesd. sum of £60 within six months to my
executor, then I give it to Samuel Stiles and Mary Stiles (his present
wife) and their heirs forever. And if the sd. John Phelps the 2nd doth
pay the sd. sum of £60, then I give to my executor £20 out of the sd. £60.
And I give to Benjamin Enno, the son of Sergt. James Enno, £20. I
also give to that part of Mr. Marsh's Society on the north side of the
Rivulet, for use and benefit of schooling, £20. My will is that my kinsman Samuel Stiles of Windsor be my sole executor.

Witness: *Israel Stoughton,*   ABRAHAM PHELPS, LS.
Jonathan Stiles, Samuel Stoughton.

An addition to invt. of Estate of Capt. Abraham Phelps formerly of
Windsor (in Vol. XXI, Page 67), which is as followeth:

						£ s d
108	acres	of	land	in	East Windsor,	179-00-00
75	"	"	"	"	Colebrook, 1st division,	41-05-00
145	"	"	"	"	" 2nd division,	61-12-06
92	"	"	"	"	" 3rd division,	16-02-00
11	"	"	"			4-02-06
76	"	"	"	"	Ellington Parish or Society,	95-00-00

Date, 2 January, 1771.   Taken by David Elsworth, Samuel Stoughton and Noah Bissell.
Court Record, Page 98—2 October, 1733: Will exhibited.
Page 104—28 December, 1733: Invt. exhibited.

Page 170.

Phelps, David, Windsor. Invt. £55-07-05. Taken by Joseph Barnard and Nathaniel Pinney.
Court Record, Page 61—19 February, 1731-2. Adms. to Thomas Phelps of Windsor.

Will and Invt. in Vol. XII, Page 246.

Phelps, Sergt. William, Windsor. Invt. taken 1st March, 1733-4, by Jacob Drake, Nathaniel Drake and Timothy Loomis. Will dated 21 September, 1733.

I, William Phelps of Windsor, do make this my last will and testament: I give to my wife Ruth the use and improvement of 1-2 of my dwelling house and homelott, 1-2 of my meadow land, and ye liberty of pasturing two cowes in my pasture on the west side of the road, all during her natural life. Also, I give unto her 1 feather bed and furniture, and a brass kettle she brought with her, and one cow, and £10 of my moveable estate (to be taken at inventory price) as she shall choose, and also £3 worth of provision and 1-2 of my wool and flax, to be to her own use and dispose forever. Also, I give unto her, for her use if she shall want the same, all the wood I have in my homelott and pasture. I give unto William Phelps, my eldest son, all the lands I have at the place called the Mill Brook. In case he have no lawfull issue, he shall have the use of sd. lands during his natural life. And if my son Ebenezer shall be helpful to him and be at cost and charge in helping of him under any difficulty he may be under by reason of his weakness and infirmity or otherwise as he may be in necessity of, that he shall be rewarded for the same out of sd. lands. And after the decease of my sd. son William, if he shall not have heirs as aforesd., not haveing necessity of spending the same, that then the 1-2 of the remainder that he shall leave I give and bequeath to my son Ebenezer and to his heirs forever, and ye other half to my two sons Caleb and Jacob forever. Also, I give to my son William all my woolen wearing apparrel. My will and pleasure is that my three sons, viz., Ebenezer, Caleb and Jacob, shall have equal share of my estate. And inasmuch as Ebenezer has already received near £80, as by my book may appear, my will is that Caleb and Jacob, and their heirs and assigns forever, shall have so much of my land (where they shall choose) as is inventoried accordingly and will amount to such sum to each of them as I have given already to Ebenezer. My will is that all the remainder of my lands shall be equally divided between my three sons, Ebenezer, Caleb and Jacob. I give unto my daughter Ruth £80, to be paid her out of my moveable estate at inventory apprisement (excepting £3 of the worst of my estate not to be forst upon her). Also, I give unto her half of my wool and half of my flax, also a pilion and pilion cloth, and 1 cotton sheet. My will and pleasure is that Ebenezer Phelps, Caleb Phelps and Jacob Phelps be my executors.

Witness: *Cornelius Brown,*   WILLIAM PHELPS, LS.
Matthew Phelps, Henry Allyn.

A codicil, dated 3 November, 1733: Wherein he gives his three sons a right to cut firewood from the land given to William; provides a special legacy to Caleb because of his service with me since he was 21 years of age; and enlarges the legacy to his daughter Ruth.

Witness: *Samuel Brown,*   WILLIAM PHELPS, LS.
Cornelius Brown, Jr., Henry Allyn.

Court Record, Page 108—5 March, 1733-4: Will proven.
Page 21 (Vol. XII) 22 February, 1734-5: Ebenezer Phelps, an heir to the estate and one of the executors, moves this Court for a distribution. This Court appoint Capt. Henry Allyn, Roger Newbery and Lt. John Cook, of Windsor, distributors.

Page 172.

Agreement on Page 190, Probate Side.

Pitkin, Nathaniel, Hartford. Died 20 February, 1731. Invt. £1348-09-00. Taken 17 March, 1731-2, by Ozias Pitkin, Nehemiah Olmsted and William Cowles. Will dated 8 October, 1730.

I, Nathaniel Pitkin of Hartford, do make this my last will and testament: I give to my wife Elizabeth Pitkin out of my moveable estate £120 at inventory price, to be at her own dispose forever; and also 1-3 part of my lands for her use during life, and the use of 1-2 of my dwelling house, barn, stable and cow house, during the time she remains my widow. I also give my wife Elizabeth the use of all the estate, real or personal, which is in this my will given to my daughter Elizabeth Pitkin, until she attain the age of 18 years, or marriage if before. And whereas, there is in my possession one great brass kettle, one two-eared silver cup and divers other small things of household stuff (all which may be found entered in the small paper book, folio the 2nd), which sd. goods were never my estate, but were given by my honoured mother-in-law, Mrs. Russell deceased, to my daughter Elizabeth Pitkin, which sd. goods I desire my wife to take into her care in trust for my sd. daughter, hereby quiting all right, title, interest and demand to the same, both to my wife and daughter aforenamed. Further, I give to my three grandchildren, viz., David, Nathaniel and Jonathan Hills, to each of them a Bible as a token of my love, if they or any of them live to the age of 8 years. Further, I give all the rest of my estate, real and personal, to be equally divided amongst my daughters, viz., Esther Pitkin, Ann Hills, Dorothy Roberts, Hannah Olcot, Deborah Pitkin and Elizabeth Pitkin, only it is to be understood that what my daughters Ann Hills, Dorothy Roberts and Hannah Olcot have already received shall be reckoned to each of them. I appoint my son David Hills, William Pitkin and my wife Elizabeth Pitkin executors.

Witness: *Timothy Cowles, William Cowles,* NATHANIEL PITKIN, LS. *Roger Pitkin, Jonathan Pitkin.*

Court Record, Page 62—7 March, 1731-2: Will proven.

Page 64—31 January, 1731-2: Elizabeth Pitkin, a minor, chose her mother, Mrs. Elizabeth Pitkin, to be her guardian. Recog., £50.

Page 190 (Probate Side):

To all people to whom these presents shall come, greeting:

Know ye that we, Esther Pitkin, Anne Hills, Dorothy Roberts, Hannah Olcott, Deborah Pitkin and Elizabeth Pitkin, all of the Town of Hartford, children and heirs of Mr. Nathaniel Pitkin:

Whereas, our honoured father having of his free will and good pleasure by his last will given and divided unto us the sd. heirs the whole of his estate, both real and personal, to be equally divided amongst us after all just debts and legacies are paid, the remaining part to be divided amounts to £1425-15-09 at inventory price, of which estate each single share is £237-12-06; and for the peaceable enjoyment of sd. estate we have agreed that the estate shall be divided amongst us, allowing each their respective portions.

In confirmation whereof we have hereunto set to our hands and seals this third day of July, 1732.

DAVID HILLS, LS.	HANNAH X OLCOTT, LS.
BENJAMIN ROBERTS, LS.	DEBORAH PITKIN, LS.
NATHANIEL OLCOTT, LS.	ELIZABETH PITKIN, LS.
ESTHER X PITKIN, LS.	OZIAS PITKIN,
ANN X HILLS, LS.	WILLIAM PITKIN,
DOROTHY X ROBERTS, LS.	ELIZABETH PITKIN,
	as Guardian.

Witness: *Eliphalet Whiting,*
Deodatt Woodbridge.

Court Record, Page 73—1st August, 1732: Agreement exhibited and accepted by the Court and ordered to be filed.

Page 289 (Probate Side, Vol. XIII): Estate of Nathaniel Pitkin, Hartford: Articles of agreement concluded between David Hills and Anne his wife, Benjamin Roberts and Dorothy his wife, Nathaniel Olcott and Hannah his wife, and Elizabeth Pitkin (daughter of Mr. Nathaniel Pitkin, late of Hartford deceased). all of Hartford, for the dividing of the estate of our sister Esther Pitkin, late of Hartford aforesd., deceased on the 27th day of February, 1732-3, and also for the dividing of the estate of our sister Deborah Pitkin, late of Hartford aforesd., who deceased on the 14th day of June, 1733:

We have, and by these presents do mutually agree, to divide the aforesd. estate: First—We do each of us above mentioned acknowledge we have received to our full satisfaction our respective parts and shares of the moveable part of the aforesd. estate, and we do now agree that each of the surviving heirs shall have their part of the real estate.

And for full confirmation of all the foregoing articles of agreement, I, Elizabeth Pitkin of Hartford, guardian to Elizabeth Pitkin, by and with the advice of Ozias Pitkin, Esq., and William Pitkin, have hereunto set our hands and seals.

DAVID HILLS, LS.,   ANNE HILLS, LS.
BENJAMIN ROBERTS, LS.,   DOROTHY X ROBERTS, LS.
NATHLL OLCOTT, LS.,   HANNAH X OLCOTT, LS.
ELIZABETH X PITKIN, LS.,   ELIZABETH X PITKIN, LS.

Witness: *Stephen Olmsted,*
Joseph Bidwell.
Before me, William Pitkin, Just. Peace.

Page 242.

Plumer, Hannah, Stafford. Will dated 18 April, 1732: I, Hannah Plumer of Stafford, in the County of Hartford, do make this my last will and testament: I give to my daughter Deborah Plumer my house and 10 acres of land of my home lott (at the north end of sd. lott, butting on the highway). I give to my daughter another tract of land containing 45 acres of meadow, butting on a brook called Roaring Brook, all which land as it is described in the Records in Stafford. I do make my daughter Deborah my sole executrix. Also do constitute her to pay all my just and honest debts, and to receive all debts due to me. I give to my son Samuel Plumer's heirs 20 acres of land in Stafford (at the south end of my homelott), or the value of it, two years after my death. I give to my son Sampson Plumer 10 acres of my homelott at the south end, or the value of it. I give to my daughter Elizabeth 10 acres of my homelott in Stafford, or the value of it. These three last parcells of land to be taken off at the south end of my homelott. I give to my son Moses Plumer 5 shillings in full as his portion. I give to my son Aaron Plumer 5 shillings. I give to my son Joseph Plumer 5 shillings. I give to my son David Plumer 5 shillings. I give to my son Eliphalet Plumer 5 shillings. I give to my son Nathaniel Plumer 5 shillings. I give to my daughter Miriam 5 shillings. I give to my daughter Hannah 5 shillings. I give to the heirs of my daughter Sarah 5 shillings. I give to my daughter Deborah Plumer and to my daughter Elizabeth Plumer all my household goods in

Haverhill and in Stafford, bedding, pewter vessels, iron, brass, wood and chests, with all manner of household stuff belonging to me whatsoever.
Witness: *Josiah Standish,*   HANNAH X PLUMER, LS.
Daniel Warner, Thomas Rood.

Court Record, Page 71—6 June, 1732: Will proven.

Porter, Daniel. Court Record, Page 77—17 November, 1732: Daniel Porter, a minor, chose Timothy Porter of Farmington to be his guardian. Recog., £100.

Page 329-30.

Porter, Samuel, Kensington. Invt. £155-05-11. Taken 28 April, 1733, by Thomas Hart and Hezekiah Hooker. Will dated 10 March, 1732-3.
I, Samuel Porter of the Parish of Kensington, son of Nehemiah Porter of Farmingtown deceased, husbandman, give to my well-beloved friend Marcy Hubbard, of sd. Kensington, daughter to Lt. George Hubbard, the full and just sum of £20 money, to be raised out of my real estate. I give unto my brother John Porter 1-6 part of the remainder of my estate. I also give unto my brother Thomas Porter 1-6 part of it. I also give unto my brother Jonathan Porter 1-6 part of it. I also give to my sister Martha Porter, alias Ashman, 1-6 part of it. I give unto my sister Hannah Porter, alias Castle, 1-6 part of it. I also give unto my sister Rachel Porter, alias Hancox, 1-6 part of it. And I appoint my friend, Lt. George Hubbard of Kensington, executor.
Witness: *Hezekiah Hooker,*   SAMUEL PORTER, LS.
Amos Porter, Isaac Peck.

Court Record, Page 89—28 April, 1733: Will now exhibited by the executor named in the will, who refused the trust, and this Court do grant letters of Adms. unto her.
Page 4 (Vol. XII) 2 May, 1734: George Hubbard, Adms. with the will annexed, exhibits as debt a legacy of £20 given by will to Mary Hubbard of Kensington, daughter to Lt. George Hubbard. Debts now amount to £62-14-11, and for the payment thereof there is nothing in the Adms. hands.
Page 10—19 September, 1734: Per act of the General Assembly of 9th May, 1734, the Adms. may sell 2 acres of land, with house and orchard thereon, in Kensington.
Page 16—13 December, 1734: Report of the sale of land by the Adms. Sold to Jonathan Porter of Farmington. Nathaniel Winchell, bidder, £48 money.
Page 22 (Vol. XIII, Probate Side): Whereas, Samuel Porter, in his will dated 10 March, 1733, gave to Mercy Hubbard, the daughter of Lt. George Hubbard, £20 money, to be raised out of his real estate if there

should not be enough of the moveables, the sd. George Hubbard in the will was named executor, which trust he refused, when the Prerogative Court for the District of Hartford did appoint him Adms., the moveables were not sufficient to discharge the debts, and of necessity the legacy should be paid out of the real estate to the sd. Mercy, who is now the wife of Daniel Smith of the Parish of Kensington, according to the true intent of the will of the sd. testator, I, George Hubbard, Adms., have set out to sd. Daniel Smith and Mercy his wife, in right of the sd. Mercy, 1-2 of a certain lott of land of which the sd. testator and one Amos Porter, of Middletown, stood seized at the death of sd. testator. The sd. Amos's share or right is now belonging to Jonathan Edwards, about 14 acres more or less. Inventory price, £18-15-00, and is to be accounted at that price in part of sd. legacy.

Witness: *Joseph Talcott,*   GEORGE HUBBARD, LS.
    Jerusha Talcott.
13 December, 1737.   *Test: Joseph Talcott, Jr., Clerk.*

Page 158.   Will on Page 188.

Primus, a Free Negro, Wethersfield.   Invt. £47-15-07½.   Taken 27 December, 1731, by Samuel Benton, Charles Bulkeley and John Crane. Will dated 17 November, 1731.   Presented in Court, 4 April, 1732.

Primus, negro man, formerly of Hatfield, in Hampshire County, in Province of Mass. Bay, in New England, and of late belonging to Wethersfield, in the County of Hartford and Colony of Connecticut, now, on the 16 day of November, about 9 of the clock in the morning, deceased being at the dwelling house of Samuel Dyx in sd. Wethersfield, and sensible his death was drawing on or near, as he supposed on sd. day before his decease, having a desire to settle and dispose of what estate he had gotten and earned in the world (Mary the wife of Samuel Dyx and Mary the wife of Jonathan Blynn being then present), declared what his mind and will was as to his estate, and they were desired to take notice thereof. The sd. Mary Dyx says that she heard sd. negro man say that he had about 5 loads of Indian corne at Bezaleel Lattemore's, and about 40 bushels of oats, and sd. Lattemore owed him £10-05-00 in money; and John Dyx owes him £5 mony, and Daniel Warner something, they could not tell what it was; and further, he said he would have Noadiah Dickinson and Daniel Warner, Jr., take care of sd. corne and mony, and git it in and pay his just debts, and the remainder they might have between them. The above written was writt on the 17th day of November, 1731, by me, *David Goodrich, Justice of the Peace.*

Before the Court of Probates holden at Hartford, 4th April, Ann. Dom. 1732, then personally appeared Noadiah Dickinson and Mary Dyx, both of lawfull age, and made oath to the truth of the above written nuncupative or verball will of Primus, negro, and it is proved and approved to be sd. negro's will so far as it relates to Daniel Warner, Jr.

                                               TALCOTT, JUDGE.
Test: Jos: Talcott, Junr., Clerk.

Court Record, Page 56—19 November, 1731: Adms. to Noadiah Dickinson.

Page 37 (Vol. XII) 10 December, 1735: Noadiah Dickinson, Adms., exhibited an account of his Adms., which is accepted by the Court.

Page 127.

Ray, James, Sen., Haddam. Died 1 March, 1730-1. Invt. £355-02-10. Taken 24 March, 1730-1, by Simon Smith, Thomas Shaylor and Joseph Arnold. Will dated 14 January, 1730-1.

I, James Ray, Sen., of Haddam, in the County of Hartford, do make and ordain this my last will and testament: Imprimis. I give and bequeath unto my beloved wife Elizabeth the use of all my household goods during her life, and do hereby bind and oblige my two sons, James Ray and Joseph Ray, at all times to take a tender and constant care of my wife, their mother, and to provide all necessaries for her comfort during her natural life. I give to my son James Ray all my land on the west side of the highway butting on the country road, which land I bought of the Ackleys, and all the land that I bought of John Kennerd on the west and east side of sd. highway or country road. Further, I conditionally give to my son James Ray my lott in the Cone Meadow, provided that he the sd. James Ray pay to my grandson Samuel Bump of Bolton £30 when sd. Bump shall arrive at the age of 21 years. But if sd. Bump should dye before that age, then my lott shall be my son James Ray's forever. I give to my son Joseph Ray 8 1-2 acres of land near or adjoining to his own land at Prospect Hill. I give to my grandson Isaac Ray my lott of land that lyes near to Benjamin Towner's, also a right of £20 in all undivided lands in Haddam West Side. I give to my daughter Anne Dunk 1 cowe and all my household goods of all sorts, as beds and bedding, woolen and linen, pewter, brass, iron and wood, to be delivered to sd. Anne or her children at the death of my wife or soon after. I give to my granddaughter Elizabeth Ray a heifer. I further give to my son Joseph Ray my plow, with the irons, chain, clevy, and all my irons belonging to the cart and wheels, as hoops, boxes or other. Under several considerations, and sufficient reasons in my own breast, I give to my son Peter Ray one shilling in money and nothing more. Further, I give to my two sons, James Ray and Joseph Ray, all my stock of creatures, as cattle, sheep and horse kind, to be equally between them two divided, except what is above disposed of. I make my son James Ray sole executor.

Witness: *Joseph Arnold,*   JAMES RAY, LS.
Nathaniel Tyler, Solomon Bates, Jr.

Court Record, Page 47—28 June, 1731: Will proven, except the testator had not given the widow her dower. The executor declined the trust.

Page 237.

Reinolds, James, Wethersfield. Invt. £612-05-11. Taken 7 December, 1732, by Michael Griswold, Ebenezer Belding and Jonathan Robbins.

Court Record, Page 68—20 May, 1732: Adms. granted to Anna Reinolds, widow, and unto John Reinolds.

Page 63 (Vol. XIII) 3 April, 1740: John Reinolds, Adms., exhibited an account of his Adms., which the Court accepted. And this Court appoint John Reinolds to be guardian unto James Reinolds, a minor, 9 years of age, son of James Reinolds, late deceased. Recog., £300.

Page 41 (Vol. XV) 7 July, 1747: Hezekiah Reinolds, a minor, 16 years of age, son of James Reinolds, chose his grandfather John Reinolds of Wethersfield to be his guardian. Recog., £500.

Page 266.

Richards, Samuel, Hartford. Invt. £483-17-06. Taken 13 February, 1732-3, by Daniel Webster and Jacob Kellogg.

Court Record, Page 81—6 February, 1732-3: Adms. granted to James and Daniel Richards, sons of the decd., who, with their uncle, Thomas Richards, recognized in £300.

Agreement on File:

An agreement, made this 5th March, 1732-3, between the heirs of Samuel Richards, concerning the estate and the widow's dowry, to which she doth agree:

	£	s	d
To the widow, Hannah,	21	14	05
To Jonah Richards, eldest son,	133	01	00
To James Richards,	135	17	06
To Daniel Richards, besides rights in land, the sum of	7	12	00

To John Merrells and Lydia his wife, their part received at marriage.
To Ebenezer Judd and Hannah his wife, their part received at marriage.
To Hannah Richards, her part to be in moveable estate.

And the foregoing parties, and each of us, subscribe and doe acknowledge ourselves fully satisfied and contented as our and each of our full part of our sd. father, Samuel Richards's, estate, and do acquit the Adms. and each other from any demands therefore from us and each of us.

JONAH RICHARDS, LS.	ESTHER X RICHARDS, LS.
JAMES RICHARDS, LS.	JOHN MERRELL, LS.
DANIEL RICHARDS, LS.	EBENEZER JUDD, LS.

Page 84—6 March, 1732-3: Agreement exhibited in Court and accepted.

Page 317.

Riley, David, Stepney. Will dated 25 November, 1730. I, David Riley, of the Parish of Stepney, in the County of Hartford, being bound on a voyage to sea, do make this my last will and testament: I give to my beloved mother, Sarah Riley, whom I constitute executrix of this my last will, all my whole estate, both real and personal, for her use during her natural life. The whole of my moveable estate she may spend if she stands in need of, for her own support in her lifetime. Next, what of my estate shall be left after my sd. mother's decease, to be divided equally between my brothers and sisters.

Witness: *Jonathan Curtis,*   DAVID RILEY, LS.
Benjamin Deming, Charles Deming.

Court Record, Page 100—6 November, 1733: Will exhibited in Court by Sarah Riley, executrix. Proven.

Page 6 (Vol. XII) 31 May, 1734: Invt. exhibited.

Page 84 (Vol. XIII) 9 March, 1740-1: Sarah Riley being deceased, Jonathan Riley was appointed Adms. on the estate of Mrs. Sarah Riley, and also upon the unfinished Adms. on the estate of David Riley. Jonathan Riley, who was appointed administrator, exhibits an account: Paid in debts, £33-04-03. Which account is accepted and ordered on file.

Page 89—20 May, 1741: An addition to the accompt of £10-10 was exhibited by Jonathan Riley, Adms., which account is accepted.

Page 91—21 June, 1741: Jonathan Riley, Adms., by act of the last General Assembly, may sell land (about 5 acres) to the value of £36-07-00, which land butts east on land of Stephen Willard and John Morton, west on a highway, north on ye heirs of Richard Robbins, south on lands of Josiah Griswold and David Wright, and make deed to him or them that shall purchase sd. land, and make return thereof to this Court.

Page 97—19 August, 1741: David Riley, by his will, after his mother deceased, gave the remainder of his estate to be equally divided among his brothers and sisters, and did not appoint by whom sd. estate should be distributed in sd. will. By request of some of the heirs, this Court appoint Deacon Benjamin Wright, Capt. Jacob Williams and Jonathan Burnham, distributors. ·

Page 49 (Vol. XVI) 7 January, 1752: John Robinson, Jr., of Wethersfield, being a purchaser of some of the lands of David Riley, now moves to this Court that dist. be made of the estate of the deceased: Whereupon this Court appoint John Stilman, Capt. Thomas Belding and Mr. Timothy Wright to dist. the estate.

Dist. File: 2 June, 1752: To Jonathan Riley, to Mehetabell, to the heirs of Jacob Riley, to Joseph Riley, and to Stephen Riley. By Thomas Belding and Timothy Wright.

Page 65—3 June, 1752: Report of the distributors.

Page 101.

Roberts, David, Middletown. Invt. £122-08-07. Taken 16 December, 1730, by Jonathan Blake and George Hubbard, Sen.

Court Record, Page 41—22 March, 1731: Adms. granted to Thankfull Roberts, widow. Recog., £200, with Samuel Bow.

Page 29 (Vol. XII) 1st July, 1735: Thankfull Roberts, Adms., exhibited an account of her Adms., which is accepted.

Page 30 (Vol. XIV) 4 October, 1743: Thankfull Roberts, alias Cooper, who was the widow and relict of David Roberts, having administered on the estate, now moved to this Court for a dist. The Court so ordered, viz., to the widow, Thankfull, and to Jabez, the eldest son, to each of them £11-04-04; and to Elias Roberts and Jacob Roberts, younger children, to each of them their single portion, which is £5-12-02. And appoint William Rockwell, George Hubbard and Samuel Bow, of Middletown, distributors.

Page 33—16 November, 1743: Report of the distributors.

Page 123.

Robbins, Joshua, Wethersfield. The will of Joshua Robbins, Sen., dated 26 March, 1730: I have already given unto my eldest son, Joshua Robbins, my lot at Stepney, where he dwells, together with all the buildings that I erected thereon; also my lot that I bought of Phillip Goff and Naomy his wife, my lot in Beaver Meadow and my lots that I had of Theophilus Sherman, Joseph Barnard and John Adgit. I do further give to my son Joshua Robbins my division lot att Newington, about 75 acres; also my five-acre lot in Mile Meadow; also that part of my lot in the Wet Swamp that I bought of Joseph Wolcott; also my right in a tract of land lying on the back side of Rockey Hill, in Wethersfield. I have already given unto my youngest son, Jonathan Robbins, half my homestead where I now dwell, with half my new house and half my barns that are upon it; also half my lot in ye Heither Plain, half my lot in the Dry Swamp that I had of Jonathan Colefax, half my lot at Smith's Landing, purchased of John Waddoms, half my lott in the Great Meadow that I had of Graves, upon the Westfield Hill, half my lot at Two Stone, purchast of Mr. Chester, half of my two lots that I had of David Tryon, and half my 50-acre lot. I do hereby give unto my said son Jonathan Robbins, only reserveing ye improvement thereof dureing the natural life of his mother, ye other half of my homestead where I now dwell, together with ye other half of my barns, with all other buildings and things that are erected thereon, also the other half of the lots above mentioned. I do hereby further give to my said son Jonathan Robbins my lot I bought of Ensign Michael Griswold, by Tryall's lot; the remaining part of the lot I had of George Kilbourn, on Vexation Hill; my four acres I had of Samuel Benton, in the Wet Swamp, and the other half of my lot of 50 acres lying next to Farmington line. Also, I give to my son Jonathan Robbins my right in a piece of land that I bought of Martin Kellog, on the burying hill, only ordering him said Jonathan Robbins and his successors to set out thereof unto the rest of my children and their heirs as they have need for burying their dead. I do further give unto my son Jonathan Robbins the one-half of all my right in or to the commons or undivided lands in Wethersfield. Also, my will is that my five daughters, vizt., Elizabeth the wife of Nathaniel Talcott, Hannah the wife of Joseph Wells, Mary the wife of Joseph Treat, Abigail the wife of Silas Belding, and Comfort the wife of John Coleman, shall each of them have £150 of my personal estate with what each of them have already received, and the rest of my personal estate which I have not already given away I leave in the hands of my well-beloved wife to improve for her comfortable subsistence and maintenance. And also I give £100 of it to Elizabeth, my wife, to do as she pleaseth with it if I die before she doth. I do hereby give unto my son Joshua Robbins the one-half of all my right in or to the commons or undivided lands in Wethersfield. Also, I do further give unto my son Jonathan Robbins my coper still and worm, together with all things provided for the work of stilling, only reserving the improvement thereof of the one-half of the suitable seasons for stilling in each year dureing the natural life of his mother. I do appoint my wife and my two sons to be executors.

Witness: *David Goodrich,*   JOSHUA ROBBINS, LS.
Joshua Robbins, 2nd,
Daniel Warner.

Court Record, Page 95—3 July, 1733: Will exhibited in Court by Sarah Robbins and Nathaniel Robbins, executors named in sd. will Proven.

Page 41 (Vol. XIII) 6 February, 1738-9: Will now exhibited by Jonathan Robbins, who accepted the trust of executorship. Ordered recorded and kept on file.

Page 297-8.

Rockwell, Joseph, Windsor. Will dated 12th June, 1733: I, Joseph Rockwell of Windsor, do make this my last will and testament: I give to my wife Elizabeth 1-3 part of my personal estate, and also the use of my houseing and lands in Windsor during the term of her widowhood. And in case she marry, then after that only 1-3 part of my houseing and land during the term of her natural life. I give to my son Joseph Rockwell my lott at Podunk, as also my lott laid out to me in Windsor in the Mile and 1-2 Division, and also the lott I bought of Benedict Alford, to my son Joseph and his heirs forever. I give to my son Benjamin Rockwell 5 shillings besides what I have already given him. I give to my son James Rockwell all that part of the lott I dwell upon, the whole breadth from the street eastward to a pond on the south side of sd. lott, about 100 rods east of the street, with the buildings thereon standing, as also the north half of sd. lott from sd. pond eastward to the end of the lott, as also the north half of sd. lott from the drain to the river. I give to my son Job Rockwell the lott that I now dwell upon, the whole breadth on the street west to the drain called the middle drain, with the buildings thereon standing, as also the south half of sd. lott from sd. drain to the river, as also the south part or moiety of sd. lott from the pond aforesd. eastward to the end of the lott, to be to my son Job and his heirs forever. I give to my daughter Elizabeth Rockwell £200, to be paid and delivered to her out of my moveable estate at inventory price or in money. I give all my other lands (undivided and right to lands) to my 3 sons, Joseph, James and Job, to their heirs forever, and to be equally divided between them. I appoint my wife Elizabeth and my son Joseph Rockwell sole executors.

Witness: *Roger Wolcott,*   JOSEPH ROCKWELL, LS.
Timothy Edwards, Josiah Rockwell.

Court Record, Page 96—29 June, 1733: Will exhibited by Elizabeth and Joseph Rockwell, executors.

Page 213.

Rollo, William, Hebron. Died 30th May, 1732. Invt. £129-09-00 (personal estate only), taken by Samuel Rowlee, Ebenezer Wilcox and Obadiah Dunham. Will dated 14 May, 1731.

I, William Rollo of Hebron, do make this my last will and testament: I give to Patience, my wife, the use of all my homestead, both lands and buildings, for the space of 10 years next ensueing the date hereof, and the use of 1-2 of sd. land and buildings after the sd. 10 years, so long as she remains my widow. I will that 1-3 part of all my personal and moveable estate be at her own dispose forever. Having given already to my son Zerubbabell 40 acres of land out of my own lott, secured by a deed, I do moreover give and bequeath to him 10 acres of land, to be taken off at the north end of my 30-acre division in Hebron. To my beloved son Ellexander I give 42 acres of land at East Haddam, to be taken off on the north side of the certain division of land that I have there, the whole containing 84 acres, Also, I give him 1-2 of my common right there. I give to my beloved son Ebenezer the other half of my division of land at East Haddam, 42 acres on the south side of it, and the 1-2 of the abovesd. common right. I give to my son John the whole of this my homestead, both land and buildings, to be his at the age of 21 years, that is to say, that he then shall have the improvement of the 1-2 at the age aforesd., and the other half when his mother shall either decease or marry. Moreover, I will and bequeath to him 10 acres of land on the south side of my 30-acre division in Hebron, provided that he shall pay certain legacies to his sisters: that at the age of 23 years he shall pay to his sister Elizabeth £10 in money; at the age of 25 years, £10 money to his sister Hannah; at the age of 27, £10 to his sister Mary; at the age of 29 years, £10 to his sister Patience; at the age of 31 years, the sum of £10 to his sister Eunice; and finally, at the age of 32 years, shall pay to his sister Abigail the sum of £10 as abovesd. Besides the several legacies to be paid to my daughters, Elizabeth, Hannah, Mary, Patience, Eunice and Abigail, I give to them 2-3 of my personal and moveable estate, to be equally divided to each of them as they come of age. I give to my daughter Elizabeth 10 acres out of my 30-acre division of land in Hebron. I do hereby appoint my wife Patience arid my son Zerubbabell sole executors.

Witness: *Nicholas Bond,*　　　　　　　　WILLIAM ROLLO, LS.
Daniel Bushnell, Obadiah Dunham.

Court Record, Page 72—27 June, 1732: Will and invt. exhibited.

Page 95—6 August, 1733: This Court appoint Zerubbabell Rollo to be guardian to Patience Rollo, age 11 years, Eunice 9, Abigail 7 years, children of William Rollo. Recog., £300.

Page 136-9.

Root, Jacob, Hebron. Invt. £235-00-08. Taken 1st September, 1731, by Ebenezer Wilcox, Hezekiah Gaylord and Joseph Phelps. Will dated 19 June, 1728.

I, Jacob Root of Hebron, in the County of Hartford, do make this my last will and testament: I give to my wife Mary her (dower rights). I give unto my son Daniel and to my son Jacob Root my lott called the "Old 100 Acres", together with what land I have since laid adjacent on the east side of the sd. 100 acres, and so bounded east on Benoni Trumbull's 100-acre lott. I give unto my son Nathaniel that part of my farm which lyeth to the west of Fawn Brook, and bounds east on sd. brook, west on the common lands, and south on land belonging to Mr. Timothy Steven's heirs. I give to my son Jonathan Root the remaining part of the pond which lyeth to the east of sd. Fawn Brook, and bounds west on sd. brook, east on Mr. Skinner's land, and on common land betwixt Mr. Skinner's and Mr. Trumbull's. As also I further give unto my sons Nathaniel and Jonathan my 50-acre lott lying on Blackledge's River. I give to my son William Root my old homelott of about 30 acres, which butts south on Daniel Barbour's land, north on Nathaniel Man's land, and east on a highway. Also, I give to my sd. son William my dwelling house and barn, together with all my homestead, excepting 20 acres on the north side, which 20 acres I yet reserve to myself. I give to my granddaughter Johanna Pummery £20, to be paid out of my estate, and my granddaughter Hepzibah Pummery I will £10, and to my grandson Caleb Pummery I will £10. These three last mentioned being the children of my daughter Johanna, and the respective bequests made to them to be paid within one year after my decease. I will to my grandchildren, the children of my daughter Mary, viz., Joseph Man, Nathaniel Man, Benjamin Man, John Man, Nathan Man and Mary Man, to each and every of them £5 as they shall come to the age of 21 years. I give to my daughter Margaret, wife to John Warner, £23; but if my daughter Margaret shall decease leaving no surviving heirs, then the sd. £23 to return to my daughter Ruth. And to my daughter Ruth aforesd. I will the sum of £40. It is hereby further to be understood that the lands which I have given to my son Jacob Root shall remain unto him and his heirs forever, with the condition that he shall render up unto my brother Jonathan Root and my nephew Hezekiah Root and Thomas Sheldon what right he may have in the lands I sold to them at Northampton, and on no other conditions. I appoint my wife Mary and my son Daniel Root executors.

Witness: *Stephen Post,*   JACOB ROOT, LS.
David Barbour, Nathaniel Phelps.

Court Record, Page 57—10 August, 1731: Will proven.

Will in Vol. XII, Page 243.

Sage, Benoni, Middletown. Invt. £1020-13-06. Taken 3 January, 1733-4, by Samuel Gipson, John Sage and John Warner. Will dated 20 December, 1733.

I, Benoni Sage, husbandman, of Middletown, do make this my last will and testament: I give to my wife her dower rights. I give to my sons Benjamin Sage and Allen Sage all my real estate, to be theirs equally between them, their heirs and assigns. I also give to my two sons before named all the rest of my moveable estate not disposed of, and do hereby order them to pay unto my daughter Sarah Sage, when they come to the age of 21 years, the just sum of £50 in money, or that which shall be in equal vallue to £50 in money. And I do hereby constitute and appoint my brother David Sage to be my executor of this my last will and testament. I give to him so much out of my moveable estate as may be reasonable to reward him for his trouble (and this is to be lookt upon as a debt).

Witness: *John North,*   BENONI SAGE, LS.
Hezekiah Hooker, Nathaniel Beckley.

Court Record, Page 108—5 March, 1733-4: Will exhibited by Benoni Sage, executor, who, with the widow, exhibited an invt. Proven. This Court appoint Mary Sage to be guardian unto her children, viz., Benjamin, age 9 years, Allen 4 years, and Sarah 6 years, children of Benoni Sage, late decd. Recog., £150.

Page 20 (Vol. XII) 4 February, 1734-5: David Sage, executor, exhibits an account, which was accepted in Court and ordered to be kept on file. Whereupon this Court appoint Capt. Isaac Hart, Deacon Thomas Hart and Leut. Isaac Norton distributors. The return, dated 7 March, 1734-5 (on file):

	£ s d
To the widow, Mary Sage,	36-08-00
To Allen Sage,	254-01-04
To Benjamin Sage,	254-01-04

20 January, 1745: Benjamin Sage gives *Thomas Hart,* ⎱
to his uncle, David Sage, a receipt for   *Isaac Norton,* ⎰ *Distributors.*
his full share of the estate.   *Isaac Hart,* ⎰

October, 1749: Ebenezer Steele and Sarah Steele give receipt for theirs.

18 February, 1750-1: Allen Sage gives to his uncle, David Sage, a receipt for his full share of the estate of his late honoured father, Benony Sage, deceased.

Page 48 (Vol. XIII) 12 April, 1739: Benjamin Sage, age 16 years, chose his uncle David Sage to be his guardian. Recog., £400.

Page 54 (Vol. XIV) 5 February, 1744-5: Allen Sage, a minor 15 years of age, son of Benoni Sage, chose his uncle David Sage to be his guardian. Recog., £800.

Page 186-7.

Sawyer, Moses, Hebron. Invt. £150. Taken 29 February, 1731-2, by John Taylor and Samuel Waters.

Court Record, Page 63—4 April, 1732: Adms. granted to Thomas Lewis of Colchester.

Page 72—27 June, 1732: This Court appoint Thomas Lewis of Colchester to be guardian to the children of Moses Sawyer, viz., to Sarah, age 11 years, to Nathan 9 years, Moses 4, and Mary Sawyer, one year old. Recog., £200.

Page 105—5 February, 1733-4: Thomas Lewis, Adms., exhibited an account of his Adms: Paid debts amounting to the sum of £28-05-03. Which account is accepted and allowed, and there remains yet due from the estate the sum of £5-17-00.

Page 7-8-9.

Schovell, Benjamin, Haddam. Died 13 August, 1729. Invt. £432-13-06. Taken by Ebenezer Cone, Samuel Ackley and Daniel Cone.

Court Record, Page 3—7 October, 1729: Adms. granted to Amy Schovell, the widow, on the estate of John (Benjamin) Schovell, late decd.

Page 19—5 May, 1730: An addition to the invt. of £26-04-00 was exhibited in this Court by the Adms. Accepted.

Page 106 (Probate Side, Vol. XIII) 7 November, 1738: Know all men by these presents: That we, the subscribers, being the sole and only surviving heirs to the estate of Benjamin Schovell of East Haddam, in the County of Hartford, being the widow and children of the sd. deceased, do by these presents jointly and severally agree that the following disposition of the estate of sd. decd. shall be a final settlement of sd. estate: First—We agree that our brother Edward shall have and hold all the land that did or doth belong to the estate of our honoured father, Benjamin Schovell, and shall be and remain our sd. brother Edward's, to be at his dispose forever, provided he pay to the other heirs and widow aforesd. the following sums hereafter in this instrument particularly described:

	£ s d
First to Benjamin Schovell,	100-00-00
" Lemuel "	62-10-00
" Nathan "	62-10-00
" Sarah (Schovell) Spencer,	52-10-00
To Amy Schovell,	52-10-00
To Kezia Schovell Steward,	52-10-00

And we mutually agree and covenant, for ourselves and heirs, with our mother Amy Schovell, that we will each of us pay our sd. mother the sum of ten shillings apiece yearly during her widowhood. Then the widow quitclaims any right of hers to the real estate.

Signed: EDWARD SCHOVELL, LS.   SARAH SPENCER, LS.
         AMY X SCHOVELL, LS.   HEZEKIAH SPENCER, LS.
         AMY X SCHOVELL, 2nd, LS.   JAMES STEWARD, LS.
         BENJAMIN X SCHOVELL, LS.   KEZIA X STEWARD, LS.

Test: Jos: Talcott, Jr., Clerk.

Court Record, Page 35—7 November, 1738: Agreement exhibited in Court and accepted. Lemuel Schovell, age 19 years, and Nathan, 14 years, chose their brother Edward Schovell to be their guardian. Recog., £300.

Will and Invt. in Vol. XII, Page 234.

Sheldon, Capt. John, Hartford. Invt. £2569-07-07. Taken 20 March, 1733-4, by John Marsh, John Whiting and Jos. Talcott, Jr., for Hartford. Taken 13 March, 1733-4, for Windsor, by Samuel Strong, Thomas Filer and Timothy Loomis. Taken 5 March, 1733-4, for Deerfield, by Samuel Field, Joseph Sever and Jonathan Hoit.

Will dated 13 April, 1726: I, John Sheldon of Hartford, do make this my last will and testament: I give to my two grandsons, John and Charles Sheldon, the 1-2 of my lands in Deerfield (except the wanting lands), to them and their heirs forever, they paying to their sister Hannah Sheldon £20, as also £30 to their aunts (my daughters), Hannah Clark and Mary Clapp, being an addition to what I have already given them. I give to my son Ebenezer Sheldon the other half of my lands in Deerfield, with all the wanting lands there, to him and his heirs forever, he paying to my two daughters, Hannah Clark and Mary Clapp, £15 apiece, and also to my son Remembrance Sheldon the sum of £10. I give to my son Remembrance Sheldon all my houseing and lands in Windsor (excepting that tract of land I bought of Zechariah Sanford), to him and his heirs forever. I give to my beloved wife 1-3 part of all my real and personal estate lying in Hartford, that is to say, my houseing and lands lying in Hartford, with 1-3 part of that tract of land I bought of Zechariah Sandford lying in Windsor, during her natural life, which third part of houseing and lands after her decease to return to my son John Sheldon and his heirs. I give to my wife my negro boy named Coffe during her widowhood, then to return to my son John Sheldon or to my daughter Abigail Sheldon, to which their mother shall please to give it. I give to my son John Sheldon all my houseing and lands in Hartford, with that tract of land I bought of Zechariah Sandford, and to his heirs forever, excepting the use I have above given to his mother. I give to my daughter Abigail Sheldon £150, to be paid out of my moveable estate by my executors hereafter named, at the age of 18 years or day of marriage. If my moveable estate doth arise considerably higher than what I have above given, I then give to my son Remembrance Sheldon the sum of £5 in money or of my goods, as my executrix shall choose. And further, my will is that my beloved wife take the care of the education of my children, and for that end I give her the use of my lands given to my son John till he come of age, with the improvement of all my personal estate, the over-plus to her. Lastly, I do hereby appoint my beloved wife, with my son Remembrance Sheldon, to be executors.

Witness: *Joseph Colyer,*   JOHN SHELDON, LS.
John Colyer, William Andrews.

Court Record, Page 107—26 February, 1733-4: The last will and testament of Capt. John Sheldon of Hartford was exhibited by the widow and Remembrance Sheldon, son of the decd. John Sheldon, son of the decd., of Deerfield, and grandson of Capt. John Sheldon, and the Rev. Mr. Elis of Enfield in right of his wife, sister of John Sheldon of Deerfield, was present when the will was approved.

Page 1 (Vol. XII) 1st April, 1734. Executors exhibit an inventory

---

Page 77.

Shailor, Timothy, 2nd, Haddam.   Died 4 September, 1730.   Invt. £260-01-10. Taken 1st October, 1730, by Thomas Shailor, Thomas Selden and Joseph Arnold. Will dated 14 September, 1730.

I, Timothy Shailor of Haddam, in the County of Hartford, do make this my last will and testament: I give to Deborah, my wife, her thirds during life. If she bear me a son after my decease, then I give him a double portion of my estate; but if she bear me a daughter after my decease, then I give to her a double portion with her sister. To my two daughters Abigail and Jerusha I give all my estate not above disposed of, to be equally divided between them. I appoint Deborah, my wife, sole executrix.

Witness: *Phineas Fisk,*   TIMOTHY SHAILOR, LS.
Joseph Arnold, Caleb Cone.

Court Record, Page 30—3rd November, 1730: Will and invt. exhibited by Deborah Shailor, widow, executrix named in the will.

Page 18—15 April, 1730: Report of the distributors.

Page 85 (Vol. XIII) 7 April, 1741: Abigail Shailor, age 14 years, chose Thomas Brooks of Haddam to be her guardian. Recog., £150. Jerusha Shailor, age more than 12 years, this Court do appoint Abraham Brooks to be her guardian. Recog., £150.

Page 276-7.

Shepherd, Susannah, Hartford. Died 26 July, 1732. Invt. £81-16-01. Taken by William Gaylord and Elizabeth Hopkins.
Court Record, Page 91—5 June, 1733: This Court grants Adms. on the estate of Susannah Shepherd, late of Hartford decd., unto Daniel Shepherd, brother of the sd. decd., who gave bond with Deacon William Gaylord. Exhibit of an inventory. Accepted and ordered on file.

Page 29 (Vol. XII) 1st July, 1735: Ephraim Tucker appeared in Court and desired to be guardian to Ephraim Tucker, a minor, age 2 years, the son of Susannah Shepherd of Hartford decd. The sd. Susannah was daughter of Thomas Shepherd of Hartford, and the sd. Ephraim Tucker acknowledged in Court that the sd. minor was his child. Yet notwithstanding, sd. Thomas Shepherd, grandfather to the sd. minor, objected against the motion of sd. Ephraim Tucker being guardian to sd. minor: Whereupon this Court appoint the sd. Thomas Shepherd guardian to sd. minor. Recog., £100.

Page 16 (Vol. XIII) 1st November, 1737: Ephraim Tucker, son of Susannah Shepherd of Hartford: Thomas Shepherd, sometime ago appointed his guardian, is now willing to be discharged and is willing that his son Daniel Shepherd be appointed guardian to the sd. Ephraim Tucker, and he is appointed. Recog., £200.

Page 107-8-9-10.

Smith, Benjamin, Glastonbury. Invt. £953-03-06. Taken 17 February, 1730-31, by Samuel Gains and David Hubbard. Will dated May, 1727.

I, Benjamin Smith of Glastonbury, husbandman, do make this my last will and testament: I give to Hannah, my wife, two cows for her use, all the moveable estate which she brought with her that is now in being, my bay ambling horse, the bed I lodge on with its furniture, my biggest brass kettle and least brass kettle, my warming pan and porridge pot and pot hooks, two iron kettles, a paire of cob irons, two trammells, a slice and a paire of tongs, as also the chaires belonging to the house, all the meat that is in the house, all my hoggs, all the corne and grain that is in the house, two cow calves, and all the syder and beere barrels. I give unto my son Richard Smith my yoke of oxen, trammel, bedd he lodges on, and its furniture, a horse and cowe and farming tools, and the plow chain that belonged to his uncle Joseph. And after my two sons Jeduthan and Manoah and my daughter Dorothy have had each of them 150 acres of land out of my right of land in the Five-Mile Purchase of Glastonbury, I give and devise the remainder of the sd. right to my sd. son Richard. I give to my son, Jeduthan Smith, cattle and farming tooles, tackling for a cart that belonged to his uncle Joseph, and 150 acres of land to be laid out to him out of my right of land in that part of Glastonbury called the Five-Mile Purchase. I give unto my son, Manoah

Smith, cattle and farming tooles, a bedd that formerly belonged to his aunt Bethiah, and 150 acres of land laid out to him out of my right of land in that part of Glastonbury called the Five-Mile Purchase. I give unto my daughter, Dinah Smith, a wainscott cupbard outstanding in my new house, and the sum of 5 shillings in money. And the reason that my sd. daughter Dinah hath no more by this my will is because I have lately given her by deed the homelott of 22 acres of land at the Town Street of Colchester, and have delivered to her as gifts several other things. I give unto my daughter Dorothy 150 acres of land laid out to her out of my right of land in that part of Glastonbury called the Five-Mile Purchase, a wainscott chest, and £16 in money or money's worth. As to the remainder of my land at the Wigwam Hill in Glastonbury which I have not given by deed to my son Manoah, which remainder goes from the east bound of my sd. son Manoah's land (so given by deed) to the end of the Three Miles eastward into the woods, to be reckoned from the Great River, I give the sd. remainder to my three sons, Richard, Jeduthan and Manoah, equally to be divided among them. As to the rest and residue of my moveable estate not hereinbefore given, I give and devise it unto Hannah, my beloved wife. I appoint my son Richard to be executor.

Witness: *John Sparks,*   BENJAMIN SMITH, LS.
Samuel Gains, John Lynn.

Court Record, Page 45—4 May, 1731: Will and inventory exhibited.

Smith, John. Court Record, Page 89—4 July, 1732: Whereas, the last will of John Smith, late of Hartford, dated in Cork, Ireland, on the 18th day of November, One Thousand Seven Hundred and Thirty-One, proved and allowed in London before William, Archbishop of Canterbury, Primate and Metropolitan of England: a duplicate of which, with the probate thereof as aforesd., being exhibited in this Court by Ann Smith, executrix to sd. will, and the sd. Anne Smith accepted the trust.

Page 12 (Vol. XII) 6 October, 1734: David Williams, executor to the last will of the decd., made oath to the invt. as containing all that he knew of in New England.

Page 9 (Vol. XIV) 6 July, 1742: George Smith, a minor, 15 years of age, son of John Smith, late of Hartford, chose Col. John Whiting and Capt. George Wyllys of Hartford to be his guardians. And the Court appoint sd. Whiting and Wyllys guardians to Mary Smith, age 13 years, and William Smith, age 11 years, children of John Smith. Recog., £10,000.

Page 112 (Vol. XIII) 16 October, 1752: A discharge from the heirs of John Smith, sometime of Hartford, merchant, to their honoured mother, Anne Smith, now Anne Morrison, with Capt. David Williams of Wethersfield, executors, the heirs now being of lawful age and having each received £1,000 bills of credit in hand paid or secured to be paid by our honoured father and mother, Normand and Anne Morrison, both of

Hartford, do exonerate and discharge them from all claims or demands; also discharge our guardians, Col. John Whiting and Col. George Wyllys.

Witness: *Roderick Morrison,*   GEORGE SMITH, LS. |ROBERT NEVINS, LS.
        Alexander Campbell. MARY NEVINS, LS. |WILLIAM SMITH, LS.

Hartford, 27 November, 1761: Then personally appeared Alexander Campbell, now of Oxford, in the County of Worcester, Province of Massachusetts Bay, physition, and made solemn oath that, on the day of the date of the within written instrument or discharge, he saw George Smith, Robert Nevins, Mary Nevins and William Smith, the ensealers thereof, severally sign, seal and execute and deliver the same as their voluntary act and deed, and that at the same time he set to his hand as witness, together with Roderick Morrison, then of sd. Hartford, since deceased.

Sworn before me, John Ledyard, J. P.

Page 230.

Smith, Joseph, Haddam. Died 23 July, 1732. Invt. £713-10-00. Taken 15 September, 1732, by Simon Smith, Joseph Arnold and Thomas Brooks, Jr. Will dated 23 July, 1732.

To all Christian People to whom these presents shall come, greeting:
Know ye that I, Joseph Smith of Haddam, in the County of Hartford, do make this my last will and testament: I give to Elizabeth, my wife, the use of my dwelling house, barn and lott, and all improvable lands, so long as she remains my widow or till my eldest son John shall come of age, and 1-2 of my moveables forever. And when John comes of age she shall deliver up to him his part of the estate. I give to my son John Smith all my land at Beaver Meadow which was formerly Capt. James Bate's, and the black pacing horse that is now called John's horse. I give to my daughter Elizabeth all that land which I had of Thomas Smith, and all my interest on the Island, and an equal interest in all my moveable estate, towards bringing her up. I give to my sons, Jos: Smith and Jethro, my dwelling house and barn and homelott, and all my land in the home meadow and the Creek land and swamp land at the lower end of sd. meadow, to be divided equally between them. Sd. Joseph and Jethro shall pay to their sisters Else and Hannah, when they come of age, £10 in money to each. I give to my two daughters, Else Smith and Hannah, all my land and rights in undivided land not yet disposed of, to be divided equally between them. I ordain my wife Elizabeth and her brother, Samuel Smith, sole executors.

Witness: *Simon Smith, Jr.,*   JOSEPH SMITH, LS.
Jacob Smith, Caleb Cone, Jr.

Court Record, Page 78—5 December, 1732: Will and invt. exhibited by Samuel Smith, executor named in the will.

Page 308.

Smith, Nathaniel, Hartford. Invt. £405-01-00. Taken 31 August, 1733, by Jonathan Sedgwick and Daniel Webster.

Court Record, Page 96—4 September, 1733: Adms. granted to Mary Smith, widow, who gave bond with David Ensign, £300.

Page 50 (Vol. XII) 3 August, 1736: This Court appoint Mary Smith, widow, to be guardian to Justes Smith, age 8 years, Nathaniel 3 years, Elizabeth 7 years, and Hannah 5 years, all children of the sd. decd. Recog., £200.

Page 252, 260.

Smith, Samuel, Glastonbury. Invt. £1742-11-02. Taken 14 December, by Nathaniel Talcott and Joseph Fox. Will dated 19 September, 1727.

I, Samuel Smith, husbandman, of Glastonbury, do make my last will and testament: I give unto my son Samuel Smith my Great Bible, and the reason why my sd. son has no more of my estate is because I have given him by deed my homelott in Glastonbury. I give unto my daughter Rachel Smith a certain tract of land belonging to me, lying at or neare a pond neare the east bounds of Glastonbury, called Dickeson's Pond. I give all my cattle, horse kind, sheep, swine, bedding, pewter, plate, brass, linen, casks, and all my household goods, as also my books and all other chattel or moveable estate whatsoever, unto my daughters Rachel and Dinah, except only my cart and cart tackling, plows, harrows, etc., and other husbandry tools, which I give unto my son Joseph Smith. I give all my land and rights of land, laid out or not laid out, to me in the land called the Five-Mile Land, in Glastonbury, unto my son Joseph and to my daughters Rachel and Dinah, to be divided among them share and share alike, and the reason why my sd. son Joseph has no more of my estate is because I have formerly given him by deed two lotts of land in Glastonbury. I do hereby appoint my daughter Rachel Smith to be executor.

Witness: *Elizabeth Hills,*   SAMUEL SMITH, LS.
Thomas Brewer, John Lynn.

Memorandum: That at the sealing of my within written will I do give and devise a certain tract or parcell of land belonging to me below Naug, in Glastonbury, containing 80 acres of my lott, unto Thomas Buck of Glastonbury, husbandman, for and during the term of his natural life, and after his death and decease then to the use and behoof of Thomas Buck, an infant now living in the house with me, and to the heirs and assigns of the sd. infant Thomas Buck, if he attain the age of 21 years. If he should die before that age, then after his father's decease, said land to return to my heirs.

Witness: *Elizabeth Hills,*   SAMUEL SMITH, LS.
Thomas Brewer, John Lynn.

Memorandum: Dated 21 September, 1730: All my land laid out or not laid out in Glastonbury, in that part called the Five-Miles Land, I give the same unto my daughter Rachel Smith and to her heirs forever. I also give unto my daughter Rachel my great silver tankard in respect of her tending me in my sickness, and all legacies given to my daughter Dinah I do order that my daughter Rachel have the possession, keeping and disposal of after my decease, to be given by her to my sd. daughter Dinah and her child or children as my daughter Rachel shall think fit.

Witness: *John Sparks,*   SAMUEL SMITH, LS.
Jean Lynn, John Lynn.

Court Record, Page 81-2—6 February, 1732-3: Will exhibited by Rachel Smith, executrix named in sd. will, and desired it approved. Enoch Lyman, an heir to the estate in right of his wife Dinah, appeared in Court against the alteration wherein the part given to Dinah is put into Rachel's hands, etc. Case continued.

Page 82—6 February, 1732-3: According to the continuance of the case respecting the objection made against the last codicil to the will of Samuel Smith of Glastonbury decd., from Tuesday the 6th of this instant February to this time, the parties were heard thereupon, and this Court having considered that sd. will with the codicil made at the time of the testator sealing his will (with a gift to Thomas Buck), and the codicil made the 21st day of September, 1730, wherein the parties were at variance as aforesd., are all proved to be the will of the testator: Approved by the Court and ordered to be recorded and kept on file. Enoch Lyman, an heir in right of his wife Dinah to the estate of Samuel Smith, appealed from the judgement of this Court respecting the probation of the last codicil to the will of the sd. deceased, unto the Superior Court. Recog., £20.

Dist. File, 1st May, 1734: Estate Samuel Smith, Glastonbury: To Rachel Smith, to Enoch and Dyna Lyman. By Abner Moseley and Nathaniel Talcott.

Page 283.

Southmayd, Margaret, Middletown. Will dated 5 December, 1728: I, Margaret Southmayd, of Middletown, widow and relict of William Southmayd, sometime of the aforesd. Middletown, decd., do make this my last will and testament: I give to my son Joseph Southmayd that lottment of land on the east side of the Connecticut River in Middletown in the last division laid out, about 30 acres. I give to my son William Southmayd a large family Bible and also my best bed with all the furniture properly belonging to it. I give to my two daughters, Margaret Gaylord and Anne Stilman, all my wearing apparell. I give to my granddaughter Millicent Gaylord my small brass kettle. I give unto my granddaughter, Anne Gaylord, my smallest bell-mettal skillett. I give to my three sons, Allyn, Joseph and William Southmayd, with my two daughters, Margaret Gaylord and Anne Stilman aforesd., the lower lott in the Long Meadow in

Hartford, which formerly did belong to my honoured father, Cololl. John Allyn of Hartford decd., and also the 1-5 part of the houseing and homestead formerly belonging to my honoured father, Col. John Allyn of Hartford, now in the possession of Mrs. Martha Cooke of Hartford, together with all my bills, bonds, money, debts, and all my moveables and household goods, to be divided equally among my five children above named (except) my cobirons, fire slice and tongs in the outer room, which I give unto my son Joseph Southmayd. And I do hereby oblige my sd. children to purchase out of sd. estate 5 pieces of plate of equal value, that is, with what I now have to be part, and marke them thus, "W. S. M.", to be kept by each of them in memory of their father and myself. And I hereby appoint my two sons, Joseph Southmayd and William Southmayd, executors.

Witness : *Thomas Allyn,*   MARGARET SOUTHMAYD, LS.
Joseph Rockwell, William Rockwell.

Codicil, dated 28 August, 1731 : My two daughters and my youngest granddaughter being now deceased, I see cause to make this alteration in my will : that which was given to my two daughters and to my granddaughter, Anna Gaylord, I now give to my son Joseph's wife and my son William Southmayd.

Witness : *Joseph Rockwell,*   MARGARET X SOUTHMAYD, LS.
William Rockwell, John Rockwell.

Page 339.

Spelman, Daniel, Middletown. Invt. £102-00-11. Taken 28 January, 1733-4, by Richard Spelman, Benjamin Cornwall and Samuel Cotton.

Court Record, Page 104—5 February, 1733-4: Adms. to Annah Spelman, widow, who, with Benjamin Cornwall, gave bond.

Page 18 (Vol. XV) 7 May, 1746: Thomson Spellman, a minor, 16 years of age, and Daniel Spellman, 15 years, children of Daniel Spellman, chose their uncle Benjamin Cornwell of Middletown to be their guardian. Recog., £500 for each minor.

Spencer, Joseph, Haddam. Court Record, Page 23—5 June, 1730 : Joseph Spencer, a minor, 18 years of age, chose Samuel Ackley of East Haddam to be his guardian. Recog., £50.

Page 33—5 January, 1730-1 : Samuel Ackley, guardian, shows this Court that some land in Haddam (one parcell in the first division, 15 acres, adjoining William Spencer, Lt. Knowlton and James Bates; one other piece of land in Haddam in the second division, 30 acres, the width of the lott is 20 rods, 12 of them is part of sd. William Spencer's own dwelling lott, the other eight he had of his brother Daniel Brainard) was given to Joseph Spencer and to Elizabeth Spencer, now come of age to inherit. This Court appoint Capt. Daniel Brainard and Capt. Samuel Olmsted to assist Samuel Ackley, guardian, to make a division of sd. land.

Page 226.

Spencer, Timothy, Haddam. Died 29 March, 1732. Invt. £872-02-06. Taken 26 April, 1732, by Joseph Arnold, James Brainard and Caleb Cone. Will dated 27 March, 1732.

I, Timothy Spencer of Haddam, in the County of Hartford, do make this my last will and testament. I give to Abigail, my wife, the use of my homelott, house, barn, and the lott adjoining Capt. Brainard's woodlott, and 2 acres of grass land in the home meadow in grandfather's lott next the swamp, so long as she remains my widow, and 1-3 part of all my moveable estate. I give to my son Timothy Spencer all my homelott, and the house, and the barn and the lott the barn stands upon, and the lott joining to Capt. Brainard's woodlott, and the 2 acres of mowing land in my own meadow, when his mother hath done with it; and also, to be at his own use forthwith, all my land in the home meadow and 7 acres of land lying on the heather end of the Streights, and 10 acres of land lying below the Streights (partly improved), and a third part of all my right of undivided land, and no more of my estate shall be his. I give to my son Jonathan Spencer that lott in the woods that was Sergeant Daniel Hubbard's, and that lott I had of Deacon Brooker, be it more or less, and 35 acres of land in the lott that I had of Isaac Spencer, and 1-3 part of my right in the undivided land, and no more of my estate shall be his. I give to my son Simeon Spencer all that land which is several pieces joined together neare Benjamin Spencer's house, which is partly improved, and all that part of the lott I had of Isaac Spencer which I have not given away already, be it more or less, and a third part of my right in the undivided land. I give to my daughters, Abigail, Hannah, Deborah, Elizabeth and Martha, all my estate in lands and moveables not already disposed of, to be divided equally between them, excepting that Hannah shall have £10 more than any of the rest of the daughters, and Abigail to be equal to them with what she hath had already. My will is that my wife and my son-in-law, Richard Wakeley, be my executors.

Witness: *James Brainard,*   TIMOTHY SPENCER, LS.
Daniel Brainard, Caleb Cone, Jr.

Court Record, Page 71—6 June, 1732: Will exhibited by Abigail Spencer and Richard Wakeley, executors named in sd. will. This Court appoint Mrs. Abigail Spencer to be guardian to Symon Spencer, 8 years of age, and Martha Spencer, 11 years, children of the decd. Recog., £100.

Page 82—13 February, 1732-3: Jonathan Spencer, age 9 years, and Elizabeth, age 15 years, chose their mother, Abigail Spencer, to be their guardian. Recog., £100.

Page 83—22 February, 1732-3: Richard Wakeley, in right of his wife Abigail, a daughter to Timothy Spencer, showing to this Court that he has a right in several parcels of land by the will of the sd. decd., in common with divers others of the daughters (2 of which are under age and so not able to come to a partition amongst themselves), and the sd. Richard Wakley moves to this Court that freeholders may be appointed to divide sd. lands with the assistance of the guardian of sd. minors: Whereupon this Court appoint Lt. Hezekiah Brainard and Thomas Brooks, of Haddam, with Abigail Spencer, guardian to sd. minors, to divide sd. lands among the daughters according to the sd. will.

Dist. File: 10 May, 1733: To the five daughters: to Abigail, wife of Richard Wakeley, to Hannah, to Deborah, to Elizabeth, and to Martha Spencer. By Thomas Brooks and Hezekiah Brainard.

Page 97—4 September, 1733: Report of the distributors.

Page 267.

Stanly, Lydia, Mrs., Hartford. Invt. £29-16-05. Taken 7 March, 1732, by William Cadwell and James Church.

Court Record, Page 84—28 February, 1732-3: Adms. to Richard Seamore of Hartford, who, with Capt. Thomas Seamore of Hartford, gave bond.

Page 189.

Steward, Ellexander, East Haddam. Invt. £150. Taken 28 February, 1732, by Isaac Spencer, John Church and Thomas Millard.

Court Record, Page 73—1st August, 1732: Adms. to Margaret Steward, widow.

Page 124.

Steele, Sarah, Farmington. Invt. £744-00-06. Taken 16 April, 1731, by Isaac Cowles, Sen., and Daniel Judd.

Court Record, Page 42—6 April, 1731: Adms. to Thomas Smith of Farmington.

Stocking, Daniel, Middletown. Court Record, Page 83—22 February, 1732-3: Jane Stocking, widow, and Joseph Stocking refuse to take Adms., whereupon Adms. is granted to John Stocking, one of the sons of the deceased, who gave bond with Joseph Stow of Middletown.

Stocking, Elisha. Court Record, Page 80—1st February, 1732-3: Elisha Stocking, son of the deceased, 19 years of age, chose Nicholas Ayrault of Wethersfield to be his guardian. Recog., £100.

Page 48-9.

Stow, Thomas, Middletown.   Invt. £696-01-06.   Taken 29 April, 1730, by John Warner, John Shepherd and Hugh White.   Will dated 12 March, 1728.

The last will and testament of Thomas Stow, late of Middletown: I give to my wife, Bethiah Stow, so much of my estate to be to her use as she shall find useful during her natural life. I give to my wife, to be at her sole disposal, all my stock of creatures which I shall leave, as also my right of land on the east side of the Great River that is lying in that tract of land belonging to Middletown which is called the last division, which sd. stock of creatures and land is to be at her dispose, so much of it as is left after my just debts are paid out. I give to my son Samuel the whole of my homelott, with that part of the building which belongs to me, as also I give him all my part of the land called the Island, in Pistol Pint, as also 3-4 of my boggy meadow lott, as also I give him that part of my brother John Stocking's lott in the west quarter which fell to my wife, called the mountain; also I give him so much of what remains of the sd. lott that is not before disposed of and which lyes this side ye mountain, that is to say, on the east side of the mountain, as shall be in proportion a third part of sd. land; all this besides which I have formerly given him by deed of gift. I give to my son Thomas Stow 1-4 part of my boggy meadow lott, as also 1-3 part of the lottment of land in the west quarter which fell to my wife by Brother John Stocking, that is to say, 1-3 part of what belongs to me of sd. lott on the east side of the mountain and which is not before disposed of; this besides which I have formerly given him by deed of gift. I give to my son Joseph Stow half my pasture in Burch Swamp, my land in Wongogue Meadow, all my land at Timber Hill, and 1-3 part of my right of land in the lottments of John Stocking's, 1-3 part of what remains east side of the mountain; this I give to my son Joseph, he paying £10 to his sisters. I give to my two daughters, Bethiah and Hannah, each of them 1-3 part of my household goods after my wife's decease. I give to my daughter Bethiah £10 in money. I give to my daughter Hannah my right of land in John Stocking's lottment in the west quarter that remains undisposed of and lies on the west side of the mountain. I give to my daughter Mary's children 1-3 part of my household goods after my wife's decease; also give them £10 in money. I give to our present minister, Joseph Smith, 20 shillings.

Witness: *John Shepherd,*   THOMAS STOW, LS.
Thomas Johnson, Samuel Shepherd.

Court Record, Page 13—3 March, 1729-30: Thomas Stow, a minor, 12 years of age, this Court appoint Thomas Stow of Middletown to be his guardian.
        Page 18—5 May, 1730: Will exhibited and proven.
        Page 34 (Vol. XII) 7 October, 1735: Thomas Stow, an orphan, 17 years of age, chose William Rockwell of Middletown to be his guardian. Cert: *Jabez Hamlin, J. P.*

Page 113-14.

Taintor, Michael, Esq., Colchester. Invt. £181-01-08. Taken 2 April, 1730, by Samuel Loomis and William Roberts. Will dated 9 February, 1729-30.

I, Michael Taintor of Colchester, in the County of Hartford, do make this my last will and testament: I give to my two daughters, Mary and Sarah, to each of them, £20 out of my moveable estate. All the rest of my moveable estate I give to my wife during her lifetime. I give to my wife and son John the use of all my lands, viz., my homelotts, the whole about 60 acres, together with my dwelling house, barn and orchards, during the time of both of their natural lives; also my 100-acre lott lying on the east side of the Town Platt. And after the decease of my wife and my son John, I give unto John Taintor, son to my son Michael Taintor, and Michael Taintor, son to my son Joseph Taintor, late of Brandford decd., all my aforementioned houseing and lands and orchards, to be equally divided between them; also to each of them a £50 right in the commons and undivided land in Colchester. I hereby make my wife sole executrix. I give to my son Michael £100 right in the commons and undivided lands in the Township of Colchester. I give to my son John all my wearing apparell. I give to my son Michael and my daughter Mary and my daughter Sarah all my right in the commons and undivided lands in the Township of Windsor which ought or doth accrue to me by virtue of the Pattin (patent) granted by the General Assembly in the Town of Windsor.

Witness: *David Hamilton,*   MICHAEL TAINTOR, LS.
Samuel Knight, George Holmes.

Court Record, Page 46—4 June, 1731: Will now exhibited by the widow, executrix named in the will, who declined the trust. Proven. This Court grant Adms. to Mabell Taintor, widow relict, who recog. in £360 with Nathaniel Clarke of Colchester.

Taylor, Hannah. Court Record, Page 41—22 March, 1731: Hannah Taylor of Long Island, in the Province of New York, widow relict of John Taylor, late of Huntington decd., formerly of Windsor, Conn., to be guardian to her children, viz., John, 8 years of age, Nehemiah 6, Medad 4, Mary 1½ years of age. Recog., £200.

Page 125.

Thrall, Aaron, Windsor. Died 7 July, 1731. Invt. £171-01-09. Taken 26 July, 1731, by Samuel Strong, Peletiah Allyn and Israel Stoughton.

Court Record, Page 49—3 August, 1731: Invt. exhibited by Moses Thrall, Adms.

Page 199-200.

Thrall, Sergt. John, Windsor. Died 18 April, 1732. Invt. £856-16-06. Taken 15 May, 1732, by Jonathan Stiles, Peletiah Allyn and Job Drake. Will dated 18 April, 1732.

I, John Thrall of Windsor, do make this my last will and testament: I give to my wife Mindwell my house and homestead, with the barn, and the land adjoining running to the Great River, and three acres of land south of the highway, which was Grandfather Gun's, and the syder press, during her widowhood, and after to return to my sons, Joseph, Daniel, Joel and Charles, equally to be divided among them. Also I give to my wife £20 out of the moveables, she takeing her choice, and the feather-bed and bedding. I give unto my son John all my right in the 1½-mile lott lately laid out, known as Town Commons, and also all my right in the equivalent land. I give unto my daughter Amy £20 out of my move-ables, also ye youngest cow, six sheep and five gees(e). I give unto my youngest daughter Jerusha £60 and one cow. I give unto my sons, Joseph, Daniel, Joel and Charles, all my right in the western lands, equally to be divided between them; also my lott at Hoit's meadow, ye pasture, and my lott at Sandy Hill, and my lott which I bought of Fits John Allyn, equally to be divided between them. I give to my son John my lott at Turkey Hill, provided he pay to my daughter Ammey £10 towards the £20 above named. I give to my son Moses 1-3 part of all my right in the undivided lands in Windsor, and ye remainder to be equally divided between Joseph, Daniel, Joel and Charles. My wife and son Moses Thrall to be executors.

Witness: *Israel Stoughton,*   JOHN THRALL, LS.
Samuel Stoughton, John Allyn.

Court Record, Page 66—9 May, 1732: Joel Thrall, a minor, age 16 years, chose John Thrall of Windsor to be his guardian. Recog., £200.

Page 69—6 June, 1732: Will exhibited by Mindwell Thrall and Moses Thrall, executors. Mrs. Mindwell Thrall refused the trust.

Page 70—6 June, 1732: This Court appoint Mrs. Mindwell Thrall to be guardian to Jerusha Thrall, age 9 years. Recog., £100. And Moses Thrall is appointed guardian to Charles Thrall, a minor son of Sergt. John Thrall. Recog., £100.

Page 39 (Vol. XII) 3 February, 1735-6: John Thrall of Windsor, guardian to Joel Thrall, one of the heirs to the estate of Sergt. John Thrall, moves this Court for a division of the real estate of the sd. decd. according to the will. This Court appoint Lt. Joseph Barnard, Lt. James Enno and John Stoughton, distributors.

Page 51—5 October, 1736: Report of the distributors of the estate to the Court. Accepted and ordered on file.

Page 86.

Tryon, David, Glastonbury, Wethersfield. Invt. £45-16-10. Taken 23 December, 1730, by Samuel Boardman of Middletown and Benjamin Rose of Glastonbury.

Court Record, Page 35—5 January, 1730-1: Adms. granted to Hannah Tryon, the widow.

Page 108—5 March, 1733-4: Benjamin Tryon, a minor, 18 years of age, son of David Tryon, chose Ebenezer Dickinson of Wethersfield to be his guardian. Recog., £100.

Page 3 (Vol. XII) 25 April, 1734: Ezra Tryon of Wethersfield, age 14 years, son of David Tryon, chose his brother Jonathan Tryon to be his guardian. Allowed. Recog., £100.

Page 166.

Inventory in Vol. XII, Page 390.

Wadsworth, Capt. Joseph. Invt. £968-07-06.   Taken 24 March, 1730, by Nathaniel Marsh and John Cook. Will dated 6 July, 1723.

I, Joseph Wadsworth, do make this my last will and testament. And having given a jointure in full satisfaction to my wife Mary, I proceed to bequeath my estate to my children. And I give to my son Joseph the upper Neck lott of land where his dwelling house stands, with all the buildings, orchards, priviledges and appurtenances, to him and his heirs forever. Also I give to my son Joseph my upper lott in the long meadow, and the 5-acre lott that I bought of Capt. Nathan Gold, and the 4 acres of land at Brother Talcott's upper lott, which I have by agreement with Brother Talcott; and also give to my son Joseph all my land in Coventry. This I give to him besides what he hath formerly had or improved of my estate. I give to my son Jonathan and his heirs forever a woodlott butting east on the road to Windsor, with all the buildings thereon, with all the priviledges and appurtenances thereunto belonging. Also I give him my Neck lott of land lying over against the aforesd. woodlott, butting west on the road leading to Windsor, that was bought of Thomas Thomlinson. Also I do give him the lott of land which the half-way tree stands on, in the long meadow. I do give to my son Ichabod the lower houselott, so called, that butteth west on a highway and north on Joseph Barnard's land, with the mansion house, barn, and all the priviledges and appurtenances thereunto belonging. Also my 4 acres in the south meadow and 6 acres in the Soldier's Field, bounding south on Richard Goodman's land. Also my 3 acres at the lower end of the long meadow, and the acre lott nigh the lower end of sd. meadow. Also my woodlott of 60 acres lying on the west side of Mill River, nigh the road leading to Simsbury. And I order Ichabod to pay to Jonathan 40 shillings yearly so long as my wife continues my widow. And my will is that if I dye before my present wife, that my sons aforenamed do allow to her the improvement of all such lands as by joynture I have given her to use, according to the true intent of sd. instrument, without any let or hindrance whatsoever. I do give to my three grandchildren, children of my daughter Elizabeth Marsh, viz., Jonathan Marsh, Joseph Marsh and Elizabeth Marsh, £10, to be paid to them as they come to lawful age, each of them £3-06-08, to be paid them by my three sons, Joseph, Jonathan and Ichabod, in equal parts. This I give to them besides what I gave to their mother and what she hath had of my estate formerly. I do give unto my daughter Hannah Cook £10 besides what she hath formerly had. I appoint my son Joseph Wadsworth my executor.

Witness: *Joseph Talcott,*   JOSEPH WADSWORTH, LS.
Joseph Farnsworth, Mary Farnsworth.

Court Record, Page 39—2 March, 1730-1 : Will proven.

Page 143, 148.

Wadsworth, Lt. Samuel, Farmington. Invt. £675-10-03. Taken September and 6 December, 1731, by Isaac Cowles and Daniel Wadsworth.

Court Record, Page 51—7 September, 1731 : Adms. to Samuel Wadsworth, a son of the decd., who, with Thomas Hooker of Hartford, recog. in £300.

Page 79.

Ward, Thomas, Middletown. Invt. £1389-17-08. Taken 5 October, 1730, by William Whitmore, Daniel Hall and James Ward. Will dated 6 July, 1729.

I, Thomas Ward of Middletown, do make this my last will and testament : I give to my wife all that she brought with her that is in being, and one-third part of the rest of my moveable estate besides what I have already given to my two daughters, Rebeckah and Sarah, only the team and tackling I give to my son Thomas and my wife to improve together so long as she remains my widow. I also give to my wife half the home-lott and house and barn and 1-2 of all my land to improve with my sons, Thomas, Tappin and Fenner, so long as she remains my widow and no longer. I also give to my wife and my son Thomas 1-2 of my part of the incomes of the land and stock which I have leased out for the term of 7 years, and the other half I reserve to pay my just debts. I give to my son Thomas my wearing apparel and that Bible which was my honoured father's. I give to my son Tappin the remainder of my Hill lott and 1-3 part of my land at West Swamp, and 2 acres of meadow, and one equal half of that farm which was my honoured father's, to be equally divided between him and his brother Thomas, and 1-3 part of common and undivided land, when divided. I give to my son Fenner 1-3 part of my land at West Swamp, and all my land lying west of that, after my wife's decease or marriage, and 3 acres of meadow and 1-3 part of my undivided land or common, when divided. I do call all that land West Swamp which lyeth on the homeward side of West Swamp Brook and eastward with Brother William's land. I give to my daughter Rebeckah 1 equal third part of my moveables which I have not disposed of before. I give to my daughter Sarah also one equal third part. And further, it is my will that ·whatsoever estate of my first wife's heirs doth fall to them, that it be equally divided between my two daughters, Rebeckah and Sarah, from their grandfather Burnham's estate. And I do constitute my wife and my son Thomas Ward sole executors, and do put Brother William Ward and Brother James Ward to be overseers, and Brother Daniel Hall and Brother Richard Burnham to be guardians for my first wife's children, and Brother Hugh White for my son Fenner.

Witness: *John Elton,*   THOMAS WARD, LS.
Nathaniel Bacon, Jr., Daniel Hall.

Court Record, Page 30—3 November, 1730: Will exhibited by Deborah and Thomas Ward. This Court appoint Daniel Hall of Middletown guardian to Thomas Ward, age 15 years, and Tappan Ward, Rebeckah Ward and Sarah Ward, minor children of Thomas Ward decd. Recog., £200. This Court appoint Hugh White guardian to Fenner Ward, age 5 years. Recog., £50.

Warner, Daniel, Jr. Court Record, Page 8 (Vol. XII) 6 August, 1734: Daniel Warner now appeared before this Court with Joshua Robbins the 2nd, who was his guardian, and the sd. Daniel Warner, being of age, now releases his guardian. Allowed.

Page 340.

Warner, Jonathan. Middletown. Invt. £368-03-09. Taken 4 November, 1733, by Nathaniel Savidge and Nathaniel White. Will dated 22 May, 1733.

I, Jonathan Warner of Middletown, in the County of Hartford, do make this my last will and testament. I give to Elizabeth, my wife, 1-2 of my moveable household goods, two heifers, and likewise I give to my wife my dwelling house, barn and homelott and all the land joining thereto. This I give to my wife and her heirs and assigns forever. And likewise I give to my wife the use of all the remainder of my land and other moveable estate, excepting £10 worth, during her life. But it is and must be understood that debts and necessary charges are first of all to be paid. I give to Abigail Harris, now dwelling in my house, after my wife decease, I give to the sd. Abigail Harris 1-2 of my moveable household goods, and to her heirs forever. I give to the Rev. Mr. Moses Bartlett, if he shall be settled in the work of the ministry on the east side the Great River in Middletown, I give to him £10 as money, to be paid out of my moveable estate. I give to my own relations, after my wife's decease, all my lands excepting my homelott, together with what moveable estate is not given away and shall remain. This I give to my own relations, to be divided amongst them as the law directs intestate estate should be. And I do make Elizabeth, my wife, to be sole executor, and Deacon White to be overseer.

Witness: *Joseph White,*   JONATHAN WARNER, LS.
Nathaniel Savidge, William Kesson.

Court Record, Page 105—5 February, 1733-4: Will exhibited by Elizabeth Warner, widow.

Court Record, Page 2—3 January, 1758: Richard Coleman and Ebenezer Ranny, two of the heirs to the estate of Jonathan Warner, late of Middletown deceased, moves to this Court that freeholders may be appointed to distribute the estate: Whereupon this Court appoint Mr. Sampson How, David Sage and Noadiah White, of Middletown, distributors.

Page 21—26 May, 1758: Report of distribution.

Dist. File, 3 January, 1758: Estate Jonathan Warner, Middletown: To Ebenezer Ranny, to Richard Coleman, to Jabez Warner. By Samson How and David Sage.

Page 86-7.

Warner, Hannah, Middletown. Invt. £240-06-05. Taken 25 December, 1730, by John Collins, Joseph Rockwell and Jacob Cornwall.

Court Record, Page 32—9 December, 1730: Adms. to John Warner of Middletown.

Page 35—5 January, 1730-1: Invt. exhibited by the Adms., who also exhibited in the same inventory the estate of Lt. Andrew Warner that was given to Hannah Warner and left by her at her decease, both in one.

Page 69.

Warner, Mary, widow of Seth Warner, Middletown. Invt. £24-14-06. Taken 12 August, 1729, by John Collins and Joseph Rockwell.

Court Record, Page 7—2 December, 1729: Adms. to Robert Warner of Middletown.

Page 228.

Warner, Lt. Robert, Middletown. Invt. £996-02-03. Taken 10 November, 1732, by John Collins, Joseph Rockwell and William Rockwell. Will dated 15 August, 1732.

I, Robert Warner of Middletown, do ordain this my last will and testament: My will is that my estate be settled according to the laws of this Colony relating to intestate estates. And do ordain my wife Isabell sole executrix.

Witness: *Francis Whitmore, Jacob Cornwall,*   ROBERT WARNER, LS.
Samuel Warner, William Rockwell.

Court Record, Page 77—13 November, 1732: Will exhibited by Isabell Warner, executrix. This Court appoint Isabell Warner to be guardian to Daniel Warner, age 14 years, Stephen 11, Joseph 8, and Mary Warner, children of the decd. Recog., £200.

Page 94—3 July, 1733: Robert Warner, a minor, 16 years of age, son of Lt. Robert Warner, chose his uncle Francis Wetmore to be his guardian. Recog., £100.

Page 31 (Vol. XII) 26 August, 1735: Isabell Warner, the executrix, not having fully administered on sd. estate, being now deceased, this Court grant Adms. unto Samuel Warner of Middletown, who recog. in £200, with Isaac Lane.

Page 5 (Probate Side, Vol. XIII): An invt. of lands valued at £819-08-00, and also of goods at Isaac Lane's aprised at £40-03-02. Taken 11 May, 1736, by John Collins, Joseph Rockwell and William Rockwell.

Court Record, Page 54 (Vol. XII) 28 December, 1736-7: An account of Adms. was now exhibited in Court by Isaac Lane, one of the executors of the last will of the decd., whereby it appears he has with the other executrix, his wife (who was the widow of the decd. Robert Warner), paid the sum of £36-15-06, which is allowed them. Account accepted, ordered recorded and kept on file.

Page 6 (Vol. XIII) 3 May, 1737: An invt. was now exhibited by Samuel Warner the 2nd, Adms., who made oath that sd. invt. contained all the estate that he knew of, which belonged to sd. estate, since he took Adms. Also he exhibited an account of debts due from the estate amounting to the sum of £110-10-04.

Page 7—18 May, 1737: Samuel Warner, Adms. with the will annexed, exhibited a further account of Adms. of debts due, amounting to the sum of £100-07-00.

Page 15—4 October, 1737: Samuel Warner, Adms. with the will annexed, may sell land to procure the sum of £66-05-08.

Page 42—23 February, 1738-9: Daniel Warner, son of Lt. Robert Warner, chose Jacob Cornwell the 2nd to be his guardian. Recog., £300. This Court appoint Samuel Warner to be guardian to Mary Warner, a minor, 6 years of age. Recog., £300. Stephen Warner, age 16 years, and Joseph Warner, age 14 years, sons of Robert Warner, chose Samuel Warner to be their guardian. Recog., £600. Cert: *Jabez Hamlin, J. P.*

Page 43—8 March, 1738-9: Samuel Warner, Adms., exhibits an account of the sale of lands to Lt. John Bacon of Middletown.

Page 44—8 March, 1738-9: Samuel Warner, Adms., moves to this Court for a dist. of the estate according to the will: Whereupon this Court appoint Lt. John Bacon, Seth Wetmore and William Rockwell, of Middletown, distributors.

Dist. File: 29 March, 1739: To Robert Warner, eldest son, £332-12-11; to Daniel Warner, 2nd son; to Stephen Warner, 3rd son; to Joseph Warner, youngest son; and to Mary Warner, only daughter, to each, £166-06-03½. By Seth Wetmore, William Rockwell and John Bacon. Report accepted.

Page 206.

Warner, Samuel, Middletown.   Invt. £440-03-09. Taken 8 June, 1732, by Joseph Rockwell, Edward Foster and Samuel Hall.
Court Record, Page 72—27 June, 1732: Adms. to Susannah Warner, widow.

Page 9-10-11.

Warner, Seth, Middletown. Invt. £529-11-10. Taken 28 November, 1729, by John Collins and Joseph Rockwell. Will dated 8th July, 1729.
I, Seth Warner of Middletown, do make this my last will and testament: I give to my brother Robert Warner the eastern end of my lott at Three-Mile Hill, so far westward as the west side of the small swamp that lies southward of the Burnt Swamp. And the remainder of my lands there westward in the sd. lott I give to my brother Samuel Warner and my sister Mary Whitmore to be equally divided between them. And I give to my brother Robert Warner the whole of my right and title to and in the homestead and land in the lott whereon my brother Robert now dwells, that is to say, my reversion right in sd. land, and also my reversion right in the pasture land so called, and also my right that I had or have in Wongum lands, and my whole right in all other lands whether divided or undivided. All which I give to my brother Robert Warner. I give to my brother Samuel Warner all my wearing apparrell. I give to my brother Robert Warner the whole of my stock of creatures, both horse kind and neat cattle, also my tools of what name soever, he paying to my sister Mary 20 shillings money. I also give to my brother Robert Warner my chest and my saddle. I give to my dearly beloved friend Phebe Hubbard £35 current money, the whole £35 to be paid within three years after my decease. I do hereby appoint my brother Robert Warner executor.

Witness: *Abel Tryon,*   SETH WARNER, LS.
John Brown, Joseph Rockwell.

Court Record, Page 5—4 November, 1729: Will exhibited.

Waters, Elizabeth. Court Record, Page 50—7 September, 1731: Gideon Waters of Hebron to be guardian to his daughter Elizabeth Waters, one and one-half years old. Recog., £100.

Page 309-345.

Watson, Nathaniel, Windsor. Invt. £441-12-08. Taken 1st October, 1733, by James Enos, Timothy Loomis and William Thrall. Land belonging to sd. estate in Harwinton was not apprised.

Court Record, Page 98—2 October, 1733: Adms. granted to Nathaniel Loomis of Windsor, brother-in-law to the decd. Recog., £400, with Samuel Stoughton of Windsor.

Page 103—1st January, 1733: Nathaniel Loomis, Adms., exhibits an account of his Adms., and he reports the estate insolvent. This Court appoint Sergt. James Enno and Lt. Roger Newbery, of Windsor, commissioners.

Page 13 (Vol. XII) October, 1734: This Court direct Nathaniel Loomis, Adms., per act of the General Assembly and by advice of the Court of Probate, to sell a right of land in Harwinton and some in Windsor, to procure the sum of £132-05-00 and charges of sale.

Page 335.

Welles, Samuel, Hartford. Will dated 29 June, 1733: I, Samuel Welles of Hartford, do make this my last will and testament: I give to my wife Ruth Welles the use of 1-2 of my dwelling house and barn, and 1-2 of my improved land, including what I have given by deed to my daughter Sarah Welles. I do give unto my wife 1-3 part of all my moveable estate properly belonging within my dwelling house, and 1-3 of all my moveable estate whatsoever, and 1-2 of my negro man called Jack, to be her own, to her, her heirs and assigns forever. I also give unto my wife 50 acres of upland forever. I give to my son Samuel Welles, he paying such legacies as are hereafter expressed and my just debts out of my estate, all my estate, both real and personal, except what is in this my last will and testament otherwise disposed of, or shall be in my lifetime, to be to him sd. Samuel Welles, his heirs and assigns forever. I hereby give unto my sd. son the priviledge of fruit enough in my orchard for makeing 10 barrells of syder, on each other year when the orchard bears most fruit, notwithstanding the improvement given to my wife and daughter Sarah. I give unto my daughter Sarah Welles the use and improvement of 1-2 of my dwelling house and barn and 1-2 of my improved upland on the west side of the country road, with what is included in my deed of gift to her, during the time she shall remain unmarried. And if she marry, to have the improvement thereof six years after marriage, and no longer. I hereby give unto her the use of my improved lands eastward of the country road, to make up with what I have given her by deed of gift; also three acres of my meadow lott lying in Hockanum meadow, so long as she shall live unmarried. I do give unto my daughter Sarah Welles 1-2 of my negro man Jack, and 2-3 of all the moveables belonging within my dwelling house, and 1-3 of all my other moveable estate whatsoever. I give unto my three grandchildren, Samuel Bewell, Thomas Pitkin and Hannah Bewell, to each of them £30 money. I give unto my grandson Welles Ely, if he shall live to the age of 21 years, 1-2 of my right in the western land which was given to the Towns of Hartford and

Windsor. I appoint my wife Ruth Welles and son Samuel Welles executors.

Witness: *Joseph Hollister,*   SAMUEL WELLES, LS.
Joseph Pitkin, John Risley, Jr.

Court Record, Page 99—6 November, 1733: Will exhibited. Proven.

Page 338.

West, Benjamin, Middletown. Invt. £103-19-00. Taken 9 January, 1733-4, by Daniel Prior, Francis Wetmore and George Hubbard.

Court Record, Page 104—5 February, 1733-4: Adms. granted to Hannah West, widow, who gave bond with Lemuel Lee of Middletown. Abigail West, a minor daughter, chose her mother Hannah West to be her guardian. Recog., £50.

Page 14 (Vol. XII) 3 December, 1734: Hannah West, Adms., exhibited an account of her Adms., which is accepted by the Court.

Page 117.

West, Francis, Tolland. Will dated 9 April, 1731: I, Francis West of Tolland, in the County of Hartford, do make this my last will and testament: I give to my wife Mercy all my moveable estate, both within doors and without doors, reserving to my son Amasa West all my wooden and iron tackling for teaming, ordering my wife to pay out of this my estate £15 in bills of credit to my granddaughter Zurvia Wales when she come to the age of 18 years, which I give to her as her mother's portion of my estate, and also to pay to my granddaughter Susannah Wales £15 in bills of credit. Also I give to my wife Mercy 1-3 part of my homestead farm whereon I now live, with 1-3 of the house, during the time of her life. To my son Samuel West I have already given him his portion by deed of land on record. Also, to my son Joseph West I have already given him his portion by deed of land on record. Also to my son Zebulon West I have already given him his portion by deed of land on record. To my son Peletiah West I have already secured him his portion by bond given him from mv son Amasa West bearing date with these presents. I give to my son Amasa West 1-2 of my homestead farm whereon I now live, with the house and barn, reserving to my wife 1-3 part as aforesd., which farm is bounded on the north of land I once gave to my son Amasa West and on the west by Scongamock River, lving part in Tolland and part in Coventry, to him my sd. son Amasa West, his heirs and assigns forever, willing him to pay to my granddaughter Jerusha Wales £20 in bills of credit when she comes to the age of 18 years, which I give to her as her part of her mother's portion. I give to my son Christopher West 1-2 of my farm. I give all my wearing apparrell and books to my six sons, to be equally divided between them, reserving my Great Bible, which I give to my son Samuel West. I give to my son Christopher West one whole right in the undivided land in Tolland, and also one right in the Cedar Swamp in Tolland. I give to my son Peletiah one whole right in the undivided land in Tolland, and also one right in the Cedar Swamp. I appoint my wife and my son Amasa West executors.

Witness: *John Crane, Jr.,*   FRANCIS WEST, LS.
John Poalk, Samuel West.

Court Record, Page 47—4 June, 1731: Will exhibited by Mercy West.

Page 2-3.

Wetmore, Sergt. Joseph, Middletown. Invt. £879-02-10. Taken 1st August, 1729, by John Warner, Samuel Gipson and William Whitmore.

Court Record, Page 1—5 July, 1729,: Adms. granted to Mrs. Mary Wetmore and Francis Wetmore.

Page 34—5 January, 1730: Hannah Wetmore, a minor daughter of Joseph Wetmore, with her mother's consent chose her uncle Francis Wetmore to be her guardian. Recog., £50.

Page 71—6 June, 1732: Joseph Wetmore and Abigail, both 20 years of age, chose their uncle Francis Wetmore to be their guardian. Recog., £100.

Page 5 (Vol. XIII) 12 April, 1737: Seth Whitmore, age 20 years, chose Joseph Savage to be his guardian, and also to be guardian to Francis Whitmore, 11 years of age. Recog., £400.

Page 6—12 April, 1737: Martha Whitmore, age 17 years, chose her brother Joseph Whitmore to be her guardian, also to be guardian to Samuel Whitmore, both sons of Joseph Whitmore decd.

Page 117 (Probate Side): We, the subscribers, being desired and impowered by Joseph Whitmore and the rest of the heirs of Joseph Whitmore and Mary his wife, late of Middletown decd., to divide the estates of our sd. father and mother, have done the same this 22 February, 1737-8, in the following form, viz.:

	£ s d
To Joseph Whitmore, eldest son,	270-18-08
To Seth Whitmore, 2nd son,	100-07-06
To Samuel Whitmore, 3rd son,	100-07-06
To Francis Whitmore, 4th son,	100-07-06
To Abigail Clark, eldest daughter,	100-07-06
To Hannah Whitmore, 2nd daughter,	100-07-06
To Martha Whitmore, 3rd daughter,	100-07-06

Agreement exhibited in Court by Joseph Whitmore and William Rockwell, 22 February, 1738-9. Accepted.

Court Record, Page 42—23 February, 1738-9: Martha Whitmore, age 19 years, chose Joseph Savage of Middletown to be her guardian. Recog., £300. Samuel Whitmore, age 14 years chose Seth Whitmore to be his guardian. Recog., £300.

Page 99.

Wetmore, Margaret (alias Gaylord), late of Middletown decd. Invt. £19-19-09. Taken 10 March, 1730-1, by Israhiah Wetmore, Joseph Southmayd and Joseph Rockwell.
Court Record, Page 38—12 February, 1730-1: Adms. to Seth Wetmore.

Page 4-5-6.

Whaples, John, Wethersfield. Invt. £301-06-08. Taken 2 July, 1729, by John Camp and Josiah Willard. Will dated 11 July, 1728.
I, John Whaples of Wethersfield, do make this my last will and testament: I give to Sarah, my wife, my house, barn and homelott until my son Reuben comes to be 21 years of age, and after to have 1-2 of my house, barn and homestead during life. I give to my wife one yoke of oxen, one horse and a cowe to dispose of as she thinks best, and the use of the team tackling during her life. I give to my wife the choice of my beds and furniture belonging to it. My will is that my son Reuben shall have the whole of my homelott after the death of my wife, with the buildings. I give to my son Jonathan Whaples, in addition to what I have already given him by deed of gift, 5 shillings. I give to my son Jacob Whaples the remainder of my lott on the Plain adjoining Jonathan Whaples, west on Ephraim Whaples, he paying £10 current money of this Colony or bills of credit (£6 to my daughter Sarah Whaples, £2 to Marah Whaples, and £2 to Lois Whaples). I make my sons Jonathan Whaples and Jacob Whaples executors. I give to my son Reuben my gunn. And my will is that the remainder of my moveable estate be equally divided amongst my 3 daughters above named.
Witness: *John Camp,*   JOHN WHAPLES, LS.
David Griswold.

Court Record, Page 2—2 August, 1729: Will exhibited and proven.

Invt. in Vol. XII, Page 249.

Whaples, Thomas, Glastonbury. Invt. £166-08-11. Taken 30 November, 1733, by Robert Loveland, Jr., and Alexander Brewer.
Court Record, Page 107—5 March, 1733-4: Adms. granted to Elizabeth Whaples, widow, who recog. with her father, James Hannison of Hartford.

Page 10 (Vol. XII) 19 September, 1734: Elizabeth Whaples, widow, is appointed guardian to her son Joseph Whaples, age 6 years, and Gideon Henderson of Hartford is appointed guardian to Samuel Whaples, age 4 years, sons of the decd. Recog., £50.

Page 11 (Vol. XIII) 13 June, 1737: This Court do appoint Elizabeth Whaples to be guardian to Samuel Whaples, 7 years of age. Recog., £50.

Page 291, 344.

White, Ebenezer, Hebron. Invt. £108-12-10. Taken by Ebenezer Wilcock and Matthew Ford. Will dated 14 May, 1733.

I, Ebenezer White of Hebron, in the County of Hartford, do make this my last will and testament: I give to Hannah, my wife, all my lands lying and being in the Township of Middlebury, in the County of Plymouth and Province of Massachusetts Bay, to be at her own dispose forever. Likewise I give to Hannah, my wife, the use and improvement of my dwelling house, together with the improvement of all my lands in Hebron, during her natural life, unless she shall change her condition by marriage, then my will is that each of my sons enjoy and possess the same according to this my last will. I give to Obadiah, my son, my dwelling house with 18 acres of land adjoining thereto. I give and bequeath unto my two sons, Ebenezer and Joseph, all the rest of my land within the bounds of Hebron, to be equally divided between them. I give unto Rebeckah, my daughter, £5, to be paid to her out of my moveable estate, at 21 years of age. Having given the principal part of my estate to my wife, I leave the care of my three youngest daughters, Hannah, Cheanna and Mehetabell, with her, to provide for them as God shall enable her. I appoint Hannah, my wife, only and sole executrix.

Witness: *Ebenezer Wilcock,*   EBENEZER WHITE, LS.
Samuel Filer, Matthew Ford.

Court Record, Page 94—3 July, 1733: Will exhibited by the executrix.

Page 27 (Vol. XII) 17 May, 1735: Rebeckah White, age 16 years, and Hannah White, age 14 years, children of Ebenezer White, chose Capt. Hezekiah Gaylord to be their guardian.

Page 41—11 March, 1735-6: Account of Adms. accepted.

Page 167.

White, Mary, widow of Joseph White, Middletown.

Middletown, August 5th, 1730: We whose names are underwritten were present at the house of the Widow Mary White, relict of Joseph White, late of Middletown decd., and did hear her say that after her decease she gave to her son Ebenezer £3 in money that she had lent him, and her right in the bay horse between them. And she gave her daughter Martha Stow a Bible, and the rest of her estate she gave equally to her four daughters after her daughter Jerusha had had £5. And desired us to bear witness of it.   ELIZABETH WHITE.

HUGH WHITE.

Mr. Hugh White and Elizabeth White, both of Middletown, made oath to the above written: That Mrs. Mary White, their aunt, while she lay sick, desired them to be witnesses to the above, which this 31st day of August they gave oath to before me.   *Giles Hall, J. P.*

Court Record, Page 27—1st September, 1730: Mrs. Mary White did make a verbal will, now exhibited in Court by Thomas Stow and John Bacon, wherein she gave away all her estate, so that there is nothing left to pay the debts. The sd. Thomas Stow and John Bacon recog. in £100 that they will pay all the debts, whereby the will is proven.

Page 61, 71.

White, Martha, Middletown. Invt. £35-04-03. Taken 22 June, 1730, by John Warner and Samuel Gipson, which includes 2 bonds of £10 each in the hands of Solomon and Daniel Coit of New London.

Susannah White, the wife of Ensign Daniel White of Middletown, and her daughter, Ruth Stone of Gilford, testifyeth that about February, 1729-30, at the house of sd. Ensign White, proposed to her mother (Mrs. Martha White, widow) to give to her daughter Esther her kettle, her bed, one pillow, two blankets and her curtains. The sd. widow, her mother, replyed: "She may have them if she will. I do desire it." Further saith not.

Test: before John Hamlin, J. P.

Court Record, Page 21—2 June, 1730: Adms. to Daniel White and Samuel Stow.

Page 48—6 July, 1731: Adms. account accepted and *Quietus Est.* granted.

Page 59.

Wickham, Thomas, Wethersfield. Died 30 April, 1730. Invt. £61-06-02. Taken by Martin Kellogg and Joseph Woodhouse.

Court Record, Page 22—2 June, 1730: Adms. to Gideon Wickham of Southold, in the Province of New York, on the Island of Nassau.

Page 23—16 June, 1730: Gideon Wickham, Adms., exhibits account which was accepted, and he was discharged from his bond and Adms. granted to Benjamin Deming of Wethersfield.

Page 332.

Wilcox, Sergt. William, Simsbury. Died 22 March, 1733. Invt. £438-09-07. Taken 19 April, 1733, by Samuel Pettebone, William Alderman and Joseph Case, Jr. The legatees of the estate of the decd. are his wife Elizabeth and his sons: William, 30 years, Azariah 27, Amos 24, Daniel 16; and his daughters: Elizabeth, 32, and Mary, 20 years of age. Will dated 19 March, 1732-3.

I, William Wilcox of Simsbury, do make this my last will and testament: Imprimis. For the love that I bear to my dear wife Elizabeth I give to her the improvement of 1-2 of my dwelling house, 1-2 of my barn, and 1-3 part of my orchard, and 1-3 part of the homelott, during her natural life; and also 1-3 part of my moveable estate forever, after my debts are paid out of them. And also my sons shall pay her, if she demand it, the sum of £3 annually during life, to be paid in equal shares by William, Azariah, Amos and Daniel. To my son William, my eldest son, I give, over and above an equal share of my real estate, all that charge that I have been at in helping him to build his house. I give and confirm to my sons, William, Azariah and Amos, what I have already given them by deed of gift, only it is to be recorded to them as part of their shares and part of their portions hereafter mentioned according to its value in sd. deed. I give to my sons William and Azariah one acre of land (where they choose to take it) in my meadow lott in Farmingtown bounds. I give all my lands to my sons, William, Azariah, Amos and Daniel, except as before is expressed, to hold in equal shares. But I order that my son Amos shall hold, sole seized, the 1-2 of a grant of land I have in a place called the Great Swamp, and also my son Daniel shall hold, sole seized, the homestead and ye lott and orchard that I had of my father. And if the value of them should exceed his portion, or 4th part, he shall pay his brothers the amount of sd. excess equally. I order my sons William, Azariah and Amos to pay to my son Daniel, when he comes of age, the sum of £6, or so much as the 1-2 of that grant of land at ye Great Swamp shall be prised, at the sd. Daniel's election. I give to my two daughters, Elizabeth and Mary, with what they have already had, the sum of £40 money to each of them, to be paid out of the moveable estate; or, if not sufficient, shall be paid by my four sons equally. I appoint my wife Elizabeth and my son William executors.

Witness: *Timothy Woodbridge,*   WILLIAM WILCOX, LS.
Samuel Pettibone, Samuel Humphrey, 2nd.

Court Record, Page 89—1st May, 1733: Will proven. Daniel Wilcox, a minor, chose his mother Elizabeth Wilcox to be his guardian.

Page 306.

Winchell, John, Windsor. Invt. £110-00-00. Taken 5 July, 1733, by Jonathan Stiles and Samuel Stoughton.

Court Record, Page 98—2 October, 1733: Adms. granted to Martha Winchell, widow, who recog. in £400 with Jonathan Stiles.

Page 44 (Vol. XII) 4 May, 1736: A discharge was now exhibited in Court by Martha Winchell under the hands and seals of John Winchell, Samuel Winchell, Simon Chapman, Silence Chapman and Hannah Winchell, heirs to the estate, who acknowledge the receipt of their portions of the estate of John Winchell, their father, deceased.

Page 45—19 May, 1736: Ebenezer Winchell, age 14 years, son of John Winchell, late decd., chose John Stoughton of Windsor to be his guardian. Recog., £100.

Page 68.

Wolcott, Anna, Wethersfield. Invt. £105-17-10. Taken 30 June, 1730, by Samuel Curtis and Joseph Woodhouse. She was 3rd daughter of Mr. George Wolcott, late of Wethersfield decd.

Court Record, Page 24—7 July, 1730: Adms. to Mrs. Elizabeth Wolcott.

Page 48—6 July, 1731: Account exhibited.

Page 237.

Wolcott, Simon, Windsor. Invt. £196-03-09. Taken 27 November, 1732, by Hezekiah Porter and Joshua Loomis.

Court Record, Page 78—5 December, 1732: Adms. granted to Simon and James Wolcott, sons of the decd., who, with John Loomis, recog. in £300.

Page 81—6 February, 1732-3: An agreement to settle the estate of Symon Wolcott was exhibited in Court by the heirs of that estate under their hands and seals, and they acknowledged sd. agreement to be their free act and deed, which agreement is to be recorded in Windsor Town Book of Records.

Wood, John. Court Record, Page 30—3 December, 1730: John Curtis to be guardian to John Wood, a minor, 2 years of age, his mother consenting. Recog., £50.

Page 216.

Woodbridge, Rev. Timothy, Hartford. Invt. £756-18-09. Taken 10 October, 1732, by Cyprian Nichols and Joseph Skinner. Will dated 1st April, 1732.

I, Timothy Woodbridge, of Hartford, do make this my last will and testament: I give to my wife, Abigail Woodbridge, my team and furniture belonging thereunto, and the improvement of John Wobbin during the time he is bound to serve me at my present rates, and the provisions that are now in the house, and my negro girle named Lydia, desireing, if my wife should incline to it, that my daughter Susannah Treat may have said negro girle, paying a reasonable price for her. And whereas, I have disposed of the principal part of my real estate to my three sons by deeds of gift, my mind and will is that the remainder of my estate, both real and personal, shall be disposed of in the following manner: Whereas, I have given to my daughter Mary Pitkin that I account to the value of £105 money, I give her £5 more out of my real estate. I give to my daughters Ruth Pierson and Susannah Treat, with what each of them have already received, so much out of my estate as to make up the value of £110 money to each of them. And whereas, my son Theodore is under tuition at Yale College, I give £100 out of my estate to defray the charge of his education there. I do appoint my son Timothy Woodbridge sole executor of this my last will and testament, and do hereby authorize and impower my executor to make sale of my farm at Stafford and my interest in the western lands, or any part thereof, to enable him, with my moveable estate, to pay my just debts and legacies herein given. And what estate shall remain after my just debts and legacies are paid, shall be divided to and amongst my children, viz: to my three sons, Timothy, Ashbell and Theodore, and to my three daughters, Mary, Ruth and Susannah, in equal proportion.

Witness: *Hezekiah Wyllys,*   TIMOTHY WOODBRIDGE, LS.
Samuel Woodbridge, Cyprian Nichols.

Court Record, Page 74—2 September, 1732: Will exhibited by the executor, Rev. Timothy Woodbridge of Simsbury.

Page 94—3 July, 1733: Theodore Woodbridge, son of Rev. Timothy Woodbridge, chose his mother Abigail Woodbridge to be his guardian. Recog., £300.

Page 183.

Woodruff, Sergt. Joseph, Farmington (son to John Woodruff). Invt. £1002-09-07. Taken 24 March, 1732, by Joseph Hawley, Daniel Judd and John Merrells. Will dated 16 January, 1729-30.

I, Joseph Woodruff of Farmingtown, son of John Woodruff, do make this my last will and testament: Unto my wife Elizabeth Woodruff, to her, her heirs and assigns forever, I give one certain parcel of land in Farmingtown containing 10 acres more or less, and also 1-3 part of all my personal estate. And further, I give her the use, improvement and profit of my homestead where I now live, with all the buildings thereon standing, and all other of my lands lying on the east side of the river in sd. Farmingtown. This during her widowhood and bearing of my name. Unto my son Josiah Woodruff I give the 1-2 part of my team and team tackling. Unto my five sons, viz., Josiah Woodruff, Jonathan

Woodruff, Joseph Woodruff, Zebulon Woodruff and Judah Woodruff, to them and their heirs forever, in equal proportions between them, I give all my real estate of houseing and lands, whatsoever and wheresoever it may be found, they not to injoy that part thereof willed to their mother for her use until the term therein set be expired, and the 10 acres given her for her own is excepted. Unto my daughter Hannah Clark, besides what I have already given her, I give her 30 shillings. Unto my three daughters, viz., Lydia Woodruff, Phebe Woodruff and Abigail Woodruff, I give to each of them of my personal estate to the value of £30 as current money. And all the residue and remainder of my personal estate, whatsoever and wheresoever, not before disposed of, I give unto my three youngest daughters in equal proportions between them. I appoint my wife Elizabeth Woodruff and Josiah Woodruff executors.

Witness: *John Hooker, Sen.*,   JOSEPH WOODRUFF, LS.
Joseph Hooker, Roger Hooker.

Court Record, Page 66—2 April, 1732: Will exhibited by Elizabeth Woodruff and Josiah Woodruff, executors named in the will. Josiah Woodruff refused the trust. Jonathan, Joseph and Zebulon Woodruff, minor children of Joseph Woodruff, chose their mother Elizabeth Woodruff to be their guardian, and she was also appointed guardian to Abigail and Judah, all children of the sd. decd. Recog., £300.

Page 243.

Woodruff, Ensign Samuel, Farmington. Invt. £2649-13-02. Taken 26 December, 1732, by Isaac Cowles, Daniel Judd and Anthony Judd. Will dated 8 February, 1730-1.

The last will and testament of Samuel Woodruff is as follows: I give to my wife Mary Woodruff, besides her thirds, the use of 1-3 part of my house, orchard and barn. Also, I give to my wife £10 in money besides her thirds in the moveables. I give to my eldest son, Ezekiel Woodruff, his heirs and assigns forever, my new house and all the nails, boards and logs that I have prepared for the same; also 100 acres of land where the house standeth, to be taken on the north side of the lott, extending eastward to the west end at a place where the old bars were; but if the lott should be moved west, then to extend west accordingly; also my lott of land in the first tier in the west division, which was my grandfather Woodruff's lott firstly; also my great Bible. I give and bequeath to my son James Woodruff my house and homestead, with the buildings thereon, and all the remainder of my lott at Burnt Hill. I give unto my son Robert Woodruff my lott of land at the Green Swamp by David Curtice, and also all my right in ye lott that was my father Judd's in the division of land against Hartford, and also 1-4 part of the lott that was Mr. Anthony Howkins's in sd. division. I give unto my son Samuel Woodruff my lott in the southward division, which lott was firstly John

Warner's, Sen., and also the whole of my land lying in that division of land against Waterbury. I give unto my daughter Mary Woodruff my lott of land against Hartford, that lott that was firstly John Scovell's, and also 3-4 part of that lott which was firstly John Higginson's in the Shuttle Meadow division. I give unto my daughter Abigail my lott of land in the division against Hartford, that lott that was firstly Jonathan Smith's, and also 1-4 part of my grandfather Woodruff's lott in Shuttle Meadow division. I give unto my daughter Sarah Woodruff my lott of land lying in the north division on the west side of the river at Nod, that lott that was firstly Thomas Newell's. I give unto each of my daughters so much of the remainder of my estate as to make them, with what I have given them in lands, worth the sum of £150 to each of them. The remainder of my estate, both personal and real, I give unto my sons to be equally divided between them. I appoint my wife Mary Woodruff and my loving son Ezekiel Woodruff executors.

Witness: *John Hart,*   SAMUEL WOODRUFF.
Matthew Woodruff, Jr., Samuel North.

Court Record, Page 82—6 February, 1732-3: Will now exhibited by the executors. Abigail Woodruff, a minor, 14 years of age, chose her mother Mary Woodruff to be her guardian. The widow was also appointed guardian to Samuel Woodruff, age 10 years, and Sarah Woodruff, age 7 years, children of the sd. decd.

Page 207.

Wright, Capt. Samuel, Wethersfield. Invt. £2222-07-02. Taken 28 June, 1732, by Daniel Wright and Jonathan Belding.

Court Record, Page 72—27 June, 1732: Adms. granted to Abigail Wright, the widow.

Page 93—3 July, 1733: Abigail Wright, Adms., exhibited an account of her Adms., which is accepted.

Page 96 (Vol. XIII) 13 August, 1741: Abigail Wright (alias Dickinson), Adms., having finished her account, exhibits it as followeth:

	£ s d
Paid in debts and charges the sum of	139-05-02
Inventory of the moveable estate,	1573-16-15
There remains for distribution to the widow and children,	1434-11-03
To Abigail Wright, alias Dickinson,	478-03-09
To Samuel, eldest son,	318-15-10
To Abigail, to Rebeckah, to Lucy and Moses Wright, to each,	159-07-11

Noadiah Dickinson, in right of his wife Abigail, moves this Court that her right of dowry may be set out to her. This Court appoint Capt. Eleazer Goodrich, Lt. Jonathan Belding and Benjamin Stilman to set out to the sd. Abigail Dickinson her 1-3 part of the houseing and lands of her deceased husband's estate. Moses Wright, age 10 years, son of Capt.

Samuel Wright, chose Noadiah Dickinson to be his guardian. Recog., £200.

Page 95—7 July, 1741: Samuel Wright, age 19 years, chose Jonathan Goodrich to be his guardian. Recog., £500. Rebeckah Wright, age 14 years, chose her father-in-law Noadiah Dickinson to be her guardian. Recog., £500. Noadiah Dickinson, guardian to Moses Wright, having resigned, this Court appoint the sd. *Moses** Wright to be guardian to sd. minor, the sd. Moses Wright. Recog., £500. Abigail Wright, age 17 years, chose Ebenezer Wright to be her guardian. Allowed.

Page 1 (Vol. XIV) 6 April, 1742: Timothy Wright of Wethersfield, who was guardian to Lucy Wright, a minor daughter of Samuel Wright, now resigns the trust, whereupon sd. minor made choice of Rev. Daniel Fuller to be her guardian. Recog., £500.

Page 7—9 June, 1742: A return of the widow's dowry was exhibited in Court under the hands of Eleazer Goodrich, Jonathan Belding and Benjamin Stilman. Accepted.

Page 70.

Wyott, Israel, Colchester. Invt. £1121-05-07. Taken 2 May, 1729, by William Roberts and Nathaniel Foote. An addition to the invt. of a mare, a colt, a broad ax, a hand-saw, drawing knife and several other small things not yet apprised. Taken by Ephraim Welles, John Skinner and Isaac Jones.

Court Record, Page 4—4 November, 1729: Will not proven (not found on file or record). Adms. granted to Sarah Wyott, the widow, who recognized with Noah Welles. Mary Wyott, a minor daughter of Israel Wyott, chose her mother, Mrs. Sarah Wyott, to be her guardian.

*Note: A recorder's error is apparent in the appointment by the Court of a guardian to Moses Wright after the refusal or resignation of his father-in-law Noadiah Dickinson. Probably Timothy Wright was appointed. Moses the minor could not be guardian to himself.

PROBATE RECORDS.

VOLUME XII.

1732 to 1737.

Page 380.

Ackley, Sergt. John, East Haddam. Died 25 August, 1736. Invt. £383-04-06. Taken by Henry Chapman, Jeremiah Gates and Thomas Cone.

Court Record, Page 50—22 September, 1736: Adms. to John Ackley, son of the decd., who gave bond with Bartholomew Foster of Wallingford for £500.

Page 52—2 November, 1736: Exhibit of inventory.

Page 370.

Andrews, John, Middletown. Invt. £1687-07-08. Taken 1st September, 1736, by John Sage, Solomon Adkins and Joseph Rockwell. Will dated 31 July, 1736.

I, John Andrews of Middletown, doe make this my last will and testament: I give unto Rachel, my wife, 1-3 part of my real estate during her natural life, and 1-3 part of all my personal estate to be at her own dispose. I give to my son Thomas Andrews £10, which is his full portion of my estate with what I have already given him. I give to my daughter Abigail Porter £24-13-00 added to what I have already given her, which makes the sum of £60. I give unto my daughter Hannah Johnson £22-11-00. I give to my daughter Sarah Gillum £28-18. I give to my daughter Mary Tryon £28—which makes to each the sum of £60. I give to my two sons, Joseph and Benjamin, 2-3 of all my real estate for their present improvement, and 2-3 of all my personal estate also; and the other third of my real estate to them after their mother's decease, equally to be divided between them, accounting £130 which I have already given to Joseph and £120 which I have already given to Benjamin. And my will is my son Benjamin shall have the dwelling house that I built for my son Samuel, and half an acre of land adjoining thereto, as part of his portion. I give to my two daughters, Jane and Elizabeth, to each £60. I give to my granddaughters, Lois and Lucia (the daughters of my son Samuel Andrews deceased), to each of them £70. I ordain my two sons, Joseph and Benjamin, executors.

Witness: *Thomas Johnson, Jr.,*   JOHN ANDREWS, LS.
Samuel Lucas, William Rockwell.

Court Record, Page 50—7 September, 1736: Will proven.

Page 59 (Vol. XIV) 4 June, 1745: Rachel Andrews, widow and relict, moves to this Court that her right of dower in the real estate of the sd. decd. may be set out to her according to the last will and testament of the sd. decd. Whereupon this Court appoint William Rockwell, Robert Johnson and Joseph Johnson to set out to the widow her right of dower by bounds and marks, and make return to this Court.

Page 288-9.

Barnard, Sergt. John, Hartford. Invt. taken 30 January, 1734-5, by William Pratt, Thomas Sanford and Joseph Talcott, Jr. Will dated 30 May, 1732.

I, John Barnard of Hartford, doe make this my last will and testament: I give to my cousin Jonathan Olcott of Hartford a tract of land in Hartford where his dwelling house now is, being part of my house lott, the northwest corner of it, bounded north by the Town Street 14 rods, and west by the Town Street 12 rods, south by my own land 14 rods, and east by my own land 7 rods. I give to my cousin Joseph Olcott all the rest of my land and buildings, and also all my husbandry tools, with 2 yoke of oxen and two horse kind. I give to Sarah, my wife, the use of 1-3 part of my land and buildings during her natural life, and all her goods and estate that was her own before our marriage, one cow and one three-year-old heifer, to her forever. I make Joseph Olcott my executor.

Witness: *Daniel Burr,*   JOHN BARNARD, LS.
Nathaniel Goodwin, Richard Abbe.

Court Record, Page 21—12 February, 1734-5: Will exhibited by Joseph Olcott, executor. Joseph Barnard, a brother of the deceased, objected against the proof and approbation of the will. It was approved, and Joseph Barnard appealed to the Superior Court.

Page 24—1st April, 1735: Sarah Barnard, widow of Sergt. John Barnard, moves this Court to set out her dower. John Marsh, John Skinner and Obadiah Spencer were appointed.

Page 36—13 November, 1735: Report of the dower set out according to the will.

Page 362.

Beckley, Benjamin, Wethersfield. Will dated 28 June, 1728: I, Benjamin Beckley of Wethersfield, think it my duty to make this my last will and testament. I give to my eldest son, John Beckley, the house he now lives in, with 1-2 of all my land. I give to my other son, Benjamin Beckley, the house I now live in, and barn, and the other half of all my land. I give to my daughter Martha Hart, over and above what I have already given her, 5 shillings money. I give to my younger daughters, Miriam and Hannah, all my remaining moveables, to be divided to them equally after the decease of my wife. I give to my wife, during the time she shall continue my widow, one convenient room in my dwelling house and the comfortable and honourable subsistence to be contributed to her (with her own labour) by my sons in equal proportions. And in case my sd. sons shall neglect or refuse, my will is that my sd. wife shall have the improvement of 1-3 part of my lands while she continues my widow. My wife and my sons John and Benjamin to be executors.

Witness: *Nathaniel Burnham,*   BENJAMIN BECKLEY, LS.
Joseph Flower, Henry Hills.

Court Record, Page 46—1st June, 1736: Will proven.

Page 261.

Bidwell, Mary, Middletown. Invt. £22-18-08. Taken 13 September, 1734, by Nathaniel White and Richard Goodrich.

Court Record, Page 9—3 September, 1734: Adms. granted to Hezekiah Sumner of Middletown.

Page 32—2 September, 1735: Hezekiah Sumner, Adms., exhibited an account of his Adms., which is accepted by the Court.

Page 238-9, 251.

Bissell, David, Windsor. Invt. £523-09-08. Taken 8 March, 1733-4, by Job Elsworth, Joseph Phelps and Joshua Loomis.

Court Record, Page 2—1st April, 1734: Adms. granted to Nathaniel Bissell, Jr., and David Bissell, who recog. in £800 with John Burroughs of Windsor.

Bissell, Nathaniel, Windsor. Court Record, Page 40—23 February, 1735-6: Adms. granted to David Bissell, who gave bond with Moses Cook of Hartford.

Page 367.

Blake, Elizabeth, Middletown. Invt. £87-07-06. Taken 23 March, 1736, by Daniel Hall and Stephen Blake. Will dated 4 February, 1735-6.

I, Elizabeth Blake, widow relict of John Blake the 2nd, late of Middletown, do make my last will and testament as follows: What right I have in lands in Woodstock shall be equally divided among my foure sons, viz., Richard, John, Joseph and Freelove. And that my moveable estate shall be equally divided among my fower sons, except one pair of steers 3 years old next spring, which steers I give to my son Freelove besides his equal quarter-part of all my estate whatsoever. I also give unto my son Freelove that gun which I bought with my own money. The reason why I give the above particulars to my son Freelove is because he hath taken care of me and my creatures and wrought for a great part of them. It is my will that what right I have in lands descending to me in right of my father shall be equally divided amongst my four sons. I give to Mary Bevin, who liveth with me, one cow. I appoint my son Richard sole executor.

Witness: *Elizabeth Kent,*   ELIZABETH X BLAKE, LS.
Esther Blake, Joseph Rockwell.

Court Record, Page 47—6 July, 1736: Will exhibited by Richard Blake, executor. Proven.

Invt. in Vol. XIII, Page 19-20.

Blynn, Deliverance, Wethersfield.   Invt. £1256-02-03.   Taken 11 December, 1736, by Nathaniel Stilman, Hezekiah May and John Stilman.

Court Record, Page 53—4 January 1736-7: Adms. granted to Benjamin Stilman of Wethersfield.   Recog., £800, with John Stilman.

Page 47 (Vol. XIII) April, 1739: George Blynn, a minor, 14 years of age, son of Deliverance Blynn, chose his uncle Nathaniel Stilman to be his guardian.   Recog., £200.

Page 348-9.

Booge, Richard, East Haddam.   Invt. £177-16-06.   Taken 6 March, 1733-4, by John Spencer, John Church and Jabez Chapman.   The apprisement of the house, barn, orchard and appurtenances, with the lott of land given by Mr. John Booge to his son Richard Booge, was taken 23 April, 1734, being valued by the apprisers at £400, with right in the undivided lands of £5-03-00.   Total, £405-03-00.   By John Spencer, John Church and Jabez Chapman.

Court Record, Page 1—1st April, 1734: Adms. granted to Joanna Booge, the widow, who recog. in £200 with Jonathan Mark of Lyme.

Page 13—13 November, 1734: John Booge of East Haddam is appointed guardian to Sarah Booge, a minor daughter of Richard Booge decd.   Recog., £100.

Page 385-6-7.

Brainard, William, Jr., Haddam.   Died 18 March, 1736.   Invt.
£636-18-06. Taken 31 March, 1736, by Joseph Arnold, Ebenezer Smith
and Thomas Sheldon. Will dated 4 March, 1735-6.

I, William Brainard, Jr., of Haddam, do make this my last will and
testament: I give unto my wife Esther her dower rights. I give to my
only son Jonathan Brainard and his heirs and assigns forever, my dwelling house, barn, and two acres of land takeing in sd. house and barn, and
1-2 of all my lands, be the same more or fewer acres, besides the sd. two
acres, in consideration that he pay to my three daughters hereinafter mentioned, within one year after he shall arrive to the age of 21 years, 1-2 of
what there shall be wanting of £150 of my personal estate after my debts
are paid and my wife shall have had her thirds out of the sd. personal estate. I give to my three daughters, to Esther, to Prudence, and to Elizabeth, £50 to each. And for one that may be born provision is made in the
will, whether it be a son or a daughter. I make my wife Esther Brainard
and my brother Josiah Brainard executors.

Witness: *Chileab Brainard,*   WILLIAM BRAINARD, JR., LS.
Daniel Bidwell, Hez: Brainard.

Court Record, Page 51—5 October, 1736: Will and inventory exhibited by the executors. Proven.

Page 256.

Brooks, Deacon Thomas, Haddam.   Died 6 April, 1734.   Invt.
taken 28 June, 1734, by Joseph Arnold, Caleb Cone and Thomas Sheldon. Will dated 24 February, 1728-9.

I, Thomas Brooks of Haddam, do make this my last will and testament: I give and bequeath to Susannah, my wife, the use of my dwelling
house, barn and shop, and all that part of land hereinafter given to my
son Jabez as his portion, for and until he shall attain to the age of 21
years if he live so long, or till she shall be married again, which shall happen first. I also give her 1 weaving loom, together with half the tackling
belonging to two looms, and if sd. Jabez arrive at the age aforesd. and she
remain still my widow, I give her the use of one end of my dwelling house
(which she shall choose), viz., two rooms, so long as she shall continue
my widow. I give to my wife ye third part of all my moveable estate forever. As touching my eldest son Thomas, I have already by deed of gift
settled his inheritance upon him, reserving £8 to be paid by him to me or
my order. As to my son Abraham, I have already by deed of gift settled
his inheritance upon him, reserving £9 to be paid by him to me or my order. Item. I give to my son Jabez, and to his heirs and assigns forever,
all my land lying southwestward on his brother Abraham's land, butting
thereon northwesterly, butting northeast partly on the Great River and
partly on land of Capt. James Welles, and butting on land of Capt. Caleb

Cone southeast, he to pay to his only sister Eunice £10 in money at the age of 18 years. I give to my son Joseph all my lands and rights of land, divided and undivided, within the bounds of Haddam, be the same more or less, which is not by me already disposed of, except the sixth division lott laid out upon my list which lyes near Flag Swamp. I give to my daughter Mary, over and above what I have already given and done for her, 20 shillings of money. I give to my other five daughters, viz., Elizabeth, Susannah, Thankfull, Sarah and Eunice, all my moveable estate not hereinbefore disposed of, and also £8 in money to be paid them by their brother Thomas, and £9 in money to be paid them by their brother Abraham. And whereas, two of my sd. daughters, viz., Elizabeth and Susannah, are deceased, I do will and determine that their children, viz., Elizabeth Lester and Susannah Smith, shall have their mother's part of my estate, and that the £17 in money last mentioned be equally divided and paid to my sd. daughters and sd. grandchildren, Mary and Eunice not to have any part thereof, but are hereby exempted. Finally, I do appoint my loving wife Susannah and my loving son Thomas executors.

Witness: *Caleb Cone,*　　　　　　　　　　THOMAS BROOKS, LS.
Caleb Cone, Jr., Elisha Cone.

Court Record, Page 8—6 August, 1734: Will proven.

Page 319-20. Will in Vol. XXII, Page 77.

Brown, Nathaniel, Middletown. Invt. £129-14-05. Taken 15 July, 1735, by John Collins, Joseph Rockwell and Robert Hubbard. Will dated 20 September, 1731.

I, Nathaniel Brown of Middletown, being sicke and weak in body, doe make this my last will and testament: I give to Sarah, my wife, the whole of my household goods and all other moveable estate (as stock of creatures and other utensils of what kind soever), to be for her comfort and at her dispose forever (excepting my gun and sword and amunition, which, if my daughter Sarah Beckwith should have a son and they call him after my name, I give the sd. arms and amunition unto that child). It is my will that my Wongunk land and my lott in the last division of land on the east side of the Connecticut River, which was laid out in the name of Jasper Clemens, and also my 15-acre lott by Capt. Daniel Hall's, each lott shall be made sale of by my executors after named, for the payment of my just debts and funeral charges, and for the procuring of two silver cups, to be marked with the two first letters of my name, and to be of £12 price each of them, the one of which cups I give to the First Church in Middletown, and the other of them I give unto that church in Lyme which my son George Beckwith is now the pastor of. I give unto Sarah, my wife, for her comfort so long as she shall continue my widow, my dwelling house and barn and homestead, and my two acres of Long Meadow and my Boggy Meadow land. I give unto my only daughter Sarah, now the wife of George Beckwith, and to her issue, all other of my lands in Middletown which are not above mentioned, as specified of record, and also all my above-mentioned buildings and lands granted to my wife, when her right therein shall expire. I give to my son George Beckwith and to my daughter Sarah, now his wife, all my right in Lyme, to be wholly at their dispose. I give to my son and daughter above named my griss mill and my right there, they allowing and paying to my wife the 1-6 part of their income from time to time therefrom for her support and comfort, excepting my executors shall see cause to sell sd. mill and keep the lands above mentioned for sale, or any parts of sd. lands, then the sd. lands to be theirs. I give to my daughter and son all my rights in Middletown. I constitute my wife and George Beckwith and Sarah his wife my executors.

Witness: *Giles Hall,*   NATHANIEL BROWN, LS.
Joseph Rockwell, Joseph Southmayd.

Page 320 (Probate Side, Vol. XII): An agreement, dated 14 July, 1735, made by and between Mrs. Sarah Brown of Middletown, widow and relict of Mr. Nathaniel Brown decd., and the Rev. Mr. George Beckwith of Lyme, in the County of New London, and with Sarah his wife, daughter of them the aforesd. Nathaniel and Sarah Brown. It is mutually agreed by the parties aforesd. that the sd. Sarah Brown shall have, hold and injoy to her, her heirs and assigns forever, all the personal or moveable estate which Mr. Nathaniel Brown was possessed of at the time of his death, excepting only ye gun and sword and amunition accutrements for war, with the use and improvement of the dwelling house, barn and homested, his 2 acres of Long Meadow and the Boggy Meadow land, during the terme that sd. Sarah Brown remains a widow. It is further agreed that Adms. of the estate shall be granted to the Rev. George Beckwith, and that after paying all just debts the remainder and residuary of the estate of sd. Nathaniel Brown, with the reversion thereof, be and remain unto her the sd. Sarah Beckwith, her heirs and assigns forever, so that neither the sd. Sarah Brown nor any other from or by her shall have any rights whatsoever in the residuary and remainder of the estate aforesd. under colour of dowry or priviledge of thirds, but that she and they and each of them shall be secluded and barred forever.

SARAH BROWN, LS.
GEORGE BECKWITH, LS.
SARAH BECKWITH, LS.

Court Record, Page 30—14 July, 1735: Adms. granted to George Beckwith of Lyme, who recog. with John Brown of Middletown. An agreement for the settlement of the estate was now exhibited in Court and accepted. Ordered recorded and kept on file.

Page 39 (Vol. XXII) 23 March, 1775: At a Court of Probates, held at Hartford, the last will and testament of Nathaniel Brown of Middletown, who died about the year 1731, was exhibited by Nathaniel Brown Beckwith, son of the sd. George Beckwith of Lyme, who reported

146   PROBATE RECORDS.   VOL. XII,

that sd. will had for some time been secreted. Sd. will being proved by
the witnesses thereto, taken by *John Hamlin, J. P.*, is by this Court approved and ordered to be recorded and kept on file.

Page 254.

Buck, Benjamin, Farmington. Invt. £53-05-10. Taken 6 June,
1734, by Isaac Cowles and William Porter.
Court Record, Page 5—4 June, 1734: Adms. granted to John Rue,
who recog. in £200 with Stephen Buck.
Page 7—2 July, 1734: The Adms. reports the estate insolvent, and
this Court orders that necessaries be set out to Mary Buck, the widow.
Page 11—8 October, 1734: John Rue, Adms., exhibits an account
of his Adms. Accepted.
Page 26—6 May, 1735: By an act of the General Assembly, this
Court direct the Adms. to sell land at vandue to the value of £38-10-00.
Page 30—1st July, 1735: A return of the sale of land by John Rue,
Adms. Accepted.

Buck, Thomas. Court Record, Page 28—3 June, 1735: Thomas
Buck, a minor, age 16 years, chose John Benjamin of Hartford to be his
guardian. Recognized in £100.

Page 268.

Buell, Jonathan, Simsbury. Invt. £335-08-09. Taken 8 November,
1734, by Joseph Humphrey, Joseph Hoskins and Andrew Robe.
Court Record, Page 14—19 November, 1734: Adms. to Abigail
Buell, widow. Recog., £300, with Jonah Case.

Page 269.

Buell, William, Simsbury. Invt. £565-01-09. Taken 30 October,
1734, by Joseph Humphrey and Andrew Robe. Will dated 9 September,
1734.
I, William Buell of Simsbury, see cause to make this my last will
and testament: I give unto my brother Jonathan Buell my house and
homelott with my barn and lott of land on the west side of the street
where the barn standeth, with all my lands in Hop Meadow, and with
all my other outlands that I shall die possessed of, to him and his heirs
and assigns forever. I give to my brother Jonathan my horse, mare and
colt, one yoke of oxen, two calves, two cows, and my cart and plow, and
all my team tackling, corn on the ground and hay in the barn, with all

my other moveable estate. Only I give to my sister Miriam Stephens one cow and calf. I also give unto my sister Esther Buell 3 sheep, and also order my brother Jonathan to pay unto my sister Esther £30 as money. I appoint my brother Jonathan Buell sole executor.

Witness: *Joseph Humphrey,*   WILLIAM BUELL, LS.
John Hilyer, Andrew Robe, Jr.

Court Record, Page 14—19 November, 1734 : Will now exhibited. Proven. But the executor being dead, this Court grant Adms. with the will annexed, to Thomas Stephens and Samuel Buell.

Page 293.

Burr, Jonathan, Middletown. Died 1st February, 1734-5. Invt. £963-03-03. Taken by Philip Goff, George Hubbard and Daniel Prior. Will dated 27 January, 1734-5.

I, Jonathan Burr of Middletown, doe make and ordain this my last will and testament: I give to my wife Abigail Burr the improvement of 1-3 part of my whole estate during life, and 1-3 part of my moveable estate forever. I give to my sons Ebenezer, Jonathan and Nathaniel, all of them an equal share in my dwelling house and in my barn. To my eldest son, Ebenezer, I give out of my real estate, over and above an equal part, £30 as money. My three sons shall have all of my lands equally alike, except Ebenezer to have £30 more. Nextly, my will is that my three sons shall pay to my six daughters as they come of age, Marcy, Elizabeth, Abigail, Thankfull, Hannah and Martha, £50 to each. I ordain my wife Abigail and my son Ebenezer to be my executors.

Witness: *Philip Goff,*   JONATHAN BURR, LS.
John Swadell, Nathaniel Goff, Jr.

Court Record, Page 24—1 April, 1735: Will proven. Abigail accepts the trust. Ebenezer Burr refused to be executor.

Page 3 (Vol. XIV) 13 December, 1742: Martha Burr, daughter of Jonathan Burr, chose Mr. Jacob Whitmore to be her guardian. Recog., £300.

Page 278.

Caldwell, John, Hartford. Invt. £5405-10-10. Taken 9 December, 1734, by Benjamin Stilman, John Edwards and John Skinner.

Court Record, Page 11—28 September, 1734: Adms. granted to Mrs. Hannah Caldwell, widow, who gave bond with Nathaniel Stilman of Wethersfield in £8000.

Page 18—7 January, 1734-5: Invt. exhibited by Hannah Caldwell.

Page 349-50.

Carter, Joshua, Hartford. Invt. £1521-10-01. Taken 26 February, 1735-6, by John Skinner and Joseph Skinner. Will dated 22 May, 1733.

I, Joshua Carter of Hartford, doe make this my last will and testament: I give unto Mary, my wife, 1-3 part of my moveable estate forever, and 1-3 part of my houseing and lands during life. I give to my son John all my land, with the buildings thereon, in the west division of lotts in sd. Hartford, so-called, and £30 to be paid by my son Joshua for what is hereafter mentioned as given to him sd. Joshua. I give to my son Joshua my dwelling house, barn, orchard and 16 acres in the homested, more or less, adjoining, and also my cow pasture in Wethersfield butting on Hartford line, containing 10 acres more or less, he paying £30 to my son John. I give to my son Gideon all my land in Hartford that lyeth on the west side of the highway opposite from my house, and also all the houseing and land that fell to me from the estate of Robert Shirley decd. I give to my daughter Mary £5. I give to my daughter Sarah £5. I give to my daughter Ruth £50. I give to my granddaughter Abigail Benton £10 if she continue to live in my family with her grandmother till she be 18 years of age. After my debts are paid, the remainder of my estate, if any, I give to my 4 children, John, Joshua, Gideon and Ruth. I appoint my son Joshua and my wife Mary to be sole executors.

Witness: *Thomas Richards,*   JOSHUA CARTER, LS.
Thomas Seymour, Jr., Hepzibah Seymour.

Court Record, Page 41—2 March, 1735-6: Will proven.

Page 238.

Case, Peletiah, Simsbury. Invt. £43-08-04. Taken March, 1734, by Joseph Cornish and Benajah Humphrey.

Court Record, Page 2—1st April, 1734: Adms. to Jonah Case, a brother. Recog., with Samuel Case. Estate insolvent. Michael Humphrey, Joseph Cornish and Samuel Pettebone 2nd appointed commissioners.

Page 359.

Center, John, Middletown. Invt. £143-11-00. Taken 21 April, 1736, by George Hubbard, Nathaniel Johnson and Stephen Blake.

Court Record, Page 45—11 May, 1736: Adms. to Hannah Center, widow. Recog., £300, with James Brainard of Haddam.

Page 15 (Vol. XIII) 6 September, 1737: Hannah Center, Adms., exhibited an account of her Adms. Accepted.

Dist. File: 7 January, 1745: To Hannah Center, alias Turner, sometime widow of the decd., and to Hannah Center, only daughter. By William Whitmore and William Rockwell.

Page 2 (Vol. XV) 7 January, 1745: This Court appoint Mr. James Brainard of Haddam to be guardian unto Hannah Center, a minor, 13 years of age, daughter of John Center, late of Hartford deceased.

Page 11—6 May, 1746: Report of the distributors.

Page 370.

Chapman, William, Sen., Colchester. Will dated 21 August, 1724: Whereas, in time past, by a deed of guift, I have given to my son Solomon the farm which I now live upon, and have given to each of my other children what I designed they shall have of my estate saving the small legacies hereafter mentioned, I give unto Lydia, my wife, all my personal estate which I have now or may have at the time of my decease, to her only and sole use and disposal forever, with this proviso, that in a seasonable time after my decease she pay to each of my sons and daughters, both by my former and present wife, the sum of 5 shillings in money, which shall be in full of their several portions of my estate. I appoint my wife Lydia sole executor.

Witness: *John Bulkeley,*   WILLIAM X CHAPMAN, LS.
Nathaniel Bosworth, Benj. Taylor.

Court Record, Page 49—3 August, 1736: Will proven.

Invt. in Vol. XIII, Page 26-7.

Chenevard, John Michael, Hartford. Invt. £856-19-10. Taken 19 June, 1735, by Timothy Woodbridge and Cyprian Nichols.

Court Record, Page 26—22 April, 1735: Adms. granted to Margaret Chenevard, widow, who gave bond with John Beauchamp of £1000.

Page 12 (Vol. XIV) 5 October, 1742: An account of Adms. was now exhibited in Court by Margaret Chenevard, widow and Adms: Paid in debts and charges, £1322-09-10. Which account is accepted and ordered to be kept on file.

Page 54—5 February, 1744-5: Pursuant to an act of the General Assembly, holden at New Haven on the 2nd Thursday of October, 1742, directing Mrs. Margaret Chenevard, Adms., and Mr. Amos Church, of Hartford, to make sale of so much real estate of the deceased as may be necessary to answer the sum of £466-17-03 and the necessary charges, this Court do direct sd. Mr. Church and the Adms. to set up advertisements on the sign post in Hartford, 20 days before the sale, signifying that there is to be sold at publick vandue, such a day, time and place, the home-lott of the deceased in Hartford, on the east side of the Great River, which land bounds west on a highway, east on land of Richard Burnham, south on land of John Goodwin, and north on land of Elisha Burnham; or so much thereof as shall procure sd. sum and charges of sale.

Page 337-8-9.

Church, John, Hartford.   Invt. £1166-06-09.   Taken 30 October, 1735, by John Marsh, John Skinner and Jos: Talcott, Jr.   Will dated 5 June, 1735.

I, John Church of Hartford, doe ordain this to be my last will and testament: I give to my eldest son, John Church, these several pieces of land as followeth, viz.: one piece of meadow land lying at the north end of the long meadow in Windsor bounds; 1 parcel of land called the Blue Hill lott; one piece of land lying in sd. long meadow. These three pieces of land is all that my son John shall have of my estate. I give to my son Caleb Church 4 acres of land upon the south side of my lott where his house stands, and also one parcel of land lying in Windsor. I give unto my son Joseph Church all the remainder of the lott I live upon, with all the buildings thereon standing; and one piece of land lying on the Brickhill Swamp in Hartford bounds. I give unto my son Daniel Church £60 in money or moveables. I give to my two daughters, Abigail Church and Mary Church, £100 apiece. I appoint my sons Caleb and Joseph Church executors.

Witness: *John Marsh,*   JOHN CHURCH, LS.
Ozias Pratt, Susannah Pratt.

Court Record, Page 55—19 February, 1735-6: Receipt exhibited in Court from Abigail, Mary and Daniel Church, acknowledging their several legacies. (See the last page but one of Court Records.)

Page 252.

Churchill, Jonathan, Wethersfield.   Invt. £346-04-05.   Taken 3 June, 1734, by Joseph Goodrich, James Butler and Nathaniel Wright. An addition to the inventory of £9-00-00, taken in Bolton 23 May, 1734, by William Howard and John Bishop.

Court Record, Page 3—29 April, 1734: Adms. granted unto Samuel Churchill, who gave bonds with David Churchill of £600.

Page 6—4 June, 1734: This Court appoint Samuel Churchill guardian to Jonathan Churchill, a minor, 10 years of age. Recog., £100.

Page 15—3 December, 1734: This Court also appoint the sd. Samuel Churchill guardian to William Churchill, a minor, 7 years of age. Recog., £100.

Page 49 (Vol. XIII) 1st May, 1739: Samuel Churchill, Adms., exhibited an account of his Adms: Paid in debts and charges, £43-01-07; and received in credit 5 shillings. Account accepted by the Court.

Inventory on File.

Churchill, Nathaniel, Wethersfield.   Invt. taken 4 June, 1734, by Joseph Goodrich, James Butler and Nathaniel Wright.   Invt. exhibited in Court by John Cole, Adms.   Accepted.

Page 290.

Clark, Benoni, Windsor.   Invt. £26-11-08.   Taken by Isaac Skinner and John Eglestone.

Court Record, Page 22—4 March, 1734-5: Adms. granted to Solomon Clark on the estate of Benoni Clark, late of Windsor, alias Enfield,
in Hampshire County, in the Province of Massachusetts Bay.

Inventory on File.

Cole, Lydia, Wethersfield. Invt. £321-11-04. Taken 31 December,
1734, by Gideon Goodrich, David Goodrich and Benjamin Wright.

Court Record, Page 23—18 March, 1734-5: Adms. granted unto
her son John Cole, who gave bonds with John Riley of £100.

Page 43—13 April, 1736: John Cole, Adms., exhibited an account
of his Adms. Accepted.

Cole, Lydia. Court Record, Page 55—1st June, 1737: This Court
appoint David Goodrich, Jr., to be guardian unto Lydia Cole, daughter of
Joseph Cole, late of Stepney Parish, in Wethersfield, decd. Recog., £100.

Inventory on File.

Cole, Lydia, Middletown. Invt. £32-09-08. Taken 3 June, 1735,
by Nathaniel White and Eleazer Gaylord.

Page 308-9.

Coleman, Capt. Thomas, Wethersfield. Invt. £1912-15-03. Taken
by Thomas Curtis, Benjamin Stilman and Hezekiah May.

Court Record, Page 27—6 May, 1735: Adms. granted to Martha
Coleman, widow, who recog. in £2000 with Nathaniel Stilman.

Page 59 (Vol. XIII, Probate Side): We, the subscribers, co-heirs
to the estate of Capt. Thomas Coleman, late of Wethersfield deceased,
having on the 26th and 27th of June, Anno. Dom. 1735, distributed to
ourselves, by full and free consent and agreement of sd. co-heirs to the
estate, do acknowledge the receipt of the severall sums annexed to our
severall and respective names as followeth:

	£ s d
Received by John Coleman, Junr., the sum of	268-05-00
Received by Elisha Coleman the sum of	268-05-00
Received by Nathaniel Coleman the sum of	268-05-00
Received by Ebenezer and Hannah Sage the sum of	268-05-00
Received by Jonathan and Tabitha Biggelow the sum of	268-05-00
Received by Mary Owen, wife and attorney of Aaron Owen, the sum of	268-05-00

In testimony that we, sd. subscribers, have received the before written sums, or the just value thereof, from the aforesd. estate, being annexed to our severall and respective names, we do hereto set our hands severally and respectively. As witness oure hands this 27th day of June, Anno. Dom. 1735.

MARY OWEN, as atty. to AARON OWEN.

JOHN COLEMAN, JUNR., LS.

NATHANIEL COLEMAN.

NATHANIEL BURNHAM, JR., in behalf of JOHN COLEMAN, JR.

ELISHA COLEMAN, LS.

NATHLL BURNHAM, in behalf of NATHLL COLEMAN.

EBENEZER SAGE, LS.

JONATHAN BIGGELOW, JR., LS.

At a Court of Probate held at Hartford, for ye district of Hartford, on the 14th day of February, 1737-8, then the severall heirs to the estate of Capt. Tho. Coleman exhibited the foregoing agreement or receipts, and signed and sealed and acknowledged the same in Court.

Test: Jos. Talcott, Junr., Clerk.

Page 353.

Colyer, John, Hartford. Invt. £299-12-08. Taken 2 August, 1734, by Nathaniel Goodwin and Jos: Talcott, Jr.

Court Record, Page 6—17 June, 1734: Adms. granted to William Goodwin. Recog., £600, with Joseph Olcott.

Page 44—13 April, 1736: William Goodwin, Adms., exhibited an account of his Adms. Accepted.

Page 130 (Probate Side, Vol. XIII): *Know all men by these presents:* That we, William Goodwin and Elizabeth Goodwin, Joseph Olcott and Eunice Olcott, Thankfull Colyer and Mary Colyer, all of Hartford, being heirs to the estate of our brother John Colyer deceased, and there having been no legal partition yet made of our interest in sd. estate, we do now mutually agree in dividing our respective interest in the following manner: Firstly, that William Goodwin and Elizabeth his wife, and their heirs, shall have the upper lott and the long meadow, 7 acres more or less, butting north on land of John Skinner and Mrs. Woodbridge, and on William Day south; and also £27-14-02 interest in the lands belonging to the aforesd. estate in New Hartford, valueing the whole interest

in New Hartford at £90. Secondly, that Joseph Olcott and Eunice his
wife, and their heirs, shall have that lott over Brick Hill bridge, esteemed
to be 21 acres, butting west on land belonging to the heirs of Elisha Lord
and east on land of Obadiah Spencer; and also £6-06-08 interest in the
lands at New Hartford. Thirdly, that Thankfull Colyer and her heirs
shall have the homestead and the buildings thereon, butting east and
north on a highway, south on Daniel Colyer's land, and west on Jonathan
Burr's. Fourthly, that Mary Colyer shall have a lott on the east side of
the Great River, esteemed to be about 2½ acres more or less, butting
south on James Easton's land and north on the heirs of Daniel Clark;
and also one small lott in the long meadow containing ¾ of an acre, butting north on Abigail Woodbridge's land and south on Samuel Cadwell's
land; and also £56-04-02 interest in the lands at New Hartford. Fifthly:
We, William Goodwin, Joseph Olcott and Thankfull Colyer, do agree
and oblige ourselves in the defense of that lott on the east side of the
Great River from the demands of Joseph Clark's heirs, promising for
ourselves and heirs to be at our proportionable cost in case any suit shall
arise, and bear our part of the damage that the sd. Mary or her heirs
shall sustain for want of a good title to the described land. In confirmation of the foregoing agreement, we sett to our hands and fixed our seals
this 27th day of March, 1739.

WILLIAM GOODWIN, LS.	ELIZABETH X GOODWIN, LS.
JOSEPH OLCOTT, LS.	EUNICE OLCOTT, LS.
THANKFULL COLYER, LS.	MARY COLYER, LS.

Court Record, Page 46—27 March, 1739: An agreement now exhibited by the heirs to the estate of John Colyer, Jr., and accepted.

Page 382.

Cowles, Abigail, Kensington. Invt. £49-12-09. Taken 25 November, 1736, by Anthony Judd and John Cowles.

Court Record, Page 53—8 December, 1736: Invt. exhibited by
Samuel Cowles, Adms.

Page 9 (Vol. XIII) 7 June, 1737: Samuel Cowles, Adms., exhibits
an account of his Adms. Accepted.

Page 381.

Cowles, Hezekiah, Kensington. Invt. £366-07-08. Taken 25 November, 1736, by Anthony Judd and John Cowles.

Court Record, Page 53—8 December, 1736: Adms. to Samuel
Cowles of Farmington. Recog., £200, with Nathaniel Hart.

Page 375-6.

Cowles, Timothy, Hartford. Died 30 August, 1736. Invt. £126-05-05, personal estate. Taken 2 November, 1736, by Joseph Pitkin and Nehemiah Olmsted. Will dated 31 March, 1728.

I, Timothy Cowles of Hartford, do make this my last will and testament: I give to my son William Cowles (besides what I have already given him) the 1-2 of my land in the lott whereon he dwells, which now remains undisposed of, and 10 acres toward the east end, lying east of the road, excepting 10 acres which I do hereafter give unto my son Joseph Cowles, and my part of the land within the meadow fence, which I do herein except, to be divided equally between him and my son Joseph Cowles, which land I give to the sd. William Cowles forever. I give unto my son Joseph Cowles, he paying £10 of the legacies given to my daughters hereafter named, severall parcells of land as follows: That is, 10 acres of the upland lott whereon my son William Cowles now dwells, butting west on 10 acres toward the east and belonging to my son William above given; also all my part of the sd. lott lying within the meadow fence, butting west on land of the heirs of Deacon Joseph Olmsted; and also the whole of my land lying within the meadow which is bounded north on land of the heirs of Deacon Joseph Humphrey, south on land of Richard Case and the heirs of Deacon Daniel Bidwell, west on land of Daniel Bidwell, and east on a highway; and 1-2 of my land in the lott whereon my son William dwells, to be divided equally with the sd. William Cowles; and also all my part of the team tackling; all which I give to my son Joseph Cowles forever. I give to my daughter Elizabeth Wells, besides what she hath already received, 20 shillings. I give unto my daughter Hannah Hubbard so much as to make up, with what she hath already, £40. I give to my daughter Abigail Cowles £40. I give to my daughter Martha Cowles £40. I give all the remainder of my estate, after the legacies are paid, unto my two sons, William Cowles and Joseph Cowles, to be equally divided between them. And I make my two sons, William Cowles and Joseph Cowles, executors.

Witness: *Joseph Pitkin,*   TIMOTHY COWLES, LS.
Nehemiah Olmsted, Isaac Olmsted.

Court Record, Page 50—22 September, 1736: Will proven.

Page 302-3.

Dyxx, Samuel, Wethersfield (yeoman). Invt. £516-13-11. Taken 9 May, 1735, by Jonathan Belding, David Goodrich and Ebenezer Belding, Jr. Will dated 21 February, 1733-4.

I, Samuel Dyxx of Wethersfield, do make this my last will and testament: I give unto Mary, my wife, all my real and moveable estate, both house and negro man named Ruben, during their natural life. And after the decease of my sd. wife, I will and bequeath all my house, land and moveable estate to my grandson Charles Nott, with the negro man, except £5 to be given my daughter Sarah Nott. And further I give to Mary, my wife, one cow and one horse kind forever for her own. And I likewise constitute, make and ordain Mary Dyxx, my wife, to be sole executrix of this my last will and testament, all and singularly my land, messuages and tenements by her freely to be possessed and enjoyed during her sd. life. And after her decease I ordain Jonathan Nott of Wethersfield to be my executor for to pay and deliver to my sd. daughter Sarah Nott the sd. £5, and the lands and moveable estate (with the sd. negro man) to Charles Nott. I do hereby utterly disanull and revoke all and every other former testament, legacies, bequests and executor by me in any way before named, willed and bequeathed, ratifying and confirming this and no other to be my last will and testament. In witness whereof I have hereunto set my hand and seal the year and day above written. Signed, sealed, published, pronounced and declared by the sd. Samuel Dyxx as his last will and testament in the presence of the subscribers.

Witness: *Aaron Goff,*   SAMUEL DYXX, LS.
Stephen Hollister, Henry Grimes.

Court Record, Page 26—22 April, 1735: Will proven.

Page 363.

Doud, Sergt. Jacob, Middletown. Invt. £672-00-00. Taken 27 April, 1736, by Benjamin Cornwell, Stephen Turner and John Bartlett.

Court Record, Page 46—17 June, 1736: Adms. granted to Elizabeth Doud, the widow. Recog., £1000, with John Bartlett of Middletown.

Page 17 (Vol. XIII) 6 December, 1737: John Doud, a minor, 20 years of age, son of Jacob Doud, late of Middletown, chose Edward Higbee of Middletown to be his guardian. Recog., £100.

Page 19—3 January, 1737-8: Adms. account was now exhibited in Court by Isaac Lane and his wife, who was the widow and relict of sd. Doud, which account is accepted. Isaac Lane, the present husband to Elizabeth Lane, alias Doud, the relict of Jacob Doud, with his sd. wife, moved to this Court that a right of dower in the estate of the sd. deceased may be set out to her, whereupon this Court appoint Deacon Solomon Adkins, William Rockwell and Jonathan Allin, of sd. Middletown, to set out to the sd. Elizabeth 1-3 part of the real estate of the decd. by bounds, and make return of their doings thereupon to this Court. This Court appoint Isaac Lane to be guardian to 3 of the children of Jacob Doud, viz., Sarah, 10 years of age, Rachel 7 years, and Lois, age 4 years. Recog., £300. Esther Doud, 16 years of age, and Jacob Doud, 13 years, children of Jacob Doud, chose Edward Higby of Middletown to be their guardian. Recog., £200.

See File: We, the subscribers, being by the honourable Court of Probate for the County of Hartford, on the 26th day of February, 1745-6, appointed to make division and partition of the lands of Jacob Doud, late of Middletown, in sd. County of Hartford, have with the partners and guardians done the same. We have set off to Joseph Tibbals, Jr., in right of Esther his wife, to Rachel Doud, to Lois Doud, to Samuel Green, Jr., in right of his wife Sarah, to the heirs of John Doud, eldest son, decd., to Jacob Doud, youngest son, to each of them their respective portion in lands belonging to the estate of the decd. By *Nathaniel Bacon, William Rockwell* and *John Warner,* distributors.

We, the subscribers, being partners and guardians to the heirs of the within mentioned estate, do agree with and consent to the within division and settlement thereof. As witness our hands.

> EDWARD HIGBEE,
> *Guardian to the heirs of* JOHN DOUD
> *decd., and to* JACOB DOUD.
> ISAAC LANE,
> *Guardian to* RACHEL *and*
> LOIS DOUD.
> SAMUEL GREEN,
> JOSEPH TIBBALS, JR.

Page 26 (Vol. XV) 29 October, 1746: Report of the distributors. Accepted.

Easton, Susannah. Court Record, Page 36—13 November, **1735:** At the request and by the desire of Susannah Easton, widow relict of Joseph Easton, Jr., deceased, this Court appoint Michael Burnham of Hartford to be guardian to three of the children of the deceased, viz., James Easton, age 7 years; Susannah, age 5 years in July last, and Eliphalet, age 3 years 9th of August last. Recog., £200.

Inventory on File.

Eaton, Samuel, Tolland. Invt. £155-04-02. Taken by Samuel Chapman and Joseph West.

Court Record, Page 55—8 February, 1736-7: Adms. granted to Ebenezer Heath, the widow desiring the same.

Page 2 (Vol. XIII) 4 March, 1736-7: Inventory exhibited.

Page 3—22 March, 1737: Jemima, age 7 years, Bethia 5 years and Samuel 3 years of age, children of Samuel Eaton, upon the desire of the widow the Court appoint Samuel Chapman to be their guardian. Recog., £200.

Page 34—5 October, 1738: Ebenezer Heath, Adms., having first taken the advice of the Judge of the Court of Probates in the County of

Hartford to sell so much of the real estate as will raise the sum of £47-17-05 with the necessary charges, whereupon this Court now directs the sd. Adms. to sell the dwelling house of the sd. decd., and so much of the land adjoining to sd. house, as will raise the sum aforesd, first setting up advertisements 20 days before the sale of the land, on the sign posts in the Town of Windsor, on the east side of the Great River, and on the sign posts in the Towns of Tolland and Stafford, signifying the place and time of day such estate will be sold, at the beat of the drum, to the highest bidder.

Page 62—4 March, 1739-40: Samuel Chapman desires to be discharged as guardian to the children of Samuel Eaton, whereupon this Court appoints Joshua Wills of Tolland, father-in-law, to be guardian to sd. children, viz., Samuel, age 5 years; Aaron 3 years, Jemima 9 years, and Bethia 6 years.

Page 96 (Vol. XVI) 13 April, 1753: Aaron Eaton, a minor, 16 years of age, son of Samuel Eaton, chose Mr. Joshua Wills to be his guardian. Recog., £200.

Page 101—1st May, 1753: David Bates of Kent, in the County of Litchfield, showing to this Court that there are several pieces of land lying in the Town of Tolland that lies in common to the heirs of Samuel Eaton, which heirs (Samuel and Aaron) are minors, and that the sd. Bates has purchased the right of Jemima and Bethia Eaton, heirs to the sd. deceased, moves to this Court for freeholders to assist sd. minors in dividing sd. land: Whereupon this Court appoints Zebulon West, Barnabas Delano and Eleazer Steele, of Tolland, to divide sd. land.

Dist. File: We, the subscribers, being appointed by the Judge of Probate to make a distribution of the lands of Samuel Eaton, do distribute as follows: To Samuel Eaton, eldest son, 17½ acres of land, which we judge a double portion; to Bethia Crandall, the daughter, 5¼ acres; to Jemima West, the daughter, 5½ acres; and to Aaron Eaton, youngest son, 5½ acres. Distributed 28 May, 1753, by us: Barnabas Delano and Eleazer Steele.

Will and Invt. in Vol. XIII, Page 33-4.

Eglestone, Samuel, Middletown. Invt. £76-04-15. Taken 10 January, 1736-7, by Solomon Adkins and William Rockwell; and in Guilford by Judah Everts, Ebenezer Chittenden and Samuel Chittenden. Will dated 13 April, 1736.

I, Samuel Eglestone of Middletown, in the County of Hartford, being advanced to the age of 73 years, and being very infirm in body, do make this my last will and testament: I give to Patience, my wife, the use of my dwelling house and all my homelott (being about 20 acres) during her natural life or so long as she remains my widow; and 1-3 part of my moveable estate to be at her own dispose. I give to my son Samuel what I have already given him, and likewise all my land, divided and undivided, on the east side of the Great River in Middletown, forever. I give to my son-in-law, John Benton, and Abigail his present wife, my dwelling house and the south side of my present homelott, to lie 15 rods wide from end to end, and the equal half of my land on the east side of Hop Swamp Brook, to lye on the north side, to them and their heirs forever, provided my sd. son-in-law doth comfortably maintain my wife until her decease or marriage, and my son Joseph during his natural life. And the remainder of my homelott and the southern half of my land on the east side of Hop Swamp Brook I give to my daughters, Susannah, Sarah, Patience and Mary, they paying to my son Samuel the sum of £20; each to pay £5, Susannah and Sarah to pay the sum of £10 within 12 months after my decease, and my daughters Patience and Mary each £5 after they arrive to lawfull age. And further, my will is that my beloved wife Patience shall have a decent mourning suit and pay for the same out of my moveable estate after she hath received her thirds thereof. And what remains of my moveable estate I give equally to my daughters, Susannah, Abigail, Patience and Mary. And the reason why I don't give any of the moveable estate to my daughter Sarah is because I have already given her in moveables £10-11. And I hereby constitute my son-in-law John Benton and my friend Stephen Blake executors.

Witness: *Jabez Brooks,*   SAMUEL EGLESTONE, LS.
Roberts Johnson, William Rockwell.

Court Record, Page 55—1st February, 1736-7: Will proven.

Page 277.

Gates, Capt. Thomas, Haddam East. Invt. £780-08-01. Taken 13 May, 1734, by Isaac Spencer, Matthew Smith and Jabez Chapman.

Court Record, Page 10—10 September, 1734: Adms. granted to Thomas Gates, son of the decd. Recog., £1500, with his brother Daniel Gates.

See File: An agreement, dated at Haddam, 7 September, 1734, made by and between the surviving heirs for the dividing and full settlement of the estate of Capt. Thomas Gates, was by us the heirs, who acknowledge it to be our free act and deed, signed and sealed in presence of

HANNAH GATES, THE RELICT, LS.	DAVID GATES, LS.
THOMAS GATES, LS.	MARY BRAINARD,
JEREMIAH GATES, LS.	only daughter, LS.
BEZALEEL BRAINARD, LS.	JOSHUA GATES, LS.

Witness: *Samuel Olmsted,*
Dorothy Olmsted.

Page 9—10 September, 1734: Agreement exhibited in Court and accepted.

Page 372-392.

Gilbert, Ebenezer, Farmington. Invt. £3824-12-08. Taken by Samuel Hooker, Samuel Cowles and Jonathan Lewis. Will dated 17 July, 1726.

I, Ebenezer Gilbert of Farmington, do make this my last will and testament: I give to my wife Esther Gilbert £300 and the use and improvement of 1-2 of my eastermost dwelling house in Farmington. I give to my 3 sons, Moses, Ebenezer and Jonathan Gilbert, all my house and lands in Farmingtown, Hartford and Simsbury, all in sd. County, to be equally divided amongst them, excepting that my eldest son Moses shall have my sd. dwelling house in Farmingtown abovesd. and beyond his other brothers' parts. To my daughter Sarah I give and bequeath £200, reckoning what she hath had already as part thereof, to be paid to her within the space of 4 years after my decease. And if her children all die without issue, then her portion is to return to her surviving brother or brethren or their heirs after her decease. And my will is that the cloth I have now at the clothiers shall be for clothing for my sd. three sons, and not be inventoried as part of my estate. I appoint my wife and eldest son Moses Gilbert executors.

Witness: *William Burnham,*   EBENEZER GILBERT, LS.
John Woodruff, Dinah Deming.

Court Record, Page 50—3 August, 1736: Will exhibited in Court and proven.

Page 113 (Probate Side, Vol. XIV): Articles of agreement made and concluded by Moses Gilbert, Jonathan Gilbert and Ebenezer Gilbert, sons and heirs to the real estate of Mr. Ebenezer Gilbert, late of Kensington, in Farmingtown, decd., made and concluded this 12th day of April, Anno. Dom. 1743, is as follows: To Moses Gilbert the dwelling house; also 4 acres of land bought of Thomas Hancox and Stephen Post; also the lott bought of Benjamin Judd south on land bought of Seymour; and half that land I bought of Doctor Timothy Porter; and 30 acres that I had of Benjamin Loomis; and 9 acres that I had of Mr. Wyllys; and half that house and land and barn that I had of Stephen Andrews; and that land that I had of Thomas Rowley and John Steadman; and the 1-2 of the farm that my father bought of Daniel Clark (the east side of sd. farm); and also half of that land father bought of Richard Seymour. We are now to understand that the aforesd. Moses Gilbert doth firmly agree that his brother Jonathan Gilbert and any after him shall have a liberty of 1½ rods or 2 rods in breadth from the east side of his part in the farm to the west side of sd. land, beginning at the street and so running by the fence that runs near east and west on the south side of the orchard on which my dwelling house stands, and from that fence to run southwest or west in the most direct and convenient way to pass in to come to the sd. Jonathan Gilbert's land in sd. farm. And further, I, the sd. Jonathan Gilbert, do hereby firmly agree that the sd. Moses Gilbert shall have the

same quantity of land that the sd. way takes up, out of my part in sd. farm, and be added adjoining to his, running north and south the whole length of the farm. And further, I, the sd. Jonathan Gilbert, do hereby promise to make all the fence on the south side that shall be occasioned in fencing off the sd. passway from the rest of the farm forever. Now the term of time that the whole of this agreement hath reference to, is to be understood is forever. As witness our hands, 9th day of April, 1737.   MOSES GILBERT,
              JONATHAN GILBERT, EBENEZER GILBERT.

And to Jonathan Gilbert 1-2 of the farm that was Daniel Clark's, the west side of sd. farm; also 7½ acres on the east side of the highway, with the barn on the sd. lott; and that 50 acres, be it more or less, that I bought of Edward Allyn; and half of that land that I bought of Doctor Timothy Porter; and half that house and barn and land that I bought of Stephen Andros (Andrews).

                                          EBENEZER GILBERT,
                                          MOSES GILBERT.

To Ebenezer Gilbert the house and land that I had of Mr. Wyllys, and my division of land over the Great River, and also the land that 1 bought of Cyprian Watson.

                                          MOSES GILBERT,
                                          JONATHAN GILBERT.

And further, there is one certain piece or tract of land in sd. Farmingtown bounds, butted and bounded south on land of Gershom Hollister, west on a highway, north and east on Col. John Chester's land, within which boundaries is contained about 3½ acres, which sd. piece of land shall remain to each of us as tenants in common. To which agreement we the sd. heirs have hereunto set our hands and seals, and acknowledge the same before the Court of Probate in Hartford on the 3rd day of April, 1743.

                                          MOSES GILBERT, LS.
              JONATHAN GILBERT, EBENEZER GILBERT.

4 April, 1741: Then received of Moses, Jonathan and Ebenezer Gilbert, in notes to the value of £109-10-00, payable to me, which is in full for the remaining part of the legacy due to my children by virtue of ye will of Mr. Ebenezer Gilbert decd. I say received by me.
Witness: *Esther* X *Gilbert,*   GERSHOM HOLLISTER.
         Elizabeth X *Gilbert.*

Gilbert, Allin, Middletown. Court Record, Page 2—1st April, 1735: Nathaniel Gilbert to be guardian to his sons, Allin Gilbert, age 17 years, and Nathaniel Gilbert, age 11 years.

Gillett, William, Simsbury (an idiot).   Court Record, Page 54—
1st February, 1736-7: Adms. to Samuel Pettebone, Jr.   Recog., £100,
with John Edwards of Hartford.

Page 260-1.

Goff, David, Wethersfield (Stepney Parish).   Invt. £333-04-08.
Taken 2 August, 1734, by John Dyxx, Ephraim Williams and Jonathan
Belding.   Will dated 5 March, 1734.

I, David Goff of Stepney Parish, do make my last will and testament: I give to Lydia, my wife, whome I constitute, with Daniel Andrews, of Wethersfield, executors.   That is to say, I give to my wife the
use of my whole estate till my children come to lawfull age, and £50
money then to her out of my estate to be paid.   Next, I give to my beloved son Moses £10 more than to my other son, which first being done,
I will that all my estate and lands be equally divided between him and my
son Elijah, excepting my daughter Jerusha, which I will that she shall
have 2-3 as much as my son Moses.

Witness: *Benjamin Wright,*   DAVID GOFF, LS.
Jonathan Renals, Ephraim Goff.

Court Record, Page 11—1st September, 1734: Will proven.

Page 35 (Vol. XV) 14 March, 1746-7: Elijah Goff, a minor, 17
years of age, son of David Goff, chose his father Noadiah Taylor of
Wethersfield to be his guardian.   Recog., £300.

Page 118—1st March, 1749-50: Moses Goff of Wethersfield now
moves to this Court that distribution be made of the estate of David Goff,
his father, according to his last will: Whereupon this Court appoint
Jonathan Belding, Ephraim Williams and John Warner, of Wethersfield,
distributors.   And also direct them to set out to Lydia Goff, alias Taylor,
relict, 1-3 part of the real estate for her improvement during life.

Will on Page 295-7.   Inventory on Page 385.

Grant, Matthew, Windsor.   Invt. £1641-12-10.   Taken 20 March,
1734-5, by Joseph Phelps, Joseph Loomis and Timothy Loomis; and 26
November, 1736, by Joseph Loomis and Timothy Loomis (page 385).
Will dated 5 May, 1732.

I, Matthew Grant of Windsor, do make this my last will and testament: I give to my wife Hannah, during the term of her natural life, all
that land which was formerly Deacon Samuel Baker's, from the highway on the east to the river on the west, with the buildings and fences
thereon standing; and also, on the east side of the way, a parcel of land
that was Samuel Baker's, bounding north at the north side of the land I
have that was sd. Baker's, south on my own land by a line drawn ac-

cording to the south bounds of my lott, sd. line to run from the highway eastward through the barn at the south side of the barn floor, and so further eastward till it extends 40 rods from the street, at which distance of 40 rods east of the highway this parcel of land now given to my wife is to terminate; this parcel of land I give her during her natural life, and that part of the barn standing on the same. I also give her £150 out of my personal estate forever, to take it at inventory price in such things as she shall choose. I give to my son Daniel Grant 1 parcell of land where I dwell, east on the highway, north on land of Thomas Sadd, south on the land of Samuel Grant, and west on the drain, with the fences and buildings thereon standing. Also, one parcell of meadow land, being 17 rods and 1-2 in breadth north and south, as the same is bounded east by the drain, north on Daniel's own land, west on the river, and south on my own land. Also, 1 piece of land on the east side of the highway, bounded west on the highway, partly on the land of John Mackenstry, east on my own land by a line drawn from John Mackenstry's southeast corner across my lott, and south on the land of Daniel Grant. This I give my son Daniel Grant, with the barn thereon standing. Also, another parcell of land on the east side of the way, to be 22 rods and 1-2 in width north and south, bounding north on land of Thomas Sadd, east on land of John Rockwell, south on my own land, and west on John Mackenstry's. All the above parcells of land I give to my son Daniel and his heirs forever, saving only to his mother her right in it given in this will, and upon condition that he execute a deed for the ample passing over in the law to my son William and his heirs forever that parcell of land where he the sd. Daniel now liveth, with the buildings thereon standing, within the bounds following, that is to say, west on the street, north on my own land, south on the land of Samuel Grant, and east on Dracke's Brook, and on the east side of Dracke's Brook the south half of his sd. lott on the south side, from the sd. Dracke's Brook on the west to the Town Commons on the east, however his sd. lott may be otherwise bounded. I give to my son William Grant 1 parcell of meadow land 6 rods in breadth, as the same is bounded, east on the drain, north on land of Samuel Grant, west on the river and south on the land of Grace Grant. Also another parcell of meadow land, being 14 rods in breadth. I also give to my son William one parcell of land on the east side of the high-way, being 10 rods in breadth, south on Daniel Grant, east on John Rockwell, west on my own land. I also give to my son William 2-3 parts of my right, interest and share in the large tract of land pattened (patented) to sundry proprietors in Hartford and Windsor, called the western lands. These parcells of land I give to my son William and his heirs forever, saving his mother's right. I give to my daughter Hannah Sadd one parcell of land westward of the highway westward of Thomas Sadd's land, and also 1-3 part of my right or share in the western land, and all my right or share in the "equivalent land." These parcells of land I give to my daughter Hannah Sadd and her heirs forever. I further give her £300 out of my personal estate with what she hath already had (reckoning the land at £135 at inventory price). I give to my daughter Mary Grant all the land I bought of Ebenezer Bliss, to her and her heirs forever, and £100 out of my personal estate at inventory price. I give to my daughter Rachel and to my daughter Sarah the lands I bought of Capt. Job Elsworth, with the buildings, and all the land I bought of Jonathan Elsworth, to them and their heirs forever, to be equally divided between them. And further, I give them, the sd. Rachel and Sarah, £300 each out of my personal estate, at inventory price, with what they have had, reckoning their land at £135 each.

Witness: *Samuel Grant,*   MATTHEW GRANT, LS.
Ebenezer Grant, Timothy Grant.

Court Record, Page 24—1st April, 1735: Will exhibited by Hannah Grant, widow, and Daniel Grant, executors.

Page 273.

Grimes, Joseph, Stepney. Invt. £943-00-06. Taken 21 November, 1734, by Benjamin Wright, David Boardman and David Goodrich. Will dated 19 April, 1733.

I, Joseph Grimes of Stepney, in Wethersfield, do make and ordain this my last will and testament: I give to my son Henry Grimes 1-2 of my lott at Copse Hill, the whole lott containing 30 acres more or less, and is butted as followes: On the highway north, and east, south and west on the land of Richard Robbins and on land formerly Noah Waddams's, now David Stoddard's (south end of sd. lott) ; as also 1-2 of my lott bounded as follows: West on Beaver Brook, north on land of the Widow Edwards, south on land of Samuel Dix, and east on land of Ebenezer Belding, the whole lott containing three acres more or less (the north side of the sd. lott) ; these to him and his male heirs forever. I give to my son Josiah Grimes my homelott with all the buildings on it, bounded west on a highway and east on a highway, south on the land of the heirs of Aaron Goff, north on land of Capt. Joshua Robbins and on lands of Theophilus Sherman's. Also, I give to my son Josiah (one-half) of my lott at Drye Swamp, which lott is bounded east on a high (way), north on land of Joseph Cowles, west on land of John Reinolds and on land of Widow Edwards, south on land of Ebenezer Belding, the south side of sd. lott ; and also another piece of land containing about 4 acres more or less, bounded as followeth: south on lands of the heirs of Zachariah Seymour and east on a ditch, north on his own land and west on a highway ; these to him and his male heirs forever. I give to my son Hezekiah Grimes, besides what I have already given him by deed of gift, and besides what money I have paid out for him, which amounts to near £50, I give him (stil) my son Hezekiah the other half of my lott in Dry Swamp described as above to Josiah. I give to my son Christopher Grimes the other half of my lott at Copse Hill described as above to

Henry, the north end of sd. lott; and also the other half of my lott at Beaver Brook bounded as above mentioned (to Henry), the south side of sd. lott; these pieces of land to him and his male heirs forever. I give to my daughter Mary, besides what she hath already received, the sum of £40 in good lawful money. I give to my daughter Deborah, besides what she hath already received, 20 shillings in money. The remainder of my moveable estate I order should be equally divided between my two sons, Henry and Josiah Grimes, whom I constitute and appoint executors.

Witness: *Daniel Russell,*   JOSEPH GRIMES, LS.
Joshua Robbins ye 3d, Jonathan Riley.

Court Record, Page 14—3 December, 1734: Will exhibited by the executors.

Hale, Daniel. Court Record, Page 47—17 June, 1736: Daniel Hale, 18 years of age, son of John Hale of Glastonbury, chose Ensign John Gains of Middletown to be his guardian.

Page 302.

Ham, James, Hartford. Will dated 13 December, 1734: I, James Ham of Hartford, doe make this my last will and testament: I give, devise and bequeath to my beloved sister Mary Ham, now living at Hartford, all my estate, both real and personal. I doe hereby ordain and appoint the sd. Mary Ham to be my executrix.

Witness: *William Keith,*   JAMES HAM, LS.
William Tiley, Joseph Gilbert, Jr.

Court Record, Page 26—25 April, 1735: Will proven.

Page 335.

Harris, Daniel, Middletown. Invt. £1008-04-00. Taken 20 November, 1735, by Abijah Moore, Jonathan Allin and William Rockwell.

Will dated 22 March, 1734-5: I, Daniel Harris, being advanced in age to fourscore years, do make this my last will and testament, in manner and form following: I give to my wife Elizabeth my silver spoon, Bible, bellows, and whatsoever goods or household stuff she brought to my house when I marryed her, my best bed with furniture, and £20. I give to the First Church of Christ in Middletown my silver cup (inventoried at £18). I have already given my two sons, Daniel and Joseph, their full portions by deeds of gift. I give to the children of my daughter Abigail Cornell deceased, viz., to Abigail Miller, the wife of Amos Miller, my brass kettle; to Elizabeth Cornell, my silver salt cellar; to Joseph,

Daniel and Nathaniel, to each, two acres of my boggy meadow. I give to my son-in-law Ezekiel Gilbert two acres of my boggy meadow. And to my grandson Jonathan Gilbert I give four acres of the western part of my home lot. I give to my son Daniel Harris my cloak, and to my grandson Daniel Harris I give the remainder of my home lot and the buildings thereto belonging. I give to my sons-in-law, Joseph Cornell and William Ward, all my rights of land on the east side of the Great River, divided or undivided, especially my Wongunk swamp. I give to my grandsons, the sons of my daughter Mary Ward, all my husbandry utensils. I give to my wife the use of all my improveable estate so long as she continues my widow, except the silver cup, brass kettle and silver salt cellar before mentioned. I give to my daughters, Mary Ward and Patience Gilbert, all my household stuff and stock that shall remain after my wife's decease or marriage. I give to my grandsons, Jonathan Gilbert, Daniel Harris and Moses Harris, all my right in the commons or undivided land, to be equally divided. I give my gun to my grandson Joseph Harris. I give my gold ring to my granddaughter Abigail Harris, the daughter of my son Joseph Harris deceased.

I ordain my wife Elizabeth to be sole executrix.

Witness: *Nathaniel Starr,*   DANIEL HARRIS, LS.
James Ward, William Rockwell.

Court Record, Page 336—13 November, 1735: Will proven.

Page 382.

Hart, Matthew, Kensington. Invt: realty, £1406-00-00. Taken 29 November, 1736, by Anthony Judd and Samuel Lanckton.

Court Record, Page 53—8 December, 1736: Adms. to Sarah Hart, widow, and Nathaniel Hart, of Farmington.

Page 20 (Vol. XIII) 3 January, 1737-8: Nathaniel Hart, Adms., exhibited an account of his Adms., which is accepted.

Page 24 (Vol. XVII) 25 April, 1754: Oliver Hart, aged 20 years, and Matthew Hart, about 17 years of age, children of Matthew Hart, late of Farmington deceased, chose their uncle John Hooker to be their guardian. Recog., £300.

Page 252-3-4.

Holmes, Capt. John, Haddam East. Invt. £1279-17-00. Taken 17 June, 1734, by Isaac Spencer, John Church and Jabez Chapman. Will dated at Hartford, 7 November, 1733.

I, John Holmes of Haddam, do make this my last will and testament: I give to Mary, my wife, the use of my house and barn, and also the use and improvement of 1-3 part of all my real estate during her widowhood, and 1-3 part of my moveable estate forever. I give to my eldest son Thomas so much more of my lands and right in commons, with that lott which I have already given him by deed, which I value at £100, as to make him equal with either of his three brothers, and whom I make my executor. I give to my son John so much more of my lands and right in commons, with the land which I have already given him, as to make him equal with all the rest of his brothers. The land which I have heretofore given him, together with that right which I bought of Mr. Skinner, is to be considered at £100 money, whom also I make my executor. I give unto Christopher and Eliphalet, my two youngest sons, £100 apiece as money out of my lands more than Thomas or John, under the consideration of my having given them as is above mentioned. And my will is that my interest in the New London Society be equally divided between my four sons, namely, Thomas, John, Christopher and Eliphalet, and the land also which lies in security for the same. I give to my daughter Leucrese £30 as money besides what I gave her at her marriage. I give to my other four daughters, Mary, Grace, Sarah and Abigail, all the remainder of my moveable estate to be equally divided between them, and what that wants of makeing them £70 as money apiece, my will is that their four brothers make it up and pay them as they come of age. Or if any or either of my daughters should remain single after the expiration of their mother's widowhood, my will is that they have the use of 1-2 of my house during their single life, and after that my will is that my house and barn return to my son Christopher.

Witness: *Moses Nash,*　　　　　　　　　　JOHN HOLMES, LS.
Henry Brace, Ebenezer Sedgwick.

Court Record, Page 7—2 July, 1734: Will now exhibited by Thomas and John Holmes, executors. Proven. Mary Holmes, widow, relict, to be guardian to three of the children of the deceased, viz., Eliphalet, age 12 years, Sarah 8 years, and Abigail 5 years. Recog., £150.

Dist. File: 23 October, 1734: Estate Capt. John Holmes, East Haddam: The lands to sons Thomas, John, Christopher and Eliphalet Holmes. The moveable estate to the widow Mary Holmes; to Lucretia Willey, wife of Joseph Willey; to Mary, to Grace, to Sarah, and to Abigail Holmes. By Matthew Smith and Jabez Chapman.

Page 241.

Hoskins, John, Sen., Windsor. Invt. £248-16-06. Taken 8 March, 1733-4, by Jonathan Stiles and Samuel Stoughton. Will dated 21 March, 1722.

I, John Hoskins, Sen., of Windsor (yeoman), being of perfect health and memory, do make this my last will and testament: I give my wife Ruth Hoskins 1-3 of my house and homelott, 1-3 of my meadow land and barn on the east side of the highway, all this to injoy during her natural life and then to return to my two sons John and Jonathan. I have given unto my son Thomas already a house and homestead, with all my lands in Pine Meadow, to him and his heirs forever, and also at my death 5 shillings. I give unto my other two sons (viz.), John and Jonathan, all my other land in Windsor, namely, those lands mentioned in a deed of trust bearing date 7 April, 1718, with that house and homelott which I bought of my son Thomas Hoskins. I give unto my daughter Elizabeth 5 shillings; I have given her £31 already. I give unto my daughter Susannah a feather bed and with it the furniture that she now has, and my will further is that by reason of the weakness of her body and mind I ordain my three sons, Thomas, John and Jonathan, to maintain her during her natural life with decent apparrel, necessary food and physick, and that at an equal proportion between my three sons, and also a Christian burial at death. I give unto my other daughters (viz.), Mary, Abigail and Margaret, £20 to each of them, and each of these legacies to be paid by my two sons John and Jonathan. I give unto my wife Ruth Hoskins all the rest of my estate that I have not yet disposed of, and that for her to injoy during her natural life, and then to dispose of it as she sees cause amongst her children that she hath by me. I make my wife Ruth Hoskins sole executrix.

Witness: *John Hill,*   JOHN X HOSKINS, LS.
Andrew Robe, Mary Gaylord.

Court Record, Page 2—1st April, 1734: Will proven.

Page 1 (Probate Side, Vol. XIV): Articles of agreement made the 12th day of August, Anno. Dom. 1742, between John Hoskins 2nd, Jonathan Hoskins, David Pinney and his wife Abigail, all of Windsor, in Hartford County, and Henry Veats of Simsbury and his wife Margaret. They and each of them have mutually agreed, being the heirs of the estate of John and Ruth Hoskins, late of Windsor decd., as followeth: First, the sd. John Hoskins and Jonathan Hoskins shall pay unto the sd. Daniel Pinney and his wife Abigail the sum of £80 out of the estate of John Hoskins and his wife Ruth, late of Windsor decd. Second, that the sd. John Hoskins and Jonathan Hoskins shall pay unto ye Henry Veats and his wife Margaret the sum of £50 out of ye estate aforesd. Thirdly, that the sd. Daniel Pinney and his wife Abigail, Henry Veats and his wife Margaret shall give a good and well executed quitclaim deed of 20 acres of land lying in Windsor, butted and bounded at large as may appear by one certain writing or ffeoffe of trust upon record, unto ye sd. John Hoskins and Jonathan Hoskins, to them, their heirs and assigns forever, with all the rest of the moveable estate which belonged unto the sd. John Hoskins and Ruth Hoskins at their decease. In witness whereof we have hereunto set our hands and seals this 12th day of August, A. D. 1742.

JOHN X HOSKINS, 2nd, LS.   JONATHAN X HOSKINS, LS.
DANIEL X PINNEY, LS.   ABIGAIL X PINNEY, LS.
HENRY VEATS, LS.   MARGARET X VEATS, LS.

At a Court of Probates held at Hartford, 13 August, 1742: Then the several signers and sealers to this instrument personally in Court acknowledged their hand and seals, and the foregoing agreement to be their free act and deed.

Test: Joseph Talcott, Clerk.

Court Record, Page 2—13 August, 1742: This agreement was accepted in Court and ordered to be recorded and kept on file.

Page 290-1.

Hoskins, Mary, Windsor. Invt. £133-07-11. Taken 25 February, 1734-5, by John Cook, Jr., Ebenezer Phelps and Timothy Loomis. Will dated 14 July, 1716.

I, Mary Hoskins of Windsor, do make this my last will and testament: I give to my eldest son John Wilson my great Bible. I give to my son Samuel Wilson my best bed and bedstead, feather boalster and pillow, curtains and vallients, bed roap, my best kersey blankett and best coverlid, with 1 paire of sheets, and one of my best swine, and a gunn, and a paire of weaver's looms and so much of the tackling proper to sd. looms as did belong unto me. I give to my daughter Mary Filley the use of a cow during her natural life, then to be divided among her children. I give to my grandson Job, who has lived with me, $5 in money, to be paid to him at the age of 21 years; but in case he die before he arrive thereunto, then sd. £5 shall be equally divided among my five children, John, Samuel, Elizabeth, Mary and Abigail, or their legal representatives. My will is that my son Samuel Wilson shall have my house and homested in Windsor which formerly was Nicholas Sention's, to be and remain to him and his heirs forever. But it is to be understood I give to son Samuel clearly but 1-5 part of the sd. houseing and land, and therefore he shall pay what I am behind of the purchase money for sd. houseing and land, which I suppose is about £10, which being taken out of the inventory price, sd. Samuel shall pay 1-5 part of the remainder to his brother John Wilson, 1-5 to his sister Elizabeth Wilcoks, 1-5 to his sister Mary Filley, and 1-5 part to his sister Abigail Alford, all to be paid within 18 months after my decease. And further, my will is that if my son Samuel do at any time make sale of sd. houseing and lands, his brother John Wilson shall have it, paying therefore as much as another would give. My will is that the rest of my estate, both real and personal, be equally divided amongst my five children above named. I constitute my two sons, John and Samuel Wilson, executors.

Witness: *William Phelps,*   MARY X HOSKINS, LS.
Matthew Allyn.

Court Record, Page 22—4 March, 1734-5: Will proven.

Will and Invt. in Vol. XIII, Page 24-5.

Humphrey, Lt. Samuel, Simsbury. Died 15 June, 1736. Invt. £228-08-07. Taken by Joseph Cornish, Benajah Humphrey and Samuel Pettibone. Will dated 22 July, 1734.

I, Samuel Humphrey, of the Town of Simsbury, in the County of Hartford, do make this my last will and testament: I do give unto my daughter Mary £39-06-08. I give unto my daughter Elizabeth £33-06-08. I give unto my daughter Abigail £24-06-08. And my will is that my three daughters shall have their portions paid unto them out of my moveable estate, and that the goods which I have delivered to them since the decease of my wife Mary (as shall appear by the account thereof that I have kept) shall be accounted to them as part of their portion. And in case my moveable estate, with the goods above mentioned, be not sufficient to pay unto them their portions, then my sd. daughters to have the remaining part of their portion set out to them in my land in that tract commonly called the Ash Swamp, unless my sons hereafter named shall pay unto them the remaining part of their portions. And in case my sons shall pay unto my sd. daughters the remaining part of their portions, then the sd. tract of land to be divided amongst my sons. I give unto my four sons, to Samuel, Jonathan, Charles and Noah, all the right that I have in ye common and undivided lands lying in sd. Simsbury, and also in Windsor, to be equally divided amongst them. Also, I do give unto my forenamed four sons that tract of land before mentioned called the Ash Swamp, upon condition that they will pay unto my three daughters so much money as shall be sufficient to make up to them what shall be wanting in my moveable estate to make up to them their portions. I give unto my son Noah that tract of land of mine lying on the side of the hill eastward from the house, bounding westerly part on his house lott, part on my son Samuel's land, part on land of Hannah Cornish, and part on land of Abraham Sidervelt, northerly on my son Samuel's land, eastward on land of Joseph Phelps, and south on the highway. I do give unto my granddaughter Sarah Case £19, to be paid unto her out of my moveable estate. I appoint John Humphrey of Simsbury and my son Jonathan Humphrey and my daughter Mary Case to be executors.

Witness: *John Mills,*   SAMUEL HUMPHREY, LS.
Benjamin Mills, Michael Humphrey.

Court Record, Page 48—30 June, 1736: Will proven.

Page 380-1.

Hubbard, William, Kensington. Invt. £449-13-10. Taken by Samuel Peck and Caleb Galpin. Will dated 31 August, 1736.

I, William Hubbard of Kensington, in the County of Hartford, do make this my last will and testament: I give to my wife, Sarah Hubbard,

1-3 part of my moveable estate forever, and the use of 1-3 of my lands during her naturall life, and so much of my moveable estate as shall amount to £30 for the bringing up of my children, and the use of one room in my house during her widowhood. To my son William Hubbard I give 8 acres of land on which my buildings stand and that my father gave me by deed of gift, with the buildings, the house and barn. I likewise give to him 1 yoke of oxen, 2 young creatures and 1 heifer, each coming two years old. I likewise give to him my gunn. To my two daughters, Sarah and Ruth, I give one certain parcell of land containing 7 acres, bounded on land of my own east, and north on land of Daniel (Blake)? Blague, to be equally divided between them. And the rest of my moveables that is not given to my wife and son I give to my daughters, to be divided equally between them. I do hereby appoint my beloved wife sole executrix.

Witness: *Caleb Galpin,*   WILLIAM HUBBARD, LS.
Zebulon Peck, Richard Hubbard.

Court Record, Page 51—5 October, 1736: Will proven. Mrs. Sarah Hubbard to be guardian to Sarah Hubbard, age 7 years, William Hubbard, age 3 years, and Ruth Hubbard, age 9 months, children of William Hubbard decd. Recog., £150.

Page 54 (Vol. XV) 5 January, 1747-8: William Hubbard, a minor, 14 years of age, son of William Hubbard, late of Farmington deceased, chose his father-in-law Samuel Andruss to be his guardian. Recog., £300.

Page 332.

Hungerford, Green, East Haddam. Invt. £1549-10-06. Taken 27 August, 1735, by Samuel Andrews, Henry Champlin and Noadiah Brainard. Will dated 29 April, 1735.

I, Green Hungerford of East Haddam, do make this my last will and testament: I give to my wife Jemima the use of all my moveable estate, and 1-3 part of my house and barn and orchard, and all my improved lands, during her widowhood. And if my wife, after my decease, shall see cause to marry, my will is that she shall have and enjoy as her own proper estate all the estate that I have received by her that did acrue to her by her parents. And my will is that my wife shall doe her endeavour to bring up my children with the use of my moveable estate, until they shall come to lawfull age. 2ndly, I give to my three sons, viz., Green, Lemuell and Stephen Hungerford, all the farm or lot of land on which I now dwell, to be equally divided between them in quantity and quality, excepting only that I give to my eldest son Green Hungerford 10 acres, to be first taken off from sd. farm on that side that joyns to Benjamin Graves his land. 3rdly, I give to my son Nathaniel Hungerford one lot of land adjoining to the land of Allin Willey and the land of Mr. Alexander Steward, containing 40 acres be it more or less, and one lott of land neare the northwest corner of the lott on which I now dwell, adjoining to the land of John Sharrard; also another lot of land partly adjoyning to the land of Jabez Chapman, not far from a pine swamp. Furthermore, I give to my four above sd. sons, viz., Green, Lemuell, Stephen and Nathaniel, all my rights in all the undivided land in East Haddam, to be equally divided amongst them; all which lands and rights I give to my four sons and their male heirs. I give to my five daughters, viz., Jemima, Mary, Rachell, Esther and Elizabeth Hungerford, £40 to each of them, to be paid to them severally as they come of age or are married, that is to say, to Jemima £40 with what she hath already received. I hereby authorize and appoint my wife sole executrix.

Witness: *Stephen Cone,*   GREEN HUNGERFORD, LS.
Jabez Chapman, Noadiah Brainard.

Court Record, Page 32—7 October, 1735: Will and invt. exhibited by Jemima Hungerford, widow and executrix. Will proven.

Page 90 (Vol. XIII) 2 June, 1741: This Court appoint Green Hungerford to be guardian unto Elizabeth Hungerford, a minor, age 11 years, Lemuel and Nathaniel, each 8 years, children of Green Hungerford deceased. Recog., £500.

Page 330.

Hurlbut, Stephen, Farmington. Invt. £141-19-06. Taken 1st September, 1735, by Daniel Hall and William Whitmore of Middletown.

Court Record, Page 30—1 July, 1735: Adms. to Hannah Hurlbut, widow. Recog., £300, with Daniel Hall of Middletown.

Page 32—Moveables set out to the widow.

Page 34—7 October, 1735: An account of debts due from the estate, £57-01-06, was exhibited.

Page 40—9 February, 1735-6: Adms. may sell land in value £47-00-00. This Court directs Capt. Hall to set up an advertisement on the door of the dwelling house of Jonathan Yeomans, tavern keeper at a place called Maromas in Middletown, and on the sign post at the lower housing in Middletown, signifying there is to be sold so much of the lot of land at sd. Romas, belonging to the estate of the sd. deceased, lying neare to Nathan Sayers, as would produce the sum of £47, etc.

Page 59 (Vol. XIV) 24 May, 1745: Jonathan Hurlbutt, a minor, age 17 years, son of Stephen Hurlbutt deceased, chose his uncle Daniel Hall of Middletown to be his guardian. Recog., £500.

Page 325.

Jones, Samuel, Hebron. Invt. £2860-00-00 in real estate, £344-06-08 in personal estate. This includes goods from New London Society per John Curtis.

Received by me, Rachel Kneeland, alias Jones, Adms., £24-00-00.
                              Signed: RACHEL KNEELAND.

Invt. taken 7 November, 1735, by Hez: Gaylord, Nathaniel Phelps and Joseph Kellogg.

Court Record, Page 36—13 November, 1735: Adms. to Rachel Jones, widow. Recog., £500, with her father Ebenezer Dibble of Colchester. The widow prays that necessaries be set out for her use, which this Court allow to the value of £49-01-11.

Page 44—13 April, 1736: Account exhibited and accepted.

Page 5 (Vol. XIII) 1st April, 1737: Rachel Jones, Adms., recog. with Nathaniel Dunham of Hebron. Per act of the General Assembly, this Court directs Rachel Jones to sell land to the value of £400.

Page 22—14 February, 1737-8: This Court, on the 1st day of April, directed the widow, Rachel Jones, to sell lands with Joseph Phelps at inventory price, and having sold to the value of £200, they could not sell more at invt. price, and was directed to sell at vandue to the highest bidder.

Page 28—2 May, 1738: This Court appoint Rachel Jones to be guardian to four of the children of Samuel Jones, viz., to Mary, age 12 years, Ezekiel 7, Joel 5, and Samuel 3 years. Recog., £400.

Page 29—2 May, 1738: Report of the sale of land by Rachel Jones, 20 April, 1738, at vandue: 100 acres, butting on Chapwell's land, sold to Nathaniel Man at £223-10-00; 8 acres to Abraham Blanchard, £16-00-00; and 100 acres to Samuel Fyler for £100-00-00. Account accepted by the Court.

Page 90 (Vol. XVI) 6 March, 1753: Rachel Jones, alias Man, Adms., showing to this Court that she hath fully made up her account of Adms., now moves that distribution may be made: Whereupon this Court appoint and impower Alexander Phelps, Deacon Joseph Kellogg of Hebron and Daniel Addams of Colchester to distribute the estate, viz.: To the sd. Rachel, relict, 1-3 part of the personal estate; to Ezekiel, the eldest son, a double share; and to Joel and Samuel Jones, younger sons, an equal single share of sd. estate; and make return thereof to this Court.

Page 334.

Joyner, William, East Haddam. Died 29 November, 1734. Invt. taken 26 December, 1734, by Samuel Emmons, Jr., James Cone and Joseph Fuller.

Court Record, Page 23—7 October, 1735: Adms. granted to Elizabeth Joyner, widow, who gave bonds with Joseph Fuller of £200.

Page 14 (Vol. XIII) 6 September, 1737: Elizabeth Joyner, Adms., exhibited an account of her Adms., by which account it appears she has paid in debts and charges the sum of £5-10-04. Accepted and ordered on file.

Page 93—1st July, 1741: William, Robert and Elizabeth Joyner, being more than 14 years of age, children of William and Elizabeth Joyner decd., chose Samuel Fuller, Jr., of Colchester, to be their guardian. Recog., £100. Cert: *John Bulkeley, Jr., J. P.*

Page 255.

Judd, Ebenezer, Hartford.   Invt. £605-06-04.   Taken 26 June, 1734, by Isaac Merrells and Timothy Seymoure.

Court Record, Page 7—2 July, 1734: Adms. to Hannah Judd, widow. Recog., £500, with Thomas Judd of Farmington.

Page 25—22 April, 1735: Hannah Judd, widow, informs this Court that the moveable estate is not sufficient to pay the debts, and prays that necessaries be set out to her.

Page 50—7 September, 1736: Hannah Judd, Adms., exhibited an account of her Adms. Accepted.

Page 2 (Vol. XIII) 1st and 4th March, 1736-7: Thomas Judd and Joseph Judd, being notified, appeared before this Court by their attorney, Daniel Judd, to object to the account of Adms. of Hannah Judd on the estate of Ebenezer Judd decd. Hannah Judd had charged 7 shillings and 6 pence per week for the maintenance of her children. The Court allows but £0-04-06 per week (102 weeks in the whole). Account allowed. Lt. Isaac Merrells, Timothy Seymour and Lieut. John Newell were appointed to set out the widow's dower from the estate of Ebenezer Judd decd.

Page 11—13 June, 1737: The Adms., Hannah Judd and Deacon Thomas Richards, may sell land, £48-08-08, per act of the General Assembly of 14 October, 1736.

Page 13—2 August, 1737: A return of the sale of the land of Ebenezer Judd which was ordered to be sold by the General Assembly to answer the debts due from sd. estate, was now exhibited in Court by Hannah Judd and Deacon Thomas Richards, appointed to sell sd. land, and the contents of the land sold:

First, we set up 2-3 of the four-acre lott in Farmingtown:

	£ s d
Sold to Timothy Merrells for	6-19-06
Secondly: 6 acres at Three-Mile Hill in Farmingtown:	
Sold to Samuel North for	25-15-00
Thirdly: 57¼ acres in the third division in Farmington:	
Sold to Joshua How of Wallingford, 33 acres 20 rods at 12 shillings 6 pence per acre, for	20-12-10
Total,	£53-08-12

We, the subscribers, being at the dwelling house of Mr. Timothy Seymour in Hartford, 19th of July, 1737, at 2 of the clock afternoon, we then saw the above pieces of land sold at the beat of the drum.

Test: *Thomas Richards,*
David Ensign.

And also an accott. of the charge of the sale of sd. land, £5-16-10, which return is accepted by the Court.

Judd, Jonathan. Court Record, Page 31—5 August, 1735: An account of Adms. on the estate of Jonathan Judd of Middletown decd. was now exhibited in Court by Hannah Judd, Adms., whereby it appears she had paid in debts and charges £69-13-04, and received £0-16-00, which account is accepted and ordered upon file.

Page 383.

Langton, Joseph, Sen., Farmington. Invt. £711-01-03. Taken 9 April, 1736, by Isaac Cowles, Sen., Nathaniel Wadsworth and Thos. Wadsworth. Will dated 3 September, 1733.

I, Joseph Langton, Sen., of the Town of Farmingtown, do make this my last will and testament: Unto my wife Mary Langton (provided she survive me) I give to her the use, improvement and profit of 1-3 part of my house and lott where I now live, so long as she shall see cause there to live, reside and personally to dwell a widow bearing my name, and no longer; and also the use and profit of 1-3 part of all other of my real estate during her natural life. Also unto her my wife I give, to be at her own dispose, all the estate she brought with her and became mine by virtue of my marriage with her, and an addition of £8 of my personal estate. Unto my son Joseph Langton, besides what I have formerly given him, I give to him 1 suit of my wearing clothes, he to choose. And to my grandson Thomas Langton, son to the sd. Joseph Langton, to him and his heirs and assigns forever, I give and bequeath the 16th lot of land lying in the division of land in Farmingtown between Southington and Waterbury bounds, laid out on the right of my father Deacon John Langton decd., containing by estimation 148 acres. Unto my son John Langton, besides what I have already given him, I give to him and his heirs and assigns forever the 25th lott in the division of land in sd. Farmingtown on the range of Blew Mountain, laid out on the right of my aforesd. father, containing by estimation about 107 acres. Unto my son Samuel Langton, besides what I have already given him, I give to him the 67th lott of land in the division of land in sd. Farmingtown, lying north of the reserved land and on the west side of the river, laid out on my sd. father's right, containing 98 acres. Unto my three sons, viz., John Langton, Samuel Langton and Ebenezer Langton, I give and bequeath all the remainder of my wearing clothes in equal proportion. Unto my daughter Sarah Woodruff, besides what I have already given her, I give to her the sum of £40 in money. Also my will further is, that my sd. daughter shall have the liberty of living in my now dwelling house and have room for her comfort therein so long as she liveth unmarried. Unto my daughter Susannah Langton I give the sum of £60 in money. Unto my son Ebenezer Langton, now living with me, and on whose help the comfort of my present life much depends, besides what I have already given him, I give to him the residue and remainder of my estate, both real and personal, with the reversion thereof, not before in this instrument disposed of, wheresoever it is or may be found or whatsoever it be, he paying my debts and legacies aforesd. And I do hereby ordain my son Ebenezer Langton sole executor.

Witness: *John Hooker, Sen.,*   JOSEPH X LANGTON, LS.
Gershom Lewis, Stephen Bissell.

A codicil, dated 31 January, 1735, made the legacies to Sarah Woodruff and Susannah Langton to each £60 as money.

Witness: *John Hooker, Sen.,*   JOSEPH X LANGTON, LS.
Joseph Rootes, Samuell Nash.

Court Record, Page 43—13 April, 1736: Will proven.

Lane, John. Court Record, Page 1—28 March, 1734: John Lane, son of John Lane, late of Middletown, chose Nathaniel Bacon to be his guardian.

Page 266-7-8.

Lathrop, Corp. Hope. Invt. £489-02-36. Taken 25 November, 1734, by Ichabod Hinkley, Peter Emmons and John Lathrop. Will dated 6 March, 1731-2.

I, Hope Lathrop of Tolland, in the County of Hartford, do make this my last will and testament: I give to my wife Elizabeth 1-3 part of my household goods. I give to her 1-3 part of my neat cattle and sheep. I give to my sd. wife the use of 1-2 of my homestead and the use of 1-2 of my building during the time she shall remain my widow; this in lieu of her dower. I give to my wife the use and improvement of my great Bible during her natural life. I give to my son Benjamin Lathrop my great Bible and cane, the cane to be his at my decease and the Bible to be his after the decease of my sd. wife. I give to my son Ichabod Lathrop 1-2 of my right in the Cedar Swamp that is in sd. Tolland. I give to my son Solomon Lathrop 1-2 of my right in sd. swamp. I give to my son Solomon Lathrop all my homested, that is to say, all but what I have given to my son Ichabod Lathrop by a deed of gift and by a deed of sale. That which I give to my son Solomon bounds east on Willimantic River, south on my son Ichabod Lathrop's land which was part of sd. homested as well, as largely will appear upon Tolland Records, together with all my buildings and fences on that part of sd. homested. And my will is that my sd. son Solomon enter into the possession of what I have herein given in the following manner: 1-2 of sd. homested and buildings upon my decease, and the other half when my sd. wife ceases to be my widow, if my sd. son Solomon shall pay or cause to be paid the full sum of £75 in manner as followeth, viz., the sum of £50 in money unto my son Melatiah Lathrop at the age of 21 years, and £25 unto my son Joseph Lathrop at the age of 21 years. I give to my son John Lathrop 10 shillings. I give to my son Ebenezer Lathrop the sum of 10 shillings. I give to my son Melatiah Lathrop 1 feather bed and boalster. I give to my son Melatiah a paire of 3 (years) and vantage steers. I give to my son Joseph Lathrop £25 in money. I give to my son Joseph the bed we lodge on, after the death of my wife. I give to my son Joseph my riding beast. I give to my daughter Rebeckah Lewis £10. I give to my daughter Elizabeth Lathrop £30. I give to my daughter Mary Lathrop £30. I give to my daughter Sarah Hammond 10 shillings. Further, my will is that all my moveable estate, except what I have already disposed of, be equally divided to my four daughters, Rebeckah Lewis, Sarah Hammond, Elizabeth Lathrop and Marah Lathrop. I appoint my wife Elizabeth and my son Solomon Lathrop to be executors.

Witness: *Ichabod Hinkley,*   HOPE LATHROP, LS.
Benjamin Hinkley, David Hinkley.

Court Record, Page 14—19 November, 1734: Will proven.

Page 30—1st July, 1735: It was certified to this Court by *John Huntington, J. P.*, that Joseph Lathrop, a minor, 14 years of age, son of Capt. Hope Lathrop decd., chose his brother Ebenezer Lathrop of Mansfield to be his guardian. Recog., £50.

Lester, Elizabeth. Court Record, Page 34—5 November, 1735: Abraham Brooks of Haddam is appointed guardian to Elizabeth Lester, age 8 years, daughter of John Lester decd. Recog., £50.

Lewis, Deborah. Court Record, Page 11—1st September, 1734: Joseph Lewis of Haddam to be guardian to two of his children, viz., Deborah, age 12 years, and John, age 11 years. Recog., £100.

Invt. in Vol. XIII, Page 48.

Lewis, Noadiah, Farmington. Invt. £435-02-02. Taken 24 December, 1736, by Giles Hooker, Daniel Lewis and John Newell.

Court Record, Page 54—4 January, 1736-7: Adms. granted to Elisha Lewis of Faimington, who recog. in £200 with Joseph Hooker.

Page 14 (Vol. XIII) 12 August, 1737: Elisha Lewis, Adms., now wishes to resign, and this Court grant letters of Adms. unto Elizabeth Lewis, widow of sd. decd., who recog. in £200 with Elisha Lewis.

This Court appoints Elizabeth Lewis of Hadley to be guardian to Noadiah Lewis, a minor, about 9 months old. Recog., £100, with Elisha Lewis.

Page 34—5 October, 1738: Elizabeth Lewis, Adms., exhibits now an account of her Adms: Paid in debts and charges, £68-06-04, and an addition to the estate of £24-12-00. Account accepted.

Page 6 (Vol. XVI) 4 December, 1750: Noadiah Lewis, a minor, 14 years of age, son of Noadiah Lewis, chose Elisha Lewis of Farmington to be his guardian. Recog., £500.

Page 46.

Lewis, William, Farmington. Will dated 7 January, 1733-4: I, William Lewis, of the Town of Farmingtown, being stricken in years, do make this my last will and testament: Unto my son Isaac Lewis, besides what I have formerly given him, I give him all my right to lands in ye division of lands in Farmingtown laid out on the range of Blue Mountains; also all my right in lands in sd. town in the divisions of lands laid out between Southington and Waterbury, contained in 3 lotts, about 150 acres in the whole. To my son Daniel Lewis, besides what I have formerly given him, I give him all my land in the common field in Farmingtown, and all the land I have near home at a place called New Field, 4 or 5 acres; also all my land that I have at or near a place called ye Great Hill in sd. town, about 13 acres; also all my right to land that I have at a place called the Great Brook in sd. town. The 1-2 that I here give to my son Daniel Lewis is by way of portion to him; the other half is on the account of what support and sufferance I expect from him in my old age, if needed. Unto my two sons, Daniel Lewis and Jonathan Lewis, besides what I have formerly given them, I give them my lott in the north division on the west side of the river, containing 130 acres and 3 roods. Unto my aforesd. three sons, and to their heirs and assigns forever, I give and bequeath all my right in the several divisions of land in sd. Farmingtown accruing to me from my father-in-law Isaac More. My will further is, that in case my sons shall neglect to settle their estates by deed or by will, or either of them shall so neglect as to die intestate, then in that case the younger sons of him or them so neglecting their heirs and assigns shall have, hold and injoy in fee simple the lands that in this will I have given to him or them that shall so neglect to settle his estate. Unto my daughter, Mary Lewis, single woman, besides what in time past I have given her, I give to her the sum of £14 money, to be paid out of my personal estate. Unto my daughters, viz., Ruth Brounson and

Sarah Smith, I give to each of them the sum of £3 in money or as money. All the residue of my personal estate I give unto my aforenamed son Daniel Lewis, whome I constitute sole executor.

Witness: *John Hooker, Sen.*,   WILLIAM LEWIS, LS.
Asahel Strong, Asahel Strong, Jr.

Court Record, Page 54—1st February, 1736-7: Will now exhibited by Daniel Lewis, executor. Proven.

Invt. and Agreement in Vol. XIII, Page 36-7-8.

Lord, Sergt. William, East Haddam. Died 29 October, 1736. Invt. £260-03-06. Taken by Samuel Emmons, Jr., John Lord and Thomas Cone.

Articles of agreement, made by us whose names are hereunto subscribed, in the following manner, viz.: William Lord, Mary Lord, Joseph Crouch and his wife Hannah Crouch, Sarah Lord, John Sheppason and Hepsibah Sheppason, Mehetabell Lord and Susannah Lord, all heirs of William Lord, Sen., of East Haddam, our honoured father, for the division and settlement of his estate to us the surviving heirs, to each of us our respective portions thereof: We do all agree that we have received the whole of our portions to our full satisfaction, and do acquit and discharge our brother William Lord, Jr., of any further demand of any of the estate of our honoured father William Lord decd., whether real or personal.

HANNAH LORD, LS.	SARAH LORD, LS.
WM. LORD, LS.	JOHN SHEPPASON, LS.
MARY LORD, LS.	HEPSIBAH SHEPPASON, LS.
JOSEPH CROUCH, LS.	MEHETABELL X LORD, LS.
HANNAH CROUCH LS.	SUSANNAH X LORD, LS.

Witness: *William Olmsted,*
Dorothy Olmsted.

Court Record, Page 54—28 December, 1736: Adms. granted to William Lord, son of the decd., who recog. in £500 with Jonathan Lord of Colchester.

Page 17 (Vol. XIII) 6 December, 1737: William Lord, Adms., exhibits an account of his Adms. Accepted. Also, an agreement is exhibited and confirmed by the Court.

Page 351.

Man, William, Wethersfield. Will dated 2 March, 1735-6: I, William Man of Wethersfield, brasier, as to my estate my will and testament is as followeth: I give unto my grandchildren, Thomas Man, Hannah Man, Rebeckah Man, William Man, Mary Man and Sarah Man, all children of my son William Man of Marblehead decd., the sum of £10 money or bills of publick credit to each of them severally, to be paid to them by my executor hereafter named, viz., to Thomas Man and Hannah Man I order my executor hereafter named to pay the sum of £10 to each of them immediately after my decease, and £10 to each of the other of the four remaining children of my sd. son William Man upon their arriving to lawfull age. I give to my granddaughter Rebeckah Lupton the sum of £10 money, to be paid within three years after the date hereof. I give to my three grandchildren, John Rennals, Hannah Rennals and William Rennals, £10 money to each of them at lawfull age. I give to my law son John Reinalds (Rennals), Junr., and to my daughter Rebeckah, the wife of sd. Rennals, the remaining part of my estate, vizt., brasier's tools, pewter tools, brass ware, puter ware, money, bills, bonds, notes, and my estate remaining in Boston, personal or real, be it what it is. Finally, and to conclude, I give to my sd. son-in-law John Rennals, Jr., of Wethersfield, all my estate, whether real or personal, of what name, nature or denomination soever, excepting the legacies by me before ordered and given. I appoint my sd. son-in-law, John Rennals, Jr., to be sole executor.

Witness: *Nathaniel Burnham,*   WILLIAM MAN, LS.
Jonathan Williams, Elizabeth Warner.

Court Record, Page 41—19 March, 1735-6: Will now exhibited by John Rennals, executor.

Page 341-2.

Marshall, Deacon Thomas, Windsor. Invt. £178-09-08. Taken 1st December, 1735, by Nathaniel Drake, Roger Newbery and Timothy Loomis. Will dated 5 June, 1734.

I, Thomas Marshall, of the Town of Windsor, do make and ordain this my last will and testament: My will is, that what I have obliged myself, my heirs, etc., to pay to or allow my present wife Elizabeth, by a bond bearing date 13 November, 1729, that she shall have the full and free liberty of 1 room in my dwelling house, which of them she shall choose, and the use and improvement of 8 or 10 rods of ground near my house for a garden plott, and to pasture a cow for her during her natural life, provided she survive and continue to dwell in this town, is the whole she shall have out of my estate. I give to my son Samuel Marshall, more than I have given him by deed of gift, my orchard and six acres of upland adjoining to John Graham's land. Also I give him all my right and share I have or ought to have in Torrington, in the County of Hartford, lying in common and undivided with the rest of the proprietors of sd. Torrington. And further, I give him all my right and share in the mile and 1-2-mile division of sd. Windsor Town Commons, being the lott numbered 239. And lastly, I give him 1-8 part of the whole of the grist mill (in which I have a part), except he shall allow of or give liberty for the setting up of another grist mill on the same brook on which this stands. If so, then my will is that my son Daniel shall have it, he not paying anything for it to him the sd. Samuel Marshall, his heirs and assigns forever. I give to my son Thomas Marshall, more than I have already given him, my lott in the second meadow, also my lott in the first meadow, and my five acres of upland lying by the wayside as you go to the 2nd meadow. Also, I give him my right and share in the equivalent land lying northeast of the township of Windsor. I give to my grandchildren, Ichabod and Eunice Marshall, or their guardian for their use, more than I have given to their father my son John Marshall decd., £10 money, to be paid them in equal shares by my son Daniel Marshall. I give to my son Daniel Marshall my dwelling house and homested, with the upland east of my house, and my pasture which I bought of Cornelius Gillett, reserving only to my wife Elizabeth the use of one room in the house, which she shall choose, and about 8 or 10 rods near the house, and pasturing for a cow, for her use during her natural life if it please God that she survive me and continue to dwell in this town. Also, I give him one part of the grist mill (of which I have a part) and that broken time in it of 16 hours. And further, I give him my pasture west of the grist mill forever, he paying the sum of £10 money to my grandchildren, Ichabod and Eunice Marshall, or to their guardian; and to my grandchildren, Esther, Katharine and Ann Fowler, or their father Fowler, to be paid them in equal shares when they come of age, £10 money in the whole, to be paid by the sd. Daniel Marshall; and also to my two daughters, Mary Wilson and Eunice Marshall, £10 money each. I appoint my son Samuel Marshall executor.

Witness: *Timothy Loomis,*   THOMAS MARSHALL, LS.
Mary X Soper, Hannah Loomis.

Court Record, Page 37—10 December, 1735: Will exhibited.

Page 388.

Meakins, Mary, Hartford. Invt. £60-00-04. Taken 30 November, 1736, by Samuel Welles and John Pratt, Jr.

Court Record, Page 53—28 December, 1736: Adms. to Thomas Miller, Jr., of Springfield. Recog., with Samuel Welles of Farmington.

Page 19—(Vol. XIII) 3 January, 1737-8: Thomas Miller, Adms., exhibits an account of his Adms., by which account it appears he has paid in debts and charges the sum of £10-13-09; credit received, 10 shillings. Account accepted and ordered on file.

Page 328-9.

Merrells, Caleb, Hartford. Invt. £230 in realty. Taken 3 November, 1735, by Moses Nash and Martin Smith. Will dated 22 September, 1735.

I, Caleb Merrells of Hartford, do make this my last will and testament: First, I give to my wife Mercy 1-3 part of all my moveable estate, to be at her own dispose forever. The other two-thirds of my moveable estate I give to my son Abijah and to the other child (whether son or daughter) which my wife now goes withall, provided always, if either of them die before the other comes of age, his or her share to be for the use and benefit of sd. survivor. And if they both live to be 21 years of age, then to be equally divided betwixt them. And my real estate, that is, the house and land I live on, I give and bequeath in manner following: First, I hereby authorize and fully impower my executors hereafter named to sell and dispose of so much of the land as shall be sufficient to pay Samuel Culver of Wallingford about £130 money which I owe him for the purchase of sd. house and land I live in, as also ye house and whole lot, if lots be not sufficient to pay sd. debt, and to make ample deeds of conveyance for the same. And what shall remain, if any, after sd. debts are paid, of the homestead and house, I give one-third of it to my wife Mercy, and the other 2-3 to be equally divided between my son Abijah and the child my wife now goes withall. And if either of them die before they arrive to 21 years, to be to the survivor. I appoint my brother Jonathan Sedgewick, Cyprian Merrells, and my wife Mercy, or any two of them, to be my executors.

Witness: *Daniel Hooker, Jr.,*   CALEB MERRELLS, LS.
Ebenezer Smith, Elisha Smith.

Court Record, Page 33—7 October, 1735: Will proven.

Page 6 (Vol. XIII) 3 May, 1737: An addition to the estate of Caleb Merrells was exhibited in Court by Mercy Merrells, executrix, amounting to the sum of £13-11-11.

Page 7—3 May, 1737: The children, Abijah Merrells now 3 years of age, and Mercy, one year, this Court appoint their mother Mercy Merrells to be their guardian. Recog., £100.

Page 62 (Vol. XIV) 6 August, 1745: Jonathan Sedgewick of Hartford, executor to the last will of Caleb Merrells, moves this Court that distributors may be appointed to distribute the estate according to the will: Whereupon this Court appoint Capt. Daniel Webster, Moses Nash and Stephen Hosmer, of Hartford, distributors.

Page 64 (Vol. XV) 3 May, 1748: Abijah Merrells, a minor, 14 years of age, son of Caleb Merells, chose Moses Nash of Hartford to be his guardian. And this Court appoint the sd. Moses Nash guardian to Mercy Merrell, a minor, 12 years of age. Recog., £300.

Page 75—5 September, 1748: Ebenezer Mix being brought before *Joseph Talcott, J. P.,* and being bound over to this Court, now appeared and under oath answered to sundry questions with respect to his withholding and concealing part of the moveable estate of Caleb Merrell, of Hartford, deceased.

Page 320.

Miller, Jonathan, Glastonbury. Invt. £820-02-03. Taken 1st August , 1735, by Nathaniel Talcott and William Miller.

Court Record, Page 31—5 August, 1735: This Court grant Adms. unto Elizabeth Miller, widow and relict of sd. deceased, who gave bond, with Deacon Nathaniel Talcott of sd. Glastonbury, of £400.

Page 344.

Inventory on Page 369.

Miller, Thomas, Middletown. Invt. £175-12-10. Taken 8 November, 1735, by John Warner, Samuel Gipson and Stephen Miller.

Court Record, Page 46—1st June, 1736: Account of Adms. now exhibited by Ephraim Squire, Adms. Accepted.

Page 49—3 August, 1736: Stephen Miller and James Miller exhibit an agreement for a final settlement under their hands and seals.

Page 369—3 August, 1736: *To all people to whom these presents shall come, greeting:* Whereas, we, Stephen Miller and James Miller, both of Middletown, are by heirship and quitclaims from the other heirs of our honered father, Thomas Miller, late of Middletown deceased, the lawfull owners of the real estate of our sd. father lying and being in sd. Middletown, which we do agree to divide as followeth: We do agree to improve the mill joyntly, each one to hold an equal share therein, with all the priviledges and appurtenances thereof, except the mill land. And the said James Miller, in consideration that the sd. Stephen Miller doth give me a lawfull quitclaim of all his right to the dwelling house and three acres of land that we bought of our uncles, Benjamin, John and Elijah Miller, do agree that he the sd. Stephen Miller shall have and hold all the dwelling house that did belong to our said father, and one acre and half more than half the lot on which said house standeth, to lye on the northern side thereof, which land contains in the whole lot about eighteen acres. And all that piece of land that lies on the hill called Captain's Hill, being westward from the mill, and all that piece of land that lies on the northern side of ye path or highway from the mill to the sd. dwelling house, unto all which I, the sd. James, do quitclaim to him the sd. Stephen, his heirs and assigns forever. And I, the sd. Stephen, do agree that he the sd. James shall have and hold all the remainder of sd. eighteen-acre lott, to lye on the southern side thereof, being the equall half of it wanting one acre and a half acre ; and all that piece of land that lyeth southward of the sd. path or highway that leads from the mill to the dwelling house abovesaid, unto all which I, the sd. Stephen, do quitclaim to him the sd. James, his heirs and assigns forever.

In presence of: STEPHEN MILLER, LS.
Lamberton Cooper,   JAMES MILLER, LS.
William Rockwell.
And acknowledged.
Acknowledged in Court, **3 August, 1736.**
           Test: *Jos: Talcott, Jun'r, Clerk.*

Page 13 (Vol. XIII) 2 August, 1737: Ephraim Squire, Adms., exhibited an account of his Adms. Pursuant to an act of the General Assembly, 12 May, 1737, this Court direct the Adms. to sell land to the value of £29-14-01.

Page 29—2 May, 1738: Return of the sale of land by Ephraim Squire, Adms. All except the mill platt not being sufficient to pay all the debts, the mills, house and utensils ordered to be sold.

Page 96—21 July, 1741: Moses Miller, age 18 years, son of Thomas Miller, chose Ephraim Squire of Durham to be his guardian. Recog., £100. Cert: *Giles Hall, J. P.*

Page 286.

Mitchelson, William, Simsbury. Invt. £41-12-10. Taken 6 January, 1734-5, by Samuel Griswold and John Enos.

Court Record, Page 20—4 February, 1734-5: Adms. to Mary Mitchelson, widow.

Page 298-9-300.

Moore, Capt. Thomas, Windsor. Invt. taken 18 February, 1734-5, by Nathaniel Drake and Timothy Loomis. In this inventory appears the following: In coined silver, 30s-8d at 15d weight, £4-03-00; a silver drinking bowl, two silver dram cups and three silver spoons weighing 16 ounces averdupoise weight, £14-00-00. Will dated 20 April, 1733.

I, Thomas Moore, do make this my last will and testament: I give unto my beloved wife Deborah Moore 1-3 part of all my moveable estate forever, and also the use and improvement of 1-3 part of all my real estate during her natural life; and also the use and improvement of all the lands and buildings given unto my son Thomas in this my will, untill he shall arrive at the age of 21 years, provided she keep the buildings in repair and maintain the fences inclosing the lands. I give unto my son Thomas my home lott and the buildings thereon standing, and the 3 acres in Bowfield lying at the west end thereof; also my pasture on the east side of the country road (3 acres), being part of my father's homelott; also my little meadow lott, 6 acres, and also 4 acres in the Great Meadow, bounded west on the Rivulett; and also my lott at a place called Garson, 45 acres, bounding west on the country road; also my Mill Brook lott that I bought of John Graham, 17 acres; also all my land lying in Torrington, being a right I bought of my brother Josiah Moore; and also 1-5 part of all the common and undivided land belonging to me in the Township of Windsor, with my saws and 2 best broad axes, and all my other necessary shop tools, all which shall be set out to him, by my executor hereafter named, when he arrives at the age of 21 years. I give to my daughter Hannah 1-2 of the lott called Moses' lott, at Greenfield, containing in the whole 20 acres; and also the other half of sd. lott I give and bequeath unto my grandson Isaac Skinner, to be his at the age of 21 years, and until then his father to have the use of it. I give unto my sd. daughter Hannah 1-5 part of my right in the common and undivided land at Windsor, and also 1-4 Town Commons division that is already made, with 1-4 part of all my land lying in Barkhamstead. I give unto my daughter Abiah £60 at inventory price out of my moveable estate, and 1-5 part of my common and undivided land in the Township of Windsor, and 1-4 part of my Town Commons division that is already laid out, and also 1-4 part of my lands lying in Barkhamstead. I give to my daughter Keziah £60, 1-5 part of my common and undivided land, and 1-4 part of my Town Commons division, and 1-4 part of my land at Barkhamstead. I give unto my daughter Deborah £10 besides what I have already given her, also 1-5 part of my common and undivided land, and 1-4 part of my Town Commons division, and 1-4 part of my lands in Barkhamstead. The remainder of the moveables, if any, shall be equally divided unto my four daughters. I appoint Roger Newbery and my wife executors.

Witness: *Matthew Allyn,*   Thomas Moore, ls.
Josiah Drake, Martha Drake.

Court Record, Page 25—1st April, 1735: Will now exhibited by Capt. Roger Newbery and Mrs. Deborah Moore, executors.

Orvice, Azuba, Farmington. Court Record, Page 31—5 August, 1735: Rachel Orvice, Farmington, to be guardian to Azuba Orvice and Oliver Orvice, children of Samuel and Rachel Orvice. Recog., £100.

Page 366-7-8-9, 392.

Osborn, Samuel, Sen., Windsor. Invt. £501-13-06. Taken 19 July, 1736, by John Cady, John Stiles and Jacob Osborn. Will dated 7 June, 1736.

I, Samuel Osborn, Sen., of Windsor, do make this my last will and testament: I give to my loving wife so much out of my estate as shall be comfortable maintenance for her under her circumstances. My will is that my son Samuel Osborn shall have the care and oversight of it and see it done; and in consideration of that and the great love and affection that I have for him, I give him all my lands, divided and undivided, excepting land that doth belong to me by the death of my brother-in-law John Denslow, only I order him, and my will is, that he should pay to my daughter Rebeckah £100 money worth in cattle, or part cattle and part money, within one year after the death of my wife. My will further is yt what belongs to me by the death of my brother-in-law John

Denslow shall be equally divided between my son and daughter, both lands and moveables. My will further is, that my son should have all that is due to me, and also the moveables that I now have, only he shall pay to my daughter £4 in money within two years from the date hereof. My son Samuel to be sole executor.

Witness: *John Stiles,*   SAMUEL OSBORN, LS.
John Morris, Jacob Osborn.

Court Record, Page 47—6 July, 1736: Will proven.

Will and Invt. in Vol. XIII, Page 10-11.

Owen, Isaac, Simsbury. Invt. £940-06-04. Taken 5 January, 1736-7, by Peletiah Allyn, Benjamin Griswold, Jr., and Jonathan Stiles. Will dated 26 February, 1734-5.

I, Isaac Owen of Simsbury, in the County of Hartford, do make this my last will and testament: I give to my wife Sarah 1-3 part of my personal estate, and likewise 1-3 part of my real estate, during her natural life, and the use of 1-2 of my dwelling house during her widowhood. I give to my eldest son Isaac Owen all that remains of that lott that I bought of John Lewis, which joins partly on Josiah Hinkley's land and partly on land I had of John Owen. I give to my son Isaac 6 acres of my mowing pasture lying in Suffield, in the County of Hampshire and Province of Massachusetts Bay, which mowing pasture is bounded west on Simsbury, east and north on land I bought of Capt. Joseph Winchell of Suffield, and on the south side lyes partly in Windsor Township, which 6 acres is the south side of sd. pasture. I give to my son Isaac Owen all that lott I bought of Nathaniel Hamlin of sd. Suffield. I give to my son Elijah Owen, after my decease, my homelott as it is butted and bounded east on the present road, north on Isaac Gillett's land, south on land I bought of John Lewis, west on Turkey Hills, with all the accommodations to the same, after my decease, excepting what may be his mother's dowry. Also I give to my son Elijah Owen all the remaining part of my sd. mowing pasture in Suffield, besides sd. six acres given to my son Isaac, together with all the other land I have in Suffield. I give to my daughter Sarah Phelps £20 besides what she hath already. I give to my daughter Rebeckah £60. I give to my daughter Deborah Eno £35 besides what she hath already had. I give to my daughter Anne £50. I appoint my two sons, Isaac and Elijah Owen, my executors.

Witness: *John Hunt,*   ISAAC OWEN, LS.
Benjamin Owen, John Lewis.

Court Record, Page 55—1st February, 1736-7: Will proven.

Page 35 (Vol. XIV) 6 December, 1743: Isaac Owen, one of the executors, moves to this Court that the widow's dowry in the estate of the sd. decd. given her in sd. will may be set out to her according to the will, viz., in the estate of Elijah Owen, one of the sons of the sd. decd., who is also deceased: Whereupon this Court appoint Joshua Holcomb, Isaac Gillett and Samuel Owen, of Simsbury, to set out to Sarah Owen, widow, the relict, her legacy or dowry in the estate of sd. Isaac Owen decd., viz., Elijah Owen's estate, by bounds, according to sd. will, and make return of their doings to this Court.

Page 301.

Peirce, Edward, Simsbury. Invt., 2 parcels of land, £30-00-00. Taken 31 March, 1735, by Samuel Bemon, Jr., and Gillet Addams.

Court Record, Page 12—5 November, 1734: Adms. to Nathaniel Pinney of Windsor. Recog., £100, with Wm. Pratt of Hartford.

Page 37—15 December, 1735: Nathaniel Pinney, Jr., Adms., being now deceased, not having finished his Adms., this Court appoint Samuel Pettebone, 2nd, Adms. Recog., £100, with John Pettebone, Jr.

Page 321.

Pelton, John, Middletown, East. Died 15 July, 1735. Invt. £225-11-06. Taken 20 August, 1735, by Nathaniel Nichols and John Penfield. Will dated July, 1735.

I, John Pelton of Middletown, do make this my last will and testament: I give to my wife Jemima all my household goods, to be her estate forever. I also give to her the use of 1-2 of my house in Middletown, and the use of 1-3 part of my 400-acre farm called the School lott, during the time she continues my relict and widow. I give to my eldest son John, besides what I have advanced toward his settlement, my £50 right in Potopogue Quarter in Saybrook, together with the divisions and allottments of land that have been laid out thereupon and have not been by me conveyed, and also that shall hereafter be laid out upon sd. right or belong thereto. To my son James (besides what I have already given him) I give him 5 shillings. And upon condition that my son James shall discharge my executors from all claims and demands which he may pretend to have against my estate, and, as he ought to do, shall resign up his claims and interest in two yoke of my oxen (which I heretofore mortgaged to him) unto my executors that the sd. oxen may by them be disposed of as in this my will I shall order, then my will is that he shall have £40 paid to him, as I shall hereafter direct, within four years after my decease. To my two sons, Phineas and Johnson, I give the 1-2 of my abovesd. 400 acres called the School lott, together with the 1-2 of my dwelling house thereon standing, to them, their heirs and assigns forever, on condition that they pay out such legacies as I shall hereafter order. To my other two sons, Joseph and Josiah, and to my daughter Mary, I give the other half of my sd. 400 acres, to be between them three equally divided, to be to them, their heirs and assigns forever, upon condition that they pay out such legacies as I shall hereafter order. I give to my daughter Jemima £20. To my other three daughters, Sarah, Elizabeth and Ketureh, I give to each of them £20. To my four sons, Phineas, Johnson, Joseph and Josiah, I give and bequeath all my cattle, husbandry tools and utensils, to be equally divided between them. I give and bequeath my 200 acres of land in Middletown, which I bought of Mr. Woodward, to my executors hereafter named, to be by them sold for the payment of my debts and for no other purpose. My wife Jemima and my son Phineas Pelton to be executors.

Witness: *Hez: Buckingham,*   JOHN X PELTON, LS.
Solomon Wheat, Samuel Williams.

Court Record, Page 32—2 September, 1735: Will proven.

Page 6 (Vol. XV) 1st March, 1746: Joseph Pelton of Middletown, one of the heirs to the estate of John Pelton, moved to this Court that freeholders may be appointed to divide one certain piece of land lying in Middletown, containing about 400 acres, and is on the east side of the Great River, being one of the long lotts, so called, the executors neglecting and refuseing to divide the same: Whereupon this Court appoint Joseph Frary, William Rockwell and Samuel Wadsworth, of Middletown, to make division and partition of sd. land according to the last will and testament of the sd. deceased to the heirs, and make return of their doings to this Court.

Page 339-40.

Pinney, Nathaniel, Jr., Windsor. Invt. £880-06-06. Taken by Samuel Bemon, Jr., Gillett Addams and Lemuel Roberts. Add to the invt. 59 acres of land in Colchester, land bought of Thomas Crow in Colebrook, and a £2-06-00 right in Barkhamsted. Will dated 27 June, 1735.

I, Nathaniel Pinney, Jr., of Windsor, being very sick and weak in body, but of present mind and memory, do make this my last will and testament: I give to Elizabeth, my wife, the use of all my land in the mile and 1-2-mile division in Windsor, and of all my land in Simsbury, until my eldest son Darius come to the age of 21 years, and the use of 1-3 during her natural life, and one-third part of moveables forever. I give to my eldest son Darius £20 more than the 1-2 of my land in the mile and 1-2-mile division in Windsor, and 1-2 of all my land in Simsbury. I give to my youngest son Filander the other half of the above sd. land, excluding the £20 which my eldest son Darius shall have more than the 1-2, to him and his heirs forever. Furthermore, that if either of my sons shall die before he shall come to the age of 21 years, the other son shall have all his lands before mentioned, provided he shall, in the term of 6 years after he comes to the age of 21 years, pay each of my daughters in equal share the price of land as it shall be inventoried, that is to say, he having an equal share with them. Furthermore, my will is that all my lands in Barkhamsted and Colchester and Peller Hill shall be sold by my executrix hereafter named to pay my debts, and what remains more than to pay my debts be divided in equal share amongst my daughters. Also, I give the remainder of my estate in equal share to my daughters, viz., to Martha Addams, to Ruhama, to Lurana, to Elizabeth and to Sarah, to them and their heirs forever, excluding my buildings. My will is that my sons Darius and Filander shall have an equal share of my house and barn. I appoint my wife Elizabeth sole executrix.

Witness: *Thos. Griswold,*   NATHANIEL PINNEY, JR., LS.
Joseph Barnard, Nathaniel Griswold.

Court Record, Page 34—7 October, 1735: Will exhibited by Elizabeth, the widow, executrix.

Page 61 (Vol. XIII) 19 February, 1739-40: Darius Pinney, age 16 years, son of Nathaniel Pinney, chose his mother Elizabeth Pinney to be his guardian. Recog., £100.

Page 353.

Porter, John, Kensington. Invt. £887-11-06. Taken 16 March, 1736, by Isaac Hart and Caleb Galpin. Will dated 18 February, 1735-6.

I, John Porter of Kensington, in the County of Hartford and Colony of Connecticut, do make this my last will and testament: I give to Hannah Porter her dower rights, and also the use of all my real estate until my only son shall come to the age of 21 years. I give to my only son John Porter all my real estate in houseing and lands, and to his heirs and assigns forever, he paying to my eldest daughter Ann Porter £30 in current money of sd. Colony within the space of 3 years after he shall come to be of the age above mentioned, and also £30 in sd. specie to my second daughter Abigail Porter within the space of four years after he shall come to the sd. age, and also £30 in sd. specie to my youngest daughter Jerusha Porter within the space of five years after he shall come to be of the age above mentioned. All the rest of my estate I give to my three daughters above mentioned, to be equally divided among them. And I do hereby appoint my well-beloved wife above named sole executrix.

Witness: *Isaac Lee,*   JOHN PORTER, LS.
Daniel Hancox, Josiah Hurlbut.

From File:

DISTRIBUTION OF THE ESTATE OF JOHN PORTER.

Know all men by these presents: That we, Ann Porter, Abigail Brownson and Jerusha Porter, all of Farmington, in ye County of Hartford and Collony of Connecticut, being heirs and equal sharers in the estate of our beloved brother John Porter, late of the parrish of Kensington, in sd. Farmington, deceased, do by these presents, each of us for ourselves and for our heirs, fully and finally agree to divide all ye lands accrueing to us from our said brother in manner and form following, that is to say, in ye first place we all agree that the said Ann Porter shall for her share in sd. lands have full nine acres of the west side of the house lot that did belong to our sd. brother, runing throw from ye highway to the river, being eighteen rods in breadth east and west; and also foer acars and one-halfe acar of the east end of the lot called ye lot at Two-Mile Brook, runing across sd. lot and buting east and north with highway. And 2nd, we all agree that Abigaile Brownson shall for her share of sd. lands have full thirteen acars of the northeast corner of ye abcve sd. house lott, buting east with highway, west with ye above sd. nine acars sett out to Ann, and north with ye river called Betses' Branch; and also foer acars and one-halfe acar of the lot called ye lot at Two-Mile Brook, buting east with ye above described piece of sd. lot sett to Ann Porter, north with highway, and south with Jonathan Edwards. And 3dly, we all agree that the above sd. Jerusha Porter shall for her share in sd. lands have full thirteen acars of the southeast corner of the above described house lot, buting south and east with highways, and north and west with Ann and Abigail's parts of sd. house lot; and also all the rest of the sd. lot at Two-Mile Brook, on each side of the highway that parts ye west end of sd. lot. And now, for a final confirmation of the above writen division of the lands accruing to us as heirs to our sd. brother's estate, we have hereunto severally set to our hands and seals the second day of February, and in ye 15th yeare of ye reign of our souereign lord George the Second, of Great Britaine, etc., King. *Annoqui domini* 1741-2.

ANN PORTER (her mark) LS.

ABIGAILL (her mark) BROWNSON, LS.

AARON BROWNSON, LS.

JERUSHA (her mark) PORTER, LS.

Endorsement:
At a Court of Probate held at Hartford,
2nd February, 1741-2: Then Ann Porter,
Abigail Brownson and Jerusha Porter
acknowledged their hands and seals.
       Test: *Jos: Talcott, Clerk.*
Ordered to be recorded.

Court Record, Page 108 (Vol. XIII) 2 February, 1741-2:
This agreement was accepted in Court and ordered to be recorded and kept on file. [*It is not found recorded.*]

Page 355-6.

Porter, Doctor Samuel. Invt. £1364-00-06. Taken by John Porter, Isaac Cowles and Nathaniel Wadsworth. Will dated 21 June, 1735.

I, Samuel Porter, doctor, of Farmingtown, do make this my last will and testament: I give unto my wife Abigail Porter, to be at her own dispose forever, 1-2 part of all my household goods and two cowes, also one horse (which she shall choose). I give unto her, during her natural life, the use and profit of 1-2 part of all my lands now under improvement. I give her 1-2 part of all my buildings. Unto my three daughters, viz., Abigail Thomas, Sarah Lee and Eunice Wadsworth, I give and bequeath all the rest of my household goods, to be equally divided between them. Unto my son, Ezekiel Porter, besides what I have already given him, I now give to him the 51st lott in number in the fourth division of lands in Farmingtown, laid out on the right of my father, about 103 acres. Unto my son Thomas Porter I give severall parcels of land within the bounds of the Township of Farmingtown, viz., all the lands laid out in my father's right, and half the land laid out on the right of Mr. Newton as is contained in the 6th allottment in the division of lands lying against Hartford and Windsor, about 125 acres; also all the land laid out on my father's right in the 11th allottment in the 2nd division of land in Farmingtown, 103 acres more or less. Unto my son Hezekiah Porter I give all the lands that was laid out on the right of Capt. John Stanly in the 9th allottment in the 2nd division in Farmingtown, 150 acres more or less; also the 10th lott in number in the 6th division, containing 103 acres more or less, which lott was laid out on my father's right. Unto my son Samuel Porter I give lands and buildings in sd. Farmingtown as followeth, viz., my homelott where I now live, with all the buildings thereon standing; also my pasture at ye place called ye Mill Swamp; also my pasture across the way against my house; also all my land that I have in the common field; also all my land at a place called ye Long Swamp; also all my land at a place called White Oak Plaine. My wife to have the use as is before willed to her. My will further is, that all the remainder of my personal estate, after the foregoing legacies and debts are paid, shall belong to and be equally divided among my three youngest sons, James Porter, Hezekiah Porter and Samuel Porter. I will and bequeath my right lying in common in the reserved lands in Farmingtown to be equally divided among my four sons. I make my son Ezekiel Porter and my son-in-law Hezekiah Lee to be executors.

Witness: *Giles Hooker,*   Samuel Porter, ls.
Gershom Lewis, Thomas Smith.

Court Record, Page 43—6 April, 1736: Will proven. Hezekiah Porter, age 19 years, and Samuel Porter, age 17 years, chose Ezekiel Porter to be their guardian.

Page 238.

Purple, Edward, Haddam. Invt. £143-15-00. Taken 21 February, 1733-4, by John Gates, David Cone and Bezaleel Brainard.

Court Record, Page 2—1st April, 1734: Elias Purple, son of Edward Purple, chose Joseph Gates to be his guardian. Recog., £100.

Page 4—7 May, 1734: Adms. granted to Edward Purple of Haddam, who gave bonds of £200 with Moses Cook.

Page 27—6 May, 1735: Edward Purple, Adms., exhibited an account of his Adms., which is accepted. And John Purple, son of Edward Purple, age 17 years, chose Lt. Jabez Chapman to be his guardian.

Page 346.

Robe, Andrew, Sen., Simsbury. Invt. £124-00-00. Taken 27 November, 1735, by Samuel Buell and Joseph Humphrey. Will dated 26 August, 1729.

I, Andrew Robe, Sen., of Simsbury, do see cause to make this my last will and testament: I give unto my wife Sarah, during her natural life, the use of 1-2 of my house lott, with 1-2 of my meadow lott lying in Hop Meadow, with the east end of my now dwelling house, with so much cellar room as she needs from year to year, and also so much barn room as to keep stover for two cowes and sheltering in bad weather. And also I oblige my son Andrew Robe to keep his mother's buildings and fences in repair during the time of her widowhood. And also I give her 1-2 of my moveable estate forever, but the houseing and land for life, unless she see cause to marry, then she shall move off with only 1-3 of these lands and 1-3 of my moveable estate, and shall not bring any man into my son's possessions which may cause differences to arise between him and his mother. I give unto my son Andrew Robe all my lands that I now possess, excepting what I have given to my wife during her natural life, which he is not to enter into possession of until her decease, and then he is to enjoy the same and all other my land, both divided and undivided land, to him, his heirs and assigns forever. Also, I give unto my son Andrew Robe the other half of my moveable estate to pay debts and legacies withall unto his sisters. I give and bequeath unto my three daughters, namely, Mary, Elizabeth and Amy, unto each of them so much as to make up, with what they have already received, £20 to each of them. I appoint my son Andrew Robe sole executor.

Witness: *Josiah Alford,*   ANDREW ROBE, LS.
Jacob Case, Abigail Case.

Court Record, Page 37—28 November, 1735: Will proven.

Page 304-5.

Roberts, John, Simsbury. Invt. £34-16-00. Taken 5 May, 1735, by Andrew Moore and Samuel Bemon, Jr.

Court Record, Page 23—26 March, 1735: Adms. to Nathaniel Roberts. Recog., £200, with Gillet Addams.

Page 26—6 May, 1735: Exhibit of personal inventory.

Page 302.

Roberts, Nathaniel, Middletown. Invt. £68-13-06. Taken 1st April, 1735, by Stephen Blake, Jabez Brooks and John Roberts.

Court Record, Page 25—14 April, 1735: Adms. to Mehetabell Roberts, widow. Recog., with John Roberts of Middletown.

Page 35 (Vol. XIII) 7 November, 1738: Mehetabell Roberts, widow, exhibited in Court an account of her Adms., which this Court do see cause to accept. This Court also appoint Mehetabell Roberts, widow, to be guardian to her children, viz., Deborah, age 6 1-2 years; Mehetabell, age 4 years, and Nathaniel, age 3 years, all children of Nathaniel Roberts, late decd. Recog., £150.

Page 225.

Root, Thomas, Jr., sometime of Lebanon, late of Farmington, decd. Invt. £83-10-05. Taken 24 June, 1734, by Daniel Judd and John Newell.

Court Record, Page 8—22 July, 1734: Invt. exhibited by Joseph Hawley, Adms.

Page 38 (Vol. XIII) 5 December, 1738: Eleazer Root, age 9 years, Hannah age 7, and Sarah age 5 years, children of Thomas Root: this Court appoint Ebenezer Hawley, with their mother Hannah Root's consent, to be guardian to sd. minors. Recog., £300.

Page 40—6 February, 1738: Joseph Hawley, Adms., exhibits an account of his Adms., whereby it appears he has paid in debts and charges the sum of £100-07-05, which account is accepted, ordered recorded and kept on file.

Page 323.

Rowlandson, Wilson, Wethersfield. Died 3 July, 1735. Invt. £438-06-09. Taken 18 August, 1735, by Thomas Deming, William Blin and Joseph Flower. Will dated 17 May, 1735.

I, Wilson Rowlandson of Wethersfield, do make this my last will and testament: I give to my two sons, Phineas and Wilson, my land in Stepney Parish in sd. Wethersfield, bounding north on a highway, east on land of Samuel Deming, south on a highway, west on land of John Reinolds, containing about 20 acres, together with the house and barn thereon standing, after the payment of my debts and funeral expenses as above mentioned. Then the residue of my moveable estate I give to Mary, my loving wife, 1-3 part forever. Then what remains I give and bequeath to my two daughters, Thankfull and Hannah. To Mary, my wife, I give and bequeath the use and improvement of the land, house and barn above bequeathed as long as she shall remain my relict, provided that it exceed not the time of my two sons their arrival at the age of 21 years. I appoint and desire Josiah Churchill at Wethersfield and Mary my wife to be executors.

Witness: *Richard Lord,*   WILSON ROWLANDSON, LS.
Joseph Woodhouse, Timothy Baxter.

Court Record, Page 32—2 September, 1735: Will proven. Josiah Churchill declines, and the widow Mary Rowlandson is appointed Adms. with the will annexed.

Page 50—3 August, 1736: This Court do appoint Mary Rowlandson to be guardian to Phineas Rowlandson, age 5 years, Wilson 3 years, and Hannah 7 years of age, all children of Wilson Rowlandson decd. Recog., £100.

Page 4 (Vol. XIII) 29 March, 1737: Mary Rowlandson, widow, Adms., exhibited an account of her Adms.: Paid in debts and charges, £98-03-05; credited with £7-04-00. Which account is accepted and ordered to be kept on file. Thankfull Rowlandson, age 9 1-2 years, daughter of Wilson Rowlandson, chose her mother Mary Rowlandson to be her guardian. Recog., £50.

Page 9 (Vol. XV) 1st April, 1746: Phineas Rowlandson, a minor, 14 years of age, son of Wilson Rowlandson, late of Wethersfield deceased, chose Jacob Gibbs, his father-in-law, to be his guardian. Recog., £500.

Page 330.

Rowley, Moses, East Haddam. Invt. £33-12-05. Taken 19 August, 1735, by Thomas Gates and John Fuller. Will dated 24 March, 1734-5.

I, Moses Rowley, of the Town of East Haddam, in the County of Hartford, do make and ordain this my last will and testament: I give to my loving sons, viz., Moses, Samuel, Ebenezer and Jonathan Rowley, all my lands known by the name of the Purchase Land or Lotts, equally to be divided among them, that is to say, if the sd. purchasers are pleased to divide the same, then I do give it them and their heirs as in manner abovesd.; but if the sd. purchasers should not divide the sd. land, but let it lie for the use first intended, then I do give and bequeath it to that use for the Gospel in this place. Secondly, I do give and bequeath to my loving son John Rowley all my carpenter's tools. I give to my son Jonathan Rowley my cart boxes and bands, my small axe and broad hoe. I give to my daughter Hannah Rowley that cowe that my son John Rowley now hath, and six sheep, my bed that I now lye on and all the bedding belonging to the same, and all the household goods that I now have. I give my wearing clothes to my sons, Moses, Samuel, John, Ebenezer and Jonathan Rowley. And whatsoever else which I shall have, at my decease, of estate that I have not disposed of as above sd., to be equally divided among them, excepting 20 shillings apiece to be paid out of the same to my three daughters, viz., Mary Olmsted, Nein Fuller and Mehetabell Chapman. Furthermore, my will is that my sons Samuel Rowley of Hebron and Ebenezer of East Haddam be executors.

Witness: *John Fuller,*   MOSES ROWLEY, LS.
John Persival, Ebenezer Fuller.

Court Record, Page 33—7 October, 1735: Will now proven. Moses Rowley, one of the sons, appealed from the decision of this Court approveing the will.

RECEIPTS RECORDED ON PAGE 56, THEY BEING THE LAST OF THE COURT ENTRIES IN VOL. XII:

2nd January, 1733-4: I, Mary Rowlee, the wife of Moses Rowlee, Sen., of Haddam, do acquit my husband and his heirs, executors, administrators or assigns, from all joyntures, dowryes and agreements whatsoever hereafter may arise, having received the full sum of ten pounds.
Witness: *Thomas Fuller,*   MARY ROWLEE, *her mark.*
          Nathaniel Stocking.

We, the subscribers, do acknowledge ourselves satisfied, having received in full what was due to us from the estate of our hon'd father Moses Rowley decd., and do acquit and discharge brothers Samuel and Ebenezer Rowlee, executors, this 17th February, 1736-7.
Witness: *Charles Williams,*   MOSES ROWLEE,
          Moses Roberts.   JOHN ROWLEE,
                                     JONATHAN X ROWLEE.

We, the subscribers, do hereby acquit and discharge brothers Samuel and Ebenezer Rowlee, executors to the last will and testament of our honoured father Moses Rowlee deceased, having received in full of what belonged to us of the estate by said will. In witness whereof we have hereto set our hands this 17th day of February, 1736-7.
                    HENRY CHAMPEN (CHAMPION),
                    MEHETABELL CHAMPEN.

Page 284.

Savage, Lt. Nathaniel, Middletown. Invt. £982-13-00. Taken 30 January, 1734-5, by Nathaniel White and Samuel Shepherd. Will dated 25 April, 1733.

I, Nathaniel Savage of Middletown, do make this my last will and testament: I give to Esther, my beloved wife, whom I likewise ordain my sole executrix, 1-4 part of all my moveable estate, likewise the use of 1-2 of my dwelling house, with half the cellarage, with half the barn, and the use of half that part of my lott on which my dwelling house stands, 1-2 of the orchard and other conveniences belonging thereto, and likewise the use of half of all my improveable meadow; all this during her life. I give to my eldest son John Savage the whole of that part of my lott against my dwelling house, east of the highway, his mother's interest excepted; and likewise all the west end of that lott on which my house stands, running east so far as the cross fence as it now stands, with liberty to pass and re-pass to and from it where it may be convenient at least damage to the rest of the lott; and likewise that part of my meadow land in Wongunk which lyeth above the crick; and likewise 1-2 of all my meadow land in sd. Wongunk meadow below the sd. crick, excepting half an acre lying next to his Uncle Jonathan's meadow, and his mother's interest excepted; and likewise all that piece of land which I bought of Nathaniel Stocking lying by Richard Gill's land; and likewise my interest in the last three miles granted to the Town of Middletown, together with half my right in the common or undivided land in the town, and likewise half of both parts of my half-mile lott lying near Shamger Bernis (Barnes or Bourne?), and over the hill, however it may be butted and bounded; and likewise the use of half my dwelling house and barn, with yarding convenient, until his brother comes of age. I give to my son Jabez Savage my dwelling house and barn and the land on which it stands, running westward until it comes to his brother John's part, with a half acre in Wongunk meadow, lying next his uncle Jonathan Warner's land. I give to my daughters, Esther, Abigail, Susanah, Mary and Elizabeth, 1-2 of all my rights in the last three miles granted to the Town of Middletown, together with 3-4 of all my moveable estate (excepting one pair of 3-year-old steers and husbandry tools), to be divided thus, viz., my daughters Susanah, Mary and Elizabeth first of all to have each of them as much as their sisters Esther and Abigail have each of them had, and then the remainder to be equally divided among the five children. This I give to my five daughters and their heirs forever. And further, I give to my two sons, John and Jabez, one paire of 3-year-old steers and all my husbandry tools, to be divided equally between them.

Witness: *Joseph White*,   NATHANIEL SAVAGE, LS.
John McCleane, William Kesson.

Court Record, Page 19—4 February, 1734-5: Will now exhibited by Esther Savage, widow, who declined to be executrix. Adms. to the widow with the will annexed.

Page 303.

Sedgewick, Capt. Samuel, Hartford. Invt. £2190-04-06. Taken 10 April, 1735, by Martin Smith, Daniel Webster and Moses Nash. Will dated 21 June, 1722.

I, Samuel Sedgewick of Hartford, do make this to be my last will and testament: I do give to my wife, the time of her natural life, half my dwelling house and half of my celler, and half of my barn and outhouses, and half my orchards. And I also give my wife the improvement of 1-3 part of all my land during her natural life, and also 1-3 part of my moveable estate to be at her own dispose forever. I give unto my son Samuel Sedgewick's children, besides what I have already given by deeds of gift, 5 shillings apiece. I give unto my son Jonathan Sedgewick the

house he now lives in, and all the land on the east side of the brook be-
tween him and where I now live, butting on the land of Lt. Gillett south.
I also give my son Jonathan all my plain lott, butting upon his brother
Joseph's land east, and upon Lt. Gillett's south. Also, I give to my son
Jonathan my old and new swamps, being known by that name, butting on
Lt. Gillett's house partly, on land west belonging to the heirs of my son
Samuel Sedgewick, partly on land formerly belonging to Jared Spencer,
and east on land hereafter given to my son Benjamin. I also give unto
my son Jonathan, after my son Stephen hath had 55 acres out of it, the
rest of my mountain lott, to be equally divided between him and Benjamin, provided that my son Jonathan pay to his four sisters, Abigail,
Mary, Elizabeth and Mercy, 50 shillings apiece within a year after my
decease. I give unto my son Ebenezer Sedgewick that house and lands
I bought of John Peck and 40 shillings more. I give unto my son Joseph
Sedgewick 15 acres of land where his house now stands, butting on his
brother Jonathan's land west and on land of Lt. Gillett's south, besides
what I have already given him. I give to my son Stephen Sedgewick that
lott I bought of John Andrews, and the house he now lives in, and 55
acres of land on which his house now stands, and he shall have liberty
to take the 55 acres in one piece, either east and west or north and south.
I give unto my son Benjamin Sedgewick my dwelling house, barn and all
of my outhouseing and all my land at home, butting on his brother
Jonathan's land east, and on Lt. Gillett's south. I also give unto my
son Benjamin my hill, butting on the heirs of my son Samuel's children
east and on land given to Jonathan west, and on Lt. Gillett's south. I
also give unto my son Benjamin my Jared lott and swamp, being known
by that name, and I give unto my son Benjamin the half of my mountain
lott above mentioned, to be equally divided between him and his brother
Jonathan, and provided he pay, when he comes of age, to his four sisters
50 shillings apiece, unto Abigail, Mary, Elizabeth and Mercy. I give to
my daughter Abigail 50 shillings, to my daughter Mary 50 shillings, to
my daughter Elizabeth Sedgewick £40, to my daughter Mercy Sedgewick £40. I appoint my two sons, Jonathan and Ebenezer, with my wife,
executors.

Witness: *Caleb Watson,*   SAMUEL SEDGEWICK, LS.
Ebenezer Smith, Caleb Merrells.

Court Record, Page 24—1st April, 1735: Will exhibited. Benjamin
Sedgewick, age 18 years, chose his mother Mary Sedgewick to be his
guardian. Samuel Sedgewick, a grandson, age 15 years, chose his uncle
Jonathan Sedgewick to be his guardian. (A son of Samuel Sedgewick
deceased, who was a son of Capt. Sedgewick decd.)

Page 30—14 July, 1735: Jonathan Sedgewick moves this Court
for a distribution of the estate. This Court appoint Moses Nash and
Martin Smith, of Hartford, distributors.

Dist. File, 7 February, 1737-8: Estate of Capt. Samuel Sedgewick:
To the widow Mary Sedgewick, to Samuel, Jr., decd. (his 5 children),
to Ebenezer, to Abigail Sedgewick alias Kellogg, to Mary Sedgewick

alias Kellogg, to Elizabeth Sedgewick alias Orton, to Mercy Sedgewick alias Merrells. By Martin Smith and Moses Nash.

Page 359.

Shepherd, Deacon John, Hartford. Invt. £557-00-07. Taken 7 April, 1736, by Benjamin Catling and John Skinner, Jr. Will dated 1st August, 1728.

I, John Shepherd of Hartford, do make this my last will and testament: I give to my wife, besides the joynture I gave her at marriage, 20 loads of wood a year, yearly, during her naturall life or so long as she remaineth my widow, to be paid by my executors hereafter named. I give to the children of my son John Shepherd, late of Milford decd., £30, that is to say, to his eldest son John £10, and to his daughter Rebeckah £5, and to his daughter Abigail £5, and to his son Timothy £5, and to his daughter Hannah £5, to be paid by my executors hereafter named. I give to my son Samuel my lot called the wood lott, containing three acres; and my swamp lott in the south meadow, containing two acres and a rood; and also I give to my son Samuel the 1-2 of my tools. I give to my grandson John, the eldest son of my son Samuell Shepherd, my now dwelling house, shop, barn and orchard, and two acres of land at home, he paying £80 to his father, my executor, only the widow is to have her part of it during her life. I give to my son Joseph a piece of land called my lower lot, neare home, containing foure acres and a half; also I give to my son Joseph my lot at the Sands in the south meadow, containing 2 1-2 acres, and my tools. Also, I order my executors to pay to him £30. I give to the children of my daughter Hannah, besides what she formerly received, £15, that is to say, to her eldest daughter Jane £5, and to her son Charles £5, and to her daughter Hannah £5. Also, I give to Mehetabell £5. I give to my son Samuell Shepherd, after my just debts are paid and funerall charges discharged, all the rest of my moveable estate. And I likewise constitute, make and ordain my son, Samuell Shepherd, and Thomas Richards, to be my sole executors.

Witness: *Jonathan Butler,*   JOHN SHEPHERD, LS.
Thomas Burkett, Elizabeth Wyllys.

Court Record, Page 46—6 April, 1736: Will now exhibited by Samuel Shepherd and Thomas Richards, executors. Proven.

Page 45—6 April, 1736: John Shepherd of Milford, son of John Shepherd decd., appeals from the judgement of this Court in the approbation of this will of the sd. John Shepherd of Hartford decd., unto the Superior Court at Hartford, 2d Tuesday of September next.

Invt. on File. Will on Page 275.

Smith, Hannah, Widow, Glastonbury. Invt. taken December, 1734, by Samuel Gains and Gershom Smith. Will dated 17 September, 1731.

I, Hannah Smith of Glastonbury, in the County of Hartford, do make and ordain this my last will and testament: I give unto my son Richard Smith my biggest brass kettle. I give unto my two sons, Jonathan and Manoah, all my swine of what sort soever, to be equally divided betwixt them. I give unto my son Jeduthan Smith my little or least brass kettle and my warming pan, frying pan, little iron kettle, and my bell-metal morter and pestle. I give unto my son Jeduthan Smith, and his heirs and assigns forever, all my land or rights of land whatsoever in Middletown, in the aforesd. County of Hartford. I give unto my son Manoah Smith my middle brass kettle, my silver spoon, and my bay horse. I give unto my daughter-in-law, Dorothy Boardman, one of my trammels, and a pine chest that stands in my leanto, and also my iron porridge pot and my biggest iron kettle. I give unto my son Jeduthan Smith my feather bed which I lye on, with the bedstead, covering and all furniture belonging to the same. And as for all the rest of my estate whatsoever belonging unto me at my decease and not before herein mentioned, as cattle, pewter, iron ware, bees, or any other estate whatsoever not before mentioned as aforesd., I give and bequeath the same unto my three sons, Richard, Jeduthan and Manoah, to be equally divided among them, share and share alike. And I do hereby appoint my two sons, Richard and Jeduthan, to be executors of this my last will.

Witness: *Samuel Gains,*   HANNAH X SMITH, LS.
Abraham Kilbourn, John Lynn.

Memorandum: That whereas, I have above given and bequeathed unto my son Richard Smith my great brass kettle, and to my son Jeduthan Smith my little or least brass kettle and my warming pan, frying pan and little iron kettle, I do now make this alteration, that the sd. great brass kettle I bequeath it to my son Jeduthan, and I bequeath my little or least brass kettle and my sd. warming pan, frying pan and little iron kettle to my son Richard.

Witness: *Samuel Gains,*   HANNAH X SMITH, LS.
Abraham Kilbourn, John Lynn.

Court Record, Page 15—3 December, 1734: Will now exhibited by Jeduthan Smith, executor named in said will, who accepted the trust of being executor to sd. will, which being proven, was ordered recorded, etc.

Smith, Hannah, Glastonbury. Court Record, Page 19—27 January, 1734-5: This Court grant Adms. on the estate of Hannah Smith, late of Glastonbury deceased, unto Francis Smith of Bolton, father of the deceased, who gave bond of £50 with Jonat: Olcot of Hartford, and took letters of Adms.

Page 344.

Smith, Jacob, Haddam. Died 9th June, 1735. Invt. £153-19-08. Taken 5 August, 1735, by Joseph Arnold, Caleb Cone and Thomas Brooks.

Court Record, Page 33—7 October, 1735: Adms. to Sarah Smith, widow. Recog, £200, with Thomas Brooks.

Page 2 (Vol. XIV) 13 August, 1742: Eliphalet Smith, a minor, 9 years of age, son of Jacob Smith: this Court do appoint Joseph Smith of Haddam to be his guardian. Recog., £200.

Page 278.

Smith, James, Haddam. Died 15 September, 1735. Invt. £40-19-06. Taken 3 December, 1734, by Joseph Arnold, Caleb Cone and Thomas Brooks.

Court Record, Page 12—5 November, 1734-5: Adms. granted to Abraham Brooks of Haddam.

Page 34—4 November, 1735: Abraham Brooks, Adms., exhibits an account of his Adms. Accepted. This Court appoint Abraham Brooks to be guardian to Susannah Smith, daughter of James Smith, late of Haddam deceased, she being 9 years of age. Recog., £50.

Inventory in Vol. XIII, Page 8-9.

Smith, Rev. Joseph, Middletown. Invt. £1368-13-04. Taken 29 November, 1736, by John Warner, Samuel Gipson and Samuel Stow. An invt. was taken of his books, which amounted to the sum of £43-07-10, by William Russell and Jabez Hamlin.

Court Record, Page 53—28 December, 1736: Adms. granted to Esther Smith, widow, who recog. in £100 with Edward Bulkley of Wethersfield.

Smith, Mary, Estate, Hartford. Court Record, Page 9—17 August, 1734: Adms. to Nehemiah Smith, son of the decd. Recog., £150, with Benjamin Roberts.

Page 237.

Smith, Nathan, Wethersfield. Will dated 11 December, 1733: I, Nathan Smith of Wethersfield, being very sick but of sound memory, doe make this my last will and testament: I give to my honoured mother, Widow Hannah Smith, the use and improvement of all my estate, both reall and personal, during the term of her natural life, except £10, which

I will and bequeath to Sarah Norton as a token of my good will, to be paid to her by my executrix. I give to my two sisters, Hannah Smith and Abigail Grimes, all my lands and real estate which my father died seized of and descended to me, and which I have since possessed or otherwise whatsoever, to be equally divided between them, and to be possessed by them during life, and after their decease to the heirs of their bodies lawfully begotten, and to their heirs and assigns forever, and to be the estate of the children of sd. Abigail in fee simple, to be not possessed till my mother's decease. Lastly, I do hereby constitute and ordain my honoured mother Hannah Smith to be sole executrix of this my will during the term of her natural life, and after her decease I appoint my sister Hannah Smith to be executrix instead of my sd. mother.

Witness: *Benjamin Strong,*   NATHAN SMITH, LS.
John Bishop, Samuel Hill.

Court Record, Page 1—1st April, 1734: Will proven.

Page 49—3 August, 1736: Invt. exhibited and accepted by this Court. Hezekiah Grimes, in right of his wife, appeals from the judgement of this Court in accepting of the inventory, to the Superior Court, 2d Tuesday of September next.

Page 7 (Vol. XIII) 18 May, 1737: An account of Adms. on the estate of Nathan Smith was now exhibited in Court by Widow Hannah Smith, who was appointed sole executrix. Accepted, ordered recorded and kept on file.

Page 310.

Smith, Samuel, Kensington, tanner and cordwainer. Invt. £2124-03-00, lands and realty. Taken 27 May, 1735, by Thomas Curtis, Joseph Smith and Jonathan Lewis. Will dated 29 April, 1735.

I, Samuel Smith of Kensington, do make my last will and testament: I give to my wife Sarah Smith, her heirs and assigns forever, 1-3 part of all my personal estate forever, and the use and improvement of 1-3 part of my real estate during her natural life. I give to my eldest son, Noah Smith, his heirs and assigns forever, all the land I bought of Deacon Thomas Hart and the land adjoyning thereto, which I bought of the heirs of Samuel Gridley; and also the frame for a dwelling house standing thereupon; and all my right and interest in the undivided land lying to the southward of the above-mentioned; and also the use and improvement of 1-4 part of all my mowing lands, and 1-4 part of all the fruit of my orchards, for the space of 8 years next ensueing after the date hereof. And also I give him one yoke of my oxen, and all the money due to me from Jonathan Worthington of Springfield, and half the money due to me from Ebenezer Orvis of Farmingtown, and also all the bricks, boards and timber which I have prepared for his frame above mentioned. I give to my son Daniel Smith, his heirs and assigns forever, besides the money I paid to purchase that three acres of land which he hath a deed of from Ens. Samuel Hart, (nigh to which his frame for a dwelling house standeth), my tan house, and all my instruments and conveniences for tanning, and all my leather and instruments for a cordwainer, and so much of the southward part of my homelot as may, together with the three acres above mentioned, by an indifferent apprisement be reckoned of equall vallue with the remainder of my sd. home lott and ye buildings thereon; and also 1-2 of all my right in the division of upland belonging to the great swamp in Farmington, except my 16-acre lot lying between land belonging to Hezekiah Hart and the heirs of Jonathan Hurlbut; and also 1-2 of the money due to me from Ebenezer Orvis, and also all the bricks, boards and timber I have prepared for the frame last mentioned. I give to my youngest son Samuel Smith, his heirs and assigns forever, my dwelling house and barn and all the remainder of my homelott and of my right in the sd. division of upland belonging to the great swamp besides what I give to my son Daniel as is above expressed. And moreover my will is that if by my wife and my two eldest sons, or any two of them, it be thought best that my sd. son Samuel should be brought up to college learning, I do hereby impower them or any of them to sell so much of his estate, real or personal, as shall be needfull to obtain sd. learning, and to lay out the product thereof according to their discretion. All the rest of my estate, real and personal, I give to my three daughters, Eunice, Phebe and Sarah, to be equally divided among them. And provided the whole hereof shall not by an indifferent apprisement amount to the value of 1-6 part of all that I have given to my three sons above mentioned, then my will is that my sd. sons shall in an equal proportion pay to my daughters (which shall be equally divided among them) so much as may, with the part of real and personal estate last mentioned, make all my daughters' portions together equal to 1-6 part of the total of all my sd. sons' portions reconed together. And moreover I do hereby appoint my wife above named and eldest son aforesd. executors to this my will.

Witness: *Isaac Norton,*   SAMUEL SMITH, LS.
Isaac Norton, Jr., Elizabeth Norton.

    Court Record, Page 28—3 June, 1735: Will proven. This Court appoint Mrs. Sarah Smith to be guardian to her son Samuel Smith, age 12 years.
    Page 8 (Vol. XIV) 6 July, 1742: Sarah Smith, widow and one of the executors, prays that distributors may be appointed by this Court to divide the real estate of the sd. decd. given to her and the sons of the sd. decd. by sd. will: Whereupon this Court appoints Isaac Daniels and Jonathan Lewis, of Farmington, distributors.

Page 357.

Spencer, John, Jr., Haddam. Died 26 April, 1735. Invt. £460-09-04. Taken 13 June, 1735, by Joseph Arnold, Benjamin Smith and Gideon Arnold. Will dated 7 February, 1734-5.

I, John Spencer, Jr., of Haddam, do make this my last will and testament: I give to my wife Elizabeth the use of 1-3 part of all my real estate in buildings and land during life, and 3-4 part of all my personal estate to her forever, except such things as I have otherwise disposed of or for the payment of debts. I give to my eldest son Jeremiah my dwelling house and homestead, viz., all the land which I have there adjoining, be it more or 4 acres, and my barn and part of that lott on which my sd. barn stands, and 2 acres and 1-2 of land given me by the proprietors of Haddam, and 8 acres of land formerly belonging to Nathaniel Spencer, late of Haddam decd., adjoining to sd. two acres and 1-2 of land. All which I give him in consideration that he pay to my daughter Deborah the sum of £25 in money when she shall arrive at the age of 18 years. I give to my son James Spencer the remainder of that lott that the barn stands on, and 15 acres of land adjoining, abutting on a highway southerly and upon land of Joseph Clark. Also, I give to sd. James my largest chain. All which I give him in consideration that he pay to my daughter Deborah £5 in money within one year after his arriving at the age of 21 years. I give to my son Joseph Spencer 18 acres of land lying on the south side of the highway and near my dwelling house, butting north on the sd. highway, easterly on land formerly Nathaniel Bailey's, south on land of Benjamin Spencer; and 4 acres more or less of land abutting north on land of Daniel Spencer, Jr., south on land of Daniel Clark, east on land of Jared Spencer, Jr., and west on land of Benjamin Spencer. Also, I give the sd. Joseph a draft chain. All which I give him in consideration that he pay to my daughter Deborah £5 within one year after he shall arrive at the age of 21 years. I give to my daughter Deborah Spencer, besides what I have herein ordered my three sons to pay her, 1-4 part of my personal estate, excepting the gunn and 2 chains and what shall be needful for paying my debts. I make my wife Elizabeth sole executrix.

Witness: *Daniel Hubbard, Jr.,*   JOHN SPENCER, JUN., LS.
Jeremiah Hubbard, Hez. Brainard.

Court Record, Page 44—4 May, 1736: Will proven.

Page 24 (Vol. XIV) 24 May, 1743: James Spencer, a minor son of John Spencer, chose Timothy Olcott of Bolton to be his guardian. Recog., £200.

Page 331.

Spencer, Jonathan, Haddam. Died 23 April, 1735. Invt. £227-06-01. Taken 22 May, 1735, by James Brainard, Joseph Arnold, Jr., and Abraham Brooks.

I, Jonathan Spencer of Haddam, do make and ordain this my last will and testament: I give to my honoured mother out of my estate £20 in money; to my brother Timothy £4 in money; to my three eldest sisters I give £4 to each in money; to my brother Simeon I give 2-3 of the remainder of my estate as it shall be apprised. I give to my sister Elizabeth £4 in money. Lastly, I give all the remainder of my estate to my sister Martha. I appoint Thomas Brooks and Caleb Cone, Jr., both of Haddam, to be the sole executors.

Witness: *Phineas Fiske,*   JONATHAN SPENCER, LS.
Abraham Brooks, Joshua Cone.

Court Record, Page 33—7 October, 1735: Will proven.

Page 44—4 May, 1736: Thomas Brooks, executor, now moves for a distribution of the estate. This Court appoint James Haseltine, Hezekiah Brainard and Abraham Brooks to divide the real estate.

Page 345.

Standish, Thomas, Wethersfield. Died 3 September, 1735. Invt. £396-16-06. Taken 14 September, 1735, by Nathaniel Wright, Jonathan Goodrich and Samuel Hunn.

Page 284. Invt. on Page 290.

Steadman, John, Wethersfield. Invt. £6-15-00. Taken 22 January, 1734-5, by Gershom Nott and Joseph Curtice. Testimony dated 9 April, 1731. Will nuncupative: He declared his will was that his estate after his decease should be divided equally between his two sons, Thomas and Samuel Steadman, his son Thomas being present.

Witness: *James Butler,*
Mehetabell Goodrich, Joseph Curtice.

Court Record, Page 17—6 January, 1734-5: Will now exhibited. Proven. Adms. with the will annexed to Thomas Steadman.

Page 20—4 February, 1734-5: Thomas Steadman made complaint against Samuel Steadman for concealing some of the goods of the estate of John Steadman decd.

Page 22—25 February, 1734-5: Samuel Steadman appeared and showed that he had none of the estate of John Steadman in his hands.

Page 364.

Stoddard, David, Wethersfield. Died 14 May, 1736. Invt. £711-00-05. Taken 10 July, 1736, by Thomas Deming, Gideon Goodrich and Ebenezer Wright. Will dated 12 May, 1736.

I, David Stoddard of Stepney, in Wethersfield, do make this my last will and testament: I give to my wife Keziah 1-3 part of my moveable estate for her own, and the use and improvement of 1-3 part of my buildings and lands during her natural life. I give the remainder of my estate to be equally divided, both buildings, moveables and lands, among my children, both sons and daughters, viz., to David, Samuel, Stephen, John, Keziah and Jerusha, excepting to my son David I give 10 acres of land on the east side of my homelott over and above his equal part with the rest of my children. Lastly, I appoint my beloved wife Keziah Stoddard and Deacon David Goodrich to be executors.

Witness: *Josiah Churchill,*   DAVID STODDARD, LS.
Samuel Belding, Jr., Abraham Goodrich.

Court Record, Page 48—6 July, 1726: Will proven. David Stoddard, son of David Stoddard, made choice of his mother Keziah to be his guardian. Recog., £50.

Page 24 (Vol. XIII) 7 March, 1737-8: Keziah Stoddard, age 15 years, daughter of David Stoddard, chose her mother Keziah Stoddard to be her guardian. And this Court appoint Keziah to be guardian to Samuel Stoddard age 12 years, Jerusha 8, Stephen 5 years and John 2 years of age, children of David Stoddard. Recog., £500.

Page 45 (Vol. XV) 1 September, 1747: Keziah Stoddard, widow and executrix to the last will and testament of David Stoddard, late of Wethersfield decd., moved to this Court that her right of dowry in the real estate of the sd. decd. may be set out to her, together with the moveable estate; and also that the estate remaining be divided to the heirs of sd. estate according to sd. will: Whereupon this Court appoint Deacon Benjamin Wright, Ebenezer Wright and Thomas Curtiss, of Wethersfield, to dist. and set out to the sd. widow 1-3 part of the moveable estate when the debts are taken out, to be her own forever, and 1-3 part of the lands and buildings to sd. widow for her improvement during life; and also set out to David or his heirs and to Samuel, Stephen, John and Jerusha Stoddard, heirs to the sd. estate, their proportional part of sd. estate according to the sd. will, and make return of their doings to this Court.

Page 123—3 April, 1750: Stephen Stoddard, a minor, 17 years of age, son of David Stoddard, chose his mother Keziah Stoddard to be his guardian. Recog., £600.

Page 376.

Stoughton, Sergt. Israel, Windsor. Invt. £2070-19-11. Taken 26 October, 1736, by Peletiah Allyn, Samuel Stoughton and Jonathan Stiles. Will dated 20 June, 1735.

I, Israel Stoughton of Windsor, do make this my last will and testament: I give to my wife Mary (her dower rights). I give to my only son Israel Stoughton lands I bought of the following persons, viz., from my sisters Elizabeth and Rebeckah Stoughton, Mr. Atherton Mather, Samuel Stoughton, John Bissell, John Hoskins and Timothy Hosford; also land from my father Thomas Stoughton's estate, and the deeds on record which I had of the before mentioned persons; also 1 1-2 acre of land bought of Jacob Gibbs, bounded east on the Great River, south on Eliakim

Marshall, north on Winchell's lands, and west on Giles Elsworth's land which I sold him. Also, I give him a bond I have from Enock Phelps, with the condition thereof; also a yoke of oxen, a horse, with all my team tackling; also the still with the appurtenances thereof. And lastly, I give him an equal share with my daughters in my negro man Ceazer, to him and his heirs forever, he paying to my eight daughters, to Mary, to Elizabeth, to Hannah, to Rebeckah, to Sarah, to Lucie, to Jemima and to Abigail Stoughton the sum of £96 in the whole, they to be residuary legatees. I appoint my wife Mary and my son Israel Stoughton executors.

Witness: *John Gaylord*,   ISRAEL STOUGHTON, LS.
Samuel Stoughton, Timothy Loomis.

Court Record, Page 52—2 November, 1736: Will proven.

Page 59 (Vol. XIII) 17 January, 1739-40: Mary Stoughton, widow, moves this Court for a dist. of the residue of the estate to her 8 daughters, to Mary, Elizabeth, Hannah, Rebeckah, Sarah, Lucie, Jemima, and to Abigail Stoughton. This Court appoint Capt. Peletiah Allyn, James Enno and Samuel Stoughton distributors. This Court appoint Mary Stoughton, widow, to be guardian to Jemima age 11 years and Abigail age 9 years, children of Israel Stoughton. Recog., £500. Sarah Stoughton, age 15 years, and Lucie, 13, chose their mother Mary Stoughton to be their guardian. Recog., £300.

Page 313.

Stow, Samuel, Jr., Middletown. Invt. £543-07-11. Taken 14 May, 1735, by John Sage, John Warner and Jonas Green.

Court Record, Page 26—6 May, 1735: Adms. to Ebenezer Sage. Recog., £2000, with Elisha Coleman of Wethersfield.

Page 43—6 April, 1736: Account exhibited by Ebenezer Sage, Adms., and moves that a sufficiency of moveables be set out to the widow for her necessity. Set out £60-14-02 by order of the Court.

Page 52—2 November, 1736: These may certify to all whom it doth concern: That we, the subscribers, being present at the sign post in the North Society in Middletown on the 23 day of June, 1736, did then see Ebenezer Sage of Middletown, administrator on the estate of Samuel Stow, late of Middletown deceased, set up at public vandue the house and so much of the land of sd. decd. as to make £104-19-10, with costs and charges: And the house and other buildings sold for £50 to Ebenezer White, the highest bidder, and the land belonging to sd. house was sold to sd. White for £60, he being the highest bidder. Charges of sale, £5-08-01.

Signed: CHARLES BULKLEY,
JOHN SAGE, JUN: R.

Page 11 (Vol. XVI) 1 January, 1750-1: Submit Stow, 15 years of age, only daughter and sole heir to the estate of Samuel Stow, Jr., chose her father-in-law Lt. Joseph Savage of Middletown to be her guardian. Recog. £400. Certified to this Court by *Thomas Johnson, J. P.*

Page 389.

Taylor, Nathaniel, Windsor. Invt. £37-05-11. Taken 31 May, 1736, by John Boughers, Daniel Elsworth and Nathaniel Grant.

Court Record, Page 45-46—19 May, 1736: Adms. to John Stiles, Jr. Recog., £300, with Enock Lyman of Tolland. This Court appoint Ruth Taylor, widow of Nathaniel Taylor, to be guardian to Margaret Taylor, age 11 years, and Keziah Taylor, age 8 1-2 years; and Stephen Taylor, age 18 years, chose John Stiles, Jun:r, of Windsor, to be his guardian.

Page 49—3 August, 1736: John Stiles, Jun:r, now Adms., reports the estate insolvent. Daniel Bissell and Abraham Foster appointed commissioners.

Page 315.

Thompson, Joseph, Farmington. Invt. £381-16-04. Taken 26 June, 1735, by John Steele, John Newell and Nathaniel Newell.

Court Record, Page 26—6 May 1735: Adms. to Ezekiel Thompson, a brother of sd. deceased.

Page 28—1st July, 1735: Invt. exhibited.

Page 54—4 January, 1736-7: Adms. account accepted.

Page 305.

Thompson, Thomas, Farmington. Invt. £1018-10-06. Taken 23 April, 1735, by Isaac Cowles, William Porter and John Newell. Will dated 17 March, 1734-5.

I, Thomas Thompson of Farmingtown, in the County of Hartford and Colony of Connecticut, in New England (son to Thomas Thompson decd.), being sick and weak in body but of sound mind and memory, do make this my last will and testament: I give unto Elizabeth, my wife, the use and improvement and profit of 1-3 part of my real estate during her natural life. And if my son Timothy do proceed to build a new house, for which I have prepared timber, my will then is that my wife shall have the use of 1-3 part of sd. building and as part of sd. thirds. My will is that she shall have the use of 1-3 part of my four-acre lott lying by the highway leading towards Symsbury, and 1-3 part of 4 acres of land which I have lying by the common land; also I give to her my sd. wife, to be at her own dispose forever, 1-3 part of all my personal estate, my debts being first paid. Unto my eldest son Timothy Thompson, and to his heirs forever, I give him of sd. estate in Farmington as followeth, viz., all my buildings and all my homelott, viz., that part by my house and that part by the river, and all the timber of all sorts which I have prepared towards the building of a new house; also all my land lying within the common field; also my 4-acre lott and my 5 acres of land above mentioned; also all my right of land which I have purchased in the fourth lottment in the first division of land lying west from the reserved land, containing about 52 acres, laid out in the right of my father Thomas Thompson decd.; also the 33rd lott in number in the division of land lying north from the reserved land on the west side of the river, containing about 42 acres, laid out on my sd. father's right; also the 62nd lott in number in the division of land lying north from the reserved land on the east side of the river, containing about 15 acres, laid out on my sd. father's right; also I give unto my sd. son Timothy Thompson 1-3 part of my team of oxen and horses; also 1-3 part of my team tackling and tools for husbandry business; also 1 gunn. My sd. wife to enjoy her right of improvement, use and profit of 1-3 part of my houseing and lands as above I have given her. And further, that the sd. Timothy shall have my loom and weaving gears, he to instruct my son Thomas Thompson in the art of weaving, provided that he the sd. Thomas inclines to learn that trade and will live with his brother untill he arrives at full age. Unto Thomas Thompson, his heirs and assigns forever, I give of real estate in Farmington as followeth, viz., the 15th lott of land in the division of land lying southward from the reserved land between the mountains, laid out on the right of my father Thomas Thompson decd., and it containeth about 108 acres; also all my right in the 21st lottment of land in the 2nd division of land lying west from the reserved land, containing about 53 acres, laid out on the right of my sd. father; also 1-3 part of my team of oxen and horses and 1-3 part of my team tackling, and my silver spoon; also 1 gunn and a sword. Unto my aforenamed sons Timothy and Thomas Thompson I give all my right lying in common with the rest of the proprietors in the common and undivided land in sd. Farmington. Unto my daughter Elizabeth Hart, besides what I have already given her, I give her 5 shillings, to be paid to her by my executor out of my personal estate. Unto my daughter Abigail Hart, besides what I have already given her, I give her 5 shillings. Unto my daughter Phebe Thompson, now living with me, I give her the sum of £50 money. Unto my granddaughter Abigail Hawley I give her the 23rd lot in number lying in the 4th division of land in Farmington, about 53 acres, laid out on my father's right. Unto my daughter Elizabeth Hart I give the 61st lott in the 3rd division of land in Farmington, containing about 53 acres, which was laid out on my sd. father's right. Unto my daughter Abigail Hart I give the 35th lott in the 5th division of land, containing about 53 acres, laid out on my father's right. Unto my aforesd. daughter Phebe Thompson I give the 24th lott in the 6th division of land, containing about 53 acres, laid out on my father's right. My will further is that my daughter Phebe shall have liberty to live in my now dwelling house, or in the sd. new house when built, so long as she continueth unmarried. And I do hereby constitute my son Timothy Thompson to be sole executor.

Witness: *Joseph Hooker,*   THOMAS THOMPSON, LS.
Timothy Hart, Ezekiel Thompson.

Court Record, Page 26—6 May, 1735: Will proven.

Page 307.

Treat, Samuel, Wethersfield. Invt. £1507-16-03. Taken 27 April, 1733, by Nathaniel Burnham, Benjamin Smith and D(avi)d Boardman. Court Record, Page 28—3 June, 1735: Adms. to Sarah Treat, widow. Recog., £600, with Nathaniel Burnham. Mrs. Sarah Treat to be guardian to her son Samuel Treat, age 11 years. Recog., £100.

Invt. in Vol. XIII, Page 69.

Tuttle, Stephen, Farmington. Invt. £102-09-02. Taken 27 August, 1735, by Josiah Hart and John Newell. Court Record, Page 31—5 August, 1735: Adms. granted to Sarah Tuttle, widow, who recog. with her father Nathaniel Stanly of Farmington (who is joyned as Adms.) and Samuel Pettebone the 2nd, of Simsbury.

Page 25 (Vol. XIII) 14 March, 1737-8: Invt. exhibited.

Page 73—2 September, 1740: Nathaniel Stanly, Adms., exhibited an account of Adms., by which account it appears he has paid in debts and charges the sum of £24-13-05. Accepted.

Page 10 (Vol. XV) 1st April, 1746: An account of Adms. was now exhibited in Court by Nathaniel Stanly, Adms. Accepted.

Page 327.

Webster, Deacon Jonathan, Sen., Hartford. Invt. £533-02-04. Taken 23 July, 1735, by James Ensign and Thomas Richards. Will dated 7 April, 1732.

The last will and testament of Jonathan Webster, Sen., of Hartford: I confirm to my wife all which before I have made over to her by an instrument under my hand and signed by my own handwrighting. I give to my three daughters all my moveable estate (namely, Susannah Steele, Mary Brace and Mehetabell Bidwell), to be equally divided between them. And also I give unto each of my before named daughters the sum of £10, to be paid unto them in money apiece by my executor within 12 months after my decease. I give unto my son Benjamin all the land that I have within the south meadow. I confirm unto the heirs of my son Stephen decd. the land which I made over to him in his lifetime and to have at my decease. I give unto my son Jonathan my homelott, together with the buildings standing thereupon, except the use of what I have given to my wife. And lastly I constitute and appoint my son Jonathan executor.

Witness: *John Marsh,*   JONATHAN WEBSTER, LS.
Elizabeth X Marsh, John Marsh, Jr.

Court Record, Page 31—5 August, 1735: The will proven.

Page 258.

White, Hannah, Widow, Hebron. Invt. £109-00-02. Taken 26 September, 1734, by Ebenezer Wilcox and David Porter.

Court Record, Page 9—10 September, 1734: Hannah White, executrix to the will of Ebenezer White, her husband decd., being deceased and not having made any account of what she had done, and there being a necessity of an administrator on the estates of Ebenezer White and his wife Hannah White deceased, the biggest creditor and nearest relations having refused to take Adms., this Court grant letters to Joseph Phelps of Hebron. Obadiah White, age 17 years, and Chene White, age 12 years, children of Ebenezer White, chose Joseph Phelps to be their guardian. Certified: *Nathaniel Foote, Justice of the Peace.*

Page 44 (Vol. XIII) 13 March, 1738-9: Joseph Phelps, who is Adms. of the estate of Hannah White, late relict of Ebenezer White, both of Hebron deceased, did on the 11th day of March, 1735-6, exhibit his account of Adms. on sd. estate of Hannah White: Paid in debts and charges, £46-15-04; inventory, £103-00-00; subtracting £46-15-04, there remains £54-00-04 to be distributed as follows:

	£ s d		£ s d
To Obadiah White,	15-06-08	To Hannah White,	7-13-04
To Ebenezer White,	7-13-04	To Chene White,	7-13-04
To Rebeckah White,	7-13-04	To Mehetabell White,	7-13-04

Which is the whole of the moveable estate to be distributed to the children and the heirs of the sd. deceased. And this Court do appoint Nathaniel Phelps, Deacon Benjamin Skinner and David Porter, of sd. Hebron, distributors.

Page 287.

White, Jacob, Jr., Middletown. Invt. £581-14-10. Taken 12 July, 1732, by Daniel White, Thomas Johnson and Samuel Shepherd.

Court Record, Page 20—4 February, 1734-5:. Adms. granted to Martha White, widow. Recog., £300, with Samuel Shepherd of Middletown.

Page 43—6 April, 1736: Martha White, Adms., exhibited an account of her Adms., which was accepted.

Page 4 (Vol. XIII) 29 March, 1737: Martha White now exhibited a further account of her Adms., which was also accepted.

Page 259.

Whittlesey, Ruth, Wethersfield. Invt. £128-00-10. Taken 11 June, 1734, by Samuel Jones and William Tulley. In Wethersfield by James Francis and Caleb Andrews.

Court Record, Page 8—6 August, 1734: Adms. to Jabez Whittlesey.

Page 316.

Williams, John, Middletown. Died 6 May, 1735. Invt. £323-11-02.
Taken 23 May, 1735, by Solomon Adkins, Ephraim Adkins and Joseph
Rockwell. Will dated 27 February, 1721-2.

I, John Williams of Middletown, do make this my last will and
testament: I give unto my wife Abigail £20 current money, to be paid
out of moveable estate at inventory price. And also I give unto my
wife the improvement of all my homestead and all the homelott from
east to west highways, with all the buildings thereon, as dwelling house
and barn and all the appurtenances thereon, the whole term of her
natural life. I give unto my daughter Mary the one equal half of the
Hunting Hill, so called and known, the quantity as pr record doth appear; and also 1-2 of the meadow land which I bought of Sergt. Whitmore and John Gilbert, the quantity as pr record; these two parcels of
land to be equally divided between Mary and Martha. I give unto my
daughter Martha the 1-2 of my Hunting Hill lot, so called, and also the
1-2 of my meadow land which I bought of Sergt. Whitmore and John
Gilbert; these two parcels to be equally divided between Martha and
Mary. I give unto my daughter Dorothy my homestead whereon I now
dwell, the land being butted on the highways easterly and westerly, and
sideing by the Halls' land north and the Wards' land south, be the acres
more or less, together with all the buildings and fences thereon, as dwelling house and barn, and all other my meadow land which I bought of my
son-in-law Ambrose Clark; the whole of both these lotments of land and
buildings abovesaid I give unto my daughter Dorothy. And as to my
moveable estate, after my wife hath had £20 and my just debts and
funerall charges are all paid, it is my will that what remaineth shall be
equally divided between my three daughters, Mary, Martha and Dorothy,
excepting one of my best feather beds with all the needful bedding and
furniture to it, which I give unto my daughter Dorothy. And I do also
give unto my three daughters above named my lotment of land on the
east side the Great River, lately laid out, containing 68 acres, bounded
as per record, with this promise, if I do not see cause to dispose thereof
in my lifetime; if not, to be equally divided between them. I appoint
my wife Abigail, my daughters Martha and Dorothy, and my son-in-law
Stephen Smith executors.

Witness: *Joseph Rockwell,*   JOHN WILLIAMS, LS.
Joseph Rockwell, Jr., William Rockwell.

Court Record, Page 28—3 June, 1735: The last will of John Williams, late of Middletown deceased, was now exhibited in Court by
Stephen Smith, one of the executors, which will being proven, was
ordered to be recorded.

Page 31—26 August, 1735: Dorothy Warner, daughter to the deceased, being appointed an executrix, with her husband Samuel Warner
now accepted the trust, and also brought in an addition of £10-14-00 to
the inventory.

Page 266.

Wolcott, Oliver, Wethersfield. Invt. £41-13-00. Taken 21 November, 1734, by Jonathan Belding, Elizur Goodrich and Nathaniel Stilman. Court Record, Page 12—8 November, 1734: Adms. granted to Samuel Wolcott. Page 15—13 November, 1734: Invt. exhibited.

Page 261.

Wolcott, Samuel, Wethersfield. Invt. £4400-12-03. Taken 18 November, 1734, by Nathaniel Stilman, Elizur Goodrich and Jonathan Belding. Will dated 29 August, 1734.

I, Samuel Wolcott of Wethersfield, do make and ordain this my last will and testament: I give to Abigail, my wife, all such and so much estate, goods and chattels which pertained unto her at the day of our intermarriage and which by virtue thereof hath been brought into my family (viz.) her proper portion which I received with or by her, to have and to hold sd. estate (both real and personal) to her and her heirs forever. I also give to my wife aforesd. 1-3 part of the residue of my moveable and personal estate herein nextly devised (that is to say), 1-3 part of my household goods, quick or live stock, and utensils and implements of husbandry, to have and to hold the same to her and her heirs forever. I give and bequeath to my aforesd. wife the use and improvement of 1-2 of my present mansion house wherein I now dwell, to be to her use during such time she shall survive as my widow, sole and unmarried againe, and also the improvement of 1-3 part of my real estate. I give unto my sons, Oliver, Samuel, Elisha and Josiah Wolcott, after the abovesd. bequest is made out and lawful debts by me contracted satisfied and paid, all the residue of my estate, both real and personal or mixt, to be equally divided amongst my sons, saving and excepting my son Elisha, whose part and portion in the premises is to be £60 less than an equal part in regard of his advancement in a trade, and saving and excepting my eldest son Oliver, whose portion is to be double the sd. share and part of ye aforesd. So have Oliver, Samuel, Elisha and Josiah Wolcott in such their respective portions, and to their heirs and assigns forever. Furthermore, my will is that the partition of the above divided premises to my sons be made by them or their guardians. I give to my aforesd. sons all the reversion and remainder of that estate, goods and chattels afore divided and bequeathed to my wife for and during the term of her natural life, to be divided amongst them at her decease, according to the rule and in proportion as above. I give to my two daughters, Abigail, the wife of Abraham Waterus, and Mehetabell, the wife of Jonathan Russell, £100 apiece, and to each of them in addition to what they have already received, to be paid either in money or out of the moveable part of my estate at inventory price, at the election of my sons, to be borne and paid by them or their legal representatives. Lastly, I hereby constitute and appoint Oliver, my eldest son, sole executor. I entreat the Rev. William Burnham of Kensington and Mr. John Stilman of Wethersfield to oversee the execution of my will.

Witness: *William Burnham,*   SAMUEL WOLCOTT, LS.
Amasa Adams, Abraham Harris.

Court Record, Page 11—1 September, 1734: Will proven.

Page 261-2: An Agreement.

To all people to whom these presents shall come: Abigail Wolcott of Wethersfield, in the County of Hartford and Colony of Connecticut, in New England, relict of Mr. Samuel Wolcott of Wethersfield aforesd., late deceased, sendeth greeting:

Whereas, my late well-beloved husband, the sd. Samuel Wolcott, did in and by his last will and testament, bearing date the 29 of August, Anno. Dom. 1734 (which hath been proved and approved according to the direction of the law), give, devise and bequeath unto me the sd. Abigail Wolcott all such estate, goods and chattells as were mine at the day of my intermarriage with him, to be to my use and the use of my heirs forever; also 1-3 part of his household goods, quick and live stocks, and utensils and implements of husbandry, in like manner to me and my heirs, &c., forever; also the improvement of 1-2 of his mansion house and one-third of his real estate, &c., as is in sd. will more at large expressed:

Know ye therefore that I, the said Abigail Wolcott, in consideration of the severall divisions and bequests mentioned, do acknowledge that I am fully and entirely satisfied and contented, and do therefore remise and release to the children and heirs of my sd. husband, and to the executor of the sd. last will and testament aforesd., all my right and title to the remainder of the estate of my sd. deceased husband, real and personal, together with my dower or power of thirds therein, with all my claim therein or thereto, what is given me in sd. will only excepted, *provided always,* that the sd. executor, children and heirs do never hereafter contradict or deny my injoying the severall above-mentioned legacies. In witness whereof I have hereunto set my hand and seal this first day of October, Anno. Dom. 1734.

Witness: *Joseph Andrews,*   ABIGAIL WOLCOTT, LS.
William Burnham.

Page 12—8 November, 1734: Adms. to Samuel Wolcott with will annexed. Recog., £500, with John Stilman.

Page 39—3 February, 1735-6: Samuel Wolcott now moves for a distribution of the estate of his late father, Capt. Samuel Wolcott. This Court appoint Capt. Thomas Curtice, Lt. Jonathan Belding and John Stilman to make a division.

Page 40—9 February, 1735-6: Elisha Wolcott, age 18 years, chose John Stilman of Wethersfield to be his guardian. Josiah Wolcott, age 15 years, chose Rev. William Burnham of Kensington Parish to be his guardian.

Page 256.

Wood, James, Middletown. Invt. £29-08-04. Taken 23 July, 1734, by John Tiley and Seth Wetmore.

Court Record, Page 8—22 July, 1734: James Wood, a transient person, late of Middletown decd.: Adms. to John Keith, sometime of Hartford, who gave bond of £100 with George Sutton of New London. Inventory exhibited.

Page 271, 301.

Wright, Sergt. Samuel. Died 12 October, 1734. Invt. £1845-12-10. Taken 12 November, 1734, by David Wright, Nathaniel Burnham and Jonathan Williams. Will dated 8 April, 1734.

I, Samuel Wright of Wethersfield, in the County of Hartford, in Connecticut, in New England, do make and ordain this my last will and testament: I give to Samuel Wright, the eldest son of my son Samuel Wright lately deceased, the northeast part of my homelott, viz., 7 rods and a half in breadth and 7 in length, beginning at the street and bounded north on John Stilman's land, which dimensions take in the house and other buildings which his father possessed. This land and buildings I give to him and his heirs and assigns forever. I give to Moses Wright, the younger son of my sd. son Samuel Wright decd., the other part of my homelott from 7 rods and from the street, that is to say, from the west end of what I have given to his eldest brother Samuel Wright to the southwest corner of the homelott of Mr. Samuel Wolcott deceased, and to hold 9 rods in breadth for this length from what I gave his brother above to sd. Mr. Wolcot's rear, and then 1 rod and 1-2 in breadth up to the street by the side of his brother Samuel as above. I give to the sd. Moses Wright half my pasture which I purchased partly of Daniel Boardman and partly of Mr. Ephraim Woodbridge; both these pieces to him and his heirs and assigns forever; of the pasture the eastern part or half. I give to my son Ebenezer Wright, besides what I have given by deeds of gift, one acre in Beaver Meadow, the west side of my land, these to be to him and his heirs and assigns forever. I give to my son Timothy Wright my dwelling house and other buildings pertaining to me, with part of my homelott, bounded east on the street, south by Thomas Boardman's land, west by lands on the homelott that a few years since pertained to Thomas Griswold decd., and north on the land I have of my homelott given to abovesd. Moses Wright, till we come to the west end of sd. land given to abovesd. Moses Wright, and then east on sd. Moses' land 9 rods till we come to sd. Mr. Wolcott's corner, so that this land given to my son Timothy contains the remaining part of my homelot. I give to my sd. son Timothy 1-2 of my pasture, viz., the western part thereof, the 1-2 of my land there which I purchased partly of Daniel Boardman and partly of Mr. Ephraim Woodbridge. I give to Timothy my son my four-acre lot in the Great Meadow of Wethersfield, bounded north on land of Lt. John Coleman, on a way east, and on a highway west, and south on land belonging to Mr. James Treat and Nathaniel Boardman. Also, I give to my son Timothy my back lot, all of it excepting 1 acre at the north end. These several pieces of land I give to him, his heirs and assigns forever, and the use of the lands given to Moses Wright till he arrive to the age of 21 years. I give the sd. Timothy the abovesd. land, he paying to my daughter Mary Stanly £70 in money or bills of publick credit, and £70 in such money to my daughter Abigaill Miller, within the space of 1 year after my decease. Also, to the children of my son Crafts Wright decd., viz., Cauly Wright and Martha Wright, to each of them 1 acre of land in Beaver Meadow, bounded west on land above given to Ebenezer Wright, east on land hereafter given to my daughter Mabel Belding, on a highway north, and on land of the heirs of Capt. Samuel Talcott south. To Stephen Wright, my son, I give the 1-2 of my 2-stone lott at or near the place so called, the east side of my land there, and my 3-acre lott in the Great Meadow. To my daughter Mabel Belding I give 1 acre of land in Beaver Meadow, on the side east on land of Daniel Wright, west on land given to the children of my son Crafts Wright, on a highway north, and on land belonging to the heirs of Capt. Samuel Talcott south, to be to her and her heirs forever. To my daughter Sarah Flowers and to Joseph Flowers, to them I give 1 acre of my back lot next to or adjoining to what he purchased of either Josiah Buck or his father. I give to Abigail Wright, my wife, the use of 1-2 of my dwelling house, cellar and garden, and the use of 1-2 of my household goods, as pewter, brass and iron, during her continuance as my relict. Also, I give to my wife one cow and the pastureing and keeping winter and summer during the term above mentioned, which my son Timothy shall yearly provide. I give to my sd. wife the use of my 4-acre lot in the Great Meadow which I gave to my son Timothy, for her use during her continuing my relict. I also give my wife the use of five apple trees at the end of my lott next the cider mill. I give to my 4 daughters, Mabel Belding, Mary Stanly, Abigail Miller and Sarah Flowers, all my remaining moveable estate except such as I give to my son Timothy hereafter named, to be equally divided among them. I give to my son Timothy out of the moveables all my tackling, as cart, plows belonging thereto, and harrow, all my chains of plow and horse chains. Lastly, I desire and appoint my two sons, Ebenezer Wright and Timothy Wright, to be the executors of this my last will and testament.

Witness: *Jonathan Williams,*   SAMUEL WRIGHT, LS.
Thomas Fox, Elisha Griswold.

Court Record, Page 12—5 November, 1734: Will proven.

Page 365.

Yeomans, Elisha, Tolland. Invt. £699-14-04. Taken 24 June, 1736, by John Lathrop, Nathaniel Bery and Zebulon West. Will dated 19 May, 1736.

I, Elisha Yeomans of Tolland, do make and ordain this my last will and testament: My will is that my wife Mary Yeomans should have the use and improvement of my house, farm and all my estate, excepting my mother's interest in the same, her lifetime or during the time that she shall continue my widow; and all my moveable estate, after my debts are paid as aforesd. (except two heifers which shall be hereafter mentioned) I give unto my sd. wife to be at her use and dispose forever. And my house and land I give unto my five children, to be unto them, their heirs and assigns forever, to be divided amongst them in manner and form as followeth: I give unto my eldest son, Daniel Yeomans, the 1-2 of my land yt lyeth on the north side of the highway that runeth east by my house, and also my house, and two acres of land to be laid out in some convenient form about the house. I give these unto my eldest son, Daniel Yeomans, to him, his heirs and assigns forever. I give unto my son Jonathan Yeomans the 1-2 of my land that lyeth on the north side of the highway aforementioned, to be unto him, his heirs and assigns forever. My will is that all my land that lyeth on the south side of the aforementioned highway should be equally divided between my five children, viz., my two sons Daniel Yeomans and Jonathan Yeomans, and my three daughters, viz., Jerusha Yeomans, Mary Yeomans and Hannah Yeomans, to be to them, their heirs and assigns forever. I give unto my two daughters, Jerusha Yeomans and Mary Yeomans, the two heifers before mentioned, namely, two three-year-old heifers. Lastly, I constitute, ordain and appoint my well-beloved wife Mary Yeomans to be the sole executrix of this my last will and testament.

Witness: *Samuel Hare,*   ELISHA YEOMANS, LS.
Samuel Eaton, Zebulon West.

Court Record, Page 48—6 July, 1736: Will proven.

PROBATE RECORDS.

VOLUME XIII.

1737 to 1742.

Page 223.

Addams, Edward, Middletown. Invt. £317-12-06. Taken 11 June, 1740, by George Hubbard, Daniel Starr and William Rockwell.

Court Record, Page 71—5 August, 1740: Adms. granted to Mary Addams, the widow, who recog. in £300 with William Rockwell.

Page 26 (Vol. XIV) 5 July, 1743: Mary Addams, Adms., exhibited an. account of her Adms.: Paid in debts and charges the sum of £146-13-00, and credit received to the amount of £34-07-00. Which account is accepted. This Court appoint Mary Addams to be guardian to her children, viz., Leah Addams, 10 years, Edward 7, Margaret 5, and Ebenezer 3 years of age, children of Edward Addams deceased.

Page 50 (Vol. XVI) 12 December, 1751: Edward Addams, a minor, age 16 years, son of Edward Addams, late of Durham deceased, made choice of William Rockwell to be his guardian. Recog., £500.

Page 110—7 November, 1753: Mary Addams, alias Mary Arnold, Adms., haveing finished her account of Adms., which is accepted by the Court, now moves for a distribution of the estate. This Court so order: To Mary the relict, 1-3 part of the real estate for her use during life; and to Edward Addams, eldest son, a double share of the remaining estate; and to Ebenezer, Leah and Margaret Addams, the rest of the children, to each of them their single shares. And appoint Joseph Johnson, Return Meigs and Mr. James Ward, of Middletown, distributors.

Page 283.

Addams, Joseph, Simsbury. Died 26 March, 1741. Invt. £2577-03-04. Taken 17 April, 1741, by Joshua Holcomb, Joseph Case 2nd and Jonathan Cole. Will dated 7 December, 1736.

I, Joseph Addams of Simsbury, in the County of Hartford, do make this my last will and testament: I give to my wife Mary 1-3 part of my now dwelling house and barn, and 1-3 part of my now improvable lands, during the time of her widowhood; and also 1-4 part of my moveable estate forever. I give to my two sons, Joseph and Matthew, all my lands with all the buildings thereon contained, and the rest of my moveable estate, to be equally divided between them my two sons Joseph and Matthew. And further, I appoint my trusty friend James Case, with my wife Mary, to be executors.

Witness: *Benjamin Addams,*   JOSEPH ADDAMS, LS.
Martha Addams, Reuben Slater.

Court Record, Page 88—5 May, 1741: Will proven.
Page 37 (Vol. XIV) 7 February, 1743-4: An account of Adms. was now exhibited in Court by the executors. They have paid in debts and charges £24-13-03, and credit received of £5-06-00. Account is allowed and ordered to be kept on file. The executors now move this Court for a dist. according to the will. This Court appoint Jonathan Case, Joseph Case and Josiah Holcomb, distributors.

Page 128.

Additional Inventory on Page 333.

Allyn, Thomas, Windsor. Inventory taken 16 February, 1738-9, by Nathaniel Drake, John Palmer, Jr., and Timothy Loomis.
Court Record, Page 44—13 March, 1738-9: Adms. to Elizabeth Allyn, widow, who recog. in £500 with Nathaniel Drake.
Page 119 (Vol. XV) 6 March, 1749-50: An account of Adms. was now exhibited in Court by Elizabeth Allyn, widow and Adms., which account is accepted. And this Court order that the estate be dist., viz.:

	£ s d
To Elizabeth Allyn, widow, her thirds,	113-17-10
To Thomas Allyn, eldest son,	56-19-06
To Theophilus, Jonah and Joseph Allyn, to each,	28-09-09
To Elizabeth, Eunice and Azuba Allyn, to each,	28-09-09

And appoint Deacon John Cook, Ensign John Palmer and Deacon Nathaniel Drake, of Windsor, distributors.
Page 29 (Vol. XVI) 2 July, 1751: Jonah Allyn, a minor, age 16 years, son of Thomas Allyn of Windsor, chose his mother Elizabeth Allyn to be his guardian. Recog., £500.
Page 20 (Vol. XVII) 26 March, 1754: Joseph Allyn, a minor, 16 years of age, son of Thomas Allyn, chose his mother Elizabeth Allyn to be his guardian. And Theophilus Allyn of sd. Windsor acknowledged himself bound in a recog. of £500 money.
Dist. File: 24 April, 1772: Distribution of Thomas Allyn his estate, viz.: To Elizabeth Allyn, widow; to Jonas, to Thomas, to Joseph, to Azuba Warner, wife of Ely Warner, to Eunice Sheldon, wife of Epapharas Sheldon, to the Widow Elizabeth Birge, to the heirs of Theophilus Allyn. By Josiah Bissell, Phineas Wilson and Edward Moore.

Page 47.

Andrews, Elijah, Hartford. Invt. £490-01-06. Taken 7 February, 1737, by John Skinner and John Edwards in Hartford, and by Edward Cadwell and David Ensign in New Hartford.

Court Record, Page 12—5 July, 1738-9: Adms. to John Cole, the widow desireing the same. Recog., £600, with Ozias Goodwin.

Page 255.

Andrews, John, Kensington. Died 16 June, 1740. Invt. £676-04-04. Taken 6 October, 1740, by Daniel Andrews, Thomas Deming and Elihu Dickinson.

Court Record, Page 13—2 August, 1737: An addition to the invt. of the estate of John Andrews was now exhibited in Court by Joseph Andrews, which addition amounts to the sum of £8-02-11, which invt. is accepted.

Page 81—20 January, 1740-1: This Court grant letters of Adms. to Mary Andrews, widow, and David Andrews, son of the decd.

Page 50 (Vol. XIV) 4 December, 1744: Mary Andrews, Adms., exhibited an account of her Adms., by which account it appears she has paid in debts and charges the sum of £59-16-04. Accepted. Abraham Andrews, a minor, 16 years of age, son of John Andrews of Wethersfield, made choice of his brother Moses Andrews to be his guardian. Recog., £500. Esther Andrews, age 12 years, chose her mother Mary Andrews to be her guardian. Recog., £500. And the sd. Mary Andrews, Adms., moves this Court for a dist. of the moveable estate of the sd. deceased:

	£ s d
The moveable part of the invt.,	189-18-10
Subtracting the debts and charges,	59-16-04
There remains to be distributed,	130-03-06
To the widow,	43-07-06
To David, eldest son,	28-18-04
To Mary, Moses, Abraham and Esther, children of the deceased, to each of them,	14-09-02

And appoint Joseph Beckley, Isaac North and Benjamin Beckley, of Wethersfield, distributors.

Page 277.

Andrews, John, Hartford. Invt. £876-16-01. Taken 23 April, 1741, by William Day, Joseph Day and Timothy Andrews. Will dated 13 March, 1741.

I, John Andrews of Hartford, do make this my last will and testament: I give to my wife Lydia the whole use of my estate during her natural life for her subsistence. I give to my two sons Silvanus and

Ithamer all the lands belonging to me in Hartford aforesd., and also my lands that belong to me in New Hartford, to be equally divided between them. I give to my wife Lydia all my moveable estate to dispose of as she shall think meet and to pay my just debts. And I appoint my wife Lydia to be executrix.

Witness: *Timothy Andrews,*　　　　JOHN ANDREWS, LS.
Thomas Andrews, Jr., James Ensign.

Court Record, Page 94—7 July, 1741: Will exhibited in Court and proven, ordered recorded and filed.

Page 63 (Vol. XIV) 3 September, 1745: Ithamer Andrus, age 16 years, chose his uncle James Ensign to be his guardian. Recog., £400. Silvanus Andrews, age 20 years, chose his uncle William Bacor of Hartford to be his guardian. Recog., £200.

Page 134.

Arnold, Samuel, East Haddam. Invt. £441-06-00. Taken 27 April, 1739, by Joshua Brainard, Henry Chapman and Noadiah Brainard. Will dated 3 November, 1738.

I, Samuel Arnold of East Haddam, husbandman, do make this my last will and testament: I give unto my beloved wife Abigail 1-3 part of my moveable estate (excepting my negro slaves), to her, her heirs and assigns forever, and also the use of 1-3 part of my lands, house, barn, orchard or other commodity appertaining to my sd. land, to use and improve during her natural life. I give to my son Samuel Arnold one lot of land lying in the 3rd division of land in East Haddam, 43 1-2 acres more or less, north on the land of Sergt. Samuel Andrews, and east and west on highways or commons, and south on a highway, to him, his heirs and assigns forever, as his or their own proper inheritance in fee simple, and also my negro man servant named Prince, ye 5th son of my eldest man servant named Prince and of Cate his wife, and also my will is that the aforesaid servant shall at my decease be in the hands of my executors and by them to be put in the hands of my son Samuel if they shall judge it best for him to have the sd. servant; but if my sd. executors shall judge it best to sell the sd. servant and my sd. son to have ye money, then my will is that my executors shall sell my sd. servant in the following manner, viz.: to such suitable master as will give most for my sd. servant, and to pay £10 a year annually until the payment be out; and also my will is that my sd. son shall have the money according to the foregoing proposal of payment, provided my sd. servant shall not be sold to any master living out of this town; and also £100 to be paid to him by my two sons, viz., Josiah and John, and in the following manner, viz., that Josiah Arnold shall pay unto his brother Samuel Arnold £3 a year annually for the space of 20 years next after my decease, and John Arnold shall pay unto his brother Samuel Arnold 40 shillings a year for the space of 20 years next after my decease. I give unto my son Joseph Arnold 1 lott of land in the fourth division of land in East Haddam joining land of Sergt. Samuel Ackley, containing about 60 acres be it more or less; and also 20 acres out of two lotts of land in the 5th and 8th divisions, to him and his heirs forever; and also my negro man servant named Sampson. I give unto my son Enoch Arnold 120 acres of land laid out to me in the 5th and 8th divisions, to him, his heirs and assigns in fee simple; and also my negro man servant called Ceaser. And further, my will is that my son Enoch shall have his 120 acres where it shall best suit him in the sd. two division lotts. I give to my son Josiah Arnold my dwelling house and homelott, with all the fences, orcharding, buildings or other appurtenances thereto belonging; and also 1 small piece of land lying in the 6th division, containing about 4 1-2 acres, lying west of the great highway; and also the west half of a small lott lying in the 2nd division; and also 4 negro servants, viz., my eldest man servant named Prince, and Cate his wife, and my man servant named Japhet and my woman servant named Rose. And further, my will is that my sd. son Josiah shall pay unto my son Samuel £3 a year for the space of 20 years after my decease, and also £5 a year for the space of 20 years annually after my decease to my daughter Mary Bates. I give to my son John Arnold 1 certain lott or tract of land lying partly on the hill called Bold Hill, being by estimation 40 acres be it more or less, and also the east half of a small lott lying in the 2nd division, to him and his heirs forever; and also my negro man servant named Peter. And further, my will is that my son John Arnold shall pay unto my son Samuel Arnold 40 shillings a year annually for the space of 20 years after my decease. I give to my daughter Mary Bates 6 1-2 acres of land butting west on Connecticut River, south on the land of Jabez Chapman, east on a ledge of rocks, being half a certain tract of land laid out to me in the 6th division of land in East Haddam; and also £100 in money or bills of public credit, to be paid to her £5 a year annually, for the space of 20 years after my decease, by my son Josiah Arnold. I give unto my daughter Abigail Arnold 6 1-2 acres of land butting west on Connecticut River, south on land above given to Mary Bates, east on the great rock, and north on the commons, being 1-2 of a certain tract of land laid out to me in the 6th division of land in East Haddam. I give to my sd. daughter Abigail my negro maid servant named Lois. I give my right in the undivided land, also the rest of my moveable estate, to be equally divided among my children. I appoint Ensign Daniel Cone and Sergt. Bezeleel Brainard, both of East Haddam, executors.

Witness: *Noadiah Brainard,*   SAMUEL X ARNOLD, LS.
Henry Chapman, Thomas Smith.

Court Record, Page 49—1st May, 1739: Will proven. The executors refused the trust and were appointed Adms. with the will annexed.

Page 57—4 December, 1739: The executors exhibit an account, which is accepted.

Page 57—4 December, 1739: John Arnold, age 18 years, and Abigail Arnold, age 14 years, chose their mother to be their guardian. Recog., £400.

Page 273-4.

Arnold, Simon, Haddam. Died 9 May, 1741. Invt. £1077-04-06. Taken 26 May, 1741, by James Hazeltine, Thomas Brooks and Abraham Brooks. Will dated 24 April, 1741.

I, Simon Arnold of Haddam, in the County of Hartford, do make this my last will and testament: I give to Hannah, my wife, 1-3 part of my dwelling house and barn and 1-3 part of all my lands, the use thereof so long as she continues my widow; and 1-3 part of all my moveable estate forever. I give to my son Joseph Arnold my dwelling house and barn and all my farm sd. house stands on, as it butts easterly on the Great River, southerly on land of Nathaniel Tyler, north on land that is or lately was John Schovel's, and south on the country road, containing by estimation 66 acres more or less, to sd. son Joseph, his heirs and assigns forever. And that 2-3 parts of my moveable estate shall be equally divided to my three children, viz., Joseph, Hannah and Susannah. And further, it is my will that my two daughters, Hannah Arnold and Susannah Arnold, shall have a lottment of my land called the new pasture, lying by Roaring Brook, and what land I bought of the Bates's, viz., the 8th division lott set out to the original right of Mr. James Bates deceased (sd. 8th division lot should contain 32 acres in land more or less), both the two lotts as butted and bounded in the records, to be equally divided amongst my two daughters Hannah and Susannah. My son Joseph shall have my gun. I appoint my brother Joseph Arnold executor.

Witness: *Aaron Cleaveland, Clerk,*   SIMON ARNOLD, LS.
David Smith, Joseph Welles.

Court Record, Page 95—21 July, 1741: Will proven.

Page 84.

Bacon, Daniel, Middletown. Invt. £691-12-03. Taken 20 June, 1738, by Solomon Adkins, Nathaniel Bacon and Wm. Rockwell.

Court Record, Page 30—27 June, 1738: Adms. to Hannah Bacon, widow. Recog., with Josiah Beardslie of Stratford.

Page 50—5 June, 1739: Hannah Bacon, Adms., exhibits an account of her Adms. Accepted.

Page 19 (Vol. XIV) 13 May, 1743: Hannah Bacon, alias Fairchild, Adms., having finished her account of Adms., moved for a distribution of the moveable part of the estate: Whereupon this Court appoint Nathaniel Bacon, Benjamin Adkins and William Rockwell distributors. Invt. on record with additions and £6-16-06 as per credit on the Adms. account, £669-13-09. The real estate subtracted, there remains £161-09-05. Debts and charges, with allowance for bringing up the children, £127-06-09, which being subtracted from the moveable part of the invt., there remains £44-02-08 to be distributed. This Court order 1-3 part to Hannah Bacon, alias Fairchild, and the remainder to Mary and Hannah Bacon, minor children.

Page 36—16 January, 1743-4: Report of the distributors accepted and filed.

Page 212.

Barnard, Joseph, Hartford. Will dated 30 December, 1737: I, Joseph Barnard of Hartford, do make this my last will and testament: I will that my loving wife Lydia have the use of my homelott I now live on, the lower room and chamber in the south end of my dwelling house, 1-3 part of my cellar, the use of the oven as she may have occasion, and 1-3 part of all my moveable estate after my debts are paid; the moveables for her own forever, the rest for her improvement during her natural life. And that my son Joseph pasture one cow for her during life. I give to my son Joseph Barnard all my lands, both in possession and reversion, divided and undivided, with all the rights, priviledges and appurtenances, to him, Joseph Barnard, and his heirs and assigns forever, he paying all my debts and the legacies hereafter given by me to his sisters, that is to say, to my daughter Lydia Barnard I give £200 in money. I give to my daughter Elizabeth King, besides what I have formerly given her, £50 money. I appoint my son Joseph Barnard sole executor.

Witness: *Joseph Talcott,*   JOSEPH BARNARD, LS.
John Wadsworth, Ichabod Wadsworth.

Codicil, dated 25 January, 1739-40: I, Joseph Barnard of Hartford, now considering that my estate is much involved in debt, do order this codicil to my foregoing will, that is to say, that whereas in my will I did give unto my daughter Lydia £200, I now see cause to alter sd. legacy, and do will and declare that my daughter Lydia (now Goodwin) shall have and I do give her £40, and no more, besides what she hath already received, and that my executor shall pay unto sd. Lydia Goodwin, in money or moveable estate at inventory price, £40 within 14 months after my decease. And although in my will I did will that my daughter Elizabeth King shall have £50 paid to her out of my estate, I now see cause to alter sd. legacy, and do will and declare that my sd. daughter Elizabeth King shall have but £40 besides what she hath already had.

Witness: *Thomas Burr,*   JOSEPH BARNARD, LS.
John Wadsworth.

Court Record, Page 76—24 November, 1740: Will exhibited by Joseph Barnard, executor. Proven.

Bartlett, Robert, Estate, Hartford. Court Record, Page 32—26 September, 1738: Adms. to Walter Henderson of Hartford. Recog., £2000 money.

Page 285.

Bartlett, Samuel, Jr., Bolton. Will dated 3 July, 1740: I, Samuel Bartlett, Jr., of Bolton, in the County of Hartford, do make this my last will and testament: I give to my wife Margaret Bartlett 1-2 of my estate during the term of her natural life, and then to descend to my daughter Abigail Bartlett. In case of her death before the decease of my wife Margaret Bartlett, she shall have the whole of my estate, she paying my hond. mother, Sarah Bartlett, £100 in money or out of my estate at inventory price. The other half of my estate I give to my daughter Abigail Bartlett. I appoint Rev. James White, of Bolton, executor.

Witness: *John Bissell,*   SAMUEL BARTLETT, LS.
Joseph Olmsted, Martha Olmsted.

Court Record, Page 86—7 April, 1741: Will now exhibited by the executor, who refused the trust. Adms. to Margaret Bartlett, widow, with the will annexed. Recog., with Theophilus Smith of Bolton.

Page 90—2 June, 1741: The Adms. reports the estate insolvent. Commissioners appointed, Capt. John Bissell, Jonathan Rennolds and Jonathan King, of Bolton.

Beacraft, Thomas. Court Record, Page 58—1st January, 1739-40: Jonathan Beacraft, age 14 years, son of Thomas Beacraft, late of Wethersfield decd., chose Josiah Griswold of Wethersfield to be his guardian. Recog., £100.

Page 213, 227.

Beauchamp, John, Hartford. Invt. £5835-08-09 1-4 (exclusive of debts due to the estate). Taken 1st December, 1740, by John Potwine, J. Gilbert, Jr., and William Keith. Will dated 8 February, 1738-9.

I, John Beauchamp of Hartford, do make this my last will and testament: I give to the children of my son John Beauchamp, in South Carolina, £5 in money to be equally divided between them, to be paid on demand. I give to my son Adam Beauchamp £100, to him and his heirs forever. I give to my granddaughter, Mary Sigourney, daughter to my daughter Mary Rauchon, £10, to be paid on demand. I give to my daughter Katharine Laitail, or her heirs, the sum of £450, to be paid £50 a year, to begin 12 months after my decease, and my executrix to give her a full discharge of all former debts and dues from her to me, as well for the rent of my house as all other contracts between me and her. And in case the sum aforesd. is not sufficient to maintain her, or after the expiration of the 9 years that she is to have £50 a year, should she stand in need of help, I order, and it is my will, that my daughter Mary Ann Lawrence should help her (in case she be in a capacity) to what she shall stand in need for her necessary support. I give to my son Isaac £400 (£100 a year, to begin 12 months after my decease), to him and his heirs forever. I also discharge him from all debts due from him to me upon any matter of account whatsoever. I give to the French Church in Boston, to the use of the poor, £10, to be paid 12 months after my decease. I give to my granddaughter Margaret, daughter of my daughter Katharine Latail, all my household goods that are now in my house at Boston. And in case my sd. granddaughter Margaret should dye before she marry, then I give the above sd. household goods to my granddaughter Marianne, daughter to my daughter Mary Ann Lawrence. I give to my grandson John Lawrence all my wearing apparrell of what kind, sort or denomination whatsoever. To my daughter Margaret Chenevard I give £1500, to her and her heirs and assigns forever, she allowing what she shall be in my debt at my decease to be a part thereof. To my daughter Susannah Beauchamp I give £1000, giving my executrix Mary Ann Lawrence the liberty, if she see cause, to add £500 more to make her equal with her sister Margaret Chenevard, to her the sd. Susannah and her heirs forever. I give to my daughter Marianne Lawrence all the remainder of my estate, both real and personal, wheresoever the same may be, to be to her and her heirs and assigns forever. And I do hereby appoint the sd. Marianne Lawrence to be my sole executrix to this my last will and testament.

Witness: *Abraham Foster, Daniel Skinner,*   JOHN BEAUCHAMP, LS.
Joshua Matson, Samuel Filley.

Court Record, Page 76—24 November, 1740: Will proven.

Page 324.

Belding, Mary, Wethersfield. Will dated 10 March, 1735-6: I, Mary Belding, widow of Deacon Jonathan Belding of Wethersfield, do make and ordain this to be my last will and testament: As touching such worldly estate as it hath pleased God to bless me with, I give and bequeath the whole of it (reserving only so much as shall be sufficient to bear my funeral expenses and to pay all my just and lawfull debts) to my two daughters, viz., Mary, the wife of David Wright, and Elizabeth, the wife of Ezra Belding. I say the whole of my worldly estate, whether it lies in money, debts, household goods, creatures, clothes, and whatsoever thing else it consists in, my will is that it be equally divided by my executors to my sd. daughters, to be to them, their heirs and assigns forever. And I constitute, make and ordain my sons-in-law, David Wright and Ezra Belding, executors.

Witness: *Elisha Micks,*   MARY BELDING, LS.
Thomas Belding, Mary Belding.

Court Record, Page 105—5 January, 1741-2: The last will and testament of Widow Mary Belding, late of Wethersfield decd., relict of Jonathan Belding, was now exhibited in Court by David Wright, one of the executors. Proven.

Will on File. Agreement on Page 317.

Belding, Mary, Wethersfield. Will dated 12 March, 1740: I, Mary Belding of Wethersfield, being very sick and weake, doe make this my last will and testament: Imprimis: I give and bequeath to my three daughters, Sarah Burnham, Mary Boardman and Esther Wolcott, all my moveable estate to be equally divided between them (excepting one sorrill mare which was of the estate of my brother John Meakings, which I give to my daughter Mary Boardman). And also all my land I give to my 6 children, Joseph Belding, Thomas Belding, Amos Belding, and the sd. daughters, Sarah Burnham, Mary Boardman and Esther Wolcott, to be equally divided between them all (excepting one small woodlott in the bounds of East Hartford, which I give to my cousin Aaron Burnham, son to my daughter Sarah). And my will is that my three daughters shall pay all my debts and all charges that shall arise upon my sisters. And my will further is, that my son Amos Belding shall have liberty to pay for them creatures of mine which are in his custody. I make my daughter Mary Boardman sole executrix.

Witness: *Jonathan Belding,*   MARY X BELDING.
Ephraim Willard, Stephen Russell.

Will exhibited in Court, 8 April, 1740, and proven.

AN AGREEMENT.

We, the subscribers, being the only heirs of the widow Mary Belding, late of Wethersfield decd., who by her last will and testament gave and bequeathed unto us her children (viz) all her land (excepting one small woodlott in the bounds of East Hartford), to be equally distributed among us all, and all her moveable estate to be equally divided among her three daughters: We, the sd. three daughters, viz., Sarah Burnham, Mary Boardman and Esther Wolcott, have received our full part of the moveable estate of our mother aforesd. of Joseph Belding and Mary Boardman, Adms. with the will annexed, and have also all of us agreed and are fully satisfied with ye division of her land in manner and form following: That is to say, the two acres of land in the Mile Meadow into six equal parts, Amos Belding on the north side, Thomas Belding next south, Sarah Burnham next south, Mary Boardman next south, Joseph Belding next south, and Esther Wolcott last south. And ye upland at East Hartford to be likewise equally divided, Joseph Belding lying on the west side, Thomas Belding, Amos Belding, Sarah Burnham, Mary Boardman and Esther Wolcott all lying successively eastward from ye sd. Joseph. And also the lott in the Meadow at East Hartford to be also equally divided, Joseph Belding first lying on the south side, Amos Belding, Mary Boardman, Thomas Belding, Sarah Burnham and Esther Wolcott lying successively northward from Joseph, the first south in the order above written. And upon the Honourable Court's acceptance and confirmation of the same, we shall acknowledge ourselves fully satisfied and shall forever quit and discharge ourselves from any further demands upon the sd. estate of the Adms. aforesd. whatsoever. In witness hereof we have set to our hands this 4th day of August, 1740.

RICHARD BURNHAM, *2nd,*	SARAH BURNHAM,
JOSHUA WOLCOTT,	ESTHER WOLCOTT,
AMOS BELDING,	THOMAS BELDING,
JOSEPH BOARDMAN,	MARY BOARDMAN,

JOSEPH BELDING.

Witness: *Jonathan Belding,*
Jonathan Boardman.

Page 119-20.

Belding, Samuel, Sen., Wethersfield. Died 27 December, 1738. Invt. £381-16-01. Taken 25 January, 1739, by Josiah Churchill, Ebenezer Wright and Ichabod Welles. Will dated 25 December, 1738.

I, Samuel Belding, Sen., of Wethersfield, do make this my last will and testament: I give unto Hannah, my wife, the use of all my personal or moveable estate during the time of her natural life or widowhood, and at my wife's decease or marriage I give my son Matthew 20 shillings and no more, and the remaining part of my moneys, goods or chattels I give to the rest of my children to be equally divided among them, or to their heirs. And further, as an addition to my son Samuel and to my son Daniel, I give to each of them and to their heirs all my right and title in or to the commons or undivided lands in Wethersfield or elsewhere.

And my will is that my wife and my son Daniel be my executors.

Witness: *Josiah Churchill,*   SAMUEL BELDING, LS.
John Crane, Jr., Ichabod Welles.

Court Record, Page 40—2 February, 1738-9: Will proven.
Recorded: Samuel Curtiss (L. S.)

Invt. in Vol. XIV, Page 34-5-6-7-104.

Belding, Silas, Wethersfield. Invt. £2248-08-10. Taken 2 October, 1741, by Jonathan Robbins, Jonathan Belding and Josiah Smith. An invt. of real and personal estate in Caanan, £2452-09-11, taken 23 September, 1741, by Josiah Walker, Augustin Bryan and Andrew Stevens. An addition to the invt. taken 10th May, 1742, and also a further addition of £175, taken at Wethersfield on the 19th day of May, 1742, by the above-named apprisers, Jonathan Belding, Josiah Smith and Jonathan Robbins.

Court Record, Page 98—21 December, 1741: Adms. granted to Abigail Belding, widow, who gave bonds, with Jonathan Belding of Wethersfield, of £600.

Page 102—1st December, 1741: Joshua Belding, a minor, age 16 years, son of Silas Belding, chose his mother Abigail Belding to be his guardian. And this Court appoint her guardian to Charles Belding, age 13 years, Oliver 9 years, Jonathan 4 years, and Lydia 11 years, all children of the sd. Silas Belding decd. Recog., £3600.

Page 39 (Probate Side, Vol. XIV): Agreement, dated 19 May, 1742: Know all men by these presents: That we, Abigail Belding of Caanan, in the County of Hartford, in the Colony of Connecticut, in New England, widow and relict of Silas Belding, late of Wethersfield, in sd. County, for myself and as I am a guardian to Joshua Belding, Charles Belding, Oliver Belding, Jonathan Belding and Lydia Belding, minor children of the sd. deceased, and Silas Belding of sd. Caanan and Abigail Belding, eldest son and daughter of the sd. deceased, do for ourselves and heirs forever make the following agreement for the settlement of the real estate of the sd. deceased: First: We agree that Silas Belding, eldest son of the sd. deceased, shall have his double portion and part in sd. real estate of the sd. deceased, which is or shall fall to the estate of the sd. deceased, wherever it may fall, and that the rest of the above-named children of the sd. deceased shall each of them have their single share, that is, 1-2 so much as Silas Belding, their abovesd. elder brother. And that it is and shall be in the power of our elder brother Silas to sell and dispose of the homelott of the deceased in Wethersfield, containing about 3 acres of land, together with all the buildings and appurtenances thereunto, which sd. lands and buildings was prised at £900, and that if it amount to more than a double portion of the real estate of the sd. deceased, then he the sd. Silas Belding shall and is hereby obliged to refund and pay back the over-plus to the rest of the children, and then sd. homelott in Wethersfield is and shall be accounted for him our brother Silas and his heirs forever, except the over-plus of his part, if any there be, and the widow's dowry in sd. homelott. And that by virtue of these presents it shall be in the power of any one of the heirs of the sd. deceased to apply themselves to any proper Judge of Probates to appoint freeholders to cut off and make division and partition of any of the lands and real estate of the sd. deceased to such heir or heirs together or respectively as shall then be thought most proper. And that I, the sd. Silas Belding, for myself and heirs, do by these presents forever quitclaim of all the real estate of the sd. deceased to my aforesd. brethren and sisters, except my double share and part of the estate of our father Silas Belding, and that the remainder, exclusive of my double share, shall be to my sd. brothers and sisters and at their dispose forever. In witness whereof, and in full confirmation of the foregoing agreement, we, the subscribers, have hereunto set our hands and seals in Hartford before the Court of Probate this 19th day of May, in the 15th year of His Majestie's Reign, George the 2nd, King of Great Britain, &c., Anno. Dom. 1742.

SILAS BELDING, LS.

ABIGAIL BELDING, LS.   ABIGAIL X BELDING, LS., *and as guardian to the several minors in this instrument above named.*

Court Record, Page 5—19 May, 1742: An agreement was exhibited in Court and accepted.

Page 24—24 May, 1743: An account of Adms. on the estate of Silas Belding, late of Caanan, formerly of Wethersfield decd., was now exhibited in Court by Abigail Belding, Adms. Accepted.

Invt. in Vol. XIV, Page 28.

Bement, Samuel, Simsbury. Died September, 1741. Invt. £773-05-02. Taken 1741, by Joshua Holcomb, Reuben Slater and James Case.

Court Record, Page 111—6 March, 1741-2: Adms. granted to Samuel Bement of Simsbury. Recog., £1000, with Aaron Cooke of Hartford.

Page 38 (Vol. XV) 5 May, 1747: William Enos, Jr., of Simsbury, showing to this Court that he hath purchased the homelott and buildings of Samuel Bemon, of Simsbury, in Scotland Parish, decd., of Roberts & Moses, who purchased of the heirs of the sd. decd., and prays this Court to appoint freeholders to set out to the widow of the decd. her right of dowry in the sd. homelott and buildings, as he may improve separate from sd. widow: Whereupon this Court appoint James Case, William Case and John Case, of Simsbury, to set out to the sd. Margaret Bemon, widow of the deceased, 1-3 part of homelott and buildings for her improvement during life.

Page 69 (Vol. XVI) 18 July, 1752: Margaret Beman, the relict of Samuel Beman, late of Scotland, in Simsbury, in the County of Hartford, deceased, now moves to this Court that her right of dowry be set out to her: Whereupon this Court appoint Stephen Goodwin, William Manly and Samuel Foot, of Simsbury, to set out to said Margaret Beman by bounds and monuments one-third of the lands and real estate of the said deceased for her improvement during life.

Page 14.

Bird, Sarah, Farmington. Will dated 29 March, 1737: I, Sarah Bird of Farmingtown, widow, do make this my last will and testament: I give to Thomas Day, my grandchild, a note given me by Jonathan Arnold, allowing the sd. Arnold 4 years time to pay what is due upon it; also my old Bible and all my debts remaining after the payment of my own debts. To my grandchild Sarah Day I give my bed with the furniture belonging to it, and a new Bible and a trunk. To my grandchild Eunice Day I give a chest with drawers. To my grandchild Mary Day I give a chest and a glass bottle and a little box. To my three grandchildren, Sarah, Eunice and Mary above named, I give a brass kettle, an iron kettle, my linen (namely, two towels, 2 napkins, 1 table cloth and 3 pillowbeers), 2 jugs, a chamber pot, my books not already given, and all my clothing, to be equally divided among them; also 1 towel, a pot and a dish. To my daughter Hannah Bird I give a muff and a brush and a lute-string. And I appoint my son Jonathan Bird sole executor.

Witness: *Samuel Whitman,*   SARAH X BIRD, LS.
Stephen Sedgewick, Nathaniel Thompson.

Court Record, Page 7—3 May, 1737: The last will and testament of Sarah Bird of Farmingtown was now proven.

Page 13—21 July, 1737: This Court grant letters of Adms. on the estate of Sarah Bird, widow, late of Farmingtown decd., with the will annexed, unto Richard Seymour.

Page 52.

Birge, Daniel, Hebron. Invt. £556-16-08. Taken by Samuel Watters and Benjamin Taylor. Signed by Simon Baxter as witness that the appraisers had taken the oath.

Court Record, Page 17—6 December, 1737: Adms. to Rebeckah Birge, widow. Recog., £300, with Simon Baxter of Hebron.

Page 43—6 March, 1738-9: The Adms. may, with Jonathan Root, sell land (£44-05-08 in value) by advice of Capt. Nathaniel Phelps, Joseph Phelps and Deacon Benjamin Loomis of Hebron.

Dist. File: 1761: Estate of Daniel Birge: To Rebeckah, the relict, to Daniel Birge, to Jonathan Birge, to Rebeckah Burroughs a daughter, to Sarah Taylor, to Deborah Haldrige, to the heirs of Eleanor Howard, to Lydia Root. By Israel Root, Daniel Foot and Joel Jones, distributors.

Page 121-2.

Bissell, Cornet Daniel, Windsor. Invt. taken 5 February, 1738-9, by Samuel Strong, Ebenezer Heydon and Roger Newbery. Will dated 25 November, 1738.

I, Daniel Bissell of Windsor, do make this my last will and testament: I give to my wife Elizabeth Bissell the use of one-third part of my real improveable estate during widowhood. Also, one-quarter part of my moveable estate, excepting her proportion of what I shall give more to my daughter Anne than one-quarter part of my moveable estate. I give unto my son Daniel Bissell all my right and proportion in the land called the equivalent land at Windsor, and also 3 1-2 acres of land at Bissell's farm, lying on the west side of Pine Meadow, and also one full half of all my remaining undisposed-of-lands, wheresoever and howsoever the same is butted and bounded, excepting ye lands I shall hereafter give to my daughters and brother Jeremiah Bissell. I give unto my son Ezekiell Bissell one full half of all my undisposed-of lands excepting what is above especially given to my son Daniel Bissell and shall hereafter give to my brother Jeremiah Bissell and to my daughters. I give to my daughter Margaret Levet and to her heirs 1-4 part of my moveable estate, only excepting out of her 1-4 part so much as to allow her proportion of the £5 I shall hereafter give to my daughter Anne. But it is to be understood that what my daughter Margaret hath already had is to be accounted as part of her portion. I give to my daughter Mary Bissell 1-4 part of my moveable estate, only excepting out of her 1-4 part so much as to allow her proportion of the £5 I shall hereafter give to my daughter Anne. I give unto my daughter Anne Bissell 1-4 part of my moveable estate, and also £5 thereof which I have above excepted and provided for her more than her sisters. I give unto my daughters, Margaret Levet, Mary Bissell and Anne Bissell, and their heirs and assigns forever, 150 acres of land lying on the east side of the Great River on the east part of the three-mile lott which was Father Bissell's, to be to my daughters in equal proportion, only they paying in equal shares to my son Daniel Bissell £5 money. I give unto my brother Jeremiah Bissell my right in the 1 1-2-mile division of the commons that came from my brother Samuel Bissell's estate to me. I hereby appoint my two sons Daniel Bissell and Ezekiel Bissell executors. I would further signify to my son Ezekiel that my desire is that he would show himself kind to my wife and my two younger daughters with respect to household, and give them kind entertainment or allowance to be with him under his *ruff*, till God in his providence shall otherwise provide for them.

Witness: *Henry Allyn,*   DANIEL BISSELL, LS.
Benjamin Bissell, Miriam Bissell.

Court Record, Page 40—6 February, 1738-9: Will proven.

Page 49.

Bissell, John, Windsor. Invt. £332-14-06. Taken 29 August, 1737, by Job Elsworth, Joseph Harper and Ebenezer Watson, Jr.

Court Record, Page 15—6 September, 1737: Adms. to Hannah Bissell, widow. Recog., £500, with Jeremiah Bissell of Windsor.

Page 39 (Vol. XVI) 5 November, 1751: Hezekiah Bissell, a minor, 14 years of age, son of John Bissell, late of Windsor decd., made choice of his father-in-law Jonathan Bartlett of Windsor to be his guardian. Recog., £600.

Blackbourn, Samuel. Court Record, Page 87—20 April, 1747: This Court grant Adms. on the estate of Samuel Blackbourn, late of Canaan, a transient person deceased, unto Richard Seymour of sd. Canaan, who gave bond with Stebbin Wilson of Hartford for £50.

Page 91.

Blake, Richard, Middletown. Invt. £809-14-03. Taken 7 August, 1738, by Francis Whitmore, Jacob Cornwall and William Rockwell.

Court Record, Page 7—10 May, 1737: Adms. to Abigail Blake, widow. Recog., £300, with William Whitmore of Middletown.

Page 3 (Vol. XV) 7 January, 1745-6: Hannah Blake, a minor, 15 years of age, daughter of Richard Blake, chose William Rockwell to be her guardian. Recog., £500.

Page 46—6 October, 1747: Abigail Blake, a minor, chose her uncle Stephen Blake to be her guardian. Recog., £500.

Page 47—29 September, 1747: Elizabeth Blake, a minor, 11 years, chose Jonas Green of Middletown to be her guardian. Recog., £300.

Page 30 (Vol. XVI) 2 July, 1751: Abigail Green, alias Blake, the relict of Capt. Richard Blake, now moves to this Court for a dist. of the estate: To Abigail Green, alias Blake, her 1-3 part in moveables, £204-08-11. And to Hannah, Abigail and Elizabeth Blake their equal shares. And also set out to Abigail Green one-third part of the real estate for her improvement during life. And this Court order set out to the abovesd. heirs, Hannah, Abigail and Elizabeth Blake, children of the sd. decd., their part fallen to them in the dist. of the estate of their uncle Freelove Blake. And appoint Joseph Southmaid, Esq., Jonathan Allin and James Wood, distributors.

Blynn, John. Court Record, Page 38—2 January, 1738-9: John Blynn, age 14 years, son of John Blynn, late of Wethersfield, chose Thomas Harris of Wethersfield to be his guardian. Recog., £200.

Inventory on File.

Boardman, Abia, Wethersfield. Invt. £130-19-08. Taken by Jacob Goodrich, Timothy Baxter and Benjamin Stilman.

Court Record, Page 84—9 March, 1740-1: Adms. granted to Thomas Boardman, Jr., and Thomas Fox. Recog., £200, with Jacob Goodrich.

Page 105—5 January, 1741-2: Thomas Boardman, Adms., exhibited an account of his Adms. Accepted. This Court order the estate dist., viz., to the heirs of Isaac Boardman, to heirs of Samuel Boardman, to Thomas Boardman, to Sarah Boardman alias Frary's heirs, to Eunice Boardman alias Williams, to each, £12-11-09. By Jacob Goodrich, Timothy Baxter and Benjamin Stilman.

Page 67.

Boardman, Moses, Middletown. Invt. £450-00-00. Taken 24 January, 1737-8, by Stephen Stocking and Janna Wilcock.

Court Record, Page 24—7 March, 1737-8: Adms. granted to Silence Boardman, widow. Recog., £600, with John Penfield of Middletown.

Page 29 (Vol. XV) 2 December, 1746: Joseph Washburn, in right of his wife Lucy Boardman, alias Washburn, daughter of Moses Boardman, moved to this Court for a dist. of the moveable estate: Whereupon this Court appoint Janna Wilcocks, of Middletown, and John Penfield, distributors, to distribute the estate, as followeth:

	£ s d
Inventory of moveables and credits,	205-03-09
The debts allowed,	9-09-09
The debts subtracted, there remains to be distributed,	196-03-09
To Silence Boardman, widow,	65-07-10
To Samuel Boardman, eldest son,	65-07-10
To Moses Boardman and Lucy Washburn, to each,	32-13-11

Page 44.

Booge, William, East Haddam. Invt. £432-11-08. Taken 17 August, 1737, by Joshua Brainard, Jabez Chapman and Ephraim Griswold. Court Record, Page 15—4 October, 1737: Adms. granted to Dorothy Booge, widow. Recog., £800, with Samuel Ingram of West Haddam.

Page 89—2 June, 1741: William Booge, age 18 years, chose his uncle John Booge to be his guardian. Recog., £300. Elizabeth and Dorothy Booge chose their mother Dorothy Booge to be their guardian, and she was appointed guardian to Ephraim Booge, age 5 years. Recog., £200.

Page 90—2 June, 1741: Dorothy Booge, Adms., exhibited an account of her Adms., which account is accepted.

Page 42 (Vol. XIV) 10 May, 1744: Dorothy Booge, widow, having administered on the sd. estate, the heirs, viz., William and Elizabeth, now moved to this Court for a dist., which this Court grant:

	£ s d
To Dorothy Booge, widow,	124-10-05
To William Booge, eldest son,	71-02-10
To Jonathan, Timothy, Dorothy, Ephraim and Elizabeth Booge, to each of them their single portion,	35-11-05

And appoint Lt. John Brockway, Ensign John Comstock and Mr. William Comstock, of Lyme, distributors.

Page 278.

Bradley, George, Tolland. Invt. £2800-00-00. Taken by George Hall, Samuel Dimock and Zebulon West. Will dated 13 January, 1740-1.

I, George Bradley of Tolland, in the County of Hartford, do make this my last will and testament: I give to my wife Hannah Bradley all and the whole of my household goods whatsoever, to be to her use and dispose forever; and the use of the lower room in the east end of my house and 1-3 part of the cellar during the time she shall remain my widow, and also the use of 1 cow, to be kept for her out of my estate, during the time she remains my widow. And further, my will is that my sd. wife shall have an honourable maintenance out of my estate during widowhood. I give to my eldest son George Bradley the west end or part of my dwelling farm joining the heirs of Deacon John Huntington decd. All that part of my dwelling farm, together with my dwelling house and barn, I give to my son George and to his heirs (male) forever in fee tail. And also I give to my sd. son George all the remaining part of my personal estate except what I have given to my wife, ordering and requireing him to maintain and support his mother while she remains my widow, and also to pay out further according as my will is and is hereafter mentioned. My will is and I give to my son Jabez Bradley all that part of my homestead lying eastward of the line running from the white oak tree, and to his heirs (male) in fee tail. My will is that all the remaining part of my lands, both that which lyeth in Tolland and Stafford, and wheresoever, shall be equally divided between my three sons, viz., Henry Bradley, Josiah Bradley and Jonah Bradley, to them and their heirs and assigns forever. Also I give to my sd. three sons, Henry, Josiah and Jonah, £30 in money each, which I order my sd. son George to pay unto them as they come of the age of 21 years old. My will is and I give to my daughter Hannah Bradley the sum of £65 money, to be paid to her within one year after my decease, which I order my son George Bradley to pay unto the sd. Hannah. My will is and I give to my daughter Mary Bradley the sum of £50 money, to be paid to her out of my estate within two years after my decease, which I order my son George to pay to the sd. Mary. My will is and I give to my daughter Jean Bradley the sum of £40 money, to be paid to her out of my estate within three years after my decease, which I order my son George to pay to the sd. Jean. I appoint my son George Bradley sole executor.

Witness: *George Hall,*   GEORGE BRADLEY, LS.
Aaron Cady, Jr., Zebulon West.

The day of the date above written I, Hannah Bradley, wife to the signer, George Bradley, hereby signify my acceptance of and full contentment with the dower that is above mentioned and given to me by my sd. husband in this his last will, as the full of my dower or third of his estate. As witness my hand:

Witness: *George Hall,*   HANNAH X BRADLEY.
Aaron Cady, Jr.

Court Record, Page 91—15 June, 1741: Will proven.

Page 5 (Vol. XIV) 19 May, 1742: Jabez Bradley, age 16 years, son of George Bradley, chose John Paulk of sd. Tolland to be his guardian. Recog., £600.

Page 49—12 August, 1744: Josiah Bradley, 14 years of age, son of George Bradley, also made choice of John Paulk to be his guardian. Recog., £500.

Page 92 (Vol. XV) 7 March, 1748-9: George Bradley, executor to the last will of Mr. George Bradley, late of Tolland, now moved this

Court for a dist. of the real estate given by the sd. George Bradley to his 3 sons, Henry Bradley, Josiah Bradley and Jonah Bradley, which this Court grant (sd. Jonah being deceased). This Court appoint Joshua Wills, Christopher West and John Starr, distributors.

Page 125.

Brainard, Rev. Chileab, Glastonbury. Invt. £551-12-11. Taken 22 January, 1738-9, by Jonathan Hale, Abner Moseley, John Fisk and James Brainard. Will dated 18 August, 1738.

I, Chileab Brainard of Glastonbury, do make this my last will and testament: I give to my wife Abigail all my moveable estate, together with the 100 acres of land given to me by the proprietors of sd. Glastonbury on consideration of my settling in the work of the ministry in this place, and also an equal part of the house and land wherein I dwell with my daughter Abigail. In case my wife have another child by me, it shall share equally with my sd. daughter Abigail. I give and release to the Society of Eastbury the £100 due to me as part of my settlement in sd. Society, and what little part of sd. £100 that I have had, my mind and will is that it be paid back again with my just debts out of what I have already given to my wife Abigail. I give to my sd. wife Abigail (as part of my moveable estate) £42-10-00, being the 1-2 of my salary for this present year from the aforesd. Society, and the remaining part I give and release to sd. Society. And whereas, sundry persons promised me several days work for my encouragement in the work of the ministry in this place, I do hereby give and release sd. persons from any further demands for sd. days work. And I appoint my brother Josiah Brainard, with my wife Abigail, to be executors.

Witness: *Thomas Wells,*   CHILEAB BRAINARD, LS.
Ashbel Woodbridge, John Waddams.

Court Record, Page 40—6 February, 1738-9: Will proven.

Page 66—25 April, 1740: This Court appoints Abigail Brainard, widow, to be guardian to her daughter Abigail Brainard, age 2 years and 8 months. Recog., £300.

Page 215-216.

Brainard, Elijah, Haddam. Died 20 April, 1740. Invt. £1963-15-03. Taken 13 June, 1740, by Joseph Arnold, Caleb Cone and Thomas Brooks. Will dated 24 May, 1739.

I, Elijah Brainard, in the County of Hartford, do make this my last will and testament: I give to my wife Margaret Brainard (her dower rights). I give to my eldest son Joseph Brainard the 1-2 of the 8th division lott in Haddam, laid out on the right of Abraham Dibble, containing in the whole 30 acres, and the 8th division lott laid out on the right of Moses Pond, containing 12 acres, and my inhabitant right (being £77-11-00) in all the undivided land on the west side of the Great River. I give to my 2nd son Elijah Brainard, Jr., 23 acres and 56 rods of the 4th division lott in sd. Haddam, laid out on the right of Capt. Gates, late of sd. Haddam deceased, and £55-06 right in all the undivided land on the west side of the Great River, being 1-5 part of the original rights of Richard Piper, Abraham Dibble and my honoured father Daniel Brainard, late of sd. Haddam decd. I give to my 3rd son Jabez Brainard all my land on the south side of the country road opposite my homestead, be the same more or four acres, and all my land lying on the southeast side of the highway that goeth from Jabez Brainard's house to Purcel (?) and my lott in the upper meadow, with the upland adjoining thereto, and one piece of land of about 4 acres on the northwest side of Higanum Cove, and all my right in the undivided land on the east side of the Great River in Haddam. I give to my 4th son Phineas Brainard, his heirs and assigns forever, my dwelling house, barn, and homestead, viz., all my land there adjoining, and 1-2 of the warehouse standing thereon, and the 5th division lott laid out upon the right of the aforesd. Abraham Dibble, containing 50 acres, and about 3 acres of land adjoining thereto, and a right of £40 (the right of Moses Pond) in all the undivided land on the west side of the Great River. I give to my four daughters, viz., Mary Pond, Abigail Arnold, Thankfull Brainard and Esther Brainard, and to my granddaughter Rachel Bailey, all my personal estate of all sorts not otherwise disposed of in this will, equally to be divided to and amongst them five. And I make my two sons, Elijah Brainard and Jabez Brainard, executors.

Witness: *William Porter,*   ELIJAH BRAINARD, LS.
Abraham Brooks, Hez: Brainard.

Court Record, Page 70—5 August, 1740: The last will and testament of Elijah Brainard, late of Haddam, exhibited in Court by Elijah Brainard and Jabez Brainard, executors. Will proved and ordered recorded.

Inventory on File.

Brunson, Samuel, Kensington. Invt. £231-07-06. Taken February, 1741, by William Burnham, Jr., and Ebenezer Hart. At a Court of Probate this invt. was exhibited by Hezekiah Brunson, executor, and accepted.

Court Record, Page 110—2 March, 1741-2: Will now exhibited by Hezekiah Brunson, son of the deceased. Proven. (Will not found.)

Page 250.

Bull, Nehemiah, Westfield (Mass.). Invt. 4 tracts of land in New Hartford (Ct.) 109 acres, £163-10-00 as money. Taken by Joseph Gilbert and Peletiah Mills. Will dated 28 February, 1739-40.

I, Nehemiah Bull of Westfield, in the County of Hampshire and Province of Massachusetts Bay, in New England, clerk, do make this my last will and testament: Imprimis. I ordain and appoint that my debts and funeral charges be discharged and payd by my executor in convenient time after my decease, and that my house lott in Westfield with the buildings thereon be sold by my executors, part of the products of which to be employed in the discharging of my debts. I give to my wife Elizabeth Bull 1-2 of my personal estate to her own dispose forever, and also 1-2 of the produce of my house lott and buildings aforesd., when sold, to be improved for her maintenance, comfort and support so long as she shall continue my widow, and what remains thereof afterwards to be equally divided among my children. I give and bequeath to my loving and dear children, William Bull, John Partridge Bull, Justin Bull and Nehemiah Bull, all the remaining part of my estate, whether real or personal, to be equally divided among them, to be to them and their heirs forever. And my will is that my son William be well educated in the Latin and Greek tongue and natural philosophy whilst he come to be of a suitable age to live with a doctor, and that then he be put to some skillful physician; and that my other children be well educated for such imployment as shall be found agreeable to their genious and dispositions. I ordain my dearly beloved wife and my brother Oliver Partridge, of Hatfield, executors.

Witness: *John Root,*   NEHEMIAH BULL, LS.
Edw. Martindale, Moses Root.

A codicil: I, Nehemiah Bull, &c., do by these presents approve, ratify and confirm my last will and testament, and now do by this my codicil or schedule impower and fully authorize my brother Mr. Oliver Partridge (who was one of my executors) to act and transact for me and my heirs as fully and amply as if I myself were living and present, in giving a deed of my land that I bought (with some others) of Joikim Vanvaulkenburk to the Indians of Stockbridge to fullfill the conditions of a grant made by the Great and General Court, and what he shall transact shall be as valid as if it were done by myself. I also fully impower him to join with Ephraim Williams, Esq., and Company in dividing our land near Stockbridge. The date, 9 April, 1740.

Witness: *John Root,*   NEHEMIAH BULL, LS.
Moses Root.

Test: Timothy Dwight, Register.

Court Record, Page 82—3 February, 1740-1: Will now exhibited by Oliver Partridge, one of the executors. Proved at Court of Probate at Northampton, 13 May last (1740), and ordered to be recorded.

Attested by Timothy Dwight, Regstr.

Page 68-9.

Bunce, Ann, Hartford. Invt. £56-10-00. Taken 17 February, 1737-8, by Hezekiah Goodwin and Jonathan Olcott.

Burr, John, late of Farmingtown. Court Record, Page 98-99—21 September, 1741: An agreement of the heirs for the settlement of the estate: We, John Burr, Noadiah Burr, Stephen Burr, Nathaniel Burr and Ebenezer Burr, of Farmington, Gideon Burr of Goshen, Sarah Gillett of Hartford, Eunice Case of Simsbury, Thankfull Brown and Miriam Case of Farmington, being the only children and heirs of the estate of our father John Burr of sd. Farmington decd., do hereby acknowledge that we have received our full part and portion of our sd. father's estate, and do hereby quitclaim respectively to each other, and do hereunto set our hands and seals this 21 September, 1741.

JOHN BURR, LS.	EBENEZER BURR, LS.	SARAH GILLETT, LS.
NATHANIEL BURR, LS.	JOSEPH GILLETT, JR., LS.	MIRIAM CASE, LS.
THANKFULL X BROWN, LS.	NATHANIEL CASE, LS.	SARAH BURR, LS.
EUNICE CASE, LS.	STEPHEN BURR, LS.	EPHRAIM BROWN, LS.
NOADIAH BURR, LS.	GIDEON BURR, LS.	SAMUEL CASE, LS.

Then they 15 subscribers personally appeared and acknowledged their hands and seals.

Test: Jos: Talcott, Jr., Clerk.

Butfield, William. Court Record, Page 36—7 November, 1738: William Butfield, age 16 years, chose Ephraim Shaylor of Bolton to be his guardian. Recog., £300.

Cert: John Bissell, J. P.

Inventory on File.

Butler, Joseph, Middletown. Invt. taken 21 January, 1740-1, by Samuel Shepherd and John Kirby. Also an addition of £28-03-00 to be added to the inventory.

Court Record, Page 81—27 January, 1740-1: Adms. granted to Benjamin Butler of Middletown, who gave bond with Edward Higby of £300.

Page 103—1st December, 1741: Benjamin Butler, Adms., exhibited an account of his Adms.; also an additional invt. of £28-03-00. Accepted.

Invt. in Vol. XIV, Page 28.

Cadwell, Aaron, Hartford. Invt. £356-19-02. Taken 28 May, 1740, by Joseph Talcott, Jr., and William Keith.

Court Record, Page 65—22 April, 1740: Adms. granted to Rachel Cadwell, widow, who recog. in £500 with John Butler, Jr.

Page 6 (Vol. XIV) 4 May, 1742: Rachel Cadwell, Adms., exhibited an account of her Adms. Accepted. Also, this Court do set out for the widow her necessity, £17-11-06.

Page 22—3 May, 1743: Rachel Cadwell, Adms., exhibited a further account of her Adms. Accepted.

Page 17 (Vol. XVII) 22 April, 1754: Mr. Ebenezer Williamson of Hartford, in right of his wife Rachel, the relict of Aaron Cadwell, late of Hartford deceased, moves to this Court that her right of dowry be set out to her: Whereupon this Court appoints Jonathan Seymour, John Skinner and Daniel Steele to set out the widow's thirds.

Page 34—8 July, 1754: Report of the distributors.

Page 36—6 August, 1754: Jonathan Cadwell, for himself and in behalf of his brethren, moves for a distribution of the estate of their brother Aaron Cadwell: Whereupon this Court appoint Daniel Goodwin, Stephen Hosmer and Ozias Pitkin to make an equal distribution, viz., to Thomas Cadwell, Jonathan, James and Moses Cadwell, the heirs of Hannah Chappell deceased, and Lois Bliss, alias White, to each of them their equal shares.

Page 203-4.

Cadwell, Leah, wife of Jonathan Cadwell, Hartford. Will dated 23 May, 1740: I, Leah Cadwell of Hartford, do make this my last will and testament: I give to Jonathan Cadwell, my husband, and to his heirs and assigns, 10 acres of land lying and being in the west division of Hartford, being part of a piece of land given to me by my honoured father Thomas Morgan, late of Hartford decd., by his last will and testament, which by sd. will may more fully appear, which 10 acres shall begin at the east end of sd. lott and extending the whole breadth of sd. lott westward until it shall take in the full of sd. 10 acres. And further, I give unto my sd. husband the remaining part of sd. lott, to be for his use during his natural life. And I do hereby ratify and confirm this to be my last will and testament.

Witness: *Moses Nash,*   LEAH X CADWELL, LS.
Gideon Butler, Simon Mors.

Court Record, Page 73—2 September, 1740: Will now exhibited by Jonathan Cadwell, executor, who was the husband of the deceased. Proven.

Page 176, 185.

Cadwell, Lt. Thomas, Hartford. Invt. £300-17-02. Taken 21 February, 1739-40, by William Gaylord, William Cadwell and Nathaniel Jones. Will dated 30 December, 1737.

I, Thomas Cadwell of Hartford, do make and declare this my last will and testament: I give to my wife Hannah 1-3 part of all my personal estate, to her and her heirs forever. I also devise to the use of my sd. wife one end of my present dwelling house in Hartford, which she shall choose, with a proportional part of the cellar and garden and well, to be hers during life. And also, for her more comfortable support, my will is that my sons shall pay to her annually during her life the sum of £10 money as I hereafter shall order. I give to my eldest son Thomas all that my farm at the west division in Hartford which is bounded north on the lands of Samuel and Thomas Shepherd and Daniel Ensign, south on his own land, east on Hartford commons, and west on Farmingtown bounds, with the house and all other buildings thereon erected, part whereof I have already given him by deed, my son Thomas paying to my wife the sum of £4 annually during her life in part of the legacy of £10 I have herein before given her, and also what I shall hereinafter order him to pay to my two daughters, Hannah and Lois. I give and devise to my two sons, Jonathan and James, the lott which I bought of Thomas Sadd in the aforesd. west division according as I have already given the same to them by deeds of gift. Also, I give to them, the sd. Jonathan and James, a lott of land in Farmingtown which I bought of Samuel Wadsworth, and also the southward part or all the remainder of a lott of land lying in Farmingtown that I bought of Capt. Hart, which remainder is not contained in my deed of part of sd. lott to the Burrs, the aforesd. land to be equally divided between them my sd. sons Jonathan and James, each of my sd. sons Jonathan and James paying to my wife each 40 shillings annually in part of the aforesd. legacy of £10, and also paying what I shall hereafter order them to pay to my aforesd. two daughters. As to my son Moses, I have already given him the full portion of my real estate, that is to say, what part of my estate I did intend he should have. By his desire I have sold and have given him the money for which the same was sold, so that he has had a full single portion of my estate. Yet my will is that my executors shall pay to him the sd. Moses out of my personal estate at inventory price to the value of 30 shillings, and no more. I give to my son Aaron my present dwelling house, homelott, barn and orchard thereon, also my meadow land lying in the North and South Meadow, and my pastureland lying in the Ox Pasture, and my lott called the Brickiln lott, all lying in Hartford aforesd., to be to him, his heirs and assigns forever, of all which I have heretofore given him a deed of gift, reserving to the use of my wife only what I have hereinbefore given to her in my sd. house, &c., for life, the same to be to him, his heirs and assigns forever, he paying to my sd. wife 40 shillings annually during her life in part to make up the aforesd. legacy of £10, and also what I shall hereafter order him to pay to my aforesd. daughters. As to my daughter Hannah Chappell, I have already given her £30-04, and my will is that she shall have out of my estate, more than what she hath already had, the sum of £69-16, to her and her heirs forever. As to my daughter Lois Bliss, I have already given her £48-06, and I will that she shall have out of my estate, more than what she hath already had, £51-14, to her and her heirs forever. If there be not sufficient personal estate to pay sd. sums to my daughters, what part thereof is wanting I hereby order to be paid to them by my four sons, Thomas, Jonathan, James and Aaron, my son Thomas to pay 2-5 part thereof, and Jonathan, James and Aaron each 1-5 part thereof. I hereby appoint my two sons, Thomas and Jonathan, to be executors.

Witness: *Daniel Smith,*   THOMAS CADWELL, LS.
Jos: Gillett, Jr., Margaret Butler.

Court Record, Page 61—4 March, 1739-40: Will proven.

Page 35 (Vol. XIV) 6 December, 1743: Thomas Cadwell and Jonathan Cadwell, executors to the last will and testament of Thomas Cadwell, now exhibited an account of debts and charges due from the estate and legacies paid, in all amounting to £6-01-06 more than to discharge the legacies in sd. will.

Page 61 (Vol. XVII) 6 May, 1755: William Cadwell and Joseph Dickins of Windsor, in right of his wife Mary Cadwell, alias Dickins, cited the rest of the heirs to the estate of Thomas Cadwell of Hartford aforesd. deceased, grandfather to the sd. William and Mary, to appear before the Court and show cause why the undivided lands belonging to Thomas Cadwell his estate should not be divided. The above cited parties did not appear to make any objections, whereupon this Court, on the motion of the sd. William Cadwell and Joseph Dickins, order that a dist. be made of land lying in Hartford on the east side of the river, in that land lying in the Five-Miles, so-called, viz., 2-9 parts thereof to the heirs of Edward Cadwell deceased; to the heirs of Thomas Cadwell deceased, 1-9 part; to the heirs of Matthew Cadwell deceased, 1-9 part; to the heirs of Samuel Cadwell of sd. Hartford deceased, 1-9 part; to the heirs of Mary Cadwell (alias Dickins) of Windsor, 1-9 part; to the heirs of Abigail Cadwell (alias Church) of Hartford deceased, 1-9 part; to the heirs of Hannah Cadwell (alias Bliss) of Springfield, in the County of Hampshire, 1-9 part; to Mehetabell Cadwell (alias Boardman) deceased, her heirs, 1-9 part. And this Court appoint Samuel Welles of Hartford, Erastus and Gideon Wolcott of Windsor to distribute the lands accordingly.

Page 87—17 November, 1755: Report of the distributors accepted.

Page 184.

Carrier, Thomas, Colchester. Invt. £659-15-11. Taken 28 March, 1740, by Michael Taintor, John Bigelow and Elnathan Rowlee.

Court Record, Page 64—11 April, 1740: Adms. to Thomas Carrier, son of the deceased. Recog., £500, with Isaac Carrier. Jeremiah Carrier, age 14 years, son of Thomas Carrier, chose his brother Thomas Carrier to be his guardian. Recog., £100. *Cert: Nathaniel Foot, J. P.*

Page 10 (Vol. XIV) 1st September, 1742: Thomas Carrier, Adms., exhibited an account of his Adms.: Paid in debts and charges, £78-08-01; credit received, £2-06-00. Account accepted.

Page 13.

Carter, Gideon, Hartford. Invt. £749-16-05. Taken 4 April, 1737, by Zachariah Seymour and Joseph Skinner, Jr.
Court Record, Page 5—5 April, 1737: Invt. exhibited.

Page 267.

Case, Moses, Hebron. Invt. £3285-03-01. Taken 21 September, 1741, by Nathaniel Phelps, Joseph Phelps and Joel White. Will dated 4 September, 1741.

I, Moses Case of Hebron, in the County of Hartford, do make and ordain this to be my last will and testament: I give to my wife Mary, after my debts are discharged, 1-3 part of my house moveable estate to be to her own dispose forever, whom, with my son Moses Case, I ordain to be my executors. I give to my wife the use and improvement of 1-3 part of my lands during life or while she remains my widow, as also one room in my dwelling house. I give to my two sons, namely, Moses and Josiah, all my houseing and lands in Hebron to be equally divided betwixt them, only my son Moses shall have 10 acres of land more than Josiah. In the division regards shall be had both to quantity and quality, sd. division to be made by indifferent men. Sd. division to be made when my sd. son Moses shall come of full age of 21 years. I give to my 4 daughters, namely, to Patience, Lois, Alice and Hannah, to each of them £100, to be paid to them when or as they arrive to the age of 18 years. And whereas, my daughter Patience has had already near £100, the remaining 2-3 of my house moveables I give to my three younger daughters, Lois, Alice and Hannah, equally to be divided. And as to my debts and charges aforesd., my will is that they be paid out of my cattle, horses, sheep, &c., and not out of my house moveables, having given them to my sd. wife and daughters. And the remaining part of my horses, cattle, sheep and tools for husbandry I give to my sd. sons Moses and Josiah, equally to be divided, and my joiner tools I give to my sd. son Moses. I give to Eliphalet Case, son to my sd. wife, £5, to be paid him out of my estate when my sd. son Josiah shall come of full age to 21 years, &c., whereas I am apprehensive. But if my wife yet bring forth a son and he survive, he shall have out of my estate £600; but if she bring forth a daughter that shall survive until she comes to the age of 18 years, sd. daughter shall be paid £100 with lawfull interest thereon from the day of her birth. I appoint my wife and my son Moses Case executors.
Witness: *Ebenezer Case,*   MOSES CASE, LS.
Jonathan Case, Nathaniel Phelps.

The inventory shows debts due to the estate from the following persons:

David Barbour,	Samuel Darbe,	Caleb Strong,
John Barley,	Thomas Dewey,	William Sumner,
Simon Baxter,	Jabez Dunham,	Joseph Swetland,
Benjamin Beach,	Matthew Ford,	Eleazer Tappany,
Samuel Bewell,	Ebenezer Fuller,	Benjamin Thompson,
John Bliss,	Samuel Gilbert, Jr.,	Jonathan Tillotson,
Oliver Bly,	Thomas Goldwaite,	Peter Urtwell,
Gershom Bulkeley,	Joseph Kellogg, Jr.,	Jonathan White,
Philip Bump,	Amos Owen,	Joseph White,
John Burchard,	Josiah Owen,	Aaron Wright,
Samuel Calkin, Jr.,	John Pengilly,	Jabez Wright,
Joseph Chamberlain,	Elnathan Rowley,	Samuel Wright,
Noah Clark,	Nathan Rowley,	Ephraim Youngs.
Samuel Curtiss,	Job Stiles,	

Court Record, Page 100—3 September, 1741: Will proven.

Page 91, 105.

Chapman, Lydia, East Haddam. Invt. £414-01-06. Taken 31 August, 1738, by Joshua Brainard, John Spencer and Bezaleel Brainard.

Know all men by these presents: That we, the subscribers, being the only surviving heirs of our sister Lydia Chapman, late of East Haddam decd., according to the statute of this Colony as it is explained in page 330 of our Law, do, with the approbation of his Honr. the Gouernour and Judges of the Court of Probate for the County of Hartford, agree that the land and moveable estate that did belong to our deceased sister aforesd. shall be divided equally according to the quality thereof into five parts, and that the children of our sister Elizabeth Chalker, late of Saybrook decd., shall hold, possess and enjoy 1-5 part to them, their heirs and assigns forever, and the rest to be held by us the sd. subscribers in equal proportion. And in confirmation of the written agreement we have hereunto sett our hands and seals this 7th day of November, Annoque Dom. 1738, and the 12th yeare of His Majestie's reign.

Signed and sealed in the   JABEZ CHAPMAN, LS.
presence of us: SAMUEL CHAPMAN, LS.   ANN SELDEN, LS.
Edward Schovill,   JOHN WARNER, LS.   MEHETABELL WARNER, LS.
Esther Talcott.

Court Record, Page 32—1st August, 1738: Adms. to Jabez Chapman. Recog., £200, with John Fisk.

Page 35—7 November, 1738: Account exhibited and allowed.

Page 36—7 November, 1738: An agreement by the heirs to divide the estate now exhibited and accepted.

Page 1-2.

Chapman, Simon, Jr., Windsor. Invt. £668-10-11. Taken by Jonathan Stiles and John Stoughton. Will dated 4 March, 1736-7.

I, Simon Chapman, Jr., of Windsor, husbandman, do make this my last will and testament: Imprimis. I give to Samuel Chapman, son of Samuel Chapman of Tolland, my beloved cosen, if he live until the age of 21 years, all my houseing and land in Ellington in Windsor, with this proviso, that within two years after he is 21 years of age that he pay in good lawful money of this Colony to my wife Silence Chapman £100; provided sd. Samuel Chapman do not live to the age of 21 years, then to the next male heir; or whosoever shall have my land and buildings shall pay sd. £100, and £50 more to my brother Samuel Chapman's son Simon Chapman. I give to my wife the 1-2 of my moveable estate, and 1-2 to my brother Samuel Chapman's daughters. I appoint my brother Samuel Chapman of Tolland and my wife Silence Chapman executors.

Witness: *John Stoughton,*   SIMON CHAPMAN, JR., LS.
Asahel Bissell, John MacMorran.

Court Record, Page 9—7 June, 1737: Inventory exhibited.

Page 83-4.

Chester, Stephen John. An agreement, made 27 June, 1738, by Martin Kellogg and Dorothy his wife, of Wethersfield, and by Joseph Lamb and Sarah his wife, of Southold, L. I., County of Suffolk, in the Province of New York, and Mercy Chester of Wethersfield, the only surviving heirs and co-heirs of Stephen John Chester deceased: First: That we, the aforesd. heirs to the estate of the sd. deceased Stephen John Chester, do for ourselves and heirs mutually agree that the aforesd. Martin Kellogg and Dorothy his wife shall have to their portion in and of the estate of the sd. decd. 100 acres of land, more or less, lying in Wethersfield in the tier of lotts commonly called the 50-acre lott, butted and bounded as followeth: east on a highway, west on the line dividing between Wethersfield and Farmington, north on land belonging to Capt. John Chester, south partly on land belonging to John Kelsey and partly on land belonging to Stephen Kelsey, to their heirs and assigns forever in full of their part or portion of sd. estate. We, the heirs, do mutually agree that the aforesd. Joseph Lamb and Sarah his wife shall have for their part and portion in and of the estate of the sd. decd. the southern half of 300 acres of land, more or less, lying in the Town of Glastonbury, butting and bounded as followeth: east on undivided land, west on Connecticut River, north on land belonging to Capt. Thomas Wells, south on land belonging to Samuel Hale; also a certain tract of land lying in Wethersfield, containing 4 acres more or less, bounded east on a highway, west on land belonging to Timothy Wright, north on land be-

longing to John Smith, south on land belonging to Ebenezer Belding,
to them and their heirs and assigns forever in full of their part or
portion of sd. estate. We, the heirs, do agree that Mercy Chester
aforesd. shall have for her part and portion of the estate of the sd.
decd. ye northern half of 300 acres of land, more or less, lying in the
Town of Glastonbury, bounded as followeth: east on undivided land,
west on Connecticut River, north on land belonging to Capt. Thomas
Wells, south on land belonging to Samuel Hale; as also a house and
barn standing on sd. land, to her, her heirs and assigns forever, in full
of her part and portion of sd. estate. And the above-named parties, for
themselves, their heirs and assigns forever, have given, granted and released unto each other by these presents the several claims or demands
that they have or might have in or to the estate aforesd., or any part
thereof, other than what in the above distribution or partition is to them
set out. In witness whereof the parties to these presents have hereunto
sett their hands and seals.

MARTIN KELLOGG, LS. | DOROTHY KELLOGG, LS.
JOSEPH LAMB, LS. | SARAH LAMB, LS.
MERCY CHESTER, LS.

Acknowledged in Court. *Test: Jos: Talcott, Junior, Clerk.*

See File.

Church, Joseph. We, the subscribers, have agreed upon the division
of the estate of our honoured brother Joseph Church, late of Hartford
decd., according as it is hereafter mentioned, and as to the moveables
we have each of us already received accordingly, and as to the housing
and lands to be divided as followeth: To John Church, all that right of
land called the western land, which lyeth in the township commonly
called Middle West. And to Caleb Church, in the homelott, 9 1-2 acres
of land; to Daniel Church, in the homelott, 3 1-2 acres; to Abigail
Church and Mary Church, in the homelott, 7 acres; and the Brickill
Swamp, 5 1-2 acres, bounding north by John Spencer, east on Moses
Dickinson, west on a highway, and south by land divided to Daniel
Church. And for the full and absolute confirmation of the above-mentioned division, according as it is therein entered to us, we have hereunto
subscribed our hands and seals this 8th of April, 1743.

Witness: *John Marsh,* JNO. CHURCH, LS. | ABIGAIL CHURCH, LS.
Zebulon Spencer. CALEB CHURCH, LS. | MARY X CHURCH, LS.
DANIEL CHURCH, LS.

*April the 20th, 1750: Before the Court of Probate in Hartford the
heirs to this agreement appeared and acknowledged the same to be their
free act and deed.*

Test: Joseph Talcott, Clerk.

Page 110.

Churchill, Mary, Widow, Wethersfield. Invt. £39-11-03. Taken 4 July, 1738, by Richard Boardman, Henry Kirkham and David Wright, Junr.

Court Record, Page 31—4 July, 1738: Adms. to Samuel Churchill. Recog., with Daniel Churchill.

Page 110-111.

Coe, John, Wethersfield. Invt. £121-05-05. Taken by Samuel Curtiss, Samuel Butler and Joseph Flower.

Court Record, Page 33—3 October, 1738: Inventory exhibited by Jonathan Carter, Adms.

Page 286.

Coleman, Ebenezer, Colchester. Invt. £131-19-08. Taken 28 April, 1741, by John Johnson and John Strong.

Court Record, Page 90—2 June, 1741: Adms. to Ruth Coleman, widow. Recog., £200, with her son Niles Coleman of Colchester.

Page 150.

Colt, Benjamin, Hartford. Invt. £322-04-06. Taken 30 June, 1739, by Richard Gilman and Caleb Pitkin. Will dated 16 March.

I, Benjamin Colt of Hartford, do make this my last will and testament: Imprimis. I give to Joanna, my well-beloved wife, and Lucy, my daughter, all my moveable estate excepting one cowe, which I give to my daughter Anne Hopkins. I give to my son John Colt 20 shillings in money. I give to my daughter Lucy all my right in the equivalent land in Windsor, by her freely to be possessed and injoyed. I make my wife Joanna Colt and William Williams, Jr., of Hartford, to be sole executors.

Witness: *John Morton,*   BENJAMIN X COLT, LS.
Richard Gilman, Samuel Williams.

Court Record, Page 52—7 August, 1739: Will exhibited 5 June last, now proven.

Page 99-100-101.

Colyer, Joseph, Hartford. Invt. taken by Edward Cadwell, Jos. Talcott, Jr., and Daniel Butler. Will dated 16 July, 1733.

I, Joseph Colyer of Hartford, being desirous that what worldly goods or estate God hath bestowed upon me may be disposed of before

I die, I do make the following disposition of them: I give to my wife Hannah the use of 1-3 part of my improveable land during life, and 1-3 part of my dwelling house in case she shall see cause to live in it; but if she doth not live in it, then I dispose of it otherwise; and 1-3 part of my moveables I give to her to dispose of as she shall think best. I give to my son Joseph Colyer my right of land at Coventry which I gave him a deed of gift of, which is his whole portion except 20 shillings. I give to my son Hezekiah Colyer half the lott I bought of Capt. Stoughton, bounded south on Capt. John Sheldon's land and east on Windsor Road, 4 acres, which I give him by deed of gift when he desires it, as he may build thereon. I give to my son Daniel my house and homelott, only my wife to have her part therein as above mentioned, with all my buildings and appurtenances thereunto belonging, and the other half of my land at Blue Hills, and at my Brick Hill Bridge lott the 1-2 thereof; also my orchard on the land known by the name of Douglass's lott, provided he, within two years after my decease, pays £20 to my son Abell; also I give Daniel 1-2 of the lott I bought of Capt. Stoughton. I give to my daughters Mary Foote and Sarah Olcott £30 apiece with what they have already had, and to my daughter Abigail Colyer I give £30 of money or goods at inventory price. And I do hereby make my son Daniel to be my sole executor.

Witness: *Isaac Butler,*   JOSEPH COLYER, LS.
Jonathan Olcott, John Colyer.

Court Record, Page 37—7 November, 1738: Will proven.

Invt. in Vol. XIV, Page 83-4.

Cooke, Moses, Hartford. Invt. £2179-00-08. Taken 16 November, 1738, by William Cadwell, Ozias Pitkin and Joseph Talcott, Jr.

Court Record, Page 41—15 February, 1738-9: Adms. granted to Deborah Cooke, widow, who recog. with her father Edward Cadwell. This Court appoint Mrs. Deborah Cooke to be guardian to her daughter Martha, 3 years and 8 months of age. Recog., £300.

Page 17 (Vol. XIV) 15 February, 1742-3: Invt. exhibited by Mrs. Deborah Cooke, relict, alias Deborah Bicknall, Adms. Also, the sd. Adms., with her husband James Bicknall, exhibited an account of their Adms.: Paid in debts and charges, £147-01-11. Which account is allowed. More, £5-10-12 paid Dr. Morrison.

Page 224-5-6.

Cornish, James, Simsbury. Invt. £866-14-06. Taken 25 April, 1740, by Joseph Pettibone and Samuel Pettibone, Jr. Will dated 8 February, 1739-40.

I, James Cornish of Simsbury, in the County of Hartford, do make this my last will and testament: I do give unto my wife Hannah, whom I constitute to be the sole executrix of this my will, the sole use of all my lands and goods and chattells during her life, and also 1-3 part of my personal estate to be her own and at her own dispose forever. Also, I give unto my son Gabriel my meadow lott with the adjoining land, to be to him and his heirs forever, upon condition that my sd. son Gabriel shall, before he enters into the possession thereof, give unto my son Jabez a well executed deed whereby he shall become seized of 1-2 of the division lott lying in the Half-Mile tier at the West River, which was laid out to me and which I have conveyed to sd. Gabriel by a deed of gift. And in case the sd. Gabriel doth not give unto my son Jabez a deed as aforesd. of 1-2 of sd. division lott, then the sd. division lott to be to my son Gabriel, and to be his whole portion of my estate. Also, I give unto my son Jabez my dwelling house and barn and homelott, and also all my land lying westward from my homelott, bounded west by the river, south and east by land of John Mills, and so to the northerly bounds of sd. lands (the last-mentioned piece contains about 14 acres), to be to him my sd. son Jabez and to his heirs forever. And also about 5 acres of land which I bought of Jonathan Humphrey, lying southward from my wife's land, on Weatogue Plain, on the east side of the river, to him and his heirs forever. And also my land on the hill which I bought of Thomas Humphrey, lying eastward from my house and lying near the foot of the mountain, adjoining to my wife's land. And also the land which I have bargained for, lying on the hill eastward from my house, part of the 20 acres of land which was formerly granted unto John Humphrey in lieu of 20 acres of land granted to sd. Humphrey on the hill north of Mill Swamp Brook, upon any deed or deeds of sd. land, or any part thereof, executed to me any time hereafter, I give the same to my son Jabez and to his heirs and assigns forever. I do give unto my son Jabez my meadow lott (before mentioned and damnified to my son Gabriel upon conditions before mentioned), provided my son Gabriel doth not fulfill the condition on which it is given to him, then to be and remain to my son Jabez and to his heirs forever. I give unto my daughter Jemima 1-2 of my lott of land lying in the Half-Mile tier of lotts at the West Mountain and south by Joseph Case's house (the whole lott contains about 124 acres more or less), to be to her and her heirs forever; and also £10, to be paid to her out of my personal estate, to be at her own dispose forever. I give to my daughter Mary the 1-2 of my division lott at the West Mountain, lying in the Half-Mile tier of lotts south from Joseph Case's house, 124 acres, and also the sum of £30, to be paid to her out of my personal estate. Further, my will is that whereas, my sons James and Joseph and my daughters Elizabeth, Phebe and Sarah, have already received their portion of my estate, I do give unto each of them in severallty what they have already received, to be to each of them their full portions of my estate. And further, my will is that my above-named children, Gabriel, Jabez, Jemima and Mary, shall not receive or enter into the possession of any parts of their portions above mentioned until after the death of my wife Hannah, unless my executrix shall think fitt to pay them or any of them their portions sooner.

Witness: *John Humphrey,*   JAMES CORNISH, LS.
Jacob Pettibone, Abigail X Butler.

Court Record, Page 37 (Vol. XIV) 20 January, 1743-4: Jabez Cornish, a minor, 17 years of age, son of Deacon James Cornish decd., before *John Humphry, Just. Peace.* on the 24th day of February, 1742-3, made choice of Thomas Marvin of Simsbury to be his guardian, which choice this Court allows. The said Marvin before this Court acknowledged himself bound to the Judge of this Court that he will faithfully discharge the trust, etc.

Page 304-5.

Cornwell, Capt. Joseph, Middletown. Invt. £804-03-02. Taken 26 March, 1741, by Nathaniel Gilbert, William Rockwell and Jonathan Allin. Will dated 22 October, 1740.

I, Joseph Cornwell of Middletown, in the County of Hartford, do make this my last will and testament: I give to Elizabeth, my wife, all and every part of the estate that did belong to her when I married her, and the equal half of all my household goods that have been added to my estate since our marriage. I also give to her one horse kind, which (of mine) she shall choose, and 1-3 of my stock of neat cattle and sheep, after two oxen, two 3-year-old heifers and six sheep are taken out of the whole, to be to her, her heirs and assigns forever. I also give to my wife, for and during the time she shall remain my widow, the liberty of part of my dwelling house, cellar, oven, barn, well and a garden plat, as I have reserved the same for her in my deed of gift to my youngest son Nathaniel Cornwell. And I do hereby oblige my three sons, Joseph, Daniel and Nathaniel, to find and provide suitable and convenient firewood and bread corne, and both winter and summer keeping sufficient for one horse and one cowe, or for 2 cows (she shall choose), during the time she remains my widow. I give to my eldest son, Joseph Cornwell, what I have already given him by deed of gift, and 1-4 part of my right in the land and buildings that did belong to my brother William Cornwell, and 1-3 part of all my husbandry tools and utensils, and 1-3 part of my horse kind (after my wife hath taken one). I give to my 2nd son, Daniel Cornwell, what I have already given him by deed of gift, and 1-4 part of my right in the land and buildings that did belong to my brother William Cornwell, and 1-3 part of all my husbandry tools and utensils, and one 3-year-old heifer (which of mine he shall choose), and 1-3 of my horse kind (after my wife hath taken one). I give to my youngest son, Nathaniel Cornwell, what I have already given him by deed of gift, and 1-2 of my right in the lands and buildings that did belong to my brother William Cornwell, and 1-3 part of all my husbandry tools and utensils, and the benefit of the payment that I have made to my brother John Cornwell and his son John for about 1-2 an acre of land, desireing them to pass a deed thereof to my son Nathaniel. I also give to my sd. son two oxen, 6 sheep (which he shall choose) and one 3-year-old heifer, and all the remainder of my family provisions after enough thereof is taken to support my wife and family that shall remain to dwell in my house one whole year. My meaning is, that all my swine, corne, cyder, &c., be accounted family provisions, only I reserve so much syder as to pay John Kirby for 6 black chairs which I have agreed with him for for my daughter Abigail Miller. I also give to my son Nathaniel all my money and credit by book, bonds or notes of hand, which is in consideration that I have given him my dwelling house in which I now dwell, which will in a short time want repairing, and that I do hereby oblige my sd. son to pay all my just debts and funeral charges and provide for my wife a decent mourning gown, scarf and veil, and for my other two sons to each of them a mourning weed, and for my two daughters to each a mourning scarf and veil. I give to my daughter Abigail Miller, besides what I have already given her, one chest of drawers and a round table which I have paid Waitstill John Plumb for, and the six black chairs above mentioned, and the equal half of all the household goods that were mine before my last marriage, and 1-4 part of all my household goods that have been added since my last marriage. I also give her 1-3 of all my stock of neat cattle and sheep after the above-mentioned 2 oxen, 2 heifers and 6 sheep are taken out. I give to my daughter Elizabeth Bacon, besides what I have already given her, the equal half of all the household goods that were mine before my last marriage, and 1-4 part of all my household goods that have been added since my last marriage, and also give her 1-3 of all my stock of neat cattle and sheep after the above-mentioned 2 oxen, 2 heifers and 6 sheep have been taken out. I do give to my three sons all my wearing apparrell. I appoint my youngest son Nathaniel Cornwell sole executor.

Witness: *Nathaniel Bacon,*   JOSEPH CORNWELL, LS.
William Ward 3rd, William Rockwell.

Court Record, Page 86—7 April, 1741: Will proven.

Page 77.

Cotton, Samuel, Sen., Middletown. Invt. £620-11-05. Taken 28 April, 1738, by Benjamin Adkins, Jonathan Allyn and William Rockwell. Will dated 16 November, 1737.

I, Samuel Cotton, Sen., of Middletown, in the County of Hartford, do make this my last will and testament: I give unto Experience, my wife, all my household goods of what name soever which she brought with her when we were married, and 1 cow, 1 heifer and my iron kettle, to be at her own dispose. I give to my son Samuel 1 equal third part of my right in the piece of land that is laid out in the third division to the heirs of my mother Mary Cotton deceased, and 4 acres of land called the Indian Point, which 4 acres shall lye next to the Boggy Meadow; and a large sermon book which was my father John Cotton's, entitled "Gospel Conversation." I give to my son Ebenezer 1-3 part of my right in the piece of land that is laid out in the third division to the heirs of my mother Mary Cotton deceased, and 3 acres more of land called Indian Point, to lye next to Samuel's 4 acres, and the equal half of all my carpenters' and joyners' tools after John hath taken the tools I have particularly mentioned hereafter, only I give to Ebenezer my 2-inch augur. I give to my son John my broad axe, vears, adice, inch and a half augur and inch augur, and 2 or 3 old narrow chisells, and a piece of a square, and the equal half of all the remainder of all my carpenter and joyner tools except my 2-inch augur. I give to my sons John and William my dwelling house and homelott and all the remainder of my land at Indian Point, and the other third part of my right in a piece of land that was laid out in the third division to the heirs of my mother Mary Cotton deceased, and all my stock and husbandry tools and utensils except the cow and heifer I have given to my wife. And my will is that my two sons John and William shall pay all my just debts and funeral charges. And further, I give to my two sons John and William all my boggy meadow, they paying to my two daughters, Mary and Elizabeth, to each £6-10 money, and to the two children of my daughter Prudence, to each of them 20 shillings. I further give to my daughter Mary my cubboard, and to my daughter Elizabeth my chest. And my will is that my sons John and William shall pay to my daughter Lydia 20 shillings money. I make my wife Experience and my brother-in-law Samuel Hall executors.

Witness: *John Elton,*   SAMUEL COTTON, LS.
John Chivers (Cheever?), William Rockwell.

Court Record, Page 28—2 May, 1738: Will proven.

Page 286.

Cotton, Samuel, Middletown. Invt. £162-13-03. Taken 18 May, 1741, by Nathaniel Gilbert, Benjamin Cornell and Jonathan Allyn.

Court Record, Page 65 (Vol. XV) 12 May, 1748: Elihu Cotton, a minor, age 17 years, son of Samuel Cotton, Jr., chose Capt. Jonathan Allin of Middletown to be his guardian. Recog., £500.

Page 57-8.

Cowles, Isaac, Jr., Farmington (Southington Parish). Invt. £976-03-06. Taken 15 November, 1737, by Isaac Lewis and Thomas Hart. Will dated 24 September, 1737.

I, Isaac Cowles of Southington, in Farmington, in the County of Hartford, do make this my last will and testament: I give unto my wife Jerusha Cowles 1-3 part of all my estate excepting what came by my first wife. I give to my son Isaac Cowles, and to his heirs and assigns forever, all my estate excepting what came by my first wife and £40 of my estate, and also excepting what is not already given for the use of my wife, unless that I have a son by my present wife, and if I have a son by her, I give and bequeath unto him, and to his heirs and assigns forever, 1-2 of what I gave to my son Isaac excepting £40; but if I have a daughter by my present wife, I give unto her out of what I gave to my son Isaac as much as I give to my present daughter Mary Cowles, hereafter named, excepting £30. I give unto my daughter Mary Cowles all the estate that came by my first wife and £40 of my estate. And I, Isaac Cowles, do constitute and appoint my wife Jerusha Cowles to be my executrix, and my brother-in-law Samuel Root executor.

Witness: *Jeremiah Curtiss,*   ISAAC X COWLES, LS.
Daniel Hooker, Daniel Andrus.

Court Record, Page 17—6 December, 1737: Will proven.

Page 18—6 December, 1737: Samuel Root, of the Parish of Southington, is appointed guardian to Isaac Cowles, son of Isaac Cowles, Jr. Recog., £100. And this Court do appoint Capt. Isaac Cowles of Farmington to be guardian to Mary Cowles, age 6 years, daughter of sd. decd. Recog., £100.

Page 26—17 March, 1737-8: Ruth Cowles, age 6 months, a posthumous child of Isaac Cowles, this Court do appoint Jerusha Cowles, widow, to be guardian. Recog., £100.

Page 70 (Vol. XVI) 4 August, 1752: Isaac Cowles, a minor, now 16 years of age, chose Samuel Root to be his guardian. Recog., £500.

Page 108—2 October, 1753: Ruth Cowles, a minor, 16 years of age, daughter of Isaac Cowles, chose Eldad Lewis to be her guardian. Recog., £300.

Page 157-8.

Curtiss, Richard, Hebron. Invt. £1825-17-10. Taken 26 June, 1739, by Jordon Post and Obadiah Dunham. Will dated 8 May, 1739.

I, Richard Curtiss of Hebron, in the County of Hartford, do make this my last will and testament: Imprimis. I give to Abigail, my wife, 1-3 part of my moveable estate forever, whom likewise I make, with my son Richard, the sole executors. I give to my son Richard all my other lands whereon I now dwell, with all the appurtenances, he paying to his brethren such legacies as I do herein give and bequeath, viz.: I will that my sd. son Richard shall pay or cause to be paid the sum of £100 money or chattells to each of my three youngest sons, viz., Jonathan, John and Henry, as they or each of them come to the age of 21 years, that is to say, each of their legacies to be £100 as aforementioned. I give to my son David one certain tract of meadow land lying near a meadow commonly called Major's Meadow, with all the appurtenances, and also my youngest horse colt, which colt shall be kept by Richard his brother if my sd. son David sees cause to abide in subjection unto his brother Richard until the age of 21 years, which is my great desire. I give to my daughter Abigail my weaving loom, together with 1-2 of my weaving gears or tackling, also one set of bed curtains which is now almost completed or made by preparing for the same. I give to my daughter

Mehetabell my wool combs, together with all the things thereunto belonging, for the combing of wool, and a set of curtains, in the same manner as to Abigail. I give to my daughter Deborah the 1-2 of my weaving gear or tackling, that is, the other half thereof, and a set of curtains, in the same manner as to Abigail. I give to my daughter Dorothy, the wife of Azariah Brown, 4 sheep over and above of what I have already given them heretofore, which amounted to £38-16-00. And all the rest of my moveable estate I give, devise and dispose to and amongst all my daughters, viz., Abigail, Mehetabell, Deborah, Dorothy, Hannah and Elizabeth, equally to be divided as they shall come to lawfull age or marry, these particulars only excepted: my cart, sled, one plow, two draft chains and all my axes and hoes, one yoke and horse harrow, which shall be to and for the use of my sd. executrix and executor. And also my sd. son Richard to have my smallest gunn, and my son David to have my other gunn and sword. That is to say, that which I have already give to my daughter Dorothy shall be included in the equal division to and with her sisters. I do here in my last will and testament give free liberty unto my sd. wife and each of my sd. daughters to abide and remain in my now dwelling house until marriage, viz., my wife to have free use and liberty therein during her widowhood; and daughters to use and have liberty in my westerly room until they marry, and not otherwise.

Witness: *John Birchard,*   RICHARD CURTISS, LS.
Jordon Post, Jr., Edmund Wells.

Court Record, Page 53—7 August, 1739: Will proven.

Page 186-7.

Curtiss, Samuel, Hebron. Invt. £127-15-02, personal estate. Taken 4 April, 1740, by Hez: Gaylord, Jonathan White and Joseph Phelps. Will dated 24 May, 1733.

I, Samuel Curtiss of Hebron, do make and ordain this my last will and testament: I give to Caleb, my eldest son, 1-3 part of all my tools over and above of what I have heretofore given him in land, which may fully appear by a deed of gift, and also 1-3 part of the fruit of my orchard for 10 years after my death, whome I likewise make my sole executor. I give to Samuel and Hosea, my sons, all my other lands and buildings, equally to be divided between them, Samuel to have the south part of my land, and Hosea to have the north. I give to Sarah, my daughter, my loom and all my weaving tackling. And all the rest of my moveable estate I will and give to all my daughters, viz., Mary, Elizabeth, Abigail, Sarah and Dinah, equally to be divided amongst them all. And I will and hereby order that Joel my son shall have £20 money for his legacy (to be paid to him by my son Caleb) within one year after he comes to lawfull age. And I will and hereby order that Naniard, my son, shall have £20 money for his legacy (to be paid to him by my sons

Samuel and Hosea equally) within one year after he comes to lawfull age. And it is my desire and will that my brother Richard Curtiss shall, by this my last will and testament, oversee and have special charge to oversee that every one of my children have their legacy well distributed, and that every one of my children yt lives to lawfull age and receives their legacy, it shall be to them and their heirs and their assigns forever. And further, it is my will that Caleb, my son and executor, shall have power and authority, and I do by this my will impower and give him, my sd. son and executor, authority (by and with the advice of Richard, overseer) to put out Naniard my sd. son as an apprentice, so that he may learn some good trade, until he be 21 years of age.

Witness: *Joseph Porter,*   SAMUEL CURTISS, LS.
John Sprage, Samuel Heton (Eaton?), Jr.

Court Record, Page 65—6 May, 1740: Naniard Curtiss, age 15 years, son of Samuel Curtiss, chose his brother Caleb Curtiss to be his guardian. Recog., £50.

Page 66—6 May, 1740: Will proven. Invt. of personal estate exhibited and accepted.

Page 290.

Curtiss, Capt. Thomas, Wethersfield. Invt. £1231-07-06. Taken 23 March, 1734, by John Stilman, Josiah Talcott and Samuel Woolcott. Will dated 3 August, 1734.

I, Thomas Curtiss of Wethersfield, marriner, do make this my last will and testament: First: I give to my eldest son Ambrose my dwelling house and barn and so much of my land as shall make him a double share of the rest of my children. I give to my son James and to my son Waitstill the rest of my land, all my real estate to my three sons, to them and their heirs and assigns forever, with this intention and on this condition, that they and each of them pay their equal parts of £80 to my daughter Experience and £80 to my daughter Rachell as soon as they arrive at lawfull age. I give and devise to my daughter Experience the half of my moveable estate, which I esteem at £40, and £80 to be paid to her by her three brothers when she comes at the age of 18 years. I give to my daughter Rachel the other half of my moveable estate and £80 money, to be paid her by her three brothers, Ambrose, James and Waitstill, when she comes to be 18 years of age. I appoint Mr. Ebenezer Deming, Sen., with my eldest son, executors.

Witness: *Benjamin Deming,*   THOMAS CURTISS, LS.
Robert Mackee, Elizabeth Mackee.

Whereas, our honoured father, Capt. Thomas Curtiss, aforesd., made and declared the foregoing writing to be his last will and testament, and two of the witnesses to the foregoing will being removed out of the County of Hartford and not likely to be come at or their evidencing to sd. will, we, the subscribers, being the only heirs to the sd. estate, do

hereby actually agree for ourselves and heirs forever that the foresd. will of the sd. Capt. Thomas Curtiss shall be a final settlement of his estate, and that we and every of us do hereby acknowledge that we accept of what is given us in sd. writing or will as our whole share of the estate of our honoured father as aforesd., and do hereby discharge each other of any further demand of sd. estate, and that our brother James Curtiss take Adms. on sd. estate of our father aforesd., and when he hath finished his Adms. that then the remainder of sd. estate shall be distributed to each of us respectively according as is expressed or set forth in the aforesd. writing or will. Also, we agree that Mr. Ebenezer Deming, who was appointed an executor to the aforesd. will, be Adms. with our brother as aforesd. And in confirmation that the foregoing is our mutuall agreement, we have hereunto sett our hands and seals in Hartford this 17th day of April, 1741.   EXPERIENCE CURTISS, LS.
          JAMES CURTISS, LS.   AMBROSE X CURTISS, LS.
          JOHN STILMAN, LS., GUARDIAN TO WAITSTILL CURTISS, LS.
          JOSIAH TALCOTT, LS., GUARDIAN TO RACHELL CURTISS, LS.

Court Record, Page 87—7 April, 1741: A writing called the last will and testament of Capt. Thomas Curtiss, agreed upon by the severall heirs to the estate, was now exhibited in Court, and the severall heirs acknowledged their hands and seals to sd. agreement was their voluntary act and deed. Also, this Court grant Adms. on sd. estate unto James Curtiss, son of the sd. deceased, and Ebenezer Deming of sd. Wethersfield, who gave bonds accordingly. Rachel Curtiss, age 17 years, chose Josiah Talcott to be her guardian. Recog., £300. Waitstill Curtiss, age 17 years, chose John Stilman of Wethersfield to be his guardian. Recog., £300.

Page 107—26 January, 1741-2: James Curtiss, Adms., exhibited an account of his Adms., he being appointed Adms. with the will annexed, by which account it appears he has paid in debts and charges £29-16-00, and received £11-10-03, which account is accepted and ordered on file. James Curtiss, Adms., now moves this Court for distribution: Whereupon this Court appoint John Stilman, Josiah Talcott and Samuel Wolcott distributors.

Page 2 (Vol. XIV) 6 April, 1742: Report of the distributors.

Page 143 (Vol. XIV).

Curtiss, William, Jun., Wethersfield. Invt. £239-17-08. Taken 13 April, 1744, by Jonathan Belding and John Warner. Personal estate apprised in old tenor.

Court Record, Page 27—10 April, 1738: Adms. on the estate of William Curtiss, Jun., late of Wethersfield decd., to William Curtiss, father of the decd., who gave bond with James Michell of Wethersfield in £400.

Page 41 (Vol. XIV) 17th March, 1743-4: This Court grants Adms. on the estate of William Curtiss, late of Wethersfield decd., unto John Crane of Wethersfield and Lydia Crane, his wife. Recog., £500, with Thomas Harris of Wethersfield.

Page 45—3 July, 1744: Inventory exhibited, approved, and ordered recorded and kept on file. (No further record found of this estate.)

This record may be considered as two estates, that of father and son, the father having been administrator upon the son's estate and dying before having made any report of his accounts to the Court, and the recorded inventory being accepted as the estate of the father. Supposing this Lydia Crane to have been the wife or sister of William Curtiss, Jun., and only heir to this property, the case would appear as settled out of Court.

Page 273, 331.

Day, John, Hartford. Invt. £62-18-02 in Hartford, £18-11-02 in Killingworth. Taken 19 May, 1741, by William Pratt and Jos: Talcott, Jr., in Hartford. Taken 17 July, 1742, by John Stephens and Daniel Redfield in Killingworth.

Court Record, Page 83—25 February, 1740-1: Adms. to Ensign James Church. Recog., £200, with Maynard Day.

Page 89—20 May, 1741: Exhibit of account.

Page 97—15 August, 1741: The Adms. may sell land, per act of the General Assembly, May, 1741.

Page 109—16 February, 1741-2: The Adms. reports the estate insolvent, and this Court appoint John Edwards and Nathaniel Hooker commissioners.

Page 55 (Vol. XIV) 4 February, 1744-5: James Church, Adms., exhibits an account of his Adms., whereby it appears he has paid in debts and charges £12-17-00, which account is allowed. Also exhibited a report of the commissioners, which report is likewise approved. And this Court now order the Clerk of this Court to make an average on sd. estate so that the creditors may have their just proportion thereof.

Page 179.

Deming, Noadiah, Wethersfield. Invt. £681-12-00. Taken 23 August, 1739, by Joseph Curtiss, Nathaniel Wright and Joseph Goodrich.

Court Record, Page 54—4 September, 1739: Adms. granted to Ruth Deming, widow. Recog., £500, with Nathaniel Wright.

Page 114 (Vol. XV) 2 January, 1749-50: An account of Adms. was now exhibited in Court by Ruth Deming, Adms. Accepted. This Court do order the estate to be dist. as follows:

£ s d
To the widow Ruth Deming in moveables, 50-04-06
To Solomon Deming, eldest son, 183-09-06
To Hezekiah, Dudley, Zachariah and Dorothy Deming, to each, 91-14-06

And appoint Lt. Joseph Goodrich, Joseph Curtice and Hezekiah Butler distributors.

Page 137—7 August, 1750: Zachariah Deming, 15 years of age, son of Noadiah Deming, chose his uncle Gideon Deming to be his guardian. Recog., £500.

Denslow, George, Windsor. Court Record, Page 24—7 March, 1737-8: Adms. granted on sd. estate unto William Alderman of Simsbury. Recog., £30, with Samuel Allyn of Windsor.

Page 296.

Dix, Leonard, Wethersfield. Invt. £838-11-05. Taken 6 October, 1741, by Thomas Hurlbutt, Timothy Wright and Timothy Baxter.

Court Record, Page 101—30 November, 1741: Adms. granted to Elisha Griswold of Wethersfield, who gave bond with Elisha Boardman of Wethersfield of £500.

Page 108—2 February, 1741-2: Elisha Griswold, Adms., exhibited an account of his Adms. Accepted by the Court and ordered to be recorded and kept on file.

Page 326 (Probate Side): An agreement, made this 2nd day of February, 1741-2, for the distribution of the estate of Leonard Dix decd., concluded and consented unto and by the heirs and guardians to the minors and their heirs to sd. estate, is that what particulars follow to each name of such heirs hereafter respectively annexed shall be such heir's part or portion of sd. estate:

£ s d
To Elisha Griswold and Abigail his wife, 242-12-03
To Elisha Boardman and his wife, 226-10-08
To Rebeckah Dix, 139-00-09
To Jacob and to Charles Dix equally together, 278-08-00

The foregoing concluded and consented the day of the date above-written. Signed, sealed and acknowledged before the Court of Probate.

ELISHA GRISWOLD, LS.	REBECKAH DIX, LS.
ABIGAIL GRISWOLD, LS.	ELISHA GRISWOLD, GUARDIAN
ELISHA BOARDMAN, LS.	TO CHARLES DIX, LS.
HANNAH BOARDMAN, LS.	ELISHA BOARDMAN, GUARDIAN
	TO JACOB DIX, LS.

Page 109: An agreement for the settlement of the estate of Leonard Dix, late of Wethersfield decd., and of his son Leonard Dix of said Wethersfield, was now exhibited in Court by the heirs to said estates under their hands and seals, who acknowledged said agreement to be their voluntary act, etc.

Page 89.

Dodd, John, Hartford. Invt. £73-12-10. Taken 12 April, 1738, by Jonathan Butler and John Skinner, Jr.
Court Record, Page 27—10 April, 1738: Adms. to Edward Dodd. Recog., £300, with John Spencer.

Page 241.

Doud, David, Middletown. Invt. £1234-19-04. Taken 20 November, 1740, by Nathaniel Gilbert, William Rockwell and Joseph Clark. Will dated 19 July, 1740.

I, David Doud of Middletown, in the County of Hartford, do make this my last will and testament: My will is that my estate be settled according to the antient custom of this Colony relateing to intestate estates, and appoint my wife Mary and my eldest son Cornwell Doud executors.

Witness: *Joseph Clark,*   DAVID DOUD, LS.
Miriam Clark, William Rockwell.

Court Record, Page 80—6 January, 1740-1: Will proven.
Page 24 (Vol. XIV) 7 June, 1743: Mary Doud and Cornwell Doud, executors to the last will and testament of David Doud, late of Middletown, presented an account of £121-06-02. Allowed and ordered on file. And they move this Court that the estate be distributed according to the will, whereupon this Court appoint Lt. Nathaniel Gilbert, William Rockwell and Jonathan Allyn, of Windsor, distributors. This Court appoint Cornwell Doud of Middletown to be guardian to Giles Doud, age 8 years, and Ebenezer Doud, age 4 years, children of David Doud. Recog., £200.
Page 25—7 June, 1743: This Court appoint Mary Doud, widow, to be guardian to Desiah Doud, Hannah and Jane Doud, minor children of David Doud. Recog., £200. And Richard Doud, age 19 years, Benjamin 17, and Mary 15, chose their uncle Joseph Clarke of Middletown to be their guardian. Recog., £500.
Dist. File: 7 June, 1743: To Mrs. Mary Doud, widow; to Cornwell, to David, to Richard, to Benjamin, to Giles, to Ebenezer, to Mary, to Desiah, to Hannah, and to Jane Doud. By Nathaniel Gilbert and William Rockwell.
Page 29—6 September, 1743: Report of the distributors.

Inventory on File.

Eaton, Daniel, Windsor. Inventory taken 27 January, 1738-9, by John Burroughs, Daniel Elsworth and Isaac Davis. Abigail Eaton, executrix, exhibited the inventory in Court. Accepted.

Page 111.

Eaton, William, Tolland. Invt. £491-05-06. Taken 15 February, 1737-8, by John Lathrop and Zebulon West.

Court Record, Page 28—13 April, 1738: Adms. to Rachel Eaton, widow. Recog., £300, with John Polk of Tolland.

Page 103 (Vol. XVII) 6 April, 1756: An account of Adms. was now exhibited in Court by Nathan and Rachel Wheeler, Adms., which account is accepted by the Court.

Page 247-8-9.

Emmons, Peter, Tolland. Invt. £833-10-06. Taken by Edy Hatch and Ichabod Lathrop. Will dated 30 October, 1740.

I, Peter Emmons of Tolland, in the County of Hartford, do make this my last will and testament: After my just debts and funeral charges are paid, what remains of my real and personal estate I do give and bequeath to my grandson Daniel Brown, who lives with me, to him and his heirs forever, upon the following conditions: 1st. That he live to the age of 21 years. 2nd. That he pay these following legacies to my grandchildren hereafter named successively as they arrive at the age of 21 years; and although some of the legatees are older than the sd. Daniel, and, if they live, will arrive to 21 years before the sd. Daniel, yet my will is that neither of sd. legacies be payable until the sd. Daniel arrive to the age of 22 years; then the sd. Daniel to pay the following legacies one year after another to my grandchildren as they come of age: to pay Cornelius Brown, his brother, £40; next year, to his sister Mehetabell Brown, £40; nextly, to Ebenezer Brown, his brother, £40; nextly, his sister Elizabeth Brown £50; nextly, to his brother Emmons Brown £50; all to be paid in bills of credit of the old or present tenor and made equal unto silver at eight and twenty shillings per ounce. Should sd. Daniel die before the age of one and twenty years, or without issue, the estate to vest in Emmons Brown, he paying the legacies aforesd. In case of the death of both Daniel and Emmons, then the estate in the hands of the executors to be improved for the heirs as they shall think proper. I appoint Capt. Samuel Chapman and Lt. Ebenezer Nie executors.

Witness: *Stephen Steele,*   PETER X EMMONS, LS.
Shubael Sterns, Ichabod Hinckley.

Court Record, Page 79—6 January, 1740-1: Will proven.

Page 55-6.

Ensign, Thomas, Hartford. Invt. £916-06-01. Taken 20 January, 1737-8, by Thomas Richards and Benjamin Catling. Will dated 9 January, 1737-8.

I, Thomas Ensign of Hartford, do make this my last will and testament: I give and bequeath to my loving wife Hannah Ensign the 1-2 of the houseing and homestead whereon I now dwell, and also 20 acres of meadowland for her improvement during her natural life, and also the free use of all my moveables within doors, and the provisions that shall be laid in and left at my decease, and half my stock of creatures, for her comfortable support during life. I give to my son Thomas Ensign 1-4 part of my right in the western land, which in the whole is 530 acres, and lyeth undivided in the northeast township, to be for him and his heirs forever. And further, I give him my stake and round knife. I give to my son John Ensign 1-4 of my western land before described. I give to my son Daniel Ensign the free use of the dwelling house and land at the west division, bounded east on John Skinner, Jr.'s land and west on a highway, north on land of Thomas Sanford and south on land of Thomas Cadwell; and also 1-4 of my western land before described. And further, my will is that after my sd. son Daniel Ensign's decease, sd. land at the west division and western land shall be equally divided to his surviving sons. I give to my son Moses Ensign 1-4 part of my western land before described, and also all my shop tools not before disposed of. I give to my daughter Hannah Ensign, alias Benton, the free use and improvement of all such household goods within doors (excepting books), viz., bedds, bedding, furniture, linen, woolen, tables, cupboards, chaires, desks, boxes, pewter, brass, iron or other household goods whatsoever that shall be left after the decease of myself and my wife. And also my will is that my sd. daughter Hannah shall have free liberty to dispose of sd. goods to her children after her decease as she will. And further, I give to my sd. daughter Hannah Benton 40 shillings money. I give all my goods to be equally divided amongst all my children. I appoint my two sons, Thomas Ensign and Moses Ensign, executors.

Witness: *Samuel Shepherd,*   THOMAS ENSIGN, LS.
William Andrews, Moses Nash.

Court Record, Page 23—28 February, 1737-8: Will proven.

Invt. in Vol. XIV, Page 16-21.

Farnsworth, Joseph, Hartford. Invt. £256-16-02. Taken 7 January, 1741-2, by John Edwards and James Bicknell.

Part of the invt., £230-02-04, is real estate belonging to sd. estate, which lyes in the Township of Stoughton, in the County of Suffolk,

260 PROBATE RECORDS. VOL. XIII,

within His Magestie's Province of the Massachusetts Bay in New England. Taken 7 January, 1742, by James Blake and Thomas Wiswell. Suffolk, S. S.: Dorchester, 17 January, 1742: The above written James Blake and Thomas Wiswell, sufficient freeholders in the Town of Dorchester, within the County of Suffolk, personally appearing made oath that the above apprisement is just and true according to their best skill and judgement. Before me, *Benjamin Bird, J. P.*

Farmington, 22 April, 1743: We, the subscribers hereof, being desired to apprise some part of the real estate belonging unto Joseph Farnsworth, do apprise as followeth: To 1 piece or parcel of land lying and being within the bounds of Farmington, in the 6th and last division of land, lying west from the reserved land in the abovesd. town, which is part of the 2nd lott in number drawn upon the original right of John Warner, Sen., decd., and as it appears to us upon record the number of acres 41 3-4, apprised at £52-10-06 by us: *Isaac Cowles and Giles Hooker.*

Court Record, Page 103—23 December, 1741: Christian Farnsworth, 13 years of age, daughter of Joseph Farnsworth decd., Mr. Thomas Wells of Hartford to be her guardian. Recog., £100. Abigail Farnsworth, one of the daughters, and Elizabeth Farnsworth, age 14 years, chose Deacon John Edwards of Hartford to be their guardian; also to be guardian to James Farnsworth, age 7 years. Recog., £100. This Court do appoint Timothy Biggelow of Hartford guardian to Samuel Farnsworth, age 9 years. Recog., £100. All children of Joseph Farnsworth deceased.

Page 109—10 February, 1741-2: Adms. on the estate of Joseph Farnsworth to Thomas Wells of Hartford, who gave bond with John Edwards of Hartford. Also, the administrator, with Joseph Farnsworth of Wethersfield and Mary Nichols of Hartford, exhibited an inventory. Accepted, ordered recorded and filed. The administrator informs this Court that he suspects said estate is insolvent: Whereupon this Court appoint Messrs. James Bicknell and Joseph Talcott commissioners to adjust the claims of the several creditors.

Page 17 (Vol. XIV) 15 February, 1742-3: A report of the commissioners on sd. estate was now exhibited in this Court under the hands of James Bicknall and Joseph Talcott, commissioners appointed by this Court, which report is accepted and ordered to be kept on file.

Page 33—6 December, 1743: Whereas, the General Assembly holden at Hartford on the 2nd Thursday in May, 1743, impowered Thomas Welles, Adms. on the estate of Joseph Farnsworth, to sell the land of the sd. deceased, that so the creditors may have their just proportions on sd. estate as the law directs, takeing the advice of the Court of Probates in the District of Hartford aforesd.: Whereupon this Court directs the sd. Adms. to set up advertisement in the towns of Hartford and Farmingtown signifying that there is to be sold at publick vandue, at the beat of the drum, one parcell of land within the bounds of Farmingtown, in the 6th and last division of land, lying west from the reserved lands in Farmingtown, which is part of the 2nd lott in number drawn upon the original right of John Warner decd., and appears by record to be 41 3-4 acres, to be sold to the highest bidder at such a day and time of day by sd. Adms.

Page 35 (Vol. XV) 11 May, 1747: Samuel Farnsworth, age 14 years, son of Joseph Farnsworth, chose his uncle William Nichols of Hartford to be his guardian. And this Court appoint the sd. William Nichols guardian to Elizabeth Farnsworth and James Farnsworth, also children of sd. decd., their former guardian John Edwards desiring to be dismissed of his guardianship. And the sd. William Nichols recog. in £500.

Page 16.

Filley, John, Windsor. Invt. £248-06-02. Taken 6 January, 1736-7, by Roger Newbery, John Cook, Jr., and Timothy Loomis, and was presented to the Court by the widow and John the son.

Court Record, Page 3—8 March, 1737: This Court grant Adms. on the estate of John Filley, late of Windsor deceased, unto Mary Filley, widow, who gave bond with Benedict Alverd of Windsor. Also exhibited an inventory, which was ordered recorded.

Page 120 (Vol. XV) 6 March, 1749-50: This Court now grant Adms. unto David Filley of Windsor, who gave bond with Caleb Phelps.

Page 123—3 April, 1750: An account of Adms. was now exhibited by David Filley, Adms. Account accepted, and this Court order that the real estate be dist., viz., to John Filley, grandson of the deceased, a double portion, and to Joseph Filley, Amos Filley, David Filley and Daniel Filley, sons of the deceased, to each of them their single portions of sd. estate. And appoint Henry Allyn, Esq., Capt. Peletiah Mills and Richard Cook, of Windsor, distributors.

Filley, Mary. Court Record, Page 131 (Vol. XV) 5 June, 1750: This Court grant Adms. on the estate of widow Mary Filley, late of Windsor decd., unto David Filley, son of the deceased, who gave bond with Capt. Peletiah Mills in £500.

Page 14 (Vol. XVI) 5 February, 1750-1: David Filley, Adms. having finished his account of Adms., now moves for a dist. of moveable estate. Whereupon this Court appoints Richard Cook, Return Strong and Samuel Stoughton to dist. the estate: To the heirs of John Filley, which was the eldest son, now deceased, £7-06-02, it being their double share of sd. estate; and to Joseph, Amos, David and Daniel Filley, to each of them £3-13-01, which is their single share of sd. estate; and make return of their doings to this Court.

Page 16—6 March, 1750-1: Report of the distributors accepted.

Page 51.

Filley, John, Windsor. Invt. £249-12-00. Taken 16 August, 1737, by John Wilson, John Cook and Timothy Loomis.

Court Record, Page 13—5 July, 1737: This Court grant Adms. on the estate of John Filley, late of Windsor deceased, unto Rebekah Filley, widow relict of the said deceased, who gave bond with Nathaniel Drake of Windsor.

Page 15—6 September, 1737: Rebekah Filley, Adms., exhibited an inventory. Accepted and ordered recorded.

Page 82—3 February, 1740-1: An account of Adms. was now exhibited in Court by Nathaniel Drake, who was bondsman for Rebeckah Filley, she being deceased. This Court appoint Nathaniel Drake to be guardian to John Filley, a minor son of the deceased. Recog., £300.

Page 244.

Filley, Jonathan, Windsor. Inventory taken 4 June, 1740, by Nathaniel Drake, John Cook 2nd and Timothy Loomis. Will dated 5 December, 1739.

I, Jonathan Filley of Windsor, do make this my last will and testament: I give to my wife the use of 1-3 part of all my lands, and also the use and benefit of the north end of my dwelling house, and the north end of the house in which my son Jonathan lives, and the north half of the house in which my son Nathaniel lives, during the term of her natural life. Also, I give to her and her heirs forever, one cow and £30 at inventory price. I give to my son Jonathan the house in which he lives and the land thereunto adjoining; also 1-2 of the house in which my son Nathaniel lives, and 1-2 of the land that adjoins thereto; also 4 acres on the west side of my lower lott in the Great Meadow; and 4 acres of land in the north side of my 10-acre lott near Bowfield, bounding north and west on my brother Josiah Filley's land; and 1-2 of my town common division, and 1-2 of all my common and undivided land in the Town of Windsor, and 1-2 of the common and undivided land in the Township of Colebrook, to him and his heirs forever. Also, I give to my son Jonathan the looms that he hath at the house where he lives, and 1-2 of my weaver's tackling, excepting my blanket slay. I give to my son Nathaniel my house in which I live and all my lands thereto adjoining, and 1-2 of the house in which he lives, and 1-2 the land adjoining thereto, and my lott in the first meadow and 2nd meadow, and my lott in the Great Meadow, and that part of my lott in the Great Meadow not bequeathed to my son Jonathan, and the remainder of my 10-acre lott not given to my son Jonathan, and all my land at Newell Swamp, and 1-2 of my town commons division, and 1-2 of my common and undivided land in the Town of Windsor, and 1-2 of my common and undivided land in the Township of Colebrook, to him and his heirs forever. Also, I give to my son Nathaniel my gunn and my blanket slay, and 1-2 of all the remainder of my weaver's tackling, and all my loom tackling. I give to my daughter Deborah Palmer £70 out of my moveable estate. I give to my daughter Anne Gillett the sum of £70 out of my moveable estate. All the remainder of my estate, both real and personal, after my debts and legacies are paid, I give to my two sons, Jonathan Filley and Nathaniel Filley, and appoint them to be my executors.

Witness: *Roger Newbery,*   JONATHAN FILLEY, LS.
John Roberts, John Hoskins.

Court Record, Page 68—10 June, 1740: Will proven.

Page 249.

Filley, Rebeckah, Widow. Invt. £21-17-07. Taken 23 January, 1740-1, by John Cook, John Brace and Henry Allyn.

Court Record, Page 82—3 February, 1740-1: This Court grant letters of Adms. unto Nathaniel Drake, who recog. in £50 with Timothy Mather.

Page 101.

Fiske, Rev. Phineas, Haddam. Died 14 October, 1738. Invt. £2736-09-09. Taken 13 November, 1738, by John Fisk and Gideon Brainard. Books valued at £52-09-03. Taken by William Russell and David Eells. Will dated 18 September, 1738.

I, Phineas Fiske of Haddam, in the County of Hartford, do make this my last will and testament: Imprimis. I give to my wife Lydia Fiske 1-3 part of all my personal estate of all sorts (exclusive of my negro woman and her child), which third part of my personal estate and the sd. negro woman and her child I give to my sd. wife to be her own forever; also I give to my sd. wife the use and improvement of 1-3 part of all my real estate and buildings and lands during her natural life. I give to my only son Samuel Fiske, his heirs and assigns forever, my dwelling house with the lott it stands upon, and my lott before my door, with the barn and orchard upon it, be the sd. pieces of land more or 4 acres, and all my land in the Town Meadow (both what I had of Mr. Noyes and what I had of Sarah Smith), and all my land upon Long Hill, and all my land on or neare Parsonage Brook, and all my right and title in and to the undivided land, and my library (except my sermon books), and my best horse and two yoke of oxen, with all my tackling proper for a team, and all my husbandry tools of all sorts, and one piece of land in the upper meadow which I bought of Benjamin Bailey, Jr. I give to my 4 daughters, viz., Lydia Bartlett, Mary Brainard, Abigail Brainard and Elizabeth Fiske, and their heirs and assigns forever, all my land (which I have not in this will given to my son Samuel) to be equally divided amongst them, excepting a lott in the third division in the Neck, on the east side of the Great River, in Haddam, drawn on my right but not laid out, which lott I give to the sd. Mary Brainard besides 1-4 part of the other land. I give to my sd. 4 daughters all my personal estate which I have not otherwise disposed of in this will, equally to be divided among them all, excepting Elizabeth, to whome I give the sum of £150 more than her sisters, she having had nothing yet. I ordain my loving wife Lydia Fiske and my son-in-law Hezekiah Brainard executors.

Witness: *John Fiske,*   PHINEAS FISKE, LS.
Daniel Smith, Sarah Fiske.

Court Record, Page 37—5 December, 1738: Will proven.

Page 44—13 March, 1738-9: Whereas, the Rev. Phineas Fiske, in and by his last will, gave to his four daughters all his lands which he had not in and by sd. will given to his son Samuel, to be equally divided amongst them, and not appointing any persons to make a division of sd. lands: Whereupon this Court appoint Capt. John Fiske, Deacon Joseph Arnold and Mr. Thomas Brooks, of Haddam, to divide and make partition of sd. lands to and amongst the sd. daughters.

Page 202.

Foote, Daniel, Simsbury. Died 15 July, 1740. Invt. £1567-15-08. Taken 3 November, 1740, by John Hubbard, Stephen Goodwin and Thomas Humphrey.

Court Record, Page 72—2 September, 1740: Adms. granted to Mary Foote, widow, who recog. in £800 with Jonathan Olcott of Hartford. Daniel Foote, age 16 years, and Joseph Foote, age 14 years, chose their mother Mary Foote to be their guardian. And this Court appoint her guardian to John, age 11, Sarah 8, and Rachell 2 1-2 years, children of Daniel Foote. Recog., £1000.

Page 54.

Forbes, James, Jr., Hartford. Died 9 January, 1736-7. Invt. £251-00-04. Taken 23 February, 1736-7, by Joseph Cowles, Thomas Spencer, Jr., and Samuel Roberts.

Court Record, Page 28—3 May, 1738: Ann Forbes, widow, who was appointed Adms., exhibited an account of her Adms., which is accepted. This Court also appoint Ann Forbes to be guardian to James Forbes, age 9 years, Ann 6 years, Aaron 4, Moses 2 years of age, and Silas 9 months. Recog., £500.

Page 4 (Vol. XIV) 13 December, 1742: James Forbes, a minor, now 14 years of age, chose his mother Ann Forbes to be his guardian. Recog., £200.

Page 106 (Vol. XV) 5 September, 1749: Ann Forbes, alias Ann Keney, the wife of Joseph Keney of Hartford, Adms. on the estate of James Forbes, Jr., by her son James Forbes moves this Court for a dist. of the real estate: Whereupon this Court appoint Jonathan Hill, Lt. Samuel Welles and Timothy Williams, of Hartford, distributors: To James Forbes, eldest son, 1-2 of the real estate; and to Moses Forbes, 1-4 part thereof; and to Ann Forbes, daughter, 1-4 part; which is each one's part of sd. estate. And also this Court order set out to the relict 1-3 part for her improvement during life.

Page 108—3 October, 1741: Report of the distributors.

Page 86-7-8.

Forward, Samuel, Simsbury. Invt. £1787-00-04. Taken 15 June, 1738, by Isaac Gillett, John Lewis and Benjamin Griswold, Jr. Will dated 10th April, 1738.

I, Samuel Forward of Simsbury, in the County of Hartford, do make this my last will and testament: Imprimis. I give to my wife Martha one room in my dwelling house, the use and the liberty to live in it during the time she shall continue my widow (which room is the outer north fire room), my eldest son Samuel Forward to have the liberty to live there with her in sd. room; and the use of my well and cellar. I bequeath unto her likewise the use of my little bedroom in the north-west part of my house, to her own use; and likewise I bequeath and ordain that she shall have the use of 1 1-4 acres of plowing land and 1 1-4 acres of grass land and pasturing for 1 cow during the whole time she shall continue to live my widow. And it is to be understood that it is my will and I ordain that whereas, there was a joynture made with my sd. wife Martha and myself before our marriage, wherein I was obliged to let her have the use of one room in my house and ye use of 1 acre of grass land and 1 acre of plowing land, ye liberty of pasturing one cow, and ye use of my cellar and well, and the apples to fill two barrels of syder, and apples for her own use, all what she should have occasion for during the full term of two years after my decease, and likewise in sd. joynture I was to give her £20 money to be hers forever as her own property: I therefore ordain that, whether she remains my widow or not, she shall have the use of one room in the house, the use of my well, the use of my cellar, apples to eat winter and summer, and apples to fill two barrels for the full term of two years after my decease, which is included in our sd. joynture made before marriage; and as, according to sd. joynture, I was to give her the sd. £20 to be her own property forever, I hereby confirm unto her and ordain she shall have sd. £20 money with this addition, viz., three of my sheep forever, for her own dispose after my decease. I give unto my eldest son Samuel Forward 1-4 part of all my lands and 2-5 part of my dwelling house, 2-5 part of my barn, 2-5 part of my well (reserving the above priviledges to his mother-in-law allowed her as a dowry during her widowhood). And I ordain that he shall have his liberty to have my lands in Suffield as part of his portion if he please, and it is to be deemed or reckoned to him as rough land, except 3 1-2 acres that was formerly cleared. I give unto my 2nd son Joseph Forward the 1-4 part of all my land, to-wit, my home-lott and other land, with 1-5 part of my dwelling house, of my barn and of my well, to be to him forever after my decease. I give to Abell Forward, my third son, 1-4 part of my homelott, together with 1-4 part of all my other land, with 1-5 part of my house and barn and well, for-ever after my decease. I give unto John Forward, my fourth and young-est son, 1-4 part of all my lands, to-wit, 1-4 part of my homelott, with 1-4 part of all the rest of my land, with 1-5 part of my house and barn and well, that is to say, on this consideration: that whereas he is very sick and in a lanquishing condition, therefore it is my will and I ordain that he, my youngest son, John Forward, shall have the sd. 1-4 part of my aforesd. lands and 1-5 part of my house and barn and well, provided he ever lives and continues in this world to have any heirs of his own. I give unto my daughter Rachell Hawley £70 with what she hath had of my estate, deemed to be £60-04-00. And my will is she should have towards her portion my great brass kettle. I give all the rest of my per-sonal or moveable estate to my four sons, provided they pay their sister Rachell Hawley £15 money. I appoint my three sons, Samuel Forward, Joseph Forward and Abell Forward to be sole executors.

Witness: *John Holcomb,*   SAMUEL FORWARD, LS.
John Lewis, James Enno, Junr.

Court Record, Page 31—4 July, 1738: Will proven.

Page 157.

Fowler, Benjamin, Simsbury. Died 14 May, 1739. Invt. £85-10-02. Taken by Jacob Read, Amos Wilcockson and Joseph Case.

Court Record, Page 52—3 July, 1739: Adms. to Lydia Fowler, widow. Recog., £200, with Timothy Case.

Page 71—5 August, 1740: Account exhibited by Lydia Fowler, Adms. Accepted. Paid out in debts and charges, £11-10-11; and re-ceived 15 shillings.

Page 114.

Francis, John, Jr., Wethersfield. Invt. £781-11-02. Taken 26 De-cember, 1738, by Joseph Flowers and Thomas Curtiss.

Court Record, Page 35—7 November, 1738: Adms. granted to Mary Francis, widow. Recog., £1000, with Samuel Curtiss.

Page 102 (Vol. XV) 17 May, 1749: John Francis, age 16 years, son of John Francis, chose his father-in-law Peter Ayrault of Wethers-field to be his guardian. Recog., £600.

Page 119—9 February, 1749-50: Josiah Francis, age 15 years, son of John Francis, Jr., chose his father-in-law Peter Ayrault to be his guardian. And this Court appoint the sd. Ayrault to be guardian to Charles Francis, 13 years of age, and Mary Francis, 11 years. Recog., £400 for each minor.

Invt. in Vol. XIV, Page 30.

Gains, John, Jr., Middletown. Invt. £370-18-03. Taken 25 November, 1741, by Nathaniel White and William Rockwell.

Court Record, Page 103—1st December, 1741: Adms. granted to Susannah Gains, the widow, who recog. in £700, with William Rockwell.

Gains, Daniel, Hartford. Court Record, Page 39—2 January, 1737-8: Henry Gains, a minor, 15 years of age, son of Daniel Gains of Hartford, chose Joseph Roberts of sd. Hartford to be his guardian. Recog., £200.

Page 40—7 July, 1747: This Court appoint Sarah Gains, the widow of Daniel Gains, late of Hartford deceased, to be a guardian to her son Stephen DeWolph; and the sd. widow with John Clark, Jr., of Middletown, recog. in £500.

Page 23.

Gains, Simon, Glastonbury. Invt. £127-15-09. Taken 1st July, 1737, by Gershom Smith and Richard Smith.

Court Record, Page 12—5 July, 1737: Adms. granted to Samuel Gains. Recog., £300, with Samuel Price.

The widow moves to this Court that a sufficiency of moveables be set out for her necessities, amounting to the sum of £9-16-01: This Court so order. This Court appoint Amy Gains, widow, to be guardian to Timothy Gains, a minor, 10 1-2 years of age, Mindwell 7 1-2, Rachel 5, and Simon 2 years of age, children of Simon Gains decd. Recog., £100.

Page 28—2 May, 1738: An account of Adms. on the estate of Simon Gains deceased was now exhibited by Samuel Gains, Adms. There is due from sd. estate in debts and charges, £80-13-00. Which account is accepted in Court and ordered on file.

Page 66—7 April, 1740: Amy Porter, formerly the widow of Simon Gains of Glastonbury decd., moving to this Court that the third part or dower of houseing and lands that her husband Simon Gains died seized of may be ordered by this Court to be set out to her: This Court do therefore appoint Capt. Nathaniel Talcott, Lt. Abner Moseley and William House, of Glastonbury, to set out to the sd. Amy Porter, alias Amy Gains, her right of dower on the estate of the decd.

Page 65—6 May, 1740: A return of the setting out of the widow's dowry was now exhibited in Court and accepted. Also a further ac-

count of Adms. of £3-16-10 charges allowed the Adms., and also receipts
to prove this full accompt, whereby it appears that there is allowed in
with this former account the sum of £83-01-00. Account accepted.
See Estate of Simon Gains, on page 402.

Page 30-31.

Gates, Sergt. Samuel, East Haddam. Died 31 July, 1737. Invt.
£848-12-06. Taken 12 October, 1737, by Daniel Brainard, Jabez Chapman and Daniel Cone.

AGREEMENT:

This agreement, made the 7th day of December, 1737, being joyntly,
severally and unanimously agreed to by the heirs and co-heirs and relict
of Mr. Samuel Gates, late of East Haddam decd., by and with the consent of the guardians to the sd. heirs which are yet in their minority:
First: That whereas, we, Samuel Gates, Stephen Gates, James Gates
and Jonah Gates, being the only surviving children male heirs, and Sarah
Gates, Hannah Gates, Esther Gates and Mary Gates, the only surviving
daughters and co-heirs of the estate of our honoured father, do hereby
covenant and agree to and with our honoured mother Esther Gates,
relict of the sd. decd., that after the debts due from sd. estate are paid
she shall have and injoy 1-3 part of all the personal estate, and 1-3 part
of all the real estate of the sd. decd., viz., the buildings, orchards and
lands, during her natural life. 2ndly: We, the aforementioned heirs
of the estate of the sd. decd., do for ourselves and heirs agree that the
sd. Samuel Gates shall have for his part and portion in and of the
estate, the house, barn, orchards and homelott, bounded as appears on
record, with all the priviledges and appurtenances thereunto belonging,
together with 1-4 part of all ye right in undivided lands in East Haddam
or elsewhere belonging to the estate, to him the sd. Samuel, his heirs
and assigns forever, in full of his part of sd. estate. Thirdly: That the
sd. James Gates shall have and hold to the use of himself and his heirs
forever, for his part and portion, a certain tract or parcell of land in
the first division in East Haddam, containing by estimation 60 acres,
butteth and bounded south on land belonging to Ensign Daniel Cone and
Sergt. Bezeleel Brainard, north on land belonging to Capt. Joshua Brainard and the heirs of Daniel Brainard, Jr., decd., east and west on a highway; and 1-4 part of all the right in the undivided lands in East Haddam
or elsewhere belonging to the estate, with all the priviledges and appurtenances thereunto belonging, which is his share of sd. estate.   Fourthly:
That Stephen Gates shall have and hold to the use of himself and his
heirs, for his portion of the estate, one tract or parcell of land lying in
the Parish of Millington, in East Haddam, containing by estimation 75
acres, being butted and bounded as appears in the survey upon record,
together with the 1-4 part of all the right in the undivided lands in East
Haddam or elsewhere belonging to sd. estate, with all the priviledges

and appurtenances thereunto belonging. Fifth: That Jonah Gates shall have and hold to the use of himself, his heirs and assigns forever, for his part and portion of the sd. estate, one tract of land in the Parish of Millington, in East Haddam, containing by estimation 30 acres, butted and bounded as appears on record; also one tract or parcell of land containing by estimation 24 acres, be it more or less, being butted and bounded east on the land of Joshua Gates, south on land of Mr. Hosmer, west and north on common land; also one tract or parcell of land in the Cone Meadow, containing 6 acres by estimation, butted and bounded southeast on land of Bezeleel Brainard, southwest on the Great River, northwest on the land of William Schovill, and east on the Cove; together with 1-4 part in all the right in the undivided lands in East Haddam or elsewhere belonging to sd. estate, with all the priviledges and appurtenances belonging to the severall parcells of land agreed he should have. Sixthly: That Sarah, Hannah, Esther and Mary Gates shall, after all the debts due from sd. estate are paid, have all the personal estate belonging to the sd. deceased, to be equally divided amongst them and set out by such persons as the Honourable Court of Probates in Hartford shall appoint, which moveable estate shall be their full part and portion, excepting 1-3 part of sd. personal estate, which shall be to their honoured mother Esther Gates as aforesd. And the above named parties, for themselves and with the consent of their guardians which represent them, have given, granted and released unto each other the severall claims or demands that they have or might have unto the estate aforesd., or any part of them, other than what in the above distribution or partition is to them set out, as before in this instrument agreed to, and particularly and severally apportioned and set out, and that the above distribution, division or partition shall forever hereafter be and remain a full and final settlement of the estate. In witness whereof the parties to these presents have hereunto set their hands and seals this 7th day of December and 10th day of January, 1737.

JAMES GATES, LS.	ESTHER X GATES, LS.
SAMUEL GATES, LS.	JONAH GATES, LS.
SARAH GATES, LS.	STEPHEN GATES, LS.
ESTHER GATES, LS.	HANNAH GATES, LS.
	MARY GATES, LS.

Court Record, Page 17—6 December, 1737: Adms. to Esther Gates, widow, and Samuel Gates, a son. Recog., £1500, with Bezaleel Brainard of Haddam. James Gates, age 16 years, chose his mother Esther Gates to be his guardian. And this Court appoint the widow guardian to Jonah Gates, age 12 years. Recog., £200. Stephen Gates, age 14 years, son of Samuel Gates, chose his brother Samuel Gates to be his guardian. Recog., £100.

Page 20—7 December, 1737: Agreement exhibited in Court, accepted and ordered to be recorded and kept on file.

Page 37—5 December, 1738: A discharge by the heirs, viz., Sarah Gates, Mary Gates, Esther Gates, Thomas Smith and Hannah Smith alias Hannah Gates, to their mother Esther Gates and Samuel Gates, Adms., having received the sum of £113 money.

Page 256-7, 259-60.

Gaylord, John, Windsor. Invt. £2883-09-09. Taken 4 December, 1740, by Jonathan Stiles, Samuel Stoughton and Peletiah Allyn. Will dated 18 September, 1739.

I, John Gaylord of Windsor, do make this my last will and testament: I give to my wife Elizabeth Gaylord 1-2 of my moveable estate to be her own forever. I also give unto my wife Elizabeth ye use and improvement of 1-2 of my dwelling house and 1-3 part of all my improved land during her natural life, and after her decease my will and pleasure is that the thirds of the lands and half of the house aforesd. which I gave to my wife during her natural life shall return unto my son William Gaylord in the form it may be hereafter expressed. I give to my daughter Mary Gaylord, alias Mary Copley, 10 shillings in money. I give to my daughter aforesd. the 1-2 of my right which I have in the Township of Harwington, to be to the sd. Mary Gaylord, alias Copley, during her natural life, then to be to her heirs forever during their natural life, and then to descend to their heirs, and so from generation to generation. I give unto my loving daughter Elizabeth MacMoran 10 shillings in money. I give unto my daughter aforesd. the 1-2 of my right which I have in the Township of Harwington, to be to her the sd. Elizabeth MacMoran during her natural life, and then to be to her heirs during their natural life, and then to descend to their heirs, and so from generation to generation. Furthermore, my will and pleasure is that my sd. daughter Elizabeth MacMoran shall have all the moveable estate which she hath in her hands or custody which I formerly lent unto her, which then amounted to the sum of £64-03-00 money, to be to her my sd. daughter's use during her natural life, and after her decease to be to her heirs forever. I give unto my son William Gaylord all the remainder of my estate, both real and personal, not above disposed of, viz., all the lands which are improved in the Township of Windsor, I give unto my sd. son William, during his natural life, then to his heirs, etc., forever. I give unto my sd. son William Gaylord all the improved lands in Windsor with all the rights and improvements I have in the common and undivided lands in Windsor, with all the rights and priviledges that I have or may hereafter have in the equivalent land that may or shall hereafter be laid out to me, to be to him my sd. son William and to his heirs forever. My will is that my son William Gaylord be executor.

Witness: *Peletiah Allyn,*   JOHN GAYLORD, LS.
Israel Stoughton, John Allyn.

Court Record, Page 76—2 December, 1740: Will now exhibited by William Gaylord, executor. Proven.

Page 92 (Vol. XVII) 5 February, 1756: Mrs. Gaylord, the relict of John Gaylord, late of Windsor deceased, showing to this Court that her dowry in the real estate of the deceased has never been set out to her: Whereupon this Court appoint Peletiah Allyn, Samuel Stiles and Josiah Bissell to set out to the widow her thirds.

Invt. in Vol. XIV, Page 37-8.

Gaylord, Josiah, Windsor. Invt. £1204-19-02. Taken 8 October, 1741, by Peletiah Allyn, Josiah Phelps the 3rd and John Allyn.

Court Record, Page 102—1st December, 1741: Adms. granted to Naomi Gaylord, widow, and Josiah Gaylord, son of sd. deceased, who recog. in £1000, with Peletiah Allyn.

Gilbert, Amy, Estate, Wethersfield. Court Record, Page 58—1st January, 1739-40: Adms. granted to Jacob Williams of Wethersfield. Recog., £200, with Ephraim Williams.

Page 315-322.

Gillett, Jonathan, Hartford. Invt. £452-06-01, taken 6 June, 1741, and £303-02-08 taken 4 May, 1741, by Isaac Kellogg, Moses Nash and John Ensign.

Court Record, Page 79—6 January, 1740-1: Adms. to Joseph Gillett of Hartford and Caleb Andrews of Wethersfield. Recog., £500, with John Ensign of Hartford.

Page 103—1st December, 1741: This Court appoint Moses Dickinson of Hartford to be guardian to Mehetabell Gillett, age 8 years, Mary age 6, and Jonathan age 4 years, children of Jonathan Gillett, late deceased. Recog., £300.

Page 17 (Vol. XIV) 7 February, 1742-3: Caleb Andrews and Joseph Gillett, Adms., exhibited an account of their Adms.: Paid in debts and charges the sum of £160-02-09; received £18-06-00. Which account is accepted.

Page 5 (Vol. XVI) 13 November, 1750: Mary Gillett, a minor daughter, now 15 years of age, chose Stephen Goodwin of Simsbury to be her guardian. Recog., £500.

Page 54—11 February, 1752: Jonathan Gillett, a minor, age 14 years, son of Jonathan Gillett, made choice of his uncle Joseph Gillett to be his guardian. Recog., £600.

Page 58—7 April, 1752: Joseph Gillett, Adms., having made up his account of Adms., now moves that dist. be made of the estate, viz.: To Jonathan Gillett, only son, a double share; and to Mehetabell and Mary Gillett, to each of them a single share; and also to dist. to the sd. children of Jonathan Gillett what was given to them in and by the last will and testament of their grandfather Joseph Gillett of sd. Hartford deceased. And appoint Capt. Daniel Webster, Moses Nash and Abraham Merrell, of Hartford, distributors.

Page 6 (Vol. XVII) 1st November, 1753: Report of the distributors.

Page 222.

Goodale, Richard, Middletown. Invt. £230-14-05. Taken 16 June, 1740, by Nathaniel White and William Rockwell.
Court Record, Page 71—5 August, 1740: Adms. to Daniel Brewer. Recog., £500, with William Rockwell.

Page 13.

Goodrich, Isaac, Wethersfield. Invt. £130-12-00. Taken by Thomas Welles, Joseph Allyn and John Deming.
Court Record, Page 10—7 June, 1737: Adms. granted to Mary Goodrich, widow.
Page 15 (Vol. XIV) 4 January, 1742-3: Isaac Goodrich, 17 years of age, son of Isaac Goodrich of Wethersfield, chose Josiah Griswold of Wethersfield to be his guardian. Recog., £500.

Page 114-15-16.

Goodrich, Lt. William, Wethersfield. Invt. £3079-05-03. Taken 27 December, 1737, by Ephraim Goodrich, Isaac Riley and David Wright. Will dated 27 December, 1737.
I, William Goodrich of Wethersfield, do make this my last will and testament: I give to my wife Mary Ann the 1-2 of my negro man George, and so much right and interest in my west swamp pasture as will suffice to pasture well 2 milch cowes (this last article I give to my sd. wife during the time she remains my widow, and no longer; the first to be to her, her heirs and assigns forever). I give to my son Benjamin one acre of my land lying in Wethersfield Plain, commonly called the Great Plaine, and 5 roods of my land lying in ye west swamp of Wethersfield, to be to him, his heirs and assigns forever. I give and bequeath to my son Joseph 10 acres of land lying in that part of Wethersfield commonly called the west swamp, to be to him, his heirs and assigns forever, provided that he maintain the fence and suffer my wife to pasture two cows there during the time she remains my widow. Also, I give to my son Joseph one acre of my land lying in Wethersfield Plain, and the 1-2 of my negro man George, to be to him, his heirs and assigns forever. I appoint my son Joseph to be my only executor.
Witness: *David Goodrich,*   WILLIAM X GOODRICH, LS.
Gideon Welles, Elisha Micks.

Court Record, Page 18—7 December, 1737: Will now exhibited.
Page 28—7 March, 1737-8: Joseph Goodrich, executor, made application for the probate of the will. The rest of the heirs appeared and objected, viz., William Goodrich, Benjamin Goodrich, Marian Goodrich the widow, William Goodrich, attorney for the heirs of Ephraim Good-

rich decd., the relict of Isaac Goodrich decd., Robert Powell in right of his wife Ann, Noadiah Dickinson, attorney for Elizabeth Goodrich, Lucenia and Eunice Goodrich, daughters of the sd. deceased, and being severally heard, the case was continued.

Page 32—1st August, 1738: Exhibit of inventory. Accepted.

Page 33—3 October, 1738: Mary Ann Goodrich, widow, asks for her dower. This Court appoint Capt. Thomas Welles, Lt. Elizer Goodrich and Deacon Thomas Wright to set out her dower by meets and bounds.

Page 50—5 August, 1739: The set out of dower not accepted, and Deacon Thomas Wright, Jonathan Burnham and Benjamin Stilman are appointed to set out her dower anew.

Page 60—5 February, 1739-40: Adms. on the intestate estate of William Goodrich decd. granted to Joseph Goodrich, one of the sons of the deceased. Recog., £500, with Benjamin Goodrich.

Page 61—5 February, 1739-40: Report of the administrator accepted and ordered to be kept on file.

Page 181-2.

Grant, Daniel, Windsor. Inventory taken 14 March, 1739-40, by Henry Wolcott, Joseph Phelps and Joseph Loomis. Will dated 14 January, 1739-40.

I, Daniel Grant of Windsor, do make this my last will and testament: I give to my wife Sarah my sheep and 3 cows and all the rest of my personal estate, except the remainder of cattle, horse and my swine and my credits, which are to be apprised at their worth in current money, and what they fall short in the sum of £300 at apprisement, my will is that it should be paid to my wife in current money within 12 months after my decease by my three sisters, Hannah, Mary and Sarah, so as to make up the whole sum of £300 in current money. I also give to my wife during her widowhood the west part of the dwelling house that faceth to the south, 1-2 of the cellar, the full part of my homestead in breadth from ye south bounds to the south end of the house, and so to extend from ye street to the sd. west part of the dwelling house, and from thence 1-3 part of the homestead on the south side to the west bounds; as also 1-3 part of the pasture on the east side of the way from the street to the brook, and the south half of the barn and the buildings adjoining to it; as also 1-3 part of my meadow lott that is 18 rods wide. I give to my honoured mother the sum of £18, to be paid within one year after my decease. I give to my brother William and to my sister Rachel £40 in current money to each of them, to be paid within one year after my mother's decease. I give to my brother Burt's children, Daniel and Silence, the sum of £20. I give to Asa West the sum of £20, to be paid when he shall come to the age of 21 years. My will is that the legacies abovesd. given to my mother, sister Rachel, brother William, Daniel and Silence

Burt and Asa West, shall be paid by my three sisters, Hannah, Mary and Sarah, in equal parts. And all the rest and residue of my estate, be it now in possession or in remainder, as also the lands and buildings given to my wife during her widowhood, after her widowhood I give to my three sisters, Hannah, Mary and Sarah, share and share alike, to them and their heirs forever, excepting only that Sarah shall have £20 more than an equal part. I appoint my brother Thomas Sadd and Daniel Bissell executors.

Witness: *Roger Wolcott,*   DANIEL GRANT, LS.
Samuel Grant, Thomas Drake.

Court Record, Page 63—3 April, 1740: Will proven.

Page 189-190.

Gridley, John, Kensington. Invt. £1004-14-06. Taken 4 January, 1740, by John Hooker, Samuel Lankton and Nathaniel Hart. Will dated 13 April, 1739.

I, John Gridley, of the Parish of Kensington, in the Township of Farmington, do make this my last will and testament: I give to my wife Dorothy Gridley 1-3 part of all my personal estate forever, and 1-3 part of my real estate and buildings during her natural life. I give to my son John Gridley one lott of land which lyeth in a division of land east of the Blue Mountain, which lott was laid out to Daniel Andrews and contains about 32 acres; also one parcell of land in sd. division lying near a place called Pike Island, 11 acres, and one piece of 6 acres, which piece of land is part of the lott on which my house now stands, butting west on a highway and south on land now belonging to Elisha Brownson. I give to my son John my gunn. I give to my son Andrew Gridley 50 acres lying in the lott on which my house standeth, butting west on the 6 acres I have willed to my son John; also I give to my son Andrew 1-2 of my buildings. Also I give to my son Amos Gridley 44 acres of land lying in the lott on which my house standeth, and on the north side of the sd. lott, to extend the length of sd. lott; also I give to my sd. son Amos my loom with all the tackling belonging thereto. I give to my daughter Mary Evans 5 shillings, which 5 shillings makes it up £55 with what I have already given her. I give to my daughter Mercy Gridley £55, to be taken out of my personal estate. My will further is that my two sons, John and Andrew, shall pay in equal proportion to my daughter Mercy aforesd. so much as I shall want of my personal estate till it amount to the full sum of £55. And I appoint my wife Dorothy and my son John executors.

Witness: *John Hooker, Jr.,*   JOHN GRIDLEY, LS.
Thomas Gridley, Andrew Hooker.

Court Record, Page 63—1st April, 1740: Will proven.

Dist. File: 29 April, 1757: To Andrew Gridley. to Marah Evans, to Mercy Manross, and to Amos Gridley. By Ebenezer Gridley and Seth Hooker.

Page 20-1.

Griswold, Jacob, Sen., Wethersfield.   Died 22 July, 1737.   Invt. £268-17-09.   Taken 18 August, 1737, by John Stilman, Jonathan Williams and Jonathan Belding.   Will dated 10 February, 1735-6.

I, Jacob Griswold, Sen., of Wethersfield, do make this my last will and testament: I give to my son Josiah Griswold the whole of my lott lying in Newington Parish, in that tier of lotts called the half-mile tier, containing 29 1-2 acres, butted east on commons or a highway and also west, north on the heirs of Capt. Robert Welles, and south on a highway, to be to him my son Josiah and his heirs forever. I also give my son Josiah 3 1-2 acres of land lying in the south part of Wethersfield, in the Great Meadow, butted east on a highway, west on land of my son Josiah Griswold, north on land of Ephraim Williams, and south on land of the heirs of Eliphalet Dickinson, with this condition, that he the sd. Josiah Griswold pay and make out these sums following to the persons next mentioned: To the heirs of my eldest son John Griswold deceased: To Jeremiah, the eldest son of the deceased, £10 in money; to John, 2nd son of ye deceased, £5 in money; to Hannah, a daughter of the deceased, £5; to Thankfull, another daughter of the decd., £5 in money; to Mabell, another daughter of the decd., £5 in money; also that my sd. son Josiah pay to my eldest son now surviving, Jacob Griswold, £35 money to complete his portion. My son Ebenezer Griswold has already been advanced in portion and settlement, as appears by record, equal with his brethren. To my son Ephraim Griswold I give 8 acres of land, part of my homelott, butted east on a highway, west on my son Josiah's land, north on land of Michael Griswold, and south on common land. I give to my eldest daughter, Mary Ellis, £110, to be her portion, of which she hath already received £100. I give to my daughter Sarah £110 in moveable estate, of which she has already received £75-18-11. I give to my daughter Esther £110, of which she hath already received £77-04-09. I give to my daughter Lydia £110 in moveable estate, of which she hath already received £66-02-08. I appoint my son Josiah Griswold to be sole executor.

Witness: *Thomas Wright,*   JACOB GRISWOLD, LS.
Elisha Micks, Joseph Pynchon.

I, the sd. Jacob Griswold, by this present codicil, do ratify and confirm my last will and testament, and do give unto my beloved son Ephraim Griswold, besides what I have given him in the will abovesd., 8 acres of pasture land, butted east on the heirs of Jonathan Belding decd., west on land of my son Josiah Griswold, north on the land of Capt. Joshua Robbins, and south on common land.

Witness: *Thomas Wright,*   JACOB GRISWOLD, LS.
Elisha Micks, Joseph Pynchon.

Court Record, Page 14—2 August, 1737: Will proven.

Page 117-118-119.

Griswold, Sergt. John, Windsor.   Invt. £1585-04-10.   Taken 17 January, 1738-9, by Thomas Griswold, Nathaniel Griswold and Nathaniel Pinney.

Court Record, Page 39—18 January, 1738-9: Adms. to John Griswold, son of the decd. Recog., with Nathaniel Griswold.

Page 39.

Griswold, Lieut. Matthew, Windsor.   Invt. £2125-02-05.   Taken 18 November, 1737, by Nathaniel Pinney, Josiah Phelps 3d and John Owen, Jr. Will dated 16 September, 1737.

I, Matthew Griswold of Windsor, do make this my last will and testament: Imprimis. I give to my wife Mary 1-3 part of my moveable estate, also £40 money, and the use of 1-3 part of my lands during her natural life. I give to my eldest son Matthew £20 more than 1-2 of my lands and buildings. I give to my son Noah the remainder of my lands and buildings, that is to say, 1-2 of my lands excepting £20 worth which I give to my son Matthew more than half, as above expressed. I give to my three daughters, to Mary, to Jerusha and to Lucy, six score pounds to each, together with what they have had already, to be raised and levied out of my estate in two years after my decease. I give to my youngest daughter Lydia six score pounds, to be paid at the age of 18 years. I appoint Mary, my beloved wife, to be my sole executrix.

Witness: *Nathaniel Griswold,*   MATTHEW GRISWOLD, LS.
Martha Holcomb, Rebeckah X Loomis.

Court Record, Page 22—14 February, 1737-8: Will proven.

Page 42—15 February, 1738-9: Noah Griswold, a minor, 17 years of age, chose Daniel Phelps to be his guardian. Recog., £200.

Page 47—3 April, 1739: Upon motion of Matthew Griswold, son of Matthew Griswold, late deceased, that there being no person especially appointed in his sd. father's will to dist. the deceased's land or estate, and that there being minors concerned in sd. estate so that the heirs cannot come to portion amongst themselves, sd. Matthew now standing in need of the division of sd. estate that he may be able to improve the land that falls to him by sd. will: This Court therefore appoint Lt. Nathaniel Pinney and Ensign Nathaniel Griswold, together with Daniel Phelps (guardian to Noah Griswold), to make the division and partition of the estate according to the last will of the deceased.

See Estate of Matthew Griswold, on page 409.

Gross, Freeman, Hartford. Court Record, Page 111—6 April, 1742: Adms. granted to Susannah Gross, widow. Recog., £1000, with Ensign James Church.

Page 88 (Vol. XV) 23 January, 1748-9: Freeman Gross, a minor, 16 years of age, chose his mother Susannah Gross to be his guardian. Recog., £500.

Page 55 (Vol. XVII) 24 March, 1755: Thomas Gross, a minor, 17 years of age, son of Freeman Gross, chose his mother Susannah Gross to be his guardian. Recog., £100.

Page 141—14 February, 1757: Jonathan Gross, a minor son of Freeman Gross, appeared before this Court and made choice of his brother Freeman Gross to be his guardian. Recog., £300.

Distribution from file.

Pursuant to an order of the Court, we, the subscribers, have made a distribution of the real estate of Freeman Gross, Sen., late of Hartford decd.: To the heirs of Thomas Gross for their share of the estate, the north side of the home lot, next to the land sd. Thomas Gross purchased of William Hooker, and adjoins land of Jonathan Butler; to Susannah Bunce, a daughter of the decd., land next to the heirs of Thomas Gross, on the south; to Experience Ensign, wife of Thomas Ensign, a daughter of the decd., land south of the land set out to Susannah Bunce, and adjoins land of Capt. Aaron Bull on the south; to the heirs of Jona: Gross decd., all that remains of the lot that has not been set out to the others.

> Joseph Church,   ⎱
> Barnabas Hinsdale,   ⎰ Distributors.
> John Skinner,   ⎰

Dated 14 March, 1777.

Page 323.

Hale, Nathaniel, Wethersfield. Invt. £567-07-06. Taken 5 February, 1738-9, by Thomas Curtice, John Stilman and Robert Francis.

Court Record, Page 41—6 February, 1738-9: Adms. granted to Abigail Hale, widow. Recog., with Oliver Deming of Wethersfield.

Page 52 (Vol. XIV) 5 February, 1744-5: Abigail Hale, widow and Adms., exhibited an account of her Adms. Accepted. The widow moves to this Court that a dist. be made of the moveable estate, which is £335-07-04; the debts and charges being subtracted, there remains £167-08-09 of moveable estate to be dist.: To the widow, £55-16-03; to Ebenezer Hale, eldest son, £44-13-00; to Justus Hale, Hezekiah Hale and Lucy Hale, to each, £22-06-06. And appoint John Stilman, Nathaniel Stilman and Hezekiah May distributors. Hezekiah Hale, age 16 years, son of Nathaniel Hale, chose Robert Francis of Wethersfield to be his guardian. Recog., £500.

Page 221.

Hall, Samuel, Sen., Middletown. Will dated 26 April, 1739: I, Samuel Hall, Sen., of Middletown, in the County of Hartford, do make this my last will and testament: Imprimis. I give to my wife Phebe the use of 1-2 of my buildings and the use of 1-2 of my lands on this side of the Great River so long as she continues my widow; also the use of 1-2 of my stock during her life, and at her death what is left to be equally divided amongst my daughters; also I give her as much of my household goods as she shall need for her conveniency during her life, and at her death what remains to be equally divided among my daughters; also I give my six acres of land I pitcht for near Two Sticks Brook to her to dispose of as she shall see good. I give to my son Samuel Hall all my lands on the west side of the Great River, with all the buildings thereon, excepting and reserving what I have given to his mother, and the use of 1-2 the buildings and lands which I have given her, and also the use of half the orchard near Long Hill, which I give to my daughter Mary during her life, part of which buildings and lands I have already given him by deed of gift; also I give him all my husbandry tools and utensils and the 1-2 of my stock. And I do appoint him to be sole executor of this my last will and testament. And I do order and it is my will that out of what I have given him he pay all my just debts and funeral charges and the legacy of £60 and one cow, which I give to my daughter Mary, and to procure for my daughters Phebe and Susannah, each of them, a brass kettle about the bigness of that I gave to my daughter Mary. To my four daughters, Experience, Phebe, Susannah and Mary, besides what I have already given them, I give them all my lands on the east side of the Great River, divided or undivided, or rights of lands, to be equally divided among them. To my daughter Experience I give one iron pott she hath now in use. To my daughter Phebe I give a brass kettle, to be procured by my executor as above. To my daughter Susannah I give one brass kettle, to be procured by my executor. To my daughter Mary I give £60 in money and a cow, to be paid her by my executor, and the use of 1-2 of my orchard near Long Hill, during her life; also I give her the use of the room in my house so long as she continues single. I give to my four daughters above named all my household goods that remain after my wife hath taken what is needful for her use, to be equally divided among them.

Witness: *John Wallis,*   SAMUEL HALL, LS.
Obadiah Mors, James Appleby.

Court Record, Page 70—5 August, 1740: Will of Samuel Hall, Sen., Middletown, exhibited by Samuel Hall, executor. Proven before *Jabez Hamlin, J. P.* Approved by the Court at Hartford.

Will copied from File. Inventory on Page 319.

Hall, Deacon Samuel, East Middletown. Died 6 March, 1739-40. Invt. £1707-14-07. Taken by Nathaniel White and Thomas Johnson. Will dated January, 1732.

The last will and testament of Deacon Samuel Hall of East Middletown, in the County of Hartford: Though at present being under bodily illness, yet sound in mind and reason and memory, and calling to mind the mortality of my body, knowing that it is appointed for all once to dye, do therefore in the fear of God appoint and ordain this to be my last will and testament: I give to my wife Elizabeth my dwelling house, orchard and homestead, to be hers during the time she abide my widow, excepting my youngest son Samuel, when he arrives to the suitable discretion, to have the improvement of the 1-2 of the land. To my eldest son John I give the house that he now dwells in, together with the land appertaining thereunto, and all my land eastwardly adjoining thereunto, together with all my meadow land lying south from the path to the river, and 2-3 of my lott of land in the 1-2-mile lottment, and my ploughing land in the common field eastward from the ditch to the river, together with my right of land laid out in the last division of land (excepting 50 acres), and Mr. Farrend's "Comment upon the Revelations." To my third son Isaac I give 40 acres of land adjoining eastwardly of land of John Churchill and westward adjoining land of heirs of Beriah Bacon, together with all my swamp and upland on the north of my land in the common field. To my 2nd son Thomas I give 3 acres of swamp land lying in a place commonly called by the name of Pasmachaug, adjoining southwardly on my own land, northerly on land given to my son John Hall, together with £78 in money. My fourth son Samuel I give about 4 acres in swamp land lying in the common field, adjoining south on Deacon White and west upon land given to Thomas Hall, together with 1-3 part of my lott of land lying in the 1-2-mile lottment, and 16 roods of land in breadth across the north end of my meadow land running from the ditch to the common passing road, together with my house and homestead, to descend to him at the decease of his mother, and also my great Bible. To daughter Elizabeth I give 50 acres of land lying in my lottment in the last division of land, together with all my household goods and stuff, and 3 cows. The remainder of my books I give to be equally divided and distributed among all my children respectively. And lastly I do ordain and appoint my wife Elizabeth and my eldest son John Hall to be the executors.

Witness: *Daniel White,*   SAMUEL HALL, LS.
Thomas Johnson, Moses Bartlett.

Middletown, March ye 31st, 1740: Then personally appeared the Rev. Mr. Moses Bartlett, one of the witnesses to the within written will, and made solemn oath that he did see Deacon Samuel Hall, the testator, sign and seal to the within written will, and that ye sd. testator did dictate to him in the writing of the same, and that he set his hand thereto as a witness in his presence, and that at the same time he judged the testator to be of a sound, disposeing mind.

Before me: Joseph White, Justice of Peace.

Middletown, March ye 31st, 1740: Then personally appeared Mr. Daniel White, one of the witnesses to the within written will, and made solemn oath that he was fully satisfied that he did set his hand to the within written will in the presence of the testator; and although sd. White was accidentally there at that time, yet, with some considerable discourse that he had with him at the same time, he judged the sd. testator to be of a sound, disposeing mind.

Before me: Joseph White, Justice of Peace.

Middletown, March ye 31st, 1740: Then personally appeared Copr. Thomas Johnson, one of the witnesses to the within written will, and made solemn oath that he being informed that he was one of the witnesses to the within written will, upon the view of the same he was fully satisfied that his name there written was his own handwriting, although he had but little remembrance of the transaction.

Before me: Joseph White, Justice of Peace.

Last will of Deacon Samll. Hall to lie on file, by the desire of the heirs. 1740.

Court Record, Page 65—6 May, 1740: Samuel Hall. son of Deacon Samuel Hall, chose Ensign Stephen Stocking to be his guardian.

Page 86—7 April, 1741: This Court grant Adms. to John Hall, executor named in the writing called the last will of sd. deceased, which will not being proved according to law, is not approved; and the sd. John Hall desired sd. will might be lodged in the files of this Court, which writing is accordingly filed as aforesd. And the sd. John Hall gave bond with Joseph White of Middletown, of £500.

Page 9 (Vol. XIV) 1st June, 1742: John Hall, Adms., exhibited an account of his Adms.: Paid in debts and charges, £27-05-09. Which account is accepted, ordered recorded and kept on file.

Page 42-3.

Hancox, Rachel, single woman, Kensington. Invt. £414-07-10. Taken 19 December, 1737, by John Norton, Samuel Lancton and Daniel Hancox. Will dated 15 October, 1737.

I, Rachell Hancox of Kensington, in the County of Hartford, do make and ordain this my last will and testament: I give to my well-beloved brothers, John Hancox of Springfield and Daniel Hancox of the aforesd. Kensington, and to my only sister Mabel Barnes, the wife of Ebenezer Barnes, Sen., of Farmingtown, their heirs and assigns forever, all my personal and moveable estate that shall remain after my debts and funeral charges are paid, to be equally divided amongst them. All my real estate, lands, tenements and hereditaments, I give to my friends, Mr. John Hooker and William Burnham, Jr., both of Kensington, to their heirs and assigns forever, whome I now appoint executors. And my will and desire is that my executors should sell or otherwise dispose of the whole or any part of the sd. real estate so as to pay to my sister above named the value of £100 in such bills of public credit as have commonly passed and been current in this Colony, and that the payment thereof should be made either in land or in bills of credit aforesd., as my sd. executors shall think best, within one year after my decease. And if any of my real estate remain after the sd. payment, and after my executors are recompensed for their necessary charge and trouble about my estate, that they would sell or otherwise dispose of the whole remainder for the relief of poor persons either in Kensington aforesd. or elsewhere, and distribute it to sd. poor persons according to their discretion.

Witness: *William Burnham,*   RACHEL HANCOX, LS.
Isaac Norton, Isaac Hart.

Court Record, Page 16—1st November, 1737: Will proven.

Page 20—3rd January, 1737-8: John Hooker and William Barnard, Jr., of Farmingtown, now appeared in Court and accepted the trust of being executors to the last will of Rachel Hancox, late of Farmingtown deceased, and exhibited an inventory, which was ordered on file. And the sd. executors informed this Court that they doubted the estate of the sd. deceased is "insolvent." Whereupon this Court allows the sd. executors 3 months to inquire into and get an accot. of the debts due to the sd. estate.

Harris, Joseph. Court Record, Page 27—10 April, 1738: Abigail Harris, a minor, 14 years of age, daughter of Joseph Harris, late of Litchfield decd., chose Stephen Sedgewick of Farmington to be her guardian. Recog., £300.

Page 110—2 March, 1741-2: Asa Hopkins and Abigail Harris, alias Hopkins, the wife of sd. Asa Hopkins, acknowledged before this Court that they have received of Stephen Sedgewick, guardian to the sd. Abigail in her minority, the whole of the moveable estate of Joseph Harris, late of Litchfield deceased, which belonged to them.

Page 288.

Harrison, Edmond, Middletown. Invt. £130-12-04. Taken 20 January, 1740, by John Warner, Hugh White and Joseph Ranny, Jr.

Court Record, Page 94—7 July, 1741: Estate insolvent. John Wilcocks and Hugh White appointed commissioners.

Page 110—2 March, 1741-2: John Wilcocks refuses to act, and this Court appoint Capt. Thomas Johnson and Isaac White, with sd. Hugh White, to act as commissioners.

Page 9 (Vol. XIV) 3 August, 1742: A report of the commissioners was now exhibited in Court by Thomas Johnson and Hugh White, commissioners, and accepted. The Court now order that the Clerk of this Court make a rule of average on sd. estate, that the creditors may have their proportion of sd. estate.

Page 67.

Hart, Hannah, Farmington. Will dated 31 August, 1737: Note: Whereas, Lt. John Hart of Farmington hath by an instrument under his hand and seal bearing date 8 April, 1734, given considerable of moveable estate unto his deare wife Hannah Hart to be at her dispose in life and at death, and obliged himself not to hinder or frustrate any disposition the sd. Hannah shall make of sd. estate, either by deed of gift or will, but by all suitable means to endeavor that the same may be confirmed and take effect, all which by sd. instrument (reference thereunto being had) may more fully appear: Therefore she, the sd. Hannah Hart, being encouraged to make disposition of sd. estate, do proceed to do the same: I will as followeth: I, Hannah Hart, being of ordinary health of body but stricken in years and crazy, but of sound mind and memory, do make this my last will and testament: I give to Richard Treat, son to Thomas Treat, £5. I give to my kinswoman Mary Judd, wife of John Judd, one chest of draws. I give to my kinswomen, viz., to Mary Hart, wife of Deacon Thomas Hart, Mary Warner, Prudence Deming and Mary Smith, wife of Thomas Smith, in equal porportions, all the residue of my estate. I appoint Joseph Hooker of Farmington sole executor.

Witness: *John Hooker,*   HANNAH X HART, LS.
Joseph Hooker, Elisha Lewis.

Court Record, Page 23—7 March, 1737-8: Will proven.

Page 263.

Highstead, Edward, Caanan. Invt. £45-14-00. Taken 9th April, 1741, by Samuel Bryon, Ephraim Fellows and Isaac Lawrence.

Court Record, Page 88—23 May, 1741: Adms. granted to David Whitney of sd. Caanan, who gave bond with George Holloway of Cornwall, by request of the widow, to whome necessaries are set out.

Page 91—2 June, 1741: Elizabeth Highstead, age 8 years, and Abigail, 5 years, and Edward 3, children of Edward Highstead: This Court appoint David Whitney to be their guardian. Recog., £60.

Page 5 (Vol. XIV) 19 May, 1742: David Whitney exhibited an account of Adms. Accepted.

Page 309-10.

Higley, John, Simsbury. Will dated 24 October, 1741: In the name of God, amen: I, John Higley of Simsbury, in the County of Hartford and Colony of Connecticut, being in a weak and languishing condition of body, yet of sound mind and memory, and of a disposing capacity, blessed be God therefor, and calling to mind that I must shortly die, do make and constitute this my last will and testament, in manner and form following: Imprimis: I give and bequeath my soul to God that gave it, and my body to the earth to be decently buried at the discretion of my executor in hopes of a glorius resurrection. And for the worldly goods that God hath given me, I dispose of after the following manner, viz.: I give unto my brother Brewster Higley of Simsbury all my whole estate, as well real as personal, all which I now have in my actual possession. I constitute my sd. brother executor.

Witness: *Thomas Holcomb,*   JOHN HIGLEY, LS.
Daniel Holcomb, Joseph Wilcockson.

Court Record, Page 106—5 January, 1741-2: Will proven.

Page 3-4.

Higley, Doctor Samuel, Simsbury. Invt. £299-09-06, personal estate. Taken 4 June, 1737, by James Case, Samuel Griswold and Joshua Holcomb. Will dated 30 April, 1733.

I, Samuel Higley of Simsbury, do make this my last will and testament: I give to my wife Abigail Higley all my moveable estate excepting books, chymacall tools, and a white-faced heifer; also the improvement of all my lands and mines if she continueth my widow, until my son Jonathan comes to the age of 21 years, and one-half until my daughter Ann comes to the age of 16 years, and from that time one-fourth until my daughter Abigail comes to the age of 16 years. I give to my son Jonathan Higley half my books and all my chymacall tools, etc., provided he pay to his two sisters, Ann and Abigail Higley, £250 to each. I appoint my wife Abigail Higley sole executrix.

Witness: *Samuel Griswold,*   SAMUEL X HIGLEY, LS.
Elizabeth X Griswold, Elizabeth Griswold, Jr.

Court Record, Page 9—7 June, 1737: Will now exhibited by Abigail Higley, widow. Jonathan Higley, a minor, 16 years of age, chose his mother Abigail Higley to be his guardian. And this Court appoint the sd. Abigail guardian to Anne, age 11 years, and Abigail, 4 years of age. Recog., £200.

Page 60 (Vol. XIV) 22 June, 1745: Report of the distributors on the estate of Doctor Samuel Higley, under the hands of Samuel Griswold and James Case, distributors. Accepted and ordered upon file.

Page 149.

Higley, Sarah, Widow, Windsor. Invt. £38-01-00. Taken 4 December, 1739, by Jacob Drake, Job Loomis and Timothy Loomis. Presented by Jonathan Loomis and Sarah his wife.

Court Record, Page 57—4 December, 1739: Adms. granted to Nathaniel Higley. Recog., £60, with Jonathan Loomis of Windsor.

Page 92 (Vol. XV) 7 March, 1748-9: Nathaniel Higley, Adms., exhibited an account of his Adms. Accepted. This Court order the estate distributed, viz., to Benoni Bissell, Nathaniel Higley, Josiah Higley, Isaac Higley, Sarah Loomis, Susannah Blackman, and to the heirs of Abigail Thorp their mother's part, to each of them £1-05-03. And appoint Job Loomis and Ephraim Loomis distributors.

Page 253-325.

Hill, John, Simsbury. Died 1st November, 1740. Invt. £1339-09-07. Taken 25 November, 1740, by Joseph Case, Joseph Case, Jr., and Michael Humphrey.

Court Record, Page 78—3 December, 1740: The widow, Sarah Hill, having been notified that Adms. would be granted, and not appearing, letters of Adms. were granted to John Hill and Ephraim Wilcockson of Simsbury. Recog., £600, with Jacob Read.

Page 86—7 April, 1741: Sarah Hill, the widow, asked this Court to set out her dower. And this Court appoint John Humphrey, James Case and David Holcomb to set out 1-3 part of the lands and buildings of sd. deceased.

Page 8 (Vol. XIV) 6 July, 1742: John Hill and Ephraim Wilcock, Adms., exhibit an account of their Adms. Accepted. Order to distribute as follows:

	£ s d
To Sarah Hill, the widow, her thirds,	71-06-02
To John Hill, eldest son, his double part,	47-10-08
To the heirs of Sarah Strickland,	23-15-05
To Mary Read, to Hannah Wilcock, and to Elizabeth Hoskins, to each of them the sum of,	23-15-05

And appoint James Case, Jonathan Case and Andrew Robe distributors.

Page 133-137-8.

Hinsdale, Isaac, Hartford. Invt. £1073-18-04. Taken 30 March, 1739, by Timothy Seymour, Joseph Skinner, Jr., and Jacob Kellogg. Will dated 6 April, 1733, with addition, 23 February, 1739.

I, Isaac Hinsdale of Hartford, do make this my last will and testament: I give to my wife Lydia Hinsdale (her dower rights). I give to my eldest son, Isaac Hinsdale, 1-2 of my homelott at the west division in Hartford, on the north side thereof, with the buildings thereon, forever. I give to my two sons, Joseph and Jonathan Hinsdale, the other half of my sd. homelott, lying on the south side thereof, and also my meadow land lying in Hartford, the South Meadow, containing 3 1-2 acres, to be equally divided between them. I give my interest or allottments of land in the western lands, so called, and also in the Five Miles of land on the east side of the Connecticut River in Hartford, to my three sons, Isaac, Joseph and Jonathan, to be equally divided between them, for them, their heirs and assigns forever. I give to my daughter Lydia Hinsdale to the value of £70 money out of my moveable estate. And it is my will that my three sons shall pay annually unto their mother, after my decease, for 2-3 of my homelott and meadow land as the same shall come under their respective improvement, after the rate of 3 shillings per acre for her more comfortable support than I have provided for in this my will. And she shall require it of them during the time she shall remain my widow. I appoint my wife Lydia and my son Isaac to be executors.

Witness: *Nathaniel White,*   ISAAC HINSDALE, LS.
Joseph Skinner, Daniel Richards.

In addition to this will, I, Isaac Hinsdale of Hartford, being at this time in perfect memory, under the consideration of my daughter Lydia's infirmity of body, do order each of my sons, Isaac Hinsdale, Joseph Hinsdale and Jonathan Hinsdale, to pay or cause to be paid to my daughter Lydia Hinsdale £1-13-04 apiece yearly during the time of her infirmity.

If the sd. Lydia shall change her conditions by marriage, then the addition to be of non-effect.

Witness: *Joseph Skinner,*   ISAAC HINSDALE, LS.
Daniel Kellogg, Timothy Merrells.

Court Record, Page 49—1st May, 1739: Will proven.

Page 127.

Hinsdale, Martha, Hartford.   Invt. £120-08-00.   Taken January, 1738-9, by John Skinner, Jun., and Thomas Seymour, Jr.

Court Record, Page 38—2 January, 1738-9: Adms. to Daniel Hinsdale. Recog., £100, with Obadiah Spencer.

Page 51—15 June, 1739: Account of Adms. on the estate of Martha Hinsdale, widow of Barnabas Hinsdale, was exhibited in this Court by Daniel Hinsdale, Adms.: Paid in debts and charges, £41-09-07; received 10 shillings. Which account is accepted and ordered on file. Sd. Adms. moved to this Court for a distribution of sd. estate. Invt. £120-15-06; subtracting £41-09-07, there remains £79-05-11 to be distributed, excepting 5 shillings 11 pence to be left in the Adms. hands *for further trouble.* Order: To Hannah and Mary Hinsdale, children of Barnabas Hinsdale, Jr., of Tolland, decd., £15-16-00, it being a double part or portion of sd. estate; to Martha Bull, £7-18-00; to Jacob Hinsdale, £7-18-00; to Sarah White, £7-18-00; to Elizabeth Benton, £7-18-00; to Mary Skinner, £7-18-00; to John Hinsdale, £7-18-00; to Daniel Hinsdale, £7-18-00; to Amos Hinsdale, £7-18-00. And appoint Thomas Seymour, Jr., and John Skinner, Jr., of Hartford, distributors.

Hodge, Catharine. Court Record, Page 51—15 June, 1739: Catharine Hodge, age 15 years, chose Giles Hall of Middletown to be her guardian. Recog., £200. *Cert: Jabez Hamlin, J. P.*

Page 51.

Holcomb, Jacob, Simsbury. Died 13 July, 1737. Invt. £78-07-05. Taken 14 October, 1737, by James Hillier, James Smith and John Willcoxson 2nd.

Court Record, Page 16—1st November, 1737: Adms. to Margaret Holcomb, widow. Recog., £200, with Joseph Wilcockson of Simsbury.

Page 35—7 November, 1738: Account of Adms. exhibited by Margaret Holcomb, widow and relict and Adms.: Paid in debts and charges, £10-17-03; received, 3 shillings. Which account is accepted and ordered on file. Invt. £78-07-05; subtracting £10-17-03, there remains £67-10-02 to be distributed. Order: To Margaret Holcomb, widow relict, £33-15-01; to Azariah Holcomb, £11-05 1-3d; to Damarus Ward, alias Holcomb, £11-05 1-3d; to Mary Holcomb, £11-05 1-3d. And appoint James Smith, Jr., Nathaniel Holcomb 3rd and Joshua Holcomb, of Simsbury, distributors.

Page 49.

Holcomb, Jonathan, Jr., Simsbury. Invt. £346-08-09. Taken by James Hillier, James Smith and John Wilcockson 2nd.

Court Record, Page 16—1st November, 1737: Adms. granted to Amey Holcomb, widow. Recog., £500, with Azariah Holcomb of Simsbury.

Page 94 (Vol. XV) 8 March, 1749: Jonathan Holcomb, a minor, 14 years of age, son of Jonathan, chose Mr. Joshua Boardman of Sheffield, in Hampshire County, to be his guardian. Recog., £1000.

Page 300.

Holcomb, Nathaniel, Simsbury. Invt. £100 plus. Taken 2 April, 1741, by Elias Slater and Jno. Owen, Jr. Will dated 7 February, 1740-1:

I, Nathaniel Holcomb, Sen., of Simsbury, do make this my last will and testament: Imprimis. To my wife, besides what I have already secured for her before marriage, I give her the sum of 20 shillings. Item. I give to my sons, Nathaniel, Jonathan, John and Benjamin, that lott of land of 150 acres that lyeth near the northwest corner of the Town bounds, to be equally divided between them. Also, to my sons, Nathaniel, Jonathan and John, I give the 1-2 of my propriety in Windsor of undivided land. To my son Nathaniel I also give my right and interest in the Copper Hill, the whole of it, and also that addition of land that was made to my lott at Raven Swamp. To Jonathan I give further 10 acres of land lying on Salmon Brook Plaine. To John I give 12 acres of land lying at Barn Door Hills. I give to my son Benjamin the other half of my right in Windsor undivided lands, the house and homestead I now dwell on, being about 3 acres, with the orcharding standing on it; also 14 acres of land at the head of Owen's Brook, as it was layd out, be it more or less; also the remainder of my home division lott that I am now possessed of; also 10 acres of land at a place called Slater's Swamp, bounded south in part on Elias Slater's land. Also, I give to Benjamin the 1-2 of my copper's (cooper's?) tools and my best gunn, and the other half to my sons Nathaniel, Jonathan and John. To my five daughters, Mary, Katharine, Hester, Sarah and Margaret, I give, after debts and legacies are paid out of them, the remainder of my moveable estate, to be divided equally amongst them. And to the son of my daughter Martha deceased I give 20 shillings, to be paid him by my sons Nathaniel, Jonathan and John, to buy him a Bible. To my daughter Mary I give her a cow in particular, to be taken out of my moveables before the division is made. And ordain my son Benjamin to be my sole executor.

Witness: *Elias Slater,*   NATHANIEL HOLCOMB, LS.
Ephraim Bewell, Timothy Woodbridge.

Court Record, Page 86—7 April, 1741: Will proven.

Invt. in Vol. XV, Page 414.

Holman, Katherine, Windsor. Invt. £76-09-06. Taken 30 June, 1740, by Samuel Strong, Jonathan Stiles and Samuel Stiles.

Court Record, Page 67—3 June, 1740: Adms. granted to Benjamin Roberts of Hartford, who recog. in £500, with Joseph Roberts.

Page 132 (Vol. XV) 5 June, 1750: An invt. of Katherine Holman's estate, widow of Samuel Holman, was now exhibited in Court by Benjamin Roberts, Adms. Accepted, ordered to be recorded and kept on file.

Will and Invt. in Vol. XIV, Page 56-7-8.

Hollister, John, Glastonbury. Died 31 December, 1741. Invt. £1182-17-00. Taken by Thomas Welles and Jonathan Hale. Will dated 25 November, 1741.

I, John Hollister of Glastonbury, do make and ordain this my last will and testament: I give to my son Benjamin Hollister 5 shillings. I give to my daughters Sarah Judd and Prudence Miller 5 shillings apiece. I give to my son Jeremiah Hollister and my daughter Abigail Loveland all the rest of the land of the lott whereon I now dwell, both meadow and upland, besides what I have formerly by deed of gift given to my son Abraham, he my sd. son and daughter Jeremiah and Abigail, with her husband Benjamin Loveland, to pay to my beloved wife Susannah £8 annually during the term of her natural life. And also I give to my sd. son Jeremiah and daughter Abigail my team horse and all my team tackling, viz., cart, plows, harrows, chains, traces, &c., and all my right in the undivided lands in the Town of Glastonbury. And also I give to my sd. son Jeremiah my oldest bay mare. I give to my daughter Sarah Judd all my rights in Wethersfield Commons belonging to me from my uncle Lazarus Hollister deceased. I give to my son Abraham Hollister, besides what I have already given him by deed of gift, the sum of 20 shillings, to be paid out of my moveable estate. I give to my daughter Abigail Loveland about 35 acres of land which I lately bought of Ephraim Goodrich, lying near Pail Brook so called. I give to my wife Susannah all the remaining part of what moveable estate she brought with her when I married her, besides what I have already disposed of, and also 1-3 part of all the rest of my moveable estate after my just debts and legacies are paid. I give to my sd. daughter Abigail Loveland the 2-3 of my moveable estate after my just debts and legacies are paid. I give to my daughter Martha Hubbard £10, to be paid out of my moveable estate. I appoint my son Jeremiah Hollister and my kinsman Josiah Hollister to be sole executors.

Witness: *Thomas Welles,*   JOHN HOLLISTER, LS.
Penelopy X Tryan, Thomas Treat.

Court Record, Page 106—5 January, 1741-2: Will proven. Jeremiah and Josiah Hollister, executors. Benjamin Hollister of Oblong, New York, and John Miller, of Glastonbury, appeal from the probate of the will to the Superior Court, and each recog. in £40 money.

Page 264-5.

Horsford, Capt. Obadiah, Hebron. Invt. £2589-09-07. Taken 16 March, 1741, by Hezekiah Gaylord, Jonathan White and William Buell. Will dated 14 September, 1737.

I, Obadiah Horsford of Hebron, in the County of Hartford, do make this my last will and testament: I give to my wife Mindwell £80, to be paid her out of my moveable estate, to be to her own dispose; also the use of 1-3 part of my dwelling house and barn; also the 1-3 part of all my improveable lands, my houselott, house, barn and lands, that is, 1-3 part thereof during her natural life or so long as she shall remain unmarried. I give to my four sons, Daniel, Joseph, Aaron and Obadiah, and to my two daughters, Ann and Mindwell, all the rest of my estate, both lands and moveables, in manner following, only my son Daniel shall have £50 more out of my estate than any of my three sons shall have; and to my two daughters I give to each of them the 1-2 so much as my sd. son

Daniel's portion shall amount unto; but what I have already paid out to my daughter Ann is to be reckoned as part of her portion. My will is that my son Daniel shall have the liberty of takeing his choice where he shall like best to settle, either at Burnt Hill or on my homelott or the land near adjoining, with that condition that he make his choice within three months after the date hereof. I appoint Mindwell, my sd. wife, and my son Daniel to be sole executors.

Witness: *Nathaniel Phelps,*   OBADIAH HORSFORD, LS.
John Taylor, Israel Dewey.

Court Record, Page 98—21 September, 1741: Will proven.

Page 311.

Hossington, Elizabeth, Farmington.   Invt. £33-01-03.   Taken 22 August, 1740, by Samuel Peck and Joseph Hopkins.

Court Record, Page 79—6 January, 1740-1: Adms. to John Hossington of Farmington. Recog., £100.

Hubbard, Martha, widow, late of Middletown.   Court Record, Page 94—7 July, 1741: Adms. to John Stow of Middletown. Recog., £500, with Joseph Savage of Middletown.

Page 80-81.

Hubbard, Nathaniel, Sen., Middletown.   Invt. £341-09-03.   Taken 2 June, 1738, by Solomon Adkins, Ephraim Adkins and Wm. Rockwell. Will dated 6 March, 1734-5.

I, Nathaniel Hubbard, Sen., of Middletown, in the County of Hartford, being sensible by my great age and weakness through it that my departure is at hand, do make and ordain this my last will and testament: I give to my son Nathaniel Hubbard what I have given him by deed of gift and £10 in money more, and 1-2 of my land on the west side the mountain, belonging to the lott my son Ebenezer liveth on. I give to my son John Hubbard what I have given him by deed of gift and £5 in money more, and the 1-2 of my land on the west side of the mountain, belonging to the lott my son Ebenezer liveth on. I give to my son Ebenezer Hubbard what I have given him by deed of gift and 10 shillings more. I give to my daughter Mary what I have given her by deed of gift and a share in the remainder of the homelott, so much as with the 1-2 acre already given her to make her part equal in value with her sisters' part in the homelott, except Sarah; and also a pewter platter which her mother designed for her. I give to my daughter Abigail £10-

15-00 in money, which is to make her equal with the rest of them, and an iron kettle and an old brass kettle which her mother designed for her. I give to my daughter Elizabeth £10-15 in money, which is to make her equal with Esther, and my feather bed and blankets. I give to my daughter Sarah 1-2 of an acre of land at the southeast corner of my homelott, to lye square, and my new brass kettle, and my iron pott, and a pewter platter, which her mother designed for her. I give to my daughter Thankfull £7-15-00 in money to make her equal with Esther, and my hetchell between her and her sister Hannah. I give to my daughter Hannah £7-15-00 in money to make her equal with Esther, and 1-2 of my hetchell and my chest. I give to my daughter Esther my warming pan. My will is that my debts, funeral charges and ye legacies above mentioned to be paid to my children be paid out of my household stuff not here disposed of, and out of my stock so far as they will go, and the rest to be made up out of my homelott. And what remains of my homelott and buildings upon it I give to my 7 daughters, to Abigail, Elizabeth, Sarah, Thankfull, Hannah and Esther equal parts in it, and to Mary such a part as with the half acre I have already given her to make her part equal in value with her sisters' parts except Sarah, who is to have the half acre above mentioned besides her equal part in the rest. I appoint my sons Nathaniel and John Hubbard executors.

Witness: *William Rockwell,*   NATHANIEL X HUBBARD, SEN., LS.
Benjamin Hand, Jr., Ebenezer Rockwell.

Court Record, Page 30—5 June, 1738: Will proven.

Page 53.

Hunn, David, Wethersfield. Died 8 September, 1737. Invt. £333-03-06. Taken 20 December, 1737, by Joseph Woodbridge, Peletiah Buck and Josiah Riley.

Court Record, Page 17—6 December, 1737: Adms. to William Smith of Farmington, who married one of the sisters of the decd. Samuel Hunn, Jr., eldest brother of sd. deceased, refused Adms. William Smith recog. in £200 with Samuel Hunn, Jr.

Page 19—3 January, 1737-8: Exhibit of inventory, which was ordered on file.

Page 20—18 January, 1737-8: Upon complaint of William Smith, administrator, Samuel Hunn and Gideon Hunn was by special writ brought before this Court to be examined upon oath for concealing divers goods of the deceased and bills, notes of hand, etc., from the Adms. And the sd. Gideon and Samuel Hunn before this Court plead that they are not held to answer to any interrogatories, etc., but ought to be dismist in that they have not been bound over to this Court by an Assistant or Justice, etc. This Court having considered the pleas of the parties: and that the rule and practice of this Court upon the law even this thirty years past, and as long as this Court can remember, hath been that the Court have generally made this the rule (and it is always supposed) that when the administrator chose it, etc., the circumstances were such as not to enhance the cost nor hazzard the estate being lost, that in such cases the parties complained of as offenders in concealing the estate of decd. intestates, etc., should be and have been from time to time immediately brought before this Court and obliged to answer. And this Court being of opinion that the law and reason of it in this and many cases will admit of, and that the cost will be less, the parties offending as well as the estate sooner secured, the case less circular, and all that the law intends as effectually answered: This Court do judge that the pleas made against the proceeding are insufficient, and order that the case proceed and the offenders answer. Samuel and Gideon Hunn appealed from this decree to the Superior Court. Recog., £50.

Page 38—5 December, 1738: Samuel and Gideon Hunn were, upon complaint of the Adms. to *John Hooker, justice of the peace,* bound with surety to appear before this Court to be examined as the law directs. The parties now appeared in Court and under oath were particularly examined respecting said goods or estate.

Page 41—6 February, 1739-40: Account now exhibited by William Smith, and allowed.

NOTE: *In some part of the Court record the name Sarah Hunn appears instead of Samuel Hunn.*

Page 333.

Hunn, Samuel, Wethersfield. Invt. £925-09-06. Taken 26 April, 1739, by Martin Kellogg and John Camp.

Court Record, Page 47—3 April, 1739: Adms. to Gideon Hunn. Recog., £500, with Jonathan Whaples of Wethersfield.

Page 18.

Huntington, John, Tolland. Invt. £1971-04-06. Taken 23 May, 1737, by Samuel Chapman, John Lathrop and Ebenezer Stiles.

Court Record, Page 9—7 June, 1737: Adms. to Thankfull Huntington, widow. Recog., £200, with Capt. Samuel Chapman of Tolland.

Page 32-33 (Vol. XIV) 16 November, 1742: John Huntington, age 18 years, and Samuel Huntington, age 15 years, sons of John Huntington, chose William Marsh of Plainfield to be their guardian. Recog., £200. Cert: *Timothy Peirce, Assistant.*

Page 57—2 April, 1745: Andrew Huntington, a minor, 15 years of age, and Abigail, 13 years, children of John Huntington, also chose Mr. William Marsh of Plainfield to be their guardian. Recog., £1000.

Page 46 (Vol. XV) 13 September, 1747: An account of Adms. was now exhibited by Mr. William Marsh and Thankful his wife. Accepted. They move this Court for a dist. of sd. estate, both real and personal, to be divided among the heirs of the deceased, viz., to Thankfull Marsh, alias Huntington, the relict of sd. deceased, 1-3 part of the moveable estate for her own, and 1-3 part of the real estate for her improvement during life; and to John Huntington, eldest son, a double share; and to Samuel, Andrew, Abigail and Deborah, to each of them their single shares of sd. estate. And appoint John Lothrop, Joshua Wills and Zebulon West distributors.

Dist.: Page 109 (Vol. XVI) 2 October, 1753: It was certified to this Court by *Zebulon West, J. P.,* that Deborah Huntington, a minor, 17 years of age, daughter to John Huntington, made choice of Mr. John Huntington of Tolland to be her guardian. Recog., £300.

Page 7.

Hurlbut, Daniel, Middletown. Invt. £384-11-00. Taken 15 December, 1736, by Joseph Starr, Jr., William Rockwell and Charles Hamlin.

Court Record, Page 10—7 June, 1737: Adms. granted to Esther Hurlbut, widow, who recog. with Charles Hamlin.

Page 15—4 October, 1737: Esther Hurlbut, Adms., exhibited an account of her Adms. Accepted. And the sd. Esther moves to this Court that her right of dowry may be set out to her. This Court appoint Joseph Southmayd, Lt. John Bacon and Jacob Cornwell to set out to the widow her right of dowry in sd. estate.

Page 18—13 December, 1737: This Court allow Esther Hurlbut and Jabez Hamlin to sell land to pay the debts.

Husket, Martha, Middletown. Court Record, Page 27—13 April, 1738: Martha Husket, a minor, 14 years of age, chose John Whitmore of Middletown to be her guardian. Recog., £50.

Hutchens, Edward. Court Record, Page 61—19 February, 1739-40: Edward Hutchens, a minor, 12 years of age, son of Henry Hutchens, late of Rhode Island decd., chose James Garrel (Garret?) of Hartford to be his guardian. Recog., £100.

Page 239-40.

Johnson, Mary, Sen., Middletown, widow of Isaac Johnson of Middletown decd. Invt. £120-06-02. Taken 18 August, 1740, by George Hubbard, Solomon Adkins and William Rockwell. Will dated 16 May, 1720.

I, Mary Johnson of Middletown, doe make this my last will and testament: Imprimis: I give to my three sons, namely, to my son Isaac,

Daniel and Joseph Johnson, and to the male heirs of my son Nathaniel Johnson decd., all my half of the household goods willed to me by my deceased husband, and all the stock and husbandry utensils which was left to my dispose, except some reservation of each which after followeth, that is to say, I give to my grandson Nathaniel Johnson my oxen and yoke, chains and plow, with the utensils thereunto belonging. Item. I give to my daughter Elizabeth Johnson, of my household goods, a Bible and belmettle morter, a great wheel and reel, fire shovel and tongs, and an iron trammel and lamps. I also give to my abovesd. daughter a colt and a year's provision for herself, and also a sound living sheep and a small iron kettle. Item. I give to my daughter Mary Blake my Dutch wheel. It is also concluded and intended that the abovesd. stock and moveables given to my three sons and grandson mentioned should be equally divided between them. I give my wearing clothes and linen to be equally divided between my daughters Elizabeth Johnson and Mary Blacke, and do constitute my three above mentioned sons to be executors.

Witness: *William Harris,*   MARY X JOHNSON, LS.
John Harris, William Harris, Jr.

Whereas, I, Mary Johnson, the above testator, did many years ago make and execute the above-written instrument to be my last will and testament: I do, this 21st day of February, Anno. Dom. 1739-40, ratify and confirm the same to be my last will and testament, with this addition or codicil: That whereas, my son Joseph Johnson is now deceased, I do hereby declare that what of my estate I have given to my son Joseph above named, my will is that the same shall be equally divided to and among the children that my sd. son had by his first wife. And I appoint my grandson Nathaniel Johnson executor with my two sons Daniel and Isaac Johnson.

Witness: *William Harris,*   MARY X JOHNSON.
John Harris, William Rockwell.

Court Record, Page 79—25 December, 1740: Will now exhibited by Daniel and Nathaniel Johnson, two of the executors; the third (Isaac Johnson) not able to appear, but accepts the trust. Will proven.

Page 174.

Johnson, Joseph, Middletown. Invt. £1911-10-08. Taken 13 December, 1739, by William Prout and William Rockwell.

Court Record, Page 57—4 December, 1739: Adms. to Joseph Johnson, son of the decd. Recog., £600, with Jabez Hamlin.

Page 77—10 December, 1740: Account exhibited by Joseph Johnson, Adms. Order to distribute as follows:

	£ s d
To the widow, Elizabeth Johnson,	141-10-07 1-2
To Joseph, eldest son,	66-03-01 1-2

To Richard, to Ebenezer, to Samuel, to Edward, to Oliver Johnson, to Elizabeth Harris, to Thankfull Hubbard, to Martha Gilbert, to each,

£33-01-09 3-4. By Solomon Adkins, William Rockwell and William Prout. Ebenezer Johnson, age 17 years, chose his mother Elizabeth Johnson to be his guardian. Recog., £500. Edward Johnson, a minor, chose Capt. Henry King of Middletown to be his guardian. Recog., £500. This Court appoint Elizabeth Johnson to be guardian to Oliver, Jemima and Mary Johnson, *all children of Joseph Johnson.* Recog., £500. Samuel Johnson, age 17 years, chose his brother Return Meggs of Middletown to be his guardian. Recog., £500. *Cert: Giles Hall, J. P.*

Page 204.

Jones, Daniel, Colchester. Invt. £1106-06-07. Taken 3 July, 1740, by Israel Newton, Isaac Jones and Daniel Worthington. Debts were collected from Daniel Daniels, David Graves, Nathaniel Gove, John Chapman, Jonathan Kilborn, John Skinner, Samuel Chapman and Tanstum Blustos.

Court Record, Page 72—2 September, 1740: Adms. to Mary Jones, widow. Recog., £1800, with Daniel Worthington of Colchester.

NOTE: *"This original inventory is transmitted to the Probate Office in Colchester by order."*

Page 83 (Vol. XV) 29 December, 1748: Account of Adms. was now exhibited by Capt. Benjamin Lothrop and Mary his wife, administrators: Paid in debts and charges, £595-02-01. The account allowed and ordered on file. Distribution ordered. Inventory of moveable estate, £1850-17-07; debts and charges subtracted, there remains £1255-15-06 to be distributed, as follows:

	£ s d
To Mary Jones, alias Lothrop,	418-11-10
To Amasa Jones, only son,	279-01-02
To Mary, Abigail, Ann and Elizabeth Jones, to each,	139-10-07

And that there be also distribution of real estate as follows: To Mary Jones, alias Lothrop, one-third of land and buildings during life, and to Amasa Jones his double share; to Mary, Abigail, Ann and Elizabeth Jones, to each their single share: To be set out by bounds. And appoint Messrs. James Treadway, James Jones and Israel Foot, distributors.

Inventoried in this estate was an old negro man, £40; a boy, £25; a young man, £150; a negro wench, £150. The three youngest daughters to have each a £20 right in the negro wench.

Page 262.

Joyner, Elizabeth, East Haddam. Invt. £34-15-00 personal estate, taken 15 April, 1741, by Jabez Rowley and Daniel Skinner.

Court Record, Page 93—1st July, 1741: Adms. granted on the estate of Elizabeth Joyner, who was Adms. on the estate of her husband

William Joyner, unto Samuel Fuller, Jr., of Colchester, who recog. in £70 with Ensign James Church of Hartford. Exhibit of an inventory. Accepted.

Page 10 (Vol. XV) 1st April, 1746: Samuel Fuller, Adms., exhibited an account: Paid in debts and charges, £20-16-03. Which account is by this Court allowed and ordered on file.

Page 28.

Judd, Ebenezer, Hartford. Whereas, our brother Ebenezer Judd of Hartford deceased leaving no heirs to inherit his estate, we, his surviving brothers and sisters, covenant and agree for the settlement thereof, viz.: Thomas Judd and Joseph Judd shall have their part in Hartford bounds, with the lott adjoining thereto lying in Farmingtown bounds; and that James Williams and Sarah his wife, and William Scott and Joanna his wife, and Joshua How with Elizabeth his wife, and Joseph Hull* with Abigail his wife, and Samuel Moss with Mary his wife, and Rachel Judd, for their parts, have all the outlands, divided or undivided, in Farmingtown bounds, with the right in Hartford that belongs to the estate of our deceased brother Ebenezer Judd, and shall peaceably and quietly enjoy and improve the same. And that this is our firm covenant and agreement, we who are here above named, Thomas Judd and Joseph Judd, do relinquish our right, title, interest or claims that we have or should have to the above named land in Farmingtown or Hartford, divided or undivided, unto the above named James Williams and Sarah his wife, William Scott and Joanna his wife, Joshua How and Elizabeth his wife, Joseph Hull and Abigail his wife, Samuel Moss and Mary his wife, and Rachel Judd, and that they shall injoy and improve the same peaceably to their own proper use and behoof without any molestation or trouble from us or our heirs or assigns forever. And we, the above named James Williams and others, do relinquish all our right, title, interest or claims that we have or should have unto the above named lands in Hartford bounds, with the lott in Farmingtown bounds adjoining thereto, unto the above named Thomas Judd and Joseph Judd, to them and their heirs forever. Whereunto we bind ourselves, our heirs, executors, etc., by these presents, whereunto we have set our hands and seals. Dated in Wallingford, 18 October, 1737.

THOMAS JUDD, LS.

JOSEPH JUDD, LS.	JAMES WILLIAMS, LS.
SARAH X WILLIAMS, LS.	WILLIAM SCOTT, LS.
JOANNA SCOTT, LS.	JOSHUA HOW, LS.
ELIZABETH HOW, LS.	JOSEPH HALL.
ABIGAIL HALL, LS.	SAMUEL MOSS, LS.
MARY MOSS, LS.	RACHEL JUDD, LS.

Witnesses: *Asahell Hall,*
Ephraim Rice, Thomas Clark,
Sarah Clark.

---

*Written Joseph Hull and signed Joseph Hall.

Wallingford, 21 Jan., 1737-8: Ap'rd. Samuel Moss and Mary his wife before Benj. Hall, J. P.

Wallingford, 23 Jan., 1737-8: Ap'rd. Joseph Hall and Abigail his wife before Benj. Hall, J. P.

Wallingford, 23 Jan., 1737-8: Ap'rd. Joshua How and Elizabeth his wife before Theophilus Yale, J. P.

Hartford, 9 Feb., 1737-8: Ap'rd. Thomas Judd and acknowledged this to be his free act and deed. Before Jos: Talcott, Clerk.

Exhibited in Court, 9 February, 1737-8. Accepted and ordered to be recorded. *Test: Jos: Talcott, Jr., Clerk.*

Page 138-9-40.

Judson, Mrs. Ann, Wethersfield. Invt. £219-13-10. Taken 19 April, 1739, by Benjamin Smith, Joseph Hurlbut and Isaac Riley. Will dated 12 January, 1738-9.

I, Ann Judson, widow and relict of Mr. James Judson of Stratford deceased, of Fairfield County, but now resident in Wethersfield, in Hartford County, do make this my last will and testament: I give to my son Samuel Steele of Wethersfield one silver cup of two handles, and one large case of bottles, one long table and one bellmetle mortar, one trammel, one paire of tongs, and a small guilded trunk. I give to my son Joseph Steele of Kensington, in Farmingtown, of Hartford County, one yoak of oxen and £7 in money already received, and I do acquit him of all demands due to me. I give to my son-in-law Josiah Deming and daughter Prudence Deming and their heirs, of Wethersfield, one silver tankard and one brass kettle already received, also one featherbed, the best sort, pillows and boulster, curtains, and one green rug, two sale white blanketts, one green graset suit of apparrell, one black calliminco frock, and two undercoats (one black silk and the other flowered brown silk), one green salone quilt, a lutstring, hood and scarf, a silk bonnet, a silk apron, 1 paire of green silk gloves, 5 paire of sheets, 4 paire of pillow beers, a Holland table cloth, 4 pewter platters (ye middling size), 4 plates, 2 basins with brim, one warming pan, one brass skillett, a paire of sad-irons, one iron pott, one peel, one trunk, one chest of drawers, one looking-glass, one round table, two chaires, one candle-stick, and one pillion and pillion cloth. I give to my son Ephraim Goodrich and daughter Hannah Goodrich of Glastonbury one featherbed, five blanketts, two paire of sheets, one iron kettle, one brass skillett, a brass pan, quart pott, one small bed and furniture, one small table and one joynt stool, the above already received. And I give to my daughter Hannah two paire of sheets, two pillow beers, one silk creep caliminco frock, a flowered undercoat, black damask, two pewter platters, one iron skillett, a trundel bedstead and featherbed, one boulster and two pillows, two blanketts and two chairs, one looking-glass with a block frame, and one trunk. I give to my son David Steele of Wethersfield a certain tract of land that was my uncle Lazarus Hollister's of Wethersfield, that fell to me by division of his estate, namely, his homestead of land in Wethersfield; also £3 money received to pay a debt that he owed to Bazaleel Lattimore of Wethersfield. Furthermore, I leave in the hands of my son Josiah Deming and Prudence Deming my daughter, for the defraying the necessary charges of my sickness and trouble that they have been att for me, a large trunk, large brass pan, three brass kettles, two large pewter platters, some more pewter if need be, and, further, anything that is not mentioned, to be equally divided between my two daughters, Prudence Deming and Hannah Goodrich.

Witness: *John Deming,*   ANN X JUDSON, LS.
Joseph Hurlbut, Jedediah Deming.

Court Record, Page 49—1st May, 1739: Will exhibited by Josiah Deming and Samuel Steele, who were appointed Adms. with the will annexed.

Page 57—4 December, 1739: Account exhibited and accepted.

Page 260-1.   Invt. on Page 314-15.

Kilbourn, George, Wethersfield.   Invt. £1604-00-04.   Taken 31 March, 1741, by Nathaniel Stilman, William Manly and Joseph Flower. Will dated 5 April, 1739.

I, George Kilbourn of Wethersfield, think it my duty to settle my temporal estate. My will is as followeth: I give to my son Hezekiah Kilbourn £100 money toward the payment of a certain debt due from him to one Peter Schuyler of New York, and to no other use or intent, which sum, with what he hath already received, shall be the whole of his portion. I give to my son Peletiah Kilbourn 2 acres of land exactly, and to be set out to him at the west end of my pasture in Hartford bounds, near Penny Wise, by line directly crossing sd. pasture, and that to be the whole of his portion. I give to my daughter Abigail the 1-2 of my homelott, lying on the south side thereof. Also I give to sd. Abigail my houseing and edifices, well, and their appurtenances, standing on sd. lott (excepting the barn only), also all my stock of creatures, household goods, and all other my personal or moveable estate of what name, nature or denomination soever it may be. Also I give to sd. Abigail the use of the northern half of sd. homelott and the barn until my grandson Hezekiah Kilbourn shall arrive to the age of 21 years, but not longer without his consent. I give to my grandson Hezekiah Kilbourn the northern half of my home-lott and my barn, with liberty to enter and possess and move off sd. barn, upon his arrival at the age of 21 years, and not before. Furthermore my will is, and I do hereby order, that my land at a place called Poke Hill, viz., ye orchard and that part of my pasture there not given to my son Peletiah, shall be in the hands and at ye disposal (in way of sale) of my executors hereafter named, for the payment of all my just debts, funeral expenses and charges of executing this my last will, and also for a stock or fund for the payment of sd. £100 due to sd. Schuyler as aforesd. And further, whatsoever surplusage there be after sd. payments are made by my executors shall remain in their hands, and they shall deliver the same to my grandchildren, Keturah Kilbourn and George Kilbourn, in equal proportion, upon the sd. George Kilbourn coming to the age of 21 years. And I appoint Jacob Goodrich and my daughter Abigail Kilbourn executors.

Witness: *Daniel Williams,*   GEORGE KILBOURN, LS.
Nathaniel Burnham, Mehetabell Burnham.

Court Record, Page 83—3 March, 1740-1: Will proven. Abigail Kilbourn executrix, Jacob Goodrich refused.

Kilbourn, John. Court Record, Page 89—26 May, 1741: John Kilbourn, age 15 years, son of John Kilbourn of Whippenny, decd., on 29 December, 1740, chose Josiah Kilbourn of Glastonbury to be his guardian. Recog., £300.

Will in Vol. XIV, Page 55-6.

Kilbourn, John, Hartford. Will dated 7 December, 1741: I, John Kilbourn of Hartford, do make this my last will and testament: My will is that my just debts and funeral expenses be well and truly paid and discharged by my executor hereafter mentioned. My will is that my executor take care and provide all things necessary for my wife during her life. I give unto my daughter Mary Kilbourn £40 in current money. I give unto my daughter Sarah Kilbourn £40 in current money. I give to my daughter Susannah Kilbourn the sum of £50 in current money, to be paid to each of them at the age of 18 years. I give and confirm all the remaining of my estate, both real and personal, unto my son John Kilbourn, to be his own forever, at his own dispose. And I appoint my sd. son John Kilbourn to be my executor.

Witness: *John Hills,*   JOHN KILBOURN, LS.
Samuel Roberts, Jonathan Hills.

Page 108—2 February, 1741-2: Will of John Kilbourn now exhibited by John Kilbourn, executor.

Page 64 (Vol. XIV) 20 September, 1745: Sarah Kilbourn, daughter of John Kilbourn, made choice of Capt. Jonathan Hill to be her guardian. Recog., £500.

Page 21 (Vol. XVII) 2 April, 1754: Simon Strickland, in behalf of ——— Kilbourn, the relict of John Kilbourn, late of Hartford deceased, now moves to this Court that the relict's dowry be set out to her as the law directs: Whereupon this Court appoints William Wells and Josiah Benton, of Glastonbury, and David Porter, of Hartford, to set out by bounds 1-3 part of the buildings and lands for the widow's improvement during life, and make return thereof to this Court.

Page 293.

King, Deacon Hezekiah, of Dutchess County, New York, and estate in Sharon, Conn., £703-03-08. Inventory taken 19 December, 1740, by Jabez Cripen and James Smith, appointed and chosen by Samuel King, son of sd. deceased and executor. Estate in Tolland, Bolton, and at Hockanum, £231-17-06. Taken 19 November, 1740, by Nathaniel Allis and Benjamin Talcott, being appointed and chosen by Samuel King, son of sd. deceased, male executor of his last will. Will dated 8 October, 1740.

I, Hezekiah King, of Dutchess County, in the Province of New York: I will that my wife Sarah, with my son Samuel, with the help and assistance of Capt. Jonathan Dunham of Sharon, shall be executors. I give to my wife Sarah all my household goods, a yoke of oxen and three cows forever; also the improvement of my land in Bolton. To my eldest son Hezekiah I have already given by deed of gift. I give to my son Samuel the half of a six schore acre lott in Sharon, which is my home lot, to take his choice in it, the other half my executors to sell for the payment of £4 to my eldest daughter Sarah, to Esther £13, to Mary £20, and to Bathsheba £20, these sums to be the remaining portions of my estate to each of sd. daughters added to what they have already received. The remainder of the money sd. land shall be sold for to be for the payment of my debts. I give to my two youngest sons, William and John, my land in Bolton after their mother's decease, they to pay to their youngest sisters, Mary and Alice, £20 apiece. All notes of hand due to me I order my executors to make use of for the payment of my debts. And as to the place I now live upon, I give my wife the improvement of it so long as she is pleased to live upon it, and my interest shall hold good. If she move, then my interest to Samuel. My right of land in Sharon not already laid out I order my executors to dispose of for the payment of my obligations to the Country. I give all the overplus to my wife and my son Samuel, only I oblige them to reward Capt. Dunham for his service and help.

Witness: *Samuel Chapman,*   HEZEKIAH KING, LS.
Joseph Parke, Alexander Spencer.

Court Record, Page 102—1 December, 1741: Will of Hezekiah King, of Dutchess County, New York, late of Bolton and Hartford, proven.

Page 12.

Lamb, Samuel, Glastonbury. Invt. £59-02-00. Taken 9 March, 1736-7, by Josiah Hollister and Thomas Treat.

Court Record, Page 11—13 June, 1737: Adms. to Mercy Lamb, widow. Recog., £100, with Josiah Hollister.

Page 15—6 September, 1737: Account of Adms. on the estate of Samuel Lamb, late of Glastonbury decd., exhibited in Court by Mercy Lamb, Adms.: Paid in debts and charges, £5-01-03. Which accott. is accepted and ordered on file.

Launcelet, Samuel. Court Record, Page 108—26 January, 1741-2: Samuel Launcelet, 17 years of age, son of Samuel Launcelet, a transient person, chose Isaac Hubbard of Windsor to be his guardian. Recog., £300.

Page 223-224.

Lee, Sargt. Thomas, Farmington. Invt. £943-09-09. Taken 28 October, 1740, by Isaac Cowles, John Hart and Joseph Judd.

Court Record, Page 76—2 December, 1740: Adms. granted to Jared Lee, who recog. in £500 with Joseph Lee.

Page 106—5 January, 1741-2: Ebenezer Lee, a minor, age 14 years, son of Sergt. Thomas Lee, chose his brother Joseph Lee to be his guardian. Recog., £200. Cert: *John Hooker, J. P.*

Page 56 (Vol. XIV) 2 April, 1745: Jared Lee, Adms., exhibits an account of his Adms. Accepted.

Dist. File: 1st April, 1746: Distribution as followeth:

	£ s d		£ s d
To the widow,	58-13-06	To Joseph Lee,	156-11-00
To Lydia Norton,	64-02-06	To John Lee,	156-11-00
To Ebenezer Lee,	156-11-00	To Thomas Lee,	156-19-00
To Jared Lee,	30-00-00	To James Lee,	156-11-00

April the 1st, 1746: We, the subscribers, do mutually agree that the foregoing writing shall be a final distribution of the estate of our honrd. father Thomas Lee, late of Farmington deceased, and have hereunto set our hands and seals in Hartford before the Court of Probate; and that we are fully satisfied and contented for our part with what is in this agreement set out to us, and doe discharge all other demands on sd. estate.

JARED LEE, LS.   THOMAS LEE, LS.
JOSEPH LEE, LS.   EBENEZER LEE, LS.
JOHN LEE, LS.

Page 62—14 August, 1745: At a Court of Probate holden at Hartford, for the District of Hartford, on the 22nd day of January, A. D. 1760: Present, Joseph Buckingham, Esq., Judge; J. Talcott, Clerk: Jared Lee, Esq., Adms. on the estate of Mr. Thomas Lee of Farmington deceased, having finished his account of Adms. on sd. estate, and sd. estate has since been settled by an agreement under hand and seal of the heirs of sd. estate: Whereupon this Court grant to the sd. Adms. a *Quietus Est.*

Page 155-6-7.

Lewis, Rev. Judah, Colchester. Invt. £1300 in real estate, taken by Jonathan Dunham and Stephen Brainard. Will dated 31 March, 1739.

I, Judah Lewis of Colchester, in the County of Hartford, do make this my last will and testament: I give to my wife Mercy 1-3 part of my moveable estate and make her my sole executrix, and give her £150 more of my moveable estate to bring up my children with. And also I give unto my wife Mercy the use of all my real estate until my son Ephraim comes to the age of 14 years, capable to choose a guardian. And also my wife to have the use of which room in my house she pleases so long as she remains my widow. Nextly, my will is that my daughter Sarah have all the things that was her mother's apprised to her, and also that she have so much more paid to her out of my estate as to make up that £200. And also I give her a fine satin blanket which was bought for her, which I order not to be apprised, and £5 money to buy her a mourning suit withall. Nextly, I give unto my two sons Ephraim and Judah all my real estate whatsoever, to be divided in this manner: Ephraim to have £200 more than Judah, as shall be apprised by indifferent men. Nextly, I give to my daughter Lydia £200; and if there be not enough of the moveable estate left to pay it, then it shall be made up out of my two sons' estate in equal porportion, to be paid her at 18 years of age or when married, which shall happen first. I appoint my wife Mercy sole executrix.

Witness: *Nathaniel Foote,*   JUDAH LEWIS, LS.
Benjamin Lewis, Jonathan Dunham.

Court Record, Page 52—3 July, 1739: Will proven. This Court appoint Nathaniel Kellogg, Jr., to be guardian unto Sarah Lewis, a minor, 9 years of age, daughter of Judah Lewis deceased. Recog., £300.

Page 332 (Probate Side) March the 28th, 1748: Then received of Mrs. Mercy Biggelow, executrix to the estate of my honoured father Judah Lewis, late of Colchester deceased, all the things that were my mother's (Sarah Lewis decd.) which my honoured father gave me in his last will, which amounted to £75-11-00. I also received £124-09-00 in bills of the old tenor, it being in full £200 with the things that I received, it being the full of my portion that my honoured father gave me by his will, as may appear by sd. will. I say received pr me.

Witness: *John Hopson,*   SARAH LEWIS.
Aaron Kellogg.

Court Record, Page 152 (Vol. XVII) 31 May, 1757: Mr. Ephraim Lewis, one of the sons of the Rev. Judah Lewis, now moves to this Court that the real estate of the sd. deceased given him the sd. Ephraim and his brother Judah Lewis by the last will and testament of the deceased, may be set out to them according to sd. will: Whereupon this Court appoint Israel Foot and David Day, of Colchester, and Daniel Horsford, of Hebron, to make a division of the real estate and make return thereof to this Court.

Page 153—10 June, 1757: Report of the distributors. Accepted.

Page 112 (Vol. XVIII): Colchester, April the 18th, 1761: Then received of David and Mercy Biggelow, executrix, the full of our demands as heirs of the estate of Mr. Judah Lewis deceased exhibited in Court of Probates. We say received per us: JOSEPH CROCKER, EPHRAIM LEWIS,
Witness: *Aaron Kellogg.*   SARAH CROCKER, JUDAH LEWIS.

Page 217-18.

Loomis, Sergt. Daniel, Windsor. Inventory taken 10 July, 1740, by Jacob Drake, Aaron Loomis and Timothy Loomis. Will dated 26 February, 1731-2.

I, Daniel Loomis of Windsor, do make this my last will and testament: I give to Hannah my wife my best bedd and such sheets, blankets and other furniture thereunto belonging or is needful as she shall choose. I also give her a brass kettle that we have of Jonathan Loomis. I further give her a red heifer as her own estate. Also I give unto her the use of my dwelling house and so much of the barn as she shall stand in need of, and suitable land about each for convenience of gardening and other necessary occasions. And also the use of so many of the household goods and utensils thereof as are needful in order to her keeping house, and also the use of about 13 1-2 acres of land I had partly of David Porter and partly of Robert Westland. And the sd. use and improvement of sd. building and household goods, &c., she is to have freely during her natural life. I give unto my four sons, Daniel, Job, John and Isaac, and to their heirs forever, about 13 1-2 acres of land which I purchased partly of David Porter and partly of Robert Westland, to be divided among them in equal parts, reserving the use thereof to my wife as aforesd. I give to my son Josiah all my part and share of the western lands, sometimes called New Bantums, which was by Assembly granted to Hartford and Windsor. I give unto my 7 sons, Daniel, Josiah, Job, John, Isaac, Abraham and Benjamin, all my share or right in the commons or proprietors' land being in the Township of Windsor, and also my right or share in the land called equivalent land, lying between Windsor, Enfield, Tolland, Bolton and Willimantic River, to be divided among them in equal share both for quantity and quality. I give unto my daughter Mary Barbour £5, to be paid unto her out of my moveable estate at inventory prices. All the residue of my estate, if any there be, I give to all my forementioned children in equal shares. I appoint my sons Daniel Loomis and Job Loomis to be the only executors.

Witness: *Matthew Allyn,*   DANIEL LOOMIS, LS.
Henry Allyn, Timothy Loomis.

Court Record, Page 71—5 August, 1740: Will proven.

Page 136-7.

Loomis, Gershom, Windsor. Invt. £990-04-10. Taken 16 February, 1738-9, by Hezekiah Porter, Joseph Loomis, Jr., and Timothy Loomis.

Court Record, Page 47—3 April, 1739: Adms. to Mary Loomis, widow. Recog., £500, with David Bissell.

Page 163-4.

Loomis, Joseph, Windsor. Invt. £38-12-00. Taken 5 October, 1739, by Hezekiah Porter and William Wolcott. Will dated 17 January, 1733.

I, Joseph Loomis of Windsor, being advanced to a great age, do make my last will and testament: I give to my wife Abigail what I have obliged myself to give her by joynture made to her on our marriage, which was £20, and also that piece of land which we bought of the heirs of Daniel Birge, to be at her own dispose. I give to my son Joseph Loomis one acre of swamp land lying the whole breadth of my lott next west to the land which he bought of me. I give to my son Enoch Loomis my division of land laid out in ye outer commons, known by the name of the mile and half-mile, also my right in Tolland. My will is that my debts and funeral charges be paid out of my moveable estate and that part of my land which I do in this my will give to my son Isaac Loomis. I give to my son Isaac Loomis all my meadow land which I have not disposed of already, and also 1-4 of my right in land known by the name of the equivalent land, and also 1-2 of my right in Windsor Proprietors' undivided land. Further, I give to my son Joseph Loomis 1-4 of my right known by the name of the equivalent lands or land, and also 1-2 of my right in Windsor Proprietors' undivided land. Further, it is my will that my six children that I had by my former wife, viz., Joseph Loomis, Enoch Loomis, Lydia Hinsdale, Martha Bissell, Rachel Lombard and Phebe Munsell, shall have 1-2 of my right to the land known by the name of the equivalent land in recompense for the land I sold to Daniel Loomis. Further, I give to my daughter Lydia Hinsdale £13. Further, I give to my daughter Martha Bissell £12-06. Further, I give to my daughter Rachel Lombard £15. Further, I give to my daughter Phebe Munsell £13-03-00. Further, I give to my daughter Abigail Loomis £20. Further, it is my will that if any or so many of my children as shall endeavor to disturb Daniel Loomis about the land I sold him, they shall have of the estate but 5 shillings apiece. I appoint my son Isaac Loomis to be executor.

Witness: *William Wolcott,*   JOSEPH X LOOMIS, LS.
Simon Wolcott, Joseph Newbery, Jun.

Court Record, Page 59—11 January, 1739-40: Will proven.

Inventory on File.

Loomis, Timothy, Windsor. Inventory taken 1740, by Nathaniel Drake, John Cooke and Henry Allyn.

Court Record, Page 71—5 August, 1740: Adms. granted to Hannah Loomis, widow, who recog. in £800 with Timothy Phelps of sd. Windsor.

See page before the index to Vol. XIV for the following item:

I, Timothy Loomis of Windsor, in Hartford County, and Esther Loomis of Hartford, in sd. County, heirs to the estate of Timothy Loomis,

late of Windsor, hath received of our honoured mother Hannah Burnham of Hartford, Adms. to the sd. estate, our full proportionable part of
all the real and personal estate that did belong to us as heirs to sd. estate,
to the sum of £1075-01-08 at inventory price, for which we do fully acquit
and discharge our honoured mother Hannah Burnham aforesd., Adms.
on sd. estate, from all demands on sd. estate whatsoever. As witness our
hands this 4th day of April, Anno. Dom. 1755.　　　TIMOTHY LOOMIS,
　　　　　　　　　　　　　　　　　　　　　　ESTHER LOOMIS.

Page 207-8.

Lord, Nathaniel, East Haddam. Died 12 June, 1740. Invt. £355-18-
03. Taken 14 July, 1740, by Henry Chapman, Joseph Gates and Bezaleel
Brainard.
　　Court Record, Page 73—2 September, 1740: Adms. to Hannah Lord,
widow. Recog., £500, with Samuel Emmons.
　　The inventory includes 50 acres of land at £5 per acre, £250.

Page 242-3.

Lord, Richard, Wethersfield. Invt. £3592-14-08. Taken 24 December, 1740, by Eleazer Goodrich, Benjamin Stilman and Noadiah Dickinson. Will dated 19 July, 1740.
　　I, Richard Lord of Wethersfield, do make this my last will and testament: I give to my wife Ruth Lord all my moveable estate which properly
belongs within my dwelling house, viz., all my household stuff and
utensils and implements used in housekeeping, to be her own forever.
And I give her also the use of 1-3 part of all my real estate during her
natural life. I give my four children, Richard Lord, George Lord, Ruth
Lord and Mary Lord, all the remainder of my estate, real and personal
(under the proviso hereafter mentioned), to be divided among them after
the following manner, that is to say, that Richard Lord shall have the
sum of £800 of my estate, and George £600. Ruth Lord and Mary Lord
shall have each of them the sum of £400 of my estate, or in that proportion to each of them, as my estate shall arrive, be it more or less, at inventory price, to be distributed so as may least break up my land into
pieces and best accommodate my children. I do also further provide that
my executrix hereafter named shall have full power to sell so much of
my land as shall be sufficient to pay my just debts, after my moveable
estate is disposed of, so far as my executrix shall think best. And I do
herein fully impower her so to do. And further, my will is that the use
and improvement of my sons' part of my estate shall be for the support
of my family until they shall be put out to some trade as apprentices, and
the use of my daughters' portion for the same use until they shall come
to the age of 18 years. I appoint my wife Ruth Lord to be my executrix.
Witness: *Joseph Pitkin,*　　　　　　　　RICHARD LORD, LS.
Timothy Wright, John Stilman, Jr.

Court Record, Page 77—10 December, 1740: Will proven.
Page 14 (Vol. XVII) 5 March, 1754: Mrs. Ruth Lord, alias Belding, the relict of Mr. Richard Lord deceased, and executrix to the last will and testament, now exhibited an account of sundry debts and charges due from the estate, amounting to the sum of £639-01-01. Account accepted. Also, the sd. executrix now moves that distribution be made according to the last will of her deceased husband: Whereupon this Court appoint Elizur Goodrich, Hezekiah May and John Stilman distributors.

Dist. File: 5 March, 1754: To the widow Ruth Lord (now Belding), to George Lord and to Mary Lord, children of the deceased. By Elizur Goodrich, Hezekiah May and John Stilman, distributors.

Page 31—22 April, 1754: Report of the distribution according to the last will of the deceased.

Page 57—6 March, 1755: Report of the distribution of part of the real estate of the deceased. Accepted.

Page 111.

Lothrop, Solomon, Tolland. Will dated 15 February, 1737-8: I, Solomon Lothrop of Tolland, in the County of Hartford, do make this my last will and testament: After my just debts and funeral charges are paid out of my personal or moveable estate, I give the remainder unto my wife Susannah to be to her only use and dispose forever. I give to my daughter Mercy £100. Should my wife bear me a son, my will is that my sd. son yet to be born should have all my real estate, houseing and lands, buildings, orchards, &c. And I do order that he pay unto my daughter Mercy, before mentioned, £100 money or bills of public credit, one year after my sd. son shall arrive to the age of 21 years. But if my wife bear me a daughter, then my will is that all my real estate as aforesd. be equally divided between my two daughters. And also my will is that my wife have all the use and improvement of my real etsate, as well buildings as lands, to and for herself for the maintenance of my child or children until my son (if God bless me with one) shall arrive to the age of 21 years. I do hereby appoint my wife Susannah sole executrix.
Witness: *Stephen Steele,*   SOLOMON LOTHROP, LS.
Thomas Barnard, Ichabod Lothrop.

Court Record, Page 91 (Vol. XV) 22 February, 1748-9: Joseph Lothrop, a minor son of Solomon Lothrop, late of Bolton decd., chose his father-in-law Matthew Loomis of Bolton to be his guardian. Recog., £1000.

Mathews, William. Court Record, Page 30—5 June, 1738: William Mathews, a minor, 17 years of age, of Wethersfield, chose John Reinolds of Wethersfield to be his guardian. Recog., £50.

Page 148-9.

Meakins, Lt. John, Hartford. Died 28 August, 1739. Invt. £595-18-02. Taken 27 November, 1739, by Nehemiah Olmsted, John Pitkin and Stephen Olmsted. Will dated 18 August, 1739.

I, John Meakins of Hartford, do make this my last will and testament: I give unto my four sisters £20 apiece, namely, Mary Belding, Sarah Spencer, Rebeckah Holeburd and Hannah Arnold, to be paid to them by my executor out of my moveable estate; and also to pay unto my sisters aforesd. £10 apiece which I am indebted unto them for their part of the negro man called Sharper. I give to my brother Joseph Meakins's daughters £10 apiece in moveables, namely, to Mary and Sarah Meakins, Hannah Olmsted, Abigail and Rebeckah Meakins. I give to my cousins Mary and Sarah Meakins a small piece of meadow land commonly called Ensign's lott, to be equally divided between them. If my moveable estate shall fall short of paying all my just debts and legacies herein given, my will is that my cousin Joseph Meakins shall pay the rest within one year after that he comes of age. I give to my cousin Joseph Meakins (my brother Joseph Meakins's son) all the rest of my estate, houseing, lands and moveables, and especially my negro man Sharper, to be servant unto my cousin Joseph Meakins until the sd. Sharper is 45 years of age, and no longer: at that time the sd. Sharper to be free. I appoint Mr. William Pitkin executor.

Witness: *Roger Pitkin,*   JOHN MEAKINS, LS.
Ozias Pitkin, William Bidwell.

Court Record, Page 56—2 October, 1739: Will proven.

Page 180-1.

Merrells, Noah, New Hartford. Invt. £177-13-04. Taken 25 July, 1739, by Martin Smith and Joseph Merrells.

Court Record, Page 53—7 August, 1739: Adms. granted to Esther Merrells, widow, who recog. in £300 with Isaac Merrells of Hartford.

Page 110 (Vol. XV) 14 November, 1749: Joseph Merrells, age 18 years, Mehetabell 15 years, and Esther 19 years of age, children of Noah Merrells of New Hartford deceased, chose Matthew Gillett of sd. New Hartford to be their guardian. Recog., £500 for each minor.

Page 59 (Vol. XVII) 1st April, 1755: Ichabod Merrill of New Hartford, guardian to Noah Merrells, son of Noah Merrells, showing to this Court that there are several pieces of land that lie in common or joynt tenancy between sd. minor and the rest of the heirs to sd. estate, and desires sd. land may be distributed according to a law impowering freeholders to assist guardians in dividing such lands: Whereupon this Court appoint Capt. Matthew Gillett, Israel Loomis and Eleazer Goodwin to assist sd. guardian in dividing sd. lands, and make return to this Court.

Page 167-8-328-331.

Merrells, Samuel, Hartford. Invt. £1020-14-02. Taken 21 November, 1739, by Joseph Cooke, James Church and Thomas Sanford.

Court Record, Page 58—1st January, 1739-40: Invt. exhibited by Gideon Merrells, Adms.

Page 17 (Vol. XIV) 7 February, 1742-3: Gideon Merrells, Adms., exhibited an account of his Adms. Accepted.

Page 18—11 April, 1743: Gideon Merrells having exhibited an account of his Adms. to the acceptance of this Court, now moves that distributors may be appointed by this Court to divide the real estate of the sd. deceased that lyes within the bounds of the Township of New Hartford, the half part thereof to Gideon Merrells and the other half part to Hannah Merrells alias Hannah Butler, the wife of Daniel Butler of Hartford aforesd., they being sole heirs to the estate of the deceased. This Court do appoint David Ensign and Isaac Kellogg of Hartford distributors.

Page 40—6 March, 1743-4. An addition to the invt. of the estate of Samuel Merrells was now exhibited by Gideon Merrells. Also, he exhibited a further account of his Adms. Also, report of the distributors. Allowed.

Page 142.

Micks, Elisha, Wethersfield. Invt. £4704-01-07. Taken 31 August, 1739, by Nathaniel Burnham, Thomas Goodwin and Josiah Griswold. Will dated 18 May, 1737.

I, Elisha Micks of Wethersfield, do make this my last will and testament: Imprimis. I give £20, or what shall be sufficient to procure a decent tombstone for the grave of my honoured father, to be disposed of by my executor for that purpose. I give to my four sisters now living in the house with me all my lands in Wethersfield, except three acres, which I give to my sister Belding; also 1-5 of all my books, except my physickall books, which I give to my cousin John Goodrich. I give to my sister Goodrich all my father's wearing apparell and my own, with all my deer's leather and £20 money (this last upon condition that she maintains and take care of my negro maid Betty), and my old bay mare, to be to her, her heirs and assigns forever. I give to my sister Rebeckah all my drugs and a silver cup which fell to my lot of the things which came from Northampton. I appoint Mr. Thomas Curtis, Mr. Hezekiah May and my sister Goodrich executors.

Witness: *John Deming,*   ELISHA MICKS, LS.
Jonathan Goodrich, Elizabeth Goodrich.

Court Record, Page 53—7 August, 1739: Will now exhibited by Thomas Curtis and Sarah Goodrich, executors.

Page 55—13 September, 1739: Invt. exhibited by Sarah Goodrich.
Page 32 (Vol. XV) 3 February, 1746-7: Mr. Hezekiah May of Wethersfield, one of the executors to the last will and testament of sd. deceased, now moves this Court to make a division of one certain piece of land in Middletown, according to the will of the sd. deceased, viz., to the heirs of Mary Belding 3-8 part of sd. lott, excepting 3 roods of the low land, and the rest of the sd. lott to be divided to all his sisters and to all the heirs of the sd. Mary Belding: Whereupon this Court appoint Return Meigs, William Rockwell and Lt. Jacob Whitmore, of Middletown, distributors.

Micks, Rev. Stephen. Court Record, Page 39—23 January, 1738-9: Whereas, Rev. Stephen Micks of Wethersfield decd., by an instrument under his hands and seal, did convey all his estate to his son Elisha Micks, sd. instrument bearing date 12 August, 1738, and there being no provision made whereby the debts due the estate can be recovered, or for the creditors to receive their dues from the estate: This Court grant administration to Elisha Micks of Wethersfield, who gave bond, etc.

Page 34-5.

Miller, Nathaniel, Middletown. Invt. £656-06-07. Taken 24 December, 1736, by Benjamin Adkins, Joseph Miller and William Rockwell.

Court Record, Page 1—10 December, 1736: This Court appoint Elizabeth Miller to be guardian to Elizabeth Miller, a minor, 9 months of age. Recog., £100.

Page 24—7 March, 1736-7: Elizabeth Miller, Adms., exhibited an account of her Adms. Accepted.

Page 7 (Vol. XIV) 1st June, 1742: This Court appoint Elijah Miller to be guardian to Elizabeth Miller, a minor, now 7 years of age, daughter of Nathaniel Miller, late of sd. Middletown deceased. Recog., £100.

Page 8—6 July, 1742: Caleb Hubbard of Middletown, Adms. in right of his wife Elizabeth Miller (alias Hubbard) on Nathaniel Miller his estate, showing to this Court that his sd. wife is also deceased, and that there has been an account of Adms. rendered to this Court and accepted, and that his sd. wife now deceased hath not had her part of the moveable estate distributed to her: Whereupon this Court do appoint and impower William Rockwell, Benjamin Adkins and Joseph Miller, of Middletown, to distribute and divide the moveable estate to the sd. Nathaniel Miller in the proportion hereafter set forth. Paid in debts and charges, £72-06-00; invt. of the moveable estate, £217-11-05; debts and charges subtracted, £72-06-00; there then remains to be distributed the sum of £145-06-00. This Court order 1-3 part thereof to be distributed to Caleb Hubbard in right of his wife Elizabeth, and 2-3 thereof to Elizabeth Miller, the only child.

Page 2—23 September, 1742: Report of the distributors.

Page 82, 152-3.

Miller, Samuel, Middletown. Invt. £1068-05-00. Taken 18 May, 1738, by Solomon Adkins, Hezekiah Sumner and William Rockwell. Will dated 8 March, 1737-8.

I, Samuel Miller of Middletown, in the County of Hartford, do make this my last will and testament: I give unto Marcy my wife the use of 1-3 part of my buildings and of my improved land during the time she shall remain my widow; 1-3 part of my household goods and stock to be at her dispose forever. I give to my son Samuel my buildings and homelott and all my lands at Pegowset. I give to my son Nathan all that piece of land I bought of Mr. Woodbridge, and my will is that what my son Nathan wants to be equal with my son Samuel shall be made to him in out-land. And then all the remainder of my land, divided and undivided, and my interest in Hop Swamp Stream, and all my carpentry tools and husbandry tools, shall be equally divided between my two sons, only it is to be understood that I give my son Samuel all my buildings more than to equal him with my son Nathan. In consideration whereof my will is that my son Samuel shall pay all my just debts and funeral charges. And my will is that my two sons shall equally pay to my two daughters, Esther and Sibell, as their full portion of my estate, to each the sum of £40 in or as money. I appoint my son Samuel sole executor.

Witness: *James Miller,*   SAMUEL MILLER, LS.
Jared Miller, William Rockwell.

Court Record, Page 30—5 June, 1738: Will and invt. exhibited. Will proven.

Page 152—28 September, 1739: We, the subscribers (at the desire of the executors of the last will and testament of Samuel Miller, late of Middletown decd.), have this 28th day of September, 1739, divided the estate of the sd. decd. according to his last will and testament, as follows:

	£ s d
To the widow, 1-3 of the household goods and stock,	42-10-10
To Samuel Miller, eldest son, household goods and stock and husbandry tools,	99-09-03
To Nathan Miller, 2nd son, household goods and stock and husbandry tools,	99-09-03
To Samuel Miller, in real estate,	515-11-07
To Nathan Miller, in real estate,	415-11-07

We, the subscribers, being the widow and sons of the aforesd. Samuel Miller, do agree with, consent to and promise, for ourselves and our heirs, to abide by the foregoing distribution. As witness our hands this 2nd October, 1739.

Witness: *Charles Hamlin,*   MARCY MILLER,
Wm. Rockwell.   SAMUEL MILLER,
                                         NATHAN MILLER.

Dist. accepted in Court and ordered to be recorded.

Test: Joseph Talcott, Jr., Clerk.

Page 261.

More, William, Simsbury. Died 29 January, 1738-9. Invt. £95-14-02. Taken 25 January, 1739-40, by Benjamin More and John Lewis. Estate of William More of Simsbury, who died 29 January, 1738-9, in East Jersey, in the Province of New York: To money in bills of New York, New Jersey, Rhode Island and New Hampshire, and in value of our bills, £24-09-06. More of public (bills) on the Province of New York, New Jersey, Rhode Island and New Hampshire, all, £24-05-00 (with personal estate taken at Simsbury).

Court Record, Page 45—19 March, 1738-9: Adms. to William More of Simsbury, father of the deceased.

Page 16 (Vol. XIV) 1st February, 1742-3: William More, Adms., exhibits an account of his Adms.: Paid in debts and charges, £135-12-11. Which account is accepted and ordered to be kept on file.

Page 136.

Morgan, Rachel, Widow of Thomas, late of Hartford decd.. We, the subscribers, being heirs of the estate, have received our several proportions by agreement this 3 April, 1739, as followeth:

	£ s d
To Leah, the wife of Jonathan Cadwell, daughter of the decd.,	16-19-00
To Hannah, the wife of Isaac Goodwin, daughter of the decd.,	16-19-00
To Rachel, wife of Abel Colyer, daughter of the decd.,	16-19-00
To Deliverance, wife of Stephen Hosmer, granddaughter of the decd.,	16-19-00

Signed: JONATHAN CADWELL, LS. | ISAAC GOODWIN, LS.
          ABELL COLYER, LS. | STEPHEN HOSMER, LS.

Court Record, Page 20—18 January, 1737-8: Estate Rachel Morgan decd.: Adms. to Isaac Goodwin and Stephen Hosmer. Recog., £400, with William Pratt.

Page 256.

Morley, Martha, Glastonbury. Invt. £61-01-07. Taken 2 January, 1740-1, by Jonathan Hale and Nathaniel Talcott.

Court Record, Page 81—20 January, 1740-1: Adms. to Ebenezer Morley. Recog., £300, with Jonathan Hale.

Page 318.

Morton, Thomas, Stepney. Will dated 28 November, 1734: I, Thomas Morton of Stepney, in Wethersfield, do make this my last will and testament: I give to Comfort Morton, my wife, the use of 1-3 part of my buildings and of all my lands during her natural life, and 1-3 of my household goods and moveable estate freely to be possessed and disposed of by her as she shall think fitt. I give to my daughter Ruth £150 in or as money, reckoning to make up the above-mentioned sum what she hath already received. I give to my daughter Sarah £150 with what she hath already received. I give to my daughter Sarah the liberty and improvement of a convenient room in my house, and also the improvement of 1-3 part of the gardens so long as she continues unmarried. I give to my son John Morton, whom I constitute my sole executor, all and singular my buildings and lands, he allowing to his mother and sister Sarah the use and improvement of such a part of the buildings and lands as above mentioned. Also, I give to my son John all the remainder of my household and moveable estate (after my wife has taken her thirds), he paying to his sisters the legacies above mentioned.

Witness: *Daniel Russell,*   THOMAS MORTON, LS.
Jonathan Riley, Daniel Deming.

Court Record, Page 71—5 August, 1740: Will exhibited by John Morton. Proven.

Page 331 (Probate Side): Whereas, our honoured father Thomas Morton, late of Wethersfield deceased, did in his last will and testament give to our honoured mother, Comfort Morton, 1-3 part of his moveable and household estate for her own, which will being made before the death of our mother and never altered by our father since her death, we, the subscribers, children and heirs of the deceased, have mutually and lovingly agreed equally to divide among ourselves that part of the moveable estate which in our father's will was to have been our mother's, and have each one received our part of sd. estate. As witness our hands and seals. Signed and sealed in the presence of the Court of Probates in Hartford on the 2nd day of March, 1741-2.

JOHN MORTON, LS.   SARAH X ROBBINS, LS.
STEPHEN RUSSELL, LS.   RUTH RUSSELL.
ZEBULON ROBBINS, LS.

Court Record, Page 111—2 March, 1741-2: Agreement exhibited in Court and accepted.

Newbery, Benjamin, Estate. Court Record, Page 51—25 June, 1739: Adms. granted to Roger Newbery and Roger Wolcott, Jr. Recog., £1000, with Peletiah Mills.

Page 312-13-14-332-3-4.

Newbery, Roger, Windsor. Invt. £4050-06-05, equal to silver at 28 shillings per ounce, taken 17 November, 1741, by John Cooke 2nd, Samuel Enno and Daniel Bissell. Additional invt., £1177-08-02. A still further addition of £362-10-00, taken 11 December, 1749. On the 14th day of December, 1755, Charles Kilby of London received £168. Will dated 5th September, 1740.

I, Roger Newbery of Windsor, in the County of Hartford, being entered into His Majestie's service against the Spanish West Indies, not knowing how God may dispose of me, do make this my last will and testament: I give to my wife Elizabeth Newbery £150 money, equivalent to silver at 27 shillings per ounce, and 1-3 part of all the remainder of my moveable estate after the sd. £150 is first deducted, to her and her heirs forever; and also the use of 1-3 part of all my real estate, both houseing and lands, so long as she shall remain my widow. I give to my son Roger £200 out of my real estate at inventory price. I give to my son Benjamin £150 out of my real estate. I give to my son Thomas £150 out of my real estate. I give to my four daughters, Elizabeth, Hannah, Abigail and Sarah, £100 to each of them. And further, my will is that all my estate, both real and personal, shall be inventoried, according to which inventory all my estate shall be distributed and equally divided amongst my children by distributors appointed by the Court of Probates (except what I have herein disposed of to my wife) in such proportion as is above mentioned. And my daughters shall take their portions out of the moveable estate so far as that will answer, which shall be paid them at marriage or when they arrive to the age of 21 years. And if the moveables are not sufficient to answer their several portions, the remainder thereof shall be set out to them in land at inventory price. My will is that my molatto servant Tony (alias Benoni), when he shall arrive at the age of 25 years, shall be released and discharged from any service or duty to any of my heirs, and also suitably clothed (out of my estate) for such person. I appoint my wife Elizabeth Newbery and my brother Roger Wolcott, Jr., to be executors.

Witness: *Matthew Allyn*,   ROGER NEWBERY, LS.
Henry Allyn, Esther Filley, Jr.

Court Record, Page 97—9th September, 1741: Will proven.

Page 59 (Vol. XVI) 7 April, 1752: Abigail Newbery, a minor, 18 years of age, Roger Newbery, 17 years, and Sarah Newbery, 15 years, children of Roger Newbery, chose their mother Mrs. Elizabeth Newbery to be their guardian. Recog., £1000.

Page 201-2.

Newell, Elizabeth, Farmington. Invt. £207-01-06. Taken October, 1740, by John Newell and John Rew. Will dated 19 December, 1739.

I, Elizabeth Newell of Farmington, doe make this my last will and testament: I give unto my son Thomas Newell my house and barn and ye lott on which they stand, and all my land adjoining thereunto, to him, his heirs and assigns forever. I give unto my son Simon Newell 40 shillings, to be paid unto him by my executor hereafter named, out of my moveable estate. I give unto my daughter Elizabeth Lewis (alias Newell) all my wearing clothes. I give unto my son Joseph Newell my feather bed with all the furniture for sd. bed. I give unto my daughter Easter Newell and to my son Thomas Newell and to my son Joseph Newell all the remaining part and residue of my estate in what kind or degree soever, to be equally divided between them. Lastly, I make my son Thomas Newell whole and sole executor.

Witness: *John Newell,*   ELIZABETH X NEWELL, LS.
Ephraim Smith, Jr., Sarah X Smith.

Court Record, Page 73—2 September, 1740: Will exhibited in Court by the executor named therein, who refused the trust and desired that his cousin James Newell of Farmington be Adms. This Court grant him letters of Adms. with the will annexed. Recog., £200, with Samuel Newell of Farmington.

Page 83—3 March, 1740-1: Jonathan Lewis of Farmington, in right of his wife, a daughter of sd. decd., now appeals from a decree of this Court granting Adms. to James Newell on sd. estate to the Superior Court. Recog., £10.

Page 90—2 June, 1741: James Newell, Adms., exhibited an account of his Adms., which account is accepted. Also, the sd. Adms. moves for a dist., whereupon this Court appoints Capt. John Newell and Lt. John Rew, of Farmington, distributors.

Distribution from File, date 2 June, 1741: To Elizabeth Lewis, alias Newell, to Joseph Newell, to Simon Newell, to Thomas Newell, to Easther Newell. *By John Newell and John Rew, Distributors.*

Nichason, Henry, Estate, Hartford. Court Record, Page 54—13 September, 1739: Adms. to Hannah Nichason, widow, and Peletiah Mills of Windsor. Recog., £100, with Disbrow Spencer of Hartford.

Page 69—23 June, 1740: Estate insolvent. This Court appoint Ensign James Church, Ensign Daniel Goodwin and Walter Henderson commissioners.

Page 44-5-6.

Nott, William, Stepney. Invt. £229-18-01. Taken 14 December, 1737, by Benjamin Wright, Gideon Goodrich and Jonathan Boardman. Will dated 9 November, 1737.

I, William Nott of Stepney, do make this my last will and testament: I give to my wife Abigail Nott the use and improvement of one-third part of my house, barn, cyder mill press and all my other buildings; also the improvement of one-third part of all my cleared lands during her widowhood: Also, I give to my beloved wife all the moveable estate that she brought with her when I married her, and all that remains due to her from her first husband's estate, to be her own property and at her own dispose. Also, I give to her for her own property one-third part of my moveable estate in my house, allowing to her first choice, particularly that she shall have in her part a midling iron pot. I give to my son Thomas Nott 21 1-2 acres of land which I bought of Samuel Benton, lying near Daniel Belding's; also 4 acres of land in the meadow near Beaver Brook, that I bought of John Russell. I give to my son Abraham Nott 6 acres of land adjoyning to the heirs of Eliphalet Dickinson decd. Also, I give him my lot lying at the head of Hog's Brook, which I had of Joseph Belding. Also I give to Abraham one-half of my lot bought of John Belding, lying in the meadow. These to him and his heirs forever. I give to my son William Nott the remainder of my homelott with all the buildings thereon, he paying to my wife the improvement of 1-3 part. I give to my wife's daughter Olive Nott my lott in Beaver Meadow, which lott I bought of Nathaniel Burnham. My sons to pay to their sisters, to Jemima, to Elizabeth and to Olive, to each £5. I appoint my wife Abigail and my son Abraham Nott executors.

Witness: *Daniel Russell,*   WILLIAM NOTT, LS.
Gideon Goodrich, Samuel Goffe.

Court Record, Page 19—3 January, 1737-8: Will now exhibited by the executors, who refused the trust and took Adms. with the will annexed. Recog., £500, with Benjamin Wright.

Page 22—14 February, 1737-8: An account of Adms. was exhibited by Abigail Nott, widow. Accepted.

Page 70—5 August, 1740: Abigail Nott, widow and relict of William Nott of Wethersfield decd. (alias Abigail Blynn, now the wife of Jonathan Blynn of sd. Wethersfield), now moved to this Court that suitable persons may be appointed as the law directs to set out to her her dowry in the estate of the sd. decd., whereupon this Court do appoint Benjamin Wright, Lt. Gideon Goodrich and Deacon David Goodrich to set out 1-3 part of the buildings and lands of the sd. decd. by bounds, and make return to this Court.

Page 85—17 March, 1740-1: William Nott, age 17 years, son of William Nott decd., chose Thomas Curtiss of Wethersfield to be his guardian. Recog., £100.

Page 96—13 August, 1740: Abigail Blynn, former wife of William Nott, desired this Court to appoint Elisha Boardman of Wethersfield to be guardian to Olive Nott, age 6 years. Recog., £100.

Page 110—2 March, 1741-2: Jonathan Blynn, in right of his wife Abigail, widow and relict of William Nott, late of Wethersfield decd., moves to this Court that freeholders may be appointed to set out to him and his sd. wife her dowry in that estate (the sd. decd. not having given his sd. widow her dowry in his estate by his last will), whereupon this Court appoint Jonathan Belding, Ephraim Williams and John Stilman to set out by bounds 1-3 part of the buildings and lands of the decd. for her improvement during life.

Page 2 (Vol. XIV) 13 August, 1742: A return of the dowry set out to the widow, under the hands of Jonathan Belding, Ephraim Williams and John Stilman, was now exhibited and accepted by the Court.

Page 146-7.

Olmsted, Mary, East Haddam. Invt. £102-12-10. Taken 29 October, 1739, by John Spencer, Jabez Chapman and John Willey, Jr. Will dated 23 April, 1734.

I, Mary Olmsted of East Haddam, in the County of Hartford, do make this my last will and testament: I give to my son Samuel Olmsted all my estate after my just debts are paid, except what is hereafter in this my will otherwise bequeathed. I give to my son John Olmsted my Bible. I give to my daughter Sarah Cone 1 Duroy suit of aparrel and 20 shillings in money. I give to my daughter Elizabeth Church my bed and bedstead with the furniture; also I give to her my trunk and all that is therein; also I give to her my box and all that is in it. I give to her my warming pan, my brass kettle, two pewter platters, one basin and one porringer; also I give 9 sheets and two pillow beers, also my linen wheel. I give to my above-named children and their heirs and assigns in manner as above sd. I constitute my son-in-law John Church to be sole executor.

Witness: *John* X *Spencer,*   MARY X OLMSTED, LS.
Isaac Spencer, Jabez Chapman.

Court Record, Page 57—6 November, 1739: Will proven.

Page 276-7.

Olmsted, Thomas, Hartford. Invt. £111-09-08. Taken 28 May, 1741, by David Ensign and Daniel Webster. Will dated 23 May, 1735.

I, Thomas Olmsted of Hartford, do make this my last will and testament: I give to my sons Thomas and Stephen my north lott which they have improved for some years past, to each of them an equal part of it. I give to my son Daniel 16 acres at the west end of the lott on which my dwelling house stands, the remainder of which I give to my three sons, Thomas, Stephen and Daniel, to each of them an equal part. And my will is that Thomas shall have his part on the south side of the lott, and Daniel his part next to him, and Stephen his part on the north side. This is the order in which I would have the land on the west side of the highway divided. And east of the highway Stephen's part shall be next to Thomas's, and Daniel shall have the north side of the lott. And I will have it understood that if Stephen's part east of the highway shall be found to take in the barnyard or any part of it, that Daniel shall notwithstanding have the yard entirely to himself and his own use, and shall make a proportionable allowance to Stephen out of the land that shall fall to him eastward. It is moreover my will that Thomas and Stephen shall have and injoy the buildings, viz., the houses and barns that stand upon their respective shares of land. And also I give to my son Daniel my dwelling house and barn and my team, that is to say, a yoke of oxen and the brown mare that leads the team, etc. I will 20 shillings to my daughter Sarah and 5 shillings to my daughter Damarus; and to my other daughters, viz., Rebeckah, Hannah and Jerusha, I will and bequeath £40 apiece, to be paid out of my moveable estate.

Witness: *Benjamin Woodbridge,*   THOMAS OLMSTED, LS.
Reuben Ely, Ruth Cotton.

Court Record, Page 94—7 July, 1741: Will exhibited by the witnesses, there being no executor named in the will. Adms., with the will annexed, to Thomas Olmsted. Recog., £1000, with Daniel Olmsted, son of the deceased.

Page 53-4.

Orvice, Roger, Farmington. Invt. £179-12-07. Taken by Isaac Cowles and Samuel Nash. Will dated 18 December, 1736.

I, Roger Orvice of Farmington, do make this my last will and testament: I give to my wife Miriam my estate all, both real and personal, to be at her own dispose to give to my own children. I appoint my wife Miriam Orvice sole executrix.

Witness: *Isaac Cowles,*   ROGER ORVICE, LS.
William Hooker, Ebenezer Lancton.

Court Record, Page 2—1st March, 1736-7: Will proven.

Page 151-2.

Owen, Aaron, Wethersfield. Invt. £398-06-09. Taken 3rd September, 1739, by Joshua Robbins and Timothy Boardman.

Court Record, Page 49—12 May, 1739: Adms. to John Coleman, Jr. Recog., £500, with Gershom Nott.

Page 74—4 November, 1740: James Owen, age 17 years, and Hannah Owen, age 14 years, children of Aaron Owen, chose Nathaniel Coleman to be their guardian. Recog., £400.

Page 27 (Vol. XV) 4 November, 1746: John Coleman, Adms., exhibited an account of his Adms. Accepted.

Page 84—3 January, 1748-9: John Coleman, Adms., having rendered his account of Adms. on sd. estate, now moves this Court for a distribution of the moveable estate, £312-06-06, to be distributed: to John, the eldest son, his double share; and to Aaron, James, Hannah and Prudence, to each of them their single shares. And appoint Timothy Baxter, Isaac Riley and Samuel Treat, of Wethersfield, distributors.

Page 115—2 January, 1749-50: John Coleman, Adms., now moves to this Court that distribution of the real estate might be granted to and among the heirs of the sd. deceased: Whereupon this Court appoint Isaac Riley and Samuel Treat, of Wethersfield, to distribute the sd. real estate to Hannah and Prudence, the whole of sd. estate in equal proportion, and make return of their doings thereon to this Court.

This record is unaccountable—that the whole of the real estate should be distributed to Hannah and Prudence Owen, and no mention of the sons, John, Aaron and James Owen. But no further record has been found to either prove or disprove the Court's order for distribution. —[C. W. M.

Owen, Asahel. Court Record, Page 91—2 June, 1741: Asahel Owen, a minor, age 15 years, son of Asahel Owen, late of Sheffield, in the Province of Massachusetts Bay, chose Major William Pitkin to be his guardian. Recog., £50.

Page 328.

Owen, Elijah, Windsor. Died 21 September, 1741. Invt. £1761-09-05. Taken by Isaac Gillett, Joshua Holcomb and Joseph Wilcoxson.

Court Record, Page 105—5 January, 1741-2: Adms. granted to Hannah Owen, widow. Recog., £1000, with Isaac Owen of Windsor.

Page 27 (Vol. XIV) 2 August, 1742: Peletiah Mills, Jr., of Windsor, and his wife Hannah Mills, relict of Elijah Owen, late of sd. Windsor, Adms. on the sd. estate, being cited to render an account of Adms., Peletiah Mills, Jr., appeared and rendered an account, which is accepted, and this Court order them to present a full account on the 1st Tuesday of October next.

Page 35—6 December, 1743: Rebeckah Owen, age 7 years, Elijah 5 years, and Hannah 3 years, children of Elijah Owen of Windsor: this Court appoint Brewster Higley of Simsbury to be their guardian. Recog., £500.

Pantry, John, Estate, Hartford. Court Record, Page 34—5 October, 1738: Adms. granted to Nathaniel Jones and Richard Goodman of Hartford. Recog., £500, with Matthew Talcott of Hartford, for their Adms. on the moveable estate.

Page 263.

Peck, Joseph, Tolland. Invt. £406-17-03. Taken 29 May, 1741, by Nathaniel Woodward, Joshua Wills, Jr., and Zebulon West.

Court Record, Page 91—15 June, 1741: Adms. granted to John Abbott, of Tolland, by desire of Elizabeth Peck the widow. Recog., £500, with George Bradley of Tolland.

Page 11 (Vol. XIV) 5 October, 1742: John Abbott, Adms., exhibited an account of his Adms. Accepted. The Adms. moves to this Court that the widow may have her thirds of moveables set out to her: Whereupon this Court appoint Ensign Ephraim Grant, Sergt. Samuel West and Mr. Joshua Wills, of Tolland, to set out and divide 1-3 part of the moveables to Elizabeth Peck, widow, £38-10-04.

Page 21—5 April, 1743: John Peck, a minor, 3 years of age next August, son of Joseph Peck of Tolland: this Court do appoint John Abbott to be his guardian. Recog., £100 money.

Page 47—September, 1744: A further account of allowance on the estate of Joseph Peck to John Abbott, Adms., for the maintenance of the child 2 years at £8 per year; total, £16 old tenor.

Invt. in Vol. XIV, Page 22.

Pellett, Thomas, Sen., Hartford. Died 17 August, 1741. Invt. £68-13-04. Taken 2 September, 1741, by Samuel Gains and James Porter.

Court Record, Page 97—1st September, 1741: Adms. granted to Stephen Shipman of Glastonbury, who gave bond with Samuel Shipman of Hebron, the widow desiring the same, she being very aged and infirm.

Page 9 (Vol. XIV) 3 August, 1742: Stephen Shipman, Adms., exhibited an account of his Adms., which account is accepted, ordered recorded and kept on file.

Page 15 (Vol. XV) 1st July, 1746: Stephen Shipman of Glastonbury, Adms., now exhibits a further account of his Adms. of £25-06-01; so that it appears he has paid in debts and charges more than the amount of the inventory, and is granted a *Quietus Est.*

Page 196.

Pendleton, Caleb, Colchester. Invt. £1616-01-06. Taken 28 May, 1740, by John Holmes, Jr., and Simon Miner. Will dated 15 May, 1740.

I, Caleb Pendleton of Colchester, do make this my last will and testament: I give to Marcy, my wife, 1-2 of the income of the farm I now live on, 1-2 of the house, that is to say, the west end of the house, during the term of 10 years after the 29th day of July next after the date hereof, for the bringing up of my two small children, Lydia and Elizabeth; and from the expiration of 10 years I give her 1-3 part of the income of the farm during her natural life, and also the bed that I had with her when I married her, and bedding, and all the household goods I had with her, and 1-3 part of all my household goods, and the best cow and calf that I have, and my sorril mare, and six of my middle sort of shoats. I give to my son Benajah Pendleton all my land, messuages and tenements, to him and his assigns forever, that I now have, except that piece of land I had of Capt. John Holmes, and all my utensils for husbandry, and my gunn and cane, and one large paire of stillyards, and all my wearing clothes; and it is to lye in the hands of my executors until my son Benajah comes of age. I give to my daughter Abigail Johnson 5 shillings in money; I have already paid her a portion. I give to my daughters Sarah and Mary Pendleton 2-3 parts of all my household goods and £30 in money apiece, to be paid at the age of 18 years. I give to my two youngest daughters, Lydia and Elizabeth Pendleton, £15 apiece, to be paid at 18 years of age. And I also leave all the rest of my stock and lands and servants in the hands of my brother John Randall, Jr., of Stoningtown, in New London County, for him to sell and dispose of to pay my debts and legacies, whom I ordain my sole executor.

Witness: *Clement Minor,*   CALEB PENDLETON, LS.
Richard Tozer, John Holmes, Jr.

Items from the Inventory of Caleb Pendleton's Estate:

One Indian boy servant named Samuel, inventoried at	£15
One Indian boy servant named Peter, inventoried at	£22
One Indian boy servant named Jonathan, inventoried at	£18
Notes of hand due from Ichabod Randall,	£139
Due from Benoni Smith,	£18
Due from James Tilley,	£6-06
Due from Daniel Tennant,	£5
Due from Peter Bulkley,	£12-12

Court Record, Page 67—10 June, 1740: Will now exhibited by John Randall, Jr., executor named in the will. Proven.

Page 88—5 May, 1741: Stephen Stark, in right of his wife Marcy Stark, who was widow of Caleb Pendleton of Colchester deceased, by his attorney William Treadway of Colchester, moves this Court that her dowry in the real estate may be set out to her. This Court appoint Samuel Lathrop of Norwich, Lt. James Fitch of Lebanon and Noah Welles of Colchester to set out to the sd. Marcy Stark (alias Marcy Pendleton) one-third part of the building and lands.

In Vol. XIII, the last Court Record in regular continuation bears date 6th April, 1742. The following items were recorded upon a blank page, as will be seen, at a much later date. Otherwise it might have been recorded at Colchester.

Court Record, Page 113—10 October, 1750: Then received of Capt. John Randall £235 in full of what was due to me from him, which was left in his hands by my hond. father, late of Colchester deceased.

Witness: *John Breed,*   BENAJAH PENDLETON.
    Peter Bulkley.

17 December, 1754: Received of Capt. John Randall, of Stonington, £26-08-00, old tenor, in full of what sd. Randall was to pay to Lydia Pendleton when she comes of age.

ICHABOD RANDALL, GUARDIAN.

Stonington, 27 June, 1758: Received of Capt. John Randall £2-12-06 lawfull money, it being in full which was given me by will of my honoured father Caleb Pendleton.

ELIZABETH X PENDLETON.

We, Thomas Main, Jun., of Stonington, and Mary Main his wife, a daughter of Caleb Pendleton, late of Colchester decd., have received of Capt. John Randall, executor to the last will of the sd. Caleb Pendleton, 1-3 part of the household stuff mentioned in the inventory of the estate of the sd. Caleb Pendleton, and also £30 money, which is in full of the legacy given to the sd. Mary in sd. will. And we also have received other third part of the household stuff and £30 money, which was a legacy given to Sarah Pendleton deceased, daughter of sd. Caleb Pendleton.

Witness: *Simeon Miner,*   THOMAS MAIN, JR.,
       Thomas Wheeler, Jr.   MARY MAIN.

14 August, 1749.

Page 251.

Persivell, Elizabeth, wife of James, now deceased. Invt. £14-19-08. Taken 2 April, 1740, by Thomas Gates, John Fuller and Jeremiah Gates.

Court Record, Page 67—3 June, 1740: Adms. granted to John Persivell. Recog., £50, with Isaac Spencer.

Page 75-251.

Persivell, James, East Haddam. Invt. £856-17-06. Taken 20 April, 1738, by Thomas Gates, Jeremiah Gates and John Persivell.

Court Record, Page 28—2 May, 1738: Adms. granted to Elizabeth Persivell, widow. Recog., £500, with John Persivell.

Page 67—3 June, 1740: This Court appoint John Persivell to be guardian to the children of James Persivell, viz., Ebenezer, age 9 years, Mary 7 years, Abigail 5, and Ann 3 years of age. Recog., £500.

Page 25 (Vol. XIV) 7 June, 1743: John Persivell, Adms., exhibited an account of his Adms., which is accepted.

Page 63 (Vol. XVI) 9 April, 1752: John Persivell, Adms. on the estate of James Persivell and Elizabeth his wife, of East Haddam, having fully administered on sd. estates, now moves for a distribution. This Court so order:

£ s d

To Ebenezer Persivell, son of the deceased,   327-05-08
And to Mary, Abigail and Anna, daughters, to each of them,   163-12-10

And appoint Capt. Thomas Gates and Deacon Jeremiah Gates, of
East Haddam, and Stephen Brainard, of Colchester, distributors.

Page 79—7 November, 1752: A distribution of the estate of James
Persivell and Elizabeth his wife was exhibited in Court and accepted.

Invt. in Vol. XIV, Page 14-18.

Pettibone, John, Simsbury, in Farmington. Died 18 September,
1741. Invt. £1177. Taken by Azariah Wilcocks and James Case. Will
dated 8 February, 1733-4.

I, John Pettibone of Simsbury, in the County of Hartford, do make
this my last will and testament: Imprimis. I give unto my wife Mary 1-3
part of all my moveable estate, to be at her own dispose forever; and also
the use of my now dwelling house, and the homelott and orchard on which
my house standeth, during the term of her natural life; and also the use
of 1-3 part of all my improveable land (excepting that part of my homelott on the east side of the highway, on which my barn now standeth);
and also the use of 1-2 of my barn, and the whole of the yard by the barn,
next to David Phelps's lott, during the time of her natural life. I give
unto my daughter Catherine a feather bed with a bedstead and all the
furniture belonging to it, and also the use of 8 acres of meadow land,
to be taken out of my lott in Manto Meadow, during the time of her
natural life; also I give to my daughter Catherine £100. I give to my
daughter Sarah the sum of £100 with what I have already given her. I
give unto my daughter Abigail the sum of £100 with what I have already
given her. All the rest of my estate, real and personal, I give unto my
two sons, John and Samuel, equally divided between them, to them and
their heirs forever. I give unto my wife Mary and to my daughter
Catherine all my provisions, both corne and meat, that I shall leave at my
decease. I appoint my beloved wife Mary and my two sons John and
Samuel to be executors.

Witness: *Samuel Pettibone,*   JOHN PETTIBONE, LS.
Joseph Pettibone, John Humphrey.

Know all men by these presents: That I, John Pettibone of Simsbury, in the County of Hartford, have formerly made my last will and
testament, which is written on the other half of this sheet, dated 8 February, 1733-4, which I do hereby ratify and confirm to be my last will and
testament, and make this following codicil in addition thereto, viz:
Whereas, my beloved wife Mary is under low circumstances and unable
to provide for or help herself, I do, in addition to what I have already
given her, devise and order that my executors shall sell and dispose of

my lott of land lying on the north end of Mount Philip, in that tract of land called the Hogs-Skin, and the value or produce thereof they shall dispose and improve for the maintenance and support of my sd. wife if she shall come to want; and if not, then sd. land to be disposed of as in my will aforesd. is provided. And I do, in addition to my will aforesd., appoint my son-in-law Amos Phelps to be an executor to my sd. last will with the other executors therein named. And my will is that this codicil be and allowed to be part of my last will and testament. 31 December, 1740.

Witness: *Samuel Pettibone,*   JOHN PETTIBONE, LS.
Joseph Pettibone, John Humphrey.

Court Record, Page 104—23 December, 1741: The last will and testament of John Pettebone was now exhibited in Court by Samuel Pettebone of Goshen and Amos Phelps of Simsbury, two of the executors named in sd. will. John Pettebone, one of the executors, objected to the probate of this will, but withdrew his appeal to the Superior Court and accepted the trust of executorship, 2 April, 1742.

Will and Invt. in Vol. XIV, Page 66.

Phelps, Lt. Samuel, Windsor.   Invt. £1702 in realty.   Taken 22 December, 1741, by Thomas Griswold, John Cook 2nd and Peletiah Mills. Will dated 26 October, 1741.

I, Samuel Phelps of Windsor, do make this my last will and testament: My will is that my three sons, Samuel, James and Hezekiah, be my executors. Also, my will is, that all my lawfull debts be paid. I give to my wife Abigail 1-2 of my house, 1-2 of my homelott, and a lott in the meadow called Birge's lott, during her natural life; also the improvement of the lower pasture to cut three loads of hay annually during her natural life; also I give 1-3 of my moveable estate to my wife Abigail. I give to my son James £200 money. I give to my son Joshua £250 money. I give to my daughter Abigail £150 money. My will is that my executors shall sell 70 acres of land in the 1 1-2-mile of land in the division of Windsor and about 6 or 7 acres at the West Brook, to pay my lawful debts. Then what remains of my estate, my will is that it shall be equally divided among all my children, namely, Samuel Phelps, James Phelps, Hezekiah Phelps, Joshua Phelps and Abigail Phelps.

Witness: *Cornelius Phelps,*   SAMUEL PHELPS, LS.
Samuel Griswold, John Phelps 3rd.

Court Record, Page 104—23 December, 1741: Will proven.
Page 108—2 February, 1741-2: This Court appoint Abigail Phelps to be guardian to Joshua Phelps, age 12 years. Recog., £200.
See File: Know all men by these presents: yt I, Abigail Phelps of Windsor, widow of Samuel Phelps of sd. Windsor decd., I with all my

children have this day come to a division and distribution of all ye estate of ye abovesd. Samuel Phelps, both real and personal. First, to our honoured mother the 1-2 of ye dwelling house, 1-2 of the homested, and ye liberty of cutting 3 loads of hay annually, and 1-3 part of ye moveables forever; and the use of the abovesd. lands during life. The abovesd. lands, after ye death of our honoured mother, to be to James Phelps; to Samuel Phelps, £59 in the house and barn; to James Phelps, £27 in the house; to Hezekiah Phelps, with the lands, £27. Further, to James Phelps, part of the Brown lott, and the remainder to Abigail Grant, the wife of Jehiel Grant. To Samuel Phelps, a right in Colebrook. To Joshua Phelps, 2 rights in Torrington and £53 in the old homelott. In witness of the above-written being mutually agreed to and acknowledged, we have hereunto set our hands and seals this 11th November, 1746.

ABIGAIL X PHELPS, LS.	HEZEKIAH PHELPS, LS.
SAMUEL PHELPS, LS.	JEHIEL GRANT, LS.
JAMES PHELPS, LS.	ABIGAIL X GRANT, LS.

Page 29 (Vol. XV) 11 November, 1746: Agreement exhibited in Court and accepted.

Page 178.

Pinney, Aaron, Windsor. Invt. £298-09-06. Taken 5 November, 1739, by Thomas Griswold and George Griswold, Jr.

Court Record, Page 54—4 September, 1739: Adms. granted to Azariah Pinney, a brother of the deceased. Recog., £500, with Jacob Munsell of Windsor. And the Adms. reports the estate insolvent.

Items from the Inventory of Aaron Pinney, Deceased:

The eighth part of the sloop *Swan,* £112-10-00.

Due from Elisha Stutson,	£16-17 00	Due from Peter Bewell,	£50-00-00
Due from Daniel Tuller,	£7-00-00	Due from Thomas Barbour,	£2-00-00
Due from Edward Griswold,	£22-00-00	Due from Samuel Pettibone, Jun.,	£36-00-00

Page 68-77.

Pinney, Jonathan, Windsor. Invt. £61-16-05 (personal estate). Taken 20 April, 1738, by Jonathan Elsworth, Jonathan Stiles and Samuel Heydon, Jr. Will dated 29 June, 1736.

A memorandum concerning the disposition of Jonathan Pinney's estate: His will is that Noah Pinney (his brother) shall have his lott at Stafford with all the after divisions. And to Daniel Pinney all my right of land in Colebrook. And to my sisters, viz., Mary, Sarah and Hannah Pinney, all my right in the land called the equivalent land and commons in Windsor. And as to all the rest of my estate, I give and bequeath it to the heirs of Lt. Nathaniel Pinney to be equally divided between them, saving only two trammells, which I bequeath one of them to Margaret Marsh and the other to Dorothy Allyn.

Witness: *Timothy Loomis,* JONATHAN PINNEY.
Hannah Loomis, Rebeckah Loomis.

Court Record, Page 22—14 February, 1737-8: Noah Pinney (his brother) now exhibits a writing as the will of Jonathan Pinney deceased. Proof not now ready.

23 February: This Court consider the writing presented to be the last will, and Humphrey Pinney and Daniel Pinney, two of the brothers of Jonathan Pinney, appealed from the judgement of the Court.

Page 25—7 March, 1737-8: Adms. with the will annexed, to Noah Pinney of Windsor. Recog., £100, with William Pratt of Hartford.

Page 43—8 March, 1737-8: Account of Adms. by Noah Pinney. Accepted.

Page 75-76.

Pinney, Joseph, Windsor. Invt. £677-08-08. Taken by Joseph Phelps 3rd and Daniel Griswold. Will dated 13 December, 1737.

I, Joseph Pinney of Windsor, do make this my last will and testament: I give to Jerusha, my wife, 1-3 part of my moveable estate. My will is that my house and homelott that I bought of Mr. Dwite, which contains about 30 acres, shall be sold at the discretion of my executors. And after my debts are well and truly paid, my will is that the remainder of my estate shall be disposed of in equal shares to my three sons, viz., Joseph, Nathaniel and John. I likewise constitute my honoured father Nathaniel Pinney and Jerusha, my wife, executors.

Witness: *Matthew Griswold,* JOSEPH X PINNEY, LS.
Benjamin Barbour, Hannah X Barbour.

Court Record, Page 27—4 April, 1737-8: Will exhibited.

Page 17 (Vol. XIV) 21 February, 1742-3: Benjamin Ennos, of Windsor, moved to this Court in behalf of his wife, late widow and relict of Joseph Pinney, for a distribution to set out the sd. widow's dowry in the houseing and lands of sd. deceased: Whereupon this Court appoint Odiah Loomis, Thomas Marshal and Jonathan Wright to set out to the sd. widow (alias Jerusha Enos, the present wife of Benjamin Enos) 1-3 part of the real estate, and make return of their doings to this Court.

Page 23—3 May, 1743: Nathaniel Pinney, executor, exhibited an account of Adms. in this Court, which was accepted.

Page 42 (Vol. XV) 2 June, 1747: John Pinney, a minor son of Joseph Pinney: this Court appoints Nathaniel Pinney of sd. Windsor to be his guardian. Recog., £400.

Page 310.

Porter, John, Farmington. Invt. £813-08-10. Taken 11 February, 1740-1, by Isaac Cowles, John Hart and Nathaniel Wadsworth. Will dated 22 February, 1739-40.

I, John Porter of Farmingtown, do make this my last will and testament: I give to Martha, my beloved wife, all that remains of the household goods that she brought with her, and all the linen that was made since she came to my house by marriage, and one cow, and one heifer, and 2 silver spoons, and £40 in money that is out at interest, and the liberty of pasturing one cow, and the liberty of 1-2 of the house and homestead during her natural life. I give to my daughter Rebeckah Wadsworth £60. I give to my daughter Mary Cowles £5. I give to my daughter Hester £50. I give to my daughter Anne Porter £10. Further, I give unto my four daughters, namely, Rebeckah Wadsworth, and my daughter Mary Cowles, and Hester Porter, and my daughter Anne Porter, all the remainder of real and personal estate forever. I make my son Ebenezer Porter executor.

Witness: *Isaac Cowles,*   JOHN PORTER, LS.
Jonathan Bird, Solomon Cowles.

Court Record, Page 83—3 March, 1740-1: Will now exhibited by Ebenezer Porter. Proven.

Pratt, John, Jr. Court Record, Page 49—26 May, 1739: John Pratt, a minor, son of John Pratt deceased, chose his mother Hannah Pratt to be his guardian. Recog., £200.

Page 119 (Vol. XV) 9 February, 1749-50: Isaac Pratt, 16 years of age, son of John Pratt, chose his brother John Pratt to be his guardian. Recog., £500.

Page 4-5.

Price, John, Glastonbury. Invt. £32-05-11. Taken 25 April, 1737, by Nathaniel Talcott and Gershom Smith.

Court Record, Page 6—3 May, 1737: Adms. to Samuel Price. Recog., £70, with Jeduthan Smith. Exhibit of inventory. Estate supposed to be insolvent.

Page 12—5 July, 1737: Elizer Price, a minor, 1 year old, son of John Price: this Court appoint his grandfather Samuel Price to be his guardian. Recog., £50.

Page 29—2 May, 1738: Samuel Price, Adms., exhibited an account of his Adms., which is accepted.

Page 242.

Rice, Joseph, Tolland. Will dated 24 March, 1736: I, Joseph Rice of Tolland, do make and ordain this to be my last will and testament: I give to my wife Elizabeth all my real and personal estate, together with my buildings, fencings, orchards, and whatever appertains to me, I give to my sd. wife Elizabeth and to her heirs forever. I also appoint her to be sole executrix.

Witness: *Hezekiah Loomis,*　　　　　　JOSEPH X RICE.
Hepzibah X *Loomis, John Lothrop.*

Court Record, Page 79—25 December, 1740: The last will and testament of Joseph Rice was exhibited in Court by Capt. Samuel Chapman of sd. Tolland. Sd. will being proved by the witnesses thereto, is by this Court approved. The widow requests the Court that there might not be an invt. taken of sd. estate, as the whole estate was given to her. The Court not thinking it necessary, order that the will be recorded.

Page 63-4-5.

Riley, Lt. Isaac, Wethersfield. Invt. £2856-13-03. Taken 14 February, 1737-8, by John Rose, Joseph Goodrich and Jonathan Belding. Will dated 20 January, 1737-8. I, Isaac Riley of Wethersfield, do think it my duty to settle that temporal estate that God hath graciously given me. My will is as followeth: Imprimis: I give to my wife Ann 1-3 part of my personal estate to be at her dispose, and the improvement of 1-3 part of my real estate during life. I give to my son Josiah Riley my 50-acre lott at Newington, with the house, barn, orchard and fences thereon, excepting 10 acres of land at the west end next Farmington line, and reserving to my son Samuel the liberty of ingress and egress, he the sd. Josiah paying my debts and legacies as hereafter by me ordered. Furthermore, on the condition aforesd., I give to my son Josiah 1-4 part of my lott purchased of Josiah Crane deceased, the whole containing 3 1-2 acres. I give to my son Isaac Riley, 2nd son, 2 acres of land more or less, lying in Wethersfield, joining west on land of Richard Montague, north by land of Noadiah Dickinson, and south by land of Amasa Addams. Also, two acres of land at the lower end of the Great Plaine, bounded easterly on a highway, west and north on land of Capt. Edward Bulkeley, and south on land of Amos Belding. Also, 3 1-2 acres in Wethersfield Great Meadow, being a parcell of my six-acre lott there. Also, 1-4 part of my lott purchased of Josiah Crane, containing 3 1-2 acres more or less, he the sd. Isaac paying my debts and legacies hereafter by me ordered. I give to my son Samuel Riley, 3rd son, the 1-2 of my homelott (at the east end), together with the dwelling house, barn, corn house, orchard and other appurtenances thereon or thereunto belonging, excepting as hereafter specified. Also, 3 1-2 acres of my pasture lying near Waddams's Brook, to lye on the eastern end of sd. pasture. Also, the 1-2 of my 4-acre lott in the Great Plaine, near Capt. Chester's lott. Also, 1-2 of my five-acre lott in the Great Meadow, lying near Smith's Landing. Also, 10 acres of land lying at the west end of my 50-acre lott before given to my son Josiah, and also the liberty of passing to and from sd. 10

acres as necessity and convenience shall require. I give to my son Nathaniel Riley 1-2 of my homelott; also, 2 1-2 acres of my pasture lying near Waddams's Brook. I give to my daughter Ann £40 money, to be paid by my four sons in equal proportion, and also the liberty of improving my north chamber in my dwelling house during her unmarried state or until sd. Samuel shall actually sell sd. house, and no longer. I give to my daughter Mary £10-06-07, to be paid by my four sons. I give to my daughter Lucy £28-11-02, to be paid by my four sons. And concerning the 2-3 of my personal or moveable estate, my will is that immediately at my decease my executors shall enter upon and take possession thereof as a fund or stock out of which to pay my debts and legacies; but if not sufficient, my sd. four sons to pay the complement of my debts and legacies in equal proportions. I appoint my wife Ann and my son Samuel executors.

Witness: *Bezaleel Lattimore,*   ISAAC X RILEY, LS.
David Boardman, Nathaniel Coleman.

Court Record, Page 23—7 March, 1737-8: Will proven.

Page 251.

Riley, Joseph, Stepney Parish, in Wethersfield. Died 18 September, 1739. Invt. £982-03-05. Taken 2 November, 1739, by Peter Blynn, Josiah Churchill and Thomas Deming.

Court Record, Page 58—1st January, 1739-40: Adms. to Ann Riley, the widow. Recog., £500, with Thomas Deming.

Page 110—2 March, 1741-2: Daniel Riley, age 17 years, and Elizabeth Riley, age 12 years, chose their mother Ann Riley to be their guardian. Recog., £500. And this Court appoint her guardian to Elisha Riley, age 2 3-4 years. Recog., £100. Also Ann Riley, Adms., exhibited an account of her Adms., which this Court accepted.

Page 81 (Vol. XV) 6 December, 1748: Ann Riley (alias Goodrich), Adms. on the estate of Joseph Riley, having fully rendered an account of her Adms., prays that distributors may be appointed to distribute the moveable estate, which is granted:

	£ s d
To the widow,	29-07-02
To Daniel, the eldest son,	29-07-02
To Elizabeth and Elisha Riley, to each of them,	14-13-08

And appoint Ebenezer Wright, Thomas Deming and Nathaniel Boardman, of Wethersfield, distributors.

Page 101—6 June, 1749: James Collins, of Wethersfield, in right of his wife Elizabeth, daughter of Joseph Riley, now moves to this Court that distribution be made on the real estate: Whereupon this Court appoint Capt. Jacob Williams, Thomas Curtis and Mr. Joseph Frary distributors to divide sd. estate and set out to Ann Riley (alias Goodrich), relict of sd. deceased, her right of dowry, 1-3 of the buildings and land during life. Also, to set out to Daniel Riley, eldest son, his double part, and to Elisha Riley and Elizabeth Riley (alias Collins, daughter of sd. deceased) their single shares.

Page 102—6 June, 1749: Report of the distributors, viz., Ebenezer Wright and Thomas Deming.

Page 105—1st August, 1749: Report of the distribution of the real estate, by Joseph Frary and Thomas Curtis.

Page 180-200.

Riley, Sarah, widow, Wethersfield. Invt. £51-11-06. Taken 22 June, 1739, by David Goodrich and Gideon Goodrich.

Know all men by these presents: That I, Sarah Riley of Stepney, in Wethersfield, for the love, good will and affection that I have and do bear to my beloved daughter Mehetibell, the wife of Ephraim Griswold of Modus, and other considerations me thereto moveing, give, grant, and by these presents do freely, clearly and absolutely give and grant to the said Mehetabell Griswold (namely, at my decease), to her heirs, etc., all my wearing apparell as her proper goods forever, without any manner of condition. As I, the said Sarah Riley, have absolutely and of my own accord set and put in further testimony. In witness whereof I have hereunto set my hand and seal this 11th of June, A. D. 1739.

SARAH RILEY (HER MARK AND SEAL). Signed, sealed and delivered in the presence of
Daniel Russell, Daniel Deming, Jun'r.

Know all men: That I, Sarah Riley, for the love that I have and do beare to my granddaughter Mehetabell Riley, the daughter of Jacob Riley of Stepney, give and grant to the said Mehetabell Riley my old cow, with my poorest bed and furniture, forever, without any manner of condition.

Know all men by these presents: That I, Sarah Riley, for the love that I have and do beare to my granddaughter Grace Riley, daughter of Stephen Riley of Stepney, do absolutely give and grant to the said Grace Riley my youngest cow or heifer, with my best bed and furniture, as her proper goods forever, without any manner of condition. As I, the said Sarah Riley, have absolutely and of my own accord set and put.

SARAH RILEY (HER MARK AND SEAL).
Witness: *Daniel Russell,*
            Daniel Deming, Jun'r.

Each bequest was written out in full, signed, sealed and witnessed by the same persons and upon the same day and date.

Court Record, Page 51—25 June, 1739: Adms. granted to Jonathan Riley. Recog., £100, with Robert Powell of Wethersfield.

Page 52—3 July, 1739: This Court appoint Stephen Riley to be guardian to his daughter Grace Riley, age 10 years. Recog., £50. The Rev. Mr. Daniel Russell of Wethersfield now exhibited in this Court three deeds of gift under the hand and seal of Sarah Riley, the relict of Jonathan Riley of Wethersfield deceased.

Page 69—1st July, 1740: Account of Adms. exhibited. Estate insolvent, and Noadiah Dickinson and Daniel Deming appointed commissioners.

Page 84—9 March, 1740-1: Account of Adms. and also of commissioners. Accepted of each report.

Page 85—12 March, 1740-1: Order to distribute to the heirs of sd. estate: to Jonathan Riley, eldest son, to Jacob, to the heirs of Joseph Riley, to Stephen Riley, to the heirs of Abigail Riley (alias Cowles), to heirs of Mehetabell Riley (alias Griswold), to each, £2-11-07. By Capt. Jacob Williams, Lt. Gideon Goodrich and Stephen Williams.

Rippenear, John. Court Record, Page 87—20 April, 1741: Christopher Rippenear, age 15 years, son of John Rippenear, late of Hartford decd., chose John Potwin, goldsmith, of Hartford, to be his guardian. Recog., £50.

Page 37 (Vol. XIV) 2 February, 1743-4: Christopher Rippenear, a minor, now 18 years of age, chose Col. John Whiting to be his guardian. Recog., £50.

Page 295.

Risley, Doctor Nathaniel, Hartford. Died 30 September, 1741. Invt. £628-06-01. Taken November, 1741, by James Porter and David Hills. Will dated 28 September, 1741.

I, Nathaniel Risley of Hartford, do make this my last will and testament: Item. I give to my wife Elizabeth £50, and the use of 1-3 part of my real and personal estate so long as she remains my widow. I leave in the hands of my wife £20 to be disposed of to Elizabeth Biggelow, now living with me, if she faithfully serve out her time and my wife see cause to dispose of the same to her. My will is that my executor hereafter mentioned shall carefully dispose of £50 of my estate in schooling my three daughters hereafter mentioned, in instructing them in reading and writing. I give all my remaining estate, both real and personal, to my three daughters, Elizabeth, Zurviah and Deborah, to be equally divided between them. I make my wife Elizabeth Risley executrix.

Witness: *Jonathan Hills,*   NATHANIEL RISLEY, LS.
Jonathan Risley, Joseph Bidwell.

Court Record, Page 103—1st December, 1741: Will proven.

Page 60.

Robbins, Richard, Stepney. Invt. £4457-11-08. Taken 3 March, 1737-8, by Joshua Robbins, Benjamin Wright and Jonathan Robbins. Will dated 3 December, 1737.

I, Richard Robbins of Stepney, in Wethersfield, do make this my last will and testament: I give to my wife Martha 1-3 part of all my real estate during life, 1-3 part of my personal estate forever, and the use and profit of such lands herein devised to my children until they severally arrive to age, and also the improvement of 1-2 of my homelott and 1-2 of all my buildings during her natural life. I give to my eldest and only son John Robbins all my homelott situated in Stepney, in Wethersfield, consisting of a mansion house and barn and 20 acres of land, to him and his heirs forever, reserving 1-2 to my wife as aforesd., and reserving one room in my house to my daughters until such time as they are married. Also, 30 acres of land in sd. Stepney, lying near Samuel Belding, bought of Eliphalet Dickinson. Also, 2 acres of land in Wethersfield Great Meadow, against the Island house, which I had of my brother John. Also, a little piece of land over against the above-mentioned, which I had of Will Nott. Also, in sd. meadow, 5 acres of land more, which I bought of Nathaniel Burnham and Thomas Deming. Also, one acre of land by Goff's Bridge, which was my father's. Also, I give him my right in lands which I bought of Doctor Proutt. Also, a double part of what I may have in any after divisions of land, etc., to him and his heirs forever, reserving 3ds to my wife above mentioned. I give to my daughters, Mary, Rachel, Esther, Elizabeth, Experience and Martha, all the rest of my lands (excepting my farm at Colchester), to be equally divided among them, reserving thirds to my wife, and also all the right that may fall to me in any after divisions of land, excepting what I have already given to my son John. I give my farm at Colchester to my 7 children, John, Mary, Rachel, Esther, Elizabeth, Experience and Martha, to be equally divided among them. I appoint my wife Martha to be sole executrix.

Witness: *Josiah Churchill,*   RICHARD ROBBINS, LS.
Jonathan Warner, Elizabeth Warner.

Court Record, Page 23—7 March, 1737-8: Will proven.

Page 26—22 March, 1737-8: Upon motion of Nathaniel Robbins and Mary his wife and Rachel Robbins, heirs to the estate, showing that by the will of their decd. father considerable of the real estate was to them the sd. Nathaniel Robbins and Mary his wife and Rachel Robbins, with Experience, Martha, Esther and Elizabeth Robbins, minors, that a division be made in severalty to each except John Robbins, only son of the sd. decd., as the will directs, and the widow asks that her dower be set out to her. Joshua Robbins ye 2nd, Jonathan Robbins and John Warner were appointed to set out the dower and make report of the distribution. This Court appoint Martha Robbins to be guardian to her children, viz., Esther, 17 years of age, Elizabeth 14 years, Experience 10, and Martha 6 years, children of Richard Robbins deceased.

Page 235.

Robinson, James, Middletown. Invt. £2034-02-04. Taken 17 December, 1740, by Solomon Adkins, James Brown and Jonathan Allin. Will dated 1st October, 1740.

I, James Robinson of Middletown, in the County of Hartford and Colony of Connecticut, in New England, being advanced in years and weak in body, but of sound disposing mind and memory (thanks be giuen to God therefor), and calling to mind ye mortallity of my body, knowing that it is appointed for man once to die, do make and ordain this my last will and testament: That is to say, in the first place I giue and recommend my soul into the hands of God that gaue it when he shall see cause to call for it, and my body to the earth, to a decent buriall; hoping to haue free pardon of all my sins through the merits of Jesus Christ, my blessed Redeemer, and to inherit euerlasting life. And as touching such worldly estate wherewith it hath pleased God to bless me: After my just debts and funerall charges are first paid out of it, I giue and deuise the remainder in maner and form following, viz: Imprimis. I giue and bequeath unto Jane, my well-beloued wife, the use and improuement of all my estate, both real and personall, during the time she remains my widow; but if she shall marry, then my will is that she shall haue one-third part of my household goods to be at her dispose, and no more. Item. I giue unto my louing daughter and only child, Margaret Stuartt, and to the heirs of her body lawfully begotten, all and euery part of my estate, both real and personal, at the decease of my wife; and if my wife shall marry, then and in such case I giue to my sd. daughter and her heirs as aforesd. at sd. marriage all my estate, both real and personall, except the aforesd. 1-3 part of my houshold goods. And I do hereby nominate and constitute and appoint my beloued widow Jane and trusty friend Wm. Rockwell to be joynt executors of this my last will and testament, ratifying and confirming this and no other to be my last will and testament. In witness whereof I haue hereunto set my hand the day and year aboue writen.

Witness: *John Ward,*   JEAMS ROBINSON, LS.
Eliakim Mather, Jabez Hamlin.

Court Record, Page 79—2 December, 1740: The last will and testament of James Robinson, late of Middletown decd., was now exhibited in Court and proven.

Page 179.

Rockwell, Benjamin, Stafford. Invt. £982-18-06. Taken by Samuel Warner, Amos Walbridge and Josiah Converse.

Court Record, Page 50—5 June, 1739: Adms. granted to Margaret Rockwell, widow, who recog. in £600, with Job Rockwell of Windsor.

Page 5 (Vol. XIV) 11 October, 1743: An account of Adms. was exhibited in Court by Margaret Rockwell, Adms. Accepted.

Page 22 (Vol. XV) 2 September, 1746: Margaret Rockwell, Adms., now moves this Court for a dist. of the moveable part of sd. estate to her the sd. widow and to Samuel Rockwell, Margaret, Elizabeth, Mary and Sarah Rockwell, children of the sd. deceased. And this Court appoint Lt. Samuel Warner, Amos Walbridge and Josiah Converse, of sd. Stafford, to divide sd. estate: to the widow, 1-3 part of the moveable estate, and to Samuel a double part; and to each of the other children their single shares. And make return thereof to this Court.

Page 121—16 March, 1749-50: Margaret Rockwell now having fully finished her Adms. (estate for distribution, £901-16-01), moves that dist. be made: To the widow, 1-3 part of the moveable estate, and 1-3 part of the real estate during life; and to Samuel Rockwell his double share; to Margaret Rockwell (alias Bloggett) and Elizabeth, Mary and Sarah Rockwell, to each of them their single shares. And appoint Samuel Warner, William Orcut and ———— Olvin(?) distributors.

Dist. File, 31 August, 1761: To Margaret Rockwell, late widow, alias Avery; to Samuel Rockwell, to Margaret Rockwell alias Bloggett alias Tyler, to Elizabeth Rockwell alias Orcutt, to Mary Rockwell alias Orcutt, and to Sarah Rockwell alias Loomis. By Isaac Pinney, Josiah Converse and Daniel Alden, Jun'r.

Rose, Benjamin. Court Record, Page 95—17 July, 1741: Upon application made to this Court by Benjamin Rose, a minor, 14 years of age, that his parents are dead and that the Selectmen of Tolland had in the lifetime of his parents (they being unable to provide for him) bound him to Lieut. Josiah Converse of Stafford, whom said minor now makes choice of to be his guardian. Recog., £100.

Page 169-70-71.

Root, Joseph, Farmington. Invt. £827-02-08. Taken 3 January, 1739-40, by Isaac Cowles, Giles Hooker and Samuel Nash. Will dated 14 July, 1729.

I, Joseph Root of Farmingtown, do make this my last will and testament: I give to my wife Ruth Root the use and profit of 1-3 part of my houseing and homelott where I now live during the time of her widowhood, and also the use and profit of 1-3 part of all other of my real estate during her natural life (1 parcell of land, about 60 acres, which I have in the southward division between the mountains, only excepted); also I give to her my sd. wife, to be at her own dispose forever, £30 money or personal estate equivalent thereto. Unto my daughter Elizabeth Root, besides what she now hath and claims to call her own, I give of my personal estate (of such things as she shall choose) the value of £100 current money; also I give her the use and improvement and profit of 2-3 parts of all my real estate, viz., houseing and lands, during her natural life or day of marriage if it shall so happen; also the use and profit for the sd. term of that third part given to my sd. wife in case she be living when my sd. wife's time therein is expired. To my daughter Mary Lee, besides what I have already given her, £20 current money. Unto my five grandchildren, children of sd. daughter Mary Lee, I give to each of them £5 as current money. Unto Joseph Olmsted, now living with me, provided his life be continued until he arrive at the age of 21 years and shall during that time continue faithfully in my service or the service of my son Joseph Root after my decease, then I give him 50 acres of ye land which I have in Farmingtown and in the division of land southward from the reserved land between the mountains, land that was laid out on the west of John Brounson, Sen. deceased; and in case he the sd. Olmsted shall not have heirs, then my will is that the sd. 50 acres of land shall revert and belong unto my three children, Joseph, Elizabeth and Mary, in equal proportion. All the residue of my personal estate (except some few things I shall give unto my son Joseph Root) I give unto my two daughters, Elizabeth and Mary Lee, and my sd. five grandchildren, in equal proportion between them. Unto my only son Joseph Root, besides what I have already given him, I give all the remainder of my real estate, whatsoever it be, to him and to his heirs forever, together with the reversion and fee simple of all that real estate the use thereof for a time I have given to my sd. wife and to my daughter Elizabeth Root. I make my son Joseph Root to be sole executor.

Witness: *John Hooker,*   JOSEPH ROOT, LS.
Robert Porter, Roger Hooker.

Court Record, Page 60—24 January, 1739-40: Will exhibited.

Page 188.

Root, Sarah, Farmington. Invt. £65-19-00. Taken 22 April, 1740, by Isaac Cowles and Nathaniel Wadsworth. Will dated 21 February, 1739-40.

I, Sarah Root of Farmington, do make this my last will and testament: I give to my children, namely, son John Root, Mary Judd and Sarah Gridley, to each of them 20 shillings; and to my grandson Jonathan I give 20 shillings; and to my two grandsons Stephen Root and Timothy Root I give to each of them 10 shillings. And all the remainder of my estate I give to my daughter Hannah Root as a reward for her care and pains in careing and provideing for me in my old age. I constitute my son John Root to be my executor.

Witness: *William Wadsworth,*   SARAH ROOT, LS.
    Joseph Root.

Court Record, Page 65—6 May, 1740: Will proven.

Page 14-15.

Sawyer, Jonathan, Hebron. Invt. £365-18-02. Taken 2 May, 1737, by Nathaniel Phelps, Hezekiah Gaylord and Joseph Phelps.

Court Record, Page 11—22 June, 1737: Adms. to Joseph Phelps of Hebron. Recog., with Stephen Post.

Page 44—13 March, 1738-9: Account of Adms. accepted.

Page 219-20.

Sayer, Nathan, Jr., Middletown. Invt. £169-15-09. Taken 2 July, 1740, by Jabez Hamlin and William Rockwell. Will dated 13 June, 1740.

I, Nathan Sayer, Jr., of Middletown, in the County of Hartford, do make this my last will and testament: I give to my sister Eunice Prout 3-4 parts of my wife's wearing apparrel and household goods which she left. I give to Susannah, the daughter of William Prout, 1-4 part of my wife's wearing apparrel and household goods, also 2 gold rings. I give to my two brethren, Daniel and Matthew, two of my wearing coats and my fine shirts, to be equally divided between them. I give to my honoured father Nathan Sayer all my other clothes and all the remainder of my estate not otherwise disposed of.

N. B.: My wife's wearing apparell and household goods to be excluded and not subject to the payment of my debts.

I appoint my father sole executor.

Witness: *Samuel Green,*   NATHAN SAYER, JR., LS.
Isaac Woodward, Jabez Hamlin.

Court Record, Page 70—5 August, 1740: Will proven.

Page 15-16.

Selden, Joseph, East Haddam. Invt. £1472-08-04. Taken 1st November, 1736, by Isaac Spencer, Jabez Chapman and Abel Willey.

Court Record, Page 8—2 June, 1737: Adms. granted to Phebe Selden, widow. Recog., £1500, with Jabez Chapman.

[The settlement of this estate, with distribution, may be on record at Colchester.]—C. W. M.

Invt. in Vol. XIV, Page 85. Will in Vol. XV, Page 324-5.

Seymour, Capt. Thomas, Hartford. A true invt. of the goods, chattells, credits and all other real estate, apprised by James Ensign and Joseph Holtom.

ITEMS OF REAL ESTATE.

	£ s d
Homestead, 30 acres, with buildings,	800-00-00
Lott in the west division, called Easton's lott, 18 acres at £20,	360-00-00
To Shepherd's orchard, 6 acres at £15 per acre,	90-00-00
To his rights in Winchester, £300,	300-00-00
To 115 acres of land in Waterbury,	100-00-00
To his rights in the Old Mills in Hartford,	5-10-00
	£1655-10-00
To personal estate,	£265-10-04

To cash received from sundry persons as followeth:

	£ s d		£ s d
From Cyprian Watson,	00-22-10	Thomas Richards,	00-12-04
From Timothy Seymour,	1-16-07	Jacob Kellogg,	00-12-00
From Caleb Benton,	00-17-09	Moses Benton,	1-00-00
From William Powell,	00-13-09	Deacon Merrells,	2-08-05
From Jubert Quenipue,	2-02-01	Jed: Richards,	1-14-06

WILL DATED 4 MAY, 1738:

I, Thomas Seymour of Hartford, do make this my last will and testament: I give unto my wife Mary the north room of my now dwelling house and the northwest cellar belonging to sd. house; also I give to her the best bed and suitable furniture to sd. bed; also the use of a good cow during her natural life; also I give her £6 per annum, to be paid to her by my two daughters, Sarah and Alice, in consideration of what I shall hereafter mention to be given to them out of my estate, and the £6 to be paid in equal proportion by my two daughters Sarah and Alice aforesd. yearly during their mother's natural life. Further, I give to her 8 bushels of wheat, 16 bushels of Indian corne and 10 cords of wood a year during her natural life, all which shall be paid by my son Bevell Seymour once every year as long as she shall live or continue my widow, which is in consideration of what is hereafter mentioned to be given to him my sd. son Bevell out of my estate, all which is to be the full of her dowry from and of my whole estate. And if she my sd. wife shall not accept of what is hereafter mentioned to be given her in full of sd. dowry, then what is herein given to her before mentioned shall cease and be of no value. I give unto my son Thomas Seymour, besides what I have heretofore given him by deed of gift, all my right, interest and property in the lands called the western lands, formerly granted to the Townships of Hartford and Windsor, in whatever township the same doth or may happen to fall or lye, sd. lands to be to him my son Thomas and to his eldest male heir in a right line forever to the end of the world, without liberty to sell, convey or alter the property thereof. Also, I give unto my sd. son Thomas 10 acres of land on the north side of my lott at Four Mile Hill, called Shepherd's lott, to him, his heirs and assigns forever. Also,

I give unto my son Thomas 2 acres of woodland in my Wethersfield lott, sd. two acres to lye upon a square at the south end of Hartford's westermost highway which runs down to Wethersfield bounds, and the western part of sd. two acres to extend west as far as the west side of sd. highway. And my will is that my son Thomas shall not compel his brother Bevell to fence against him in the two acres aforesd. And further, I give unto my son Thomas my negro man named Sias, and to his heirs and assigns forever. I give unto my son Zebulon Seymour all my land in the Parish of Newington within the Township of Wethersfield after that two acres is set out to Thomas aforesd., to him and his heirs and assigns forever. Also, I give to him my lott of land in Hartford bounds adjoining to the Wethersfield land aforesd., called Easton's lott, in quantity about 18 acres. Also, I give to him the remaining part of that lott in Hartford bounds called Shepherd's lott after that my son Thomas has measured out to him 10 acres on the north end thereof. I give to my son Bevell all my lands in the Township of Waterbury, to be to him and to descend to his eldest male heir lawfully begotten in a right line forever to the end of the world, without liberty to sell, convey or alter the property thereof. And in case the sd. Bevell or his male heir aforesd. shall attempt to sell or alienate the aforementioned lands in Waterbury, that then the same shall become the estate and property of the second son surviving of my son Thomas aforesd. And further, my will is that my son Bevell do punctually pay the above-mentioned legacies of wheat, Indian corn and wood to his mother for her comfortable support during life. I give unto my daughter Mary £20 besides what I have already given her, which shall be paid to her by my two daughters, Sarah and Alice, in equal proportions when they come to the age of 20 and 7 years. I give to my daughter Ruth Seymour all my land in the 2 westermost tiers of lotts next to Farmingtown, as well that which lyeth in common with my brother John Seymour as that which butteth north on Isaac Merrells in the westermost tier of all, the same to be to my sd. daughter Ruth and to her heirs and assigns forever. I give to my three youngest daughters my house and homestead in equal proportions, and to their heirs and assigns forever, that is to say, unto Sarah, Alice and Jerusha, only reserving to my wife the use of the north room and the northwest cellar during her natural life as before mentioned, and ordering that my two daughters Sarah and Alice do pay to their mother £6 per annum, and to my daughter Mary £20, in equal proportion when they shall arrive to the age of 20 and 7 years as aforesd. And further, my will is that when my just debts and funeral expenses are paid, the remainder of my moveable estate shall be and remain to my son Thomas for redeeming of his land mortgaged to the Country on account of the New London Society. I appoint my sd. son Thomas Seymour sole executor.

Witness: ————————,   (NOT SIGNED.)

———————— ————————--.

A true copy, taken out of the original will and examined by me.

————————— —————————, ———.

Court Record, Page 7—25 December, 1740: Adms. granted to Thomas Seymour, son of the deceased. Recog., £1000, with John Seymour, Jr.

Page 88—5 May, 1741: Mrs. Mary Seymour asks that her dower be set out to her: Whereupon this Court appoint Capt. Daniel Webster, Deacon Isaac Kellogg and Joseph Holcomb to set out to the widow her thirds.

Page 94—7 July, 1741: Report of the distributors.

Page 18 (Vol. XIV) 1st March, 1743: Thomas Seymour, Adms., exhibited an account of his Adms., which account is accepted.

Page 22—3 May, 1743: A further allowance was now made to the Adms., which, together with what was allowed on sd. account 1st March, 1742-3, amounted in debts and charges to the whole sum of £599-07-07. Account accepted.

Page 43—1st May, 1744: This Court do set out to Mary Seymour, widow, the use of household goods for her necessary use.

Page 59—15 May, 1745: A further account of Adms. exhibited. Accepted.

Page 106 (Vol. XV) 13 September, 1749: Whereas, Thomas Seymour of Wethersfield and others showing to the General Assembly of the Colony of Connecticut in May, A. D. 1749, by their petition, that the last will and testament of Capt. Thomas Seymour, late of Hartford decd., which was dated 4 May, 1738, was by sd. Thomas Seymour, executor, put into the hands of the Honble. Joseph Talcott, Esq., Judge of the Court of Probates, in order for the probate thereof, and that sd. will, by some means unknown, was destroyed and lost, and that having obtained a true copy of sd. will before the loss or destruction thereof, and the sd. copy was exactly transcribed into and recited in sd. petition, and that sd. recital does intirely show the contents of the sd. last will and testament, and that sd. General Assembly did resolve that it was sufficiently proved that the sd. Capt. Thos. Seymour did so make his last will and testament, and that the sd. exhibited writing of the abovesd. form and purport, as also the recital thereof in sd. petition, do respectively contain and are fully and sufficiently proved to contain and make manifest the full and intire and sole contents of sd. original will destroyed or lost as abovesd., and therefore order that George Wyllys, Secretary of this Colony, carefully transmit sd. described writing and recitall to this Court to be recorded. In pursuance of sd. resolve, this Court order that the abovesd. copy and recital be recorded and kept on file.

Page 62—5 April, 1748: Further account of Adms. on the estate of Capt. Thomas Seymour (£338-07-02), arising on the sale of the land of the sd. decd., including the former account. Allowed. Also received former amount, £320-05-00. Which account is allowed. Also, the Adms. now exhibited an account of the sale of the lands of the sd. decd. agreeable to the order of the General Assembly and direction of this Court, which account is allowed and ordered to be kept on file.

Page 66—5 April, 1748: Hartford, 9 April, 1747: Then, pursuant to the resolve of the General Assembly in May, 1745, and by the direction of the Court of Probates of the District of Hartford, I made sale of one parcel of land belonging to the estate of Capt. Thomas Seymour decd., in quantity six acres, called Shepherd's orchard, to Bevel Seymour of Wethersfield for the price of £120-01-00 money, he being the highest bidder for sd. land, which parcel is butted east on a highway, west on land of John Carter, north on land of Moses Seymour, and south on Wethersfield north line. Also, I made sale of one other parcel belonging to the estate of the sd. decd., being about 7 acres in quantity, to Nathaniel Seymour and Ebenezer Benton, Jr., they being the highest bidders for sd. parcel, which 7 acres was a parcel of the homestead of the sd. Thomas Seymour decd., and is butted east on the other part of sd. homestead, west on the river or commons, north on the river or commons, and south on the land of Zach: Seymour, and was sold as aforesd. at the price of £198-02-00 money, the whole amounting to £318-03-00, and was for the payment of £306-18-00 debts due from the estate of the sd. decd. more than the moveable estate and incident charges.

Pr. Thomas Seymour, Administrator.

At a Court of Probate held at Hartford, 5 April, 1748, this report was allowed and ordered to be recorded and kept on file.

Test: Joseph Talcott, Clerk.

Shipman, Joseph. Court Record, Page 17—6 December, 1737: Sylvanus Shipman, a minor, 9 1-2 years of age, son of Joseph Shipman, late of Haddam, chose his mother Anne Shipman to be his guardian.

Shrigley, George. Court Record, Page 54—4 September, 1739: George Shrigley, a minor, 14 years of age, son of George Shrigley of Hartford deceased, chose Joseph Talcott, Jr., of Hartford, to be his guardian. Recog., £50.

Page 7 (Vol. XIV) 9 June, 1742: George Shrigley, a minor, desired that Joseph Talcott, his guardian, might be released from his trust of guardianship to him, and the sd. minor made choice of Capt. Peletiah Mills of Windsor to be his guardian. Recog., £200.

Page 6.

Skiff, Stephen, Tolon (Tolland), shoemaker. Will dated 22 February, 1737: I, Stephen Skiff of Tolland, shoemaker, do make this my last will and testament: I give unto my wife Elizabeth Skiff all my moveable estate in the house and out of doors, ordering her to pay unto my daughters what I shall hereafter give unto them. Also, I give unto my sd. wife Elizabeth Skiff my dwelling house and barn and about 60 acres of land on which they stand, unto her and her heirs forever; bounded partly by Willimantic River, Capt. Joseph Hatch's land, Edy Hatch's land, and land belonging to the heirs of Anthony Slafter. My will is and I give all the remaining part of my land unto my three sons, Nathan Skiff, Benjamin Skiff and Joseph Skiff, to be equally divided among them, to be to them and their heirs forever. I give to my four daughters, Sarah Skiff, Elizabeth Skiff, Hepzibah Skiff and Mary Skiff, 5 shillings in money apiece, to be paid unto them by their mother, hoping that she will also respect my sd. daughters in her will. I appoint my wife Elizabeth Skiff executrix.

Witness: *Joseph Hatch,*   STEPHEN SKIFF, LS.
Timothy Hatch, Zebulon West.

Court Record, Page 9—7 June, 1737: Will exhibited by Elizabeth Skiff, executrix. Proven.

Page 56—2 October, 1739: Nathan Skiff now moves this Court for a division of lands given by will to the three sons. This Court appoint Ebenezer Nye, John Lothrop and Edy Hatch to make the division.

2nd Tuesday of October, 1739: Distribution of land of Stephen Skiff, given by will: To Nathan Skiff, 53 acres adjoining land of Capt. Joseph Hatch, Malatiah Lothrop and Barnabas Hatch; to Benjamin Skiff, 59 1-2 acres, including 14 1-4 acres bought of Joseph Skinner, which 14 1-4 acres lyeth in common with other land belonging to the heirs of Anthony Slafter, formerly of Tolland, deceased, and 45 acres of the sd. land adjoins south upon Capt. Joseph Hatch's land, east upon land given by sd. Skiff deceased to Elizabeth his wife, north upon land of heirs of Anthony Slafter; to Joseph Skiff, 55 acres of land by meets and bounds.

Page 198-9.

Skinner, Deacon John, Colchester. Invt. £413-10-09. Taken 11 September, 1740, by Nathaniel Foot, Ebenezer Kellogg and Andrew Carrier. Will dated 12 February, 1739-40.

I, John Skinner of Colchester, in the County of Hartford, do make this my last will and testament: I give to my wife Sarah Skinner (whom I make sole executrix to this my last will and testament) 1-3 part of all my moveable estate after my just debts be paid out of the whole, then she to take ye third part for herself clear forever; and also half the use of my dwelling house and barn so long as she remains my widow; and also 1-3 of all my orcharding and improved lands during the term of her natural life. Nextly, to my son John Skinner I have given him several tracts of land by deed, which makes his full portion of my estate which belongs to him; also to my son Daniel Skinner, and to Joseph Skinner, and to Aaron Skinner, and to Noah Skinner, I have given them their portions by deed. It is to be understood that when I was in health I considered the state of my lands, and with advice and to the satisfaction of all my sons I give them each one his portion of my estate, and my will is that they shall not have any more. But the remaining part of my estate my will is that my wife shall have 1-3 part clear as is above written, and the remaining part to be paid out by my executrix in manner following, that is to say, to be divided into five equal parts according to the number of my daughters, but considering my daughter Sarah wt married to Nathaniel Loomis is dead and left three children, one daughter and two sons, my will is that the two sons shall each of them have 10 shillings paid to them by my executrix out of the 1-5 part of the whole, and the remainder of that 1-5 part to be paid to Sarah Loomis, daughter to my sd. daughter Sarah deceased. And my will is that the other four equal parts be paid out to my other four daughters now surviving, namely, Ann Dean, Joanna Loomis, Mary Kilbourn and Elizabeth Sextone, to be paid to each of them out of my estate as it shall be apprised, at the discretion of my executor. I make my wife Sarah my sole executrix.

Witness: *Nathaniel Foot,*   JOHN SKINNER, LS.
Ebenezer Kellogg, Israel Foot.

Court Record, Page 71—18 September, 1740: Will proven.

Page 53.

Slater, Elizabeth, Simsbury. Died 7 November, 1737. Invt. £40-19-00. Taken 21 November, 1737, by John Case and Joseph Cornish.
Court Record, Page 18—13 December, 1737: Adms. to Nathaniel Holcomb 3rd, of Simsbury. Recog., £60, with Roger Wolcott.

Smith, Hannah, Estate, Wethersfield. Court Record, Page 85—17 March, 1740-1: Adms. granted to Hezekiah Graham of Wethersfield, who recog. in £100, with Stephen Riley of Wethersfield.

Invt. and Will in Vol. XIV, Page 2.

Spencer, Obadiah, Hartford. Invt. £2221-14-08. Taken 4 December, 1741, by Aaron Cook and Joseph Talcott. Will dated 27 February, 1732-3.
I, Obadiah Spencer of Hartford, do make this my last will and testament: I give to my wife Ruth 1-2 of the improved lands which I shall hereafter in this my will bequeath to my son Daniel, and the use of 1-2 of my dwelling house, 2 cows and one horse, and the use of all my house-

hold stuff, so long as she remains my widow. But if my sd. wife should marry, then my will is that my son Daniel shall improve the whole of sd. house and land given as aforesd. to my sd. wife. I give to my son Obadiah Spencer one parcel of land in Hartford which I bought of Col. Whiting, Capt. Joseph Whiting and Capt. Stanly, and part of that I bought of Richard Goodman, bounded north on land of my brother John Spencer, east on the road that leads to Windsor and on the heirs of Thomas Butler decd., south in part on the heirs of Thomas Butler and part on my own land, and west partly on John Pratt's land, partly on Thomas Burr, Jr., his land, and partly on land of Thomas Sanford, about 40 acres more or less, with the buildings thereon erected; also one lott of land in the Long Meadow, bounding east on a passway, west on Neck land, north on land of Ebenezer Welles, and south on John Church's land. Also, I give to my son Obadiah all my right of land in Windsor which I now have or that may hereafter fall to me by right of my wife's father Mark Kelsey decd. Also, my joyner's tools of all sorts, to him and his heirs forever. I give to my son Stephen 10 acres of the south side of a lott of land at the Blue Hills, which I bought of Mr. John Reed, to run east and west through sd. lott, besides what I have already given him of moveables, to him and his heirs forever. I have confirmed to my son Jonathan by deed of gift a certain lott of land in the west division at Hartford which he has conveyed away for a tract of land at Enfield, which settlement or tract of land I fully confirm to him by this bequest. Also, I give him one yoke of oxen. All which land I give to him and his heirs forever. I give to my son Daniel my homelott that my now dwelling house stands on, to him and his heirs forever; and also that land in the Long Meadow I bought of Charles Kelsy, butting east on the Great River, west on Neck land, north on John Pratt, and south on land given to the First Church in Hartford; and my lott at Brick Hill Bridge, which I bought of Mr. Dodd, butting north on the country road, on a driftway and church land; and also a lott at Pitkin Swamp, butting east on the heirs of Thomas Butler decd., west on a highway, north partly on land of John Pratt and partly on my own land given in this will to my son Obadiah, south partly on Dickinson's land and partly on land of John Church, one yoke of oxen, 2 horse kind, and all my team tackling, to be to him and his heirs forever. I give to my son Caleb the house and homested where he now dwells, which I bought of my brother Disborah Spencer, and also the rest of my Blue Hills lott not before bequeathed, about 20 acres, and my lott of land in the Long Meadow called Hobs Hole, besides what of moveable estate I have already given him. All which I give to him my son Caleb and his heirs forever. I give and bequeath to four of my sons, Obadiah, Stephen, Jonathan and Caleb Spencer, all my right and interest in the lands commonly called the western lands, equally to be divided amongst them. I give to my son Obadiah my great Bible that was my father's, and my great wainscot chest, to him and his heirs forever. If what I have in this my will before given to my sd. wife be not sufficient for her comfortable maintenance or support, then

I order my five sons to pay to my sd. wife 20 shillings apiece yearly so long as she continues my widow; but if my sd. wife shall marry, then my will is that she shall have only the two cows and horse in this will bequeathed to her, and 1-3 part of my household stuff, to be at her own dispose forever. I appoint my son Obadiah and my son Daniel to be executors.

Witness: *Matthew Talcott,*   OBADIAH SPENCER, LS.
Abigail Talcott, Eunice Talcott.

    Court Record, Page 102—1st December: Will proven.

Invt. in Vol. XIV, Page 130.

Stedman, John, Sen., Farmington. Invt. £103-14-03. Taken 19 January, 1740, by Joseph Hawley, Isaac Cowles and H. Deming.

    Court Record, Page 9—7 June, 1737: Adms. granted to Abigail Stedman, widow, who recog. with Samuel Cowles of sd. Farmington.

    Page 37 (Vol. XIV) 2 February, 1743-4: Abigail Stedman, Adms., exhibited an account of her Adms., which is accepted by the Court.

Page 120-130.

Steele, Benoni, Hartford. Invt. £586-03-06. Taken 12 February, 1738-9, by Thomas Orton, Jr., and Timothy Thompson.

    We, the subscribers, being the sole heirs to the estate of Benoni Steele, late of Hartford deceased, doe by these presents covenant and agree, for ourselves and our heirs, that this agreement shall be a final settlement of the estate of the sd. decd. forever: First, we agree that Thomas Steele, Daniel Steele and Eliphalet Steele, the heirs of Samuel Steele of Hartford aforesd. deceased, shall have and hold for themselves and to their dispose one piece of land in a division against Hartford in Farmingtown bounds, being the 17th allottment (20 acres). Second, by one piece in the division of land between the mountains, 41 3-4 acres, within the bounds of the Parish of Southington, in sd. Farmingtown, with two other pieces of land, one of 18 acres and one of 14 acres, described boundries omitted. To the heirs of John Steele, late of Farmingtown decd., and to Sarah and Rachel Steele, heirs to the estate of the sd. John Steele, all the rest and residue of the lands belonging to the estate of sd. Benoni Steele deceased which is in the bounds of sd. Farmingtown, divided and undivided, to be to them the sd. Sarah Steele and Rachel Steele forever. In confirmation of the foregoing agreement, we, the subscribers, have hereunto set our hands and seals this 21st day of March, 1738-9.

THOMAS STEELE, LS.   DANIEL STEELE, LS.   ELIPHALET STEELE, LS.
JOSEPH HART, ATTY. FOR SARAH AND RACHEL STEELE.

                         Test: *Joseph Talcott, Clerk.*

    Court Record, Page 41—15 February, 1738-9: Adms. to Joseph Hart of Farmington.

Page 108-9.

Steele, John, Sen., Farmington. Invt. £991-16-00. Taken 13 September, 1738, by Joseph Judd, Isaac Cowles and Joseph Hart. Will dated 14 June, 1735.

I, John Steele, Sen., of Farmingtown, do make and ordain this my last will and testament: Unto my only son John Steele, Jr., I give the sum of 20 shillings, to be paid him out of my personal estate by my executrix, which is all I shall now give him considering the liberal donation I have formerly made him, and order him my sd. son to pasture for his two sisters, viz., Sarah Steele and Rachel Steele (so long as they shall live and bear my name) each of them a cow as I provided by a deed of gift I formerly gave him. Unto my daughter Mary Bird, besides what I have already given her, I give her my 2 lotts of land lying in the two divisions of land in Farmington which lye north from the reserved lands (one division on the west, ye other on the east side of the river), in each division one lott. Unto my daughter Ruth Thompson, besides what I have already given her, I give to her my lott of land lying at a place called and known by the name of the sixth and furthest division of land, lying west of the reserved land in Farmington. Unto my daughter Sarah Steele, now living with me, I give several lotts of land, all within the bounds of ye Town of Farmington, viz., one lott which I have in a division of land laid out on the range of Blue and Shuttle Meadow Mountain; another of sd. lotts is the lott that was laid out on my own right in a division of land lying between Panthorn Division and Waterbury bounds; another of sd. lots is in the lott that was laid out in my own right in the first division of land lying west from the reserved lands; also 2 lotts more, laid out on my right, one in the 2nd and the other in the 3rd division of land in sd. Farmingtown, lying west of the reserved land. Unto my daughter Rachel Steele, now living with me, to her and to her heirs forever, I give several pieces of land in the Township of Farmingtown, viz., two lotts of land laid out by my right, one in the 4th and the other in the 5th division of land lying west from ye reserved lands in Farmingtown; also 36 acres of land, more or less, which I have att a place called Three Mile Hills, which I purchased of my son John Steele; also 5 acres of land at a place called by the name of Judd's Hill in Farmingtown. I give to my two daughters, Sarah and Rachel Steele, all my right in the common and undivided land in sd. Farmingtown; and unto them my daughters, Sarah and Rachel, I give all the residue and remainder of my estate, both real and personal, not heretofore disposed of, whatsoever and wheresoever it be, to be divided equally between them; and also that they shall have, hold and injoy for their use the kitchen and lean-to of my dwelling house so long as they or either of them live bearing my name. And my will further is, that my sd. daughter Rachel Steele shall not have power to sell, barter or exchange the estate that I have given her in this will, or any part of it, without the approbation and allowance of my sd. daughter Sarah Steele and my grandson-in-law Joseph Hart. But at the same instant of time that she shall presume to act contrary hereunto, her right that I have given her shall cease and be void as to that part of sd. estate which she shall presume so to alienate without the aforesd. approbations and allowance, and I hereby will and bequeath the same to my sd. daughter Sarah Steele. I appoint my daughter Sarah Steele to be sole executrix.

Witness: *Joseph Woodruff,*   JOHN STEELE, LS.
Thomas Smith, Roger Hooker.

Court Record, Page 33—3 October, 1738: Will proven.

Page 164-5-6-7.

Steele, Capt. Thomas, Hartford. Invt. £2900 plus. Taken 29 January, 1739-40, by Ebenezer Sedgewick, Stephen Hosmer and Moses Nash. Will dated 20 September, 1737.

I, Thomas Steele of Hartford, do make this my last will and testament: I give to Susannah, my wife, 1-3 part of my moveable estate forever, and 1-3 part of my dwelling house, barn and all my lands during her widowhood. And provided she shall hereafter marry, my will is (she being willing) that she shall have £60 out of my moveable estate, provided she releases her right in the buildings and lands aforesd. I give to my son Samuel Steele the 1-2 of my lands which I now live upon, lying on the east side of the highway or common road running north and south to the west division (and provided my dwelling house shall be found upon the north side, that I reserve for my son John Steele; and my son Samuel aforesd. shall have his lands made up of lands eastward of sd. house). Further, I give to my sd. son Samuel my house on the west side of the highway and 3 acres of land adjoining to sd. house, and also 9 acres of land that I lately bought of the heirs of Samuel Sedgewick, Jr., late of Hartford deceased. And further, I give unto my son Samuel Steele the 1-3 part of my barn during the time it shall remain fit for service. I give to my son William Steele all my lands at New Hartford, divided and undivided. I give unto my two sons Nathaniel Steele and James Steele all my lands in Hartford in the west division west of the highway not before disposed of, to be equally divided between them. I give to my daughter Jerusha Steele, alias Mills, £40 money and one cow over and above what I have already given her. I give to my daughter Susannah Steele, alias Hosmer, £16 besides what I have already given her. Furthermore, I give unto my sons, Samuel Steele, William Steele, James Steele, Nathaniel Steele and John Steele, all my personal estate not before disposed of, to be equally divided between them. I give to my son John Steele my dwelling house and 1-3 part of my barn, and 1-2 on the south side of the land east of the highway, it being the remaining part of sd. land that I have given to my son Samuel on the east side of the highway. Further, I give all my land east of the Connecticut River to all my children, both sons and daughters, to be equally divided among them. And I appoint Susannah Steele, my wife, and Samuel Steele, my son, executors.

Witness: *Martin Smith,*   THOMAS STEELE, LS.
Adonijah Moody, Moses Nash.

Court Record, Page 60—5 February, 1739-40: Will proven. James Steele, a minor, age 20 years, and Nathaniel, age 18 years, sons of Capt. Thomas Steele, chose their mother Susannah Steele to be their guardian. John Steele, age 16 years, chose his brother Samuel to be his guardian.

Steward, John. Court Record, Page 19—3 January, 1737-8: John Steward, age 17 years, lately arrived from Great Britain, made choice of Michael Steward of Wethersfield to be his guardian. Recog., £100.

Page 324-5.

Stow, Samuel, Middletown. Will dated 26 September, 1741: I, Samuel Stow of Middletown, in the County of Hartford, shoemaker, do make this my last will and testament: I give to my wife Esther the west end of my dwelling house with the cellarage, and so much of the utensils in the house as she shall have occasion for her own use, and so much room in my barn as she shall need, and one cow (which of them she shall choose); also the use of 1-3 part of my improved land, with the 1-3 part of the orchard. This I give to my wife during her natural life or widowhood. I give to my two daughters, Esther and Bethiah, and also to my granddaughter, Submit Stow, only heir to my eldest son Samuel Stow decd., what they have already had, and nothing more at present; but after my wife's decease my will is that these three last above mentioned shall have an equal share in dividing those moveables that my wife shall leave at her decease, with my other two daughters, Abigail and Lucia. I give to my son Jerediah Stow 1-2 of my homelott, to be taken off the north side, makeing a crooked line between that north part and that on the south part so as to leave out the tan house and tan vats. Also, I give to my son Jerediah 1-3 part of my barn. I give to my son Isaac Stow all my rights of land on the east side of the Great River, also 1-2 of my boggy meadow land. I give to my son Jonathan Stow 1-2 of my homelott, to be taken on the south side, with all the buildings thereon (except 1-3 part of the barn), with the tan house and tan vats; also the cyder mill and press. Also, I give to my son Jonathan all my burnt swamp pasture; also the 1-2 of my boggy meadow; also all my land at Pistol Point; also I give to my son Jonathan all my husbandry tools; also all my tanning and shoemaker's tools. And further, my will is, that my son Jonathan shall have my yoke of oxen and my two mares and one of my cows; also my four young cattle; also a gunn. These things as above mentioned I give to my son Jonathan, obliging him to pay all my debts and funeral charges, and also to make up to his two sisters, Abigail and Lucia, what shall be wanting of £110 after my wife has spared what she can out of the utensils of the house; and further, that he shall find his mother her firewood during her widowhood. And further, I give to my son Jonathan three acres of land off from the west end of my lott at Woolph Pitt Hill, also all my sheep.

I give to my two daughters, Abigail and Lucia, £55 apiece, which is to be made up out of utensils in the house so far as my wife can spare them, and what they fall short of £110 my will is that my son Jonathan shall make up to his sisters. I give to my son Stephen Stow all my lottment of land at Woolphitt Hill, excepting the three acres given to my son Jonathan. Further, my will is that my red cow and all my swine, excepting one, and all my corne, flax and wool shall be disposed of to the present support of my family. I appoint my son Jonathan sole executor.

Witness: *John Shephard,*   SAMUEL STOW, LS.
Thomas Johnson, Jonathan Stockin.

Court Record, Page 106—5 January, 1741-2: Will proven.

Page 33 (Vol. XIV) 16 November, 1743: Stephen Stow, 18 years of age, son of Deacon Samuel Stow, chose William Rockwell to be his guardian. Recog., £200.

Page 10 (Vol. XVI) 1 January, 1750-1: An inventory of the estate of Deacon Samuel Stow, late of Middletown decd., which the said deceased gave his widow dureing life, was now exhibited in Court by Jonathan Stow, executor, which this Court accepts and order on file. The said executor now moves that distribution be made, the widow being deceased: Whereupon this Court appoint Joseph Smith, Joseph Ranny and Thomas Johnson, of Middletown, to distribute said estate to the heirs: To heirs of Esther Ranny, to Bethia Morton, to Abigail Shailor, to Luce Warren, and to Submit Stow, to each an equal fifth part of said moveable estate, agreeable to the last will of the said deceased.

Page 204.

Stow, Thomas, Jr., Middletown. Invt. £163-06-06. Taken 28 April, 1740, by William Rockwell and Seth Wetmore.

Court Record, Page 69—1st July, 1740: Adms. granted to Nathaniel Stow. Recog., £300, with Thomas Hurlbut, Jr.

Page 86 (Vol. XV) 12 January, 1748-9: Nathaniel Stow, administrator, exhibited an account of his Adms. Accepted.

Page 161.

Strong, Asahel, Farmington. Invt. £1126-13-07. Taken 31 December, 1739, by Josiah Hart and John Newell. Will dated 28 June, 1739.

I, Asahell Strong of Farmingtown, do make this my last will and testament: I give to my son John Strong, his heirs and assigns forever, all my land in that division lying in the southwest corner of Farmingtown bounds called the division on the mountain against Waterbury, that is to say, all those lands in sd. division that I bought of Roger Bronson; also that pitch of land which he hath taken up on my account at Rattlesnake Hill; also what creatures of mine shall be in his hands at my decease; also what debts shall be due from him to me upon my decease. I give to my daughter Margaret Root, alias Strong, that pilion and cloth that were her mother's. I give unto sd. Margaret Root and Mary Lewis, alias Strong, in equal degree, my two biggest brass kettles, two iron potts and two iron kettles of those that were their mother's; also, all the pewter and earthen ware that were their mother's, except an earthen dye pott; also all my wooden ware, as bowls, dishes, trenchers, wool combs and cards, warming pan, frying pan, and two brass skilletts; also each of them one trunk; to be set to them at the discretion of my son Asahell Strong. All the remainder of my estate, both real and personal, utensils both within doors and without, money, debts, dues or demands, that is to say, all ye remainder of my estate of what kind and degree soever, I give and bequeath to my son Asahell Strong and his heirs forever. I appoint my son Asahell Strong to be sole executor.

Witness: *John Hart,*   ASAHELL STRONG, LS.
Samuel Porter, John Hart, Jr.

Court Record, Page 56—6 November, 1739: Will proven.
Page 58—1st January, 1739-40: Exhibit of an inventory. Accepted and ordered to be recorded.

Will and Invt. in Vol. XIV, Page 4-5-6-7.

Strong, Samuel, Windsor. Inventory taken 8 February, 1741-2, by John Stoughton, Peletiah Allyn and John Allyn. Will dated 14 January, 1741-2.

I, Samuel Strong of Windsor, do make this my last will and testament: I give to my wife Martha Strong the right in my house and cellar during widowhood, with the use of 1-3 part of my orchard and pasture land adjoining to the house we now live in, which land I bought of Jacob Gibbs the 2nd, and land of Jonathan Elsworth, both of Middletown, so long as she shall remain my widow. My will and pleasure is that my beloved wife shall have the use of 1-3 part of all my improved lands in the Town of Windsor so long as she shall remain my widow. I give to my wife 1-3 part of all my moveable estate, except the timber and pine boards that are provided and intended for my house, to be to her forever and at her own dispose. I give unto my son Samuel Strong the house he now liveth in, and also 2-3 of the land on which the house now standeth, and the other third part of that lott of land, after the decease or marriage of his mother, to him and his heirs forever. My will and pleasure is that my son Samuel Strong shall have 1 1-2 acres of upland running from the street down to the bottom of the hill eastward, which I bought of Robert

Hoskins and Elizabeth his wife; also 4 acres of pasture land adjoining, which I bought of Dr. Samuel Mather and Hannah his wife; that is to say, 2-3 of sd. parcels or pieces of land to him at my decease, and the other third after the marriage or decease of his mother. I give unto my son Samuel Strong 2 pieces of meadow land lying in the great meadow on the west side of the Great River in Windsor, containing 4 acres in each piece, formerly belonging to my grandfather, the Rev. John Warham, to be to him, my sd. son, and his heirs forever. I give to my son Return Strong my new house in which we now dwell, and also the orchard and pasture land adjoining to sd. house, except what I have before reserved and given to my wife for her use while she remains my widow, and after that the whole tenement to be to my sd. son Return Strong, to him and his heirs forever. I give to my son Return Strong 9 acres of my meadow land lying in the great meadow in Windsor, on the west side of the Great River. My will and pleasure is that all the land that I have or may and ought to have in the commons and undivided lands in Windsor, and also in that tract of land called the equivalent land, shall be divided and shared equally unto my two sons, namely, Samuel and Return. My will and pleasure is that my lands at Torrington shall be sold by my executors towards paying my debts and the legacies to my daughters. I give and bequeath my land at Harwington, that was laid out to the heirs of my honoured father Return Strong of Windsor, unto my daughter Sarah Phelps, to be to her and her heirs forever. My will and pleasure is that my daughter Sarah Phelps shall have out of my moveable estate the sum of £110, including the land at Harwington above mentioned, and also what she hath already had. I give to my daughters, namely, Martha and Mary Strong, £110 money, to be paid to each of them out of my moveable estate. My will and pleasure is that the timber and boards intended for my new house shall be reckoned with the house to my son Return Strong. My will and pleasure is that what provisions may be in the house at my decease shall be and remain for the use of the family without price. My will and pleasure is and I hereby appoint my wife Martha Strong and my two sons, Samuel Strong and Return Strong, executors.

Witness: *Samuel Mather,*   SAMUEL STRONG, LS.
Jonathan Wright, Samuel Stiles.

Court Record, Page 109—2 February, 1741-2: Will proven.

Page 191-2.

Sumner, William, Middletown. Invt. £959-00-08. Taken 30 January, 1739-40, by Solomon Adkins, John Bacon and William Rockwell.

Court Record, Page 64—14 April, 1740: Adms. granted to Hannah Sumner, widow, and Hezekiah Sumner, who recog. in £500 with Benjamin Adkins.

Page 47 (Vol. XIV) 7 August, 1744: An account of Adms. was now exhibited in Court by Hannah Sumner, widow. Accepted. Order to distribute the estate:

	£ s d
To the widow, Hannah Sumner, her thirds,	107-12-00
To Hezekiah Sumner, eldest son,	51-16-00
To Hannah, Sarah and Mary Sumner, to each,	25-15-00¼
And to William, John and Ebenezer Sumner, to each,	25-15-00¼

And appoint Solomon Adkins, William Rockwell and Return Megs, of Middletown, distributors.

Page 55—5 March, 1744-5: Hezekiah Sumner, age 20 years, and Mary Sumner, age 15 years, chose Hezekiah Sumner of Middletown to be their guardian. Recog., £600. Hannah Sumner and Sarah Sumner chose William Rockwell to be their guardian. Recog., £500. And this Court appoint Hezekiah Sumner of Middletown to be guardian to William Sumner, age 13 years, to John, 10 years, and to Ebenezer Sumner, age 8 years, all children of William Sumner, late of Middletown. Recog., £800.

Page 125 (Vol. XV) 10 April, 1750: John Sumner, 14 years of age, chose his father-in-law, Joseph Johnson, and his mother to be his guardians. Also, this Court appoint Joseph Johnson and his wife guardians to Ebenezer Sumner, 13 years of age, both sons of William Sumner of Middletown. Recog., £300 for each minor.

Page 139—4 September, 1753: William Sumner, age 19 years, son of William Sumner, made choice of his father-in-law, Lt. Joseph Johnson, to be his guardian. Recog., £500. Cert: *John Tully, J. P. for New London County.*

Page 5 (Vol. XVI) 20 November, 1750: Hannah Sumner, widow and Adms., having finished her account of Adms. on sd. estate, now moves for a distribution. This Court so order, viz.: To Hezekiah Sumner, eldest son, a double part; to William, John and Ebenezer Sumner, and Hannah, Sarah and Mary Sumner, children of the decd., to each of them their single shares of sd. estate. And appoint William Rockwell, Return Meigs and Daniel Starr, of Middletown, distributors.

Page 103 (Vol. XVII) 17 March, 1756: Report of the dist. Accepted.

Sweet, Benjamin. Court Record, Page 104—23 December, 1741: Estate of Benjamin Sweet, a transient person, late of Hartford decd.: Adms. to Timothy Bigelow. Recog., £100, with Deacon John Edwards.

Will on Page 321. Invt. in Vol. XIV, Page 150-153.

Talcott, Joseph, Hartford. Invt. £10,979. Taken 11 and 12 November, 1741, by Nathaniel Stanly, John Edward and Ozias Goodwin.

Part of the Inventory:

Negros, males: Jupiter, £70-00-00; Prince, £120-00-00; York, £100-00-00. Females: Rose, £45-00-00; Lillie, £90-00-00.
Lands in Middletown, 100 acres, apprised by Giles Hall and George Phillips, £625.
Lands in Stafford, 100 acres, £60-00-00; 100 acres, £40-00-00; 250 acres, £220-00-00. Taken by John Warner, Samuel Warner and Samuel Chapman.
Lands in Bolton, taken by John Bissell and Daniel White, £1217-00-00.
Lands in Coventry, one piece by Mr. Brigham's and Sargt. Silas Long's, 240 acres, £600-00-00; one near Capt. Parker's and Capt. Bissell's, 15 acres, £20-00-00; one near John Robinson and Elisha Fitch, 31 1-4 acres, £187-00-00; one on Skungamug River, 146 acres, £365-00-00; one near Capt. and James Parker's and Aaron Strong, 35 acres, £100-00-00; one near Samuel Parker and Thomas Porter, 150 acres, £50-00-00. Land in the Five Miles, 45 acres, £56-00-00; 150 acres, £50-00-00. Inventory at Coventry taken by Samuel Parker and Thomas Porter; and in the Five Miles by John Pitkin and Josiah Olcott.

WILL DATED 5 MAY, 1739:

I, Joseph Talcott of Hartford, do make this my last will and testament: I give out of my estate £5 to the poor of the Parish that I belong to, such as my executors shall think to be most proper objects of our charity. I give to my daughter Abigail Wadsworth a chest of drawers that was my first wife's, not to be reckoned as part of her portion of my estate. I give of my estate for the support of my unmarried daughters at my decease, for one full year after my decease, not to be charged as portions to my daughters, they to have right in my now dwelling house that I have given to my son Samuel Talcott, either Jerusha or Helena Talcott. After debts and legacies, etc., are paid, the remaining part of my whole estate, both real and personal, shall be divided: to my eldest son John Talcott, a part or portion double to the rest of my sons (Nathan and his children excepted); and to my other sons, Joseph, Samuel and Matthew Talcott, a double part or portion to my daughters; and to my daughters, Abigail Wadsworth, Eunice Hooker, Jerusha Talcott and Helena Talcott, half so much as my three youngest and three last mentioned sons. And on consideration of the discount on oure bills of credit, and uncertainty of that currency, how they may pass at my decease, I do order and determine that all my lands that I have given by deeds to any of my children in my lifetime, together with what I shall die seized of, shall after my decease be apprised by freeholders under oath, either by Capt. Nathaniel Stanly, Capt. Ozias Pitkin and Capt. William Pitkin, or such others as the Court of Probate shall appoint. I appoint my three sons, John, Joseph and Samuel, or any two of them, executors.
Witness: *Giles Hall,*   JOSEPH TALCOTT, LS.
Joseph Farnsworth, Daniel Hinsdale.

Court Record, Page 106—5 January, 1741-2: Will proven.
Page 68 (Probate Side, Vol. XIV): Whereas, the Honourable Joseph Talcott, Esq., of Hartford, in the County of Hartford and Colony of Connecticut, deceased, did in and by his last will and testament order that after his just debts, funerall expenses, provisions for the support of Jerusha and Helena Talcott (daughters of the sd. deceased) one year, and each of his children a suit of mourning apparel out of his moveable estate, with £5 to the poor of the Parish or Society to which he belonged, had been deducted, all the rest of his estate should be divided to and amongst his children (Nathan and his children excepted), John the eldest son to have a double share, the rest of the sons half so much, and the daughters half so much as his youngest sons: The following is an account of the sundry particulars, goods, etc., received by the children and heirs of the Honoureable Joseph Talcott, Esq., late of Hartford decd., of the executors of the last will and testament of the sd. Joseph Talcott deceased:

	£ s d
Received by John Talcott,	2991-18-08
Received by Joseph Talcott,	1781-14-04
Received by Samuel Talcott,	1903-16-01
Received by Matthew Talcott,	1505-02-00
Received by Abigail Wadsworth,	838-07-06
Received by Eunice Hooker,	838-13-04
Received by Jerusha Talcott,	736-12-00
Received by Helena Talcott,	736-11-00

November, the 16th day, A. D. 1744.
We, the subscribers, do hereby acknowledge that we have each of us received oure proportionable part of the inventoryed estate of our honoured father Joseph Talcott, Esqr., of Hartford, deceased, both of real and personal estate.

> John Talcott, Joseph Talcott, Samuel Talcott,
> Matthew Talcott, Daniel Wadsworth, Abigail Wadsworth,
> Eunice Hooker, Jerusha Talcott, Helena Talcott.

Page 172.

Talcott, Ensign Samuel, Wethersfield. Invt. £3912-18-01: In personal estate, £557-15-04. In negros: one man and one woman, £200-00-00; one boy, Peter, £45-00-00; one boy, Sampson, £30-00-00. In lands, £2079-00-00. Taken 3 July, 1739, by Elizur Goodrich and John Patterson.
Court Record, Page 52—3 July, 1739: Adms. granted to Thankful Talcott, widow, and Ebenezer Belding, Jr. Recog., £300, with John Patterson.

Page 62—28 March, 1740: Samuel Talcott, a minor, 15 years of age, son of Samuel Talcott, chose Ebenezer Deming to be his guardian. Recog., £300.

Page 23 (Vol. XV) 2 September, 1746: Thankful Talcott, widow, and Ebenezer Belding, Jr., Adms., exhibited an account of their Adms. Accepted. The sd. Adms. move this Court that the moveable estate be distributed to the surviving heirs, viz.:

	£ s d
To Thankful Talcott, widow,	259-00-08
To Samuel Talcott, eldest son,	207-04-06
To Elizur, Ebenezer and Mary Talcott, to each,	103-12-00

And appoint Elizur Goodrich, Hezekiah May and Jonathan Goodrich, distributors.

Page 35—12 March, 1746-7: Elizur Talcott, a minor, 19 years of age, and Ebenezer Talcott, aged 16 years, sons of the deceased, chose their mother Thankfull Talcott to be their guardian. Recog., £500.

Page 37 (Vol. XVI) 1st October, 1751: Thankfull Talcott, Adms., now moves that the real estate be distributed: Whereupon this Court appoint Col. Elizur Goodrich, Jonathan Belding and Capt. Josiah Griswold to distribute the estate, viz.: To Thankfull Talcott, widow, 1-3 part of the buildings and lands for her improvement during life; and to Samuel Talcott, eldest son, his double share; and to Elizur, Ebenezer and Mary Talcott, their single shares of sd. real estate.

(A report of this distribution was made to the Court, but no action was taken except to order it on file.)

Page 297.

Thompson, John, Sen., Farmington. Invt. £966-02-00. Taken 26 October, 1741, by Isaac Cowles, John Hart and Thomas Wadsworth. Will dated 5 July, 1737.

I, John Thompson of Farmingtown, do make this my last will and testament: I give to my wife, Ruth Thompson, the use of 1-3 part of my dwelling house, barn and improvable lands during her natural life; also the use during life of all that estate I received with her from her father Steele; and what thereof shall remain of sd. estate to return to my heirs. Unto my son Nathaniel Thompson I give £5 out of my personal estate besides what he hath already received. To my son John Thompson I give half that part of land in sd. Farmington at a place called Crane Hall, which I bought of John Lewis; also all that land which I bought of John and Joseph Woodruff, lying in the first division west from the reserved lands; also all my right in that place called Thompson Swamp; all in sd. Farmingtown. I give unto my son James Thompson half of that land which I bought of Hezekiah Hooker; sd. half contains 50 acres and lyeth near to a place called Burnt Hill; also all my right in ye buildings thereon; also 5 acres in ye common field, which land I bought of Jonathan

Smith, butting east on the river; all in the sd. Township of Farmingtown. Unto my two sons, Solomon and Hezekiah Thompson, I give my dwelling house, barn and homestead, and also that lott I bought of Timothy Thompson, butting west on the river; also that 6 acres of land which I bought of Thomas Orton, butting south on Joseph Hawley; also that 10 acres which I bought of Joseph Hawley, butting east on a highway; all in the Township of Farmington. Unto my son Ezekiel Thompson I give all my tools properly to the trade of blacksmith belonging. Unto my three sons, Ezekiel, Solomon and Hezekiah Thompson, I give all the residue and remainder of my real estate of lands in the Townships of Farmingtown and Litchfield or elsewhere whatsoever, disposition of which hath not before in this instrument been made, to be equally divided between them. Unto my daughter Margaret Beech, besides what I have already given her, I now give her out of my personal estate £10. Unto my daughter Hannah Bird, besides what I have formerly let her have, I now give her the sum of £10. Unto my daughter Eunice Thompson I give out of my personal estate £80. All the three last legacies at inventory price. I give unto my wife and all my children above named all that shall remain of my personal estate when my debts are paid and the above named legacies are answered, that they share thereof equally. I constitute my two sons, James and Ezekiel Thompson, to be my executors.

Witness: *Nathaniel Newell,*   JOHN THOMPSON, LS.
Samuel Thompson, Daniel Thompson.

Court Record, Page 103—1st December, 1741: Will proven.

Page 15 (Vol. XIV) 4 January, 1742-3: Ezekiel Thompson, one of the executors of the last will of John Thompson, moves this Court that freeholders might be appointed to make distribution of the surplusage of the moveable estate of the sd. decd. after the debts and legacies are paid. This Court order a distribution to be made thereof according to sd. will:

	£ s d
The inventory, with additions,	574-18-06
Debts and legacies paid,	272-16-06
Which being subtracted, there remains to be distributed,	302-02-00
To the widow and Nathaniel Thompson, to each of them,	30-04-02
To Ezekiel Thompson and to Margaret Thompson, to each of them,	30-04-02
To John Thompson and to Hannah Thompson, to each of them,	30-04-02
To Solomon Thompson and to Hezekiah Thompson, to each of them,	30-04-02
To James Thompson and to Eunice Thompson, to each of them,	30-04-02

The Court appoint Capt. Isaac Cowles, Deacon John Hart and Thomas Wadsworth, of Farmingtown, distributors.

Page 19—22 March, 1743-4: Report accepted.

Invt. in Vol. XIV, Page 55.

Thompson, Joseph, Windsor. Invt. £212-01-02. Taken 28 January, 1741-2, by John Stiles, Jr., James Thompson and Ebenezer Watson, Jr.
Court Record, Page 107—11 January, 1741-2: Adms. granted to William Thompson of Windsor. Recog., £600, with James Thompson of Windsor.
Page 11 (Vol. XIV) 5 October, 1742: William Thompson, Adms., exhibited an account of his Adms., which this Court accepted.

See File:

Know all men by these presents: That it is agreed upon, by and between us the subscribers, all of the Town of Windsor, being the lawful heirs and successors of our brother Joseph Thompson, late of Windsor deceased, and we have and do by these presents give, grant, make over, convey and confirm unto our brethren, Samuel and James Thompson, all and singular the estate of our sd. deceased brother Joseph Thompson, be it either in lands, goods or chattells. We the subscribers do hereby, for ourselves and heirs, covenant to and with the sd. Samuel and Joseph Thompson and their heirs, and with either of them singly, to warrant and defend the abovesd. given and granted premises unto them or any of them against the lawful claims of us or any of our heirs or any other person. In confirmation whereof we have hereunto set our hands and seals this 6th day of July, A. D. 1747.

WILLIAM THOMPSON, ADMS., LS.	JOSEPH HARPER, LS.
SAMUEL X THOMPSON, LS.	MIRIAM X HARPER, LS.
JAMES THOMPSON, LS.	RUTH X THOMPSON, LS.
ROBERT X THOMPSON, LS.	

Witness: *William McCarty,*
Ann Grant.

Page 42 (Vol. XV) 7 July, 1747: An agreement for the settlement of the estate of Joseph Thompson was now exhibited in Court under the hands and seals of the heirs to sd. estate, and acknowledged before this Court. The Court accepts the same and orders it to be recorded and kept on file.

Page 131-2-3.

Thompson, Samuel, Farmington. Invt. £1361-07-06. Taken 23 February, 1739, by Isaac Cowles, Daniel Judd and John Newell. Will dated 17th January, 1738-9.
I, Samuel Thompson of Farmingtown, son to John Thompson, being visited with dangerous sickness, do make this my last will and testament: I give to Hannah, my wife, for her use and profit during her natural life, 1-3 part of my real estate of houseing and lands; also, 1-3 part of all my personal estate to be her own forever. To my eldest son Samuel Thomp-

son I give all my right to and in land laid out on the right of my father John Thompson, lying in the 16th allottment in the 2nd division of land lying west from the reserved land in sd. Farmingtown, together with so much of my real estate of houseing and lands, with what I have already given him, as to make his part equal with each of his three youngest brethren, not reckoning into it land in the 16th allottment. Unto my son Ebenezer Thompson, besides what I have already given him, I give him 10 shillings money. Unto my three youngest sons, Daniel Thompson, Thomas Thompson and Barnabas Thompson, I give all the residue and remainder of my real estate of houseing and land, whatsoever and wheresoever, to be equally divided to them, reserving to my wife the use of 1-3 part as before mentioned. Unto my two eldest daughters, Ruth Judd and Mary Woodford, besides what I have already given them, I give to each of them 10 shillings as money. Unto my three youngest daughters, Bethiah Thompson, Hannah Thompson and Anne Thompson, unto each of them I give £75 of my personal estate as money. And the remainder of my personal estate, if any be, my will further is that it be equally divided between my five daughters. I appoint my son Samuel Thompson to be sole executor.

Witness: *Samuel Whitman, Jr.,*   SAMUEL X THOMPSON, LS.
Gershom Lewis, Roger Hooker.

Court Record, Page 45—14 March, 1738-9: Will now exhibited by Samuel Thompson, who declined the trust. This Court appoint Hannah Thompson, the widow, and Samuel Thompson, the son, Adms. with the will annexed. Recog., £500, with Ebenezer Thompson of Farmington. Barnabas Thompson, a minor, age 15 years, and Hannah, age 13 years, chose their mother Hannah Thompson to be their guardian. Recog., £400.

Page 10 (Vol. XIV) 1st Tuesday in September, 1742: Hannah Thompson and Samuel Thompson, Adms. with the will annexed, moved this Court that distributors may be appointed to make division of the estate according to sd. will of the deceased: Whereupon this Court appoint Capt. Josiah Hart, Nathaniel Newell and Daniel Judd, of sd. Farmington, distributors.

Page 107-12-13.

Thrall, William, Windsor. Invt. 1114-02-11. Taken 19 December, 1738, by James Enno, John Stoughton and Jonathan Stiles. Will dated 9 June, 1736.

I, William Thrall of Windsor, do make this my last will and testament: I give to my honoured mother, Sarah Thrall, my negro girl called Pegg, and £20 money. I give to my wife Hannah Thrall the sum of 10 shillings money. I give to my daughter Charity Thrall the sum of £500, to be paid to her at the age of 18 years or upon marriage. I give to my sister Sarah Ward's children, viz., to Sarah, Lucy, Alice and Abigail, to each £25 when they are of lawfull age. I give to my sister Sarah Ward

£30 to be to her own use and disposal. I give to John Warham Strong's children, viz., to Elizabeth, Sarah and John Strong, £25 to each. I give to my brother Timothy Thrall all the remainder of my estate, and appoint him executor. It is my will that my brother Timothy Thrall be guardian to my daughter Charity Thrall until she comes of age, and that he shall allow for her support (until she arrive of age) out of my estate what shall be necessary, or the lawful interest for what was given her besides what I have given her by will.

Witness: *John Stoughton,*   WILLIAM THRALL, LS.
John McMorran, Ezekiel Bissell.

Court Record, Page 38—29 December, 1738: Invt. exhibited by Timothy Thrall, executor. Charity Thrall, age 13 years, daughter of William Thrall, chose her mother Hannah Thrall to be her guardian. Recog., £300.

Page 49—1st May, 1739: Hannah Thrall, the widow, complains to this Court that Timothy Thrall hath not perfected the inventory. He was cited to appear to perfect the inventory and answer to the complaint of Mrs. Thrall. Hannah Thrall with her attorney Joseph Gilbert, and Timothy Thrall, executor, appeared, with James Enno, his attorney. It appears that there was considerable of the estate that was not put into the inventory of the estate of the deceased, both bonds, notes and lands, that did belong to the estate, nor did the executor now or at no time hereafter bring the estate to this Court to be added to sd. inventory. Neither did sd. executor make any excuse to the satisfaction of this Court for his neglecting to do the same.

Page 50—26 May, 1739: Hannah Thrall moves this Court that her dower be set out. Roger Newbery, Timothy Loomis and Daniel Heydon were appointed to set out her dower.

9th of June, 1739: Timothy Loomis and Daniel Heydon decline to act, and this Court appoint Lt. Roger Newbery, Lt. Nathaniel Gaylord and Josiah Phelps, Jr., to set out 1-3 part of all the real estate of which sd. decd. died seized of.

Page 70—5 August, 1740: Hannah Thrall, widow of William Thrall, shows this Court that distribution of her dower has not been finished by reason of Capt. Newbery being appointed to go on an expedition against the Spaniards. This Court now appoint John Palmer with Lt. Nathaniel Gaylord and Josiah Phelps, Jr., to finish the distribution of dower of land, which was set out 30th April, 1739.

Toney, Betty, Negro Woman. Court Record, Page 25—17 March, 1737-8: Betty Toney of Hartford, a minor, 18 years of age, chose Deacon John Edwards to be her guardian. Recog., £50.

Page 280.

Tuller, William, Simsbury. Invt. £789-06-03. Taken by Richard Cook and Josiah Loomis, Jr. Will dated 11th June, 1740.

I, William Tuller of Simsbury, Hartford County, doe make this my last will and testament: Imprimis: My will is and I doe give to my wife one bed and covering for the same, one cow and one iron pott, together with 1-3 part of all my household stuff, 1-2 of my dwelling house during her lifetime, and 1-2 of my orchard and the piece of land where my barn now stands, being about 2 acres, and 2 acres where my house stands, and 2 acres where Nathaniel Bacon lived formerly in Windsor bounds, with ye liberty for to keep one or two cows in ye pasture, and my young pacing mare. This I freely give to my wife during her natural life. To James, my first son, I give the remaining part of sd. lott that I formerly bought of Daniel Addams, together with the part of sd. sawmill lott that I gave him by deed of gift, and one acre at the north end of my orchard next to the land above mentioned. This I give to my son James provided he make no demands on me nor on my heirs for the land that his uncle James Cornish gave him. To John, my 2nd son, I give the remaining part of the lott that I bought of John Lewis's widow. To Daniel, my third son, I give the lott that fell to me by first division, meaning the 100-acre lott that lyeth between Salmon Brook and the place called the Plaine, and my right in the sawmill that stands on Griffin's Brook. To David, my fourth son, I give one lott of land of 100 acres in my second division, lying in the west mountain, lying near the north of Bold Hill, and my longest gunn. To William, my fifth son, I give all my homelott with the house now standing on sd. land, which land I bought of Mr. Merriman, and two acres that I bought of Nathaniel Bacon, lying in Windsor bounds and joins on my homelott, and my short gunn. This I give to my son William. To Elizabeth, my first daughter, I give 1-3 part of my household goods and 1-3 part of all my moveable estate, excepting my oxen and excepting what I have given to my sons. This I give to Elizabeth, my first daughter. To Hannah, my second daughter, I give 1-3 part of my household goods and 1-3 part of my moveable estate, except my oxen and what I have given to my sons. This I give to Hannah, my second daughter. And I do order that all my notes and bonds, oxen, and 10 acres of land lying on Bear Hill, should be disposed of to pay my debts; and the overplus, if any, to be divided between my two daughters equally. And I appoint Damarus Tuller, my wife, and James Tuller, my son, executors.

Witness: *Samuel Allyn,*   WILLIAM TULLER, LS.
Abigail Loomis, Josiah Loomis, Jr.

Court Record, Page 94—7 July, 1741: Will exhibited by John and Daniel Tuller, Adms. with the will annexed. Recog., £500, with Jacob Loomis of Simsbury.

Page 7 (Vol. XIV) 1st June, 1742: Daniel Tuller, a minor, 18 years of age, son of William Tuller, chose his brother John Tuller to be his guardian. Recog., £300.

Page 11—5 October, 1742: John and Daniel Tuller, Adms., exhibited an account of their Adms. Accepted. And they moved to this Court that distribution might be granted: Whereupon this Court appoint Daniel Mills, Jacob Drake, Jr., and Richard Cook, of Windsor, distributors.

Page 12—5 October, 1742: Hannah Tuller, a minor, 15 years of age, chose her brother John Tuller to be her guardian. Recog., £300.

Page 253.

Wadsworth, Hezekiah, Farmington. Will dated 14 October, 1740: I, Hezekiah Wadsworth of Farmington, do make this my last will and testament: I give to my brother Thomas Wadsworth, and to his heirs and assigns forever, all and singular my lands, messuages and tenements, whatsoever and wheresoever (they may be found); also, lott and buildings thereon that was formerly my brother John Wadsworth's, whereon he lived only excepted. I give unto my brother Thomas Wadsworth the use and improvement and profit of sd. lott during his natural life. Also, unto my brother Thomas Wadsworth I give all my personal estate whatsoever, to be at his dispose forever. I give to my kinsman Mr. Daniel Wadsworth, pastor of the First Church of Christ in Hartford, to him, his heirs and assigns forever, the aforesd. lott in Farmington that was his father's and on which in his lifetime he lived, to be to him and his heirs after the death of his uncle Thomas Wadsworth, and not before.

Witness: *John Hart,*   HEZEKIAH WADSWORTH, LS.
Timothy Porter, Jr., Thomas Cowles, Jr.

Court Record, Page 78—28 December, 1740: Will now exhibited by Thomas Wadsworth, brother of sd. deceased, executor, who informed this Court that the estate of the deceased and his own were joynt and never any division made, and the testator had given him all his personal estate by his will. This Court thinks it unnecessary to make any apprisement of the estate.

Page 168.

Wadsworth, Sergt. Jonathan, Hartford. Invt. £991-07-00. Taken 30 August, 1739, by Joseph Cook, James Church and Thomas Sanford.
Court Record, Page 55—13 September, 1739: Adms. to Abigail Wadsworth, widow, with Capt. Peletiah Mills of Windsor. Recog., £800, with Joseph Wadsworth, a brother of the deceased.
Page 60—24 January, 1739-40: Exhibit of an inventory.
Page 14 (Vol. XV) 4 June, 1746: An account of Adms. was now exhibited in Court by Jacob Kellogg, Abigail Kellogg (alias Wadsworth) and Capt. Peletiah Mills, Adms. Account accepted. Jonathan Wadsworth, age 16 years, and Lydia Wadsworth, age 14 years, children of Jonathan Wadsworth, chose their father-in-law Jacob Kellogg of Hartford to be their guardian. Recog., £200 for each minor.

Invt. in Vol. XIV, Page 40.

Ward, Deborah, Middletown. Invt. £127-18-00. Taken 18 February, 1741-2, by Daniel Hall and William Rockwell.

Court Record, Page 108—2 February, 1741-2: Adms. granted to Hugh White. Recog., £300, with Obadiah Spencer of Hartford.

Page 29 (Vol. XIV) 6 September, 1743: Hugh White, Adms., exhibited an account of his Adms. Accepted.

Page 35—6 December, 1743: Middletown, 27th May, 1743: Received of Mr. Hugh White, Adms. on the estate of my mother, Deborah Ward, and as her being my guardian, my full part of the sd. estate after the debts and charges thereon are taken out, hereby discharging sd. White from any demands on sd. estate.

FENNAR WARD.

A true copy of the original on file: Test: Joseph Talcott, Clerk.

Will and Invt. in Vol. XIV, Page 7-8.

Wallis, Robert, Hartford. Invt. £194-08-04. Taken 19 November, 1741, by John Talcott and Thomas Pitkin. Will dated 2 October, 1741.

I, Robert Wallis of Hartford, do make this my last will and testament: After my just debts and funeral charges are well paid and answered, I give to my wife Elizabeth the use of all my lands and moveable estate of what sort or wheresoever the same may be, during the term of her natural life. I give unto my son John Wallis what I have already given him, and no more. I give unto my son William Wallis what I have already given him, and no more. My will further is that after my wife's decease my three daughters, Margaret, Elizabeth and Mary, shall have all my moveable estate that shall then be left, to be in quality divided among them; and that if Margaret, who is now in Ireland, be not come over hither at my wife's decease, that then the whole of sd. moveables shall be divided between Mary and Elizabeth. I give unto my son James Wallis all my land, to him and his heirs forever, after the death of my wife Elizabeth. And I appoint my loving wife Elizabeth to be executrix.

Witness: *John Bissell,*   ROBERT X WALLIS, LS.
Thomas Pitkin, Ann Wallis.

Court Record, Page 108—2 February, 1741-2: Will proven. William Williams of Hartford and John Wallis of Bedford, in the County of Hampshire, heirs to the estate, appeal from the probate of the will to the Superior Court at Hartford March next, and gave a bond of £50.

Will and Invt. in Vol. XIV, Page 31-213.

Warner, Elizabeth, Wethersfield. Inventory taken 4 December, 1741, by Jonathan Robbins, Jonathan Belding and Joseph Boardman. Will dated 20 October, 1741.

I, Elizabeth Warner of Wethersfield, do make this my last will and testament: I give to my daughters all the rest of my estate, both moneys, household goods and moveables, to them each alike (except 1-5 part of money, which I give to my son Daniel Warner) : To my eldest daughter, Ruth Kilbourn, 1-4; to my 2nd daughter, Elizabeth Welles, 1-4; to my 3rd daughter, Martha Kilbourn, 1-4; to my fourth daughter, Susannah Rennals, 1-4. I make my beloved brother, Joshua Robbins, of Wethersfield, sole executor.

Witness: *Niell McLean,*   ELIZABETH X WARNER, LS.
Jonathan Robbins, William Bement.

Court Record, Page 111—2 March, 1741-2: Invt. exhibited by Joshua Robbins, executor. Accepted.

Page 318.

Waters, Joseph, Hartford. Invt. £30-18-11. Taken 21 January, 1740-1, by David Ensign, Isaac Kellogg and Nathaniel White.

Court Record, Page 81—20 January, 1740-1: Adms. granted to Elizabeth Waters, widow. Recog., £100, with David Ensign. This Court appoint Elizabeth Waters to be guardian to her son Joseph Waters, a minor, 3 years of age. Recog., £500.

Page 107—6 January, 1741-2: Elizabeth Waters, widow, Adms., by her attorneys, David Ensign and Isaac Kellogg, reports the estate insolvent. This Court appoint Lt. Jonathan Steele and Jonathan Seymour commissioners.

Page 3 (Vol. XIV) 21 December, 1742: Lt. Jonathan Steele and Mr. Jonathan Seymour, commissioners appointed by this Court to adjust the claims of the creditors, not having completed their account with the creditors, this Court allow the creditors longer time to bring in their claims.

Page 17—7 February, 1742-3: An account of Adms. was now exhibited in Court by the Adms., whereby it appears the estate is indebted £10-03-04. Account allowed. Report of the commissioners accepted.

Page 131 (Vol. XV) 24 May, 1750: Abraham Waters, a minor, 16 years of age, son of Joseph Waters, chose his brother Webster Waters to be his guardian. Recog., £400.

Page 134—11 June, 1750: Elizabeth Waters, a minor, daughter of Joseph Waters, chose her mother to be her guardian. Recog., £300.

Page 325.

Watson, Jedediah, Windsor. Will dated 12 August, 1738: I, Jedediah Watson of Windsor, do make this my last will and testament: I give all my tools to Ebenezer Bliss of Windsor. I give all my lands in Torrington and all the rest of my personal estate, after my just debts are paid (excepting the legacy above sd.), to Ebenezer Bliss and to Mary Seger and to her heirs forever. I appoint Ebenezer Bliss executor.

Witness: *Roger Wolcott,*   JEDEDIAH WATSON, LS.
Sarah Ward, Mary X Hancocks.

Court Record, Page 106—5 January, 1741-2: Will proven.

Page 123.

Way, Richard, Haddam. Will dated 1st June, 1735: I, Richard Way, mariner, belonging to His Majestie's ship *Namur*, being of bodily health and of sound disposing mind and memory, and considering the perils and dangers of the seas and other uncertainties of this transitory life, do make this my will: I give such wages, sum or sums of money, lands, tenements, goods, chattells and estate whatsoever as shall be any way due, oweing or belonging unto me at the time of my decease, I do give, devise and bequeath the same unto my beloved friend John Nightingirl of the sd. ship, mariner, for my wife Hannah Way of New England. And I do hereby nominate and appoint John Nightingirl my executor of this my last will and testament. And I do ordain and ratify these presents to stand and be for and as my only last will and testament. In witness whereof to this my sd. will I have set to my hand and seal the 1st day of June, Anno. Dom. 1735, and in the 8th year of the reign of His Majestie Lord King George the 2nd, over Great Britain.   Rd. X Way.
Signed, sealed, published and declared
in the presence of us: *Rt. Sporle,*   *Examined by Robt. Bogg, Junr.*
Jos: Adkins, Bart. Pitts.

Court Record, Page 43—15 February, 1738-9: A copy of the will of Richard Way, late of Haddam, in the County of Hartford, mariner in His Majestie's ship *Namur,* deceased, with ye probation thereof by William, by Divine Providence Arch Bishop of Canterbury, Primate of all England, and Metropolitan, was now exhibited in Court by Hannah Way, widow relict of the sd. decd., which copy of sd. will is ordered to be recorded and kept on file. And the sd. widow informing this Court that there is sundry debts due to sd. estate which cannot be recovered without Adms. is granted, the executor to sd. will being gone, and not known whether he ever will (return) to this land again, and that the debts due from sd. estate may be duly paid and the credits received, Adms. is granted to Hannah Way, the relict of the decd., who gave bond, with Maynard Day of Hartford, of £200.

Page 101.

Webb, Orange, Hartford. Invt. £33-05-10. Taken 11 October, 1738, by John Skiner and Timothy Stanly.
Court Record, Page 34—5 October, 1738: Adms. to Hannah Webb of Wethersfield, sister of the deceased. Recog., £200, with Nathaniel Deming of Wethersfield.
Page 37—5 December, 1738: Exhibit of inventory.

Page 70.

Welles, Ebenezer, Hartford. Invt. £2806-07-03. Taken 14 February, 1737-8, by William Gaylord, Samuel Welles and John Whiting.

Court Record, Page 25—7 March, 1737-8: Adms. to Rachel Welles, widow.

Page 42 (Vol. XVII) 16 October, 1754: Rachel Welles, Adms., exhibited now an account of her Adms. Accepted. This Court order dist. of the estate: To the widow, her third in real and moveable estate; and to Ebenezer Welles, eldest son, a double share; and to Ashbell Welles, to Rachel Welles, alias Merrells, the wife of Elijah Merrells, and to Hannah, Mary and Sarah Welles, children of the deceased, to each of them a single portion. And appoint Thomas Hosmer, Stephen Hosmer and Thomas Shepherd, of Hartford, distributors.

Page 193, 207-8-9.

Welles, Capt. Gideon, Wethersfield. Invt. £5137 in lands and house. Taken 27 June, 1740, by Thomas Welles, Eleazur Goodrich and Hezekiah May. Will dated 26 March, 1740.

I, Gideon Welles of Wethersfield, being very sick and weake, do give and dispose of my worldly estate as follows: I give to Hannah, my wife, 1-3 part of my moveable or personal estate, and the use of 1-3 part of all my real estate. I give to my two sons, Solomon and Gideon, 2-3 parts of all my moveables or personal estate, and the whole of my real estate, land, tenants, etc., wheresoever lying and being, to them and their heirs in equal proportion, all my just debts being first paid. And that the sum of £500 money be paid to my daughter Eunice at the age of 18 years; and £500 money be paid to my daughter Sarah at 18 years of age; and the sum of £500 money to be improved by my executors in the bringing up and educating my oldest son Gideon. I say my will is that my sd. debts and the next above mentioned sums (amounting to £1500) be all paid by my executors out of the estate of my sd. sons in equal proportions. And I appoint my wife and son Solomon to be executors, with the advice, direction and assistance of my friend John Chester.

Witness: *Nathaniel Burnham,*   GIDEON WELLES, LS.
Jonathan Bull, Elizur Goodrich.

Court Record, Page 68—11 June, 1740: Will proven.

Page 32 (Vol. XV) 3 February, 1746-7: Gideon Welles, a minor, age 12 years, son of Gideon Welles: This Court appoint Col. John Chester of Wethersfield to be his guardian. Recog., £2000.

Page 63—5 April, 1748: Solomon Welles, one of the executors to the last will and testament of Capt. Gideon Welles, now moves to this Court that distributors may be appointed to distribute the estate: Whereupon this Court appoint Col. Elizur Goodrich, Capt. Thomas Belding and Hezekiah May distributors.

Page 67—27 May, 1748: Jonathan Hale, Esq., of Glastonbury, in right of his wife Hannah, who was the widow of Capt. Gideon Welles, now moves to this Court that her right of dowry in the real estate may be set out to her: Whereupon this Court appoint Col. Elizur Goodrich, Capt.

Thomas Belding and Hezekiah May, of Wethersfield, to set out to the sd. Hannah Welles, alias Hale, 1-3 part of the buildings and improveable lands of the sd. deceased for her improvement during life.

Welles, Mary, Wethersfield. Court Record, Page 72—2 September, 1740: Mary Welles, relict of Robert Welles, late of Wethersfield: Adms. to Michael Gibson of Tuoro, County of Barnstable, Province of Massachusetts Bay, attorney to Dorothy Totman and some of the rest of the heirs of the sd. deceased Mary Welles. Recog., with John Knowles of Hartford.

Page 96-7-8-9.

Welles, Capt. Robert, Wethersfield. Invt. £4147-10-00. Taken 14 September, 1738, by Thomas Curtice and John Stilman. Will dated 2 November, 1734.

I, Robert Welles of Wethersfield, do make this my last will and testament: I give to my wife Sarah my maid Moll, the silver tankard and two silver spoons, with use of lands and house during widowhood. I give to my son Robert land in Newington bought of Jonathan Goodrich, also of the Kircums, also of William Powell in Hartford Meadow; also my right in the Flats, what I have there with brother Thomas Welles. I give to my son Appleton Welles my 50-acre lott by Deacon Welles, as also 10 acres in Hartford Meadow I bought of Jonathan Steele. I give to my son Josiah 6 acres I bought of Nathaniel Nott, 1-2 the pasture I bought of William Welles, and that land I bought of Daniel Griswold; also half of that lot I bought of Lieut. Catling in Hartford Meadow—the 8-acre lot; also half of the east end of that lot by David Churchill's (the west end I have given to Robert). I order my son Josiah to pay £20 to his sister Martha when she is 18 years of age. I give to my son Hezekiah half my house and homelot, barn and pasture I bought of William Welles; also 1-2 of some land bought of Mother Wolcott, he to pay to his sister Judith £20 when she is 18 years of age. My will is that my son Hezekiah have the homelott and buildings after his mother's decease. I give to my daughter Sarah, after her mother's decease, my great Bible, my silver cup and two silver spoons. And the five girls to have £100 right in the homelott given to my son Hezekiah. I give to my five daughters, viz., Abigail, Elizabeth, Mary, Martha and Judeth, £20 to each out of my house, lott and buildings after their mother's decease. I appoint my sons Robert and Appleton to be executors, with their mother.

Witness: *Gideon Welles,*   ROBERT WELLES, LS.
Elizur Goodrich, John Stilman.

Court Record, Page 33—3 October, 1738: Will now exhibited by Sarah Welles, the widow, and Robert, the son. Proven. Adms. to Robert Welles on part of the estate intestate. Recog., with Rev. William Burnham.

Page 34—3 October, 1738: This Court appoint Mrs. Sarah Welles to be guardian to Hezekiah, Martha and Judith Welles, children of Robert Welles deceased. Recog., £600. Josiah Welles, age 17 years, chose his mother Sarah Welles to be his guardian.

Will and Invt. in Vol. XIV, Page 8-9-10.

Whaples, Jonathan, Wethersfield. Invt. £1244-12-10. Taken 10 February, 1741-2, by Martin Kellogg and David Wright, Jr. Will dated 11 September, 1741.

I, Jonathan Whaples of Wethersfield, do make this my last will and testament: I give to Sarah, my wife, the use of my houseing, stock, chattells and lands during the space or time of her remaining my widow. I give to my daughter Theodocia £100 of good and lawful money, to be raised and levied out of my estate. I give to my son Jonathan Whaples my dwelling house and barn with the 7 1-2 acres of land it stands upon; also 5 1-2 acres of land I bought of Joseph Andrews and his brethren, heirs to Benjamin Andrus decd.; also 2 1-2 acres of land at the Springs; also 15 1-2 acres at Buck's lott; all in Wethersfield. I give to my well-beloved son Daniel Whaples 30 acres of land lying in Farmingtown, which I bought of William Wadsworth partly, and part of Thomas Stanley, both of Farmingtown. I make my wife Sarah sole executrix. And in her hands I leave the disposal of my stock and moveables, as she shall think best, among my children.

Witness: *Martin Kellogg,*   JONATHAN WHAPLES, LS.
Joseph Deming, Benajah Andrews.

Court Record, Page 110—2 March, 1741-2: Will proven.

Page 288.

Wheeler, Mary, Middletown. Invt. £10-11-06. Taken by Ebenezer White, William Whitmore and John Stow.

Court Record, Page 81—27 January, 1740-1: Adms. to Edward Higbee. Recog. in £50, with Benjamin Butler, of Middletown.

Page 72-3-4.

White, Jacob, Middletown. Invt. £1629-07-10. Taken 12 April, 1738, by Thomas Johnson and Samuel Stow. Will dated 8 February, 1736.

I, Jacob White of Middletown, do make this my last will and testament: I give to my son Thomas White all my lands that I now own in the Town of Lebanon; also all my right of land on the east side of the

Great River in Middletown. I give to my son John White the whole of my homestead, viz., my now dwelling house and barn and all the land in the lot which they stand on, except one room in my dwelling house I reserve and give to my daughter Elizabeth, which room she please to choose, a convenient part in the cellar, and garden spot. I give to my cousin Isaac White of Middletown ten shillings, and make him sole executor of this my will. I give to my son John White all my improved lands in Middletown on the west side of the Great River, all my lands on the Plains, likewise the whole of a lotment of land that lies in the norwest corner of Middletown. I give to my son Joseph Frary five acres of my right in the commons in Middletown. I give to my daughter Elizabeth the improvement of one acre of land in the little meadow next to the bridge during her life (except she marry, then to return to my son John White). I give to my daughter Elizabeth two brass kettles, one large and one small, my son John to pay to my daughter Elizabeth £40 money. I will that my son John pay to my daughter Deborah £30 money, and to pay to my daughter Hannah £20 money. Also I will that my granddaughter Jerusha White have £5 out of all my estate if she live to the age of eighteen years. I give to my daughter Elizabeth all my household goods.

Witness: *Hugh White,*   JACOB WHITE, LS.
Thomas Johnson, Jun.,
Timothy White.

To this a codicil, without date, was added, giving larger benefit to his daughter Elizabeth.   Signed: JACOB WHITE, HIS MARK AND SEAL.
Witness: *Hugh White,*
Thomas Johnson, Jun.,
Timothy White.

Court Record, Page 29—2 May, 1738: Will proven.

Page 126-7-330.

Whitmore, Joseph, Middletown. Invt. £668-18-07. Taken 31 January, 1738-9, by Thomas Johnson, Hugh White and Samuel Shepherd. Will dated 21 September, 1738.

I, Joseph Whitmore of Middletown, do make and ordain this my last will and testament: My will is that after my just debts and funeral charges are paid, all my estate be distributed to and amongst my brethren and sisters, accounting the two children of my sister Abigail Clark deceased equal to one sister, in the proportion following, that is to say: To my brethren, Seth, Samuel and Francis, to each 2-9; and to my sisters, Hannah and Martha, to each 1-9; and to the two children of my sister Clark deceased 1-9, equally to be divided between them, to be paid them as they arrive to lawfull age. I appoint my brother-in-law Joseph Savage and my brother Seth Whitmore executors.

Witness: *John Gipson,*   JOSEPH WHITMORE, LS.
William Rockwell, Hannah X *Gipson.*

Court Record, Page 40—6 February, 1738-9: Will proven.

Page 14 (Vol. XIV) 24 December, 1742: Francis Whitmore, a minor, age 17 years, son of Joseph Whitmore deceased, chose his brother-in-law Thomas Savage, Jr., of Middletown, to be his guardian. Recog., £600. Cert: *Jabez Hamlin, J. P.*

Page 20—5 April, 1743: Francis Whitmore now made choice of Joseph Ranney of Middletown to be his guardian. Recog., £200.

Page 48—2 October, 1744: Joseph Savage and Seth Whitmore, executors, exhibited now an account of Adms. .Accepted.

Page 50—4 December, 1744: Joseph Savage, one of the executors on the estate of Joseph Whitmore, late of Middletown decd., showing to this Court that the General Assembly holden at New Haven on the 2nd Thursday in October, 1744, appointed him, the sd. executor, to make sale of so much of the real estate of the sd. decd. as will procure the sum of £28-16-04, with necessary charges, to pay the debts due from sd. estate: Whereupon this Court direct to set up advertisements on the several sign posts in Middletown that there is to be sold at publick vandue, at the beat of the drum, to the highest bidder, on such a day and time of day, and at such a place, one piece or part of a piece of land lying in Middletown on the west side of the Great River, in the North Society, about 2 miles west of the Meeting House, which land butts east on a highway, south on a highway, west on William Savage, Jr., his land, and north on Churchill Edwards, about 48 acres, or so much of sd. land as will raise the sd. sum, and make return to this Court to whom he sold the sd. land and for how much.

Page 53—5 February, 1744-5: An account of the sales of the land of Joseph Whitmore, late of Middletown decd., and account of the charges of the sale thereof, was now exhibited by Joseph Savage, Adms. Accepted. .Seth Wetmore of Middletown, one of the executors and an heir to the estate of Joseph Whitmore, moved to this Court that distributors may be appointed to distribute the real estate of the sd. decd. according to his last will: Whereupon this Court appoint William Rockwell, Joseph Frary and Samuel Shepherd, of Middletown, to be distributors.

Page 92-3-4-5.

Wilcocks, Israel, Middletown. Invt. £1855-08-11. Taken 25 September, 1738, by Thomas Johnson, Samuel Stow and Francis Wilcocks. Will dated 27 April, 1738.

I, Israel Wilcocks, yeoman, do make this my last will and testament: I give to Hannah, my wife, all that she brought with her which was her own proper estate before I married her, to be wholly at her own dispose. Also, I give to my wife the use of 1-2 of my dwelling house, 1-2 of the seleridge belonging to it, half of my well, 1-2 of my barn at home and the use of 1-3 part of my orchard. Also, I give to my wife the improvement of 1-3 part of all my lands so long as she remains my widow. My will is that in case she should marry, then she should have but 1-2, and release the other half to my children. I give to my wife two cows, my youngest yoke of oxen and my two old mares. I give to my son Israel Wilcocks 64 acres of land out of my right in the lottment of land lying in the northwest quarter at the turn of the river; also 1-3 part of a lottment of land I have on the east side the Great River, called the undivided land; also my Goose Delight meadow and the piece of land on the Neck which lyeth near by it; also my gunn, rapier and belt. This I give to my son Israel Wilcocks, his heirs and assigns forever. I give to my son Gideon Wilcocks all my lottments of land at the Short Hill; also all that I had of Capt. Nathaniel White near the stone quaries; also 30 acres of land out of my right in a lottment of land at the turn of the river in ye northwest quarter; also 1-3 part of a lottment of land I have on the east side of the Great River, called the undivided land; also all my right in ye round meadow. I give to my son Nathaniel Wilcocks 55 acres of land on the northwest quarter; also my right in the boggy meadow; also 1-3 part of a lottment of land on the east side of the Great River, called the undivided land. I give to my son Charles Wilcocks all my homelott which my house stands on, with the buildings upon it; also I give him all my pasture; also all my lottment of land at ye Plaines or Pines. I give to my daughter Ruth Wilcocks £70; also my bigest brass kettle besides the £70. I give to my daughter Mary Wilcocks £55. I give to my daughter Jerusha £60. I give to my daughter Hannah Wilcocks £60. And further, my will is that my two eldest daughters, Ruth and Mary, shall have my right in the half-mile lott on the east side of the Great River also my Fourth Division Lott on the east side of the Great River at inventory price. And it is to be understood these two pieces of land is to be counted for part of the sums above mentioned for my two eldest daughters' portions. And further, I give to my two youngest daughters, out of my stock of sheep, 12 good sheep. And my will is that my wife shall have the improvement of them until my two youngest daughters come of age, and then my wife shall make them good to my sd. daughters according to inventory price. I give to my daughter Jerusha my brown two-year-old heifer. Also I give to my daughter Hannah my pied heifer calf. And further, my will is that my two sons, Israel and Nathaniel, shall be put out to prentice as soon as may be with conveniency, and that my son Gideon shall live at home with his mother until he shall arrive to the age of 21 years, and that my son Charles shall live with his mother until he comes to the age of 15 years, if his mother finds it will be for the best. And upon consideration that my wife has small children to bring up, I think it proper to make her these following considerations on that account: My will is that my son Gideon shall work with his mother until he is 21 years old, and that my wife, with my son Gideon, shall have the improvement of all my improvements at home and of my pasture at Siding Hill, and of all my mowing land and that part of my lott at the turn of the river which is contained between the ledges and the river: all these, except my wife's right of thirds, I give my wife and my son Gideon the use of until my son Gideon comes to the age of 21 years, and no longer. Further, I give my son Gideon the use of my oldest yoke of cattle until 3 years is

expired from the date of this will, and no longer. And further, my will is
that my wife and my son Gideon shall have the use of all my husbandry
tools until my son Gideon comes of age, then it shall be divided
equally between my four sons. Also, that my son Gideon shall
take the whole care of all the husbandry business for his mother,
as giting of wood and looking after creatures, etc.; and that my
son Gideon shall have for his encouragement 1-2 of the grain
which he raiseth off of the land, to be at his own dispose; and also,
when business will allow to go out to work with a team, my son
Gideon shall have 1-2 of what he gits; also that my wife shall find Gideon
his victuals and clothes until he comes of age. Also, my will is that the
provision in house and the pied cow and all my swine shall be improved
to the use of my family without being accountable for to any; and also
so much of my English grain on the ground as the family shall need, and
the remainder to go to pay debts or legacies. I make my brother John
Wilcocks sole executor.

Witness: *John Shepherd,*   ISRAEL WILCOCKS, LS.
John Clark, Thomas Johnson.

Court Record, Page 32—1st August, 1738: Will proven. This Court
appoint Hannah Wilcocks to be guardian to Charles Wilcocks, age 9
years, Jerusha, age 4 years, and Hannah, one year old, children of Israel
Wilcocks deceased. Recog., £400.

Page 33—3 October, 1738: Nathaniel Wilcocks, age 15 years, and
Israel, age 18 years, sons of Israel Wilcocks, chose Joseph Savage of Middletown to be their guardian. Recog., £300.

Page 46—3 April, 1739: Mary Wilcocks, age 14 years, daughter
of Israel Wilcocks, chose her uncle John Wilcocks to be her guardian.
Recog., £200.

Page 47—3 April, 1739: Gideon Wilcocks, son of Israel Wilcocks,
chose his uncle John Wilcocks to be his guardian. Recog., £400. John
Wilcocks of Middletown informs this Court that he has a right in a parcell of land lying in Middletown, which lies in common and joynt tenantcy with heirs of Thomas Wilcocks, viz., with Thomas and Jonathan
Wilcocks, minors, and with heirs of Israel Wilcocks, viz., Israel and
Nathaniel Wilcocks, minors, and also with Daniel and Josiah Wilcocks,
heirs of Samuel Wilcocks of Middletown deceased. Sd. Wilcocks desires
this Court to appoint persons to divide sd. lands. This Court appoint
John Shephard, Hugh White and Joseph Frary to make the division
with guardians to the minors.

Page 85—7 April, 1741: Hannah Wilcocks, widow, moves to this
Court that the estate given her by will may be set out to her: Whereupon
this Court appoint Capt. Thomas Johnson, Mr. Joseph Frary and Francis
Wilcocks to set out the widow's estate.

Page 101—1st December, 1741: Israel Wilcocks moves this Court
for a division of lands lying in joynt tenantcy between sd. Israel Wilcocks
and Nathaniel Wilcocks. This Court appoint Lt. Samuel Shepherd,
Thomas Savage and Joseph Frary to divide sd. lands.

Page 173-4.

Wilcocks, Ruth, Middletown. Invt. £127-04-07. Taken 20 February, 1738-40, by Samuel Stow, Francis Wilcocks and Thomas Johnson.
Court Record, Page 58—1st January, 1739-40: Adms. to John Wilcocks. Recog., £200, with Josiah Griswold.
Page 61—4 March, 1739-40: Exhibit of an inventory.
Page 73—4 November, 1740: Account of Adms. now exhibited in Court by John Wilcocks, Adms.: Paid in debts and charges, £17-01-04. Which account is accepted and ordered on file. Inventory, £120-10-06; real estate, £25-00-00; subtracted from the moveable estate, there remains £95-10-00; the aforesd. Adms. account subtracted therefrom, there remains £75-13-08 of moveable estate to be distributed as follows to the brothers and sisters of deceased:

	£ s d
To Israel Wilcocks, eldest of the brethren,	12-12-02
To Gideon,	12-12-02
To Charles,	12-12-02
To Nathaniel,	12-12-02
To Mary,	12-12-02
To Jerusha,	12-12-02
To Hannah Wilcocks,	12-12-02

And appoint Samuel Stow, Francis Wilcocks and Thomas Johnson of Middletown, distributors.

Page 287-308.

Willard, Stephen, Wethersfield. Invt. £4112-03-11. Taken 30 October, 1741, by Jonathan Belding, Joseph Boardman and Thomas Belding. Will dated 8 November, 1728.
I, Stephen Willard, do think it my duty to settle that temporal estate which God hath given me. First, I give unto my nephew Ephraim Willard, the fifth son to Simon Willard of Wethersfield deceased, all my estate, both personal and real, that I shall die seized of, in the tenour following, viz.: I give to the sd. Ephraim Willard all my personal or moveable estate, and also all my lands lying without the bounds of the Township of Wethersfield, to be to the sd. Ephraim Willard, his heirs and assigns forever, upon and after my decease, in and according to the most free tenour of East Greenwich, in the County of Kent, in the Kingdom of Great Britain. But my lands within the bounds of the Township of sd. Wethersfield I give, grant and bequeath unto the sd. Ephraim Willard in fee tail, that is, to him the sd. Ephraim Willard and upon his decease to the eldest son lawfully begotten of the body of the sd. Ephraim Willard, and, upon the decease of the eldest son of the sd. Ephraim, to the eldest son of the sd. Ephraim Willard's eldest son, and this in like manner successively (such issue being continued) forever. And in default of such

issue, to descend to the next of kin bearing the name of Willard, according to the laws of England relateing to inheritance of intestate estate real.
Witness: *Nathaniel Burnham,*   STEPHEN WILLARD, LS.
Isaac Riley, Sen., Josiah Willard.

Part of Stephen Willard's Inventory:	£ s d
First, a negro man named Shampane,	100-00-00
The homelott with all the buildings thereon,	900-00-00
11 acres of land formerly Buttles's,	330-00-00
8 acres of pasture land at Southfield,	400-00-00
7 acres of land at Great Plaine,	375-00-00
3 1-2 acres of land at Stepney,	140-00-00
2 acres of land in the meadow formerly David Steele's,	60-00-00
2 acres ditto formerly Michael Griswold's,	70-00-00
2 acres of do. near Hubbard's Pond,	80-00-00
3 acres ditto called Lare's lott,	120-00-00
2 acres ditto at the willow tree,	70-00-00
2 1-2 acres at Send Home,	137-10-00
1 1-2 roods at the Whirlpool,	6-00-00
10 acres of land formerly Saltonstall's,	550-00-00
2 acres of land in ye Mile Meadow,	50-00-00

Court Record, Page 97—1st September, 1741 : Will proven. Adms. granted to Ephraim Willard with the will annexed.

Page 195-6.

Williams, Charles, Colchester. Invt. £193-08-01. Taken 10 June, 1740, by Joseph Wright and Joseph Chamberlain. Will dated 3 February, 1740.

I, Charles Williams of Colchester, do make this my last will and testament: I give to my wife Priscilla, with her joynture, all she brought to me, what she has got since, my brown cow, and the piece of gold which she wears about her neck. I have given to my sons by deed of gift. Yet my son John Williams deceased and my son William Williams had the better part of my estate. My will is to make it up to the rest so far as I can. And having but one daughter already set off comfortably, I give to the child of my son John 1 shilling, and to William Williams 10 shillings, and the rest of my estate in equal portions to the rest of my children, viz., to Charles Wix and to Nathan Williams and Elizabeth Kellogg. I appoint Nathaniel Foot and my son Nathan Williams executors.
Witness: *Alexander Rollo,*   CHARLES X WILLIAMS.
Samuel Northam, Charles Foot.

Court Record, Page 68—10 June, 1740 : Will proven.

Page 90-91.

Williams, Jonathan, doctor, Wethersfield. Invt. £171-07-06. Taken by Elisha Micks, Nathaniel Stilman and Timothy Baxter.

Court Record, Page 31—24 July, 1738: Adms. to Isaac Riley and Timothy Wright. Recog., £200, with Samuel Riley.

Page 40—2 February, 1738-9: The Adms. exhibit account of debts, £348-01-02. Estate insolvent.

Page 45—16 March, 1738-9: This Court appoint Lt. Jonathan Belding and Mr. Timothy Baxter, of Wethersfield, commissioners on the insolvent estate.

Page 140-1-2.

Williamson, Capt. Caleb, Hartford. Invt. £1154-11-05. Taken 14 February, 1738-9, by John Skinner, James Church and J. Gilbert, Jr. Will dated 29 June, 1734.

I, Caleb Williamson of Hartford, do make this my last will and testament: I give to my wife Mary all my houseing, lands, chattels, household goods, everything that I die possessed of, for her proper use and benefit so long as she live, only my daughter Mercy is to live with her and partake of the benefit with her. After my wife is dead, my will is and I give to my daughter Martha Goodwin land I bought of George Sextone, up Neck. I give to my daughter Sarah and Martha's children what is given to Mercy in case she die childless. I give to Ebenezer Williamson for his use so long as he live, and no longer; then to his heirs; but if he die without issue, then to the children of my daughters Sarah and Martha. I give a £24 right I have in Hartland to my two grandsons Samuel and Ebenezer Barnard, equal alike forever. I give my working tools to my grandson Samuel Barnard, my carbine to Ebenezer Barnard, and the rest of my armour to my son Ebenezer Williamson and two gold rings. I order my son Ebenezer to pay to my grandson Samuel Barnard £20 money, to Ebenezer Barnard £20, and to my granddaughter Rebeckah Barnard £10. I order my son Ebenezer to pay them three children; otherwise, I give them liberty to come upon the land for it, that is, the land I gave my son for his life. I give my little grandson Ebenezer Barnard to Caleb Church. I make my son Ebenezer Williamson and my son-in-law Ozias Goodwin executors. Now I declare that the above-written is my will, and all my will; and that I am now in my right mind as well as ever; and he or they that try to break or disannul this my sd. will, judgement will follow them.

Witness: *John Butler,*   CALEB WILLIAMSON, LS.
Mary X Butler, John Butler, Jr.

Court Record, Page 46—3 April, 1739: Will proven.

Page 273.

Wilson, Samuel, Middletown. Will dated 29 July, 1740: I, Samuel Wilson of Middletown, being engaged in the expedition against the Spaniards, and considering the uncertainty of my temporal life, do make this my last will and testament: After my just debts are paid, my will is that all my estate be equally divided to and among my brothers and sisters. And I appoint my brother John Wilson sole executor.

Witness: *John Bacon,*   SAMUEL WILSON, LS.
Josiah Wetmore, John Deliber.

Page 285.

Winchell, Nathaniel, Sen., Farmington. Invt. £14-15-09. Taken 5 May, 1741, by Samuel Cowles, Nathaniel Hart and Samuel Lankton.

Court Record, Page 84—17 March, 1740-1: Adms. granted unto Nathaniel Winchell, who gave bond of £200 with Samuel Hooker of sd. Farmington.

Page 12 (Vol. XIV) 2 November, 1742: Nathaniel Winchell, Adms., exhibited an account of his Adms., which this Court accepts.

Page 258.

Wolcott, Judith, Wethersfield. Whereas, Mrs. Judith Wolcott, late of Wethersfield, did give by her will her whole estate to her five surviving daughters and unto the sons and daughters of her deceased son Capt. Samuel Wolcott, late of Wethersfield, to be divided among them as in sd. will expressed; and whereas, her son Josias Wolcott did likewise give by his will some part of his estate to his brother, the aforesd. Capt. Samuel Wolcott, and his sisters, to be equally divided among them after the death of his mother, Mrs. Judith Wolcott: Now, know all men by these presents: That we, William Burnham and Hannah his wife of Kensington, Sarah Welles, relict of Capt. Robert Welles, late of Wethersfield deceased, Samuel Robbins and Lucy his wife, Elizabeth Wolcott, John Stilman and Mary his wife, Abigail Wolcott, relict of Capt. Samuel Wolcott deceased, Samuel Wolcott, Elisha Wolcott and Josiah Wolcott, all of Wethersfield, Abraham Waterhouse and Abigail his wife of Saybrook, and Jonathan Russell and Mehetabell his wife of Wethersfield, all the parties that are interested in either of the estates given as above said, have agreed upon a division and final settlement of both the estates aforesd. Signed and sealed, 12 March, 1740-1.

JOHN STILMAN, LS.	MARY STILMAN, LS.
ABIGAIL WOLCOTT, LS.	SAMUEL WOLCOTT, LS.
ELISHA WOLCOTT, LS.	SARAH WELLES, LS.
WILLIAM BURNHAM, LS.	HANNAH BURNHAM, LS.
SAMUEL ROBBINS, LS.	LUCY ROBBINS, LS.
ELIZABETH WOLCOTT, LS.	JOSIAH WOLCOTT, LS.
ABIGAIL WATERHOUSE, LS.	ABRAHAM WATERHOUSE, LS.
JONATHAN RUSSELL, LS.	MEHETABELL RUSSELL, LS.

Witness: *William Burnham, Jr.,*
Josiah Welles.

Court Record, Page 84—12 March, 1740-1: Agreement accepted.
Joseph Talcott, Esq., Judge.

Page 17.

Wolcott, Peter, Middletown. Invt. £63-08-00. Taken 21 February, 1736-7, by Joseph Starr, Jr., and William Rockwell.

Court Record, Page 6—3rd May, 1737: Adms. to Samuel Dwight, the widow desireing the same.

Page 12—5 July, 1737: Invt. exhibited. Report estate insolvent. James Hamlin and Seth Wetmore appointed commissioners.

Page 76—2 December, 1740: Commissioners report.

Page 1 (Vol. XVII) 21 November, 1753: Pursuant to an act of the General Assembly held at New Haven on the 12 of October, 1753, impowering Samuel Dwight, Adms., to make sale of so much land as would procure the sum of £85-06-01, this Court now orders the sd. Adms. to make known the day of sale and set up advertisements.

Wood, Moses. Court Record, Page 13—2 August, 1737: Moses Wood, a minor, 17 years of age, chose his uncle Robert Johnson of Middletown to be his guardian. Recog., £100. Cert: *Giles Hall, J. P.*

Page 79.

Woodruff, Capt. Joseph, Farmington. Invt. £728-03-05. Taken 21 February, 1737-8, by Isaac Cowles, Giles Hooker and John Newell.

Court Record, Page 28—2 May, 1738: Adms. granted to Elizabeth (File: *Esther*) Woodruff, widow, who recog. in £1000 with Ebenezer Moodey of Farmington.

Page 28—2 May, 1738: Thomas Woodruff, a minor, age 13 years, and Sarah, age 9 years: this Court appoint their mother Elizabeth (*Esther*) Woodruff to be their guardian.

Page 1 (Vol. XIV) 6 April, 1742: An account of Adms. on the estate of Capt. Joseph Woodruff was now exhibited in Court by Esther Woodruff. Accepted.

Page 66—19 November, 1745: A further account of Adms. was exhibited, which was also accepted: The Court order and copy for distribution of the moveable estate, £1-00-00; the Adms. journey to Hartford and attendence in Court, £0-14-00; return of the distributors, £0-04-00. Accepted.

Page 15 (Vol. XV) 1st July, 1746: Esther Woodruff, the widow, having rendered to this Court an account of Adms., moves that the moveable estate be distributed as follows:

	£	s	d
To the widow her thirds,	22	01	06
To Thomas Woodruff, only son, his double share,	17	13	02
To Martha, Esther and Sarah Woodruff, to each,	8	16	07

And appoint Hezekiah Lee, Lt. Joseph Hooker and Robert Porter distributors.

Page 81—6 December, 1748: Report of the distributors. Accepted.

Will and Invt. in Vol. XIV, Page 41-2.

Woodruff, Samuel, Southington. Inventory taken 1st day of April, 1742, by Samuel Root and Jared Lee. Will dated 7 August, 1739.

I, Samuel Woodruff, Sen., of Farmingtown, do make this my last will and testament: I give unto my son Samuel Woodruff, besides what I have already given him, a feather bed, a boulster and two pillows; also my steel trap; also my right in two lotts laid out in two small divisions butting north on the reserved land laid out on the right of my father Matthew Woodruff decd. Unto my son Ebenezer Woodruff, besides what I have already given him, I give the sum of 20 shillings. Unto my son Daniel Woodruff, besides what I have already given him, 20 shillings. Unto my son David Woodruff, besides what I have formerly given him and his heirs and assigns forever, all my right in the 62nd lott of land laid out on my sd. father's right in the division of land in sd. Farmingtown lying on the range of Blue and Shuttle Meadow Mountains, and my right in sd. lott is the 1-2 part thereof. Unto my son Hezekiah Woodruff, besides what I have formerly given him, I give unto him, his heirs and assigns forever, 1-4 part of my lott laid out on my sd. father's right in the division of land lying between Southington Parish and Waterbury bounds, the whole lott containing about 114 acres; also all my right included in the 12th lottment in the 2nd division west of the reserved lands. Unto my son John Woodruff, besides what I have formerly given him, I give him a certain gunn that was once William Smith's. Unto my two daughters, Rebeckah Pike and Rachel Bell, besides what I have formerly given them, I now give unto each of them £4, to be paid to them out of my personal estate. Unto all my aforenamed sons I give all my sermon books, to be equally divided between them. Also, unto my forenamed son Samuel Woodruff, I further give unto him all my right in a certain tract of unlotted land in Farmingtown, lying eastward from that called the Blue Hill division, and by upland to the great swamp. Unto my aforenamed son Hezekiah Woodruff, I further give unto him all the residue and remainder of my estate, real and personal, not before in this my will disposed of, whatsoever and wheresoever the same may be found, always provided that the aforesd. debts and legacies be by him paid. And I appoint my son Hezekiah Woodruff to be my only and sole executor.

Witness: *John Hooker,*   SAMUEL WOODRUFF, SEN., LS.
Thomas Smith, Elisha Lewis.

Court Record, Page 110—2 March, 1741-2: Will proven.

Page 210-11.

Wright, Jonathan, Wethersfield. Invt. £296-01-05. Taken 14 July, 1740, by Jabez Whittlesey and Martin Kellogg. Will dated 29 March, 1740.

I, Jonathan Wright of Wethersfield, do make and ordain this my last will and testament: I give to my wife Anne 1-3 part of my moveable estate, as household goods, &c. I give to my son Judah Wright, whome I make and ordain my only and sole executor, all and singular my land and 2-3 of my stock and cattle, by him freely to be possessed and injoyed, only that part I now order him my sd. executor to distribute to some of the rest of my dear children out of my estate, to say: First, I order my executor to pay £15 money to my daughter Thankfull. 2ndly, I order him to pay £15 to my daughter Elizabeth. Also, that he pay £15 to my daughter Mary. Also, that he pay £5 money to my daughter Jane. Also, I order him to pay to my granddaughter Damarus £4 money. Also, I order him my abovesd. executor that he pay to my two grandsons, Jonathan and Josiah Wright, £4 money each, when the eldest of them comes to age.

Witness: *Martin Kellogg,*   JONATHAN WRIGHT, LS.
Joseph Andrews, Joseph Benton.

Before signing and sealing, the following was written and is part of the will of the above mentioned Jonathan Wright, to say: that 2-3 of my household goods to be equally divided among my daughters.

Witness: *Martin Kellogg,*   JONATHAN WRIGHT, LS.
Joseph Andrews, Joseph Benton.

Court Record, Page 73—2 October, 1740: Will exhibited by Judah Wright. Proven.

Yeomans, Thomas, Estate, Tolland. Court Record, Page 70—5 August, 1740: Adms. to Joseph Yeomans, a brother of sd. deceased. Recog., £500, with Benjamin Hutchins of Tolland. Exhibit of an inventory.

PROBATE RECORDS.

VOLUME XIV.

1742 to 1745.

Page 112-113.

Abborn, Samuel, Tolland, Hartford County. Invt. £821-01-09. Taken 30 November, 1742, by Jonathan Ladd, Samuel Dimock and John Sterns. Will dated 1st November, 1743.

I, Samuel Abborn, of the Town of Tolland and County of Hartford, yeoman, do ordain this my last will and testament: I give to my wife Martha the 1-3 part of all my personal estate forever, and the use and benefit of 1-3 part of my dwelling house, barn and all my improved land during her natural life. My will is and I do give my land (the whole thereof) to my two sons, John Abborn and Samuel Abborn, together with the buildings thereon, to be equally divided between them, they paying out legacies as I shall hereafter order. I give to my daughter Elizabeth Woodward £50 of the old tenor. I give to my daughter Abigail Abborn the sum of £150 old tenour at the age of 21 years or at her marriage. I give to my son John Abborn 2-3 parts of my personal estate, and do appoint him to be my executor.

Witness: *Stephen Steele,*   SAMUEL ABBORN, LS.
Jonathan Mackindiah, Zebulon West.

Court Record, Page 34—6 December, 1743: The will and inventory now exhibited in Court. Proven, allowed and ordered on file. Samuel Abborn, 17 years of age, son of Samuel Abborn, late of Tolland decd., chose John Sterns of Tolland to be his guardian. Recog., £100. John Abborn of Tolland, executor to the will of Samuel Abborn, and John Sterns, guardian to the minor Samuel Abborn, moves to this Court that freeholders be appointed to make division of the real and personal estate of the sd. deceased. This Court appoint Samuel Chapman, Esq., Joseph West and Solomon Loomis, distributors.

Page 49—10 September, 1744: A report of the distributors was now exhibited in Court, accepted and ordered on file.

Page 12-13.

Allin, Alexander, Windsor. Inventory taken 7 May, 1742, by Jonathan Stiles, Samuel Stoughton and Peletiah Allyn. Will dated 27 February, 1741-2.

I, Alexander Allin of Windsor, do make this my last will and testament: I give to my beloved wife Hannah Allin my dwelling house, barn and shop, with ye homestead and ye upland I bought, which was Mr. Samuel Gibb's, about an acre adjoining my homelott, and also 4 acres of land in the meadow against my pasture or homelott, with the third part of my moveable estate, to be to her and to her use and dispose forever. I give unto my son Alexander Allin the house and homestead which I bought of Lt. Jonathan Elsworth, formerly Mr. James MackJerrew's, with all the rest of my outside lands in Windsor or elsewhere, already laid out or which shall or may be laid out. My will is that if my son Alexander shall have a mind to dispose of sd. house and homestead which I bought of Lt. Jonathan Elsworth, yt he first give his mother the offer or refusal thereof. I give unto my two daughters, Mary Allin and Hannah Allin, to each of them the sum of £80 out of my moveable estate; and also I give unto my three daughters, Abigail Elsworth, Mary Allin and Hannah Allin, all the remainder of my moveable estate, if any there be, to be equally divided amongst them; also I give unto my three daughters aforesd. the land which I bought of Jacob Gibbs in the Great Meadow, 4 acres more or less. My will is that my wife Hannah Allin be sole executrix.

Witness: *Jonathan Stiles,*   ALEX: X ALLIN, LS.
Samuel Stoughton, John Allin.

Court Record, Page 6—4 May, 1742: Will exhibited and proven.

Agreement on File.

Allyn, Joseph, Wethersfield. Whereas, Mr. Joseph Allyn, late of Wethersfield deceased, died intestate, wee, the heirs to the estate of sd. Allyn, have agreed (some by themselves and others by their lawfull attorneys) to divide and settle sd. estate, both personal and real, in manner following: Imprimis: To Samuel Allyn, the homested, containing 6 or 7 acres more or less, with the buildings and appurtenances. 2ly. To Hezekiah Kilbourn and Elizabeth his wife, to sundry moveables as per agreement; allso the 6th part of a pasture in Hartford township, of 20 acres; allso 9 1-2 acres in Wethersfield meadow; amounting to the sum of £274-19-08. 3ly. To James Otis and his wife Mary, sundry moveables and 1-6 part of the abovesd. 20-acre pasture in Hartford township; amounting in all unto the sum of £224-19-08. 4ly. To Ebenezer Wright and his wife Hannah, sundry moveables and the 6th part of the abovesd. pasture; allso 5 acres of land in Hartford meadow, a warehouse, and lott in Wethersfield; all amounting unto the sum of £224-19-08. 5ly. To Nathaniel Stilman and his wife Sarah, sundry moveables and 1-6 part of sd. pasture; all amounting unto the sum of £224-19-08. 6ly. To James Knowles and Martha his wife, sundry moveables and 1-6 part of sd. pasture; allso sundry parcels of land in Killinsworth bounds near Durham; amounting in all unto £224-19-08. 7ly. To Ephraim Bostwick and his wife Abigail, sundry moveables and 1-6 part of the pasture abovesd.; all amounting unto the sum of £224-19-08. The above divisions and settlements were consented and agreed to by the parties in their own persons and by their lawfull attorneys this 24th day of January, A. D. 1743-4. In testimony whereof we have hereto set our hands and seals.

SAMUEL ALLYNE, LS.
HEZEKIAH KILBORN, ELIZABETH KILBORN, LS.
JAMES OTIS AND MARY OTIS
HIS WIFE, JAMES KNOWLES, LS., ATTORNEY.
EBENEZER WRIGHT AND HANNAH
HIS WIFE, EPHRAIM BOSTWICK, LS., ATTORNEY.
EPHRAIM BOSTWICK AND
ABIGAIL BOSTWICK, LS.
NATHANIEL STILLMAN AND SARAH STILLMAN, LS.
JAMES KNOWLES AND MARTHA KNOWLES, LS.

In presence of us:
Alexander Mackey,
Samuel Pitkin.

25 January, 1743-4: Before this Court of Probate the above named subscribers appeared and acknowledged the agreement to be their free act and deed. Accepted by the Court.

Page 54, 78.

Allyn, Samuel, Windsor. Invt. £2856-06-06. Taken 27 January, 1742-3, by Jacob Drake, Samuel Enno and Jacob Phelps. Will dated 16 August, 1742.

I, Samuel Allyn of Windsor, do make this my last will and testament: I give unto my son-in-law John Wells, late of Deerfield, now of Windsor aforesd., the 1-2 of my farm at Scotland in Simsbury, exclusive of my marsh called Gillet's marsh, in consideration of sums of money by him paid for me already, and in consideration of his sd. Wells paying to my daughter Mary £20 money in the space of one year next after my decease, 1-2 of the farm to be to him, his heirs and assigns forever. I give unto my daughter Mary the bedd I now lye on, with all the furniture thereto belonging; also I give her the £20 above mentioned, to be paid by my sd. son Wells. My just debts and funeral expenses and the above legacies being paid, the remainder of my estate, both real and personal, to be equally divided to and amongst my four daughters, to Sarah the wife of John Wells, Mary Allyn, Jane Loomis the wife of Odiah Loomis, and Elizabeth the wife of Nathaniel Mather; only the negro boy yt my daughter Wells had I account and reckoned to her as £50 money in the division of my estate, amongst my daughters. My will is that my servants, Cyrus and William, inventoried at £100 each, be not sold, but serve my heirs; and also I give them the liberty of choosing which of my heirs they will serve. And it is also further my pleasure that when they have served my heirs 10 years after my decease, that upon their providing and giving good security that my estate nor heirs shall ever be burdened by their support or maintenance, they shall be made free men and set at liberty from service to my heirs. I appoint my sons-in-law, John Wells, Odiah Loomis and Nathaniel Mather, and also Mr. Samuel Bemon, of Simsbury, to be the executors.

Witness: *Jacob Drake,*   SAMUEL ALLYN, LS.
John Palmer, Jr., Henry Allyn.

Court Record, Page 11—5 October, 1742: Will exhibited by the executors and proven.

Page 22—3 May, 1742: William, a man servant, before this Court declared he made choice to live with Mary Allyn, one of the daughters of Mr. Samuel Allyn of Windsor decd., during his servitude with sd. Mr. Allyn's heirs according to the will of the sd. decd.

Page 43—14 May, 1744: Account of debts and charges paid, with what is due from the estate of Mr. Samuel Allyn, was now exhibited: Paid in debts and charges, £1060-06-06: and credit received £101-01-07. Account allowed and ordered on file.

Page 47—4 September, 1744: Pursuant to an act of the General Assembly, 2nd Thursday in May, 1744, the executors to the will of Samuel Allyn, late of Windsor, allowed to make sale of so much of the real estate to make the sum of £368-03-09, takeing advice of the Court of Probates at Hartford, the executors to look for chaps: one lott of land in Simsbury, about 10 acres, that lies in that part of the town called Scotland; and also in Harwington the whole lott of sd. deceased.

Page 59—4 June, 1745: A report of sale of some land.

Page 65—12 November, 1745: A report of the executors that they have sold land as directed, which amounted to no more than £214-15-06. They moved for directions to sell more.

Page 1—13 December, 1745: Noadiah Loomis and Nathaniel Mather, two of the executors to the last will and testament of Samuel Allin, late of Windsor decd., moves to this Court for a distribution of the estate: Whereupon this Court appoint Peletiah Allyn, Daniel Bissell and John Wilson, of Windsor, distributors.

Dist. File: 13th December, 1745:

	£	s	d
To Sarah Wells, the wife of John Wells,	159	18	11
To Mary Pinney her heirs,	159	18	11
To Jane Loomis and Elizabeth Mather, to each,	159	18	11

By John Wilson, Peletiah Allyn and Daniel Bissell, distributors.

Page 93.

Andrews, Benjamin, Middletown. Invt. £1998-16-01. Taken 14 November, 1743, by Solomon Adkins and Joseph Johnson. Will dated 1st October, 1743.

I, Benjamin Andrews of Middletown, in the County of Hartford, do make this my last will and testament: I give to Tabitha, my wife, the use of all and every part of my estate, both real and personal, until my children arrive to lawful age (only reserving to my aged mother the use of 1-3 part of my dwelling house); and when my two children shall come to lawfull age, my will is that my wife shall have 1-3 part of my personal estate to be at her dispose, and the use of 1-3 part of my real estate during her natural life; and the other 2-3 to be equally divided between my two children (being sons) when they shall come to lawfull age; and the third part of my real estate to be equally divided between them at the decease of their mother. And my will is that my executors after named particularly perform my obligation to my mother by a lease in the keeping of William Rockwell. And further, my will is, concerning the payment of my just debts, that my executors, whome I do hereby fully impower to do the same, do sell and give legal conveyance of so much of the southern part of my farm as to pay my debts due to the Governor and Company of this Colony, and that all my other debts be paid out of my personal estate. And I appoint my wife Tabitha and my friend William Rockwell executors.

Witness: *William Harris,*   BENJAMIN ANDREWS, LS.
Seth Wetmore, Henry Hedges.

Court Record, Page 32—16 November, 1743: Will proven.

Invt. in Vol. XV, Page 59.

Andruss, Mrs. Lydia, Widow. Invt. £638-17-03. Taken 9 September, 1745, by Thomas Andruss and William Day.

Court Record, Page 63—3 September, 1745: Adms. granted to Ebenezer Ensign of Hartford, who gave bond with James Ensign of Hartford in £400 money.

Page 117—6 February, 1749-50: Ebenezer Ensign, Adms., exhibited an account of his Adms. Accepted.

Page 187.

Andrews, Nathaniel, Hartford. Will dated 25 November, 1742: I, Nathaniel Andrews of Hartford, do make this my last will and testament: I give to my wife during her natural life the whole of my estate to improve for herself, and at her decease my will is that my eldest son Timothy shall have the whole of my estate, real and personal, he paying to my son Nathaniel Andrews £5 in money, and also to pay to my daughter Deborah £20 money, and to Jacob, the son of my daughter Deborah,

£10 money. And also I give to Jacob my gunn. And to my son William I do give and confirm my right of land at New Hartford. And do appoint my beloved wife executrix.

Witness: *Jared Spencer,*   NATHANIEL ANDREWS, LS.
Thomas Andrews, Jr., Ithamer Andrews.

Court Record, Page 62—6 August, 1745: The last will of Nathaniel Andrews was now exhibited by Susannah Andrews, widow and executrix, who accepted the trust. Will proven and ordered recorded.

Page 31.

Arnold, John, Hartford. Will dated 14 November, 1741: I, John Arnold of Hartford, do make this my last will and testament: I give unto my daughter Hannah, the wife of Ebenezer Hills, Jr., the sum of £10 over and above what I have given her already, to be as money, and to be her own forever and at her own dispose. I give to my daughter Mary, the wife of John Vibbard, the sum of £10 as money over and above what I have before given her, and at her own dispose. I give to my daughter Sarah, the wife of Thomas Wadsworth, the sum of £10 as money over and above what I have given her already, to be her own forever and at her own dispose. I give unto Hannah, my well-beloved wife, the use of about 2 acres of land commonly called Kenney Point, and the use of 1-3 part of the dwelling house wherein I now live, and the use of 1-3 part of all my improvable lands, and the free liberty of giting firewood and timber on any part of my land, what she stands in need of for her own use during widowhood. And further, I freely give to my wife 1-3 part of all my moveable estate, to be her own forever and at her own dispose. I give unto my son John Arnold the new house built by brother Henry Arnold deceased, and the 1-2 of my barn, to be his own forever and at his dispose. I give unto my son Henry Arnold the house wherein I now live and the 1-2 of my barn, to be his own forever. I give all the remaining part of my estate, real and personal, unto my two sons, John Arnold and Henry Arnold, to be equally divided between them, to be their own forever. I hereby appoint my two sons, John Arnold and Henry Arnold, executors.

Witness: *John Kilbourn,*   JOHN X ARNOLD, LS.
Joseph Smith, Jonathan Hills.

Page 43.

Aspenwell, Eliezur, Kensington Parish. Invt. £930-09-04. Taken 2 July, 1742, by Caleb Galpin and William Burnham, Jr.

Court Record, Page 8—6 July, 1742: This Court grant Adms. on the estate of *Ebenezer* Aspenwell, late of Farmingtown decd., unto Aaron and Mary Aspenwell, son and widow of the sd. decd., who gave bond, with Peletiah Mills, of Windsor, of £1000 money and took letters of Adms. this day.

Page 29—17 August, 1743: Account of Adms. on the estate of Eliezur Aspenwell, late of Farmingtown deceased, was now exhibited in Court by Mary Aspenwell and Aaron Aspenwell, Adms., which account is allowed and ordered on file. Adms. now moved for a distribution of the moveable estate: To Mary Aspenwell, widow, her thirds; to Aaron Aspenwell his double share; to Mary Adkins, to Hulda Cotton and Anna Nott, to each of them their single shares. And appoint Amos Porter, Samuel Hart and David Sage, of Middletown, distributors.

Page 91-2.

Austin, John, Hartford. Will dated 19 February, 1741-2: I dispose of my worldly goods as followeth: To my dear and good and beloved wife I give £300 (as money), to be paid out of my moveable estate or in money as soon as it can be conveniently raised out of my estate off the currency as it now passess; as also one cow and the time or service of one of my servants (which she shall chose) to serve her during her natural life; as also the profits arising from 1-2 of my land and houseing in Hartford, for her benefit for the term of her natural life. I give my dear dater, Mary Ellery, the use or profit of the other half of my land and houseing in Hartford during her natural life, and at her mother's decease the other half for sd. term. All the remainder of my moveable estate I give to my daughter Mary Ellery, to her and her heirs forever. At the decease of my dear wife and dater, I give to my dear grandson Johnny Ellery all my land and houseing in Hartford, to be to him and his heirs forever. The use or profit arising from any other of my lands, wheresoever they be, I give to my dater Mary Ellery during her natural life, and at her decease I give my grandson William Ellery all my land in Litchfield and New Hartford, to be to him and his heirs forever. And the remainder of my lands, wheresoever they be, I give to be equally divided to and amongst the rest of my dear dater's children (if any there be born), whether male or female, share and share alike; and for want of such children, to be divided between my grandsons Johnny and Billey Ellery equally, to them and their heirs forever. And I do hereby appoint my son John Ellery and my daughter Mary to be executors.
Witness: *James Church,*   JOHN AUSTIN, LS.
John Potwin, Joseph Church.

Court Record, Page 30—20 September, 1743: The last will of Mr. John Austin was now exhibited in Court by John Ellery and Mary his wife. Will proven and ordered to be recorded.
Page 38—15 February, 1743-4: Capt. Nathaniel Hooker of Hartford, in behalf of his mother, Mrs. Mary Austin, the relict of Mr. John Austin, late of Hartford decd., appeals from the judgement of this Court in approveing the last will and testament of the late deceased unto the Superior Court to be holden at Hartford on the first Tuesday in March. Recog. in £10 lawfull money that the sd. Mary Austin shall prosecute this her appeal to effect, or answer all damages if she make not her plea good.

Dist. File:

To the Honourable Judge of Probate for the District of Hartford:

We, the subscribers, being appointed by the said Judge of Probate to make a distribution of the outlands of the estate of Mr. John Austin, late of Hartford deceased, to the children of his daughter Mary Ellery, given to the said Mary's children by the last will of the said John Austin deceased, in pursueance we have distributed the estate as follows:

To Jane Ellery, two lots in Harwinton, one containing 100 acres at 24s per acre, £120-12-00; one of 87 acres at 18s per acre, £78-06-00; also, lot in Winchester laid out to Thomas Whaples, 26 acres at 16s per acre, £20-16-00.

To Austin Ledyard, 176 acres of the farm of land at New Preston at 24s per acre, £211-04-00; he to pay to his sister Nancy £00-10-04 1-2 penny, it being so much more than his equal share, it being £210-13-07 1-2 pence.

To Lucy Ledyard, 54 acres of the farm of land at New Preston at 24s per acre, £64-16-00; and the third lot in the first division of lots in Farmington adjoining the reserved land, 110 acres at 14s per acre, £132-00-00; also, one lot in Winchester, in the first division of lots, laid out to Daniel Smith, 23 acres at 15s per acre, £17-05-00; she to pay to Nancy Ledyard £3-07-04 1-2 penny.

To Abigail Talcott, wife of Samuel Talcott, Jun., one lot in Winchester, in the second division of lots, laid out to Wilterton Merrels, 134 acres at 16s per acre, £107-04-00; also, 3 lots in Hartland which were laid out to John Austin's heirs: one lot in the first division, 42 3-4 acres at 11s per acre, £29-10-03; and one lot, the 43d, in the second division, 52 3-4 acres, £52-15-00; and the other lot, the 41st in the third division, 81 acres at 6s per acre, £24-06-00; she to receive of her sister Lucretia Ledyard £2-18-04 1-2 penny.

To Lucretia Ledyard, one lot in Farmington, 77 1-2 acres at 24s per acre, £93-00-00; and one lot in Winchester, laid out to Wilterton Merrells in the first division, 134 acres at 18s per acre, £120-12-00; she to pay to her sister Abigail Talcott £2-18-04 1-2 penny.

To Nancy Ledyard, a lot in Winchester, in the last division, 183 1-2 acres at 17s per acre, £155-19-06; also, two lots laid out to Thomas Whaples, 26 acres, £23-08-00; the other laid out to Daniel Smith, 23 acres at 16s per acre, £18-08-00; and that the said Nancy may be made to share equal with the other heirs, she is to receive of Austin Ledyard £00-10-04 1-2 penny; to receive of Jane Ellery £9-00-04 1-2 penny, and of Lucy Ledyard £3-07-04 1-2 penny.

29 April, 1775.   *Daniel Skinner,* } *Distributors.*
                                   Joseph Church, }

Accepted by me: J. Talcott, Judge of Probate.

384 PROBATE RECORDS. VOL. XIV,

Page 112.

Bacor, Daniel, Tolland. Invt. £142-00-05. Taken 16 February, 1742-3, by Samuel Chapman and Samuel Dimock.

Court Record, Page 14—24 December, 1742: Adms. on the estate of Daniel Bacor unto Heman Bacor of sd. Tolland, who gave bond with Niel McLean of Hartford.

Page 34—6 December, 1743: An account of Adms. now exhibited in Court by Heman Bacor, Adms.: Paid in debts and charges, £75-18-06; received, £12-12-09. Account allowed and ordered on file. Adms. moves this Court for a distribution: Inventory, £142-05-00, to which is added £12-12-09; amounts to £154-13-02; paid in debts and charges, £75-18-06; there remains £78-14-08 to be distributed: To Joseph, Samuel, John and Heman Bacor, and to Hannah Bacor, alias Gurley, and Abigail Bacor, brethren and sisters of the sd. deceased, to each of them £13-02-04 in moveable estate; and what real estate shall appear to belong to the estate of sd. deceased to be divided in an equal proportion to and amongst sd. heirs, brethren and sisters. And this Court appoint John Bissell, Esq., of Bolton, and Samuel Chapman and Zebulon West, of Tolland, to make a distribution.

Page 64—5 November, 1745: Report of the distributors.

Page 30.

Bacor, Jacob, Tolland. Invt. £265-16-09. Taken 1st July, 1742, by Samuel Chapman, Daniel Cook and Samuel Dimmock.

Court Record, Page 7—1st June, 1742: Adms. of the estate of Jacob Bacor, late of Tolland decd., unto John Bacor of Tolland, who gave bond with Niel McLean of Hartford, £700.

Page 27—2 August, 1743: Account of Adms. exhibited in Court by John Bacor, Adms.: Paid in debts and charges, £104-19-02; received, £85-11-04: Which account is allowed.

Dist. File: Whereas, we the subscribers have been appointed to distribute the real and personal estate of Mr. Jacob Baker of Tolland, we do distribute the personal estate this 14th December, 1743, as followeth:

	£ s d
To Samuel Baker,	38-18-11
To John Baker,	38-19-00
To Hannah Gurley, alias Baker,	38-18-11
To Heman Baker,	38-18-11
To Abigail Baker,	38-18-11

By John Bissell, Samuel Chapman and Zebulon West.

Page 81-2.

Bancroft, Samuel, Windsor. Inventory taken 17 January, 1742-3, by William Woolcott, Jr., Nathaniel Loomis and David Smith. Will dated 19 November, 1742.

I, Samuel Bancroft of Windsor, do make this my last will and testament: I give to my wife Joanna all the estate that I receiyed with her in marriage, and so much more of my moveable estate as will make up 1-3 of my moveable estate at inventory price, to be to her own use forever; and also all the meat, butter and cheese that then I shall leave in the house at my decease, with my largest swine, and all the corne that is now in the east chamber and garret of my house; and also the use of the three lower rooms and cellar of my house during her widowhood, with 1-3 part of my homelott (with the north side thereof), she to have the use of it during her life provided that she does not make any lease of the house to any person whatsoever. I give to my daughter Margaret 40 acres on the north side of my Town Common lott on the east side of the Great River, and the remainder of sd. lott I give to my daughter Eunice, or £60 out of my moveable estate at inventory price. I give to my daughter Elizabeth £50, to be paid to her out of my moveable estate at inventory price; or, if she shall choose, £50 in the bills of credit of the old tenour. And all the rest of my estate, both real and personal, I give to my son Nathaniel and to his heirs forever. I hereby make my son Nathaniel sole executor.

Witness: *Roger Wolcott, Jr.,*　　　Samuel Bancroft, ls.
Zachariah Long, Joseph Dickins.

Court Record, Page 16—1st February, 1742-3: The last will of Samuel Bancroft was now exhibited in Court. Proven and ordered recorded.

Page 76 (Vol. XVI) 25 October, 1752: Joanna Bancroft, widow and relict, now moves that her right of dowry may be set out to her: Whereupon this Court appoint Matthew Rockwell, Ebenezer Grant and Moses Loomis to set out the widow's dowry in sd. estate.

Barnard, Samuel. Court Record, Page 30—6 September, 1743: Ebenezer Barnard, a minor, 18 years of age, son of Samuel Barnard, chose Caleb Church of Hartford to be his guardian. Recog., £200.

Page 143.

Barnes, Thomas, Farmington. Invt. £727-01-06. Taken 12 April, 1744, by James Pike and Samuel Niel.

Court Record, Page 45—3 July, 1744: Adms. on the estate of Thomas Barnes, late of Farmingtown, unto Hannah Barnes, widow, who gave bonds with Ebenezer Barnes of Farmingtown, £300.

Page 59—4 June, 1745: Account of Adms. exhibited in Court by Hannah Barnes, Adms.: Paid in debts and charges, £97-14-02. Account allowed and ordered to be kept on file. Phineas Barnes, a minor, 15 years of age, son of Thomas Barnes, chose his mother Hannah Barnes to be his guardian.

Page 34 (Vol. XVI) 3 September, 1751: Hannah Barnes, alias Beckwith, Adms., having finished her account of Adms., which this Court accepted, now moves for a distribution as follows:

	£ s d
To Hannah Barns, alias Beckwith,	44-13-04
To Phineas Barns, eldest son,	113-16-08
To Timothy and Nathaniel Barns, to each of them,	56-18-04
And to Ann Hart, alias Barns, Irene, Lydia and Mary Barns,	56-18-04

And appoint Nathaniel Hitchcock, Samuel Niel and John Bell, of Farmington, distributors.

Page 41—5 November, 1751: Mary Barns, a minor, 15 years of age, daughter of Thomas Barns, chose her brother Phineas Barns to be her guardian. Recog., £400. Lydia Barns, a minor, 17 years of age, chose her brother Phineas Barns to be her guardian; also to be guardian to Timothy Barns, age 14 years, and Nathaniel, 9 years. Recog., £400.

Page 198.

Barton, William, Kensington. Inventory taken 28 December, 1745, by Caleb Galpin and Daniel Hancox.

Court Record, Page 1 (Vol. XV) 3 December, 1745: Adms. granted unto Sarah Barton, widow, who gave bonds with Daniel Hancox of Farmington, of £300.

Page 30—6 January, 1746-7: Sarah Barton, widow, exhibited an account of her Adms. Accepted.

Page 113 (Vol. XVII) 1st June, 1756: William Barton, a minor, aged 16 years, son of William Barton, late of Wethersfield deceased, appeared before this Court and made choice of Josiah Burnham to be his guardian. Recog., £200.

Beckley, Miriam. Court Record, Page 10—13 September, 1742: Adms. on the estate of Miriam Beckley, late of Wethersfield, unto John Beckley of Wethersfield, who gave bonds with Timothy Baxter, £100.

Page 79-80.

Beckley, Richard, Wethersfield. Died 27 September, 1741. Invt. £1997-13-11. Taken by Thomas Deming, Elihu Dickinson and Joseph Beckley.

Court Record, Page 16—1st February, 1742-3: Adms. granted to Nathaniel Beckley of Wethersfield, who gave bond with Abraham Beckley in £200.

See File: We, the subscribers, Nathaniel Beckley, Abraham Beckley and Elizabeth Beckley, children of Richard Beckley, late of Wethersfield deceased, who died intestate; we, the sd. Nathaniel, Abraham and Elizabeth, considering the difficulties and trouble that sometimes arise on such estate, have convenanted and agreed each with the other that the sd. Nathaniel and Abraham shall inherit all the lands and equally divided them, and also to divide all the buildings equally between them; and that the sd. Nathaniel and Abraham shall and will set out 1-3 part, both real and personal, of the estate of the aforesd. deceased unto their mother, to be to her proper use and benefit during the whole term of her natural life or widowhood; and that the sd. Nathaniel and Abraham shall pay or cause to be paid unto Elizabeth, their sister, out of the moveable estate at inventory price or in money (old tenor), the sum of £350. We do further covenant with and promise each to the other that our above agreement and partition of our deceased father's estate shall stand good and be and remain forever, without any lett, suit, molestation or denial from us or from any persons from, by or under us. And for the further confirmation of every of the above agreed and covenanted premises, have set our hands and seals this 1st day of February, 1742-3.

NATHANIEL BECKLEY, LS.
ABRAHAM BECKLEY, LS.
ELIZABETH X BECKLEY, LS.

Test: Joseph Talcott, Clerk.

Page 16—1st February, 1742-3: Agreement exhibited in Court and accepted, and by them ordered to be recorded and kept on file.

Belding, Samuel. Court Record, Page 20—5 April, 1743: Whereas, this Court did on the 2nd day of December, 1735, pursuant to an act of the General Assembly held at New Haven October the 9th, 1735, direct Samuel Belding of Wethersfield to set up advertisements signifying that there is a certain piece or tract of land lying toward the northwest corner of Coventry, within the bounds of sd. Coventry, of 25 acres, to be sold at publick vandue, the sd. Mr. Belding attended sd. direction, and no person appeareing to purchase sd. land, this Court do now direct the sd. Samuel Belding to look for a chap to purchase sd. land, and if he can find a chap that will purchase sd. land or so much thereof that will answer the sum of £22-18-06 with incident charges of sale, then the sd. Samuel Belding is to give a deed of sd. land to such person or chap, and report to this Court to whom he sold the sd. land and for how much.

[This refers to estate of Gideon Belding of Wethersfield, on page 11 of this volume.]

Bignall, Abigail. Court Record, Page 28—17 August, 1743: Abigail Bignall of Sheffield, in the Colony of Massachusetts Bay, age 13 years, daughter of Mark Bignall of sd. Sheffield deceased, chose Joseph Forward of Simsbury to be her guardian, her father-in-law Jedediah Moore of Simsbury and her mother Dorothy Moore (who was the relict of sd. Mark Bignall) desireing the same. Recog., £200.

Page 65.

Bliss, Jonathan, Windsor. Will dated 29 October, 1737: I, Jonathan Bliss of Windsor, in the County of Hartford, yeoman, being weak of body but of sound mind and memory, doe make this my last will and testament: I give to my wife Sarah Bliss 1-3 part of my personal estate, to her own dispose, and 1-3 part of all my real estate during her natural life, and that my executors find and procure firewood fit for use sufficient for my sd. wife Sarah Bliss during and as long as she continues my widow. I give to my daughter Sarah Mugglestone, alias Sarah Bliss, 40 shillings, to be paid out of my estate by my executors at my decease. I give to my only and well-beloved son Jonathan Bliss all my real and personal estate, to him, his heirs and assigns forever, whome I make my sole executor.

Witness: *Ebenezer Terry,*   JONATHAN BLISS, LS.
Josiah Hadlock, Israel Bissell.

Court Record, Page 15—4 January, 1742-3: The last will and testament of Jonathan Bliss, late of Windsor deceased, was now exhibited in Court by Jonathan Bliss, executor. Proven and ordered to be recorded.

Bolman, Moses. Court Record, Page 49—6 November, 1744: Moses Bolman, a minor, 15 years of age, son of Moses Bolman decd., chose his mother Silence Bolman to be his guardian. Recog., £1000.

Page 63.

Brainard, Nehemiah, Glastonbury. Invt. £737-13-07. Taken 24 November, 1742, by Gideon Hollister and Robert Loveland, Jr. Will dated 5 October, 1742: I, Nehemiah Brainard of Glastonbury, do make this my last will and testament: I give to my son Nehemiah Brainard and to his heirs all that tract of land that I bought of Edward Boardman, lying and being in Glastonbury. I give to my wife, and to her heirs and assigns, that 50 acres of land that the proprietors of the Town of Glastonbury gave to me at their meeting, 3 March, 1739-40, and also all my moveable estate. I also relinquish all my rights to Eastbury Parish of £100 that they are obliged to pay me towards my settlement in the work of the ministry amongst them. I appoint my brother John Brainard to be my executor.

Witness: *Jonathan Hale,*   NEHEMIAH BRAINARD, LS.
Daniel Wright, Jonas X Strickland.

Court Record, Page 2—25 November, 1742: The last will of Rev. Nehemiah Brainard of Glastonbury decd. was now exhibited in Court by John Brainard, executor. Proven and ordered to be recorded. This Court appoint John Brainard to be guardian unto Nehemiah Brainard, a minor, one year old, son of Rev. Nehemiah Brainard deceased. Recog., £500.

Page 43—2 May, 1744: John Brainard now resigns his guardianship to sd. minor unto his mother, widow of the sd. deceased. Recog., £200.

Page 173.

Brown, John, Middletown. Invt. £878-18-06. Taken 31 October, 1744, by Samuel Warner, Benjamin Miller and Joseph Miller.

Court Record, Page 49—12 August, 1744: This Court grant Adms. unto Nathaniel Brown of Middletown, who gave bond with Jeremiah Guild of sd. Middletown of £1000 money.

Dist. File: Distribution of the estate of John Brown, late of Middletown, 1st July, 1745, viz.:

	£ s d
To Nathaniel Brown,	22-16-00
To Lydia Brown,	36-02-03
To Mary Brown,	36-08-02

The dwelling house and barn we agree to hold in common. To our sister Dorothy Hurlbutt a full fifth part. In witness whereof we have hereunto set our hands and seals, 23 March, 1745.

JONATHAN COLE, LS. | LYDIA X BROWN, LS.
NATHANIEL BROWN, LS. | MARY X BROWN, LS.

Witness: *John Bartlett,*
William Rockwell.

Middletown, 1st July, 1745: Then Mary Brown, since the above signing and sealing, being married to one Jonathan Cole, Jr., of Hartford, the sd. Jonathan and Mary Cole acknowledged this instrument to be their free act and deed before me.   *Giles Hall, J. P.*

Page 149.

Buck, David, Wethersfield. Died 23 August, 1744. Invt. £1538-00-00. Taken 25 September, 1744, by Nathaniel Wright and Josiah Goodrich.

Court Record, Page 48—2 October, 1744: Adms. granted to Josiah Buck of Wethersfield, who gave bond of £2000.

Page 58—15 May, 1745: Josiah Buck, Adms., exhibited an account of his Adms.: Paid in debts and charges, £256-01-04. Which account is accepted.

Page 66.

Buckland, Thomas, Windsor. Will dated 30 June, 1737: I, Thomas Buckland of Windsor, do make this my last will and testament: I give to my wife Abigail Buckland the use of all my estate, real and personal, during her widowhood; and after her decease my will is that all my sd. estate I give and bequeath unto my son Joseph Gaylord and to his wife, to them and their heirs forever. I give unto Mary Hannum £10, that is, out of the moveable estate. After the decease of my wife, my will is that if my son Joseph Gaylord should die before my daughter Sarah, that then she the sd. Sarah Gaylord shall have all my estate, both real and personal; and in case my daughter Sarah should die before my sd. son Joseph, then my will is that my son Joseph shall have all my sd. estate, both real and personal, to be at his own use and to his heirs forever, he paying out the aforesd. legacy unto Mary Hannum. I make my son Joseph Gaylord executor.

Witness: *Daniel Bissell,*   THOMAS BUCKLAND, LS.
Josiah Bissell, Benjamin Bissell.

Court Record, Page 1—6 April, 1742: The last will and testament of Thomas Buckland, deceased, now exhibited in Court by Joseph Gaylord, executor. Proven and ordered to be recorded.

Butler, Peter. Court Record, Page 46—7 August, 1744: Mary Butler, a minor, 18 years of age, and Lucy Butler, 14 years of age, daughters of Peter Butler decd., chose Edward Hamlin of Middletown to be their guardian. Recog., £500.

See page 21.

Page 100-1.

Candee, Zacheus, Middletown. Invt. £3038-16-10. Taken 18 August, 1743, by Jonathan Allin, Joseph Clark and William Rockwell. Will dated 10 October, 1734.

I, Zacheus Candee of Middletown, in the County of Hartford, do make this my last will and testament: I give unto Sarah, my wife, the use of the 1-2 of my now dwelling house and barn, or so much as she shall see cause to improve for her comfort during her natural life or so long as she shall continue my widow; and also the yearly benefit of 1-3 part of my improved lands during widowhood. I give my wife the 1 equal third part of my moveable estate, to be at her whole dispose. I give to my son Zacheus Candee the 1-3 part of my homelott or farm whereon I now dwell, that is to say, the westernmost end of sd. lott. I give to my other two sons, Isaac and Theophilus, the other 2-3 of my home lands, at the eastermost end of my lott whereon I now dwell, in equal part to each of them; also to each of them my dwelling house and barn and buildings on sd. land (only reserving to my wife as abovesd. in houseing and lands). And it is my will that if I should be removed by death before I make up to my four daughters equally to each of them, namely, Sarah, Hannah, Abigail and Mary, in their portions in part of what I have formerly given to some of them, that they shall be made up equal one with another out of my other estate and not out of any part of my homelott. The remainder of my estate shall be divided equally among all of my seven children. I appoint my sons Zacheus Candee and Theophilus Candee my executors.

Witness: *Joseph Rockwell,*   ZACHEUS CANDEE, LS.
Edward Rockwell, Lamberton Cooper.

Court Record, Page 29—6 September, 1743: Will exhibited by Zacheus and Theophilus Candee, executors. Proven and ordered to be kept on file.

Page 29.

Case, Elizabeth, Simsbury. Died 12 July, 1742: Inventory taken 7 September, 1742, by Benajah Humphrey, Jacob Tuller and Amos Wilcockson.

Court Record, Page 10—1 September, 1742, Adms. granted to Thomas Case, who gave bond with Isaac Case of £700.

Page 4—1st February, 1742-3: Thomas Case, Adms., now exhibited an account of his Adms.: Paid in debts and charges, £19-12-09; received in credit, £8-19-06. Accompt accepted and ordered on file. Inventory, £117-02-11; credit per account, £8-19-06; added to the inventory, £126-02-05; debts and charges subtracted, there remains £106-09-06. Real and personal estate to be distributed and divided, viz.: to Thomas Case, Amos Case, Isaac Case, Abraham Case, Sarah Case, alias Higley, and to the heirs of Abigail Case, alias Abigail Slaughter, to each of them an equal sixth part of the sum of £106-09-06. This Court appoint Jacob Tuller, Benajah Humphrey and Amos Wilcox distributors.

Page 147.

Case, Jonah, Windsor. Invt. £1771-07-13. Taken 19 April, 1744, by Joseph Hickcox and Josiah Phelps 3rd.

Court Record, Page 41—17 March, 1743-4: Adms. on the estate of Jonah Case, sometime of Simsbury, late of Windsor decd., unto Martha Case, widow and relict of sd. decd., who gave bonds with Joseph Heacok of Windsor, £500.

Page 109.

Case, Thomas, Hartford. Died 1742. Invt. £61-11-08. Taken 5 December, 1742, by Nehemiah Olmsted and Stephen Olmsted.

Court Record, Page 35—6 December, 1743: An inventory of the estate of Thomas Case, late of Hartford deceased, was now exhibited in Court by Joseph Cowles, Adms. Approved and ordered on file.

Page 47—7 August, 1744: Account of Adms. was now exhibited by Joseph Cowles, Adms. Account accepted.

Inventory in Vol. XV, Page 10-11.

Clapp, Ensign Thomas, Hartford. Invt. £957-07-01. Taken 13 January, 1745-6, by Joseph Cooke and Jonathan Steele. An additional inventory of lands in New Hartford, valued at £174-18-06. Taken 31 October, 1745, by Samuel Messenger and David Ensign, Jr. Also, another piece of land lying in New Hartford, being 6 acres and 30 rods. Apprised 30 December, 1745, by William Baker and David Ensign at £6-02-06.

Court Record, Page 49—18 August, 1744: Adms. granted unto Mary Clapp, widow and relict, who gave bonds with Robert King, of Hartford, of £600.

Page 63 (Vol. XV) 15 April, 1748: An account of Adms. was now exhibited in Court by Mary Clapp, widow. Accepted. This Court order distribution, viz.:

	£ s d
To Mary Clapp, the widow,	40-06-05
To the heirs of Oliver Clapp, their double share,	32-05-03
To Elijah and Thomas Clapp, to each,	16-02-08
And to the heirs of Mary Clapp, alias Waters,	16-02-08

And appoint Thomas Richards, Jonathan Steele and Thomas Wells, distributors. Also, this Court order the sd. distributors to set out to Mary Clapp, widow, her dowry, and make return to this Court.

Page 172.

Cole, John, Hartford. Inventory taken 30 November, 1744, by John Edwards and John Skinner.

Court Record, Page 52—20 December, 1744: This Court grants Adms. on the estate of John Cole, late of Hartford decd., unto Elizabeth Cole, widow, who gave bonds with Ozias Goodwin of Hartford for £600.

Page 65 (Vol. XVI) 3 June, 1752: An account of Adms. was exhibited in Court by Elizabeth Cole, Adms. Accepted.

Page 67—20 June, 1752: Elizabeth Cole, Adms., now moves for a distribution of the estate: Whereupon this Court appoint Joseph Talcott. Joseph Holton and John Skinner, of Hartford, to distribute the sd. estate to the heirs.

Page 81 (Vol. XVII): Articles of Agreement, made and concluded upon this 3 day of December, A. D. 1754, by and between the heirs of Mr. John Cole, late of Hartford deceased, are as follows:

AGREEMENT.

Imprimis: We, Jonathan and Elizabeth Nobles, Jonathan and Jerusha Easton, Timothy and Lydia Shepherd, Daniel Goodwin, guardian to and in behalf of Nathaniel, Daniel, Dorothy and Sarah Goodwin, heirs of Dorothy Cole (alias Goodwin) deceased, Mary Cole, Stephen and Sarah Hopkins, and Thomas and Susannah Nobles, for ourselves and our heirs, do covenant, promise and agree, to and with Phineas Cole and John Cole, that for and in consideration of the sum of £22 old tenor by them to us in hand paid or secured to be paid, we do remise, release and forever quitt claim unto them the sd. Phineas Cole and John Cole, and to their heirs and assigns forever, all the parts and parcels of the homested lately the property of our honoured father John Cole of Hartford deceased, which was set out and distributed to them by order of the Court of Probates, by Mr. Joseph Talcott and John Skinner, according as the same is butted and bounded in the distribution dated August 22nd, 1752, and accepted by sd. Court, with the mansion house and all other buildings erected thereon, and with the appurtenances and priviledges thereunto belonging.

2nd. We, the said Phineas Cole and John Cole, do covenant and agree that for and in consideration of the full performance of the above recited premises, we do forever quitclaim unto the above named Jonathan *et. als.* all the right, title and interest that we have, etc., in a lot of land in Hartford called Jones's lot, 3 acres more or less, bounded east on Joseph Sheldon, Daniel Wells and Isaac Sheldon's land, north and south on highways, and west on John Skinner's land, with all the priviledges and appurtenances thereof, etc.

In confirmation thereof we have hereunto mutually set to our hands and affixed our seals the day and year above named.

DANIEL GOODWIN, *Guardian to* NATHANIEL,
DANIEL, DOROTHY *and* SARAH GOODWIN, *heirs*
of DOROTHY GOODWIN *deceased*, LS.

		PHINEAS COLE,	LS.
MARY X COLE,	LS.	JOHN COLE,	LS.
STEPHEN HOPKINS,	LS.	JONATHAN EASTON,	LS.
SARAH HOPKINS,	LS.	JERUSHA EASTON,	LS.
THOMAS NOBLE,	LS.	TIMOTHY SHEPHERD,	LS.
SUSANNAH NOBLE,	LS.	LYDIA X SHEPHERD,	LS.

Acknowledged in Court, 3 December, 1754.

Test: Jos: Talcott, Clerk.

Page 89-90.

Cole, Nathaniel, Kensington. Inventory taken 29 June, 1743, by Isaac Hart and Samuel Lankton. Will dated 20 March, 1738-9.

I, Nathaniel Cole, Sen., of Kensington, in the Township of Farmingtown, do make this my last will and testament: I give to my wife Lydia Cole the use of 1-3 part of all my real estate during her natural life, and 1-3 part of all my personal estate I give to her, her heirs and assigns forever. I give to my eldest daughter Lydia, the wife of Zebulon Curtiss, and her heirs forever, besides what I have already given her, £30 in moveables, to be reckoned according to the value of the bills of credit that now pass among us. I give to my second daughter Rachel, now the wife of Josiah Boardman, and her heirs forever, besides what I have already given her, £30 in moveables, to be reckoned as aforesd. I give to my third daughter Eunice Cole and her heirs forever, £130 in moveables, to be reckoned as aforesd. All the rest of my estate, real and personal, I give to my four sons and their heirs forever, namely, Nathan, Job, Nathaniel and Elisha Cole, to be equally divided among them. I appoint my two eldest sons, Nathan and Job Cole, executors.

Witness: *William Burnham,*   NATHANIEL COLE, LS.
John Root, Nathaniel Roberts.

Court Record, Page 26—5 July, 1742: Will now exhibited in Court by Nathan and Job Cole, executors. Proven. Exhibit of an inventory, which is ordered on file.

Page 134.

Collier, Daniel, Hartford. Invt. £1184-01-07. Taken 28 September, 1743, by Joseph Talcott and Daniel Goodwin.

Court Record, Page 40—6 March, 1743-4: This Court grant Adms. on the estate of Daniel Collier (supposed to be) deceased unto Thankfull Collier, widow and relict of sd. deceased, and Daniel Goodwin, who gave bond with John Rue of Farmington for £500 lawful money.

Page 78 (Vol. XVII) 2 September, 1755: Sarah Colyer, aged 19 years, daughter of Daniel Colyer of Hartford deceased, chose Capt. Daniel Goodwin of Hartford to be her guardian. Recog., £300.

Page 83—18 November, 1755: Daniel Goodwin, guardian to Sarah Colyer (alias Sheldon), Thankfull and Susannah Colyer, children and heirs to the estate of Daniel Colyer, now moves for a distribution of the estate: Whereupon this Court appoint Richard Goodman, Joseph Wadsworth, Jr., and Moses Dickinson to distribute the estate equally to and among the heirs. Also to set out the widow's dowry, and make return of their doings to this Court.

Page 95—9 February, 1756: Report of the distributors accepted.

Page 10.

Cornwall, John, Middletown.   Invt. £106-19-00.   Taken 9 March, 1742, by William Rockwell, Nathaniel Gilbert and Jonathan Allyn.

Will dated 26 February, 1738-9: I, John Cornwall, Sen., of Middletown, in the County of Hartford, do make this my last will and testament: I give unto Mary, my wife, my sheep's wool and all my wool combs and all my sheep's wool that shall be mine at my decease, and 1-3 part of my household goods, and one cow, all of which I give her. Also, I give her the use of 1-2 of the boggy meadow that belongs to me and my son John, and of my sheep, during the time she shall remain my widow. I give unto my son John Cornwall my gunn, with what I have already given him by deed of gift. I give unto my two grandsons, John and Abijah, the two sons of my son John Cornwall, all my part of the boggy meadow land above mentioned, to be to them in equal parts at their grandmother's decease or marriage. I give unto my daughter Eunice my brass kettle. I give unto my daughter Hannah one cow, to be paid to her out of my estate by my executor hereafter named, except I shall do it myself before my decease. I also give to my son John all my part of our team and team tackling, provided he shall supply his mother with convenient firewood during her widowhood. And my will is that what I shall have growing at my decease, of the fruits of the earth, with what shall be provided for my family or creatures, as corne, meat, syder, swine, and other family necessaries, and hay and other provisions for creatures, shall be for the use of my wife and son John and their families. And my will is that what then remains of my personal estate shall be equally divided to and among all my children. And whereas, in my deed of gift to my son John, dated 26 February, 1723-4, I did oblige my sd. son to pay to my three younger daughters to each the sum of £10 money as they come to lawful age if not done by me before my decease, I do hereby declare that I have fully done the same. I appoint my only son John Cornwall, Jr., executor.

Witness: *Joseph Rockwell,*   JOHN CORNWALL, LS.
Ebenezer Rockwell, William Rockwell.

Page 49-50.

Cornwall, Capt. Waite, Middletown. Invt. £1208-06-07. Taken 14 October, 1742, by William Rockwell and John Hubbard.

Court Record, Page 3—13 December, 1742: Adms. on the estate of Waite Cornwall, late of Middletown, unto Jacob Whitmore of Middletown, who gave bond with John Hubbard of Middletown for £500. Timothy Cornwall, a minor, 20 years of age, and Abigail, 18 years of age, children of Waite Cornwall, chose John Hubbard of Middletown to be their guardian. Recog., £300. And it was also further certified by *Jabez Hamlin, J. P.,* that Susannah, another daughter of sd. deceased, made choice of Mr. Jacob Whitmore to be her guardian, which this Court allow. And it was further certified by sd. Justice that the widow and relict of sd. deceased desired that Jacob Whitmore might be guardian to Mabell, age 12 years, and Sarah, age 10 years, daughters of Waite Cornwall deceased. Recog., £1000.

Page 66 (Vol. XV) 15 May, 1748: An account of Adms. was now exhibited in Court by Jacob Cornwall, Adms. Accepted. This Court order distribution as followeth:

	£ s d
To Mercy Cornwall, the widow, her thirds,	83-15-10
To Timothy Cornwall, only son, his double part,	47-16-10
To Millicent, Mercy, Mary, Abigail, Susannah and Sarah Cornwall, to each of them,	23-18-05

And appoint Jonathan Allin, John Hubbard and Ephraim Adkins, distributors.

Page 70—25 May, 1748: Sarah Cornwall, a minor, age 15 years, daughter of Waite Cornwall: her brother-in-law Nathaniel Cornwall to be her guardian. Recog., £500.

Page 113-145-146.

Crozier, James, Simsbury. Invt. £612-19-06. Taken 7 December, 1743, by James Cornish, Michael Humphrey and John Case. Additional inventory:

	£ s d
1 box of glass, cost £25; 1 horse, prised by Nichols & Ashley at £7; 1 silver box, 4 oz. 16 dwt., 5 qr., by Potwin & Whiting, £7-04-03,	39-02-03
1 coat and breeches, by 3 tailors, viz., Nichols, Muckelrey & Lord,	5-10-00
Added to Mr. Crozier's inventory by Samuel Griswold, one of the administrators, 16 November, 1744,	945-16-02
Total inventory,	£1114-16-05

NOTES OF HAND: from

	£ s d		£ s d	£ s d
Ebenezer Hurlbut,				1-13-00
Joseph Forward,	3-01-00	Joseph Atwell,	5-11-01	8-12-01
John Drake,	8-00-00	Martin Winchell,	10-10-00	18-10-00
Benajah Loomis,	7-02-00	Ebenezer Loomis,	5-00-00	12-02-00
Joseph Forward,	5-07-02	John Lewis,	1-08-10	6-16-00
John Dimaway,	8-12-10	Israel Gosward,	3-15-04	12-08-02
John Matson,	2-00-00	David More,	1-10-00	3-10-00
David Enos,	4-10-00	William Keith,	6-08-06	10-18-06
John Lewis,	0-06-06	Abell Forward,	3-09-04	3-15-10
Henderson & Bartlett,	18-12-03	Dudley Woodbridge,	40-00-00	58-12-03

To certain instruments used in surveying land, belonging to the estate of James Crozier,   9-10-00

Jonathan Burnham, Appriser.

Court Record, Page 5—11 October, 1743: Adms. on the estate of James Crozier, late of Simsbury, unto Norman Morrison of Hartford and Samuel Griswold of Simsbury, who gave bond with Christian Miller of Simsbury for £1000.

Page 49—12 August, 1744: An inventory of the estate of James Crozier was now exhibited in Court by Norman Morrison and Samuel Griswold, Adms. Approved and ordered to be recorded and kept on file.

Memorand: 3rd March, 1762: Then Samuel Griswold, in Hartford County, one of the Adms. on the estate of Mr. James Crozier, late of Simsbury decd., by an agreement between himself and Mr. Lancelet Crozier, heir to the estate of the sd. deceased, in the full balance of the moveable estate surmounting the debts of the sd. decd., has given his note of £12-00-00 lawfull money to pay to sd. heir as a final discharge of everything relative to the moveable estate of the sd. decd.

Witness: Witness our hands:
George Stean,   SAMUEL GRISWOLD,
J: Talcott.   LANCELET CROZIER.

A true copy of the original, examined by me. *Joseph Talcott, Clerk.*
NOTE: *See page before the index, in Vol. XIV.*

Daviss, William. Court Record, Page 40—6 March, 1743-4: This Court appoint Mary Daviss of Simsbury, widow and relict of William Daviss of Simsbury, in Hartford County (lately of Summers in Hampshire County), to be guardian to the children of the sd. decd., viz., William and Samuel, both aged 1 year and 7 months. Recog., £400.

Deliber, James. Court Record, Page 41—17 March, 1743-4: James Deliber, 17 years of age, son of James Deliber decd., chose his brother John Deliber to be his guardian. Recog., £200. Cert: *Jabez Hamlin, J. P.*

Page 75-6-7.

Deming, Ephraim, Wethersfield. Inventory taken 17 December, 1742, by Josiah Belding, Jonathan Belding and John Deming. Will dated 16 June, 1742.

I, Ephraim Deming of Newington, in Wethersfield, do make this my last will and testament: I give to Hannah, my wife, 1-3 part of my houseing to use and improve during the time of her widowhood; also 1-3 part of my land to use and improve for and during the time of her natural life; also 1-3 part of my goods and chattells to use as she shall see fit and dispose of forever. Also, my will is that all my land be prised and divided into five parts equally, and two parts thereof I give to my eldest son Janna Deming; also the other three parts equally divided between my two youngest sons, to say, 1 1-2 parts I bequeath to my son Stephen Deming, and 1 1-2 parts to my youngest son Waitstill Deming. Also, my will is that my daughters, Dorothy Willard, Honour Deming, Hannah Deming and Lydia Deming, have half as much of my estate, even, to each of them, as will come to each of my two youngest sons, Stephen and Waitstill Deming's parts, to be raised and levied out of my estate with all my household goods, debts and moveable effects, stock, &c. Now if my household goods, debts and moveable effects, stock, &c., should prove not enough to make each of my daughters above mentioned equally to have half what shall come to my son Stephen Deming or my son Waitstill Deming, my will is that my sons, Janna, Stephen and Waitstill Deming, shall pay (each in his proportion) to my daughters above mentioned until each has their part as above sd., always to be understood that my daughter Dorothy Willard has had £150 already, which is to be accounted to her as part of her part above given. I ordain my wife Hannah and my son Janna Deming executors.

Witness: *Martin Kellogg,*   EPHRAIM DEMING, LS.
John Deming, Elisha Deming.

Court Record, Page 16—1st day of February, 1742-3: The last will and testament of Ephraim Deming was now exhibited in Court by Hannah Deming and Janna Deming, son and widow of the sd. decd. Will proven and ordered to be recorded.

See File:

Wethersfield, in Hartford County, October the 28th, 1765: We, the subscribers, viz., Stephen Deming, Waitstill Deming, Dorothy Willard, Honour Steele, Hannah Burnham and Lydia Wells, all children and heirs of our honoured father Ephraim Deming of sd. Wethersfield deceased, having received our full part, share or portion of our sd. father's estate from our honoured mother Hannah Deming, executrix, and Janna Deming, executor to our sd. father's estate or last will, wee are fully satisfied and do hereby aquit and discharge our sd. mother and brother Jannah Deming from any further demands on the account of sd. estate from the beginning of the world to this day and hereafter. As witness our hands the day and date abovesaid.

STEPHEN DEMING,	HANNAH BURNHAM,
DANIEL WILLARD,	WAITSTILL X DEMING,
DOROTHY WILLARD,	SAMUEL AND HONOUR
LYDIA WELLS,	STEELE HIS WIFE.

In presence of:
Josiah Willard, Dorothy Willard,
Hannah Brown, Abigail Goodrich,
Mary Lusk, Jedediah Deming.

Denslow, Samuel. Court Record, Page 32—16 November, 1743: This Court grants Adms. on the estate of Samuel Denslow, late of Windsor, unto John Bissell, Esq., of Bolton, who gave bond with Joseph Bacor of Tolland for £200.

Page 179.

Dickinson, Noadiah, Wethersfield. Invt. £2200-09-03. Taken 11 July, 1745, by Nathaniel Baldwin and Nathaniel Stanly.

Court Record, Page 61—6 August, 1745: This Court grant Adms. on the estate of Noadiah Dickinson to Abigail Dickinson, widow and relict, who gave bond with Samuel Wright of Wethersfield for £800 old tenour.

Page 6 (Vol. XV) 4 March, 1746: Benoni Hills, of Goshen, was before this Court interrogated with respect to his withholding and concealing some of the moveable estate of Noadiah Dickinson of Wethersfield decd. (See file.)

Page 60—1st March, 1747-8: An account of Adms. was now exhibited in Court by Abigail Dickinson, Adms. Accepted.

Page 63—5 April, 1748: Abigail Dickinson now moves to this Court that her right of dowry of the real estate be set out to her: This Court appoint Capt. Jonathan Deming, Lt. Jonathan Robbins and Deacon Hezekiah May of Wethersfield to set out to the sd. widow 1-3 part of the buildings and lands of the sd. deceased for her improvement during life.

Page 73—22 August, 1748: Eliphalet Dickinson of Wethersfield now appeals from the judgement of this Court in allowing Adms. account on the estate of the sd. deceased unto the Superior Court, and Eliphalet Dickinson is bound for £50.

Page 74—6 September, 1748: Return of the dowry set out to Abigail Dickinson, relict. Accepted and ordered to be kept on file.

Agreement on File.

Diggins, Jeremiah, Windsor. An agreement for the final settlement of the estate of Jeremiah Diggins, late of Windsor deceased, by us the subscribers and heirs: First, we agree that Rebeckah Diggins, the widow, shall have the improvement of the parlor of the dwelling house, with 1-4 part of the cellar, for the widow's improvement during her widowhood; and 1-3 part of all the residue of the personal estate, after the debts are paid. To John Diggins £45 in addition to what he has already received, and the land that lyes in Barkhampsted. To Mary Diggins, alias Kilbourn, £62 money, old tenor, besides what she hath already received. Jeremiah Diggins has, by legal conveyances or otherwise, received of the sd. estate his full part. That Joseph Diggins shall have all the residue of sd. estate, whether real or personal, in possession or reversion, be it more or less, to him and his heirs forever. In confirmation that the foregoing writing is our actual agreement, we have hereunto set our hands and seals this 2nd April, 1745.

| REBECKAH X DIGGINS, LS. | JOHN DIGGINS, LS. |
| JEREMIAH DIGGINS, LS. | THOMAS KILBOURN, LS. |

Court Record, Page 56—2 April, 1745: An agreement for the settlement of the estate was now exhibited in Court by the heirs of the sd. estate under their hands and seals. Accepted by the Court.

Page 157.

Doud, Cornwell, Middletown. Invt. £478-02-09. Taken 19 May, 1744, by Nathaniel Gilbert, Joseph Clark and William Rockwell. Will dated 5 April, 1744.

I, Cornwell Doud, of Middletown, in the County of Hartford, do make this my last will and testament: I give unto my honoured mother Mary Doud my cow and calf, my best barrow swine and my sow and all the family provisions. I give these for the use of my sd. mother and the family now dwelling with her, and also so much of my grain as they may have occasion to use till the next crop comes in. I also give my sd. mother 1-2 of the grain that I now have growing, and 1 hive of bees, and all my apparrel (except my two best sutes); also, I give her my silver shirt buttons and a silver shilling, all my part of the wool and flax, and ye woolen and linen yarn. I give to my brother David Doud my mare. And all other of my estate, both real and personal, I give to and among all my brethren and sisters in the following proportions, viz.: To each of my brothers (being five) 1-7, and to each of my sisters (being four) 1-14. And my will is that my brother David shall have all my real estate, provided he will pay to my other brothers and my sisters their proportion thereof according as the same was valued and set in the inventory of the estate of my honoured father David Doud decd., 2-3 thereof within 12 months after they shall severally arrive to lawfull age, and the other third after the decease of my sd. mother. I appoint my brother David Doud sole executor.

Witness: *Janna Meigs,*   CORNWELL DOUD, LS.
Joseph Clark, William Rockwell.

Court Record, Page 45—5 June, 1744: Will proven.
Page 59—4 June, 1745: Account of Adms. was now exhibited by David Doud, executor. Accepted.

Invt. in Vol. XV, Page 8.

Doud, Sergt. John, Middletown. Invt. £563-19-03. Taken 31 October, 1745, by Nathaniel Bacon, Joseph Adkins and John Warner.

Court Record, Page 64—5 November, 1745: Adms. granted to Edward Higbee of Middletown, who gave bond with Henry King of Middletown for £600.

Page 5 (Vol. XV) 26 May, 1745-6: This Court appoint Mr. Edward Higbee of Middletown to be guardian to the children of John Dowd, late of Middletown decd.: to Elizabeth, 8 years of age, John 6 years, Rebeckah and Mary Dowd, all children of John Dowd, late of Middletown decd. Recog., £1000. And the sd. Edward Higbee, guardian to the aforesd. children, showing to this Court that there is one piece or parcel of land in sd. Middletown belonging to the heirs of Jacob Dowd, which lyes in common or joynt tenancy between Joseph Tibbals, Jr., of Durham, in New Haven County, in right of his wife Esther Dowd, alias Tibbals, daughter of Jacob Dowd, and Samuel Green, Jr., of sd. Middletown, in right of his wife Sarah Dowd and as he is guardian to Rachel and Lois Dowd, children of sd. Jacob Dowd decd., which land is butted and bounded north on Jacob Strickland, south on Nathaniel Bacon's land, east on the commons, and west supposed to be on the town line: And this Court do appoint and impower William Rockwell, Nathaniel Bacon (carpenter) and John Warner, of Middletown, or any two of them, with the sd. guardian, to make divisions and partitions of sd. lands, and make return of their doings to this Court.

Page 11—13 May, 1746: Edward Higbee, Adms., exhibited an account of his Adms. Accepted.

Page 25—7 October, 1746: Some further addition to the account of Adms. was exhibited, which was also accepted by the Court.

Page 27—13 November, 1746: Whereas, at the General Assembly holden at New Haven the 2nd Thursday of October, Anno. Dom. 1746, Edward Higbee of Middletown, in the County of Hartford, Adms. on the estate of John Dowd, obtained liberty of sd. Assembly to sell so much of the real estate of the sd. decd. as will pay the sum of £404-08-08 with incident charges, taking advice of the Court of Probate in Hartford, this Court directs sd. Adms. to set up advertisements on the sign posts in Middletown, etc., etc., etc.

Page 39—2 June, 1747: Edward Higbee, Adms., now exhibits an account of the sale of the lands pursuant to the direction of this Court on the 13th of November, 1746, as follows:

		£ s d
Sold to Jacob Dowd, of Middletown, 3 acres at		47-00-00
" " Jacob Dowd " " " 9 acres and 54 rods,		100-00-00
" " Moses Persons " " 6 acres and 86 rods,		76-15-00
" " Jacob Dowd " " 4 acres,		45-00-00
" " Jacob Dowd " " 2-7 parts of 1 acre of land and buildings,		60-00-00
Credits received,		7-10-00
Also, the Adms. exhibits a further account of debts due from the sd. estate,		25-13-00
Account of incident charges arising on the sale of land,		7-09-06

All which is by this Court allowed.

Page 156. Inventory on Page 148.

Drake, Moses, Bolton. Invt. £74-00-00. Taken 20 August, 1744, by John Bishop and Simon Atherton. Will dated 16 June, 1740.

I, Moses Drake of Bolton, in Hartford County, do make this my last will and testament: I give unto my friend, Mr. Thomas Loomis of Bolton, all my lands in the Township of Bolton, and also what land shall or may descend to me by the will of James Loomis of sd. Bolton, or from Nathaniel Loomis of sd. Bolton. And in case any lands do descend to me as aforesd., then my will is that the sd. Thomas Loomis shall pay unto my kinsman Matthew Loomis of sd. Bolton the sum of £20 money, and to Lois Loomis the sum of £10. And in case nothing shall descend to me as aforesd., then I give all the land I have in Bolton as aforesd. unto the sd. Thomas Loomis and to his heirs forever. I appoint the sd. Thomas Loomis sole executor.

Witness: *John Bissell,*   MOSES DRAKE, LS.
Lucy Bissell, Jane Bracey.

Court Record, Page 49—12 August, 1744: An invt. of the estate of Moses Drake, late of Bolton decd., was now exhibited in Court by Thomas Loomis, executor. Accepted and ordered to be recorded and kept on file.

Elger, Thomas. Court Record, Page 11—5 October, 1742: Ezra Elger, a minor, 14 years of age, son of Thomas Elger, late of Windsor decd., chose his mother Rachel Elger to be his guardian. Recog., £200.

Page 167.

Fairbanks, Jonathan, Middletown. Invt. £131-12-10. Taken in Middletown 10 November, 1744, by Solomon Adkins and William Rockwell. Also, £315-17-00, being his part of the interest in the iron works. Taken 8 January, 1744-5, by John Sprague and John Adams.

Court Record, Page 55—5 February, 1744-5: This Court grant Adms. on the estate of Jonathan Fairbanks, late of Middletown, unto Jabez Hamlin, Esq., of Middletown, who gave bonds with Joseph Talcott of Hartford.

Gains, Simon. Court Record, Page 36—16 January, 1743-4: Mindwell Gains, a minor, 14 years of age, daughter of Simon Gains, chose Josiah Griswold of Wethersfield to be her guardian. And this Court appoint Mr. Samuel Wolcott of sd. Wethersfield to be guardian to Rebeckah Gains, a minor, 12 years of age, daughter of sd. deceased.

Page 138 (Vol. XV) 6 June, 1750: Samuel Gains, a minor, 15 years of age, son of Simon Gains, late of Glastonbury deceased, chose Ezekiel Webster of Hartford to be his guardian. Recog., £400.

See Estate of Simon Gains, on page 267.

Page 177-8-184.

Gillett, Nathan, formerly of Windsor. Invt. £403-03-01. Taken 22 July, 1745, by John Edwards and John Pottwine. To his right of land in Torrington, amounting to £70. Taken 22 November, 1745, by Jonathan Coe and Abel Beach.

Will dated 10 June, 1745: I, Nathan Gillett, formerly of Windsor, in the County of Hartford and Colony of Connecticut, in New England, late of St. Thomas in the East, on the Island of Jamaica, in the West Indies, but now resideing in Lebanon, in the County of Windham and Colony aforesd., do make this my last will and testament: I give to my honoured father Nathan Gillet, of Windsor, £50, to be paid him out of my estate. I do give unto my brothers Isaac Gillett and Noadiah Gillett and my sister Dinah Higley all my wearing apparrel that I have in New England, to be divided equally among them. I give and bequeath all the rest of the residue of my estate, after my debts and funeral charges are paid, unto my son George Gillett, wheresoever and of what kind soever it be, whether in New England or on the Island of Jamaica. And in case my sd. son George Gillett should die before he arrives to the age of 21 years, it is my will that whatsoever of estate shall remain or be left at his death shall be divided equally between my two brothers and my sister above named. I appoint my two brothers above named, Isaac and Noadiah Gillett, to be executors.

Witness: *Josiah Strong,*   NATHAN X GILLETT, LS.
Ebenezer Gray, Thomas Coit.

Court Record, Page 61—9 July, 1745: The last will and testament of Nathan Gillett, formerly of Windsor, lately resideing at Lebanon, in the County of Windham, decd., was now exhibited in Court by Isaac and Noadiah Gillett, executors. Proven.

Page 190.

Gleason, Thomas, Simsbury. Died 8 May, 1745. Invt. £288-09-06. Taken 12 June, 1744, by Samuel Pettebone, James Cornish and Benajah Humphrey.

Court Record, Page 61—9 July, 1745: This Court grant Adms. on the estate of Thomas Gleason, late of Simsbury decd., unto Elizabeth Gleason, widow of the sd. decd., and Thomas Gleason of sd. Simsbury, who gave bond with Joseph Tuller of Simsbury for £600.

Page 76 (Vol. XVI) 1st November, 1752: Isaac Gleason, a minor, about 15 years of age, son of Thomas Gleason, late of Simsbury deceased, made choice of his uncle Ezekiel Thompson to be his guardian. Recog., £500.

Page 165-6.

Goff, Ephraim, Wethersfield. Invt. £861-18-11. Taken 24 January, 1745, by Benjamin Wright, David Goodrich and Josiah Grimes.

Court Record, Page 54—5 February, 1744-5: This Court grant Adms. on the estate of Ephraim Goff, late of Wethersfield decd., unto Mary Goff, widow, who gave bond with Aaron Goff of Wethersfield for £1000. Exhibit of an inventory, which was ordered on file. And this Court appoint Mary Goff to be guardian to Ephraim Goff, age 12 years; to Mercy Goff, age 10 years; to Mary Goff, age 8 years; to David Goff, age 7 years; and to Jacob Goff, age 5 years; all children of Ephraim Goff decd. Recog., £1000.

Page 99 (Vol. XV) 2 May, 1749: Ephraim Goff, age 16 years, chose John Taylor, of Wethersfield, to be his guardian. Recog., £800.

Distribution of the real estate, 13 May, 1757. Report on file:

To Ephraim Goff, eldest son,	To Mercy Goff,
To David Goff,	To Mary Goff,
To Jacob Goff,	To the widow, Mary Goff.

By *Josiah Griswold,* ⎫
   Jonathan Belding, ⎬ *Distributors.*
   John Warner, ⎭

Page 160.

Goodale, Ebenezer, Glastonbury. Died 2 May, 1744. Invt. £242-17-10. Taken 10 May, 1744, by Stephen Andrews and Alexander Brewer.

Court Record, Page 44—5 June, 1744: This Court grant Adms. on the estate of Ebenezer Goodale unto Joseph Brewer of Glastonbury, who gave bond with Benjamin Brewer. Thomas Goodale, a minor, 15 years of age, son of Ebenezer Goodale, chose Benjamin Brewer to be his guardian. Recog., £200.

Page 45—3 July, 1744: Sarah Goodale, age 15 years, daughter of Ebenezer Goodale, chose her brother Joseph Goodale to be her guardian. Recog., £200.

Dist. File: 13 July, 1744: To Sarah Goodale, the widow; to Joseph Goodale, to Benjamin Goodale, to Isaac Goodale, to Thomas Goodale and to Sarah Goodale. By Col. Thomas Wells, John Holden and Job Risley.

Page 51—11 December, 1744: Isaac Goodale, a minor, 19 years of age, son of Ebenezer Goodale, chose Job Risley to be his guardian. Recog., £200.

Page 59—4 June, 1745: A distribution of the moveable estate of Ebenezer Goodale under the hands of Col. Thomas Wells, John Holden and Job Risley, distributors, was now exhibited in Court and accepted.

Codicil on Page 73-4. Will is found on File only.

Goodrich, Benjamin, Wethersfield. Inventory taken 10 and 11 June, 1742, by Jonathan Belding, John Deming and Samuel Churchill. Will not dated.

I, Benjamin Goodrich of Wethersfield, in Hartford County, in Connecticut, in New England, in health of body and sound in mind, knowing myself mortal and in consideration of my death, make the following disposition of that outward estate God hath or shall while I am here bestow upon me: I give to my wife Grace 1-3 part of my moveable estate and 1-3 part of my houseing and lands during her natural life, and of each and every of my children their portions in my estate till my sons arrive at the age of 21 years, and my daughter at 18 years, or until they marry, that is to say, the use of each child's portion until that child comes of age. The names of my children now living are as followeth: Benjamin the eldest, the next Ebenezer, the next Timothy, the next Daniel, the next Waitstill, and my daughter Sarah Goodrich.

Witness: *Elisha Micks,*   BENJAMIN GOODRICH, LS.
Sarah Goodrich, Rebeckah Micks.

Be it known to all men by these presents: That whereas I, Benjamin Goodrich of Newington, in Wethersfield, have made and declared my last will and testament in writing: I, the sd. Benjamin Goodrich, by this present codicil do ratify and confirm my last will and testament. And my will and meaning is that this codicil be and be adjudged to be part and parcel of my last will and testament, and that my son Benjamin Goodrich, Jr., in addition to my last will, be executor. This above writing was drawn from and are the words of his own mouth voluntarily, and is drawn within 4 and 20 hours after the sd. Goodrich deceased, he being in his sound mind and memory, 11th May, 1742, about 1 or 2 of the clock in the night.

Witness: *Ebenezer Goodrich,*
Timothy Goodrich, John Deming.

Court Record, Page 8—6 July, 1742: The last will of Benjamin Goodrich was exhibited in Court by Grace and Benjamin Goodrich, widow and son, executors by his nuncupative will, who accepted the trust. Sd. will not being fully proven, the eldest son of sd. decd. and the widow made an agreement in writing and exhibited it in Court, how they would have the estate distributed, which agreement is ordered to be recorded and kept on file.

Page 12—2 November, 1742: Timothy Goodrich, 18 years of age, chose Josiah Lee of Farmington to be his guardian; and Daniel Goodrich, 16 years of age, chose Josiah Lee to be his guardian. Recog., £500.

Page 16—1 February, 1742-3: Waitstill Goodrich, 14 years of age, chose George Kilborn of Wethersfield to be his guardian. Recog., £50.

Page 23—24 May, 1743: An agreement for the settlement of the estate of Benjamin Goodrich, under the hands and seals of the heirs, was now exhibited in Court for the settlement of that estate, which this Court accepts and orders to be recorded.

Page 42—April, 1744: An account of Adms. on the estate of Benjamin Goodrich was now exhibited by Grace Goodrich and Benjamin Goodrich, administrators, which account is accepted.   Grace Goodrich

now moves that her dowry be set out to her. This Court appoint Capt.
Thomas Curtiss, of Farmington, Capt. Jonathan Belding and John Stilman, of Wethersfield, to set out one-third part of the moveable estate; the
whole being £410-13-03, one-third of which is £133-07-05, to be hers forever, and one-third part of the real estate for her use.

Page 47 (Vol. XV) 3 July, 1746: A return of the distribution accepted by the Court and ordered on file. This agreement also on file, as
follows:

AGREEMENT.

Whereas, Mr. Benjamin Goodrich made a writing under his hand
and seal, exhibited unto the Court of Probates 6 July, 1742, supposed to
be his last will and testament, and the evidences to sd. will not being able
to make oath thereto in the usual form, the widow and relict of the sd.
deceased, with the rest of the heirs to sd. estate, viz., Grace Goodrich,
the relict of the sd. decd., and Benjamin Goodrich, Ebenezer Goodrich,
Timothy Goodrich, Daniel Goodrich, Waitstill Goodrich and Sarah Goodrich, widow, children and heirs to the estate of the sd. Benjamin Goodrich, of sd. Wethersfield decd., do hereby mutually agree, for ourselves
and our heirs forever, that sd. writing called the will of the sd. Benjamin
Goodrich decd. shall be the rule by which sd. estate shall be divided to
and amongst us, the widow, children and heirs before mentioned, and
that we, the sd. heirs, etc., do hereby ratify and confirm sd. will to be our
agreement, and shall be binding to us, our heirs and assigns forever. And
that sd. writing or will be offered to the Court of Probate for our agreement, with only these reserved or excepted, viz: That our brother Benjamin Goodrich shall have, more than his proportion given him in sd.
writing or will, one acre off of the front of the homelott of sd. decd., on
the north side, to be 12 rods in breadth and to extend east so far as the
sd. decd. died seized of, and westward so far as to make an acre of land;
and that the sd. widow Grace does hereby quit her right of dowry in and
to sd. acre of land, except so much as shall be judged a reasonable garden platt for her, with liberty also of passing and repassing to the house
and barn as occasion shall require. And that after the sd. widow hath
her thirds set out to her, the daughter shall have set out to her 1-6 part
of the moveable estate as part of that proportion of the estate given to her
by the will as aforesd., and the remainder to be made up to her by her
eldest brother out of the houseing and buildings at inventory price. And
that the sd. widow shall hold out of the buildings 1-3 part of the sd.
daughter's right (which the eldest son is to pay the sd. daughter) during
her natural life. For full confirmation of all the foregoing agreement, we
have hereunto set our hands and seals this 3rd day of May, in the 16th
year of His Majestie's Reign, Anno. Dom. 1743.

GRACE GOODRICH, LS.	BENJAMIN GOODRICH, LS.
EBENEZER GOODRICH, LS.	TIMOTHY GOODRICH, LS.
DANIEL X GOODRICH, LS.	WAITSTILL GOODRICH, LS.
——————— ——————— LS.	

Waitstill Goodrich signed, sealed and acknowledged the within written agreement before the Court of Probate in Hartford, the 22 day of January, A. D. 1749-50.   *Test: Joseph Talcott, Clerk.*

Page 125—3 April, 1750: Grace Goodrich, Adms. on the estate of Benjamin Goodrich, late of Wethersfield, having finished her account of Adms., now moves that distributors may be appointed to distribute sd. estate according to an agreement well executed under the hands and seals of the heirs, and approved by this Court. And appoint John Stilman, Peletiah Buck and Capt. Jonathan Belding, distributors.

Page 1.

Goodwin, Elizabeth, Widow. Will dated 10 July, 1738: I, Elizabeth Goodwin, do make this my last will and testament: I give to my son William 5 shillings, to be paid to him after my decease. I give to my two daughters, viz., Vilot Goodwin and Susannah Goodwin, my two cows, for them and their heirs and assigns forever, equally between them. And all the rest of my real and personal estate I give to my five daughters, to be equally divided amongst them, only the two cows afore mentioned. And I appoint William Cadwell executor.

Witness: *Esther Talcott,*   ELIZABETH X GOODWIN, LS.
Agniss X *Nichols, Cyprian Nichols, Jr.*

Court Record, Page 11 (Vol. XV) 6 May, 17 (46): William Cadwell, in right of his wife Rebeckah deceased, moves to this Court that freeholders may be appointed to make division and partition of the land belonging to the estate of Elizabeth Goodwin, the widow of Mr. Wm. (Goodwin), late of Hartford deceased, according to her last will: Whereupon this Court appoint [Record gone].

Distribution on file, 11 June, 1746: Set out to the heirs of Elizabeth Goodwin decd., one lot of land in the south meadow in Hartford, bounded east on a pond, west on an old ditch, north on land of Samuel Howard, and south on land of Col. David Goodrich; sd. land is in length 64 rods, in breadth 5 1-2 rods. Set out on the north side to Sarah Clark, alias Goodwin, one rod and 2 links wide the whole length of the lot; to Mary Goodwin, alias Savage, one rod and 2 links wide; to Rebeckah Goodwin, alias Cadwell, or her heirs, one rod and 2 links wide; to Vilet Goodwin one rod and 2 links wide; and to Susannah Goodwin one rod and 2 links wide the whole length; which includes the whole lot.

Garrard Spencer, }
John Wadsworth, } *Distributors.*

Page 195.

Goslee, Henry, Glastonbury. Died 25 August, 1745. Invt. £375-17-02. Taken 7 October, 1745, by Daniel Hubbard and Eleazer Crocker.

Court Record, Page 65—5 November, 1745: This Court grants Adms. on the estate of Henry Goslee, late of Glastonbury decd., to Elizabeth Goslee, widow of sd. decd., and William House, of Glastonbury, who gave bond with Mathias Treat of Hartford for £300 money. Exhibit of an inventory, which was ordered on file.

Page 3 (Vol. XV) 7 January, 1745: This Court appoint and impower Elizabeth Goslee, widow and relict of Henry Goslee, to be guardian to the children of the sd. Henry Goslee, viz., to John age 12 years, Sarah 9 years, Thomas 7, Timothy 4, and James about 15 months. Recog., £500.

Page 11—13 May, 1746: An account of Adms. was now exhibited in Court by William House and Alpheus Gustin (in right of his wife Elizabeth Goslee, alias Gustin), Adms. on sd. estate. Account accepted.

Page 23—2 September, 1746: Pursuant to an act of the General Assembly, holden at Hartford on the 2nd Thursday of May, 1746, authorising William House and Alpheus Gustin, Adms., to sell so much of the real estate as may be sufficient to pay the sum of £110-01-10 with necessary charges of sale, taking the advice of the Court of Probates in the District of Hartford thereon: This Court direct the Adms. to set up advertisements on the sign posts in Wethersfield and Glastonbury that there is to be sold so much of the east end of the 1-70 acre lott lying in sd. Glastonbury, in the Parish of Eastbury, at publick vandue, etc., etc., etc.

Page 60—1st March 1747-8: Report of the Adms. that they sold to John Wavels of Glastonbury 20 acres at 35 shillings per acre, bounded as followeth: East on common land, west on land of the heirs of Henry Goslee decd., south on land of the aforesd. heirs, and north on land to be sold to John Gustin, Jr. Then adjourned until the 25th day of the abovesd. month, and then sold to John Gustin, Jr., 30 acres at 30 shillings per acre, bounded as follows: East on common or undivided land, west on land of the aforesd. heirs, north on land of Capt. Thomas Belding, and south on lands to be sold to the aforesd. John Wavels. Then they adjourned the sale of the rest until the 9th day of October next ensuing, and then they sold to the abovesd. John Gustin, Jr., 6 1-4 acres more at £6-08 per acre, bounded as follows: North on land of the aforesd. Belding, east on land of Gustin, west on land of the aforesd. heirs, and south on land sold to the abovesd. Wavels. All at publick vandue, at the beat of the drum, to the highest bidder. Charges of sale, £8-19-02. Allowed.

Page 90 (Vol. XVI) 6 March, 1753: Thomas Goslin, a minor, 14 years of age, son of Henry Goslin, chose Jonathan Strickland of Bolton to be his guardian. Recog., £300.

Page 95.

Griffin, Stephen. Died 30 March, 1743. Invt. £160-01-00. Added a negro man called Sambo, £50 silver; negro woman called Susan, prised at £90 old tenour. Taken 2 May, 1743, by Nathaniel Holcomb 2nd, Joshua Holcomb and James Case.

Court Record, Page 22—3 May, 1743: This Court grant Adms. on the estate of Stephen Griffin, late of Simsbury deceased, unto Mary Griffin, widow and relict of the sd. deceased, who gave bond with Joshua Holcomb of Simsbury for £100.

Page 27—2 August, 1743: Stephen Griffin, age 4 years, and Martha, age 6 years, children of Stephen Griffin: this Court appoint Mary Griffin, widow, to be guardian to them. Recog., £200.

Griswold, Matthew. Court Record, Page 15—4 January, 1742-3: This Court grant Adms. on the estate of Matthew Griswold, late of Windsor decd., unto James Phelps of Windsor, brother to the sd. decd., who gave bond with David Ensign of Hartford for £50.

See Estate of Lieut. Matthew Griswold, on page 276.

Page 24-25.

Griswold, Michael, Wethersfield. Invt. £96-12-03. Taken 24 August, 1742, by Timothy Baxter, Timothy Wright and Thomas Hurlbut. Will dated 9 October, 1741.

I, Michael Griswold of Wethersfield, being far advanced in years, do make this my last will and testament: I give to my son Stephen one acre of land lying on the northward side of my homelott, butting northerly on my son Stephen's homelott. I give to my sons Caleb and Elisha my land lying on the west side of the highway near my homelott, being 9 1-2 acres, to be divided in equal proportion between them. I give to my son Jonathan all my right, share or interest in and to the commons and undivided lands lying within the bounds of the Township of Wethersfield aforesd., and £25 in money. I give to my son David my best Bible. I give to my sons Jonathan, Caleb and Elisha, all my wearing apparrel, to be divided equally between them. I give to my son Caleb £15 in moveable estate. I give to my son Nathaniel £30 in moveable estate. I give to my son Joseph my loom and bedd and furniture. I give to my daughter Elizabeth, the wife of Zachariah Bunce, £5 in moveable estate. I give to my daughter Anne, the wife of [   ], £20 in moveable estate. And if any of my moveable estate be left or remaining after my debts, funeral expenses and legacies are paid, I give the same and all of it to my sd. daughter Anne. I do hereby appoint my sons Caleb and Elisha Griswold executors.

Witness: *Samuel Deming,*   MICHAEL GRISWOLD, LS.
Timothy Wright, Isaac Riley.

Court Record, Page 10—1st Tuesday in September, 1742: The last will and testament of Michael Griswold was now exhibited in Court by Caleb and Elisha Griswold, executors. Proven. Also, exhibited an inventory, which was ordered on file.

Page 12—5 October, 1742: Caleb and Elisha Griswold, executors to the last will of Michael Griswold, moved to this Court that freeholders may be appointed to distribute the moveable estate: Whereupon this Court appoint Thomas Hurlbut, Timothy Wright and Timothy Baxter, of Wethersfield, distributors.

Page 31—4 October, 1743: Zachariah Bunce of Wethersfield, in right of his wife Elizabeth Griswold (alias Elizabeth Bunce), one of the daughters of Michael Griswold, late decd., not being notified nor present at the probation of the last will and testament of the sd. decd., and being agreaved with the probation of sd. will, appeals from the decree and probation of this Court in approving sd. will unto the Superior Court to be holden in Hartford on the 1st Tuesday of March next. Recog., £10.

Page 34—6 December, 1743: Report of distributors.

Dist. of the estate of Michael Griswold on file without date: To Caleb, to Nathaniel, to Zachariah Bunce in right of Elizabeth his wife, and to Dositheus Humphrey in right of his wife Ann. By Timothy Wright and Timothy Baxter, distributors.

Page 156.

Griswold, Phineas, Wethersfield. Invt. £397-04-00. Taken 3 January, 1743-4, by Thomas Hurlbut and Timothy Baxter.

Court Record, Page 45—5 June, 1744: This Court grant Adms. on the estate of Phineas Griswold, late of Wethersfield decd., unto Martha Griswold, widow, who gave bonds with William Hurlbut of Wethersfield for £200.

Page 128 (Vol. XV) 1st May, 1750: William Griswold, age 13 years, son of Phineas Griswold of Wethersfield: This Court appoint Benjamin Griswold of Wethersfield to be his guardian. Recog., £300.

Dist. File: 4 October, 1758: To William Griswold, to Phineas, to Miles Griswold, to Martha Griswold alias Benton, and to Martha Griswold the widow. By John Smith and Joseph Richards.

Page 102.

Haford, John, Farmington. Died 16 October, 1742. Invt. £356-09-00. Taken by Nehemiah Manose and Ebenezer Hamlin.

Court Record, Page 31—4 October, 1743: This Court grant Adms. on the estate of John Haford, late of Farmingtown decd., unto Thankfull Haford, widow and relict of the sd. decd., who gave bond with Ebenezer Hamlin of Farmingtown for £300. Exhibit of an inventory, which was ordered upon file.

Page 51—8 October, 1744: Account of Adms. on the estate of John Haford was now exhibited in Court by Thankfull Haford, Adms.: Paid in debts and charges, £39-06-02. Which account is allowed and ordered on file. This Court do appoint Thankfull Haford to be a guardian to one of the sons of John Haford, aged 5 years, and also to John Haford, aged one year and five months, another of the children of sd. deceased. Recog., £300.

Page 65 (Vol. XV) 3 May, 1748: Thankfull Haford, alias Carrington, Adms. on the estate of John Haford, late of Farmington decd., now moves to this Court that distribution be made of the moveable estate of sd. deceased, which this Court order. Inventoried, £134-02-00; debts and charges allowed, £61-14-11; being deducted, there remains £72-07-01 to be distributed: To Thankfull, the relict, £24-02-00, which is her third part, to be her own forever; and to Joseph Haford, eldest son, £32-03-02; and to John Haford, £16-01-00. And appoint Deacon Hezekiah Rue, Ebenezer Barns and Joseph Gaylord distributors. (This record was interlined on page 51: "May 3rd, 1748: Allowed to Thankfull Haford, Adms., to keeping child 3 years, the sum of £21.")

Page 74—6 September, 1748: Report of the distributors.

Page 124-125.

Hale, Thomas, Middletown. Invt. £2933-03-02. Taken 27 July, 1743, by John Hall and John Hale. Will dated 3rd June, 1743.

I, Thomas Hale of Middletown, do make this my last will and testament: I give to Mary, my wife, 1-3 part of my moveable estate forever. And further, I give to her the use of my dwelling house and barn and all the lots that they stand on, that now belong to me, with all the appurtenances thereof, and likewise all that lott of land which I bought of Mr. Israhiah Wetmore, and likewise that which I bought of Joshua Gill, lying near by it, and likewise liberty of having her firewood and fencing stuff, &c., on any part of that land which I bought of Robert Warner. This priviledge I give to Mary my wife during her natural life, excepting only a liberty of necessary and comfortable house room, &c., for my daughter Sara during her natural life. Further, I give to my wife the use of 6 acres of meadow land at Pecowsit, of that side next to the Great River, during her natural life. I give to my granddaughter Abigail Hale what remains of that lott which I bought of Robert Warner, which I now possess, and likewise 4 acres of meadow land at Pecowsit, takeing of it next to the parsonage, this excepting her grandmother's interest, if the sd. Abigail shall live to the age of 20 years; this I give to my granddaughter Abigail Hale and to her heirs and assigns forever. I give to my grandson George Ranney two yoke of oxen and all my team tackling, as cart, plows, harrows, etc., only he shall do all his grandmother's team work; and likewise I give to my sd. grandson all that lottment of land that I bought of Mr. Israhiah Wetmore, his grandmother's interest excepted; this I give to my grandson George Ranney and to his heirs and assigns forever. Likewise I give to my sd. grandson all my interest in the Wongunk meadow, and on the Island, and on Indian Hill, viz., all that land which I bought of Lt. Samuel Frary. Likewise I give to sd. George Ranney the care of my negro man, and to manage my wife's business with him as well as his own; but if sd. negro proves ungoverned, so that it be thought best to sell him, then my wife and daughters to have the effect of him equally among them. I give to my two daughters, Mary Ranney and Sara Hale, my dwelling house and barn and all the particular lottment that it stands on, and all the appurtenances thereto belonging, and all my interest in Pecowsit meadow, excepting the abovesd. 4 acres and 2 acres more excepted, and excepting their mother's interest; this I give to my sd. two daughters equally divided between them. And the abovesd. two acres at Pecowsit I give to my sd. granddaughter Abigail Hale when she comes to the age of 21 years. I give that 14 acres of land which I bought of Joshua Gill for the use of my daughter Sary Hale. If she live to need to spend it, it may be sold for her use; but if Sary do not live to need it, I give the sd. 14 acres of land to my daughter Mary and to her heirs forever. I give to my grandson Hozial Smith all my interest in the undivided land in Middletown not yet laid out, and likewise £50 old tenor money, to be paid to him by my executors next March come 12 months; this I give to my sd. grandson Hozial Smith, to his heirs and assigns forever. I give to my granddaughter Mary Ranney £50 in old tenor money, to be paid to her by my executors next March if she needs it, upon this condition, that she will discount £50 with her brother as paid to her towards her portion of her father's estate. Likewise I give to my sd. granddaughter £50 worth, old tenor, in moveable estate; this I give to my granddaughter Mary Ranney and to her heirs forever. I give to the Rev. Mr. Moses Bartlett £10 old tenor money. I give the remainder of my moveable estate to my wife and my two daughters, equally amongst them. And my will is that my grandson George Ranney, whom I make sole executor, shall take care of my daughter Sarah and see that what I have bequeathed to her be laid out and used for her as she shall need it.

Witness: *Joseph White,*   THOMAS X HALE, LS.
John Hale, Marcy Miller.

Court Record, Page 28—2 August, 1743: The last will and testament of Thomas Hale was now exhibited in Court by George Ranney, executor. The will being proven is by this Court approved. Now exhibited an inventory. Proven and ordered on file.

Invt. in Vol. XV, Page 78.

Ham, Mrs. Mary, Hartford. Invt. £349-06-12. Taken by Thomas Hooker and Samuel Flagg. Invt. in New Hartford, £217-04-00. Taken 24 October, 1745, by Joseph Merrells and Samuel Messenger.

Court Record, Page 58—7 May, 1745: Adms. granted unto Col. John Whiting of Hartford, who gave bonds with Jonathan Olcott of sd. Hartford for £1000.

Page 74 (Vol. XVI) 3 October, 1752: An account of Adms. was now exhibited in Court by Col. John Whiting, Adms., by which account he has paid in debts and charges £345-19-10. Account accepted.

Harris, William, Jr. Court Record, Page 41—17 March, 1743-4: Joseph Harris, age 16 years, son of William Harris, Jr., late of Middletown decd., chose Seth Wetmore of Middletown to be his guardian. Recog., £200. Cert: *Jabez Hamlin, J. P.*

Page 114.

Hatch, Jonathan. Will dated 27 January, 1742-3: I, Jonathan Hatch, being distempered in body but sound in intellectuals, do ordain and confirm this to be my last will and testament: First of all, I recommend my soul to God who gave it, and my body to the dust from whence it sprang. Imprimis: It is my will that my land at Kent be sold and all my lawfull debts and dues be paid, and my funeral charges to be paid out of it. I give and bequeath unto my well-beloved wife Thankfull Hatch the 1-2 of my farm at Lambstown, to her own use and behoof forever. I give unto my wife all my moveable estate and creatures, and all that remains of the sale of my land at Kent after my just dues and charges are paid. I give and bequeath unto my two daughters, Rebeckah and Thankfull, the 1-2 of my farm at Lambstown, to be divided between them when they shall come to full age. My will also is that my honoured father-in-law, Ichabod Hinckley, be my sole Adms. to this my last will and testament.
Witness: *Ebenezer Nyes (Nye)*,   JONATHAN HATCH, LS.
Jonathan Delano, Joseph Hatch, Jr.

Court Record, Page 21—5 April, 1743: The last will and testament of Jonathan Hatch, late of Tolland decd., was now exhibited in Court by Ichabod Hinckley of Tolland, executor. Proven and ordered to be recorded and kept upon file.
Page 190 (Probate Side, Vol. XV) 1st May, 1748: Know all men by these presents: That whereas, Ichabod Hinckley of Tolland, in the County of Hartford, executor to the last will and testament of Jonathan Hatch decd., has fully and absolutely, to the satisfaction of us the subscribers, the only persons concerned, to all intents and purposes answered the intentions of the testator as well as our expectations and the obligations he lay himself under by virtue of his accepting the business of executorship in the case: these are therefore to certify all persons whom it may concern, that we the subscribers hereafter named do for ourselves, our heirs and assigns, fully, freely and absolutely acquitt and discharge the abovesd. Ichabod Hinckley, executor as aforesd., of and from all and all manner of debts, dues, bills, bonds, law suits, executions or rewards that shall or may arise unto him the sd. Hinckley, executor as aforesd. In

witness whereof we the subscribers have hereunto set our hands ye day and date above.

N. B.—The particular account of what the sd. Ichabod Hinckley, executor, has to do and has done is as follows:

	£ s d
The sum total of the inventory,	97-09-03
Land sold by order of will,	275-09-00
Total sum of what the executor held to dispose of,	372-09-03

The full sum of £372-09-03 has been paid out or otherwise accounted for to the satisfaction of the parties concerned.

Witness: *Nehemiah Parker,*   GEORGE NYE, LS.
          Samuel Cobb.   THANKFULL NYE, LS.

Page 160.

Hayes, Benjamin, Simsbury. Died 19 October, 1744. Inventory taken 17 November, 1744, by Joshua Holcomb, David Holcomb and James Smith.

Court Record, Page 52—20 December, 1744: This Court grant Adms. on the estate of Benjamin Hayes unto Ann Hayes, widow and relict, who gave bond with Othniell Gillett of Simsbury for £800. Exhibit of an inventory, which was ordered on file.

Page 128 (Vol. XV) 1st May, 1750: An account of Adms. on the estate of Benjamin Hays, late of Simsbury, was now exhibited by Ann Hays, widow. Account allowed.

Page 89 (Vol. XVII) 6 January, 1756: Ann Hays, Adms., having finished her account of Adms. on sd. estate, now moves for a distribution: Whereupon this Court appoint Jonathan Holcomb, Judah Holcomb and Ebenezer Lampson, of Simsbury, to divide the estate, viz.: To Ann Hays, widow, her right of dowry; to Zedekiah Hays, the eldest son, his double share of the estate; and to Zadock and Zenus, sons of the deceased, and to Hannah Hays (alias Graham) and to Anna Hays, daughters, to each of them their single share.

Page 60.

Heydon, Samuel, Harwinton. Invt. £237-02-07. Taken 5 November, 1742, by Nathaniel Davis, Jacob Benton and Ciprian Webster. Inventory of estate taken in Windsor, 18 November, 1742, by Daniel Bissell and Ebenezer Heydon.

See File:

Articles of agreement, made this 29th day of November, 1742, between Samuel Heydon and Nathaniel Heydon, both of Windsor, and Joseph Heydon and William Heydon of Harwinton, in Hartford

County, heirs to the estate of Samuel Heydon, late of Windsor deceased, is as followeth, viz.: That Samuel Heydon and Nathaniel Heydon of sd. Windsor, and Joseph Heydon and William Heydon, have mutually agreed each with the other that we will share equal in proportion as to quantity and quality in real estate of our honoured father's yet undivided, and also equal in his personal estate undivided. And to the true performance of the above written we bind ourselves, our heirs, executors and Adms. each to the other in the sum of £100 money, conditioned that if either one of the sd. party shall not agree and performe that above agreement, that he or they that fall therefrom shall pay unto them that stand to and abide thereby that aforesd. sum within one year from the date thereof. As witness our hands this 29th November, 1742.

SAMUEL HEYDON, LS.	JOSEPH HEYDON, LS.
NATHANIEL HEYDON, LS.	WILLIAM HEYDON, LS.

Witness: *Josiah Bissell,*
    Henry Gains.

Articles of agreement, made and concluded between Samuel Heydon and Nathaniel Heydon, both of Windsor, and Joseph Heydon and William Heydon, of the one part, and Abraham Addams and his wife Ann Addams of Suffield, in Hampshire County, and Moses Lyman and his wife Sarah Lyman of Goshen, in Hartford County, of the other part, witnesseth: That ye sd. Abraham Addams and Ann his wife and Moses Lyman and Sarah his wife shall have out of the moveable estate of our honoured father Samuel Heydon, late of Harwinton deceased, or in publick bills of credit of the old tennour, the sum of £480-00-00, viz: To Abraham Addams and his wife, £240; and to Moses Lyman and his wife Sarah, £240; with which the sd. Abraham Addams and his wife Ann and Moses Lyman and his wife Sarah are fully satisfied and contented. And in confirmation hereof we have hereunto set to our hands and seals this 30th day of November, 1742.

ANN HEYDON, LS.	WILLIAM HEYDON, LS.
SAMUEL HEYDON, LS.	ABRAHAM ADDAMS, LS.
NATHANIEL HEYDON, LS.	MOSES LYMAN, LS.
JOSEPH HEYDON, LS.	ANN ADAMS, LS.

Witness: *Benony Denslow,*
    Henry Gains.

Furthermore, we covenant and agree with our honoured mother Ann Heydon that she shall have 1-3 part of the moveable estate that was our honoured father's forever; as also her thirds of dowry in the lands during her natural life.

Court Record, Page 14—7 December, 1742: Adms. granted to Samuel Heydon of Windsor and William Heydon of Harwinton. Agreement exhibited in Court and acknowledged by the heirs to be their free act and deed. Accepted by the Court and ordered to be recorded and kept on file.

Page 146, 159.

Holcomb, John, Simsbury. Died 11 July, 1744. Invt. £362-01-09. Taken 27 August, 1744, by Isaac Gillett, Joshua Holcomb and Abell Forward. Will dated 20 May, 1743.

I, John Holcomb of Simsbury, in the County of Hartford, do make and ordain this my last will and testament: I give to my wife Ann the 1-3 part of all my real estate (the use thereof) during her life, and the 1-3 part of my personal estate that I leave undisposed of at the time of my decease to be her's forever. I hereby give to my son John the south side of my homelott, from Windsor bounds to the west end of the same (5 and 20 rods, called the old lot), of which piece I have already given him a deed. I also give him my lott at the place called Barn Door Hill which my honoured father Nathaniel Holcomb decd. gave me in his last will. I give to my son Asahell and his heirs forever my lott of land at Turkey Hill, bounded east and south on a highway, extending west to Griffen's upper marsh lot, and northward to the upper side of Sergant Gillett's lot; and also all my right to the lot my father gave me in his last will with my brethren, in common and undivided. I give and bequeath to my son Moses and his heirs forever all my homelot with the buildings thereon standing, orcharding, etc., excepting the 25 rods on the south side already given to my son John by deed, and my lot at the east end of my homelot, lying in Windsor bounds. I also give to my two sons Asahell and Moses all the rest of my lands, wheresoever lying and being, to be equally divided between them and their heirs; and also all the moveable estate, namely, oxen, cows and horses, sheep, swine, &c., with all the team tackling, &c., as also cooper's tools, with the gunns, axes, howes, etc., to be theirs. I give to my four dafters now living, viz., Dinah, Esther, Martha and Sarah, as is hereafter expressed, and I had in the lifetime of my daughter Ann decd. given her her portion: I give the aforesd. four daughters now surviving £60 to each of them, to be paid them or their heirs out of my estate at inventory price according to the old tenor bills of credit, accounting what they have as part of the £60. I give to my son Moses my Bible, and the Lord be with him. My will is and I hereby give to my son Moses full liberty to use the 1-2 of my part of the sawmill standing on the lot given to Asahell, with full liberty to pass to and from the same; and also I give him 1-2 of my part of the irons of sd. mill and saws, the other part to be to Asahell with the land as aforesd. I appoint my two sons, Asahell and Moses, executors.

Witness: *Samuel Forward,*   JOHN HOLCOMB, LS.
Joseph Phelps 3rd, Peletiah Mills.

Court Record, Page 46—7 August, 1744: The last will and testament of John Holcomb of Simsbury was now exhibited in Court by Asahell and Moses Holcomb, executors. Will proven and ordered to be recorded.

Page 175.

Holcomb, Mary, Simsbury. Invt. £138-03-11. Taken 27 May, 1745, by Joseph Hoskins and Daniel Addams. Will dated 22 December, 1744.

I, Mary Holcomb, in the Town of Simsbury, do make this my last will and testament: I give unto my brother Benjamin Holcomb my Bible, to be his forever, and the Lord be with him. I give unto my sister Esther Higley my best quilt and a pair of silver clasps, to be hers forever. I give unto my four sisters, viz., Esther aforesd., Katharine Messenger, Margaret North and Sarah Barbour, all the rest of my estate which I shall leave after my decease, after debts and charges are paid, to be theirs forever, to be equally divided between them. And my will further is, that the aforenamed Katharine and Margaret shall have their part or proportion in bedds, bedding and wearing apparrel. I constitute my brother Benjamin to be sole executor.

Witness: *Brewster Higley, Jr.,*   MARY X HOLCOMB, LS.
Joseph Higley, John Higley.

Court Record, Page 59—4 June, 1745: Will proven.

Page 116-17.

Hubbard, Ebenezer, Middletown. Invt. £1152-18-05. Taken 31 May, 1743, by Solomon Adkins and William Rockwell. Will dated 23 January, 1742.

I, Ebenezer Hubbard of Middletown, being advanced in years, do make this my last will and testament: Imprimis: I give to Ebenezer Sage and Hannah his wife, and to their heirs forever, one acre of land at the west end of my homelott, to run across ye lott and to extend so far east as to make up one acre. Also, I give them free liberty to use and improve the well where he hath digged it in my land forever. Also, I give to the sd. Hannah Sage my silver cup after my decease. And this I give them in consideration of the great kindness they have exercised toward me ever since they have dwelt near me. I give to my loving cousins, Daniel Stow and Azuba his wife, that now dwell with me, all the remainder of my estate, both real and personal, that is not disposed of in this my last will and testament, to them and their heirs forever. I appoint my cousins, Daniel Stow and Azuba his wife, to be executors. And I do hereby order my sd. cousin Daniel Stow to pay 40 shillings to the Church of Christ over which the Rev. Mr. William Russell is pastor.

Witness: *Matthew Talcott,*   EBENEZER HUBBARD, LS.
Mary Talcott, Jabez Hamlin.

Court Record, Page 24—7 June, 1743: The last will and testament of Ebenezer Hubbard, late of Middletown deceased, was now exhibited in Court and proven. Also, exhibited an inventory, which was ordered recorded.

Page 39—15 February, 1743-4: Daniel Stow of Middletown, executor to the last will and testament of Ebenezer Hubbard, late of Middletown deceased (being also deceased), and there being no executor to sd. will, this Court grant Adms. on the estate of the sd. Ebenezer Hubbard, with the will annexed, unto Isaac Lee of Middletown, who gave bond with Ebenezer Sage of sd. Middletown.

Page 185-6.

Hubbard, Samuel, Sen., Middletown. Invt. £2310-18-11. Taken 18 June, 1745, by Caleb Galpin, Daniel Smith and Elisha Peck. Will dated 15 April, 1743.

I, Samuel Hubbard, Sen., of Kensington, in the Township of Middletown, do make this my last will and testament: I give to my wife Martha Hubbard forever 1-3 part of my personal estate, and the use and improvement of 1-3 part of my real estate during her natural (life). Further, I give peculiarly to my wife one featherbed and furniture, with one great brass kettle, and all the linen, and one certain great puter platter, besides her thirds. To my eldest son now living, Samuel Hubbard, I give, besides what I have heretofore given him by deed of gift, one parcell of land I bought of John Gilbert, near to Mattabesick River, bounded as follows: East upon the river, south upon his own land, north upon Henry Johnson, and west upon a highway. To my second son, Timothy Hubbard, besides what I have already given him, I give him one certain parcell of land bounded as follows: Near Henry Johnson's, butteing east upon a highway, west upon a run of water or brook, south upon John Sage and Samuel Hubbard, and north upon Henry Johnson. Further, I give to him a certain parcell of land lying in my houselott, bounded as follows: South on a highway, north upon George Hubbard, east upon his brother Samuel Hubbard, and west upon Stony Swamp Brook. Further, I give to him one certain parcell of land lying partly upon the ledge and partly upon low land or swamp, bounded as follows: South upon a highway, north upon George Hubbard, east upon a fence now standing in my mowing land, and west extending half across the ledge. Further, I give to him the fruit of 25 apple trees for the term of 15 years, standing upon the north end of my orchard. To my third son, Watts Hubbard, I give one certain parcell of land bounded south upon a highway, north upon George Hubbard, east upon Stony Swamp Brook, and west upon a fence now standing butting upon his brother Timothy. Further, I give to him a certain parcell of land bounded as follows: West on a highway, south upon a highway, north upon George Hubbard, and east upon the middle of the ledge, butting upon his brother Timothy, with the dwelling house and barn standing upon the sd. land. Further, I give to him one certain parcel of land bounded as follows: East upon the country road, west upon Lt. Isaac Norton, north upon Nathaniel Edwards, and south upon John Hinsdale. To my grandson William Hubbard, the only son of my son William Hubbard decd., I give, besides what I gave to my son his father in his lifetime, a certain parcel of land near to his dwelling house, bounded as follows: West upon a highway, south upon John Sage his land, north upon Samuel Hubbard, Jr., and Henry Johnson, and east upon the 2nd fence now standing, which sd. land is part upland and part swamp. Unto my daughter Sarah, the wife of Joseph Francis, and unto her heirs forever, I give one certain parcel of land bounded as follows: East upon William Hubbard, south upon John Sage, west upon Timothy Hubbard, and north upon Henry Johnson. Unto my grandson Matthew Cole, his heirs and assigns forever, I give £5 money, old tenour. All the rest of my personal estate I give to my three sons, Samuel, Timothy and Watts, to be equally divided among them, and appoint my wife and my son Watts executors.

Witness: *Caleb Galpin,*   SAMUEL HUBBARD, LS.
William Andrus, Abijah Peck.

Court Record, Page 62—6 August, 1745: The last will and testament of Samuel Hubbard, late of Middletown decd., was exhibited in Court by Martha Hubbard, widow, and Watts Hubbard, executor. Proven. Inventory exhibited and ordered to be recorded.

Page 180.

Ingraham, Joseph, Middletown. Invt. £1206-19-10. Taken 19 July, 1745, by William Rockwell, Isaac Lee and Joseph Gleason. Will dated 31st March, 1745.

I, Joseph Ingraham of Middletown, in the County of Hartford and Colony of Connecticut, do make this my last will and testament: Imprimis. I give unto Hannah, my wife, 1-3 part of all my estate forever, to be at her dispose; and the other 2-3 thereof during the time she remains my widow and until my children shall arrive to lawfull age, provided she shall take the care of them and bring them up. I give to my only son Joseph Ingraham all my apparrell and £20 more of my estate. And what then remains of my estate I give to my three children, Martha, Joseph and Hannah, equally to be divided among them. I appoint my wife Hannah and Mr. Thomas Goodwin executors.

Witness: *Philip Mortimer,*   JOSEPH INGRAHAM, LS.
John Storer, William Rockwell.

Court Record, Page 58—28 May, 1745: The last will and testament of Joseph Ingraham, late of Middletown, was now exhibited in Court by Hannah Ingraham, widow, and Thomas Goodwin, executor. Proven and ordered to be recorded. Thomas Goodwin refused the trust in Court.

Page 66—18 November, 1745: An inventory was now exhibited by Hannah Ingraham, widow and executrix, which was accepted and ordered to be kept on file. And the sd. Adms. informs this Court that she supposes sd. estate to be insolvent, and prays commissioners may be appointed to examine the claims of creditors: Whereupon this Court appoint William Rockwell, William Brintnall and Joseph Gleason commissioners.

Page 31 (Vol. XV) 8 January, 1746-7: The commissioners who were ordered to adjust the claims of the creditors not having finished their report, now move to this Court to lengthen out the time: Whereupon this Court allow 6 months from the date hereof to sd. commissioners to finish their report. And whereas, Joseph Glesson, one of the commissioners, being bound to sea, this Court appoint Mr. Ebenezer Sage of Middletown to be commissioner in the room of Joseph Glesson, to adjust accounts.

Page 128.

Jackson, Eunice, Middletown. Invt. £391-14-10. Taken 9 June, 1743, by Cheney Clark and William Rockwell.

Court Record, Page 25—13 June, 1743: This Court grant Adms. on the estate of Eunice Jackson, late of Middletown, unto Ambrose Clark of Middletown, who gave bonds with Samuel Pelton for £100 money.

Page 26—13 June, 1743: Ann Jackson, a minor, 12 years of age, chose her uncle Ambrose Clark to be her guardian. Recog., £100.

Page 28—17 August, 1745: Eunice Jackson, 15 years of age, chose Alexander Douglas of Wallingford to be her guardian. Recog., £200.

Page 9 (Vol. XV) 1st April, 1746: An account of Adms. was now exhibited by Ambrose Clark, which account is accepted by this Court and ordered on file.

Page 31—8 January, 1746-7: Elizabeth Jackson, 20 years of age, and Eunice Jackson, 18 years of age, children of Eunice Jackson decd., chose William Rockwell to be their guardian. Recog., £200. *Cert: Jabez Hamlin, J. P.*

8 January, 1746-7: Ambrose Clark of Middletown, Adms. on the estate of Eunice Jackson, late of Middletown decd., and William Rockwell, guardian to Elizabeth and Eunice Jackson, and Samuel Roberts, son of the sd. decd., and the sd. Ambrose Clark as guardian to Anne Jackson, moved to this Court that the moveable estate of the sd. decd. may be distributed to the heirs of the sd. estate.

	£	s	d
The moveables, now the debts and charges are paid, amount to the sum of	40	05	00
To the eldest son,	16	02	00
And to each of the three daughters, to Elizabeth, Eunice and Anne Jackson, to each of them,	8	01	00

And appoint Capt. Daniel Hall, Capt. Joseph Southmayd and Ephraim Adkins, of Middletown, distributors.

And whereas, the heirs to the estate of the sd. decd., by an agreement under their hands, as may appear in the files of this Court, have agreed that the real estate of the sd. decd. shall be distributed with the guardians to sd. minors, this Court directs the sd. distributors to make division by bounds of the lands of the sd. decd. to sd. heirs: To Samuel Roberts, son of sd. decd., a double share; and to the three above named daughters their single shares; and make return of their doings to this Court.

Page 99—23 March, 1747: Then received of Ambrose Clark, Adms. on the estate of my mother, Eunice Jackson decd., £16-02-00 in full of my part of sd. estate.

Witness: *Ambrose Clark,*   SAMUEL ROBERTS.
Samuel Roberts.

23 January, 1747: Received of my honoured uncle, Ambrose Clark, Adms. on the estate of my honoured mother Eunice Jackson decd., £8-01-00 in full of my part of sd. estate; also the sum of £11 old tenor in full for a cow of sd. estate belonging to me, in the hands of my sd. uncle.

Witness: *William Rockwell.*   ELIZABETH X JACKSON.

20 April, 1747: Received of Ambrose Clark, Adms. on the estate of my mother Eunice Jackson decd., £8-01-00, which is in full of my part of sd. estate.

Witness: *Thomas Stevens,*   EUNICE X JACKSON.
Samuel Clark.

3 August, 1748: Received of Ambrose Clark, Adms. on the estate of my mother Eunice Jackson decd., £8-01-00, which is my part of sd. estate.

Witness: *Daniel Ward,*   ANNE X JACKSON.
Isaac Barnes.

Page 140-1-2.

Johnson, Isaac, Middletown. Invt. £475-03-00. Taken 12 April, 1744, by Jacob Whitmore and William Rockwell. Will dated 1 January, 1739-40.

I, Isaac Johnson of Middletown, being advanced to the age of 70 years, do make and ordain this my last will and testament: Imprimis: I give unto Margaret, my wife, 1-3 part of all my household goods and stock to be at her own dispose, and the use of so much of my real estate that I have by deed of gift given or shall herein give to my son Stephen, as she shall have occasion for during her natural life. I give to my son John all that piece of land on which he now dwells, and all that piece of land on which his barn now stands, running eastward to the extent of my land there, which, with what I have already given to my sd. son by deed of gift, is his full portion of my estate. I give to my son Isaac 10 shillings, which, with what I have already given him by deed of gift, is his full portion of my estate. I give to my son Thomas all that piece of land on which he now dwells, supposed to contain about 40 acres, which makes his full portion of my estate. I give to my son Henry 10 shillings, which, with what I have already given to him by deed of gift, is his full portion of my estate. I give to my son William all my wearing apparrel, which, with what I have already given him by deed of gift, makes his full portion of my estate. I give to my son Stephen all of one piece of land lying near Thomas Tryon's, containing about 8 acres more or less, bounded east on the Town highway, west on the Mill Brook, north on Abell Tryon's land, and south on Nathaniel Johnson's land. I also give him the other 2-3 of my stock and all my husbandry tools and utensils whatsoever, which, with what I have already given him by deed of gift, makes his full portion of my estate, only it is to be observed that I have allowed to my wifa Margaret the improvement of so much of the real estate (that I have given my sd. son Stephen) as she shall have occasion for during her natural life. It is to be understood, and my will is, that my sd. son shall have the improvement thereof so long as he shall provide for my sd. wife comfortable and honourable maintenance. I give to my daughter Sarah the sum of £38. I give to my daughter Margaret the sum of £35. I give to my daughter Content the sum of 10 shillings. I give to my daughter Tabitha the sum of 50 shillings. I give to my daughter Mary the sum of £11-02-00. I give to my daughter Hannah the sum of £50. Which sums, with what I have already given to my daughters above named, makes them their full portions of my estate. And my will is that the above-mentioned legacies of my sd. daughters be paid out of the other 2-3 of my household goods. I appoint Stephen Johnson sole executor.

Witness: *Ebenezer X Robberds,*   ISAAC JOHNSON, LS.
Giles Hamlin, William Rockwell.

Court Record, Page 42—1st day of May, 1744: The last will of Isaac Johnson, late of Middletown, was now exhibited in Court by Stephen Johnson, executor. Will proven. Exhibited an inventory, which was proven and ordered on file.

Page 98-9-100.

Johnson, James, Middletown. Died 18 March, 1743. Invt. £332-15-00. Taken by Philip Goff, Benjamin Harris and Benjamin Smith. Will dated 14 March, 1743.

I, James Johnson of Middletown, in the County of Hartford, do make this my last will and testament: I give to my wife Anne Johnson the 1-3 part of my estate, both real and personal, during her natural life. I give to my son James Johnson and to my son Caleb Johnson and to my son Joseph Johnson all my lands, 150 acres, equally to be divided between them, only my son James Johnson shall have 10 acres more than either of the other two sons. Sd. lands I give to them and their heirs forever. I give to my daughter Anne Johnson and to my daughter Elizabeth Johnson £40 money, or as money, apiece. I give to my daughter-in-law Mercy

Johnson, widow and relict of John Johnson decd., all the moveable estate that my son died seized of, within doors or without, forever. I appoint my wife Anne Johnson and my son James Johnson only and sole executors.

Witness: *Philip Goff,*   JAMES JOHNSON, LS.
Benjamin Harris, Daniel Young.

Court Record, Page 30—4 October, 1743: Will proven. Caleb Johnson, age 19 years, Anne Johnson, 17 years, and Elizabeth Johnson, 13 years, children of James Johnson, chose their brother James Johnson to be their guardian. Recog., £500.

Page 106-7.

Jones, Stephen, Bolton. Will dated 25 March, 1735-6: I, Stephen Jones of Bolton, in the County of Hartford, being in old age, do hereby make my last will and testament: I give to my wife Jane sufficiency for her comfortable maintenance after my decease during her natural life, which is already secured to her by obligation to my two sons Benjamin and Stephen for 2-3 thereof, and the other third secured in this testament in what I have given to my son Hugh. I give unto my son Benjamin Jones all that which I have already given him by a deed of gift and not yet recorded. I give unto my son Stephen Jones what I have already given him by a deed of gift not yet recorded. I give unto my son Hugh Jones my 50 acres of land, or half a lott which I purchased of the committee for settling Bolton, and laid out to me by Joseph Pitkin, and lyeth southward of my other half lott. Secondly, I give him my orchard adjoining to my dwelling house, commonly called Hugh's orchard, bounded north half a rod northward of the trees and west on a brook. Thirdly, I give him 1-3 part of sundry parcels of land laid out in the undivided land in Bolton by the committee for laying out divisions in Bolton, and laid out by sd. committee the last winter, except his third part of 7 1-2 acres, and also 3 acres of sd. land which are contained in my deed of Stephen Jones above named. Also I give unto Hugh Jones 1-3 part of all my undivided lands in Bolton not yet laid out. All the aforesd. parcels of land I do hereby will and dispose unto my son Hugh Jones, only upon this condition and proviso, that if he the sd. Hugh Jones shall well and truly pay or cause to be paid to my executors hereafter named £7-10-00 annually from the time of my decease to my executor, to be by him disbursed unto my wife towards her comfortable maintenance and subsistence annually to her from the time of my decease during her natural life. I appoint Mr. John Bissell of Bolton my sole executor.

Witness: *John Bissell,*   STEPHEN X JONES, LS.
Moses Thrall, John Millington.

See File:

Judd, Ithiel, Farmington. 30 April 1742: Know all men by these presents: That I, Mary Judd of Farmington, widow and relict of Ithiel Judd, late of Farmington decd., for a valuable consideration to me in hand well and truly paid by the heirs and administrators of the estate of Nathaniel Judd of Wallingford, in the County of New Haven, late decd., for the receipt whereof I bind myself, my heirs, executors, etc., forever from the date of these presents to remise, relinquish and quit my claim unto the estate of Ithiel Judd, my husband, of Farmington decd., and all right and title to any part of the estate of Mr. Nathaniel Judd of said Wallingford, either lands or moveables, and that the said heirs shall possess quietly all the said estates, personal and real, forever hereafter, without any molestation or disturbance from me or my heirs: provided that the said Mary Judd is to have the use and improvement of part of the house that was her husband Ithiel Judd's during the time she goes by the name of Ithiel Judd's widow; and that she shall have all the stock and moveables that belonged unto the said Ithiel Judd, provided she payes the debts that her husband Ithiel Judd did owe or that is due from his estate to any person or persons. And that I do forever acquit and discharge the heirs, etc., of the said Nathaniel Judd decd., excepting the last proviso, I bind myself, my heirs, executors, etc., firmly by these presents, and have hereunto set my hand and affixed my seal in Wallingford this 30th day of April, A. D. 1742.

Signed, sealed and
delivered in presence of:
Joseph Buckingham,
Joseph Judd,
Edmund Scott,
Daniel Merwin,
Isaac Curtis.

MARY X JUDD, LS.
NATHAN HUBBARD, LS.
LYDIA HUBBARD, LS.
MARY X JUDD, LS.
ELIZABETH X JUDD, LS.
SARAH X JUDD, LS.
NATHANIEL X JUDD, LS.
IMMER X JUDD, LS.

Elizabeth Judd and Sarah Judd sign with the consent of their guardian.

Page 188.

Keith, William, Hartford. Invt. £1353-08-00. Taken 30 July, 1745, by Thomas Seymour and Roderick Morrison.

Court Record, Page 62—6 August, 1745: This Court grant Adms. on the estate of William Keith, late of Hartford decd., unto Mariane Keith, widow, who gave bond with John Lawrence of Hartford for £1000. Also, presented an inventory, which was ordered to be recorded and kept on file.

Page 197-8.

Kelsey, Abigail, Farmington. Invt. £116-10-08. Taken 29 October, 1745, by Giles Hooker and Elisha Lewis.

Court Record, Page 65—5 November, 1745: This Court grants Adms. on the estate of Abigail Kelsey, late of Farmingtown, unto Joseph Root of sd. Farmingtown, who gave bond with Stephen Root of sd. Farmingtown, for £400.

Page 191-2-3.

Kelsey, Stephen, New Hartford. Invt. £273-05-01. Taken 17 May, 1745, by Isaac Kellogg, Eliphalet Ensign and John Spencer. Will dated 8 December, 1744.

I, Stephen Kelsey of New Hartford, in the County of Hartford, do make this my last will and testament: . Imprimis. I give to Dorothy, my wife, her thirds of my moveable estate, one room in my dwelling house and her thirds of income of my estate during life, and 1 chest. I give to my eldest son Stephen Kelsey, of Waterbury, 1-2 of a £40 note payable to me by my son Timothy Kelsey of Kensington, dated 9 October, 1744. I give my gunn to his eldest son Daniel Kelsey. I give to my son Jonathan Kelsey, of Woodbury, the other half of the before mentioned £40 note, to his own proper use and benefit after my decease, and to his heirs forever. To Nathan, one heifer calf, one year old. I give to my son Ebenezer Kelsey, of New Hartford, my tools for makeing syder press, my new broad axe, a square and twy bill, 1-2 of the team and tackling, cart and plow and chains, 1-2 of the wheat fan, half of the carpenter's tools and half of (a) half bushel; whom I appoint one of my executors. I give to my son Timothy Kelsey, of Kensington, besides what I have already given to him, a five quarter augur. I give to my son Samuel Kelsey, of New Hartford, my sword and broad axe and 1-3 of my lott laid out in New Hartford, bounded south upon land now belonging to Sarah Kelsey and north upon land belonging to Joseph Webster's heirs. This land I give to his son Daniel and to his heirs forever. To Samuel, 1-2 of the team and team tackling, cart and plow and chain, 1-2 of the wheat fan, and half of (a) half bushel; whom I appoint one of my executors. I give to Ebenezer Kelsey, son of Ebenezer Kelsey of New Hartford, a certain parcel of land lying in New Hartford, it being my last division, bounded north by Ebenezer Kelsey's land and south by land belonging to Abell Merrells. I give to my daughter Dorothy, above what she has already received, 1 hive of bees. To my daughter Esther Kelsey, of New Hartford, a featherbed and bedding and 1-2 of a lott bounded on the north by land belonging to Thomas Olcott, south by John Spencer's land, east and west upon a highway. These I give to her and her heirs forever; also a red chest with one drawer, peal, tongs, trammell, brass kettle and a puter platter. I give to my daughter Sarah, of Farmingtown, above what she has already received, a good weaver's loom and tackling, a frying pan, one box, (a) featherbed and bedding, and one puter platter. I give to my daughter Abigail, of Farmingtown, above what she has already received, a good new bedd tick, a warming pan and one bed blankett. I give to my daughter Eunice Church, of New Hartford, above what she has received already, 1-2 of a piece of land bounded by John Spencer's land on the south and on the north by land belonging to John Olcott, and one pewter platter.

Witness: *John Spencer,*   STEPHEN KELSEY, LS.
Eliphalet Ensign, William Day, Jr.

Court Record, Page 62—6 August, 1745: The last will and testament of Stephen Kelsey, late of New Hartford decd., was now exhibited in Court by Ebenezer and Samuel Kelsey, executors. Proven. Exhibit of an inventory, which was approved, recorded and kept on file.

Page 193.

Kelsey, Timothy, Wethersfield. Died 15 August, 1745. Invt. £606-12-10. Taken by Joseph Beckley and William Burnham, Jr.

Court Record, Page 63—3 September, 1745: Adms. granted unto Eunice Kelsey, widow of sd. deceased, who gave bond with Jacob Barnes of Farmington for £1000.

Page 24 (Vol. XV.) 26 September, 1746: An account of Adms. was now exhibited in Court by Daniel Andruss in right of his wife, the widow and Adms. of the deceased. Account accepted.

Page 33—3 March, 1746-7: Pursuant to an act of the General Assembly holden at New Haven on the 2nd Thursday of October, 1746, directing Daniel Andruss and Eunice Andruss, Adms. on the estate of Timothy Kelsey, late of Wethersfield decd., to sell so much of the real estate of the sd. decd. as will procure the sum of £182-11-05 with incident charges, land being in Kensington Parish.

Page 103—4 July, 1749: In pursuance to an act of the General Assembly and direction of the Court of Probate held at Hartford for Hartford County on the 3rd day of March, 1746-7, we did set up advertisements and sold land of the estate of Timothy Kelsey decd., viz: On the 25th day of March, 1746-7, we sold at publick vandue to Martin Kellogg, Jr., of Wethersfield, 2 1-2 acres and 11 rods of land being in Wethersfield in Kensington aforesd., the east end of a lott there, which land sold by us bounded east on land of John Kelsey or Enoch Kelsey, west on a highway, north on a highway, and south on Daniel Andruss' land; sold for £66-16-06. Also, we sold part of the west end of sd. lott to James North of Farmingtown, 7 1-2 acres and 23 rods of land, for £25-18-09. And gave deeds accordingly. Signed: *Daniel Andruss and Eunice Andruss.* The charges of the sale of land is £10-13-10.

Page 77 (Vol. XVII) 2 September, 1755: Elizabeth Kelsey, a minor, aged 13 years, daughter of Timothy Kelsey, made choice of Lt. Hezekiah Deming to be her guardian. Recog., £300 money.

Page 169-70-71.

Lane, Isaac, Middletown. Invt. £1880-09-02. Taken 28 February, 1745, by Nathaniel Gilbert, Jonathan Allin and William Rockwell. Will dated 15 December, 1744.

I, Isaac Lane of Middletown, in the County of Hartford, do make this my last will and testament: Imprimis: I give to my wife Elizabeth Lane 1-3 part of all my personal estate (except my apparrel) after my just debts and funeral charges are paid out of it, to be at her dispose; and the improvement of 1-3 part of my buildings and half an acre of land adjoining, to lye in convenient form, so long as she continues my widow and see cause to dwell in my house; but if she shall marry after my decease or shall leave my house, my will is that she then quit her right to any of my real estate. I give to my four sons, Nathaniel, Cornelius, Zacheus and Ashbell, all my lands, part whereof I have already given by deed of gift to two of my sons, namely, Nathaniel and Cornelius, which shall be accounted to them as so much of their part of my estate. I give to my youngest son Ashbell all my buildings and all my apparrel more than to my other children. I give to my three daughters, Mary, Mindwell and Hannah, the other 2-3 of all my personal estate (except my apparrel). And further, my will is that my two daughters, Mindwell and Hannah, shall have liberty to dwell in my house so long as they shall remain single. And I appoint my two eldest sons, Nathaniel Lane and Cornelius Lane, executors.

Witness: *Jonathan Doolittle,*   ISAAC LANE, LS.
William Rockwell, Jonathan Doolittle, Jr.

Court Record, Page 55—5 March, 1744-5: Will proven.

Zacheus Lane, a minor, 20 years of age, and Ashbell Lane, age 16 years, chose Jonathan Allyn of Middletown to be their guardian. Recog., £600.

Page 178, 183.

Lattimore, Bezaleel, Wethersfield. Invt. £4236-01-06. Taken 25 June, 1745, by Jonathan Belding and John Stilman:

	£ s d
The homelott and buildings thereon,	1300-00-00
33 1-2 acres of land in a division lott called Vexation,	500-00-00
10 acres of pasture land at the South Field,	500-00-00
2 acres of land at the South Field,	100-00-00
8 acres of land in the Great Plaine,	400-00-00
5 acres of land in the meadow leading to Smith's Landing,	250-00-00
7 1-2 acres of land in the meadow at Foot lott,	350-00-00
6 acres of land in the meadow in the dry swamp,	300-00-00
1 silver cup, 10 oz. 2d. weight at 35s per ounce,	17-13-06

Will dated 10 May, 1745:

I, Bezaleel Lattimore of Wethersfield, do make this my last will and testament: Imprimis: I give to Sibell, my wife, the free use and improvement of 1-3 part of my buildings and lands during the term of her natural life; and also 1-2 of all my moveable estate, after my just debts and funeral charges are paid, I give to my sd. wife to be at her only and sole dispose forever. I give to my son Samuel Lattimore the 1-2 of my homelott, it being on the north side of sd. lott, with all the buildings thereon, excepting some priviledge in the buildings hereafter given to my son Solomon. I also give to my sd. son Samuel 2 acres of land in the South Field, on the south side of the 10-acre pasture. I give to my son Solomon Lattimore the 1-2 of my homelott, it being on the south side of sd. lott. I also give to my sd. son the 1-2 of my division lott at Vexation, on the south side thereof. My will also is that my son Solomon shall have liberty to live in the house now given to my son Samuel during the space of 7 years after he shall arrive to the age of 21 years. I give to my son Bezaleel Lattimore 4 acres of land at the South Field, on the north side of my pasture; also 5 acres in the Plaine, on the south side, being all that land bought of Paterson and Coleman; and so much on the south side of sd. land that I bought of Porter as to make up the sd. 5 acres; also half my lott in the meadow on the way leading to Smith's Landing, and on the west side of sd. lott; also half of my Foot lott in the meadow, on the north side thereof. I give to my son John Lattimore 4 acres of land in the South Field, on the south side of the land now given to my son Bezaleel and on the north side of the land now given to my son Samuel; also the remaining part of my lott in the Plaine besides what I now have given to my son Bezaleel; also half of my lott in the meadow butting on the way leading to Smith's Landing, being on the east side of sd. lott; also half of my Foot lott in the meadow, on the south side thereof. I give to my son Hezekiah Lattimore 2 acres of land in the South Field. lying on the north side of John Rennolds his homelott; also 6 acres of land in the meadow called dry swamp, being the whole of that lott; also half of my division lott at Vexation, on the north side thereof. I give to my daughter Abigail Lattimore £50 out of my moveable estate, old tenor. My will further is that after all my just debts and funeral charges are paid, and my wife Sibell hath received her half of the remainder of the moveables, and my sd. daughter Abigail the aforementioned sum of £50 in moveable estate, then my will is that the remainder of the moveables shall be equally divided between my five sons. I appoint my wife Sibell Lattimore and my son Samuel Lattimore executors.

Witness: *Jonathan Belding,*   BEZALEEL LATTIMORE, LS.
John Smith, Josiah Smith.

Court Record, Page 60—22 June, 1745: The last will and testament of Bezaleel Lattimore, late of Wethersfield decd., was now exhibited in Court by Sibell and Samuel Lattimore, executors. Will being proven, an inventory was presented, which was ordered recorded and kept on file.

Page 20 (Vol. XV) 5 August, 1746: Bezaleel Lattimore, a minor, 16 years of age, chose his mother Sibbell Lattimore to be his guardian. Recog., £500. Solomon Lattimore, a minor, 18 years of age, son of Bezaleel Lattimore, chose his brother Samuel Lattimore to be his guardian. Recog., £500.

Page 46 (Vol. XVII) 3 December, 1754: Sibbell Lattimer, guardian to Hezekiah Lattimer, a minor son of Bezaleel Lattimer, showing to this Court that there is several pieces of land in sd. Wethersfield that is in common or joynt tenancy among the heirs of John Lattimer deceased, and desires freeholders may be appointed to divide sd. lands, with the assistance of sd. guardian, that each heir may know and improve separate: Whereupon this Court appoint Capt. Jonathan Belding, Josiah Smith and Ebenezer Belding to divide sd. lands.

Page 115.

Lay, Thomas, Middletown. Invt. £136-18-07. Taken 29 March, 1743, by George Hubbard and Daniel Starr. Will dated 2nd March, 1743.

I, Thomas Lay of Middletown, do make and ordain this my last will and testament: Imprimis. I give and bequeath unto Mary, my wife, all and every part of my household goods, to be at her dispose, and the equal half of all my stock after the legacies herein mentioned are paid out of it. I give unto my sons-in-law, Eleazer Gilbert and Jonathan Roberts, all my husbandry tools and utensils and the equal half of my stock after the legacies hereinafter mentioned are paid out of it, provided they do well and truly perform the condition of one obligation by them jointly and severally given to me bearing date even with these presents. And whereas, my former wife Rachel (from whom I obtained a bill of divorcement) had one child (before) I obtained sd. bill, called Dorothy Lay, I give to the sd. Dorothy the sum of 5 shillings, old tenor money, to be paid out of my stock estate by my executor after named, on her demand, within 12 months after my decease. And I do appoint my friend William Rockwell sole executor, to whom I give the sum of £10 old tenor money, to be taken out of my stock estate.

Witness: *Daniel Johnson,*   THOMAS LAY, LS.
Nathaniel Johnson, Elisha Sayer.

Court Record, Page 21—4 April, 1743: The last will and testament of Thomas Lay, late of Middletown, was now exhibited in Court by William Rockwell of Middletown, executor. Proven and ordered to be recorded.

Page 98.

Lee, James, Farmington. Invt. £18-17-02. Taken 26 January, 1741-2, by Hez. Lee and Joseph Hooker. Will dated 22 October, 1741.

I, James Lee of Farmingtown, do make this my last will and testament: I give unto my five brethren, Jared Lee, Joseph Lee, John Lee, Thomas Lee and Ebenezer Lee, all my real and personal estate that I have in the world, to be equally divided amongst them, and to their heirs and assigns forever, in whose hands, custody and possession soever the same may be found, after that my sister Lydia Norton is first paid out of my sd. estate the sum of £10 money by my executor hereafter named. I hereby appoint my brother Jared Lee sole executor.

Witness: *Daniel Hooker,*   JAMES LEE, LS.
Isaac Graham, Abigail X Wadsworth.

Court Record, Page 31—4 October, 1743: The last will and testament of James Lee, late of Farmingtown, was now exhibited in Court by Jared Lee, executor. Proven and ordered to be recorded.

Page 111.

Lewis, Shubael. Invt. £12-06-02. Taken by Jonathan Wood and Ebenezer Clark.

Page 110-111.

Lewis, Thomas, Middletown. Invt. £210-12-00. Taken 16 November, 1743, by Jonathan Wood and Ebenezer Clark.

Court Record, Page 34—6 December, 1743: This Court grant Adms. on the estate of Thomas Lewis and Shubael Lewis of Middletown decd. (father and son) unto Elnathan Rowley of Colchester, who gave bonds with George Sexton, Jr., of sd. Colchester, for £500 for their faithfull Adms. Exhibited an inventory, which is approved, ordered to be recorded and kept on file. Also, the sd. Adms. informed the Court that the estate of the sd. deceased was insolvent, and prays commissioners may be appointed to adjust a claim of creditors: Whereupon this Court do appoint and impower Jonathan Wood and Ebenezer Clark of Middletown to receive and adjust the claim of the creditors. Also, this Court have set out a list of moveables of the estate of the sd. decd. to Mary Lewis, widow of the sd. decd. The particulars amount to the sum of £13-12-00, which account is on file.

Page 51—11 December, 1744: Whereas, the General Assembly holden at New Haven on the 2nd Thursday of October, 1744, appointed Elnathan Rowley of Colchester to sell so much of the real estate of Thomas Lewis, late of Middletown decd., as should procure the sum of £82-12-01 bills of credit of the old tenor, together with incident charges arising, and by the direction of the Court of Probate in Hartford County: whereupon this Court directs the sd. Adms. to make sale of the lands of the sd. decd., viz., one certain piece of land lying in the three-mile division of land on the east side of the Connecticut River in sd. Middletown, being the 38th

lottment of sd. division, containing 35 1-2 acres and 30 rods of land, or
so much of sd. land as will procure sd. sum and charges of sale. And the
Court directs the Adms. to set up advertisements in some publick places
in Middletown 20 days before the sale, signifying that there is to be sold
such piece or parcell of land, such a day and time of day, to the highest
bidder at publick vandue and at the beat of the drum, and make report to
this Court.

Page 133.

Logan, James. Invt. £160-09-00. Taken 15 February, 1743-4, by
John Edwards and James Church.
Court Record, Page 36—20 January, 1743-4: This Court grant
Adms. on the estate of James Logan, late of Hartford decd., unto John
Logan of Charlestown, in the County of Middlesex, in the Province of
Massachusetts Bay, who gave bond with Jonathan Steele of Hartford for
£200.
Page 38—15 February, 1743-4: John Logan, Adms. on the estate
of James Logan, late of Hartford, informed this Court that he sup-
poses the estate is insolvent, and prays that commissioners may be appointed to adjust the claim of the creditors: Whereupon this Court appoint James Church and John Edwards, of Hartford, commissioners.

Page 86.

Loomis, Elizabeth, Widow, Windsor. Invt. £287-00-00. Taken 28
May, 1743, by William Wolcott, Jr., and Moses Loomis, Jr.
Court Record, Page 25—7 June, 1743: Inventory of the estate of
widow Elizabeth Loomis, late of Windsor decd., was now exhibited in
Court by Jacob Osborn and David Skinner, Adms. Accepted and ordered
on file.
Page 38—9 February, 1743-4: Account of Adms. on the estate of
widow Elizabeth Loomis was now exhibited in Court by Jacob Osborn
and David Skinner, Adms.: Paid in debts and charges, £155-07-08. Which
account is allowed and ordered to be kept on file. Adms. now moved for a
distribution of the sd. estate:

	£ s d
Inventory,	280-09-00
Subtracting the amount paid in debts and charges,	155-07-08
There remains to be distributed,	125-01-04
To the heirs of Josiah Elsworth,	18-00-00
To Sergt. Thomas Elsworth,	18-00-00
To the heirs of Lt. John Elsworth,	18-00-00
To Capt. Job Elsworth,	18-00-00
To Martha Osborn,	18-00-00
To the heirs of Mary Loomis deceased,	18-00-00
To Lt. Jonathan Elsworth,	18-00-00

Which is their equal share of the sum of £125-01-04. And this Court appoint Samuel Watson and Jonathan Bliss, of Windsor, distributors.

Page 49—6 November, 1744: Distributors report, and are granted a *Quietus Est.*

Page 144.

Marsh, John, Hartford. Will dated 17 September, 1741 : Whereas, I, the subscriber, being at the present time sound in mind and memory, take this opportunity to put this my last will and testament into this writing: Unto my beloved wife I give 100 acres of land lying in the Township of Litchfield, it being the first 100-acre piece laid out to me in the 2nd going over, and is laid out near Waterbury River; and also the whole of my household goods; and likewise the 1-2 of my stock, that is to say, cattle, horses, sheep and swine, together with all the provisions in the house provided for food, to be at her dispose forever, she paying the legacies to my daughter Elizabeth Cook hereafter mentioned. And further, I give unto my wife the use of 1-3 part of my dwelling house and barn, together with 1-3 part of all my lands in Hartford, during her natural life. And further, I give unto my sd. wife Elizabeth the use of the 1-2 part of all my houseing and lands in Hartford during the time she remains my widow. Secondly, I give unto my sons living at Litchfield, that is, Ebenezer, William, George, Isaac and John Marsh, all my lands in sd. Litchfield which I have not before disposed of, to be divided as followeth : after Ebenezer hath £20 set out to him out of the whole, the remainder to be equally divided between them as they shall agree, or to be so divided by indifferent men as they shall choose; and also ratifying unto them all the lands I have already given to each of them by deed or otherwise, as appears in the Records of Land in the sd. Litchfield Town Book. Third, I give unto my son Hezekiah the whole of my homelott, together with all the buildings and orchard thereon, to be unto him, his heirs and assigns forever. I give unto my son Timothy Marsh and my son Hezekiah all the remaining of my lands in Hartford, to be equally divided between them, to be unto them, their heirs and assigns forever. Fifth, I give to my daughter Elizabeth Cook £30, to be paid within 12 months after my decease. The remainder of my moveable estate not before disposed of I give to my executors in order to pay my just debts and funeral charges. My well-beloved wife Elizabeth Marsh to be executrix, and my son Hezekiah Marsh, whom I do hereby constitute and appoint to execute this foregoing will and testament.

Witness : *Nathaniel Stanly,*   JOHN MARSH, LS.
Sarah Stanly, Susannah Stanly.

Page 167.

Marshall, Samuel, Hartford. Invt. £191-16-03. Taken by Thomas Hopkins and Jonathan Steele.

Court Record, Page 50—4 December, 1744: This Court grant Adms. on the estate of Samuel Marshall, late of Hartford, unto Patience Marshall, widow of the sd. decd., who gave bond with Thomas Hopkins of Hartford for £500 money.

Page 60—12 June, 1745: An account of Adms. on the estate of Samuel Marshall, late of Hartford decd., was now exhibited in Court by Patience Marshall, Adms.: Paid in debts and charges, £47-07-09. Accepted and ordered on file. Also, moved to this Court for a distribution of the moveable estate: Whereupon this Court appoint Lt. Jonathan Steele and Mr. Daniel Steele, of Hartford, distributors:

	£ s d
The moveable estate amounted to	81-06-03
Subtracting the debts,	47-07-09
There remains to be distributed,	38-18-06
To Patience, the widow, 1-3 thereof,	11-06-02
To Joel, only son, his double part,	15-01-08
To Sarah, daughter of sd. decd.,	7-10-10

Which sums include the whole of the moveable estate.

Page 60—22 June, 1745: This Court appoint widow Patience Marshall to be guardian to Joel Marshall, age 12 years, and to Sarah Marshall, age 7 years, children of Samuel Marshall decd. Recog., £200. A report of the distributors is by this Court approved and ordered on file.

Page 27.

Merrells, Lt. Isaac, Hartford. Invt. £981-18-09. Taken 2 December, 1742, by Daniel Webster, Joseph Skinner, Jr., and Jacob Merrells.

Court Record, Page 13—7 December, 1742: Adms. granted unto Sarah Merrells, widow and relict, who gave bond with Thomas Judd of Hartford for £900.

Page 25—7 June, 1743: Isaac Merrells, a minor, now 15 years of age, son of Isaac Merrells of Hartford, chose his mother Sarah Merrells to be his guardian. Recog., £50.

Page 332 (Vol. XV, Probate Side): Articles of agreement made and agreed upon this 15th November, Anno. Dom. 1749, between Ichabod Merrells and Mehetabell, children of Noah Merrells decd., Esther Merrells, guardian to Noah Merrells, son of sd. Noah Merrells, Timothy Merrells, Eliakim Merrells and Sarah Clark (by and with the consent of her husband Matthew Clark) for the settling and dividing of the estate of Isaac Merrells, and are as followeth, viz: The lot that the house and barn stands on, butting south on Farmingtown road, shall be divided as follows, viz: Timothy Merrells shall have 1-4 part and half an acre on the east side of sd. lott; the heirs of Noah Merrells shall have 1-4 part and half an acre of sd. lott next to Timothy's part; Eliakim Merrells shall have 1-4 part of sd. lott wanting half an acre, lying next west of sd.

heirs' land; and Sarah Clark shall have 1-4 part of sd. lott wanting half
an acre, on the west side of sd. lott. It is to be understood to be divided
exclusive of the house and barn and half an acre of land butting south
on a highway, extending along sd. highway by the east end of sd. house
north 4 rods, and then extends westward 16 rods, and from thence to the
sd. highway southward 6 rods, which half an acre and buildings is left
undivided. And further, it is agreed that widow Sarah Merrells shall
have her thirds in sd. lott. Further, we agree that the lott butting east
on the aforesd. lott extending west shall be divided as followeth, viz:
Timothy shall have 1-4 part, Eliakim 1-4, Noah's heirs shall have 1-4
part, and to Sarah 1-4 part. The lott on the south side of Farmington
road shall be divided as followeth, viz: to Timothy 6 acres, and Sarah
Clark shall have 13 acres and 30 rods next west of Moses Seymour. In
witness to each of the aforesd. articles each one have hereunto set their
hands and seals the day above written.

SARAH X MERRELLS, LS.	TIMOTHY MERRELLS, LS.
ICHABOD MERRELLS, LS.	ELIAKIM MERRELLS, LS.
ESTHER X MERRELLS, LS.	SARAH X CLARK, LS.
MATTHEW GILLETT, GUARDIAN, LS.	MATTHEW CLARK, LS.

Witness: *Bevel Seymour,*
    Moses Nash.

Merrells, Jacob. Court Record, Page 14—7 December, 1742:
Joshua Merrells, a minor, son of Jacob Merrells of Hartford decd., and
Abigail, 20 years of age, daughter of the sd. decd., chose Jacob Merrells
of Hartford to be their guardian. Recog., £600.

Page 174.

Miller, John, Middletown. Invt. £600-03-06. Taken 14 May, 1745,
by John Wood, Stephen Johnson and Deliverance Warner. Will dated
1 May, 1745.

I, John Miller of Middletown, do make this my last will and testament: Imprimis: I give to Mercy, my present wife, all the remainder of
my moveable estate, excepting one gunn, after debts and necessary
charges are paid. This I give to Mercy, my wife, and to her heirs forever. And further, I give to Mercy, my wife, the use of all my lands,
excepting 4 acres where my son Asa now lives on, and excepting my interest in the land in the last three miles on the east side of the Great
River in Middletown. I give the use of all the remainder of all my lands
to Mercy, my wife, during her natural life. I give to Ebenezer Miller,
my eldest son, 10 shillings in old tenor money. I give to Benjamin Miller,
Jr., of sd. Middletown, all my interest in the middle tier of land laid out
in the last three miles granted to the Town of Middletown, which is partly for value already received of sd. Benjamin Miller. This I give to sd.

Benjamin Miller, his heirs and assigns forever. I give to Margery Ranney, my daughter, the 1-2 of the half-mile lott which she now dwells upon, takeing half the quantity of sd. lott, at the north end. This I give to my daughter Margery Ranney and to her heirs forever. I give to my daughter Margaret Presson about 3 acres laid out to me in the fourth division on the east side of the Great River, near a place called Joshua's Rock. This I give to my sd. daughter Margaret and to her heirs forever. I give to my son Asa Miller the house that he now lives in, and likewise 4 acres of land athwart my lott where sd. house stands. This I give to my son Asa Miller and to his heirs forever; also one gunn. And further, I give to my son Asa Miller and my daughter Ann Crowe and my daughter Mercy Butler and my daughter Martha Ranney and my daughter Margery Ranney and my daughter Margaret Presson all the remainder of all my land, to be divided amongst them, after their mother's decease, namely: my son Asa Miller to have a double share of the whole, and all my daughters to have all that they have formerly had of my estate counted, and likewise all which I have now given any of them counted, so that each of my daughters shall be equivalent (or made equal?) by this land. This I give to my sd. son Asa and sd. daughters, and to their heirs and assigns forever. But nevertheless my will is that my son Asa, if he shall pay to his sisters for their part or to any of them their proportionable part of sd. land according to the apprisement, then he shall have the liberty of the same and hold the land or their part of the same for himself and his heirs forever. I ordain my son Asa Miller sole executor.

Witness: *Joseph Bartlett,*   JOHN X MILLER, LS.
John Gains, John Wood.

Court Record, Page 59—4 June, 1745: Will proven.

Mitchell, James. Court Record, Page 60—22 June, 1745: James Mitchell, a minor, 12 years of age, and Mabell Mitchell, 9 years of age: This Court appoint their father James Mitchell of Wethersfield to be their guardian. Recog., £500.

Invt. in Vol. XV, Page 297.

Moody, Ebenezer, Farmington. Invt. £1132-07-00. Taken 19 July, 1748, by Hezekiah Lee, Joseph Hart and Ebenezer Orvis.

Court Record, Page 44—5 June, 1744: This Court grant Adms. unto Ann Moody, widow of the sd. deceased, who gave bonds with David Porter of Farmington for £200.

Page 97 (Vol. XV) 2 May, 1749: An account of Adms. was now exhibited in Court by Annah Moody, alias Porter. Account accepted. This Court order distribution as followeth:

£　s　d
To Samuel Moody, eldest son, in real estate,　　　　510-11-00
To Zimri Moody and Lurenia Moody, to each of them,　255-05-06

And this Court order that 1-3 part of the real estate be set out to the widow for her improvement during life. And appoint Joseph Hart, Hezekiah Lee and William Judd, of Farmington, distributors.

Page 26 (Vol. XVI) 4 June, 1751: Samuel Moodey, a minor, son of Ebenezer Moodey, late deceased, chose Joseph Hooker of Farmington to be his guardian. Recog., £300.

Inventory in Vol. XV, Page 9.

Nichols, Cyprian, Jr., Hartford. Invt. £244-08-08. Taken 26 November, 1745, by Joseph Talcott and Michael Burnham.

Court Record, Page 63—1st Tuesday of October, 1745: Adms. granted to Agnes Nichols, widow and relict of sd. deceased, who gave bonds with Capt. Joseph Cook of Hartford.

Page 2 (Vol. XV) 2 January, 1745-6: An inventory was exhibited in Court by Agnes Nichols and Dositheus Humphrey, Adms. Inventory accepted.

Page 25—7 October, 1746: An inventory of the lands of Cyprian Nichols which lye in New Hartford was now exhibited in Court by Isaac Seymour and Agnes his wife, Adms. Accepted. Also, they exhibit an account of their Adms. Also, this Court do order that the moveables for the widow's necessary use be set out to her, which amounts to the sum of £30-17-00.

Page 40—10 June, 1747: Pursuant to an act of the General Assembly holden at New Haven on the 2nd Thursday of October, 1746, directing Dositheus Humphrey and Isaac Seymour, Adms. on the estate of Cyprian Nichols, Jr., to sell so much of the real estate as shall be sufficient to pay the sum of £303-05-03 with necessary charges of sale, taking the advice of the Court of Probate in the District of Hartford therein.

Page 58 (Vol. XVI) 7 April, 1752: A further account of Adms. was exhibited by the Adms. Accepted.

Page 153 (Vol. XVII) 12 July, 1757: George Nichols, a minor, age 15 years, son of Cyprian Nichols of Hartford deceased, made choice of his mother Agnes Seymour to be his guardian. And the sd. Agnes Seymour recog. in £200 with Dositheus Humphrey.

Page 176-7.

North, John, Farmington. Invt. £261-10-06. Taken 14 May, 1745, by John Hart, Thomas Wadsworth and Elisha Lewis. Will dated 26 April, 1737.

I, John North of Farmingtown, do make this my last will and testament: I give to Abigail North, my wife, the use of 1-3 part of my houseing and lands, and also the use of 1-3 part of my moveable estate, so long as she bears my name. And my eldest son Jonathan North and my youngest son Samuel North having already received their portions, or is otherwise secured to them, therefore I give them nothing by this will. I give to my daughter Anna Coleman, and to the children of my daughter Mary Wilson decd., £70 to Anna aforesd., and £70 to the children of Mary aforesd., with what Anna and Mary has already received in way of portion from me. And what they the sd. Anna and Mary has had from their grandfather's estate at Middletown to be reckoned and accounted as part of the £70. I give to my daughter Margaret Prior the sum of £70 with what she hath already received. I give to the children of my daughter Ruth Cowles £70 with what my daughter Ruth has already received. I give to my daughter Eunice Hawley £70 with what she hath already received. I give to my son Josiah North my homestead whereon I now dwell, both houseing and lands; also 20 acres of land in the 2nd lottment in the division butting on Hartford and Windsor bounds; also about 7 acres of land in the great meadow, with all the rest of my estate, both real and personal, I give to him and his heirs forever. I appoint my son Josiah North executor.

Witness: *Joseph Hawley,*   JOHN NORTH, LS.
John Newell, Abell Hawley.

Court Record, Page 58—7 May, 1745: The last will and testament of John North, late of Farmingtown deceased, was now exhibited in Court by Josiah North, executor. Will proven and ordered to be recorded.

Page 22.

Norton, Gideon, Kensington. Invt. £1513-15-03. Taken by John Cowles, Joseph Porter and William Burnham, Jr.

Court Record, Page 1—6 April, 1742: This Court grants letters of Adms. on the estate of Gideon Norton, late of Farmingtown, unto Samuel Thompson of Farmingtown, who gave bonds with Anthony Judd of Farmington for £150.

Page 198.

Norton, Samuel, Simsbury. Invt. £109-10-00. Taken 7 November, 1745, by Jacob Tuller, Thomas Marvin and David Phelps.

Court Record, Page 65—5 November, 1745: This Court grants Adms. on the estate of Samuel Norton, late of Simsbury, unto Lydia Norton, widow of the sd. decd., who gave bonds with John Norton of Farmingtown for £300.

Page 3 (Vol. XV) 7 January, 1745: This Court appoint Lydia Norton, widow, to be guardian to her children, viz., Matthew Norton, age 7 years, Hannah 5 years, Abigail 3 years and John Norton 12 months. Recog., £500.

Page 25—7 October, 1746: An account of Adms. on the estate of Samuel Norton was now exhibited in Court by Lydia Norton, Adms. Accepted.

Page 26—31st October, 1746: Pursuant to an act of the General Assembly holden at New Haven on the 2nd Thursday of October, 1746, directing Lydia Norton, Adms., to sell so much of the real estate as will procure the sum of £62-02-04 with incident charges, taking the advice of the Court of Probates in the District of Hartford therein, this Court now direct the sd. Adms. to sell the real estate of the deceased.

Page 51—6 November, 1747: A return of the sale of land by Lydia Norton, widow. Accepted by the Court, and the Adms. is granted a *Quietus Est.*

Page 74 (Vol. XVII) 5 August, 1755: Matthew Norton, a minor, 16 years of age, son of Samuel Norton, made choice of his uncle Ebenezer Lee to be his guardian. Recog., £300.

Page 158.

Olmsted, James, Hartford. Died 11 April, 1744. Invt. £2389-16-04. Taken 7 August, 1744, by Nehemiah Olmsted and Joseph Cowles.

Court Record, Page 45—5 June, 1744: This Court grant Adms. on the estate of James Olmsted, late of Hartford decd., unto James Olmsted of Hartford, son of the sd. decd., who gave bonds with Ozias Pitkin for £300.

Page 109.

Orvis, Charles, Farmington. Invt. £261-00-14. Taken 14 November, 1743, by Samuel Lankton and John Hooker.

Court Record, Page 34—6 December, 1743: This Court grant Adms. on the estate of Charles Orvis, late of Farmingtown, unto Elizabeth Orvis and Ebenezer Gridley of Farmingtown, who gave bonds of £300 with Thomas Gridley of Farmingtown.

Page 43—14 May, 1744: An account of Adms. on the estate of Charles Orvis was now exhibited in Court by Ebenezer Gridley and Elizabeth Orvis, Adms.:

	£ s d
Paid in debts and charges,	160-01-07
Credit received,	3-09-00

Which account is allowed and ordered on file. Also, this Court have set out to the widow, of moveable estate of sd. decd. for her necessity, £9-05-11. A list thereof is on file.

Page 44—5 June, 1744: Ebenezer Gridley and Elizabeth Orvis, Adms. on the estate of Charles Orvis, late of Farmingtown, show to this Court, by a copy of record, that the General Assembly in Hartford, at their session in May last, granted liberty to the Adms. to make sale of so much of the real estate of the sd. decd. as may be sufficient to pay the sum of £11-18-04 old tenor with incident charges, taking the advice of the Court of Probate in Hartford therein.

Page 21 (Vol. XV) 6 May, 1746: A further account of debts due on the estate of Charles Orvis, late of Farmington, was now exhibited in Court by Ebenezer Gridley and Elizabeth Orvis, Adms., which amounts to the sum of £9-04-03. Account allowed.

Page 87.

Palmer, Stephen, Windsor. Invt. £186-12-05. Taken 25 March, 1743, by Josiah Phelps 3rd and George Griswold, Jr.

Court Record, Page 18—1st March, 1743: This Court grant Adms. on the estate of Stephen Palmer, late of Windsor decd., unto Timothy Palmer of sd. Windsor, brother of the sd. decd., who gave bond with Josiah Phelps of Windsor for £200 of money.

Page 89 (Vol. XV) 7 February, 1748-9: Whereas, this Court did grant Adms. unto Timothy Palmer, who now being deceased and never having rendered an account of his Adms. to this Court, and the relict of sd. deceased now being married to Joshua Case, Jr., of Simsbury, and they both appearing in Court and desiring the Court to appoint Samuel Palmer Adms., this Court do so order. And the sd. Samuel Palmer gave bond with Capt. Peletiah Mills of sd. Windsor for £1000.

Page 95—1st Tuesday of April, 1749: Capt. Peletiah Mills of Windsor, attorney in behalf of Joshua Case, Jr., and his wife Lydia, the relict of Stephen Palmer of Windsor, moves to this Court that her right of dowry may be set out to her: Whereupon this Court appoint and impower Josiah Phelps the 3rd and Nathaniel Loomis the 3rd to set out to the sd. Lydia 1-3 part of the lands of the deceased.

Page 61.

Peck, Abell, Doctor, Kensington. Invt. £160-18-03. Taken 3 December, 1742, by Samuel Bronson, David Sage and William Burnham, Jr.

Court Record, Page 12—2 November, 1742: Adms. granted to Elisha Peck of Middletown, who gave bond with Samuel Peck of Farmington for £500.

Perry, William. Court Record, Page 40—6 March, 1743-4: This Court grant Adms. on the estate of William Perry, late of Hartford decd., unto Jonathan Merrells of New Hartford, who gave bonds with Hezekiah Merrells of Hartford for £100.

Page 171.

Persons, Aaron, Kensington, in Farmington. Invt. £417-09-09. Taken February, 1744-5, by Samuel Peck and Joseph Hopkins.

Court Record, Page 55—5 March, 1744-5: Adms. granted unto Sarah Persons, widow and relict of sd. deceased, who gave bonds with Joseph Hills of Wallingford, in the County of New Haven, for £500.

Page 41 (Vol. XV) 7 July, 1747: Sarah Persons, Adms., exhibited an account of her Adms. Account allowed. This Court appoint Sarah Persons, widow, to be guardian to her children, viz., Lois Persons, age 6 years, and Content Persons, age 4 years, children of Aaron Persons, late deceased. Recog., £200 for each minor.

Will on Page 53-4. Invt. on Page 58-9.

Phelps, Cornelius, Windsor. Inventory taken 10 December, 1742, by John Cook 2nd, Samuel Enno and William Barbour:

	£ s d
The moveables, exclusive of notes and bonds, is	509-09-05
The house, £40; barn, £60; 30 acres of land, £24 per acre, £720,	820-00-00
To 18 acres of land on which Cornelius's house stands,	200-00-00
12 acres at £17 per acre, £200; 12 acres, £190,	390-00-00
6 1-2 acres at £28 per acre,	182-00-00
5 acres of land at £30 per acre,	150-00-00
8 1-2 acres of land at £32-10 per acre,	275-05-00
1 1-2 acre of land at £12 per acre,	18-00-00
15 acres of land at £12 per acre,	275-00-00
34 acres at Milbrook, £204; 106 acres, £200,	404-00-00
A lott of land in Torrington and another in Barkhampsted,	200-00-00
To 7 acres of land at £4 per acre,	28-00-00
Some money due by notes and bonds.	

Will dated 8 March, 1741-2:

I, Cornelius Phelps of Windsor, do make this my last will and testament: Imprimis: I give unto my wife Sarah forever 1-3 part of my moveable estate; also the use of 1-2 of my houseing and lands during her natural life. I give to my son Cornelius lands I have already given him, and the residue of a bond given me by Jacob Phelps obliging him to give me a deed of land. I give unto my son John 1 parcel of land containing 12 acres, lying on the west side of the street and bounding south on the heirs of Samuel Phelps decd. I give unto my son Timothy 2 pieces of land, one lying at the old house and the other across the way near to it, both containing about 12 acres. I give to my son Isaac my dwelling house, barn and homestead, containing about 26 acres, bounding north by ye street, on the heirs of Samuel Phelps, and to go east as far as Peter Brown's acre as it is called. Also I give to my son Isaac, as a peculiar gift, my tools and provisions made for a blacksmith. Also, whereas I have hereby given to my son Isaac in houseing and lands to a greater value than to the rest of my sons, my will is that my three sons, Cornelius, John and Timothy, shall have in my other lands indifferently taken till each of them be made equal at inventory apprisement with Isaac's houseing and lands, only excepting from all my sons my wife's improvement as given to her. I give unto my daughter Sarah Hutchingson, and to her heirs and assigns forever, £120, to be paid to her in moveable estate. My will is that my four sons aforenamed shall in equal share be at the trouble, cost and charge of providing for Samuel Mansfield during his natural life for ye necessaries thereof. And in case that they or either of them neglect or refuse to do the same, that then he or they shall fall short in his or their portions accordingly, and the same be improved for the support and comfort of the sd. Samuel Mansfield from time to time. Lastly, my will is that after my funeral charges, just debts and legacies are paid and Samuel Mansfield duly provided for, that the residue of my estate, both real and personal, shall be equally divided among my four sons in equal shares. I appoint my sons Cornelius, John and Timothy to be executors.

Witness: *Henry Allyn,*   CORNELIUS PHELPS, LS.
Hezekiah Phelps, Abigail Phelps.

Court Record, Page 11—5 October, 1742: The last will and testament of Cornelius Phelps, late of Windsor deceased, was now exhibited in Court by the executors. Accepted and ordered to be recorded.

Page 130-1.

Phelps, Ephraim, Simsbury. Invt. £641-17-04. Taken 2 December, 1743, by Isaac Gillett, Joshua Holcomb and Samuel Owen. Will dated 18 July, 1740.

I, Ephraim Phelps of Simsbury, in the County of Hartford, being occasionally called to go into His Majestie's service in an expedition against some of the Spanish settlements in the West Indies, in America, do therefore make this my last will and testament: I give to my eldest son, Asa Phelps, the sum of £5 within one year after he arrives to the age of 21 years. I give to my 2nd son, David Phelps, £5 money or the value thereof when he shall arrive to the age of 21 years. I give to my 3rd son, Jonathan Phelps, £5 out of my estate when he arrives at the age of 21 years. I give to my 4th son, Elihu Phelps, at age of 21 years, the sum of £5. I give to my little daughter, Sarah Phelps, the sum of £5 when she shall arrive to the age of 18 years. All the remainder of my estate that I have or shall die possessed of, both real and personal, lands, money, goods, chattells, and all my estate whatever, I give to Sarah, my true and loving wife, to be to her own use and behoof forever after my decease. I nominate Elijah Owen and my wife Sarah Phelps to be sole executors.

Witness: *Isaac Gillett,*   EPHRAIM PHELPS, LS.
John Holcomb, Jr., John Loomis.

Court Record, Page 37—7 February, 1743-4: The last will and testament of Ephraim Phelps, late of Simsbury decd., was now exhibited in Court by Sarah Phelps, widow and relict. Will proven. Exhibit of an inventory. Ordered recorded and kept on file.

Page 135.

Pike, James, Southington. Invt. £48-18-11. Taken 21 July, 1743, by Hezekiah Lee and Thomas Barnes.

Court Record, Page 26—5 July, 1743: This Court grant Adms. on the estate of James Pike, late of Farmingtown decd., unto Sarah Pike, widow, and John Rue, who gave bond with William Rockwell of Middletown.

Page 41—April, 1744: John Rue, of Farmingtown, Adms. on the estate of James Pike, late of Farmingtown decd., informs this Court that he suspects the estate insolvent, and prays commissioners may be appointed: Whereupon this Court appoint Capt. John Webster and Mr. Robert Cook, of sd. Farmingtown, commissioners.

Page 42—April, 1744: This Court have set out a list of moveables out of the estate of James Pike to his widow, to the value of £12-13-00, old tenor, and an account thereof is on file.

Page 47—7 August, 1744: An account of Adms. on the estate of James Pike, late of Farmingtown, was now exhibited in Court by John Rue, Adms.: Paid in debts and charges, £6-19-06. Which account is allowed and ordered to be kept on file. Also, now exhibited a report of the commissioners appointed to adjust the claims of the creditors, which report is accepted and ordered to be kept on file.

Page 194.

Pinney, Lurane, Windsor. Invt. £30-15-03. Taken 4 November, 1745, by Gillet Addams and Daniel Tuller.

Court Record, Page 61—6 August, 1745: This Court grant Adms. on the estate of Lurane Pinney, late of Windsor, unto her mother Elizabeth Pinney, who gave bonds with Azariah Pinney of sd. Windsor for £300.

Will on Page 65. Invt. on Page 80-81.

Plumb, Joseph, Farmington. Invt. £401-03-01. Taken 29 June, 1742, by John Hickox and Gideon Peck. Names and ages of the children as followeth: Lois Plumb, 13 years old 8 November, 1741; Thankfull

Plumb, 11 years old 29 day of January last; Amariah Plumb, 8 years old 6 September, 1741; Sibell Plumb, 6 years old 5 June, 1741; Simeon Plumb, 3 years old 10 October, 1741; Gamaliel Plumb, one year old 20 April, 1742; Susannah Plumb, one year old 20 April, 1742. Will dated 22 September, 1741.

I, Joseph Plumb of Milford, East Farm, in the County of New Haven and Colony of Connecticut, being in health of body and mind but sensible of my mortality, not knowing how soon I may die, I am desirous that what God has given me in this world may be disposed of according to my mind after my decease. I make this my last will and testament: Whereby I bequeath my soul to God who gave it and my body to the earth by a decent burial, in sure hope to receive the same at the general resurrection. After just debts and funeral charges are paid, I give, bequeath and dispose of my estate in manner and form following, viz.: To my wife Thankfull Plumb 1-3 part of my land during her natural life, and 1-3 of my moveable estate forever. And the other 2-3, both real and personal, to be equally divided both for quantity and quality between all the surviving children that I had by my sd. wife Thankfull Plumb; and at her decease the other third of land to be divided after the same manner to the sd. children; for all the children I had by my former wife have already had their portions in full. And I do put, constitute. and appoint my present wife Thankfull Plumb my sole executrix of this my last will and testament. In confirmation thereof I have set to my hand and fixed my seal.

Signed and sealed in   JOSEPH PLUMB, LS.
presence of *Israel Baldwin,*
Abigail X *Beech, Thomas Beech.*

Court Record, Page 7—9 June, 1742: The last will and testament of Joseph Plumb, late of Farmingtown deceased, was now exhibited in Court by Thankfull Plumb, executrix, said will being proven and ordered recorded.

Page 16—1st February, 1742-3: An inventory of the estate of Joseph Plumb, late of Farmingtown, was now exhibited in Court by Thankfull Plumb, widow and executrix, which inventory is approved and ordered to be recorded.

Page 31—4 October, 1743: A list of debts due from the estate of Joseph Plumb, late of Farmingtown decd., was now exhibited in Court by Hezekiah Rue, executor by marriage with his wife, the widow and relict of the sd. decd. (viz., Thankfull Plumb, executrix to the last will and testament of the sd. decd.), which account is accepted and ordered to be kept on file.

Page 41—1744: Whereas, the General Assembly at New Haven, on the 2nd Thursday of October, 1743, did appoint Mr. Joseph Gaylord of Farmingtown to make sale of so much of the real estate of Joseph Plumb, late of sd. Farmingtown decd., as will raise the sum of £51-17-11 old tenor, with incident charges, taking advice of the Court of Probate in the County of Hartford: Whereupon this Court direct Mr. Gaylord to make sale of the whole of the land of the sd. decd. that is in sd. Farmingtown, which land butts north on Huss River so called, being at or near the place where a grist mill is erected, being about 4 1-2 acres. And that sd. Joseph Gaylord set up advertisements on some publick places in sd. Farmingtown 20 days before the sale, signifying sd. land will be sold at publick vandue at such a day and time of day, to the highest bidder at beat of the drum.

Page 43—14 May, 1744: Lois Plumb, a minor, 15 years of age, daughter of Joseph Plumb, chose Samuel Gaylord of Farmington to be her guardian. Recog., £200.

Page 46—7 August, 1744: A return of the sale of land of Joseph Plumb was now exhibited in Court by Joseph Gaylord, whereby it appears they sold 4 acres of land and a mill place, upon which a sawmill is now erected, for £77-04-00, which was sold to John Rue of sd. Farmington. Account accepted.

Page 103 (Vol. XV) 15 June, 1749: Amariah Plumb, a minor, 16 years of age, son of Joseph Plumb, chose his uncle Joseph Gaylord to be his guardian. Recog., £500.

Page 109—31 October, 1749: Sibbel Plumb, a minor, 14 years of age, daughter of Joseph Plumb, chose Deacon David Gaylord to be her guardian. Recog., £500.

Page 24 (Vol. XVII) 25 April, 1754: Simeon Plumb, a minor, 15 years of age, son of Joseph Plumb, chose Deacon David Gaylord to be his guardian. Recog., £300.

Page 84—29 October, 1755: Gamaliel Plumb, a minor, 15 years of age, son of Joseph Plumb, chose Deacon David Gaylord to be his guardian. Recog., £100.

Page 25-6-7.

Porter, Joseph, Windsor. Invt. £228-02-02. Taken 29 January, 1742, by Hezekiah Porter and Joseph Phelps. Will dated 20 April, 1734.

I, Joseph Porter, of the Town of Windsor, do make this my last will and testament: I give to my wife Hannah 1-3 part of my houseing and lands, to be to her use during her natural life; and 1-3 part of my moveable estate forever. I give to my son Joseph Porter, besides what I have already given him, my lower lott in the meadow which I bought of my brother Nathaniel Porter, and also the upper lott, bounding south on Joseph Newbery's land; the 1-2 part of my rights in Torrington, the 1-2 of my lott in the 1 1-2-mile division, the 1-2 part of the equivalent lands, and the 1-2 of the commons and undivided lands in the Township of Windsor, to him, his heirs and assigns forever, he paying to my daughters Hannah and Mehetabell his equal part with my son Nathaniel so much as to make them up £150 each with what I have already given them. I give to my son Nathaniel Porter my homelott on which I dwell, the whole of it, with my dwelling house and barn and all other buildings thereon erected; also the 1-2 part of my right and share in Torrington,

1-2 part of my lott in the 1 1-2-mile division, 1-2 part of the equivalent land, and the 1-2 part of my right in the common and undivided land in the Township of Windsor, to him and his heirs forever, he paying to my daughters Hannah and Mehetabell his equal part with my son Joseph so much as to make them up £150 each with what I have already given them. I give to my daughter Hannah Watson so much of my estate, to be paid by my executors hereafter mentioned, as to make up with what I have already given her the sum of £150 in money. I give to my daughter Mehetabell Lyman so much of my estate as to make with what I have already given her the sum of £150 as money. I appoint my two sons, Joseph Porter and Nathaniel Porter, executors.

Witness: *Odiah Loomis,*   JOSEPH PORTER, LS.
Timothy Loomis, Hannah Loomis.

Court Record, Page 1—6 April, 1742: The last will and testament of Joseph Porter, late of Windsor, was now exhibited in Court by Joseph and Nathaniel Porter, executors. Proven and ordered to be recorded.

Page 23—3 May, 1743: Widow Hannah Porter, relict of Joseph Porter, late of Windsor decd., moved to this Court that her right of dower may be set out to her, and also that her right in the moveable estate be distributed to her according to the will: Whereupon this Court appoint Joshua Wolcott, Jr., Capt. Joseph Loomis and Moses Loomis, of Windsor, to be distributors.

Page 102.

Porter, Timothy, Farmington. Invt. £3030-00-00. Taken 4 February, 1743, by John Hart and Elisha Lewis.

Court Record, Page 29—6 September, 1743: This Court grant Adms. on the estate of Timothy Porter, late of Farmington, unto Timothy Porter of Farmington, who gave bond with Jonathan Olcot of Hartford for £500. Exhibited an inventory, which is ordered recorded.

Page 162-3.

Price, Zachariah, Glastonbury. Died 31 May, 1744. Invt. £174-10-00. Taken by Hezekiah Wright and Elizur Talcott.

Court Record, Page 53—5 February, 1744-5: An inventory of the estate of Zachariah Price, late of Glastonbury, by Samuel Price, Adms., which inventory is accepted and ordered to be recorded. Also, the sd. Adms. now exhibited an account of Adms.: Paid in debts and charges, £13-08-10. Adms. moves for a distribution of the estate.

	£ s d
Inventory,	174-10-00
Debts subtracting,	13-08-10
There remains to be distributed,	£160-11-02

To Samuel Price, to the children of John Price, to Ebenezer, to Robert, to John, to Francis, to Zachariah Price, to heirs of Dorothy Price (alias Colt), to Sarah Price, alias Hollister, to Elizabeth Price and to Mary Price, to each of them the sum or value of £14-11-11 to be their own forever. And this Court appoint Elizur Talcott, Samuel Talcott and Josiah Benton, of Glastonbury, distributors.

Page 7 (Vol. XV) 4 February, 1745-6: Report of the distributors:

From File:

	£ s d
To Robert Price, part of a hogs'd of rhum,	17-06-00
To Elizabeth Price, part of a hogs'd of rhum,	17-06-00
To Mary Price, part of a hogs'd of rhum,	17-06-00
To John Price the remaining part of the hogs'd of rhum,	8-02-00
Sundry goods,	9-04-00
To Francis Price, sundry goods,	17-06-00
To Zachariah Price, in sugar, cash and goods,	17-06-00
To Elizur Price,	17-06-00
To Ebenezer Price,	17-06-00
To Jabish Coult and Dority his wife, cash, £11-04-06,	17-06-00
To William Hollister's wife Sarah,	17-06-00
To Samuel Price, Jr.,	32-13-03

20 December, 1745.   Samuel Talcott, } Distributors.
                            Elizur Talcott, }

Page 182-3.

Ranny, Joseph, Middletown. Will dated 1st July, 1740: I, Joseph Ranny of Middletown, in the County of Hartford, being advanced in years, do make this my last will and testament: Imprimis: I give unto Mary, my wife, 1-3 part of all my household goods, and one good cow, six sheep and one swine, all which to be at her own dispose. I also give her the use of 1-3 part of all my buildings and improved lands (and for wood which I have reserved for her in the deed which I have given to my son) during the time that she shall remain my widow. And whereas, I have by deeds of gift disposed of all my real estate to and among my three sons, Joseph, Daniel and Jonathan, I also hereby give them all and every part of my personal estate whatsoever that I have not herein given to my wife, hereby also obliging my sd. three sons to pay all my just debts, funeral charges and legacies after mentioned, viz.: To Edward Shepherd and Mary Shepherd, the only children of my daughter Mary Shepherd decd., £40 money; to my daughter Abigail Stocking, £40 money; to my daughter Sibell Porter, £40 money; and to Lucia Stocking and Grace Stocking, the only children of my dafter Rachel Stocking decd., the sum of £40 money; which my sd. sons shall pay in the parts following: Joseph, £45; Daniel, £45; and Jonathan the remaining £70;

which legacies my sd. sons shall pay to such of my sd. daughters and grandchildren as shall be at lawfull age at my decease; 1-2 thereof within three months after my decease, and the other half within 9 months after my decease. And those of my sd. grandchildren that shall not be of lawful age at my decease shall receive their legacies as they come to lawful age. I appoint my three sons, Joseph Ranny, Daniel Ranny and Jonathan Ranny, executors.

Witness: *Isaac White,*   JOSEPH RANNY, LS.
John Schovell, William Rockwell.

Court Record, Page 57—2 April, 1745: The last will and testament of Joseph Ranny, late of Middletown decd., was now exhibited in Court by Joseph and Daniel Ranny, which will being proven, was ordered to be recorded.

Read, Joseph. Court Record, Page 48—8 October, 1744: Pursuant to an act of the General Assembly holden at Hartford 10th May, 1744, impowering Ebenezer and Sarah Humphrey, Adms. on the estate of Joseph Read, late of Oxford, to sell the 100 acres of land mentioned in the memorial of the sd. Adms., or so much thereof as may be necessary to pay and discharge the debts due from the estate of the sd. decd. and the necessary charges thereof, at the direction of the Court of Probate in the District of Hartford: Whereupon this Court directs the sd. Adms. to set up advertisement at some publick places in the towns of Wethersfield, Glastonbury and Hartford, on the east side of the Great River, signifying that there is to be sold at such a day and time of day, at the beat of the drum, to the highest bidder, such a piece or parcel of land lying and being in the Township of Glastonbury, in ye Parish of Eastbery.

NOTE: The debts exceed the personal estate £488-19-06 old tenor.

Page 52—20 January, 1744-5: An account of sundry charges against the estate of Joseph Read, late of Oxford, in the County of Worcester, decd., arising on the same, a piece of land in Glastonbury was now exhibited in Court by John Holden, attorney to Ebenezer and Sarah Humphrey, Adms. on sd. estate, by which account it appears the charges aforesd. in the whole amount to £22-17-00, which account is allowed and ordered to be kept on file. Also, the sd. John Holden made it appear to this Court that he sold sd. land at publick vandue according to the directions of this Court, and that he sd. Holden bid £176-10-00 money, old tenor, which was 25 shillings more than any other person bid on sd. land, which return of the sale of the sd. land is approved and ordered on file.

Inventory in Vol. XV, Page 2.

Reave, Robert, Hartford. Invt. £830-14-08. Taken 5 November, 1745, by Thomas Seymour, Joseph Skinner, Jr., and Moses Seymour.

Court Record, Page 65—5 November, 1745: Adms. granted unto Sarah Reave, widow, on the estate of Robert Reave, late of Hartford deceased, and unto Timothy Seymour, who gave bond with Michael Burnham for £500.

Riley, Jonathan. Court Record, Page 14—24 December, 1742: This Court appoint Jonathan Riley to be guardian to his sons, viz., Jonathan, a minor, 14 years of age, and Charles Riley, 13 years. Recog., £300.

Page 122-3.

Roberts, John, Middletown. Invt. £130-08-00. Taken 13 September, 1742, by Jabez Brooks and Stephen Blake.

Court Record, Page 21—5 April, 1743: It was certified to this Court by *Giles Hall, J. P.,* that Giles Roberts, Huldah Roberts and Sibbel Roberts chose their uncle William Roberts of Middletown to be their guardian. Recog., £200. And this Court appoint the widow Martha Roberts, the relict of John Roberts of Middletown decd., to be guardian to Jonathan Roberts, age 12 years; David, age 10 years; Gideon, age 8 years; Ruth, age 5 years; Sarah, age 4 years; and Annah, age 2 years. Recog., £200.

Adms. to Martha Roberts, widow, who gave bond with William Roberts for £400.

Page 19 (Vol. XV) 5 August, 1746: Martha Roberts, Adms., exhibited an account of her Adms. Accepted. Order distribution of the estate as followeth:

	£ s d
To Martha, the widow, her thirds,	10-03-00
To John Roberts, the eldest son, his double part,	3-02-06
To Simeon, Giles, Jonathan, David and Gideon Roberts, to each,	1-11-03
And to Martha Roberts (alias Brooks), Hulda, Sibbell, Ruth, Sarah and Hannah Roberts, daughters, to each,	1-11-03

And appoint William Rockwell, Joseph Johnson and Henry Hedges, of Middletown, distributors. Also the Court order that the 1-3 of the lands and buildings be set out to the widow for her improvement during life.

Page 27—4 November, 1746: Jonathan Roberts, a minor, 16 years of age, and David Roberts, age 14 years, sons of John Roberts, chose their uncle Samuel Lewcas of Middletown to be their guardian. Recog., £300.

Page 80—6 December, 1748: Gideon Roberts, age 14 years, son of John Roberts, chose his uncle Jonathan Roberts to be his guardian. Recog., £500.

Will from File.

Robbins, Joshua, Wethersfield. Will dated 4 April, 1733. No inventory or distribution found.

I, Joshua Robbins of Stepney, in Wethersfield, do make this my last will: I give to Sarah, my wife, the improvement of one-third part of my buildings and lands (excepting my lands at Newington). I give to my wife one-third part of all my moveable estate, and twenty pounds in money, to be her own property; also, one-fourth part of what my grist mill brings in yearly. I give to my son Nathaniel Robbins (several tracts of land) and order that he shall pay to my daughters, Sarah and Hannah Robbins, the sum of two hundred pounds (to each of them one hundred pounds), to be paid at or before their marriage. I give to my son Zebulon Robbins my land at Newington. I give to my son John Robbins my home lot and grist mill. (And other tracts.) And order that he shall pay to my daughters, Elizabeth and Abigail Robbins, the sum of two hundred pounds (to each of them one hundred pounds), at or before their marriage. I give to each of my daughters, Sarah and Hannah Robbins, one hundred pounds in money, to be paid by my son Nathaniel Robbins as before mentioned, together with what moveable estate is called hers. I give to my daughters, Elizabeth and Abigail Robbins, the sum of two hundred pounds in money (to each of them one hundred), to be paid by my son John as above mentioned. I further order that the remainder of my moveable estate, not disposed of as above mentioned, be equally divided among my sons. I constitute and appoint my wife Sarah Robbins and my son Nathaniel Robbins to be executors.

Witness: *Daniel Russel,*   JOSHUA ROBINS, LS.
        Joseph Grimes,
        Jonathan Rily.

Court Record, Page 95 (Vol. XI) 3 July, 1733: Will exhibited in Court by Sarah Robbins and Nathaniel Robbins, executors named in sd. will. Proven.

Page 46-7.

Rockwell, Josiah, Windsor. Invt. £359-16-11. Taken 21 December, 1742, by Joseph Stedman, Joshua Loomis and Nathaniel Loomis. Will dated 2nd day of July, 1742.

I, Josiah Rockwell, being old and infirm, do make this my last will and testament: I give to my wife Rebeckah my best bedd and furniture, this to be over and above her right of dowry in my houseing and lands and moveables. I give to my son Josiah Rockwell the 1-2 of the western half of that piece or parcel of land on which I now dwell, together with the buildings thereon standing, to him and his heirs forever. I give to my son Ezra Rockwell the other half, viz., the eastern half of that piece or parcel of land on which I now dwell, to him and his heirs forever. I give to my son Josiah Rockwell and to my son Ezra Rockwell all my right, interest, share and part to and in the land called the equivalent land; also all my right, interest, share and part to and in the common land in Windsor, to them and their heirs forever, share and share alike. My will is that my son Josiah Rockwell shall pay to my daughter Rebeckah, the wife of Andrew Carrier, the sum of £1, 7 shillings and 9 pence besides what she hath already had. And to my daughter Ruth Rockwell, £18-15-00 besides what she hath already had. And to my daughter Waitstill Rockwell the sum of £18-15-00 besides what she hath already had. And to my daughter Eunice Rockwell £25. All current money or bills of publick credit according to the old tenor. After my just debts and funeral expenses are paid, all the rest of my estate, both real and personal, I give to my two sons and four daughters, Josiah Rockwell, Ezra Rockwell, Rebeckah (the wife of Andrew Carrier), Ruth Rockwell, Waitstill Rockwell and Eunice Rockwell, to them and their heirs forever, share and share alike. I appoint my two sons, Josiah Rockwell and Ezra Rockwell, to be executors.

Witness: *Ebenezer Warner,*   Josiah Rockwell, ls.
Matthew Rockwell, Ebenezer Stedman.

Court Record, Page 3—21 December, 1742: The last will and testament of Josiah Rockwell, late of Windsor decd., was now exhibited in Court by Josiah Rockwell and Ezra Rockwell, executors, which, being proven, was ordered to be recorded. Exhibited an inventory, which was ordered on file.

Page 196.

Root, Timothy, Farmington. Invt. £2498-16-05. **Taken 31 Oc**tober, 1745, by Isaac Cowles, Elisha Lewis and Samuel Nash. Will dated 2 April, 1745.

The last will and testament of Timothy Root: First, I give and bequeath unto my loving wife Mary Root the 1-2 part of all my moveable estate; also, I give unto my wife the improvement of my estate so long as she bear my name or until my children come of age. Second: I give my house and homestead unto my eldest son Timothy Root. Third: I give unto my 2nd son Theodore Root all the remainder of my lands. Fourth: I give unto my daughter Esther Root the other half of my moveable estate. Fifth: I do hereby ordain my brother Stephen Root, with my wife Mary Root, to be sole executors to this my last will and testament.

Witness: *Samuel Wadsworth,*   Timothy Root, ls.
Stephen Root, Samuel Nash.

Court Record, Page 96 (Vol. XV) 10 April, 1749: This Court appoint Mary Root, widow, to be guardian to her children, viz., Theodore Root, age 7 years, and Esther Root, 5 years, children of Timothy Root. Recog., £800 for each minor.

Page 97—10 April, 1749: This Court appoint Stephen Root to be guardian unto Timothy Root, a minor, age 8 years, son of Timothy Root deceased. Recog., £800.

Page 93 (Vol. XVI) 3 April, 1753: Stephen Root, guardian to Timothy Root, son of Lt. Timothy Root decd., being deceased, this Court now appoint the Rev. Mr. Samuel Newell of sd. Farmington guardian to sd. minor. Recog., £200.

Page 73.

Russell, Abell, Southington. Invt. £891-06-06. Taken 25 July, 1742, by Isaac Lewis and Samuel Root.

Court Record, Page 9—3 August, 1742: This Court grants Adms. on the estate of Abell Russell, late of Farmingtown decd., unto Eunice Russell, widow and relict, who gave bonds with Joshua Porter of Farmingtown for £500. Exhibited an inventory, which was ordered on file. Also, the Court set out to the sd. widow, of moveables of sd. estate, £21-06-10. A list thereof is on file.

Page 11—5 October, 1742: Eunice Russell, Adms., exhibited an account of her Adms., by which account it appears she has paid in debts and charges, £569-08-03. Account is accepted and ordered to be kept on file.

Page 12—2 November, 1742: Samuel Newell of Farmingtown being appointed with Eunice Russell, widow and Adms. on the estate of Abell Russell, late of Farmingtown decd., by the General Assembly holden at New Haven the 2nd Thursday of October, 1742, to sell so much of the land of the sd. decd. as shall procure the sum of £487-11-00, and by a mistake it appearing to this Court that the debts due from sd. estate do not surmount the moveable part of the inventory but the sum of £282-11-00: Whereupon this Court do direct the sd. Adms. with the sd. Samuel Newell to sell a piece of land in East Haven which belongs to the estate of the sd. decd., provided it be come into the possession of the heirs of the sd. decd., and so much of the land in Southington (in Farmingtown) which is butted and bounded south on Lt. Isaac Norton, west on a highway, east on a highway, and sd. lott contains about 130 acres more or less. And the Court direct the sd. Adms. and the sd. Mr. Newell to sell so much of either or both pieces of land as shall procure the sum of £282-11-00 with necessary charges thereon.

Page 40—6 March, 1743-4: Eunice Russell (alias Clark), with her present husband, Enos Clark, Adms. on the estate of Abell Russell, late of Farmingtown decd., have rendered to this Court an account of their Adms.:

	£	s	d
Paid in debts and charges,	40	15	09
There remains to be divided,	68	02	00
1-3 thereof to Eunice Russell (alias Clark),	22	13	05
And the remaining 2-3 to Abell Russell, only child,	45	06	09

And the Court appoint Samuel Newell and Eldad Lewis of Farming-town to make division of the estate and set out to the sd. Eunice Russell her right of dower in the real estate for her improvement during life. This Court do appoint John Chidley of East Haven, in the County of New Haven, to be guardian to Abell Russell, a minor, age 3 years, son of Abell Russell, late of Farmington decd., the mother consenting. Recog., £200.

Page 40—2 November, 1744: Then received of Enos Clark the sum of fourty-five pounds, six shillings and eight pence (£45-06-08) old tenor money on the account of money due from the administrator of the estate of Abell Russell, decd., unto Abell Russell his son. By me, guardian.

Witness: *Joshua Porter,*   JOHN CHEDSEY.
   Silas Clark.

Test: Joseph Talcott, Clerk.

Sage, Mary. Court Record, Page 53—5 February, 1744-5: This Court grant Adms. on the estate of Mary Sage, late of Wethersfield decd., unto Mary Stedman, the wife of Thomas Stedman of sd. Wethers-field, who gave bond with sd. Thomas Stedman for £300.

Page 92.

Savage, Jabez, Middletown. Invt. £654-15-01. Taken 19 October, 1743, by John Hall and Andrew Cornwall.

Court Record, Page 31—4 October, 1743: This Court grant Adms. on the estate of Jabez Savage, late of Middletown decd., unto John Savage of sd. Middletown, who gave bond with Niel McLean of Hart-ford for £500.

Page 48—2 October, 1744: An account of Adms. on the estate of Jabez Savage was now exhibited by John Savage, Adms.:

	£	s	d
Paid in debts and charges,	45	04	09
Credit received,	29	00	00

Which account is allowed and ordered on file.

Page 184-5.

Seager, Joseph, Simsbury. Invt. £1218-00-04. Taken 18 July, 1745, by Thomas Addams, James Cornish and Richard Cook. Will dated 6 May, 1745.

I, Joseph Seager, of Simsbury, in the County of Hartford, do make this my last will and testament: I give to my wife Mary 1-3 part of all my personal estate forever, and the improvement of all my improvable lands and buildings during life. I give to my son Joseph his double portion of all my estate, what I have already given to him to be accounted as part of his double portion. I give unto my son John and to my daughters Amy, Jemima, Mary, Anne and Rachel, to each of them an equal share of my estate, viz., to each of them £10 in value more than to my two youngest daughters. Also, I do give unto my two youngest daughters, Mehetabell and Elizabeth, to each of them an equal portion to be £10 in value less than my other daughters, the sd. £10 to be in value equal to bills of credit of the old tennor. And further, my will is that my two sons shall have all my real estate and that they pay to my daughters respectively so much as the personal estate shall want of making up to them each of their portions and to be paid by my two sons. I appoint my son Joseph, Mr. Lemuel Roberts and my wife Mary to be the executors.

Witness: *John Humphrey,*   JOSEPH SEAGER, LS.
Robert Hoskins, Timothy Addams.

Court Record, Page 61—6 August, 1745: The last will and testament of Joseph Seager, late of Simsbury, was now exhibited in Court by the executors. Proven. Exhibited an inventory, which was proven and ordered to be kept on file.

Page 62—6 August, 1745: Mehetabell Seager, age 15 years, and Elizabeth Seager, age 12 years, children of Joseph Seager, chose their brother Joseph Seager to be their guardian. Recog., £400. John Seager, age 17 years, son of Joseph Seager, chose Thomas Addams to be his guardian. Recog., £300.

Page 17 (Vol. XV) 7 July, 1746: Joseph Seager, who was appointed guardian to Elizabeth Seager and Mehetabel Seager, minor children, now for divers reasons desires to be dismissed from the trust of guardian to the sd. minors: Whereupon this Court do dismiss the sd. Joseph from the trust thereof, and the sd. minors, Mehetabell, 16 years, and Elizabeth, 13, made choice of John Brown of Windsor to be their guardian. Recog., £500.

Page 19—5 August, 1746: Thomas Addams of Simsbury, guardian to John Seager, desires to be discharged from his guardianship: Whereupon this Court discharges sd. Addams, and the sd. minor now made choice of Capt. James Goodrich of sd. Simsbury to be his guardian. Recog., £500.

Page 21—7 May, 1746: Joseph Seager, Mary Seager and Lemuel Roberts, executors to the last will of the deceased, moved to this Court for a distribution of sd. estate according to the will: Whereupon this Court appoint Capt. James Case, John Case and Michael Humphrey, of Simsbury, distributors.

Page 133—15 June, 1750: Report of the distributors. Accepted.

Page 107-8-9.

Sedgwick, Mary, Hartford. Inventory taken 25 November, 1743, by Daniel Webster and Moses Nash. Will dated 20 April, 1743.

I, Mary Sedgwick, relict of Samuel Sedgwick of Hartford decd., do make this my last will and testament: I give to my son Jonathan all my rights in the lands in Hartford on the east side of the Great River. Also, a meat barrel and a suet tub and 2 meal barrells and my great glass bottle. To my son Ebenezer I give one feather bed with 3 blankets, and my chest of drawers; also my old great kettle and my little iron pott. To my son Joseph I give a chest, bed and bedsted, and one blankett; also I give him the £6-10-00 which he borrowed of me some time ago; also a trammell, frying pan, a meat barrel and suet tub and the old worm tub. I give him my cow and 3 chaires; also I give him my iron mortar and pestle; also, one paire of shoes. To my son Stephen I give the bed on which I have been used to lye, with the bedsted and furniture, one trammell, one paire of hand irons, also ye fire shovel and tongs, and a meat barrel. To my son Benjamin I give all my right in the still; also my measures, viz., quart, pint and half-pint, he paying 20 shillings to his brother Joseph, old tennor. I give to Benjamin all the cooper's tools and my great Bible. And the rest of my books I would have divided among my children, also all my right in the undivided lands in Farmingtown. To the children of my daughter Abigail decd., my colliminco frock and Barcelona handkerchief and Druget petticoat. To the children of my daughter Mary decd., I give my best silk crape frock and sassenet handkerchief. To the children of my daughter Elizabeth decd. I give my other silk crape frock and a gause handkerchief and a paire of red gloves, also a red quilt. To my daughter Mercy I give my mourning crape frock, my black quilt and green riding hood. My blue cloak I give to my granddaughter Mercy Merrells. I give to my daughter Mercy my scarf and my silk apron, and my largest earthern pott, and my right in the side saddle. And my will is that if my daughter Mercy shall be taken away by death, my granddaughter Mercy Merrells shall have all I have bequeathed to her mother. To my granddaughter Ann Sedgwick I give my new chest and old box and great chest with one drawer, my silk hood, a paire of new silk gloves, and my box iron and heaters, my great pott, quart skillett, and little brass kettle, also my chafing dish and half a dozen chaires, 4 new chaires and two high table chaires, all my pewter (excepting the measures which I have given to Benjamin), also all that earthenware not before disposed of, my cheese tub and churn and pilion, as also my table and looking-glass. Moreover, my will is that my sons, Jonathan, Joseph, Stephen and Benjamin, have and injoy equally my right in the Farmingtown land butting on Hartford; as is also my will that my syder barrells be divided equally abong my sons. My will further is that my linen and wearing apparrel not already disposed of be equally divided among the children of my three daughters decd. and my daughter Mercy. Further, it is my will that my heifer and stilyards be sold to pay my debts. I give to the children of my son Samuel decd. 20 shillings old tennor, 5 shillings to each of them, and order my hetchel be sold to pay the same. I appoint my sons, Jonathan and Benjamin, executors.

Witness: *Benjamin Colton,*   MARY X SEDGWICK, LS.
Caleb Watson, Anne X Flower.

Court Record, Page 35—6 December, 1743: The last will and testament of Mary Sedgwick of Hartford, relict of Capt. Samuel Sedgwick of Hartford, was now exhibited in Court by the executors. Proven. Exhibit of an inventory, which was proven and ordered to be kept on file.

Page 149. Invt. in Vol. XV, Page 95.

Shailer, Abiell, Bolton. Invt. £105-11-00. Taken by Thomas Loomis and Matthew Loomis. Will dated 20 December, 1742.

I, Abiell Shailer of Bolton, in the County of Hartford, do make this my last will and testament: I give to my wife Hannah 1-3 part of my moveable estate, and one cow over and above sd. third part, to be to her and her heirs and assigns forever. Also, I give her the use of my 50 acres of land I now live on, with the buildings and appurtenances, so long as she continues my widow. And in case she should see cause to marry again, then I will her £10 money, to be paid her by my executor. I give to my grandson Abraham Hills £20, to be paid him as hereafter provided. I give to my daughter Jemima Dart £30. I give to my daughter Mary Grover £30. I give to my daughter Sarah Fitch no more than what I have already given her. I give to my son Ephraim Shailer 5 shillings with what I have already given him. I give to my son Reuben 5 shillings besides what I have given him. I give unto my daughter Hannah £26 to be paid her as hereafter provided. I give to my daughter Miriam £30, to be paid her as hereafter provided. I give to my daughter Thankfull £30. I give to my son Timothy my 30 acres lying in what is called Allin's farm, and also my 10-acre division called the 6th division. I give to my son Ebenezer my 50 acres I live on, with the orchard, buildings and appurtenances, after my wife's marriage or death. My will further is, that all my just debts be paid out of my moveables, and the remainder of the moveables, besides my wife's third part, be paid and distributed to pay the above named legacies so far as they will extend. And the remainder of sd. legacies I do hereby order my son Ebenezer to pay. I hereby order my friends, Mr. John Bissell and Sergt. Francis Smith, both of Bolton, executors.   ABIEL SHAILER, LS.

Witness: *John Bissell,*
Hannah Bissell, Lucy Bissell.

Court Record, Page 50—6 November, 1744: Will proven.

Page 58—15 May, 1745: Timothy Shailer, a minor, age 16 years, son of Abiell Shailer of Bolton, chose Thomas Pitkin of Bolton to be his guardian. Recog., £500.

Page 14 (Vol. XV) 3 June, 1746: An inventory of sd. estate was exhibited in Court by John Bissell, executor. Accepted. Also, the sd. executor informs this Court that he suspects the estate insolvent, and prays that commissioners may be appointed to adjust the claims of the creditors: Whereupon this Court appoint Ichabod Welles, William Cole and Isaac Griswold, of Bolton, commissioners.

Shaw, John. Court Record, Page 57—2 April, 1745: John Shaw, a minor, 11 years of age, son of John Shaw, late of Hartford decd.: His mother, Martha Shaw, to be his guardian. Recog., £300.

Sheilds, Bryant. Court Record, Page 35—6 December, 1743: Jerusha Sheilds, a minor, 13 years of age, daughter of Bryant Sheilds of Glastonbury deceased, chose Ebenezer Kilbourn of sd. Glastonbury to be her guardian. Recog., £100.

Page 112 (Vol. XV) 3 June, 1749: Daniel Shields, a minor, 16 years of age, son of Bryant Sheilds, chose his brother-in-law Alpheus Gustin to be his guardian. Recog., £500.

Page 186-7, 194.

Shepherd, Samuel, Hartford. Invt. £453-07-00. Taken by Thomas Hosmer and Stephen Hosmer. Will dated 1st February, 1741-2.

I, Samuel Shepherd of Hartford, do make this my last will and testament: I give to Ephraim, son to Susannah Shepherd decd., if he live to the age of 21 years, my house and land in the west division, from the highway running north and south to my bounds, and extending westward to the ditch or drain about 80 rods in length, excepting about 2 1-2 acres I have already given to Zebulon Shepherd. I give to Rebeckah Shepherd, daughter of my brother Thomas Shepherd, 6 1-2 acres butting east upon the abovesd. land or ditch, north on Timothy Skinner's land, south on my brother Thomas Shepherd's land, and west on my own land. My will is that if my executor see cause to keep the two above described pieces of land, paying to each of them the sum of £72 in bills of credit of this Colony, he shall have power so to do and hold it to himself and assigns forever. I give all the remainder of my lands in sd. township to my brother Thomas Shepherd in consideration of his two children, namely, Ebenezer and Jane, being uncapable of any service, to be at his dispose for the above named children forever. My will is that if the above named Ephraim doth not arrive to the age of 21 years, the above demised shall be and remain for the use of Ebenezer and Jane, or the money. I appoint my kinsman Zebulon Shepherd, son of my brother Thomas Shepherd, to be my executor.

Witness: *William Gaylord,*   SAMUEL SHEPHERD, LS.
William Kelsey, John Whiting.

Whereas, Samuel Shepherd, late of Hartford decd., by his last will gave to Ephraim Tucker, son to Susannah Shepherd decd., the sum of £72 in bills of credit of this Colony, which sum I have received to my full satisfaction of Zebulon Shepherd, executor to sd. will, I do discharge sd. executor from any demands relateing to the same. As witness my hand this 18th day of February, 1754.

Witness: *Daniel Ensign,*   EPHRAIM TUCKER, JR.
John Whiting, Jr.

Court Record, Page 56—2 April, 1745: The last will of Samuel Shepherd, late of Hartford decd., was now exhibited in Court by Zebulon Shepherd, executor. Proven and ordered to be recorded.

Page 134, 138-9.

Shepherd, Thomas, Hartford. Invt. £657-09-11. Taken 13 March, 1744, by William Gaylord, John Whiting and Timothy Skinner. Will dated 2 February, 1741-2.

I, Thomas Shepherd of Hartford, do make this my last will and testament: Imprimis: I give to my daughter Deborah £80. I give to my daughter Sarah £80. I give to my daughter Mary £80. All which sums annexed to their names I order my executors to pay the same either in money (or lands at £10 per acre) as he thinks fit, as soon as with conveniency it may be. I give the remainder of my lands in the Township of Hartford, or in the Township of Windsor, or in any other places as if particularly mentioned, after my sd. daughters' legacies are paid into the hands of my executors, to be disposed of for the payment of my just debts and for the maintenance of my wife Jane, and my loving brother Samuel Shepherd, and my son Ebenezer and my daughter Jane, both of sd. children being uncapable of takeing care of themselves. And that my sd. land may be kept together, I give my executor full power to pay £10 per acre and hold the lands to himself and his heirs and assigns forever, that is to say, so much as is of necessity to be sold for the abovesd. use by the judgement of my friends or neighbors. And if it should be so ordered by Providence that they should not continue in the world to expend the whole of my estate left, then my will is that for what remains my exectuor shall pay the sum of £10 per acre and hold the same to himself forever, which money shall be equally divided amongst all my children excepting my son Thomas Shepherd, to whom I have already made a deed of land equivalent. I appoint my son Zebulon Shepherd to be sole executor.

Witness: *William Gaylord,*   THOMAS SHEPHERD, LS.
William Kelsey, John Hubbard.

Court Record, Page 39—6 March, 1743-4: The last will and testament of Thomas Shepherd, late of Hartford, was now exhibited in Court by Zebulon Shepherd, executor. Proven and ordered to be recorded.

Page 41—April, 1744: Zebulon Shepherd, executor to the last will of Thomas Shepherd, moved to this Court that freeholders may be appointed to set out to the widow and relict of the sd. decd. her dowry in sd. estate: Whereupon this Court appoint Colonel John Whiting, Deacon William Gaylord and Timothy Skinner, of Hartford, to set out to the widow 1-3 part of the real estate of the sd. decd. for her improvement during life, and make return thereof to this Court. Also, the executor exhibited an inventory, which was accepted and ordered on file.

Page 11 (Vol. XV) 6 May, 1746: A return of the setting out of the widow Jane Shepherd's dowry, under the hands of Col. John Whiting, William Gaylord and Timothy Skinner, distributors, was exhibited and accepted.

Page 45—1st September, 1747: An account of Adms. was exhibited by Zebulon Shepherd, executor. Accepted.

Page 129.

Skinner, John, Hartford. Will dated 19 September, 1741: I, John Skinner of Hartford, do make this my last will and testament: I give to my wife Rachel Skinner the 1-3 part of my moveable estate forever, and the use and improvement of all my houseing and lands which I have not already disposed of during her natural life. I give unto my eldest son John Skinner my lott at Rocky Hill, and my lott at the South Meadow which I bought of Hezekiah Hopkins, and also my lott in the sd. meadow which I bought of John Easton, together with my right in the land commonly called the Five-Miles, lying on the east side of the Great River, to be unto him, his heirs and assigns forever. I give unto my son Timothy Skinner 2 lotts in the Long Meadow, viz., my lott which I bought of Mr. Isaac Burr and my lott that I bought of Hezekiah Talcott, together with my right in the lands called the western lands, to be to him and his heirs forever. I give unto my son Daniel Skinner my homelott with all the buildings thereon, together with all my working tools and husbandry implements, also my upper lott and lower lott in the Long Meadow, and in the South Meadow my upper lott, and also that lott that I bought of Paul Peck, together with my lott in the Neck and my lott commonly called the Cow Pasture, to be to him and his heirs forever. I give unto my daughter Rachel Welles £200, including what she hath already received. I give unto my daughter Mary Skinner the sum of £200. My will is that after my just debts and funeral charges are paid, and also legacies, that the remainder of my moveable estate shall be equally divided amongst my sons and daughters. I appoint my wife Rachel Skinner, with my son John Skinner, executors.

Witness: *John Marsh,*   JOHN SKINNER, LS.
Mehetabell Bushnell, Elizabeth X Marsh.

Codicil, dated 25 February, 1742-3: I, John Skinner, the above subscriber, do make this following addition to this my last will and testament, namely: I add to my daughter Rachel Welles the sum of £50, and also to my daughter Mary Skinner the sum of £100, to be paid by my executors, said legacies to be paid according to the value of the old tennor bills as they commonly pass in the country. I do hereby ratify and confirm this addition, with the foregoing instrument, as my last will and testament.

Witness: *John Marsh,*   JOHN SKINNER, LS.
John Pantry Goodwin, John Jones.

Court Record, Page 36—16 January, 1743-4: The last will and testament of John Skinner, late of Hartford decd., was now exhibited in Court by Rachel Skinner, widow and relict, and John Skinner, executors. Proven and ordered to be recorded.

Page 164-200.

Standish, Josiah, Wethersfield. Invt. £2004-00-08. Taken 13 December, 1744, by Nathaniel Wright and Joseph Goodrich. Additional inventory of £332-00-00, taken at New Hartford 15 November, 1745, by Martin Smith and Matthew Gillett.

Court Record, Page 53—5 February, 1744-5: Adms. granted to Hannah Standish, widow, who gave bond with Hezekiah Butler for £500.

Page 3 (Vol. XV) 7 January, 1745: John Standish, a minor, 11 years of age, Hannah, 7 years, and James, 4 years, children of Josiah Standish: this Court do appoint Hannah Standish, widow, to be their guardian. Recog., £2000.

Page 11—6 May, 1746: Hannah Standish, Adms., exhibited an account of her Adms. Accepted.

Page 138-39-40.

Stow, Daniel, Middletown. Invt. £1372-17-01. Taken 2 February, 1744, by Solomon Adkins and William Rockwell. Will dated 13 January, 1744.

I, Daniel Stow of Middletown, in the County of Hartford, do make this my last will and testament: Imprimis: I give to my eldest son Daniel Stow and to his heirs and assigns forever the equal half of all my estate, both real and personal, after my just debts and funeral charges are paid. I give to my other two children, Rebeckah Stow and George Stow, in equal parts forever, all the other half of my estate, both real and personal. And my will is that my eldest son shall have all my homelott with the buildings thereon, as all my lands on the east side of the Connecticut River; and what that amounts to more than an equal half of my estate he shall pay the 1-2 thereof to his sister within one year after he shall attain to lawful age, and the other half to his brother within one year after he shall attain to lawful age. And I do hereby order and impower my executor to sell my part of the sloop *Sarah* (if I do not do it before my decease) and such other of my personal estate as will be likely to waste or decay, in particular my stock and provisions, and what of the produce thereof shall remain after my just debts and funeral charges are paid shall be let out on interest for my children when they come to lawful age. And whereas, I have agreed to sell to my brother Samuel Stow my right in the land where he now dwells, and have received some part of the pay for the same, I do hereby impower my executor after named to pass a legal conveyance thereof to my sd. brother upon his paying what is now coming or due for the same. I appoint my worthy friend Dr. Isaac Lee sole executor.

Witness: *Ebenezer Sage,*   DANIEL STOW, LS.
Nathaniel Stow, William Rockwell.

Court Record, Page 38—15 February, 1743-4: Will proven.
Page 39—15 February, 1743-4: Daniel Stow, a minor, 17 years of age, son of Daniel Stow, chose Dr. Isaac Lee to be his guardian. Recog., £300. Rebeckah Stow, age 16 years, chose Ephraim Adkins to be her guardian. And the Court appoint Ephraim Adkins guardian to George Stow, a minor son of Daniel Stow. Recog., £500.
Page 49 (Vol. XV) 6 June, 1748: Report of the distributors.

Page 168.

Sydervelt, Abraham, Simsbury. Will dated 2 March, 1735: I, Abraham Sydervelt, in the Township of Simsbury, gentleman, do make this my last will and testament: Seeing I have no heirs of my body, I give to my wife Martha Anero, now Sydervelt, my whole, sole and real and personal estate forever. I do give unto my brother Anthony Sidervelt his children, Mary, Jacob and Ann Sydervelt, to each of them 1 gold mourning ring with my name inscribed thereon. It is my will and I do order my dearly and well-beloved wife Martha Sydervelt to be my whole and sole executrix.

Witness: *Joseph Phelps,*   ABRAHAM SYDERVELT, LS.
Mary X Phelps, Andrew Fresneau.

Court Record, Page 56—15 March, 1744-5: The last will and testament of Abraham Sydervelt, late of Simsbury, was now exhibited in Court by Martha Sydervelt, widow and relict. Proven, approved and ordered to be recorded and kept on file.

Page 195.

Talcott, Capt. John, Glastonbury. Invt. £3121-08-03. Taken 3 October, 1745, by Thomas Wells and Abner Moseley:

Court Record, Page 64—5 November, 1745: This Court grant Adms. on the estate of John Talcott, late of Glastonbury decd., unto Lucy Talcott, widow of the sd. decd., and Elizur Talcott, of sd. Glastonbury, who gave bonds with Thomas Wells of sd. Glastonbury for £4000 money. Exhibit of an inventory. Accepted and ordered to be filed.
Page 17 (Vol. XV) 9th July, 1746: An account of Adms. was now exhibited in Court by Elizur Talcott and Lucy Talcott, Adms. Accepted.

The sd. Lucy Talcott moves to this Court that the moveable estate may be distributed to the widow and children:

	£ s d
To Lucy Talcott, her thirds,	578-11-00
To John Talcott, his double part,	578-12-05
And to Sarah and Mary Talcott, to each,	289-06-03

And appoint Col, Thomas Wells, Abner Moseley and James Cole, of Glastonbury, distributors.

Page 24—26 September, 1746: John Talcott, a minor son of John Talcott, chose Samuel Talcott of Glastonbury to be his guardian. Recog., £600. Cert: *Jonathan Hale, J. P.*

Page 86—17 January, 1748-9: Motion is now made to this Court that the widow's dowry of the estate of Capt. John Talcott may be set out to her: Whereupon this Court appoint Col. Thomas Wells, Abner Moseley and James Cole, of Glastonbury, to set out to Lucy Talcott (alias Root) 1-3 part of the buildings and lands by bounds for her improvement during life.

Page 90—10 February, 1748-9: Mr. Elizur Talcott, one of the Adms. on the estate of Capt. John Talcott, late of Glastonbury, now moves to this Court for a distribution of the real and personal estate of the sd. decd. And whereas, this Court, on the 7th day of July, 1746, made an order of the distribution of the moveable estate to the widow and children of the sd. decd. with their proportion thereof (with an account of the sum of the buildings and lands of the sd. decd); and also this Court gave order for the widow's dowry on sd. estate to be set out to her, on the 17th day of January, 1748-9: This Court therefore, on the abovesd. motion, do appoint Col. Thomas Wells, Abner Moseley and James Cole, of Glastonbury, to finish the distribution of sd. estate to the widow and children, the son to have a double portion and the daughters a single share of sd. estate, both real and personal, and make return thereof to this Court.

Page 118 (Vol. XVII) 8 June, 1756: Whereas, this Court, on the 10th of February, 1748-9, granted an order of distribution and appointed James Cole, Thomas Wells and Abner Moseley to make sd. distribution, and they never returned sd. distribution to this Court, and one of the daughters of the deceased being now dead and left no issue, this Court direct the distributors to distribute sd. estate: to John Talcott, only son, his double share; and to Sarah Wilcock (alias Talcott) a single share. And this Court now appoint Robert Loveland, Benjamin Trumble and John Rowley, of Hebron, distributors.

Page 121.

Tappin, James, Middletown. Invt. £1584-09-00. Taken 14 January, 1743, by Solomon Adkins and Daniel Hall. Will dated 1st December, 1739.

I, James Tappin of Middletown, in the County of Hartford, being advanced to ye age of 74 years, do make this my last will and testament: Imprimis: I give unto my wife Ann the use of all and every part of my estate, both real and personal, after my just debts and funeral charges are paid, during the time she shall remain my widow. But if she should marry after my decease, my will is that she should have the use of my homelott and buildings thereon during her natural life, and 1-3 part of my personal estate to be at her own dispose. And further, my will is that if she wants sustainance during the time she shall remain my widow, I do hereby grant unto her free liberty to sell any part of my estate, either real or personal, as her own for her support (my homelott and buildings thereon only eccepted). I give to my only child Ann Bacon (after the decease of my wife) the use of all my estate, both real and personal, that my wife shall leave at her decease, during the time my sd. daughter shall remain the widow of Andrew Bacon, Jr., decd. I give to my only grandchild Andrew Bacon, the only child of my sd. daughter (after the decease of my wife and daughter), all the remainder of my estate, whatsoever shall remain at their decease, only I would be understood and my will is that if my sd. daughter should again marry and have any other child or children, my sd. grandson shall have no more of my estate than a double share with the other children that my sd. daughter may have. I appoint my well-beloved wife Ann Tappin and my trusty friend William Rockwell executors.

Witness: *Ephraim Done,*   JAMES TAPPIN, LS.
John Whitmore, William Southmayd.

Court Record, Page 22—3 April, 1743: Will proven and, with inventory, ordered on file.

Page 190.

Taylor, Stephen, Hartford. Invt. £47-19-01. Taken 17 August, 1745, by Joseph Cook and Daniel Seymour.

Court Record, Page 62—14 August, 1745: This Court grants Adms. on the estate of Stephen Taylor, late of Hartford, to Violet Taylor, widow of the sd. decd., who gave bond with Stephen Taylor, son of the sd. decd.

Page 9 (Vol. XV) 1st April, 1746: Violet Tailor, Adms., exhibited in this Court an account of her Adms., and the sd. Adms. reports the estate insolvent and prays that commissioners may be appointed to adjust the claims of the creditors: Whereupon this Court appoint Lt. Jonathan Steele and Ensign Jonathan Seymour, of Hartford, commissioners.

Page 23—2 September, 1746: This Court now set out to Violet, the widow of Stephen Tailor, £17-04-10 in moveable estate for her necessity. An account thereof is on file.

Taylor, William. Court Record, Page 7—1st June, 1742: Stephen Taylor, a minor, now 17 years of age, son of William Taylor, late of New York deceased, chose Joseph Stedman of Windsor to be his guardian. Recog., £200.

Page 199.

Terry, Samuel, Middletown. Invt. £778-10-03. Taken 14 November, 1745, by Solomon Adkins, Ephraim Adkins and Jonathan Allyn.

Court Record, Page 66—18 November, 1745: Adms. granted unto Martha Terry, widow of the deceased, who gave bond with Richard Strickland of sd. Middletown for £600.

Page 11 (Vol. XV) 13 May, 1746: Samuel Terry, a minor, age 16 years, son of Samuel Terry, chose his mother Martha Terry to be his guardian. Recog., £800.

Page 80—6 December, 1748: An account of Adms. was now exhibited in Court by Martha Terry, Adms. Accepted. Sarah Terry, a minor, 14 years of age, daughter of Lt. Samuel Terry, chose Mrs. Martha Terry to be her guardian. Recog., £300.

Page 42 (Vol. XVII) 16 October, 1754: Martha Terry, Adms., having exhibited an account of her Adms., now moved for a distribution of sd. estate: Whereupon this Court appoint Jonathan Allyn, Ephraim Adkins and Philip Mortimer, of Middletown, to distribute the estate to the heirs, viz.:

	£ s d
To Samuel Terry, eldest son,	73-18-02
To John, Josiah and William Terry, to each of them,	36-19-01
To Abigail, Mary, Sarah, Ann and Martha Terry, to each,	36-19-01

Page 82—10 October, 1755: Report of the distributors.

Page 128—10 November, 1756: Whereas, the General Assembly holden at New Haven on the 2nd Thursday of October, 1756, directed Martha Terry, Adms., with Mr. John Bacon, of sd. Middletown, to make sale of so much of the real estate of the sd. deceased as will procure the sum of £207-09-07 old tenor bills with incident charge of sale, taking the advice of the Court of Probate for the District of Hartford therein: Ordered, to sell the west end of the homelott.

Page 198-199.

Terry, Zachariah, Middletown. Invt. £162-12-08. Taken 17 October, 1745, by Solomon Adkins and William Rockwell. Also an addition was added to the inventory of £53-10-01.

Court Record, Page 66—18 November, 1745: Adms. granted unto Sibell Terry, widow, who gave bond with Samuel Miller of sd. Middletown for £300.

Page 13 (Vol. XV) 3 June, 1746: Sibbell Terry, Adms., exhibited an account of her Adms. Accepted. This Court appoint Sibbell Terry, widow, to be guardian to her children, viz., Elizabeth Terry, age 5 years, and Sibbell, age 3 years, children of Zachariah Terry deceased. Recog., £700 for each minor.

Page 61.

Treat, Charles, Wethersfield. Inventory taken 20 October, 1742, by Jonathan Belding, Bezaleel Lattimore and Joseph Boardman.

Court Record, Page 12—12 October, 1742: This Court grant Adms. on the estate of Charles Treat, late of Wethersfield decd., unto Joseph and Oliver Treat of Wethersfield, who gave bonds with Wait Welles of Wethersfield for £2000.

Page 19—22 March, 1743: Joseph Treat and Oliver Treat, Adms. on the estate of Charles Treat of Wethersfield, now exhibited an accot.: Debts and charges due from the estate, £152-07-06. Which account is allowed and ordered to be kept on file. And moves to this Court that distributors may be appointed to distribute the estate. This Court so order distribution, viz.: To James and Oliver Treat, to Abigail Boardman alias Treat, to Prudence Treat, and to the heirs of Eunice Riley alias Treat, to Jerusha Welles alias Treat, to each of them an equal share of the sum of £3057-00-07. And appoint Capt. Jonathan Belding, Sergt. Bezaleel Lattimore and Corporal Joseph Boardman distributors.

Page 20—4 April, 1742: Josiah Buck of Wethersfield, guardian to David Buck, a minor, son of David Buck, late of Wethersfield, shows to this Court that the sd. minor is a co-heir to the estate of Charles Treat. and moves to this Court that suitable persons may be appointed to assist him in a division of the real estate of the sd. Charles Treat, as the sd. guardian and minor may improve separate from the sd. minor's brethren and sisters, children of Eunice Riley deceased; and also set out and make distribution of that part of the moveable estate of the sd. Charles Treat which falls by distribution to sd. Eunice Riley alias Treat in the estate of the sd. Charles Treat, viz., an equal share with the rest of the children of the sd. Eunice Riley deceased. And this Court appoint and impower Jonathan Belding, Bezaleel Lattimore and Joseph Boardman to make distribution accordingly.

Page 27—5 July, 1743: Report of the distribution of part of the estate to David Buck. Accepted.

Page 48-9.

Treat, James, Wethersfield. Will dated 31 August, 1739: I, James Treat, Sen., of Wethersfield, being greatly advanced in years, do make this my last will and testament: Imprimis: I give to my eldest son Charles Treat and to his heirs forever the following pieces or parcels of land lying in Wethersfield: one piece where the sd. Charles's dwelling house now stands, containing 32 acres more or less; also one piece in the great meadow, at a place called the dry swamp; also, 1 1-2 acres upon the north side of my lott called Send Home; also one acre on the west side of my lott called Nine Acres; also half an acre on the south side of my lott in sd. meadow called Fill Barn; also 2 acres of my lott in West Swamp butted east on land of John Edwards, west on the Great Plaine, south on John Rose and north on land in this my will given to my son James Treat; also the 1-2 of my right in and to all the common and undivided land lying within the Township of Wethersfield. I give to my 2nd son James Treat (various parcels of land). I give to my youngest son Oliver Treat (various parcels of land); also all that part of my lott lying in the Parish of Newington not before given to my son James Treat; also 1-4 part of my right in and to the common and undivided land lying in Wethersfield; also I give to my son Oliver one yoke of oxen, one team horse and all my team tackling and husbandry implements. I give to my daughter Abigail £31 in money. I give to my daughter Prudence £100 in money. I give to my daughter Jerusha, the wife of Wait Wells, the sum of £50 money; which sums of £50 to my daughter Jerusha and £31 to my daughter Abigail makes them equal, with what they have already received, with my daughter Prudence. I give to Eunice, the daughter of my daughter Eunice Riley decd., £10 money, to be paid her at the age of 18 years. I appoint my sons, Charles, James and Oliver, to be executors to this my will.

Witness: *Jonathan Burnham,*   JAMES TREAT, SEN., LS.
Ephraim Willard, John Chester.

Court Record, Page 5—19 May, 1742: The last will of James Treat, late of Wethersfield decd., was exhibited in Court by Charles, James and Oliver Treat, executors. Proven and ordered to be recorded.

Page 165.

Treat, Prudence, Wethersfield. A distribution of the estate of Prudence Treat, late of Wethersfield decd., made and agreed to by the heirs of sd. estate this 5th day of February, Anno Dom. 1745:

	£ s d		£ s d
To Abigail Boardman,	109-17-00	To James Treat,	104-01-09
To Eunice Riley, her heirs,	108-18-06	To Oliver Treat,	120-16-09
To Jerusha Wells,	108-17-09		

At a Court of Probate held at Hartford, in the County of Hartford, on the 5th day of February, A. D. 1744-5: Then James Treat, Oliver Treat, Daniel Boardman, Abigail Boardman, Jonathan Riley, Wait Wells and Jerusha Wells, signers and sealers to this instrument, acknowledged the same to be their free act and deed before this Court, and set to their hands and seals in Court. *Test: Joseph Talcott, Clerk.*

JAMES TREAT, LS.
OLIVER TREAT, LS.
DANIEL BOARDMAN, LS.
ABIGAIL BOARDMAN, LS.
JONATHAN RILEY, GUARDIAN TO EUNICE RILEY, LS.
WAIT WELLS, LS.
JERUSHA WELLS, LS.

Court Record, Page 53—5 February, 1744-5: An agreement under the hands and seals of the heirs of the estate of Prudence Treat, late of Wethersfield decd., acknowledged before this Court for the settlement of sd. estate. Approved and ordered to be recorded and kept on file.

Page 103.

Tuller, John, Simsbury. Invt. £816-17-06. Taken 28 January, 1741-2, by John Brown and Gillet Addams.

Court Record, Page 31—10 October, 1743: Inventory of the estate of John Tuller, late of Simsbury deceased, was now exhibited in Court by Jacob Tuller, Adms. Inventory was ordered recorded and kept on file. An account was now exhibited in Court by Jacob Tuller, of Simsbury: Paid in debts and charges, £88-09-09. Which account was accepted and ordered on file.

Page 36—27 December, 1743: Jacob Tuller, Adms. on the estate of John Tuller decd., showing to this Court that the General Assembly, holden at New Haven on the 2nd Thursday of October, 1743, impowered him the sd. Adms. to make sale of so much of the real estate as will procure the sum of £65-19-03 in old tenor bills for the payment of debts due from sd. estate with the necessary charges arising thereon, taking the directions of the Court of Probate in the County of Hartford: Whereupon this Court direct Jacob Tuller, Adms., to set up advertisements, etc., etc., etc.

Page 50—6 November, 1744: Pursuant to the direction of the Court of Probate in Hartford, in October, 1743, for the sale of the real estate of John Tuller, late of Simsbury decd., for paying the debts due from sd. estate, I did according to sd. direction make sale of one piece of land in Simsbury, of 104 acres of land, on the 15th day of May last, to Ambrose Ladow, for £61-00; and also one piece of land in sd. Simsbury I sold on the sd. day to Isaac Tuller of Simsbury for £11-15-00 old tenor; charge of sale amounted to £2-02-00. An account of the sale and charge ordered to be kept on file.

Twist, Benjamin. Court Record, Page 21—5 April, 1743: It was certified to this Court by *Thomas Hart, J. P.,* that Desire Twist, a minor daughter of Benjamin Twist of Wallingford, in the County of New Haven, decd., before the sd. Justice on the 28th day of February, 1742-3, made choice of Benjamin Gray of Southington Parish (in Farmington) to be her guardian. Recog., £50.

Page 19.

Waddoms, John, Glastonbury. Invt. £961-13-10. Taken by Abraham Skinner and David Dickinson. Will dated 31 October, 1741.

I, John Waddoms of Glastonbury, in the County of Hartford, do make this my last will and testament: When my just debts are paid I give to my wife Charity 1-3 part of my estate during her natural life. I will to my four sons, Caleb, John, Enos and Daniel, the remainder of my estate, Caleb having a double portion, they paying £60 to each of my daughters, whose names are Susannah, Mary, Charity and Sarah, and £60 to an unborn child. I will that my provision, cloth and wearing clothes be for the use of my family without being put in the inventory. I leave this as my last will and testament, making my wife Charity executrix and my son Caleb executor.

Witness: *Benjamin Hubbard, Jr.,*   JOHN WADDOMS, LS.
David Dickinson, Abraham Skinner.

NOTE:—The following is part of John Waddom's inventory:

	£	s	d
To 1 house and 1 barn, £40 each,	80-00-00		
To 19 acres of land at £9 per acre,	171-00-00		
9 acres of subdued pasture land at £9 per acre,	81-00-00		
To 2 acres of young orchard at £8 per acre,	16-00-00		
To 7 acres of pasture land, partly subdued, at £7 per acre,	49-00-00		
To 4 acres of pasture land, partly subdued, at £5-10 per acre,	22-00-00		
To 3 acres of plow land at £6 per acre,	18-00-00		
To 156 acres of unimproved land at £2 per acre,	312-00-00		

£749-00-00

Court Record, Page 6—4 May, 1742: Will exhibited in Court and proven.

Page 137 (Vol. XVII) 1st March, 1757: Ichabod Waddoms, a minor, 15 years of age, son of John Waddoms, chose his brother John Waddoms to be his guardian. Recog., £200.

Page 33-4.

Ward, Abigail, Middletown. Will dated 2 November, 1741: I, Abigail Ward of Middletown, spinster, do make this my last will and testament: Imprimis: I give to my cousin Abigail Ranny, the wife of Lt. Joseph Ranny, 1-3 part of my linen, 1-3 part of my household stuff, and 1-4 part of my money, after all lawful debts and necessary charges are paid. I give to my well-beloved cousin Anne Clark, the wife of Ebenezer Clark, and her heirs, my bedd and furniture and half of my wearing apparrel, 1-3 part of my linen, 1-3 part of my household stuff, and 1-2 of my money that remains after the abovesd. Abigail Ranny has taken her fourth part. I give to my cousin Andrew Warner £30 in money, which he has now in his hands. I give to my well-beloved cousin Mary Sage, wife of Timothy Sage, and her heirs, 1-2 of my wearing apparrel, 1-3 part of my linen, 1-3 part of my household stuff, and 1-2 of my money after the abovesd. Abigail Ranny hath taken her fourth part. I give to my cousin John Knott £5 in money, the old currency, on condition he live with his uncle, Capt. John Warner, until he is 21 years of age; but if he does not fulfill this condition he shall not be entitled to ye money. I give to my cousin Mary Warner a suit of apparrel out of a piece of Druget that is prepared to be wove. I give to my cousin Hannah Warner, wife of Jabez Warner, my box iron and heaters. I appoint my beloved brother Capt. John Warner and his son John Warner, and likewise Jabez Warner, to be my executors.

Witness: *Edward Eells,*   Abigail X Ward, ls.
Nathaniel Ranny, Thomas Savage, Jr.

Inventory in Vol. XV, Page 418.

Ward, William, Middletown. Invt. £4942-17-00. Taken 15 May, 1745, by George Philips, Ephraim Adkins and James Ward.

Court Record, Page 58—25 May, 1745: Adms. granted unto Daniel Ward and Jonathan Ward of Middletown, who gave bond with William Whitmore for £2000 money, old tenor.

[The settlement of this estate not found: It may be on record at Middletown.]

Inventory on Page 104. Will on Page 114.

Warner, Capt. John, Middletown. Invt. £62-06-00. Taken 2nd September, 1741, by Hugh White and Thomas Johnson. Will dated 29 June, 1736.

I, John Warner, Sen., of Middletown, in the County of Hartford, being advanced to the age of 77 years, do make this my last will and testament: I give to my son John Warner and to his heirs forever my dwelling house, barn and homelott and my pasture at Siding Hill so called, about 7 acres, and one piece of land at a place called Pistol Point, about 3 acres, and my land at Wongunk (as well what is my own property inheritance as also what right I have in any lands there or that did belong to my brother Jonathan Warner decd.), and also all my right in the common and undivided land in Middletown, otherwise called the 3rd division of land on the west side and the fourth division of land on the east side of the Great River; also I give him all my husbandry tools of all sorts, and also all my stock of cattle, horses, sheep and swine, except what I shall in this will otherwise dispose of. I give to the heirs of my daughter Mary Wilcock decd., and to their heirs forever, one cow and one feather bed; and the reason why I give them no more now is because I have given my daughter Mary, by deed of gift and otherwise, her full portion of my estate. I give to my daughter Hannah, and to her heirs forever, all my right and title in any part of the three-mile division of land so called, on the east side of the Great River in Middletown, and all my household utensils of all sorts that is not already disposed of in this will; also I give her 2 cows, 10 sheep and my sorrell mare (four years old last spring). And further, my will is that the remainder of the rest of my estate, after my just debts, funeral charges and legacies are paid, be divided between my son John and daughter Hannah, 2-3 to John and 1-3 to Hannah. And I hereby ordain my son John Warner sole executor.

Witness: *Joseph Rockwell,*   JOHN WARNER, LS.
William Rockwell, Edward Rockwell.

Court Record, Page 21—5 April, 1743: The last will and testament of John Warner, late of Middletown decd., was now exhibited in Court by John Warner, son of the sd. decd. and an executor. Will proven and ordered recorded.

Page 116.

Warner, John, Middletown. Invt. £161-04-05. Taken 2 June, 1743, by Thomas Johnson and Joseph Ranny, Jr.

Court Record, Page 28—17 August, 1743: This Court grant Adms. on the estate of Capt. John Warner, late of Middletown, unto Jabez Warner of Middletown, son of the sd. decd., who gave bond with John Bacor of Middletown.

Page 29—6 September, 1743: An inventory of the estate of Capt. John Warner, late of Middletown decd., was now exhibited in Court by Jabez Warner, Adms. Accepted and ordered to be recorded and kept on file.

Page 193-4.

Warner, Joseph, Middletown. Invt. £601-00-00. Taken 29 June, 1745, by Ebenezer Hurlbut and John Clark. Will dated 21 March, 1745.

I, Joseph Warner of Middletown, in the County of Hartford, do ordain this my last will and testament: I give unto Sarah, my wife, after my just debts and funeral charges are paid, 1-3 part of all my personal estate, and the use of 1-3 part of all my real estate during her natural life. I give to my kinswoman Mary Churchell, the daughter of John Churchell, who now dwells with me, £200 old tenor money, including the cow lately given her, which I value at £12. I give to each of the children of my brother John Warner decd. and my sisters Mary Bartlett and Rebeckah Hurlbut decd., accounting the children of Daniel Hurlbut decd. one, the sum of 40 shillings old tenor bills, in the whole £28, the number of children being 14, all to be paid by my executor within four years after my decease. I give to the Church of Christ in the Society to which I do belong, the sum of £5 old tenor bills, to be paid to the pastor or deacons of sd. church within one year after my decease, to be laid out in some vessel or vessells for the use of sd. church. And all other of my estate, both real and personal, I give to my nephew David Sage, Jr., whom I appoint sole executor to this my last will and testament.

Witness: *Isaac Lee,*   J OSEPH W ARNER, LS.
John Clark, William Rockwell.

Court Record, Page 63—3 September, 1745: The last will and testament of Joseph Warner, late of Middletown decd., was now exhibited in Court by David Sage of Middletown. Will proven. Inventory exhibited and ordered to be recorded and kept on file.

Page 16 (Vol. XV) 1st July, 1746: Sarah Warner, widow of Joseph Warner, now moves to this Court that 1-3 part of the real estate of the sd. deceased may be set out to her in severallty according to the last will of the deceased: Whereupon this Court appoint William Rockwell, Return Meigs and John Bacon distributors.

Page 53.

Warren, Abraham, Jr., Newington. Invt. £392-01-00. Taken 24 August, 1742, by Caleb Andrews and Edward Walker.

Court Record, Page 8—6 July, 1742: This Court grant Adms. on the estate of Abraham Warren, late of Wethersfield, unto William Warren of Wethersfield, who gave bonds with Benjamin Goodrich for £500.

Will on Page 123. Inventory on Page 137.

Waters, Sarah, Hartford. Invt. £149-10-09. Taken by Joseph Holtom and John Skinner, Jr. Will dated 25 May, 1736.

I, Sarah Waters of Hartford, widow and relict of Mr. Bevil Waters of Hartford, late decd., do make this my last will and testament: Imprimis: I give unto my daughter Mary one of my silver spoons, which she shall choose. I give to my daughter Dorothy the other of my silver spoons after that my daughter Mary has had her first choice. I give unto my three daughters, Mary, Sarah and Dorothy, all my linen, woolen and silk clothing of what kind so ever it be, likewise all my household goods, to be equally divided amongst them. My daughter Mary shall have her first choice. I acquit and discharge Jacob Mygatt, my grandson, all that money which he borrowed of me. I give unto my grandson Joseph Mygatt £3 money, to be paid within 12 months after my decease. I give unto my two granddaughters, Mary and Sarah, the two daughters of my son Joseph Mygatt decd., each of them a Bible, to be procured for them after my decease by my executor. I give unto my four children, Zebulon, Mary, Sarah and Dorothy, all the remainder of my estate (after that my just debts, funeral expenses and the forementioned legacies are paid) in equal proportion, saving only that my daughter Sarah shall have 25 shillings less than an equal part on account of what I have before given to her. I appoint my brother John Seymour to be sole executor.

Witness: *Timothy Seymour,*   SARAH X WATERS, LS.
Nathaniel Seymour, Thomas Seymour, Jr.

Court Record, Page 39—6 March, 1743-4: An inventory of the estate of Mrs. Sarah Waters, widow and relict of Bevil Waters decd., was now exhibited in Court by Jonathan Steele of Hartford, Adms. with the will annexed, which inventory is by this Court accepted and ordered on file.

Page 55 (Vol. XV) 11 January, 1747-8: Jonathan Steele, Adms., exhibited an account of his Adms. Accepted. The sd. Adms. now moves for a distribution of sd. estate according to the will: Whereupon this Court order that distribution be made accordingly, viz., to Mary, Sarah and Dorothy, daughters of sd. deceased, all the wearing apparrell and household stuff, according to the direction of sd. will; and to Zebulon Mygatt or his heirs and to the sd. Mary, Sarah and Dorothy, also, all the residue and remainder of sd. moveable estate after the debts and charges are paid and the abovesd. legacies discharged. And appoint John Skinner and Joseph Holtom, of Hartford, distributors.

Page 171.

Watson, Sarah, Hartford. Invt. £12-05-00. Taken 26 February, 1744-5, by David Ensign and Thomas Olmsted.

Court Record, Page 54—5 February, 1744-5: This Court grant Adms. on the estate of Widow Sarah Watson, late of Hartford decd., unto Lamrock Flowers of sd. Hartford, who gave bonds with David Ensign of Hartford for £200 money.

Page 161-2.

Webster, Robert, Hartford. Invt. £467-00-00. Taken 8 October, 1744, by John Seymour and Thomas Richards. Will dated 14 September, 1743.

I, Robert Webster of Hartford, do make this my last will and testament: Imprimis: I give to Susannah my wife all the estate she brought with her and 40 shillings per year during the time of her widowhood. I give to my grandson Justus Webster 100 acres of land in the Township of Hartland. I give to my son Abraham £15. I give to my son Caleb 1-2 of my dwelling house and 35 acres of land on the north side of my lott adjoining to my house, also 100 acres of land in the Township of Hartland, to him and his heirs forever. I give to my son Joseph 150 acres of land lying in the Township of Hartland, to him and his heirs forever. I give to my grandson Medad Webster 100 acres of land lying in the

Township of Hartland, to him and his heirs forever. I give to my grandson Ebenezer Webster 100 acres of land lying in the Township of Hartland, to him and his heirs forever. I give to my daughter Hannah £10. I give to my daughter Abigail 1-2 of my dwelling house so long as she bear my name of Webster, and also 10 acres of land lying on the south side of my homelott, for her to hold and for her heirs forever. I give to my executors hereafter named, after my debts, legacies and funeral charges are paid, all my personal estate. I make Ebenezer Webster and Abigail Webster to be my sole executors.

Witness: *John Seymour,*   ROBERT WEBSTER, LS.
Thomas Richards, Ebenezer Ensign.

Court Record, Page 51—4 December, 1744: The last will and testament of Robert Webster, late of Hartford decd., was now exhibited in Court by Ebenezer Webster and Sarah* Webster, executors named in sd. will, who also exhibited an inventory, which will and inventory are proven and ordered recorded.

Page 61—9 July, 1745: A return of the setting out of the dowry of Susannah Webster, under the hands of David Ensign and Nathaniel Seymour, distributors, was by this Court accepted and ordered to be kept on file.

Page 136-137.

Webster, Lt. Samuel, Hartford. Invt. £205-09-07. Taken 15 February, 1743-4, by Thomas Richards and James Ensign. Will dated 9 November, 1738.

I, Samuel Webster of Hartford, carpenter, do make this my last will and testament: Imprimis: I give to Elizabeth, my wife, the 1-2 of my dwelling house, 1-3 part of my barn and 1-3 part of my real estate so long as she liveth my widow. And also I give to her 1-3 part of all my personal estate (excepting 4 brass pans), and also all the estate which she brought with her, forever. I give to my cousin Ebenezer Webster's two eldest sons, Matthew and Medad, my dwelling house and homestead, barn and other buildings on it, after my wife's decease, to be equally divided between them. I give to my cousin Samuel Webster £5. I give to my cousin Ann, the wife of Thomas Olmsted, the sum of £15. I give to my above-named cousin Ebenezer Webster all the rest of my estate, personal and real, besides that which I have disposed of as above, whom I likewise constitute my sole executor.

Witness: *Joseph Cook,*   SAMUEL WEBSTER, LS.
Michael Burnham, John Whiting.

Court Record, Page 39—6 March, 1743-4: The last will and testament of Samuel Webster, late of Hartford, was now exhibited in Court by Ebenezer Webster, executor. Proven and ordered recorded with the inventory.

---

*Evidently intended for Abigail, an error of the Recorder.

Page 166. Invt. in Vol. XV, Page 264-5.

Welles, Joseph, Wethersfield. Invt. £2121-07-09. Taken 28 January, 1749, by Joseph Hurlbut and Samuel Robbins.

The last will and testament of Joseph Welles of Wethersfield is as followeth: Imprimis: I give to my wife Hannah the 1-3 part of my moveable estate which I shall die seized of, to be at her own disposeing forever; and also 1-3 part of all my real estate for her improvement during the time of her natural life or so long as she remains my widow. 2ndly, I give to my two sons, John Welles and Joshua Welles, my now dwelling house and barn, with all my lands on the north side of the highway, to them and their heirs forever, to be equally divided between them. Thirdly, I give to my son Joseph Welles all the land that I bought of John Rose and my lott lying on the south side of the highway, to him and his heirs forever. Fourth, my Cow Plain lott, so called, I give to my three sons, John Welles, Joshua Welles and Joseph Welles, to be equally divided between them. Fifthly, I give to my two sons, Joshua and Joseph Welles, my 50-acre lott, to be equally divided to them and their heirs forever. Sixthly, my two swamp lots I also give to my three sons, John, Joshua and Joseph Welles, to be equally divided among them. Seventhly, I give to my son John Welles my land in Eastbury, to him and his heirs forever. Eighthly, my eastward land which I bought of Timothy Boardman and Gershom Not, my will is it shall be sold by my executors for the payment of my debts. And if any money remain, to be at my wife's disposal. Ninthly, as to my three dafters, Prudence, Esther and Hannah, I give them what they have received of my estate, and that is to be their portion. And my will is that my three sons shall equally give to my daughter Eunice Welles so much out of their parts as to make her equal with either one of my other daughters which are married. I appoint my wife Hannah and my son Joseph Welles executors.

Witness: *David Goodrich,*   JOSEPH WELLES, LS.
Joseph Andrews, Solomon Welles.

Court Record, Page 54—5 February, 1744-5: The last will and testament of Joseph Welles, late of Wethersfield, was now exhibited in Court by Hannah Welles and Joseph Welles, widow and son, executors. Proven and ordered to be recorded.

Page 1 (Vol. XV) 13 December, 1745: Joshua Welles, a minor son of Joseph Welles, chose Joseph Hurlbut of Wethersfield to be his guardian. Recog., £200 money.

Page 142.

Welles, Ruth, Hartford. Will dated 9 September, 1741: I, Ruth Welles of Hartford, do make this my last will and testament: My debts and necessary charges being paid, I give to my grandson Samuel Bewell £30, to be paid to him when he arrives at the age of 30 years or shall be settled in the work of the ministry. This I give to my grandson Samuel Bewell and to his heirs forever. I give to my granddaughter Hannah Pitkin £30 of money, and to her heirs forever. I give to my grandson Thomas Pitkin £30, to be paid to him at the age of 22 years, to him and his heirs forever. I give to my grandson Welles Ely £30, to be paid to him at the age of 22 years. I give to my son Samuel Welles and my daughter Sarah Clark, after my four grandchildren above mentioned have each of them £30 as above mentioned, all the remainder of my moveable estate, equally divided between them. I appoint my son Samuel and my son-in-law John Clark executors.

Witness: *John White,*   RUTH WELLES, LS.
John Cornwell, Sarah Burton.

Court Record, Page 47—4 September, 1744: The last will and testament of Mrs. Ruth Welles, widow of Mr. Samuel Welles, late of Hartford decd., was now exhibited in Court by Samuel Welles of Hartford and John Clark of Middletown, executors. Will proven and ordered to be recorded and kept on file.

Page 163.

Welles, Sarah, Widow of Capt. Thomas Welles, late of Wethersfield. Invt. £487-18-03. Taken 2 January, 1744-5, by Jonathan Robbins, Benjamin Wright and Joseph Goodrich.

Court Record, Page 53—5 February, 1744-5: An inventory of the estate of Mrs. Sarah Welles, late of Wethersfield decd. (the widow of Capt. Thomas Welles of sd. Wethersfield decd.), was now exhibited in Court by Nathaniel Robbins of sd. Wethersfield, which inventory is accepted and ordered recorded and kept on file.

West, Hannah, Windsor. Court Record, Page 27—5 July, 1743: Hannah West, 15 years of age, daughter of Samuel West of Kingstown, in Hampshire County, decd., chose Capt. Ebenezer Grant of Windsor to be her guardian. Recog., £50.

Page 118.

Wetmore, Ebenezer, Middletown. Invt. £2385-10-08. Taken 22 February, 1743, by Solomon Adkins and Samuel Shepherd. Will dated 11 January, 1743.

I, Ebenezer Wetmore of Middletown, in the County of Hartford, do make this my last will and testament: Imprimis: I give unto Elizabeth, my wife, the 1-3 part of all my personal estate, and the use of 1-2 of my dwelling house, barn, and the southern 1-2 of my homelott during the time she remains my widow. I give to my only son John Wetmore all my lands and buildings on the west side of the Great River. I also give him my gunn, sword and amunition, and my team and husbandry tools and eutensils and joinery tools, he paying to my eldest daughter Mary Wetmore the sum of £50 old tenor money within 12 months after he shall attain to lawful age. I give to my four daughters all the remainder of my personal estate, and all my lands in the great lott on the east side of the Great River which was my grandfather Savidge's, to be equally divided among them (besides the sd. £50, which I particularly give to my daughter Mary, and except my old gunn, which I give to my daughter Elizabeth). And my will is and I do hereby impower my executors after named to sell my land at Wongunk and in the three miles division to pay my just debts and funeral charges; and what remains to be divided equally among my four daughters. And I appoint my wife Elizabeth and my friend William Rockwell executors.

Witness: *Isaac Lee,* EBENEZER X WETMORE, LS.
Nathaniel Stow, Susannah Lee.

Court Record, Page 22—5 April, 1743: The last will and testament of Ebenezer Wetmore of Middletown was exhibited in Court by Elizabeth Wetmore, widow and relict of sd. decd., and executrix. Will being proven and inventory exhibited, they were ordered recorded and kept on file.

Page 2 (Vol. XVI) 26 September, 1750: An account of Adms. was exhibited in Court by Elizabeth Wetmore, Adms. to the last will of the decd. Accepted. This Court appoint Jonathan Allin, Ephraim Adkins and Nathaniel Gilbert, of Middletown, to distribute the estate.

Dist. File: To the widow Elizabeth Wetmore, to John, to Mary, to Sarah Wetmore, to Elizabeth Wetmore alias Lattimer, to Lois Wetmore. By Ephraim Adkins and Jonathan Allin.

Page 33—6 August, 1751: Report of the distributors. Accepted.

Page 87-8-9.

Wetmore, Israhiah, Middletown. Invt. £281-08-07. Taken 28 June, 1743, by Solomon Adkins and William Rockwell. Will dated 26 March, 1741.

I, Israhiah Wetmore of Middletown, in the County of Hartford, do make this my last will and testament: I give to my beloved wife Hannah the improvement of so much of my dwelling house as she shall have occasion for during her continuance there, and also a comfortable maintenance during her continuance under my roof, to be performed by my executor after named; but if she shall see cause to remove from under my roof, then my will is that she shall have a bed, bedding and furniture that we usually lodged on, and also the chest and box that she brought with her, with the lining and other things therein, and also half the pewter, brass and iron and other moveables that she brought with her, to be to her and her heirs forever. And further, my will is that in case she departs from my house, my executor shall pay her £3 per annum so long as she remains my widow. And whereas it has pleased the sovereign God to smite her with the numb palsy, under which difficulty she now labors, whereby an extraordinary charge is brought upon my son Josiah for her support and comfort, my will is that the 50 shillings per annum that my son Seth and Jeremiah promised to give me when I gave them deeds of land (of which I have received none) shall be paid to Josiah, and what that falls short of paying the extraordinary charge he shall be at in paying doctors, nurses, etc., for my wife, shall be paid out of my moveable estate before any distribution thereof be made. To my son Israhiah's heirs I give and bequeath what I gave their father by deed of gift, and also 1-6 part of my lott in the third division of land on the east side of the Great River; this I give them and their heirs forever. To my son James Wetmore I give and bequeath, besides what I have already given him, 1-6 part of my lott in the third division of land on the east side of the Great River. To my son Seth Wetmore, besides what I have already given him, I give and bequeath 1-6 part of my lott in the third division on the east side of the Great River. And also, on consideration of the lawsuit he maintained against Hope Hawley, I give him 1 equal half of my lott called the new lott; but in case he sells it, my will is that Josiah can have the refusal of it. I give to my son Jeremiah, besides what I have already given him, my bond lott on the east side of the Great River; also 1-6 part of my lott in the third division of lands there. I give to my son Caleb, besides what I have already given him, 1-6 part of my lott in the third division of land on the east side of the Great River; also 1-4 and 1-2 quarter of my interest in the sawmill and half the land adjoining. I give to my son Josiah Wetmore the remainder of my homelott after Seth and Jeremiah hath measured off to them what I gave them by deed, together with all the buildings standing thereon; and also the whole of my two meadow lots, viz., my lott just within the meadow gate and that near the Ferry River; and also the equal half of my lott called the new lott; and also my pasture at Indian Hill; and also 1-6 part of my lott in the third division of land on the east side of the Great River; 1 and 1-2 quarter of my interest in the sawmill, also 1-2 of the land adjoining. Also, I give him all my husbandry tools and carpentry tools and tackling of what name soever, obliging him to pay all my just debts, funeral charges, and legacies to my wife, except the extraordinary charge of my wife's illness, for which I have made some provisions in this will. And I do hereby order him to pay to Sara, the wife of Daniel Prior, Jr., £5 money within one year after my decease. I give to my grandson Israhiah Wetmore 1-4 of my interest in the sawmill. And further, my will is that what shall remain of my moveable estate (two notes under Josiah's hands: the one dated 15 April, 1736, for the sum of £60 money, the other dated 9 May, 1737, for the sum of £30 money, and my stock in Josiah's hands, viz: two oxen, two cows, one horse valued at £10, two swine and 15 sheep) shall be equally divided among my sons,

accounting Israhiah's heirs in his stead. And I appoint my son Josiah to
be sole executor to this my last will, and desire Mr. Jabez Hamlin to be
overseer.

Witness: *Henry King,*   ISRAHIAH X WETMORE, LS.
Ebenezer Sage, Charles Hamlin.

Codicil, dated 26 August, 1742: I, Israhiah Wetmore, before named
testator, being at this time (through the goodness of God) of sound and
disposing memory, and observing a disposition in my grandson Israhiah
Wetmore before named to learning, and considering the disadvantage
that it will be to the sawmill to be sub-divided into so small rights, do
see cause to make this following alteration in my before going will.
Whereas, I have given to my grandson Israhiah Wetmore 1-4 of my interest in the sawmill and yard, my will now is that the sd. 1-4 belong to
my two sons, Caleb and Josiah; and I do now give unto my two sons,
Caleb and Josiah, and their heirs forever, equal parts in the sd. quarter of
my interest in the sawmill and yard, they paying unto my grandson
Israhiah Wetmore each £8 money, which is £16 in the whole, within a
reasonable time after my decease, to help him forward in his learning. And
this alteration is agreeable to my mind and will, and is a part thereof.

Witness: *Henry King,*   ISRAHIAH X WETMORE, LS.
Ebenezer Sage, Charles Hamlin.

Court Record, Page 26—5 July, 1743: Will proven.

Inventory on Page 105. Will on Page 126.

White, Capt. Nathaniel, Middletown. Invt. £647-03-07. Taken 14
June, 1743, by John Hall and John Clark. Will dated 22 April, 1743.
I, Nathaniel White of Middletown, in the County of Hartford, do
make this my last will and testament: Imprimis: I give to Mehetabell
my wife 1-3 part of all my moveable estate besides what I have ordered
for her use by deed in houseing and land: this I give to Mehetabell my
wife and to her heirs forever. I give to my eldest son Nathaniel White,
besides what I have given him by deed of gift, all my interest in the last
three miles granted to the Town of Middletown, and likewise one mare
which he has in possession, he paying £4 in old tenor money to his sisters Abigail and Sarah: this I give to my son Nathaniel and to his heirs
forever. I give to my son Elijah White one mare which he has in his
possession, and 6 sheep, besides what I have already given him by deed
of gift: this I give to my son Elijah White and to his heirs and assigns
forever. I give to my son Noadiah White, besides what I have already
given him by deed of gift, one mare and 6 sheep, and 2-3 of my carpenter's tools, he taking care of his mother. And it is my will that my son
Noadiah shall provide for his own mother all that she needs for her comfortable subsistence during her natural life: this I give to my son Noadiah
White and to his heirs forever. I give to my daughter Sary White, out of

the remaining part of my moveable estate, first of all, so much as to make
her up equal with what her sister Abigail has already had, and then, after
Sary is made even with her sister Abigail, the remaining part of all my
moveable estate I give to my two daughters, Abigail and Sary, equally
divided between them: this I give to my two daughters, Abigail and
Sary, and to their heirs forever. And I make my son Noadiah White sole
executor.

Witness: *Joseph White,*   NATHANIEL WHITE, LS.
John Shepherd, John Hall, Jr.

Court Record, Page 27—5 July, 1743: The last will and testament
of Nathaniel White, late of Middletown decd., was now exhibited in
Court by Noadiah White, son and executor. Will proven. Exhibit of
an inventory; ordered to be kept on file.

Whitmore, Francis, Jr. Court Record, Page 27—5 July, 1743:
Isabell Whitmore, a minor, 14 years of age, daughter of Francis Whitmore, Jr., late of Middletown, chose her grandfather, Mr. Francis Whitmore of Middletown, to be her guardian. Recog., £200. Cert: *Jabez
Hamlin, J. P.*

Page 18 (Vol. XV) 15 May, 1746: Francis Whitmore, a minor, 15
years of age, son of Francis Whitmore, Jr., chose his grandfather Francis
Whitmore to be his guardian. Recog., £300.

Page 126-7.

Whitmore, John, Middletown. Invt. £700-01-03. Taken 16 June,
1743, by Jabez Hamlin and William Rockwell. Will dated 25 May, 1743.

I, John Whitmore of Middletown, in the County of Hartford, do
make and ordain this my last will and testament: I give, bequeath, demise
and dispose of all and every part of my estate, both real and personal
(after my just debts and funeral charges are paid), unto Ruth, my dearly
beloved wife, and to her heirs and assigns forever. And I do hereby
nominate, constitute and appoint my loving wife, Ruth Whitmore, sole
executrix to this my last will and testament.

Witness: *Samuel Cravath,*   JOHN WHITMORE, LS.
George Phillips, Jr., William Rockwell.

Court Record, Page 28—2 August, 1743: The last will and testament of John Whitmore, late of Middletown decd., was now exhibited
in Court by Ruth Whitmore, executrix. Will proven. Inventory exhibited and ordered on file.

Page 47—7 August, 1744: William Rockwell, one of the commissioners on the estate of John Whitmore, late of Middletown decd., moves to this Court for longer time to adjust the claims of the creditors on the sd. estate. He was allowed 6 months.

Page 54—5 February, 1744-5: Report of the commissioners on the estate of John Whitmore, late of Middletown decd., under the hands of William Southmayd and William Rockwell, commissioners, which report is accepted and ordered to be kept on file.

Page 83.

Whittlesey, Jabez, Jr., husbandman, Newington. Invt. £776-14-01. Taken 17 January, 1742-3, by James Francis and Caleb Andrews.

Court Record, Page 17—1st February, 1742-3: This Court grant Adms. on the estate of Jabez Whittlesey, Jr., of Wethersfield, decd., unto Sarah Whittlesey, widow and relict, who gave bonds with Jabez Whittlesey of Wethersfield for £400. Exhibited an inventory, which is ordered recorded.

Page 44—5 June, 1744: Sarah Whittlesey, Adms., exhibited an account of her Adms.: Paid in debts and charges, £131-15-04; and received, £67-08-00. Account accepted and ordered on file. This Court appoint Sarah Whittlesey, the relict, to be guardian to Sarah Whittlesey, age 8 years; to Ezra Whittlesey, age 6 years; to Lydia Whittlesey, age 5 years; and Lois Whittlesey, age 6 years. Recog., £500.

Page 86 (Vol. XV) 12 January, 1748-9: Sarah Whittlesey, alias Jones, Adms., having fully rendered her account of Adms., now moves that distribution may be made. This Court so order:

	£ s d
To the widow, her thirds in moveables,	91-18-02
To Ezra Whittlesey, only son,	274-06-06
His part in the moveable estate being,	73-10-06
And to Sarah, Lydia and Lois Whittlesey, to each,	137-03-03

And appoint Caleb Andrus and Joseph Andrus, of Wethersfield, distributors. Also, they are ordered to set out to the widow 1-3 part of the buildings and lands for her improvement during life.

Page 77-8.

Wilcock, William, Middletown. Invt. £776-05-04. Taken 26 January, 1742-3, by Thomas Johnson, Jabez Edwards and John Wilcock.

Court Record, Page 13—7 December, 1742: This Court grant Adms. on the estate of William Wilcock, late of Middletown decd., unto Rebeckah Wilcock, widow and relict of the sd. decd., who gave bonds with Francis Wilcock of Middletown for £800.

Page 32—16 November, 1743: An account of Adms. on the estate of William Wilcock, late of Middletown, was now exhibited in Court by Rebeckah Wilcock, Adms.: Paid in debts and charges, £103-17-04. Which account is allowed and ordered to be kept on file.

Invt. in Vol. XV, Page 60.

Williams, David, Wethersfield. Invt. £76-17-04. Taken 25 August, 1746, by Joseph Farnsworth and John Burnham.

Court Record, Page 64—5 November, 1745: Adms. granted unto Ephraim Williams, who gave bond with Daniel Williams of Wethersfield for £1000.

Page 23 (Vol. XV) 2 September, 1746: Inventory exhibited.

Page 39—2 June, 1747: Ephraim Williams, Adms., exhibited an account and informs this Court that he suspects the estate insolvent, and prays that commissioners may be appointed to adjust the claims of the creditors. This Court appoints Jonathan Burnham and Timothy Baxter, of Wethersfield, to adjust the claims of the creditors.

Page 123—3 April, 1750: Absalom Williams, a minor, 15 years of age, son of David Williams, chose Elisha Williams, Jr., to be his guardian. Recog., £500.

Page 19 (Vol. XVI) 2 April, 1751: Othniel Williams, a minor, 14 years of age, son of David Williams of Wethersfield deceased, chose Daniel Williams to be his guardian. Recog., £500.

Page 132.

Williams, Elizabeth, Middletown. Invt. £205-15-00. Taken June, 1743, by Francis Whitmore and Joseph Ransom. Will dated 1st December, 1742.

I, Elizabeth Williams of Middletown, in the County of Hartford, do make this my last will and testament: Imprimis: I give unto my four sons, Daniel Clark, Francis Clark, Elisha Clark and Joseph Clark, equally about £60 money, which I paid as debts due from the estate of my former husband Daniel Clark decd., which my sd. sons have received the benefit of. I also give to my sd. sons, to each, the sum of 5 shillings money. I give to my three daughters, Hannah Sumner, Abigail Green and Martha Clark, in equal parts, all my negro girl and all other of my personal estate whatsoever, after my just debts, funeral charges and legacies and particular estate herein particularly mentioned are first taken and paid out of it. I give to my daughter Martha Clark my best bedd, bedsted, curtains, and all other furniture thereto belonging, and my chest with drawers. I give to my granddaughters, Elizabeth and Katharine Codner, the only children of my daughter Elizabeth Codner decd., £10 money, to each of them the sum of £5 when they arrive to lawfull age. Also, I give to my sd.

granddaughters, equally, about £40 money which is due to me from their father, my son-in-law John Codner, for 5 years rent of the priviledges left to me by my late husband John Williams decd. I appoint my son Francis Clark sole executor.

Witness: *Francis Whitmore,*   ELIZABETH X WILLIAMS, LS.
Elizabeth Rockwell, William Rockwell.

Page 190-1.

Invt. in Vol. XV, Page 60-1.

Williams, Samuel, Stepney Parish, Wethersfield. Died 23 July, 1745. Invt. £300-10-11. Taken 8 and 13 August, 1745, by Jacob Williams and Jonathan Belding. Will dated 1st February, 1742-3.

I, Samuel Williams of Stepney Parish, in Wethersfield, do make this my last will and testament: I give to my beloved wife Abigail 1-3 part of my moveable estate forever, and 1-3 part of my houseing and lands during widowhood. I give to my son Amos Williams 2 acres of land on which he now liveth; also 6 1-2 acres of land bought of Jacob Riley; also 4 acres in the cow pasture; also 8 acres of land in my great pasture; 1 acre of land lying in Smith's meadow which I bought of Noadiah Dickinson; 2 acres of land in Wethersfield meadow; the 1-2 of land of 4 acres which I bought of Jonathan Boardman, lying next to Deacon Goodrich's land. Also, I give to my son Amos Williams 10 acres of land lying on the east side of the Connecticut River in the bounds of Glastonbury, which I bought of Samuel Lucas. Nextly, I give to my son Joseph Williams 3 acres of land in my great pasture; also 1-2 of my right in the east end of Middletown lott which I bought of my second wife's brothers and sisters. Nextly, I give to my son Benjamin Williams 6 acres of land with my house and barn thereon standing, and my orchard thereon growing; and three acres of land in my great pasture next to that piece given to my son Joseph Williams; and the rest of my great pasture I give to my three sons, Amos, Joseph and Benjamin, to be equally divided among them. Also, I give to my son Benjamin 1 acre of land in the great meadow which I bought of Silas Belding; also I give to my son Benjamin another part of my Middletown lott lying on the east side of Besit River. Nextly, I give to my son Elisha Williams all my Middletown lott of land lying on the west side of Besit River. Nextly, I give to the heirs of my son Samuel Williams decd., if any there be, £20 apiece old tenor, to be paid to them by my four sons, Amos, Joseph, Benjamin and Elisha Williams, in equal proportions. Nextly, I give to the heirs of my daughter Elizabeth, besides what she had in her lifetime, £20 old tenor. Nextly, I give to my two daughters, Sarah and Martha Williams, 2 acres of land in the great meadow, in that lott I bought of Jonathan Boardman, lying next to them 2 acres I gave to my son Amos Williams. It is to be understood that that half acre of land I bought of Joseph Cole is to be included in the 2 acres aforesd., Sarah taking her acre next to Amos. Nextly, I give to my daughter Deborah Williams 1 1-2 acres of land I bought of Samuel Dix, lying in the lower swamp, in the great meadow. Nextly, I give to my dafter Susannah one acre of land in the great meadow, that I bought of Samuel Williams. Nextly, I give to my daughter Mary Dixx one acre of land in the great meadow which I bought of Noadiah Dickinson. Nextly, I give to my daughter Rachel Williams one acre of land in Smith's meadow which I bought of Samuel Williams. Nextly, with respect of my moveables that I have not herein disposed of, my will is that it be equally disposed of between my six daughters, Deborah, Susannah, Mary, Martha, Sarah and Rachel, excepting only that I give to Rachel £10 more than any one of the rest. I hereby appoint Edward Bulkeley and my son Amos Williams executors.

Witness: *David Goodrich,*   SAMUEL X WILLIAMS, LS.
Edward Bulkeley, Ephraim Goodrich.

Court Record, Page 61—9 July, 1745: The last will and testament of Samuel Williams, late of Wethersfield decd., was now exhibited in Court by Capt. Edward Bulkeley and Amos Williams, executors. Proven and ordered to be recorded.

Page 9 (Vol. XV) 1st April, 1746: Upon complaint of Edward Bulkeley, Esq., and Amos Williams, executors to the last will and testament of Samuel Williams, late of Wethersfield, to Thomas Johnson, one of His Majestie's Justices of the Peace of Hartford County, that Elisha Williams, son of sd. decd., concealed considerable of the moveable estate and was bound over to this Court by sd. Justice to be examined as the law directs, accordingly the sd. Elisha Williams appeared before this Court and under oath made answer to sd. questions as the Court put to him with respect to sd. moveable estate. An account thereof is on file.

Page 23—2 September, 1746: An inventory of the estate of Samuel Williams, late of Wethersfield, was now exhibited by Amos Williams, one of the executors, which inventory this Court accepts, orders recorded and kept on file.

Page 24—1st Tuesday of October, 1746: Amos Williams of Wethersfield and William Rockwell of Middletown, guardians to Isaac Williams, a minor son of Joseph Williams decd. (which Joseph Williams decd. was son to Samuel Williams decd.), now moves to this Court that the homelott of the sd. Samuel Williams decd. in Wethersfield may be divided according to the last will of the sd. decd., and also the sd. William Rockwell and Ebenezer Belding of Wethersfield moves to this Court that the lott of land in Middletown, in the Northwest Quarter, which did belong to the sd. Samuel Williams and his 2nd wife Elizabeth, be divided to the several heirs, viz., 3-4 of sd. lot to be divided according to the will of the sd. decd., and the other quarter part of sd. lott as follows: to Isaac Williams, a minor as aforesd., a double share of sd. 1-4 part of sd. lott; and to Ebenezer Belding, who purchased the right of Martha Williams (alias Sanborn) and also Benjamin his right, and to Elisha Williams, Susannah Williams (alias Hollister), Mary Williams (alias Dix), Sarah Williams and Rachel Williams, their single shares of sd. lott. And this

Court appoint Capt. Isaac Hart of Farmingtown, Jonathan Belding of Wethersfield, and Joseph Frary of Middletown, distributors.

See File:

Partition of the homelott of Samuel Williams: 3-4 to the heirs of Samuel Williams, and 1-4 to the heirs of Elizabeth Williams, 2nd wife: to Isaac Williams, a minor son of Joseph Williams decd., who was eldest son to the sd. Elizabeth, a double share of sd. quarter part of sd. lot; to Ebenezer Belding, who purchased the right of Martha Williams (alias Sanborn) and also Benjamin Williams's right, and to the heirs of Elisha Williams (Susannah Williams alias Hollister, Mary Williams alias Dix), Sarah Williams and Rachel Williams, their single shares of sd. quarter; Amos Williams and Sarah Williams alias Lattimer decd.

From File:

And whereas, the said Sarah Williams (alias Lattimer) is decd. since the above-mentioned order of distribution was granted, whereby her interest in said quarter of said Middletown lot comes to her brothers and sisters of the whole blood, vizt., to Isaac Williams, to the heirs of Benjamin Williams, to the heirs of Elisha Williams, to Susannah Williams (alias Hollister), to Mary Williams (alias Dix), to the heirs of Martha Williams (alias Sanborn), and to Rachel Williams, in equal parts, to each one-seventh.

3 February, 1753. By *Isaac Hart,* }
Jonathan Belding, } *Distributors.*
Joseph Frary, }

WILLIAM ROCKWELL, *Guardian to*
ISAAC WILLIAMS.

Williams, Thomas. Court Record, Page 61—9 July, 1745: Prudence Williams, a minor daughter of Thomas Williams, late of Wethersfield, chose Mr. David Goodrich, Jr., of Wethersfield, to be her guardian. Recog., £500.

Page 28 (Vol. XV) 2 December, 1746: Hannah Williams, 10 years of age, and Gideon, 7 years of age, children of Thomas Williams, late of Wethersfield: this Court appoint Deacon David Goodrich to be their guardian. Recog., £300.

Page 96-7-8.

Williams, William, Hartford. Invt. of moveable estate, £54-08-00. Taken 1st September, 1743, by Jonah Williams and Richard Gilman, Jr. Will dated 24 January, 1737-8.

The last will and testament of me, William Williams, being advanced in years, is as followeth: After my just debts are paid, I give to my wife Sarah a third part of all my real estate for her improvement during her natural life, and 1-3 part of all my personal estate for her use and to dispose of as she shall see cause. I give to the children of my daughter, Sarah Forbes decd., besides what I gave her in my lifetime, £20, to be divided equally among them; and to my granddaughter, Sarah Forbes, besides her part of the £20, a heifer (in consideration of her living with me as she hath done); and to my daughter Rachel, besides what she has already received, £20 for her children; to be paid out of my personal estate to the value of sd. sums, or in money, which my sons William, and Daniel shall see cause to do, they paying it in equal parts between them. I give to my son Jonathan, if he be living and come to demand it, £5, to be paid by my son William out of that part of the estate which I give him, or in money. To my son William I give that meadow lott, which contains about 10 acres, that lyes south of the drain and north of James Forbes's lott, together with another piece of meadow land containing about 2 acres at the great elm tree, butted west on the Great River, south on land of my brother Gabriel Williams, north on land of the heirs of my brother John Williams, and runs eastward as far as the drain; likewise my dwelling house and 1-2 of my upland lott whereon my dwelling house stands, and 1-2 of my barn, and 1-2 of my personal estate (excepting what is given to my wife as above), to be and remain to my son William and his heirs forever. To my son Daniel I give my lower meadow lott, containing about 6 acres, which lyes north of and adjoining Deacon Olmsted's pasture and south of James Forbes's lott; also another piece of meadow land, about 3 acres; likewise I give him the remaining half of my homelott, 1-2 part of my barn, the whole of my right in the Five Miles, viz., that which I have on my own right and that which came to me by my father's right, with the remaining half part of my personal estate (excepting as above); to my son Daniel and his heirs forever.

Witness: *Samuel Woodbridge,*   WILLIAM X WILLIAMS, LS.
Benjamin Colt, John Gilman.

Page 44-5.

Wills, Joshua, Tolland. Invt. £540-15-02. Taken 12 February, 1741-2, by Nathaniel Woodward, John Lothrop and Zebulon West. Will dated 27 May, 1736.

I, Joshua Wills of Tolland, in the County of Hartford, do make this my last will and testament: My estate I give, demise and dispose of in the following manner: First, my will is that all those debts that I do owe to any person or persons shall be well and truly paid within a convenient time. Nextly, I having given unto my eldest son Joshua Wills his portion already by deed of gift, I come to my second son Jonathan Wills, to whom I give 10 shillings money. I give to my son Lamson Wills 10 shillings money. I give to my daughter Elizabeth Allyn 20 shillings money. My will is that my beloved wife Mercy shall have the use and benefit of all the rest of my estate so long as she shall continue to remain my widow, and 1-2 of the same during her life. Also, I give to my wife 1-3 part of my moveable estate forever, whom I make sole executrix. Further, I impower her, in case she want or need be, to sell such a part of my land as shall be necessary for the payment of my debts or legacies or bringing up my children. And all the rest of my estate I give to be equally divided amongst my 4 daughters which I had by my last wife Mercy, viz., Martha Wills, Zerviah Wills, Azuba Wills and Hannah Wills.

Witness: *Zebulon West,*   JOSHUA WILLS, LS.
Christopher West, Peletiah West.

Court Record, Page 10—1st Tuesday in September, 1742: The last will and testament of Joshua Wills, late of Tolland decd., was now exhibited in Court by Mercy Wills, widow and executrix. Proven. Inventory exhibited and ordered to be kept on file.

Page 18—1st March, 1743: Joshua Wills of Tolland and Jonathan Wills of Wethersfield appealed from the judgement of this Court in approving the last will and testament of Joshua Wills, late of Tolland, unto the Superior Court to be holden at Hartford the first Tuesday of March next. Recog., £30 money.

Page 1.

Wolcott, Simon, Windsor. Will dated 6 April, 1742: I, Simon Wolcott of Windsor, do make this my last will and testament: My worldly estate I give and bequeath as follows: My will is that my just debts and funeral expenses be paid. I give to my brother James Wolcott all my estate, both real and personal, to him and his heirs forever. I make my brother James Wolcott executor to this my last will.

Witness: *Roger Wolcott,*   SIMON WOLCOTT, LS.
John Loomis, Jr., Abiah Wolcott.

Court Record, Page 9—3 August, 1742: The last will and testament of Simon Wolcott, late of Windsor decd., was now exhibited in Court by James Wolcott, executor. Will proven, ordered to be recorded and kept on file.

Wood, Obadiah. Court Record, Page 47—4 September, 1744: Timothy Wood, a minor, about 5 years of age, son of Obadiah Wood, late of Hartford decd.: Mehetabell Wood, widow and relict of Obadiah Wood, to be his guardian. The widow and Thomas Spencer, Jr., joyntly recog. in £100.

Page 56—2 April, 1745: Abigail Wood, a minor, 14 years of age, daughter of Obadiah Wood, late of Hartford, chose Jonathan Webster of Hartford to be her guardian. Recog., £200.

Page 2 (Vol. XVI) 2 October, 1750: Martha Wood, a minor, age 14 years, daughter of Obadiah Wood, late of Hartford deceased, made choice of Thomas Hosmer to be her guardian. Recog., £300.

Page 63.

Woodbridge, Timothy, Sen., Simsbury. Will dated 15 February, 1736-7: I, Timothy Woodbridge, Sen., of Simsbury, in the County of Hartford, do make and ordain this my last will and testament: Imprimis: I give unto my wife Dorothy the use of my house and homested at Hartford during the time of her widowhood. And also I order my three eldest sons, Timothy, Haynes and Theophilus, to pay unto my wife Dorothy £15 a year to their mother during the time of her widowhood. And if she see cause to marry, then I order my three sons above mentioned to pay my wife Dorothy £100 money, she then to move out of these my possessions. And if she should marry and be left a widow, then to return into these my possessions as afore bequeathed during that state. I also give her the use of the best bed and furniture, silver tankord, best cup, pott, kettle, and two cows, with pewter necessary for housekeeping, and chairs. I give unto my eldest son Timothy, besides his college education, my library and an equal share of my estate, real and personal, with the rest of my children. I give unto my son Haynes an equal share of my estate, real and personal, with the rest of my children (over and above his clothes during the time of his prentiship yet remaining). I give unto my son Theophilus an equal share with the rest of my children in my estate, both real and personal, and £25 more, which I order my executors to provide for him in his apprenticeship. I give unto my son Joshua the sum of £50 in case his uncle Lamb shall settle him well in the world, which, if Providence prevents, then I give him an equal share of my estate, both real and personal, with his brother last mentioned. I give unto my daughter Mary an equal share of my estate, both real and personal, with each of her brothers, except as before excepted. Further, my will is to make my well-beloved wife Dorothy and my eldest son Timothy to be executors. And I impower these my executors to sell of my outlands at Stafford and Hartland to pay my debts that shall arise; and if need be, to sell other outlands at their discretion elsewhere.

Witness: *Theodore Woodbridge,*   TIMOTHY WOODBRIDGE, LS.
Andrew Robe, Jacob Pettebone.

Court Record, Page 4—20 November, 1742: The last will and testament of the Rev. Mr. Timothy Woodbridge, of Simsbury, was now exhibited in Court by Dorothy Woodbridge and Timothy Woodbridge, widow and son of the sd. decd. Will proven and ordered to be recorded.

PROBATE RECORDS.

VOLUME XV.

1745 to 1750.

Page 281-2-3.

Adkins, Solomon, Middletown. Invt. £953-05-03. Taken 16 November, 1748, by Ephraim Adkins, Jonathan Allin and William Rockwell. Will dated 13 September, 1748.

I, Solomon Adkins, of Middletown, in the County of Hartford, do make this my last will and testament: I give unto my eldest son, Samuel Adkins, 46 acres of land, lying in the south range of lotts, that is to say: that part of my land there that did belong to Richard Hubbard decd. and Samuel Cornwell, Sen., decd., together with the dwelling house and barn that I built on sd. land, to him forever. I give unto my 2nd son, Solomon Adkins, the equal half of my land that lyes in the third division, on the west side of the Great River, that I bought of James Ward, Sen., and Ephraim Wilcocks; and the equal half of my land in sd. division that lyes by the West River, and of that land that I bought of Charles Hamlin. and of the remaining 8 acres that I bought of Deacon Joseph Tibbals, of Durham, lying in the south tier of lotts, and of my 2 bogg meadow lotts, each containing 1 1-2 acres, one lying at a place called Brown's Point and the other lying near Bacon's Landing so called; and the whole of eight acres of land which I bought of Giles Hall, Esq., and the dwelling house and barn where my sd. son Solomon now dwells, to him, his heirs and assigns forever. I give to my youngest son, Jabez Adkins, and to his heirs forever, all my land called my pasture, containing 8 acres, lying between the land of Jabez Hamlin, Esq., and James Ward, Sen.; and the equal half of the land that lyes in the west division, on the west side of the Great River, that I bought of James Ward, Sen., and Ephraim Wilcocks; and ye equal half of my land in sd. division that lyes by the West River, and of that land that I bought of Charles Hamlin; and the remaining 8 acres that I bought of Deacon Joseph Tibbals of Durham, lying in the south tier of lotts above mentioned. I also give to my two youngest sons, Solomon and Jabez, all my husbandry tools and utensils, to be equally divided between them. I further give to my son Jabez Adkins, and to his heirs and assigns forever, all my land called barn lott, as well what is in my improvement as what is in the improvement of my son-in-law Allin Ward, together with the dwelling house standing thereon, in which my sd. son-in-law now dwells. And the reason why I have not given to my sd. son-in-law the land now under his improvement and the dwelling house where he now dwells, is because I have been obliged to advance a considerable sum of money to answer his obligations. I give to my wife Phebe all and every part of my household goods and family provisions and stock of creatures, to be at her dispose. I give to my four youngest daughters, Rebeckah, Phebe, Esther and Abigail, to each the sum of £100 old tenor, including about £40 or £50 which will appear by my account which I have given to my daughter Rebeckah and shall be accounted as so much of her £100, to be paid by my sd. three sons in equal parts. And I do hereby authorize and fully impower my two eldest sons, Samuel and Solomon, to sell and give lawful conveyance of all my homelott and buildings thereon, and divide the produce thereof among themselves and all the rest of my children, to each an equal share, including my daughter Hannah (not to debar my wife having the improvement of my dwelling house during her pleasure). And further, I do hereby give to my youngest son Jabez Adkins all my apparrel and my gunn, sword and amunition. I appoint my eldest sons, Samuel Adkins and Solomon Adkins, executors.

Witness: *Ebenezer Rockwell,*   SOLOMON ADKINS, LS.
Simon DeWolfe, William Rockwell.

Court Record, Page 80—6 December, 1748: The last will and testament of Solomon Adkins, late of Middletown decd., was now exhibited by Samuel and Solomon Adkins, executors, with inventory. Proven and ordered to be recorded.

Page 43 (Vol. XVI) 28 November, 1751: Solomon Adkins, one of the executors to the last will and testament of Solomon Adkins decd., exhibited an account of debts and charges, which account this Court allowed. The sd. executors now move that distribution be made: Whereupon this Court appoint William Rockwell, Jonathan Allen and Samuel Merriman, of Middletown, to make distribution of the real and personal estate according to the last will of the deceased.

Dist. File: 26 March, 1753: To the widow, to Rebeckah Plumb, to Phebe Adkins, to Esther, to Abigail, to Solomon, and to the heirs of Jabez Adkins. By William Rockwell and Jonathan Allen.

Page 92—26 March, 1753: Report of the distributors.

Alderman, William. Court Record, Page 104—4 July, 1749: Patience Alderman, age 4 years, daughter of William Alderman of Simsbury: her father, William Alderman, Jr., to be her guardian. Recog., £50.

Page 290.

Andruss, Daniel, Wethersfield. Died 3 October, 1748. Invt. £33-10-03. Taken by Elihu Dickinson and Nathaniel Dickinson.

Court Record, Page 76—4 October, 1748: Jacob Andruss, age 20 years, son of Daniel Andruss, chose his brother Daniel Andruss to be his guardian. Recog., £500. Hezekiah Andruss, a minor, 17 years of age, chose Charles Kelsey of Wethersfield to be his guardian. Recog., £500.

Page 77—4 October, 1748: Daniel Andruss, Adms. on the estate of Daniel Andruss, late of Wethersfield, having exhibited an inventory, and showing to this Court that there is no debts due from the estate (except the charge of taking the inventory and looking after the estate, £6-17-08), as follows:

	£ s d
The inventory being	104-16-00
The charge aforesd. deducted, there remains to be divided	97-19-04
To the widow,	32-12-08
To Daniel,	18-12-10
To Mabel, to Eunice, to Hannah Andruss, to each,	9-06-05
To Jacob and to Hezekiah Andruss, to each,	9-06-04

And appoint Elihu and Nathaniel Dickinson distributors.

Page 405-6.

Andruss, Capt. Elisha, Glastonbury. Died 28 January, 1749-50: Invt. £1322-04-05. Taken 1st March, 1749-50, by Ephraim Hubbard and David Hubbard.

Court Record, Page 123—3 April, 1750: Elisha Andruss, age 20 years, and Robert Andruss, age 15 years, sons of Elisha Andruss of Glastonbury, chose David Hubbard, Jr., of sd. Glastonbury, to be their guardian. Recog., £600.

Page 134—3 July, 1750: Adms. granted unto Benjamin Andruss, son of the deceased, who gave bonds with Abraham Fox of £700.

Page 351.

Andruss, John, Hartford. Will dated 19 February, 1739: I, John Andruss of Hartford, being far advanced in age, do make this my last will and testament: Imprimis: I give unto my son Asahell Andruss all my houseing and land where I now live, be the same more or less, together with all the benefits and appurtenances to the same belonging, to him and his heirs forever. I give unto my two daughters, Elizabeth Carpenter and Abigail Richard, in equal proportion, all my personal and moveable estate, to them and their heirs forever. I appoint my son Asahell to be my sole executor, appointing him to pay and satisfy all my just debts and funeral expenses out of the estate I have bequeathed to him and not out of the moveables, which I intend shall remain whole and entire to my two daughters.

Witness: *Ebenezer Webster,*   JOHN ANDRUSS, LS.
Daniel Seymour, Thomas Seymour, Jr.

Court Record, Page 109—21 October, 1749: The last will and testament of John Andruss was now exhibited in Court by Asahell Andruss, son and executor. Will proven and ordered to be recorded.

Page 129-30.

Andruss, Joseph, Glastonbury. Invt. £235-01-06. Taken 24 August, 1745, by Thomas Wells and Jonathan Hale.

Court Record, Page 45—1st September, 1747: Daniel Andruss, a minor, 13 years of age, son of Joseph Andruss: Joseph Hollister of sd. Glastonbury appointed to be his guardian. Recog., £500.

Page 73—12 August, 1748: Daniel Andruss, now 14 years of age, made choice of Benjamin Abby of Middletown to be his guardian. Recog., £500.

Page 78—1st November, 1748: Joseph Hollister, Adms., exhibited an account of his Adms. Accepted. Also, the sd. Adms. moves for a distribution:

	£ s d
To Theoda Andruss, widow,	27-09-00
To Daniel Andruss, eldest son,	27-09-00
To Joseph and John Andruss, to each,	13-14-06

And appoint Charles Treat, Benjamin Hale and William Goodrich distributors.

Page 45 (Vol. XVI) 21 December, 1751: This Court appoint Samuel Brooks to be guardian to Joseph Andruss, a minor, age 6 years, son of Joseph Andruss. Recog., £500.

Arnold, Jonathan. Court Record, Page 113—22 December, 1749: David Arnold, a minor, 11 years of age, son of Jonathan Arnold, late of Middletown: James Pike of Farmingtown to be his guardian. Recog., £500.

Page 37.

Ashley, Lieut. Ezekiel, Hartford. Will dated 28 June, 1745: I, Ezekiel Ashley of Hartford, do make this my last will and testament: I give to my wife Hannah all my estate, both real and personal, and to her heirs and assigns forever, she paying only the several legacies herein mentioned to my several children. I give unto my son Ezekiel £20 money, to be paid at the age of 21 years. And my will further is, that my son Ezekiel shall take to himself and have all the benefit of his own wages until he shall come of age. I give unto each of my daughters £5 money, to be paid when they arrive to the age of 18 years, viz., to my daughter

Hannah £5 when she shall be 18 years old, and to my daughter Grissill £5 when she shall come to the age aforesd. I appoint my wife Hannah sole executrix.

Witness: *Joseph Talcott,*   EZEKIEL ASHLEY, LS.
Ozias Goodwin, Moses Butler.

Court Record, Page 20—5 August, 1746: The last will and testament of Lt. Ezekiel Ashley was now exhibited in Court by Hannah Ashley, widow. Will proven and ordered to be recorded.

Page 2, Ante.

Ashley, Jonathan, Hartford. Will dated 23 September, 1745: I, Jonathan Ashley of Hartford, do make this my last will and testament: I give to my son Jonathan Ashley all my estate, both real and personal, to him my sd. Jonathan, his heirs and assigns forever, always provided that my son do pay unto my daughters the several sums hereafter mentioned. And my will is and I do order and direct him to pay sd. sums as followeth: To my daughter Sarah Ashley, £8 sterling or its equivalent in bills of publick credit, at the time of my decease. To my daughter Elizabeth Olcott, £8 sterling or its equivalent in bills of publick credit, at the time of my decease. To my daughter Mary Gaylord, £8 sterling. To my daughter Abigail Ashley, £8 sterling. To my daughter Rachel Turner, £8 sterling. To my daughter Eunice Ashley, £8 sterling or its equivalent in bills of publick credit, at the time of my decease. My will is that my daughters, Sarah, Abigail and Eunice, shall have liberty to dwell in and use the south lower room, and the liberty to use my cellar, well and garden, so long as they or either of them shall remain unmarried. I appoint my son Jonathan Ashley sole executor.

Witness: *Daniel Wadsworth,*   JONATHAN ASHLEY, LS.
Jonathan Olcott, Abigail Woodbridge.

Court Record, Page 137—7 August, 1750: The last will and testament of Jonathan Ashley, late of Hartford, was now exhibited in Court by Jonathan Ashley, executor. Proven and ordered to be recorded.

Page 15-28.

Bacon, Abigail, Middletown. Invt. £279-06-03. Taken 6 March, 1746, by Ephraim Adkins and Abijah Moore. Will dated 10 April, 1745.

I, Abigail Bacon of Middletown, in the County of Hartford, do make this my last will and testament: I give the whole of my estate, real and personal, unto Frances, wife of Richard Anthony; and I order Frances, the wife of Richard Anthony, to pay out of my estate £1-04-00 to the Church of Christ of Middletown, that the Rev. Mr. Russell is pastor of. And I appoint my friends Frances Anthony and Isaac Lee executors to this my last will.

Witness: *Daniel Hall,*   ABIGAIL BACON, LS.
Esther Blake, Lament Gilbert.

Court Record, Page 7—4 February, 1745-6: The last will and testament of Abigail Bacon, late of Middletown, was now exhibited in Court by Isaac Lee and Frances Anthony, executors named in the will. Proven and ordered to be recorded.

Page 10—1st April, 1746: Inventory of the estate of Abigail Bacon was now exhibited in Court by Frances Anthony, executor, which inventory this Court accepts and order recorded.

Page 11-12-13, 278.

Bacon, Jeremiah, Middletown. Invt. £2245-07-03. Taken 24 and 31st day of January, 1746, by Benjamin Adkins, Nathaniel Gilbert and Jonathan Allin. Additional inventory, £613-08-06.

Court Record, Page 7—4 February, 1745-6: This Court grant Adms. on the estate of Jeremiah Bacon, late of Middletown, unto Elizabeth Bacon, widow of sd. decd., and Nathaniel Bacon of Middletown, who gave bond with Richard Anthony of Middletown of £2000. Inventory approved and ordered to be kept on file.

Page 113—2 January, 1749-50: Elizabeth Bacon, alias Miller, Adms. on the estate of Capt. Jeremiah Bacon, late of Middletown, having finished her account of Adms., now moves to this Court for a distribution of the estate of sd. decd.: Whereupon this Court appoint Capt. Jonathan Allin, Nathaniel Gilbert and Benjamin Adkins of Middletown to make distribution:

	£ s d
Inventory, both real and personal, with addition,	3189-04-07
The debts allowed,	843-15-01
Which being subtracted, there remains,	2345-09-06

To Elizabeth, the relict, 1-3 part of moveable estate; to Jeremiah Bacon, son of the sd. decd., 1-2 of the remainder of the estate; to Elizabeth and Abigail Bacon, daughters, the remainder in equal proportion. If there is not moveables enough, then to make up their portions in real estate.

Inventory on File.

Bacon, Nathaniel, Middletown. Invt. £19-02-06. Taken 2 December, 1747, by Benjamin Adkins and Thomas Candee.

Court Record, Page 51—2 December, 1747: Adms. granted unto Maschell Bacon of Simsbury, who gave £500 bonds with George Hubbard, Jr., of Middletown.

Dist. File: 7 April, 1752: To Beriah Bacon, to Andrew Bacon, and to John Bacon. By Benjamin Adkins and Joseph ffrary.

Page 215-16.

Bacor, Nathaniel, Windsor. Invt. £1160-08-03. Taken 11 December, 1747, by Daniel Elsworth, Henry Wolcott and Timothy Nash. Will dated 29 October, 1747.

I, Nathaniel Bacor of Windsor, do make this my last will and testament: I give to my wife Mary the use and improvement of the west room in my house, half my cellar and chamber, and all my household goods, and the east half of my barn, during her widowhood after my decease; and the use of 1-3 part of my real estate in land as long as she lives. And lastly, I give her 1-3 part of my moveable estate to be her own forever. I give to my son Simon my dwelling house and barn, and so much of my land as with the house and barn shall make him a double portion with the rest of my sons, with my cart, plows and all my husbandry tools, he paying as hereafter I shall will. I give to my sons, Daniel, Bezaleel and Benjamin, the rest of my real estate in lands besides what I have given to my son Simon, to be divided in equal portions between them, they paying as hereafter I shall will. I give to my daughter Ann £100 money. I give to my daughter Elizabeth, besides what she has had, £10 money. I give to my daughter Abigail £50 money. I give to my daughter Hannah £100 money. My will is that my moveable estate (besides what I have given away), if any remains more than enough to pay my debts, be disposed of by my executors to pay the abovesd. legacies, and that my sons aforesd. to whom I have willed my land shall pay in equal proportion between themselves to the full answering of sd. legacies by my executors in this my last will, whom I hereby appoint and constitute thereunto. In confirmation whereof I have hereunto set my hand and seal.

Witness: *John McKinstry,*   NATHANIEL BACOR, LS.
Henry Wolcott, Jr., Timothy Green.

Page 126—16 April, 1750: Daniel Bacor, age 16 years, son of Nathaniel Bacor, chose Ephraim Pierson of Windsor to be his guardian. Recog., £500. Cert: *William Wolcott, J. P.*

Page 74 (Vol. XVI) 19 October, 1752: Benjamin Bacor, a minor son of Nathaniel Bacor, made choice of Timothy Nash of sd. Windsor to be his guardian. Recog., £500.

Page 109.

Bailey, David, Middletown.   Invt. £562-07-06.   Taken 30 September, 1747, by Isaac Smith, Ebenezer Clark and William Bevin.   Will dated 16 August, 1747.

The last will and testament of David Bailey: I give to my wife Jane £10 to be her estate forever, and the use of my whole estate so long as she remains my widow relict, whom I do appoint to be my executrix. I also appoint Samuel Wadsworth to be executor with my wife Jane. To my son David I give my gunn. To my son David and to my son Joshua and to my son Elijah and to my son James, besides what I have already given to my son David, I give to each of them 2-12 parts of my estate. To my daughters, Phebe and Elizabeth, I give to each of them 1-12 part of my estate. The foregoing legacies to my four sons I order to be paid unto each of them when they arrive to the age of 21 years, paying to their mother the lawful interest provided she remains my widow and relict. And likewise the legacies to my daughters, Phebe and Elizabeth, to be paid when they arrive to the age of 18 years, paying to their mother lawful interest. The foregoing instrument I declare to be my last will and testament.

Witness: *Ebenezer Clark,*   DAVID BAILEY, LS.
Joseph Parks, Isaac Smith.

Court Record, Page 47—6 October, 1747: The last will and testament of David Bailey, late of Middletown, was now exhibited in Court by Jane Bailey, widow and executrix, and Samuel Wadsworth, executor. Jane Bailey alone accepted the trust. Will proven and ordered to be recorded and kept on file. And whereas, there is 2-12 part of the estate intestate: therefore this Court grant Adms. on the 2-12 of sd. estate unto Jane Bailey, widow, who gave bond with Ebenezer Clark of Middletown of £500. This Court appoint Jane Bailey, widow, to be guardian to her children, viz., Joshua Bailey, 13 years of age; Elijah Bailey, 9 years; James Bailey, about 5; and Phebe and Elizabeth, 7 years of age, children of David Bailey. Recog., £300.

Page 130—2 May, 1750: Jane Bailey, Adms., exhibits an account of her Adms. Accepted.

Page 131—14 May, 1750: David Bailey, a minor, 16 years of age, son of David Bailey, chose his mother Jane Bailey to be his guardian. Recog., £500. Cert: *Epapharus Lord, J. P.*

Banks, Jonathan. Court Record, Page 58—2 February, 1747-8: Daniel Banks, 17 years of age, son of Jonathan Banks, late of Middletown, chose Jabez Hamlin to be his guardian. Recog., £300. Cert: *Seth Whitmore, J. P.*

Page 70-1.

Barbour, Jonathan, Simsbury. Invt. £1065-04-06. Taken 17 May, 1747, by James Cornish, Benajah Humphrey and Hez: Humphrey.

Court Record, Page 36—7 April, 1747: This Court grant Adms. on the estate of Jonathan Barbour, late of Simsbury deceased, unto Jemima Barbour, widow, who gave bond with Jonathan Pettibone of Simsbury of £800.

Page 348-9.

Barbour, Joseph, Windsor. Invt. £2790-15-03. Taken May, 1749, by Samuel Enno, John Wilson and John Cook.

Court Record, Page 91—22 February, 1748-9: Adms. granted unto Mary Barbour and Jonah Barbour of Windsor, who gave bonds with Samuel Barbour of sd. Windsor of £1000.

Page 92—7 March, 1748-9: Joseph Barbour, a minor, 20 years of age, son of Joseph Barbour, chose Capt. Peletiah Mills of Windsor to be his guardian. Recog., £500.

Page 120—6 March, 1749-50: Mary Barbour, the relict, moves by her son Jonah Barbour that her right of dowry and 1-3 of the moveable estate be set out to her: Whereupon this Court appoint Job Loomis, Isaac Loomis and Seth Youngs of Windsor to set out 1-3 of the buildings and land for her use during life, and 1-3 part of the moveable estate when the debts are paid.

Page 128—16 May, 1750: Jonah Barbour, Adms., having exhibited an account of his Adms., now desired to be discharged from his Adms.: Whereupon this Court grant him a *Quietus Est.*

Page 81 (Vol. XVI) 24 December, 1752: Eliakim Marshall of Windsor, in Hartford County, guardian to Lucy, Lydia and Mary Barbour, heirs to the estate of their grandfather Joseph Barbour, late of Windsor, showing to this Court that some of the real estate in lands of the deceased lies in common or joynt tenancy with other of the heirs to sd. estate, moves to this Court that sd. estate may be divided: Whereupon this Court appoint Capt. Samuel Enno, Nathaniel Loomis the 3rd and John Wilson to assist the guardian to sd. minors in the division of sd. land.

Page 83—26 December, 1752: It was certified to this Court by *Henry Allyn, J. P.,* that Lucy Barbour, a minor, aged between 18 and 19 years, and also Lydia Barbour, 14 years, made choice of Eliakim Marshall, Jr., of sd. Windsor, to be their guardian, which choice this Court accepts. Also, this Court appoints sd. Eliakim Marshall, Jr., to be guardian to Mary Barbour, a minor, aged 11 years. Recog., £300 money.

Distribution File: 28 April, 1755: John Wilson and Samuel Eno, both of Windsor, appointed by the Court to assist Eliakim Marshall, Jr., guardian to Lucy Barber, Lydia Barber and Mary Barber, minors, to distribute some estate that fell to Joseph Barber, of Windsor, and Elizabeth Drake, wife of Joseph Drake, of Torrington, in the County of Litchfield, and to said Lucy, Lydia and Mary Barber, out of the estate of their grandfather, Mr. Joseph Barber, late of Windsor decd., the whole being apprised at £1157-00-04 as money. We set out to Joseph Barber, he being eldest son to Joseph Barber, Jr., and to Elizabeth Drake, etc. Signed 28 April, 1755.

	SAMUEL ENO, LS.
	JOHN WILLSON, LS.
	ELIAKIM MARSHALL, LS.
Samuel Eno,	JOSEPH BARBER, LS.
John Willson.	ELIZABETH X DRAKE, LS.

Page 62 (Vol. XVII) 6 May, 1755: Report of the distributors.

Page 129.

Barbour, Thomas, Windsor. Invt. £134-13-08. Taken 29 August, 1746, by John Hubbard and Jonathan Filley.

Court Record, Page 22—2 September, 1746: Inventory of the estate of Thomas Barbour, late of Windsor, was now exhibited in Court by Samuel Barbour and Isaac Butler, Adms. Inventory proven and ordered on file.

Page 81—6 December, 1748: An account of Adms. on the estate of Thomas Barbour was now exhibited by Isaac Butler and Samuel Barbour, Adms.:

	£ s d
Paid in debts and charges,	26-03-00
Credit received,	13-04-06
Inventory, with credits,	145-18-01
Debts subtracted, there remains to be distributed,	116-10-04
To Samuel Barbour, eldest son,	29-00-07
To Ezekiel, to Mary, to Hepzibah Barbour, to each,	29-13-03

And appoint John Hubbard and Jonathan Filley, distributors.

Page 167-8, 177. Will on Page 228.

Barnard, Abigail, Widow, Windsor. Inventory taken by Nathaniel Pinney, Noadiah Phelps and Isaac Phelps. Will dated 5 December, 1747.

I, Abigail Barnard of Windsor, do make this my last will and testament: I give unto Joseph Barnard, my son, whom I constitute to be my only and sole executor, one certain piece of land called the Indian Field lott, two acres more or less; also 16 acres of woodland lying north of the Strawberry Meadow. I give to my son Edward Barnard 3 1-2 acres of land bounded east on the lott called 6-acre lott, north on Capt. Thomas Griswold's land, and south on Capt. George Griswold's land. My sd.

son Edward Barnard, on the receipt of sd. land in his possession after my decease, to pay the several sums of money following: To my beloved son Francis Barnard, and to each of my beloved daughters, that is to say, Abigail, Sarah, Ann and Rebeckah, the sum of £10 money to each of them a half a year after my decease. Also, I give all my team tackling to my son Edward Barnard. I give my wearing apparrel to my daughters above mentioned, in equal share; also all my household goods to my sd. daughters in equal shares, excepting £10 worth to my son Joseph and £10 worth to my son Francis Barnard. Also, my will is that £50 money which I lent to my son Francis Barnard and £50 that I lent to my son Edward Barnard shall be divided amongst my above-mentioned children, except any part of it that may be laid out for my necessary support.

Witness: *Nathaniel Griswold,*   ABIGAIL BARNARD, LS.
Gideon Case, Zerviah Griswold.

Court Record, Page 58—16 February, 1747-8: The last will and testament of Abigail Barnard, late of Windsor, was now exhibited in Court by Joseph Barnard, executor. Will proven and ordered recorded.

Beauchamp, Isaac. Court Record, Page 139—20 July, 1750: Elizabeth Beauchamp, a minor, 17 years of age, daughter of Isaac Beauchamp, late of Boston, now of Middletown, chose her father Isaac Beauchamp to be her guardian. Also, this Court appoint him guardian to his daughter Mary Beauchamp, 10 years of age. Recog., £500.

Belding, Josiah. Court Record, Page 60—1st March, 1747-8: This Court grant Adms. on the estate of Josiah Belding, late of Wethersfield, unto Solomon Belding of Wethersfield, who gave bonds with Josiah Belding of £300.

Page 327.

Benjamin, David, Hartford. Invt. £211-17-00. Taken 4 September, 1749, by Jonathan Hills and David Hills.

Court Record, Page 101—6 June, 1749: This Court grant Adms. on the estate of David Benjamin, late of Hartford, unto Ruth Benjamin, widow of the sd. decd., who gave bonds with Samuel Burnham of Hartford of £1000.

Page 107—1st Tuesday in September, 1749: The inventory of the estate was presented, accepted and ordered on file.

Page 51 (Vol. XVI) 4 February, 1752: This Court appoint Ruth Benjamin of Hartford to be a guardian to Samuel Benjamin, about 7 years old, David Benjamin, about 4 years, and Jonathan, 2 years of age, children of David Benjamin decd. Recog., £500 for each minor.

Page 29 (Vol. XVII) 29 May, 1754: An account of Adms. was exhibited by Ruth Benjamin, alias Ashman, Adms., which account this Court accepts.

Page 44—25 November, 1754: Whereas, the honourable General Assembly, holden at New Haven, 2 October, 1754, impowered Capt. Jonathan Hills of Hartford, on the memorial of Amariah Ashman of Caanan, Adms. on the estate of David Benjamin, to sell so much of the real estate as will procure the sum of £69-04-02.

Page 48-50—December, 1755: I, the subscriber, after 20 days of advertisements being set up, did on the 26th day abovesd., at the dwelling house of Russell Woodbridge, sell to the highest bidder about 20 rods of land with part of the dwelling house, being in Hartford, east side, formerly belonging to David Benjamin, for £110-03-00 to Gideon Benjamin of Hartford. Sd. land butted west and north on land of Timothy Williams, east on a highway, and south on Gideon Benjamin his land.

Signed: JONATHAN HILLS.

Page 262-3.

Benton, Ephraim, Glastonbury. Invt. £4521-03-06. Taken 28 December, 1748, by Josiah Benton and Elizur Talcott.

Court Record, Page 89—7 February, 1748-9: This Court grant Adms. on the estate of Ephraim Benton, late of Glastonbury, unto Hannah Benton, widow, who gave bonds with Josiah Benton of Glastonbury of £2000 money.

Page 86 (Vol. XVI) 6 February, 1753: An account of Adms. was exhibited in Court by Hannah Benton, widow and Adms. Accepted. Order to distribute the estate as followeth:

	£ s d
To the widow, Hannah Benton,	310-04-01
To Ebenezer Benton, only son of the decd.,	1154-11-04
To Hannah, Ruth, Abigail, Sarah and Ann Benton, to each,	577-05-08

And appoint Jonathan Hale, Esq., Capt. Abner Maudsley and Elizur Talcott distributors.

Page 102—3 July, 1753: Report of the distributors.

Page 58.

Benton, Jonathan, Tolland. Invt. £27-01-00. Taken by John Brace and Ezekiel Ladd.

Court Record, Page 25—7 October, 1746: This Court grant Adms. on the estate of Jonathan Benton, late of Windsor, unto Timothy Benton of Tolland, who gave bond with Moses Benton of Hartford of £100.

Page 28—2 December, 1746: Timothy Benton of Tolland, Adms., informs this Court that the estate of the decd. is insolvent, and prays that commissioners may be appointed: Whereupon this Court appoints Samuel Dimmock, Esq., and Mr. Jonathan Ladd, of Tolland, commissioners.

Page 42—2nd June, 1747: Medad Benton, a minor, 14 years of age, son of Jonathan Benton, chose Jacob Benton to be his guardian. Recog., £300.

Page 50—3 November, 1747: An account of Adms. on the estate of Jonathan Benton was now exhibited in Court by Timothy Benton, Adms.:

	£ s d
Paid in debts and charges,	17-15-04
Credit received,	26-15-00

Also exhibited a report of the commissioners to adjust the claims of the creditors, which is allowed. Also the Court made an averidge on sd. estate, which is on file.

Page 32-3.

Benton, Samuel, Hartford. Will dated 4 April, 1744: I, Samuel Benton of Hartford, being advanced in years even to old age, do make this my last will and testament: I give to my wife Sarah 1-3 part of my moveable estate forever; also I give her 1-3 part of my real estate for her improvement during her natural life. I give unto my son Samuel Benton, besides what I have formerly given to him by deeds of gifts, a certain piece of land containing 8 acres more or less, lying in Hartford, in the west division, butted north on land of Jonathan Easton, west on land of Samuel Benton, east and south on a highway and on the commons, to be to him and his heirs forever. I give to my son Caleb, besides what I formerly gave him, £120 money I paid towards the purchase of his house, barn and homelott. Also, I give to my sd. son Caleb Benton and to his heirs forever 40 acres of land in my western right at Harwington. My will is that the land in Tolland I formerly gave my son Daniel Benton by a deed shall be in full of his portion of my estate. I give to my son Jacob Benton, besides what I have formerly given him, all the remainder of my western right of land in Harwington, to him and his heirs forever. I give to my son Moses Benton, and to his heirs forever, all the land belonging to me in Hartford (excepting what I have before disposed of), with all the buildings thereon and appurtenances thereto belonging; also I give him two oxen, two horses, cart and plow, harrow, timber chain, plow chain, and all tackling belonging to the same; also I give him a cow and axe, a hoe and a spade; also I give him a weaver's loom and tackling belonging to the same. I give to my daughter Sarah 20 shillings old tenor. I give to my daughter Lydia Benton one featherbed and furniture to it, blankets and sheets. I also give her one cow and 6 sheep. Also I give her one room in my house to live in so long as she shall remain unmarried. Also my will is that all the remainder of my moveable estate not already given away be equally divided among my three daughters, Hannah, Abigail and Lydia, at inventory price. I appoint my son Moses Benton and Lydia Benton to be sole executors.

Witness: *Joseph Buckingham,*   SAMUEL BENTON, LS.
Thomas Richards, Jonathan Ensign.

Court Record, Page 13—3 June, 1746: The last will and testament of Samuel Benton, late of Hartford, was now exhibited in Court by Moses Benton, one of the executors named in sd. will. Approved and ordered to be recorded and kept on file.

Page 366.

Bevin, Stephen, Middletown. Invt. £1131--plus. Taken 30 January, 1749-50, by John Fisk and John Cooper.

Court Record, Page 117—6 February, 1749-50: This Court grant Adms. on the estate of Stephen Bevin, late of Middletown, unto William Bevin of Middletown, who gave bonds with Ebenezer Clark of Middletown.

Page 31.

Bidwell, Joseph, Glastonbury. Invt. £415-13-06. Taken 30 October, 1745, by James Wright, Jr., and Samuel Kimberly.

Court Record, Page 13—3 June, 1746: This Court appoint Ephraim Bidwell of Glastonbury to be guardian to Rachel Bidwell, a minor, 8 years of age, Joseph 6, Benjamin 3 years and Mary Bidwell, children of Joseph Bidwell, late of Glastonbury deceased.

Page 14—6 June, 1746: Adms. granted unto Mary Bidwell, widow, who gave bonds with James Wright, Jr., of Wethersfield, of £500 money.

Page 41—7 July, 1747: An account of Adms. was now exhibited in Court by Mary Bidwell, which account is by this Court accepted.

Page 126—16 April, 1750: Mary Bidwell, the relict, now moves that her right to dowry be set out to her in the estate of the sd. deceased: Whereupon this Court appoint Jonathan Hale, Esq., John Fox and Joseph Fox, of Glastonbury, to set out to the sd. Mary 1-3 part of the buildings and lands for her improvement during life.

Page 100 (Vol. XVI) 5 June, 1753: Gideon Hale of Middletown, in Hartford County, for himself and as he is attorney to several of the heirs to the estate of Joseph Bidwell, appeals from the judgement of this Court, in not appointing freeholders to divide the real estate of the sd. deceased, unto the Superior Court.

Page 10 (Vol. XVII) 5 February, 1754: Mary Bartlett, the relict of Joseph Bidwell, now moves to this Court that Ephraim Bidwell of Glastonbury may be appointed a guardian to her three children, viz., Joseph Bidwell, about 13 years, Benjamin, about 12 years, and Mary, about 10 years of age, children of the sd. Joseph Bidwell deceased. The sd. Ephraim Bidwell recog. in £300 for each minor.

Page 115—16 June, 1756: Joseph Bidwell, a minor, son of Joseph Bidwell, now appeared before this Court and made choice of Ephraim Bidwell to be his guardian. Recog., £300.

Page 53-4.

Bidwell, Thomas, New Hartford. Invt. £1674-13-09. Taken 14 January, 1746-7, by Matthew Gillett and Elijah Flower. Will dated 7 December, 1746.

I, Thomas Bidwell of New Hartford, in the County of Hartford, do in this my last will and testament give to my wife the use and improvement of 1-3 of my land and the use of 1-3 of the buildings during her natural life, and 1-3 part of all my moveable estate I give free and clear to my wife Ruhamah's own disposal. Likewise I give to my sons, Thomas and Jehiel, all my lands and estate, personal and real, to them and their heirs (excepting what I gave to my wife above mentioned), ordering my sons Thomas and Jehiel to pay unto my four daughters, Abigail, Prudence, Ruhamah and Martha, £100 in money to each daughter as their full portion in this form: £50 to be paid at the day of my dafters' marriage, and £50 more to be paid to my dafters when my sons come of age. And appoint Deacon Martin Smith to be my administrator and my wife as administratrix.

Witness: *Daniel Hooker,*   THOMAS X BIDWELL, LS.
Nathaniel Wilcocks, Philip Harris.

Court Record, Page 34—3 March, 1746-7: The last will and testament of Thomas Bidwell, late of New Hartford, was now exhibited in Court by Martin Smith and Ruhamah Bidwell, executors. Will proven, accepted and with the inventory ordered to be recorded and kept on file.

Page 74 (Vol. XVI) 9 October, 1752: This Court appoint Ephraim Wilcox of New Hartford to be a guardian unto Thomas and Jehiel Bidwell, minor children of Thomas Bidwell deceased. The sd. Ephraim Wilcocks gave bond with Philander Pinney of Windsor of £500.

Page 75—19 October, 1752: Timothy Skinner of Hartford, showing to this Court that he has land in New Hartford, in the County of Litchfield, that lies in common or joynt tenancy with Thomas and Jehiel Bidwell, minors and heirs to Thomas Bidwell his estate, now moves to this Court that freeholders may be appointed to assist the guardian to sd. minors in the division of sd. land: Whereupon this Court appoint Matthew Gillett, Elijah Flowers and Abraham Kellogg, of New Hartford, to assist Ephraim Wilcox in the division of sd. land.

Page 87 (Vol. XVII) 17 November, 1755: Thomas Bidwell, a minor, age 16 years, son of Thomas Bidwell of New Hartford deceased, chose Francis Barnard of Windsor to be his guardian. Recog., £200.

Page 110—4 May, 1756: This Court understanding that Ephraim Wilcock of New Hartford, guardian to Jehiel Bidwell, son of Thomas Bidwell, being convicted of uttering false bills in lieu of true bills of credit, and thereby disinabled to act as guardian to sd. minor: Whereupon this Court appoint Francis Barnard of Windsor to be guardian to sd. minor, he being about 13 years of age. Recog., £200.

Page 105—4 May, 1756: Timothy Skinner of Hartford, showing to this Court that he has land in New Hartford, in the County of Litchfield, that lies in common or joint tenancy with Thomas Bidwell and Jehiel Bidwell, minors and heirs to the estate of Thomas Bidwell, late of said New Hartford deceased, now moves this Court that freeholders may be appointed to assist Francis Barnard, guardian to said minors, in the division of said land: Whereupon this Court appoints Matthew Gillet, Elijah Flower and Abraham Kellogg of New Hartford, or any two of them, to assist said guardian to make portion of said lands and ascertain the bounds between said Skinner and the said minors, that said parties may improve separate, and make return of their doings to this Court.

Page 114—1st June, 1756: A distribution of some of the lands of Thomas Bidwell that lay in common between the heirs of sd. Thomas Bidwell and Timothy Skinner was now exhibited in Court. Accepted.

At a Court of Probate holden at Hartford, 8 April, 1768:
Whereas, there has been no distribution made of the estate of Thomas Bidwell, late of New Hartford decd.: Whereupon this Court appoint Daniel Case of Simsbury, Seth Smith and Thomas Olcott, Jr., of New Hartford, to make distribution of the estate of the said decd.

To Ruhamah Wilcocks, relict of said decd., and to Thomas Bidwell, one-half of the real estate. And whereas, Jehiel Bidwell, the other son, is deceased and left no issue, this Court direct that the estate given to him by will be equally divided to Thomas, Abigail, Prudence, Ruhamah and Martha Bidwell, sisters of said decd., or to their legal representatives.

This Court Record was ordered   *J. Talcott, Judge of Probate.*
to be returned to the Court   NOTE: *Luhamah* was the name as
because it was not recorded.   written in the will.

Page 345.

Bigelow, Jonathan, Hartford. Inventory taken October, 1749, by Thomas Wells and John Cole. Will dated 16 December, 1738.

I, Jonathan Bigelow of Hartford, do ordain this my last will and testament: I give to my wife Mabel 1-3 part of my moveable estate forever, besides one cupboard, 3 pewter platters she bought of John Edwards, and a small desk she bought of Barret; and the use and improvement of 1-3 part of my real estate during her natural life. I give unto my daughter Jerusha of my homelott (the north side) the whole breadth from the highway to the meadow ditch, and to extend sd. width southward from White's land 15 rods. I give to my daughter Rebeckah Bigelow of sd. homelott 21 rods the whole width from the highway to sd. meadow ditch, and a line parralel to sd. ditch, and to extend southward 21 rods from the land I have given to Jerusha the breadth aforesd. Always provided my wife's dowry be holden in sd. land her life. The abovesd. lands to be to my daughters Rebeckah and Jerusha and their heirs forever. Also, I give unto my daughters each of them a cow, and to my daughter Jerusha the use of my north chamber and the garrett over it, and of 1-4 of the cellar and use of the well till she shall be married. Also I give unto my daughter Rebeckah the use of one acre of the south side of my wood lott I bought of Jonathan Bunce, to cut wood as she shall (need) during her life, and the privilege of pasturing one cow in the pasture I bought of Col. Whiting her life. I give unto my loving friend Mr. John Bissell of Bolton £10. Further, my will is that after just inventory and apprisement of my whole estate, both real and personal, be made and known, and my just debts and all the above-named legacies be answered and subtracted therefrom, that then the remainder of my estate, both real and personal, be equally divided to and among my six children, with the proviso hereafter named, that whereas Timothy Bigelow has already received £100, Jonathan £150, Mabel £35, and Irene £45, that sd. sums so by them received shall be reckoned as so much of their portions in the divisions of the whole as abovesd. I appoint my two sons Timothy Bigelow and Jonathan Bigelow executors.

Witness: *Joseph Cook, John Bissell,*   JONATHAN BIGELOW, LS.
Ebenezer Dart, Isaac Graham.

Court Record, Page 109—3 October, 1749: The last will and testament of Jonathan Bigelow, late of Hartford, was exhibited in Court, of which Jonathan Bigelow was appointed executor. Will proven and ordered to be recorded.

Page 112—12 December, 1749: This Court appoint Joseph Talcott, Esq., and Mr. Joseph Holtom to make distribution of the moveable estate of Jonathan Bigelow according to his last will.

Page 126—27 April, 1750: Jonathan Bigelow, executor to the last will and testament of Jonathan Bigelow, late of Hartford, now moves this Court that distribution be made of the real estate of the sd. decd.: Whereupon this Court appoint Ozias Goodwin and Joseph Holtom distributors.

Page 35 (Vol. XVI) 3 September, 1751: Mabel Bigelow, the widow of Jonathan Bigelow, moves to this Court that her dowry given her by the last will of the deceased be set out to her: Whereupon this Court appoint Capt. John Knowles, Jonathan Seymour and Daniel Steele to set out the widow's dowry.

Page 76—25 October, 1752: Daniel Marsh, in right of his wife, one of the heirs to the estate of Jonathan Bigelow, moves that distribution of the real estate be made: Whereupon this Court appoint John Skinner, Daniel Steel and Daniel Sheldon to make division of sd. estate.

Dist. File, February, 1759: To Rebeckah Bigelow, to Jonathan, to heirs of Irene Marsh decd. (wife of Daniel Marsh), to Timothy Bigelow, to Jerusha (wife of Elisha Butler), to heirs of Mabel Seymour deceased (late wife of Daniel Seymour, Jr.) By Joseph Holtom, John Skinner and William Wadsworth.

Page 326.

Bigelow, Samuel, Middletown. Invt. £3023-02-02. Taken 23 February, 1748-9, by Ebenezer Dart and Benjamin Harris. Will dated 14 October, 1748.

I, Samuel Bigelow of Middletown, in the County of Hartford, do make and ordain this my last will and testament: I give to Mehetabell, my wife, the sole improvement of my house and land whereon I now dwell so long as she shall remain my widow, and also all my moveable estate to be at her dispose, she paying those legacies hereafter named. I give to my sons, Timothy, Isaac and Samuel, all my land, to be equally divided between them (they providing for and supporting their mother in case she be reduced to want), to them and their heirs forever. I give to my daughter Abigail £30 old tenor, to be paid by my executrix in convenient time after my decease. I give to my daughter Mary £30 old tenor, to be paid by my executrix. I give to Elizabeth Spencer, my wife's daughter, £15 old tenor, to be paid by my executrix. I also make Mehetabell, my wife, sole executrix to this my last will.

Witness: *Francis Whitmore,*   SAMUEL BIGELOW, LS.
Warren Green, James Green.

Court Record, Page 107—1st Tuesday in September, 1749: The last will and testament of Dr. Samuel Bigelow, late of Middletown, was now exhibited in Court by Mehetabell Bigelow, widow and executrix. Proven. Also exhibited an inventory. Both accepted and ordered to be recorded.

Page 115.

Inventory on Page 154.

Bigelow, Lieut. Timothy, Hartford. Inventory taken by Thomas Welles and John Edwards. Will dated 9 July, 1746.

I, Timothy Bigelow of Hartford, do make this my last will and testament: I give to my wife Abigail Bigelow, and to her heirs forever, my servant maid Ann and 12 sheep, with 3 of my beds and the furniture thereof, and also £100 worth of moveable estate (to be delivered to her out of my moveables as she shall choose at inventory price). I also give her the use of one piece of land on which I now dwell, with the buildings thereon standing, sd. land I bought of Daniel Edwards of Hartford; with the use of one other piece of land bounding east on the Great River, west on the road, north on the land belonging to the heirs of Moses Cook decd., and south on the land of Thomas Hooker; and also my lott of land that I bought of Joseph Farnsworth of Hartford, commonly called my Brick Hill lott; and also the use of my team and team tackling. All this I give her the use of during the time she shall remain my widow. I give to my son Hezekiah my yearling colt. I also give to my four sons, Hezekiah, Timothy, John and James, and to their heirs forever, £180 each at inventory price, only my will is that what shall be expended on my son Timothy for his support during the time of his apprenticeship shall be paid out of his portion. I also give to my three daughters, Abigail, Ann and Martha, £60 each, all which shall be paid to them at the age of 21 years or marriage. And that all the residue of my estate, after the legacies aforesd. have been first paid, shall be divided amongst all my children in proportion to the legacies heretofore given to them. I appoint my wife Abgail Bigelow sole executrix.

Witness: *Roger Wolcott, Jr.,*   TIMOTHY BIGELOW, LS.
Rebeckah Bigelow, Mary Nichols.

Court Record, Page 42—7 July, 1747: The last will and testament of Lt. Timothy Bigelow was now exhibited by Abigail Bigelow, widow and executrix. Will proven and ordered to be recorded.

Page 15 (Vol. XVI) 22 February, 1750-1: Capt. Daniel Goodwin, in right of his wife Abigail, executrix to the last will and testament of Lt. Timothy Bigelow, now moves to this Court that freeholders may be appointed to distribute the real estate of the sd. deceased: Whereupon this Court appoint Roger Wolcott, Jr., Joseph Talcott, Esq., and Mr. Ozias Goodwin, of Hartford, to distribute the estate to the heirs according to the will of the decd. Also, set out to the widow her dower, and make return of their doings to this Court.

Page 86—6 February, 1753: Report of the distributors.

Page 190.

Bingham (John) James, Windsor. Inventory taken 17 November, 1747, by Jacob Redington and Timothy Nash.

Court Record, Page 49—3 November, 1747: This Court grant Adms. on the estate of James Bingham, late of Windsor, unto Ithamer Bingham, son of the sd. deceased, who gave bonds with Timothy Nash of Windsor of £500.

Page 64—3 May, 1748: An inventory of the estate of James Bingham, late of Windsor, was now exhibited by Ithamer Bingham, Adms., which inventory this Court accepted and ordered to be recorded and kept on file.

Page 93—7 March, 1748-9: An account of Adms. on the estate of James Bingham was now exhibited by Ithamer Bingham, Adms.: Paid in debts and charges, £278-06-09. Which account is allowed and ordered to be kept on file.

Page 106 (Vol. XVII) 10 March, 1756: John Bingham, a minor, 17 years of age, son of John (James) Bingham, chose his brother Ithamer Bingham to be his guardian. Recog., £200. Cert: *Timothy Nash, J. P.*

Page 241-2-436.

Bird, Jonathan, Farmington. Invt. £1640-08-09. Taken last day of March, 1748, by Elisha Hart and Isaac Lee.

Court Record, Page 63—5 April, 1748: This Court grant Adms. on the estate of Jonathan Bird of Farmington unto Hannah Bird, widow of the sd. decd., who gave bond with Elisha Hart of Farmingtown of £800.

Page 57 (Vol. XVII) 1st April, 1755: An account of Adms. was now exhibited in Court by Hannah Bird, alias Webster, Adms. on sd. estate. Account accepted.

Page 64—11 April, 1755: This Court appoint Ezekiel Thompson of Farmington to be a guardian to Lydia Bird, a minor, 11 years of age, daughter of Jonathan Bird deceased. Recog., £200. Mehetabell Bird, a minor, age 17 years, and Hannah Bird, age 14 years, children of Jonathan Bird, chose their uncle Ezekiel Thompson to be their guardian. Recog., £200. This Court appoint Daniel Webster of Hartford to be guardian to Jonathan Bird, a minor, about 8 years of age, son of Jonathan Bird deceased. Recog., £200.

Dist. File: 6 May, 1755: To the relict, to Zurviah, eldest daughter, to Mehetabell, to Hannah, to Lydia, and to Jonathan, only son. By Isaac Lee and Moses Andrus, distributors.

Page 160.

Blake, Freelove, Middletown. Invt. £1414-19-00. Taken 17 November, 1747, by Daniel Hall, Stephen Blake and William Rockwell.

Court Record, Page 48—3 November, 1747: This Court grant Adms. on the estate of Freelove Blake, of Middletown, unto John Blake of Middletown, who gave bond with Joseph Ranny of Middletown of £500.

Page 70—14 June, 1748: Whereas, John Blake and Joseph Blake and William Rockwell, guardian to Hannah Blake, and Jonas Green, guardian to Elizabeth Blake, all of Middletown, now move to this Court that freeholders may be appointed to make distribution of the real estate of Freelove Blake, late of Middletown, supposed to be deceased, viz., to sd. John and Joseph Blake, to each of them 1-3 part of the real estate of the sd. deceased, and to Hannah Blake, Abigail Blake and Elizabeth Blake, minors, children of Richard Blake of sd. Middletown decd., the other third part of the sd. real estate, in severalty by bounds, as each of sd. heirs may improve separately: Whereupon this Court appoint Ephraim Adkins, James Ward and Jabez Brooks, of Middletown, distributors.

Page 353.

Blin, John, Jr., Wethersfield. Invt. £33-12-06. Taken 20 December, 1749, by William Bement and John Robbins, Jr.

Court Record, Page 114—2 January, 1749-50: This Court grants Adms. on the estate of John Blin, Jr., late of Wethersfield, unto Jonathan Warner of Wethersfield, who gave bonds with surety. Exhibit of an inventory, which is accepted and ordered to be kept on file.

Page 117—6 February, 1749-50: An account of Adms. on the estate of John Blin was now exhibited in Court by John Warner, Adms.: Paid in debts and charges, £21-07-09. Which account is allowed and ordered to be kept on file.

Bloys, Richard. Court Record, Page 21—5 August, 1746: Richard Bloys, a minor, 18 years of age, son of Richard Bloys of Killingley decd., on the 1st day of August, 1746, at New Hartford, made choice of Joseph MacIntire of New Hartford to be his guardian. Recog., £300.

Page 315.

Bow, Samuel, Jr., Middletown. Inventory taken 6 May, 1749, by Josiah Churchill and Deliverance Warner. Will dated 22 March, 1748-9.

I, Samuel Bow, Jr., of Middletown, do make this my last will and testament: I give to Elizabeth, my wife, all and every part of that estate that she brought to me at our marriage and since, as also what she has received or is like to receive of the estate of our honoured father Thomas Wright decd., together with 1-3 part of my personal estate after my just debts and funeral charges are paid out of it. I also give to my sd. wife the improvement of all my real estate during the term of her natural life. I give to all my brethren and sisters the other 2-3 of my personal estate, and, at the decease of my wife, all my real estate, to be equally divided amongst them. Only it should be understood that if my wife shall have a child by me, my will is that my estate be settled according to the ancient custom of this Colony of settling intestate estates. And I appoint my wife Elizabeth and my brother Amos Bow executors.

Witness: *Aaron Griswold,*   SAMUEL BOW, JR., LS.
William Ward, William Rockwell.

Court Record, Page 105—1st August, 1749: The last will and testament of Samuel Bow, late of Middletown, was now exhibited in Court by Elizabeth Bow, widow. Will proven and ordered to be recorded.

Page 136—7 August, 1750: An account of Adms. on the estate of Samuel Bow, Jr., was now exhibited in Court by Elizabeth Bow, executrix: Had paid in debts and charges, £74-07-10. Which account is allowed and ordered on file. Now moves to this Court that distribution may be made of the estate according to the last will: Whereupon this Court appoint William Rockwell, Lt. Return Meigs and Isaac Lee, of Middletown, distributors.

Dist. File: Estate of Samuel Bow, Jr., Middletown: 7 August, 1750 (per the will): To the widow, to the brothers and sisters of sd. decd., to Elisha Bow, to Amos Bow, to Hannah Bow, to Phebe Bow (alias Miller), to Eleazer Bow. By William Rockwell.

Brenon, Timothy. Court Record, Page 70—14 June, 1748: Timothy Brenon, 15 years of age, son of Rachel Foster, alias Spencer, chose William Rockwell of Middletown to be his guardian. Recog., £500.

Page 373.

Brewer, Alexander, Glastonbury. Invt. £109-08-06. Taken 19 December, 1749, by Elisha Andrews and Benoni House.

Court Record, Page 112—5 December, 1749: This Court grant Adms. on the estate of Alexander Brewer of Glastonbury unto Thankfull Brewer, widow, who gave bond with Ebenezer Kilbourn of Glastonbury of £500.

Page 1 (Vol. XVI) 4 September, 1750: An account of Adms. was now exhibited in Court by Thankfull Brewer, Adms. Accepted.

Page 11—1st January, 1750-1: Thankfull Brewer, Adms., having finished her account of Adms. on sd. estate, now moves for a distribution: Whereupon this Court appoint Col. Thomas Wells, Jonathan Hale and Mr. Samuel Talcott of Glastonbury to distribute the estate, viz., to Thankfull, the widow, her thirds of sd. real estate for her improvement during life, and to Thomas, Hezekiah, Joseph, Benjamin and Daniel Brewer, and to the heirs of Mary Brewer (alias Dix), and to Sarah Goodale, Lydia Loveland and Amy Porter their equal share, and make return thereof to this Court.

Page 16—8 March, 1750-1: Report of the distributors. Accepted.

Page 106-145.

Brown, Daniel, Tolland. Invt. £1044-14-05. Taken 17 July, 1747, by Peletiah West and Joseph Hatch, Jr.

Items from the Inventory, Recorded on Page 145, Probate Side:

	£	s	d
To one bond on Capt. Nathaniel Kingsbury, due December, 1747,	201-06-00		
To one bond on Capt. Nathaniel Kingsbury, due May next,	300-00-00		
To one bond on Capt. Nathaniel Kingsbury, due May, 1749,	215-00-00		
To one note on Zebulon West, due December,	61-00-00		
To one note on Daniel Lathrop,	23-06-08		
To one note on Verny Fellows,	22-03-04		
To one note on Solomon Millington,	19-07-00		
To one note on Christopher West,	19-01-11		
To one note on Ebenezer Nye,	7-10-00		

Will dated 8 May, 1747:

I, Daniel Brown of Tolland, in the County of Hartford, do make this my last will and testament: My will is that out of my estate, after all my just and honest debts and funeral charges are paid, the several legacies that my honoured grandfather, Peter Emmons decd., gave to my brothers and my sisters and ordered me to pay, should be well and truly paid out of my sd. estate according to the order and direction of my sd. grandfather in his last will and testament. And what remains my will is and I do give and dispose of as followeth: First, I give to my brother Cornelius Brown all my wearing clothes and apparrel whatsoever, and also the sum of £120 money, to be paid out of my estate. My will is and I give to my brothers Ebenezer Brown and Emmons Brown £120 money each, to be paid out of my estate severally when they shall arrive to the age of 21 years. I give to my sister Elizabeth Brown £80, to be paid when she arrive at the age of 21 years. My will is and I do give to the three children that are the son or sons and daughter of my father Moses Brown decd. by his last wife Phebe the sum of 40 shillings in money, to be paid out of my estate at the time when my brother Emmons Brown is to receive what I have given to him. And it is my will that if my estate shall be more than sufficient for the payment of the several sums which I have given, that then there shall be an addition to each one of those that are the children of my mother decd. in just proportion as I have given them. I appoint Deacon John Lothrop and Joshua Wills, both of Tolland, executors.

Witness: *Peletiah West,*　　　　　　　　DANIEL BROWN, LS.
Joseph Lothrop, Sarah West.

Court Record, Page 41—7 July, 1747: The last will and testament of Daniel Brown, late of Tolland, was now exhibited in Court by John Lothrop and Joshua Wills, executors. Will proven, inventory exhibited, and ordered to be recorded.

Page 424-5.

Brown, Ebenezer, Middletown. Died 28 September, 1749. Invt. £1093-13-00. Taken 14 December, 1749, by Philip Goff and Ralph Smith.

Court Record, Page 131a—5 June, 1750: This Court grant Adms. on the estate of Ebenezer Brown unto Rebeckah Brown, widow, who gave bonds with Philip Goff of Wethersfield of £1,000.

Brown, Moses. Court Record, Page 53—1st December, 1747: Elizabeth Brown, age 16 years, daughter of Moses Brown of Tolland, made choice of Thomas Eaton of Tolland to be her guardian. Recog., £500.

Page 122—3 April, 1750: Emmons Brown, a minor, 15 years of age, son of Moses Brown, late of Kingstown in Hampshire County, the sd. minor now living at Willington, in Hartford County, chose John Farle of Willington to be his guardian. Recog., £500.

Page 116-17-18.

Brown, Jonathan, Windsor. Inventory taken 28 October, 1747, by Jonathan Filley, Jacob Drake, Jr., and Silas Fyler. Will dated 2 June, 1743.

I, Jonathan Brown of Windsor, in Hartford County, do make this my last will and testament: I give to my wife Mindwell one bed and suitable furniture belonging to the same, to be to her and to her own use and dispose forever, and also her wearing apparel; also, I give unto her the use of 1-2 of my dwelling house and as many of the utensils thereof as she shall need for her own personal use and support during her natural life. And considering her age and bodily weakness, I have thought it would be difficult for her to improve lands and stock, etc., therefore have taken bond of security of my son Benjamin to support her with all the comforts of life, both in sickness and health, through the course of her natural life. I give to my son David Brown and to his heirs, besides what I have given him, £5 in old tenor bills. I give unto my son Ephraim Brown and to his heirs, besides what I have given him, 5 shillings in old tenor bills, or equivalent in moveables at inventory price. I give unto my son Jonathan Brown and his heirs, besides what I have given him, £5 in bills of old tenor, or equivalent in moveables. Also, I give him the use of 1-4 of my barn for four years next after my decease, with liberty of passing and repassing. I give unto my son Benjamin and to his heirs forever the 1-2 of my dwelling house and barn, and homestead lying on the south side thereof, excepting the use of the half of the house and 1-4 of the barn for a team as abovesd., &c., the other half of the sd. house and barn I have conveyed to him by deed (the north half), he the sd. Benjamin paying my debts and legacies as hereafter mentioned. I give unto my dafter, Ruth Barnard, and to her heirs, 50 shillings, and to her two daughters, Ruth and Anne, £5 to each of the sd. daughters, all old tenor, to be paid to my daughter Ruth her 50 shillings in two years after my decease, and to my two granddaughters to receive their £5 each at their arrival to 18 years of age or marriage, to be all paid in bills of old tenor, or moveables at inventory price. I give to my daughter Martha Brown and to her heirs, besides what I have already given her, £10 money, old tenor. I give unto my daughter Eunice Rowell and to her heirs, besides what I have already given her, £10 old tenor. My will and pleasure is that if I shall not sell my right in the lands called the equivalent lands for the payment of my debts, that my executors shall sell the same for the payment of my debts and legacies, and if the money from the sale of sd. land and my moveables shall not be sufficient to pay my funeral expenses, just debts and legacies, then my will is that the remainder be paid out of the homested given to my son Benjamin, so that Benjamin, my son and executor, is to have the liberty of selling my equivalent land (if I do not sell the same) and with the money and my moveables to pay all my debts and legacies, etc., if sufficient; but if not, to be made up out of my homested unless he pays the same; but if there be over-plus, to be

to my son Benjamin forever (only excepting what my wife shall use during her natural life). I hereby ordain my son Benjamin Brown to be the sole executor to this my last will.
Witness: *Matthew Allyn,*   JONATHAN BROWN, LS.
Henry Allyn, Esther Filley.

Court Record, Page 46—6 October, 1747: The last will and testament of Jonathan Brown, late of Windsor, was now exhibited in Court by Benjamin Brown, son and executor. Will proven, inventory exhibited, and both ordered recorded and kept on file.

Page 49—3 November, 1747: Robert Barnett (or Barnard?) of Windsor appeals from the judgement of this Court in approveing the last will and testament of Jonathan Brown unto the Superior Court, and recog. in £50.

Page 50—3 November, 1747: Mindwell Brown, widow and relict of Jonathan Brown, moved to this Court that her right of dowry in the real estate of the sd. decd. may be set out to her: Whereupon this Court appoint Nathaniel Case, Stephen Goodwin and Solomon Clark, of Simsbury and Windsor, to set out to the widow her right of dowry by bounds, and make return to this Court.

Page 328-9-30.

Brownson, John, Farmington. Inventory taken 25 August, 1749, by Samuel Andruss and Jonathan Andruss. Will dated 21 June, 1749.

I, John Brownson of Farmingtown, do make this my last will and testament: I give unto my wife Mary Brownson 1-2 of my real and moveable estate, except particulars given to David and James Brownson, and 1-2 of the use of my house and barn, and 1-3 of the use of all my improved lands during her life. I give unto my beloved son David Brownson and his heirs forever the south half part of my homelott with the house and barn, and 1-2 of all my land in the Shuttle Meadow Mountain division, and one yoke of oxen, and 1-2 the cart, and all plow irons and team tackling and half the tools and half the swine, with a gunn and amunition. Unto my son Jonathan Brownson I give him £1 money old tenor besides what he has already received. Unto my son Joseph Brownson and to his heirs forever I give my land at Misery Meadow. Unto my son James Brownson I give the north half part of my homelott, and half my land in Shuttle Meadow division, and half the cart, and half the carpenter's tools, and half the other tools proper for husbandry. Unto my three daughters, Rachel Fery, Mary Peck and Ruth Barnard, all my land in the west woods, with half the moveable estate, my wife first having her part. And I appoint my two sons, David and James Brownson, executors.
Witness: *Jonathan Andrus,*   JOHN BROWNSON, LS.
James Brownson, Sarah Peck, Thomas Hart.

Court Record, Page 108—3 October, 1749: The last will and testament of John Brownson, late of Farmingtown, was now exhibited by David and James Brownson, executors. Will proven. Exhibited an inventory. Both ordered to be recorded and kept on file.

Page 140-1, 294.

Buell, Ephraim, Simsbury. Died 13 October, 1747. Inventory taken by Andrew Robe, Joseph Mills and Abraham Case.

Court Record, Page 48—3 November, 1747: Adms. granted unto Isaac and Thomas Barbour of Simsbury, who gave bond with William Barbour of Simsbury of £500.

Page 49—4 November, 1747: Mercy Buell, 2 years of age: this Court appoint Caleb Case of Simsbury to be her guardian. Recog., £500. This Court appoint Thomas Barbour of Simsbury guardian to Mindwell Buell, a minor, age 4 years. Recog., £500.

Page 13 (Vol. XVI) 5 February, 1750-1: An account of Adms. was exhibited in Court by Thomas and Isaac Barbour, Adms., by which account they have paid in debts and charges the sum of £266-09-06, which account is allowed.

Buell, Peter. Court Record, Page 91—7 March, 1748-9: Solomon Buell, age 15 years, son of Peter Buell, late of Simsbury, chose Dudley Case of Simsbury to be his guardian. Recog., £500. Cert: *John Humphrey, J. P.*

Page 248-9.

Bulkeley, Capt. Edward, Wethersfield. Will dated 24 August, 1748.
I, Edward Bulkeley of Wethersfield, having attained to the age of seventy-one years, do make this my last will and testament: I give to my wife the improvement of 1-3 part of my land during her natural life, and 1-3 part of my moveable estate forever; and also £5 a year (annually) of the incomes of my corn mill in wheat at 4 shillings per bushel, and Indian corn 2s 6d per bushel, and rye at 3 shillings per bushel, in equal proportion. Also, I give to my wife the improvement of 1-3 part of my dwelling house and my barn so long as she lives my widow, and also Prince, my negro man, so long as she lives my widow. And as to my eldest son Charles Bulkeley, I having given to him and his heirs forever my house and several pieces of land in the old or First Society in Wethersfield by a deed of gift wherein as I judge fully contains a double portion of my whole estate as it was before I gave any of it to my children, so that hereby I give to my son Charles no more but my silver headed cane and my law books which I lent to my cousin John Bulkeley of Colchester, namely, "Complete Attorney," "Shepherd's Abridgments" in 4 parts, the "English Liberties," "John Godolphin (alias) the Orphan's Legacies," to

dispose of as he pleases. In the next place my will is that my six daughters, viz., Elizabeth Smith, Sarah Stow, Rebeckah Treat, Dorothy Curtiss, and Abigail and Lucy Bulkeley, shall have paid to each of them out of my moveable estate £150 as money, old tenor, at an equal apprisement with what my eldest daughter hath received at the time of her marriage. And it is hereby to be understood that what my eldest daughters receive at the time of their marriage is to be part of their portion of £150. And my will is that when the legacies herein given to my wife and six daughters is paid to them, if there be any left of my moveable estate, that then it shall be given out and distributed to my six daughters in equal proportions. In the next place, there being a considerable part of my farm at Dividend besides what I have given to my three sons, Peter, Gershom and Jonathan Bulkeley, by deeds of gifts, my will is that the remaining part of my farm at Dividend aforesd. shall be equally divided to my three sons, Peter Bulkeley, Gershom Bulkeley and Jonathan Bulkeley. And with respect of my corn mill, my will is that my three sons, Peter Bulkeley, Gershom Bulkeley and Jonathan Bulkeley, shall have the improvement of sd. mill in equal proportions during their natural life, they being at the charge in equal proportion in maintaining and keeping the mill in repair. Also, they paying to their mother annually her legacy out of sd. mill as hereinbefore mentioned, their equal part thereof. And after the decease of my three sons aforesd., the sd. mill, with the liberty of makeing a dam to raise a pond, and other privileges for promoting the interest of the sd. mill, shall pass to the male heirs of him, viz., either Peter, Gershom or Jonathan Bulkeley (that) shall be the longest liver in the world, and the bolting mill also shall go with the corn mill as aforesd. In the next place, I give that lott of land I bought of Stephen Willard, which lyeth in Wethersfield great meadow, to my two sons, Peter and Jonathan Bulkeley, to be equally divided between them; and that lott of land I bought of Samuel Curtiss, in sd. Wethersfield meadows, after my son Peter has the £20 right set out to him, I give the remaining part to my son Gershom Bulkeley. Also, I give to my son Gershom that lott of land I bought of Henry Grimes. I appoint my wife Dorothy, with my 3 sons, Peter, Gershom and Jonathan Bulkeley, to be executors.

Witness: *Daniel Russell,*   EDWARD BULKELEY, LS.
Benjamin Wright, Isaac Lee.

Court Record, Page 76—4 October, 1748: The last will and testament of Capt. Edward Bulkeley was now exhibited in Court by Dorothy Bulkeley and Peter Bulkeley, executors. Proven and ordered to be recorded.

Bull, Moses. Court Record, Page 26—20 October, 1746: Jonathan Bull, a minor, age 12 years, son of Moses Bull: this Court appoint Mabel Bull, the widow, to be his guardian. Recog., £300.

Page 137—7 August, 1750: Jonathan Bull, a minor, 16 years of age, now makes choice of Major Jabez Hamlin of Middletown to be his guardian. Recog., £500.

Page 86 (Vol. XVI) 6 February, 1753: Moses Bull, a minor, age 16 years, son of Moses Bull, late of Bolton deceased, now appeared in Court and made choice of Joseph Talcott to be his guardian. Recog., £300.

Page 296.

Bull, Sibell, Hartford. Will dated 21 February, 1747-8: I, Sibell Bull of Hartford, do make this my last will and testament: I give to my brother Jonathan Bull all my land, wheresoever the same may lye, to be to him and his heirs and assigns forever. I give to my brother Jonathan Bull all my moveable estate and also my wearing apparrel. I appoint my brother Jonathan Bull, executor.

Witness: *Roger Hooker,*   SIBELL X BULL, LS.
Daniel Sheldon, Joseph Bunce.

Court Record, Page 95—18 March, 1748-9: The last will and testament of Sibell Bull, late of Hartford decd., was now exhibited in Court by Jonathan Bull, brother and executor. Will proven and ordered to be recorded and kept on file.

Page 124-5.

Bump, Samuel, Bolton. Invt. £630-08-06. Taken 20 March, 1747, by Reynold Beckwith, Samuel Carver and Thomas Pitkin, Jr. Will dated 15 April, 1730.

I, Samuel Bump of Bolton, in the County of Hartford, do make this my last will and testament: I give to my eldest son Matthew Bump 50 acres of land in the Township of Bolton which I bought of Lt. John Talcott of Bolton, bounded north on Joel White's homelott, east on a highway, south on Daniel Clark's land, and west on a highway. And further, I give to the sd. Matthew all my moveable estate which did once belong unto my first wife, the mother of sd. Matthew. I give to my other son, Samuel Bump, 50 acres of land in the Township of Bolton, bounded north on Joel White's homelott, east on a highway, south on land belonging to Abraham Foster, and west on undivided land—to him the sd. Samuel and his heirs forever. And further, I give to the sd. Samuel all that moveable estate which did once belong unto my 2nd wife, the mother of the sd. Samuel. Further, my will and pleasure is that the money which I owe to Lt. John Talcott of Bolton should be paid out of the money due from Moses Goodrich of Wethersfield. Further, my will is that after all my just debts are paid and what is necessary to be expended for the bringing up of my two sons, that then all my moveable estate not before disposed of in this will be divided between my two sons, my eldest son

Matthew £10 more than his other brother. Further, my will is that Edward Rose of Bolton shall be guardian to my eldest son Matthew till he come to the age of 21 years. Further, my will is that Sergt. Abell Shailer of Bolton shall be guardian to my son Samuel till he come to the age of 21 years. Further, my will is that Deacon Samuel Brown, Jonathan Strong and Joel White, all of Bolton, be executors.

Witness: *Thomas White,*   SAMUEL X BUMP, LS.
Abell Shailer, Elisha White.

Court Record, Page 41—7 July, 1747: The last will and testament of Samuel Bump, late of Bolton, was now exhibited in Court by Jonathan Strong and Joel White. Will proven. Exhibit of an inventory. Both ordered to be recorded and kept on file.

Invt. in Vol. XVI, Page 250.

Bunce, Joseph, Hartford. Invt. £2703-18-02. Taken 13 July, 1750, by James Church and Thomas Seymour.

Court Record, Page 135—11 July, 1750: Adms. granted to Amy Bunce, widow, who gave bonds with William Hooker of Hartford.

Page 1 (Vol. XVI) 10 August, 1750: Amy Bunce, Adms., exhibited an inventory. Accepted.

Agreement, from File.

We, the subscribers, being the only heirs to the estate of Mr. Joseph Bunce, late of Hartford decd., do mutually agree to divide the estate, real and personal, as followeth:

To Abijah Bunce (lands by deeds of guift from his father).

	£ s d
To Gideon Bunce (in lands valued at)	1200-00-00
To William Hooker and Jerusha his wife (lands value)	283-16-06
To John Bunce and his wife Ann,	283-15-06
To be paid them by Gideon Bunce.	
To Ebenezer Deming, Jr., and his wife Amy,	283-16-06
To Martha Bunce,	283-16-06
To Mary Bunce,	283-16-06
To Patrick Barmingham and his wife Abigail,	283-16-06
To Susannah Bunce,	283-16-06

Signed:

MARTHA BUNCE, LS.   ABIJAH BUNCE, LS.
MARY BUNCE, LS.   GIDEON BUNCE, LS.
ABIGAIL BARMINGHAM, LS.   WILLIAM HOOKER, LS.
SUSANNAH BUNCE, LS.   JERUSHA HOOKER, LS.
    alias STANCLIFT,   JOHN BUNCE, LS.
JAMES STANCLIFT, LS.   ANNE BUNCE, LS.
AMY BUNCE, LS.   EBENEZER DEMING, LS.
AMY DEMING, LS.

And the widow shall have £20 old tenor a year paid to her during her natural life, for which the heirs have given security.

Witness: *Joseph Talcott,*
Ozias Goodwin,
Joseph Holtom.

Page 88-89.

Bundy, John, late of Stafford. Invt. £147-05-06. Taken 28 May, 1746, by Samuel Warner and Jonathan Whitaker.

Court Record, Page 16—1st July, 1746: This Court grant Adms. on the estate of John Bundy, late of Stafford, unto James Bundy of Preston, in the County of New London, who gave bonds with Mr. Ebenezer Preston of New London of £200.

Page 38—14 September, 1747: An account of Adms. on the estate of John Bundy, late of Stafford, was now exhibited in Court by James Bundy, Adms.: Paid in debts and charges, £69-00-01. Which account is allowed and ordered to be kept on file.

Burk, Ruth. Court Record, Page 61—1st March, 1747-8: Ruth Burk, a minor, age 12 years, daughter of John Burk, late of Hatfield, in the County of Hampshire, decd., chose her father-in-law Daniel Griswold of Bolton, in the County of Hartford, to be her guardian. Recog., £300.

Burn, Francis. Court Record, Page 12—3 June, 1746: Charles Burn, a minor, 16 years of age, son of Francis Burn of Middletown, chose William Rockwell of Middletown to be his guardian. Recog., £500. Cert: *Giles Hall, J. P.*

Inventory in Vol. XVI, Page 24.

Burnham, Caleb, Hartford. Died 13 April, 1750. Invt. £1942-03-06. Taken by John Wood and William Cowles.

Court Record, Page 131—4 May, 1750: This Court grant Adms, unto Sarah Burnham and Jabez Burnham of Hartford, who gave bonds with Joseph Pitkin of £1000 money.

Page 9 (Vol. XVI) 1st January, 1750-1: Invt. exhibited.

Page 3 (Vol. XVII) 9 October, 1753: This Court appoint Sarah Burnham, widow, to be guardian to Isaac Burnham, a minor, 12 years of age, son of Caleb Burnham deceased, and Sarah Burnham, 10 years of age, Anne 5, and Jemima Burnham, 3 years of age, children of the sd. decd.

Dist. File: 3 June, 1769: To the widow, to Sarah Woodworth, eldest daughter, to Isaac Burnham, to Anne, to Jemima Burnham. By Daniel Burr and Thomas Foster.

Page 302-3-4.

Burnham, Capt. William, Jr., Kensington. Invt. £8246-10-11. Taken 12 March, 1748-9, by Isaac Norton and Josiah Burnham. Will dated 17 January, 1748-9.

I, William Burnham, Jr., of Kensington, do make this my last will and testament: I give to my wife Ruth Burnham and to her heirs and assigns forever 1-6 part of all my real estate, land, tenements and hereditaments, and 1-3 part of all my moveable estate. I give to my only son Elisha Burnham and to his heirs and assigns forever 1-2 of all my real estate and 1-2 of the remainder of all my moveable estate after my wife's thirds are taken out. To my eldest daughter Sarah Burnham I give 1-6 part of all my real estate and 1-4 part of all my moveable estate after my wife's third part is taken out. To my youngest daughter Ruth Burnham I give 1-6 part of all my real estate and 1-4 part of all my moveable estate after my wife's third part is taken out. I appoint my wife and my only son above named to be executors.

Witness: *William Burnham, Sen.,*   WILLIAM BURNHAM, JR., LS.
Isaac Norton, Josiah Burnham.

Court Record, Page 96—5 April, 1749: The last will and testament of Capt. William Burnham, Jr., of Farmingtown, was now exhibited in Court by Ruth Burnham and Elisha Burnham, executors. Will proven and inventory exhibited. Both ordered to be kept on file. Elisha Burnham, a minor, 19 years of age, and Sarah Burnham, age 15 years, children of William Burnham, chose their mother Ruth Burnham to be their guardian. Recog., £600.

Page 54 (Vol. XVII) 7 February, 1755: Elisha Burnham and Ruth Burnham, executors to the last will and testament of William Burnham, now move for a distribution of the real estate: Whereupon this Court appoint Capt. Isaac Hart of Middletown and Daniel Dewey and Jonathan Gilbert of Farmington to distribute the sd. estate.

Page 122—9 August, 1756: Report of the distributors.

Page 140—2 April, 1757: On the motion of Ruth Burnham, widow of Capt. William Burnham, showing that there is one piece of land lying in Farmington, in the 2nd division west of the reserved lands, lying in common between Hezekiah Woodruff, Nehemiah Lewis, John Clark and Ruth Burnham, a minor daughter of the sd. deceased, and the foresd. widow being guardian to sd. minor: Whereupon this Court appoint and impower Jared Lee, Esq., Jonathan Root and Elijah Porter to make division of the aforesd. lands.

Page 158.

Burroughs, David. Invt. £376-11-06. Taken by Joshua Booth and Daniel Elsworth.

Court Record, Page 57—2 February, 1747-8: Adms. granted unto Sarah Burroughs, widow, who gave bonds with John Tyler of Tolland.
Page 101—6 June, 1749: Sarah Burroughs, widow and Adms., exhibited an account of her Adms. Accepted.
Page 102—6 June, 1749: This Court appoint widow Sarah Burroughs of Windsor to be guardian to Anna Burroughs, a minor, 4 years of age, and David Burroughs, two years of age, children of David Burroughs. Recog., £500, with John Tiler of Tolland.

Page 349.

Bush, Joseph, Middletown. Invt. £103-05-00. Taken 26 October, 1749, by Amos Bow and John Cooper.
Court Record, Page 110—7 November, 1749: This Court grant Adms. on the estate of Joseph Bush, late of Middletown decd., unto Mary Bush, widow, who gave bonds with John Cooper of Middletown of £500.

Page 82.

Butler, Joseph, Middletown. Invt. £131-00-00. Taken 22 December, 1746, by Francis Whitmore and Francis Clark.
Court Record, Page 22 (Vol. XVI) 7 May, 1751: Whereas, Adms. was granted on the estate of Joseph Butler unto Francis Whitmore, which Francis is now deceased and not having finished his Adms., this Court now grant letters unto Benoni Horton of Middletown, who gave bond with Jacob Whitmore of sd. town.
Page 23—12 May, 1751: This Court appoint Benoni Haughton to be a guardian to Haughton Dorne Butler, aged 9 years, and Mary Butler, aged 11 years, children of Joseph Butler decd. Recog., £500.
Page 35—24 September, 1751: Patience Butler, alias Crosman, relict of Joseph Butler, now moves to this Court that her thirds or right of dowry in the real estate be set out to her: Whereupon this Court appoint Mr. William Rockwell, Joseph Hubberd and Daniel Johnson to set out to the widow her thirds.
Page 59—5 March, 1752: Report of the distributors. Accepted.

Butler, John. Court Record, Page 61—1st March, 1747-8: Peter Butler, age 15 years, son of John Butler, late of Middletown decd., chose his grandfather Edward Foster of Middletown to be his guardian. Recog., £500.

Page 41.

Cadwell, John, Hartford. Died 2nd April, 1746. Invt. £306-03-02. Taken by John Abby and Joseph Cowles.

Court Record, Page 15—1st July, 1746: This Court grant Adms. on the estate of John Cadwell, late of Hartford, unto Dorothy Cadwell, widow, who gave bonds with Joseph Cowles of Hartford of £200. Exhibit of an inventory, which was ordered recorded.

Page 120—6 March, 1749-50: An account of Adms. on the estate of John Cadwell was now exhibited in Court by Dorothy Cadwell, Adms.: Paid in debts and charges, £47-10-01. Which account is allowed. Now moves for a distribution:

	£ s d
Inventory amounts to	306-03-02
Debts and charges subtracted,	47-10-01
There remains of real and personal estate,	258-13-01
Moveable estate,	47-13-00
1-3 thereof to the widow,	15-17-08
To John Cadwell, eldest son, his double part,	53-10-00
To Matthew Cadwell,	26-15-00
To Ann, Abigail, Ruth, Dorothy, Susannah and Lucy Cadwell, daughters of the sd. deceased, to each of them the sum of	26-15-00

Which is their single part of sd. estate. And also set out to the widow 1-3 part of the real estate. And appoint David Hills, Jonathan Stanly and Jonathan Olmsted, distributors.

Page 37—7 April, 1747: This Court appoint Dorothy Cadwell, widow, to be guardian to John Cadwell, a minor, 13 years of age, and Dorothy Cadwell, 11 years of age; also to be guardian to Matthew Cadwell, 7 years, Susannah, age 4 years, and Lucy Cadwell, age 2 years, children of John Cadwell deceased. Recog., £300.

Page 147 (Vol. XVII) 23 March, 1757: Matthew Cadwell, a minor, age 17 years, son of John Cadwell, chose his brother John Cadwell of Hartford to be his guardian. Recog., £200.

Page 359-60-61.

Calder, John, Wethersfield. Invt. £836-16-09. Taken 28 November, 1749, by Thomas Wright and John Stilman.

Court Record, Page 113—2 January, 1749-50: This Court grant Adms. on the estate of John Calder, late of Wethersfield, unto Hannah Calder, widow, who gave bonds with John Warner of Wethersfield of £2000.

Page 73 (Vol. XVI) 1st September, 1752: Thomas Calder, a minor, 14 years of age, son of John Calder, chose Capt. John Knowles of Hartford, his father-in-law, to be his guardian. Recog., £500.

Page 125 (Vol. XVII) 18 November, 1756: John Calder, a minor, age 15 years, son of John Calder, late of New London, appeared before this Court and made choice of his uncle John Wells of Wethersfield to be his guardian. Recog., £300.

Page 222-3-4.

Camp, Capt. John, Wethersfield. Died 4 February, 1746-7. Inventory taken 26 February, 1746-7, by Peletiah Buck, John Gillett and Robert Welles. Will dated 18 April, 1741.

I, John Camp of Wethersfield, do make this my last will and testament: I give to Rebeckah, my wife, 1-3 part of my house and 1-2 of my land during her natural life. I give to my son John Camp, whom I make my only and sole executor, my dwelling house and barn, with all my lands which I have any right or title to. I give to my son John Camp all my utensils and household goods and two gunns. I give to my wife two feather beds and furniture belonging to them, and 1-2 of the remainder of my moveable estate. Further, my will is that my son John Camp shall have the other half of my moveables. Further, my will is that my son John Camp shall pay to my daughter Mary £10 in addition to what she hath already had (which I have given her).

Witness: *John Gillett,*   JOHN CAMP, LS.
Jonathan Devereaux, Isaac Hinsdell.

Court Record, Page 34—3 March, 1746-7: The last will and testament of Capt. John Camp was now exhibited in Court by John Camp, son and executor. Also exhibited an inventory. Both proven and ordered to be recorded.

Inventory in Vol. XVI, Page 108.

Case, Alpheus, Hartford. Died 26 November, 1749. Invt. £392-05-09. Taken 20 November, 1751, by Joseph Cowles and David Hills.

Court Record, Page 132—5 June, 1750: Adms. granted unto Timothy Case of Hartford, who gave bonds with Joseph Keney, Jr., of Hartford.

Record of Distribution from File. Date, January, 1752:
To John Barnard there was a note of hand due of £50, which was included.

	£ s d
To John Barnard and Mary his wife, land in Hartford,	82-05-00
To John Barnard and Mary his wife, land in Branford,	19-10-00
To Uriah Austin and Abigail his wife,	50-00-00
To Timothy Case,	50-00-00
To John Arnold and Lucy his wife,	50-00-00
To Isaac Tucker and Sarah his wife,	50-00-00
To the heirs of John Case,	50-00-00

NOTE: It is to be understood that the wife of Desborah Spencer is to have her thirds for her improvement as dowry set out to her in the distribution of her former husband John Case. After the sd. Sarah Spencer's decease, John Arnold and Lucy his wife to have the north part, Isaac Tucker and Sarah the middle part, and the south part to the heirs of John Case deceased. By Joseph Cowles and David Hills, distributors.

Page 52 (Vol. XVI) 4 February, 1752: Report of the distributors.

Page 99-106.

Case, Caleb, Simsbury. Invt. £531-13-03. Taken by Isaac Butler, Samuel Roberts and Silas Fyler. Will dated 19 October, 1745.

I, Caleb Case of Simsbury, in the County of Hartford, do make this my last will and testament: I give £50 old tenor to the poor of the church in Wintingbury, to be distributed at the discretion of my brother Samuel Case and David Brown. Secondly, I do give to the heirs of my brother Ebenezer Case £40 old tenor. Moreover, I give to my brother Ezericom Case his son Samuel £20 old tenor. I likewise give to my brother Samuel Case his two daughters £40 old tenor. 3rdly, I do give to my sister Mary Alvord her children £20 old tenor. Next, I do give to my sister Mercie Barbour her children £30 old tenor. I likewise give to my sister Eunice Stratton £20 old tenor. I likewise give a certain debt to my brother Stratton which he owes me, and the rest of my estate I give to my brother Nathaniel Case. And I do appoint my brother Samuel Case and my brother Nathaniel Case to be executors.

Witness: *Josiah Alvord,*   CALEB CASE, LS.
William Manly, George Manly, Noadiah Burr.

Court Record, Page 14—10 June, 1746: This Court grant Adms. on the estate of Caleb Case, late of Simsbury, unto Samuel Case of Simsbury, who gave bonds with Nathaniel (——————————) of Simsbury of £700.

Page 22—2 September, 1746: The last will and testament of Caleb Case, late of Simsbury decd., was now exhibited in Court by Samuel and Nathaniel Case, executors. Proven and ordered to be recorded and kept on file.

Page 89.

Case, Edward, Simsbury. Invt. £221-14-06. Taken 23 June, 1746, by Jacob Reed, Azariah Wilcocks and Michael Humphrey.

Court Record, Page 15—1st July, 1746: This Court grant Adms. on the estate of Edward Case, late of Simsbury, unto Timothy Case of Simsbury, brother of the sd. decd., who gave bonds with Samuel Case of £200.

Page 306.

Case, John, Glastonbury. Invt. £48-10-03. Taken 1st July, 1749, by Jonathan Webster of Glastonbury and Timothy Porter, Jr., of Hartford.

Court Record, Page 104—4 July, 1749: An inventory of the estate of John Case was now exhibited in Court by Sarah Case, Adms. Accepted and ordered to be recorded and kept on file. The sd. Adms. now informs this Court that the estate is insolvent. Also, this Court have now set out to the widow of the sd. decd., for her necessary use, £24-07-06. Account allowed and is on file.

Page 137—7 August, 1750: Whereas, the estate of John Case, late of Glastonbury decd., is rendered insolvent, this Court do appoint Timothy Porter and James Porter of Hartford to be commissioners to adjust the claims of the creditors.

Page 206-7.

Case, Joseph, Simsbury. Died 11 August, 1748. Inventory taken 1st September, 1748, by Jonathan Pettebone, Amos Wilcocks and David Phelps. Will dated 17 February, 1742-3.

I, Joseph Case, Sen., of Simsbury, in the County of Hartford, do make this my last will and testament: Imprimis: I do give unto my beloved wife Ann 10 acres of land, to be taken on the south side of my part of that land that I bought of Capt. James Cornish in company with my son Jacob Case and his wife Abigail, to be to her my sd. wife Ann and to her heirs and assigns forever. Also, I do give unto my wife the use of 1-3 part of all my improveable land and buildings during her life. Also, I do give unto my wife Ann the 1-2 of all my personal estate, to be her own forever. I do hereby give unto my son Joseph and to his heirs and assigns forever all the remainder of the land which I have in Nod meadow that I have not already disposed of by deed, and also all the remainder of my land that I have lying in the meadow plaine within the field which my sd. son's house stands on, lying south on the road. I give to my son Jacob a tenth part of all my homelott lying at Weatogue, on the west side of the river, be the same more or less, with 1-5 part of the dwelling house standing thereon; also 32 acres and 1-2 of land to be taken in my lott lying on the Bauld Hill in the 1st half mile tier of lotts within the west mountains, and also 9 1-2 acres of land in the first mile tier of lotts west of the meadow plain, next to Joseph Mills's lott. Also, I do give to my sons, Josiah and Joel, to each of them in equal shares, 19 1-2 acres of land to be taken off the north side of my lott lying on the Bauld Hill, in the 1st mile tier; and also 6 acres of the land that I bought of my son Jacob in that lott that I bought of Capt. Cornish in company with my sd. son Jacob and his wife Abigail; and also 58 acres of land to be taken on the north side of the same lott; and also 33 acres of land (being my lott lying in the 2nd mile tier in the Weatogue division) at a place called Rail Hill; and also 2-10 parts of my homelott lying at Weatogue, on the west side of the river. Also, I give to my son Benajah 1-4 part of all my personal estate. And I also give to my son Joel 1-8 part of all my personal estate. All the rest of my estate, real and personal, I give to my sons (if I have any real estate not disposed of), to be equally divided between my sons Joseph, Jacob, David and Josiah. I appoint my wife Ann and my son Joseph executors.

Witness: *John Humphrey,*   JOSEPH CASE, LS.
John Hoskin, Rhoda X *Alvord.*

Court Record, Page 74—6 September, 1748: The last will and testament of Joseph Case, late of Simsbury decd., was now exhibited in Court by Anne Case and Joseph Case, executors. Proven. Exhibit of an inventory. Both ordered to be recorded and kept on file.

Page 36.

Case, Penelope, Simsbury. Died 27 June, 1746. Widow of Daniel Case of sd. Simsbury decd. Invt. £223-15-11. Taken 1st September, 1746, by James Case and Andrew Robe.

Court Record, Page 25—7 October, 1746: An account of Adms. on the estate of Penelope Case, late of Simsbury, was now exhibited in Court by Daniel Case, Adms.:

	£ s d
Paid in debts and charges,	60-14-03
Credit received,	1-10-06
Inventory with credit,	223-02-04
Debts and charges subtracted,	60-14-03
There remains to be distributed,	162-09-00
To Daniel Case, eldest son, his double part,	46-08-04
To Dudley Case, to Zaccheus Case, to Ezekiel Case, to each,	23-04-02
To Mindwell Case alias Addams, to Susannah Case, to each,	23-04-02

And appoint Joshua Holcomb, Andrew Robe and Capt. Nathaniel Holcomb, of Simsbury, to be distributors.

Page 54-5-6-7.

Case, Richard, Simsbury. Invt. £603-06-08. Taken 23 June, 1746, by Jacob Reed, Michael Humphrey and Azariah Wilcocks. Will dated 18 April, 1740.

I, Richard Case of Simsbury, in the County of Hartford, do make this my last will and testament: I give to my wife Amy 1-2 of my homelott and orchard, that is, 1-2 of my tract of land that my house and barn stand upon. I give her the use of sd. homelott during her life, after my decease, with the use of the whole house and barn, for her use and profit during the term of her natural life; and also give to her 1-3 part of my moveable estate. I give unto my son Timothy 1-2 of the forementioned homelott where my house and barn stand upon, after my decease, and the other half with the house and barn I give to my son Timothy after the decease of his mother, my wife Amy, to him and to his heirs forever. I also give unto my son Timothy all my lands that belong unto me whereon he now lives, except 40 rods on the north side through the sd. lott and one mile in length, which I reserve for my son Edward. I also give unto him, his heirs and assigns forever, 1-2 of my woodlott against Hazel Meadow, provided he pay his double part to my daughters with my two other sons

Edward and Richard, provided my daughters have not their portion paid out of the moveables; or if I leave not moveables enough for their legacies or portions. I give unto my son Richard all the remaining part of that lott of land upon Chesnut Hill where he now lives (that part which now belongs unto me), I give it unto him after my decease, provided he pay 1-4 part of that which is wanting in my moveables in my daughters' portions. I give unto my son Edward the remaining part of that lott by my son Timothy, which is on the north side, 40 rods in width and one mile in length, taking in that piece of land that I have bought of Amos Case and Isaac Case. I also give unto him and his heirs and assigns forever, after my decease, a certain tract or piece of land lying upon Calf's Tongue Brook, where my old barn was. Furthermore, I give unto my son Edward the 1-2 of that aforesd. woodlott lying against Hazel Meadow, to him and his heirs forever, provided he pays 1-4 part of what is wanting in my moveable estate to make up my daughters' portions which I shall give them. I give unto my daughter Amy £30 besides what she has already had, to be paid unto her out of my moveable estate. I give unto my other three daughters, Margaret, Lydia and Mary, £40 to each of them, to be paid out of my moveable estate. I appoint my wife Amy and son Timothy to be executors.

Witness: *Samuel Pettebone,*   RICHARD CASE, LS.
Hepzibah Pettebone, Benajah Case.

Court Record, Page 17—16 July, 1746: The last will and testament of Richard Case, late of Simsbury, was now exhibited in Court by Amy Case and Timothy Case, executors. Will proven.

Page 38-9.

Chapman, Samuel, Tolland. Will dated 25 June, 1745. I, Samuel Chapman of Tolland, having undertaken an expedition against our enemies whereby I look upon myself as more immediately exposed than in my common business, do make this my last will and testament: I give to my wife Hannah Chapman, in lieu of her dowry, 1-3 part of the improvement of all my improved lands, together with the use of two rooms in my dwelling house as she shall choose, and the use of 1-4 part of my barn so long as she shall remain my widow. And when the time shall commence, either by the death or marriage to another, my will is that the use of the sd. land, house and barn shall belong to those of my children that I shall hereafter give the same unto. And also I give to my sd. wife 1-3 part of my moveable estate to be at her own dispose forever. Item. I give to my son Samuel Chapman, he paying the several sums hereafter ordered to him, my house and barn with other housing, together with that part of my homestead lying on the north side of the road, beginning at a cross fence about 30 rods west of my house and running the range of the sd. fence until it come to the land I lately bought of Mr. Dimmock, and to extend east of Mr. Dimmock's land; only reserving 1 acre on the north side to my son Simon as shall be most convenient for him for his building, if he live to have occasion therefore. And also I give to my son Samuel all my lands lying on the south side of the road on which my dwelling house stands, being about 220 acres; and also 100 acres of land lying near the northeast corner of Tolland, together with 38 acres of land lying at Wintonbury in Windsor; and also about 70 acres of undivided land in sd. Tolland. Item. I give to my son Elijah Chapman, when he shall come to the age of 21 years, 210 acres of land lying on the westerly end of my farm adjoining John Bacor's, and land I bought of Col. Whiting; also the lott called Whipple lott. Item. I give to my son .Simon, when he shall come to the age of 21 years, the remaining part of the lands I bought of Col. Whiting, with 20 acres I lately purchased of my neighbor Dimmock, and the acre I reserved on the north side of Samuel's land, he my son Simon discharging (when he comes of age) my son Samuel of a legacy of £50 given to him by his uncle Simon Chapman, which Samuel by sd. will is obliged to pay. I give to my daughter Sarah Kingsbury, to be paid by my son Samuel, £160 old tenor money. I give to my daughter Hannah Chapman £400, which I order my son Samuel to pay. Item. I give to my daughter Mary Chapman £400, which I order my son Samuel to pay unto her. Item. I give to my daughter Ruth Chapman £400, which payment I order my sons Samuel and Elijah to pay. Item. I give to my daughter Margaret £400, which I order my sons Samuel and Elijah to pay in equal proportions. And whereas, it is apparent that our paper currency is of uncertain value, I order that the above sd. legacies be paid to my daughters at the rate of silver at 33 shillings the ounce. I appoint my wife Hannah Chapman and son Samuel Chapman and my son Elijah Chapman executors.

Witness: *Stephen Steele,*   SAMUEL CHAPMAN, LS.
John Lothrop, Daniel Benton.

Court Record, Page 21—5 August, 1746: The last will and testament of Capt. Samuel Chapman, late of Tolland decd., was exhibited in Court by Samuel Chapman, one of the executors. Will proven, approved and ordered to be recorded and kept on file.

Inventory in Vol. XVI, Page 209.

Chapman, Simon, Windsor. Invt. £4620-05-07. Taken 16 January, 1750-1, by Joshua Wills and Joseph West.

Court Record, Page 112—12 December, 1749: Adms. granted to Samuel Chapman of Tolland, who gave bond with Niel McLean of Hartford of £2000.

Page 86-105.

Charter, George, Hartford. Died 6 November, 1745. Invt. £833-05-09. Taken 26 June, 1746, by Joseph Cowles and Samuel Smith.

Court Record, Page 16—1 July, 1746: Adms. to John Charter, son of the said deceased, who gave bond with Samuel Smith of Hartford of £500.

Page 90—23 January, 1748-9: An account of Adms. was now exhibited in Court by John Charter, Adms. Accepted.

Page 112—5 December, 1749: This Court appoint Sarah Charter, widow, to be guardian to Archibald Charter, 13 years of age, Ann 10, James 8, and Mary 6 years of age, children of George Charter deceased. Recog., £300.

Page 10 (Vol. XVI) 1st January, 1750-1: John Charter, Adms., exhibited a further account of his Adms. Accepted. This Court order distribution, viz., to Sarah Charter, widow, 1-3 of the moveable estate to be her own forever, and 1-3 of the real estate during life; to John Charter, eldest son, his double share; and to George, Archabel, James and Sarah Charter, Elizabeth, Ann and Mary Charter, children of the deceased, their single shares. And appoint Jonathan Hills, Samuel Smith and Timothy Williams, of Hartford, to distribute the estate accordingly.

Page 352. Additional Invt. on Page 357.

Chester, Mercy, Wethersfield. Invt. £1837-01-06. Taken 5 December, 1749, by John Lusk and Jno. Paterson.

Court Record, Page 110—7 November, 1749: Adms. granted unto Eliphalet Whittlesey, Jr., who gave bond with Zachariah Seamore of Hartford of £2000.

Page 117—6 February, 1749-50: An account of Adms. was exhibited by Eliphalet Whittlesey, Adms., which account is accepted. This Court order the estate distributed as follows: To Dorothy, the wife of Capt. Martin Kellogg, and to Widow Sarah Lamb, the only surviving heirs, to each of them £794-08-18 1-2. And appoint John Paterson and John Lusk, of Wethersfield, distributors.

Page 122—12 March, 1749-50: Report of the distributors.

Page 159.

Clark, Berzillai, Hartford. Invt. £917-16-01. Taken 3 November, 1747, by John Cook and William Day.

Court Record, Page 52—1st December, 1747: Adms. granted unto Sarah Clark, widow, who gave bond with William Day of £700.

Page 63 (Vol. XVI) 5 May, 1752: Josiah Clark, a minor, age 15 years, son of Berzillai Clark, late of Hartford decd., chose Ithamer Andruss to be his guardian. Recog., £500.

Page 23 (Vol. XVII) 2 April, 1754: An account of Adms. was exhibited in Court by William Day, attorney to the Adms. on sd. estate. Accepted. This Court order distribution of the estate, viz.: To Sarah

Clark, widow, her thirds of real and personal estate; to Josiah Clark his double share; to Elisha, Samuel and Timothy Clark and Hannah Clark alias Cadwell (see file: wife of Nehemiah Cadwell) and Sarah Clark, the rest of the children, to each of them their single shares. And appoint Richard Edwards, Joseph Church and Daniel Butler distributors. Sarah Clark, daughter of Berzillai Clark, made choice of her aunt Mary Butler to be her guardian.

Clark, Jonathan, Middletown. Court Record, Page 47—6 October, 1747: This Court grant letters of Adms. on sd. estate unto Cheny Clark, who gave bond with Samuel Pelton of £300.

Clark, Joseph, Hartford. Court Record, Page 12—13 May, 1746: Joseph Clark, a minor, age 19 years, son of Joseph Clark, late of Hartford deceased, chose Elisha Smith to be his guardian. Recog., £500.

Page 377.

Clark, Samuel, Simsbury. Invt. £2560 in land; £55-10-00 in silver. Taken 25 December, 1749, by Isaac Gillett, Joseph Cornish and Samuel Owen.

Court Record, Page 113—22 December, 1749: Adms. granted unto Joel Clark and Samuel Clark of Northampton, in Hampshire County, sons of the deceased, who gave bonds with Timothy Adams of sd. Simsbury of £2000.

Page 53 (Vol. XVI) 4 February, 1752. Symsbury, 5 April, 1750: Then we, William Ross and his wife of Simsbury, David Clark, and Charles Thrall of Windsor in right of his wife, have received of Joel Clark, Adms., the sum of £104-15-06 apiece in money, which is our part in full of the deceased his estate. And we do discharge all demands on sd. estate. In witness whereof we have set to our hands in presence of

Samuel Clark, Samuel Owen,	WILLIAM ROSS,
Samuel Clark, William Ross,	DAVID CLARK,
Samuel Clark, David Clark.	CHARLES THRALL.

Page 419.

Collins, Daniel, Middletown. Invt. £887-13-10. Taken 26 May, 1750, by Isaac North, Richard Hubbard and Abraham Harris.

Court Record, Page 131—5 June, 1750: This Court grant Adms. on the estate of Daniel Collins, late of Middletown decd., unto Hannah Collins, widow, who gave bond with Charles Nott of Wethersfield of £500.

Page 64 (Vol. XVI) 3 June, 1752: An account of Adms. on the estate of Daniel Collins was now exhibited in Court by Hannah Collins, widow. Accepted by the Court.

Page 123.

Collier, Abell, Hartford. Invt. £63-12-10. Taken 1st December, 1747, by Moses Nash and Thomas Hosmer.

Court Record, Page 13—3 June, 1746: Thomas Collier, a minor, 16 years of age, son of Abell Collier, chose Jonathan Olcott to be his guardian.

Page 28—2 December, 1746: Adms. granted unto Stephen Hosmer of Hartford, who gave bonds with David Ensign of £200.

Page 53—1st December, 1747: The Adms. reports the estate insolvent and prays that commissioners may be appointed: Whereupon this Court appoint Moses Nash and John Whitman, of Hartford, commissioners.

Page 59—1st March, 1747-8: Report of the commissioners.

Page 77—4 October, 1748: This Court appoint John Whitman of Hartford guardian to Joseph Collier, a minor, 11 years of age, son of Abell Collier. Recog., £500.

Page 90—7 February, 1748-9: An averidge was now made to the creditors.

Page 69 (Vol. XVI) 7 July, 1752: Joseph Collier, a minor, son of Abell Collier, now 14 years of age, chose his brother Thomas Collier to be his guardian. And this Court appoint the sd. Thomas Collier guardian to Rachel Collier, aged 11 years, daughter of the deceased. Recog., £300 for each minor.

Page 177-345.

Collyer, Rachel, Hartford. Invt. £1216-08-03. Taken 16 May, 1748, by Ebenezer Sedgewick and Moses Nash. Will dated 6 February, 1747-8.

I, Rachel Collyer of Hartford, doe make this my last will and testament: I give to my son Thomas 5 and 1-2 acres of land formerly mortgaged with Stephen Hosmore, being the west part of my homelott; likewise 10 1-2 acres of the remaining part of my land; also my dwelling house. Item. I give to my son Joseph the other half of my land exclusive of the 5 1-2 acres above mentioned. Item. I give my gristmill to my three daughters, viz., Sarah, Rachel and Mary; and if either of them shall die before they come of age, provision shall be made for the other two. Item. I give to my two sons, Thomas and Joseph, equal liberty of redeeming the above-mentioned mill, giving to their sisters the proportion as it shall be set in the inventory and making the money as good to them as money shall be when this mill is inventoryed. Item. It is my will further, that proper measures be taken whereby the earnings of the mill be disposed of to pay for rebuilding; and it is to be understood that my daughters take the benefit by the mill till that be paid. And I do hereby appoint my good friend Henry Brace, Jr., to be my executor.

Witness: *Isaac Goodwin,*   RACHEL X COLLYER, LS.
Stephen Hosmer, Lydia Merry.

Court Record, Page 98—2 May, 1749: Invt. exhibited by Stephen Brace, Jr.

Colwell (Caldwell), John. Court Record, Page 59—10 February, 1747-8: Charles Colwell, a minor, 15 years of age, son of John Colwell decd., chose his father-in-law Niel McLean of Hartford to be his guardian. Recog., £500.

Page 146-7-8-9.

Cook, Capt. Joseph, Hartford. Invt. £1517-00-02. Taken 24 December, 1747, by Joseph Talcott and Joseph Hosmer. Will dated 17 June, 1729.

I, Joseph Cook of Hartford, do make this my last will and testament: I give to my wife Rachel all my moveable estate and all my housing and lands to improve for her own proper use during the term of her natural life. 2ndly: My will is that my wife give some of my wearing clothes to my two brothers, Noah Cook and Eliakim Cook, according to her discretion. 3rd: I give to Dositheus Humphrey, son of Nathaniel and Agnes Humphrey, that houseing and land that was my brother Aaron Cook's. And also I give to him, the abovesd. Dositheus Humphrey, 1-2 of the lott adjoining, which land I bought of my brother Isaac Merrells, splitting that lott east and west. And I give to the abovesd. Dositheus Humphrey 1-2 of that land at Rocky Hill which I bought of John Grave and his heirs. 4th: I give the house that I now live in, and all the land adjoining to it not already given to Dositheus Humphrey, with 1-2 of the Rocky Hill lott which I bought of John Graves's heirs, and all my land in the South Meadow, unto Joseph Cook, son of my brother Noah Cook of North Hampton, in the County of Hampshire and the Province of Massachusetts Bay, in New England. And it is to be understood that I give the houseing and lands above mentioned to Dositheus Humphrey and Joseph Cook, to them and their heirs forever. 5th: I give to the abovesd. Joseph Cook my gunn and my sword and belt. 6th: I give to Agnes Humphrey, dafter of Nathaniel and Agnes Humphrey, £60 money, to be paid out of my stock or money by my executrix as she can conveniently pay it to her. 7th: I give to my sister Esther Wright £10 money, to be paid out of my moveable estate if there be any left after my wife's death. 8th: All my moveable estate, both stock and debts due to my estate, and moneys, I give to my wife Rachel Cook to dispose of forever as her own proper estate. But if my wife does not dispose of my moveables nor live to spend them, then my will is that they shall be equally divided between the three above legatees, that is to say, Dositheus Humphrey, Joseph Cook and Agnes Humphrey. 9th: Further, my will is that all my undivided land shall be equally divided between the two legatees, Joseph Cook and Dositheus Humphrey above mentioned. I appoint my wife Rachel Cook to be my executrix.

Witness: *James Handerson,*   JOSEPH COOK, LS.
John Knowles, John Whiting.

Court Record, Page 53-4—1st December, 1747: The last will and testament of Capt. Joseph Cook, late of Hartford, was now exhibited in Court by Rachel Cook, executrix. Will proven and ordered recorded.

Page 156.

Cook, Lydia, Tolland. Invt. £79-09-01. Taken 7 November, 1747, by John Abbot and Ephraim Grant.

Court Record, Page 48—3 November, 1747: This Court grant Adms. on the estate of Lydia Cook, late of Tolland, unto Joshua Wills of Tolland, who gave bonds with John Brace of Tolland.

Page 82—22 December, 1748: An account of Adms. on the estate of Lydia Cook, late of Tolland decd., was now exhibited in Court by Joshua Wills, Adms.: Paid in debts and charges, £64-16-07. Account accepted and ordered on file. Moved for distribution:

	£	s	d
Moveable estate by record,	79	09	00
Debts and charges subtracted,	64	16	07

	£	s	d
There remains to be distributed,	14	12	06
To Richard Cook, Joseph Cook and Benjamin Cook, to each,	2	01	09
To the heirs of Mary Cook alias Gilbert, to Abigail Cook alias Yeomans, to Elizabeth Cook alias Barbour, and to Jemima Cook alias Wills, to each of them the sum of	2	09	01

And appoint John Abbott, Samuel West and Lt. Ephraim Grant, of Tolland, distributors.

Invt. on File. Add. Invt. in Vol. XVI, Page 166-333.

Cook, Robert, Blandford. Invt. £39-17-00. Taken 25 July, 1746, by Nathaniel Hitchcock and Eldad Lewis.

Additional inventory: An account of debts due to my father's estate, which I have received, and are to be added to his inventory, viz.: Of Daniel Matthews, £10-17-00; of Widow Nichols, £11-11-00; of Widow Rice, £1-07-00; of Ebenezer Kimbal, £82-02-00; of Mr. Clenacan, £4-00-00; total, £99-00-00.   ROBERT COOK, *Adms.*

Court Record, Page 25—7 October, 1746: Adms. granted to Robert Cook on the estate of Robert Cook, late of Blandford, in the County of Hampshire and Province of Massachusetts Bay, of all the estate that the sd. deceased died seized of in sd. County of Hartford. And Robert Cook, Adms., gave bonds with Isaac Newell of Farmington of £500.

Page 95.

Cornwell, John, Middletown. Invt. £1356-07-00. Taken 29 May, 1746, by Benjamin Cornwell and Jonathan Allyn.

Court Record, Page 12—3 June, 1746: This Court grant Adms. on the estate of John Cornwell, of Middletown, unto William Rockwell of Middletown, who gave bonds with Daniel Warner of Middletown of £500.

Page 93—20 March, 1748-9: William Rockwell, Adms. on the estate of John Cornwell, late of Middletown, now exhibits an account of Adms.: Paid in debts and charges and spent in the family, £139-16-02. Which account is allowed. Now moves for a distribution, as follows: To Mary Cornwell, widow, to John Cornwell, eldest son, to Abijah Cornwell, Thomas Cornwell, Samuel Cornwell, Sarah Cornwell, alias Harris, Mary Cornwell and Hannah Cornwell. And appoint Capt. Jonathan Allin, Lt. Nathaniel Gilbert and Mr. Joseph Wright, of Middletown, distributors. And also to set out the widow's dowry to her.

Page 29 (Vol. XVI) 2 July, 1751: Report of the distributors.

Page 59—5 March, 1752: Abijah Cornwell, aged 14 years, son of John Cornwell, made choice of William Rockwell to be his guardian. Recog., £600.

Cornwell, William. Court Record, Page 21—5 August, 1746: This Court grant Adms. on ye part of the estate of William Cornwell, late of Newport, in the Colony of Rhode Island, decd., as now is in the Colony of Connecticut, unto Samuel Macky of Middletown, in the County of Hartford, who gave bonds with Benjamin Cornwell of Middletown of £500.

Page 284-5.

Cowles, John, Farmington. Inventory taken 5 December, 1748, by Thomas Wadsworth and John Newell. Will dated 8 January, 1746-7.

I, John Cowles of Farmingtown, do make and ordain this my last will and testament: I give to my wife Experience Cowles, alias Chapwell, one cow, one three-year-old heifer and 10 sheep, provided I do leave such creatures at my decease, otherwise I do not give them to her; also 1-2 of my wearing apparrel and all my bedding and furniture (excepting one bedd and a boulster), all my pewter, brass and iron in the house (except 1 iron pott), and all my linen; also all my earthern and wooden moveables in the house; also one book. 2nd, I give to my cousin Anne Porter, wife of Samuel Porter, one feather bed, one boulster, and one iron pott called Anne's. 3rd, I give to my cousins Caleb and Daniel Cowles, sons of Caleb Cowles decd., £10 to each of them, old tenor; and to my cousin Esther Cowles, dafter of Nathaniel Cowles, Jr., decd., £10 old tenor: all to be paid within one year after my decease. 4th, I give to my cousin Nathaniel Cowles, now dwelling with me, all my land and buildings, cattle, horses and sheep (except what is above mentioned), all my team tackling and tools whatsoever, yea, all my real and personal estate whatsoever (except what is above mentioned). And I do hereby constitute my cousin Nathaniel Cowles executor.

Witness: *Thomas Wadsworth,*   JOHN X COWLES, LS.
Timothy Porter, Samuel Porter.

Court Record, Page 81—6 December, 1748: The last will and testament of John Cowles, late of Farmingtown, was now exhibited by Nathaniel Cowles, executor. Proven. Also exhibit of an inventory, which was ordered to be recorded and kept on file.

Page 96-7-8.

Cravath, Samuel, Middletown. Invt. £960-17-09. Taken 13 November, 1746, by Samuel Starr and William Rockwell.

Court Record, Page 29—24 November, 1746: This Court grant Adms. on the estate of Samuel Cravath, late of Middletown, unto Eunice Cravath, widow of sd. deceased, who gave bonds with Jeremiah Markham of Middletown of £1000 money.

Page 37—16 April, 1747: This Court appoint Eunice Cravath, widow, to be guardian to her children, viz., Samuel, age 11 years, James 9 years, Eunice 4 years, Abigail 2 years of age and Ezekiel 7 months, children of Samuel Cravath. Recog., £200.

Page 37—16 April, 1747: Elizabeth Cravath, a minor, age 13 years, chose her mother Eunice Cravath to be her guardian. Recog., £300.

Page 72—6 July, 1748: Eunice Cravath, Adms., exhibits an account of her Adms. Accepted.

Page 110—14 November, 1749: Samuel Cravath, a minor, 14 years of age, chose Jonathan Allin of Middletown to be his guardian. Recog., £500.

Page 115—2 January, 1749-50: Eunice Cravath, Adms. on the estate of Samuel Cravath, late of Middletown, now moves to this Court for a distribution of the moveable estate of the sd. decd. (to her): Whereupon the Court appoint William Rockwell and Samuel Starr of Middletown to distribute to the sd. Adms. 1-3 of the moveable estate:

	£ s d
Inventory with credit received,	1020-05-04
The real part,	380-00-00

	£ s d
There remains,	640-05-04
Debts and charges allowed,	112-15-06

There remains to be divided,	527-09-10
Of which the widow's thirds thereof is in moveables,	175-16-07

Page 122—12 March, 1749-50: A distribution of the estate of Samuel Cravath, late of Middletown, was now exhibited and accepted.

Page 128—10 May, 1750: Capt. Jonathan Allin of Middletown, guardian to Samuel Cravath of Middletown, now moves to this Court for a distribution of the estate of the sd. decd.: Whereupon this Court appoint William Rockwell, Samuel Starr and Jacob Whitmore of Middletown to distribute the real and personal estate to and among the widow and heirs, viz.: To Samuel, eldest son of the said deceased, his double share or part, to be set to him in the real part; and to James Cravath a single part; and to Eunice, Elizabeth and Abigail Cravath, daughters of the sd. decd., their single portions of the sd. estate. And also set out to Eunice Cravath, alias Miller, relict of the sd. decd., for her improvement during life. (Sd. relict has already received her part of the moveable estate distributed to her.)

Page 137—7 August, 1750: Elizabeth Cravath, a minor, 15 years of age, daughter of Samuel Cravath, chose William Rockwell of Middletown to be her guardian. Recog., £300.

Page 59 (Vol. XVI) 5 March, 1752: James Cravath, a minor, age 14 years, son of Samuel Cravath, chose Capt. Jonathan Allen of sd. Middletown to be his guardian. Recog., £600.

Page 40.

Croswell, Thomas, Hartford. Invt. £149-19-09. Taken 24 April, 1746, by John Edwards and Samuel Flagg.

Court Record, Page 10—1st April, 1746: This Court grant Adms. on the estate of Thomas Croswell, late of Hartford, unto Hannah Croswell, widow, and John Hart of Hartford, who gave bond with Thomas Seymour and Hezekiah Colyer of Hartford of £500 money.

Page 31—23 January, 1746-7: John Hart, Adms. on the estate of Thomas Croswell, presented to this Court a list of debts due from sd. estate, whereby it appears the estate is insolvent. And this Court now appoint Deacon John Edwards and Mr. Samuel Flagg commissioners to adjust the claims of the creditors.

Page 47—6 October, 1747: This Court now have set out of moveables of the estate of Thomas Croswell to Hannah, his widow, for her necessary use, £36-14-08. The amount thereof is on file.

Page 134—11 June, 1750: Caleb Croswell, a minor, 17 years of age, son of Thomas Croswell, chose Isaac Kellogg of New Hartford to be his guardian. Recog., £400.

Page 135—2 August, 1750: Joseph Croswell, 9 years of age: this Court appoint Hannah Croswell to be his guardian, who acknowledged herself bound with Jonathan Olcott of Hartford in £500.

Crow, Christopher. Court Record, Page 35—30 March, 1747: Eunice Crow, 6 years of age, daughter of Christopher Crow, late of Hartford decd.: this Court appoint Ann Crow to be her guardian. Recog., £100.

Page 85 (Vol. XVI) 6 February, 1753: Reuben Crow, a minor, age 14 years, son of Christopher Crow, late of Hartford deceased, chose Josiah Bigelow of Hartford to be his guardian. Recog., £300 money.

Page 415-16.

Crowell, John, Middletown. Invt. £1362-19-00. Taken 5 June, 1750, by John Hubbard, Samuel Adkins and William Rockwell.

Court Record, Page 136—7 August, 1750: This Court grants Adms. on the estate of John Crowell, late of Middletown, unto Sarah Crowell, widow, who gave bonds with surety as the law directs. This Court appoint Sarah Crowell, widow, to be guardian to her children, viz., John Crowell, age 9 years, Samuel 8 years, Daniel 6 years, Abigail 4, Seth 2 years, and Mary about 7 months old, children of John Crowell. Recog., £400.

Page 344.

Curtiss, Eleazer, Wethersfield. Invt. £89-19-06. Taken 25 September, 1749, by Gideon Goodrich and Thomas Curtiss.

Court Record, Page 108—3 October, 1749: This Court appoint Elizabeth Curtiss, widow, to be guardian to her children, viz., Jonathan Curtiss, age 7 years, and Elizabeth Curtiss, age 5 years, children of Eleazer Curtiss decd. Recog., £500.

Page 89-91.

Curtiss, Samuel, Wethersfield. Invt. £1556-07-02. Taken 12 February, 1746, by Samuel Buck, Samuel Butler and Joseph Woodhouse.

Court Record, Page 4—4 March, 1745-6: Adms. granted unto Samuel Curtiss, son of the deceased, who gave bond with Caleb Griswold of £2000.

Inventory on File.

Cusshaw, Benjamin (Indian), late of Wongunk, in Middletown, in the County of Hartford, deceased. Invt. £59-10-00. Taken 13 March, 1746-7, by John Fisk and Jeremiah Goodwin.

Court Record, Page 21—6 May, 1746: Adms. granted unto Hugh White of Middletown, who gave bond with Jonathan Olcott of Hartford of £400.

Page 40—10 June, 1747: Hugh White, Adms., exhibited an account of his Adms.: Paid in debts and charges, £17-07-11. Which account is accepted.

Daily, Joseph. Court Record, Page 88—28 January, 1748-9: Field Daily, 14 years of age, son of Joseph Daily, late of Middletown decd., made choice of Joseph Daily of Middletown to be his guardian. Recog., £500. Cert: *Seth Wetmore, J. P.*

Page 1.

Damon, Timothy, Hartford. Invt. £280-05-02. Taken 3 December, 1745, by Nathaniel Olcott and Josiah Olcott.

Court Record, Page 1—3 December, 1745: This Court grant Adms. on the estate of Timothy Damon, late of Hartford, unto Susannah Damon, widow of sd. decd., who gave bonds with her father-in-law Benjamin Damon of £500.

Page 77 (Vol. XVI) 7 November, 1752: Susannah Deming, Adms., exhibited an account of her Adms. Accepted. (*Deming,* as recorded.)

Page 13-16.

Deming, Daniel, Stepney Parish, Wethersfield. Died 20 October, 1746. Invt. £278-09-06. Taken 6 January, 1745-6, by Josiah Churchill, Samuel Belding and Henry Grimes.

Court Record, Page 7—4 February, 1745-6: This Court grant Adms. on the estate of Daniel Deming, of Wethersfield, unto Eunice Deming, widow, who gave bond with Thomas Deming of Wethersfield of £700.

Page 72—6 July, 1748: Eunice Deming, Adms., exhibited an account of her Adms. Accepted and ordered to be recorded.

Page 234, 241, 293.

Deming, Daniel, Stepney Parish, Wethersfield. Invt. £3870-00-00 (£60 in Goshen, all in land). Taken 8 August, 1748, by Gideon Goodrich, Samuel Smith and Josiah Willard. And in Goshen by Gideon Hurlbut and Benjamin Phelps (no date).

Will dated 3 August, 1747. I, Daniel Deming of Wethersfield, do make this my last will and testament: I give to my wife Mehetabell Deming my riding mare and my great silver cup, together with 1-3 part of all my household goods and moveable estate. I give to my wife the use of 1-3 part of my house and the rest of my buildings, as also the use of 1-3 of all my lands, during her natural life. I give to my wife the use of the whole of my garden adjoining to the shop, as also the use of my *still*, so long as she remains my widow. I give to my son Jonathan Deming my house and homelott with all the buildings thereon standing, together with all the rest of my lands lying within the present bounds of Stepney Parish, he allowing to my wife the improvement of her thirds as before mentioned. Further, I give to my son Jonathan a cow I bought for him instead of the colt given him by his uncle Charles. Also, I give to him a yoke of steers that come of sd. cow, or another yoke, which he shall choose. Also, I give to my son Jonathan my cart, chains, plows, with all my husbandry utensils; also one featherbed and furniture. I give to my son my *still* after my wife shall have done with it, he paying to his sisters 2-3 of the value of it at inventory price. Also I give to my son all the right and title that I have or may have in the common and undivided lands in Wethersfield. I give to my daughters, Abigail and Lydia Deming, the remainder of all my household goods and moveable estate, together with the remainder of all my lands (not disposed of as before mentioned), to be equally divided between them, they allowing to my son Jonathan this liberty and privaledge with respect unto that lott I bought of Jonathan Riley, that when they shall be minded to sell sd. lott, if my son be able and have a desire to purchase sd. lott to keep for his own use, they shall let him have it at inventory price, he making good to them a sinking of the money from the time it was inventoried. Furthermore, I give to my two daughters, Abigail and Lydia, the liberty, use and improvement of the little bed room in the kitchen, together with the 1-2 in the south chamber in the house, so long as they shall remain unmarried. Furthermore, I give to my two daughters, equally to be divided between them, 2-3 of what my *still* shall be valued at at inventory price. I appoint my wife Mehetable to be sole executrix.

Witness: *Josiah Griswold,*   DANIEL DEMING, LS.
Ebenezer Kilby, Ebenezer Goodwin.

Court Record, Page 72—2 August, 1748: The last will and testament of Daniel Deming, late of Wethersfield decd., was now exhibited in Court by Elizabeth (Mehetabell), widow. Proven.

Page 74—5 September, 1748: An inventory of the estate of Daniel Deming, late of Wethersfield, was now exhibited in Court by Mehetabell Deming, executrix, which this Court accepts and orders to be kept on file. Jonathan Deming, a minor, 18 years of age, and Abigail Deming, chose their mother Mehetabell Deming to be their guardian. And this Court appoint the sd. Mehetabell, widow, to be guardian to Lydia Deming, a minor, 9 years of age, children of Daniel Deming. Recog., £1000.

See File:

Wethersfield, November 16th, 1761: An agreement made by John Goodrich of Glastonbury, now resident of Wethersfield, and Abigail his wife, of the one party, and Ebenezer Goodrich and Lydia his wife of the other party, of the aforesd. Wethersfield, concerning the division of land given to the aforesd. Abigail, wife of John Goodrich, and Lydia, the wife of Ebenezer Goodrich, by their honoured father Daniel Deming, late of Wethersfield deceased, to be equally divided. To this agreement wee have set to our hands and seals.

| JOHN GOODRICH, LS. | EBENEZER GOODRICH, LS. |
| ABIGAIL GOODRICH, LS. | LIDIA GOODRICH, LS. |

Witness: *John Robbins, Jr.,*
Jonathan Deming.

At a Court of Probate held at Hartford, 2nd February, 1762, this agreement was exhibited in Court and accepted to be recorded.

Test: Joseph Talcott, Clerk.

Page 112-13.

Deming, Hezekiah, Farmington. Invt. £1348-07-04. Taken 3 July, 1747, by Isaac Cowles and John Hart. Will dated 10 June, 1747.

The last will and testament of Hezekiah Deming of Farmingtown: I give to my three sons, Elisha, Eliakim and Samuel Deming, all my land lying on the north side of the river, being part of my farm on which I now live, only reserving to my wife her thirds of the improvements of the same during the time of her widowhood, to be divided equally between them. The remaining part of my farm not disposed of on the south side of the river I give to my son Elisha Deming. Also a yoke of oxen I give unto my son Samuel Deming. Also I give unto my daughter Sarah Deming the sum of £100 out of my moveable estate. Also I give unto my daughter Eunice £5 old tenor. Also I give unto my daughter Lois £5 old tenor. Also I give unto my son Benjamin Deming £5 old tenor. Also I give unto my son Zebulon Deming £10 old tenor. Also I give my wife and Samuel my saddle horse. Also I give unto my son Hezekiah Deming £70 old tenor. Also my youngest yoke of cattle I give unto my two sons Elisha and Samuel, with my cart and team tackling, plows, harrows and other furniture belonging thereto. The remainder of my estate I give unto my three sons, namely, Elisha Deming, Eliakim Deming and Samuel Deming, whom I appoint sole executors.

Witness: *John Hart,*   HEZ: DEMING, LS.
Joseph Newell, John Stedman.

Court Record, Page 41—7 July, 1747: The last will and testament of Hezekiah Deming, late of Wethersfield decd., was now exhibited by Eliakim Deming, Elisha Deming and Samuel Deming, executors. Proven and with the inventory ordered recorded.

Page 20.

Deming, Isaac, Wethersfield. Invt. £429-18-06. Taken 23 November, 1741, by Joseph Goodrich, Gideon Deming and Joshua Stoddard.

Court Record, Page 4—4 March, 1745-6: This Court grant administration on the estate of Isaac Deming, late of Wethersfield decd., unto Lydia Deming, widow, who gave bond with Gideon Deming of Wethersfield of £500. Exhibit of an inventory.

Page 105—1st August, 1749: Lydia Deming, the widow of Isaac Deming, late of Wethersfield, now moves to this Court to make distribution of his estate, both real and personal: Whereupon this Court appoint Joseph Goodrich, Joshua Stoddard and Hezekiah Butler, of Wethersfield, distributors to make distribution of the estate to the widow and children —the eldest son a double share and the younger children each a single share of the estate. The sons to have their portions in real estate. Also to set out to the sd. widow 1-3 part of the moveable estate for her own forever, and 1-3 part of the buildings and lands for her improvement during life, and make return of their doings to this Court.

Page 322.

Deming, Nathaniel, Wethersfield. Invt. £1425-09-02. Taken 31 January, 1748-9, by Jonathan Belding and Ephraim Williams.

Court Record, Page 81—6 December, 1748: This Court grant Adms. on the estate of Nathaniel Deming, late of Wethersfield, unto Mary Deming, widow, who gave bonds with Charles Deming of Wethersfield.

Page 127—1st May, 1750: An account of Adms. on the estate of Nathaniel Deming was now exhibited in Court by Mary Deming, Adms., which was allowed. Also, this Court set out to the sd. widow a list of moveables for her necessary use.

Page 134—3 July, 1750: Whereas, the General Assembly holden at Hartford on the 2nd Thursday in May, 1750, resolved that Capt. Jonathan Belding of Wethersfield should make sale of so much of the real estate of Nathaniel Deming, late of Wethersfield, as will be sufficient to pay the sum of £231-18-06 with incident charges, taking the direction of the Court of Probate in the District of Hartford thereon: Whereupon this Court directs the sd. Capt. Jonathan Belding to make sale of the land.

Page 57 (Vol. XVI) 7 April, 1752: Widow Mary Deming now moves to this Court that distribution be made of the real estate, the moveables being spent in debts and charges: Whereupon this Court appoint Capt. Jonathan Belding, Ephraim Williams and Abraham Crane, of Wethersfield, to distribute the estate, viz.: To the widow her thirds in land, and to the heirs of Charles Deming deceased their double part, and to Lois Deming alias Belding, Eunice Deming alias Churchill, Hannah Deming alias Belding, and Sarah Deming, to each of them their single shares.

Page 63—9 April, 1752: Sarah Deming, a minor, aged 14 years, daughter of Nathaniel Deming, chose her mother Mary Deming to be her guardian. Recog., £300.

Page 66—3 June, 1752: Report of the distributors.

Page 69, 232.

Deming, Thomas, Stepney Parish, Wethersfield. Invt. £322-03-03. Taken 31 March, 1747, by Jacob Williams and David Goodrich. Will dated 1st March, 1746.

I, Thomas Deming of Wethersfield, do make and ordain this my last will and testament: My will is that my wife shall have the use of 1-3 part of all my lands, together with the buildings thereon standing, house, barn, sawmill and whatever other buildings that I shall die seized of, during her natural life; and 1-3 part of my moveable estate forever. In the next place, I give to the heirs of my son Daniel decd., Giles and Abraham Deming, my grandsons, my dwelling house, barn and orchard as it is now fenced, and syder mill, half my plow land in my homelott, that is to say, the east part thereof, and also 1-2 of my mowing pasture on the north end thereof, and also 1-2 of my cow pasture on the west side. Also I give to my grandsons aforesd. a part of a lott of land I bought of the heirs of Joseph Crane of Wethersfield decd. Also I give to my grandsons aforesd. a certain tract of land known by the name of my sawmill lott, to begin at a cross highway and to extend southward until it comes to a 20-rod highway (excepting only a liberty to make a pond to maintain ye going of the sawmill). And also I give to my grandsons aforesd. all my right in the undivided land in the Township of Wethersfield aforesd., and also all my creatures that I wrought in the team in partnership with my son Daniel in his lifetime, and also a small gunn, a sword and belt, and also all my wearing apparrel and half of my team tackling. In the next place, I give to my daughter Eunice, the widow of my son Daniel decd., 2-3 of the lands and buildings herein given to my grandsons aforesd. as long as she continues my son's widow, on consideration of bringing up his children. In the next place, I give to my son Samuel Deming 1-2 of my homelott, with the house thereon standing, whereon he now liveth, viz., on the west side of sd. lott, with the orchard thereon growing, and also 1-2 of my mowing pasture on the south side thereof, and 1-2 of my cow pasture lying on the east side thereof; also certain tracts of land I bought of the heirs of Joseph Crane decd. Also, I give to my son Thomas Deming the north end of my meadow lott with my sawmill thereon standing, with the liberty of making the dam on sd. sawmill brook sufficient for the driving of sd. mill, and all the utensils belonging to the sd. mill, and also 1-2 of my team tackling; and also I give to my son Thomas Deming my bigest gunn. In the next place, I give to my son-in-law Joseph Belding 10 shillings money, old tenor, besides what I gave to him at the time of his marriage. Also, I give to my son-in-law Samuel Williams 10 shillings money, old tenor, besides what I gave him at the time of his marriage. In the next place, I give to my daughter Lucy Dickinson 1-2 of my moveable estate. Also, I give to my daughter Lucy one feather bed, with the furtniture thereto belonging, after my wife's decease; sd. bed stands in the chamber. In the next place, I give to my daughter Mary Hurlbut the other half of my moveable estate and one great Bible, after my wife's decease. I appoint my wife Mary and son Thomas Deming executors.

Witness: *Edward Bulkeley,*   THOMAS DEMING, LS.
Jonathan Bulkeley, Abigail Bulkeley.

Court Record, Page 37—7 April, 1747: An inventory of the estate of Thomas Deming, late of Wethersfield, was now exhibited, ordered recorded and kept on file.

Page 51—10 November, 1747: An account was now exhibited in Court by Thomas Deming, executor on the estate of Thomas Deming, late of Wethersfield deceased:

	£ s d
Paid in debts and charges,	46-08-02
Credit received,	3-10-04

Account is allowed and ordered to be kept on file. Now moves to this Court to distribute the moveable estate. And appoint Josiah Churchill, Ebenezer Wright and Gideon Goodrich distributors.

Dist. File: 1st March, 1748-9: To the widow, to Lucy (the wife of Elihu Dickinson), to Mary (wife of Gideon Hurlbutt), to each of them the sum of £50-19-00. By Gideon Goodrich and Ebenezer Wright.

Page 138—6 June, 1750: Report of the distributors. Accepted.

Page 362-3-4.

Denslow, Joseph, Windsor. Invt. £5362-09-10. Taken 2nd January, 1749-50, by David Elsworth, Eliakim Gaylord and Nathaniel Owen.

Court Record, Page 115—6 December, 1749: This Court grant Adms. on the estate of Joseph Denslow, late of Windsor, unto Ann Denslow, widow, and John Olds of Suffield, late of Windsor.

Page 85 (Vol. XVI) 6 February, 1753: An account of Adms. was now exhibited by John Olds and Anne Denslow alias Winchell, Adms. Accepted. This Court order the estate distributed, as follows:

	£	s	d
To Anne Denslow, alias Winchell,	389	04	11
To Joseph Denslow, eldest son,	2363	05	00
To Martin Denslow and Anne Denslow, to each,	1181	12	06

And appoint David Elsworth, Erastus Wolcott and Eliakim Gaylord distributors. This Court appoint John Olds of Suffield to be a guardian to Joseph Denslow, a minor, age 11 years, and Martin Denslow, aged 7 years, children of Joseph Denslow deceased.

Page 93—26 March, 1753: Ann Denslow, a minor, age 17 years, chose Mr. John Olds of Suffield to be her guardian. Recog., £300 for each minor.

Page 165-66-67.

Dickinson, Thomas, late of Hartford. Invt. £632-08-06. Taken 19 November, 1747, by Joseph Talcott and William Pratt.

Court Record, Page 49—3 November, 1747: This Court grants Adms. on the estate of Thomas Dickinson, late of Hartford, unto Ann Dickinson, widow, and Caleb Turner, of sd. Hartford, who gave bonds with Richard Goodman of £500.

Page 121—6 March, 1749-50: An account of Adms. on the estate of Thomas Dickinson was now exhibited in Court by Ann Dickinson, Adms.: Paid in debts and charges, £95-08-02. Which accot. this Court allows and ordered to be kept on file.

Page 48 (Vol. XVI) 3 December, 1751: Thomas Dickinson, a minor, about 15 years of age, son of Thomas Dickinson, chose his mother Ann Dickinson to be his guardian. Recog., £600.

Page 317.

Dix, John, Jr., Wethersfield. Invt. £995-05-00. Taken 12 May, 1749, by Ephraim Williams and Joseph Boardman.

Court Record, Page 95—1st Tuesday in April, 1749: This Court grant Adms. on the estate of John Dix, late of Wethersfield, unto Samuel Dix of Wethersfield, who gave bonds with Charles Deming of Wethersfield of £600.

See File:

AN AGREEMENT FOR THE SETTLEMENT OF AN ESTATE.
Know all men by these presents: That whereas wee, Moses Dix, Samuel Dix, Benjamin Dix and Sarah Smith, the wife of Joseph Smith,

all of Wethersfield (which Sarah aforesd. is natural sister in the whole
blood to the aforesd. Moses, Samuel and Benjamin Dix), are the only,
sole and proper heirs-in-law to the estate in lands of John Dix, Jr., late of
sd. Wethersfield deceased.
In witness whereof we have hereunto set our hands and seals this
7th day of July, 1752.   SAMUEL DIX, LS. | JOSEPH SMITH, LS.
                                MOSES DIX, LS. | SARAH X SMITH, LS.
                                BENJAMIN DIX, LS. |

At a Court of Probate holden at Hartford, 7th July, 1752, the above-
named heirs appeared and acknowledged the foregoing agreement to be
their free act and deed.   *Test: Joseph Talcott, Clerk.*

Done, Joseph.   Court Record, Page 6—4 March, 1746: This Court
grant Adms. on the estate of Joseph Done, late of Middletown decd.,
unto Deborah Done, widow, who gave bonds with Thomas Rich of Middletown of £1000.

Page 372.

Doolittle, Jonathan, Middletown.   Invt. £2094-02-11.   Taken 15
January, 1749-50, by Jonathan Allyn, Joseph Wright and Willet Ranney.
Court Record, Page 116—6 February, 1749-50: This Court grant
Adms. on the estate of Jonathan Doolittle, late of Middletown, unto Re-
beckah and Jonathan Doolittle, who gave bonds with Willet Ranney of
Middletown of £1000.   Thomas Doolittle, a minor, 19 years of age, Joel
Doolittle, age 17 years, Rebeckah 15 years, and George 14 years, chil-
dren of Jonathan Doolittle, chose their mother Rebeckah Doolittle to be
their guardian.   Recog., £200 for each minor.
Page 123—3 April, 1750: An account of Adms. on the estate of
Jonathan Doolittle, late of Middletown, was now exhibited in Court by
Jonathan Doolittle and Rebeckah Doolittle, Adms.: Paid in debts and
charges and provisions spent in the family, £184-07-02; credit received,
£43-13-10.   Which account is allowed and ordered to be kept on file.
Now moves for a distribution:

	£	s	d
Inventory,	2094	02	11
Credits,	43	13	10
Debts and charges subtracted,	184	07	02
There remains in real and personal estate,	1956	09	07

1-3 part of the moveable estate to the widow forever; to Jonathan
Doolittle, eldest son, a double share; to Samuel, Thomas, Joel and George
Doolittle, to each of them their single share; and to Rebeckah Doolittle,
the daughter, her single share.   And appoint Jonathan Allin, Nathaniel
Gilbert and Joseph Wright, of Middletown, distributors.

Page 87-8, 93-4.

Drake, Jeremiah, Windsor. Inventory taken by Ebenezer Moore, Thomas Drake and David Bissell. Will dated 15 November, 1746.

I, Jeremiah Drake of Windsor, do make this my last will and testament: I give to my wife Hannah 1-3 part of my moveable estate. I give her 1 room in my dwelling house (that is, a parlour) and free liberty to use the cellar and kitchen, and use of the well, and one rood of land for a garden plot, during her widowhood. I give to my son Jonathan all my land that was my father's, lying east of the country road, bounded north partly on Thomas Drake's land and partly on Eliakim Cook's land, south on Joseph Drake's land, and east on Lt. Thomas Grant, only reserving to my sister Rebeckah Drake the use of the old house during her natural life. I give to my daughter Elizabeth £100. I give to my daughter Ann £100. I give to my son Gideon all that lott of land I bought of Dr. Matthew Rockwell, with the house thereon standing. I give to my son Gideon the north half of my meadow lott, to be to him and his heirs forever. Further, my will is that my son Gideon shall pay unto my son Job, after he comes of age, £300 money in old tenor; also to my dafter Hannah £25, and to my daughter Nancy £100—each to be paid after he comes of age. I give to my son Job £500 money, to be paid to him as aforementioned. I give to my daughter Hannah £25, to be paid her as above described. I give to my daughter Elizabeth £100, to be paid her as above sd. I give to my daughter Ann £100, to be paid as abovesd. by Jonathan. I give to my daughter Nancy £100 money, to be paid her by my son Gideon. I hereby appoint my son Jonathan Drake and my son Ebenezer Bissell executors.

Witness: *Samuel Skinner,*   JEREMIAH DRAKE, LS.
Eliakim Cook,
Ebenezer Grant.

Court Record, Page 30—6 January, 1746-7: The last will of Jeremiah Drake, late of Windsor, was now exhibited in Court by Jonathan Drake and Ebenezer Bissell, executors. Proven.

Page 81.

Eglestone, James, Windsor. Invt. £326-07-04. Taken 13 January, 1746-7, by Peletiah Mills, Joseph Colyer and Nathaniel Case.

Court Record, Page 32—3 February, 1746-7: An inventory of the estate of James Eglestone, late of Windsor, was now exhibited by Elizabeth Eglestone, Adms., which inventory was accepted.

Page 36—7 April, 1747: Elizabeth Eglestone, the widow, late of Windsor, now moves to this Court that her right of dowry in the real estate of the sd. James Eglestone, late of Windsor, may be set out to her:

Whereupon this Court appoints Capt. Peletiah Mills, Joseph Colyer and Nathaniel Case, of Windsor, to set out to the sd. widow 1-3 part of the lands and buildings of the sd. decd. for her improvement during life.

Page 38—5 May, 1747: Abigail Eglestone, 14 years of age, daughter of James Eglestone, chose her mother Elizabeth Eglestone to be her guardian. Recog., £200.

Page 55—20 January, 1747-8: Abigail Eglestone, 14 years of age, now made choice of Jonah Gillett of Windsor to be her guardian. Recog., £300. An account of Adms. on the estate of James Eglestone, late of Windsor, was now exhibited in Court by Elizabeth Eglestone, Adms.: Paid in debts and charges, £100-00-01. Account is allowed and ordered to be kept on file. Now moves this Court for distribution of moveable estate:

	£ s d
Inventory,	216-07-04
Debts and charges subtracted,	100-00-01
There remains to be distributed,	116-07-03
To Elizabeth Eglestone, widow, her third part,	38-15-09
And to Elisha, eldest son, his double part,	38-15-09
To James and Abigail, to each of them,	19-07-10

And this Court appoint Lt. John Hubbard, Deacon Isaac Butler and Mr. Nathaniel Case, of Wintingbury, distributors.

Page 17-18.

Ellery, John, Hartford. Will dated 5 September, 1744: I, John Ellery of Hartford, do make this my last will and testament: I give to my honoured mother-in-law, Mrs. Mary Austin, £100 old tenor to furnish herself with a suit of mourning if she survive me. I give to my wife Mary Ellery all my household furniture, except one silver tankard; also all my servants; also £1000, old tenor, of my moveables, in such things as best suits her, to be apprised at cash price; also £1000 old tenor to be hers and her heirs forever. I give unto the South Church in Hartford, of which the Rev. Mr. Whitman is at present pastor, my largest silver tankard (which was formerly my late honoured father's, Capt. John Ellery, of Boston, decd.) for the use of the Sacrament of the Lord's Supper. I give unto the North Church in sd. Hartford, of which the Rev. Mr. Daniel Wadsworth is at present pastor, £30 old tenor, to be laid out in plate for the use of the Sacrament of the Lord's Supper. I give to Harvard College in Cambridge, in New England, £150 old tenor, to be disposed of by the Overseers or Trustees towards the maintenance of any of the students that may stand in need of such help, to be paid by my executors in convenient time after my decease. I give to Yale College

in New Haven, in Connecticut, £100 money, old tenor, to be disposed of
by the Trustees towards the maintenance of any students designing for
the work of the ministry and that may stand in need of such help. I
give to the poor Indians under the care of the Rev. Mr. Sergant of Hous-
tennock or Sheffield, the value of £120 old tenor in books, clothing, or
any other of my goods out of my trading stock, at my ordinary selling
price as they are marked, to be by my executors delivered to him the
aforesd. Mr. Sergant as soon as may be convenient, that he may be disposeing thereof as he shall judge most conducive to the comfort and
good of sd. Indians, both spiritual and temporal. I give to my honoured
uncle, Capt. John Bonner of Boston, £50 old tenor to put himself in
mourning, or otherwise dispose of as he shall think best. I give to my
honoured uncle, Joseph Clark of Boston, £20 money, old tenor. I give
for the use and benefit of poor, pious and faithful ministers in Connecticut, £250 old tenor in books, clothing or other things out of my trading
stock, at my general selling price as marked; also, £100 old tenor for the
use and benefit of any object of charity in Connecticut, in goods as above
expressed: all to be delivered by my executors to the Rev. Mr. Marsh
of Windsor, or the Rev. Mr. Wheelock of Lebanon, and the Rev. Mr.
Lockwood of Wethersfield, in an equal proportion, to be by them disposed
of as above mentioned. By the death of my late honoured grandmother,
Mrs. Mary Ellery of Glosester, I have something coming to me, but
what or what value I am not yet informed. However, be it more or less,
real or personal, whatsoever and wheresoever it be found, I give the same
to be disposed of by my honoured uncles, Capt. Nathaniel Ellery and
Capt. William Ellery of Glosester aforesd., for the sole use and benefit
of my poor relations in or about sd. Glosester, to be distributed among my
sd. poor relations by my sd. uncles according to their best judgement.
I give £200 old tenor to be by my executors delivered in convenient time
to Mr. Samuel Grant of Boston, shopkeeper, and Mr. Samuel Savage of
Boston, merchant, and Mr. John Welch of Boston, carver, to be by them
disposed of for pious and charitable uses in such a method as they shall
think to be most for the glory of God and interest of our holy religion. I
give to the poor of the Town of Hartford, out of my trading stock, in
any suitable articles, at my ordinary selling price as marked, £50 old
tenor to be distributed by my executors as they shall judge best for sd.
poor. My will is, and I hereby order, that my negro man Glocester be
manumitted or have his freedom (if he desires it) on the 19 day of July
in the year of our Lord 1749, agreeable to the will of my late deceased
father, Capt. John Ellery, whose servant he formerly was. Also, I give
my negro Glocester, at the time of his being made free, the value of £10
old tenor in tools or instruments, at cash price, suitable for the business
he may follow for an honest livelihood; also the value of £10 more old
tenor in wearing apparel suitable for him, according to the judgement
of my executors. I give to each of my sons £1000 old tenor, in value
equal to silver at 32 shillings per ounce. And then all the remainder of

my estate, whether real or personal, wheresoever it may be found, I give, devise and bequeath unto all my children, whether male or female, to be equally divided among them all. And the reason I give my eldest son no more is because his late honoured grandfather, Mr. John Austin, has by his last will made so much larger provision for him than for the rest of my children. And I hereby appoint my wife Mary Ellery my executrix, and Mr. James Church and Mr. Thomas Seymour, of Hartford, my executors.

Witness: *James Church,*   JOHN ELLERY, LS.
John Potwin, Abigail Church.

At a Probate Court held at Hartford, within and for the County of Hartford, on the 1st day of December, Anno. Dom. 1746: Present, Joseph Buckingham, Esq., Judge; Jos: Talcott, Clerk: The last will and testament of Mr. John Ellery, late of Hartford decd., was now exhibited by Mrs. Mary Ellery, relict of sd. decd., Capt. James Church and Mr. Thomas Seymour, executors named in sd. will, who accepted the trust hereof. Sd. will being proven, is by this Court approved and ordered to be recorded and kept on file. [This record is on the page following will.]

Eliot, Mrs. Mary. Court Record, Page 7—4 February, 1745-6: This Court grant Adms. on the estate of Mrs. Mary Eliot of Windsor decd. unto Isaac Burr and Ann Eliot, who gave bonds with David Elsworth of sd. Windsor of £2000.

Page 343.

Invt. in Vol. XVI, Page 214-333.

Elsworth, Lt. Jonathan, Windsor. Inventory taken 29 December, 1749, by Peletiah Allyn, Samuel Stoughton and Josiah Bissell.

Will dated 29 December, 1747. I, Jonathan Elsworth of Windsor, do make this my last will and testament: I give to my wife the improvement of my dwelling house and homestead during her life, and after that to be equally divided to my sons, Giles, David and Jonathan, or their heirs. I give to my wife all my personal estate after my just debts that are now due and funeral expenses be first paid. I give unto my son Giles Elsworth, his heirs and assigns forever, one certain piece of land lying in the great meadow, bounded as followeth: north and east on land of the Deputy Governor's, south on John Warham Strong, and west on his own land, containing about one acre and 1-4. I give unto my three sons, Giles Elsworth, David Elsworth and Jonathan Elsworth, and to their heirs and assigns forever, all my real estate, to be equally divided between them, only what is before given to Giles in particular, they paying unto my daughter Sarah Allyn £100 in old tenor bills, and to my daughter Mary Owen £100 in old tenor bills, and to my daughter Hannah Allyn £100 in old tenor bills. I appoint my sons Giles Elsworth and David Elsworth executors.

Witness: *Pelatiah Allyn,*   JONATHAN X ELSWORTH, LS.
Joseph Gaylord, Daniel Bissell.

Court Record, Page 108—3 October, 1749: The last will and testament of Mr. Jonathan Elsworth, late of Windsor, was now exhibited in Court by Giles and David Elsworth, executors. Proven and ordered to be kept on file.

Page 365.

Elsworth, Mrs. Mary, Windsor. Inventory taken by John Palmer, 2nd, and John Roberts, apprisers.

Court Record, Page 116—6 February, 1749-50: This Court grant Adms. on the estate of Mary Elsworth, late of Windsor decd., unto Gideon Barbour of Windsor, who gave bonds with Capt. Peletiah Allyn of Windsor of £500.

Emmes, John. Court Record, Page 78—1st November, 1748: Benjamin Emmes, 16 years of age, son of John Emmes, chose his brother Joseph Emmes to be his guardian. Recog., £500. Cert: *Giles Hall, J. P.*

Page 60.

Enno, David, Simsbury. Invt. £84-13-00. Taken 1st September, 1746, by James Hillyer and Daniel Addams.

Court Record, Page 22—2 September, 1746: Adms. granted unto Mary Enno, widow, who gave bonds with Andrew Robe of Simsbury of £400.

Page 72—2 August, 1748: David Enno, a minor, age 14 years, son of David Enno, chose Deacon Michael Humphrey of Simsbury to be his guardian. Recog., £500.

Page 98—2 May, 1749: Mary Enno, Adms., exhibited an account of her Adms. Accepted. This Court appoint Mary Enno, widow, to be guardian to Roger Enno, a minor, 12 years of age, Jonathan 9 years, and Abigail Enno 6 years of age, children of David Enno. And the sd. Mary Enno recog. with John Case in £100 for each minor.

Page 51 (Vol. XVI) 4 February, 1752: Roger Eno, a minor, now 14 years of age, son of David Eno, chose Capt. Samuel Eno to be his guardian. Recog., £600.

Page 419-20.

Eno, James, Simsbury. Invt. £174-03-06. Taken 10 April, 1750, by James Cornish and Samuel Owen.

Court Record, Page 125—5 April, 1750: This Court grants Adms. on the estate of James Eno, late of Simsbury decd., unto Deborah Eno, widow of sd. deceased, who gave bond with Samuel Phelps of Windsor of £500.

Page 131a—5 June, 1750: Deborah Eno, widow and relict of James Eno of Simsbury decd., represents to this Court that the estate is insolvent and prays that commissioners may be appointed to adjust the claims of the creditors: Whereupon this Court appoint Isaac Gillett and Samuel Owen, of Windsor, commissioners.

Page 382-3-4.

Farle, John, Willington. Invt. £1868-15-00. Taken 30 March, 1750, by John Merrick, Abner Barker and George Sawin. Will dated 2 March, 1749-50.

I, John Farle of Willingtown, in the County of Hartford, do make this my last will and testament: I give to my wife Mary the use of the south room in my dwelling house, and the use of 1-2 of the chamber over the sd. room, and of 1-2 of the cellar under it, so long as she shall remain my widow; and 10 score weight of beef and pork annually. It is my will that my executor, for the support of my sd. wife Mary, give her annually, so long as she remains my widow, 10 bushels of Indian corne, 4 bushels of rye, 1 bushel of wheat, 4 barrells of cider, 4 bushels of apples, and 1 bushel of malt. And furthermore it is my will that my executor keep a cow for my sd. wife and find her a horse to ride on so long as she remains my widow, and that he find her 25 cords of wood a year during the abovesd. term. I give and bequeath to my wife Mary the use and improvement of all my household goods that shall remain after my debts are paid, during her natural life. I give and bequeath to my son John Farle all my land and buildings and all my stock of creatures and all my husbandry tools, he paying yearly to his mother what I have above ordered to be paid to her. I give all my household goods that my wife shall leave at her death to my daughter Prudence Fisk, and that with what she hath already had shall be her portion of my estate. It is my will that if my executor neglect or refuse to give to my sd. wife Mary the articles abovesd. for her support and comfort, that then she shall have the use of 1-3 part of my real estate so long as she shall remain my widow. And I appoint my son John Farle, Jr., sole executor.

Witness: *Mirriam Whitney,*   JOHN X FARLE, LS.
Deborah Lampkin, Amos Richardson, Daniel Fuller.

Court Record, Page 123—3 April, 1750: The last will and testament of John Farle, late of Willington, was now exhibited by John Farle, son of the sd. decd., executor. Proven. An inventory was also exhibited. Both ordered recorded and kept on file.

Page 390-1-2.

Filley, Josiah, Windsor. Invt. £2688-17-06. Taken 14 April, 1750, by Ebenezer Phelps, Nathaniel Mather and John Cook. Will dated October, 1748.

I, Josiah Filley of Windsor, do make this my last will and testament: I give to my wife Esther, and to her heirs forever, the north half of my dwelling house, half the cellar, 1-3 part of my homclott, and 1-3 part of my lott at Clayey Swamp, and 1-3 part of my land that my son Josiah improves, and 1-3 part of my land that my son William improves; also I give her 2 cows and all my household stuff, meaning ye utensils thereof. I give to my son Josiah the house and all the lands where he dwells and improves, except the 1-3 part of which I have given to my wife. I give unto my son Samuel the house and land at Blue Hills as it is called, where he lives, or my right and claim thereto, and also 40 shillings money, old tenor, to be paid him by my executor. I give unto my son William Filley the houseing and all the land where he dwells and improves, being about 35 acres and 1-2, except 1-3 part of it, which I have given to my wife. I give unto my son Erasmus Filley the south half of my dwelling house and half the cellar, with the liberty of passing and repassing thereto and therefrom; also all my homelott and my lott at Clayey Swamp, except 1-3 part of them lands which I have given to my wife. And whereas my son Erasmus is often disturbed in his brain and under distraction, and unfit to bargain and trade, therefore my will is that he shall not alienate and sell the houseing and land, but they shall be to him for life and for his heirs and assigns forever; and I do, under his circumstances, nominate and appoint my son William as an overseer to take care of him and his estate if he continues in his disorder and is not well able to take good care of himself and estate. I give to my sd. son Erasmus all my moveable estate, except what I have given to my wife as above; but he shall not sell or bargain away the same without the advise and consent of my son William or other overseers as may be appointed. I give unto my daughter Esther Filley £50 money, old tenor. I give unto my daughter Dorcas Allyn £40 money, old tenor. I give unto my daughter Deliverance Holliday £40 money, old tenor. I give to my daughter Abigail Wood £40 old tenor. I give to my daughter Mary Rowley £40 money, old tenor. My will is that the legacies given to my five daughters as above shall be paid them or their heirs (the one full half in the space of three years next after my decease, and the other half shall be paid them in full within the

space of six years next after my decease) out of the bonds or the money
due thereby which Will, my son, gave me for my land over the Great
River; and if that be not sufficient, the residue out of book debts. I make
my son William Filley sole executor.

Witness: *Henry Allyn,*   JOSIAH FILLEY, LS.
Daniel Gillett, Jr., Anna Gillett.

Court Record, Page 127—1st May, 1750: The last will and testament of Josiah Filley, late of Windsor, was now exhibited in Court
by William Filley, executor. Will proven.

Page 32 (Vol. XVI) 6 August, 1751: Invt. exhibited and accepted.

Page 11 (Vol. XVII) 5 February, 1754: An account of debts paid
by William Filley, executor, was now exhibited in Court, which account
this Court accepts. This Court order that the estate be distributed among
the heirs of the deceased, and appoint Samuel Enno, Capt. Peletiah Mills
and Ebenezer Phelps, of Windsor, distributors to distribute the estate
according to the last will of the deceased.

Dist. File: 7 July, 1761: To Mrs. Esther Filley, widow; to Josiah,
to Samuel, to the heirs of William Filley, to Esther Gillett, to Dorcas
Mott, to Deliverance Halliday, to Abigail Forbes, and to Mary Rowell.
By Job Drake, Nathaniel Filley and Henry Allyn.

Page 388.

Foster, Edward, Jr., Middletown. Invt. £845-08-00. Taken 7 February, 1749-50, by Edward Foster, William Whitmore and William Rockwell.

Court Record, Page 127—1st May, 1750: This Court grant Adms.
on the estate of Edward Foster, Jr., late of Middletown decd., unto [*no
record written in here*], who gave bonds with William Whitmore of Middletown of £1000. Exhibit of an inventory, which this Court accepts and
orders it to be recorded and kept on file.

Dist. File: 21 April, 1763: Distribution of the estate of Edward
Foster, Jr., viz.: to Martha Foster alias Robberds, to William Foster, to
Jonathan, to Thomas, to Jedediah Foster. Also, estate as comes to them
from their grandfather Edward Foster, viz.: to William, Thomas and
Jedediah Foster. By Jabez Brooks and William Rockwell.

Page 341-2.

Francis, John, Wethersfield. Invt. £6069-03-04. Taken 6 November, 1749, by Jonathan Belding, John Stilman and Gershom Nott.

Court Record, Page 110—14 November, 1749: This Court grant
Adms. on the estate of John Francis, late of Wethersfield, unto Elisha

Francis and Eunice Francis, son and widow of the sd. decd., who gave bonds with Jonathan Belding of Wethersfield of £2000.

Page 119—1st February, 1749-50: This Court appoint Eunice Francis, widow, to be guardian to her children, viz., Lydia Francis, 11 years; Eunice, 8 years; and John Francis, 5 years of age, children of John Francis, late deceased. Recog., £300 for each minor.

Page 10 (Vol. XVI) 1st January, 1750-1: An account of Adms. on the estate of John Francis was now exhibited in Court by Eunice and Elisha Francis, Adms. Account accepted. And this Court order the estate distributed, viz: to Eunice Francis, widow, 1-3 part of the moveable estate to be her own forever, and 1-3 part of the real estate for her improvement during life; and to the heirs of John Francis, Jr., a double part and share of sd. estate; and to Elisha and John Francis (as recorded) and to Mary Bassit, Lydia Francis and Eunice Francis, to each of them their single shares. And appoint Capt. Jonathan Belding, Capt. Samuel Butler and Mr. John Stilman distributors.

Page 318.

Freeman, Samuel, Middletown. Died 5 May, 1749. Invt. £1188-00-06. Taken by Philip Goff and Thomas Rogers, Jr.

Court Record, Page 105—6 June, 1749: This Court grant Adms. on the estate of Samuel Freeman, late of Middletown decd., unto Elizabeth Freeman, widow, who gave bonds with Cornelius Knowles of Middletown of £100. Exhibit of an inventory. Accepted and ordered to be recorded and kept on file.

Page 127—1st May, 1750: An account of Adms. on the estate of Samuel Freeman, late of Middletown, was now exhibited in Court by Elizabeth Freeman, Adms.: Paid in debts and charges, £40-00-04. Account is allowed and ordered to be kept on file.

Page 99 (Vol. XVI) 1st May, 1753: A further account of Adms. was exhibited in Court by the sd. Adms. Accepted. This Court order distribution of the estate, viz.: to James Freeman, eldest son, his double share; and to Gideon Freeman and Elizabeth Snow, Alice Brown, Rebekah Walker, Mary Freeman, Priscilla Freeman and Abigail Freeman, children of sd. deceased, to each of them their single shares. And appoint Robert Youngs, Philip Goff and Jonathan Smith, of Middletown, distributors. Also this Court direct them to set out to Elizabeth, the relict, her thirds, and make return of their doings to this Court.

Page 34.

Gains, Henry, Windsor. Invt. £39-07-07. Taken 6 June, 1746, by Samuel Heydon, Nathaniel Heydon and Josiah Bissell.

Court Record, Page 12—3 June, 1746: This Court grant Adms. on the estate of Henry Gains, late of Windsor decd., unto Agnes Gains, widow, who gave bonds with Josiah Bissell of Windsor.

Page 202-5.

Gains, Deacon John, Middletown. Invt. £2318-18-06. Taken 23 August, 1748, by John Hall, Benoni Hale and John Gill. Will dated 14 September, 1744.

I, John Gains of Middletown, in the County of Hartford, do make and ordain this my last will and testament: I give to Naomy, my wife, the use of all my moveables, by what name soever called, during her natural life, and likewise the use of all my lands during her natural life. I give to my grandson John Gains 41 acres of land, be it more or less, lying on the east side of the Great River (it is the same piece of land which for some years I lived upon), with all I had adjoining thereto. Further, I give to my sd. grandson John Gains 6 acres of pasture land in sd. town which I bought of John Penfield. These two pieces of land (his grandmother's interest excepted), if sd. John Gains shall live to the age of 21 years, I give the same to him and to his heirs and assigns forever. I give to my daughter Annah Bartlet 4 1-2 acres of land in Middletown, lying in Wongunk meadow, be it more or less, lying siding by John Warner's land and Deliverance Warner's land: this I give to my daughter Annah Bartlet and to her heirs forever. I give to my grandson James Ackley £40 old tenor money as it passes at this day, to be paid to him if he shall live to the age of 21 years. I give the remainder of all my moveable estate, or what shall be left of it when my wife shall have done with it, I give the same to my daughter Anna and my daughter Sary and my grandson John Gains, to be equally divided amongst them. I give to my daughter Sary Gains 4 acres of land which I had of Job Pain, and lyes by a highway both west and north, and on land that did belong to Thomas Hale deceased both south and east. I give the same to my daughter Sary and to her heirs forever. I ordain my wife Naomy to be sole executrix.

Witness: *Joseph White,*   JOHN GAINS, LS.
Jer: Goodrich, Ebenezer White, Jr.

Court Record, Page 74—5 September, 1748: The last will and testament of John Gains, late of Middletown, was now exhibited by Naomy Gains, executrix. Will proven.

Page 296.

Gardner, Benjamin. Invt. £113-13-08. Taken 6 April, 1750, by Eliphalet Carpenter and Daniel Lyman.

Court Record, Page 109—7 November, 1749: This Court grant Adms. on the estate of Benjamin Gardner, late of Hartford decd., unto Ebenezer Brown of Coventry, in Windham County, who gave bonds with Noah Grant of Tolland, in Hartford County, of £200.

Page 125—10 April, 1750: An inventory of the estate of Benjamin Gardner, late of Hartford, was now exhibited in Court by Ebenezer Brown, Adms. Accepted.

Inventory in Vol. XVI, Page 332.

Gilbert, Joseph, Jr., Hartford. March the 30th, 1753: Upon motion of Theodore Gilbert, Adms., we the subscribers have apprised the lands of sd. deceased being in Harwington, in the County of Litchfield, as followeth: To a certain piece of land lying in the town aforesd., containing 106 acres, at £7-00-00 per acre one with another, £742-00-00. By Jacob Hinsdell, Ebenezer Hopkins and Jonathan Brace.

We the subscribers, being appointed by the Judge of Probates to apprise the real estate of Mr. Joseph Gilbert, Jr., have this 8th day of August, 1750, apprised the house and homelott, barn and all priviledges to sd. lott at £1900-00-00 bills, old tenor. By Jos: Talcott, John Edwards and Daniel Goodwin.

To one piece of land lying in the meadow in Hartford, £350-00-00; to a lott of land in Hartford at Brickhill Swamp lot, £1450-00-00. This apprisement made by us: Thomas Sandford and Jos: Talcott.

Court Record, Page 133—15 June, 1750: Adms. granted unto Theodore Gilbert of New Hartford, son of the deceased, who gave bonds with William Menthorn of Hartford of £1000. Isaiah Gilbert, a minor, 17 years of age, son of Joseph Gilbert, chose his brother Theodore Gilbert of New Hartford to be his guardian. Recog., £500.

Page 138—8 August, 1750: Theodore Gilbert, eldest son of Mr. Joseph Gilbert, and Adms., represents to this Court that the real estate, and especially the dwelling house and homelott of the deceased, containing 1 1-2 roods of land, if distributed to the heirs of the estate, would be very preyudicial. Theodore Gilbert having given sufficient bond with surety to the Judge of this Court or his successors that he will pay to the rest of the heirs to sd. estate a full amount of their just and equal sum which by law is their part of the price and value of the house, barn and land as above apprised, this Court do therefore set out the whole of the land of the homested of the deceased, with the dwelling house, barn, etc., being about 60 rods of land on which the sd. Joseph Gilbert, Jr., lived and died, to be to him the sd. Theodore Gilbert and his heirs forever.

Page 101 (Vol. XVI) 1st June, 1753: Elias Gilbert, a minor, aged 16 years, before this Court made choice of his brother Theodore Gilbert to be his guardian. Recog., £500.

Page 101—6 June, 1753: Joseph Gilbert, a minor, aged 17 years, son of Joseph Gilbert, Jr., late decd., also made choice of his brother Theodore Gilbert to be his guardian. Recog., £300.

Distribution from File:

To Theodore Gilbert,	£1434-06-04	To Joseph Gilbert,	£717-03-04
To Isaiah Gilbert,	717-03-04	To Elias Gilbert,	717-03-04
	To Lydia Gilbert alias Hopkins, £717-03-04.		

By Joseph Talcott and John Haynes Lord, 25 May, 1754.

Page 226-7.

Gillet, Cornelius, Windsor. Invt. £616-17-05. Taken by Robert Barnet, John Loomis and Nathaniel Cole. Will dated 23 August, 1746.

I, Cornelius Gillet of Windsor, do make this my last will and testament: I give to my son Benjamin Gillet all my real estate. I give to my son Cornelius Gillet 10 shillings old tenor. I give to my son Daniel Gillet 10 shillings old tenor. I give to my son Samuel Gillet 10 shillings old tenor. I give to my son Thomas Gillet 10 shillings old tenor. I give to my son Jonathan Gillet 10 shillings old tenor. I give to my son David Gillet 10 shillings old tenor. I give to my daughter Elizabeth Matson 10 shillings old tenor. I give to my daughter Deborah Talcott 10 shillings old tenor. I give to my daughter Phebe Gillet 10 shillings old tenor. And the rest of my moveable estate I leave to the disposal of my loving wife and my son Benjamin Gillet. I appoint my son Jonathan Gillet and my son Benjamin Gillet to be the executors.

Witness: *Samuel Rowell,*   CORNELIUS GILLET, LS.
Daniel Rowell, Robert Barnet.

Court Record, Page 33—3 March, 1746-7: The last will and testament of Cornelius Gillet, late of Windsor, was now exhibited in Court by Benjamin Gillet, one of the executors. Will proven. Exhibit of an inventory. Both accepted and ordered recorded.

Page 125—3 April, 1750: Deborah Gillet, the widow and relict of Cornelius Gillet, now moves to this Court that her right of dowry be set out to her in the estate of the sd. decd. according to law: Whereupon this Court appoints Lt. Solomon Clark, Alexander Hoskins and Stephen Goodwin, in Wintingbury Parish, to set out 1-3 of the lands and buildings of the sd. decd. for her improvement during life.

Page 25-6-7-8.

Gillet, Joseph, Gentleman, Hartford. Invt. £2246 plus. Taken 4 March, 1745-6, by David Ensign, Jonathan Sedgewick and Moses Nash.

Also some real estate at Deerfield, in the County of Hampshire and Province of Massachusetts Bay, £100. Taken 1 April, 1746, by Elijah Williams, Benjamin Mun and John Catlin. Will dated 9 July, 1743.

I, Joseph Gillet of Hartford, do make this my last will and testament: I give to Elizabeth, my wife, all that estate that she brought with her when she became my wife, and one cow, to be at her dispose forever. Further, I give to my wife, during the time she remains my widow, the free use of 1-2 of the house I now live in, and also the use of 5 acres of land in my west division lott on the east side of the highway, and the use of half of my land on the west side of the highway, and the use of an iron pott and brass kettle, during sd. term that she remains my widow. I give to my son Joseph Gillet the dwelling house he now lives in and all that part of my west division lott that lyes on the east side of the highway, and also the one moiety or half of my sd. lott on the west side of sd. highway, being the north side, to be so laid out as not to interfere on my tan houses and fats, which I reserve for the heirs of my son Jonathan decd., he doing the duties hereafter enjoyned him to do. And provided my sd. son should die before me, or survive me and not make a will, then what I have hereby given to him I do hereby give and bequeath to his two sons, Stephen Gillet and Asa Gillet, they doing the duties hereafter enjoyned to my son Joseph Gillet to do. I give to my beloved grandchildren, the children of my son Jonathan Gillet decd., viz: Jonathan Gillet, Mehetabel Gillet and Mary Gillet, the house I now live in, my tan yard and tan houses, and 20 acres of land joining to sd. house and tan. yard, to be divided as followeth: my grandson Jonathan to have the 1-2, and the other half to be divided equally to my sd. granddaughters. I give to my grandson Jonathan Gillet the remaining part of my land in the lott I now live on that is not before disposed of, he paying, when he arrives at the age of 22 years, the following legacies, viz., to my daughter Sarah Goodwin £10, and to the heirs of my daughter Abigail Smith deceased £10., and to my daughter Dorothy Bewell £10. Further, my will is that my son Matthew Gillet shall take the whole care to improve what is above given to my grandchildren, Jonathan Gillet and Mary and Mehetabell Gillet, for their best advantage until they arrive to lawfull age to receive the same, he being paid out of the income for his care and trouble. I give to my beloved son Matthew Gillet, over and above what I have done by deed of gift, my lott of land in New Hartford lately purchased of Eliakim Merrell, containing 56 3-4 acres, and also a yoke of cattle that he has now in his hands or keeping of mine, and also my cane and my long hunting gunn (not to be disposed of out of my line of heirs), all which I give to him, he paying to my granddafter Rhoda Andrews £10 old tenor when she arrives to the age of 18 years or marry. I give to my beloved daughters Elizabeth Marsh, Mary Andrews, Esther Bancroft, Hannah Burr, Sarah Goodwin, the heirs of Abigail Smith decd., and Dorothy Bewell, all my moveable estate after my debts are paid, to be equally divided amongst them, the heirs of my daughter Abigail Smith to have but 1-7 part and that to be equally divided amongst them. I give to my sd. 7 daughters (the heirs of Abigail decd. looked upon as one) £10 money to each, old tenor. I give to my 7 daughters, in equal proportion, all my land in Deerfield. I appoint my sons Joseph Gillet and Matthew Gillet to be executors.

Witness: *John Ensign,*   JOSEPH GILLET, LS.
Jacob Ensign, Moses Nash.

Court Record, Page 6—4 March, 1746: The last will and testament of Joseph Gillet of Hartford decd. was now exhibited in Court by Joseph and Matthew Gillet, executors. Proven.

Page 35.

Gillet, Stephen, Windsor. Invt. £94-01-06, including £59-15-00 Cape Breton wages. Taken 20 June, 1746, by Jacob Drake and Robert Barnet.

Court Record, Page 14—26 June, 1746: This Court grant Adms. on the estate of Stephen Gillet, late of Windsor decd., unto Ann Gillet, widow of the sd. decd., who gave bonds with Jonathan Gillet of £500.

Page 19—5 August, 1746: An inventory was exhibited by Ann Gillet, Adms., which this Court accepts. Now informs this Court that she suspects the estate is insolvent, and prays that commissioners may be appointed: Whereupon this Court appoint Robert Barnet and Nathaniel Case of Windsor to adjust the claims.

Page 36—7 April, 1747: Report of the commissioners, which is accepted and ordered on file.

Page 46—1st September, 1747: Report of the commissioners was now approved, and an averidge made of sd. estate, which is now on file.

Page 219-20-292.

Gipson, Samuel, Middletown. Invt. £664-16-06. Taken May, 1748, by Willett Ranny, Malatiah Lewis and Joseph Ranny. Will dated 5 May, 1747.

I, Samuel Gipson of Middletown, in the County of Hartford, do make this my last will and testament: I give to my wife Margaret Gipson all the household goods she brought with her at our marriage, and I give her the use and improvement of my great brass kettle during her natural life; also I give her one of my cows, which she shall choose; this I give above what I have reserved for her in a deed given to my son John Gipson bearing date 6 November, 1742. I give to my son John Gipson all and everything belonging to my estate, both personal and real, besides what I have given away by this my last will. I have already given to my son Jonathan Gipson what I mainly designed for his portion.

I give him now £5 old tenor. I give to my daughter Hannah Sage, over and above what I have already given her, all the abovesd. goods that was her own mother's, and also my great brass kettle, after my present wife's decease. I appoint my son John Gipson sole executor.

Witness: *Edward Eels,*   SAMUEL GIPSON, LS.
John Schovell, Gideon Sage.

Court Record, Page 64—3 May, 1748: The last will and testament of Samuel Gipson, late of Middletown, was now exhibited in Court by John Gipson, son and executor. Will proven, ordered to be recorded and kept upon file.

Page 78—1st November, 1748: An inventory of the estate of Deacon Samuel Gipson was now exhibited by John Gipson, executor. This Court accepts same and orders it to be recorded and kept on file.

Glesson (Gleason), David. Court Record, Page 20—5 August, 1746: This Court grant Adms. on the estate of David Glesson, late of Simsbury, unto Katharine Glesson, widow, who gave bonds with Thomas Glesson of Simsbury of £500. Now exhibit an inventory, which inventory this Court accepts and ordered to be recorded.

Page 5-6-7.

Goodrich, Jacob, Windsor. Invt. £3589-10-05. Taken by Isaac Butler, John Hubbard and William Manley.

Court Record, Page 2—7 January, 1745: This Court grant Adms. on the estate of Jacob Goodrich, late of Windsor decd., unto Benedict Goodrich, widow, and Elijah Goodrich, son of the sd. decd., who gave bonds with Stephen Goodwin of Simsbury of £3000 money.

Page 187-8-9.

Goodrich, Sarah, Wethersfield. Invt. £3272-01-07. Taken 16 December, 1747, by Nathaniel Stilman, Thomas Welles and Jonathan Goodrich. Will dated 9 November, 1747.

I, Sarah Goodrich of Wethersfield, widow, do make this my last will and testament: I ordain the Rev. Mr. James Lockwood, Col. Elizur Goodrich and Hezekiah May sole executors to this my last will, enjoyning them to receive all my just debts, dues, my bonds, notes or otherwise, and also to pay and defray all my just debts and funeral charges due from my estate. I give to my beloved sons John and David Goodrich all my lands lying in the Townships of Wethersfield and Middletown which descendeth to me by my brother Elisha Mix decd. and which I purchased of my sister Christian Mix, to be equally divided between them. I give to my son David my silver tankard. I give to my son John so much out of my moveable or personal estate as shall be equivalent to the tankard I have given to my son David. I give to my son Samuel Goodrich 3 pewter basins, one square table, half a dozen chaires, a paire of hand irons, a fire shovel and tongs, a pewter pott, a pillion and an old trunk. I give to my sd. sons John and David all my moveable or personal estate not yet mentioned that shall be remaining after my just debts are paid, equally between them.

Witness: *Charles Goodrich,*   SARAH GOODRICH, LS.
Samuel Stoddard, Honor Perrin.

Court Record, Page 62—17 March, 1748: The last will and testament of Sarah Goodrich was now exhibited in Court by Col. William Goodrich and Hezekiah May, executors. Will proven. Exhibit of an inventory. Both proven and ordered to be recorded and kept on file.

Page 19.

Goodwin, Nathaniel, Hartford. Will dated 19 April, 1742: I, Nathaniel Goodwin of Hartford, do make this my last will and testament: I appoint my son Daniel sole executor. I give to my son Daniel all my lands and real estate, divided and undivided, to him and to his heirs forever. I give to my daughter Lois Hart, besides what she hath already had, £15 in bills of old tenor or other money according to the value thereof. I give to my daughter Eunice £15, in such money to be paid as is ordered to be paid my daughter Lois. The reason why I give her my sd. daughter Eunice no more is because she hath already had my first wife's portion. I give to my daughter Thankfull Colyer £15 in bills of old tenor or other money in value thereto. I give to my daughter Rachel Seymour £15 bills of old tenor money. I order my son Daniel to pay all the foregoing legacies within two years after my decease. I give to my grandson Samuel Marsh, son of my daughter Thankfull, my gunn and sword. All the rest of my estate, whether real or personal, I give to my sd. son Daniel, to be at his dispose forever.

Witness: *John Pratt,*   NATHANIEL GOODWIN, LS.
Ozias Goodwin, Esther Talcott.

Court Record, Page 17—16 July, 1746: The last will and testament of Ensign Nathaniel Goodwin, late of Hartford deceased, was now exhibited in Court by Daniel Goodwin, executor. Will proven and ordered to be recorded and kept on file.

Page 130.

Goodwin, Nathaniel, Hartford. Will dated 6 September, 1738: I, Nathaniel Goodwin of Hartford, do make this my last will and testament: I give to my son Hezekiah Goodwin all my houseing and lands in Hartford, to him and to his heirs forever, excepting the use and improvement of one of the rooms in my dwelling house, which I give to my daughter Johanna, which she shall choose, as also all needfull use of the cellar and so much of the gardens as she shall have occasion to improve, with the profits of 2 apple trees standing or growing in the garden, so long as she continues unmarried. I give all my wearing apparrel to my five sons, Hezekiah, Isaac, Abraham, Stephen and Eliezur Goodwin, to be equally divided among them. I give to my son Eleazer Goodwin my team and all the tackling belonging thereto, also one cow. I give to my daughter Johanna all my household goods excepting one bed, viz., the bed and furniture I now lye on, which I give to my daughter Bennet Goodrich. I give to my daughter Johanna Goodwin one cow, which she shall choose. I give to the eldest son of Jacob Goodrich, my son-in-law, a mare and sucking colt. I give to my five daughters, Metetabell Goodrich, Bennet Goodrich, Johanna Goodwin, Ruth Bird and Alice Cadwell, all of my money, with what is due to me by bonds or notes, to be equally divided among them (except to my daughter Bennet, so much to be subtracted out of her part as the featherbed and furniture before mentioned shall be valued at). And further, my mind and will is that what money is due to me from my sons Isaac and Stephen Goodwin may still lye in their hands for the space of two years from the date hereof before they pay the same, if they or either of them desire the same so long. I appoint Nathaniel Stanly, Esq., and my son Hez: Goodwin to be executors.

Witness: *Nathaniel Stanly,*   NATHANIEL GOODWIN, LS.
Jared Spencer, John Spencer.

Court Record, Page 53—1st December, 1747: The last will and testament of Deacon Nathaniel Goodwin, late of Hartford decd., was now exhibited in Court by Hezekiah Goodwin, son and executor. Will proven, ordered to be recorded and kept on file.

Page 365-6-379.

Graham, George, Hartford. Invt. £111-10-06. Taken 16 April, 1750, by James Church and John Edwards. Will dated 30 October, 1749.

I, George Graham of Hartford, do make this my last will and testament: I give to my honoured father, Samuel Graham, all my carpenter's tools. I give unto my brother, James Graham, my gunn. And after my just debts and funeral charges are paid, I give 2-3 of the remaining part of my estate (debts due to me and all other estate that I have not disposed of) to my honoured mother, Sarah Graham, to be disposed of by my executor hereafter mentioned for her benefit according to his discretion. And the remaining third part of my estate, not otherwise disposed of as above, I give unto my sister Abigail Graham alias Seymour. I appoint Richard Edwards of Hartford to be my executor.

Witness: *Edward Dorr,*   GEORGE X GRAHAM, LS.
Hezekiah Colyer, Hannah Kelsey.

Court Record, Page 119—20 February, 1749-50: The last will and testament of George Graham was now exhibited in Court by Richard Edwards, executor. Proven, ordered to be recorded and kept upon file.

Page 77.

Griswold, Benjamin, Windsor. Invt. £311-15-09. Taken 13 June, 1747, by Nathaniel Griswold and Samuel Eno.

Court Record, Page 38—18 May, 1747: This Court grant Adms. on the estate of Benjamin Griswold, late of Windsor, unto Benjamin Griswold and Isaac Gillet, who gave bonds with Capt. Peletiah Allyn of Windsor of £500.

Page 48—3 November, 1747: An account of Adms. on the estate of Benjamin Griswold was now exhibited in Court by Benjamin Griswold and Isaac Gillet, Adms.: Paid in debts and charges, £69-00-01. Account allowed. Adms. move for a distribution, and this Court appoint Nathaniel Griswold, Samuel Enos and Isaac Owen, of Windsor, to divide the moveable estate among the heirs.

	£ s d
Inventory,	167-14-06
Debts and charges subtracted,	69-00-01
There remains to be distributed,	98-14-05
To widow Elizabeth, the relict,	32-17-09
To Benjamin Griswold, eldest son,	14-14-10
To Zacheus and Moses Griswold, and Elizabeth (wife of Isaac Gillet), to Hannah Wright (wife of Capt. Joseph Wright), to Zerviah the wife of George Griswold, to Azuba the wife of John Warham Strong, and to Ann the wife of Josiah Phelps, and to Esther the wife of Nathaniel Copley, all children of the sd. decd., to each of them the sum of	7-07-05

Page 279-80-1.

Griswold, George, Windsor. Invt. £2972-17-09. Taken by Nathaniel Pinney, Noadiah Gillet and Isaac Phelps. Will dated 25 November, 1746.

I, George Griswold of Windsor, do make this my last will and testament: I give unto my cousin Hezekiah Griswold the whole of the lott that I now live upon, with all the buildings and appurtenances thereof, also the pasture on the west side of the street, likewise the whole of my round swamp; also my will is that sd. Hezekiah have my two lotts in the Indian field and also my island; likewise to the sd. Hezekiah all my land at Barkhamsted. My will also is that the sd. Hezekiah have all my part in the corn mill; also that he have 1-2 of my moveable estate. I give unto Peletiah Griswold my south lott in the fourth meadow during his natural life, and after Peletiah's death my will is that the same lott return to the abovesd. Hezekiah Griswold. Also, that the sd. Peletiah have 1-2 of the last division of land laid out to me in the town commons during his natural life, and after Peletiah's death my will is that it shall return to cousin John Griswold. I give unto Joseph Barnard all my land in the Quarry Field. I give unto George Griswold, 2nd, of Windsor, my north lott in the fourth meadow. I give unto Jacob Griswold my Wash Brook lott. I give George Griswold, son of Daniel Griswold of Bolton, my right in the equivalent land. I give unto Isaac Griswold the other half of the last division of land laid out to me in the town commons, together with Peletiah Griswold, to be divided between them, viz., Peletiah and Isaac. I give to Zerviah, Sergt. George Griswold's wife, the other half of my moveable estate, together with Hezekiah Griswold, to be divided between them. I appoint my cousin Hezekiah Griswold sole executor.

Witness: *Samuel Tudor,*   GEORGE X GRISWOLD, LS.
Isaac Phelps, David Marshall, Jr.

Court Record, Page 59—16 February, 1747-8: The last will and testament of George Griswold, late of Windsor decd., was now exhibited in Court by Hezekiah Griswold, executor. Proven and ordered to be recorded and kept on file.

Page 73—19 August, 1748: Nathaniel Griswold and Edward Griswold, of Windsor, appealed to the Superior Court against the probation of the will.

Page 93—7 March, 1748-9: Peletiah Griswold and Isaac Griswold, two of the legatees of George Griswold, now moved to this Court that distribution be made of the last division of land of the town commons in Windsor according to the last will and testament of the sd. decd.: Whereupon this Court appoint Capt. Ebenezer Grant, Lt. Nathaniel Pinney and Ensign Samuel Phelps distributors.

Page 97—24 March, 1749: A report of the distributors was accepted.

Page 101—30 May, 1749: Mary Loomis, daughter of Mary Griswold and sister of Capt. George Griswold, being heir-in-law, appeals from the judgement of this Court in approving the last will of the sd. decd. unto the Superior Court.

Page 2.

Gross, Capt. Jonah, Hartford. No inventory found. Will not dated.
I, Jonah Gross of Hartford, do make this my last will and testament,
hereby revoking all former wills by me made and done: First, recom-
mending my soul unto the hands of God, and my body to the grave either
in the land or sea, hoping for the pardon of all my sins through ye merits
of Jesus Christ, not doubting of the resurection of my body on the last
day, and touching my worldly goods God has given me: First and prin-
cipally, I give my well-beloved wife Susannah Gross my house and land
in Hartford, to be to her and her heirs and assigns forever, she paying my
just debts and legacies. And also I give to my sd. wife my interest in the
sloop *Rebeckah*, and all my moveable estate of what kind soever, to be to
her and her heirs forever. I give to each of my children, Samuel, Susannah, Lucretia, Rebeckah and Lorenzo, each of them 20 shillings money,
to be paid them by my wife. It is my will that my wife do her best endeavor to bring up my children until they arrive to be able to shift well
and get a living for themselves. And I do hereby constitute and appoint
my wife Susannah Gross to be sole executrix to this my last will and testament. As witness my hand and seal this day.

JONAH GROSS, LS.

Signed, sealed, delivered, published and declared by Capt. Jonah
Gross to be his last will, before us:
John Austin, Abigail Howard,
    Ruth Howard.

Court Record, Page 1—3 December, 1745: The last will and testa-
ment of Capt. Jonah Gross, late of Hartford, was now exhibited by
Susannah Gross, widow and executrix. Will proven.
Page 5—26 February, 1745-6: Lorenzo Gross, a minor, 16 years of
age, son of Capt. Jonah Gross decd. (at Cape Breton), now before this
Court made choice of his mother Susannah Gross to be his guardian.
Recog., £500.

Page 191.

Gustin, Amos. Invt. £107-15-00. Taken 29 February, 1747-8, by
Isaac Coult and Joseph Brewer.
Court Record, Page 51—12 January, 1747-8: This Court grant
Adms. on the estate of Amos Gustin, late of Glastonbury, unto Alpheus
Gustin of Glastonbury, who gave bonds with Eliphalet Gustin of Glaston-
bury of £500.
Page 64—3 May, 1748: An account of Adms. on the estate of Amos
Gustin was now exhibited in Court by Alpheus Gustin, Adms.: Paid in
debts and charges, £78-01-02. Which account is allowed and ordered to
be kept on file.

Page 32.

Hadlock, John. Invt. £35-02-02. Taken by John Burroughs and Isaac Hubbard.

Court Record, Page 18—4 June, 1746: This Court grant Adms. on the estate of John Hadlock, late of Windsor, unto Hannah Hadlock, widow, who gave bonds with Josiah Hadlock of Windsor of £500.

Page 22—2 September, 1746: An account of Adms. on the estate of John Hadlock was now exhibited in Court by Hannah Hadlock, Adms., which account is allowed and ordered to be kept upon file.

Will and Invt. in Vol. XVI, Page 112-113-174.

Hale, Josiah, Suffield. Invt. £2416-14-03. Taken 20 August, 1750, by Daniel Spencer, Joseph King and Benjamin Kent. An inventory as shown by the widow, of moveables valued at £202-c6-00. Taken 3 September, 1750, by James King, Abraham Burbank and Jonathan Rising. Additional inventory of £93, sundry creatures in partnership with Lemuel Granger. Will dated 4 June, 1750.

I, Josiah Hale of Suffield, in the County of Hartford, husbandman, think it fitt to make this my last will and testament: I give to Hannah, my wife, 1 cow, together with all my household goods. I give to my cousin John Hale, son to my brother Timothy Hale, late of Suffield deceased, and my cousin Sarah Hale, daughter to my sd. brother Timothy, my homelott, part of which is called the Great Hollow, lying north of John Norton's homelott, about 40 acres, together with my pasture that I had of Joseph Rising, lying south of my homelott, about 14 acres, with my house and barn and all that appertains to sd. land, by them peaceably to be possessed and enjoyed, they paying to other persons whose names shall be hereafter mentioned in this my will what I shall order and appoint, my just debts being paid. I give to my cousin John Hale my meadow lying upon Stony Brook, as also a parcel of land that I have in the swamp called Huxley's, about 13 acres; also a parcel of land lying east from John Granger's homelott. It is my will that there shall be raised out of my estate by my executors, and given to my sister Hannah Hale, widow, £3 old tenour; also £3 old tenour, which I give to my cousin Joseph Hale. Also, it is part of my last will that Thomas Hale shall have £3. Also I give to Mary Hale, my cousin, £10. Also I give to my daughter Hannah Granger £40 old tenour. It is part of this my last will that Viah Granger shall have £50 old tenor. Likewise I give to Thankful Hathaway, wife of Jacob Hathaway, £30 old tenour. Also I give to my sister Hannah Remington £20 old tenor. It is to be understood as part of this my last will that my 2 faithful friends, Samuel Hathaway and Joshua Austin, both of Suffield, shall be executors. It is to be understood that my above willed estate is leased out to Limus Granger, which lease will be

out the 15th June, 1752; that then the above-mentioned heirs shall have the peaceable possession of what is above willed and bequeathed to them.
Witness: *Nathaniel Austin,*   JOSIAH HALE, LS.
John Granger, Mary Copley.

Court Record, Page 137—7 August, 1750: Will proven.
Page 1 (Vol. XVI) 4 September, 1750: This Court grant Adms. on the intestate estate of Josiah Hale, late of Suffield decd., unto Hannah Hale, widow of sd. decd., who gave bond. Also the Adms. exhibited an inventory of ye sd. intestate estate, which is accepted by the Court.

Page 3—2 October, 1750: An inventory of the estate of Josiah Hale given by his last will was now exhibited in Court by Joshua Austin, one of the executors.

Page 409-10-11.

Hale, Samuel, Suffield. Invt. £2389-03-03. Taken by Samuel Hathway, Jonathan Rising and Joshua Austin. Will dated 19 September, 1748.
I, Samuel Hale of Suffield, in the County of Hampshire and Province of Massachusetts Bay, in New England, husbandman, do make and ordain this my last will and testament: I give and bequeath to my two cousins, Timothy Hale and Thomas Hale, both of Suffield aforesd., my house and barn and homelott, and also three rights of land I bought of three of my brother Timothy Hale's heirs, John Hale, Joseph Hale and Hannah Hale alias Austin, and also 13 acres of land that lyeth southward of the place where the sd. John Hale now liveth, together with all my right and undivided land in Suffield, to be divided equally between them. I give to my well-beloved sister-in-law, the Widow Hannah Hale, £30 old tenor, to be levied out of my estate. I give to my cousin Sarah Hale £30. I give to my cousin Mary Hale £20 old tenor. I give to my cousin John Hale's 2nd son Samuel Hale £20 old tenor. And as to the remainder of my estate which may appear over and above what is already bequeathed, and all my debts being paid, it is my will and pleasure that the same may be equally divided between the abovewritten Timothy Hale and Thomas Hale. I do likewise appoint the aforenamed Timothy Hale and Thomas Hale my only executors to this my will.
Witness: *Jonathan Rising,*   SAMUEL X HALE, LS.
Joshua Austin, Lemuel Granger.

Page 422-3.
Invt. in Vol. XVI, Page 308-12.

Hall, Giles, Esq., Middletown. Invt. £35,944-00-08½. Taken 31 March, 1753, by Jabez Hamlin, William Rockwell, Isaac Smith and Ebenezer Clark. Will dated 9 January, 1749-50.

I, Giles Hall of Middletown, in the County of Hartford, doe make this my last will and testament, in manner and form following: Item: I give and bequeath to my wife Esther the improvement of my dwelling house and homelott with the buildings thereon, and also my meadow called Smith's meadow in the long meadow, and also liberty to get her own firewood and fencing stuff on any of my woodland where she shall see cause; also liberty to pasture three cows in Hunting Hill pasture or Crowel pasture, so-called; all this I give to her during the term of her natural life. Also I give to my sd. wife my negro boy Cesar and the mullatto girl Else. I give her 1-3 part of my personal and moveable estate to be to her and to her heirs forever. I give to my eldest son Giles the lott whereon he has built his house, and also 1-2 of the land at the shipyard that I bought of Leonard White, to lye on the northward side of the lott; also part of my meadow called Bacon's meadow, to extend from the Great River west to the drain; also all my right in the land I bought of the heirs of Sergt. William Ward in the year of 1746, of which purchase my sd. son paid a considerable part though I took the deed to myself; also I give him 4 acres of land adjoining eastward out of my Hunting Hill lott, to lye the length of the before-mentioned land; also one equal quarter part of my stone quarry and land adjoining on the east side of the Great River; all this I give to him and his heirs forever. I give to my sons Hamlin John, Richard and Jabez to each of them one equal quarter part of my stone quarry, and land adjoining, to them and their heirs forever. And further, my will is that my house and lott that I bought of Giles Hamlin, and the remainder of my land in the North Society that was granted by the proprietors in part pay for my Durant lott, containing about 70 acres, be sold by my executors as soon as may be, and the produce thereof to be added to the two remaining thirds of my moveable estate, out of which my will is that, my just debts and funeral charges being first paid, the remainder to be added to the remainder of my real estate after the before-mentioned legacies are taken out, of which my will is that my daughter Mary shall have £500 old tenor at the apprisement, and the remainder to be equally divided to and amongst my six children, Esther, Giles, Hamlin John, Richard, Jabez, and Mary, to be to them and their heirs forever. I have three small lotts in the third division on the east side of the Great River, commonly called the apprentice's lott, and my will is that my grandson John Hall shall have one of them, and grandson Giles Hall shall have the other two, to be to them and their heirs forever. Also I give unto the Church of Christ, of which I am a member, 5 flaggons for the use of the Communion table, to be procured by my executors. And further, I appoint my beloved wife Esther and my son Richard Hall to be executors.

Witness: *Joseph Southmayd,*   GILES HALL, LS.
Matthew Talcott, Jabez Hamlin.

16 January, 1749-50: I, Giles Hall before named, having maturely considered my will, do approve thereof this addition or alteration written in this schedule or supplement: My will is that the charges of my son Richard's education, what remains, and the charge of his taking his de-

gree at college, shall be taken out of that part of my estate that I have assigned for the payment of my debts and funeral charges before there be any division thereof among my children. And that this is a part or supplement to my before-mentioned will, I signify by setting to my hand and seal.

Witness: *Joseph Southmayd,*   GILES HALL, LS.
Matthew Talcott, Jabez Hamlin.

Court Record, Page 130—14 May, 1750: The last will and testament of Giles Hall, Esq., late of Middletown decd., was now exhibited in Court by Esther Hall and Richard Hall, executors. Proven and ordered to be recorded and kept on file.

Handerson, James. Court Record, Page 7—4 March, 1746: This Court grant Adms. on the estate of James Handerson, late of Hartford decd., unto James Handerson, son of sd. decd., who gave bond with John Shepherd of sd. Hartford of £500.

Hamlin, Jabez. Court Record, Page 87—2 February, 1748-9: John Hamlin, age 11 years, and George, 9 years of age: this Court appoint and impower Jabez Hamlin, Esq., of Middletown, to be guardian to his children. Recog., £1000.

Harris, Benjamin. Court Record, Page 111—16 November, 1749: An inventory of the estate of Benjamin Harris, late of Middletown, was now exhibited in Court by Benjamin Harris, Adms., which inventory is accepted, ordered recorded and kept on file.

Page 288-9.
Hart, Timothy, Farmington. Invt. £2778-04-0ɔ. Taken 2nd December, 1748, by Isaac Cowles, Robert Porter and Joseph Hooker.

Court Record, Page 82—6 December, 1748: This Court grant Adms. on the estate of Timothy Hart, late of Farmingtown, unto Mary Hart, widow, who gave bonds with Solomon Cowles of Farmingtown of £1000.

Page 433-4.
Hatch, Capt. Joseph, Tolland. Will dated 2nd April, 1750: I, Joseph Hatch of Tolland, in the County of Hartford, do make this my last will and testament: I give to my wife Rebeckah, whom I make my sole executrix, my best riding horse; also all my moveable estate, both without doors and within; and also all the debts due to my estate; to her and her heirs forever, my sd. wife paying all lawful debts due from my estate, and also paying such legacies as I shall hereafter mention to be paid out of my moveable estate. I give to my wife the sole improvement

of my houses and lands during her widowhood. It is also my will that if my sd. wife should marry or be taken away by death before my three youngest sons come of age to inherit what I shall hereafter give them, that then my sd. houses and lands shall be improved for the bringing up or profit of my three youngest sons, to whom I give my houses and lands as followeth: I give to my son Samuel Hatch 1-3 part of all my houses and lands, to him and to his heirs forever. I give to my son Ebenezer Hatch the 1-3 part of all my houses and lands forever. I give to my son Timothy Hatch 1-3 part of my houseing and lands forever. And this division of my houseing and lands is to be made when my youngest son comes to the age of 21 years. I give to my son Joseph Hatch one small Bible, I haveing already given him his portion in land. I give to my granddaughter Thankful Hatch 1 small Bible, having given to her father Jonathan Hatch in his lifetime his portion of my estate. I give to my daughter Amey West the sum of £10 in money of the old tenor, and one small Bible, to be paid to her two years after my decease. I give to my daughter Elsie Case one small Bible, I having given her her portion already. I give to my daughter Mercy Shiverick one small Bible, she having had her portion already. I give to my daughter Lois Hatch £80 old tenor value in moveables and £120 money of the old tenor. to be paid her by my executrix at her marriage day or in three years after my decease.

Witness: *Samuel Palmer,*   JOSEPH HATCH, LS.
Moses Swift, Jr., Mary Swift.

Court Record, Page 133—15 June, 1750: The last will and testament of Capt. Joseph Hatch, late of Tolland decd., was now exhibited in Court by Rebeckah Hatch, executrix. Proven and ordered to be recorded.

Page 18 (Vol. XVI) 29 March, 1751: Samuel Hatch, a minor, age 16 years, son of Joseph Hatch, chose his mother Rebeckah Hatch to be his guardian. Also, this Court appoint the sd. Rebeckah guardian to Ebenezer Hatch, about 11 years, and Timothy Hatch, 9 years of age. Recog., £400 for each minor.

Hatch, Zephaniah. Court Record, Page 52—1st December, 1749: Zephaniah Hatch, a minor, 17 years of age, chose Nathaniel Hurlbut of Wethersfield to be his guardian. Recog., £300.

Hawley, Thomas. Court Record, Page 4—4 March, 1746: Thomas Hawley, a minor, age 14 years 8 months, son of Timothy Hawley of Farmingtown, chose Capt. John Newell of Farmingtown to be his guardian. Recog., £1000. (The father of the minor, being present, consented to this choice.)

Page 65.

Hickcox, Ensign Joseph, Windsor. Invt. £638-02-04. Taken 9 February, 1746-7, by Jonathan Stiles and Joseph Hart.

Court Record, Page 32—2 February, 1746-7: Adms. granted unto Ezekiel Thompson of Farmington, who gave bonds of £1000.

Page 44—1st September, 1747: James Hickcox, a minor, 14 years of age, son of Joseph Hickcox, chose his brother Ezekiel Thompson of Farmington to be his guardian. Recog., £500.

Page 49—3 November, 1747: Hannah Hickcox, the widow, moved to this Court that her right of dowry may be set out to her: Whereupon this Court appoint Lt. Samuel Stiles, Samuel Stoughton and Giles Elsworth, of Windsor, to set out to the widow 1-3 part of the real estate by bounds.

Page 100—17 May, 1749: An account of Adms. was now exhibited by Ezekiel Thompson, Adms. Accepted.

Page 111—5 December, 1749: Pursuant to an act of the General Assembly holden at New Haven on the 2nd Thursday of October, 1749, directing Ezekiel Thompson, Adms., to make sale of so much of the real estate of the sd. deceased as will procure the sum of £127-10-03 with incident charges, this Court so order the Adms.

Page 125—3 April, 1750: Ezekiel Thompson, Adms., having rendered to this Court an account of the Adms. to the acceptance of this Court, now moves that distribution be made of the real estate (the moveables being expended to pay the charges due from sd. estate, and some of the lands sold by order of the General Assembly, as directed by this Court): Whereupon this Court appoint Lt. Joseph Hart, Asahell Strong, Esq., and Mr. Hezekiah Lee, of Farmington, to set out to Joseph Hickcox, eldest son, a double part of the real estate, and to James and Benjamin Hickcox, Jerusha Roberts alias Hickcox, Katharine Thompson alias Hickcox, and Hannah Hickcox, children of the sd. deceased, their single shares of sd. real estate; and also to set out to Hannah Hickcox, widow, 1-3 part of the real estate for her improvement during life; and make return thereof to this Court.

Page 409.

Higgins, Daniel, Middletown. Died 8 October, 1749. Invt. £551-04-00. Taken by Cornelius Knowles and Lazarus Griffeth.

Court Record, Page 134—3 July, 1750: This Court grant Adms. on the estate of Daniel Higgins, late of Middletown, unto Ruth Higgins, widow of the sd. decd., who gave bond as the law directs. Exhibited an inventory, which this Court accepts and ordered to be kept on file.

Page 367-8.

Hills, Ebenezer, Sen., East Hartford. Will dated 19 May, 1732: I, Ebenezer Hills, Sen., of Hartford, do make this my last will and testament: I give to Abigail, my wife, the use of one room in my dwelling house and so much of the cellar as she shall stand in need of, with the improvement of 1-3 part of my barn. My will is that my wife have the

1-3 part of all my moveable estate to improve and also to dispose of if need be for her comfortable support, together with the improvement of 1-3 part of all my lands during her life. I give to my son William Hills all the right and title I have in and unto a large tract of land commonly called the Western lands, belonging unto the Towns of Hartford and Windsor, to be his own forever, which is his full portion. I give unto my daughter Abigail, the wife of Joseph Dewey, £5 out of my moveable estate, which is her full portion. I give unto my daughter Sarah, the wife of Samuel Roberts, £5 out of my moveable estate, being her full portion. I give unto my daughter Esther, the wife of Joseph Case, £5 out of my moveable estate, it being her full portion. I will unto my daughter Hannah Hills £40 out of my moveable estate, it being her full portion. I give unto my son Ebenezer Hills one piece of land within the bounds of Hartford (East Side), butts west on my son's own land, to run east half a mile the full breadth of my lott, lying on the north with the land belonging unto the heirs of Jonathan Hills decd., on the south with the land of John Arnold, east on my own land, to be his own forever. I give unto my son Abraham Hills sundry pieces of land lying in the Town of Hartford (East Side): 4 acres in Hocanum meadow, and buts west partly on John Risley, partly on the school land, south on the way into the meadow, north on David Hill's land; one piece, 12 acres, butts east on the school land, west on the meadow, north on John Wadsworth, south on Mr. Porter his land; one piece more, about one acre, butts west on a highway, south on the school, north on John Arnold, with the dwelling house and barn standing on the same; one piece more, butting west on John Kilbourn's land, east on my son Ebenezer Hills's land, north on land belonging to the heirs of Lt. Jonathan Hills decd., south on John Arnold his land, being half a mile in length the whole breadth of my lott. I give all the rest of all my estate, real and personal, to my two sons Ebenezer and Abraham Hills, to be equally divided between them. I make and appoint Jonathan Hills and my son Ebenezer Hills executors.

Witness: *John Arnold,*   EBENEZER X HILLS, SEN., LS.
Jonathan Hills, John Vibbard.

Court Record, Page 119—6 March, 1749-50: The last will and testament of Ebenezer Hills, late of Hartford decd., was now exhibited in Court by Capt. Jonathan Hills and Ebenezer Hills, executors. Will proven, ordered to be recorded and kept on file.

Page 221.

Hinckley, Benjamin, Willington. Invt. £109-15-06. Taken 1st June, 1748 (moveable estate) by Simon Kinsbury and Samuel Cobb.

Court Record, Page 65—3 May, 1748: This Court grant Adms. on the estate of Benjamin Hinckley, of Willington decd., unto Deborah Hinckley, widow, who gave bonds with Ichabod Hinckley of Tolland of £500. This Court appoint Deborah Hinckley, widow, to be guardian to her children, viz., Ichabod Hinckley, 12 years of age, Betty 11 years,

Mary 9, Ann 8, Deborah 4, and Benjamin 3 years of age, children of Benjamin Hinckley, late deceased. Recog., £300 for each minor.

Page 68—6 June, 1748: An inventory of the estate of Benjamin Hinckley, late of Willington, was now exhibited in Court by Deborah Hinckley, widow. Accepted and ordered to be recorded. Estate is insolvent. This Court appoint Ichabod Lothrop and Simon Kingsbury of Tolland to adjust the claims of the creditors and set out a list of moveables to the widow for her necessary use of £39-12-06, which account is on file.

Page 79—1st November, 1748: A report of the commissioners on the estate of Benjamin Hinckley, late of Willington, under the hands of Ichabod Lothrop and Simon Kingsbury, commissioners, which report is accepted and ordered to be kept on file.

Page 106 (Vol. XVI) 4 September, 1753: Ichabod Hinckley, a minor, now 18 years of age, son of Benjamin Hinckley, chose his grandfather Ichabod Hinckley to be his guardian. Recog., £100.

Hogens, James. Court Record, Page 97—24 March, 1748-9: It was certified to this Court by *John Chester, Assistant,* that James Hogens, a minor, born, as pr record appears, 14 March, 1734-5, son of James Hogens and Mary his wife, before him sd. Assistant on the 24th day of March, 1748-9, made choice of his uncle Peter Hurlbut of Wethersfield to be his guardian, which choice this Court allows. Recog., £500.

Page 68.

Hollister, Joseph, Glastonbury. Invt. £997-02-10. Taken 6 August, 1746, by Thomas Welles and Jonathan Hale.

Court Record, Page 26—29 October, 1746: This Court grant Adms. on the estate of Joseph Hollister, late of Glastonbury decd., unto Timothy Hollister of Wethersfield, who gave bonds with Ebenezer Webster of Hartford of £600.

Page 37—7 April, 1747: An inventory exhibited by Timothy Hollister. Ordered to be recorded and kept on file.

Dist. File: To Sarah Hollister, the widow; to Joseph Hollister, Jr., his heirs; to Timothy Hollister, to Mary Hollister, wife of Joseph Shelton; to Ann White, to Esther the wife of Thadius Shelton. By Josiah Benton and Samuel Talcott, distributors. 5 September, 1757.

Page 102.

Hollister, Joseph, Jr., Glastonbury. Invt. £3138-00-00. Taken 17 December, 1746, by Thomas Welles and Abraham Kilbourn.

Dist. File: 4 October, 1748:

	£ s d
To Mary Hollister, widow,	339-04-04
To Mary Kilbourn, daughter,	161-10-06
To Abigail Hollister,	162-04-09

By Thomas Welles and Benjamin Hale.

Court Record, Page 76—4 October, 1748: A return of the distribution of the moveable estate of Joseph Hollister, Jr., under the hands of Thomas Welles and Benjamin Hale, distributors, was exhibited in Court and accepted. And Mary Hollister, widow, having fully administered on sd. estate to the acceptance of this Court, is now granted a *Quietus Est.*

Page 333.

Hollister, Zephaniah, Glastonbury. Invt. £2535-12-06. Taken by David Goodrich and Samuel Kimberly.

Court Record, Page 106—5 September, 1749: This Court grant Adms. on the estate of Zephaniah Hollister, late of Glastonbury, unto Ruth Hollister, widow, who gave bonds with Samuel Kimberly of sd. Glastonbury of £1000.

Page 31 (Vol. XVII) 22 April, 1754: An account of Adms. was now exhibited in Court by Ruth Hollister, Adms., which account is accepted. This Court order distribution of sd. estate, viz.: To the widow 1-3 part of the moveable estate and 1-3 part of the real estate for her improvement during life; and to Ruth, Hulda and Damaris Hollister, to each of them an equal share. And appoint Jonathan Hale, Esq., Lt. Samuel Kimberly and Mr. Richard Smith distributors.

Page 72—14 July, 1755: Ruth Hollister, a minor, 17 years of age, daughter of Zephaniah Hollister, made choice of Hope Fox of Glastonbury to be her guardian. Recog., £300.

Page 358.

Holman, Thomas, Middletown. Inventory £45-15-06. Taken by Jeremiah Spicer and Cornelius Lane. Will dated 17 August, 1749.

I, Thomas Holman of the Town of Middletown, in the County of Hartford, do make this my last will and testament: I give to Hannah, my beloved wife, 1-3 part of all my estate during her life, and also all my household moveables. I give to my son Thomas Holman, whom I constitute my only and sole executor, all and singular my lands and tenements, by him freely to be possessed and injoyed. Also I give to my son Thomas all my cattle and team tackling and husbandry tools, freely to injoy after my and my wife's decease. I give to my daughter Abigail

£10. I give to my daughter Hannah £10. I give to my daughter Abigail and my daughter Hannah all my household moveable estate after my and my wife's decease, to be equally divided between them.

Witness: *John Shepherd,*   THOMAS HOLMAN, LS.
Thomas Rogers, Ebenezer Brown.

Court Record, Page 113—2 January, 1749-50: The last will and testament of Thomas Holman, late of Middletown decd., was now exhibited in Court by Thomas Holman, executor. Proven. Exhibited an inventory. Both ordered to be recorded and kept on file.

Page 62.

Holton, Eleazer, Simsbury. Invt. £1075-03-08. Taken 11 March, 1746-7, by John Humphrey, Jonathan Case and Andrew Robe.

Court Record, Page 35—12 March, 1746-7: This Court grant Adms. on the estate of Eleazer Holton of Simsbury decd. unto John Case and John Owen, Jr., of Simsbury, who gave bonds with Thomas Seymour of Hartford of £1000.

Page 305-6.

Hooker, Mrs. Mehetabell, Hartford. Invt. £360-04-00. Taken 15 May, 1749, by Samuel Lee, Thomas Welles, John Nichols and John Wadsworth. Will dated 21 May, 1748.

I, Mehetabell Hooker of Hartford, being aged and infirm, do make this my last will and testament: I give to my sons Samuel Hooker, Giles Hooker, Thomas Hooker and William Hooker, each of them 20 shillings in bills of credit of the old currency. I give my daughters, Mrs. Esther Stiles and Mrs. Mehetabell Coit, all my interest, right or property in the mill, the stream and the land that belongs to me on the east side of the Great River at Hartford (called Pitkin's Mills). Also I give my aforesd. daughters all my lands and right of lands, whether divided or undivided, in Middletown. I give my aforesd. two daughters all my moveables or personal estate (excepting the use of my thirds or dowry left me by my husband, which was to be paid to me by my son Giles, which I give to my daughter Coit over and above the 1-2 of the rest). And lastly I make and appoint my son Thomas Hooker and my son-in-law Daniel Coit, Esq., executors.

Witness: *J: Hempstead.*   MEHETABEL X HOOKER, LS.
Mary Hooker, Mary Ellery.

Court Record, Page 94—10 March, 1748-9: The last will and testament of Mrs. Mehetabel Hooker, late of Hartford decd., was now exhibited in Court by Thomas Hooker and Daniel Coit, executors. Will proven and ordered to be kept on file.

Page 29.

Hooker, John, Farmington. Invt. £1551-15-02. Taken by Isaac Cowles, John Newell and Robert Porter on the 19th day of March, 1745-6. Will dated 6 September, 1745.

I, John Hooker, Sen., of the Town of Farmingtown, do make and ordain this my last will and testament: I give to my son Hezekiah Hooker, besides what I have formerly given him, all my wearing clothes of all sorts whatsoever. Unto my son John Hooker, besides what I have formerly given him, two parcels of land in sd. Farmington, my right in 30 acres of land near the place called Shuttle Meadow Mountain, which my sd. right is 10 acres, also 10 acres of land laid out to me at a place called Plow Hill. Unto my son Joseph Hooker, besides what I have formerly given him, I give him one parcel of land in the Great Meadow of 5 acres, at a place called Pine Orchard; one percel of five roods in Pequabuck Meadow, against a place called Higgason's Cart Way; also 1-2 part of my right in that called the Great Swamp, which half part is about 33 acres. Unto my son Roger Hooker, with whom I now dwell, who hath for some time been the staff of my age, besides what I have formerly given him, I give as followeth: one parcel of land in Farmingtown Great Meadow containing waste land (in all about 20 acres), bounded west on the river, east on a small highway, south with land of Asahell Strong; also one parcel of land, 4 1-2 acres, lying between the homestead of Josiah North and Widow Mary Bird; also one parcel of land which I have on the side of the mountain westward from the place called Norton's Swamp, the whole thereof, the quantity I do not certainly know; also the remainder of my right in that called the Dead Swamp grants; also all my right in the team and team tackling and all implements or tools for husbandry. Unto my aforenamed sons I give all the remainder of my right to lands already laid out, and may hereafter be laid out, to be to them in equal proportions between them. I give unto my four daughters, Abigail Hart, Mary Hart, Sarah Strong and Ruth Strong, besides what I have formerly given them, I give unto them in equal proportion all the residue and remainder of my personal estate not in this instrument before disposed of. I appoint my aforenamed son Roger Hooker to be sole executor.

Witness: *William Judd,*   JOHN HOOKER, LS.
Timothy Hart, David Porter.

Court Record, Page 10—1st April, 1746: The last will and testament of John Hooker, Esq., late of Farmingtown decd., was now exhibited in Court by Roger Hooker, executor. Will proven. Exhibited an inventory, which, with the will, was ordered recorded and kept on file.

———————

Page 81.

Hopkins, Deborah, Middletown. Invt. £20-00-00. Taken 29 May, 1746, by John Markham and Ebenezer Clark.

574 PROBATE RECORDS. VOL. XV,

Court Record, Page 13—3 June, 1746: This Court grant Adms. on the estate of Widow Deborah Hopkins, late of Middletown decd., unto Moses West of sd. Middletown. Exhibit of an inventory. Accepted and ordered to be kept on file.

Will on File.

Hopkins, Hannah, Hartford. Will dated 17 December, 1744: In the name of God, amen. I, Hannah Hopkins, being week in body but at present of sound mind and memory, and knowing not the day of my death, do make this my last will and testament, that is to say: First, I commit my soul to God who gave it, and my body to the grave to be decently buried, assuring myself I shall receive the same at the resurrection. And as for what goods and estate God hath been pleased to bless me with, I give and bequeath in the following manner: First, I give and bequeeth to my loving daughter Mary Hopkins, wife to my son Thomas Hopkins, one brass kettle. 2ly, I give and bequeath to grandafter Abigail Hopkins one feather bed, bolster, rugs, coverlids and sheets belonging to the same, with the bedsted and cord, to her and her heirs forever. 3ly, I give to my grandafter Mary my copper kettle, to her and her heirs forever; and also all my pewter to said Mary and her heirs forever; and also my box, with what is in it, and my chest to sd. Mary. And if any one of my 2 grandchildren die before they come to age or be married, then the whole to go to the surviving grandafter. 4ly, I give to my grandson Steven my gun, to him and his heirs forever. 5ly, I give to Ann Flowers, wife to Lamrock Flowers, 30 shillings old tenor: 6ly, I give to five of my grandsons, namely, Thomas Hopkins, Moses Hopkins, Aaron Hopkins, Elisha Hopkins and Benjamin Hopkins, one cow to them equally divided. 7ly, I give to my granddafter Sarah Shepard 30 shillings old tenor. 8ly, I give to my dafter Mary all my wearing clothes. All the rest of my estate I give to my son Thomas Hopkins and his heirs forever, he to pay all my just debts and legacies. I also appoint my son Thomas Hopkins to be the sole executor of this my last will and testament. In witness whereof I have hereunto set my hand this 17th day of December, 1744, in presence of

Witness: *John Shepard,*   HANNAH X HOPKINS.
Isaac Bunce, Jonathan Steel.

Court Record, Page 1—3 December, 1745: Will proven.

Page 236.

Hosford, Samuel, Windsor. Invt. £70-15-09. Taken 24 May, 1746, by John Allyn, John Palmer, Jr., Peletiah Allyn and John Stoughton.

Court Record, Page 33—3 March, 1746-7: This Court grant Adms. on the estate of Samuel Hosford, late of Windsor decd., unto Jesse Hosford of Windsor, who gave bonds with John Palmer of sd. Windsor of £700.

Page 60—3 March, 1747-8: This Court grant Adms. on the estate of Samuel Horsford, late of Windsor decd., unto John Cook 2nd of Windsor, who gave bonds with Phineas Drake of Windsor of £300. Exhibit of an inventory, which was ordered recorded and kept on file.

Page 191.

Hoskins, Anthony, Windsor. Will dated 24 September, 1744: I, Anthony Hoskins of Windsor, do make this my last will and testament: I having made provision for my loving wife Hannah during her life already, I further give her 1-3 of all my estate. And as I have already given to each of my children, Anthony, Alexander, Joseph, Hannah, Mabel, Amey, Sarah, Jane and Dorcas, by way of portion and settlement, what I have been able to, I have nothing further to give or bequeath to either of them. And therefore my son Zebulon Hoskins, in consideration of my love to him and in respect that he is under some obligation further to do for his mother, and also for that he payed more than £40 in old tenor money to the heirs of Samuel Allyn decd. for a debt which I owed to the sd. Allyn in his lifetime (and to secure the same to sd. Allyn I had given him a bond to secure to him the 5th part of the estate of my brother Joseph Hoskins at his decease, which £40 was paid by my son Zebulon to redeem the same), I therefore hereby give and bequeath to him, his heirs and assigns, all my right, title and interest that I have to and in the lands now belonging to my brother Joseph Hoskins, or that I ever may have at his decease, the whole thereof, that my heirs may or might by any way or means claim or challenge to the same, the whole is to be to my son Zebulon and his heirs forever. I appoint my son Zebulon to be my executor, and order him out of my estate to pay all my just debts.

Witness: *Timothy Phelps,*   ANTHONY X HOSKINS, LS.
Isaac Skinner, Peletiah Mills.

Court Record, Page 64—3 May, 1748: Will proven.

Page 81—6 December, 1748: Zebulon Hoskins, executor to the last will of Anthony Hoskins, now informs this Court that he cannot find any estate, either real or personal, belonging to the estate of the sd. deceased.

Page 233-4.

Hossington, Elisha, Farmington. Invt. £3871-17-08. Taken by Huit Strong, Ephraim Boardman and Nathaniel Judd. Will dated 11 January, 1748.

I, Elisha Hossington of Farmingtown, do make this my last will and testament: I give to Hannah, my wife, whom I make sole executrix, all and singular my lands, messuages and tenements, together with all my houshold goods, debts and moveable estate (except my best beaver hat and 20 shillings more), to be by her freely possessed and injoyed. I give to my brother James Hossington my best beaver hat. The rest of my brethren and surviving sister I give 5 shillings.

Witness: *Hewitt Strong,*   ELISHA HOSSINGTON, LS.
Ephraim Boardman, Nathaniel Judd.

Court Record, Page 77—4 October, 1748: The last will and testament of Elisha Hossington, late of Farmingtown, was now exhibited by Hannah Hossington, executrix. Will proven and with the inventory was ordered recorded and kept on file.

Page 417.

Howard, Samuel, Hartford. Invt. £4400-00-00. Taken January, 1749-50, by Thomas Hooker and Thomas Welles.

Court Record, Page 122—22 March, 1749-50: This Court grant Adms. on the estate of Samuel Howard unto Alice Howard, widow. Recog., £1000, with Nathaniel Hooker.

Page 31 (Vol. XVI) 13 July, 1751: Pursuant to an act of the General Assembly held at New Haven on the 2nd Thursday of October last, directing Alice Howard, Adms., to make sale of so much of the real estate as will pay the sum of £179-00-11 due from sd. estate, with necessary charges: Whereupon this Court direct sd. Adms. to make sale of so much of a lot of land to pay sd. sum, and make return to this Court to whom sd. land is or may be sold, and for how much.

Page 33—20 August, 1751: Alice Howard, Adms., having finished her account of Adms., now moves to this Court that freeholders may be appointed to distribute the real estate (the moveable part being spent): This Court appoint and impower John Skinner, Jonathan Seymour and Joseph Holtom to distribute the real estate, viz., to Samuel Howard, only son of the deceased, a double part, and to each of the daughters an equal or single share, and also to set out to sd. Alice Howard, widow, 1-3 part of the real estate for her improvement during life, and make return thereof to this Court.

Hunlock, Jonathan. Court Record, Page 6—4 March, 1746: Jonathan Hunlock, a minor, 16 years of age, son of Jonathan Hunlock, late of Wethersfield, chose Francis Hanmore of Wethersfield to be his guardian. Recog., £500.

Page 91-2.

Johnson, William, Middletown. Invt. £517-15-00. Taken 11 June, 1746, by William Rockwell, Jacob Whitmore and Daniel Whitmore.

Court Record, Page 15—1st July, 1746: This Court grant Adms. on the estate of William Johnson, late of Middletown, unto Martha Johnson, widow of sd. decd., who gave bonds with Stephen Johnson of Middletown of £500.

Page 77—4 October, 1748: An account of Adms. on the estate of William Johnson was now exhibited in Court by Martha Johnson, Adms.:

	£ s d
Paid in debts and charges,	111-15-04
Received,	5-00-00

Which account is allowed and ordered to be kept on file.

Jones, John. Court Record, Page 28—2 December, 1746: Thomas Jones, a minor, 16 years of age, son of John Jones, late of Hartford deceased, chose Stephen Hosmer of Hartford to be his guardian. Recog., £200.

Page 216-17-18.

Judd, Daniel, Farmington. Invt. £2280-00-00. Taken 2 June, 1748, by John Newell, Hezekiah Lee and Joseph Hooker. Will dated 14 October, 1746.

I, Daniel Judd of Farmingtown, do make this my last will and testament: Imprimis: I do give and bequeath unto my wife Mercy Judd, if she shall survive me, the use of all my meadow land within the common field in Farmingtown, and 1-3 part of the remainder of my land in sd. Farmingtown; and also 1-3 part of all my moveable estate to her own use and disposal of as she shall see cause; and also the use and service of John Barnes's labor during the time he is bound to me for. Also one year's provision for her and those that shall live with her. I give unto my son Matthew Judd, besides what I have given him already, all my right of land that I have in that lot at the Bass River, 2nd branch, and all my right in land in the old farm meadow, and on the Great Plaine, and on the Two-Mile Plaine, forever; and also all my wearing clothes. I give unto my son James Judd, besides what I have already given him, all my land at the place called 2½-Mile Hill, with what land adjoins thereto, going down to Two-Mile Meadow Brook; also the 6 1-2 acres of land I bought of my son Matthew Judd, being part of my home-lott, only reserving liberty for my daughter Rachel Judd to pasture a cow or a horse during the time she live a single life; also one piece of land in the Indian Meadow, and one piece being part of that called Webster's farm; one piece in the Little Meadow, to be possessed by him after the decease of his mother. I give unto my daughter Rachel Judd so much of my moveable estate as shall make her full equal with what I gave unto her sister Mary Thompson, alias Judd; also the £20 due from my son James Judd to me; and all the remainder of my moveable estate I give unto my two daughters, Mary Thompson and Rachel Judd, to be equally divided between them. I give unto Daniel Judd, my grandchild, son to Matthew Judd my son, 3-4 parts of that lott lying in the fifth division west of sd. Farmingtown, drawn and laid out on the right of my honoured grandfather, Thomas Judd, Sen., late of Farmingtown deceased. Also, all the remainder of my land, divided or undivided, I give in equal degree to my two sons, Matthew Judd and James Judd, and to their heirs forever. I ordain my son James Judd to be sole executor.

Witness: *John Hart,*   DANIEL JUDD, LS.
Ebenezer Barnes, Eli Andruss.

Court Record, Page 71—6 July, 1748: The last will and testament of Daniel Judd, late of Farmingtown deceased, was now exhibited in Court by James Judd, executor. Proven. Exhibited an inventory. Both ordered recorded and kept on file.

Page 214-215.

Kelsey, William, Hartford. Invt. £1873-13-00. Taken 17 March, 1747-8, by John Whiting and Moses Nash. Will dated 7 November, 1747.

I, William Kelsey of Hartford, do make this my last will and testament: I give to my beloved son Zachariah all my estate, both real and personal, he doing the duties hereafter enjoyned him to do: First of all, that he pay all my debts. Second, that he maintain and honourably support Rebeckah, my beloved wife, during her natural life. Third, that he pay out to my four daughters what I have hereafter given to them. I give to my beloved daughter Jerusha Kelsey, alias Fyler, £100 old tenor besides what I have already given to her, to be paid in four years after my decease. I give to my daughter Damarus Kelsey, alias Drake, £100 in old tenor bills besides what I have given her already, to be paid within six years after my decease. I give to my daughter Esther Kelsey £200 in old tenor, viz., £100 in one year after my decease, the other £100 in seven years after my decease. I give to my daughter Rebeckah Kelsey £200 in old tenor, £100 to be paid within one year and the other £100 within 7 years after my decease. I appoint my son Zachariah Kelsey to be sole executor.

Witness: *Moses Cadwell,*   WILLIAM KELSEY, LS.
Moses Nash, Elizabeth X Flower.

Court Record, Page 59—1st March, 1747-8: The last will and testament of William Kelsey, late of Hartford decd., was now exhibited in Court by Zachariah Kelsey, executor. Will proven and ordered to be recorded. Jeremiah Fyler and Asahell Drake of Windsor now appeal from the judgement of this Court, in approveing the last will and testament of William Kelsey, unto the Superior Court, and jointly and severaly bound themselves in a recog. of £50.

Page 62—1st April, 1748: Rebeckah Kelsey, the widow of William Kelsey, late of Hartford decd., now moves to this Court that her right of dowry in the real estate of the sd. decd. shall be paid out to her as the law directs: Whereupon this Court appoint Col. John Whiting, Moses Nash and Thomas Cadwell distributors.

Page 65—3 May, 1748: An inventory of the estate of William Kelsey, late of Hartford deceased, was now exhibited by Zachariah Kelsey, executor. Accepted and ordered to be recorded and kept on file. Also the sd. executor now exhibited a return of the widow's dowry, under the hands of Col. John Whiting and Moses Nash, distributors. Accepted and ordered on file.

Page 242-3.

Kendall, Ebenezer, Simsbury. Died 1st August, 1748. Invt. £564-13-03. Taken 29 September, 1748, by Isaac Dewey and Return Holcomb.

Court Record, Page 76—4 October, 1748: This Court grant Adms. on the estate of Ebenezer Kendall, late of Simsbury decd., unto Mehetabel, relict of sd. decd., who gave bonds with Return Holcomb of Simsbury of £500.

Page 94 (Vol. XVI) 3 April, 1753: This Court appoint Mehetabell Kendall, the wife of John Kendall of Hartland, to be guardian to the children of Ebenezer Kendall, late of Simsbury decd., viz., Ebenezer, age 9 years, Noadiah 8 years, and Mercy 4 years; and the said John Kendall and his wife joyntly recog. in £100 for each minor. An account of administration on the estate of Ebenezer Kendall decd. was now exhibited in Court by Mehetabell Kendall and John Kendall (her present husband), administrators: Paid in debts and charges, lost estate, and spent in the family, £308-11-00. Which account this Court allows and orders on file.

Page A (Vol. XVII) 6 December, 1757: Ebenezer Kendall, age 14 years, son of Ebenezer Kendall decd., chose his grandfather John Kendall of Suffield to be his guardian. And the said Joshua (John) Kendall recog. in £300.

Kilbourn, Thomas. Court Record, Page 50—19 April, 1747: Susannah Kilbourn, a minor, 15 years of age, daughter of Thomas Kilbourn, late of Hartford decd., chose Capt. Jonathan Hills of Hartford to be her guardian.

Page 245-6.

Kilbourn, Thomas, Hartford. Died 8 April, 1748. Invt. £4635-19-08. Taken 3 October, 1748. This foregoing inventory was taken by us the subscribers, which we computed equivalent to silver at 55 shillings per ounce, old tenor: Jonathan Hills, David Hills and Samuel Smith.

Court Record, Page 76—4 October, 1748: Adms. granted unto Mary Kilbourn, widow, who gave bonds with Samuel Smith of sd. Hartford of £1000 money.

Page 103—4 July, 1749: Mary Kilbourn, Adms., exhibited an account of her Adms. Accepted.

Page 75 (Vol. XVI) 24 October, 1752: Mary Kilbourn, the widow and Adms., having finished her account of Adms., now moves to this Court for a distribution of sd. estate to the heirs, viz.:

	£ s d
To Mary Kilbourn, widow,	212-03-10
To Thomas Kilbourn, eldest son,	1405-06-06
To Nathaniel, Jeremiah, Russell and Jerusha Kilbourn, to each of them their single portions,	702-13-03

And appoint Jonathan Hills, David Hills and Samuel Smith, of Hartford, distributors.

Page 86—6 February, 1753: Report of the distributors.

Page 277-8.

Kimberly, Elizabeth, Glastonbury. Invt. £570-00-00. Taken by Abraham Kilbourn and Abner Moseley. Will dated 9 August, 1746.

I, Elizabeth Kimberly, do make this my last will and testament: I give to my nephews, Samuel Kimberly and John Kimberly, my land at the lower end of Wethersfield meadow, to be equally divided between them; and to sd. Samuel Kimberly all my right in the lott of land which I now dwell on, that was my honoured father's Eleazer Kimberly, Esq., in the Town of Glastonbury decd., to be to the sd. Samuel Kimberly and to his heirs forever. I give to my niece Elizabeth Kimberly my best feather bed and furniture. I give unto my niece Anne Kimberly my best chest which has two drawers, and my table and best pottage pott. I give to my niece Sarah, the wife of Thomas Welles of Colchester, my bed with straked tickin and furniture, and my pide cow. I give to John Hubbard, Jr., Mary Richman and Sarah, the wife of Abraham Hollister, my red cow, and I also give to sd. Mary Richman my two poorest pewter platters. And to sd. Sarah Hollister I give my riding hood, silk crape frock, and my two bigest pewter platters. And to the sd. Mary Richman and Sarah Hollister I give 14 acres of land in the Five Miles, to be equally divided between them, and to them and their heirs and assigns forever. I give to Samuel and John Kimberly, Ruth the wife of Samuel Mears, and Elizabeth the wife of Oliver Dudley, the sum of £2 money, old tenor, each to be paid by my executor out of my moveable estate. And my will is that Ruth the wife of Jeremiah Goodrich, Mary the wife of Jeduthan Smith, Elizabeth and Anne Kimberly, and Sarah the wife of Daniel House, have all the rest of my moveable estate to be equally divided between them. I do appoint Samuel Kimberly to be my executor of this my will.

Witness: *Abner Moseley,*   ELIZABETH X KIMBERLY.
William Miller, Elizur Hale.

King, Capt. Henry. Court Record, Page 94—10 March, 1748-9: This Court grant Adms. on the estate of Capt. Henry King, late of Middletown decd., to Mary King, widow, who gave bonds with Return Meigs of Middletown of £2000.

King, Mary. Court Record, Page 115—2 January, 1749-50: This Court grant Adms. on the estate of Mary King, late of Hartford decd., unto Thomas Burr, Jr., of Hartford, who gave bonds as the law directs.

King, James. Court Record, Page 135—3 July, 1750: James King, a minor, age 15 years, son of James King, late of Suffield deceased, chose Isaac King of sd. Suffield to be his guardian. Recog., £500.

Page 35 (Vol. XVII) 31 July, 1754: Sarah King, a minor, age 16 years, daughter of James King of Suffield, chose her uncle Aaron Risum (Rising?) of Suffield to be her guardian. Recog., £300.

Page 45 (Vol. XVII) 8 November, 1754: Jonah King, a minor, 14 years of age, son of James King, chose his brother Isaac King to be his guardian. Recog., £300.

Page 328.

King, Robert, Hartford. Wee whose names are underwritten, being appointed by the Court of Probates to apprise the real estate of Robert King of Hartford, lately deceased, wee do apprise as followeth:

	£ s d
The house and homelott,	690-00-00
The oxpasture lott, at £65 per acre,	211-05-00

Apprised September 13th, 1749, by Ozias Goodwin, William Pratt and Thomas Welles.

Court Record, Page 69—6 June, 1748: Mary King, a minor, age 18 years, daughter of Robert King, chose her mother Elizabeth King to be her guardian. And this Court appoint the sd. Elizabeth guardian to Lydia King, about 12 years of age. Recog., £300 for each minor.

Page 104—6 July, 1749: James Bunce and his wife Elizabeth now move to this Court that her right of dowry may be set out to her in the estate of Robert King, late of Hartford deceased: Whereupon this Court appoint Jonathan Seymour, Daniel Bull and Timothy Marsh of Hartford to set out to the sd. Elizabeth 1-3 part of the buildings and lands of the deceased for her improvement during life.

Page 106—13 December, 1749: Whereas, it is represented to this Court by the heirs of Robert King, late of Hartford, that the real estate of the sd. deceased cannot be divided without great prejudice to the heirs and spoiling the whole of sd. estate, and this Court being sensible thereof, do order and set out the whole of sd. real estate to Elizabeth King alias Burr, eldest daughter of the deceased (there being no sons) and to Moses Burr, husband to sd. Elizabeth in her right, and they accepting thereof and having given security to pay unto the co-heirs, viz., Sarah King alias Sarah Burr, wife of Thomas Burr, Jr., Mary King and Lydia King their equal proportionable shares of the house and land according to the apprisement of 3 sufficient freeholders appointed for that end under oath, in such convenient time as this Court hath limited, with reasonable allowances.

Page 115—2 January, 1749-50: This Court now grant Adms. on sd. estate unto James Bunce and Thomas Burr, Jr., who gave bonds with Moses Burr of sd. Hartford of £200.

Page 133—15 June, 1750: Lydia King, now 14 years of age, daughter of Robert King, chose Ensign Jonathan Seymour to be her guardian. Recog., £800.

Page 15 (Vol. XVI) 22 February, 1750-1: An inventory of the moveable estate of Robert King was now exhibited by Thomas Burr, Jr., and James Bunce, Adms. Also the Adms. exhibit an account of their Adms. Accepted. Order the estate distributed to the heirs, viz.: To Elizabeth Bunce, the relict, her thirds; and to Elizabeth Burr and Sarah Burr, children of sd. deceased, their single shares. And appoint John Cook, Joseph Talcott and Mr. Joseph Holtom distributors.

Page 103—6 June, 1753: A distribution of the estate of Robert and Mary King, late of Hartford deceased, was now exhibited in Court under the hands of Joseph Talcott and Joseph Church, distributors. Accepted.

Page 219.

Lee, Jedediah, Willington. Invt. £925-13-00. Taken 11 April, 1748, by Benjamin Sibley and William Tyler. Will dated 7 October, 1747.

I, Jedediah Lee of Willington, in the County of Hartford and Colony of Connecticut, do make this my last will and testament: I give to my beloved wife Leusee Lee £20 New England old tenor and the improvement of the house and lands whereon she lives, and all our moveable estate, as long as she remains my widow; and then all that part of the moveable estate that she brought to her own proper use forever. To my eldest son Elias Lee I give 5 shillings. I give to my other five sons, Josiah, Jedediah, Oliver, Zebulon and Simon, all my lands, buildings and fences, to be divided equally among them. I give to my daughters,

Lydia and Jerusha, all the rest of my moveable estate, to be divided equal-
ly between them. And I do by these presents make my well-beloved **wife**
Lewce Lee and my eldest son Elias Lee my executors.
Witness: *Nicholas Whitmarsh,*   JEDEDIAH X LEE, LS.
Timothy Buck, John Calkin.

Court Record, Page 67—13 May, 1748: The last will and testament of Jedediah Lee of Willington, in the County of Hartford, was now
exhibited in Court by Luce Lee, one of the executors. Will proven and
ordered to be recorded and kept on file.

Page 70—30 May, 1748: An inventory of the estate of Jedediah
Lee, late of Willington decd., was now exhibited in Court by Lucee Lee,
one of the executors, which this Court accepts and orders on file.

Page 71—30 May, 1748: Josiah Lee, age 12 years, Jedediah 10
years, Oliver 8 years, Zebulon 6, and Simon 4 years of age, sons of
Jedediah Lee: this Court appoint Widow Lucy to be their guardian.
Recog., £300 for each minor.

Page 133—15 June, 1750: This Court appoint Elias Lee of Willington guardian to Josiah Lee, age 13 years, Jedediah 12 years, Oliver 10
years, Zebulon 8, and Simon about 5 years of age. Recog., £300 for
each minor.

Page 90.

Lee, John, Farmington. Invt. £802-18-00. Taken 1st January,
1746-7, by Isaac Cowles and Joseph Hooker.

Court Record, Page 76—4 October, 1748: Pursuant to a resolve of
the General Assembly held at Hartford on the 2nd Thursday in May,
1748, Mr. William Porter of Farmingtown is directed to make sale of
so much of the real estate of John Lee of sd. Farmingtown decd. as will
procure the sum of £145-04-04 with necessary charges arising therefrom, taking the direction of the Court of Probate of the District of
Hartford thereon.

Lee, Lucy, Farmington. Court Record, Page 133—15 June, 1750:
Adms. on the estate of Lucy Lee, late of Farmington deceased, unto Elias
Lee of said Farmington, who gave bond with David Ensign of Hart-
ford.

Page 381-2.

Leet, John, Middletown. Invt. £2090-15-06. Taken 3 April, 1750,
by Jeremiah Goodrich, Phineas Pelton and Joseph Washburn. Will dated
16 March, 1750.

I, John Leet of Middletown, in the County of Hartford, do appoint
this my last will and testament: I give to my wife Elizabeth Leet the

1-2 of my dwelling house (in such part of it as she shall choose), with my barn and one acre of land on which they stand, next adjoining thereunto; this I give to her and to her heirs forever, to be at her own disposal. And furthermore I give to her the use and improvement of 1-3 part of my whole estate, both real and personal, so long as she remains my widow and bear my name. Also I give to her my riding mare and one cow to be hers at her disposal. Second, the remainder of my estate, both real and personal, I give to be equally divided amongst all my children, except £20 in old tenor to be paid out of my estate to my eldest daughter Ann Leet. And furthermore I ordain and appoint, if there be need of it, that the north part of my lott of land lying and adjoining to a lott of land belonging to Sergt. Ebenezer Gibbs be sold to pay my just debts; and if that be not sufficient to answer my debts, that then to have so much sold from the south part of my lott yt lyeth the other side of the highway from my house, the sale of which to be made at the discretion of my executor, and title to be given and confirmed. I appoint my faithful and trusty friend John Churchill to be my executor.
Witness: *Moses Bartlett,*   JOHN LEET, LS.
Joseph Washburn, John Shepherd.

Court Record, Page 126—10 April, 1750: The last will and testament of John Leet, late of Middletown decd., was now exhibited in Court by John Churchill. Will proven.

Page 38 (Vol. XVI) 3 October, 1751: It was certified to this Court by *Joseph White, J. P.,* that Submit Leete and Hannah Leete, the eldest 14 years and the other 13, made choice of their mother, Widow Elizabeth Leete, to be their guardian. Recog., £400 for each minor.

Page 41—5 November, 1751: John Church (Churchill), executor, exhibited an account of Adms. Accepted. Also the sd. Adms. moves that distributors may be appointed to distribute the estate according to the will of the deceased: Whereupon this Court appoint William Rockwell, Capt. Jeremiah Goodrich and Mr. Phineas Pelton distributors.

Dist. File: 5 November, 1751: To the widow, Elizabeth Leete; to Ann Leete, alias Stocking; to Chloe, to Phyllis, to Submit, to Hannah Leete. By William Rockwell, Joseph Goodrich and Phineas Pelton.

Page 69—10 July, 1752: Report of the distributors.

Loomis, Ezra. Court Record, Page 50—3 November, 1747: This Court grant Adms. on the estate of Ezra Loomis, late of Windsor deceased, unto Jonathan Gillet of Windsor, who gave bonds with Robert Barnett of Windsor.

Page 53—1st December, 1747: An inventory of the estate of Ezra Loomis was now exhibited by Jonathan Gillet, Adms., which the Court accepts and orders to be recorded and kept on file. Also, the Adms. informs this Court that the estate of the sd. decd. is insolvent: Whereupon this Court appoint Deacon Isaac Butler and Nathaniel Case, of Windsor, commissioners to adjust the claims of the creditors.

Page 77—4 October, 1748: A report of the commissioners was now exhibited, accepted and ordered to be kept on file.

Page 209-10-11-12.

Loomis, Joseph, Windsor. Invt. £2802-03-05 in lands. Taken 29 June, 1748, by Matthew Rockwell, Peletiah Bliss and David Bissell. Will dated 20 January, 1747-8.

I, Joseph Loomis of Windsor, do make this my last will and testament: I give to my wife the improvement of all my buildings and lands in Windsor lying on the east side of the Connecticut River and west on the street, with half of the lott I live on on the east side of the street from the butternut tree to the east end of the bush pasture, and liberty to get wood on the rest of the lott eastward and away through the lott, where it may be most convenient, and the use of my moveable estate as long as she remains my widow; and if she marrys, then 1-3 part of my moveables to be hers forever, and the use of 1-3 part of my real estate during her life. My will is that my eldest daughter Mabel Hollibert shall have £190, and my second daughter Keziah King £150, paid to them after their mother's decease or marriage, out of my estate. My will is that my granddaughter Mary Fitch be maintained out of my estate according to my obligation to her father Elijah Fitch, that is to say, if she lives with her grandmother Loomis aforesd. or her Aunt Mabel or Keziah aforesd. till she comes of age or marrys, then the expense of her maintenance to be paid out of my whole estate; but if her father shall please to dispose of her otherwise before that time, then my will is that the cost of her bringing up shall be deducted out of the part or portion of the estate I give her. My will is that after my debts and legacies are paid, that my moveable estate, if any remains, and my land or real estate be equally divided between my daughter and granddaughter aforesd., to them and their heirs forever. I appoint my wife Mary and my son-in-law John Hollibert to be my executors.

Witness: *John Anderson, Jr.,*   JOSEPH LOOMIS, LS.
Joel Loomis, Thomas Stoughton.

Court Record, Page 73—12 August, 1748: The last will and testament of Capt. Joseph Loomis, late of Windsor decd., was now exhibited in Court by Mary Loomis, widow, and John Hollibert, executors. Will proven. Exhibited an inventory. Both ordered to be recorded and kept on file.

Page 83—28 December, 1748: John Hurlbut, one of the executors to the last will and testament of Capt. Joseph Loomis, now moves this Court that distribution be made of the sd. estate: Whereupon this Court appoint Matthew Rockwell, Peletiah Bliss and David Bissell, of Windsor, distributors.

Dist. File: 27 December, 1748: To Mabel, the wife of John Hollibert; to Keziah, the wife of Zebulon King; to Mary Fitch, granddaughter of Capt. Joseph Loomis decd. By David Bissell, Nathaniel Rockwell
and Peletiah Bliss.

Lord, John. Court Record, Page 26—20 October, 1746: Jane Lord,
a minor, 10 years of age, and John Lord, about 7 years of age, children
of John Lord, late of Hebron deceased: this Court appoint Ephraim
Hubbard of Glastonbury to be their guardian. Recog., £300 for each
minor.

Page 27—4 November, 1746: Delight Lord, a minor daughter of
John Lord, supposed to be deceased, made choice of Ephraim Hubbard
to be her guardian. Recog., £300.

Lord, Samuel Phillips. Court Record, Page 91—22 February, 1748-
9: Samuel Phillips Lord, a minor, 15 years of age, son of Epaphrus
Lord and Hope his wife, chose his father Epaphrus Lord to be his guardian. Recog., £1000. Cert: *Jabez Hamlin, J. P.*

Marks, William. Court Record, Page 54—5 January, 1747-8: William Marks, a minor, age 14 years, son of William Marks of Killingworth, chose his uncle Daniel Doolittle of Middletown to be his guardian. Recog., £500. Cert: *Seth Wetmore, J. P.*

Page 33 (Vol. XVI) 20 August, 1751: Margaret Marks, a minor,
15 years of age, daughter of William Marks, late of Middletown deceased,
chose her brother Samuel Marks to be her guardian. Recog., £400.

Page 252.

Marsh, Elizabeth, Hartford. Will dated 30 November, 1748: I,
Elizabeth Marsh of Hartford, widow and relict of John Marsh, late of
sd. Hartford, do make this my last will and testament: I give to my
daughter Elizabeth Cook and to her heirs, to be at her and their own
dispose forever, all my wearing apparel of what sort and denomination
soever, all my cloth, wool, yarn, flax, and all my bedding and the furniture belonging thereto, as also my pewter, brass, iron and the whole of
my household goods and linens, and one cow, and £20 in bills of publick
credit of the old tenor, to be paid her by my executor hereafter named.
I give to my son John Marsh and his heirs £100 in old tenor bills of
credit. And further, my will is that my son Hezekiah Marsh shall have
the lands I lately bought of John Marsh and Daniel Marsh, he paying
for it the just value thereof to my executor or to the rest of my chil-

dren. And what remains of my estate, whether real or personal, after the before-mentioned legacies are paid, I give to be equally divided to my sons, Ebenezer Marsh, William Marsh, Isaac Marsh, George Marsh, John Marsh, Timothy Marsh and Hezekiah Marsh, and to their heirs forever. I constitute my son Timothy Marsh to be my executor.

Witness: *William Pitkin,*   ELIZABETH X MARSH, LS.
Sarah Catlin, Abigail Church.

24 December, 1748: Then Timothy Marsh, executor to the will above written, exhibited the same in Court, which was proved and approved, and the sd. executor accepted the trust thereof. Sd. will is ordered to be recorded and kept on file. [This Court Record follows the will, upon the same page of manuscript.]

Page 142-3-4-5.

Marsh, Jonathan, Windsor. Invt. £3495-17-05. Taken 28 October, 1747, by Jonathan Stiles, Samuel Stoughton and Return Strong. Will dated 7 September, 1747.

I, Jonathan Marsh of Windsor, in Hartford County, clerk, do make this my last will and testament: I give unto my wife Margaret Marsh £300 money, old tenor, besides her thirds of my real and personal estate, and also my great Bible. I give unto my three daughters, Margaret Roberts, Mary Eaton and Dorcas Bissell, £300 old tenor each, including what they have had already. I give unto my daughter Hannah Marsh and my daughter Ann Marsh £300 each, old tenor, and a piece of gold which I have, to be equally divided between them. I give unto my two sons, Jonathan Marsh and Joseph Marsh, all the remainder of my estate, both real and personal, equally to be divided, excepting my son Jonathan is to have £50 less than my son Joseph, my son Jonathan taking all my library at £50. My will and pleasure is that my family remaining here shall have out of my whole estate one year's provision, that is to say, corne and meat sufficient. My will is that my wife Margaret Marsh and my son Jonathan Marsh shall be executors.

Witness: *Samuel Stoughton,*   JONATHAN MARSH. LS.
Return Strong, John Allyn.

Court Record, Page 47—6 October, 1747: The last will and testament of the Rev. Mr. Jonathan Marsh, late of Windsor decd., was now exhibited by the Rev. Mr. Jonathan Marsh of New Hartford and Mrs. Margaret Marsh, executors named in the will. Will proven and ordered to be recorded and kept on file.

Page 178-9-294.

Marsh, Mrs. Margaret, Windsor. Inventory taken in Windsor, 14 May, 1748, by Jonathan Stiles and Samuel Stoughton. Will dated 6 December, 1747.

A nuncupative will of Mrs. Margaret Marsh of Windsor, the relict of the Rev. Mr. Jonathan Marsh, late of Windsor decd., in the following way and manner:

I being at the house of Mrs. Margaret Marsh to visit her, in the evening of the day above named, who had been sick several days, being weak in body but of a disposeing mind and memory, there being present Mrs. Ann Loomis and Mrs. Hannah Allyn, the Mrs. informed me that Mrs. Marsh had several times that day and evening signified her uneasiness about disposeing of her worldly goods and estate. I was desired to make mention unto her whether or no that she had a desire to dispose of her estate according to her own mind. Accordingly I did, and her reply was that she intended the next day to send for her brother Whiting. I replied that our time was uncertain as to us, and I further said unto her whether or no it would not be best for her to make a *"verbile"* will, and she replyed and said that it was her intent that her three youngest children should have what she had, vizt., Joseph, Hannah and Ann. I further asked whether she declared it before us three there present as witnesses, and she said and declared that it was her will and pleasure that her three youngest children before named should have what estate she had, equally to be divided between them three. The above written was declared in the presence of us witnesses:

Jonathan Stiles,
Ann Loomis, Hannah X Allyn.

Court Record, Page 60—1st March, 1747-8: The last nuncupative will of Mrs. Margaret Marsh, the widow of the Rev. Mr. Jonathan Marsh decd., was now exhibited in Court, which will being proven and by this Court approved, was ordered to be recorded and kept on file. This Court grant Adms. on the estate of the sd. Mrs. Margaret Marsh, to the Rev. Mr. Jonathan Marsh of New Hartford, who gave bonds with John Cook of Windsor of £900 money.

Page 250-1-350.

Marsh, Lt. Nathaniel, Hartford. Invt. £483-14-03. Taken 2nd September, 1748, by John Cook and Benjamin Allyn.

I, Nathaniel Marsh of Hartford, do make this my last will and testament: this 19th day of July, 1736: I will unto my beloved wife £30 to be at her own dispose, and also 1-3 part of my house and lands during her natural life, together with 1-3 part of my moveable estate and her choice of any room in my house. I give unto my daughter Hannah Marsh £70, to be paid in money or moveables at inventory price within one year after my decease. I give unto my grandchildren, Samuel and Nathaniel Marsh, £130, equally to be divided between them if they live to the age of 21 years. I give unto my son Daniel Marsh the house and lott where he now dwells, reckoned to him at £130. I give unto my son Lemuel Marsh £130 in houseing and lands laid out to him at inventory price.   I give the remainder of my estate that is not above disposed of to be equally divided, that is to say, the 1-3 part to my grandchildren before named, and the remainder to my sd. sons, Daniel and Lemuel. And also I do order and appoint my sons Daniel and Lemuel, with my wife, to be executors.

Witness: *William Bushnell,*   NATHANIEL MARSH, LS.
William Bushnell, Jr., John Marsh.

Whereas, I, Nathaniel Marsh of Hartford, made and declared my last will and testament, bearing date 19 July, 1736, as on the other side of this sheet may appear; and whereas, I did in sd. will give my daughter Hannah £70 moveables, etc., I hereby ratify sd. will, and now declare and order that whatsoever my sd. daughter hath received of me or my wife before my decease shall be accounted to her as part of sd. £70 as portion.   And whereas, by deed of gift, I have given my son Lemuel my house and homestead in Hartford, it shall be accounted to him my sd. son Lemuel as his full portion of my estate. And my will further is that my grandson Samuel Marsh shall have the £130 given him by my aforesd. will as our bills of currency was valued in the year 1736, set out in land at inventory price. And then the remainder of my lands not given by deed of gift shall be equally divided between my sd. son Daniel Marsh and my sd. grandson Samuel Marsh, equally to them and their heirs forever. And I do hereby declare that this addition is part and parcel of my last will and testament.

Signed 19 day of January, 1748.

Witness: *Joseph Talcott,*   NATHANIEL MARSH, LS.
Joseph Barrett, William Wadsworth.

At a Court of Probate holden at Hartford, 2nd Tuesday of August, 1748: The last will and testament of Nathaniel Marsh, late of Hartford decd., was now exhibited in Court by Daniel Marsh, one of the executors. Will being proven and inventory exhibited, both were ordered to be recorded and kept on file. [This record follows the will, upon the same page.]

Court Record, Page 107—26 September, 1749: Samuel Marsh, a minor, son of Nathaniel Marsh, Jr., chose his uncle Daniel Goodwin of Hartford to be his guardian. Recog., £500.

Page 355-6-7.

Marshall, Samuel, Windsor. Invt. £4790-15-00. Taken by Daniel Phelps, Caleb Phelps and John Roberts. Will dated 3 April, 1749.

I, Samuel Marshall, of the Town of Windsor, do make this my last will and testament: I give to my wife 1-3 part of all my moveable estate, to be to her own use and benefit forever; one acre of land in the marsh, butting north on Capt. Eno's land, to be to her own use and benefit and also to dispose of it forever to which of my children she shall please. And furthermore I do give to my wife the use and improvement, so long as she shall remain my widow and no longer, of my house and barn and house lott till it come over the brook to the little hill where the fence now standeth, reserving liberty for the fulling mill and a way to it; and also 1-2 of the upper pasture that I bought last of Deacon Brown; and of all the apples, and likewise the use of 4 acres of plow land lying south upon William Cook and west on William Filley's land; and also of getting wood upon any of my lands for her use.

Item: I give to my son	Samuel Marshall	£80	out of my estate
" " " " " "	Noah Marshall	£60	" " " "
" " " " " "	Eliakim Marshall	£60	" " " "
" " " " " "	Abner Marshall	£60	" " " "
" " " " " "	Amasa Marshall	£60	" " " "
" " " " " "	Joseph Marshall	£60	" " " "
" " " " " "	Aaron Marshall	£60	" " " "
Item: I give to my daughter	Abigail Marshall	£40	" " " "
" " " " " "	Rachel Marshall	£40	" " " "
" " " " " "	Mary Marshall	£40	" " " "
" " " " " "	Asenath Marshall	£40	" " " "

And my mind and will further is that all my estate, except what I have given or otherwise disposed of in this my last will and testament, my just debts being paid, shall be divided in the foregoing proportions to my children, as well my real as my personal estate. I hereby nominate and appoint my wife Abigail, with my son Samuel Marshall and my son Eliakim Marshall, to be executors.

Witness: *Daniel Marshall,*   SAMUEL MARSHALL, LS.
Martha Marshall, Eunice Eno.

Court Record, Page 114—2 January, 1749-50: Joseph Marshall, a minor, 19 years of age, Aaron Marshall 14, and Asenath 16 years, children of Samuel Marshall, chose Abigail Marshall to be their guardian. Recog., £500 for each minor.

Page 117—6 February, 1749-50: Mary Marshall, a minor, daughter of Samuel Marshall, chose her brother Abner Marshall to be her guardian. Recog., £500. Abigail Marshall and Abner Marshall, guardians to Joseph, Aaron, Asenath and Mary Marshall, minors and children of Samuel Marshall, showing to this Court that sd. minors are tenants in common with the rest of the heirs to the estate of the sd. deceased, now moves to this Court that suitable persons may be appointed to assist sd. guardians in dividing sd. estate: Whereupon this Court appoint Capt. Samuel Enno and Mr. Seth Youngs of Windsor to assist sd. guardians in dividing sd. estate.

Page 42-3-4-5-6-7-8-9-51-2-135.

Mather, Capt. Samuel, Windsor. Inventory taken 6 March, 1745-6, by Samuel Culver, Edward Phelps and Joshua Garret. Will dated 10 August, 1741.

I, Samuel Mather of Windsor, do make this my last will and testament: I give to my wife Hannah Mather the use of my house we now live in, together with lands adjoining and barn, even the whole tenement, if she shall see cause to dwell in the house and use and improve the same for her own use and benefit, so long as she shall remain my widow. She, my wife, is to keep the sd. house and fences about sd. tenement in good repair during the time she useth and improveth the same, so long as she shall remain my widow; and after that my will is that the sd. house and barn and tenements shall belong to my children and be distributed with my other estate amongst them. I give unto my wife Hannah Mather £100 in bills of credit or other goods at inventory price. I give unto my wife Hannah Mather one year's provision out of my estate after my decease, that is to say, meat and corn for herself and our children that are under age. My will is that my wife Hannah Mather shall also have all the lands, or ye lands which descendeth to her by the death of her father, except what we sold to Mr. Samuel Strong; also that my wife shall have two cows, to be for her and her heirs forever. And I give unto my three daughters, Hannah Mather, Lucy Mather and Elizabeth Mather, all my child bed ornaments, such as blankets, etc., commonly called christening garments, to them and to their heirs forever as a gift without price. I give unto my daughter Lucy Mather, as a gift, one certain piece of gold called Moider, which she useth to wear about her neck, to be to her use forever. I give unto my loving son Samuel Mather all my physicall books, with my chirurgicall instruments, as a gift to him. And also my will is that my son Samuel Mather shall have so much out of my estate as to make him equal with the rest of my children besides what I have bestowed upon him for his education. I give unto my children hereafter named, Samuel Mather, Timothy Mather, Nathaniel Mather, Eliakim Mather, Hannah Mather, Lucy Mather and Elizabeth Mather, all the remainder of my estate, both real and personal, not particularly disposed of in the aforementioned will, to them in equal parts with what some of them have already had, viz., Timothy Mather, which I have given him a deed of sale of Benjamin Gibbs's house, barn and land at Litchfield, bought of sd. Gibbs, and also another deed of sale which I have given him of land at Litchfield at the price of £80, for which I have received no satisfaction therefor, all which maketh £380 which he hath received already, which I intend shall be as part of his portion which must be included to make him equal with my other children. And Nathaniel Mather having had and received already the sum of £350 which I have given him by deed of gift already of the house and barn and land and orchard which I bought of Samuel Denslow, Jr., lying on the west side of the street in Windsor, he hath already received, which shall be included to make him equal with my other children. My will is that my son Eliakim Mather shall receive his portion when he arrives at the age of 21 years, and that the rest of my children that are under age shall receive their portions at the age of 21 years or upon marriage, to be to them and their heirs forever. My will and pleasure is, and it is my true intent and meaning, yt all and each of my children share alike in my estate, including what they have already received as abovesd., to be to them and their heirs forever, except my granddaughter Abigail Wolcott, to whom I give only £10 money. My will and pleasure is and I appoint my wife and our brother-in-law, Mr. Samuel Strong, to be guardians to my children that are under age. My will is that my three sons, Samuel Mather, Timothy Mather and Nathaniel Mather shall be my executors.

Witness: *Jonathan Stiles,* SAMUEL MATHER, ĻS.
Jonathan Wright, John Allyn.

Court Record, Page 7—18 March, 1745-6: The last will and testament of Capt. Samuel Mather, Esq., was now exhibited in Court by Samuel Mather, Timothy Mather and Nathaniel Mather, executors. Proven and ordered to be recorded and kept on file.

Whereas, Capt. Samuel Mather of Windsor, in his last will appointed his wife and brother-in-law, Mr. Samuel Strong of Windsor, to be guardian to his children that are under age, his sd. wife, now his widow, appeared in Court and gave bond with Daniel Phelps of Windsor joyntly and severally in a recog. of £4000 as guardian.

Page 10—1st April, 1746: Mrs. Hannah Mather, widow of Samuel Mather, Esq., late of Windsor, moved to this Court that freeholders may be appointed to set out her right of dowry in the real estate of the sd. decd.: Whereupon this Court appoint Ebenezer Hayden, Deacon John Cook and Mr. Thomas Moore of sd. Windsor to set out 1-3 part of the buildings and lands by bounds.

Page 22—6 May, 1746: Exhibited an inventory. The executors of the last will and testament of Samuel Mather, Esq., moved to this Court to make distribution of the real and personal estate, excepting the widow's dowry, for which a particular order has been moved already: Whereupon this Court appoint Jonathan Stiles, Peletiah Allyn and Samuel Stoughton, of Windsor, distributors.

Page 34—9 March, 1746-7: Whereas, this Court in May last, upon the motion of Mrs. Hannah Mather, the widow of Samuel Mather, Esq., late of Windsor decd., did appoint freeholders to set out to the sd. widow her right of dowry in the real estate of the sd. decd. (she not accepting of the dowry or legacy given her in the will of the sd. decd.), and pursuant to the sd. order sd. freeholders set out to her her right of dowry, yet notwithstanding the sd. widow has quit her right of dowry in the real estate of the sd. decd. to all the heirs to the estate of the sd. decd., as appears to this Court by a quitclaim deed dated 5 August, 1746, acknowledged and recorded in Windsor Town Book of Record, the 7th Book, Folio 297, except 1-3 part of the house and homestead of the sd. decd., which in sd. quitclaim the sd. widow has reserved to herself during life, and the sd. widow and Nathaniel Mather now move to this Court that the sd. estate, both real and personal, be distributed and divided to the several heirs to the estate according to the last will of the sd. decd., this Court appoint Capt. Peletiah Allyn, Samuel Stoughton and Jonathan Stiles of Windsor to make distribution to the heirs according to sd. will (except the above reservation to sd. widow of 1-3 part of the house, barn and homelott), and make return of their doings to this Court.

Page 3.

Matson, Joshua, Simsbury. Died 6 November, 1745. Invt. £881-08-06. Taken 3 December, 1745, by James Smith, Daniel Hayes and Azariah Holcomb. Will dated 2 October, 1745.

I, Joshua Matson of Simsbury, in the County of Hartford, do make this my last will and testament: I give the use of all my estate whatsoever, both real and personal, to my wife Amy during her widowhood, with the use of 1-3 part of my houseing and land during her natural life, and 1-3 part of my moveable goods to be at her dispose forever. My will is and I do hereby give and devise all my houseing and land, with the appurtenances, to my sons Joshua Matson and Isaac Matson, viz., my son Joshua to have £30 more than my son Isaac, provided always, and it is my will, that they pay and make up to their sisters, Amey Matson and Lucy Matson, my daughters, their portions, viz., 1-3 so much as my son Isaac apiece, to be paid within three years after my sons come to the age of 21 years. And my will is that my sons shall equally pay their sisters the use of their portions until their legacies be paid. And my will is that my executors shall set up a head and foot stone upon my grave, with my name and the date of my birth and death written thereon. And I appoint my wife Amy to be my executrix, and my brother Edward Matson and my trusty friend Judah Holcomb to be my executors.

Witness: *James Smith,*   JOSHUA MATSON, LS.
Nehemiah Lee, Isaac Dewey.

Court Record, Page 3—7 January, 1745: The last will and testament of Joshua Matson, late of Simsbury. was now exhibited in Court by Amy Matson, Edward Matson and Judah Holcomb, executors. Will proven and inventory exhibited. Both approved and ordered to be recorded and kept on file.

Page 101—6 June, 1749: This Court appoint Edward Matson of Simsbury to be guardian to Lucy Matson, a minor, 9 years of age, daughter of Joshua Matson.

Page 124—3 April, 1750: Mr. Judah Holcomb of Simsbury, one of the executors, moved to this Court that distribution may be made of the real estate: Whereupon this Court appoint Joseph Wilcockson, Daniel and William Hays, of Simsbury, distributors. This Court appoint Edward Matson guardian to Joshua Matson, a minor, 14 years of age. Recog., £500. Isaac Holloday of Suffield is appointed guardian to Isaac Matson, age 6 years, son of Joshua Matson deceased. Recog., £500.

Maulbe, Joseph. Court Record, Page 132—5 June, 1750: John Maulbe of Brandford, 12 years of age, son of Joseph Maulbe: this Court appoint Elizabeth Maulbe of Hartford to be his guardian. Recog., £500.

McCleod, Daniel. Court Record, Page 135—3 July, 1750: Daniel McCleod, 7 years of age, son of Daniel McCleod, late of Norwalk decd.: Elizabeth McCleod, late of Norwalk, now of Wethersfield, appointed to be his guardian. Recog., £400 money, with John Welles of Wethersfield.

Page 57 (Vol. XVII) 1st April, 1755: Anne McCloud, a minor, aged 14 years, daughter of Daniel McCloud of Norwalk deceased, made choice of her father Samuel Buck of Wethersfield to be her guardian. Recog., £100.

McMoran, John. Court Record, Page 10—1st April, 1746: John McMoran, 15 years of age, son of John McMoran, late of Windsor decd., made choice of his mother Elizabeth McMoran to be his guardian. Recog., £300. Cert: *Henry Allyn, J. P.*

Page 220-1.

Merrell, Aaron, Hartford. Inventory taken October, 1747, and 30 August, 1748, by David Ensign, Thomas Seymour and Daniel Kelsey.

Court Record, Page 47—6 October, 1747: This Court grant Adms. on the estate of Aaron Merrell, late of Hartford decd., unto Esther Merrell of Hartford, who gave bonds with John Merrell of New Hartford of £300.

Page 59—1st March, 1747-8: Exhibited an inventory, which was accepted and ordered recorded and kept on file.

Page 149-50.

Merrell, Deacon Abraham, Hartford. Will dated 11 December, 1735: I, Abraham Merrell of Hartford, do make this my last will and testament: I give to my wife Prudence the free use of 1-3 part of my real estate for her maintenance and support during her natural life. I also give her £30 more than 1-3 part of my moveable estate to be at her own dispose forever. I give unto my son Abraham all my houseing and land within the Township of Hartford, and all my land within the Town of Farmingtown, and all the sums of money that he hath already had of me from time to time. And further, I give unto my son Abraham all the remaining part of my moveable estate. All to him, his heirs and assigns forever, he paying the several legacies hereafter mentioned in this my will. I give unto my son Joseph all my land and property in the

Township of New Hartford, in sd. County, and £50 in money which I do hereby order to be paid him by my son Abraham, to him and his heirs forever. I give unto each of my daughters, viz., Prudence, Abigail, Margaret, Jerusha and Joanna, £110 apiece, including the several sums that I have already given or that I shall or may hereafter give unto any or either of them, after my decease, or to be paid them by my son Abraham after my decease. And I appoint my son Abraham to be sole executor.

Witness: *George Wyllys,*   ABRAHAM MERRELLS, LS.
John Dodd, Mehctabel Wyllys.

Court Record, Page 53—1st December, 1747: The last will and testament of Deacon Abraham Merrell, late of Hartford decd., was now exhibited by Abraham Merrell, son and executor. Proven and ordered to be recorded and kept on file.

Page 412-13-14.

Merrells, Daniel, Hartford. Invt. £10,698-07-00. Taken 27 August, 1750, by Daniel Seymour and Dositheus Humphrey. Will dated 26 December, 1745.

I, Daniel Merrells of Hartford, do make this my last will and testament: I give to my wife Mindwell Merrells the use of 1-3 part of all my moveable estate during her natural life or so long as she remains my widow. Also, that my wife Mindwell shall have the use of 1-3 part of my dwelling house and land, with the appurtenances thereof, during her natural life and also so long as she shall remain my widow. I give to my son Moses Merrells my lott of land called my mountain lott in the Township of Farmingtown, on which he now dwells, containing 150 acres more or less, to him, his heirs and assigns forever. I give to my son Jonathan Merrells, besides what I have already given him in New Hartford by deed of gift, the negro girl Phebe that now lives with him, in lieu of £100 money; also £60 money, to be paid him by my executor within two years after my decease, as also what I charge in debts against him in my book, to be to his own use and benefit forever. I give to my son Israel Merrells my whole farm of land lying and being in a place called the west division in Hartford, with the mansion house and all other buildings erected thereon, with all the appurtenances, to be to him and his heirs forever. I give to my son Israel my lott of land at a place commonly called the Blue Hills in Hartford, containing 15 acres more or less, to be to him and his heirs forever. I give to my son Israel my negro man servant Peter, to be to him and to his heirs forever. I give to my son Hezekiah Merrells the whole remainder of all my lands, houseing and buildings, wheresoever they lye or be (he well and truly paying the legacies and performing what is mentioned and injoyned him in this my will), the same to be and remain to him and his heirs forever. I give to my daughter Susannah Steele £10 in money besides what I have already given her. I give to each of my sd. daughter Susannah's children, viz., John, Mary, Daniel, Susannah, Hulda, Meletiah, Bradford and Elisha, £5 in money apiece. I give to my grandson Daniel Easton £20 money, to be paid him by my executor. I give to my daughter Hephzibah Seymour £50 money besides what I have already given her. I give to my daughter Rachel Shephard £50 money besides what she has already received. I give the remainder of all my moveable estate, if any there be, to my executor hereafter named. I appoint my son Hezekiah Merrells to be sole executor.

Witness: *J: Buckingham,*   DANIEL MERRELLS, LS.
Thomas Warren, Susannah Warren.

Court Record, Page 137—7 August, 1750: The last will and testament of Deacon Daniel Merrells was now exhibited in Court by Hezekiah Merrells, executor. Will proven and ordered to be recorded and kept on file.

Page 239-40-1.

Merrell, John, Hartford. Inventory taken 4 July, 1748, by Jacob Kellogg and Abraham Merrell. Will dated 9 May, 1748.

I, John Merrell of Hartford, do make this my last will and testament: I give to Sarah, my wife, 1-3 part of my moveable estate to be at her dispose forever, and the use of 1-2 of my houseing and lands during her natural life. I give to my son John Merrell my 1st and 2nd pitch of land in New Hartford, saving what I have heretofore disposed of by deed of gift, to be at his dispose forever. I give to my son Ebenezer Merrell my homelott at New Hartford, as also a pitch of land in sd. New Hartford lying in the Mast Swamp and runs in the forks, to be at his dispose forever. I give to the heirs of my son Aaron Merrell decd. 1-3 of my lands lying in Hartford, including what I have already given him by deed of gift, to be at their dispose forever. I give to my son Cyprian Merrell 1-3 part of my houseing and land in Hartford, to be at his dispose forever. I give to my son Benjamin Merrell 1-3 part of my land at Hartford to be at his dispose forever, he paying to my grandson and granddaughter, Abijah and Mercy, the children of my son Caleb Merrell decd., when they come of age to receive it, unto Abijah £10 money, and to Mercy £5. I give to the children of my daughter Sarah decd., viz., Roger Olmsted, Irene and Damaras Olmsted, each £5 money. I give to my daughter Lydia Merrell £50. I give to my daughter Ann Merrell, alias Gillet, 10 shillings money. I give to my son Nathaniel Merrell 5 shillings money. Furthermore, my will is that what moveable estate is left after the above legacies are paid and my just debts, shall be for the use of my wife forever. I do appoint my two sons, Cyprian and Benjamin Merrell, executors.

Witness: *Daniel Hooker,*   JOHN X MERRELL, LS.
John Steele, Moses Nash.

Court Record, Page 69—6 June, 1748: The last will and testament of John Merrell, late of Hartford decd., was now exhibited in Court by Cyprian Merrell and Benjamin Merrell, executors. Will proven and ordered to be recorded and kept on file.

Page 81—6 December, 1748: Cyprian and Benjamin Merrell, executors to the last will of John Merrell, late of Hartford, now moved to this Court that distribution be made of the estate of the sd. decd. according to his last will: Whereupon this Court appoint Thomas Hosmer, Stephen Hosmer and Isaac Goodwin distributors.

Messenger, Nathaniel. Court Record, Page 46—1st September, 1747: Nathaniel Messenger, 14 years of age, son of Nathaniel Messenger, late of Farmington decd., made choice of Mr. James Beckwith of Farmington to be his guardian. Recog., £400.

Page 127.

Miller, Asa, Middletown. Invt. £281-01-08. Taken 12 June, 1747, by Josiah Churchill and Deliverance Warner. Will dated 28 November, 1746.

I, Asa Miller of Middletown, in the County of Hartford, being bound to sea, do make this my last will and testament: I give and bequeath unto Martha, my well-beloved wife, all and every part of my estate whatsoever, both real and personal. I do hereby constitute, nominate and appoint her, my sd. wife, sole executrix to this my will.

Witness: *John Rockwell,*   ASA MILLER, LS.
Hannah Rockwell, William Rockwell.

Court Record, Page 43—15 June, 1747: The last will and testament of Asa Miller, late of Middletown decd., was now exhibited in Court by Martha Miller, executrix. Proven. Inventory exhibited. Both ordered to be recorded and kept on file.

Page 150-1-160-1-2-261.

Miller, Benjamin, Middletown. Invt. £5332-12-11. Taken 18 and 19 January, 1747-8, by John Bacon, Jacob Whitmore and Jonathan Allyn. Additional inventory, £312-10-00. Taken 17 November, 1748, by Giles Hooker and Thomas Stanly. Will dated 14 April, 1746.

I, Benjamin Miller of Middletown, do make this my last will and testament: I give to my wife Mercy, and to her heirs forever, all that my farm or parcel of land whereon I dwell, with all the buildings thereon, containing 80 acres be the same more or less, as the same will be found butted and bounded; I say the whole of sd. farm I give to my wife

Marcey and her heirs forever. And I do give to my sd. wife Marcey all my household furniture, be it of what use soever, together with all the stock and provision and grain that shall be found in my house, barn or buildings at the time of my decease. I do also give to my wife three of my cows, such as she shall choose out of my stock; and also I give to my wife that mare I bought of my son Ichabod, with her colt; all which moveables I grant to my wife to be to her use and disposal as she shall think proper; and declare that what I have above granted to my wife and to her heirs forever is for that she brought £60 in silver money to me, which I laid out for land to my great profit. Secondly: I give unto my two sons, Benjamin Miller and Ichabod Miller, all that my lott or farm of land, containing 200 acres, that I bought of Jeremiah Hall, late of Wallingford, lying in the Parish of Southington, in Farmingtown bounds, being butted and bounded as appeareth of record; always provided, and it is my will, that my two sons Benjamin and Ichabod, in order to have and hold sd. 200 acres of land, shall pay £50 in old tenor bills of credit: £10 to my daughter Mary Spencer, £10 to my daughter Rebeckah Robinson, £10 to my daughter Hannah Coe, £10 to my daughter Mehetabell Barnes, and to the children of my late daughter Sarah, sometime the wife of Joseph Heikcox, I say to the children of sd. Sarah, £10. Thirdly: I will and bequeath to my sd. son Benjamin, and his heirs forever, all my quarter part of the lott lying on the east side of the Great River that was laid out on my honoured father Miller's right. Fourthly: I give to my sons, Benjamin Miller, Ichabod Miller, Amos Miller and David Miller, and to their heirs forever, also that my lott lying on the east side side of the river commonly called the Three-Mile Division, which is laid out upon my own right, etc. Fifthly: I give to my three youngest daughters, viz., Lydia Stow, Martha Adkins and Rhoda Bacon, £10 apiece in money, in bills of old tenor. Sixthly: I give all my living stock not before disposed of, with my negro man called Sharp, together with my tools and utensils not before herein disposed of, to all my children above named. And my sd. dafter Sarah Heikcox's children to be accounted one, and to have one share equal with one of my children. Seventhly: I give to my son David Miller, and to his heirs forever, all that land (containing about 60 acres) bounded southerly on a highway, north on Amos Miller's land, east on Simeon Persons's and Timothy Persons's land and partly on sd. David's land, and westerly on Joseph Coe's land. Moreover, I will and bequeath unto my sd. wife (when my debts are paid) what money and credits I have and possess at the time of my decease or that shall be due to me at sd. time. I appoint my sons Benjamin Miller and Amos Miller to be executors.

Witness: *James Wadsworth,*   BENJAMIN MILLER, LS.
Moses Persons, William Rockwell.

Court Record, Page 54—5 January, 1747-8: The last will and testament of Benjamin Miller, late of Middletown, was now exhibited in Court by Benjamin and Amos Miller, executors. Ordered to be recorded and kept on file.

Page 56—26 January, 1747-8: Amos Miller, one of the sons and executors of the last will of Benjamin Miller, moves to this Court that distribution be made of the estate of Benjamin Miller according to his last will: This Court appoint John Bacon, Jacob Whitmore and Jonathan Allyn, of Middletown, distributors.

Page 98—2 May, 1749: Distribution of the estate of Benjamin Miller, late of Middletown, was now exhibited in Court by John Bacon and Jacob Whitmore. Ordered recorded and kept on file.

Miller, Caleb. Court Record, Page 82—3 January, 1748-9: John Miller, a minor, 14 years of age, son of Caleb Miller, chose his father-in-law Samuel Williams of Wethersfield to be his guardian. Recog., £500.

Page 91—7 March, 1748-9: Betty Miller, a minor, 13 years of age, also made choice of Samuel Williams for her guardian. Recog., £300.

Page 432-3.

Miller, James, Wethersfield. Invt. £449-16-07. Taken 2nd May, 1750, by Jedediah Sanborn and Thomas Harriss in Wethersfield. Additional inventory in Middletown, £149-04-00. Taken 2nd June, 1750, by Ambross Clark and Samuel Barnes.

Court Record, Page 132—5 June, 1750: The last nuncupative will of James Miller, late of Wethersfield decd., was now exhibited in Court and proven, and by this Court approved and ordered to be recorded and kept on file, and is there recorded.

HARTFORD, SS.
Wethersfield, 17 April, 1750.

John Welles the 2nd, Ebenezer Griswold and Jacob Dix, all personally appeared before me the subscriber and made oath that in the night next after the 15th day of April inst., being at the dwelling house of James Miller, late of sd. Wethersfield decd., they heard the sd. Miller declare, some hours before his death, that it was his will that his then wife Eunice should have all the estate that she brought when they married together. And that when he so declared, he was, in their opinion, of sound mind and memory.

Witness: *Ebenezer Griswold,*   JOHN CHESTER, ASSISTANT.
Jacob Dix, John Welles, 2nd.

At a Court of Probate held at Hartford, 7th June, 1750: Then the witnesses to the above written note made oath to the truth thereof before this Court.   *Test: Joseph Talcott, Clerk.*

Page 133—5 June, 1750: The inventory of the estate of James Miller, late of Wethersfield decd., was now exhibited in Court by William Miller, Adms., which inventory is accepted, ordered to be recorded and kept on file.

Page 26 (Vol. XVI) 4 June, 1751: An account of Adms. was now exhibited in Court by William Miller, Adms. Accepted. Sd. Adms. moves for a distribution: Whereupon this Court appoint Joseph Southmayd, William Rockwell and John Hubbard distributors.

Inventory, £853-05-06; paid in debts and charges, £423-10-01; there remains for distribution, £429-15-05, as follows:

	£ s d		£ s d
To William Miller,	171-18-02	To Mary Belding,	85-19-01
To James Miller,	85-19-01	To Phebe Miller,	85-19-01

Order to distribute, and make return of your doings to this Court.

Page 128-9.

Miller, Joseph, Wethersfield. Will dated 11 May, 1747: I, Joseph Miller of Wethersfield, do make this my last will and testament: I will that my funeral charges and other just debts be well and truly paid in convenient time after my decease: and in particular, £36 in money, old tenor, to my son John Miller; £20 in money of old tenor to my cousin John Miller, and £6 to my cousin Elizabeth Miller; which money was left in my hands for them by their deceased father. Second: I give to my wife Abigail Miller the sole use of all my buildings, together with my homelott, during the term of her widowhood; and also the improvement of 1-3 of all my lands during her natural life. Furthermore, I give to my wife the 1-2 of all my household goods; also one cow and one 2-year-old heifer, and also 5 sheep. Third: I give to my sons John and Joseph Miller my buildings with all my lands, to be equally divided between them, my son John having his first choice in the division, they allowing to my wife the improvement of what I have given to her during the term above mentioned. I give to my daughter Rebeckah the other half of my household goods not given to my wife, and also one cow and one 2-year-old heifer, together with 20 sheep. Furthermore, I give to my son John Miller my two horses, my bay and black horse. The remainder of my stock, together with all my husbandry utensils, I give to my two sons John and Joseph Miller, to be equally divided between them. I appoint my wife Abigail Miller and my son John Miller to be executors.

Witness: *Thomas Butler,*   JOSEPH MILLER, LS.
Return Belding, Baley Barnd.

Court Record, Page 43—2 June, 1747: The last will and testament of Joseph Miller, late of Wethersfield, was now exhibited in Court by Abigail Miller, one of the executors named in sd. will. Will proven and ordered to be recorded and kept on file.

Page 38.

Miller, Thomas, Middletown. Will dated 22 February, 1746: Know all Christian people whom these presents may concern: That I,

Thomas Miller, a soldier in the honourable Brigr. Waldo's regiment, and in that company of which John Huston is captain, being sick and weak of body, but of sound sense and memory, and considering the certainty of death and the uncertainty of its coming, do now make this my last will and testament in manner and form as followeth:

*   *   *   *   *   *   *   *   *

Third: and lastly, I give to my well-beloved brother Moses Miller all my goods or estate I have here present with me, or shall appertain or fall to me by virtue of the expedition against this Island of Cape Breton, and also all my goods and estate I have or ever shall fall to me in any part of New England, after my just and lawful debts are paid. And I do constitute him the sd. Moses Miller to be my lawful and sole executor of this my last will and testament.

Witness: *Samuel Green,*   THOMAS MILLER, LS.
William Kellog, John Sacket.

Court Record, Page 20—5 August, 1746: A copy of the last will and testament of Thomas Miller, late of Middletown, in the County of Hartford (decd. at Lewis Bourg), was now exhibited in this Court by Moses Miller, executor named in sd. will, which will is by this Court approved, ordered to be recorded and kept on file. Which sd. copy came attested by *B: Green, Secretary,* of Lewis Bourg, in which office the original will is filed.

Page 127—1st May, 1750: This Court grant Adms. on the estate of Thomas Miller, late of Middletown, unto William Miller of Middletown, who gave bond with William Whitmore of Middletown of £500.

Page 76-134-5.

Moody, Adonijah, New Hartford. Invt. £695-09-00. Taken 4 March, 1746-7, by David Ensign, Jr., Matthew Gillet and Elijah Flower. Will dated 25 December, 1746.

I, Adonijah Moody of New Hartford, in the County of Hartford, do make this my last will and testament: I give to Sarah, my well-beloved wife, my riding mare, my red white-faced cow, my great spinning wheel and little spinning wheel, my andirons, a certain quantity of wool that we now have in the house, and all the moveable estate that belonged to my wife when she first became my wife, to be my wife's forever; and all that houseing stuff that was mine to have the improvement of during the time that she remaineth my widow; and 1-3 part of my land during the time that she remains my widow. I give to my son Ebenezer Moody my lott of land lying on the hill called the Town Hill, containing about 50 acres of land, he performing the duties hereafter mentioned. And to my daughter Susannah Moody all that housing stuff that was mine before marriage to Sarah my last wife, to be *"hurn"* forever, and my alottment of land that I purchased of Thomas Easton, containing about 28 acres; always provided that my sd. wife should not have a male heir by me. And if she should have another child by me, if it should be a son, he shall have the abovesd. lott that I purchased of sd. Easton, to be his forever; or if a daughter, it shall have 18 acres of said Easton lot. And furthermore, I do hereby order my executors that may hereafter be appointed to make sale of the following particulars to pay my debts, viz.: my sorril catle, being two years old past, and my oxen and team tackling, and brown cow, and a paire of horse chains, and beem knife. And I do hereby appoint my wife Sarah Moody and my brother Samuel Moody and Abraham Kellogg to be my executors.

Witness: *Martin Smith,*   ADONIJAH MOODY, LS.
Daniel Hooker, Matthew Gillet.

Court Record, Page 37—16 April, 1747: The last will and testament of Adonijah Moody, late of New Hartford decd., was now exhibited in Court by Sarah Moody, Samuel Moody and Abraham Kellogg, executors. Will proven and ordered recorded and kept on file.

Page 164-5.

Morley, Ebenezer, Glastonbury. Invt. £1094-03-00. Taken 30 November, 1747, by Josiah Benton and Elizur Talcott. Will dated 16 September, 1747.

I, Ebenezer Morley of Glastonbury, do make this my last will and testament: I give to my wife Susannah, after my just debts are paid, 1-3 part of my moveable estate forever, and the use of all my houseing and lands until my only son shall come of age, and then only 1-3 part of it as long as she shall remain my widow. I give to my only son John my homelott, with the buildings thereon, where I now dwell, and all that land in the Three-Mile lott which I bought of my daughter-in-law Margery Spencer alias Wickham. I give to my three daughters, Martha, Susannah and Prudence, forever, all that lott of land lying at Little Nipsick in Glastonbury, to be equally divided between them. I give to my sd. son and dafters the remaining part of my moveable estate. And I appoint my sd. wife Susannah to be sole executrix.

Witness: *Thomas Welles,*   EBENEZER MORLEY, LS.
John House, Richard Fox.

Court Record, Page 58—26 January, 1747-8: The last will and testament of Ebenezer Morley, late of Glastonbury, was now exhibited by Susannah Morley, executrix. Will proven and ordered to be recorded and kept on file.

Page 61—8 March, 1747-8: This Court appoint Susannah Morley, widow, to be guardian to John Morley, a minor, son of Ebenezer Morley. Recog., £500.

Moore, Jonathan. Court Record, Page 34—4 March, 1746-7: An inventory of the estate of Jonathan Moore, late of Simsbury, was now exhibited in Court by Jonathan Moore, Adms. Accepted.

Inventory in Vol. XVI, Page 6.

Moore, Return, Windsor. Invt. £2678-03-06. Taken 6th February, 1748-9, by Ebenezer Grant, Matthew Rockwell and Wm. Wolcott.

Court Record, Page 84—3 January, 1748-9: Adms. granted unto Samuel Goff Moore of Windsor, who gave bonds with Daniel Carpenter, of Windsor, of £700.

Page 30 (Vol. XVI) 2 July, 1751: An account of Adms. was now exhibited in Court by Philip (Samuel) Goff More, Adms. Accepted. And the sd. Adms. moves to this Court that distribution be made: Whereupon this Court appoint William Wolcott, Ebenezer Grant and Matthew Rockwell distributors. Inventory, £2672-03-06, with credits; the debts and charges subtracted, there remains £2450-04-05 to be distributed, viz.: To Samuel Goff Moore, to Damaras Moore, and to the heirs of Esther Heyden alias Moore, heirs to the estate, to each of them £816-13-04. To distribute the estate according to the foregoing order, and make return of their doings to this Court.

Page 100—1st June, 1753: Report of the distributors. Accepted.

Page 56.

Moore, Zebulon, Simsbury. Died at Newark in the Jerseys. (Recorded in New York?) Invt. £67-09-06. Taken 14 January, 1746-7, by Joseph Alderman and Reuben Slater.

Court Record, Page 28—2 December, 1746: This Court grant Adms. on the estate of Zebulon Moore of Newark, in the County of Middlesex, formerly of Simsbury, in the County of Hartford, of all the estate of the sd. decd. in the County of Hartford aforesd., unto Jonathan Moore, Jr., of Simsbury, who gave bond with David Ensign of Hartford of £500.

Page 52—1st December, 1747: Jonathan Moore, Adms. on the estate of Zebulon Moore, late of Simsbury, informs this Court that the estate of the sd. decd. is insolvent, and prays commissioners may be appointed to adjust the claims of the creditors. This Court appoint Lt. Abel Forward and Ensign Martin Winchell, of Simsbury, commissioners.

Page 65—12 May, 1748: A report of the commissioners, under the hands of Martin Winchell and Abel Forward. Accepted and ordered to be kept on file.

Page 32.

Morton, William, Farmington. Invt. £204-05-02. Taken 31st May, 1746, by John Newell, Ephraim Treadwell and James Judd; and 3 June, 1746, by James Smith, Daniel Hayes and David Holcomb.

Court Record, Page 13—3 June, 1746: This Court grants Adms. on the estate of William Morton, late of Farmingtown, unto Jeremiah Wilcockson 2nd of sd. Simsbury, who gave bonds with Peletiah Mills of Windsor of £600.

Page 252-3.

Moses, William, Simsbury. Died 14 July, 1745. Invt. £201-11-00. Taken by Samuel Pettebone, Benajah Humphrey and Noah Humphrey.

Court Record, Page 84—3 January, 1748-9: This Court grant Adms. on the estate of William Moses, late of Simsbury, unto Jonathan Pettebone of sd. Simsbury, who gave bonds with Jonathan Olcott of Hartford of £500.

Page 89 (Vol. XVI) 6 March, 1753: This Court appoint Jabez Cornish to be guardian to David Moses, a minor, age 11 years, son of William Moses. Recog., £300.

Page 285.

Mygatt, Jacob, Hartford. Invt. £1901-06-00. Taken 10 October, 1748, by Josiah Olcott and Nathaniel Olcott. Will dated 9 August, 1748.

I, Jacob Mygatt of Hartford, do make this my last will and testament: I give to my wife Elizabeth Mygatt 1-3 part of my moveable estate forever, and the use of my dwelling house until my son comes of age, and the use of the north room during her natural life, and the use of half the cellar, and use of the oven, and use of the west end of my lott whereon my dwelling house now stands. I give to my only son Jonathan Mygatt all the remainder of my estate, both real and personal, to be to him and his heirs forever. And in case my sd. son shall die before he attain the age of 21 years without issue, then I give to my beloved wife Elizabeth Mygatt 1-3 part of the estate which I have given to my sd. son, and 1-3 part thereof to her brother Daniel Butler, and the other third part to my sister Mary Stanly, and to their heirs and assigns forever. I appoint my wife Elizabeth executrix and my son Jonathan Mygatt executor.

Witness: *Joseph Pitkin,*   JACOB MYGATT, LS.
Thomas Morley, Mindwell X *Morley.*

Court Record, Page 79—1st November, 1748: The last will and testament of Jacob Mygatt, late of Hartford decd., was exhibited in Court by Elizabeth Mygatt and Jonathan Mygatt, executors, widow and son. Will proven and, with the inventory, ordered to be kept on file.

Mygatt, Zebulon. Court Record, Page 18—7 May, 1746: Austin Mygatt, a minor, 14 years of age, son of Zebulon Mygatt, late of Hartford deceased, chose Joseph Hosmer of Hartford to be his guardian. Recog., £200.

Page 75—20 July, 1748: Rachel Mygatt, a daughter of sd. deceased, also made choice of Joseph Hosmer to be her guardian. And this Court appoint sd. Hosmer guardian to Roger Mygatt, 11 years of age, and Thomas Mygatt, 9 years of age, all children of Zebulon Mygatt deceased. Recog., £200 for each minor.

Page 200-1-398.

Nelson, Dr. John, Simsbury. Died 29 February, 1747-8. Invt. £861-13-04. Taken 14 April, 1748, by James Cornish, Abel Forward and Joseph Phelps.

Additional Invt. £800. Taken 3 June, 1748, by Medad Pomeroy, Jonathan Sheldon, Jr., and Reuben Harmon. Being 44 acres of land bounding west on Simsbury line, north on land of Ebenezer Southwell, east on land of Jonathan Sheldon, Jr., and south on land of Rev. Mr. John Graham.

Court Record, Page 62—5 April, 1748: This Court grant Adms. on the estate of Dr. John Nelson, late of Simsbury deceased, unto Hannah and John Nelson, widow and son of the said decd., who gave bond with Joseph Cornish of Simsbury.

Page 23 (Vol. XVI) 7 May, 1751: An account of administration was now exhibited in Court by Hannah and John Nelson, Adms. James Nelson, age 19 years, and David Nelson, age 14 years, children of Dr. John Nelson, chose their mother to be their guardian. And this Court appoint Hannah Nelson to be guardian to Isaac, age 13 years, and to Rhoda, age 9 years, children of the said deceased. Recog., £500. The Adms. now move for a distribution of the estate of the decd. The amount, less debts and charges, to be distributed is £1551-15-02: To Hannah, the widow, her third part of the personal estate forever, and one-third part of the real estate during life; to John Nelson, eldest son, a double portion; and to James, David, Isaac, Hannah and Rhoda Nelson, to each a single share. And this Court appoint Medad Pomeroy of Suffield, Ens. Isaac Owen of Windsor and Joseph Cornish of Simsbury distributors.

Page 408-9-436.

Newbery, Mrs. Hannah, alias Merriman, Windsor. Invt. on page 408 of personal estate, including John Easton's note for £100 and a bond of Thomas Phelps of £166. On page 436, lands in western towns belonging to the estate of Mrs. Newbery, as follows:

To one lot in Simsbury, by deed from John Hoskins, 100 acres, £200
To one lot in Simsbury, by deed from John Hoskins, 20 acres, £80
To one lot in Simsbury, by deed from John Hoskins, 70 acres, £140
To one lot in Simsbury, by deed from Thomas Phelps, 160 acres, £960
To one lot in Barkhamsted, deed from Joseph Stedman, 62 acres, £186
To undivided land in Barkhamsted, £240
To her first division in Torrington, 30 acres, £150
To her second division in Torrington, 30 acres, £120
To her undivided land in Torrington, £60
To one lot in Harwinton, by deed from Nathaniel Drake, 36 acres, £234
To one lot in Harwinton, by deed from Nathaniel Drake, 71 acres, £244
To Nathaniel Drake's last division in Harwinton, 17 acres, £25-10
To one lot in Windsor, equivalent lands, 37 acres, £74
To two acres in the little meadow in Windsor, £130
To two acres behind Mrs. Newbery's house, in Windsor, £50
To 11 acres of land on Tucker's Plain, in Windsor, £190
To 35 acres of land in Wintonbury, in Windsor, £700
To land in Colebrook, by deed from J. P. Anderson, £230

Taken 11 January, 1749-50, and 20 November, 1750, by Matthew Rockwell, Moses Loomis, Jr., and Erastus Wolcott.

Court Record, Page 113—26 December, 1749: This Court grant Adms. on the estate of Mrs. Hannah Newbery, late of Windsor, unto Roger Wolcott and Elizabeth Newbery.

Page 15 (Vol. XVI) 22 February, 1750-1: Report of the administrators, and no debts being due, move for a distribution of the estate.

Page 53—4 February, 1752: An account of administration was now exhibited by Roger Wolcott and Elizabeth Newbery, which account is accepted. The Court now appoint Matthew Rockwell, Erastus Wolcott and Moses Loomis, Jr., distributors to distribute the estate to the surviving heirs, as follows:

	£ s d
Inventory,	5894-03-08
The debts subtracted therefrom,	907-02-04
There remains to be distributed the sum of	4989-01-04
Viz: To the heirs of Capt. Roger Newbery,	3326-00-10
To Roger Wolcott, Jr., Esq., and his wife Marah,	1663-00-05

And make return thereof to this Court.

Page 388-9, 390.

Newell, James, Farmington. Invt. £1779-06-00. Taken 6 April, 1750, by John Newell and Joseph Hooker. Will dated 9 March, 1749-50.

I, James Newell of the Town of Farmingtown, do make this my last will and testament: I give unto my wife Dinah Newell the use of 1-3 part of my lott of land on which I now dwell, with 1-3 part of my house, barn and all appurtenances, privileges and conveniences thereunto belonging, with 1-3 part of all my improveable lands, and this during the term of her natural life; and also I give to my wife 1-3 part of my personal estate forever. Unto my eldest son James Newell I give to him 2-3 parts of the lott of land on which I now dwell, lying at the north end of sd. lott, with my dwelling house and barn thereon standing. I give unto my two sons, James Newell and Thomas Newell, to them and their heirs forever, all my lands at a place called Cox Crank, to be equally divided between them, they paying to my two daughters in equal proportions, namely, Jerusha Newell and Mehetabell Newell, when they come to the age of 21 years, £50 to each of them in old tenor bills. To my 2nd son, Thomas Newell, I give the remaining third part of my homelott and all the residue of my real estate in lands, wheresoever it may be found, to him and to his heirs forever. I do hereby constitute my brother-in-law, Mr. Solomon Cowles, to be sole executor.

Witness: *John Newell,*   JAMES NEWELL, LS.
Joseph Hooker, Jonathan Gridley.

Court Record, Page 127—1st May, 1750: The last will and testament of James Newell, late of Farmingtown decd., was now exhibited in Court by Solomon Cowles, executor. Proven. Exhibited an inventory. Both accepted and ordered recorded and kept on file.

Page 37 (Vol. XVI) 1st October, 1751: This Court appoint Dinah Newell, the widow, to be guardian to Mehetabel Newell, a minor, aged 8 years, and Thomas Newell, aged about 6 years, children of James Newell. Recog., £400.

Page 14.

Northway, George, Farmington. Will dated 8 September, 1736: I, George Northway, of the Town of Farmingtown, doe make this my last will and testament: I give unto Hannah Northway, my wife, the improvement of 1-3 part of all my houseing and lands during her natural life, and also 1-3 part of my moveable estate and one cow to be to her and her heirs forever. I give unto my sons, John Northway, Samuel Northway and Josiah Northway, all my lands within the bounds of Farmington, to be equally divided between them, except my eldest son John Northway, to him I give in value £20 of my land more than to my other 2 younger sons—which I give to them and to their heirs forever. I give to my eldest daughter Hannah Tryall 5 shillings besides what she hath already received. To my daughter Mary North I give the sum of £10 besides what she hath already received. To my daughter Sarah Northway I give the sum of £30, to be paid her at the age of 18 years. Also, my will is that my just debts be duly paid by my executors; and if there is any moveable estate left, then my will is that it be

divided between my two youngest daughters, viz., Mary North and
Sarah Northway. I appoint my wife Hannah Northway and my eldest
son John Northway executors.

Witness: *Joseph Hawley,*   GEORGE NORTHWAY, LS.
Joseph North, Samuel Woodford.

Court Record, Page 8—4 February, 1745-6: The last will and
testament of George Northway was exhibited in Court by Hannah
Northway, widow, and John Northway, executors. Proven.

Page 45—1st September, 1747: John Northway, executor, moved
to this Court for a division of the lands of sd. deceased to and amongst
the sons of the sd. deceased according to the last will: Whereupon this
Court appoint Asahell Strong, Capt. Hezekiah Lee and Joseph Hooker,
of Farmington, distributors.

Page 295-6.

Northway, Josiah, Farmington. Invt. £101-03-00. Taken by
Samuel Buell and Joseph Woodford, Jr. Will dated 9 December, 1748.

I, Josiah Northway of Farmingtown, do make this my last will and
testament: I give to my mother, Hannah Northway, all my moveable
estate, with all my part of the building. I give unto my two brothers,
John Northway and Samuel Northway, all my lands within the Town of
Farmingtown, to be equally divided between them both. Also my will
is that my just debts be duly paid by my executors. And I appoint my
two brothers, John Northway and Samuel Northway, executors.

Witness: *John Norton,*   JOSIAH NORTHWAY, LS.
Lydia X Hart, Anna X Hart.

Court Record, Page 92—7 March, 1748-9: The last will and testament of Josiah Northway, late of Farmingtown, was now exhibited in
Court by John Northway and Samuel Northway, executors. Will
proven. Exhibited an inventory. Both to be recorded and kept on file.

Page 407.

Norton, Ebenezer, Farmington. Invt. £3823-15-00 in lands, and
£530-16-06 in personal estate. Taken 16 May, 1750, by John Norton,
Thomas Norton and Isaac Newell.

Court Record, Page 134—3 July, 1750: This Court grant Adms.
on the estate of Ebenezer Norton, late of Farmingtown, unto Sarah Norton, widow, who gave bonds with Isaac Norton of Farmingtown of £1000.

Page 94 (Vol. XVI) 3 April, 1753: An account of Adms. was now
exhibited in Court by Sarah Norton, Adms. Accepted. Also, the sd.
Adms. moves to this Court that distribution be made: Whereupon this

Court appoint John Hungerford, Stephen Barns and Jonathan Root distributors to distribute the estate to the heirs, viz., to the sd. widow 1-3 part of the buildings and lands, and the rest of the estate to be distributed: to the eldest son a double share, and the rest of the children an equal share. This Court appoint Sarah Norton guardian to Martha Norton, 9 years, Ebenezer 7, and Isaac Norton about 4 years of age, children of Ebenezer Norton. Recog., £300.

Page 96—16 April, 1753: This Court appoint Matthew Clark to be guardian to Ashbell Norton, a minor, about 11 years of age, son of Ebenezer Norton deceased. Recog., £300.

Page 13 (Vol. XVII) 7 February, 1754: Bethias Norton, a minor, age 14 years, son of Ebenezer Norton of Farmington, chose Isaac Newell to be his guardian. Recog., £300.

Page 157.

Olcott, Timothy, Jr., Bolton. Invt. £1016-14-00. Taken 29 October, 1747, by Matthew Loomis and Jonathan Strong.

Court Record, Page 57—2nd February, 1747-8: This Court grant Adms. on the estate of Timothy Olcott, Jr., late of Bolton decd., unto Timothy Olcott and Eunice Olcott of Bolton, widow and father of the sd. decd., who gave bonds with David Porter of Hartford of £1000.

Page 122.

Orcutt, Nathan, Stafford. Invt. £631-06-00. Taken 2nd October, 1746, by Josiah Converse, Eleazer Hammond and Bennet Field.

Court Record, Page 44—4 August, 1747: This Court grant Adms. on the estate of Nathan Orcutt, late of Stafford decd., unto Phebe Orcutt, widow, who gave bonds with William Orcutt of sd. Stafford of £600 money, and exhibited an inventory. Accepted.

Page 103—4 July, 1749: This Court appoint John Cross and Phebe his wife, both of Stafford, to be guardian unto Nathan Orcutt, 12 years, Hannah, 10 years, and Phebe Orcutt, 8 years of age, children of Nathan Orcutt deceased. John Cross and Phebe his wife, and Stephen Cross, all of Stafford, recog. in £500 for each minor.

Page 19 (Vol. XVI) 2 April, 1751: Nathan Orcutt, a minor, 14 years of age, chose Henry Lad of Coventry, in the County of Windham, to be his guardian. Recog., £500.

Page 27—21 June, 1751: John Cross, in right of his wife Phebe Orcutt (alias Cross), Adms., now moves to this Court for distribution of the estate, which this Court grant and appoint and impower Josiah Converse, Timothy Edson and Uriah Richardson, of Stafford, to distribute the estate, viz:

£ s d

To Phebe, the relict, 81-01-11
To Nathan Orcutt, only son, 229-01-08
To Hannah and Phebe Orcutt, daughters, to each, 114-10-11

Page 92—26 March, 1753: Report of the distributors.

Page 387-8.

Orviss, Samuel, Farmington. Will dated 6 August, 1740: I, Samuel Orviss of Farmington, doe make this my last will and testament: I give unto my brother William Orviss of Winchester, in the County of Hampshire and Province of the Massachusetts Bay, all my right of land in the new township called No. 4, on the east side of the Connecticut River, above the Great Falls, in the County of Hampshire and Province aforesd., to hold to him the sd. William, his heirs and assigns forever. I give unto my brother Charles Orviss of Farmingtown, to him and his heirs forever, 2-5 parts of all my land in Farmingtown. I give my horse to my sd. brother Charles Orviss. I give unto my brother Gershom Orviss of Farmingtown, to him his heirs and assigns forever, 2-5 parts of all my land in Farmingtown. I give unto my sd. brother Gershom Orviss my saddle, bridal, axe and hoe. I give unto my brothers, Charles and Gershom, all my wearing apparrell, equally divided between them. I give unto my sister Deborah Orviss of Farmingtown 1-5 part of all my lands in Farmingtown. I appoint my brothers, Charles Orviss and Gershom Orviss, executors to this my will.

Witness: *Daniel Wadsworth,*   SAMUEL ORVISS, LS.
Samuel Flagg, Abigail Wadsworth.

Inventory on Page 136. Will on Page 225-6.

Palmer, Timothy, Windsor. Invt. £52-10-06. Also, 21 dollars at 5 shillings sterling, 3 dollars at 6 shillings sterling, four half-dollars at 2s 6d, and one pistareen at one shilling. Taken by John Cook 2nd, Pelatiah Allyn and Noadiah Gillet. Will dated 15 November, 1745:

I, Timothy Palmer of Windsor, do make this my last will and testament: I give to Benjamin Palmer, Jr., son of John Palmer, Jr., of Windsor, one certain right of land in one of the western towns called Colebrook. The sd. right of land came by my father Stephen Palmer of Windsor decd. Also, I give to the sd. Benjamin Palmer another right of land in sd. Colebrook that I bought of Noadiah Gillet of Windsor, in Hartford County. I give unto my brother and sisters, that is, Isaac Phelps, Sarah Phelps, Rebeckah Phelps and Mary Phelps, children of Isaac Phelps of Westfield, in the County of Hampshire, the remainder of my estate. I appoint Ensign John Palmer, Jr., of Windsor, and Mr. Ebenezer Weller, of Westfield, in the County of Hampshire, to be my executors.

Witness: *Joseph Talcott,*   TIMOTHY PALMER, LS.
William Pratt, Mary Talcott.

Court Record, Page 33—3 March, 1746-7: The last will and testament of Timothy Palmer, late of Windsor decd., was now exhibited in Court by John Palmer, Jr., of Windsor, and Ebenezer Weller, of Westfield, in the County of Hampshire, executors. Will proven and ordered to be kept on file.

Page 43—5 May, 1747: Inventory exhibited.

Page 291.

Peck, Isaac, Kensington. Invt. £981-02-07. Taken by Caleb Galpin, Samuel Thompson and John Hinsdale.

Court Record, Page 80—6 December, 1748: This Court grant Adms. on the estate of Isaac Peck, late of Middletown, unto Abijah Peck and Lois Peck of Middletown, who gave bonds with Lt. George Hubbard of Middletown of £1500.

Page 6 (Vol. XVI) 4 December, 1750: Lois and Abijah Peck, Adms., exhibited an account of their Adms. Accepted.

Page 9—25 December, 1750-1: Jabez Peck, son of Isaac Peck, chose Joseph Porter of Farmington to be his guardian. Recog., £500.

Page 406-7.

Peese, Abraham, Enfield. Invt. £5251-17-00. Taken 30 June, 1750, by Joseph Olmsted and Benjamin Meachum.

Court Record, Page 134—3 July, 1750: This Court grant Adms. on the sd. estate unto Abigail Peese, widow, who gave bonds with surety.

Page 22 (Vol. XVI) 7 May, 1751: Abigail Peese of Enfield, administratrix on the estate of Abraham Peese, late of Enfield decd., now moves to this Court for a distribution of the real estate of the sd. decd.: Whereupon this Court appoint and impower Messrs. Joseph Olmsted, Benjamin Mecham and Thomas Jones of Enfield, or any two of them, to divide, portion, make and ascertain the bounds to each heir, vizt., to the widow of the said decd. one-third part of the buildings and lands during life; and to John, the eldest son, a double share; and to Abraham Peese, Samuel, Joel, Nathan, Gideon, Josiah, William and Zebulon, Mary and Desire Peese, children of said deceased, their single share of said estate, and make return thereof to this Court.

Distribution on file (of lands), 4 December, 1754:

To John Peese, eldest son,	To Moses Peese,
To Abraham Peese,	To Samuel Peese,
To Mary, eldest daughter,	To Joel Peese,
To William Peese,	To Nathan Peese,
To Zebulon Peese,	To Gideon Peese,
To Desire Peese, 2nd daughter,	To Josiah Peese,

And to Abigail Peese, the widow, her third part of buildings and land during life.

Page 32—6 August, 1751: Moses Peese, a minor, 17 years of age, and Samuel Peese, 14 years, sons of Abraham Peese, chose their mother Abigail Peese to be their guardian. And this Court appoint the sd. widow guardian to Joel Peese, age 13 years, Matthew 11, Desire 10, Gideon 8, Josiah 7, and William Peese, children of sd. decd. Recog., £300 for each minor.

Page 65—3 June, 1752: An account of Adms. was now exhibited by Abigail Peese, Adms. Accepted.

Page 72 (Vol. XVII) 5 August, 1755: An additional account of debts and charges from the estate of Abraham Peese was now exhibited in Court, and Abigail Peese, Adms., moves for a distribution of the moveable estate, viz:

	£ s d
To Abigail Peese, widow,	71-11-00
To John Peese, eldest son,	22-00-08
To Abraham, Moses, Samuel, Joel, Nathan, Gideon, Josiah, William and Zebulon Peese, and to Martha Peese, alias Lord, and Desire Peese, to each of them,	11-00-02

And appoint Joseph Olmsted, Benjamin Mecham and John Booth, distributors.

Peese, Joseph. Court Record, Page 27—13 November, 1746: This Court appoint Sarah Peese, now of Bolton, sometime the widow of Joseph Peese of Wethersfield decd., to be a guardian to Abigail Peese, her dafter, age 8 years: and the sd. Abigail (Sarah) Peese acknowledged bond with Stephen Goodwin of Simsbury of £300 money for her faithful discharge of the trust of a guardian to sd. minor.

Page 213.

Peese, Samuel. Inventory of the estate of Samuel Peese, late of Windsor, in the County of Hartford decd., viz: To his Cape *Brittan* (Breton) wages, £41-15-09 old tenor. 2nd February, A. D. 1747-8. Exhibited by John Thrall, Adms., on oath, etc., for record.

Test: Joseph Talcott, Clerk.

Court Record, Page 57—2 February, 1747-8: An inventory of the estate of Samuel Peese, late of Windsor, was now exhibited in Court by John Thrall, Adms. Accepted, ordered to be recorded and kept on file. Estate insolvent. This Court appoint Ensign Isaac Owen and Sergt. Isaac Gillet of Windsor commissioners to adjust the claims of the creditors.

Page 105—1st August, 1749: Report of commissioners on the estate of Samuel Peese, which report is accepted and ordered to be recorded and kept on file.

Page 406.

Penfield, Stephen, Middletown. Invt. £377-06-00. Taken 16 November, 1749, by John Shepherd and Sampson Howe.

Court Record, Page 134—3 July, 1750: This Court grant letters of Adms. unto Jerusha Penfield, widow, who gave bonds.

Dist. File: 20 May, 1762: To Jeremiah, to Benjamin, to John, to Jerusha, and to Samuel Penfield. Also distribution of lands given them by their grandfather John Penfield. By John Churchill, David Robinson and Daniel Shepherd.

Page 65-6-7.

Pettebone, Samuel, Simsbury. Died 11 February, 1747. Invt. £1172-18-03. Taken 4 April, 1747, by Joseph Case 2nd, Benajah Humphrey and David Phelps. Will dated 20 August, 1746.

I, Samuel Pettebone of the Town of Simsbury, in the County of Hartford, do make this my last will and testament: For the love I bear to my well-beloved wife Judith, I do give unto her the use and improvement of 1-2 of my dwelling house and half of my orchard and 1-3 part of all the rest of my real estate during her life; and also the sum of £30 equal to old tenor bills of credit and 1-3 part of all my personal estate to be her own forever. I give unto my son Samuel £10 in value equal to old tenor bills of credit. And all the rest of my estate, real and personal, I give to be equally divided to and amongst all my children: my sons, Samuel, Jonathan and Isaac, and my daughter Hephzibah. And my will is that my daughter Hephzibah shall have her portion paid to her out of my moveable estate if that be sufficient (after my wife's dower, before mentioned, and my debts are paid); and if that be not sufficient, then the remainder of her portion to be set out to her in my real estate or paid to her by my son Samuel one year after my decease. And whereas, I am become bound in several bonds for debts due from my son Samuel, my will is that if I or my executors are obliged to pay any money on the sd. bonds, the sum or sums which shall be so paid on sd. bonds by me or my executors out of my estate shall be accounted as part of my sd. son Samuel's portion. I appoint my sons, Samuel, Jonathan and Isaac, to be executors.

Witness: *John Humphrey,*   SAMUEL PETTEBONE, LS.
Anne Humphrey, Ruth Humphrey.

Court Record, Page 36—7 April, 1747: The last will and testament of Samuel Pettebone, late of Simsbury decd., was now exhibited in Court by Jonathan and Isaac Pettebone, executors. Proven, ordered to be recorded and kept on file. Capt. Samuel Pettebone, one of the sons and executors to the sd. will, appeals from the judgement of this Court in approving the will unto the Superior Court. Recog., £50.

Page 411-12-425.

Phelps, Abigail, Widow, Windsor. Invt. £339-18-04. Taken by John Palmer 2nd, John Wilson and John Roberts. Will dated 25 December, 1749.

I, Abigail Phelps of Windsor, do make this my last will and testament, appointing my three sons, James Phelps, Hezekiah Phelps and Joshua Phelps, sole executors: My will is that I give to my daughter Abigail Grant my green riding hood, and also my black silk crape gown and black taffety apron; and all the rest of my wearing apparrel to be equally divided between my four sons, Samuel Phelps, James Phelps, Hezekiah Phelps and Joshua Phelps. Nextly, I give to my son James one certain note due me, dated 14 April, 1749, for the sum of £28-02-00; also, one certain note due to me, dated 27 June, 1745, for the sum of £7-00-00. And one note due to me, dated 27 June, 1745, for the sum of £50-10-00, I give to my son Hezekiah. Nextly, I give to my son James my warming pan, chamber pott, my little brass kettle, and also one featherbed yt is now at his house; and all the rest of my moveable estate I give to my two sons, Hezekiah Phelps and Joshua Phelps, only they shall get my granddaughter Esther Phelps a pare of gold jewells, and my granddaughter Ellenor Phelps a silver hair pegg. Nextly: I give to my son James my right in the lottment of land I have in the Great Meadow in Windsor that was my mother's, Abigail Eno, late of Windsor decd. Nextly, I give to my son Hezekiah my right in that lott of land that I have in Wintingbury, that was my sd. mother's land. Nextly: I give to my son Joshua all my right of land that I have in Torrington, that was my sd. mother's land.

Witness: *John Palmer 3rd,*   ABIGAIL X PHELPS, LS.
Jerusha Palmer, Samuel Eno.

Court Record, Page 138—6 June, 1750: The last will and testament of Abigail Phelps, late of Windsor, was now exhibited in Court. Proved and approved.

Phelps, David. Court Record, Page 67—6 June, 1748: An inventory of the estate of David Phelps, late of Lebanon, in Windham County, decd., which lyes in Stafford, in the County of Hartford, was now exhibited in Court by Jedediah Phelps, Adms. Accepted and ordered recorded and kept on file. Now moved that distributors may be appointed. This Court appoint Zebulon West, Esq., of Tolland, John Pasco and Nathaniel Braman of Stafford, distributors: To the heirs of Joseph Phelps, late of Lebanon decd., 1-8 part; to Aaron Phelps of Hebron, 1-8 part; to Moses Phelps of Summers, Nathaniel Phelps, Sarah Phelps alias Blackman, Miriam Phelps alias Bingham, Eunice Phelps alias Peese, and to Hannah Phelps, heirs to sd. estate, to each of them 1-8 part of sd. estate; and make return of their doings to this Court.

Page 69—24 May, 1748: The inventory of lands lying in Stafford, in Hartford County, belonging to David Phelps, formerly of Lebanon decd.: We the subscribers, being appointed by the Adms., have apprised as followeth: That is to say, 182 acres of land, value £586-00-00 old tenor. John Pasco and Nathaniel Braman. The above inventory was exhibited 6 June, 1748, by Jedediah Phelps. Ordered to be recorded.

Page 108-9—3 October, 1749: Report of the distributors. Accepted and ordered on file.

Page 368-9-70.

Phelps, Joseph, Simsbury. Died 20 January, 1749-50. Invt. £1165-02. Taken by Andrew Robe, Jonathan Pettebone and Amos Wilcocks. Will dated 21st December, 1749.

I, Joseph Phelps of Simsbury, in the County of Hartford, do make this my last will and testament: After my funeral charges and just debts are paid, for the love I bear to my well-beloved wife Mary, I do give unto her my brass kettle, my great Bible, and my featherbed with the furniture thereunto belonging, viz., two pare of sheets, and with it my bed called Tom's bed, with the furniture belonging to it, to be her own forever; and also I do give unto her the use and service of my negro man Tom during her life. Also I do give unto my sd. wife 1-3 part of all my remaining personal estate, to be her own forever. Also I give unto her the use of all my buildings and improved lands during life. I give unto my son Joseph £10, to be paid unto him out of my moveable estate equal to old tenor bills, over and above what I have already given him by deed. I do give to my son Amos my lands lying in Farmingtown, viz., land that I bought of my son Joseph, and the lands that I bought of Daniel Andruss, and the land that I bought of Joseph Woodford; and also my division land lying in Simsbury, about 7 acres. I do give unto my son David 10 acres of land on the north side of my meadow lott, in breadth 20 rods and in length from the river eastward 80 rods, bounded north on land of Capt. James Cornish, west on the river, south and east upon land that I have given to my son Amos; and also all my land lying on the hill east of Weatogue House, and all my land lying on the North Mountain north of the siding way as it is called, both pieces bounding south on the road that leads to Hartford; and also my land on the hill which I bought of Samuel Pettebone the 2nd; and also my homelott with my buildings on it, and all my upland and marsh and meadowland adjoining to my sd. homelott, lying partly in Long Meadow as it is called, to be to him and his heirs forever. Also I give unto him my negro man Tom after the decease of my wife. Also, I do give unto my grandson Samuel Humphrey, son of my daughter Hannah decd., £10 in old tenor bills, out of my personal estate. Also, I do give him about 5 acres of land lately laid out to me at the north end of Whortlebury Hill as it is called, to be to him, his heirs and assigns forever. All the rest of my personal estate I give to my two daughters, viz., to Damarus and Elizabeth, to be equally divided between them. I appoint my wife Mary and my son Amos and my son David executors.

Witness: *John Pettebone,*   JOSEPH PHELPS, LS.
John Humphrey, Elijah Tuller.

Court Record, Page 116—6 February, 1749-50: The last will and testament of Joseph Phelps, late of Simsbury, was now exhibited in Court by Amos and David Phelps, executors. Proven.

Page 80-1.

Phelps, Noadiah, Simsbury.   Invt. £273-06-00.   Taken by Isaac Butler and Stephen Goodwin.

Court Record, Page 27—4 November, 1746: This Court grant Adms. on the estate of Noadiah Phelps, late of Simsbury decd., unto Joshua Case of Simsbury, who gave bonds with Stephen Goodwin of Simsbury of £500.

Page 50—3 November, 1747: An account of Adms. on the estate of Noadiah Phelps was now exhibited by Joshua Case, Adms.:

	£ s d
Paid in debts and charges,	91-19-05
Received,	21-16-00

Account allowed. Moved for distribution of the moveable estate:

	£ s d
Inventory of the moveable estate,	271-15-01
Add credit,	21-16-00
Debts and charges subtracted,	91-19-05
There remains to be distributed,	201-11-08
To the widow, Naomi Phelps, her thirds of moveable estate,	67-03-10
Unto Shubael Phelps, eldest son, his double share,	89-11-02
And to Noadiah Phelps, single share of sd. estate,	41-15-07

And appoint Deacon Isaac Butler, Mr. Stephen Goodwin and William Manly, of Simsbury, distributors.

Page 181-2-3-4-5, 432.

Phillips, Capt. George, Middletown. Invt. £24,734-13-03. Taken 5 March, 1747-8, by Benjamin Adkins, Jonathan Allin and Thomas Goodwin. Additional inventory, £2423-06-00. Taken 12 March, 1755, by Ephraim Adkins and Jonathan Allin.

Court Record, Page 62—24 March, 1748: This Court grant Adms. on the estate of Capt. George Phillips, late of Middletown, unto George Phillips, son of the sd. decd., who gave bonds with Capt. Nathaniel Hooker. Exhibited an inventory, which was ordered recorded and kept on file.

Page 87—2 February, 1748-9: Mr. George Phillips of Middletown, Adms. on the estate of Capt. George Phillips, late of Middletown, now moved for distribution of the real and personal estate: Whereupon this Court appoint Jonathan Allin, Thomas Goodwin and William Rockwell of Middletown to distribute both real and personal estate: To George Phillips, son of the sd. decd., a double share or part; and to Jabez Hamlin, Esq., in right of his wife, who survived her father the sd. decd., 1-4 part of the moveable estate; and to the heirs of Hope Phillips, alias Lord, 1-4 part of the moveable estate and 1-4 part of the real estate of the sd. decd.; and also to the heirs of Margaret Phillips, alias Hamlin, 1-4 part of the real estate; and make return of their doings to this Court.

Page 54 (Vol. XVII) 15 March, 1755: Epaphras Lord, Esq., guardian to Samuel Phillips Lord and Hope Lord (alias Jones), minors, children of Mrs. Hope Phillips, alias Lord, showing to this Court that there is in the distribution of the estate of Capt. George Phillips some lands distributed to the sd. minors which lies in common between them, moves to this Court that suitable persons may be appointed to assist him in dividing the lands: Whereupon this Court appoint Major Jabez Hamlin, Doctor Abijah More and George Philips, of Middletown, to assist sd. guardian in making division between sd. minors, dividing 2-3 thereof to the sd. Samuel Philips Lord, and 1-3 to Hope Lord alias Jones, and make return thereof to this Court. George Philips, Adms., exhibited an account of his Adms. Accepted. Order for distribution, viz.:

	£ s d
To George Philips, only son,	1153-18-00
To the heirs of Hope Philips, alias Lord,	576-19-00
To Major Jabez Hamlin, in right of his wife Margaret,	576-19-00

And appoint Jonathan Allin, William Rockwell and Abijah Moore distributors. Also, a report of the distributors, viz., Jonathan Allin and Thomas Goodwin, of their distribution of a part of the estate. Account accepted.

Page 71—23 June, 1755: Epaphrus Lord, Esq., guardian to Samuel Phillips Lord, a minor, and Hope Lord (alias Jones), heirs to one-quarter part of the estate of Capt. George Phillips, late of Middletown decd. (in right of their mother, Mrs. Hope Phillips, alias Lord, who was one of the heirs of the estate of the said George Phillips decd.), moves to this Court that the estate descended to them in right of their mother from the said George Phillips may be distributed to them according to law: Whereupon this Court appoint Major Jabez Hamlin, George Phillips and Doctor Abijah Moore distributors.

Page 178.

Pinney, Sarah, Windsor. Invt. £148-16-05. Taken 26 January, 1747-8, by Joseph Gaylord, Nathaniel Haydon and Peletiah Allyn.

Court Record, Page 56—21st January, 1747-8: This Court grant Adms. on the estate of Sarah Pinney, late of Windsor decd., unto Noah Pinney of Windsor, who gave bonds with William Pratt of Hartford of £500.

Page 88—7 February, 1748-9: An account of Adms. on the estate of Sarah Pinney was now exhibited in Court by Noah Pinney, Adms.: Paid in debts and charges, £62-01-02. Which account is allowed and ordered to be kept on file.

Page 95—1st Tuesday in April, 1749: A further account of Adms. on the estate of Sarah Pinney was now exhibited by Noah Pinney, upon which accot. this Court allow him for boarding, tendance and care of his sister Sarah decd., 23 weeks in time of her sickness at about 50 shillings per week, £60; and Court fees for trial, the case being long in debate, 12 shillings 4 pence old tenor.

Page 34 (Vol. XVI) 27 August, 1751: Noah Pinney, Adms., having finished his account of Adms., this Court do now order distribution of the moveable estate to and amongst the heirs of the deceased. And appoint Capt. Peletiah Allyn, Lt. Samuel Stiles and Return Strong distributors to distribute to the heirs, viz.: to Daniel, Noah, Isaac and Humphrey Pinney, Mary and Hannah, sisters of sd. deceased, and make return of their doings to this Court.

Page 52—4 February, 1752: Report of the distributors.

Page 72-3-4-5-114.

Pitkin, Ozias, Hartford. Died 30 January, 1746-7. Invt. £717-13-00. Taken 10 April, 1747, by Nehemiah Olmsted and Joseph Cowles. Will dated 22 November, 1746.

I, Ozias Pitkin of Hartford, do make this my last will and testament: I give unto my wife Esther Pitkin and to my daughter Ruth Pitkin, in equal parts, all my moveable goods within my house that are provided for and proper for housekeeping, and also £50 old tenor in part of what is due from Caleb Bull by note. The 1-2 of the household and of the £50 above mentioned to be set out by my sd. wife to my daughter Ruth when she shall come to the age of 18 years. Further-more, I give unto my wife my two oldest cows, the half of 2 steers, black heifer, two calves, 10 sheep, the cart, horse, saddle and bridle, 1-2 of the cart plow, and all team tackling, and so much hay as shall be sufficient to keep sd. stock through the winter now approaching, and the large Bible. I give unto my sd. wife the use of the south end of my dwelling, from the bottom to the top, and the use of the stairs to go up, and the use of half the cellar, and use of the oven as she shall have occasion, and the use of the well and of half the new barn and cow house, and the use of 1-3 part of all my improvable land during her natural life, and the liberty of cutting necessary firewood and timber on any part of my woodland during her natural life. I give to my wife the use of all the land given to my three youngest sons, Isaac, Daniel and James, until they shall be put apprentices or shall attain the age of 21 years respectively. Also, I give unto my wife and my daughter Ruth equally all the rent due to me from my estate in which I am interested on the west side of the Great River, and what is due to me for the re-building of a warehouse on that side of the river. I give unto my wife two pare of stilyards and a pare of wool cards. And being desirous that my son Ozias Pitkin and my wife and four youngest children may keep together in a family state, I commit to the care of my wife, to be im-proved in housekeeping, all the following particulars: All my English and Indian corne, barley and malt, flax and wool, woolen and linen cloth and yarn, cider and barrels, beef, pork and tallow, all sorts of tubs, and butter and cheese, and all eatables within doors, all hides and leather for shoose, with salt, and all my swine, with the forks and rakes and axes. And I leave with her all my wearing apparrel which I have not given to my two eldest sons, to be improved for my three youngest sons. And my house, especially the kitchen, being much decayed, I leave it to be sold by my sd. wife and my son Ozias. One heifer and all my sheep which I have not particularly given in this my will to be im-proved in bringing my shop over the cellar now covered with the kitchen, and conforming the cellar wall to it in finishing sd. shop within, and making a convenient way out of the east side of the south part of my house into sd. cellar, etc. And £10 more to be paid by my executors in old tenor out of my money if the former sum be not sufficient. I give to my son Samuel Pitkin several parcels of land (adjoining proprietors being Disborow Spencer, John Pitkin, Jonathan Pitkin, Nehemiah Olm-sted, Benjamin Roberts and Joseph Case). I give to my son Ozias Pitkin, besides what I have given him by deed, the 1-2 of my homestead besides what I have given to my son Samuel. I give unto my son Isaac Pitkin the remaining part of my homelott (adjoining proprietors being William Pitkin, Esq., Joseph Case, James Easton, Jonathan Stanly, Nehemiah Olmsted and the heirs of John Case). I give unto my son Daniel Pitkin in lands. I give unto my son James Pitkin in lands (some adjoining proprietors being Joseph Case, Jonathan and William Stanly, John Bidwell, Jr., Joseph and Stephen Olmsted). I give unto my daughters, Abigail Bidwell, Elizabeth Olmsted, Mary Pratt and Hannah Olmsted, each of them £10 bills of credit, to be old tenor. And whereas my daughter Martha Eels hath not had so much of my estate as my other daughters, I give unto her my youngest cow and 10 sheep, and also £10 in bills of credit of old tenor. I give unto my daughter Ruth my white-faced cow and 5 sheep besides what I have given her before, and hay to keep them through the coming winter. I give all my books of divinity to be equally divided between my wife and all my children. I appoint my son Samuel Pitkin executor and my wife Esther Pitkin executrix.

Witness: *Joseph Pitkin,*   OZIAS PITKIN, LS.
John Pitkin, Joseph Pitkin, Jr.

Court Record, Page 37—7 April, 1747: The last will and testament of Ozias Pitkin, Esq., late of Hartford, was now exhibited in Court by Esther Pitkin and Samuel Pitkin, executors.

Proven and ordered to be recorded and kept on file.

Page 261.

Pitkin, Roger, Hartford. Will dated 1st January, 1733-4: I, Roger Pitkin, Sen., of Hartford, do make this my last will and testament: I give to my son-in-law John Bidwell 2 acres of land next adjoining to his upland lott that he had of me, and on the east side of it, the breadth of sd. lott, which two acres I have reserved out of the deeds of gift of my sons Jonathan and Roger Pitkin. I give to my son Caleb Pitkin 5 shillings. I give to my two grandchildren (children of Timothy Porter which he had by daughter Mary) 5 shillings. And I give to my daughter Rachel, the wife of Joseph House, 5 shillings. I give to my daughter Mabel, the wife of James Porter, 5 shillings. I give to my son Jonathan Pitkin my meadow lott known by the name of Disbro's lott, and 1-2 of my meadow land in the pasture (the south part of it), and 1-2 of my land in the Five Miles, the whole being 25 acres. I give to my son Roger Pitkin my meadow lott that lyeth in Podunck pasture, also half of my meadow land in the pasture, and half of my lands in the Five Miles. And I give to my two sons, Jonathan Pitkin and Roger Pitkin, all my book debts and all other estate that I have that is moveable. Also I make my two sons, Jonathan Pitkin and Roger Pitkin, executors.

Witness: *Ozias Pitkin,*   ROGER PITKIN, LS.
Daniel Pitkin, Elizabeth Pitkin.

Court Record, Page 88—23 January, 1748-9: The last will and testament of Capt. Roger Pitkin, late of Hartford, was now exhibited in Court by Jonathan and Roger Pitkin. Proven.

Page 179-80-1-314.

Pitkin, Samuel, Hartford. Died 20 June, 1747. Invt. £3627-06-03. Taken 30 October, 1747, by William Cowles, David Hills and Jonathan

Stanly. Inventory reckoned equal to silver at 53 shillings per ounce. Additional inventory of land in Coventry, 19 acres, £24. Taken 29 May, 1755, by Peter Bewell and Jehiel Rose.

Court Record, Page 42—7 July, 1747: This Court grant Adms. on the estate of Samuel Pitkin, late of Hartford, unto Hannah Pitkin, relict, and Capt. John Pitkin of Hartford, who gave bonds with Peter Bewell of Coventry of £1000.

Page 95—4th April, 1749: This Court appoint Timothy Kimball and Hannah his wife to be guardians to Hannah Pitkin, a minor, 8 years, and Elizabeth, 4 years of age, children of Samuel Pitkin deceased. Recog., £600 for each minor.

Page 121—26 March, 1750: Timothy Kimball and Hannah his wife, guardians to the children of Samuel Pitkin, now moved to this Court that freeholders be appointed to assist the sd. guardians in dividing a certain lott of land in Hartford belonging to the heirs of Ozias Pitkin, which lies as tenants in common: Whereupon this Court appoint David Hills, William Stanly and Stephen Olmsted, of Hartford, to assist the sd. guardians in making division of such lands as belong to the heirs of sd. Ozias Pitkin decd. and sd. minors, that they may be able to improve such land separate, agreeable to the law of this Colony. And also set out to Hannah, the relict of Samuel Pitkin decd., now the wife of Dr. Timothy Kimball, her right of dowry, viz., 1-3 part of the buildings and lands of the sd. Samuel Pitkin decd. for her improvement during life, and make return thereof to this Court.

Page 66 (Vol. XVII) 3 June, 1755: An account of Adms. was now exhibited in Court by Col. John Pitkin and Mr. Timothy Kimball in behalf of his wife. Account accepted.

Page 139—18 March, 1757: Timothy Kimball, in behalf of his wife, Adms., now moves for a distribution: Whereupon this Court appoint Stephen Olmsted, David Hills and William Stanly, of Hartford, to distribute the estate, giving to Mrs. Hannah Kimball, wife of Timothy Kimball, 1-3 of the moveable estate, and to Hannah Pitkin, only child of the deceased, 2-3 of the estate.

Page 152-3-155.

Plumb, Benoni, Middletown. Invt. £3664-13-10. Taken 31 December, 1747, by Benjamin Adkins, Jacob Whitmore and Jonathan Allin. Additional inventory, £16-01-00. Taken 30 September, 1755, by Ebenezer Doolittle and Stephen Hotchkiss.

Court Record, Page 54—5 January, 1747-8: This Court grant Adms. on the estate of Benoni Plumb, late of Middletown decd., unto Rebeckah Plumb, widow, who gave bonds with Benjamin Adkins of Middletown of £1000.

Page 88 (Vol. XVI) 25 February, 1753: An account of Adms. was now exhibited in Court by Rebeckah Plumb, Adms. Accepted. This Court appoint Benjamin Adkins, Jonathan Allin and Jacob Whitmore to distribute the estate, viz: to Rebeckah Plumb, widow, her thirds; to Daniel Plumb, a double share; to Benoni Plumb, youngest son, his single share of sd. estate; and also set out to the widow 1-3 part of the buildings and lands for her improvement during life.

Page 111—5 November, 1754: Report of the distributors.

Porter, David. Court Record, Page 98—2 May, 1749: This Court grant Adms. on the estate of David Porter, late of Farmingtown, unto Anne Porter, widow and relict, who gave bonds with Joseph Hart of Farmingtown of £1000.

Page 317-364.

Porter, Martha, Widow, Farmington. Invt. £415-01-00. Taken 2 August, 1749, by William Wadsworth and Elisha Lewis. Will dated 3 April, 1741.

I, Martha Porter, of the Town of Farmingtown, do make this my last will and testament: All my estate whatsoever, after my just debts are paid, I give and bequeath the whole to my loving and obliging sister Ruth Root, widow, to be her own and her heirs forever. And I do hereby constitute my aforenamed sister Ruth Root and her son John Smith to be executors.

Witness: *John Hooker,*   MARTHA X PORTER.
Abigail X Hooker, Mary Hooker.

Codicil, dated 20 December, 1742: Be it known to all men by these presents: That whereas I, Martha Porter of Farmingtown, widow and relict of John Porter, lately decd., have made and declared my last will and testament in writing, bearing date the 3rd day of April, 1749, I, the sd. Martha Porter, do by this present codicil confirm and ratify my sd. last will and testament, and do make this little addition to the sd. will: I do constitute and ordain my loving kinsman Ebenezer Porter of sd. Farmingtown (with whome I now dwell) to be an executor added to the other two mentioned in my sd. will, meaning that this codicil be and be judged to be part and parcel of my sd. will.

Witness: *John Hooker.*   MARTHA X PORTER, LS.
Mercy Hooker.

Court Record, Page 105—1st August, 1749: The last will and testament of Martha Porter, late of Farmington, was now exhibited in Court by Ebenezer Porter and John Smith, two of the executors, making request to have it recorded, which this Court grant.

Page 121—6 March, 1749-50: An inventory of the estate of Widow Martha Porter, late of Farmingtown, was now exhibited in Court by Ebenezer Porter, which inventory this Court accepts.

Page 158.

Porter, Nathaniel, Hartford. Invt. £246-02-08. Taken 16 November, 1747, by Samuel Smith and Jonathan Stanly.

Court Record, Page 32—3 February, 1746-7: This Court grant Adms. on the estate of Nathaniel Porter, late of Hartford, unto David Porter of sd. Hartford, who gave bonds with John Kilbourn of £500.

Page 57—2 February, 1747-8: An inventory of the estate of Nathaniel Porter, late of Hartford decd., was exhibited by David Porter, Adms. Accepted.

Page 49.

Pratt, John, Hartford. Will dated 18 March, 1741-2: I, John Pratt of Hartford, being advanced to old age, do make this my last will and testament: Imprimis: I give to my grandson Ozias Pratt, the son of my son John Pratt decd., the house and half the homelott on which sd. house standeth (in which my sd. son John dwelt), the south side thereof, to run through sd. lott from east to west, butting east on the highway and south on the heirs of Thomas Dickinson decd. Also, I give to him my sd. grandson one lott of land on the east side of the country road in Hartford, known by the name of the Neck lott, which I bought of John Olcott. Also, I give to sd. Ozias Pratt one lott of land in Hartford in the Little Ox Pasture, butting east on a highway leading into the wilderness, north on land of Caleb Stanly decd., and south on Richard Goodwin's land. Also, I give to the sd. Ozias Pratt one lott of land in the Long Meadow, butting east on the Connecticut River, west upon land (——————————), north on land belonging to Nathaniel Goodwin, and south on land belonging to Obadiah Spencer. All which several pieces of land I give to my sd. grandson Ozias Pratt forever. I give to my grandson John Pratt, son of my son John Pratt, late of Hartford, the north half part of the homelott on which my sd. son John dwelt, butting east on the country road leading to Windsor and west on land belonging to the heirs of Thomas Butler decd. Also, I give to my sd, grandson John Pratt one piece of land in Brick Hill Swamp which I bought of Samuel Welles, butting west on a highway, running north, south and east on land belonging to Obadiah Spencer, and north on land belonging to Thomas Burr. Which sd. pieces of land I give to my sd. grandson John forever. I give to my grandson Isaac Pratt, son of my son John, all my right in that tract of land on the east side of the Great River in Hartford called the Five Miles, to be to him and at his dispose forever. I give to my son William Pratt my dwelling house and homestead in Hartford which butts east and west on a highway, north on Maynard Day's, and southerly on land I have already conveyed to him by deed, which I give to him and his eldest male heir forever. Also, I give my sd. son William my lott of land in the upper end of the North Meadow in Hartford, which butts east on land partly belonging to

Ozias Goodwin and part on Maynard Day's land, and west on upland, northerly on the heirs of Daniel Pratt decd., and southerly on the heirs of Capt. Aaron Cook decd. I give this to him my sd. son William and to his eldest male heirs successively forever. Also, I give to my son William one lott in the lower end of the North Meadow adjoining heirs of Samuel Olcott deceased. Also, I give him my son William my Blue Hill lott so called, adjoining land of the heirs of Capt. Aaron Cook and of Ozias Goodwin. I give to my son William my whole right of land in the Township of Hartland, to him and his heirs forever. Also, I give my son William my right in the old mills in Hartford. I give to my two daughters, Hannah Porter and Esther Talcott, besides what they have already had, £20 apiece in moveable estate. I give to my granddaughter Susannah Talcott my feather bed and boulster, also my warming pan, also my chest marked with "W. G. S." on the foreside thereof, which I give her as a token of my love. I appoint my son William to be sole executor, and order him to pay and discharge all my just debts and the legacies given to each of my daughters.

Witness: *Maynard Day,*   JOHN PRATT, LS.
Ozias Goodwin, Richard Goodman.

Whereas, I, John Pratt of Hartford, have made and declared my last will and testament, dated 18 March, 1741-2, as may be seen on this paper, and therein gave land to the children of my son John Pratt decd., I now make this alteration: I give to Hannah, the widow of my sd. son John decd., her right of dowry in the lands so given to the children of my sd. son, that is, 1-3 thereof, for her improvement so long as she remains his widow. And further, the legacies I ordered my son William to pay to Hannah Porter and Esther Talcott shall be reckoned and accounted to them according to the value of bills of the old tenor when my foregoing will was made and declared. 15 December, 1744.

Witness: *Nathaniel Goodwin,*   JOHN X PRATT, LS.
Maynard Day, Joseph Talcott.

Court Record, Page 38—5 May, 1747: The last will and testament of Mr. John Pratt, late of Hartford decd., was now exhibited in Court by William Pratt, son of the sd. decd. Will proven and ordered to be recorded and kept on file.

Pratt, William. Court Record, Page 17—16 July, 1746: Zachariah Pratt, 19 years of age, son of William Pratt of Hartford, chose his uncle Joseph Talcott of Hartford to be his guardian. Recog., £200.

Page 125-6-7.

Ranny, Mary, Mrs., Middletown. Invt. £313-11-11. Taken 27 October, 1747, by Joseph Smith and Joseph Savage. Will dated 23 September, 1747.

I, Mary Ranny, widow of Joseph Ranny decd., of Middletown, in the County of Hartford, do make this my last will and testament: I give to my son Joseph Ranny all my sheep and one of my hogs. My velvet hood I give to my son Joseph's wife, and also my panel. I give to my son Daniel Ranny one of my hogs. I give to my son Jonathan Ranny all the Indian corn I have growing this year. I give to my daughters, Abigail Stocking and Sibell Porter, my best bed and furniture and my other bed and furniture, and four pare of sheets, small iron pott, small iron kettle, a brass skillett, a brass kettle, a warming pan and all my pewter besides what is hereafter mentioned, with my chest of drawers and table, and also my wearing apparrel. I give to my grandchild Edward Shepherd my cow. I give to my grandchildren, Lucy Stocking and Grace Stocking, two pares of sheets to each of them, to be delivered to them when they shall arrive at the age of 18 years. I give to my daughters Abigail and Sibel, to each of them, one of my pewter platters and two plates apiece, and three spoons apiece. If there be anything I have not disposed of in this my will, I give it to my sons, Joseph, Daniel and Jonathan, to be equally divided between them, after the charges of the sickness and funeral are paid out of it. I appoint my son Joseph Ranny my executor.

Witness: *Edward Eells,*　　　　　MARY X RANNY, LS.
Isaac Lee, Francis Wilcock, Jr.

Court Record, Page 48—3 November, 1747: The last will and testament of Mary Ranny, late of Middletown, was now exhibited in Court by Joseph Ranny, executor. Proven.

Page 339-40.

Rich, David, of New Cambridge, in Farmington. Invt. £750-17-11. Taken 24 October, 1748, by Hezekiah Rew and Gershom Tuttle. Will dated 23 February, 1747-8.

I, David Rich of New Cambridge, in Farmingtown, in the County of Hartford, do make this my last will and testament: My will is that my son Samuel Rich shall have out of my farm on which I now dwell so much or so big a part as would have been valued at £45 at that time when I bought sd. farm, which sd. £45 worth of land is not to be reckoned to him as portion, but as his proper due by purchase. I give to my beloved wife Elizabeth, whom I make my sole executrix, 1-2 of my household goods and moveable estate free and clear of any incumbrances whatsoever, to dispose of as she pleaseth, and the improvement of 1-2 of the house in which I now live, and 1-3 part of my farm, so long as she remains my widow, but no longer. And also my will is that she have the ordering or disposal of all or any part of my estate until all my lawful debts are paid, and then my will is that what remains shall be returned or delivered to my children in form or manner hereafter mentioned, viz., that my son Samuel Rich and my daughter Sarah Rich shall have such a portion or proportion out of my estate as shall make them equal to the rest of my children. And then, if there should be any remaining, my will is that it should be divided amongst all my children according to the discretion of my executrix.

Witness: *Gershom Tuttle,*   DAVID RICH, LS.
James Naughton, Hezekiah Rew.

Court Record, Page 109—3 October, 1749: The last will and testament of David Rich, late of Farmingtown, was now exhibited in Court by Elizabeth Rich, executrix. Proven.

Page 36.

Richards, Jonah, New Hartford. Invt. £256-02-00. Taken 25 June, 1746, by Isaac Kellogg, Martin Smith and Ephraim Wilcocks.

Court Record, Page 20—5 August, 1746: This Court grant Adms. on the estate of Jonah Richards, late of New Hartford, unto Mary Richards, widow, who gave bonds with Deacon Thomas Richards of Hartford of £500.

Page 98—2 May, 1749: Hezekiah Richards, 17 years of age, and Amey Richards, 12 years, children of Jonah Richards, chose their mother Mary Richards to be their guardian. Also, this Court appoint the sd. Mary guardian to Hannah, 10 years of age, and Timothy, 9 years, both children of the sd. deceased. Recog., £300 for each minor.

Invt. in Vol. XVI, Page 29.

Richards, Deacon Thomas, Hartford. Invt. £252-03-01. Taken 3 September, 1750, by Ebenezer Webster and Daniel Seymour.

Court Record, Page 139—1st September, 1750: Adms. granted unto Benjamin Richards of sd. Hartford, who gave bonds.

Page 353-4.

Riley, Jacob, Wethersfield. Died 27 September, 1748. Invt. £371-03-09. Taken by Gideon Goodrich and Nathaniel Robbins.

Court Record, Page 114—2 January, 1749-50: This Court grants Adms. on the estate of Jacob Riley, late of Wethersfield decd., unto Abigail Riley, widow of the sd. decd., who gave bonds with John Warner of Wethersfield of £1000.

Dist. File: Estate of Jacob Riley, Wethersfield, 9 February, 1761: To Jabesh, to Jacob, to Ackley Riley, to Hezekiah Robbins and Mille his wife. By John Robbins, Jr., and Jonathan Deming.

Page 134.

Roberts, Samuel 2nd, Middletown. Invt. £46-11-00. Taken 4 July, 1747, by Ephraim Adkins and William Rockwell.

Court Record, Page 41—7 July, 1747: Samuel Roberts, Adms. on the estate of Samuel Roberts ye 2nd, late of Middletown, in the County of Hartford, decd., informs this Court that he suspects the estate is insolvent, and prays that commissioners may be appointed to adjust the claims of the creditors: Whereupon this Court appoint William Rockwell, Ephraim Adkins and John Bacon, commissioners.

Page 69—6 June, 1748: A report of the commissioners on the estate of Samuel Roberts 2nd, which account is accepted. Also exhibited by Samuel Roberts, Adms., an account of Adms., which is allowed and ordered to be kept on file.

Page 77—4 October, 1748: This Court appoint Samuel Roberts of Middletown to be guardian to Elizabeth Roberts, age 7 years. and Phebe 6 years, children of Samuel Roberts, Jr., deceased. Recog., £500.

Page 83-4-5-6.

Rockwell, John, Windsor. Invt. £430-07-00. Taken 18 December, 1746, by Joseph Loomis, Thomas Grant and Daniel Bissell. Will dated 31 August, 1743.

I, John Rockwell of Windsor, being old and infirm, do make this my last will and testament: I give to my wife Anne my best bed and furniture and £30 out of my personal estate at inventory price, being in such things as she is pleased to make choice of; all this to be over and above her right of dowry in my houseing and lands. I give to my son Daniel Rockwell all that parcel of land on which now he lives, being about one·mile and 3-4 in length and 31 rods in breadth (74 acres), with my house and barn thereon standing, to him and his heirs forever. I give to my son Ebenezer Rockwell 33 acres of that piece of land on which I now dwell, with the buildings thereon standing, reserving the use of the northern lower room or parlour for my daughter Anne Rockwell, which I give to her for her use so long as she remains unmarried. I give to my son Joel Rockwell all my land lying in the Township of Cornwell already laid out, also all my right, interest, share and part to and in the undivided land not yet laid out in sd. Township of Cornwell, to him and his heirs forever. I give to my sons Danied Rockwell and David Rockwell and to my son Joel Rockwell 20 acres of that parcel of land on which I now dwell, lying in the eastern part, to begin by my son Ebenezer Rockwell's land end, to them and their heirs forever, share and share alike. I give to my son Daniel Rockwell, to my son David Rockwell, to my son Ebenezer Rockwell, and to my son Joel Rockwell, all my, right, interest, share and part to and in the land called the Equivalent Land, also all my right in the common land, to them and their heirs forever, share and share alike. My will is that my son Daniel Rockwell shall pay to my daughter Anne Rockwell, £21-05-00 old tenor; and to my daughter Mary, the wife of Isaac Norton, the sum of £1 old tenor; and to my daughter Abigail, the wife of Joseph Stedman, £1 old tenor; and to my daughter Martha Rockwell, £18-15-00 old tenor; and to my daughter Rachel Rockwell, £18-15-00 old tenor. My will also is that my son David Rockwell shall pay to my daughter Anne Rockwell £21-05-00 old tenor; and to my daughter Mary, wife of Isaac Norton, 20 shillings old tenor; and to my daughter Abigail, wife of Joseph Stedman, 20 shillings; to my daughter Martha Rockwell £18-15-00 old tenor; to my daughter Rachel Rockwell, £18-15-00 old tenor. And Ebenezer Rockwell and Joel Rockwell each of them to pay such sums to each of their sisters as above mentioned. After my just debts and funeral expenses are paid, all the rest of my estate, both real and personal, I give and bequeath to my four sons and five daughters, Daniel Rockwell, David Rockwell, Ebenezer Rockwell, Joel Rockwell, Anne Rockwell, Mary the wife of Isaac Norton, Abigail the wife of Joseph Stedman, Martha Rockwell and Rachel Rockwell, to them and their heirs forever, share and share alike. I appoint my brother-in-law Joseph Stedman and my son Daniel Rockwell to be my executors.

Witness: *James Wolcott,*   JOHN ROCKWELL, LS.
Nathaniel Bancroft, Matthew Rockwell.

Court Record, Page 30—6 January, 1746-7: The last will and testament of John Rockwell, late of Windsor decd., was now exhibited in Court by Daniel Rockwell and Joseph Stedman, executors. Proven.

Rockwell, Joseph. Court Record, Page 42—2 June, 1747: Samuel Rockwell, a minor, 18 years of age, son of Joseph Rockwell, Jr., late of Windsor deceased, chose James Rockwell of Windsor to be his guardian. Recog., £400.

From Record on File:

7 June, 1764: A distribution of the real estate of Joseph Rockwell, Sen., late of Windsor, deceased, lying in the Township of Colebrook, in Litchfield County, as made by us, the subscribers, appointed thereto by an order of the Court of Probate for the District of Hartford:

Set out to the heirs of Joseph Rockwell, Jr., late of Windsor deceased, one-third part, viz.: the first division lot in sd. Colebrook laid out to the heirs of sd. Joseph Rockwell, Sen., deceased; also, 6 chains and 43 links in width to run the length of the lot in the second division, bounded south by land set out to James Rockwell, and north by land set out to Erastus Wolcott, Esq.

Set out to James Rockwell one-third part, viz.: the third division lot in sd. Colebrook laid out to the heirs of sd. Rockwell deceased; also, 5 chains and 59 links in width, to lay the length of the second division lot laid out to the heirs of said Joseph Rockwell, Sen., deceased, in Colebrook, on the south side, bounding north by land set out to the heirs of Joseph Rockwell, Jr., deceased.

Set out to Erastus Wolcott, Esq., by purchase from Charles, Benjamin and Miriam Rockwell, one-third part, viz.: 20 chains and 98 links in width on the north side of the second division lot in Colebrook, to lay the length of sd. lot, bounded south by land set out to the heirs of Joseph Rockwell, Jr. Also, the addition lot or the fourth division lot, as laid out to the heirs of Joseph Rockwell, Sen., deceased.

> *Nathaniel Loomis,* } *Distributors.*
> *John Loomis,*

From Record on File:

7 June, 1764: A distribution of the real estate of Joseph Rockwell, Jr., late of Windsor deceased, lying in the Township of Colebrook, in Litchfield County.

Set out to Nathaniel Porter, by purchase from Joseph Rockwell, Jr., one-fifth, as laid out to the heirs of Joseph Rockwell, Sen.

Set out to Samuel Rockwell two-fifths, one on his own right and one by purchase from Jonathan Rockwell, land laid out to the heirs of Joseph Rockwell, Jr.

Set out to Hannah, the wife of Joseph Bidwell, one-fifth part.

Set out to Jerusha Chapin one-fifth part.

> *Nathaniel Loomis,* } *Distributors.*
> *John Loomis,*

NOTE: The distribution of the land of Joseph Rockwell, Sen., was written upon one side of the paper, and that of Joseph Rockwell, Jr., was written upon the other side, both bearing the same date, and reported 25 June, 1764, and accepted by the Court in Hartford on the first Tuesday of July, 1764.

> Certified by *J. Talcott, Clerk.*

Page 330-1-2.

Rogers, Thomas, Middletown. Died 10 October, 1749. Invt. £4196-05-05. Taken by Philip Goff and Ralph Smith.

Court Record, Page 111—16 November, 1749: This Court grant Adms. on the estate of Thomas Rogers, late of Middletown decd., unto Benjamin Harris of Middletown, who gave bonds of £3000. Also exhibited an inventory. Accepted. Ordered to be recorded and kept on file.

Page 18 (Vol. XVI) 2 April, 1751: Benjamin Harris, Adms., showing to this Court that by reason of indisposition he is not able to finish his Adms. on sd. estate, this Court grant Adms. unto Jacob Whitmore of sd. Middletown, who gave bond with Ebenezer Eglestone of sd. Middletown.

Page 34—27 August, 1751: This Court appoint Ann Rogers, widow, to be guardian to Anna Rogers, a minor, 3 years of age, daughter of Thomas Rogers deceased. Recog., £500. Also the Adms. on sd. estate now exhibited an account of his Adms. Accepted.

Page 424.

Rogers, Thomas, Sen., Middletown. Died 23 September, 1749. Invt. £111-04-08. Taken 14 December, 1749, by Philip Goff and Ralph Smith.

Court Record, Page 132—5 June, 1750: This Court grant Adms. on the estate of Thomas Rogers, late of Middletown decd., unto Rebeckah Rogers, widow, who gave bonds with Stephen Sparrow of East Haddam of £500 money.

Page 131-2-3.

Root, Joseph, Sen., Farmington. Invt. £1988-11-07. Taken 19 November, 1747, by John Hooker, Judah Hart and Isaac Lee. Will dated 12 October, 1747.

I, Joseph Root, Sen., of Farmingtown, do make this my last will and testament: I give to my wife, Hannah Root, 1-3 part of my personal estate forever, and 1-3 part of my real estate during her natural life. I will to my eldest son, Samuel Root, £5 with what he hath already had. I give to my oldest daughter, Thankfull North, £3 with what she hath already had. I give to my 2nd daughter, Hannah, £150 old tenor, to be paid her within one year after my decease. I give to my 3rd daughter, Mary Smith, 10 shillings old tenor with what she hath already had. I give to my 4th daughter, Lydia Root, £150 old tenor. I will to my youngest daughter, Temperance Root, to be paid when she arrives to the age of 18 years, the sum of £150 old tenor. I give to my youngest son, Joseph Root, all the remainder of my real and personal estate, and appoint him to be sole executor.

Witness: *Judah Hart,*   JOSEPH ROOT, LS.
Isaac Lee, Gideon Griswold.

Court Record, Page 52—1st December, 1747: The last will and testament of Joseph Root, late of Farmingtown, was now exhibited in Court by Joseph Root, son and executor. Proven.

Page 96—10 April, 1749: Temperance Root, a minor, 15 years of age, daughter of Joseph Root, chose her mother Hannah Root to be her guardian. Recog., £500.

Page 243-4-249-50.

Root, Joseph, Farmington, son of Joseph Root of sd. Farmington decd. Invt. £2961-15-00. Taken 3 October, 1748, by John Hooker, Judah Hart and Isaac Lee. Will dated 20 May, 1748.

I, Joseph Root of Farmington, do make this my last will and testament: I will and bequeath to my honoured mother, Hannah Root, one certain piece of land lying near John Kelsey, butting east on John Kelsey, north on Ezra Belding, west on Robert Booth, and south on a highway; and my white horse, and my yearling colt, and one cow, one yoke of oxen and 8 sheep. I give to my sister Sarah Peck a silk hood. I give to my sister Mary Smith a silk hood. I will to my sister Temperance Root 18 acres of land on the west side of the lott that the new house standeth on, and 10 1-2 acres lying north of sd. lott, butting north on common land, east and south on Samuel Brounson; and two yoke of 3-year-old steers, 12 sheep, one cow, a two-year-old colt, and one-quarter of my moveables except creatures. I give to my cousins, Nathaniel North, Jr., and Abell Smith, one lott containing 12 acres north of the Mody Brook, butting west on Ensign Daniel Dewey, east and south on Isaac Lee, and north on a highway. And I give to Nathaniel my best coat and wascoat and breeches. And I give to Abell my plain cloth coat and wascoat, to be paid and delivered when they come of age. I give to my sister Hannah Root the house that I live in, and barn, and the lott that it stands on. I give to my sister Lydia Root my new house and the remainder of the lott it stands on. And further, I give to my sisters Hannah and Lydia Root all the remainder of my real and personal estate. And further, I constitute my sisters Hannah and Lydia Root to be sole executrixes of this my will.

Witness: *Elijah Hart,*   JOSEPH ROOT, LS.
Isaac Lee, Elnathan Ashman.

Court Record, Page 71—6 July, 1748: The last will and testament of Joseph Root, late of Farmingtown decd., was now exhibited in Court by Hannah and Lydia Root, executrixes. Will proven.

Page 133-4.

Root, Samuel, Farmington, son of Joseph Root, late of Farmington decd. Invt. £1910-00-00. Taken 25 November, 1747, by John Hooker, Judah Hart and Isaac Lee. Will dated 12 October, 1747.

I, Samuel Root of Farmingtown, do make this my last will and testament: I give to my sister Hannah Root £50 old tenor, to be paid one year after my decease. I give to my sister Lydia Root £50 old tenor. I give to my sister Temperance Root £50 old tenor, to be paid when she comes to the age of 18 years. I give to my brother Joseph Root all the remainder of my real and personal estate, ordaining my brother Joseph Root to be sole executor.

Witness: *Judah Hart,*   SAMUEL ROOT, LS.
Isaac Lee, Gideon Griswold.

Court Record, Page 52—1st December, 1747: The last will and testament of Samuel Root, late of Farmingtown, was now exhibited by Joseph Root, executor. Proven.

Page 71—6 July, 1748: Hannah Root and Lydia Root, heirs to the estate of Joseph Root and Samuel Root, late of Farmingtown decd., informing this Court that Joseph Root, Jr., executor to the last will and testament of Joseph Root of Farmingtown, is deceased, and there being no division of the estate of the sd. decd. made according to sd. will in the lifetime of the sd. executor, prays this Court to appoint freeholders to set out sd. estate, according to the will of the sd. decd., to the heirs of the sd. estate: Whereupon this Court appoint John Hooker, Judah Hart and Isaac Lee of Farmingtown to divide the estate according to the will of the sd. decd., and make return of their doings to this Court. And also sd. Hannah Root and Lydia Root further inform this Court that Samuel Root also appointed the sd. Joseph Root, Jr., decd., executor to his last will and has left no heirs except the sd. Joseph Root and three sisters, and desires the sd. John Hooker, Judah Hart and Isaac Lee to divide the estate according to his last will to sd. heirs mentioned in sd. will.

From File:

A distribution of the estates of Joseph Root and Samuel Root, both late of Farmington deceased. The order is dated 5 July, 1748, and was reported 4 October, 1748, by John Hooker, Judah Hart and Isaac Lee, distributors: Set out to Hannah Root, widow, her thirds of personal estate, etc. Set out to Hannah Root, the daughter, from her father's estate, £150; and from her brother Samuel Root's estate, £50, etc. Set out to Lydia Root £150 from her father's estate; and from her brother Samuel Root's estate, £50, etc. Set out to Temperance Root, from her father's estate, £150; and from her brother Samuel Root's estate, £50, etc. And further, Hannah Root and Lydia Root do promise to pay for us to their sisters: Thankfull North, £3 old tenor; and to Mary Smith 10 shillings; which is according to the wills.

> John Hooker, ⎱
> Judah Hart,   ⎬ Distributors.
> Isaac Lee,   ⎰

Page 380.

Rossiter, Timothy, Middletown. Invt. £381-16-03. Taken 13 March, 1749-50, by John Hurlbut, Jr., and William Rockwell.

Court Record, Page 121—6 March, 1749-50: This Court grant Adms. on the estate of Timothy Rossiter, late of Middletown deceased, unto Mary Rossiter, widow, who gave bonds with Briant Rossiter of Durham, in New Haven County.

Page 127—3 May, 1750: An inventory of the estate of Timothy Rossiter was now exhibited in Court by Mary Rossiter, Adms. Accepted. Ordered to be recorded and kept on file.

Page 330.

Rowell, Thomas, Windsor. Invt. £238-00-00, *computed old tenor at 56 shillings, with silver at 8 shillings per ounce Troy weight, sterling alloy, and apprised according to bills of old tenor.* Taken 27 October, 1749, by John Hubbard and Jonathan Olcott.

Court Record, Page 106—5 September, 1749: This Court grant Adms. on the estate of Thomas Rowell, late of Windsor decd., unto Thomas Rowell, son of the sd. decd., who gave bonds with Jonathan Olcott.

Page 109—7 November, 1749: An inventory of the estate of Thomas Rowell was now exhibited in Court by Thomas Rowell, son and Adms., who now moves that distribution may be made of the estate: Whereupon this Court appoint Lt. John Hubbard of Wintingbury Parish, and Jonathan Olcott, of Hartford, to distribute the sd. estate: To Thomas Rowell, eldest son, his double share; and to Samuel, John and Daniel Rowell, sons of the sd. decd., and to Hannah Rowell, daughter, their single shares and parts; and also set out to Violet, widow, 1-3 part of sd. estate for her improvement during life; and make return of their doings to this Court.

Page 131—25 June, 1750: A distribution of the estate of Thomas Rowell, late of Windsor decd., was now exhibited in Court by Jonathan Olcott and John Hubbard, distributors, which distribution this Court accepts and orders recorded and kept on file.

Dist. File: Windsor, 27 December, 1749: To Violet Rowell, the widow; to Thomas, to Sarah, to Hannah, to John, to Samuel, to Daniel. By John Hubbard and Jonathan Olcott.

Page 21-2-3.

Russell, John, Sen., Wethersfield. Invt. £1491-15-08. Taken 7 February, 1745-6, by Jonathan Belding, Joseph Boardman and William Bement. Will dated 6 April, 1745-6.

I, John Russell, Sen., of Wethersfield, being old and full of days, my will is: I give to my wife my great Bible. I give to my sd. wife the use of all my moveable estate (after my just debts are paid out of it) during the whole term that she shall continue my widow. I also give my wife the use of my now dwelling house and homelot, and the use of all my other land during the time she shall continue my widow. I give to my sons, John, Jonathan and Stephen Russell, all my real estate, my dwelling house and homelott and all my other land, to be equally divided between them, upon and immediately after the marriage of my sd. wife; but if she shall remain my widow during the full term of her natural life, then I give the sd. house and homelott and all my other land to my sd. three sons, to be divided as aforesd. upon the decease of my sd. wife. I give to my three daughters to each of them a large pewter platter, to be received by them after my decease. I also give to my sd. daughters all my moveable estate which I before gave to my sd. wife during the time she shall continue my widow, to be divided between them in equal proportion upon my wife's decease or marriage. I constitute and appoint my beloved wife and eldest son John Russell executor.

Witness: *Joshua Robbins,*　　　　　　JOHN RUSSELL, LS.
Ebenezer Belding, Joseph Boardman.

Court Record, Page 6—4 March, 1746: The last will and testament of John Russell, late of Middletown (Wethersfield) was now exhibited in Court by John Russell and Susannah Russell, widow and son. Proven.

Page 102.

Russell, William, Windsor (in the Parish of Ellington). Invt. £367-19-08. Taken by John Burroughs and Timothy Nash.

Court Record, Page 17—1st July, 1746: This Court grant Adms. on the estate of William Russell, late of Windsor decd., unto Elizabeth Russell, widow, who gave bonds with Ebenezer Russell of Windsor of £500.

Page 44—4 August, 1747: An account of Adms. on the estate of William Russell, late of Windsor, was now exhibited in Court by Elizabeth Russell, Adms.: Paid in debts and charges, £90-06-04 old tenor. Account is allowed and ordered to be kept on file.

Page 414-15.

Sabin, David, Enfield. Invt. £1087-19-06. Taken by Israel Peck and John Booth.

Court Record, Page 137—7 August, 1750: This Court grants Adms. on the estate of David Sabin, late of Enfield deceased, unto Mary Sabin, widow of the sd. deceased, who gave bonds.

Page 70 (Vol. XVI) 4 August, 1750: Thomas Sabin, a minor, about 17 years of age, son of David Sabin, chose Ezekiel Peese of Enfield to be his guardian. Recog., £500.

Page 125 (Vol. XVII) 17 September, 1756: David Sabin, a minor, age 16 years, son of David Sabin, chose his uncle Samuel Remington to be his guardian. Recog., £300.

Page 253-4-5-6.

Sage, Ebenezer, Middletown. Invt. £13,970-04-03. Taken 27 December, 1748, by Jabez Hamlin, Jonathan Allyn and William Rockwell. Court Record, Page 82—6 December, 1748: This Court grants Adms. on the estate of Ebenezer Sage, late of Middletown, unto Hannah Sage, widow, who gave bonds with William Rockwell of £500.

Page 2 (Vol. XVI) 24 August, 1750: Ebenezer Sage, a minor, son of Ebenezer Sage, chose his father-in-law, Michael Burnham, to be his guardian. Recog., £500.

Page 16—14 March, 1750-1: Capt. Michael Burnham, in right of his wife Hannah, the Adms., exhibited an account of Adms. Accepted. Amount for distribution, £19,882-13-05. This Court order a dist. of the estate, viz.:

	£ s d
To Hannah Sage, alias Burnham, relict,	4146-18-06
To Comfort Sage, eldest son,	6294-06-00
To Ebenezer, Martha and Hannah Sage, to each,	3147-03-00

And appoint Jabez Hamlin, Thomas Goodwin and Jonathan Allin distributors.

Page 18—21 March, 1750-1: Martha Sage, a minor, 14 years of age, and Hannah Sage, 12 years, children of Ebenezer Sage, chose their uncle Jonathan Bigelow of Hartford to be their guardian. Recog., £600.

Page 195.

Sallis, Richard, Hartford. Died 30 March, 1748. Invt. £78-09-00. Taken 6 April, 1748, by Benjamin Roberts and Edmund Bement.

Court Record, Page 63—5 April, 1748: This Court grant Adms. on the estate of Richard Sallis, late of Hartford, unto Joseph Cowles of sd. Hartford, who gave bonds.

Page 68—6 June, 1748: An inventory of the estate of Richard Sallis was exhibited in Court by Joseph Cowles. Accepted and ordered recorded and kept on file.

Page 75—6 September, 1748: Joseph Cowles, Adms. on the estate of Richard Sallis, late of Hartford, reports the estate insolvent and prays that commissioners may be appointed to adjust the claims of the creditors.

Page 84—3 January, 1748-9: An account of Adms. on the estate of Richard Sallis, late of Hartford, was now exhibited by Joseph Cowles, Adms.: Has paid in debts and charges, £7-18-00. Account allowed. Also this Court now have made an averidge on sd. estate. Account allowed and ordered to be kept on file.

Scott, Zacheus. Court Record, Page 20—5 August, 1746: This Court grant Adms. on the estate of Zacheus Scott, late of Farmingtown decd., unto Samuel Woodruff of Farmingtown, who gave bonds with Joseph Hart of £200.

Page 44—4 August, 1747: An account of Adms. on the estate of Zacheus Scott was now exhibited by Samuel Woodruff: Paid in debts and charges, £22-12-11. Accot. allowed and ordered to be kept on file. Also an invt. of Cape Breton wages, £21-15-07; and credit received, 3 shillings. Which is ordered to be filed.

Page 197-8-9-208.

Seymour, John, Hartford. Invt. £603-01-06. Taken 28 June, 1748, by Joseph Holtom, Jacob Kellogg and Joseph Skinner. Will dated September, 1747.

I, John Seymour of Hartford, do make this my last will and testament: I give to my wife Elizabeth Seymour the use of 1-3 part of all my lands of real estate; also 1-3 part of my personal or moveable estate, and likewise the use and improvement of one room in my present mansion house, which room she shall choose, and convenient part of the cellar under sd. house, and the privilege of my well, during the time she remains my widow. I give unto my son John Seymour, Jr., besides what I have already given him by deed of gift, those my lotts of land (excepting 75 acres) lying in the Township of New Hartford, in the County and Colony aforesd., my sd. son John to pay to my daughter Elizabeth the sum of £30. I give unto my son Timothy Seymour, besides what I have heretofore given him at Litchfield in other ways, the western part of that lott of land at the west division or 4-Mile Hill in Hartford, which I purchased of Mr. Stephen Steele of Tolland, on which my sd. son Timothy now liveth, together with the dwelling house and other buildings. I give to my son Timothy one other piece of land lying at sd. 4-Mile Hill, the northern half of that lott I purchased of my brother Thomas Seymour decd., called Clark's lotts. I give unto my son Daniel Seymour, besides what I have given him by deed of gift and otherwise, all that my tract or share of land called my furthermost west land or further lott, lying in Hartford, as yet in common and undivided with Elisha Smith and Ruth Smith his wife, in right of the sd. Ruth, daughter of my brother Thomas Seymour aforesd., joyning land of Joshua Carter's heirs and Joseph Skinner's land. I give unto my son Jonathan Seymour, besides what I have heretofore bestowed upon him, part of that my lott of land in the Township of New Hartford. I give unto my sd. son Jonathan £100 money, to be paid him by my son Richard Seymour hereafter mentioned. I give unto my son Nathaniel Seymour the western part of my homelott whereon I now live in Hartford. Also I give unto him all that my tract or parcel of land at the west division or 4-Mile Hill in sd. Hartford, usually called my Hubbard's, and 2 Benton's lotts (saving 5 acres of the same, which I purpose to give to my son Moses Seymour), bounded east on the common, north upon Robert

Reave's heirs, south upon Thomas Seymour's land, and west upon the five acres above excepted, to be to him, my son Nathaniel, his heirs and assigns forever, he paying to my daughter Susannah (now Susannah Pomeroy) the sum of £30 within two years after my decease. I give unto my son Zebulon Seymour, besides what I have already given him by deed of gift, land in the Township of New Hartford. I give unto my son Zebulon Seymour £100 money, to be paid him by my son Richard Seymour within two years after my decease. I give unto my son Moses Seymour the remaining eastern part of that my lott of land at the west division or 4-Mile Hill in Hartford, which I purchased of Mr. Stephen Steele of Tolland, my son Moses paying to my daughter Margaret (now Margaret Catlin) the sum of £30 within two years next after my decease. I give unto my son Richard Seymour the eastern part of my homelott whereon I now dwell, which comprehends 2 acres which I have sometime since given him by deed of gift, with the mansion house and all other buildings and appurtenances thereon; also about 18 acres in Hartford opposite my dwelling house, bounded east on Rocky Hill, west on a highway, north on land of sd. Richard Seymour, and south on Zachariah Seymour's land and school lott, together with the barn and appurtenances thereof, to him and his heirs forever, he, the sd. Richard Seymour, paying unto each of my above-named sons, Jonathan and Zebulon, £100 money apiece. I give unto my three daughters, Elizabeth, Susannah and Margaret, £30 in money apiece besides what I have heretofore given them. I give unto my two sons, Jonathan Seymour and Zebulon Seymour, in equal proportion, my land that is already laid out, and interest and share yet undivided, in the Five Miles of land so called, on the east side of the Great River in the Town of Hartford. I appoint my three eldest sons, John Seymour, Jr., Timothy Seymour and Daniel Seymour, executors.

Witness: *Ebenezer Webster,*   JOHN X SEYMOUR, LS.
Medad Webster, George Wyllys.

Court Record, Page 68—6 June, 1748: The last will and testament of John Seymour, late of Hartford decd., was now exhibited in Court by John Seymour, Timothy Seymour and Daniel Seymour, executors named in sd. will. Proven and ordered to be recorded.

Page 104-5-141.

Seymour, Mary, Hartford. Invt. £222-15-07. Taken 9 June, 1746, by John Gillet and Josiah Riley. Will dated 19 April, 1746.

Hartford, ss., April ye 19th, 1746: Be it remembered, that Mrs. Mary Seymour, late of Hartford, who died on the 14th day of April, 1746, some short time before her death expressed that she was sensible she was very near her end, and at the same time, in the presence and hearing of Phebe Booth, Hannah Welles and Hepzibah Seymour, did make her last will and testament, and did then and there verbally declare in their audience that it was her last will and testament that her daughter Jerusha Seymour shall have all her goods and estate that she the sd. Mary Seymour had in the world. And for perpetual memory and confirmation of the truth of what is above written, we, the sd. Phebe Booth, Hannah Welles and Hepzibah Seymour, have hereto set our hands this 19th day of April, 1746.

Witness: *Phebe X Booth,*
Hannah X Welles, Heph: Seymour.

The above was approved to be the last will and testament of Mary Seymour, and ordered to be recorded.

Test: Joseph Talcott, Clerk.

Court Record, Page 63—5 April, 1748: An account of Adms. on the estate of Mary Seymour decd., widow of Capt. Thomas Seymour, was now exhibited in Court by Bevell Seymour (see page 27) and Jerusha Seymour, with the will annexed:

	£ s d
Paid in debts and charges,	71-12-04
Credit received,	38-12-00

Which account is allowed and ordered recorded.

Page 295.

Seymour, Samuel, Jr., Kensington. Invt. £4177-18-06. Taken 21 February, 1748-9, by Isaac North and Phineas Judd.

Court Record, Page 92—7 March, 1748-9: This Court grant Adms. on the estate of Samuel Seymour, late of Farmingtown, unto Susannah Seymour, widow, who gave bonds with John Judd of Farmingtown of £1000.

Page 316.

Seymour, Sergt. Samuel, Kensington. Invt. £485-03-08. Taken by Jonathan Lewis, Isaac North and Jonathan Gilbert. Additional invt. £90-05-00. Taken by Jonathan Gilbert and Jonathan Lewis.

Court Record, Page 104—1st August, 1749: This Court grant Adms. on the estate of Samuel Seymour, late of Farmingtown decd., unto Isaac North of Wethersfield, who gave bonds with James North of Farmingtown of £1000.

Page 118—11 January, 1749-50: An account of Adms. on the estate of Sergt. Samuel Seymour, late of Farmingtown, was now exhibited by Isaac North, Adms.:

	£ s d
Paid in debts and charges,	37-09-00
And lost,	20-00-00

Which make the total,	57-17-00

Which account this Court allows.

Inventory of the moveable estate,	485-03-08
Debts and charges subtracted,	57-17-00

There remains to be distributed,	427-06-08
To Hannah Seymour, her thirds,	142-08-10

To the heirs of Samuel a double share, and the rest single shares: To Hannah, Mary, Rebeckah, Mercy, Sarah and Ruth, heirs to the sd. estate. And appoint John Hooker, Samuel Thompson and Ebenezer Hart distributors.

Dist. File: Samuel Seymour, Farmingtown, 17 January, 1749-50:

	£ s d
To Hannah Seymour, widow,	142-11-06
To Samuel Seymour's heirs,	302-13-00
To Hannah, wife of Allyn Goodrich,	151-06-06
To Mary, wife of Anthony Judd,	151-06-06
To Rebeckah, wife of Elisha Goodrich,	151-06-06
To Mercy, wife of Uriah Judd,	151-06-06
To Sarah, wife of James North,	151-06-06
To Ruth, wife of Phineas Judd,	151-06-06

26 March, 1750-1.   By *Samuel Thompson,* ⎱ *Distributors.*
Jos: Talcott, Clerk.   *John Hooker,*   ⎰

Page 426-7-8.

Seymour, Timothy, Hartford. Invt. £18,684-04-09. Taken for Hartford 30 March, 1750, by Daniel Webster, Stephen Hosmer and Joseph Skinner. In Canaan and Salisbury, half the dwelling house, half the iron works and half the coal house, which was £950-00-00. In Salisbury, 1-16 part of Ore Hill, £250. Taken 1st November, 1749, by Daniel Lawrence, Jr., and Benjamin Stevens. In Bethlehem, £61-00-00. Taken by Daniel Everit and Benjamin Woodruff.

Court Record, Page 108—3 October, 1749: This Court grant Adms. on the estate of Timothy Seymour, late of Hartford, unto Rachel Seymour and Timothy Seymour, widow and son, who gave bonds with Daniel Seymour of £2000 money.

Page 20 (Vol. XVI) 23 April, 1751: This Court appoint Rachel Seymour, widow, to be guardian to Charles Seymour, age 13 years, son of the deceased; and the sd. Rachel Seymour, with her son Timothy Seymour, acknowledged themselves bound in a recog. of £1000. Rachel Seymour and Timothy Seymour, Adms., exhibited an account of their Adms.

Accepted. This Court order the estate distributed, viz., to Rachel Seymour, widow, her thirds in moveable and real estate; and to Timothy Seymour, eldest son, his double share; and to Allyn Seymour, Charles' Seymour and Rachel Easton (daughter of the deceased), to each of them their single shares. And appoint Daniel Webster, Stephen Hosmer and Joseph Skinner distributors.

Page 94—2 April, 1753: Report of the distributors.

Page 119 (Vol. XVII) 17 June, 1756: Charles Seymour, a minor, aged about 18 years, son of Timothy Seymour, chose his brother Timothy Seymour to be his guardian.

Page 308-9-10.

Sheldon, Isaac, Hartford. Will dated 11 November, 1746: I, Isaac Sheldon of Hartford, do make this my last will and testament: I give to my wife Theoda the use and improvement of my northeast room, the middle chamber of the dwelling house wherein I now live, and the privilege in the kitchen and well belonging to the house, sufficient for her necessary household work; also the use of 1-3 part of my garden and the privilege in my barn and yard sufficient for the keeping of one or two cows for her use; only not to lease or farm-let to any other, and only during the time she remains my widow. And whereas, at the time of marriage with my sd. wife I received many valuable goods and household stuff with her, for which I gave a receipt to her mother, Mrs. Martha Hunt of Northampton, therein obliging myself and my heirs to return the same at my decease or at the decease of my wife, the wearing excepted, my will therefore is that all these goods mentioned in sd. receipt be returned accordingly immediately after my decease. And further, I give unto my sd. wife all other goods and chattells which she brought to me or that was hers at the time of our marriage, of what kind soever, they to be to her own use forever. And furthermore, provided my wife shall acquit and discharge my executor hereafter named from all claims of her right of dowry or thirds in my estate, that she may or can have thereunto, then my will is that my executors shall in equal proportion pay unto my sd. wife annually £20 money at the rate of 40 shillings per ounce, Troy weight, sterling alloy, during the whole time she shall continue my widow. To my daughter Elizabeth Marsh I give, besides what I have already given her, my homelott in New Hartford (50 acres more or less), to her and her heirs forever. Also, I give unto my daughter Elizabeth £60, to be paid in old tenor bills of credit or in moveables out of my estate equal to silver at the rate of 40 shillings per ounce, to be paid to her within seven years after my decease. Also, I give unto my daughter Elizabeth 20 sheep. To my daughter Sarah Woodbridge I give the sum of £200 besides what I have already given her, to be paid in bills of old tenor or in moveables equal to silver at the rate of 40 shillings per ounce. I give to my youngest daughters, Rebeckah and Hannah Sheldon, £800 apiece, to be paid to each of them in bills of credit in the old tenor or in moveables equal to silver at the rate of 40 shillings per ounce. I give unto my son Isaac Sheldon my dwelling house wherein I now dwell, barn and other buildings, and all that platt or piece of land whereon the sd. buildings are erected, about 5 roods more or less, butting west on a highway, north on the Little River, south on Thomas Welles's land, and extends east as far as the east side of Thomas Welles's land. I give to my three sons, Isaac, Daniel and Joseph Sheldon, besides what I have severally given and done for them, all my estate, both real and personal, not already disposed of, after my lawfull debts, legacies and funeral charges are paid, viz., all my land and right of land in the Townships of Hartford, New Hartford and Cole-brook, and my iron works and lands in the Townships of Canaan and Salisbury, all my lands and rights in the Township of Union, in the County of Windham, and at Northampton, in Hampshire County, and all other my lands and rights, whether divided or undivided; also all my moveable estate, as implements of husbandry, stock of cattle, horses, sheep and swine, and all other my goods, cattle and credits, wheresoever they may be found, they paying the above-named legacies, debts and funeral expenses, to be holden equally between them. I appoint my three sons, Daniel, Isaac and Joseph, to be my executors.

Witness: *Ann X Buckingham,*   ISAAC SHELDON, LS.
J: Buckingham, Joseph Olcott.

Court Record, Page 99—2 May, 1749: The last will and testament of Deacon Isaac Sheldon was now exhibited in Court by Isaac Sheldon and Joseph Sheldon, executors named in sd. will. Will proven. Ordered recorded and kept on file.

Page 115—30 January, 1749-50: Isaac, Daniel and Joseph Sheldon, executors and heirs to the estate of Isaac Sheldon, late of Hartford, now move for distribution of the moveable estate: Whereupon this Court appoint Thomas Welles and Ozias Goodwin distributors.

Page 307.

Shepherd, Jane, Hartford. Invt. £186-18-03. Taken 21 April, 1749, by Jeremiah Fyler and Aaron Gaylord.

Court Record, Page 96—7 April, 1749: This Court grant Adms. on the estate of Jane Shepherd, late of Hartford, unto Sarah Shepherd of Hartford, who gave bonds with Stephen Burr of Farmingtown.

Page 421-2.

Shepherd, Samuel, Middletown. Invt. £11,300 in lands. Taken 22 May, 1750, by Thomas Johnson, William Savage and Jonathan Ranny.

Court Record, Page 131—5 June, 1750: This Court grant Adms. on the estate of Samuel Shepherd, late of Middletown deceased, unto

642   PROBATE RECORDS.   VOL. XV,

Christian Shepherd, widow, who gave bonds with Will Savage of Middletown of £2000.

Page 40 (Vol. XVI) 5 November, 1751: Christian Shepherd, a minor, 16 years of age, daughter of Deacon Samuel Shepherd, chose her mother Christian Shepherd to be her guardian. Also, this Court appoint the sd. Christian Shepherd guardian to Jared Shepherd, age 13 years, and Mary Shepherd, 8 years; also, Samuel Shepherd, aged 18 years, chose his mother to be his guardian. Recog., £600.

Page 42—5 November, 1751: An account of Adms. was now exhibited in Court by Christian Shepherd, Adms. Accepted. This Court order the estate distributed (£12,286-13-11): To the widow, 1-3 part of the moveable estate; and to the heirs of Edward Shepherd, he being the eldest son, a double share of sd. estate; and to Samuel and Jared Shepherd and Christian and Mary Shepherd, to each of them their single shares of sd. estate. And appoint Capt. Jonathan Allin, Capt. Jacob Whitmore and Mr. Benjamin Adkins distributors.

Page 77—7 November, 1752: Report of the distributors.

Inventory in Vol. XVI, Page 158.

Shepherd, Samuel, Hartford. Died 5 June, 1750. Invt. £824-03-02. Taken 31 July, 1750, by Thomas Andrus, Jonathan Steele and James Burnham, Jr.

Court Record, Page 135—30 July, 1750: Adms. granted unto John Shepherd of Hartford, son of the deceased, who gave bonds with James Shepherd of £600.

Page 8 (Vol. XVI) 13 December, 1750: John Shepherd, Adms., exhibited an account of his Adms. Accepted. Now moves that distribution be made of the estate: Whereupon this Court appoint Jonathan Steele, Thomas Andrus and James Bunce, Jr., to distribute the estate, viz.: To the widow, £66 in moveables, and to Samuel £52 in moveables and in real estate; to John, the eldest son, a double portion; to James Shepherd, William and Amos Shepherd, and Hannah and Sarah Shepherd, children of the deceased, their single portions (from the sum of £1250-12-06 remaining after Samuel had received his). This Court appoint Samuel Shepherd to be guardian to Amos Shepherd, a minor, 12 years of age, son of Samuel Shepherd. Recog., £400. William Shepherd, son of Samuel Shepherd, 18 years of age, made choice of his brother Samuel Shepherd to be his guardian. Recog., £500.

Shepherdson, John. Court Record, Page 100—29 May, 1749: Dist. of the estate of John Shepherdson, late of Middletown decd., was now exhibited in Court under the hands of Joseph White, John Fiske and Jeremiah Goodrich. Accepted. Ordered to be kept on file.

Sherman, Theophilus. Court Record, Page 14—7 June, 1746: This Court grant Adms. on the estate of Theophilus Sherman, late of Wethersfield decd., unto Theophilus Nichols of Stratford, in the County of Fairfield, who gave bonds with John Robbins, Jr., of Wethersfield, of £500.

Page 141-2-224-5.

Shipman, Stephen, Glastonbury. Died 20 January, 1746-7. Invt. £131-16-11, moveable estate. Taken by Joseph Brewer and John Holdin. Will dated 1st July, 1746.

I, Stephen Shipman of Glastonbury, do make this my last will and testament: I give to my wife Mary the improvement of 1-3 part of my improved land, which I hereafter give to my son Daniel, and the 1-3 part of my house and barn, and of 1-3 part of my moveable estate while she remains my widow. I give to my four sons, Stephen, Jonathan, David and Daniel, all my lott of land on which I now dwell, containing 130 acres in the whole, that is to say, to Stephen 32 1-2 at the west end, to Jonathan 32 1-2 at the east end, to David 32 1-2 next to the land given to my son Stephen, and to Daniel 32 1-2 between the land now given to my sd. sons Jonathan and David, to be to them and their heirs forever. I give to my three daughters, Mary, Hannah and Abigail, that is to say, to my daughter Mary so much more than she has had as to make up £70, to Hannah £70, and to Abigail £70, to be paid out of my moveable estate. I give to my sd. three daughters four and 1-2 acres of land which I have on the lott of land in the Three Miles which belongs to the Rev. Mr. Samuel Smith, and also 30 acres which is of the division of land in Glastonbury made December, Anno. Dom. 1723, all which land is equally to be divided between my sd. three daughters, to them and their heirs forever. I give to the Rev. Mr. Isaac Chalker £5 money, to be paid out of my moveable estate. My will further is, that all my just debts be paid out of my estate by my executors hereafter named. My will further is, that if there be not enough of my moveable estate to pay the before named sums out of my moveable estate, it shall be made up and paid equally by my sons. My will further is, that if it be made to appear that any or either of my children aforesd. shall presume to break this my last will and testament, that they shall be debarred from any and all my estate aforementioned, except one shilling to each one that shall so presume as aforesd. I appoint my friends Lt. Elisha Andrews and Benoni House to be my executors.

Witness: *Samuel Talcott,*　　　　　STEPHEN SHIPMAN, LS.
John Kimberly, William Welles.

Court Record, Page 33—3 March, 1746-7: The last will and testament of Stephen Shipman, late of Glastonbury, was now exhibited in Court by Elisha Andrews and Benoni House, executors named in the last will. Proven and ordered to be recorded.

Page 42—2 June, 1747: Abigail Shipman, a minor, daughter of Stephen Shipman, chose William Slade to be her guardian. Recog., £300.

Page 47—5 October, 1747: An account of Adms. was exhibited in Court by the executors. Accepted.

Page 61—8 March, 1747-8: Pursuant to an act of the General Assembly at New Haven, granting liberty to Elisha Andrews and Benoni House, executors to the last will and testament of Stephen Shipman of Glastonbury, to make sale of so much of the land as will raise £73-16-01 old tenor with incident charges, taking the advice of the Court of Probates in Hartford, etc., etc., etc.

Simons, Priscilla. Court Record, Page 79—2 January, 1748-9: Priscilla Simons, 10 years of age, daughter of Philip Simons of Enfield, in the County of Hampshire: this Court appoint Edmund Bemond of Hartford to be her guardian, and the sd. Samuel (Edmund) Bemond now before this Court recog. in £300.

Page 312-13.

Skinner, Jonathan, Hartford. Invt. £803-13-04. Taken 9 April, 1748, in Hartford, by John Knowles, Ozias Goodwin and Timothy Seymour. Land in Hebron, Gilead Parish, £1860 old tenor. Taken 10 June, 1748, by Joseph Phelps, William Sumner and Benjamin Trumbull. (Adjoins land of Matthew Ford, Josiah Marks and Thomas Buck.)

Court Record, Page 50—19 April, 1747: This Court grant Adms. on the estate of Jonathan Skinner, late of Hartford, unto Stephen Skinner, brother of the sd. decd., who gave bonds with Joseph Skinner of Hartford of £1000.

Page 311-12.

Skinner, Joseph, Hartford. Inventory taken 4 April, 1748, by John Knowles, Ozias Goodwin and Timothy Seymour.

Court Record, Page 50—19 April, 1747: This Court grant Adms. on the estate of Joseph Skinner, late of Hartford decd., unto Stephen Skinner, son of the sd. decd., who gave bonds with Joseph Skinner of Hartford of £1000.

Page 100—26 May, 1749: Inventory of the estate of Mr. Joseph Skinner, late of Hartford decd., exhibited in Court by Stephen Skinner, Adms. Accepted. Ordered recorded and kept on file.

See File:

We the subscribers, the widow Elizabeth Skinner, Joseph Skinner, Stephen Skinner, Dorothy Skinner alias Olcott, and George Olcott, husband to the sd. Dorothy, and Hannah Skinner and Rebeckah Skinner, heirs to the estate of Mr. Joseph Skinner, late of Hartford deceased, in the County of Hartford, do hereby mutually agree to divide the sd. estate to and amongst ourselves in the following manner and form: First, we agree that our honoured mother Elizabeth Skinner shall have for her use, to improve during her naturall life, 1-3 part of all the buildings and lands and appurtenances of the said Joseph Skinner decd. as her right of dowry in sd. estate, and the several particulars in moveables hereafter set to her, to be her own to dispose of forever. [The space upon which the rest of the agreement should have been written is left blank. File date, 26 May, 1749.—C. W. M.]

Smith, Abigail. Court Record, Page 5—26 February, 1745-6: Abigail Smith, 16 years of age, Nathaniel 14 years, Rhoda 12, Abiel 10, Ebenezer 9, Esther 8 years of age: this Court do appoint Abiall Smith of Litchfield to be their guardian. Recog., £300 for each minor.

Page 1.

Will in Vol. XVI, Page 213.

Smith, Ebenezer, Suffield. Invt. £3715-09-00. Taken 2 February, 1748-9, by Benjamin Kent, Aaron Hitchcock and Samuel Hermon. Property in Windsor, Hartford County, valued at £1190-01-06, taken 30 June, 1749, by Samuel Owen, Martin Winchell and Aaron Phelps. Will dated 22 August, 1748.

I, Ebenezer Smith of Suffield, in the County of Hampshire, in New England, merchant, being of sound mind and memory, doe ordain this my last will and testament: I give unto my loving wife Christian the improvement of 1-3 part of all my real estate during life, and 1-3 part of my personal estate forever, and £50 old tenor, to be paid out of my personal estate. I give to my son Jedediah 20 shillings, to be paid out of my estate by my executors hereafter named. I give to my son Asa 20 shillings. I give to my son Ebenezer 20 shillings. I give my son Eliakim 20 shillings. I give to my son Elnathan 20 shillings. I give to my son Zebulon 20 shillings. I give to my son Elijah 20 shillings. I give to my daughter Dorcas 20 shillings. I give to my honoured mother, Sarah Kellogg, out of my personal estate, what shall be necessary for 1-3 part of her maintenance during her natural life. The remainder of my real and personal estate I give to my wife Christian to give and grant to my aforesd. children according to her own judgement and at her own discretion. I hereby appoint my sd. wife Christian and my sd. son Jedediah to be the executors of this my last will.

Witness: *Nathaniel Smith,*   EBENEZER SMITH, LS.
Mary Smith, Phineas Lyman.

Court Record, Page 136—7 August, 1750: A true copy of the last will of Ebenezer Smith of Suffield was now transmitted to this Court by Christian Smith, widow and one of the executors to sd. will, under the hands of Timothy Dwight, Jr., Register of Probates in Hampshire County, which being approved, was ordered recorded.

Page 136—7 August, 1750: Ebenezer Smith, Jr., age 17 years, and Eliakim Smith, 14 years of age, chose their mother Christian Smith to be their guardian. Also this Court appoint the sd. widow guardian to Elnathan Smith, 12 years, Zebulon 10, Elijah 9, and Dorcas Smith 7 years, children of the decd. Recog., £500 for each minor. Cert: *Phineas Lyman, J. P.*

Page 323.

Smith, Eleazer, New Hartford. Invt. £535-04-04. Taken 29 April, 1749, by Matthew Gillet, Elijah Flower and Consider Hopkins.

Court Record, Page 97—2 May, 1749: This Court grant Adms. on the estate of Eleazer Smith, late of New Hartford decd., unto Martin Smith of New Hartford, who gave bonds with Jonathan Seymour of Hartford of £1000.

Page 416-17.

Smith, Ichabod, Jr., Suffield. Will dated 24 February, 1748-9: I, Ichabod Smith, Jr., of Suffield, in the County of Hampshire and Province of Massachusetts Bay in New England, will: My will and pleasure is that after my just debts and funeral expenses are all paid in, my dearly beloved wife to have all my moveable estate and the improvement of my homelott on which I dwell till my son Ichabod Smith 3rd shall come to the age of 21 years, and then she my sd. wife to have the improvement of 1-2 of sd. lott and half of the house and barn during her natural life. I give to my son, Ichabod Smith the 3rd, all my homelott on which I now dwell, with all the buildings thereon and thereunto belonging, 1-2 of sd. homelott and half of the buildings as soon as my sd. son Ichabod shall come to the age of 21 years, and the other half with the rest of the buildings as soon as my wife shall decease. I give to my other two sons, Asahell Smith and Phineas Smith, the 1-2 of my other land on the east side of the country road that leads from Suffield to Windsor, being my lott called Eliott lott, bounding west on sd. road, south on Matthew Copley, Jr., north on James Smith, and east on Thrall's land; as also my Plaine lott so called, lying on the south side of sd. Copley, Jr. And the other half of the aforesd. lands I give to my four daughters, Elizabeth Smith, Jr., and Ruth Smith and Jerusha Smith, Jr., and Anne Smith, equally to be divided between them. And furthermore my will and pleasure is that my brother James Smith and my wife Elizabeth Smith be my only executors.

Witness: *Nathaniel Pumroy,*   ICHABOD SMITH, JR., LS.
Jonathan Smith, Joseph Smith.

Court Record, Page 135—7 August, 1750: The last will and testament of Ichabod Smith, late of Suffield decd., was now exhibited in Court by Elizabeth Smith, one of the executors. Will proven, ordered to be recorded and kept on file. Elizabeth Smith, a minor, aged 16 years, and Ruth, 14 years, chose their mother Elizabeth Smith to be their guardian. And this Court appoint the sd. widow guardian to Ichabod Smith, age 12 years, Asahell Smith 10, Jerusha 8, and Phineas about 4 years, children of Ichabod Smith deceased. Recog., £500.

Page 136 (Vol. XVII) 5 February, 1757: On the motion of some of the heirs to the estate of Ichabod Smith, Jr., late of Suffield deceased, this Court appoint Simon Hathaway, Uriah Austin and Nathaniel Pomroy of Suffield to distribute the estate according to his last will, viz.: to Ichabod and Asahell Smith, Elizabeth Spencer, Ruth and Jerusha Smith, their respective portions. And whereas, Phineas and Anna Smith are deceased, this Court, pursuant to law, order that the estate given them by sd. will be divided in an equal proportion to and amongst the sd. Ichabod, Asahell, Elizabeth, Ruth and Jerusha, children of the sd. decd. Also set out to the widow what is given to her by sd. will, and make return of your doings to this Court.

Page 403-4-5.

Smith, John, Glastonbury. Invt. £1472-14-00. Taken·8 May, 1750, by Thomas Welles and Jonathan Hale. Will dated 14 November, 1749.

I, John Smith of Glastonbury, do make this my last will and testament: I give to Gershom Smith, my eldest son, and to his heirs and assigns forever, 14 acres of land in the lott I now dwell upon, with the buildings thereon, being the southwest corner of the lott (being my old lott). I give unto David Smith, my 2nd son, 14 acres of land on the northwest corner of sd. lott. I give unto my 3rd son, Obadiah Smith, 14 acres of land, being the southeast corner of sd. lott. I give unto my 4th son, Israel Smith, 14 acres of land, being the northwest corner of sd. lott. I give to my three eldest daughters, Susannah Smith, Esther Smith and Dorothy Smith, 12 acres and 3-4 of land which I bought of my brother Joseph Smith. I give to my fourth daughter, Eunice Smith, £30 old tenor. I give to my 5th daughter, Anne Smith, £30 old tenor. The above legacies to be paid by my two sons, Obadiah and Israel Smith, to my sd. daughters when they arrive at the age of 18 years. I give to my wife Mehetabel Smith the 1-3 part of my moveable estate forever, and the 1-3 part of my houseing and lands so long as she shall remain my widow, and no longer. I give to my wife Mehetabel Smith and my brother Joseph Smith the use of all my houseing and lands two years upon consideration of their keeping and maintaining my three youngest children two years, viz., Obadiah, Anne and Israel. I appoint my brother Joseph Smith sole executor.

Witness: *Jonathan Hale,*   JOHN X SMITH, LS.
Richard Keney, Abigail X Gardner.

Court Record, Page 130—14 May, 1750: The last will and testament of John Smith, late of Glastonbury decd., was now exhibited in Court by Joseph Smith, executor. Will proven.

Page 15 (Vol. XVI) 13 February, 1750-1: This Court appoint Joseph Smith of Glastonbury to be a guardian to Eunice Smith, a minor, about 6 years of age, and Israel Smith, about 1 year and 8 months, children of John Smith of Glastonbury deceased. Recog., £300.

Page 21—4 April, 1751: This Court appoint Joseph Smith to be guardian to Noadiah (Obadiah) Smith, about 4 years of age, son of John Smith, and Anne Smith, 3 years, daughter of sd. deceased. Recog., £300.

Page 70—4 August, 1752: Joseph Smith, executor, exhibited an account of Adms. Accepted. Also sd. executor moves for a distribution according to the last will of the deceased: Whereupon this Court appoints Col. Thomas Welles, Jonathan Hale and Capt. David Hubbard to distribute the estate, viz: to the eldest son a double share, and to the rest of the children their single shares, and make return to this Court.

Page 85—6 February, 1753: Report of the distributors.

Page 435-6.

Smith, John, Windsor. Will dated 16 December, 1747: I, John Smith of Windsor, in the County of Hartford, being old and infirm, do make this my last will and testament: I give to my son John Smith all that parcel of land on which he now lives, with leave to cut wood and timber as long as he liveth upon this lott on which I now dwell, with half my equivalent land and half of my common land. I give to my son Samuel Smith the whole of the lott on which I now live, with half of my equivalent land and half of my common land, with all my moveable estate. My will also is that my son Samuel Smith shall pay unto my daughter Abigail, the wife of Daniel Skinner, the sum of £100 old tenor within two years after my decease. My will also is that my son Samuel Smith shall pay unto my wife Sarah the sum of £40 old tenor within two years after my decease. My will also is that my son John Smith shall pay unto my daughter Mary, the wife of Jeremiah Dickens, £50 money, old tenor, within three years after my decease, Jeremiah Dickens keeping £50 of that money of mine which he hath in his own hands and to pay the rest unto my son Samuel Smith when he shall have a deed of that land in Wintingbury, which I would have my son John Smith and my son Samuel Smith give as soon as can conveniently be done. I appoint my sons John Smith and Samuel Smith to be executors.

Witness: *Daniel Rockwell,*   JOHN SMITH, LS.
Timothy Bissell, Thomas Sadd, Jr.

Whereas, our honoured father, Mr. John Smith, late of Windsor, made his last will and testament, dated 16 December, 1747, and gave his estate as particularly set forth in sd. will, be it therefore known to all men, that we, John Smith and Samuel Smith, Daniel Skinner and Abigail Skinner alias Smith, and Jeremiah Dickens and Mary Dickens alias Smith, being sole heirs to sd. estate, do fully and absolutely agree that the aforesd. will shall be a final settlement of the estate of our father, the sd. John Smith decd., to us and our heirs forever. In full confirmation whereof we have hereunto set our hands and seals.

At a Court of Probate held at	JOHN SMITH, LS.
Hartford on the 5th day of July,	SAMLL. SMITH, LS.
A. D. 1748, then John Smith, Sam-	DANIEL SKINNER, LS.
uel Smith, Daniel Skinner in behalf	JEREMIAH DICKENS, LS.

of his wife Abigail, and Jeremiah Dickens in behalf of his wife Mary, signed, sealed and acknowledged the foregoing instrument to be their agreement and deed.   *Test: Joseph Talcott, Clerk.*

Page 19.

Smith, Nehemiah, Glastonbury. Invt. £78-09-09. Taken 2 January, 1745-6, by Abraham Fox, Gideon Hollister and Elisha Andrews.

Court Record, Page 6—4 March, 1746: This Court grant Adms. on the estate of Nehemiah Smith, late of Glastonbury, unto Ruth Smith, widow, who gave bonds with Gideon Hollister of sd. Glastonbury of £500 money. Also, the Adms. now informs this Court that sd. estate is insolvent: Whereupon this Court appoints Abner Moseley and Samuel Kimberly, of Glastonbury, commissioners to adjust the claims of the creditors.

Page 24—2 September, 1746: A report of the commissioners on the estate of Nehemiah Smith, under the hands of Abner Moseley and Samuel Kimberly, commissioners. Which report is accepted and ordered to be kept on file.

Page 46—1st September, 1748: Ruth Smith, a minor, daughter of Nehemiah Smith, late of Hartford deceased, chose Joshua Talcott of Bolton to be her guardian. Recog., £300. Cert: *Thomas Pitkin, J. P.*

Page 48 (Vol. XVII) 7 January, 1755: Elizabeth Smith, a minor, age 13 years, daughter of Nehemiah Smith, late of sd. Hartford deceased, chose her mother Ruth Smith to be her guardian. Recog., £100.

Page 318.

Smith, Richard, Glastonbury. Will dated 14 February, 1725: I, Richard Smith of Glastonbury, do make this my last will and testament: My debts and funeral expenses being paid, I give unto my brother Gershom Smith, with whom I now dwell, these four separate parcels of land lying and being in the Town of Glastonbury aforesd.: one piece, two acres, bounded east and north on Capt. Willis's land, south on a highway, west on land of Samuel Gains, Jr., which piece I bought of Jonathan Judd; also 20 acres, being part of my late honoured father's 100 acres lying northward of the Plaine, called Lubbe's land, and bounding east on Timothy Hale's land, west on David Hubbard's land, south on my brother Joseph's land, and north on sd. Gershom's land; also two pieces of land eastward of the hill called Minneochaug, containing in the whole 67 acres more or less, however the same may be butted or bounded; the which four parcels of land, together with all the rest and residue of my estate, real or personal, whatsoever and wheresoever, I give unto my sd. brother Gershom Smith and to his heirs and assigns forever. I appoint my brother Gershom Smith to be sole executor.

14th day of February, Annoqu. Dom. Ri. Rr. Georgis Magst. Brite. &c., duodecimo Annoqu. Dom. 1725-26.

Witness: *Thos. Kimberly,*   RICHARD X SMITH, LS.
Thaddeus Welles, Elizabeth X Welles.

Court Record, Page 101—6 June, 1749: The last will and testament of Richard Smith, late of Glastonbury, was now exhibited in Court by Richard Risley of Glastonbury, son-in-law to Gershom Smith, who was appointed sole executor, which executor is deceased. Will proven, ordered to be recorded and kept on file.

Page 370-1.

Soper, John, Windsor. Invt. £3524-14-03. Taken 7 December, 1749, by Solomon Clark and Abell Gillet. Additional invt. £16-00-00. Taken 6 February, 1749-50, by Jonathan Olcott and Stephen Loomis, Jr.

Court Record, Page 111—5 December, 1749: This Court grant Adms. on the estate of John Soper, late of Windsor, unto Capt. Peletiah Mills, Phineas Drake and Phebe Moore of Windsor, who gave bonds with Jonathan Olcott of Hartford.

Page 129—17 May, 1750: An account of debts and charges on the estate of John Soper was now exhibited in Court by Capt. Peletiah Mills and Phineas Drake, Adms. on sd. estate, amounting to £1965-14-03, which account is accepted and ordered to be filed.

Page 133—15 June, 1750: John Soper, a minor son of John Soper, chose Dr. Daniel Hooker to be his guardian. Recog., £500.

Page 80 (Vol. XVI) 11 December, 1752: Daniel Hooker, guardian to John Soper, a minor, about 19 years of age, desires to be discharged from his guardianship to sd. minor, and the sd. John Soper made choice of Stephen Loomis of Windsor to be his guardian. Recog., £500.

Page 82—26 December, 1752: Joel Soper, a minor, 18 years of age, made choice of his mother Phebe Soper to be his guardian. Recog., £300. And this Court appoint the sd. Phebe Soper guardian to Abigail Soper, a minor, age 11 years, daughter of sd. deceased. Recog., £300.

Page 104—7 August, 1753: Elizabeth Soper, a minor, 17 years of age, daughter of John Soper, chose her sister Phebe Soper to be her guardian. Recog., £300. Abigail Soper also made choice of her sister Phebe Soper to be her guardian. Recog., £300.

Page 113—8 February, 1754: A further account of Adms. was exhibited in Court by Capt. Peletiah Mills and Phineas Drake, Adms. Accepted. Order to distribute: To John Soper, eldest son, a double share; to Joel, David and Timothy, and to Phebe, Elizabeth and Abigail Soper, to each of them a single share of sd. estate. And appoint Jonathan Gillett, Jonah Gillett and Samuel Cutler, of Windsor, distributors.

Page 65 (Vol. XVII) 13 May, 1755: Report of the distributors.

Souerhill, Abraham. Court Record, Page 21—12 August, 1746: Samuel Souerhill, a minor, 13 years of age, and Reuben, 7 years of age, Annah 11 and Lydia 9 years of age, children of Abraham Souerhill of Simsbury decd.: this Court appoint Abraham Souerhill of Newark to be their guardian, who gave bonds with John Christian Miller of Simsbury of £300 for each minor.

Inventory in Vol. XVI, Page 206.

Southmayd, William, Middletown. Invt. £7279-07-11. Taken 26 February, 1750-1, by Jonathan Allin, Joseph Southmayd and William Rockwell.

Court Record, Page 58—2 February, 1747-8: Allin Southmayd, a minor, age 16 years, son of William Southmayd, chose Jabez Hamlin, Esq., to be his guardian. Recog., £300.

Page 64—19 April, 1748: Adms. granted unto Mehetabel Southmayd, widow, who gave bonds with Jabez Hamlin of £1000. This Court appoint Mehetabell Southmayd, widow, to be guardian to William Southmayd, a minor, 13 years of age, Giles 9, and to Patrick and Samuel, 11 years, children of William Southmayd. Recog., £500 for each minor.

Page 51 (Vol. XVI) 4 February, 1752: William Southmayd, a minor, 16 years of age, son of William Southmayd, chose his mother Mehetabel Southmayd to be his guardian. Recog., £1000.

Page 74 (Vol. XVII) 5 August, 1755: An account of Adms. was now exhibited in Court by Mehetabell Southmayd, Adms. Accepted. Order to distribute the estate, viz.: To Mehetabel Southmayd, widow, her thirds of moveable estate, and 1-3 part of the real estate for her improvement during life; also,

	£	s	d
To Allin Southmayd, eldest son,	2111	05	01
To William, Giles, Patrick and Samuel Southmayd, to each,	1155	12	06½

And appoint William Rockwell, Matthew Talcott and Abijah Moore, distributors.

Page 41.

Sparks, John, Glastonbury. Invt. £39-10-09. Taken 27 June, 1746, by Manoah Smith and William Densmore. Add Cape Breton wages, £24-15-04.

Court Record, Page 16—1st July, 1746: This Court grant Adms. on the estate of John Sparks, late of Glastonbury decd., unto Susannah Sparks, widow, who gave bonds with Ezekiel Webster of Hartford of £250. Exhibited an inventory. Accepted, ordered to be recorded and kept on file.

Page 30—6 January, 1746-7: John Sparks, a minor, and Susannah Sparks, both children of John Sparks, chose their mother Susannah Sparks to be their guardian. Also this Court appoint the sd. Susannah guardian to Jonathan Sparks, 13 years, Dorothy 10, David 7, and Eunice 3 years of age, children of John Sparks deceased. Recog., £200 for each.

Page 37—7 April, 1747: Susannah Sparks, Adms. on the estate of John Sparks, now moves to this Court that commissioners may be appointed to adjust the claims, the estate being insolvent: Whereupon this Court appoint Richard, Jeduthan and Manoah Smith, of Glastonbury, to adjust the claims of the creditors.

Page 66—11 May, 1752: This Court appoint Ezekiel Webster of Hartford to be guardian to Anne Sparks, a minor, about 6 years of age, daughter of John Sparks deceased. Recog., £300.

Page 289-90.

Spencer, Asahell, Windsor. Invt. £38-10-11. Taken 12 December, 1744, by Samuel Enno, Nathaniel Drake, John Drake and John Wilson.

Page 213.

Spencer, Samuel, Bolton. Will dated 19 January, 1742: I, Samuel Spencer of Bolton, in Hartford County, do make this my last will and testament: I give to my wife Hepzibah the use of 1-3 part of my real estate during the term of her natural life, and 1-3 part of my moveable estate to her and her heirs forever. I give to my son Caleb Spencer all my houseing and lands, either in Bolton or Hartford, to be and remain to him and his heirs forever, he paying to other of my children as is hereafter mentioned and expressed. As also I give to Caleb all my moveable estate which shall be remaining after my just debts are paid and my wife's thirds are extracted. I give to my daughter Hepzibah 5 shillings. I give to my son Samuel, besides what I have already given him, 5 shillings. I give to my son William 5 shillings besides what I have already given him. I give to my son Edward 5 shillings besides what I have already given to him. I give to my son Job 5 shillings besides what I have already given to him. I give to my son Philip the sum of 5 shillings. I give to my daughter Sarah the sum of £30, to be paid her by Caleb out of the moveable estate I have given him, or in money if the moveable estate will not extend to it, to be paid her at inventory price immediately after my decease. My will further is that Caleb pay unto Job and Philip the sums I have given them within two years after my decease. I appoint my son Caleb Spencer to be my sole executor.

Witness: *Timothy Olcott,*   SAMUEL SPENCER, LS.
Elizabeth Olcott, Eunice Olcott.

Court Record, Page 71—6 July, 1748: The last will and testament of Samuel Spencer, late of Bolton, was now exhibited in Court by Caleb Spencer, executor. Will proven, ordered to be recorded and placed on file.

Page 124.

Stanclift, William, Jr., Middletown. Invt. £177-00-03. Taken 25 November, 1746, by Noadiah White and Samuel Hall.

Court Record, Page 39—2 June, 1747: An inventory of the estate of William Stanclift, Jr., was now exhibited in Court by James Stanclift, Adms., which inventory is accepted, ordered recorded and kept on file. Estate supposed to be insolvent. Adms. prays that commissioners may be appointed to adjust the claims of the creditors. This Court appoint William Rockwell and John Gill, of Middletown, commissioners to adjust the claims of the creditors.

Page 110—7 November, 1749: Report of the commissioners on the estate of William Stanclift, Jr., under the hands of William Rockwell and John Gill, commissioners. Accepted, ordered recorded and kept on file.

Page 342.

Standish, Thomas, Wethersfield. Will dated 25 October, 1749: I, Thomas Standish of Wethersfield, do make this my last will and testament: I give to my brother Jeremiah Standish 4 acres of my homelott, more or less, together with my house and barn with all the buildings thereon standing. Sd. four acres are bounded north on the street, east on land of Col. David Goodrich, south partly on land of Peter Ayrault and partly on land of Robert Francis. Also, one piece of land lying in Wethersfield great meadow, containing formerly five acres, but now contains about 2 acres be the same more or less, butting north on a highway, east on land of Samuel Treat, west on land of Francis Hanmore, south partly on land of Nathaniel Stilman and partly on land of Samuel Riley. And also I give to my brother Jeremiah all my goods, chattells and personal estate. I give to my sister Hannah Standish and the heirs of Josiah Standish, late of Wethersfield decd., the remaining part of my homelott, containing about 2 acres more or less, which is butted east on land now given to my brother Jeremiah, south partly on land of Josiah Welles and Ebenezer Deming, Jr., and on a highway, west on the heirs of John Francis, and north on a highway. To Jacob Williams and Eunice his wife, and to the heirs of the sd. Eunice, I give one piece of land lying in Hartford south meadow, containing 7 acres more or less, and butted west on land of Jonathan Goodrich, north on land belonging to the heirs of Josiah Standish, south on land of John Welles. I give to my brother Hezekiah Butler and Rebeckah his wife, and to the heirs of sd. Rebeckah, one piece of land lying in Wethersfield containing 10 acres more or less, butted south partly on land of Wait Welles and partly on a highway, north on land of Deacon Thomas Wright, east on land of John Crane, west on land of John Welles. And I make and ordain my brother Jeremiah Standish sole executor.

Witness: *Peletiah Kilbourn,*   THOMAS X STANDISH, LS.
John Welles 2nd, Elisha Williams, Jr.

Court Record, Page 109—7 November, 1749: The last will and testament of Thomas Standish, late of Wethersfield, was now exhibited in Court by Jeremiah Standish. Will proven, ordered recorded and kept on file.

Agreement in Vol. XVI, Page 50.

Stanly, John, Kensington. *To all people to whom these presents shall come, greeting:* Know ye that we, John Stanly and Thomas Stanly, both of the Parish of Kensington, Township of Farmington and Colony of Connecticut, and Watts Hubbard and Mary Hubbard alias Stanly (his wife), of the aforesd. Parish and County aforesd., being the only children and heirs of the lands of Mr. John Stanly deceased, do all and each of us, for ourselves severally and respectively, covenant and agree to divide the sd. lands among ourselves. In witness whereof we have set to our hands and seals this 9th day of February, 1749-50.

JOHN STANLY, LS.   WATTS HUBBARD, LS.
THOMAS STANLY, LS.   MARY X HUBBARD, LS.

Court Record, Page 119—9 February, 1749-50: An agreement for the settlement of the estate of John Stanly, late of Farmington deceased, was now exhibited in Court under the hands and seals of John Stanly, Watts Hubbard and Mary Hubbard, who before this Court acknowledged the sd. agreement to be their free act and deed, which agreement this Court accepts for the settlement of sd. estate. Ordered to be filed.

Page 358-9.

Stedman, John, Middletown. Invt. £1190-19-00. Taken January, 1749-50, by Ephraim Adkins, James Ward and Elijah Treadway.

Court Record, Page 116—6 February, 1749-50: This Court grant Adms. on the estate of John Stedman, late of Middletown decd., unto

Mary Stedman, widow, who gave bonds with Ezra Roberts of Middletown of £500.

Page 7 (Vol. XVI) 4 December, 1750: Pursuant to an act of the General Assembly held at Hartford, impowering Mary Stedman with Benjamin Adkins of Middletown to make sale of so much of the real estate of John Stedman as will procure the sum of £126-00-10 money, this Court now order sd. Benjamin Adkins to set up advertisements on the sign posts on the west side of the river in Middletown.

Page 42—5 November, 1751: Return of the sale of land: sold to Fenner Ward the buildings called the kiln house, smith's shop, cole house and prui house, and about 24 rods of land lying 3 rods wide and near 8 rods long, all sold for £214-10-00. Why so much was sold: other debts appear, and the estate could not well be divided differently. Report accepted.

Page 57-58.

Steele, Ebenezer, Hartford. Invt. £158-19-06. Taken by Thomas Hosmer and Stephen Hosmer. Will dated 26 June, 1745.

I, Ebenezer Steele of Hartford, do make this my last will and testament: I give unto my wife Susannah the whole of my estate, both real and personal, to be to her use so long as she shall continue my widow after my decease. And if she shall afterward marry, then my estate shall go to my children in manner as hereafter mentioned, and my four sons, John, Daniel, Bradford and Elisha, shall pay to my sd. wife £3 money, old tenor, per annum during her natural life, to be equally divided between them. I give the whole of my land, being about 3 acres, to my four sons, to be equally divided between them: to my son Daniel Steele, 3 roods, butting west on the land of Deacon Daniel Merrells; to my son Bradford, 3 roods, butting west upon Daniel's part; to my son Elisha, 3 roods, lying next and butting west on the part of Bradford's; and to my son John I give 3 roods, being the eastern part of the sd. 3 acres. Also, I give unto my sons John and Daniel my house where I now dwell, standing on sd. 3 acres, with the privileges of the well thereto adjoining, for them to enjoy an equal right and privilege therein. I give unto my four daughters, Mary, Susannah, Huldah and Malatiah, all my moveable estate after the decease of my wife or after she shall marry, to be divided in such sort between them that my three daughters, Susannah, Huldah and Malatiah, shall have equal shares, and my daughter Mary shall have £15 less than they on account of what she has already had. I make my beloved wife Susannah sole executrix.

Witness: *Thomas Seymour,*   EBENEZER STEELE, LS.
Jarad Seymour, Eunice Seymour.

Court Record, Page 34—3 March, 1746-7: The last will and testament of Ebenezer Steele, late of Hartford, was now exhibited in Court by Susannah Steele, widow and executrix. Will proven, ordered recorded and kept on file.

Page 373.

Invt. in Vol. XVI, Page 202.

Steele, Joseph, Farmington. Invt. £6355-19-02. Taken 1st February, 1749-50, by Jonathan Lewis and Abraham Harris.

Will dated 30 December, 1747: I, Joseph Steele of Kensington, in the Township of Farmingtown, in the County of Hartford, do make this my last will and testament: I give to my wife Elizabeth Steele all my household goods and furniture and any sort of my moveable estate that shall be found in my dwelling house at the time of my decease. And also my sorrill mare and the colt that came of her, and two cows and 6 sheep during her natural life. I give to her the use of 1-3 part of my lands, and also the use of 1-3 part of my dwelling house, and liberty to get so much firewood as she shall have need of on any part of my land. To my eldest son James Steele, besides what I have already given him, I give about 15 acres of land lying next south to the homestead whereupon Nathaniel Dickinson now dwelleth, extending from sd. Dickinson's land 26 rods in breadth southward, and extending from the highway running across the 50-acre lott eastward to the place where our cartway crosseth the gutter or a small stream of water. To my second son Samuel Steele, besides what I have already given him, I give about 15 acres of land adjoining Jacob Deming's land south, and also about 5 acres more at the east end of the lott I bought of Daniel Warner. To my third son Ebenezer Steele I give 1-2 of my dwelling house and of my barn and of all my homestead lying westward of the parcel of land first mentioned, and which I gave my son Samuel; also 1-2 of a piece of land called the bush pasture, bounded east with land given to my son James, and west with land given to my son Samuel; and also 1-2 of a piece of woodland, containing about 5 acres, of the lott I bought of Daniel Warner, bounded east on land given to my son Samuel, and west with land given to my son James. To my fourth son Jonathan Steele I give an equal share with his brother Ebenezer of my dwelling house and barn, and of the westward part of my homestead, and of my bush pasture, and of the woodland above mentioned. To my fifth son Elizur Steele I give all the remainder of my lands eastward of the highway running across the 50-acre lotts in Wethersfield bounds, besides that which I have given to his elder brothers. To my three eldest daughters, Elizabeth, Sarah and Abigail, I give 5 sheep to each of them besides what I have already given them. To my daughter Anne Steele, besides what I expect my wife will do for her, I give her one cow. To my daughter Lucy Steele, besides what I expect my wife will do for her, I give one cow. All of the remainder of my estate I give to my wife, her heirs and assigns forever, whom I make my sole executrix.

Witness: *William Burnham,*   JOSEPH STEELE, LS.
Jacob Deming, Moses Deming.

Court Record, Page 121—6 March, 1749-50: The last will and testament of Joseph Steele, late of Farmingtown decd., was now exhibited by Elizabeth Steele, executrix. Will proven and ordered to be recorded. Elizur Steele, age 18 years, and Lucy Steele, 13 years, children of Joseph Steele, chose Capt. Jonathan Lewis of Farmingtown to be their guardian. Recog., £300 for each minor.

Page 12 (Vol. XVI) 25 January, 1750-1: This Court grant Adms. on part of the estate of Joseph Steele, late of Farmington deceased, unto Elizabeth Steele, widow, who gave bonds with Nathan Booth of sd. Farmington of £1000. Inventory exhibited.

Page 82—3 January, 1753: Elizabeth Steele, executrix to the last will of the decd., now moves that the real estate given her by her deceased husband in his last will may be set out to her: Whereupon this Court appoint Jonathan Lewis, Charles Kelsey and John Allis of Farmington to set out to the relict sd. real estate.

Page 265-6-7.

Stephens, Dorothy, Glastonbury. Will dated 1st May, 1744: I, Dorothy Stephens of Glastonbury, give to my grandson Isaac Hubbard all my rights of land in Glastonbury, viz., in the Five Miles, and which became mine according to the Town Votes referring to the first division of lands in sd. Five Miles, and all my rights of land in Hebron or otherwhere whatever, be it more or less, which I have not disposed of. I give to my grandson Isaac Hubbard two feather beds and two feather boulsters and two pillows, with the blankets belonging to them, and a pare of calico curtains and vallence white, a table and chest and draws, and six leather chairs and two white chaires, a trunk marked "N. R." (wherein is three suits of silk clothing and a pare of embroidered stays), all which I give to my grandson aforesd. I do give to my sd. grandson all the cattle that I shall have at my decease, all my table and bed linen (as sheets, table cloths and napkins), with all other my linen not herein disposed of, and a cradle quilt (silk on one side and calico on the other), a silver whistle, a silver spoon and a silver seal. I give to my grandson all my other household stuff or estate that shall properly belong to me at my decease that is not especially or shall appear by word of mouth to be disposed of. I do give to my son-in-law, Isaac Hubbard, 5 shillings. I do give my son Joseph Stephens, at my decease, my amber neck lace. I give to my daughter Dorothy Stephens, at my decease, my side-saddle and little wheel, and to her sister Martha Olmsted my silk hood, and to Martha Kilbourn my woosted combs, my great wheel, and my every-day clothing, and to her daughter Azuba Sheilds my black gown and one plad coat. But in case my sd. grandson Isaac Hubbard should not live to the age of 21 years, then I do give and dispose of my worldly goods (except what I have otherwise given and disposed of) in the following manner: I do give to my son Benjamin Stephens one cow, and to his wife, D. S., my imbroidered stayes and my silk suit faced with blue. To Mrs. Woodbridge my gown spotted with silver, with my cradle quilt aforesd. To Martha Kilbourn one suit grisett, with my riding hood and best quilt. To her daughter Azuba Sheilds one cow, a small featherbed and two blankets and two pair sheets. All the rest of my estate not already disposed of I give in equal proportion to my three sons-in-law, Timothy Stephens, Joseph Stephens and Benjamin Stephens, except to my son Timothy Stephens I do give ye debt which he owes me. And I appoint Mr. Ashbell Woodbridge to be sole executor.

Witness: *Abner Moseley,*   DOROTHY STEPHENS, LS.
William Miller, Susannah Miller.

Court Record, Page 42—7 July, 1747: The last will and testament of Mrs. Dorothy Stephens, late of Glastonbury decd., was now exhibited in Court by ye Rev. Mr. Ashbell Woodbridge, executor, who refused the trust, and Adms. was granted to Isaac Hubbard of Glastonbury, with the will annexed.

Page 24-5.

Stephens, Timothy, Glastonbury. Invt. £1305-10-04. Taken 20 February, 1745-6, by Thomas Welles, Samuel Kimberly and James Cole.

Court Record, Page 5—4 March, 1745-6: This Court grant Adms. on the estate of Timothy Stephens, late of Glastonbury, unto Hannah Stephens, widow, who gave bonds with Samuel Kimberly of Glastonbury of £600. Timothy Stephens, a minor, son of Timothy Stephens, chose Samuel Kimberly of Glastonbury to be his guardian. Recog., £500.

Page 16—1st July, 1746: An account of debts due from the estate of Timothy Stephens, and debts paid, amounting to £92-10-04. Accepted.

Page 32—3 February, 1746-7: This Court appoint Hannah Stephens, widow, to be a guardian to her child, Martha Stephens, a minor, age 4 months. Recog., £500.

Page 116—6 February, 1749-50: Hannah Stephens of Glastonbury, Adms., having rendered her account of Adms., is granted a *Quietus Est.*

Page 138-9.

Stephenson, John, Middletown. Invt. £2407-06-06. Taken 17 November, 1747, by Jeremiah Goodrich and John Savage.

Court Record, Page 53—1st December, 1747: This Court grant Adms. on the estate of John Stephenson, late of Middletown, unto Susannah Stephenson, widow, who gave bonds with John Savage of Middletown of £1000.

Page 80—6 December, 1748: Whereas, Susannah Stephenson, who was appointed Adms: on the estate of John Stephenson, late of Middletown decd., on the 1st day of December, 1747, and being deceased and not having finished her account of Adms., this Court grant Adms. on the estate of the sd. John Stephenson unto John Savage of Middletown, who gave bonds with George Ranney of £1000.

Page 84—3 January, 1748-9: An account of Adms. on the estate of John Stephenson was now exhibited by John Savage, Adms.: Paid in debts and charges, £106-05-05. Account allowed and ordered to be kept on file. The Adms. now moves to this Court that the moveable estate may be distributed as follows:

	£ s d
Inventory of moveable estate,	713-02-08
Debts and charges subtracted,	106-05-05
There remains to be distributed,	606-14-05
To Robert Stephenson, eldest son,	242-13-09
To Thomas, Susannah and Mary Stephenson, children of the sd. decd., to each of them,	131-06-07

And this Court appoint Joseph White, Esq., Capt. John Fiske and Capt. Jeremiah Goodrich, of Middletown, distributors.

Page 87—3 January, 1748-9: This Court appoint John Savage of Middletown to be guardian to Robert Stephenson, a minor, 12 years of age, and Thomas, 9 years, sons of John Stephenson. Recog., £200 for each minor. This Court appoint Gershom Goodrich guardian to Susannah Stephenson, 6 years of age, daughter of John Stephenson. Recog., £500.

Page 26 (Vol. XVI) 4 June, 1751: This Court appoint John Cornwell of Middletown to be a guardian to Mary Stephenson, a minor, aged 5 years, daughter of John Stephenson. Recog., £500. Robert Stephenson, a minor, 15 years of age, son of John Stephenson, chose his uncle John Savage to be his guardian. Recog., £1000 money.

Page 58—7 April, 1752: John Savage, guardian to Robert and Thomas Stephenson, minors, shows to this Court that there is one piece of land in sd. Middletown, on the east side of the river, that lies in joynt tenancy with other children of the deceased and their uncle James Stephenson, and desires suitable persons may be appointed to assist sd. guardian: Whereupon this Court appoint Joseph Frary, Joseph White and Jeremiah Goodrich distributors.

Stiles, Henry. Windsor. Court Record, Page 30—6 January, 1746-7: This Court grant Adms. on the estate of Henry Stiles, late of Windsor decd., unto Josiah Bissell of Windsor, who gave bonds with Ebenezer Bissell of Windsor of £600.

Page 49—3 November, 1747: An account of Adms. on the estate of Henry Stiles, late of Windsor, was now exhibited in Court by Josiah Bissell, Adms.: Paid in debts and charges, £48-18-06. Account allowed. Move for a distribution of moveable estate, as follows:

	£ s d
Inventory, moveable estate,	66-14-08
Debts and charges subtracted,	48-18-06

There remains to be distributed,	17-16-02
To Sarah Stiles, widow, her thirds,	18-08-00
To Thomas Stiles, eldest son, a double part,	3-13-04
To Rachel Bancroft and Sarah Osgood, to each of them,	1-19-07
And to Jonah and Amos Stiles,	1-19-07

Which includes the whole of the moveable estate. And this Court appoint Joseph Gaylord, Isaac Haydon and David Elsworth, of Windsor, distributors.

Page 109—7 November, 1749: A report of the distributors exhibited in Court. Ordered recorded and kept on file.

Page 34.

Stimpson, James, Farmington. Invt. £191-08-06. Taken 4 July, 1746, by John Newell and Joseph Hooker.

Court Record, Page 19—5 August, 1746: This Court grant Adms. on the estate of James Stimpson, late of Farmingtown decd., unto Mary Stimpson, widow, who gave bonds with Phineas Lewis of sd. Farmingtown of £300.

Page 114—2 January, 1749-50: An account of Adms. on the estate of James Stimpson, late of Farmingtown, was now exhibited in Court by Mary Stimpson: Paid in debts and charges, with bringing up one child two years, £113-00-00. Which account is allowed.

Page 384-5.

Stocking, John, Middletown. Will dated 2 December, 1746: I, John Stocking of Middletown, in the County of Hartford, being bound on a voyage to sea, do make this my last will and testament: I give and bequeath to my honoured mother Stocking the improvement of the 1-2 of my dwelling house, barn and homelott; also the use of my negro girl Rose for and during the term of my sd. mother's natural life. I give to my wife Mary all my estate, both real and personal, to be to her and her heirs forever, reserving the improvement aforesd., in case I have no child born; but in case I should have a child born, then and in such case my will is that the sd. child, whether male or female, shall have 2-3 parts of my personal estate and the whole of my real estate, to be to him or to her and to his or her heirs forever, reserving what is before reserved, and also reserving to my sd. wife the use of 1-3 part of my real estate during her natural life. And in case I should have a child born as aforesd. and the child should die before it arrive to lawful age to inherit, then my will is that my sd. wife shall have my estate as aforesd., reserving to my mother the improvement aforesd. And further, my will is that all my negro servants that shall survive my sd. wife shall go out free. And I do appoint my wife Mary to be sole executrix.

Witness: *Thomas Goodwin,*   JOHN STOCKING, LS.
Matthew Talcott, Jabez Hamlin.

Court Record, Page 129—17 May, 1750: The last will and testament of John Stocking, late of Middletown, was now exhibited in Court by Mary Stocking, widow and executrix. Will proven, ordered recorded and kept on file.

Page 35.

Stoddard, David, Wethersfield. Invt. £223-02-08. Taken the last day of July, 1746, by Josiah Griswold, Amos Addams and William Wright. (Cape Breton wages, £12-00).

We, the apprisers, being appointed and sworn according to law to apprise, or value two pieces of land lying in Goshen, belonging to the estate of David Stoddard deceased: Sd. land lyeth about half a mile south of the meeting house in sd. Goshen and on the country road, and is in quantity 30 acres, which we value at £210-00-00 money, old tenor. Signed: 11th June, 1746, by

Samuel Thompson,
Abell Phelps, Zacheus Griswold.

Court Record, Page 12—3 June, 1746: This Court grant Adms. on the estate of David Stoddard, Jr., late of Wethersfield decd., unto Keziah Stoddard of sd. Wethersfield, who gave bonds with Josiah Churchill of Wethersfield of £500 money.

Page 45—1st September, 1747: An account of Adms. on the estate of David Stoddard, late of Goshen decd., was now exhibited in Court by Keziah Stoddard, Adms., by which account she has paid in debts and charges, £76-12-05; credit received, £6-08-03. Which account is allowed and ordered to be kept on file. Keziah Stoddard, Adms. on the estate of David Stoddard, Jr., late of Goshen alias Wethersfield decd., moved to this Court that the estate of the sd. deceased may be distributed to the heirs of sd. estate: Whereupon this Court appoint Deacon Benjamin Wright, Ebenezer Wright and Thomas Curtiss, of sd. Wethersfield, to divide sd. estate, real and personal: To Samuel, Stephen, John and Jerusha Stoddard, brethren and sister of the sd. deceased, to each of them the sum or value of £107-17-03, which is their full and equal share and portion of sd. estate, and make return of their doings to this Court.

Stoddard, Joseph. Court Record, Page 19—5 August, 1746: This Court grant Adms. on the estate of Joseph Stoddard, late of Wethersfield, unto Zebulon Stoddard of Wethersfield, who gave bonds with Samuel Hunn of Wethersfield of £500 money.

Page 100-1-103.

Stoughton, John, Windsor. Invt. £2375-13-05. Taken 27 and 28 May, 1746, by Peletiah Allyn, John Palmer, Jr., and Job Drake. Additional inventory of land in Harwinton, £1260-08-09. Taken 1 September, 1746, by Peletiah Allyn, John Palmer, Jr., and Job Drake.

Court Record, Page 15—1st July, 1746: This Court grant Adms. on the estate of John Stoughton, late of Windsor, unto William Stoughton of sd. Windsor, who gave bonds with Capt. Peletiah Mills of £1000.

Page 298-9-300-1.

Stoughton, Capt. Thomas, Windsor. Invt. £980-10-06: Taken 20 March, 1748-9, by William Stoughton and James Rockwell. Will dated 14 June, 1738.

I, Thomas Stoughton of Windsor, do make this my last will and testament: I give to Abigail my wife the improvement of 1-3 part of my dwelling house, barn, shop, stable, cow house and all my improved lands (excepting that which I bought of Jonathan and David Bissell and John Moore, Jr.) during the time of her natural life, and liberty also to get firewood for her use on any of my unimproved lands; and after my just debts are paid I give unto my wife 1-3 part of the rest of my moveable estate forever. I give unto Thomas, my eldest son, all my lands in Torrington, and also all my lands in the Parish of Wintingbury, in Windsor, and also my silver-hilted sword. I give unto my son Daniel the 5th part of my right in the undivided lands in Windsor. I give unto my son Benjamin a lott of land which I bought of Isaac Phelps; also the land I bought of John Moore, Jr.; also 25 acres of land of the lott called Bissell's farm, which I bought of Jonathan and David Bissell, and my right in the undivided lands in the Township of Windsor, he paying to my daughters as I shall order hereafter in this my will. I give unto my son Timothy all my land in the Township of Tolland, divided or undivided, and also all my right, interest and share in the land called the equivalent land, and 1-5 part of my right in the undivided land in the Township of Windsor. I give unto my son David the 1-2 of the lott of land on which my dwelling house stands, on the south side of sd. lott, extending east upon the Great River to the three-mile end or undivided land, and from the old ditch, whereon the meadow fence formerly stood, to the country road, it shall extend northerly 3 feet in a straight line with sd. lott beyond the north end of the house standing on my lott on the west side of the country road; and also 15 acres of land of that lott called Bissell's farm, which I bought of Jonathan and David Bissell, to be on the north side of sd. land, together with the house standing thereon; and also 1-5 part of my right in the undivided land in the Township of Windsor, he paying to my daughters as I shall hereafter order in this my will. I give to my son Isaac 1-2 of my lott whereon my dwelling house stands, on the north side of sd. lott, extending from the Great River to the three-miles end or undivided lands, with the buildings standing thereon; and 1-5 part of my right in the undivided land in the Township of Windsor; also 10 acres of land at that lott called Bissell's farm. I give to my daughter Mary £5, to be paid by my executor out of my moveable estate. I give to my daughter Abigail 5 shillings, to be paid by my executor. I give to my daughter Mabel, besides what she hath already had, three score pounds. I give to my daughter Elizabeth the sum of £200 and the improvement of the west chamber in my dwelling house during her remaining a single woman. My will is that the remainder of my moveable estate, after my just debts and funeral expenses are paid, and what I have given to my wife and to my sons and to my two eldest daughters is subtracted, shall be delivered at inventory price to my daughters Mabel and Elizabeth toward the payment of the legacies given to them. And what my personal estate shall fall short of paying them the sums given them, my will is that my sons Benjamin and David shall in equal parts pay to them in current money or bills of publick credit within one year after my decease. I appoint my two sons Benjamin and David to be my executors.

Witness: *William Stoughton,*   THOMAS STOUGHTON, LS.
Peletiah Bliss, Rachel Stoughton.

Court Record, Page 94—10 March, 1748-9: The last will and testament of Capt. Thomas Stoughton, late of Windsor, was now exhibited in Court by Benjamin and David Stoughton, sons and executors. Will proven, ordered recorded and kept on file.

Page 100—17 May, 1749: Inventory exhibited, accepted, ordered recorded and kept on file.

Page 434-5.

Stoughton, William, Windsor. Will dated 27 April, 1750: I, William Stoughton of Windsor, do make this my last will and testament: I give to Martha, my wife, 1-2 of my dwelling house which I now live in, and 1-3 part of my barn and reasonable yard room, and the use of 1-3 part of my real estate during her natural life. Also, 1-3 part of my moveable and personal estate, to her and to her heirs forever, in lieu of dower. I give unto my son William Stoughton the half of the lott he now lives on not included in his deed, and the 1-2 of the lott which I purchased of Thomas Grant in the meadow not included in his deed; also all my land in Podunk Meadow and 1-2 of my land in Tolland, and 1-2 of my land in Barkhamsted, divided and undivided; and 1-2 of my right of land in Windsor town commons, divided and undivided, including the equivalent land; and also 1-2 of my 15-acre lott lying near Nathan Day's land; all which land to be to my sd. son William Stoughton and his heirs forever. I give to my son Oliver Stoughton the whole of my homelott which I now live on, on both sides of the highway, upland and meadow,

with the buildings and appurtenances, and also the lott which I purchased of Peletiah Bliss and the 3 small lotts which I purchased of my
sisters, and 1-2 of my land in Tolland; also 1-2 of my land in Barkhamsted, divided and undivided, 1-2 of my right of land in Windsor town
commons, divided and undivided, including the equivalent land, and 1-2
of my 15-acre lott near Nathan Day's land; all which land to be to my
sd. son Oliver, to him and his heirs forever. I give to my daughter Elizabeth 5 shillings and no more, for reasons best known to myself. I give
to my daughter Jerusha Newbery £100 money, old tenor, besides what I
have already given her. I give unto my daughter Sibell Newberry £80
money, old tenor, besides what I have already given her. I appoint my
wife Martha and my 2 sons William and Oliver Stoughton executors.

Witness: *Thomas Stoughton,*   WILLIAM STOUGHTON, LS.
Isaac Stoughton, Mary Stoughton.

Court Record, Page 136—7 August, 1750: The last will of William
Stoughton, late of Windsor deceased, was now exhibited in Court by
William and Oliver Stoughton, executors. Proven. Ordered recorded
and kept on file.

Stoughton, William. Court Record, Page 131—5 June, 1750: This
Court grant Adms. on the estate of William Stoughton, late of Windsor
decd., unto Eunice Stoughton, widow, and Capt. Peletiah Allyn of
Windsor, who gave bonds with Samuel Fyler of Windsor of £1000.

Page 237-8-307-8.

Stow, Ebenezer, Jr., Middletown. Invt. £43-10-06. Taken 5 October, 1748, by William Rockwell and William Brintnall. Additional
inventory of property in Woodbury, £400-00-00. Taken 4 October, 1748,
by Nathaniel Porter and Jonathan Kelsey.

Record follows the Inventory, on the same Page.

At a Court of Probate held at Hartford, 11 October, 1748: Then the
foregoing inventory was exhibited by Nathaniel Stow, Adms. Approved,
ordered recorded and kept on file.

Page 77—4 October, 1748: An account of Adms. on the estate of
Ebenezer Stow, late of Middletown, was now exhibited by Nathaniel
Stow, Adms.: Paid in debts and charges, £365-15-00. Account allowed
and ordered to be kept on file.

Page 85—12 January, 1748-9: Pursuant to an act of the General
Assembly holden at New Haven on the 2nd Thursday of October, 1748,
granting liberty to Nathaniel Stow, Adms. on the estate of Ebenezer
Stow, late of Middletown decd. [some part here left out by the Record-
er] as will procure the sum of £332-00-00 with incident charges of sale,
sd. land to be sold at publick vandue, so much of a piece of land in Wood-

bury North Purchase so called, belonging to the estate, in the County of Fairfield, describing the bounds, as will procure the sum and charges arising on sd. sale, to the highest bidder, etc.

Page 307-8.

Stow, Ebenezer, Middletown. Invt. £2992-18-04. Taken 18 January, 1748-9, by Jacob Whitmore and Daniel Hall.

Court Record, Page 103—17 June, 1749: This Court grant Adms. on the estate of Ebenezer Stow, late of Middletown decd., unto Elizabeth Stow, widow, who gave bonds with John Stow of Middletown of £3000.

Page 60 (Vol. XVI) 28 February, 1752: An account of Adms. on the estate of Ebenezer Stow was now exhibited in Court by John Arnold, Jr., and Elizabeth Stow alias Arnold, Adms. on sd. estate, which account is accepted.

Page 310-11-351.

Strong, John, Windsor. Invt. £449-16-00. Taken 10 October, 1749, by William Stoughton, Thomas Stoughton and Peletiah Bliss. Additional inventory of land in Bolton was taken 31 October, 1749, by Edward Spencer and Samuel *Fooler* (Fuller). Will dated 10 February, 1741-2.

I, John Strong of Windsor, do make and ordain this my last will and testament: I give to my wife Mary her (dower rights). I give to my son Jonathan Strong my division of lands in the Township of Windsor agreed to be divided by the Proprietors on the list of land given in the year 1738, to be to him and his heirs forever, with what I have advanced towards his settlement to be his portion. I give to my son David Strong all my right of land lying in Windsor called the equivalent land; this, with what I have advanced towards his settlement in Bolton, to be his portion. I give to my son John Strong all my lands and buildings and rights to land in Windsor (not before given to my sons Jonathan and David). Also I give to my son, John Strong, whom I make executor, all the residue of my estate, both real and personal, he paying the legacies hereafter mentioned. And my will is that what I have given to my son John Strong shall be to him and his heirs forever. I give to my daughter Esther Clarke the sum of £30 bills of publick credit in old tenor, and the like sum to my daughter Abigail Loomis. I give to my daughter Sarah Clarke 10 shillings. I give to the children of my daughter Elizabeth Burnham 10 shillings. I give to the two children of my daughter Hannah 30 shillings apiece, bills of the old tenor.

Witness: *Roger Wolcott,*   JOHN STRONG, LS.
Ephraim Wolcott, Ursula Wolcott.

Court Record, Page 104—4 July, 1749: The last will and testament of John Strong, late of Windsor, was now exhibited in Court by John Strong, executor. Proven and ordered recorded and kept on file.

Strong, John Warham. Court Record, Page 85—11 January, 1748-9: John Strong, age 15 years, Abigail 17 years, children of John Warham Strong and Abigail his late wife, chose their father John Warham Strong of Windsor to be their guardian. Recog., £500 for each minor. Cert: *Henry Allyn, J. P.*

Page 296-337.

Sumner, Lt. Hezekiah, Middletown. Invt. £7740-02-02. Taken 6 July, 1749, by John Bacon, Jonathan Allyn and William Rockwell.

Court Record, Page 105—5 September, 1749: Adms. granted unto Daniel Sumner, son of the deceased, who gave bonds with William Rockwell of Middletown of £1200.

On File:

We, the subscribers, being by the honourable Court of Probate for Hartford County, held at Hartford January the 1st, A. D. 1750-1, appointed to distribute the estate of Lt. Hezekiah Sumner, late of Middletown deceased, to and among his heirs, and having taken the oath appointed for the purpose aforesd., and takeing the order of sd. Court for our directions, have done the same, viz.:

	£ s d
To Abigail Sumner, the widow,	301-19-08
To the heirs of William Sumner,	4450-15-04
To Hannah Warren, eldest daughter,	2225-07-00
To Elizabeth Adkins, the youngest daughter,	2225-07-00

We, the subscribers, being heirs of the estate of sd. Lt. Hezekiah Sumner deceased, do approve of the foregoing distribution of the same, and discharge Daniel Sumner, Adms. on sd. estate, from any further demands thereon.

ABIGAIL X SUMNER, *widow,* JOSEPH JOHNSON,   } *Guardians to*
HEZEKIAH SUMNER,   HANNAH JOHNSON, } WILLIAM, JOHN AND
WILLIAM WARREN,   } EBENEZER SUMNER.
HANNAH X WARREN,   SARAH CRUTTENDEN,
SAMUEL ADKINS,   WILLIAM HARRIS,
ELIZABETH ADKINS,   MARY HARRIS.
WILLIAM BANKS,
HANNAH BANKS,

Page 9 (Vol. XVI) 1st January, 1750-1: An account of Adms. was exhibited in Court by Daniel Sumner, Adms. Accepted. Now moves that distribution be made: Whereupon this Court appoint Joseph Southmayd, Jonathan Allin and William Rockwell to distribute the estate, viz.: to the widow, 1-3 part of the moveable estate, and 1-3 part of the real during life; and to the heirs of William Sumner deceased a double share; to Hannah Warren and Elizabeth Adkins, children and heirs of sd. estate, their single shares (Daniel Sumner, one of the sons of the deceased, having received his portion of sd. estate in the lifetime of the decd.).

Page 93—27 March, 1753: Report of the distributors.

Page 195-6.

Sweeney, Mary, Widow, Simsbury (who died 26 May, 1748). Invt. £144-05-11. Taken 4 June, 1748, by Amos Wilcocks and Jonathan Pettebone. Will dated 20 May, 1748.

I, Widow Mary Sweeney, of the Town of Simsbury, in the County of Hartford, do make this my last will and testament: I give unto my son Benjamin Sweeney two swine, a silk neck cloth, a blue quilted coverlid and a blue quilted petticoat. I give unto my daughter Sarah Sweeney two gowns and a quilted petticoat. I give unto my granddaughter Patience Alderman a blue camblet riding hood, a brass kettle, a trammell, a bedstead, and a part of the wooden dishes. And also I give unto my daughter Patience Alderman a gown and a new shift. Also, I give unto my granddaughter Amey Johnson two beds, three sheets, two coverlids, a boulster and two pillers, a pewter platter, a puter plate, an iron pott, and part of the wooden dishes. Also, I do give unto my daughter Mary Lilley a blue Russell petticoat. I do give unto my son John Priest a shift, that is, a linen shift. Also, I do give unto my son Aaron Priest a chair and a bed cord. My will is that my funeral charges and just debts shall be first paid by having my cow sold to pay sd. debts. And I appoint my son Benjamin Sweeney to be executor.

Witness: *Josiah Grave,*   MARY X SWEENEY.
Jonathan Pettibone, Susannah X Alford.

Court Record, Page 69—6 June, 1748: The last will and testament of Mary Sweeney, late of Simsbury decd., was now exhibited in Court by Benjamin Sweeney, executor. Proven.

Page 104—4 July, 1749: An account of Adms. on the estate of Widow Mary Sweeney, late of Simsbury, was now exhibited in Court by Benjamin Sweeney, executor: Paid in debts and charges, £95-07-03. Which account was allowed and ordered to be kept on file.

Thomas, John. Court Record, Page 68—6 June, 1748: This Court appoint George Welton of Farmington to be guardian to John Thomas, a minor, 11 years of age, son of John Thomas of New Haven deceased. Recog., £300.

Page 73 (Vol. XVI) 3 October, 1752: John Thomas, a minor, 15 years of age, son of John Thomas of New Haven deceased, chose his uncle Richard Porter to be his guardian. Recog., £500. Cert: *Thomas Hart, J. P.*

Page 221-222.

Thompson, Phebe, Farmington. Invt. £319-15-00. Taken 5 February, 1748-9, by Isaac Cowles and Elisha Lewis.

Court Record, Page 55—20 January, 1747-8: This Court grant Adms. on the estate of Phebe Thompson, late of Farmingtown, unto Timothy Thompson, who gave bonds with Elisha Lewis of sd. Farmington of £700.

Page 72—2 August, 1748: An account of Adms. on the estate of Phebe Thompson was now exhibited by Timothy Thompson, Adms.: Paid in debts and charges, £60-15-11; credit received, £13-12-00. Account is allowed and ordered to be kept on file.

Thompson, Samuel, Farmington. Court Record, Page 100—29 May, 1749: A report of the dist. of the estate of Samuel Thompson, late of Farmington, by order of this Court, under the hands of Josiah Hart, Nathaniel Newell and Daniel Judd, distributors. Accepted and ordered to be kept on file.

Page 21-24.

Thompson, Thomas, Southington. Invt. £727-10-10. Taken 2 January, 1745-6, by John Norton, Samuel Thompson and William Burnham, Jr. Will dated 18 December, 1745.

I, Thomas Thompson of Farmingtown, do make this my last will and testament: I give unto my beloved brother Timothy Thompson, to him and his heirs, all my land with the house thereon, with my silver spoon, he paying to my sisters what I shall hereafter order. I give unto my friend Abigail Woodruff £60 old tenor out of my moveable estate, she to take her choice. Unto my beloved sister Elizabeth Hart I give £10 old tenor. Unto my sister Abigail Hart I give £10 old tenor. Unto my sister Phebe Thompson I give £20 old tenor. Further, my will is that my brother Timothy Thompson shall pay to my sisters, to each of them their part if the moveable estate don't do it. And I, Thomas Thompson, do constitute, ordain and appoint my brother Timothy Thompson to be my executor.

Witness: *Thomas Hart,*   THOMAS THOMPSON, LS.
Jonathan Woodruff, Daniel Woodruff.

Court Record, Page 9—1st April, 1746: The last will and testament of Thomas Thompson, late of Farmingtown, was exhibited in Court in January last. The evidences to sd. will have been taken since by this Court, and having now heard the pleas of the parties, do approve sd. will and order that it may be recorded and kept on file.

Page 375-6-7.

Invt. in Vol. XVI, Page 4-5-6.

Thrall, Sergt. John, Windsor. Inventory taken 30 November, 1749, by Daniel Bissell, Samuel Owen and Isaac Gillett. An addition was made to the inventory, 14 August, 1750. Will dated 29 August, 1748.

I, John Thrall of Windsor, yeoman, do make this my last will and testament: I give to Mary, my dearly beloved wife, the use of my house and barn and 7 acres of land, more or less, near the house, with orchard; likewise 5 acres of mow land joining the aforesd. 7 acres; likewise the use of 10 acres of pasture land joining to Sergt. Isaac Gillett on the west; also the privilege of cutting firewood during her widowhood anywhere on the west side of the highway. The aforesd. use of land and buildings I give to my sd. wife during the time she remains my widow. Nextly, I give to my sd. wife 1-3 part of my personal or moveable estate, within house and without, after my funeral charges and debts are paid out of it. I give unto my son John Thrall a piece of land lying on the east side of the brook called the calves' pasture, about 4 acres. I give to my son John my gunn, sword and belt, and a sorrill mare that he uses to call his, and her colt, and 4 sheep, and one sennet calf and one Mack Daniel calf. I give unto my sons, John, Samuel, Ezekiel, Benjamin and Luke, all my real estate, lands and tenements, divided or undivided, lying and being in Windsor, Ellington and Suffield, to be equally divided between them, and to their heirs and assigns forever. I give unto my loving daughters, Mary, Lucy and Mindwell, £200 old tenor money apiece, or publick bills of credit equivalent thereto, or in moveables at inventory price, according to the discretion of my executors, to be paid to them when they arrive to the full age of 18 years. I give unto John, Samuel, Ezekiel, Benjamin, Luke, Mary, Lucy and Mindwell all my lands at Penny Quid and Demmi Catsi, at the eastern country, and my right of land at No. 3 up the Great River, equally to be divided between them. Also, I give unto my aforesd. wife and executor full power to sell all my land lying in the Town of Housetonack or Sheffield, in the Province of the Massachusetts Bay, and also my part of the sawmill at Housetonack, to dispose of to pay my debts and legacies. Also, the remainder of my estate, after the debts and legacies are paid, I give unto my children abovesd., equally to be divided. Also, my will and pleasure is that my executor hereafter named shall have guardianship and oversight, and dispose of each and every of my children until they come to be of lawfull age, my sons to 21 years and my daughters to 18 years. And also my will is that in case my executor hereafter named shall bring up and take care of my sd. children, that then the aforesd. executor shall have the use and improvement of each of their estates until they come to law-full age. And furthermore I do hereby nominate and appoint my wife Mary to be sole executrix to this my last will.

Witness: *Samuel Taggert,*   JOHN THRALL, LS.
Samuel Owen, Jacob Gillet.

Court Record, Page 110—7 November, 1749: The last will and testament of John Thrall, late of Windsor, was now exhibited in Court by Mary Thrall, executrix. Proven, approved and ordered to be recorded and kept on file.

Page 124—3 April, 1750: An inventory of the estate of John Thrall, late of Windsor, was now exhibited in Court by Mary Thrall, executrix, except some things which the sd. decd. ordered should be made use of in his family, which inventory this Court accepts and orders recorded.

Thrall, Joseph. Court Record, Page 132—5 June, 1750: Mary Thrall, a minor, 12 years of age, daughter of Joseph Thrall, late of Windsor, made choice of her father-in-law, Phinehas Steadman of Windsor, to be her guardian. Recog., £300.

Page 228-9-30-31-156-204.

Thrall, Mrs. Sarah, Windsor. Invt. £859-15-09. Taken 8 January, 1746-7, by Samuel Stoughton, Josiah Bissell and Job Drake.

Court Record, Page 30—6 January, 1746-7: This Court grant Adms. on the estate of Mrs. Sarah Thrall, widow of Capt. Timothy Thrall, late of Windsor, unto Capt. Peletiah Allyn of Windsor, who gave bonds with Josiah Bissell of Windsor of £2000.

Page 60—1st March, 1747-8: An account of Adms. on the estate of Mrs. Sarah Thrall was now exhibited in Court by Capt. Peletiah Allyn: Paid in debts and charges, £62-01-06. Which account is allowed, ordered recorded and kept on file.

Page 85—3 January, 1748-9: Motion is now made that distribution be made of the estate as follows:

	£ s d
Inventory,	840-18-03
Debts and charges subtracted,	62-01-06
There remains to be distributed,	711-10-04
To Timothy Thrall,	234-03-04
To the heirs of Sarah Thrall alias Ward,	234-03-04
And to the heirs of Abigail Thrall alias Strong,	234-03-04

And this Court appoint Job Drake, Samuel Stoughton and Jonathan Stiles, of Windsor, distributors.

Dist. File: Estate of Mrs. Sarah Thrall, widow of Timothy Thrall, late of Windsor deceased:

	£ s d
To Timothy Thrall, son of Mrs. Sarah Thrall,	236-03-01
To Elizabeth Clarke, daughter of Abigail Thrall, alias Strong,	79-00-01
To Sarah Strong, daughter of Abigail Thrall,	79-00-01
To John Strong, son of Abigail Thrall,	79-00-01
To Grove Ward, son of Capt. James Ward,	39-10-06
To Timothy Ward,	39-10-06
To Alice Ward,	39-10-06
To Abigail Ward,	39-10-06
To Lucy Goodrich, alias Ward,	39-10-06
To Sarah Easton, alias Ward,	39-10-06

8 February, 1748-9.

By *Samuel Stoughton,*
Job Drake, } *Distributors.*

Tryon, Thomas. Court Record, Page 87—9 January, 1748-9: This Court appoint William Tryon of Glastonbury to be guardian to Abell Tryon, a minor, 13 years of age, and Elyard Tryon, 7 years, children of Thomas Tryon, late of Glastonbury deceased. Recog., £600.

Page 94—8 March, 1748-9: Abell Tryon, now 14 years of age, son of Thomas Tryon, late of Glastonbury, residing in Wallingford, in the County of New Haven, chose Lt. Josiah Robinson of Wallingford to be his guardian. Recog., £500.

Page 88-89.

Tuller, David, Simsbury. Invt. £252-14-06. Taken 4 August, 1746, by Samuel Bemont and Simon Moore.

Court Record, Page 27—4 November, 1746: An inventory of the estate of David Tuller, late of Simsbury decd., was now exhibited in Court by John Tuller, Adms. Accepted.

Page 89.

Tuller, Daniel, Windsor. Invt. £105-07-04. Taken 28 August, 1746, by Samuel Bemon and Gillet Addams.

Court Record, Page 24—2 September, 1746: An inventory of the estate of Daniel Tuller, late of Windsor decd., was now exhibited in Court by (   ), which inventory was accepted, ordered recorded and kept on file.

Page 63-4-123.

Tuller, Jacob, Simsbury. Died 15 June, 1746. Invt. £1427-09-06. Taken 1st August, 1746, by Benajah Humphrey, Lemuel Roberts and Timothy Moses. Will dated 26 March, 1745.

I, Jacob Tuller, of the Town of Simsbury, in the County of Hartford, and now engaged to go in the expedition against the French of Cape Breton, and being at present of perfect health, mind and memory, do make this my last will and testament: My will is that my debts and funeral charges be paid out of my estate. I give to my wife Mary 1-3 part of all my personal estate, to be her own forever; and the use and improvement of my upper meadow lott during her life; also the use of my house and homelott during the time that she remains my widow; and also the use of 1-3 part of my pasture between the Phillips's so long as she remains my widow; and also the liberty to pasture two cows in my lott on the hill so long as not to pasture or feed the mowing land. I give to my son Elijah my lott on the hill that I bought of John Moses and Caleb Moses; also all my land in the upper end of the meadow called my upper meadow lott, provided he pay to my daughters the sum of £100 money equall to the old tenor bills that now pass. I give to my son Jacob my house and homelott and my lott in the long meadow, provided he pay unto my daughters the sum of £50 money equal to old tenor bills as above mentioned. I give to my two sons Elijah and Jacob my land between the Phillips's provided they pay to my daughters their several portions hereinafter expressed. I give to my daughter Mary £10 bills of credit in the old tenor, besides what she hath already received, to be paid her by my son Elijah. I give to my daughter Sarah £60 in value of the old tenor bills, to be paid her by my son Elijah. I do give to my daughters Martha and Elizabeth, to each of them, the sum of £50 equal in value to bills of credit in the old tenor, to be paid them: £10 by my son Elijah and £50 by my son Jacob, and the remainder of their portions to be paid by my two sons equally. I give to my dafters Sibel and Ede and Deborah and Mabel, to each of them £60 in money equal to old tenor bills, to be paid them by my two sons Elijah and Jacob. I give my land in the West Mountains, in the last division, to my executors hereafter named, to be sold by them towards the paying of my debts. All the rest of my estate, real and personal, I give to all my children, to be equally divided among them. I appoint my wife Mary and my two sons Elijah and Jacob to be my executors.

Witness: *John Humphrey,*   JACOB TULLER, LS.
Charles Humphrey, Solomon Humphrey.

Court Record, Page 38—18 May, 1747: An inventory of the estate of Jacob Tuller, late of Simsbury, was now exhibited by his widow, executrix. Accepted, ordered recorded and kept on file.

Page 68—6 June, 1748: An account of Adms. on the estate of Jacob Tuller, late of Simsbury, was now exhibited in Court by Mary Tuller and Elijah Tuller, executors:

	£ s d
Paid in debts and charges,	439-07-04
Credit received,	4-00-00

Account allowed and ordered to be kept on file.

Page 43—5 May, 1747: This Court appoint Mary Tuller, widow, to be guardian to her children, viz., Elizabeth Tuller, age 14 years, Jacob 13, Sibel 11, Ede 8, Deborah 6, and Mehetabel 3 years of age, children of Jacob Tuller decd. Recog., £200 for each minor.

Page 69—6 June, 1748: Mary Tuller, widow, one of the executors, now moves that her thirds of the moveable estate may be set out to her according to sd. will. Also moves that distributors be appointed to make distribution of the estate, viz.: all the rest of sd. estate, real and personal, not disposed of before in sd. will, to all the children of the deceased equally between them: Whereupon this Court appoint Benajah Humphrey, David Phelps and Timothy Moses, distributors.

Tuller, Joseph. Court Record, Page 2—13 December, 1745: Adms. granted unto Barnabas Delano of sd. Tolland, who gave bonds with Josiah Goodrich of Tolland of £800.

Page 238-9-319-20-21-22.

Wadsworth, Rev. Daniel, Hartford. Inventory taken **January, 1747-8,** by John Edwards and Thomas Welles. Will dated 19th December, 1746.

I, Daniel Wadsworth of Hartford, do ordain this my last will and testament: I give unto my beloved wife Abigail 1-3 part of my personal estate forever, and also the use of 1-2 of my dwelling house, barn, home-lott and well during the term of her natural life. I give unto my sd. wife the value of £10 sterling out of my estate. I give unto Abigail my wife the use of 1-2 part of my lott in Hartford which I bought of Benjamin Catling. My will is that the rest of my estate, both real and personal, shall be divided among my children in the following proportion, that is to say, my son Daniel Wadsworth shall have £50 sterling and my son Jeremiah £35 sterling, and my daughters, Abigail, Eunice, Elizabeth and Ruth shall have each of them £25 sterling. And my will is that if my estate shall amount to more than the above-mentioned sums to each of my children, that then the overplus shall be divided amongst them all in the above-mentioned portions. I appoint my wife Abigail sole executrix.

Witness: *Elnathan Whitman,*　　　Daniel Wadsworth, ls.
Niel McLean, Abigail Woodbridge.

Be it known to all men by these presents: That whereas I, Daniel Wadsworth of Hartford, have made and declared my last will and testament in writing, bearing date the 19 day of December, 1746, by this present codicil I do ratify and confirm my sd. last will and testament, and do also, over and above what I have given unto Abigail Wadsworth, my wife, give unto her for her own proper use all such rates and taxes as shall at my decease be due to me from the North Society in Hartford. I do also give unto the sd. Abigail, my wife, to her heirs and assigns forever, one certain piece or parcel of land lying in the Township of Farmingtown, containing by estimation 160 acres, be it more or less, as it is bounded in the Town Records of Farmingtown, it being the lott that was drawn on the right of my honoured grandfather, John Wadsworth, Esq., decd.. in the third division westward from the Town. And my will and meaning is that this codicil or schedule be part of my last will and testament. Codicil dated 3 October, 1747.

Witness: *Edward Dorr,*　　　Daniel Wadsworth, ls.
Niel McLean, Helena Talcott.

Court Record, Page 58—2 February, 1747-8: The last will and testament of the Rev. Daniel Wadsworth was now exhibited in Court by Mrs.

Abigail Wadsworth, executrix. Will proven, ordered to be recorded and kept on file.

Page 375-399-400-1-2-3.

Wadsworth, Capt. Joseph, Windsor. Invt. £6399-07-02. Taken 7 March, 1749-50, by Jonathan Stiles, Samuel Stoughton and Alexander Allin. Inventory taken at Canterbury, 23 April, 1750, by Obadiah Johnson and Joseph Bull. Will dated 30 January, 1749-50.

I, Joseph Wadsworth of Windsor, do make this my last will and testament: I give to my wife all my household stuff, and horse and cow, and negro fellow Hazard, and the improvement of my house and homelott as long as she remains my widow. I give unto my son Joseph Wadsworth the remaining part of my estate that shall be left when he shall come of age. My mind and will is that my executors hereafter named do bring up my son Joseph Wadsworth unto the college. I appoint my honoured father, Daniel Bissell, and my beloved wife, Jerusha Wadsworth, of Windsor, my sole executors.

Witness: *Jonathan Stiles,*   JOSEPH X WADSWORTH.
Nathaniel Loomis 3rd, Ann Loomis.

Page 7-31.

Wadsworth, Lt. Samuel, Farmington. Invt. £1923-13-06. Taken 21 December, 1745, by Isaac Cowles, Giles Hooker and Stephen Root.

Court Record, Page 2—7 January, 1745: This Court grant Adms. on the estate of Lt. Samuel Wadsworth, late of Farmingtown, unto Rebeckah Wadsworth, widow, and William Wadsworth, Esq., who gave bonds with Ebenezer Porter of Farmington of £200.

Page 4—4 March, 1745-6: Rebeckah Wadsworth, widow of Lt. Samuel Wadsworth, moves this Court that her right of dowry be set out to her: Wherefore this Court appoint Capt. Isaac Cowles, Lt. Giles Hooker and Stephen Root to set out by meets and bounds one-third part of the buildings and lands of the said deceased for her improvement during life. This Court do appoint Rebeckah Wadsworth to be a guardian to Asa Wadsworth, 11 years of age, and Hannah Wadsworth, 9 years, children of the said deceased. Recog., £200 for each minor.

Page 8—20 March, 1745-6: James Wadsworth, 16 years of age, son of Lt. Samuel Wadsworth, chose his kinsman William Wadsworth to be his guardian. Recog., £500.

Page 34—10 March, 1746-7: An account of administration on the estate of Lt. Samuel Wadsworth was now exhibited in Court by William Wadsworth and Rebeckah Wadsworth, administrators, and accepted.

Page 17 (Vol. XVI) 26 March, 1751: James Wadsworth, eldest son of Lt. Samuel Wadsworth, moves to this Court that distribution be made of his father's estate: Whereupon this Court appoint Joseph Hooker, Giles Hooker and Robert Porter, of Farmington, to distribute, viz.:

	£ s d
To Rebeckah Wadsworth, widow,	116-15-00
To James Wadsworth, eldest son,	640-08-00
To Samuel, Asa and Hannah Wadsworth, to each,	320-04-00

Page 51—7 January, 1752: Report of the distributors. Accepted.

Ward, James. Court Record, Page 85—11 January, 1748-9: Abigail Ward, 13 years of age, Grove 11 years, and Timothy Ward 6 years of age, children of Capt. James Ward and Sarah his late wife: Capt. James Ward to be their guardian. Reçog., £500 for each minor. Cert: *Jabez Hamlin, J. P.*

Page 393.

Invt. in Vol. XVI, Page 123.

Warner, Daniel, Wethersfield. Invt. £284-11-14. Taken 28 May, 1750, by Ephraim Williams, Joseph Boardman and Timothy Wright. Will dated 24 March, 1750.

I, Daniel Warner of Wethersfield, do give to my wife Mary Warner the use of the house in which I now dwell, and the garden, and one negro man called Pop, during her life (and at her decease to be by her disposed of to one of my children as she shall see fit); and the improvement of 1-3 of all my lands during her natural life, and also 1-3 part of all my moveable estate except the negro. I give to my son William the house in which he now dwells, and both my barns and cow house and the yard thereto belonging, and the following pieces of land: one piece I purchased of Robert Powell, containing about 2 1-2 acres; one piece which I purchased of Capt. Martin Kellogg, about 6 1-2 acres; also 1-2 of the lott which I purchased of Mr. Benjamin Stilman; also 6 acres, more or less, in a place called South Field; also 4 acres, more or less, butted east and north on highways, west on Thomas Harris, and south on Samuel Benton; also two pieces of land lying in the Great Plaine, one piece of 6 acres, the other about 2 1-2 acres; also 3 1-2 acres, more or less, lying in the Great Meadow, butted east and south on the heirs of Samuel Talcott, west on a highway, north on David Wright; also 4 acres, more or less, lying near the middle of the meadow that I purchased of Jonathan Tryon; also one acre in the west swamp; also 1 1-2 acre, more or less, lying in the Mile Meadow, butted east on the river, west on a highway, north on John Crane, and south on the heirs of George Stilman; also 2 1-2 acres in Mile Meadow, being on the south side of the lott which is butted north and south on Thomas Harris, west partly on my own land and partly on land of Daniel Warner, Jr.; also 3 acres of land, more or less, butted east on the last-mentioned piece of land, west on a highway, north on Daniel Warner, Jr., south on Benjamin Wright; also 4 acres, more or less, lying in the lower swamp, butted east and west upon highways, north on Nathaniel Robbins, and south on Joseph Boardman; also 2 pieces of land lying in Fearful (Fairfield) Swamp, one piece containing 6 acres, the other 2 1-2 acres; also 23 acres, more or less, lying in Stepney Parish, butted north on the heirs of Joseph Riley, south on Daniel Warner, Jr., east on my own land, west on land of Josiah Wolcott; also 40 acres, more or less, which I purchased of Isaac Goodrich, adjoining to the last-mentioned piece of land; also one piece of land lying at a place called Hangdog, containing 17 acres, more or less; to him, his heirs and assigns forever. Also I give to my son William the use of the remainder of my homelott, which was my honoured father's (not before given to my wife) until my grandson Daniel Warner shall arrive at the age of 21 years. Also I give to my sd. son William two of my negros, namely, Charles and Jabez. To my daughter Sarah the following pieces of land: two pieces in Beaver Meadow, one of 2 1-2 acres, the other 1-2 an acre; also 1-2 of the lott which I purchased of Mr. Benjamin Stilman; also the south half of the 6-acre lott lying in the Great Meadow near ye gate; also one acre in Mile Meadow which I purchased of Jonathan Tryon. Also I give to my sd. daughter Sarah 2-3 of all my moveable estate (except the negros) and 2 of my negros named Cate and Betty. And also I give to my sd. daughter all the money or bills of credit which I now have or that is due to me, my just debts and funeral charges being first paid out of sd. money. I give to my grandson Daniel Warner, and to his heirs, the house I now dwell in and the homelott, which was my honoured father's, always provided that my dear wife have the use and improvement of the house during her life. And in case she die before my sd. grandson shall arrive to the age of 21 years, then my son William to use and improve the same until such time as he shall arrive to the sd. 21 years of age. I make my wife and son William executors.

Witness: *Joseph Boardman,*   DANIEL WARNER, LS.
Ebenezer Belding, Elisha Williams, Jr.

Court Record, Page 127—1st May, 1750: The last will and testament of Daniel Warner, late of Wethersfield decd., was now exhibited in Court by Mary Warner and William Warner, executors. Proven and ordered to be recorded and kept on file.

Page 131a—5 June, 1750: Mrs. Mary Warner, one of the executors to the last will and testament of Mr. Daniel Warner, late of Wethersfield, moves to this Court to make distribution of the estate according to his will: Whereupon this Court appoint Timothy Wright, Ephraim Williams and Joseph Boardman, of Wethersfield, distributors.

Page 41.

Warner, Robert, Middletown. Invt. £50-16-00. Taken 27 June, 1746, by William Brintnall and William Rockwell.

Court Record, Page 12—3 June, 1746: This Court grant Adms. on the estate of Robert Warner, late of Middletown decd., unto Daniel Warner of sd. Middletown, brother of sd. deceased, who gave bonds with Mr. William Rockwell of Middletown of £200. [Part of this record gone.]

Page 47—23 July, 1747: A report of the commissioners on the estate of Robert Warner, late of Middletown decd., was now exhibited under the hands of Nathaniel Stow and Seth Wetmore, commissioners, which report this Court accepts and order it be filed.

Page 201-2.

Waters, Samuel, Hartford. Invt. £272-03-04. Taken 4 August, 1748, by Dositheus Humphrey and John Cole.

Court Record, Page 71—6 July, 1748: Benjamin Waters, 15 years of age, and Sarah Waters, 13 years, chose their uncle Elijah Clapp to be their guardian. And this Court appoint the sd. Elijah Clapp guardian to Samuel Waters, 12 years of age, Thomas 8 years, John 6, and Bevel Waters 3 years of age, children of Samuel Waters deceased.

Page 74—5 September, 1748: An inventory of the estate of Samuel Waters was exhibited in Court by Elijah Clapp, Adms.

Page 65 (Vol. XVII) 13 May, 1755: Samuel Waters, a minor, about 17 years of age, son of Samuel Waters, made choice of Elijah Clapp to be his guardian. Recog., £300.

Page 4 and 63.

Webster, Elizabeth, Hartford. Invt. £90-06-00. Taken by Joseph Holtom and Thomas Richards. Will dated 17 January, 1743-4.

I, Elizabeth Webster, of the Town of Hartford, do give to my beloved sister Mehetabell Peck all my wearing apparel. I give all the remainder of my estate, after my just debts and funeral expenses are paid, to my brother Robert Reave and to my above-named sister and Elizabeth Benton, now the wife of Ebenezer Benton, and the two sons of Ebenezer Webster, namely, Matthew Webster and Medad Webster, to be divided unto the above named in four equal parts. And I appoint my brother Robert Reave and Matthew Webster to be my executors.

Witness: *Daniel Hooker,*   ELIZABETH X WEBSTER, LS.
James Nichols, Daniel Skinner.

This record follows the will, upon the same page:

Before the Court of Probate in Hartford, on the 30th day of December, 1745, Col. John Whiting, who was the penman of the within-written will, testifieth and saith that in the legacy wherein the testator to this will gave all the remainder of her estate, after debts and funeral charges are paid, to her brother Robert Reave and to her above-named sister and Elizabeth Benton, the wife of Ebenezer Benton, and the two sons of Ebenezer Webster, namely, Matthew Webster and Medad Webster, to be divided unto the above named in four equal parts, that Matthew and Medad were understood as one, and both to have but 1-4 part of the sd. moveable estate exclusive of the wearing apparrel. The above written was sworn to in Court on the day and date abovesd. by

COL. JOHN WHITING.
Test: Joseph Talcott, Clerk.

Court Record, Page 1—3 December, 1745: The last will and testament of Elizabeth Webster, late of Hartford decd., was now exhibited in Court by Matthew Webster, executor. Proven, ordered recorded and kept on file.

Webster, Joseph, Hartford. Court Record, Page 107—26 September, 1749: This Court grant Adms. on the estate of Joseph Webster, late of Hartford decd., unto Ebenezer Webster of sd. Hartford, who gave bonds with Caleb Webster.

Page 394-5-426.

Webster, Joseph, Hartford. Invt. £260-11-11. Taken 2 May, 1750, by Daniel Seymour and Abijah Bunce. Will dated 3 March, 1749-50.

I, Joseph Webster of Hartford, do make this my last will and testament: I give to my wife Hannah my pide cow, yearling colt and 1 sheep, to be at her own dispose forever. I also give unto my sd. wife the use of the north half of my dwelling house and 1-2 of my cellar, with an equal privilege of my well, the north half of my homelott, the north half of my barn, also the 1-2 of my cow pasture, during the term of her natural life. Also I do further give to my wife the use of my red cow and the use of all and any part of my household stuff and goods that she shall need during her natural life. I give unto my daughter Mary Kellogg, and to her heirs forever, besides what I have already given her and done for her, two acres of land in the south meadow, joining land of Jonathan Barret and John Knowls. Also I give unto my sd. daughter Mary Kellogg 1-3 part of all my moveable and personal estate that shall remain after my decease and the decease of my wife. I give unto my daughter Elizabeth Waters, and to her male heirs forever, all my dwelling house, barn and homelott with the appurtenances, all my cow pasture lying south of the land of Thomas Seymour, and all my lands in the south meadow in Hartford, more or less, excepting only the 2 acres given to my daughter Mary, only reserving the use of half of the sd. house and homestead and cow pasture to my sd. wife during her natural life. Also I give unto my sd. daughter Elizabeth 2-3 parts of all my moveable or personal estate that shall remain after the decease of my sd. wife. And I hereby appoint my son-in-law Isaac Kellogg and my wife Hannah sole executors.

Witness: *Ebenezer Webster,*   JOSEPH WEBSTER, LS.
Joseph Holtom, Asahell Andrus.

Page 128—1st May, 1750: The last will and testament of Joseph Webster, late of Hartford, was now exhibited in Court by Capt. Isaac Kellogg, executor named in sd. will, who accepted the trust thereof. Will proven, ordered to be recorded and kept on file.

Webster, Susannah. Court Record, Page 30—6 January, 1746-7: This Court grant Adms. on the estate of Susannah Webster, late of Hartford decd., unto William Bacor of Hartford, who gave bonds with David Ensign of Hartford of £500.

Page 395-6-7-8.

West, John, Hartford. Invt. £2717-12-03, and a list of notes due, £805-06-01. Taken 22 May, 1750, by John MacKnight and John Lawrence.

Court Record, Page 129—22 May, 1750: Adms. to Henry Patterson of New York, who gave bond with Normand Morrison of Hartford of £2000 money of the Colony and exhibited an inventory, which was accepted.

At Court, 24 May, 1750: Mr. Henry Patterson of New York, administrator on the estate of Mr. John West, late of Hartford, deceased, now exhibited a large amount of debts due from the estate, which surmount the inventory of the estate, whereby it appears to this Court that the estate is insolvent, and the Adms. now moves to this Court that commissioners be appointed to adjust the claims of the creditors. This Court appoint Messrs John Lawrence and John Macknight, of Hartford, commissioners.

Page 287-8.

Westover, Capt. Jonathan, Simsbury. Died 23 June, 1748. Invt. £1278-09-03. Taken by Jonathan Smith and Increase Moseley.

Court Record, Page 74—6 September, 1748: This Court grant Adms. on the estate of Capt. Jonathan Westover, late of Simsbury, unto Amy Westover, widow, who gave bonds with Stephen Pettibone of Simsbury of £1000.

Page 91—22 February, 1748-9: Jonathan Westover, a minor, 16 years of age, son of Capt. Jonathan Westover, chose Capt. James Case of Simsbury to be his guardian. Recog., £500. Cert: *John Humphrey, J. P.*

Page 118—23 February, 1749-50: An account of Adms. on the estate of Capt. Jonathan Westover, late of Simsbury, was now exhibited by Joseph Kilbourn, Adms. in right of his wife Amy, relict of the sd. decd., by which account she has paid in debts and charges, £105-18-07. Account allowed. Now moves for distribution of moveable estate: Whereupon this Court appoint Andrew Robe, John Owen and John Case, of Simsbury, distributors:

	£ s d
Inventory of the moveable estate,	1000-02-00
Debts and charges,	105-18-07
There remains,	894-03-05
To the widow her thirds,	298-01-01
To Jonathan, the eldest son,	198-14-02
And to Silas, Hannah, Joseph and David, to each,	99-07-02

To be their own forever, which includes the whole of the moveable estate.

Wetmore, Daniel. Court Record, Page 33—3 March, 1746-7: Daniel Wetmore, a minor, 16 years of age, son of Daniel Wetmore, chose his uncle Samuel Wetmore to be his guardian. Recog., £500. Cert: *Jabez Hamlin, J. P.*

Page 97—14 April, 1749: Elias Wetmore, a minor, 15 years of age, son of Daniel Wetmore, chose his uncle Benjamin Wetmore to be his guardian. Recog., £600. Cert: *Giles Hall, J. P.*

Page 162-3-4.

Wetmore, Nathaniel, Middletown. Invt. £2189-03-06. Taken 14 January, 1747-8, by Ephraim Adkins, Jonathan Allin and Nathaniel Gilbert.

Court Record, Page 56—2 February, 1747-8: This Court grant Adms. on the estate of Nathaniel Wetmore, late of Middletown, unto Ruth Wetmore, widow, who gave bonds with Joseph Wetmore of Middletown of £500.

Dist. File: Middletown, 7 January, 1755: To Ruth, the widow; to Ruth Wetmore, only child. By Ephraim Adkins and Jonathan Allin.

Page 49 (Vol. XVII) 7 January, 1755: An account of Adms. was now exhibited in Court by Ruth Wetmore, widow and Adms., which account is accepted. This Court order distribution of the estate, viz.: To the sd. widow, her thirds in the real and moveable estate; and to

Ruth Wetmore, only child of sd. deceased, all the remainder of sd. estate, real and personal. And appoint Jonathan Allin, Ephraim Adkins and Nathaniel Gilbert distributors.

Page 203-4-208-09.

White, John, Hartford. Invt. £519-17-03. Taken 23 September, 1748, by Jonathan Steele and Joseph Holtom. Will dated 7 November, 1747.

I, John White of Hartford, do make this my last will and testament: I give unto my son John White a lott of land he now lives upon, containing by estimation 18 acres more or less, with the mansion house and all the appurtenances thereunto belonging; also a lott of land on which my son Nathaniel White decd. dwelt, 19 acres more or less, with all the buildings thereon standing, only reserving for Hannah White, my daughter-in-law, the widow and relict of my son Nathaniel, the use and improvement of the full benefit of 5 acres of sd. lott of land and the use of 1-2 of the dwelling house, 1-2 the cellar, and 1-2 the barn, during the time she shall remain his widow. I give unto my son Jacob White all the lott of land I now live upon, 16 acres more or less, with the dwelling house, barn and other buildings thereon; also one piece or parcel of land lying in Hartford on the east side of Rocky Hill, butting west on Joseph Skinner's homelott and south on Wethersfield bounds, containing 15 acres more or less, to be to him and to his heirs forever. My will is that all the rest and remainder of my lands in the Township of Hartford, wheresoever and howsoever butted and bounded, be equally divided between my two sons John and Jacob White, to be to them and their heirs and assigns forever. I give unto my granddaughter Elizabeth White, the daughter of my son Nathaniel White deceased, 20 acres of land in New Hartford, being that pitch of land laid out and surveyed by William Bacor, &c. I give to my son John White one yoke of oxen, one white mare and a sorrill colt, with all my wearing apparrel. I give all my lands in Middletown and all my lands in the Five Miles (so called), on the east side of the Connecticut River, in Hartford, to my daughter Elizabeth Benton and to my daughter Ann Rust, to be equally divided between them. I give to my sd. daughters, Elizabeth Benton and Ann Rust, £10 money apiece. I give to my daughter Sarah Andruss one moiety or half part of my right of land in New Hartford (exclusive of the 20 acres already given to my granddaughter Elizabeth White), the same to be to my sd. daughter Sarah and to her heirs forever. Also I give to my sd. daughter one cow and 6 sheep. Also I give to my daughter Sarah £40 of wool that she has now in her house of mine if I shall not demand the same of her. I give to my son Jacob White all the remainder of my right of land in New Hartford not before disposed of. I give unto my granddaughter Sarah White, daughter of my son Nathaniel White decd., three score pounds money, to be paid her at the age of 18 years or day of marriage. I give unto my son Jacob White one yoke of oxen, my cart, plows, team tackling and all my husbandry tools and utensils. My will is that all the remainder of all my moveable estate, if any there be, to be equally divided to my sons, John and Jacob White, and my daughters, Elizabeth Benton, Sarah Andruss and Ann Rust. I appoint my sons John White and Jacob White executors.

Witness: *J: Buckingham,*   JOHN WHITE,' LS.
Asahell Andruss, Josiah Bigelow.

Court Record, Page 73—2 August, 1748: The last will and testament of Mr. John White, late of Hartford decd., was now exhibited in Court by John and Jacob White, executors. Proven, ordered to be recorded and kept on file.

Page 94—23 March, 1748-9: This Court, on the motion of Jacob White, one of the executors to the last will and testament of John White, appoints Joseph Talcott, Jonathan Steele and Joseph Holtom, of Hartford, to make distribution of the moveable estate of the sd. decd. according to his last will.

Page 108—3 October, 1749: Ebenezer Benton of Hartford now appeals from the judgement of this Court in aproveing the last will and testament of John White, unto the Superior Court. Recog., £100.

Page 107-8.

White, Nathaniel, Hartford. Invt. £900-00-00. Taken 11 June, 1747, by Jonathan Steele and Thomas Welles.

Court Record, Page 42—2 June, 1747: This Court grant Adms. on the estate of Nathaniel White, late of Hartford, unto Hannah White, widow, and Jacob White, of sd. Hartford, who gave bonds with Jared Spencer of Hartford of £800.

Page 52—1st December, 1747: An account of Adms. on the estate of Nathaniel White was now exhibited in Court by Hannah White and Jacob White, Adms.: Paid in debts and charges, £143-12-09. Account is allowed and ordered to be kept on file. Now move that the moveable estate be distributed to the widow and two daughters of the sd. decd.: Whereupon this Court appoint Joseph Talcott and Thomas Welles distributors.

Page 156.

White, Robert, Jr., Stafford. Invt. £452-05-00. Taken 9 October, 1747, by Samuel Warner, Richard Lord and Josiah Converse.

Court Record, Page 57—2 February, 1747-8: This Court grant Adms. on the estate of Robert White, Jr., late of Stafford decd., unto

Joseph White of Stafford, who gave bonds with Amos Walbridge of Stafford of £600 money. Exhibited an inventory, which was accepted and ordered recorded and kept on file. An account of Adms. on the estate of Robert White, Jr., was now exhibited in Court by Joseph White, Adms.: Paid in debts and charges, £20-06-04. Which account this Court allows. Ordered to be recorded and kept on file. Now moves that distributors may be appointed: Whereupon this Court appoint Amos Walbridge, Lt. Samuel Warner and Joseph Converse, of Stafford, to divide the estate, both real and personal, to Ebenezer, Samuel, William and Hugh White, and to Miriam White (alias Thompson) and Jane White, an equal part and portion of sd. estate when the sum of debts aforesd. are subtracted therefrom.

Page 429-30-1-2.

Whitmore, Francis, Middletown. Invt. £685-19-05. Taken 8 May, 1750, by Jonathan Allyn and Timo: Bigelow. Will dated 4 April, 1748.

I, Francis Whitmore of Middletown, do make this my last will and testament: I give unto Mary, my well-beloved wife, the equal third part of all my personal estate after my just debts and funeral charges are paid, and the improvement of the equal half of my dwelling house and cellar, and the use of 1-3 part of my barn and the 1-3 part of all my improved lands during her natural life. I give to my grandson Francis Whitmore, the only son of my eldest son Francis Whitmore, Jr., decd., 7 acres of land which joyns Nathan Sayre's and Hamilton's land; and to the six daughters of my sd. son, namely, Sarah, Mary, Isabel, Susannah, Zerviah and Abigail, to each the sum of £10. I give to my son Jacob Whitmore 15 acres of land joyning the Connecticut River, Harris's meadow, Lemuel Lee's land and Daniel Pryor's land; and half of the land I have in the lott that did belong to John Boarn, adjoining a highway, Daniel Lucas's land, and on my own land; and 1-5 part of all that part of my Kent lott that lyes on the west of the highway by Samuel Brooks's. I give to my son Daniel Whitmore that 6 acres of land that I bought of Samuel Hurlbut, and 4 acres adjoining Daniel Pryor's land. I give to my son Nathaniel Whitmore all that place where he now dwells, bounded west on a highway. I give to my son Ebenezer Whitmore all the land adjoining to the land where his house stands, and all the land lying between 10 acres of land that I have given him by deed of gift. I give to my son Hezekiah Whitmore, and to his heirs and assigns forever, all my dwelling house and barn and the land on which they stand, bounded northerly on Daniel Pryor's land, west on a highway by sd. highway till it comes two lotts southward of the north fence of my son-in-law John Davis. I give to my daughter Margery, the wife of John Davis, and to her heirs forever, all my land that lyes between the lands of Nathan Sayres and the land herein given to my son Hezekiah. I give to my daughter Elizabeth, the wife of Peter Morgan, and to her heirs and assigns forever, all that 25 acres of land which I bought of Zachariah Hubbard. And all the remaining part of all my personal estate (after my just debts and funeral charges and legacies are paid and 1-3 part taken out for my wife) I give to my four daughters, Margery, Hannah, Elizabeth and Abigail, in equal parts. And I further give to my daughter Hannah £100 old tenor, to be paid by my son Hezekiah aforesd. I also give to my daughter Abigail £60 old tenor, to be paid her by my son Ebenezer. I appoint my two sons, Jacob Whitmore and Daniel Whitmore, executors.

Witness: *Giles Hall,*   FRANCIS WHITMORE, LS.
George Hubbard, William Rockwell.

Court Record, Page 130—14 May, 1750: The last will and testament of Francis Whitmore, late of Middletown, was now exhibited in Court by Jacob and Daniel Whitmore, executors. Will proven.

Page 16-20.

Whitmore, Samuel, Middletown. Invt. £646-07-00. Taken 3 March, 1745-6, by Ephraim Adkins and James Ward. Will dated 17 July, 1745.

I, Samuel Whitmore of Middletown, in the County of Hartford, do make this my last will and testament: I give unto my brother Seth Whitmore all and every part of my estate, both real and personal and credit (except the legacies and particular estate herein otherwise disposed of), he paying all my just debts and funeral charges. I give to my brother Francis Whitmore all my Long Meadow lott and the sum of £60 money, old tenor, to be paid him when he shall arrive to lawful age. I give to my sister Martha Savage £100 old tenor. I give the two children of my sister Abigail Clark decd., to each of them, £5 old tenor when they shall arrive to lawful age. I give to my kinsman Daniel Warner the equal half of my mare. And I appoint my brother Seth Whitmore sole executor.

Witness: *William Brintnall,*   SAMUEL WHITMORE, LS.
Joseph Gleason, William Rockwell.

Court Record, Page 8—4 February, 1745-6: The last will and testament of Samuel Whitmore, late of Middletown, was now exhibited in Court by Seth Whitmore, executor. Proven, ordered recorded and kept on file.

Page 4—4 March, 1745-6: Seth Whitmore of Middletown, executor to the last will and testament of Samuel Whitmore, late of Middletown, showing to this Court that he has a right in a certain piece of land in Middletown which lyes in common or joynt tenantcy with Francis Whitmore, a minor son of Joseph Whitmore of Middletown decd., and Joseph

Ranney, guardian to the sd. Francis, which sd. land is at a place called Timber Hill, about 30 acres: And this Court appoint Capt. Henry King, William Rockwell and Joseph Frary of Middletown to assist the guardian of the sd. Francis in the division of the sd. lands to the sd. Seth Whitmore and sd. Francis Whitmore, and make return of their doings to this Court.

Page 11—6 May, 1746: A division of land belonging to the estate of Samuel Whitmore of Middletown decd., under the hands of Joseph Frary, distributor.

Page 67.

Whitmore, Samuel, Middletown. Invt. £135-16-06. Taken 28 June, 1746, by Joseph Miller and John Bartlett. Part in lands: two and half acres in the homestead, bounded north by Benjamin Wetmore and south by Moses Persons; three acres bounded west by Joseph Hale and east by Caleb Wetmore, south by Joseph Miller and north by a highway; four acres bounded east by Daniel Dregs; one and a half acres in the third division sold to Elisha Clark, and two acres and a half sold to John Kirbe.

Court Record, Page 15—1st July, 1746: This Court grant Adms. on the estate of Samuel Whitmore, late of Middletown, unto Samuel Whitmore, son of the sd. decd., who gave bonds with Seth Whitmore of Middletown of £500. Exhibit of an inventory, which was accepted, ordered recorded and kept on file.

Page 23—2 September, 1746: An account of Adms. on the estate of Samuel Whitmore, late of Middletown, was now exhibited in Court by Samuel Whitmore, Adms.:

	£ s d
Paid in debts and charges,	230-06-08
Received,	51-01-02

Which account is allowed and ordered to be kept on file.

Page 28—15 November, 1746: Pursuant to an act of the General Assembly holden at New Haven on the 2nd Thursday of October, 1746, Samuel Whitmore, Adms. on the estate of Samuel Whitmore of Middletown, is directed to sell so much of the real estate of the sd. deceased as will procure the sum of £172-06-11 with the necessary charges of the sale, taking the advice of the Court of Probate in the District of Hartford therein.

Page 257-8-9.

Whitmore, Seth, Middletown. Invt. £1736-10-09. Taken 20 December, 1748, by Jonathan Allin and James Ward. Will dated 21 November, 1748.

I, Seth Whitmore of Middletown, do make this my last will and testament: I give unto Elizabeth, my wife, all and every part of my household goods, as well what she brought with her by our marriage as what has been added since, and the cow that was given to her by Father Hall, these to be at her dispose. I also give her the improvement of half my dwelling house, barn, shop and homelott in the Town Platt, for and during the time she shall remain my widow. I give to my only brother Francis Whitmore, and to his heirs and assigns forever, all my half of sd. dwelling house, barn, shop and homelott (after the decease or marriage of my widow). And all my Long Meadow lott which I bought of Willet Ranny, containing 2 1-2 acres, and my horse, saddle and bridle, and all my apparel, and my trooper's tackling, and all other of my estate (as family provisions, husbandry tools, credits, and every other thing whatsoever) I give to my sd. wife and brother to be equally divided between them, after my just debts and funeral charges are paid out of it. And I appoint my kinsman Lt. Jacob Whitmore and my sd. brother Francis Whitmore executors.

Witness: *Edward Rockwell,*   SETH WHITMORE, LS.
John Mathews, William Rockwell.

Court Record, Page 88—7 February, 1748-9: The last will and testament of Seth Whitmore, late of Middletown, was now exhibited in Court by Jacob Whitmore and Francis Whitmore, executors. Will proven.

Wilkerson, Lodowick. Court Record, Page 10—1st April, 1746: This Court appoint Thomas Cannady of Bolton to be guardian to William Wilkerson, a minor, 11 years of age, son of Lodowick Wilkerson. Recog., £300.

Page 18—7 May, 1746: Mary Wilkerson, a minor, 14 years of age, chose Timothy Olcott, Jr., of Bolton, to be her guardian. Recog., £300. Cert: *Thomas Pitkin, J. P.*

Page 94—31 March, 1749: Mary Wilkerson, now 17 years of age, made choice of Thomas Pitkin to be her guardian. Recog., £300.

Page 13 (Vol. XVII) 7 February, 1754: William Wilkerson, a minor, 19 years of age, son of Lodowick Wilkerson, late of Wethersfield, now made choice of Jonathan Couch of Hartford to be his guardian. Recog., £300.

Page 313.

Williams, John, Wethersfield. Invt. £2258-03-03. Taken 26 December, 1748, by Jacob Williams and William Goodrich.

Court Record, Page 102—30 May, 1749: An inventory of the estate of John Williams, late of Wethersfield decd., was now exhibited in Court by Esther Williams, Adms. Accepted, ordered to be recorded and kept on file. An account of Adms. on the estate of John Williams was now exhibited by Esther Williams, which account is allowed and ordered to be kept on file. This Court appoint Esther Williams, widow, to be guardian to her children, viz., Mehetabell, 6 years of age, and Abigail, 1 year and 9 months, children of John Williams, late deceased. Recog., £500 for each minor.

Page 92-3.

Williams, Joseph, Middletown. Invt. £477-18-03. Taken 2 June, 1746, by William Brintnall and Samuel Wyllys.

Court Record, Page 14—24 June, 1746: This Court grant Adms. on the estate of Joseph Williams, late of Middletown, unto William Rockwell of sd. Middletown, who gave bonds with James Brown of £500.

Page 16—1st July, 1746: An inventory of the estate of Joseph Williams, late of Middletown, was now exhibited in Court by William Rockwell, Adms. Accepted.

Page 18—24 June, 1746: This Court appoint William Rockwell to be guardian to Isaac Williams, a minor son of Joseph Williams, late of Middletown decd. Recog., £500.

Page 327-8.

Williams, Sarah, Widow, Hartford. Will dated 23 May, 1744: I, Sarah Williams, widow, relict of William Williams, late of Hartford decd., do make this my last will and testament: I give to my son William Williams £10 old tenor of my estate. I give to my son Daniel Williams £10. I give to my daughter Rachel Burnham £10, in which sum I would have my wearing apparrel included. I give unto each of my grandchildren, the children of my daughter Sarah Forbes decd., 5 shillings each, in old tenor money, including the late wife of James Forbes, Jr., decd. I give the remainder of my estate, be it more or less, to my son Daniel Williams. I appoint my two sons, William and Daniel Williams, to be my executors.

Witness: *Joseph Pitkin,*   SARAH WILLIAMS, LS.
Elizabeth X *Lowheed.*

Court Record, Page 107—1st Tuesday of September, 1749: The last will and testament of Sarah Williams, widow of William Williams, late of Hartford decd., was now exhibited in Court by William and Daniel Williams, executors named in the sd. will. Will proven, ordered to be recorded and kept on file.

Page 71-2.

Williams, Stephen, Wethersfield. Invt. £1474-16-03. Taken 19 February, 1747, by Gideon Goodrich and Nathaniel Robbins.

Court Record, Page 32—17 February, 1746-7: This Court appoint Edward Bulkeley, Esq., to be guardian to John Williams, a minor, age 12 years, son of Stephen Williams. Recog., £500.

Page 36—7 April, 1747: An inventory of the estate of Stephen Williams was exhibited in Court by John Williams, Adms. Accepted.

Page 86—12 January, 1748-9: Jehiel Williams, a minor, 15 years of age, son of Stephen Williams, chose his uncle Jacob Williams to be his guardian. Recog., £500.

Page 89—7 February, 1748-9: An account of Adms. was exhibited in Court by Abigail Williams, Adms. Also, the sd. Adms. moves this Court for a distribution of sd. estate:

	£ s d
Inventory of the real and personal estate,	1575-03-03
Moveable part of the inventory,	382-03-03
Debts and charges being subtracted,	297-03-03
There remains to be distributed,	134-19-00
To Abigail the relict, her thirds,	49-19-10
To the heirs of John Williams, eldest son, in real estate,	291-10-00

Stephen having already received by deed of gift in his father's lifetime his full portion, and to Abigail Williams, alias Bulkeley, in moveable estate the sum of 145-15-00

To Jehiel Williams, in personal estate, 145-15-00

And the remainder in real estate.

And appoint Deacon Benjamin Wright, Deacon David Goodrich and Ebenezer Wright, distributors:

	£ s d
Land to be divided,	493-00-00
Moveables,	97-12-04
Both,	590-14-04
Exclusive of Stephen's,	700-00-00

Page 102—6 June, 1749: Distribution of the estate of Stephen Williams, late of Wethersfield, was now exhibited in Court under the hands of Benjamin Wright and Ebenezer Wright, distributors. Accepted and ordered to be kept on file.

Page 244-5.

Williams, Stephen, Wethersfield.   Invt. £1242-10-00.   Taken 22 September, 1748, by William Bement and Nathaniel Robbins.

Court Record, Page 72—2 August, 1748: This Court grant Adms. on the estate of Stephen Williams, late of Wethersfield decd., unto Elizabeth Williams, widow of the sd. decd., who gave bonds with John Robbins 2nd of Wethersfield of £1000.

Page 75—4 October, 1748: An inventory of the estate of Stephen Williams was now exhibited in Court by Elizabeth Williams, Adms. Accepted, ordered recorded and kept on file.

Page 90—7 February, 1748-9: An account of Adms. on the estate of Stephen Williams, late of Wethersfield, was now exhibited in Court by Elizabeth Willaims, Adms.: Paid in debts and charges and for provisions spent in the family, £111-05-01. Which account is allowed.

Page 112—5 December, 1749: This Court appoint Elizabeth Williams, widow, to be guardian to her son Oswald Williams, a minor, 3 years of age, son of Stephen Williams, late of Wethersfield deceased. Recog., £500.

Page 136-7.

Wolcott, Henry, Windsor. Invt. £447-17-10. Taken 1st January, 1747-8, by Matthew Rockwell, Joshua Loomis and Moses Loomis, Jr. Will dated 14 November, 1740.

I, Henry Wolcott of Windsor, do make this my last will and testament: I give to my son Henry Wolcott all my lands in Colebrook, and all my lands in Willingtown, and all my lands and rights to common and undivided lands in the Township of Windsor, and the lands called the Equivalent, to him and his heirs forever. I give to my grandsons, Thomas Wolcott and Luke Wolcott, 2-3 parts of my 400-acre farm in Tolland that is bounded south on Coventry, as also my three rights or lotts in the Cedar Swamp in Tolland, share and share alike, to them and their heirs forever. I give to my son Thomas his four daughters 1-3 part of my 400-acre farm in Tolland, to them and their heirs forever. And my will is that my son Thomas shall have the improvement of what land he hath before this time enclosed at any time within fence of my 400-acre farm in Tolland during his natural life. I give to my son Gideon Wolcott that lott of land in Windsor I bought of my brother Simon Wolcott, whereon I now live, from the river to the end of the three-mile lotts, bounded east on the commons, with the appurtenances, to him and his heirs forever. I give to my grandson Giles Wolcott about 300 acres of land more or less, lying in Windsor, bounded east upon Bolton, north upon land belonging to Gideon Wolcott, south upon land laid out to Joseph Barbour, and west upon a highway, or however the same may be otherwise bounded, to him and to his heirs forever. I give to my daughter Rachel my two black servants, Philehas and Scipio, and £50 more to be paid out of my personal estate at inventory price. And all the rest and residue of my estate I give to my sons, Henry, Thomas and Gideon, and to my daughter Rachel and to my grandson Giles, share and share alike, in five equal parts, my grandson Giles his part to remain in the hands of my executors until he attain the age of 21 years. I appoint my son Gideon Wolcott and my kinsman Roger Wolcott, Jr., executors.

Witness: *Roger Wolcott,*   HENRY WOLCOTT, LS.
James Wolcott, Simon Wolcott.

Court Record, Page 54—5 January, 1747-8: The last will and testament of Henry Wolcott, late of Windsor, was now exhibited in Court by Roger Wolcott, Jr., Esq., and Gideon Wolcott, executors. Will proven and exhibit of an inventory of the moveable estate. Accepted, and both ordered to be recorded and kept on file.

Page 1 (Vol. XVII) 26 November, 1753: Luke Wolcott, one of the grandsons of Mr. Henry Wolcott, now moves to this Court for a distribution of a 400-acre farm in Tolland and three rights of land in the Cedar Swamp in sd. Tolland, to be divided, viz., 2-3 to Thomas Wolcott and the sd. Luke, and 1-3 part of sd. 400-acre farm to the four daughters of the deceased, agreeable to the last will and testament of the deceased: Whereupon this Court appoint Zebulon West, Joseph West and Amasa West, of Tolland, distributors.

Dist. File: Distribution of land in Tolland: To Thomas and Luke Wolcott, grandsons (sons of Thomas Wolcott, son of the decd.) Also, four daughters of sd. Thomas Wolcott, late decd.: Miriam Wolcott, the wife of Stone Mills; Jane Katharine Wolcott, the wife of Ellis Russell; Redexalena and Rachel Wolcott. 2 May, 1754. By Joseph West, Amasa West and Zebulon West.

Page 185-186-7.

Wolcott, James, Windsor. Invt. £862-13-00. Taken 9 March, 1747-8, by Nathaniel Bancroft, Gideon Wolcott and Matthew Rockwell.

Court Record, Page 61—8 March, 1747-8: This Court grant Adms. on the estate of James Wolcott, late of Windsor decd., to Samuel Treat, late of Wethersfield, who gave bonds with Joseph Newberry of Windsor of £1000.

Page 185 (Probate Side): An agreement under the hands of William Stoughton: Whereas, there is descended to us, William Stoughton and Martha his wife, in right of sd. Martha, and to Samuel Treat of Wethersfield in his own right, on the death of Mr. James Wolcott of Windsor decd., an estate (real and personal) in such proportion that by the descent aforesd. to them, the sd. William Stoughton and Martha his wife, in right of sd. Martha, belongs one moiety or 1-2 of sd. estate, and to the sd. Samuel Treat another half thereof, they being the only heirs of sd. estate by the descent aforesd.; and whereas, we being minded to divide sd. estate according to our interest and just proportion thereof, viz: We do hereby agree to divide to sd. Samuel Treat, for his half of sd. moveable estate, viz., one negro man named Answer, £240; two horses, £106-00-00; all which amount to £346; together with some of the other articles of sd. moveable estate equally divided to sd. Samuel Treat, amounting to the sum of £380-00-00; and being the sd. Samuel Treat's proportion of sd. moveable estate. 2ndly, we do hereby devise and set out unto the sd. William Stoughton, in right of his wife Martha, for their part of sd. moveable estate, all the cattle and colt, all amounting to £202-00-00, with sundry other articles set out to sd. William Stoughton, in the whole the sum of £380. And we, the sd. William Stoughton and Martha Stoughton of the one part, and Samuel Treat of the other part, do each of us, for ourselves and our heirs, acknowledge we have received our part of sd. moveables.

     At a Court of Probate held   WILLIAM STOUGHTON, LS.
at Hartford, 3rd May, A. D. 1748:   MARTHA STOUGHTON, LS.
Then   William   Stoughton,   and   SAMUEL TREAT, LS.
Martha Stoughton his wife, and Samuel Treat, signers and sealers of this instrument, acknowledged the same to be their free act and deed, and their hands and seals.   *Test: Joseph Talcott, Clerk.*

Page 65—3 May, 1748: An agreement for the settlement of the estate of James Wolcott, late of Windsor decd., under the hands of William Stoughton and Martha Stoughton and Samuel Treat, heirs to sd. estate, was now exhibited, which agreement this Court approve, order to be recorded and kept on file.

Page 119-20-21-22-192-3-4-5.

Woodbridge, Samuel, Hartford. Died 9 June, 1746. Invt. £2311-19-02. Taken 25 July, 1746, by Nehemiah Olmsted and William Stanly. Will dated 29 May, 1746.

     I, Samuel Woodbridge of Hartford, do make this my last will and testament: I give unto my wife, Content Woodbridge, all those household goods and estate which I had with her when I married her. I say all that remains, of whatsoever denomination, and all the household goods which have been brought into the house since our marriage, and the negro woman and all her children, which are now my property, and all the debts due to me in Rhode Island, and £100 money out of a bond due to me from my son Deodat Woodbridge, and 1-3 part of my moveable goods belonging within the house, besides those before given her, and

two cows and a black mare I bought of Matthew Beel. And further I
give to my wife the use of 1-3 part of my dwelling house and barn, and
1-3 part of all my improveable lands, during her natural life. I give
unto my son Deodat Woodbridge several parcels of land joining lands of
Elisha Burnham, Allen McLean, my son Russell Woodbridge, Richard
Burnham, Daniel Bidwell, Joseph Meekin, Deacon Joseph Olmsted, Joseph and James Easton, Stephen Olmsted, John Bidwell, Nehemiah Olmsted, Samuel Pitkin, etc., all the forementioned parcels of land lying in
Hartford on the east side of the river. I also give to my son Deodat 1-2
of my lands in New Hartford, and 1-2 of my lands in Bolton, and 1-3
part of my interest in the mines there, all of which estate I give to my son
Deodat, to him and to his heirs forever, provided nevertheless that he
shall pay the sum of £206, due to me by bonds, with the interest, within
two years after the date of this my last will, to my executors. I give to
my son Russell Woodbridge several parcels of land: one parcel whereon
his dwelling house now stands, adjoining Richard Burnham, John Hurlbut, John Goodwin, John Pitkin and Joseph Meekin; also 1-2 of 20 acres
which I bought of John Hills decd.; one piece of meadow land called
Easton's Hollow, about 3 1-2 acres, adjoining Joseph Meekin and John
Bidwell, all of which pieces of land above named lye on the east side of
the Great River in Hartford. Also I give unto my son Russell Woodbridge 1-2 of all my lands in New Hartford, and 1-2 of all my lands in
Bolton, and 1-3 part of my interest in the mines there, all which parcels
of land I give to my son Russell Woodbridge and to his heirs forever.
I give to my son Samuel Woodbridge several parcels of land: I give him
my homelott butting east on the country road, west on land of William
Bidwell, north on land of Disborah Spencer, and south on land of James
Bidwell, together with my dwelling house, barn and all buildings on the
sd. land; and also one small piece of upland lying north of the road leading to the ferry, about 3 acres, bounded east on land of Thomas Spencer,
west on land of Sarah Easton, north on land of Joseph Meekin, and south
on the country road; also one piece of upland which I bought of Benjamin Cheney, about 2 1-2 acres, butting south and west on the country
road leading to the mills, north and east on land of Ozias Pitkin, Esq.
I give to my son Samuel Woodbridge 1-3 part of my interest in the mines
at Bolton, and the sum of £100 money of old tenor, in money or some
of my moveable estate. I also give him 1-2 of 20 acres of woodland
bought of John Hills. I give unto my former wife's son, Dr. George
Hubbard of New Haven, and to the heirs of Mr. Daniel Hubbard, late of
New London decd., all my land in the Township called Hartland, upon
this condition, that they give a quitclaim deed to all the lands which I
sold to their mother, unto which they have pretended some claim. I
give unto my daughter Elizabeth Little the 1-2 of all my lands at Willington, in the County of Hartford, to be divided equally with my
daughter Mabel Little. I give unto my daughter Mabel Little the 1-2 of
all my lands in Willington, to be equally divided between her and her

sister Elizabeth Little. I give unto her the sum of £50 money of the old tenor or in notes or bonds for money due, to be paid to her or delivered to her within 4 months after my decease. I give unto my wife's daughter Theadocia Bull the sum of £10 money as a token of my paternal love to her, to be paid to her within one year after my decease. I do hereby reserve for my son Samuel, provided he shall have a liberal education and settle in the work of the ministry, all my library of books, anything foregoing notwithstanding. And I herein give to my son Deodat the £50 which I lately paid to my son Nathaniel Little on his account, and release him from paying a note of £75, dated 18 November, 1743. And in case he shall by any means fail of paying what is due to me upon his bond to my executors within two years after my decease, then I do hereby fully impower my executors hereafter named to sell the 12 acres of upland given him, butting south on land of Daniel Pitkin aforesd., anything herein to the contrary notwithstanding. My will is that all the provisions in my house, of what kind soever, at the time of my decease, shall be exempted from an inventory and shall be improved by my wife at her discretion in the family. My will is that my son Samuel's estate be under the care of my executors during his minority, and that the income of it be improved by them for his support or education until he come to the age of 21 years. I hereby make my friend, Col. Joseph Pitkin, and my wife, Content Woodbridge, executors.

Witness: *Joseph Cowles,*   SAMUEL WOODBRIDGE, LS.
Aaron Benton, James Bidwell.

Court Record, Page 29—7 August, 1746: The last will and testament of the Rev. Samuel Woodbridge, late of Hartford, was now exhibited. by Joseph Pitkin and Content Woodbridge, executors. Proven, ordered recorded and kept on file.

Page 227.

Woodbridge, Theodore, Hartford. Will dated 8 August, 1740: I, Theodore Woodbridge, being bound on a voyage to sea, do make this my last will and testament: I give to my honoured mother, Abigail Woodbridge, all my lands, tenements, hereditaments, with all my goods, chattells and credits of what kind or nature soever, that is to say, all my estate, real and personal, wheresoever the same is, or however the same is or may be described, to be to her and her heirs and assigns forever. And I do hereby further will and determine that if it should so happen that my sd. mother should die after my decease without disposeing of the estate I have herein devised to her, the same estate after her death I will and devise to be to my brother-in-law Ashbell Woodbridge and my brothers-in-law Richard, Epaphras and Ichabod Lord, that is to say, in such proportion as that brother Ashbell Woodbridge shall have the full half thereof, and the other half to be divided between the sd. Richard,

Epaphras and Ichabod, to them and their heirs forever. I do appoint my mother, Mrs. Woodbridge, to be sole executrix.

Witness: *Normand Morrison,* THEODORE WOODBRIDGE, LS.
Hez: Collier, William Nichols, J: Gilbert, Jr.

Court Record (follows the will, on the same page), first Tuesday of October, 1747: The last will of Theodore Woodbridge, late of Hartford decd., was now exhibited in Court by Mrs. Abigail Woodbridge, executrix named in said will, who accepted the trust thereof. Said will being proved, is by this Court approved and ordered to be recorded and kept upon file. *Test: Joseph Talcott, Clerk.*

Woodbridge, Theophilus. Court Record, Page 110—14 November, 1749: This Court grant Adms. on the estate of Theophilus Woodbridge, late of Simsbury deceased, unto Haynes Woodbridge of Windsor, who gave bonds with Ambrose Ladou of Simsbury of £500.

Page 110-11-12.

Woodruff, Ebenezer, Southington. Invt. £2103-11-10. Taken 20 May, 1747, by Samuel Root, Nathaniel Gridley and Jarad Lee. Will dated 15 April, 1747,

I, Ebenezer Woodruff of Southington, in Farmingtown, in the County of Hartford, do make this my last will and testament: Unto my wife Esther Woodruff I give 1-3 part of my moveable estate forever, and the use of 1-3 part of my real estate during her natural life. Unto my daughter Sarah Woodruff I give £500 of money, old tenor. To my only son Asa Woodruff I give all the residue and remainder of my whole estate, real and personal, lands, tenements, hereditaments, goods and chattells that I have not already given unto my wife and daughter. And I, Ebenezer Woodruff, appoint my brother Hezekiah Woodruff to be sole executor.

Witness: *Jeremiah Curtiss,* EBENEZER WOODRUFF, LS.
Stephen Andruss, Nathaniel Gridley.

Court Record, Page 39—2 June, 1747: The last will and testament of Ebenezer Woodruff, late of Farmingtown, was now exhibited in Court by Hezekiah Woodruff, executor, who also exhibited an inventory. Both accepted, ordered recorded and kept on file.

Page 102—6 June, 1749: Sarah Woodruff, a minor, age 15 years, daughter of Ebenezer Woodruff, chose Mr. Thomas Hart of Farmington to be her guardian. Recog., £1000.

Wright, James. Court Record, Page 94—17 March, 1748-9: Adms. granted unto Isaac Wright of Wethersfield, who gave bonds with Michael Burnham of Hartford of £800.

Page 259-60.

Wright, Thomas, Middletown. Invt. £2268-06-03. Taken 28 January, 1748-9, by John Fisk and John Cooper. Will dated 26 December, 1748.

I, Thomas Wright of Middletown, do make this my last will and testament: I give to Elizabeth, my wife, 1-3 part of all my personal estate and 1-3 part of all my real estate for her improvement during her natural life. I give to my eldest son, Thomas Wright, and to his heirs and assigns forever, the equal half of all my estate, he paying to my daughters the legacies hereafter mentioned. I give to my second son, Jonas Wright, and to his heirs and assigns forever, 3-20 of all my estate, he paying to my daughters the legacies hereafter mentioned. I give to my youngest son, Earl Wright, and to his heirs and assigns forever, 7-20 of all my estate, he paying to my daughters the legacies hereafter mentioned. I do hereby give to my three daughters, Elizabeth, Mary and Hepzibah, to each so much of my estate as shall make each of them £200 old tenor with what I have already given them, which legacies shall be paid to them by my three sons in such proportion as I have herein given my estate to them. I further give to my wife a proper mourning suit besides what I have herein given her. And I appoint my two eldest sons, Thomas Wright and Jonas Wright, executors.

Witness: *Thomas Andrews,*   THOMAS X WRIGHT, LS.
Joseph Storer, William Rockwell.

Court Record, Page 89—7 February, 1748-9: The last will and testament of Thomas Wright, late of Middletown, was now exhibited in Court by Jonas Wright, one of the executors. Will proven. Exhibited an inventory. Accepted. Both ordered recorded and kept on file.

Page 385-6.

Yeomans, Elijah, Tolland. Invt. £2866-03-06. Taken 26 March, 1750, by Jabez Delano, Peletiah West and John Lothrop. Will dated 1st February, 1749-50.

I, Elijah Yeomans of Tolland, in the County of Hartford, do make this my last will and testament: I give to my wife, Abigail Yeomans, the improvement of all my estate, both real and personal, that is to say, my buildings, orcharding, plowing and grass land, together with my neat cattle, sheep, horses, and household goods and whatsoever, after all my just debts and funeral charges are paid out of the sd. moveables, then the same to remain to her, her use and improvement until my son Elijah Yeomans shall arrive to the age of 21 years, she supporting my children and paying out of it the legacies as I shall hereafter name to my eldest daughter Abigail. I give to my daughter Abigail Yeomans £200, to be paid unto her out of my moveable estate when she shall arrive to the age of 18 years. I give unto my wife Abigail 1-3 part of my moveable estate forever. And further I give unto my wife Abigail the improvement of the north room in my dwelling house, and half my barn, during the time of her widowhood. I give unto my daughter Eunice Yeomans £200, to be paid out of my moveable estate at the age of 18 years. I give to my son Elisha Yeomans 20 acres of land on the southeast corner of my farm, which is land that I bought of Joseph Chamberlain, Jr., for the bounds of which I refer to Tolland Records. I give unto my son Elijah Yeomans the 1-2 of my farm that I now live on, taking it off at the east end, reckoning what I have or shall have of my honoured mother's thirds to belong to it, exclusive of what I have given to my son Elisha. I give to my sd. son Elijah the 1-2, drawing a line across my farm north and south, giving him the east end. I give unto my son Oliver Yeomans the 1-2 of the farm of land that I now live on, taking it off at the west end. And further, my will is that my son Oliver shall have out of that part of my orchard that comes into my son Elijah's hands the improvement of the 1-2 of it for the term of 7 years next coming after the sd. Oliver shall arrive to the age of 21 years, that is to say, the profit of the 1-2 of the fruit of the trees, but not of the land to plow or feed or mow. And further, my will is that what I have given by this instrument to my two daughters, being to be paid to them some time hence, and not knowing how our paper currency may rise or fall, I order and my will is that my executors make payment thereof at the several times of payment as I have said in this instrument according to the true and just value of our present paper bills of credit, allowing silver at this time to be 55 shillings per ounce, and so to pay more or less as paper money shall rise or fall, at the discretion of my executors.

I appoint my wife Abigail Yeomans executrix.

Witness: *John Lothrop,*   ELIJAH YEOMANS, LS.
David Lothrop, Clorandy Lothrop.

Court Record, Page 126—10 April, 1750: The last will and testament of Elijah Yeomans, late of Tolland deceased, was now exhibited in Court by Abigail Yeomans, widow and executrix. Will proven. Exhibit of an inventory. Both accepted, ordered to be recorded and kept on file.

Page 60 (Vol. XVII) 24 April, 1755: Whereas, Elijah Yeomans of Tolland deceased, by his last will and testament appointed the above-named Abigail executrix to his last will and testament, and ordered his executrix to pay unto Abigail and Eunice Yeomans £200 each in old tenor bills at the rate of 55 shillings per oz. in silver (sd. Abigail, executrix, now being deceased) and the legacy not being yet paid, these are to direct sd. distributors: First, to distribute and set out to the sd. Abigail and Eunice the legacy given by sd. will, and the remaining part of sd. estate to be divided: to Elijah, the eldest son, his double share; and to Oliver and Elisha Yeomans, to each of them a single share. And appoint John Abbott, Ephraim Grant and Samuel West, of Tolland, distributors.

INDEXES.

INDEX TO ESTATES.

INDEX TO NAMES.

A

B

Benton, Abigail, 148, 158, 498, 500.
  Ann, 498.
  Caleb, 335, 499.
  Daniel, 499, 525.
  Ebenezer, 338, 498, 677, 678, 682.
  Elizabeth, 285, 677, 678, 681, 682.
  Ephraim, 498.
  Hannah, 259, 498, 500.
  Isaac, 57.
  Jacob, 414, 499.
  John, 158.
  Jonathan, 498, 499.
  Joseph, 375.
  Josiah, 298, 446, 498, 570, 602.
  Lydia, 499, 500.
  Martha, 410.
  Medad, 499.
  Moses, 335, 498, 499, 500.
  Ruth, 498.
  Samuel, 36, 57, 98, 102, 314, 499, 500, 675.
  Sarah, 498, 499.
  Timothy, 498, 499.
Bernard, see Barnard.
Bernard, Mr., 57.
Bernis, Shamger, 195.
Bery, Nathaniel, 215.
Beteille, Francis, 43.
Betty (negro), 307.
Betty (negro woman), 676.
Bevin, Mary, 142.
  Stephen, 500.
  William, 494, 500.
Bewell, see Buell.
Bewell, Dorothy, 555.
  Ephraim, 287.
  Hannah, 127.
  Peter, 323, 621.
  Samuel, 127, 242, 473, 474.
Bicknall, see Bignall.
Bicknall, Deborah, 246.
  James, 246, 260.
Bicknell, James, 260.
Bidwell, Abigail, 501, 502, 620.
  Benjamin, 500.
  Daniel, 1, 143, 154, 692.
  Ephraim, 500, 501.
  Hannah, 629.
  James, 692, 693.
  Jehiel, 501, 502.
  John, 11, 42, 619, 620, 692.
  Joseph, 96, 329, 500, 501, 629.
  Luhamah, 502.
  Martha, 501, 502.
  Mary, 141, 500.
  Mehetabell, 208.
  Prudence, 501, 502.
  Rachel, 500.

Bidwell, Ruhamah, 501, 502.
  Stephen, 11.
  Thomas, 501, 502.
  William, 11, 12, 306, 692.
  Zebulon, 11.
Bigelow, Abigail, 504, 505.
  Ann, 505.
  Hezekiah, 505.
  Irene, 503.
  Isaac, 504.
  James, 505.
  Jerusha, 502, 503.
  John, 240, 505.
  Jonathan, 502, 503, 635.
  Josiah, 534, 682.
  Mabel, 502, 503.
  Martha, 505.
  Mary, 504.
  Mehetabell, 504.
  Rebeckah, 502, 503, 505.
  Samuel, 504.
  Timothy, 349, 503, 504, 505, 683.
Biggelow, Abigail, 12.
  Daniel, 11, 12.
  David, 301.
  Elisha, 12.
  Elizabeth, 11, 12, 329.
  Hannah, 11.
  Jonathan, 152.
  Joseph, 12.
  Josiah, 12.
  Martha, 12.
  Mary, 12.
  Mercy, 301.
  Sarah, 12.
  Tabitha, 152.
  Thankful, 12.
  Timothy, 260.
Bignall, see Bicknall.
Bignall, Abigail, 388.
  Mark, 388.
Bingham, Ithamer, 505.
  James, 505.
  John, 505.
  Miriam, 615.
Birchard, see Burchard.
Birchard, John, 252.
Bird, Benjamin, 260.
  Hannah, 228, 353, 506.
  Jonathan, 228, 325, 506.
  Lydia, 506.
  Mary, 343, 573.
  Mehetabell, 506.
  Ruth, 559.
  Sarah, 228, 229.
  Zurviah, 506.
Birge, Daniel, 229, 303.
  Elizabeth, 217.

Bush, Joseph, 518.
  Mary, 518.
Bushnell, Daniel, 105.
  Mehetabell, 458.
  William, 589.
Butfield, William, 237.
Butler, Abigail, 247.
  Benjamin, 21, 237, 364.
  Bethia, 20.
  Charles, 21.
  Daniel, 19, 245, 307, 527, 604.
  Elisha, 504.
  Esther, 20, 71.
  Gershom, 21.
  Gideon, 20, 238.
  Hannah, 307.
  Haughton Dorne, 518.
  Hezekiah, 256, 459, 538, 654.
  Isaac, 246, 496, 521, 544, 557, 585, 616.

Butler, James, 150, 203.
  Jerusha, 504.
  John, 238, 371, 518.
  Jonathan, 197, 257, 277.
  Joseph, 20, 21, 35, 237, 518.
  Lucia, 22.
  Lucy, 390.
  Margaret, 240.
  Mary, 21, 22, 371, 390, 518, 527.
  Mercy, 435.
  Moses, 491.
  Patience, 518.
  Peter, 21, 390, 518.
  Phebe, 22.
  Rebeckah, 20, 22, 654.
  Richard, 21, 35.
  Samuel, 245, 534, 551.
  Thomas, 66, 341, 600, 623.
Buttolph, Mr., 23.

C

Cadwell, Aaron, 237, 238, 239, 240.
  Abigail, 240, 519.
  Alice, 559.
  Ann, 519.
  Dorothy, 519.
  Edward, 218, 240, 245, 246.
  Hannah, 239, 240, 527.
  James, 238, 239, 240.
  John, 518, 519.
  Jonathan, 238, 239, 240, 310.
  Leah, 238, 310.
  Lois, 239.
  Lucy, 519.
  Mary, 240.
  Matthew, 240, 519.
  Mehetabell, 240.
  Moses, 238, 239, 578.
  Nehemiah, 527.
  Rachel, 238.
  Rebeckah, 407.
  Ruth, 519.
  Samuel, 153, 240.
  Susannah, 519.
  Thomas, 14, 26, 238, 239, 240, 259, 579.
  William, 117, 238, 240, 246, 407.
Cady, Aaron, 233.
  John, 5, 184.
Calder, Hannah, 519.
  John, 519.
  Thomas, 519.
Caldwell, Hannah, 147.
  John, 147, 529.

Calkin, see Caulkins.
Calkin, John, 583.
  Samuel, 242.
Camp, Abigail, 22.
  Elizabeth, 22.
  John, 130, 291, 520.
  Mary, 22, 520.
  Rebeckah, 520.
Campbell, Alexander, 112.
Candee, Abigail, 391.
  Hannah, 391.
  Isaac, 391.
  Mary, 391.
  Sarah, 390, 391.
  Theophilus, 391.
  Thomas, 492.
  Zacheus, 2, 78, 390, 391.
Cannady, Thomas, 686.
Carpenter, Daniel, 603.
  Eliphalet, 552.
  Elizabeth, 489.
Carrier, Andrew, 339, 450.
  Isaac, 240.
  Jeremiah, 240.
  Rebeckah, 450.
  Thomas, 240, 241.
Carrington, Clark, 67.
  Thankfull, 411.
Carter, Gideon, 148, 241.
  John, 148, 338.
  Jonathan, 245.
  Joshua, 148, 636.
  Mary, 148.

Comstock, William, 232.
Cone, Caleb, 25, 109, 112, 116, 143, 144,
　　199, 203, 234.
　Daniel, 10, 107, 220, 268.
　David, 190.
　Ebenezer, 107.
　Elisha, 144.
　James, 1, 172.
　Joshua, 203.
　Sarah, 315.
　Stephen, 171.
　Thomas, 77, 139, 178.
Converse, Joseph, 683.
　Josiah, 331, 332, 609, 682.
Cook, Aaron, 29, 340, 529, 624.
　Abigail, 530.
　Anna, 29.
　Annah, 28.
　Anne, 29.
　Benjamin, 530.
　Daniel, 57, 384.
　Eliakim, 42, 529, 543.
　Elizabeth, 432, 530, 586.
　Hannah, 122.
　Jemima, 530.
　John, 8, 29, 94, 121, 168, 217, 261,
　　262, 263, 322, 440, 495, 526, 549,
　　575, 582, 588, 592, 610.
　Joseph, 12, 18, 28, 358, 436, 462, 472,
　　503, 529, 530.
　Lydia, 530.
　Martha, 28, 29.
　Mary, 29, 530.
　Moses, 17, 28, 29, 141, 191, 504.
　Mr., 47.
　Noah, 529.
　Rachel, 529, 530.
　Richard, 261, 356, 357, 452, 530.
　Robert, 442, 530, 531.
　William, 590.
Cooke, Aaron, 27, 28, 55, 228.
　Annah, 28.
　Deborah, 246.
　Joanna, 7, 8.
　John, 28, 40, 303, 312.
　Joseph, 42, 307, 392.
　Josiah, 7, 8.
　Martha, 28, 115, 246.
　Moses, 246.
Cooper, Abigail, 30.
　George, 30.
　John, 30, 500, 518, 695.
　Lamberton, 30, 182, 391.
　Thankfull, 102.
　Thomas, 29.
Copley, Esther, 560.
　Mary, 270, 564.

Copley, Matthew, 646.
　Nathaniel, 560.
Cornell, Abigail, 164.
　Benjamin, 250.
　Daniel, 165.
　Elizabeth, 164.
　Joseph, 164, 165.
　Nathaniel, 165.
Cornish, Benjamin, 30.
　Elizabeth, 247.
　Gabriel, 247.
　Hannah, 169, 246, 247.
　Jabez, 247, 248, 604.
　James, 30, 246, 247, 248, 357, 396,
　　403, 452, 495, 522, 548, 605, 615.
　Jemima, 247.
　Joseph, 30, 60, 73, 85, 148, 169, 247,
　　340, 527, 605.
　Mary, 247.
　Phebe, 247.
　Sarah, 247.
Cornwall, Abigail, 395, 396.
　Abijah, 395.
　Andrew, 452.
　Benjamin, 20, 115.
　Eunice, 395.
　Hannah, 395.
　Isaac, 30, 31.
　Jacob, 31, 124, 230, 396.
　John, 13, 395, 396.
　Mabell, 396.
　Mary, 395, 396.
　Mercy, 396.
　Millicent, 396.
　Nathaniel, 396.
　Phebe, 31.
　Rebeckah, 63.
　Samuel, 31, 32.
　Sarah, 396.
　Susannah, 395, 396.
　Timothy, 32, 63, 395, 396.
　Waite, 395, 396.
Cornwell, Abijah, 531.
　Benjamin, 115, 155, 531.
　Daniel, 248.
　Ebenezer, 32.
　Elizabeth, 248.
　Hannah, 531.
　Jacob, 125, 292.
　John, 248, 474, 531, 659.
　Joseph, 248, 249.
　Mary, 531.
　Nathaniel, 248, 249.
　Phebe, 32.
　Samuel, 32, 487, 531.
　Sarah, 531.
　Thomas, 531.

Curtice, Eleazer, 34, 35.
　Hepzibah, 34, 35.
　John, 33, 35.
　Jonathan, 34, 35, 65.
　Joseph, 203, 256.
　Samuel, 7, 36, 37, 51.
　Thomas, 34, 35, 87, 212, 277, 363.
Curtis, see Curtice, Curtiss.
Curtis, Isaac, 424.
　John, 134, 171.
　Jonathan, 101.
　Samuel, 6, 134.
　Thomas, 151, 200, 308, 327, 328.
Curtiss, see Curtice, Curtis.
Curtiss, Abigail, 251, 252.
　Ambrose, 253, 254.
　Caleb, 252, 253.
　David, 251, 252.
　Deborah, 252.
　Dinah, 252.
　Dorothy, 252, 513.
　Eleazer, 534.
　Elizabeth, 252, 534.
　Experience, 253. 254.
　Hannah, 252.

Curtiss, Henry, 251.
　Hosea, 252, 253.
　James, 253, 254.
　Jeremiah, 251, 694.
　Joel, 252.
　John, 251.
　Jonathan, 251, 534.
　Joseph, 255.
　Mary, 252.
　Mehetabell, 252.
　Naniard, 252, 253.
　Rachel, 253, 254.
　Rachell, 253, 254.
　Richard, 251, 252, 253.
　Samuel, 226, 242, 245, 252, 253, 266.
　　513, 534.
　Sarah, 252.
　Thomas, 204, 253, 254, 266, 314, 406,
　　534, 661.
　Waitstill, 253, 254.
　William, 254, 255.
　Zebulon, 394.
Cusshaw, Benjamin (Indian), 535.
Cutler, Samuel, 651.
Cyrus (man servant), 379.

D

Daily, Field, 535.
　Joseph, 535.
Dallison, John, 43.
Damon, Benjamin, 535.
　Susannah, 535.
　Timothy, 535.
Daniels, Daniel, 294.
　Isaac, 201.
Darbe, Samuel, 242.
Dart, Ebenezer, 503, 504.
　Jemima, 455.
Davis, Isaac, 258.
　John, 683.
　Margery, 683.
　Nathaniel, 414.
Daviss, Mary, 397.
　Samuel, 397.
　William, 397.
Day, David, 301.
　Ebenezer, 89.
　Eunice, 228.
　John, 35, 255.
　Joseph, 35, 218.
　Mary, 228.
　Maynard, 255, 361, 623, 624.
　Nathan, 663, 664.
　Sarah, 35, 228.

Day, Thomas, 228.
　William, 35, 152, 218, 380, 426, 526.
Dean, Ann, 340.
Delano, Barnabas, 157, 673.
　Jabez, 695.
　Jonathan, 56, 413.
Deliber, James, 397.
　John, 372, 397.
Deming, Abigail, 536, 537.
　Abraham, 539.
　Amy, 515.
　Benjamin, 101, 132, 253, 537.
　Charles, 101, 538, 539, 541.
　Daniel, 311, 328, 329, 535, 536, 537,
　　539.
　David, 55.
　Dinah, 159.
　Dorothy, 256.
　Dudley, 256.
　Ebenezer, 253, 254, 352, 515, 654.
　Eliakim, 537, 538.
　Elisha, 398, 537, 538.
　Elizabeth, 536.
　Ephraim, 397, 398.
　Eunice, 535, 537, 539.
　Gideon, 256, 538.
　Giles, 539.

Deming, H., 342.
  Hannah, 397, 398, 539.
  Hezekiah, 256, 426, 537, 538.
  Honour, 398.
  Isaac, 538.
  Jacob, 656.
  Janna, 398.
  Jannah, 398.
  Jedediah, 297, 398.
  John, 36, 272, 297, 308, 397, 398, 404, 405.
  Jonathan, 399, 536, 537, 626.
  Joseph, 364.
  Josiah, 296, 297.
  Lois, 537, 539.
  Lydia, 398, 536, 537, 538.
  Mary, 36, 538, 539, 540.
  Mehetabell, 536, 537.
  Moses, 656.
  Nathaniel, 36, 361, 538, 539.
  Noadiah, 255, 256.
  Oliver, 277.
  Prudence, 282, 296, 297.
  Ruth, 255, 256.
  Samuel, 34, 192, 409, 537, 538, 539.
  Sarah, 537, 539.
  Solomon, 256.
  Stephen, 398.
  Susannah, 535.
  Thomas, 11, 192, 203, 218, 327, 328, 330, 387, 535, 539, 540.
  Waitstill, 398.
  Zachariah, 256.
  Zebulon, 537.
Dennison, Anne, 36.
  Joseph, 36.
Denslow, Ann, 540, 541.
  Anne, 541.
  Benony, 415.
  George, 256.
  John, 36, 184, 185.
  Joseph, 540, 541.
  Martin, 541.
  Samuel, 399, 591.
Densmore, William, 652.
Deuplessey, Elizabeth, 43.
  Francis, 42, 43.
  Lewis, 43.
  Mary Anne, 43.
  Peter, 43.
Devereaux, Jonathan, 520.
Dewey, Abigail, 569.
  Charles, 36, 37.
  Daniel, 517, 631.
  David, 36.
  Isaac, 579, 593.
  Israel, 37, 289.

Dewey, Jabez, 37.
  Joseph, 36, 37, 569.
  Mr., 37.
  Nathaniel, 37.
  Thomas, 242.
DeWolfe, Simon, 488.
Dewolph, Charles, 37, 38.
  Elizabeth, 38.
  John, 38.
  Joseph, 38.
  Mary, 38.
  Prudence, 38.
  Rebeckah, 38.
  Sarah, 38.
  Stephen, 38.
  Symon, 38.
Dibble, Abraham, 234, 235.
  Ebenezer, 172.
Diceson, ——— 90.
Dicke, Mr., 48.
Dickens, see Diggins.
Dickens, Jeremiah, 648, 649.
  Mary, 648, 649.
Dickins, Joseph, 240, 385.
  Mary, 240.
Dickinson, ——— 90.
  Abigail, 137, 399.
  Ann, 541.
  Daniel, 48, 64.
  David, 466, 467.
  Ebenezer, 14, 121.
  Eleazer, 38.
  Elihu, 218, 387, 488, 540.
  Eliphalet, 38, 59, 275, 314, 330, 399, 304, 326, 329, 399, 481, 482.
  Eunice, 38.
  Lucy, 540.
  Moses, 244, 271, 394, 395.
  Mr., 90, 341.
  Nathaniel, 488, 656.
  Noadiah, 36, 98, 99, 137, 138, 273, 304, 326, 329, 399, 481, 482.
  Obadiah, 38.
  Rebeckah, 38.
  Sarah, 38.
  Thomas, 541, 623.
Diggins, see Dickens, Dickins.
Diggins, Jeremiah, 399, 400.
  John, 399, 400.
  Joseph, 399.
  Mary, 399.
  Rebeckah, 399, 400.
Dimaway, John, 396.
Dimmock, Mr., 524, 525.
  Samuel, 499.
Dimock, Samuel, 232, 376, 384.
Dix, see Dixx, Dyx, Dyxx.
Dix, Abigail, 39.

Dix, Benjamin, 541, 542.
   Charles, 39, 256.
   Hannah, 39.
   Jacob, 39, 256, 599.
   Jerusha, 39.
   John, 541, 542.
   Leonard, 39, 256, 257.
   Mary, 483, 508.
   Moses, 541, 542.
   Rebeckah, 39, 256.
   Samuel, 163, 481, 541, 542.
Dixwell, Bathshua, 40.
   Mr., 40.
Dixx, see Dix, Dyx, Dyxx.
Dixx, Mary, 482.
Dod, John, 8, 16, 17.
Dodd, Edward, 257.
   John, 257, 595.
   Mr. 341.
Done, Deborah, 542.
   Ephraim, 462.
   Joseph, 542.
Doolittle, Abraham, 40.
   Daniel, 586.
   Ebenezer, 40, 621.
   George, 542.
   Joel, 542.
   Jonathan, 427, 542.
   Joseph, 40.
   Martha, 40.
   Rebeckah, 542.
   Samuel, 542.
   Thomas, 542.
Dorr, Edward , 560, 673.
Doud, see Dowd.
Doud, Benjamin, 257, 258.
   Cornwell, 257, 258, 400.
   David, 257, 258, 400.
   Ebenezer, 257, 258.
   Elizabeth, 155.
   Esther, 155.
   Giles, 257, 258.
   Hannah, 257, 258.
   Jacob, 155, 156.
   Jane, 257, 258.
   John, 155, 156, 400.
   Josiah, 258.
   Keziah, 257.
   Lois, 155, 156.
   Mary, 257, 258, 400.
   Rachel, 155, 156.
   Richard, 257, 258.
   Sarah, 155.
Douglas, Alexander, 420.
Dowd, see Doud.
Dowd, Elizabeth, 401.
   Esther, 401.

Dowd, Jacob, 401.
   John, 401.
   Lois, 401.
   Mary, 401.
   Rachel, 401.
   Rebeckah, 401.
   Sarah, 401.
Dracke, Catharine, 41.
   Elizabeth, 40, 41.
   Hannah, 41.
   Jacob, 40, 41.
Drake, Ann, 543.
   Asahell, 578.
   Damarus, 578.
   Dorcas, 47.
   Ebenezer, 42.
   Elizabeth, 8, 41, 42, 495, 496, 543.
   Enoch, 9.
   Eunice, 41, 42.
   Gideon, 543.
   Hannah, 8, 543.
   Jacob, 7, 53, 93, 283, 302, 357, 378, 379, 510, 556.
   Jeremiah, 41, 42, 543.
   Job, 40, 41, 42, 120, 543, 550, 662, 670.
   John, 396, 652.
   Jonathan, 41, 543.
   Joseph, 42, 495, 496, 543.
   Josiah, 184.
   Lemuel, 42.
   Martha, 184.
   Moses, 402.
   Nancy, 543.
   Nathaniel, 8, 9, 10, 46, 47, 93, 179, 183, 217, 262, 263, 303, 606, 652.
   Phineas, 575, 650, 651.
   Rebeckah, 8, 41, 543.
   Samuel, 42.
   Sarah, 42.
   Thomas, 274, 543.
Dregs, Daniel, 685.
Dudley, Elizabeth, 580.
   Oliver, 580.
Dunham, Esther, 72.
   Jabez, 242.
   Jonathan, 299, 300, 301.
   Nathaniel, 172.
   Obadiah, 71, 72, 104, 105, 251.
Dunk, Anne, 99.
Dutton, Benjamin, 44.
   David, 44, 45.
   Joseph, 44, 45.
   Mary, 44.
   Samuel, 44, 45.
   Thomas, 44.
Dwight, Samuel, 32, 373.

Dwight, Sibbell, 61.
  Sibell, 61.
  Timothy, 236, 646.
Dwite, Mr., 324.
Dyx, see Dix, Dixx, Dyxx.
Dyx, Abigail, 39.
  John, 98.

Dyx, Mary, 98.
  Samuel, 98.
Dyxx, see Dix, Dixx, Dyx.
Dyxx, John, 161.
  Mary, 154, 155.
  Samuel, 154, 155.

E

Easton, Daniel, 596.
  Eliphalet, 156.
  James, 153, 156, 619, 692.
  Jerusha, 393, 394.
  John, 458, 605.
  Jonathan, 393, 394, 499.
  Joseph, 156, 692.
  Rachel, 640.
  Sarah, 670, 692.
  Susannah, 156.
  Thomas, 601, 602.
  Timothy, 42.
Eaton, Aaron, 157.
  Abigail, 258.
  Bethia, 156, 157.
  Daniel, 258.
  Jemima, 156, 157.
  Mary, 587.
  Rachel, 258.
  Samuel, 156, 157, 215, 253.
  Thomas, 57, 509.
  William, 258.
Edson, Timothy, 609.
Edwards, Churchill, 366.
  Daniel, 66, 504.
  Jabez, 479.
  Jerusha, 46.
  John, 17, 42, 43, 59, 147, 161, 218,
    255, 260, 261, 349, 356, 392, 393,
    403, 431, 465, 502, 504, 533, 553,
    559, 673.
  Jonathan, 98, 189.
  Mr., 45.
  Mrs., 163.
  Nathaniel, 418.
  Richard, 527, 560.
  Samuel, 35, 45, 46.
  Timothy, 42, 104.
Eells, David, 263.
  Edward, 468, 625.
Eels, Edward, 557.
  Martha, 620.
Eglestone, Abigail, 46, 544.
  Benjamin, 46.
  Dameras, 47.
  Deborah, 47.

Eglestone, Ebenezer, 629.
  Edward, 46.
  Elisha, 544.
  Elizabeth, 543, 544.
  Ephraim, 47, 48.
  Esther, 46, 47.
  Grace, 47.
  Hannah, 47.
  Isabell, 47.
  James, 46, 543, 544.
  Jedediah, 47, 48.
  John, 46, 47, 151.
  Joseph, 47, 48, 158.
  Martha, 47.
  Mary, 47, 158.
  Mindwell, 47.
  Patience, 157, 158.
  Samuel, 13, 157, 158.
  Sarah, 158.
  Susannah, 158.
  Thomas, 47, 48.
Elger, Ezra, 402.
  Rachel, 402.
  Thomas, 402.
Eliot, Ann, 546.
  Mary, 546.
Elis, see Ellis.
Elis, Mr., 109.
Ellery, Billy, 382.
  Jane, 383.
  John, 544, 545, 546.
  Johnny, 382.
  Mary, 382, 383, 544, 545, 546, 572.
  Nathaniel, 545.
  William, 382, 545.
Ellis, see Elis.
Ellis, Mary, 275.
Else (mulatto girl), 565.
Elsworth, Abigail, 377.
  Daniel, 56, 206, 258, 493, 517.
  David, 92, 93, 540, 541, 546, 547,
    660.
  Giles, 9, 85, 205, 546, 547, 568.
  Job, 141, 163, 230, 431.
  John, 431.

Elsworth, Jonathan, 163, 323, 347, 377,
 431, 546, 547.
 Josiah, 431.
 Mary, 547.
 Thomas, 13, 431.
Elton, John, 123, 250.
Ely, Reuben, 316.
 Welles, 127, 474.
Emmes, Benjamin, 547.
 John, 547.
 Joseph, 547.
Emmons, Peter, 175, 258, 259, 509.
 Samuel, 172, 178, 304.
Enno, Abigail, 547.
 Benjamin, 92.
 David, 547.
 James, 79, 92, 120, 127, 205, 266,
 355, 356.
 Jonathan, 547.
 Mary, 547.
 Roger, 547.
 Samuel, 312, 378, 440, 495, 550, 590,
 652.
Ennos, see Enos.
Ennos, Benjamin, 324.
Eno, Abigail, 614.
 David, 547.
 Deborah, 185, 548.
 Eunice, 590.
 James, 548.

Eno. Mr., 589.
 Roger, 547.
 Samuel, 496, 547, 560, 614.
Enos, see Ennos.
Enos, Benjamin, 324.
 David, 396.
 James, 126.
 Jerusha, 324.
 John, 183.
 Samuel, 560.
 William, 228.
Ensign, Daniel, 55, 239, 259, 456.
 David, 85, 113, 174, 218, 307, 315,
 360, 392, 409, 471, 472, 528, 554,
 583, 594, 601, 603, 679.
 Ebenezer, 380, 474.
 Eliphalet, 425, 426.
 Experience, 277.
 Hannah, 259.
 Jacob, 556.
 James, 48, 208, 219, 334, 380, 472.
 John, 259, 271, 556.
 Jonathan, 500.
 Moses, 259.
 Sarah, 85.
 Thomas, 17, 71, 259, 277.
Evans, Marah, 274.
 Mary, 274.
Everit, Daniel, 639.
Everts, Judah, 157.

F

Fairbanks, Jonathan, 402.
Fairchild, Hannah, 221, 222.
Farle, John, 509, 548, 549.
 Mary, 548.
Farnsworth, Abigail, 260.
 Christian, 260.
 Elizabeth, 260, 261.
 James, 260, 261.
 Joseph, 122, 260, 261, 350, 480, 505
 Mary, 122.
 Samuel, 260, 261.
Farrend, Mr., 279.
Fellows, Ephraim, 282.
 Verny, 508.
Fery, Rachel, 511.
Ffrary, see Frary.
ffrary, Joseph, 493.
Field, Bennet, 609.
 Samuel, 108.
Filer, see Fyler.
Filer, Samuel, 15, 131.
 Thomas, 9, 108.

Filley, Amos, 261.
 Daniel, 261.
 David, 261.
 Erasmus, 549.
 Esther, 46, 312, 511, 549, 550.
 John, 261, 262.
 Jonathan, 262, 263, 496, 510.
 Joseph, 261.
 Josiah, 262, 549, 550.
 Mary, 168, 261.
 Nathaniel, 262, 263, 550.
 Rebeckah, 262, 263.
 Samuel, 224, 549, 550.
 William, 549, 550.
Fisher, Nathan, 45.
Fisk, John, 2, 234, 242, 263, 500, 535, 695.
 Phineas, 109.
 Prudence, 548.
Fiske, Elizabeth, 263, 264.
 John, 264, 642, 659.
 Lydia, 263, 264.
 Phineas, 3, 203, 263, 264.

Fuller, Elizabeth, 10, 51.
   John, 1, 193, 320.
   Joseph, 172.
   Nein, 193.
   Samuel, 173, 294, 295, 665.
   Shubael, 77.
   Thomas, 194.

Fuller, Timothy, 10.
Fyler, see Filer.
Fyler, Jeremiah, 578, 641.
   Jerusha, 578.
   Samuel, 172, 664.
   Silas, 510, 521.

G

Gains, Agnes, 552.
   Amy, 267.
   Ann, 52.
   Anna, 552.
   Daniel, 267.
   Henry, 267, 415, 551, 552.
   John, 20, 52, 164, 267, 435, 552.
   Mindwell, 267, 402.
   Naomy, 552.
   Rachel, 267.
   Rebeckah, 402.
   Samuel, 110, 111, 197, 198, 267, 318,
      402, 650.
   Sary, 552.
   Simon, 267, 402.
   Susannah, 267.
   Timothy, 267.
Galpen, Caleb, 22.
   Samuel, 22.
Galpin, Caleb, 169, 170, 188, 381, 386,
      418, 419, 611.
   Samuel, 91.
Gardner, Abigail, 647.
   Benjamin, 552, 553.
Garrel, James, 292.
Garret, Francis, 51.
   James, 292.
   John, 51.
   Joshua, 590.
   Sarah, 51.
   Susannah, 51.
Garrett, Francis, 51.
   John, 51.
   Sarah, 51.
Gates, Daniel, 45, 158.
   David, 1, 158.
   Esther, 268, 269.
   Hannah, 1, 158, 268, 269.
   James, 268, 269.
   Jeremiah, 139, 158, 320, 321.
   John, 190.
   Jonah, 268, 269.
   Joseph, 190, 304.
   Joshua, 158, 269.
   Judah, 45.

Gates, Mary, 268, 269.
   Mr., 235.
   Rebeckah, 44, 45.
   Samuel, 268, 269.
   Sarah, 268, 269.
   Stephen, 268, 269.
   Thomas, 158, 193, 320, 321.
Gaylord, Aaron, 641.
   Anna, 115.
   Anne, 114.
   David, 444.
   Eleazer, 18, 151.
   Eliakim, 540, 541.
   Elizabeth, 18, 270.
   Hezekiah, 7, 105, 131, 172, 252, 288,
      334.
   John, 205, 270.
   Joseph, 390, 411, 443, 444, 547, 618,
      660.
   Josiah, 271.
   Margaret, 114, 130.
   Mary, 167, 270, 491.
   Millicent, 18, 114.
   Mrs., 270.
   Naomi, 271.
   Nathaniel, 18, 356.
   Samuel, 18, 444,
   Sarah, 390.
   William, 20, 26, 110, 238, 270, 361,
      456, 457, 458.
George the Second, King of Great
      Britaine, 189.
George the Second, King of Great
      Britain, 227.
George the Second, King of Great
      Britain, 361.
George, (negro), 272.
Gibbs, Benjamin, 591,
   Ebenezer, 584.
   Jacob, 193, 205, 347, 377.
   Ruth, 10.
   Samuel, 377.
Gibson, see Gipson.
Gibson, Michael, 363.
Gilbert, Allin, 160.

H

Hosford, Timothy, 204.
Hoskin, John, 522.
Hoskins, Abigail, 167.
  Alexander, 554, 575.
  Amey, 575.
  Anthony, 575.
  Daniel, 68, 69.
  Dorcas, 575.
  Elizabeth, 167, 284, 348.
  Hannah, 575.
  Jane, 575.
  John, 68, 69, 166, 167, 168, 204, 263, 606.
  Jonathan, 167.
  Joseph, 24, 27, 68, 69, 146, 417, 575.
  Mabel, 575.
  Margaret, 167.
  Mary, 68, 69, 167, 168.
  Robert, 68, 69, 348, 453.
  Ruth, 166, 167.
  Sarah, 575.
  Susannah, 167.
  Thomas, 167.
  Zebulon, 575.
Hosmer, Ann, 70.
  Anne, 69, 70.
  Deliverance, 310.
  John, 69, 70.
  Joseph, 69, 70, 529, 605.
  Mr., 269.
  Sarah, 70.
  Stephen, 10, 69, 70, 77, 181, 238, 310, 344, 362, 456, 528, 529, 577, 597, 639, 640, 655.
  Susannah, 344.
  Thomas, 69, 70, 362, 456, 486, 528, 597, 655.
Hosmore, Stephen, 528.
Hossington, Elisha, 575, 576.
  Elizabeth, 289.
  Hannah, 576.
  James, 576.
  John, 289.
Hotchkiss, Stephen, 621.
Houghton, see Haughton, Horton, Orton.
Houghton, Benoni, 83.
House, Benoni, 508, 643, 644.
  Daniel, 581.
  John, 602.
  Joseph, 620.
  Rachel, 620.
  Sarah, 580.
  William, 267, 408.
How, Elizabeth, 295, 296.
  Joshua, 173, 295, 296.
  Sampson, 124.
  Samson, 124.

Howard, Abigail, 562.
  Alice, 576.
  Benjamin, 91.
  Eleanor, 229.
  Ruth, 562.
  Samuel, 8, 407, 576.
  William, 150.
Howe, Sampson, 613.
Howkins, Anthony, 136.
Hubbard, Abigail, 289, 290.
  Benjamin, 467.
  Caleb, 308, 309.
  Daniel, 116, 202, 407, 692.
  David, 110, 489, 648, 650.
  Ebenezer, 289, 417, 418.
  Elizabeth, 70, 290, 308, 309.
  Ephraim, 489, 586.
  Esther, 290.
  George, 71, 97, 98, 102, 128, 147, 148, 216, 292, 418, 429, 493, 611, 684, 692.
  Hannah, 70, 154, 290.
  Isaac, 300, 563, 657, 658.
  Jeremiah, 202.
  John, 71, 264, 289, 290, 395, 396, 457, 496, 534, 544, 557, 580, 600, 633.
  Lydia, 424.
  Marcy, 97.
  Martha, 70, 71, 288, 289, 418, 419.
  Mary, 71, 97, 289, 290, 654.
  Mercy, 97, 98.
  Nathan, 424.
  Nathaniel, 289, 290.
  Phebe, 126.
  Richard, 70, 71, 170, 487, 527.
  Robert, 144.
  Ruth, 170.
  Samuel, 71, 87, 418, 419.
  Sarah, 169, 170, 289, 290, 419.
  Thankfull, 290, 293.
  Timothy, 418, 419.
  Watts, 418, 419, 654.
  William, 169, 170, 418, 419.
  Zachariah, 684.
Hubberd, Joseph, 518.
Hucheson, Hezekiah, 81.
Huchisson, Aaron, 72.
  Ann, 72.
  Hezekiah, 72.
  Israel, 72.
  Jonathan, 72.
  Joseph, 71, 72.
  Mary, 72.
  Rachel, 72.
Huffman, John Casper, 72, 73.
  Martha, 72.
Hull, Abigail, 295.

Hull, Joseph, 295.
Humphrey, Abigail, 169.
 Agnes, 529, 530.
 Ann, 410.
 Anne, 614.
 Benajah, 73, 148, 169, 391, 392, 403, 495, 604, 613, 671, 672.
 Charles, 169, 672.
 Daniel, 73.
 Dositheus, 410, 436, 529, 530, 595, 677.
 Ebenezer, 447.
 Elizabeth, 169.
 Hannah, 73, 616.
 Hezekiah, 495.
 John, 23, 24, 30, 73, 87, 169, 247, 248, 284, 321, 322, 453, 512, 522, 572, 614, 616, 672, 680.
 Jonathan, 169, 247.
 Joseph, 24, 146, 147, 154, 191.
 Mary, 169.
 Michael, 51, 73, 148, 169, 284, 396, 453, 521, 523, 547.
 Nathaniel, 529.
 Noah, 169, 604.
 Ruth, 614.
 Samuel, 133, 169, 616.
 Sarah, 73, 447.
 Solomon, 672.
 Thomas, 247, 264.
Humphris, Benajah, 69.
 Thankfull, 69.
Hungerford, Elizabeth, 171.
 Esther, 171.
 Green, 170, 171.
 Jemima, 170, 171.
 John, 609.
 Lemuell, 170, 171.
 Mary, 171.
 Nathaniel, 170, 171.
 Rachell, 171.
 Stephen, 170, 171.
Hunlock, Jonathan, 576.
Hunn, David, 290.
 Gideon, 290, 291.
 Samuel, 203, 290, 291, 661.

Hunn, Sarah, 291.
Hunt, John, 185.
 Martha, 640.
Hunting, Edward, 6.
Huntington, Abigail, 291, 292.
 Andrew, 291, 292.
 Deborah, 292.
 John, 56, 77, 176, 233, 291, 292.
 Samuel, 291, 292.
 Thankfull, 291, 292.
Hurlbut, see Holeburd.
Hurlbut, Abiah, 73, 74.
 Daniel, 62, 292, 469.
 Ebenezer, 14, 61, 396, 469.
 Esther, 62, 292.
 Gideon, 536.
 Hannah, 171.
 Isaac, 74.
 James, 74.
 John, 585, 632, 692.
 Jonathan, 73, 74, 201.
 Joseph, 296, 297, 473.
 Josiah, 73, 74, 188.
 Martha, 74.
 Mary, 74, 540.
 Nathaniel, 567.
 Peter, 570.
 Rebeckah, 84, 469.
 Samuel, 683.
 Sarah, 74.
 Stephen, 73, 171.
 Thomas, 63, 84, 346, 409, 410.
 William, 410.
Hurlbutt, Dorothy, 389.
 Gideon, 540.
 Jonathan, 171.
 Mary, 540.
 Stephen, 171.
 Thomas, 256.
Husket, Martha, 292.
Huston, John, 601.
Hutchens, Edward, 292.
 Henry, 292.
Hutchingson, Sarah, 441.
Hutchins, Benjamin, 375.

I

Ingraham, Hannah, 419.
 Joseph, 419.

Ingraham, Martha, 419.
Ingram, Samuel, 232.

J

Jabez (negro), 676.
Jack (negro), 127.
Jackson, Ann, 420.

Jackson, Anne, 420, 421.
 Elizabeth, 420, 421.
 Eunice, 420, 421.

Japhet (negro), 220.
Joanes, see Jones.
Joanes, Jabez, 74.
    James, 74, 75.
    Jonathan, 74.
    Joshua, 74, 75.
    Lewcey, 74.
    Lucy, 75.
    Lurenia, 75.
    Mary, 74, 75.
    Rachell, 74.
    Sarah, 74.
    Thomas, 74, 75.
Johnson, Abigail, 319.
    Amey, 667.
    Anne, 422, 423.
    Caleb, 422, 423.
    Content, 422.
    Daniel, 293, 429, 518.
    Ebenezer, 293, 294.
    Edward, 293, 294.
    Elizabeth, 293, 294, 422, 423.
    Hamlin, 61.
    Hannah, 139, 422, 666.
    Henry, 418, 419, 421.
    Isaac, 292, 293, 421, 422.
    James, 422, 423.
    Jemima, 294.
    John, 28, 245, 421, 423.
    Joseph, 13, 140, 216, 293, 294, 349,
        379, 422, 448, 666.
    Margaret, 421, 422.
    Martha, 577.
    Mary, 292, 293, 294, 422.
    Mercy, 423.
    Mr., 13.
    Mrs., 61.
    Nathaniel, 148, 293, 422, 429.
    Obadiah, 674.
    Oliver, 293, 294.
    Richard, 293.
    Robert, 140, 158, 373.
    Samuel, 293, 294.
    Sarah, 422.
    Stephen, 421, 422, 434, 577.
    Tabitha, 422.
    Thomas, 118, 140, 209, 278, 279, 280,
        281, 346, 364, 365, 366, 368, 369,
        421, 468, 469, 479, 482, 641.
    William, 422, 577.
Jonathan (Indian boy), 319.
Jones, see Joanes.
Jones, Abigail, 294.

Jones, Amasa, 294.
    Ann, 294.
    Benjamin, 423.
    Daniel, 294.
    Elizabeth, 294.
    Ezekiel, 172.
    Hope, 617.
    Hugh, 423.
    Isaac, 138, 294.
    James, 294.
    Jane, 423.
    Joel, 172, 229.
    John, 458, 577.
    Lucy, 75.
    Mary, 74, 172, 294.
    Nathaniel, 238, 317.
    Rachel, 171, 172.
    Samuel, 171, 172, 209.
    Sarah, 479.
    Stephen, 423.
    Thomas, 74, 75, 577, 611.
Joyner, Elizabeth, 172, 173, 294, 295.
    Robert, 173, 295.
    William, 172, 173, 294, 295.
Judd, Anthony, 136, 153, 165, 437, 639.
    Benjamin, 88, 159.
    Daniel, 33, 117, 135, 136, 173, 192,
        354, 355, 577, 578, 668.
    Ebenezer, 100, 173, 295.
    Elizabeth, 424.
    Hannah, 100, 173, 174.
    Immer, 424.
    Ithiel, 424.
    James, 577, 578, 603.
    John, 282, 638.
    Jonathan, 174, 650.
    Joseph, 173, 295, 300, 343, 424.
    Mary, 282, 333, 424, 578, 639.
    Matthew, 577, 578.
    Mercy, 577, 639.
    Mr., 136.
    Nathaniel, 424, 575, 576.
    Phineas, 638, 639.
    Rachel, 295, 577, 578.
    Ruth, 355, 639.
    Sarah, 287, 288, 424.
    Thomas, 13, 173, 295, 296, 433, 578.
    Uriah, 639.
    William, 88, 436, 573.
Judson, Ann, 296, 297.
    James, 296.
Jupiter (negro), 350.

K

Keith, John, 213.
    Mariane, 424.

Keith, William, 164, 223, 237, 396, 424.
Kellog, Martin, 103.

King, Remember, 76, 77.
　Robert, 392, 581, 582,
　Samuel, 76, 77, 299.
　Sarah, 299, 581, 582.
　William, 299.
　Zebulon, 586.
Kingsbury, Nathaniel, 508.
　Sarah, 525.
　Simon, 570.
Kinsbury, Simon, 569.
Kirbe, John, 685.
Kirby, John, 21, 237, 249.
Kircum, Mr., 363.
Kirkham, Henry, 245.

Kneeland, Rachel, 171.
Knight, Samuel, 119.
Knott, see Not, Nott.
Knott, John, 468.
Knowles, Cornelius, 551, 568.
　James, 378.
　John, 70, 363, 519, 503, 530, 644, 678.
　Martha, 378.
　Rachel, 70.
Knowlton, Hannah, 77.
　Lucy, 77.
　Mr., 115.
　Susannah, 77, 78.
　Thomas, 10, 77.

L

Labbe, Esther, 78.
　Stephen, 78.
Lad, Henry, 609.
Ladd, Ezekiel, 498.
　Jonathan, 376, 499.
Ladou, Ambrose, 694.
Ladow, Ambrose, 466.
Laitail, see Latail.
Laitail, Katharine, 223.
Lamb, Joseph, 243, 244.
　Mary, 299.
　Mercy, 299.
　Mr., 486.
　Samuel, 299.
　Sarah, 243, 244, 526.
Lampkin, Deborah, 548.
Lampson, Ebenezer, 414.
Lanckton, see Langton.
Lanckton, Samuel, 165.
Lancton, Ebenezer, 316.
　Samuel, 280.
Lane, Ashbell, 427.
　Cornelius, 427, 571.
　Elizabeth, 155, 427.
　Hannah, 427.
　Hezekiah, 17.
　Isaac, 125, 155, 156, 427.
　John, 175.
　Mary, 427.
　Mindwell, 427.
　Nathaniel, 427.
　Zacheus, 427.
Langton, see Lancton.
Langton, Ebenezer, 175.
　John, 174.
　Joseph, 174, 175.
　Mary, 174.
　Samuel, 174, 175.
　Susannah, 175.

Langton, Thomas, 174.
Lankton, Samuel, 274, 372, 394, 438.
Latail, see Laitail.
Latail, Katharine, 224.
　Margaret, 224.
Lathrop, see Lothrop.
Lathrop, Benjamin, 175.
　Daniel, 508.
　Ebenezer, 176.
　Elizabeth, 175, 176.
　Hope, 175, 176.
　Ichabod, 175, 176, 258.
　John, 175, 176, 215, 258, 291.
　Joseph, 176.
　Marah, 176.
　Mary, 176.
　Melatiah, 176.
　Samuel, 319.
　Solomon, 175, 176.
Lattemore, Bezaleel, 98.
Lattimer, Bezaleel, 429.
　Elizabeth, 475.
　Hezekiah, 429.
　John, 429.
　Sarah, 483.
　Sibbell, 429.
Lattimore, Abigail, 428.
　Bezaleel, 297, 327, 427, 428, 429, 464.
　Hezekiah, 428.
　John, 428.
　Jonathan, 38.
　Samuel, 428, 429.
　Sibbell, 429.
　Sibell, 428.
　Solomon, 428, 429.
Launcelet, Samuel, 300.
Lawrence, Daniel, 639.
　Isaac, 282.
　John, 224, 424, 679.

M

N

O

Orvice, Miriam, 316.
  Oliver, 184.
  Rachel, 184.
  Roger, 316.
  Samuel, 184.
Orvis, Charles, 438, 439.
  Ebenezer, 200, 201, 435.
  Elizabeth, 438, 439.
  Hannah, 18.
Orviss, Charles, 610.
  Deborah, 610.
  Gershom, 610.
  Samuel, 610.
  William, 610.
Osbond, Esther, 46.
  Samuel, 46.
Osborn, Isaac, 77.
  Jacob, 36, 184, 185, 431.
  Martha, 431.
  Rebeckah, 184.
  Samuel, 5, 36, 184, 185.
Osgood, Jeremiah, 91.
  Jeremiah Hubbard, 91.
  Sarah, 660.

Otis, James, 377, 378.
  Mary, 377, 378.
  Mr., 81.
  Nathaniel, 37, 81.
Owen, Aaron, 152, 316, 317.
  Amos, 242.
  Anne, 185.
  Asahel, 317.
  Benjamin, 185.
  Elijah, 185, 186, 317, 442.
  Hannah, 316, 317.
  Isaac, 185, 186, 317, 560, 605, 613.
  James, 316, 317.
  John, 185, 276, 286, 317, 572, 680.
  Joseph, 5.
  Josiah, 242.
  Mary, 152, 547.
  Mr., 68.
  Nathaniel, 540.
  Prudence, 317.
  Rebeckah, 185, 317.
  Samuel, 186, 441, 527, 548, 645, 668, 669.
  Sarah, 185, 186.

P

Pain, Job, 552.
Palmer, Benjamin, 610.
  Deborah, 263.
  Jerusha, 614.
  John, 40, 217, 356, 379, 547, 574, 575, 610, 611, 614, 662.
  Lydia, 439.
  Samuel, 439, 567.
  Stephen, 439, 610.
  Timothy, 439, 610, 611.
Pantry, John, 317.
  Mr., 48, 49.
Parke, Joseph, 299.
Parker, James, 350.
  Mr., 350.
  Nehemiah, 414.
  Samuel, 350.
Parks, Joseph, 494.
Parsons, see Persons.
Parsons, Hezekiah, 48.
Partridge, Oliver, 236.
Pasco, James, 91.
  John, 77, 91, 92, 615.
  Jonathan, 91, 92.
  Rebeckah, 77.
Passewell, Elizabeth, 4.
Paterson, Jno., 526.
  John, 526.
  Mr., 428.

Patterson, Henry, 679.
  John, 351.
Paulk, see Poulk, Poalk, Polk.
Paulk John, 233.
Peck, Abell, 439.
  Abijah, 419, 611.
  Elisha, 418, 439.
  Elizabeth, 318.
  Gideon, 442.
  Isaac, 22, 97, 611.
  Israel, 634.
  Jabez, 611.
  John, 196, 318.
  Joseph, 318.
  Lois, 611.
  Mary, 511.
  Mehetabell, 677.
  Paul, 458.
  Samuel, 169, 289, 439, 440.
  Sarah, 511, 631.
  Zebulon, 170.
Peese, Abigail, 611, 612.
  Abraham, 611, 612.
  Desire, 611, 612.
  Eunice, 615.
  Ezekiel, 634.
  Gideon, 611, 612.
  Joel, 611, 612.
  John, 611, 612.

Q

Quenique, Jubert, 335.

R

Randall, Ichabod, 319, 320.
  John, 319, 320.
Ranney, George, 411, 412.
  John, 3.
  Joseph, 366, 685.
  Margery, 435.
  Martha, 435.
  Mary, 412.
  Willet, 542.
Ranny, Abigail, 467, 468.
  Daniel, 446, 447, 625.
  Ebenezer, 124.
  Esther, 31, 346.
  Fletcher, 30.
  George, 659.
  Jonathan, 446, 447, 625, 641.
  Joseph, 30, 31, 281, 346, 446, 447, 467,
    469, 506, 556, 625.
  Mary, 31, 446, 624, 625.
  Nathaniel, 468.
  Willet, 686.
  Willett, 556.
Ransom, Joseph, 480.
Rauchon, Mary, 223.
Ray, Elizabeth, 99.
  Isaac, 99.
  James, 99.
  Joseph, 99.
  Peter, 99.
Read, see Reed.
Read, Jacob, 266, 284.
  Joseph, 447.
  Mary, 284.
Reave, Robert, 447, 448, 637, 677, 678.
  Sarah, 448.
Redfield, Daniel, 255.
Redington, Jacob, 505.
Reed, see Read.
Reed, Jacob, 521, 523.
  John, 341.
Reinalds, John, 179.
Reinolds, Anna, 100.
  Hezekiah, 100.
  James, 100.
  John, 100, 163, 192, 306.
Remington, Hannah, 563.
  Samuel, 634.
Renals, Jonathan, 161.
Rennals, Hannah, 179.

Rennals, John, 179.
  Rebeckah, 179.
  Susannah, 360.
  William, 179.
Rennolds, John, 428.
  Jonathan, 223.
Rew, see Rue.
Rew, Hezekiah, 625, 626.
  John, 313.
Rice, Elizabeth, 326.
  Ephraim, 295.
  Joseph, 57, 325, 326.
  Mrs., 530.
Rich, David, 625, 626.
  Elizabeth, 625, 626.
  Samuel, 625.
  Sarah, 625.
  Thomas, 542.
Richard, Abigail, 489.
Richards, Amey, 626.
  Benjamin, 626.
  Daniel, 100, 285.
  Esther, 100.
  Hannah, 100, 626.
  Hezekiah, 626.
  James, 100.
  Jedidiah, 335.
  John, 17.
  Jonah, 100, 626.
  Joseph, 410.
  Mary, 626.
  Samuel, 100.
  Thomas, 48, 100, 148, 173, 174, 197,
    208, 259, 335, 392, 393, 471, 472,
    500, 626, 677.
  Timothy, 626.
Richardson, Amos, 548.
  Uriah, 609.
Richman, Mary, 580.
Riley, see Ryley.
Riley, Abigail, 329, 626.
  Ackley, 626.
  Ann, 326, 327.
  Charles, 448.
  Daniel, 327, 328.
  David, 101.
  Elisha, 327, 328.
  Elizabeth, 327, 328.
  Eunice, 390, 464, 465.

Rockwell, Anne, 627, 628.
Benjamin, 92, 103, 331, 629.
Charles, 629.
Daniel, 627, 628, 648.
David, 627, 628.
Ebenezer, 290, 395, 396, 488, 627, 628.
Edward, 391, 469, 686.
Elizabeth, 103, 104, 332, 481.
Eunice, 450.
Ezra, 449, 450.
Hannah, 597.
James, 103, 104, 628, 662.
Job, 104, 331.
Joel, 42, 627, 628.
John, 61, 115, 162, 597, 627, 628.
Jonathan, 629.
Joseph, 3, 21, 29, 31, 32, 40, 42, 49,
50, 62, 70, 103, 104, 115, 124,
125, 126, 130, 139, 142, 144, 145,
210, 391, 395, 396, 469, 628, 629.
Josiah, 104, 449, 450.
Margaret, 331, 332.
Martha, 628.
Mary, 332.
Matthew, 385, 450, 543, 585, 603, 606,
628, 689, 690.
Miriam, 629.
Nathaniel, 586.
Rachel, 628.
Rebeckah, 449.
Ruth, 450.
Samuel, 332, 628, 629.
Sarah, 332.
Waitstill, 450.
William, 2, 4, 5, 6, 21, 32, 61, 62, 83,
102, 115, 118, 124, 125, 129, 140,
148, 155, 156, 157, 158, 164, 165,
182, 187, 210, 216, 221, 230, 248,
249, 250, 257, 258, 267, 271, 289,
290, 292, 293, 294, 308, 309, 310,
331, 334, 346, 348, 349, 358,
365, 366, 373, 380, 389, 390, 391,
395, 396, 400, 401, 402, 417, 419,
420, 421, 422, 427, 429, 442, 447,
448, 459, 460, 462, 463, 469, 470,
475, 478, 479, 481, 482, 483, 487,
488, 506, 507, 508, 516, 518, 531,
532, 533, 534, 550, 564, 577, 584,
597, 598, 600, 617, 627, 632, 635,
651, 653, 664, 666, 677, 684, 685,
686, 687, 695.
Rogers, Ann, 630.
Anna, 630.
Rebeckah, 630.
Thomas, 551, 572, 629, 630.
Rollo, Abigail, 105.
Alexander, 370.

Rollo, Ebenezer, 104.
Elizabeth, 104, 105.
Ellexander, 104.
Eunice, 105.
Hannah, 104, 105.
John, 104.
Mary, 104, 105.
Patience, 104, 105.
William, 104, 105.
Zerubbabell, 104, 105.
Rood, Thomas, 97.
Root, Daniel, 105, 106.
Eleazer, 192.
Elizabeth, 332, 333.
Esther, 450.
Hannah, 192, 333, 630, 631, 632.
Hezekiah, 106.
Israel, 229.
Jacob, 7, 105, 106.
John, 22, 236, 333, 394.
Jonathan, 105, 106, 229, 517, 609.
Joseph, 332, 333, 425, 630, 631, 632.
Lucy, 461.
Lydia, 229, 630, 631, 632.
Margaret, 347.
Mary, 105, 106, 450.
Moses, 236.
Nathaniel, 105.
Ruth, 106, 332, 622.
Samuel, 251, 374, 451, 630, 631, 632,
694.
Sarah, 192, 333.
Stephen, 333, 425, 450, 451, 674.
Temperance, 630, 631, 632.
Theodore, 450.
Thomas, 192.
Timothy, 333, 450, 451.
William, 105.
Rootes, Joseph, 175.
Rose (negro), 220, 350, 660.
Benjamin, 120, 332.
Edward, 515.
Jehiel, 621.
John, 326, 465, 473.
Jonathan, 11.
Ross, William, 527.
Rossiter, Briant, 632.
Mary, 632, 633.
Timothy, 632, 633.
Rowell, Daniel, 554, 633.
Eunice, 510.
Hannah, 633.
John, 633.
Mary, 550.
Samuel, 554, 633.
Sarah, 633.
Thomas, 633.

Rowell, Violet, 633.
Rowlandson, Hannah, 192, 193.
 Mary, 192, 193.
 Phineas, 192, 193.
 Thankfull, 192, 193.
 Wilson, 192, 193.
Rowlee, Ebenezer, 194.
 Elnathan, 240.
 John, 194.
 Jonathan, 194.
 Mary, 194.
 Moses, 194.
 Samuel, 72, 104, 194.
Rowley, Ebenezer, 193.
 Elnathan, 242, 430.
 Hannah, 193.
 Jabez, 294.
 John, 193, 461.
 Jonathan, 193.
 Mary, 549.
 Moses, 1, 193, 194.
 Nathan, 242.
 Samuel, 51, 71, 193.
 Thomas, 159.
Ruben (negro), 154.

Rue, see Rew.
Rue, Hezekiah, 411, 443.
 John, 146, 394, 395, 442, 444.
Russel, Daniel, 449.
Russell, Abell, 451, 452.
 Daniel, 90, 164, 311, 314, 328, 329, 513.
 Ebenezer, 634.
 Elizabeth, 634.
 Ellis, 690.
 Eunice, 451, 452.
 John, 18, 314, 633, 634.
 Jonathan, 211, 372, 633.
 Katharine, 690.
 Mehetabell, 211, 372.
 Mr., 492.
 Mrs., 94.
 Ruth, 311.
 Stephen, 225, 311, 633.
 Susannah, 634.
 William, 61, 63, 82, 87, 199, 263, 417, 634.
Rust, Ann, 681, 682.
Ryley, see Riley.
Ryley, Jonathan, 66.

S

Sabin, David, 634.
 Mary, 634.
 Thomas, 634.
Sacket, John, 601.
Sadd, Hannah, 162.
 Thomas, 162, 239, 274, 648.
Sage, Allen, 106, 107.
 Benjamin, 106, 107.
 Benoni, 106, 107.
 Benony, 107.
 Comfort, 635.
 David, 106, 107, 124, 382, 439, 470.
 Ebenezer, 152, 205, 417, 418, 420, 460, 477, 635.
 Gideon, 557.
 Hannah, 152, 417, 557, 635.
 John, 6, 14, 106, 139, 205, 418, 419.
 Martha, 635.
 Mary, 106, 452, 467.
 Sarah, 106.
 Timothy, 467.
Sallis, Richard, 635.
Saltonstall, Mr., 370.
Sambo (negro man), 408.
Sampson (negro), 220.
Sampson (negro boy), 351.
Samuel (Indian boy), 319.

Sanborn, Jedediah, 599.
 Martha, 482, 483.
Sandford, Mr., 48.
 Thomas, 19, 553.
 Zechariah, 108, 109.
Sanford, Thomas, 140, 259, 307, 341, 358.
 Zachariah, 108.
Savage, Abigail, 195.
 Elizabeth, 195.
 Esther, 194, 195.
 Jabez, 195, 452.
 John, 38, 194, 195, 452, 658, 659.
 Joseph, 129, 130, 289, 346, 365, 366, 368, 624.
 Martha, 684.
 Mary, 195, 407.
 Mr., 52.
 Nathaniel, 38, 194, 195.
 Samuel, 545.
 Susannah, 195.
 Thomas, 366, 368, 468.
 Will, 642.
 William, 366, 641.
Savidge, Mr., 475.
 Nathaniel, 123, 124.
Sawin, George, 548.
Sawyer, Jonathan, 334.

T

Thrall, Joel, 120.
  John, 85, 86, 120, 612, 613, 668, 669.
  Joseph, 120, 670.
  Lucy, 669.
  Luke, 669.
  Mary, 669, 670.
  Mindwell, 120, 669.
  Moses, 119, 120, 423.
  Mrs., 356.
  Samuel, 669.
  Sarah, 355, 670.
  Timothy, 356, 670.
  William, 126, 355, 356.
Tibbals, Esther, 156, 401.
  Joseph, 156, 401, 487.
Tiler, see Tyler.
Tiler, John, 518.
Tiley, John, 213.
  William, 164.
Tilletson, Morris, 7.
Tilley, James, 319.
Tillotson, Jonathan, 242.
Tom (negro man), 615, 616.
Toney, Betty (negro woman), 356.
Tony, alias Benoni (mulatto), 312.
Totman, Dorothy, 363.
Towner, Benjamin, 99.
Tozer, Richard, 319.
Treadway, Elijah, 654.
  James, 294.
  Josiah, 75.
  William, 75, 319.
Treadwell, Ephraim, 603.
Treat, Abigail, 464, 465.
  Charles, 390, 464, 465, 490.
  Eunice, 390, 464.
  James, 214, 464, 465.
  Jerusha, 464, 465.
  John, 33.
  Joseph, 15, 103, 464.
  Mary, 103.
  Mathias, 408.
  Oliver, 464, 465.
  Prudence, 464, 465, 466.
  Rebeckah, 513.
  Richard, 282.
  Samuel, 208, 317, 653, 690, 691.
  Sarah, 208.
  Susannah, 135.
  Thomas, 282, 288, 299.
Trot, John, 37.
Trumble, Benjamin, 461.
  Benoni, 9.
  Sarah, 9.
Trumbull, Benjamin, 644.
  Benoni, 105.
  Mr., 105.

Tryall see Thrall.
Tryall, Hannah, 607.
  Mr., 102.
Tryan, Penelopy, 288.
Tryon, Abel, 126.
  Abell, 422, 671.
  Benjamin, 121.
  David, 102, 120, 121.
  Elyard, 671.
  Ezra, 121.
  Hannah, 121.
  Jonathan, 121, 675, 676.
  Mary, 139.
  Thomas, 422, 671.
  William, 671.
Tucker, Ephraim, 84, 110, 456.
  Isaac, 520.
  Sarah, 520.
Tudor, Samuel, 561.
Tuller, Damarus, 357.
  Daniel, 323, 357, 442, 671.
  David, 357, 671.
  Deborah, 672.
  Ede, 672.
  Elijah, 616, 671, 672.
  Elizabeth, 357, 672.
  Hannah, 357, 358.
  Isaac, 466.
  Jacob, 391, 392, 437, 466, 671, 672.
  James, 357.
  John, 357, 358, 466, 671.
  Joseph, 403, 673.
  Mabel, 672.
  Martha, 672.
  Mary, 671, 672.
  Mehetabel, 672.
  Sarah, 672.
  Sibel, 672.
  William, 356, 357.
Tulley, William, 209.
  John, 349.
Turner, Caleb, 541.
  Hannah, 148.
  Rachel, 491.
  Stephen, 155.
Tuttle, Gershom, 625, 626.
  Sarah, 208.
  Stephen, 208.
Twist, Benjamin, 466.
  Desire, 466.
Tyler, see Tiler.
Tyler, Abraham, 3.
  Hannah, 3.
  John, 518.
  Margaret, 332.
  Nathaniel, 99, 221.
  William, 582.

U

Urtwell, Peter, 242.

V

W

Welles, Joseph, 221, 473.
Joshua, 473.
Josiah, 363, 364, 372, 654.
Judeth, 363.
Judith, 363, 364.
Martha, 363, 364.
Mary, 362, 363.
Mr., 363.
Noah, 138, 319.
Prudence, 473.
Rachel, 362, 458.
Robert, 275, 363, 364, 372, 520.
Ruth, 127, 128, 473, 474.
Samuel, 19, 26, 27, 127, 128, 180, 240, 265, 361, 474, 623.
Sarah, 15, 127, 362, 363, 364, 372, 474, 580.
Solomon, 362, 473.
Thaddeus, 38, 50, 650.
Thomas, 50, 76, 260, 272, 273, 287, 288, 362, 363, 474, 504, 557, 570, 571, 572, 576, 580, 581, 602, 641, 647, 648, 658, 673, 682.
Wait, 464, 654.
William, 363, 643.
Wells, Daniel, 393, 394.
Edmund, 252.
Elizabeth, 154.
Hannah, 103.
Jerusha, 465.
John, 378, 379, 519.
Joseph, 103.
Lydia, 398.
Sarah, 378, 379.
Thomas, 234, 243, 244, 260, 392, 393, 460, 461, 404, 490, 502, 508.
Wait, 465.
William, 298.
Welton, George, 667.
West, Abigail, 128.
Amasa, 36, 128, 129, 690.
Amey, 567.
Asa, 273, 274.
Benjamin, 128.
Christopher, 128, 129, 234, 485, 508.
Dorothy, 46.
Francis, 128, 129.
Hannah, 128, 474.
Jemima, 157.
John, 679.
Joseph, 128, 156, 376, 525, 690.
Mercy, 36, 128, 129.
Moses, 574.
Peletiah, 128, 129, 285, 508, 509, 695.
Samuel, 57, 128, 129, 318, 474, 530, 696.
Sarah, 509.

West, Zebulon, 56, 57, 58, 128, 157, 215, 232, 233, 258, 292, 318, 339, 376, 384, 484, 485, 508, 615, 690.
Westland, Robert, 302.
Westover, Amy, 679.
David, 680.
Hannah, 680.
Jonathan, 679, 680.
Joseph, 680.
Nathaniel, 23.
Silas, 680.
Wetmore, see Whitmore.
Wetmore, Abigail, 129.
Benjamin, 13, 681, 685.
Caleb, 476, 477, 685.
Daniel, 680, 681.
Ebenezer, 474, 475.
Elias, 681.
Elizabeth, 474, 475.
Francis, 30, 125, 128, 129.
Hannah, 129, 475.
Israhiah, 3, 130, 411, 475, 476, 477.
James, 476.
Jeremiah, 476.
John, 474, 475.
Joseph, 129, 680.
Josiah, 372, 476, 477.
Lois, 475.
Margaret, 130.
Mary, 129, 475.
Mr., 61.
Nathaniel, 680.
Ruth, 680.
Samuel, 680.
Sarah, 475.
Seth, 5, 40, 91, 125, 126, 130, 213, 346, 366, 373, 380, 413, 476, 535, 586, 677.
William, 82.
Whaples, Abigail, 47.
Daniel, 364.
Elizabeth, 130, 131.
Ephraim, 130.
Grace, 47.
Jacob, 130.
John, 130.
Jonathan, 130, 291, 364.
Joseph, 131.
Lois, 130.
Marah, 130.
Reuben, 130.
Samuel, 131.
Sarah, 130, 364.
Theodocia, 364.
Thomas, 47, 130, 383.
Wheat, Solomon, 187.
Wheeler, Mary, 364.

Wheeler, Nathan, 258.
  Rachel, 258.
  Thomas, 320.
Wheelock, Mr., 545.
Whitaker, Jonathan, 518.
White, Abigail, 477, 478.
  Ann, 570.
  Cheanna, 131.
  Chene, 209.
  Daniel, 132, 209, 279, 280, 350.
  Deborah, 365.
  Ebenezer, 131, 205, 209, 364, 552, 683.
  Elijah, 477.
  Elisha, 515.
  Elizabeth, 132, 365, 681.
  Esther, 132.
  Hannah, 131, 209, 365, 681, 682.
  Hugh, 118, 123, 132, 281, 359, 365, 368, 468, 535, 683.
  Isaac, 281, 365, 447.
  Jacob, 12, 209, 364, 365, 681, 682.
  James, 223.
  Jane, 683.
  Jerusha, 132, 365.
  Joel, 241, 514, 515.
  John, 12, 365, 474, 681, 682.
  Jonathan, 51, 242, 252, 288.
  Joseph, 4, 30, 38, 52, 61, 124, 131, 195, 242, 279, 280, 412, 478, 552, 584, 642, 659, 683.
  Leonard, 565.
  Lois, 238.
  Martha, 132, 209.
  Mary, 131, 132.
  Mehetabell, 131, 209, 477.
  Miriam, 683.
  Mr., 124, 279.
  Nathaniel, 4, 14, 19, 20, 37, 52, 61, 123, 141, 151, 194, 267, 271, 278, 285, 360, 367, 477, 478, 681, 682.
  Noadiah, 124, 477, 478, 653.
  Obadiah, 131, 209.
  Rebeckah, 131, 209.
  Robert, 682, 683.
  Samuel, 683.
  Sarah, 38, 285, 477, 682.
  Sary, 477, 478.
  Susannah, 132.
  Thomas, 38, 364, 515.
  Timothy, 365.
  William, 683.
Whiting, Charles, 8, 55, 56.
  Eliphalet, 95.
  Honor, 55, 56.
  John, 12, 26, 29, 69, 108, 111, 112, 329, 361, 412, 413, 456, 457, 458, 472, 530, 578, 579, 678.

Whiting, Joseph, 341.
  Mr., 341, 503, 525.
Whitman, Elnathan, 673.
  John, 528.
  Mr., 544.
  Samuel, 228, 355.
  Solomon, 63.
Whitmarsh, Nicholas, 583.
Whitmore, see Wetmore.
Whitmore, Abigail, 683, 684.
  Daniel, 577, 683, 684.
  Ebenezer, 683, 684.
  Elizabeth, 684, 686.
  Francis, 30, 124, 129, 230, 365, 366, 478, 480, 481, 504, 518, 683, 684, 685, 686.
  Hannah, 129, 365, 684.
  Hezekiah, 683, 684.
  Isabel, 683.
  Isabell, 478.
  Jacob, 78, 147, 308, 395, 396, 421, 518, 533, 577, 597, 599, 621, 622, 629, 642, 665, 683, 684, 686.
  John, 292, 462, 478, 479.
  Joseph, 129, 365, 366, 684.
  Margery, 684.
  Martha, 129, 130, 365.
  Mary, 126, 129, 683.
  Mr., 210.
  Nathaniel, 683.
  Ruth, 478.
  Samuel, 129, 130, 365, 684, 685.
  Sarah, 683.
  Seth, 129, 130, 365, 366, 494, 684, 685, 686.
  Susannah, 683.
  William, 29, 30, 62, 122, 129, 148, 171, 230, 364, 468, 550, 601.
  Zerviah, 683.
Whitney, David, 282.
  Mirriam, 548.
Whittlesey, Eliphalet, 526.
  Ezra, 479.
  Jabez, 209, 374, 479.
  Lois, 479.
  Lydia, 479.
  Ruth, 209.
  Sarah, 479.
Wickham, Gideon, 132.
  Margery, 602.
  Thomas, 132.
Wilcock, Ebenezer, 131.
  Ephraim, 284, 502.
  Francis, 479, 625.
  Hannah, 284.
  Janna, 231.

Y